❖ ❖❖ ❖

CUBS
JOURNAL

❖ ❖❖ ❖

Year By Year & Day By Day
With The Chicago Cubs Since 1876

CUBS
JOURNAL

JOHN SNYDER

emmis
books

Front Cover Photo Credits

(left to right)
Cap Anson (courtesy of Transcendental Graphics)
Frank Chance (courtesy of Dennis Goldstein)
Ernie Banks (courtesy of Dennis Goldstein)
Hack Wilson (courtesy of Mike Mumby)
Ron Santo (courtesy of Dennis Goldstein)
Ryne Sandberg (courtesy of George Brace)
Les Mann (courtesy of Mike Mumby)
Billy Williams (courtesy of George Brace)

Back Cover Photo Credits

(top, left to right)
Ernie Banks (courtesy of Transcendental Graphics)
Johnny Evers—sliding (courtesy of Mike Mumby)
Kerry Wood (courtesy of finalshot.com)

(below, left to right)
Three Finger Brown (courtesy of Transcendental Graphics)
Sammy Sosa (courtesy of George Brace)

For further information, contact the publisher at:

Emmis Books
1700 Madison Road
Cincinnati, OH 45206

www.emmisbooks.com

Library of Congress Cataloging-in-Publication Data

  Snyder, John, 1951-
    Cubs journal : year by year and day by day with the Chicago Cubs since 1876 / John Snyder.
      p. cm.
    ISBN 1-57860-192-4 (pbk.)
    1. Chicago Cubs (Baseball team)--History--Chronology. I. Title.
    GV875.C57S69 2005
    796.357'64'0977311--dc22

                 2005000041

Interior designed by Mary Barnes Clark
Edited by Jack Heffron
Cover designed by Steve Sullivan

About the Author

John Snyder has a master's degree in history from the University of Cincinnati and a passion for baseball. He has authored thirteen books on baseball, soccer, hockey, tennis, football, basketball, and travel. His *Redleg Journal: Year by Year and Day by Day with the Cincinnati Reds Since 1866* (Road West Publishing Company, 2000) with Greg Rhodes, won the 2001 Sporting News-SABR Baseball Research Award. He lives in Cincinnati.

Acknowledgments

This is the second book in a series that will take a chronological look at major league baseball teams. Like *Redleg Journal: Year by Year and Day by Day with the Cincinnati Reds Since 1866*, the first in the series and the winner of the 2001 Baseball Research Award issued by *The Sporting News* and SABR, *Cubs Journal: Year by Year and Day by Day with the Chicago Cubs Since 1876* is full of little known items which have never been published in book form.

Greg Rhodes was my co-author on *Redleg Journal*, in addition to publishing the book under his company, Road West Publishing. While Greg had no active participation in *Cubs Journal*, he deserves considerable credit for the success of this book because many of the creative concepts he initiated in *Redleg Journal* were repeated in this work.

The idea for turning *Redleg Journal* into a series of books goes to Richard Hunt, president and publisher of Emmis Books, and editorial director Jack Heffron. Thanks to Mary Barnes Clark and Jack Heffron, who designed and edited the book, and also to the other people at Emmis Books who helped in a variety of ways: Steve Sullivan, Steve Watkins, Andrea Kupper, Jessica Yerega, Connie Springer, and Megan Varelman.

I would also like to thank the staff at the Public Library of Cincinnati and Hamilton County. The vast majority of research for this book came from contemporary newspapers and magazines. The library staff was extremely helpful with patience and understanding while retrieving the materials for me, not only in this book, but in all of my previous endeavors as well.

My father, who passed away in 1999, instilled in me a love of both baseball and history. He grew up in the Chicago suburb of Oak Park, and during my formative years, I heard many stories about Cubs players such as Gabby Hartnett, Billy Herman, and Phil Cavaretta. Many of our family vacations were spent at the Indiana Dunes and always included a day trip into Chicago that included a morning at one of the city's world-renowned museums and an afternoon at Wrigley Field.

And finally, although they should be the first, thanks to my wife and two sons, whose encouragement and support have helped me though another book.

Contents

❖ ❖ ❖

When Does Time Begin?

The official beginning of the Chicago Cubs dates from February 2, 1876, with the creation of the National League in a meeting of representatives of eight cities in New York City. There, franchises were established in Chicago, Boston, Cincinnati, Hartford, Louisville, New York, Philadelphia, and St. Louis. Our story begins with that historic meeting.

The foundations of the franchise that would become the Cubs extend a few years earlier, however. The first professional team in Chicago was the White Stockings, created in 1870. Civic leaders raised $20,000 to organize a strong team, believing that it would help boost the city's image. Although Chicago was a booming and bustling city as a transportation hub at the beginning of the industrial revolution, it was still a relatively new municipality. As recently as 1830, Chicago was a mere village while cities in the East like Boston and New York were already 200 years old.

The first world's first professional baseball club—the Cincinnati Red Stockings—came to Chicago on September 7, 1870. The Red Stockings were created in 1869 and toured the country, including a trip to the West Coast on the newly completed transcontinental railroad. The Cincinnati club came to Chicago with an astounding two-year record of 113-2-1. The White Stockings pulled off a huge upset, defeating the Red Stockings 10-6. On October 13, the Red Stockings returned to Chicago, and the White Stockings won again 16-13. The wins were cause for a city-wide celebration.

The National Association of Professional Baseball Players—known popularly as the National Association—was formed in 1871. The White Stockings entered the league and contended for the championship until October 8, when the Great Chicago Fire destroyed their ballpark at Michigan and Randolph Streets along with most of the city. Forced to play their last three games on the road, they lost the championship.

As Chicago resurrected itself from the ashes, city residents had priorities other than baseball. The White Stockings reentered the National Association in 1874 with a new ballpark at 23rd and Clark Streets, but were a mediocre entity. All of the best players from the 1871 juggernaut had gone else-where. It was at this point that William Hulbert entered the picture.

A local coal merchant who took an aggressive role in the rebuilding of Chicago after the fire, Hulbert purchased controlling interest in the club in June 1875. Determined to build a winner, he secretly signed Boston pitching ace Albert Spalding for the 1876 season. Spalding, in turn, recruited Ross Barnes, Deacon White, and Cal McVey from Boston and Cap Anson and Ezra Sutton from Philadelphia.

The National Association had fallen on hard times. Scheduling was piecemeal, contract jumping rampant, betting was openly flaunted at the ballparks, and rowdiness abounded. Largely through Hulbert's efforts the Association was dissolved and replaced by the National League.

To counteract the problems with the National Association, Hulbert insisted that a strict schedule, drawn up by the league instead of by individual teams, was followed with heavy fines for any club that failed to play their games. Each club would respect the contracts of the other. Open betting was prohibited, along with the sale of alcohol at the ballparks.

The National League experienced some growing pains. Six of the original eight franchises folded or were expelled from the league by 1880 to be replaced by others. It was a lasting success, however. The NL started its 130th season in 2005. The Chicago Cubs are the only one of the original eight clubs still operating in the same city.

Wrigley Field 1949

THE STATE OF THE CUBS

The National League was founded in 1876, and the Chicago franchise won six of the first eleven pennants, finishing first in 1876, 1880, 1881, 1882, 1885, and 1886. Other NL pennants during the 1870s and 1880s were won by Boston (1877, 1878, and 1883), Providence (1879 and 1884), Detroit (1887), and New York (1888 and 1889).

THE BEST TEAM

The 1880 Cubs had a record of 67–17 with a winning percentage of .798 and won the NL pennant by 15 games.

THE WORST TEAM

The only losing season from 1876 through 1889 was in 1877, when Chicago was 26–33.

THE BEST MOMENT

The Cubs spread goodwill and the sport of baseball on a world tour between the 1888 and 1889 seasons.

THE WORST MOMENT

Chicago manager Cap Anson refused to play an exhibition game against a minor league team in Newark because African–American pitcher George Stovey played for the team.

THE ALL–DECADE TEAM • YEARS WITH CUBS

Silver Flint, c	1879–89
Cap Anson, 1b	1876–97
Fred Pfeffer, 2b	1883–89, 1891, 1896–97
Ned Williamson, 3b	1879–89
Tom Burns, ss	1880–91
Abner Dalrymple, lf	1879–86
George Gore, cf	1879–86
King Kelly, rf	1880–86
Larry Corcoran, p	1880–85
John Clarkson, p	1884–87
Fred Goldsmith, p	1880–84
Terry Larkin, p	1878–79

Anson, Kelly, and Clarkson are all in baseball's Hall of Fame. Other key players during the early years of the franchise were center fielder Jimmy Ryan (1886–89, 1891–1900), left fielder George Van Haltren (1887–89), and pitcher Jim McCormick (1884–85).

THE DECADE LEADERS

Batting Avg:	Anson	.333
On–Base Pct:	Gore	.395
Slugging Pct:	Anson	.475
Home Runs:	Pfeffer	69
RBI:	Anson	1,132
Runs:	Anson	1,082
Stolen Bases:	Pfeffer	196
Wins:	Corcoran	175
Strikeouts:	Corcoran	1,086
ERA:	Corcoran	2.24
Saves:	Williamson	3

THE HOME FIELD

The Cubs played in three different Chicago ballparks during the 1870s and 1880s. The club used the 23rd Street Grounds in 1876 and 1877, Lakefront Park from 1878 through 1884, and West Side Park from 1885 through 1890.

THE GAME YOU WISH YOU HAD SEEN

On May 30, 1884, Ned Williamson became the first player in major league history to hit three homers in a game. Because of the ridiculously short fences at the ballpark, there were 197 homers hit in 57 games at Lakefront Park in 1884.

THE WAY THE GAME WAS PLAYED

The first all-professional team was established in Cincinnati in 1869, and the game was still very much in the evolutionary and experimental stage during the 1870s and 1880s. National League games averaged about 11 runs per game during this period, but about half of them were unearned, as rough fields made defensive play an adventure. Fielders played bare-handed in 1876, but soon after the first gloves began to appear, although they were fingerless and meant only to protect the palm of the hand. In 1876, pitchers threw underhanded, as it was illegal to throw a pitch above the waist. By the mid-1880s, the overhand delivery was legalized, giving hurlers more speed and leverage on their curveballs. The pitching distance was forty-five feet in 1876 and increased to fifty feet in 1881 and fifty-five feet in 1887. During the 1870s, it took nine balls for a walk and three strikes for a strikeout. The number of balls required for a walk was gradually reduced until the four-ball, three-strike count was established in 1889.

THE MANAGEMENT

The three guiding lights of the early years of the Cubs franchise were William Hulbert, Albert Spalding and Cap Anson. Hulbert was the president of the Cubs from their founding in 1876 until he died in 1882. He was also the force behind the creation of the National League and served as league president from 1877 until his untimely death. Spalding was the club's manager in 1876 and 1877, in addition to being one of the top pitchers in the game. He left baseball temporarily after the 1877 season to look after his enormously successful sporting goods store, but he remained a behind-the-scenes force with the Chicago franchise. Spalding became principal owner and president of the Cubs after Hulbert's passing. Anson was acquired as a player before the 1876 season. He remained with the Cubs for 22 seasons, the last 19 as player-manager.

THE BEST PLAYER MOVE

Cap Anson was signed away from the Philadelphia Athletics before the start of the 1876 season. He was the best player for Chicago during the 19th century, and arguably the best in all of baseball. Anson is still first all-time among Cubs in career batting average (.339), runs scored (1,711), hits (3,081), singles (2,330), doubles (530), and runs batted in (1,879), second in games (2,253), at-bats (9,084), and triples (129), and third in total bases (4,149) and walks (952).

THE WORST PLAYER MOVE

Following the pennant-winning 1886 season, in which the Cubs were 90–34, Cap Anson sold top players King Kelly, George Gore, Abner Dalrymple, and Jim McCormick. After finishing third in 1887, the Cubs sold ace pitcher John Clarkson. Chicago didn't win another NL pennant until 1906.

1876

ubs

Season in a Sentence

The Cubs easily capture the championship flag in the National League's first season.

Finish • Won • Lost • Pct • GB

Second   52   14   .788   +6.0

Manager

Al Spalding

Stats   Cubs • NL • Rank

	Cubs	NL	Rank
Batting Avg:	.377	.265	1
On–Base Pct:	.353	.277	1
Slugging Pct:	.417	.321	1
Home Runs:	8		2
ERA:	1.76	2.31	4
Fielding Avg:	.899	.866	2
Runs Scored:	624		1
Runs Allowed:	257		2

Starting Lineup

Deacon White, c
Cal McVey, 1b–sp
Ross Barnes, 2b
Cap Anson, 3b
John Peters, ss
John Glenn, lf
Paul Hines, cf
Bob Addy, rf
Oscar Bielaski, rf

Pitchers

Al Spalding, sp

Attendance

65,441 (first in NL)

Club Leaders

Batting Avg:	Barnes	.429
On–Base Pct:	Barnes	.462
Slugging Pct:	Barnes	.590
Home Runs:	Anson	2
	Hines	2
RBI:	White	60
Runs:	Barnes	126
Wins:	Spalding	47
Strikeouts:	Spalding	39
ERA:	Spalding	1.75
Saves:	McVey	2

FEBRUARY 2   Chicago joins the new National League, which is officially organized during a meeting at the Grand Central Hotel in New York. The eight–team league was composed of clubs from Boston, Chicago, Cincinnati, Hartford, Louisville, New York, Philadelphia, and St. Louis. William Hulbert, who was instrumental in organizing the league, was the president of the Chicago club. A wealthy grain and coal merchant, Hulbert also served as NL president from 1877 until his death in 1882 at the age of 49. The National League was formed after the National Association folded at the end of the 1875 season. The National Association was baseball's first organized league. It was created in 1871 but was disorganized and a hotbed of rowdyism, drunkenness, and gambling. Chicago had a team in the National Association in 1871, 1874, and 1875. The two–year break was caused by the Great Chicago fire, which devastated the city in October 1871. The new National League required each team to play 70 games (an average of three games a week, generally played on Tuesdays, Thursdays, and Saturdays.) It was agreed that a pennant worth at least $100 would be awarded to the league champion. Tickets were 50 cents. No liquor was sold at the games. The pitcher's mound was forty–five feet from home plate, and the pitcher's arm could not be above his waist when delivering the ball to the plate. Games on Sunday's were prohibited.

Of the eight original clubs, only the Chicago and Boston clubs have operated continuously since 1876. Chicago is the only one to have operated in one city since the birth of the National League. The Boston club moved to Milwaukee in 1953 and Atlanta in 1966.

FEBRUARY 12   Albert Spalding, pitching star of the National Association, moves from Rockford, Illinois, with his brother, J. Walter, to Chicago to "open a large emporium where they will sell all kinds of baseball goods" at 118 Randolph Street. This was the start of the Spalding sporting goods enterprise. The business was enormously successful, and both Spalding brothers became millionaires.

Spalding played for Boston in the National League in 1875. He was lured to Chicago by club president William Hulbert, who offered Spalding $4,000 to act as manager, captain, and pitcher. Spalding convinced three other Boston stars to move to Chicago. The trio consisted of Deacon White, Cal McVey, and Ross Barnes. Boston won the National Association pennant in 1872, 1873, 1874, and 1875, and the hijacking of the four players made Chicago the best team in the new National League and created an intense rivalry between Chicago and Boston.

APRIL 8   After four great seasons with the Philadelphia Athletics, Cap Anson reports to Chicago to play third base.

Anson played 22 seasons for the Cubs through 1897, and was the manager of the club from 1879 through 1897.

APRIL 25   Six weeks after Alexander Graham Bell patents the telephone, the Cubs (then known as the White Stockings) play their first game and win 4–0 against the Louisville Grays in Louisville. Albert Spalding pitched the shutout. The lineup for the first Cubs game was Ross Barnes (2b), Cap Anson (3b), Cal McVey (1b), Paul Hines (cf), Spalding (p), Bob Addy (rf), Deacon White (c), Johnny Peters (ss), and John Glenn (lf).

The greatest acquisition of the Cubs' early years, Cap Anson began his 22-year Cubs career by leading the team to the league title.

APRIL 27   In the second game of the 1876 season, Albert Spalding pitches his second shutout, defeating Louisville 10–0 in Louisville.

Spalding shut out the opposition so often in the early going in 1876 that when any club was held without a run it was said that they were "Chicagoed." The slang term remained part of baseball's lexicon into the early part of the 20th century. In 1876, Spalding had a record of 47–12 with an ERA of 1.75. In the few games he didn't pitch, he played outfield or first base and hit .312.

MAY 2   Ross Barnes hits the first home run in National League history during a 15–9 win over the Reds in Cincinnati. The pitcher was Cherokee Fisher.

MAY 5   The Cubs suffer their first defeat, losing 1–0 to the St. Louis Brown Stockings in

St. Louis as George Bradley outpitches Albert Spalding. The lone run, scored in the first inning, was unearned because of Spalding's error on a throw to first.

MAY 10   The Cubs play a National League game in Chicago for the first time and defeat the Cincinnati Reds 6–0 at 23rd Street Grounds.

The Chicago ballpark at the corner of 23rd Street and State Street was built in 1872. It was a ramshackle facility with a wooden grandstand that could seat perhaps 1,500 fans and had a short wooden fence surrounding the playing field about six or seven feet high. The outfield dimensions are unknown, but at least two balls cleared the right field barrier at a time when a 300–foot drive was considered to be a mammoth clout. The fences in that era were not conceived as home run targets but merely as a means of ensuring that fans would have to pay to enter and see the games. The 23rd Street Grounds were used by the Cubs in 1876 and 1877.

MAY 30   The Cubs, with four former Boston stars in their lineup, play their first 1876 game in Boston. The crowd estimated at 20,000 was described as "the largest that ever attended a baseball match in the world." This was also the first game between the Cubs and the present–day Atlanta Braves franchise. Chicago won 5–1.

JULY 4   On the day of the nation's centennial and nine days after General George Custer makes his "last stand" at the Little Bighorn, the Cubs lose 3–0 to the Hartford Dark Blues in Hartford, Connecticut. The crowd was announced at 12,000.

JULY 11   The Cubs score nine runs in the third inning and defeat the Boston Red Stockings 18–7 in Chicago.

JULY 15   The Cubs wallop Boston 15–0 in Chicago.

JULY 20   The Cubs score in each of their first eight turns at bat and swamp the Louisville club 18–0 in Chicago.

JULY 22   The Cubs score ten runs in the first inning and eight in the fourth in a 30–7 rout of Louisville in Chicago. The Cubs had 31 hits in the contest.

JULY 25   Cal McVey collects six hits in seven at–bats in a 23–3 win over the Reds in Chicago. McVey also had six hits in the Cubs previous game on July 22. He is the only player in major league history with back–to–back six–hit games. In fact, the only other players with two games of six hits or more in a career are Jimmie Foxx of the Athletics in 1930 and 1932, and Kirby Puckett of the Twins in 1987 and 1991. From July 20 through July 30, McVey had 22 hits over five consecutive games.

JULY 27   Ross Barnes picks up six hits, including a double and a triple, in six at–bats during a 17–3 win over the Reds in Chicago. The Cubs scored 88 runs in four consecutive games from July 20 through July 27.

It was the third game in a row in which the Cubs had a player with six hits. No other club in major league history has had more than two games of six or more hits from an individual over an entire season. Barnes led the National League in batting in 1876 with an average of .429. Other top hitters for the Cubs were

John Peters (.351), Cal McVey (.347), Deacon White (.343) and Paul Hines (.331). Barnes also led the league in runs (126 in only 66 games), hits (138), total bases (190), and triples (14). Deacon White led the league in RBIs (60) and Paul Hines in doubles (21). Barnes accumulated his high batting average in part because of a rule that stipulated that any ball which landed in fair territory was in play. Barnes mastered a technique in which he could maneuver a ball to land fair and immediately slice foul. After the season, a change in the rules stated that for a batted ball to be called in play by the umpires it must stay within the foul lines until it crossed a base or it was fielded. Barnes's batting average fell to .272 in 1877 because of the new rule and a long illness that sapped his strength. The Cubs deducted $1,000 of his $2,500 salary because of the illness, a common practice at the time. Barnes took the club to court to regain the lost income, but he lost the case.

AUGUST 1 — The Cubs crush the Louisville Grays 15–7 in Louisville.

AUGUST 3 — Two days after Colorado becomes the thirty-eighth state in the Union and the day after Wild Bill Hickok is shot dead in Deadwood, South Dakota, a contest between the Cubs and Louisville in Louisville is declared "no game" after the Cubs walk off the field. Rain was falling heavily in the fifth inning with Chicago leading 4–1. Louisville protested to the umpire that the game be stopped, but he ordered play to continue. Louisville made error after error in order to prolong the game and prevent it from reaching the end of the fifth inning, when it would be declared a legal contest. The Cubs walked off the field. The two clubs later agreed to replay the game, and the Cubs won 9–2 on August 7.

AUGUST 8 — The Cubs wallop the Reds 13–3 in Cincinnati.

AUGUST 12 — Versatile Cal McVey plays two innings at first base, four as a pitcher, and three as a catcher during a 5–0 win over the Reds in Cincinnati.

AUGUST 21 — Trailing the Brown Stockings 7–6 in the ninth inning in St. Louis, the Cubs leave the field to protest an umpire's call. The dispute began when Mike McGreary of St. Louis started for home from third on a grounder by teammate Ned Cuthbert. The throw struck McGreary and went foul. The Cubs claimed interference, but umpire William Walker ruled that the contact was accidental and allowed the run to stand. Albert Spalding pulled his team off the field and St. Louis was awarded the game in a forfeit.

AUGUST 22 — The Cubs rebound from the previous day's forfeit to win 12–2 over St. Louis in Chicago.

AUGUST 26 — The Cubs crush St. Louis 23–3 in Chicago.

SEPTEMBER 22 — The Cubs defeat Boston 12–10 in Chicago with two runs in the ninth.

SEPTEMBER 26 — The Cubs clinch the National League pennant, defeating Hartford 7–6 in Chicago.

What is a Cub?

For the purposes of simplicity and consistency, Chicago's National League baseball team is called the "Cubs" throughout this book. A fan of the club prior to 1902 would have been thoroughly confused by the name "Cubs," however, because it wasn't until that year that the nickname was coined. The Cubs nickname first appeared in the *Chicago Daily News* of March 27, 1902, in an unsigned sports column that noted that "manager Frank Selee will devote his strongest efforts on the team work of the new Cubs this year." The "Cubs" were the many young players and rookies on the roster that season as the club was engaged in a massive rebuilding project after a losing season in 1901 and after several players jumped to the newly formed American League.

That the nickname originated in a newspaper was typical of the period. Many of the most famous nicknames in baseball, such as the Cubs, Reds, Yankees, Dodgers, Giants, Braves, Phillies, Pirates, Cardinals, Indians, Orioles, and Tigers, were created not by the clubs themselves but by an enterprising sportswriter. The name caught the imagination of the public and began to be used in everyday speech until it became part of the team's identity. The editors and authors of many baseball histories have attempted retroactively to attach a single nickname to clubs from the 19th and early 20th centuries, when in fact many of these nicknames were seldom used. Many clubs most often were called by the city, such as the "Chicagos," the "New Yorks," the "Bostons," or the "Pittsburghs." Other teams had several nicknames simultaneously.

The nicknames attached to the present-day Cubs include:

White Stockings (1876–1887)—The Chicago club was known as the White Stockings because of the color of their hosiery. The nickname passed out of use when Chicago switched to black stockings in 1888. The White Stockings nickname was revived in 1900 when a new American League club moved into the Windy City and adopted the moniker. The name White Stockings was soon abbreviated to White Sox.

Whites (1876–1887)—This shortened version of White Stockings often appeared in print in the early years of the National League.

Silk Stockings (1879)—The name Silk Stockings surfaced briefly after team owner William Hulbert adorned his club in expensive uniforms that included stockings made of silk, and because he assembled the highest-salaried team in baseball. Despite the payroll, Chicago finished in fourth place.

Black Stockings (1888–90)—A switch from white stockings to black brought a change in the team nickname as the White Stockings became known as the Black Stockings. The club was also called the Black Sox.

Colts (1890–1905)—Most of Chicago's top players defected to the newly formed Players League between the 1889 and 1890 seasons, forcing manager Cap Anson to field a team of young talent. The assortment of rookies was nicknamed the "Colts" and the name soon applied to the whole team. As the club aged, they were sometimes called the "Ex-Colts."

Orphans (1898–1901)—Cap Anson was fired in February 1898 after 22 seasons as a player and 19 as player-manager. Without Anson, who was also known as "Pop," the Chicago club was known as the Orphans for several seasons.

Rainmakers (1898)—After many early-season games were postponed by rain, the club was briefly known as the "Rainmakers."

Rough Riders (1899)—During the spring of 1899, the club trained on a ranch in remote New Mexico, which was then a territory and not yet a state in the Union. Horseback riding was part of the club's training regimen. Inspired by the training session in the "Wild West" and the success of Theodore Roosevelt's "Rough Riders" in the Spanish-American War of 1898, the Chicago club was also dubbed the Rough Riders during the 1899 season. During the spring of 1899, the club was also called the "Cowboys" and the "Desert Rangers." The Rough Riders nickname was phased out as the 1899 team was wracked by bickering and dissension.

Remnants (1901–02)—The American League

declared itself a major league between the 1900 and 1901 seasons and began raiding National League rosters for talent. Chicago's NL club lost several top players, many of them to the cross-town White Sox. What remained of the roster of the NL franchise was called the "Remnants."

Cubs (1902–present)—The nickname caught the fancy of the public almost immediately, but many of the city's newspapers, including the influential *Tribune*, weren't so enamored of the name and tried out other monikers over the next few years.

Panamas (1903)—During spring training in Los Angeles in 1903, many players purchased Panama hats.

Microbes (1903)—The Cubs of 1903 had many players of small stature, led by Johnny Evers who weighed barely 100 pounds at the start of his career, earning the nickname "Microbes."

Zephyrs (1905)—Zephyrs was stamped on the club because of Chicago's own nickname "Windy City," and the overall team speed of the club.

Nationals (1905–07)—Nationals was used simply because the Cubs were in the National League.

Spuds (1905–06)—The Spuds nickname was attached to the club because of owner Charles Murphy and the large number of players of Irish extraction on the team.

Manager Frank Chance hated the name "Spuds" and insisted in 1907 that the club be called the "Cubs" exclusively. The Chicago newspapers fell in line. The Cubs nickname was "officially" recognized during the 1907 World Series, when new coats were issued to the players sporting a large white bear figure on each sleeve. The Cubs uniforms in 1908, both at home and on the road, featured a small brown bear holding a bat inside the letter "C."

1877

Season in a Sentence

Just a year after dominating the National League, the Cubs stagger to a fifth-place finish in a six-team league.

Finish • Won • Lost • Pct • GB

Fifth	26	33	.441	15.5

Manager

Al Spalding

Stats

Stats	Cubs	NL	Rank
Batting Avg:	.278	.271	2
On–Base Pct:	.296	.289	3
Slugging Pct:	.340	.338	3
Home Runs:	0		6
ERA:	3.27	2.81	5
Fielding Avg:	.883	.884	5
Runs Scored:	366		2
Runs Allowed:	375		5

Starting Lineup

Cal McVey, c–sp
Al Spalding, 1b
Ross Barnes, 2b
Cap Anson, 3b–c
John Peters, ss
Paul Hines, lf–cf
Dave Eggler, cf
Jimmy Hallinan, rf
John Glenn, lf
Harry Smith, 2b–cf

Pitchers

George Bradley, sp
Laurie Reis, sp

Attendance

46,454 (second in NL)

Club Leaders

Batting Avg:	McVey	.368
On–Base Pct:	McVey	.387
Slugging Pct:	McVey	.455
Home Runs:	None	0
RBI:	Peters	41
Runs:	McVey	58
Wins:	Bradley	18
Strikeouts:	Bradley	59
ERA:	Bradley	3.31
Saves:	McVey	2

MAY 8 — Two months after Rutherford B. Hayes is inaugurated as president and two weeks after federal troops leave the South, ending the post–Civil War Reconstruction of the former Confederacy, the Cubs open the 1877 season with a 6–5 win over Hartford before 2,000 in Chicago.

The National League reduced its roster from eight teams to six, with New York and Philadelphia out of the circuit. Hartford remained in the league, but played no games in the Connecticut city. Hartford's home contests were held at the Union Grounds in Brooklyn. The New York and Philadelphia franchises were kicked out the league for failing to finish their schedules in 1876.

JUNE 5 — Albert Spalding pitches his last game. Spalding failed to retire any of the five Cincinnati batters he faced and was literally knocked out the box when ex–Cub Bob Addy nailed him with a line drive to the chest. Spalding was replaced by George Bradley and the Cubs went on to win 12–5 in Chicago.

JUNE 26 — The Cubs wallop the St. Louis Browns 11–0 in Chicago with Charley Jones and Jimmy Hallinan from the recently disbanded Cincinnati club.

JULY 4 — Nearly 12,000 attend a 12–2 win over Boston in Chicago. The crowd overflowed the grandstand and surrounded the outfield.

AUGUST 2 — The Cubs score seven runs in the second inning and maul the reorganized Reds 15–1 in Cincinnati.

AUGUST 6 — A dispute over the umpire highlights a 7–2 Chicago win at Louisville. The NL rule called for the home team to submit three names of approved local men for each game, with the visiting team choosing one of the three at random. Cal McVey reached into a hat and picked out a slip with Dan Devinney's name on it. Disgusted, McVey then grabbed the hat and found that all three slips had Devinney's name on them. After a long discussion, Devinney was allowed to continue as the umpire.

AUGUST 7 — The Cubs score 13 runs in the second inning and rout the Reds 21–7 in Chicago. John Peters had five hits in seven at–bats.

Top hitters for the Cubs in 1877 were Cal McVey (.368), Cap Anson (.337), and Peters (.317). Anson led the league in doubles with 19.

AUGUST 9 — The Cubs continue to wallop Cincinnati pitching, winning 13–9 in Cincinnati.

SEPTEMBER 22 — Hartford defeats the Cubs 11–9 in a game played at New Haven, Connecticut.

OCTOBER 2 — The Cubs rout the Reds 13–1 in Chicago. The only Cincinnati run was scored on a home run by Lip Pike that soared over the right field fence at the 23rd Street Grounds. It was one of seven home runs the Cubs allowed in 1877, four of which were at home. The Cubs failed to hit a single home run either at home or on the road all season.

OCTOBER 16 — In the final game of the season, the Cubs beat 1877 National League champion Boston 15–7 in Chicago. It was the last contest played at the 23rd Street Grounds.

NOVEMBER 17   The Cubs secure a lease to build a new ballpark at the southeast corner of Michigan Avenue and Randolph Street. It was on the same site as a previous ballpark that was destroyed in the Great Fire in 1871.

The new facility was called Lakefront Park. Right field extended southward along Michigan Avenue to a point midway between Washington and Madison Streets. The left field fence paralleled Randolph Street. To the east, toward Lake Michigan, lay the yards of the Illinois Central Railroad. The lake itself was just beyond the tracks. Landfills in later years pushed the lakefront farther east. The new park began with a seating capacity of 3,000. The infield was bumpy and littered with rocks, boulders, ashes, glasses, and bottles because the land previously served as a dumping ground for the debris left over from the 1871 fire. The outfield was probably the smallest in big league history because the ballpark was shoehorned into a small, narrow lot. No reliable figures exist as to the field dimensions prior to Lakefront Park's renovation in 1883, but the fences were so close to home plate that any ball hit out of the park in fair territory was a ground–rule double. In 1878, Lip Pike of Cincinnati hit a drive that cleared a freight shed and six freight cars in the railroad yards, but he earned only a two–base hit. The wind off the lake often made attending a game an unpleasant experience because of swirling dust from the infield and the nearby unpaved streets and sandy beaches. Smoke and cinders from the locomotives in the nearby railroad yards also added to the nuisances of attending games at Lakefront Park.

1878   Cubs

Season in a Sentence

The Cubs outscore every team in the league but finish with a .500 record under the uninspired leadership of new manager Bob Ferguson.

Finish • Won • Lost • Pct • GB

Fourth   30   30   .500   11.0

Manager

Bob Ferguson

Stats

Stats	Cubs	NL	Rank
Batting Avg:	.290	.259	1
On–Base Pct:	.316	.279	1
Slugging Pct:	.350	.319	1
Home Runs:	3		3 (tie)
ERA:	2.37	2.30	4
Fielding Avg:	.891	.893	5
Runs Scored:	371		1
Runs Allowed:	331		4

Starting Lineup

Bill Harbidge, c
Joe Start, 1b
Bill McClellan, 2b
Frank Hankinson, 3b
Bob Ferguson, ss
Cap Anson, lf
Jack Remsen, cf
John Cassidy, rf
Jimmy Hallinan, lf

Pitchers

Terry Larkin, sp
Laurie Reis, sp

Attendance

58,691 (first in NL)

Club Leaders

Batting Avg:	Ferguson	.351
	Start	.351
On–Base Pct:	Ferguson	.375
Slugging Pct:	Start	.439
Home Runs:	Three tied	1
RBI:	Anson	40
Runs:	Start	58
Wins:	Larkin	29
Strikeouts:	Larkin	163
ERA:	Larkin	2.24
Saves:	None	0

MAY 1   The Cubs win the season opener 5–4 in Indianapolis.

> *The National League remained a six–team circuit in 1878, with franchises in Indianapolis, Milwaukee, and Providence replacing those from Hartford, Louisville, and St. Louis. The Indianapolis franchise had trouble drawing crowds, however, and played some "home" games in St. Louis and Pittsburgh. By 1878, the only three of the original eight 1876 franchises remaining in the National League were Chicago, Boston, and Cincinnati. The Cincinnati franchise was kicked out of the NL following the 1880 season, but it returned to the league in 1890.*
>
>   *The Cubs had a new manager in 1878 with manager Bob Ferguson replacing Albert Spalding, who remained as team secretary to aid William Hulbert in the front office. Ferguson also played shortstop for Chicago.*

MAY 14   The Cubs play a regular season game at Lakefront Park for the first time and lose 5–3 to Indianapolis. Cold weather limited attendance to 2,500.

MAY 20   Terry Larkin pitches a one–hitter to beat Indianapolis 3–1 at Lakefront Park. The only Indianapolis hit was a first–inning single by Orator Shafer.

> *The Cubs played in 61 games in 1878, and Larkin was the starting pitcher in 56 of them. He pitched a complete game in all 56, hurling a total of 506 innings. Larkin had a record of 29–26 (with one start ending in a tie) and compiled an ERA of 2.24.*

JUNE 6   The Cubs outslug Providence 17–10 at Providence.

> *The leading hitters for Chicago in 1878 were Bob Ferguson (.351), Joe Start (.351), and Cap Anson (.341). Start led the league in hits with 100, and Ferguson led in on–base percentage (.368).*

JUNE 12   Behind the stellar pitching of Terry Larkin, the Cubs defeat Milwaukee 1–0 in ten innings. Chicago player–manager Bob Ferguson drove in the lone run of the game with a single. The game ended when right fielder John Cassidy caught a fly ball and threw out a runner trying to score from third base.

JUNE 15   The Cubs rout the Milwaukee Cream Citys 12–2 at Lakefront Park.

JUNE 22   The Cubs curdle the Cream Citys 14–3 at Milwaukee.

JUNE 27   The Cubs defeat Boston, a club which won the NL pennant in both 1877 and 1878, 16–5 at Lakefront Park. Chicago first baseman Joe Start collected five hits in six at–bats.

JULY 4   The Cubs celebrate the holiday with a 15–7 win over Providence before 8,000 at Lakefront Park.

JULY 6   The Cubs again take measure of Providence pitching with a 16–4 win at Lakefront Park.

JULY 15   The Cubs clobber Milwaukee 14–8 in Milwaukee.

JULY 16	The Cubs trample Milwaukee again 17–10 in Milwaukee.
JULY 29	Because of injuries to their regular catchers, the Cubs use amateur Bill Traffley behind the plate for a game against Indianapolis at Lakefront Park. Traffley was hitless in five at–bats and was credited with eight passed balls, but Chicago survived to win 12–9.
JULY 30	The Cubs defeat Indianapolis 13–3 at Lakefront Park.
AUGUST 15	The Cubs batter Providence pitcher and future Hall of Famer John Montgomery Ward to win 17–3 in Providence. According to the newspaper reports, Ward had trouble gripping the ball to throw his trademark curveball because of the wet grass due to a rain that delayed the start of the contest for twenty minutes.
AUGUST 21	The Cubs score five runs in the ninth inning to stun the Reds 7–4 in Cincinnati.
AUGUST 31	Albert Spalding comes out of retirement to play second base for the Cubs. He was 2–for–4 but made four errors as Chicago lost 5–2 to Boston at Lakefront Park. Spalding never played again in a regular season game, although he did appear in an exhibition contest two days later.
SEPTEMBER 2	The Cubs and Boston play in an exhibition to benefit victims of a yellow fever epidemic. A total of $682 was raised. Albert Spalding pitched for Chicago and 43–year–old Harry Wright for Boston. Wright was Boston's manager, and was one of the founders of the 1869 Cincinnati Red Stockings, baseball's first professional team. Wright hadn't played regularly for eight years, but he beat Spalding and the Cubs 10–5.
SEPTEMBER 16	The Cubs win an exhibition 11–8 against Boston at Lakefront Park in a test of a new rule in which players received a walk after six balls. In 1878, it took nine balls for a walk. *At the conclusion of the season, the nine–ball walk remained on the books. The number of balls necessary for a walk was gradually reduced during the 1880s until it reached the four–ball format in 1889.*
SEPTEMBER 17	Another exhibition between the Cubs and the Boston club tests the idea of the pitcher throwing from a line fifty–one feet from home plate. In 1878, pitchers delivered the ball from a distance of forty–five feet. Pitchers Terry Larkin and Tommy Bond had trouble with the new dimensions, and Chicago won 18–10 at Lakefront Park. *The pitching distance remained at forty–five feet until 1881, when it was lengthened to fifty feet. The sixty–foot, six–inch distance was established in 1893.*
SEPTEMBER 23	After making a few disagreeable calls against the Cubs, umpire Joseph Julian is nearly mobbed after a 9–7 loss to Indianapolis at Lakefront Park. Julian had to escape through the grandstand.

1879

^Cubs

Season in a Sentence

The Cubs win 35 of their first 47 games and lead the league in early August by 5 ½ games, but in what would become a familiar pattern for the franchise, the club collapses down the stretch.

Finish • Won • Lost • Pct • GB

Fourth   46   33   .582 10.5

Manager

Cap Anson

Stats

Stats	Cubs	NL	Rank
Batting Avg:	.259	.255	4
On–Base Pct:	.276	.271	4
Slugging Pct:	.336	.329	4
Home Runs:	3		7
ERA:	2.46	2.50	5
Fielding Avg:	.900	.892	4
Runs Scored:	437		4
Runs Allowed:	411		4

Starting Lineup

Silver Flint, c
Cap Anson, 1b
Joe Quest, 2b
Ned Williamson, 3b
John Peters, ss
Abner Dalrymple, lf
George Gore, cf
Orator Shafer, rf
Jack Remsen, cf

Pitchers

Terry Larkin, sp
Frank Hankinson, sp

Attendance

66,708 (first in NL)

Club Leaders

Batting Avg:	Anson	.317
On–Base Pct:	Anson	.323
Slugging Pct:	Williamson	.447
Home Runs:	Three tied	1
RBI:	Flint	41
Runs:	Williamson	66
Wins:	Larkin	31
Strikeouts:	Larkin	142
ERA:	Larkin	2.44
Saves:	None	0

MAY 1   In Cap Anson's debut as manager, the Cubs open the season with a 4–3 win over the Syracuse Stars at Lakefront Park. The Cubs broke a 2–2 tie with two runs in the eighth.

The National League increased from six teams to eight in 1879. The clubs in Indianapolis and Milwaukee folded. New teams from Buffalo, Cleveland, Syracuse, and Troy, New York, were added. The schedule was also increased from 70 to 84 games. The Cubs lineup was almost completely made over. Silver Flint, Joe Quest, Ned Williamson, and Orator Shafer came from the defunct Indianapolis club, and Abner Dalrymple was added from the Milwaukee team. George Gore was a promising rookie, and Cap Anson moved to first base, a position he held as a Cubs starter until 1897. Dalrymple, Gore, and Williamson were key members of the Chicago teams that dominated the National League during the early and mid–1880s.

MAY 6   The Cubs defeat Troy 12–1 at Lakefront Park.

MAY 10   The Cubs defeat Troy 15–8 to start the 1879 season with six straight wins. After a 14–5 loss to Providence in Chicago on May 12, the Cubs won nine in a row to run their record to 15–1.

JUNE 7   The Cubs hammer the
            Providence Grays 12–0
            at Providence.

JUNE 12   The Cubs capture the Troy
            Trojans 13–3 in Troy,
            New York.

JUNE 14   Silver Flint of the Cubs hits
            a ball over the fence in the
            ninth inning with Chicago
            trailing Troy 10–7 at Troy.
            Flint stopped at third base,
            however, because he wanted
            to force the catcher to play
            close to the batter, giving the
            hitter a better chance. The
            Cubs scored twice, but
            wound up losing 10–9.

JUNE 26   Cap Anson is arrested when
            the Cubs stop for an exhibi-
            tion game in Indianapolis.

The Cubs' 1879 team picture. The club rebounded from a mediocre 1878 season to finish 46–33.

Silver Flint and Orator Shafer, who both played baseball in Indianapolis in 1878, left the city with several unpaid bills. A constable tried to arrest Flint and Shafer at the ballpark because of the debts, but Anson talked the officer out of it, explaining that a crowd had assembled to see the pair play ball and that the arrest might cause a riot. The constable went to the hotel where the Cubs were staying to nab Flint and Shafer after the contest, but the two ballplayers escaped in a carriage that took them beyond the city limits. Anson became engaged in a heated argument with the constable at the hotel, and the Cubs skipper would up being taken to jail for profanity and resisting arrest. Anson was fined $16 by an Indianapolis judge.

The Cubs closed the month of June with a record of 24–4 and a 5½-game lead over second-place Providence.

JULY 5   The Cubs rout Boston 14–6 at Lakefront Stadium.

            *Leading hitters for Chicago in 1879 were Cap Anson (.317), Orator Shafer
            (.304), Ned Williamson (.294), and Abner Dalrymple (.291).*

JULY 11   The Cubs break a 1–1 tie with seven runs in the eleventh inning and go on to defeat
            Syracuse 8–2 at Lakefront Park.

            *The Cubs batted first despite playing at home, because in the nineteenth century
            a pre-game coin flip determined the batting order.*

JULY 15   The Cubs wallop Troy 11–0 at Lakefront Park.

JULY 22   Pitcher Terry Larkin's arm gives out in the ninth inning with the Cubs leading Providence 8–5 at Lakefront Park. The game was stopped to allow Larkin to bathe his arm in ice water for several minutes. He resumed pitching, and although he gave up two more runs, the Cubs emerged with an 8–7 win.

AUGUST 7   The Cubs score three runs in the ninth inning to beat Buffalo 3–2 at Lakefront Park. Frank Hankinson drove in the winning run with a single.

AUGUST 13   The Cubs win a game by forfeit against the Reds in Cincinnati.

At the start of the 3:00 P.M. start of the game, it was raining steadily and the field was muddy. Reds manager Cal McVey declared the field unplayable, but Chicago skipper Cap Anson insisted that the teams play to avoid issuing refunds, even though only 165 fans paid admission. At the time, umpires didn't travel from city to city. The umpires assigned to games lived in the city where the contest was played. According to the NL rules of 1879, the visiting team submitted a list of five umpires, the home team narrowed the list to two, and the visiting team chose between the remaining two. Anson refused to accept either of the men nominated by the Reds and appointed Chicago employee John A. Brown as the umpire of the game. Brown then declared the contest a forfeit because the Reds refused to play. At a league meeting the following December, it was declared a legal Chicago victory.

SEPTEMBER 17   With only eight healthy Chicago players available for a game at Troy, the Cubs borrow Herm Doscher from the Troy club in order to play the contest. The Cubs lost 5–4. Doscher played three games for the Cubs. His son Jack played one game for the Cubs in 1903. The Doschers were the first father and son to both play in the major leagues.

OCTOBER 3   The Cubs embark on a month–long tour of exhibition games in the West, playing in Dubuque, Omaha, Denver, Salt Lake City, and San Francisco.

OCTOBER 16   The Cubs sign King Kelly of the Reds.

At the time, there was no reserve system, and players were free agents at the expiration of their contracts. Cap Anson convinced Kelly to leave Cincinnati and cast his lot with the Cubs. Colorful, versatile, innovative, and immensely talented, Kelly was perhaps the best player of the nineteenth century. He was also a first–class "man about town," who often frustrated Anson with his drunken off–the–field escapades. Kelly played for Chicago through the 1886 season.

1880

Cubs

Season in a Sentence

Chicago cruises to the National League pennant with 67 victories and just 17 losses.

Finish • Won • Lost • Pct • GB

First   67   17   .798   +15.0

Manager

Cap Anson

Stats

Stats	Cubs	NL	Rank
Batting Avg:	.279	.245	1
On–Base Pct:	.303	.267	1
Slugging Pct:	.360	.320	1
Home Runs:	4		7
ERA:	1.93	2.37	3
Fielding Avg:	.913	.901	1
Runs Scored:	538		1
Runs Allowed:	317		2

Starting Lineup

Silver Flint, c
Cap Anson, 1b
Joe Quest, 2b
Ned Williamson, 3b
Tom Burns, ss
Abner Dalrymple, lf
George Gore, cf
King Kelly, rf

Pitchers

Larry Corcoran, sp
Fred Goldsmith, sp

Attendance

66,708 (first in NL)

Club Leaders

Batting Avg:	Gore	.360
On–Base Pct:	Gore	.399
Slugging Pct:	Gore	.463
Home Runs:	Gore	2
RBI:	Anson	74
Runs:	Dalrymple	91
Wins:	Corcoran	43
Strikeouts:	Corcoran	2.68
ERA:	Goldsmith	1.75
Saves:	Corcoran	2

MAY 1   Four months after Thomas Edison receives a patent for the first long–lasting light bulb, the Cubs score two runs in the bottom of the ninth inning to beat the Reds 4–3 in the season opener at Cincinnati. Chicago won the pre–game coin toss and elected to bat last, which set up the game–ending rally. Pitcher Larry Corcoran, playing in his major league debut, started the ninth with a single. Tom Burns reached base on an error that moved Corcoran to third. After Burns stole second, both he and Corcoran scored on Joe Quest's hit. It was the first "walk–off" victory in major league history. Prior to 1880, the bottom half of the last inning was played until there were three outs no matter what the score. Earlier in the contest, King Kelly hit the first Opening Day home run in Cubs history.

There was one change in the National League lineup in 1880. The franchise in Syracuse, New York, folded and was replaced by one in Worcester, Massachusetts. The 1880 season also marked the introduction of the reserve clause, which permitted teams to protect, or reserve, five players for the upcoming season. Prior to 1880, players signed one–year contracts and were free to switch teams the next season. The league adopted the reserve clause to help financially strapped clubs from losing star players to higher bidders. Since most teams began the season with a roster of 11 or 12 players, the clause essentially covered half the team. The number of players who could be reserved grew to 11 in 1883, and was soon broadened to include the entire roster and all players in a club's minor league system. It would be nearly 100 years before the reserve clause was abolished and free–agency returned to baseball.

MAY 7

In the home opener, the Cubs score ten runs in the first inning and hammer the Reds 20–7 at Lakefront Park. George Gore collected six hits in six at–bats and scored five runs, including a steal of home.

MAY 10

The Cubs score seven runs in the fourth inning and thrash the Reds again 15–1 at Lakefront Park.

Catcher Silver Flint severely injured his fingers early in the season, but in the code of the day, played through the injuries, and appeared in 74 of the 86 games. It hampered him while batting, as Flint's average dropped to .162 in 1880 after hitting .284 in 1879. Healthy again in 1881, Flint had a batting average of .310.

George Gore went 6–for–6 in the home opener in 1880 and went on to lead the league in hitting (.360), on–base percentage (.399), and slugging average (.463).

MAY 27

Fred Goldsmith pitches a two–hitter to beat Buffalo 11–0 at Buffalo. The only Buffalo hits were singles by Hardy Richardson and Davy Force.

Goldsmith had a record of 21–3 with an ERA of 1.75 for Chicago in 1880.

JUNE 4

The Cubs and the Providence Grays play sixteen innings to a 1–1 tie at Providence. The game was called by darkness. Larry Corcoran of Chicago and John Montgomery Ward of Providence both pitched complete games. There was considerable pushing and shoving on the base paths during the tension–filled game, which led to some hard feelings. After the contest, Cap Anson threatened Jack Farrell of Providence with a bat, but didn't carry out the threat.

JUNE 26

Abner Dalrymple, George Gore, and Larry Corcoran, all normally left–handed batters, cross over and bat right–handed against southpaw Lee Richmond and get one hit each as Chicago beats Worcester 4–0.

JULY 8

The Cubs win their 21st game in a row with a 5–2 decision over Providence at Lakefront Park. The victory gave Chicago a 35–3 record on the season.

This streak began on June 2. There was one tie game during the 21–game winning streak (see June 4, 1880). Chicago's 21–game streak in 1880 has been surpassed only once in major league history. The 1916 New York Giants won 26 games in a row (with two ties). The 1935 Chicago Cubs also won 21 games in a row in a streak unblemished by a tie game.

JULY 10

Cleveland snaps the Cubs' 21–game winning streak with a 1–0 decision in Cleveland. The lone run of the game was scored in the bottom of the ninth inning on a long drive by Fred Dunlap that scored Jack Glasscock from first base.

JULY 13   John Clarkson wins his 13th game in a row with a 3–0 decision over Cleveland in Cleveland.

AUGUST 5   Larry Corcoran pitches a two–hitter to beat Boston 3–0 at Boston. The only hits off Corcoran were singles by John Morrill and John O'Rourke.

AUGUST 12   In the first home loss since August 25, 1879, the Cubs drop a 6–4 decision to Providence at Lakefront Park.

AUGUST 17   The Cubs hammer Boston 14–6 at Lakefront Park.

AUGUST 19   Appearing in his third game in three days, Larry Corcoran pitches the first no–hitter in Cubs history to win 6–0 against Boston at Lakefront Park. Corcoran had no strikeouts or walks. Four Boston batters reached base on four Chicago errors.

               Corcoran, a rookie in 1880, had a record of 43–14, including a 13–game winning streak, led the league in strikeouts with 268, and compiled an ERA of 1.95. He stood only five–foot–five and weighed a mere 120 pounds, but he pitched 536⅓ innings during the season. Corcoran played for the Cubs until 1885, when his arm went dead, and compiled a record of 175–85. He ranks fourth all–time among Cubs pitchers in victories, sixth in ERA (2.26), fourth in innings pitched (2,338⅓), and sixth in strikeouts (1,086). Corcoran also added two more no–hitters, hurling one in 1882 and another in 1884. He died in 1891 from Bright's disease at the age of 32.

SEPTEMBER 1   The Cubs play two games in one day for the first time. There were two separate admissions for the morning–afternoon double–header at Lakefront Park. In the morning, Chicago defeated Troy 1–0. In the afternoon, Troy was victorious 6–1. Because of an illness to Fred Goldsmith, Larry Corcoran pitched two complete games.

SEPTEMBER 15   The Cubs clinch the 1880 National League pennant with a 5–2 win over the Reds in Cincinnati.

SEPTEMBER 22   Cubs catcher King Kelly utilizes a loophole in the rules to help defeat the Reds 5–3 at Lakefront Park.

               Kelly was a player who always looked for an edge. Beginning in 1880, the third–strike rule was adopted, requiring a catcher to catch a third strike on the fly for the batter to be retired. Cincinnati had the bases loaded with one out in the seventh when Kelly intentionally dropped the third strike, stepped on home to force the runner on third, and threw to first to complete the double play. After the season, the rule was changed stating that the batter was out if first base was already occupied to prevent a re–occurrence.

SEPTEMBER 30   The Cubs defeat Buffalo 10–8 at Lakefront Park to finish the season with a record of 67–17. The winning pitcher was Charlie Guth, who went all nine innings in what proved to be his only major league game. Guth was an amateur from the Chicago neighborhood of Lakeview, where Wrigley Field is now located. He was called on to pitch because Larry Corcoran and Fred Goldsmith were both ill. Guth died in 1883 when he was only 27.

1881   Cubs

Season in a Sentence

With the same lineup that won the pennant in 1880, Chicago takes National League honors for the second year in a row.

Finish • Won • Lost • Pct • GB

First   56   28   .667   +9.0

Manager

Cap Anson

Stats

Stats	Cubs	NL	Rank
Batting Avg:	.290	.260	1
On–Base Pct:	.325	.290	1
Slugging Pct:	.380	.338	1
Home Runs:	12		1 (tie)
ERA:	2.43	2.77	2
Fielding Avg:	.916	.905	2
Runs Scored:	550		1
Runs Allowed:	379		1

Starting Lineup

Silver Flint, c
Cap Anson, 1b
Joe Quest, 2b
Ned Williamson, 3b
Tom Burns, ss
Abner Dalrymple, lf
George Gore, cf
King Kelly, rf
Hugh Nicol, rf–cf

Pitchers

Larry Corcoran, sp
Fred Goldsmith, sp

Attendance

82,000 (first in NL)

Club Leaders

Batting Avg:	Anson	.399
On–Base Pct:	Anson	.442
Slugging Pct:	Anson	.510
Home Runs:	Burns	4
RBI:	Anson	82
Runs:	Gore	86
Wins:	Corcoran	31
Strikeouts:	Corcoran	150
ERA:	Corcoran	2.31
Saves:	None	0

APRIL 30   Nearly two months after James Garfield is inaugurated as president, the Cubs open the season with an 8–5 win versus Cleveland on a wintry day at Lakefront Park. This was the last time that the Cubs opened a season at home until 1907. Club management preferred opening the season on the road because of the often–harsh spring weather in Chicago. Beginning in 1907, the Cubs opened the season at home every other year in an alternating arrangement with the White Sox.

A new franchise in Detroit replaced the one in Cincinnati among the eight National League teams. The only two of the original eight National League franchises established in 1876 that were still in the league in 1881 were Chicago and Boston.

MAY 11   The Cubs break a 2–2 tie with six runs in the eighth inning and defeat Troy 11–3 at Lakefront Park. In the ninth inning, Troy's Roger Connor hit a long drive that became stuck in the center field fence. Connor circled the bases for a home run before the ball was dislodged.

MAY 14   A "rally hen" and the big black dog of Cubs owner William Hulbert helps Chicago win a 4–3 decision over Worcester at Lakefront Park. Cubs players believed that a black hen found near the ballpark was good luck, and in the seventh inning they let the hen run loose on the field with Worcester leading 3–2. In the ninth, the Cubs scored two runs to win 4–3. Chicago's Tom Burns drove in the winning run on a long drive toward the clubhouse, which was in play in left field. Hulbert's dog was sleeping on the clubhouse platform, and Worcester outfielder Buttercup Dickerson was afraid of the animal, or pretended to be. The dog paid no attention to Dickerson, but Worcester claimed interference, a "silly protest" that was overruled by the umpire. It was Worcester's first loss of the season after an 8–0 start.

Six days later, when Boston came to Chicago, a discussion about the dog took place prior to the game. Boston demanded the removal of the animal from the clubhouse platform and that the clubhouse doors be closed to prevent a ball being hit through the opening. "There's no rule covering dogs and doors," barked Hulbert. "But if it will make you any happier, the dog shall be bounced and the door closed."

MAY 20   Trailing 4–1, the Cubs score four runs in the seventh inning to beat Boston 5–4 at Lakefront Park. The winning run was scored when King Kelly "cut" third base by some 30 feet. Kelly was on second base when Cap Anson hit a grounder to Boston second baseman Jack Burdock, who fumbled the ball before throwing to first. There was only one umpire on the field, and he was focused on the play at first base, failing to notice Kelly rounding third well shy of the bag. The run was allowed to stand despite the protests of the Boston club.

MAY 25   Cubs catcher Silver Flint breaks his nose with a foul ball off of his own bat in the first inning of an 11–6 win over Providence at Lakefront Park.

JUNE 7   The Cubs wallop Worcester 13–1 at Worcester. The game was called after eight innings by darkness.

JUNE 13   The Cubs score seven runs in the seventh inning and win 12–5 at Providence.

JUNE 24   Returning home from a long road trip, the Cubs unveil new lavender uniforms and defeat Providence 8–0 at Lakefront Park.

JUNE 25   George Gore sets a major league record with seven steals during a 12–8 win over Providence at Lakefront Park. He reached base on three singles, a walk, and an error. Gore stole second five times, third twice, and scored five runs.

Gore was one of the fastest players of the era, despite standing five-foot-eleven and weighing 195 pounds. He was nicknamed "Piano Legs" because of his thick thighs.

JULY 5   The day after Billy the Kid is shot and killed in New Mexico by Pat Garrett, the Cubs outgun Boston 13–11 at Lakefront Park with two runs in the ninth after Boston tied the contest 11–11 with six tallies in the eighth.

JULY 12   The Cubs score nine runs in the sixth inning and defeat Worcester 12–6 at Lakefront Park. Ned Williamson had five hits, including a homer and a double, in five at-bats.

AUGUST 2   Two weeks after Sitting Bull surrenders to Army authorities, Larry Corcoran pitches a two-hitter to win 4–0 over Buffalo at Lakefront Park. The only hits off Corcoran were singles by Dan Brouthers and Davy Force.

AUGUST 11   The Cubs carve up the Detroit Wolverines 17–0 at Lakefront Park.

AUGUST 23   Pitcher Fred Goldsmith sprains his ankle in the second inning in a game against Detroit at Lakefront Park and is replaced by Larry Corcoran, who was in street clothes working at the gate. Corcoran pitched the rest of the game and was the winning pitcher in a twelve–inning, 8–6 Chicago victory.

During the nineteenth and early twentieth centuries, players who weren't in the starting lineup were expected to earn their pay by working at the turnstiles or on the grounds crew.

Cap Anson managed the Cubs from 1879 to 1897 and was a star player that entire time, leading to a Hall of Fame career.

AUGUST 25   In the final home game of the season, the Cubs lose 7–5 to Detroit amid much pre–game pomp and circumstance at Lakefront Park. The clubhouse was draped with flags. More flags flew from the fences, and engraved and perfumed cards were distributed to fans as souvenirs. The two teams came out of the clubhouse together and marched four abreast to great applause.

AUGUST 30   The Cubs score eight runs in the third inning and defeat the Wolverines 12–8 in Detroit.

SEPTEMBER 5   The Cubs outslug Cleveland 14–9 at Cleveland.

SEPTEMBER 11   The Cubs wallop Buffalo 11–1 at Buffalo.

SEPTEMBER 16   The Cubs clinch the pennant with a 4–0 win at Boston.

SEPTEMBER 27   Eight days after President James Garfield dies from wounds suffered in a July 2 assassination attempt, the Cubs defeat Troy 10–8 in a driving rainstorm at Troy in which the paid attendance was 12. The dozen fans represented the smallest attendance ever at a major league game.

SEPTEMBER 28   A month before the Earps and the Clantons stage their shoot–out at the O. K. Corral in Tombstone, Arizona, King Kelly and Cap Anson hit back–to–back homers in the first inning of a 7–6 win at Worcester. It was the first time that two consecutive Cubs batters hit homers.

DECEMBER 9   The National League votes to experiment with color–coded uniforms for the 1882 season. To help fans identify the players, each wore a uniform of a different color, according to the position they played, in various shades of red, blue, orange, yellow, green, black, and brown. Unfortunately, it was next to impossible for fans and players alike to tell friend from foe, especially on the base paths in the days when few fielders wore gloves. The innovation was scrapped before the 1882 season concluded.

1882

Cubs

Season in a Sentence

The Cubs are in seventh place in early June before surging to their third consecutive NL pennant.

Finish • Won • Lost • Pct • GB

First   55   29   .655   +3.0

Manager

Cap Anson

Stats

Stats	Cubs	NL	Rank
Batting Avg:	.277	.251	1
On-Base Pct:	.307	.279	1
Slugging Pct:	.389	.342	1
Home Runs:	15		5 (tie)
ERA:	2.22	2.89	1
Fielding Avg:	.898	.897	5
Runs Scored:	604		1
Runs Allowed:	353		1

Starting Lineup

Silver Flint, c
Cap Anson, 1b
Tom Burns, 2b–ss
Ned Williamson, 3b
King Kelly, ss–rf
Abner Dalrymple, lf
George Gore, cf
Hugh Nicol, rf
Joe Quest, 2b

Pitchers

Fred Goldsmith, sp
Larry Corcoran, sp

Attendance

128,452 (first in NL)

Club Leaders

Batting Avg:	Anson	.362
On-Base Pct:	Anson	.397
Slugging Pct:	Anson	.500
Home Runs:	Flint	4
RBI:	Anson	83
Runs:	Gore	99
Wins:	Goldsmith	28
Strikeouts:	Corcoran	170
ERA:	Corcoran	1.99
Saves:	None	0

APRIL 10   Seven days after Jesse James is shot to death by a member of his own gang, Cubs president William Hulbert dies of heart disease at the age of 49.

On April 26, the board of directors of the club named Albert Spalding to succeed Hulbert as team president. Spalding had been team secretary since resigning as field manager in 1877. He also became one of the two principal owners, the other being banker John L. Walsh. Spalding served as team president until 1891 and retained a financial interest in the club until 1902.

MAY 1   The National League season opens with the Cubs losing 7–5 to the Buffalo Bisons in Buffalo. Chicago players wore badges of mourning in honor of William Hulbert.

The National League had a rival in 1882 with the formation of the American Association as a second major league. In 1882, the AA had teams in Baltimore, Cincinnati, Louisville, Philadelphia, Pittsburgh, and St. Louis. Relations between the National League and the American Association were generally amicable, as the new league respected the contracts of the older one. The AA folded after the 1891 season.

MAY 5   Cap Anson is called out for walking back to his base instead of running as the rule specified during a 7–6 win over Cleveland at Cleveland.

MAY 10   In the home opener, the Cubs win 8–4 over Cleveland before 1,500 at Lakefront

Park. Chicago broke a 3–3 tie with five runs in the seventh inning.

Watching Cubs games from a vantage point outside the ballpark is a long–time tradition. Approximately 1,000 people viewed the opener for free from a nearby viaduct. Chicago officials unsuccessfully attempted to eliminate this "unfair opportunity to beat the gate" by petitioning City Council to pass a law banning people from stopping on the viaduct during games, but council rejected the suggestion. The Cubs responded by building a 37½–foot–high fence to block views from the viaduct.

MAY 22   The Cubs punish Detroit 12–2 at Lakefront Park.

MAY 30   The Cubs play the Troy Trojans in two different cities. In the morning, Chicago won 9–2 in Albany. The two teams traveled five miles to the town of Watervilet, just across the Hudson River from Troy, where the Cubs lost 5–4 in the afternoon.

                The Cubs were off to a poor start in 1882. The club was 9–13 on June 6 and was in seventh place.

JUNE 12   The Cubs outlast Providence 13–9 in Providence.

JUNE 19   The Cubs thrash Detroit 12–0 in Detroit.

JUNE 20   Pitcher Larry Corcoran hits the first grand slam home run in Cubs history during a 13–3 stomping of Worcester at Lakefront Park. Corcoran hit the historic homer off Lee Richmond in the ninth inning. Larry also had two doubles and a single during the afternoon.

JUNE 21   For the second day in a row, the Cubs defeat Worcester by a 13–3 score at Lakefront Park.

JULY 4   The Cubs score four runs in the fourteenth inning to beat Troy 9–5 in the second game of a double–header at Lakefront Park. Chicago also won the first game 5–1.

JULY 8   The Cubs take first place with a 3–0 win over Troy at Lakefront Park. It was Chicago's ninth win in a row and gave the club a 24–15 record.

                The Cubs held first for about a month before falling to second behind Providence in mid–August.

JULY 11   The Cubs win their tenth game in a row with an 8–3 decision over Detroit at Lakefront Park.

JULY 14   The Cubs score seven runs in the seventh inning and wallop Detroit 23–4 at Lakefront Park. A crowd of 6,000 overflowed the small grandstand and many of them lined the outfield. Balls hit into the crowd in fair territory were doubles, contributing to the high score.

JULY 24   The Cubs pummel Cleveland 35–4 at Lakefront Park. Dave Rowe pitched the complete game for Cleveland. The 35 runs he allowed is the most ever by a major league pitcher in a single game, a record that will likely stand for all eternity. The

31–run victory margin by the Cubs is also a major league record. Normally an out-fielder, Rowe was pressed into emergency service as a pitcher because of injuries to Jim McCormick and George Bradley, Cleveland's two regular hurlers.

JULY 29   Larry Corcoran earns his tenth win in a row in a 17–1 thrashing of the Wolverines in Detroit.

AUGUST 5   The Cubs win 12–2 in Boston.

AUGUST 24   Fred Goldsmith beats Worcester at Worcester for his third complete game victory in three days. He was the only pitcher available because Larry Corcoran left the club to get married.

Fred Goldsmith paced the Cubs with 28 victories in 1882 and picked up 25 more wins in 1883.

Goldsmith was the Cubs leading winner in 1882 with a 28–17 record. Corcoran was 27–12, and his 1.95 ERA led the NL.

SEPTEMBER 5   The Cubs clobber Troy 10–0 at Lakefront Park.

SEPTEMBER 9   The Cubs have a picnic at the expense of Troy, winning 24–1 at Lakefront Park in a game called after eight innings by darkness.

At the conclusion of the game, Chicago was 43–28 and in second place, three games back of Providence.

SEPTEMBER 14   The Cubs take first place by completing a three–game sweep of Providence at Lakefront Park with a 6–2 win.

Chicago remained in first place for the rest of the season and finished three games ahead of Providence. The Cubs won 15 of their last 16 games.

SEPTEMBER 20   Larry Corcoran pitches the second no–hitter of his career, beating Worcester 5–0 at Lakefront Park. Corcoran walked two and struck out three.

SEPTEMBER 22   In a special National League meeting, Troy and Worcester are kicked out the organization and are replaced by clubs from Philadelphia and New York to begin play in 1883. When the expelled teams threaten not to finish the schedule, the Cubs and Providence Grays agree to play a best–of–nine series after the season to determine the league championship.

SEPTEMBER 29   The Cubs clinch first place with an 11–5 win over Buffalo at Lakefront Park.

The Cubs finished the season three games ahead of Providence, but the undisputed league championship was still undecided pending the best–of–nine series agreed to on September 22.

SEPTEMBER 30   At the age of 16, Milt Scott becomes the youngest player in Cubs history. Batting fourth and playing first base in place of the injured Cap Anson, Scott had two hits in five at–bats. Ned Williamson collected five hits, including three doubles, in five at–bats. Larry Corcoran was the winning pitcher, his tenth victory in a row.

This was the only game that Scott played for the Cubs. From 1884 through 1887, he appeared in 340 big league games for three clubs.

OCTOBER 6   The National League champion Cubs play the American Association champion Cincinnati Reds and lose 4–0 in Cincinnati.

OCTOBER 7   The Cubs turn the tables on the Reds by winning 2–0 in the second game of two post–season exhibition contests in Cincinnati.

OCTOBER 10   The Cubs lose 11–4 to the Grays in Providence in the first game of the best–of–nine series to determine the National League champion.

Chicago lost the first three games with Cap Anson playing several regulars out of position, and many accused the club of trying to prolong the series to maximize gate receipts. The Cubs won four of the next five to even the series, with the ninth and deciding game to be played on October 24 at a neutral site in Fort Wayne, Indiana.

OCTOBER 24   The Cubs claim the undisputed NL title by slaughtering the Grays 19–7 in Fort Wayne, Indiana.

Did the Cubs Play in the First World Series?

The first post–season meeting between two first–place teams from rival major leagues took place in 1882 between the National League champion Chicago Cubs and the American Association pennant–winning Cincinnati Reds.

The American Association was formed in November 1881 as competition to the established National League, but the two organizations co-existed in a relatively peaceful fashion. NL clubs, like the Cubs, played exhibition games against many American Association clubs in 1882 during spring training and on off–days during the regular season.

When the regular season ended on October 1, more exhibition games between the two leagues were scheduled. The Cubs met the Reds in Cincinnati on October 6 and 7.

The contests against the Cubs were much anticipated in the Ohio city. Not only had Chicago won the NL pennant for the third year in a row, but Cincinnati had revenge on its mind because the Reds had been kicked out of the league at the end of the 1880 season. The games were not part of a "World Series" to determine a "world champion," however. Although the games were considered a test of the strength of the two pennant–winning clubs, only two contests were scheduled.

Rumors circulated that American Association President Denny McKnight threatened to expel the Reds from the organization if they played the Cubs, but the *Cincinnati Commercial* called the scuttlebutt "the utmost buncombe." It has often been reported in baseball histories that the Reds and Cubs planned a long series to decide the championship and that McKnight's threat stopped the series at two games, but there is no evidence in the newspapers of the day to suggest that any more than two games were planned.

Heading into the October 6 games, the National League had a record of 22–1 against American Association clubs. Given the AA's lack of success against the NL, the Reds were given little chance of standing up against the contingent from Chicago. "The Chicagos are the veteran team of the choice ball–players of the country who have won the league championship for three years," reported the *Commercial*, "and, it

would be folly for any one to expect their defeat at the hands of the Cincinnati team made up of lighter weight material."

Therefore, it was considered a stunning upset when the Reds defeated the Cubs 4–0 in the first of the two games before a crowd of 2,700. The *Cincinnati Enquirer* compared the victory to David's slaying of Goliath. The Cubs rebounded to win the second game 2–0.

There was a post–season series between the AA and NL champs from 1884 through 1890 to determine the "world champion" of baseball. The Cubs participated in 1885 and 1886 against the St. Louis Browns (today's St. Louis Cardinals). Exactly who won the 1885 series is still in dispute. The Browns took the title in 1886.

1883   Cubs

Season in a Sentence

The Cubs fail in their bid for a fourth straight National League pennant, coming in second to Boston.

Finish • Won • Lost • Pct • GB

Second   59   39   .602   4.0

Manager

Cap Anson

Stats

Stats	Cubs	NL	Rank
Batting Avg:	.273	.262	3
On–Base Pct:	.298	.290	4
Slugging Pct:	.393	.360	2
Home Runs:	13		4 (tie)
ERA:	2.78	3.14	4
Fielding Avg:	.879	.891	7
Runs Scored:	679		1
Runs Allowed:	540		4

Starting Lineup

Silver Flint, c
Cap Anson, 1b
Fred Pfeffer, 2b
Ned Williamson, 3b
Tom Burns, ss
Abner Dalrymple, lf
George Gore, cf
King Kelly, rf–c

Pitchers

Larry Corcoran, sp
Fred Goldsmith, sp

Attendance

124,880 (second in NL)

Club Leaders

Batting Avg:	Gore	.334
On–Base Pct:	Gore	.377
Slugging Pct:	Gore	.472
Home Runs:	Kelly	3
RBI:	Anson	68
Runs:	Gore	105
Wins:	Corcoran	34
Strikeouts:	Corcoran	216
ERA:	Corcoran	2.49
Saves:	Anson	1

MAY 1   The Cubs open the season at Detroit and defeat the Wolverines 7–4. Trailing 3–2, Chicago scored five runs in the seventh inning to break the game open.

Teams in New York and Philadelphia replaced those in Worcester and Troy. This was a huge boost for the prestige of the National League, as two small cities were dropped in favor of what were then the two largest cities in the United States. The two new teams are still part of the NL. The Philadelphia club has operated continuously in the City of Brotherly Love as the Phillies. The San Francisco Giants are a direct descendant of the New York franchise. The Giants moved from New York to San Francisco following the 1957 season.

MAY 5   In the home opener, the Cubs lose 3–2 to Detroit at Lakefront Park. Detroit scored two runs in the ninth to win.

Lakefront Park was extensively remodeled during the 1883 season. According to Michael Gershman in his book DIAMONDS, the ballpark was the first "marketed as an attraction in its own right" and set new standards for fan comfort. Lakefront Park had the largest seating capacity in baseball, holding 10,000, including 2,000 in the standing–room section. A pagoda built as a bandstand overlooked the main entrance and provided more room. Baseball's first "skyboxes" sat above the stands on the third–base side. The 18 plush luxury boxes featured armchairs and curtains to keep out the sun and wind. Team owner Albert Spalding had his own box, which included a telephone, an invention patented only in 1876, "to enable him to conduct the details of the game without leaving his seat" and a Chinese gong to summon his employees. (The gong later moved to West Side Park and was used to signal the start of the game.) A bicycle track surrounded the field to supplement Spalding's income on non–playing days. Lakefront Park was staffed by forty–one people, including seven ushers, six policemen, four ticket sellers, three field men, three cushion renters, six refreshment boys, and eight musicians. Despite all this comfort, Lakefront Park was hardly an ideal place to play baseball because of its absurd outfield dimensions. It had the smallest playing field in major league history. The six–foot–high left field fence was just 180 feet away down the left field line, center field was 300 feet, and right field was 196 feet, although there was a 20–foot fence in that direction topped by a 17½–foot tarpaulin to block the view of bystanders on a nearby viaduct. The power alleys were 280 feet to left–center and 252 feet to right–center. In 1883, any ball hit over the fence was a ground-rule double. In 1884, balls over the fence were home runs (see May 29, 1884).

MAY 11   The Cubs outslug Philadelphia 11–9 at Lakefront Park.

This was the first game between the Cubs and the present–day Philadelphia Phillies.

MAY 22   Outfielder Billy Sunday makes his major league debut and strikes out four times in four at–bats in a 4–3 Cubs win over Buffalo at Lakefront Park.

Sunday played for the Cubs as a reserve outfielder until 1887 and in the majors until 1890. After he quit baseball, Sunday became a fiery world–famous evangelist, spearheading the Prohibition movement and attempting to outlaw Sunday baseball. He would often "slide" onto the stage as if sliding into a base.

MAY 30	The Cubs rip the Phillies 15–8 and 22–4 in a double–header at Lakefront Park. In the second game, Chicago scored seven runs in the first inning and nine in the fifth.

JUNE 2 — The Cubs commit 20 errors and lose 22–7 to the Giants in New York.

JUNE 9 — The Cubs whitewash the Grays 11–0 at Providence.

JULY 3 — The Cubs wallop Buffalo 31–7 at Lakefront Park. Abner Dalrymple, King Kelly, and Cap Anson each had five hits, and Dalrymple scored five times. Both Dalrymple and Anson collected four doubles, and Kelly had a triple and a double. As a team, the Cubs collected a major league record 14 doubles. Chicago scored eight runs in the first inning and nine in the ninth. Buffalo pitcher George Derby pitched the complete game, allowing 32 hits along with the 31 runs.

Larry Corcoran won 34 games and struck out 216 in 1883 to lead the Cubs pitching staff.

JULY 25 — The Cubs explode for nine runs in the eleventh inning to win 11–2 at Philadelphia.

JULY 26 — The Cubs score seven runs in the ninth inning and win 17–5 at Philadelphia.

AUGUST 8 — The Cubs commit six errors in the first inning, three of them by center fielder George Gore, and lose 5–1 to the Wolverines at Detroit.

AUGUST 10 — An exhibition game between the Cubs and Toledo of the Northwestern League in Toledo is jeopardized because Cap Anson refuses to play if Toledo's African–American player, Moses Walker, appears in the game.

Toledo management noted that the team had played many other visiting major league teams without incident and declared that it would play Walker regardless of Anson's objections. Anson backed down, Walker played right field, and the Cubs won 7–6 in ten innings. A year later, Toledo joined the American Association and Walker and his brother Welday became the first African–Americans in the majors. The Cubs played another exhibition game in Toledo in 1884, and Anson gained a written guarantee before signing the contact for the game that the Walker brothers would not play. This time Toledo agreed, and the Walkers sat out that contest and all future appearances against the Cubs in the northern Ohio city. Toledo dropped out of the American Asssociation after the 1884 campaign, and Moses and Welday Walker would be the last African–Americans in the majors until the arrival of Jackie Robinson in 1947. It would not be the last time that Cap Anson's white supremacist views kept a black player off the field (see July 14, 1887).

SEPTEMBER 1 — The Cubs score 11 runs in the third inning and pound Cleveland 21–7 at Lakefront Park.

SEPTEMBER 4   The Cubs crush Detroit 13–1 at Lakefront Park.

SEPTEMBER 5   The Cubs have another easy time with Detroit, winning 14–1 at Lakefront Park.

SEPTEMBER 6   The Cubs set a major league record by scoring 18 runs in a single inning during a 26–6 win over Detroit at Lakefront Park. The eruption came in the seventh. Chicago also established records for most hits (18) and total bases (29) in an inning. A total of 23 batters went to the plate. Tom Burns, Fred Pfeffer, and Ned Williamson each had three hits in the 18–run inning to set a major league record. Burns collected two doubles and a homer, Pfeffer two singles and a double, and Williamson also had two singles and a double. Burns and Williamson both scored three runs for another big league record.

SEPTEMBER 8   The Cubs defeat Detroit 12–8 at Lakefront Park. It was Chicago's 11th win in a row. In the four–game series from September 4–8, the Cubs outscored Detroit 65–16.

The Cubs lost their next three games in Boston to eliminate any chance of winning the pennant for the fourth year in a row.

SEPTEMBER 25   The Cubs defeat the Giants 11–10 in New York. The game was called in the seventh inning by darkness.

1884

Season in a Sentence

The Cubs hit 142 homers but lose 14 of their first 20 games and are never a factor in the pennant race.

Finish • Won • Lost • Pct • GB

Fourth   62   50   .554   22.0

Manager

Cap Anson

Stats

Stats	Cubs	NL	Rank
Batting Avg:	.281	.247	1
On–Base Pct:	.324	.287	1
Slugging Pct:	.446	.340	1
Home Runs:	142		1
ERA:	3.03	2.98	4
Fielding Avg:	.886	.899	8
Runs Scored:	834		1
Runs Allowed:	647		5

Starting Lineup

Silver Flint, c
Cap Anson, 1b
Fred Pfeffer, 2b
Ned Williamson, 3b
Tom Burns, ss
Abner Dalrymple, lf
George Gore, cf
King Kelly, rf–c
Billy Sunday, rf

Pitchers

Larry Corcoran, sp
Fred Goldsmith, sp
John Clarkson, sp

Attendance

87,867 (fourth in NL)

Club Leaders

Batting Avg:	Kelly	.354
On–Base Pct:	Kelly	.414
Slugging Pct:	Williamson	.554
Home Runs:	Williamson	27
RBI:	Anson	102
Runs:	Kelly	120
Wins:	Corcoran	35
Strikeouts:	Corcoran	272
ERA:	Clarkson	2.14
Saves:	None	0

MAY 1	In the season opener, the Cubs lose 15–3 to the Giants in New York.

A third major league called the Union Association was formed in 1884 to try to compete with the National League and the American Association. At the start of the season, there were eight teams in the Union Association, including one in Chicago that played on 39th Street on the South Side adjacent to the present-day site of Comiskey Park. The Chicago franchise moved to Pittsburgh in August. The Union Association folded at the end of the 1884 season.

MAY 2	The game in New York is called in the seventh inning by high winds with the Giants leading the Cubs 12–6. The wind blew dust over the field so heavily that the outfielders couldn't see home plate.

MAY 5	The Cubs score eight runs in the third inning and win 12–7 in Philadelphia.

MAY 8	The Cubs wallop the Phillies 13–0 at Philadelphia.

MAY 23	Larry Corcoran pitches a one-hitter to beat the Cleveland Blues 5–0 at Cleveland. The only hit off Corcoran was a single by Pete Hotaling.

MAY 27	Pitcher Fred Goldsmith hits two homers in a 14–6 win over Buffalo at Buffalo.

The Cubs opened the season with a long six-city, 20-game road trip through New York, Philadelphia, Providence, Boston, Cleveland, and Buffalo. Chicago lost 14 of the 20 games.

MAY 29	The Cubs finally play their first home game and win 15–5 over Detroit at Lakefront Park before 2,000 fans chilled by a cold north wind. There were five homers hit in the game. Lead-off hitters Abner Dalrymple of the Cubs and George Wood of the Wolverines began each half of the first inning with homers.

In 1883, balls hit over the wall at Lakefront Park were doubles. In 1884 they were home runs. As a result, the Cubs hit 142 homers during the season. In 57 home games, the Cubs hit 131 homers and allowed 66. On the road, Chicago hit only 11 homers in 56 contests and the pitchers surrendered 17. The 142 homers remained a major league record for a team until the 1927 Yankees hit 158.

Abner Dalrymple, the Cubs' leadoff hitter in 1884, finished among the league leaders with 111 runs, 161 hits, and 22 homers.

MAY 30

Cubs pitcher George Crosby surrenders four runs in the top of the ninth to allow Detroit to take a 10–8 lead, then hits a walk–off homer in the bottom of the inning to cap a three–run Chicago rally that wins the game 11–10 in the first game of a double–header at Lakefront Park. Crosby played only three major league games, and this was his only home run. In the second tilt, Ned Williamson became the first player in major league history to hit three home runs in a game, leading the Cubs to a 12–2 win over Detroit. Williamson also had a double in the game. All four extra base hits came at the expense of Detroit pitcher Stump Weidman.

Williamson was the chief beneficiary of the cozy fences at Lakefront Park. He hit 27 homers in 1884, 25 of them at home. Williamson's 27 homers marked the major league record until Babe Ruth hit 29 for the Red Sox in 1919.

The Home Run Explosion of 1884

Prior to 1920, home runs were a rarity. Most of the outfield fences were much farther away from home plate than those today and weren't designed as home–run barriers. The fences surrounding the ballparks of the nineteenth and early twentieth centuries were built simply to keep out intruders, ensure that those who reached the inside of the grounds paid their way into the enclosure, and followed the often irregular plot on which the ballpark was built. The dimensions of the playing fields varied widely. Foul lines could be less than 200 feet long or longer than 500 feet. Some center field fences were more than 600 feet from home plate.

The eight National League teams in 1883 combined for a total of only 124 homers, an average of just 15.5 per team. The Cubs hit 13 homers in 98 games. A year later, the Chicago Cubs hit the astonishing total of 142 in a 113–game schedule. This was due to the peculiar dimensions of Lakefront Park, where the Cubs played their home games. The six–foot–high left field fence was just 180 feet away down the line, center field was 300 feet, and right field was 196 feet, though there was a 20–foot wooden fence topped by 17 1/2 feet of tarpaulin. The power alleys were 280 feet to left–center and 252 feet to right–center. From 1878 through 1883, any ball hit over the fence was a ground–rule double.

The Cubs decided to change the ground rule in 1884. Any ball that cleared the fence was a homer. There were 197 homers hit at Lakefront Park that season, 131 of them by the Cubs, in just 57 games. There only 28 homers in 56 Cubs road games, just 11 of them by Chicago batters. No other ballpark in the NL other than Lakefront Park in 1884 yielded more than 43 homers. In the 56 games at Recreation Park in Philadelphia, there were only two home runs. The top four home–run hitters in the league were all Cubs. Ned Williamson clouted 27, Fred Pfeffer 25, Abner Dalrymple 22, and Cap Anson 21.

The Cubs abandoned Lakefront Park before the start of the 1885 season and moved to West Side Park. That season the Cubs hit 54 homers, 88 less than in 1884, but it was still more than twice as many as any other club in the NL.

The home–run records of the 1884 Cubs stood until the lively ball was introduced in 1920 and Babe Ruth revolutionized baseball by swinging for the fences. Prior to 1920, the only other major league club to top the 100 home–run mark was the Boston Braves, with 103 in 1894. Ned Williamson's 27 homers in 1884, 25 of which were hit at Lakefront Park, stood until Ruth hit 29 in 1919. The club record of 142 wasn't surpassed until the 1927 Yankees clouted 158.

JUNE 7   The Cubs walk over Cleveland 13–6 at Lakefront Park.

JUNE 16   Suffering from an injured finger on his right hand, right–handed pitcher Larry Corcoran tries to throw left–handed before moving to shortstop in the fourth inning in a game at Buffalo. He was succeeded on the mound by King Kelly, Fred Pfeffer and Ned Williamson in the 20–9 Chicago loss. Corcoran's finger healed quickly. Eleven days later he pitched a no–hitter.

JUNE 21   The Cubs win 11–7 at Boston in a game in which the Boston club played for more than seven innings with only eight men. Under the rules of the day, no substitutions were allowed unless a player was severely injured, and then only if the umpire allowed the replacement. Boston center fielder Jim Manning sprained his ankle in the second inning and was unable to continue, but the umpire refused to allow a substitute to take the field. Boston played the rest of the way with eight men.

JUNE 24   The Cubs hit five homers and defeat Boston 13–6 at Lakefront Park. Ned Williamson hit two home runs, and Abner Dalrymple, Cap Anson, and Fred Pfeffer added one each.

          On the same day, a Chicago judge ruled that the Cubs must take down their 37½–foot right field fence at the end of the 1884 season. The fence was erected to keep fans on a nearby viaduct from watching games for free. A suit against the club claimed the barrier illegally blocked the lake view and prevented landowners to the west from enjoying the benefits of lake breezes.

JUNE 27   Larry Corcoran pitches the third no–hitter of his big league career, defeating Providence 6–0 at Lakefront Park. He struck out six and walked one.

JUNE 30   King Kelly hits a walk–off homer in the ninth inning to beat Providence 5–4 at Lakefront Park.

JULY 1   The Cubs rout Philadelphia 14–0 at Lakefront Park.

JULY 4   Ned Williamson hits a grand slam during a 22–3 win over Philadelphia in the second game of a double–header at Lakefront Park. The Cubs scored seven runs in the fifth inning. The winning pitcher was Fred Andrus, who went all nine innings in the only major league game he pitched. His only other big league experience was eight games as an outfielder with the Cubs in 1876. Chicago also won the first game 3–1.

JULY 15   The Cubs give Larry Corcoran's brother Mike a big league trial with disastrous results. In what proved to be the only major league game of his career, Mike Corcoran threw five wild pitches in a 14–0 loss at Detroit.

JULY 29   The Cubs whip Detroit 16–3 at Lakefront Park.

JULY 31   In his major league debut, John Hibbard throws a shutout to lead the Cubs to a 4–0 triumph over Detroit at Lakefront Park.

          Hibbard was a Chicago amateur pitcher who was given a chance because of injuries to the pitching staff. He appeared in only one other big league game, and was the losing pitcher.

AUGUST 5   Deaf–mute pitcher Thomas Lynch makes his major league debut with the Cubs and pitches into the seventh inning before his arm gives out. When the umpire refused to let Lynch leave the game, he switched positions with first baseman Cap Anson, who gave up four runs in the 8–5 loss to Cleveland. Lynch never appeared in another big league game. It was also the last of three games that Anson appeared in as a pitcher during his 22–year career with the Cubs.

AUGUST 6   Cap Anson hits three homers off Sam Moffett of Cleveland during a 13–4 win at Lakefront Park. Anson also hit two homers in the August 5 contest. His five homers in two consecutive games set a major league record. The only other Cubs players with five homers in consecutive games are Billy Williams in 1968 and Dave Kingman in 1979.

AUGUST 11   A crowd of 2,000 at Lakefront Park watches the Cubs lose by a forfeit and play to a tie in a double–header against Buffalo. In the first inning of the first game, George Gore was the runner on first base when King Kelly hit a grounder to second base-man Hardy Richardson. After Gore was forced out, he threw his arms around Richardson to prevent him from completing the double play. Umpire Stewart Decker declared both Gore and Kelly out. Cap Anson objected, claiming that Kelly couldn't be called out for Gore's indiscretion. After a long argument, Anson pulled his team off the field, and Decker forfeited the game to Buffalo. After a wait of a half–hour, Anson decided to play the second game, a makeup of a postponed contest from ear-lier in the season. After nine innings, the game was called on account of darkness with the score 6–6.

AUGUST 14   Five Cubs homers highlight a 17–10 win over Buffalo at Lakefront Park. Abner Dalrymple hit two homers, and Cap Anson, Fred Pfeffer, and King Kelly added one each. Kelly's homer was a grand slam in the second inning off Billy Serad.

SEPTEMBER 2   The Cubs outslug Buffalo 12–9 at West Side Park.

SEPTEMBER 10   The Cubs score seven runs in the first inning and go on to win 16–6 over the Phillies in Philadelphia.

SEPTEMBER 11   The Cubs hammer the Phillies for the second day in a row, winning 19–2 at Philadelphia. The game was called after eight innings by darkness.

SEPTEMBER 15   The Cubs play an exhibition game against the Louisville club in the American Association, drawing an astonishing crowd of 22,000 at Eclipse Park in Louisville. Chicago won the game 11–7.

SEPTEMBER 16   Fred Pfeffer collects five hits, including a homer, during a 17–0 rout of Boston at Lakefront Park.

SEPTEMBER 17   The Cubs pound on Boston again 18–9 at Lakefront Park.

SEPTEMBER 27   The Cubs, with 10 runs in the first inning, beat Providence 15–10 at Lakefront Park.

SEPTEMBER 30   John Clarkson strikes out seven batters in a row, and 13 during the game, in a 17–2 rout of the Giants at Lakefront Park. The Cubs scored nine runs in the fourth inning.

OCTOBER 2   Trailing 5–0, the Cubs score eight runs in the seventh inning and defeat the Giants 9–5 at Lakefront Park.

OCTOBER 9   Jack Manning hits three homers for Philadelphia, but the Cubs hit five home runs of their own and win 19–7 at Lakefront Park. Pitcher John Clarkson hit two homers, and Cap Anson, Fred Pfeffer, and Tom Burns added one each.

OCTOBER 3   The Cubs hammer the Giants 13–6 at Lakefront Park.

OCTOBER 10   Ned Williamson hits a walk–off homer in the ninth inning to beat the Phillies 4–3 at Lakefront Park.

The 1884 season was the last one that the Cubs played at Lakefront Park. The site was owned by the city of Chicago, and the Illinois Central made an offer of $800,000 for the land, about half of its value. The U.S. government obtained a federal court injunction against the sale because the city was prohibited from selling it. It had been given to the city by the government with the stipulation that the site not be used for a commercial venture. By the start of the 1885 season, the Cubs built a new ballpark on the West Side (see June 6, 1885).

1885   Cubs

Season in a Sentence

The Cubs win more than three–fourths of their games and nose out the New York Giants in a thrilling pennant race.

Finish • Won • Lost • Pct • GB

First   87   25   .777   + 2.0

Manager

Cap Anson

Stats

Stats	Cubs	NL	Rank
Batting Avg:	.264	.241	2
On–Base Pct:	.320	.284	1
Slugging Pct:	.385	.322	1
Home Runs:	54		1
ERA:	2.23	2.82	2
Fielding Avg:	.903	.905	4
Runs Scored:	834		1
Runs Allowed:	470		1

Starting Lineup

Silver Flint, c
Cap Anson, 1b
Fred Pfeffer, 2b
Ned Williamson, 3b
Tom Burns, ss
Abner Dalrymple, lf
George Gore, cf
King Kelly, rf–c
Billy Sunday, rf

Pitchers

John Clarkson, sp
Jim McCormick, sp
Ted Kennedy, sp
Larry Corcoran, sp

Attendance

117,519 (third in NL)

Club Leaders

Batting Avg:	Gore	.313
On–Base Pct:	Gore	.405
Slugging Pct:	Anson	.461
Home Runs:	Dalrymple	11
RBI:	Anson	108
Runs:	Kelly	124
Wins:	Clarkson	53
Strikeouts:	Clarkson	308
ERA:	Clarkson	1.85
Saves:	Pfeffer	2
	Williamson	2

APRIL 30   Eight weeks after Grover Cleveland is inaugurated as president, succeeding Chester Arthur in the White House, the Cubs open the season with a 3–2 loss at St. Louis.

The new franchise in St. Louis, nicknamed the Maroons, replaced the one in Cleveland, which folded at the end of the 1884 season.

MAY 8   The Cubs score nine runs in the fifth inning and win 13–4 at Buffalo.

MAY 19   The Cubs score six runs in the first inning and win 11–9 against the Phillies in Philadelphia.

MAY 26   The Cubs outslug the Boston Braves to win 11–10 at Boston.

Chicago opened the 1885 season with a seven–city road trip, traveling to St. Louis, Buffalo, New York, Philadelphia, Boston, Providence, and Detroit. The first home game wasn't played until June 6.

JUNE 6   The Cubs new ballpark, called West Side Park, opens with a 9–2 win over St. Louis before 10,327. George Gore had two homers, a triple, and a single.

West Side Park was located at the corner of Congress and Throop Streets. It was even more lavish than Lakefront Park, with the woodwork painted a terra–cotta shade. It was surrounded by a twelve–foot–high brick wall. The ballpark had seating for 10,000 and included private roof boxes in addition to facilities for track, cycling, and lawn tennis. It also offered a "neatly furnished toilet room with a private entrance for ladies." Spectators entered the stands by a sixteen–foot–wide stairway. The ballpark was bathtub–shaped, with 216–foot foul lines and a deep center field. Fans arriving by carriage could reach the grandstand through a covered entrance inside the grounds and park their vehicles in deep center field. The carriages were in play, although few balls were ever hit that far. West Side Park wasn't quite the home run haven that Lakefront Park provided, but it was still a relatively easy poke to pull the ball over the right and left field fences. From 1885 through 1890, Cubs batters hit 318 home runs at West Side Park, but only 92 on the road. During the same period, Cubs pitchers gave up 230 homers at home and 86 on the road.

JUNE 15   The Cubs score seven runs in the fifth inning and win 13–5 in Detroit.

JUNE 20   John Clarkson baffles Buffalo with a one–hitter to win 5–0 at West Side Park. The only Buffalo hit was a single by Bill Crowley. It was the Cubs 16th win in a row.

JUNE 24   John Clarkson tosses a two–hitter to defeat Philadelphia 12–2 at West Side Park to run the Cubs' winning streak to 18 games and the season record to 32–6. The only Philadelphia hits were a double by Joe Mulvey and a single by Al Myers.

JUNE 25   The Cubs 18–game winning streak comes to an end with a 2–0 defeat at the hands of Philadelphia at West Side Park.

JUNE 29   The Cubs outlast Boston 14–10 at West Side Park.

JUNE 30   The Cubs proceed to pound Boston pitching, winning 13–9 at West Side Park.

JULY 1   The terrific batting prowess of Chicago batters continues unabated, as the Cubs win 24–10 against Boston at West Side Park. The Cubs scored 18 runs in the last three innings, including eight in the seventh. Tom Burns hit a home run estimated at 500 feet.

JULY 9   George Gore sets a major league record (since tied) with five extra–base hits in a game. Gore had three doubles and two triples in an 8–5 win over Providence at West Side Park.

JULY 23   The Cubs splatter Boston 12–2 in Boston.

JULY 24   The Cubs score seven runs in the second inning and wallop Boston 14–5 at Boston.

JULY 27   John Clarkson pitches a no–hitter to beat the Providence Grays 4–0 at Providence. Clarkson struck out four batters and walked no one. The only three Providence base runners reached on errors, one of them by Clarkson.

JULY 29   The Cubs beat the Grays 3–2 in a fourteen–inning struggle at Providence. Clarkson and Old Hoss Radbourne, both future Hall of Famers, pitched complete games. Cap Anson drove in the winning run with a two–out sacrifice fly.

JULY 30   John Clarkson shuts out the Phillies 2–0 in Philadelphia.

In a four–day span, Clarkson pitched 31 innings and allowed only two runs and eight hits.

JULY 31   Jim McCormick pitches a one–hitter to beat the Phillies 9–0 in Philadelphia. The only hit off McCormick was a single by Jack Manning.

John Clarkson leads the league in wins with a whopping 53 and completes 68 of the 70 games in which he pitches in 1885.

AUGUST 4   A Cubs batting display results in a 13–3 win over the Phillies at Philadelphia.

AUGUST 31   The Cubs rout Detroit 16–6 at West Side Park.

SEPTEMBER 4   Buffalo plays a "home" game against the Cubs in Milwaukee. It was a makeup of a postponed game in Buffalo earlier in the season, and since the two clubs weren't scheduled there again before the season ended, they agreed to play at a neutral site in Milwaukee. The Cubs won 12–9. It was Jim McCormick's 14th win in a row.

SEPTEMBER 5   John Clarkson strikes out 13 batters to beat Buffalo 6–0 at West Side Grounds.

SEPTEMBER 16   John Clarkson wins his 50th game of the season in a 10–3 decision over Boston at West Side Park. The contest was called after seven innings by darkness.

Clarkson had a record of 53–16 in 1885, his third season in the majors and second with the Cubs. He led the National League in wins, games pitched (70), games started (70), complete games (68), innings pitched (623), shutouts (10), and strikeouts (318). Clarkson was 137–57 in four seasons with Chicago, but was sold to Boston in 1888 after demanding a salary increase. He finished his career in 1894 with 329 wins and was elected to the Hall of Fame in 1963.

SEPTEMBER 23   Short of pitchers because of injuries, Providence uses 21-year-old Chicago amateur Charlie Hallstrom to pitch a game against the Cubs at West Side Park. Hallstrom was born in Jonkoping, Sweden, and was nicknamed the "Swedish Wonder," but the Cubs knocked his pitches all over the lot. Chicago won 16–8 and Hallstrom never pitched another big league game.

SEPTEMBER 25   The Cubs play at Milwaukee again with Providence as the "home" team to make up a postponed game scheduled earlier in the year in the Rhode Island city. The Cubs won 21–3.

The Cubs won more than three-fourths of their games in 1885, but were unable to shake the New York Giants. Heading into a four-game series played between the Cubs and Giants at West Side Park on September 29 through October 2, Chicago had a two-game lead, with a total of eight contests left on the schedule. The series drew national interest. Newspapers from around the nation sent reporters to cover the games.

SEPTEMBER 29   The Cubs beat the Giants 7–4 before 10,000 at West Side Park in the first of a critical four-game series.

SEPTEMBER 30   The Cubs take the second game of the series against the Giants at West Side Park 2–1 before 11,300. There were eight future Hall of Famers in the game. Cap Anson, King Kelly, and John Clarkson played for Chicago, and Jim O'Rourke, Roger Connor, Buck Ewing, Tom Keefe, and Monte Ward for New York.

OCTOBER 1   The Cubs win their third straight over the Giants by an 8–3 score at West Side Park to all but wrap up the National League pennant. Chicago had a five-game lead with five games left to play.

The Cubs finished the season with an 87–25 record. The Giants were 85–27. The Cubs met the American Association champion St. Louis Browns to determine the "world championship" of baseball. It was the second time that the National League and American Association pennant-winners met in a post-season championship series. In 1884, the Providence Grays played the New York Metropolitans. The Browns were managed by Charlie Comiskey, who later founded the Chicago White Sox in 1900 and owned the club until his death in 1931. Comiskey was also the St. Louis first baseman. The Browns are the predecessors of the present-day St. Louis Cardinals. The Browns moved to the National League in 1892 and were renamed the Cardinals. Thus, the 1885

World Series between the two clubs was the beginning of the long–standing Cubs–Cardinals rivalry. The original schedule for the 1885 series called for one game in Chicago, three in St. Louis, and seven more in Pittsburgh, Cincinnati, Baltimore, Philadelphia, and Brooklyn. The contests in the latter three cities were never played, as the series turned into a complete fiasco.

OCTOBER 14   In game one of the 1885 World Series, the Cubs and the Browns play to a 5–5 tie, called after eight innings by darkness before a crowd of 2,000 at West Side Park. St. Louis took a 5–0 lead in the fourth and was still on top 5–1 heading into the eighth when the Cubs scored four runs on a walk, two singles, and a three–run homer by Fred Pfeffer.

The contest was preceded by field events. Ned Williamson won the throwing contest by tossing a ball 400 feet and four inches. Fred Pfeffer was the fastest circling the bases with a time of 15 ¾ seconds.

OCTOBER 15   The Cubs win game two in St. Louis by forfeit. The Cubs led 5–4 in the sixth inning when Browns manager Charlie Comiskey pulled his team off the field, objecting to the decisions of umpire David Sullivan. The crowd swarmed all over the grounds, and Sullivan needed police protection to leave the ballpark. Once in the safety of his hotel room, Sullivan forfeited the game to Chicago. He didn't umpire any more games in the series.

George Gore showed up for the second game drunk and unable to play, and was suspended for the remainder of the series.

OCTOBER 16   The Browns win game three against the Cubs, scoring five unearned runs with two out in the top of the first and holding on for a 7–4 win in St. Louis.

OCTOBER 17   The Cubs lose game four 3–2 in St. Louis. The Browns scored first with a run in the third, but Abner Dalrymple hit a two–run homer in the fifth to give Chicago a 2–1 lead. In the bottom of the eighth, however, St. Louis scored twice and held on for a 3–2 win. The right fielder for the Cubs was St. Louis amateur Bug Holliday, who was 17 years old. He was pressed into service because of injuries and the suspension of George Gore. Holliday later played in the majors from 1889 through 1898 and hit .316.

After the fourth game, the series took a five–day break. During the interruption, the Cubs played two exhibition games against the Cincinnati Reds of the American Association in Cincinnati, and the Browns played the St. Louis Maroons of the National League.

OCTOBER 22   The Cubs–Browns series moves to Pittsburgh for game five. Only 500 fans saw the Cubs win 9–2. The contest was called after seven innings by darkness.

OCTOBER 23   The Cubs win game six 9–2 in Cincinnati. Jim McCormick stopped the Browns on only two hits.

Poor crowds in Pittsburgh and Cincinnati compelled the Cubs and Browns to cancel the games at the neutral sites in the eastern cities of Baltimore, Philadelphia, and Brooklyn. It was also agreed to throw out game two, which *was forfeited to the Cubs, which left the series even with each team winning two games with the other contest a tie. The two clubs further consented to make the October 24 game in Cincinnati the last of the series, with the victor taking the championship and the winner–take–all prize money of $1,000.*

OCTOBER 24   The Browns take the 1885 championship by defeating the Cubs in a 13–4 runaway in Cincinnati. John Clarkson was scheduled to pitch, but he missed the carriage taking the club to the ballpark because he overslept. Although Clarkson arrived in another conveyance in time for the start of the game, Cap Anson put in Jim McCormick as the pitcher. McCormick pitched nine innings the day before, and wasn't up to the task. He gave up ten runs in the first four innings.

After St. Louis won the title, Cubs manager Cap Anson decided his club should retain its forfeit win after all, and a select committee agreed, leaving the series in a draw, with three wins for Chicago, three for St. Louis, and one tie. The winning prize money of $1,000 was split evenly between the two teams.

1886   Cubs

Season in a Sentence

For the second year in a row, the Cubs win more than 70 percent of their games, but they need every one of them to stave off a strong challenge from Detroit in a race that isn't decided until the final day of the season.

Finish • Won • Lost • Pct • GB

First   90   34   .726   + 2.5

Manager

Cap Anson

Stats

Stats	Cubs	NL	Rank
Batting Avg:	.279	.251	2
On–Base Pct:	.348	.300	1
Slugging Pct:	.401	.342	1
Home Runs:	53		1 (tie)
Stolen Bases:	213		2
ERA:	2.54	3.29	2
Fielding Avg:	.912	.916	4
Runs Scored:	900		1
Runs Allowed:	555		3

Starting Lineup

Silver Flint, c
Cap Anson, 1b
Fred Pfeffer, 2b
Tom Burns, 3b
Ned Williamson, ss
Abner Dalrymple, lf
George Gore, cf
King Kelly, rf–c
Jimmy Ryan, lf

Pitchers

John Clarkson, sp
Jim McCormick, sp
Jocko Flynn, sp

Attendance

142,438 (third in NL)

Club Leaders

Batting Avg:	Kelly	.388
On–Base Pct:	Kelly	.483
Slugging Pct:	Anson	.544
Home Runs:	Cap Anson	10
RBI:	Anson	147
Runs:	Kelly	155
Stolen Bases:	Kelly	53
Wins:	Clarkson	36
Strikeouts:	Clarkson	313
ERA:	Flynn	2.24
Saves:	Three tied	1

APRIL 30   The Cubs open with a 6–5, thirteen–inning win over the Kansas City Cowboys in Kansas City. The Cubs arrived in Kansas City from Hot Springs, Arkansas, where the club conducted its first out–of–town spring training.

       The franchises in Buffalo and Providence folded at the end of the 1885 season, and were replaced by new ones in Kansas City and Washington.

MAY 6   Two days after the Haymarket Riot in Chicago, which results in the death of eleven people including seven police officers, the Cubs play their first home game of the season and win 5–1 over Detroit before a crowd of 6,000 in teeth–chattering weather at West Side Park.

JUNE 14   Cubs rookie Jocko Flynn strikes out 13 batters in a 6–1 win over Kansas City at West Side Park.

       Flynn was only 21 years old when the 1886 season started. He posted a sensational 23–6 record, which included a 14–game winning streak, and also played 28 games in the outfield. The 257 innings he pitched that season ruined his arm, however. With the exception of one game as an outfielder in 1887, Flynn never played again in the majors after his rookie campaign.

JUNE 17   The Cubs score seven runs in the fifth inning and defeat the St. Louis Maroons 11–3 at West Side Park.

JUNE 22   Cap Anson is fined $110 for whining about the decisions of umpire John Gaffney during a 5–4 loss to the Wolverines in Detroit.

JULY 7   The Cubs pound the Giants 21–9 at West Side Grounds.

JULY 8   With first place at stake, 12,000 jam into West Side Park for a game between the Cubs and Detroit. The park was decorated, including an arch with the words "Welcome Detroit." At 3:00 P.M., a procession arrived, headed by a platoon of Chicago police and followed by the First Regiment Band, carriages carrying the Chicago and Detroit players, and 300 rooters who traveled from Detroit to root for their Wolverines. The Detroiters marched under the arch to great cheers from the Chicago fans. The Cubs won the game 9–4.

JULY 15   The Cubs defeat the Kansas City Cowboys 14–2 in Kansas City.

JULY 17   The Cubs down the Cowboys again 14–8 in Kansas City.

JULY 20   The Cubs score seven runs in the first inning and roll to a 20–4 win over St. Louis at West Side Park.

JULY 22   The Cubs slaughter Kansas City 14–1 at West Side Park.

       On the same day, news leaked out that Cubs owner Albert Spalding hired detectives to follow the players and report on their drinking habits. Seven players were fined $25 each.

JULY 28   The Boston Braves leave the field for fifteen minutes after a dispute with the umpires, then return to defeat the Cubs 3–2 in eleven innings in Boston. In the tenth inning with the score 2–2, John Morrill of Boston scored the apparent winning run on a sacrifice fly. Cap Anson argued that Morrill left the base early, and umpire John Eagan agreed. Angry over the decision, the Boston players left the field but were persuaded to return after a quarter of an hour with the threat of a forfeit.

AUGUST 6   The Cubs win 11–0 in Washington.

Pitcher Jocko Flynn, who finished the season with a batting average of only .200, batted leadoff. He hit at the top of the order because he was a right-handed batter and Washington started lefty pitcher Dupee Shaw. Cap Anson was among the first managers in baseball to adjust his lineup when an opposing left-handed pitcher started the game. In such games, left-handed swingers Abner Dalrymple and George Gore, who normally batted 1–2 in the order, were shifted to the bottom of the lineup.

AUGUST 17   The Cubs rout Kansas City 15–1 at West Side Park.

AUGUST 18   John Clarkson strikes out 16 batters in a 7–1 win over Kansas City at West Side Park. The 16 strikeouts was a Cubs record for a nine-inning game until Kerry Wood fanned 20 in 1998.

AUGUST 23   John Clarkson one-hits Detroit 4–0 in Detroit. The only hit off Clarkson was a single by Deacon White in the eighth inning.

Clarkson had a record of 36–17 in 1886 with an ERA of 2.41.

AUGUST 24   Cap Anson scores six runs during an 18–6 win over Boston at West Side Park. The Cubs scored seven runs in the fourth inning.

AUGUST 26   The Cubs take first place with a 10–4 win over Boston at West Side Park.

AUGUST 27   The Cubs score a baker's dozen runs and win by an even dozen in a 13–1 victory over Philadelphia at West Side Park.

The leading hitters for the Cubs in 1886 were King Kelly (.388), Cap Anson (.371), Jimmy Ryan (.306), George Gore (.304), and Tom Burns (.276). Kelly led the league in batting average, runs (155), and on-base percentage (.483), Anson in RBIs (147), and Gore in walks (102).

King Kelly led the 1886 Cubs and the NL in batting (.388), runs (155), and on-base percentage (.483).

AUGUST 30	The Cubs score seven runs in the first inning and lead 11–1 after seven, then withstand a furious Philadelphia rally to win 12–10 at West Side Park.
SEPTEMBER 1	With the help of 14 walks and five wild pitches from Washington pitcher Cannonball Crane, the Cubs win 15–2 at West Side Park.
SEPTEMBER 2	A two–run walk–off triple from Cap Anson beats Washington 5–4 at West Side Park.
SEPTEMBER 8	Jimmy Ryan hits a grand slam off Mickey Welch during an eight–run sixth inning, highlighting a 12–3 win over the Giants at West Side Park.
SEPTEMBER 10	Dan Brouthers hits three homers, a double, and a single for Detroit, but the Cubs win 14–8 at West Side Park.
SEPTEMBER 11	The Cubs rout Detroit 14–4 at West Side Park to take a 3 ½–game lead in the pennant race.
SEPTEMBER 13	The Cubs win 1–0 in St. Louis behind the pitching of Jocko Flynn. George Gore drove in the winning run with a single.
SEPTEMBER 16	Playing on a wet and muddy field after a long morning rain, the Cubs slip and slide their way to a 7–2 win at Kansas City. According to the newspaper reports, "the players looked as though they emerged from the plastering stage of a mud bath" and that the "ludicrous flounderings of the players evoked much mirth among the audience."
SEPTEMBER 22	There was trouble on the way to the Detroit ballpark, where the Cubs won 6–4 in a contest called after six innings by darkness.

During the nineteenth century, visiting players dressed at the hotel and traveled to the ballpark in full uniform in carriages. On this day, someone threw a rock into one of the carriages carrying the Cubs and hit one of the players. King Kelly and Tom Burns took off after the assailant, and Burns was hit by a man in the crowd. The assemblage closed in on them and "several umbrellas were brandished threateningly." Burns suffered a dislocated thumb during the altercation and missed three weeks.

OCTOBER 9	On the final day of the season, the Cubs clinch the pennant by routing Boston 12–3 at Boston in a contest called after seven innings by darkness. Detroit had a chance to win the pennant if it swept a double–header in Philadelphia combined with a Cubs loss. Detroit lost both games.

The Cubs played the St. Louis Browns in the 1886 World Series in a rematch of the controversial 1885 series between the two clubs. The Cubs and Browns agreed to a best–of–seven series with the winner taking all of the prize money, amounting to about $14,000.

OCTOBER 18	The 1886 World Series begins in Chicago with the Cubs defeating the Browns 6–0 behind the five–hit shutout pitching of John Clarkson.
OCTOBER 19	The Browns even the series by trouncing the Cubs 12–0 in Chicago in a game shortened to eight innings by darkness. Bob Caruthers pitched a two–hitter for St. Louis.

OCTOBER 20   The Cubs regain the lead in the series by winning 11–4 over the Browns in Chicago. King Kelly and George Gore hit home runs for the Cubs.

OCTOBER 21   The Browns break a 5–5 tie by scoring three times in the sixth inning to beat the Cubs 8–5 in St. Louis in game four. The game was called after seven innings by darkness.

OCTOBER 22   The Browns move within one win of the world championship by defeating the Cubs 10–3 in St. Louis in game five. John Clarkson, Jim McCormick, and Jocko Flynn were all unavailable because of injuries or fatigue, forcing the Cubs to use Ned Williamson and Jimmy Ryan as pitchers.

OCTOBER 23   The Browns defeat the Cubs 4–3 in ten innings in game six to win the 1886 World Series. The game was interrupted in the fifth inning with the Cubs leading 2–0 by rain and a rowdy crowd that poured onto the field. Chicago added another tally in the sixth, but the Browns tied the game with three in the eighth and won it in the tenth. The winning run was scored when Curt Welch tried to steal home and John Clarkson threw the ball past catcher King Kelly.

1887 — Cubs

Season in a Sentence

The Cubs sell four regulars, including the entire starting outfield, to rival teams and fail to repeat as National League champions.

Finish • Won • Lost • Pct • GB

Third   71   50   .587   6.5

Manager

Cap Anson

Stats

Stats	Cubs	NL	Rank
Batting Avg:	.271	.269	5
On–Base Pct:	.336	.326	4
Slugging Pct:	.412	.381	2
Home Runs:	80	1	
Stolen Bases:	382	2	
ERA:	3.46	4.05	1
Fielding Avg:	.914	.915	4
Runs Scored:	813		5
Runs Allowed:	716		3

Starting Lineup

Tom Daly, c
Cap Anson, 1b
Fred Pfeffer, 2b
Tom Burns, 3b
Ned Williamson, ss
Marty Sullivan, lf
Jimmy Ryan, cf
Billy Sunday, rf–cf
Silver Flint, c
George Van Haltren, rf –p
Dell Darling, rf–c
Bob Pettit, rf

Pitchers

John Clarkson, sp
Mark Baldwin, sp
George Van Haltren, sp

Attendance

217,070 (fourth in NL)

Club Leaders

Batting Avg: Anson	.347
On–Base Pct: Anson	.422
Slugging Pct: Anson	.517
Home Runs: Pfeffer	16
RBI: Anson	102
Runs: Ryan	117
Stolen Bases: Pfeffer	57
Wins: Clarkson	36
Strikeouts: Clarkson	237
ERA: Clarkson	3.08
Saves: Three tied	1

FEBRUARY 17   The Cubs sell King Kelly to the Boston Braves for the then–record price of $10,000.

Cap Anson and Albert Spalding were angry over the loss to the Browns in the 1886 World Series and grew tired of the drinking and insubordination of many of the players, as well as what management believed were excessive salary demands. During the 1886–87 off–season, Anson also sold Kelly's outfield mates to other clubs. George Gore was shipped to the Giants and Abner Dalrymple to Pittsburgh. Pitcher Jim McCormick also went to Pittsburgh. Chicago fans were outraged at the sale of the players, especially the enormously popular Kelly. Anson was hooted by Cubs fans all season, and many at West Side Park openly rooted for the opposition. The Cubs slipped from first place with a 90–34 record in 1886 to 71–50 and third place in 1887. Chicago didn't win another National League pennant until 1906.

APRIL 30   After two days of postponements due to rain, the Cubs open the season with a 6–2 win over the Pirates at Pittsburgh. This was the first time that the Cubs played the present–day Pittsburgh Pirates.

Pittsburgh and Indianapolis were new franchises in the National League in 1887, replacing those in St. Louis and Kansas City. The Pittsburgh club, then nicknamed the Alleghenys, was a member of the American Association from 1882 through 1886 before transferring to the National League.

MAY 7   In the home opener, Fred Pfeffer, John Clarkson, and Jimmy Ryan all hit homers, but the Cubs lose 10–8 at West Side Park.

MAY 17   Cubs left fielder Marty Sullivan hits three triples and a single, but the Cubs lose 16–6 to Washington at West Side Park.

MAY 18   Marty Sullivan ties a major league record by making five errors in left field during an 11–4 Cubs loss to Washington at West Side Park.

Second baseman Fred Pfeffer ranked among the NL's top home-run hitters in 1887 with 16.

MAY 30   Giants pitcher Bill George sets a major league record (since tied) by walking 16 Chicago batters. He also hit two batters and threw a wild pitch, helping the Cubs stage an incredible rally to win 12–11 in the first game of a double–header at West Side Park. The Cubs scored six runs in the ninth for the victory. Mickey Welch relieved George in the ninth and walked one more Chicago batter for a total of 17, which is a National League record for most walks in a game by a team. The Cubs completed the sweep with a 3–2 triumph in the nightcap.

The Cubs started the season with an 11–16 record, but they won 23 of their next 27 to leap into the pennant race in early July.

JUNE 24   Prior to his first game in Chicago since his sale to Boston the previous February, King Kelly is presented with more flowers "than a prima donna on an opening night." The Cubs won the thrilling contest 15–13. Down 5–1, Chicago scored eight runs in the sixth inning, then survived a six–run Boston rally in the ninth. Kelly made the final out with a runner on second base.

Kelly had three excellent seasons in Boston before age and alcohol abuse brought about a decline. He died from pneumonia in 1894, when he was only 36.

JUNE 27   In his major league debut, Cubs pitcher George Van Haltren ties a major league record by walking 16 batters. He also hit three batters in a 17–11 Chicago loss to Boston at West Side Park.

JUNE 28   The Cubs belt Boston 19–6 at West Side Park.

JULY 5   The Cubs score nine runs in the fifth inning and defeat the Giants 15–3 at West Side Park.

JULY 9   John Clarkson wins his 11th game in a row with a 5–3 decision over the Phillies at Philadelphia.

JULY 13   In a 3–0 loss at Washington, Cap Anson only reaches third base on a ball hit over the left field wall.

Anson hit the ball over the fence with one out in the ninth inning. Left fielder Cliff Carroll pretended that he had the ball, and Anson, who wasn't sure his drive had landed, stopped at second. Anson made a move toward third base, but Carroll made a feint to throw, and the Cubs manager–first baseman retraced his steps. This was repeated several times to the vast amusement of the crowd. Anson was finally convinced by his teammates that the ball traveled over the wall, but "for reasons best known to himself," he stopped at third base and refused to go any further.

JULY 14   Cap Anson refuses to play an exhibition game against Newark of the International League in Newark if African–American pitcher George Stovey and catcher Moses Walker appeared in the game. Newark manager Charley Hackett complied with the request. His club had financial troubles and needed the cash that an exhibition against the Cubs promised to generate.

AUGUST 1   John Clarkson pitches a shutout and hits a homer in a 13–0 win over Washington at West Side Park. The Cubs scored eight runs in the sixth inning.

Clarkson was 38–21 with a 3.08 ERA for Chicago in 1887. He led the league in wins, strikeouts (237), games (60), games started (59), complete games (56), and innings pitched (523). The leading hitters were Cap Anson (.347) and Fred Pfeffer (.276 with 16 homers).

AUGUST 6   Billy Sunday makes a remarkable catch in right field during a 9–8 loss to the Giants at West Side Park. Sunday leaped over a bench in deep right–center to pull in a long drive off the bat of Mike Tiernan. The benches ran from left–center to right–center for fans to sit on when the grandstand and the bleachers were sold out. Although the extra seats were in play, it was supposed that no one would ever hit a ball that far.

AUGUST 9   A home run by Fred Pfeffer is Chicago's only hit off Charlie Buffinton in a 17–4 loss to the Phillies in Philadelphia.

AUGUST 10   The Cubs rout the Phillies 14–3 in Philadelphia.

AUGUST 15   The Cubs defeat the Detroit Wolverines 6–4 at West Side Park. The win allowed Chicago to pull into a tie for first place with Detroit.

AUGUST 16   With a chance to take sole possession of first place, the Cubs lose 5–3 to Detroit at West Side Park. The Cubs never reached first place again and faded out of contention. By September 7, Chicago was seven games behind.

SEPTEMBER 13   Jimmy Ryan reaches base six times in six plate appearances on a homer, a double, a single, and three walks during a 16–13 slugfest against the Phillies at West Side Park. After starting the game in center field, Ryan also pitched from the sixth inning through the end of the game.

Ryan was an often–overlooked star outfielder during a career that started in 1886 and ended 1903. He was a Cub for 14 seasons and appeared in 1,660 games with the club, posting a .312 batting average, 1,409 runs, 2,126 hits, 362 doubles, 914 RBIs, 683 walks, and 325 stolen bases. Ryan's 142 career triples is the all–time club record. As he did on September 13, 1887, Ryan sometimes performed double–duty as a pitcher. He had a 6–1 lifetime record and two saves.

SEPTEMBER 14   The Cubs and Phillies stage another offensive display, with the Cubs winning 17–12 at West Side Park. Chicago scored seven runs in the seventh inning. The contest was called on account of darkness after eight innings.

SEPTEMBER 15   The Cubs win 12–8 over the Giants at West Side Park in a game called by darkness after six innings.

SEPTEMBER 29   Cap Anson hits a homer, triple, and double during a 4–0 win over the Pirates in the first game of a double–header at West Side Park. Pittsburgh won the second game 5–2.

1888

Cubs

Season in a Sentence

The Cubs hold first place for 88 days early in the season, but a 22–27 record during July and August prevents another pennant from flying over Chicago.

Finish • Won • Lost • Pct • GB

Second   77   58   .570   9.0

Manager

Cap Anson

Stats

Stats	Cubs	NL	Rank
Batting Avg:	.260	.239	2
On–Base Pct:	.308	.285	2
Slugging Pct:	.383	.325	1
Home Runs:	77		1
Stolen Bases:	287		5
ERA:	2.98	2.83	6
Fielding Avg:	.927	.921	2
Runs Scored:	734		1
Runs Allowed:	659		6

Starting Lineup

Tom Daly, c
Cap Anson, 1b
Fred Pfeffer, 2b
Tom Burns, 3b
Ned Williamson, ss
Marty Sullivan, lf
Jimmy Ryan, cf
Hugh Duffy, rf
George Van Haltren, lf–p
Duke Farrell, c–rf
Bob Pettit, rf

Pitchers

Gus Krock, sp
Mark Baldwin, sp
George Van Haltren, sp
John Tener, sp
George Borchers, sp

Attendance

228,908 (third in NL)

Club Leaders

Batting Avg:	Anson	.344
On–Base Pct:	Anson	.400
Slugging Pct:	Ryan	.515
Home Runs:	Ryan	16
RBI:	Anson	84
Runs:	Ryan	115
Stolen Bases:	Pfeffer	64
Wins:	Krock	25
Strikeouts:	Krock	161
ERA:	Krock	2.44
Saves:	Van Haltren	1

APRIL 3   The Cubs sell John Clarkson to the Boston Braves for $10,000.

Although Clarkson was one of the best pitchers in the game, Cap Anson and Albert Spalding grew tired of his temperamental nature. Clarkson was known to sulk when he was criticized or things didn't go his way. Letting him go to Boston proved to be a big mistake. Clarkson had a record of 192–120 after leaving Chicago. He spent most of the last three years of his life in a mental institution in Massachusetts and died in 1909 of pneumonia when he was 47.

APRIL 20   The Cubs win the season opener 5–4 over the Indianapolis Hoosiers at Indianapolis. In the first inning, leadoff batter Jimmy Ryan hit a home run, and after Marty Sullivan was retired, Bob Pettit followed with another homer. The Cubs won the game in the ninth inning on a double by Dell Darling and a single by Ryan.

The game was marked by fights between Darling and Paul Hines of Indianapolis in the first inning, and Sullivan and Dude Esterbrook of the Hoosiers in the fifth. Police were necessary to break up the Sullivan–Esterbrook battle, and both were arrested for disturbing the peace and fined $15 in court the following day. Umpire John Valentine also assessed a fine of $25 to each of the two players for fighting.

APRIL 23   After trailing 7–2 in the fifth inning at Indianapolis, the Cubs rally to win 11–10. The ill will between the two clubs from the opener three days ago apparently still lingered. The first pitch of the game struck Paul Hines of Indianapolis in the head and put him out of the game with a two–inch–long cut on his forehead. The pitch was thrown by Dad Clarke, who was making his major league debut.

Clarke pitched only two games as a member of the Cubs before he was released. He later pitched in the majors in 1891 and again from 1894 through 1898.

MAY 1   In the first home game of the season, the Cubs win 8–4 against Indianapolis before 3,000 at West Side Grounds.

The Cubs had a new color scheme on their uniforms in 1888 as the white stockings worn since the club's inception in 1876 were replaced by black ones. The White Stockings nickname passed out of use because of the change, and the Chicago club became known as the Black Stockings or Black Sox.

MAY 5   The Cubs rout the Washington Nationals 10–0 at West Side Park.

MAY 8   The Cubs again wallop Washington 13–2 at West Side Park.

MAY 15   John Clarkson makes his first appearance in Chicago as an opposing player and pitches Boston to a 20–5 trouncing of the Cubs at West Side Park before the contest comes to a merciful ending when it is called by rain at the end of the sixth inning.

In the tradition of the day, the two teams arrived on the field in horse–drawn carriages. One of the four–horse teams pulling the carriages became unmanageable and trampled and severly injured a policeman.

MAY 18   Playing in ankle–deep mud in a drizzling rain at West Side Park, the Cubs beat Boston 13–0 in a contest called after five innings because of the miserable conditions. Making his major league debut, George Borchers pitched the abbreviated shutout.

Borchers made 10 more big league starts, nine of them with the Cubs, and never pitched another shutout. He finished his career with a record of 4–5.

JUNE 21   George Van Haltren pitches a six–inning no–hitter to beat the Pirates 1–0 at West Side Park. The contest was cut short by rain. He struck out three and walked one.

JUNE 22   The Cubs score 11 runs in the sixth inning off Pud Galvin and win 12–6 over the Pirates at West Side Park.

At the conclusion of the game, the Cubs had a record of 33–14 and a 3 ½–game lead over second–place Detroit.

JULY 12   The Washington Nationals beat up on the Cubs 22–9 at West Side Park.

JULY 24   The Cubs drop out of first place with a 4–1 loss to the Hoosiers in Indianapolis.

JULY 28   Jimmy Ryan hits for a cycle that includes two singles in a 21–17 slugfest against Detroit at West Side Park. Ryan also pitched from the second inning through the ninth in relief of Mark Baldwin, who was shelled by the Detroit batters. It wasn't a good day for pitchers named Baldwin. The Detroit starter was Charles "Lady" Baldwin, who earned his nickname because he didn't drink, smoke, curse, or carouse.

AUGUST 14   The 19–game major league record winning streak of Giants pitcher Tim Keefe comes to an end when the Cubs beat him 4–2 in New York. The winning pitcher was Gus Krock. That night, the Cubs went to Wallack's Theater to watch actor William DeWolfe Hopper recite the poem "Casey at the Bat."

Jimmy Ryan batted for the cycle in 1888 and led the league in hits and homers.

The only other pitcher to win 19 games in a row in a single season was Rube Marquard of the Giants in 1912. The Cubs also stopped that streak (see July 8, 1912).

AUGUST 24   Cap Anson collects five hits in five at–bats during a 14–4 win over the Wolverines in Detroit.

AUGUST 30   Gus Krock pitches the Cubs to a 1–0 win over the Hoosiers at Indianapolis.

A 22–year–old rookie in 1888, Krock had a record of 25–14 and an ERA of 2.44. The 339⅔ innings he pitched that year wrecked his arm, however, and he was never successful again. Krock pitched only two more seasons with four different clubs and won just seven games. He was only 38 when he died of consumption in 1905.

AUGUST 31   Cubs pitcher John Tener makes his major league debut, and is the losing pitcher in a 14–0 decision at Indianapolis.

SEPTEMBER 7   The Cubs score four runs in the ninth inning and win 11–9 versus Boston at West Side Park. Tom Daly broke the 9–9 tie with a two–run triple.

SEPTEMBER 11   The Cubs beat the Giants 5–3 at West Side Park in a game marked by a sensational catch by right fielder Hugh Duffy. He caught the ball in deep right–center field and fell under a horse attached to a carriage parked along the outfield wall. Duffy narrowly escaped being kicked to death.

SEPTEMBER 12   The Giants are forced to forfeit to the Cubs when Buck Ewing is injured in the fifth inning and there are no uniformed substitutes available to replace him.

SEPTEMBER 18   Phillies pitcher Ben Sanders retires the first 25 Cubs batters to face him before Chicago hurler Gus Krock singles with one out in the ninth. Krock was the only Chicago base runner in a 6–0 loss to Philadelphia at West Side Park.

SEPTEMBER 20   Cubs pitcher Frank Dwyer pitches a three–hit shutout in his major league debut, defeating Washington 11–0 in the first game of a double–header at West Side Park.

The Cubs completed the sweep with a 5–1 win in the second tilt.

OCTOBER 8   The Cubs visit the White House to meet with President Grover Cleveland. Each member of the club was presented to Cleveland individually. This was followed by an informal session in which Anson told the president about the club's upcoming plans to travel around the world. (See November 4, 1888.) Later in the day, the Cubs defeated the Washington Nationals 11–6.

A month later, Cleveland lost his bid for re-election to Benjamin Harrison.

OCTOBER 9   The Cubs score seven runs in the fifth inning and defeat Washington 13–4 at Swampoodle Grounds in the nation's capital.

OCTOBER 13   The Cubs lose a game to the Phillies in Philadelphia by forfeit.

Anson looked out of his hotel window at noon and saw a steady rain. Believing that there was no chance a game would be played, Anson failed to take his club to the ballpark. The Phillies did show up, however, as did umpire Charlie Daniels, who gave Philadelphia the victory by forfeit.

NOVEMBER 4   As part of an around–the–world tour, the All–Americas defeat the Cubs 14–4 before a crowd of 10,500 in San Francisco.

The Cubs played a team of All–Stars from teams in the National League and American Association during the 1888–89 off–season in a tour that took them all over the globe. The tour began in Chicago, and the two clubs worked their way west with contests in Minnesota, Iowa, Nebraska, Colorado, Utah, and California. Before the tour ended in March 1889, games were played in Hawaii, New Zealand, Australia, Ceylon, India, Egypt, Italy, France, and England.

DECEMBER 15   The Cubs and the All–Americas play their first game in Australia, drawing 5,500 in Sydney.

1889

Season in a Sentence

The club continues to decline and barely finishes above .500.

Finish • Won • Lost • Pct • GB

Third   67   65   .508   19.0

Manager

Cap Anson

Stats

Stats	Cubs	NL	Rank
Batting Avg:	.263	.254	5
On–Base Pct:	.338	.334	3
Slugging Pct:	.377	.359	2
Home Runs:	79	1	
Stolen Bases:	243	5	
ERA:	3.73	4.02	4
Fielding Avg:	.923	.923	5
Runs Scored:	867		2
Runs Allowed:	814		6

Starting Lineup

Tom Daly, c
Duke Farrell, c
Cap Anson, 1b
Fred Pfeffer, 2b
Tom Burns, 3b
Ned Williamson, ss
George Van Haltren, lf
Jimmy Ryan, cf
Hugh Duffy, rf
Charlie Bastian, ss

Pitchers

Bill Hutchison, sp
Frank Dwyer, sp
John Tener, sp
Ad Gumbert, sp

Attendance

149,175 (fourth in NL)

Club Leaders

Batting Avg:	Anson	.311
On–Base Pct:	Anson	.414
Slugging Pct:	Ryan	.498
Home Runs:	Ryan	17
RBI:	Anson	117
Runs:	Duffy	144
Stolen Bases:	Duffy	52
Wins:	Three tied with:	16
Strikeouts:	Hutchinson	136
ERA:	Hutchinson	3.54
Saves:	Bishop	2

JANUARY 1	On New Year's Day, the Cubs defeat the All–Americas 9–8 in Melbourne, Australia.
FEBRUARY 9	In what can be described as the ultimate sandlot game, the All–Americas defeat the Cubs 10–6 in the shadow of the Pyramids outside Cairo, Egypt. Players on both teams had their photo taken sitting on the massive statue of the Sphinx.
FEBRUARY 19	The tour stages its first game in Europe, playing in Naples, Italy.
FEBRUARY 22	At the Villa Borgjesi outside of Rome, the Cubs edge the All–Americas 3–2 before a crowd that includes King Humbert of Italy.
MARCH 8	The All–Americas defeat the Cubs 6–2 at Parc Aristotique in Paris. Ned Williamson suffered a knee injury sliding into a sharp stone on the cinder playing field, disabling him until August 14 and effectively ending his days as a top player. He was only 36 when he died of dropsy of the stomach in 1894.
MARCH 12	The Cubs and the All–Americas play at the Surrey County Cricket Club in Kensington Oval in London in the presence of the Prince of Wales.
MARCH 22	The All–Americas beat the Cubs 7–6 in England's Old Trafford Cricket Stadium. The Manchester *Guardian* said the "general verdict of the more than 1,000 spectators was that the American game was slow and wanting in variety."

MARCH 27	The final game of the world tour is played in Dublin. The group sailed for America the next day after playing 28 games overseas.

APRIL 15 — Invited to the White House, the Cubs and the All-Americas meet with new President Benjamin Harrison.

APRIL 24 — Two days after the Oklahoma land rush, the Cubs lose the opener 8–6 to the Pirates in Pittsburgh. The contest was preceded by a carriage parade through the streets of Pittsburgh with both teams in full uniform. A sudden thunderstorm thoroughly soaked participants and the spectators.

The National League franchise in Detroit folded and was replaced by a new one in Cleveland.

Ned Williamson starred for the Cubs for a decade, but he hurt his knee during a game in Paris on a world tour, effectively ending his career.

MAY 8 — In the first home game of the season, the Cubs lose 3–2 when the Pirates score two fluke runs in the ninth. With one out and Pittsburgh runners on second and third in the final inning, Chicago left fielder Duke Farrell caught a fly ball just before colliding with center fielder George Van Haltren. As the two were on the ground recovering their faculties, both runners came around to score.

MAY 9 — Cubs pitcher Ad Gumbert hits a grand slam in the fourth inning off Pete Conway during a 7–6 win over the Pirates at West Side Park. According to the news reports, the ball landed "in a mangled condition among the carriages in center field."

MAY 17 — The Cubs score eight runs in the eighth inning and win 11–4 in Washington.

MAY 18 — The Cubs win 14–13 in an eleven-inning thriller against the Nationals in Washington.

MAY 23 — The Cubs win another high-scoring, extra-inning fray 18–17 in ten innings against the Giants in New York. The Cubs scored seven runs in the ninth inning to tie the game 17–17 before adding the winning run in the tenth.

The game was played at the St. George Cricket Grounds on Staten Island, a facility used temporarily by the Giants while a new ballpark was being built in Manhattan. The Staten Island ballpark was located in a beautiful setting overlooking the New York harbor and the Statue of Liberty, which was dedicated three years earlier. The playing field was far from ideal, however. The field was bare and stony from second base to center field because the 1888 stage production of NERO, THE FALL OF ROME had been held there. The scaffolding from the play remained in place, surrounding the outfield. In addition, the swampy outfield was covered with boards left over from the play, forcing outfielders to wear rubber–soled shoes.

JUNE 6 — Six days after the Johnstown, Pennsylvania, flood, which claimed the lives of 2,000, the Cubs outlast Indianapolis 11–10 at West Side Park.

JUNE 19 — The Cubs score eight runs in the fourth inning to take a 12–4 lead, but wind up losing 14–13 in ten innings to the Phillies at West Side Park.

JUNE 24 — Ad Gumbert pitches a one–hitter to beat the Giants 6–0 at West Side Park. The only New York hit was a single by Jim O'Rourke.

JULY 6 — The Cubs smack down Washington 14–6 at West Side Park.

Top hitters for Chicago in 1889 were Cap Anson (.311), George Van Haltren (.309), and Jimmy Ryan (.307).

JULY 16 — The Cubs score seven runs in the second inning to take a 7–0 lead, fall behind 10–7, then score six in the eighth to win 13–10 against the Giants in New York.

JULY 19 — The Cubs clobber the Boston Braves 13–6 in Boston.

JULY 24 — The Cubs play their first one–admission double–header in Chicago. Previous double–headers had been two–admission affairs, with one game in the morning and one in the afternoon. Playing Indianapolis, the Cubs won the first game 3–2, but lost the second 6–3. Attendance was 1,800.

JULY 25 — The Cubs allow two Indianapolis runs in the top of the eleventh to fall behind 6–4, then score three in their half to win 7–6 at West Side Park.

JULY 27 — The Cubs win a double–header 17–5 and 5–2 against Indianapolis at West Side Park.

JULY 29 — The Cubs pound the Pirates 13–8 in Pittsburgh.

AUGUST 14 — The Cubs score 10 runs in the eighth inning of a 19–6 win over the Phillies at West Side Park.

AUGUST 17 — Jimmy Ryan hits a grand slam in the sixth inning off Mike Sullivan during an 8–5 victory over Washington at West Side Park.

AUGUST 27 — The Cubs survive a four–run Cleveland ninth inning to win 12–11 in Cleveland.

SEPTEMBER 4 — The Cubs trample the Phillies 15–8 in Philadelphia.

SEPTEMBER 17 — The Cubs hand Indianapolis a 19–8 defeat at West Side Park in a game called by darkness after seven innings.

SEPTEMBER 19   The Cubs smash the Cleveland Spiders 19–10 at West Side Park.

DECEMBER 16   Six weeks after South Dakota, North Dakota, Montana, and Washington are granted
                 statehood, the Players League is formally organized.

*The new league grew out of dissatisfaction among players over their salaries
and contracts. Many top stars left their National League and American Associa-
tion teams to join the new league. The Players League located clubs in Chicago,
Boston, Brooklyn, Buffalo, Cleveland, New York, Philadelphia, and Pittsburgh.
The new organization, also known as the Brotherhood, devastated the Cubs
roster. Cap Anson lost a dozen players. Among them were front–liners Fred
Pfeffer, Jimmy Ryan, Ned Williamson, Hugh Duffy, Duke Farrell, Frank Dwyer,
John Tener, Ad Gumbert, Charlie Bastian, Dell Darling, and George Van Haltren.
The only regulars who stayed with the Cubs, besides Anson himself, were Bill
Hutchison and Tom Burns. Duffy, Pfeffer, Ryan, Farrell, Bastian, Williamson,
Darling, Bastian, and Dwyer all played for the Chicago entry in the Players
League, which was nicknamed the Pirates because of their success in "pirating"
away the best players on the Cubs roster. The Pirates, managed by Charlie
Comiskey, played at South Side Park at 35th and Wentworth streets on almost
the exact same spot as the first Comiskey Park, which existed from 1910
through 1990. With the loss of most of his roster, Cap Anson played the 1890
season with a contingent of young players. The assortment of youngsters was
called the "Colts" and the moniker soon became the team nickname. Previously,
the Chicago club was known primarily as the White Stockings from 1876
through 1887 and the Black Stockings in 1888 and 1889.*

THE STATE OF THE CUBS

The Cubs had a record of 710–654 during the 1890s, a winning percentage of .521. The club failed to win the National League pennant during the decade. NL championships were won by Brooklyn (1890, 1898, and 1899), Boston (1891, 1892, 1893, 1897, and 1898), and Baltimore (1894, 1895, and 1896).

THE BEST TEAM

The club with the best winning percentage was in 1890 when the Cubs were 83–53 and finished in second place 6½ games out. The 1891 outfit came closest to first place, landing 3½ games out with a record of 82–53.

THE WORST TEAM

The 1894 Cubs were 57–75 and finished seventh in a twelve–team league. The 1893 and 1897 Cubs both had better winning percentages than the 1894 outfit, but ended the season in ninth place.

THE BEST MOMENT

In a stunt in 1894, Cubs catcher Pop Shriver caught a ball dropped more than five hundred feet from the observation deck of the Washington Monument.

THE WORST MOMENT

Hundreds were injured on August 5, 1894, when West Side Grounds caught on fire during a game against the Reds.

THE ALL–DECADE TEAM • YEARS WITH CUBS

Malachi Kittridge, c	1890–97
Cap Anson, 1b	1879–97
Fred Pfeffer, 2b	1883–89, 1891, 1896–97
Bill Everett, 3b	1895–1900
Bill Dahlen, ss	1891–98
Walt Wilmot, lf	1890–95
Bill Lange, cf	1893–99
Jimmy Ryan, rf	1886–89, 1891–1900
Bill Hutchison, p	1889–95
Clark Griffith, p	1893–1900
Ad Gumbert, p	1888–89, 1891–92
Pat Luby, p	1890–92

Anson and Griffith are both in the Hall of Fame. Ryan and Dahlen are two of the best nineteenth–century players who haven't been enshrined at Cooperstown.

THE DECADE LEADERS

Batting Avg:	Lange	.330
On–Base Pct:	Lange	.401
Slugging Pct:	Lange	.459
Home Runs:	Dahlen	57
RBI:	Anson	747
Runs:	Ryan	911
Stolen Bases:	Lange	399
Wins:	Hutchison	184
Strikeouts:	Hutchison	1,088
ERA:	Callahan	3.09
Saves:	Hutchison	4

THE HOME FIELD

The Cubs played their home games at three different ballparks during the decade. West Side Park, opened in 1885, was used in exclusively in 1890. In an odd arrangement, games were played there on Mondays, Wednesdays, and Fridays in 1891, while Tuesday, Thursday, and Saturday contests were held at South Side Park. South Side Park was Chicago's only ballpark in 1892, and was used for all games in 1893 except for those played on Sunday, the first season that games were permitted in the Windy City on the Christian Sabbath. Sunday games in 1893 were played at West Side Grounds. That facility remained as the Cubs' home field exclusively until 1915.

THE GAME YOU WISH YOU HAD SEEN

Setting an all-time record for most runs in a game, the Cubs rout the Louisville Colonels 36–7 on June 29, 1897.

THE WAY THE GAME WAS PLAYED

In 1893, the pitcher was moved from 55 feet to 60 feet, six inches. The added pitching distance put more offense in the game. League batting averages jumped from .245 in 1892, to .280 in 1893, and to .309 in 1894. The decade is known for its rough, even dirty, baseball, with many managers encouraging players to bend every rule and challenge every call. Brawling became commonplace.

THE MANAGEMENT

Albert Spalding was the club president at the start of the decade. Spalding stepped down at the end of the 1891 season, although he remained a major stockholder until 1902. James Hart was club president from 1891 through 1905. Cap Anson was in his twelfth season as Cubs field manager in 1890, and his fifteenth as a player. He was fired at the end of the 1897 season. Tom Burns replaced Anson and served as manager in 1898 and 1899.

THE BEST PLAYER MOVE

In 1894, the Cubs acquired pitcher Clark Griffith from Oakland in the California League. Griffith won at least 21 games for the club six straight seasons beginning in 1894.

THE WORST PLAYER MOVE

After the Players League folded following the 1890 season, the Cubs failed to sign Hugh Duffy and George Van Haltren, emerging stars who played on the 1889 club. Duffy went on to the Hall of Fame, and Van Haltren had a better career than many outfielders enshrined at Cooperstown.

1890s

1 8 9 0

After losing most of their top stars to the Players League, the Cubs flounder around the .500 mark until early August, when the club jells and surges to second place.

Finish • Won • Lost • Pct • GB

First   84   53   .613   6.0

Manager

Cap Anson

Stats	Cubs	NL	Rank
Batting Avg:	.260	.254	3
On–Base Pct:	.336	.329	4
Slugging Pct:	.356	.342	3
Home Runs:	67		1
Stolen Bases:	329		3
ERA:	3.24	3.58	5
Fielding Avg:	.940	.927	2
Runs Scored:	847		2
Runs Allowed:	692		4

Starting Lineup

Malachi Kittridge, c
Cap Anson, 1b
Bob Glenalvin, 2b
Tom Burns, 3b
Jimmy Cooney, ss
Cliff Carroll, lf
Walt Wilmot, cf
Howard Earl, rf–2b
Jim Andrews, rf
Tom Nagle, c

Pitchers

Bill Hutchison, sp
Pat Luby, sp
Ed Stein, sp
Mike Sullivan, sp
Roscoe Coughlin, sp

Attendance

102,536 (fifth in NL)

Club Leaders

Batting Avg:	Anson	.312
On–Base Pct:	Anson	.443
Slugging Pct:	Wilmot	.415
Home Runs:	Wilmot	13
RBI:	Anson	107
Runs:	Carroll	134
Stolen Bases:	Wilmot	76
Wins:	Hutchison	42
Strikeouts:	Hutchison	289
ERA:	Hutchison	2.70
Saves:	Hutchison	2

APRIL 19   The Cubs collect only four hits, but win the season opener 5–4 over the Reds in Cincinnati. Bill Hutchison settled down after allowing four runs in the first three innings to earn the complete game victory. Walt Wilmot, playing in his first game as a member of the Cubs, homered in the third inning.

Both the Cincinnati Reds and the Brooklyn Dodgers moved from the American Association to the National League in 1890, replacing franchises in Washington and Indianapolis.

APRIL 22   The Cubs trounce the Reds 13–3 in Cincinnati.

APRIL 29   The Cubs win the home opener 9–4 over the Pirates before 2,365 at West Side Park.

MAY 5   On a bitterly cold and windy day when a Players League game was played at South Side Park, only 125 attend a contest between the Cubs and Reds at West Side Park. It is the smallest recorded home attendance figure in Cubs history. The game was called after nine innings by darkness with the score 2–2.

MAY 8   Trailing 9–3, the Cubs explode for 12 runs in the sixth inning and go on to wallop the Reds 18–9 at West Side Park. Howard Earl hit a grand slam in the big inning off Lee Viau. Bill Hutchison hit a homer that rolled under the horse–drawn carriages parked in the outfield.

MAY 29   The Cubs play the Dodgers for the first time and lose 8–4 in Brooklyn.

MAY 30   Bill Hutchison pitches two complete–games victories during a Memorial Day double–header, beating the Dodgers 11–7 and 6–4 in Brooklyn.

From 1889 through 1895, Bill Hutchison pitched 3,020 innings, compiling a 181–158 record.

At the age of 30, Hutchison was a work-horse in 1890, pitching 603 innings in 71 games and completing 65 of his 66 starts. He had a record of 42–25 with two saves and an ERA of 2.70.

JUNE 2   The Cubs beat the Pirates 14–1 in Pittsburgh.

JUNE 12   The Cubs again batter the Pirates 16–3 at West Side Park.

JUNE 27   The 7–2 loss to the Dodgers at West Side Park is halted briefly in the fifth inning when Cap Anson is presented with a floral horse-shoe and a huge crystal glass slipper by the manager of the Chicago Opera House.

JULY 22   Two weeks after Idaho and Wyoming are admitted to the Union as the forty–third and forty–fourth states, the Cubs topple the Giants 14–7 at the Polo Grounds in New York.

JULY 31   Just seven days after his major league debut, 20–year–old rookie Ed Stein pitches a two–hitter to beat Boston 4–1 at West Side Park. The only hits off Stein were a triple by Paul Hines and a single by Steve Brodie.

              On August 7, the Cubs had a record of 44–43. The club won 40 of its last 50 games to surge into second place by the end of the season.

AUGUST 8   Bill Hutchison comes within one out of a no–hitter in a 7–0 win over the Spiders in Cleveland. With two out in the ninth, Will Smalley hit a looping single just beyond the infield. Hutchison retired the next batter to end the contest with a one–hitter.

AUGUST 12   The Cubs win 13–12 in a twelve–inning battle with the Pirates in Pittsburgh.

AUGUST 16   The Cubs score 13 times in the fifth inning and defeat the Pirates 18–5 at West Side Park. Chicago set a major league record (since tied) by hitting two grand slams in the inning. The pair of slams were struck by Malachi Kittridge and Tom Burns, both off Pittsburgh hurler Bill Phillips.

This is the only time in Cubs history that two players hit grand slams in a single inning. The only other time that two players hit slams in the same game was during a 22–7 win over the Astros on June 3, 1987. Those were hit by Brian Dayett and Keith Moreland.

The 1890 Pittsburgh Pirates were one of the worst aggregations in National League history. The Pirates had a record of 23–113.

AUGUST 22   Ed Stein pitches a shutout and drives in the winning run in the ninth to lift the Cubs to a 1–0 win over the Dodgers in Brooklyn.

SEPTEMBER 5   Cubs pitcher Pat Luby hits three batters in the sixth inning and four in the game, but defeats the Reds 12–8 at West Side Park.

SEPTEMBER 8   Elmer Foster of the Cubs hits a grand slam in the first inning off Dave Anderson of the Pirates during a 7–3 win at West Side Park.

SEPTEMBER 9   The Cubs score seven runs in the third inning and win 13–4 over the Pirates at West Side Park.

SEPTEMBER 12   The Cubs walk away with 17–2 and 11–4 wins over the Cleveland Spiders in a double–header at West Side Park.

SEPTEMBER 22   Just before the game is called by darkness, the Cubs score seven runs in the eighth inning and defeat the Dodgers 14–1 at West Side Park.

SEPTEMBER 29   Bill Hutchison pitches a one–hitter to beat the Braves 3–0 at West Side Park. The only Boston hit was a single by Tommy Tucker.

The top hitter for the Cubs in 1890 was Cap Anson, who at the age of 38 hit .312 and drove in 107 runs. Anson led the league in walks (113) and on–base percentage (.443). Walt Wilmot led the NL in homers with 13 and Cliff Carroll was second in runs with 134.

OCTOBER 3   Pat Luby wins his 17th consecutive game, beating the Giants 3–2 at West Side Park. The contest was called after seven innings by darkness.

Luby's winning streak is the longest in Cubs history. He was a 21–year–old rookie in 1890, and he posted a 20–8 record and pitched 267 ⅓ innings. Like most young pitchers with a high workload, Luby never had any success after his first season. Over the remainder of his career, Luby won 22 and lost 35. He was only 30 when he died following a long illness in 1899.

OCTOBER 22   After only one season, the Players League folds.

Albert Spalding bought the Chicago franchise in the league for $18,000, which included South Side Park, the players contracts, and the club's equipment. Spalding failed to sign two key young outfielders, Hugh Duffy and George Van Haltren, from the 1889 team, however. Both went to the American Association, with Duffy playing for Boston and Van Haltren for Baltimore. The two players became stars and were huge losses to the Cubs.

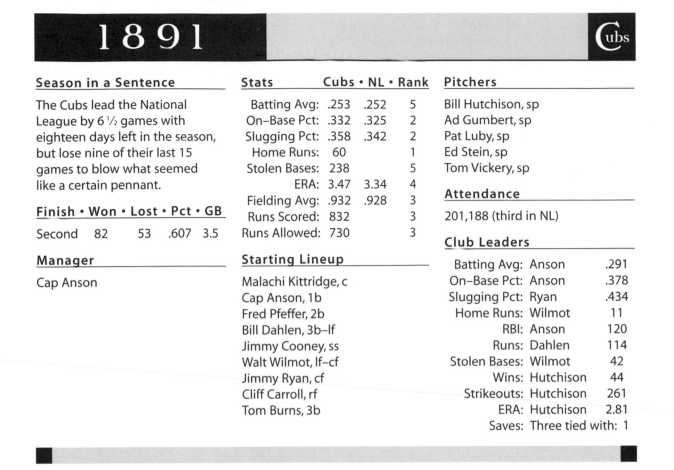

1891   Cubs

Season in a Sentence

The Cubs lead the National League by 6 ½ games with eighteen days left in the season, but lose nine of their last 15 games to blow what seemed like a certain pennant.

Finish • Won • Lost • Pct • GB

Second   82   53   .607   3.5

Manager

Cap Anson

Stats

Stats	Cubs	NL	Rank
Batting Avg:	.253	.252	5
On–Base Pct:	.332	.325	2
Slugging Pct:	.358	.342	2
Home Runs:	60		1
Stolen Bases:	238		5
ERA:	3.47	3.34	4
Fielding Avg:	.932	.928	3
Runs Scored:	832		3
Runs Allowed:	730		3

Starting Lineup

Malachi Kittridge, c
Cap Anson, 1b
Fred Pfeffer, 2b
Bill Dahlen, 3b–lf
Jimmy Cooney, ss
Walt Wilmot, lf–cf
Jimmy Ryan, cf
Cliff Carroll, rf
Tom Burns, 3b

Pitchers

Bill Hutchison, sp
Ad Gumbert, sp
Pat Luby, sp
Ed Stein, sp
Tom Vickery, sp

Attendance

201,188 (third in NL)

Club Leaders

Batting Avg:	Anson	.291
On–Base Pct:	Anson	.378
Slugging Pct:	Ryan	.434
Home Runs:	Wilmot	11
RBI:	Anson	120
Runs:	Dahlen	114
Stolen Bases:	Wilmot	42
Wins:	Hutchison	44
Strikeouts:	Hutchison	261
ERA:	Hutchison	2.81
Saves:	Three tied with:	1

MARCH 25   Three months after the massacre of Native Americans by the U.S. Army at Wounded Knee, South Dakota, Cubs President Albert Spalding retires from day–to–day participation in the affairs of the club. James Hart, a Chicago businessman, succeeded Spalding as president.

APRIL 22   In the season opener, the Cubs win 7–6 over the Pirates in ten innings in Pittsburgh. Jimmy Ryan drove in the tying run with a double in the ninth. Bill Dahlen, in his major league debut, hit a triple in the tenth and scored on Cliff Carroll's single.

This was the start of a 20–year career for Dahlen, who played for the Cubs the first eight of those seasons. As a rookie he hit .260 and scored 114 runs.

MAY 1   In the home opener, the Cubs lose 5–2 to the Pirates at West Side Park before 6,000.

The Cubs had a unique arrangement in 1891, playing in two different ballparks. On Mondays, Wednesdays, and Fridays, the club played at West Side Park, which had been the home of the club since 1885. On Tuesdays, Thursdays, and Saturdays, the Cubs' home field was South Side Park, opened in 1890 for the Players League team. National League rules prevented games from being played on Sunday. (Sunday games in the NL began in 1892, and in Chicago in 1893.)

South Side Park was located at 35th and Wentworth Streets, and overlapped part of the site on which the original Comiskey Park was located. A ten–foot–high wooden fence surrounded the ballpark. The outfield dimensions and precise seating capacity aren't known, though it was more than 10,000. The Cubs played all of their home games at South Side Park in 1892, and all games in 1893 except those played on Sunday.

MAY 5   Ed Stein pitches a two–hitter to beat the Pirates 1–0 at South Side Park. The only Pittsburgh hits were singles by Jake Beckley and Doggie Miller. Pete Browning of the Pirates bunted into a triple play in the top of the sixth inning and made an error to allow the lone run of the game in the bottom of the frame.

MAY 8   The Cubs win 14–12 against Cleveland at West Side Park. Chicago held an 11–0 lead in the sixth inning before nearly blowing the huge advantage.

MAY 15   Jimmy Ryan hits the first pitch of the game off Brooklyn's Tom Lovett setting the stage for a 12–11 win over the Dodgers at West Side Park.

           Jimmy Ryan hit 20 career lead–off homers for the Cubs, which is still the club record. Rick Monday is second in lead–off homers with 17 from 1972 through 1976.

MAY 16   Jimmy Ryan collects a triple, three doubles, and a single during an 11–9, ten–inning win over the Dodgers at West Side Park.

           During the 1891 season, Ryan hit .277 and scored 110 runs.

MAY 18   The Cubs thrash the Dodgers 13–4 at West Side Park.

JULY 1   Jimmy Ryan hits for the cycle during a 9–3 win over Cleveland at West Side Park.

           Ryan is the only Cubs player to hit for the cycle twice in his career.

JULY 2   The Cubs score 11 runs in the third inning to take a 17–0 lead and roll to a 20–5 win over Cleveland at South Side Park. For the second game in a row, Jimmy Ryan collected four hits.

JULY 16   After Boston scores two runs in the twelfth inning, the Cubs rally for three in their half for a thrilling 8–7 win at South Side Park. With two out, no one on base, and John Clarkson pitching, Cap Anson and Cliff Carroll both singled. Jimmy Cooney scored both with a double, and after Boston right fielder Harry Stovey made a bad throw, Cooney kept running and crossed the plate with a winning run.

JULY 25   The Cubs score four runs in the ninth inning to beat the Spiders 15–14 in Cleveland. The Spiders batted first, and they scored four times in the top of the ninth to take a 14–11 lead. The game ended when Cliff Carroll hit a drive over the left field fence with a runner on and the score 14–14. Under the scoring rules of the day, the contest ended when the lead runner scored, and Carroll was credited with a double instead of a homer.

JULY 27   The Cubs squash the Spiders 14–8 in Cleveland.

| AUGUST 20 | The Cubs wallop the Spiders 14–2 at South Side Park in a contest called after seven innings by darkness. |

AUGUST 20   The Cubs wallop the Spiders 14–2 at South Side Park in a contest called after seven innings by darkness.

AUGUST 22   Walt Wilmot sets a major league record by walking six times in six plate appearances during a 10–4 win over Cleveland at South Side Park. The pitchers were Lee Viau and Cy Young.

The only other major leaguer to walk six times in a nine–inning game was Jimmie Foxx of the Red Sox in 1938.

AUGUST 25   Jimmy Ryan hits the second pitch of the game for a homer, starting the Cubs on the way to a one–sided 28–5 slugging match over the Dodgers at South Side Park. Chicago had 28 hits, including four homers, five triples, and four doubles. Cap Anson collected five hits, including two triples. George Hemming pitched the complete game for Brooklyn.

AUGUST 26   The Cubs win their 11th game in a row with a 9–8 victory over the Dodgers at West Side Park.

AUGUST 31   The Cubs and the Giants battled to an 0–0 tie, called after eleven innings by darkness at West Side Park. Bill Hutchison of Chicago and Amos Rusie of New York both pitched complete games.

Hutchison won more than 40 games for the second consecutive season. His record in 1891 was 44–19 with a 2.81 ERA. Hutchison led the NL in games pitched (66), games started (58), complete games (56), and innings pitched (561).

SEPTEMBER 4   Making light of being referred to as an "old man" repeatedly in the press, 39–year–old Cap Anson wears a shaggy, gray wig and a long, gray false beard during a 5–3 win over Boston at West Side Park. Anson wore the "grandpa" costume throughout the entire contest. It didn't help him at the plate, as Anson went hitless in four at–bats.

Despite his advanced age, Anson played in 136 of Chicago's 137 games in 1891 and hit .291 with a league–leading 120 RBIs. He went on to play six more seasons in the majors.

SEPTEMBER 7   After losing the first game of a double–header 21–3 to the Dodgers in Brooklyn, the Cubs rebound to win the second tilt 9–8.

SEPTEMBER 15   The Cubs beat the Braves 8–4 in Boston.

The victory gave the Cubs a 6½–game lead over Boston and a 76–44 record with just 15 games left on the schedule. Chicago lost nine of the 15 games, however, while Boston won its next 18 contests. At the end of the season, the Cubs trailed the Braves by 3½ games.

SEPTEMBER 25   The Cubs win a game by forfeit against the Pirates at West Side Park. With the score 4–4 in the eighth inning, Pittsburgh catcher Doggie Miller vociferously objected to a decision by umpire Jack McQuaid. When Miller refused to leave the field, McQuaid forfeited the game to the Cubs.

SEPTEMBER 26   Doggie Miller of the Pirates continues to cause trouble in Chicago. During a game at South Side Park that ended after eight innings by darkness, Miller threw his glove in Cap Anson's face.

After the September 26 game, the Cubs had a 1½–game lead over Boston with six contests left on the schedule.

Tom Burns was a solid performer for years, but at 34 in 1891, his final year with the team as a player, he appeared in only 59 games.

SEPTEMBER 29   The Cubs desperately hold onto first place with a 14–13 win over the Spiders in Cleveland. After falling behind 5–1, Chicago scored seven runs in the third inning. The victory allowed the Cubs to maintain a one–half–game lead with four games left.

SEPTEMBER 30   The Cubs drop out of first place with a 12–5 loss at Cleveland in a contest called after eight innings by darkness.

On the same day, the Braves completed a five–game sweep of the Giants in Boston. Two of the five games were make–up games because of postponements during an earlier series in New York. Cubs President James Hart protested the extra make–up games. Hart and several sportswriters were convinced that the New York club purposely let Boston win the games, especially after four Giants were retired at home plate in the final game, which Boston won 5–3, and many regulars failed to play with dubious injuries.

OCTOBER 1   Boston clinches the NL pennant with its 17th consecutive victory, a 6–1 decision over the Phillies. On the same day, the Cubs lost 6–1 to the Reds at South Side Park.

The late–season collapse that cost the Cubs a pennant was a crushing blow for Cap Anson, the players, and the fans. The Cubs weren't in contention for a pennant in September again until 1906.

1892

Cubs

Season in a Sentence

The Cubs win 13 straight in May, but wind up with a losing record for the first time since 1877.

Finish • Won • Lost • Pct • GB

Seventh   70   76   .479 30.0

Manager

Cap Anson

Stats

Stats	Cubs	NL	Rank
Batting Avg:	.235	.245	10
On–Base Pct:	.299	.317	12
Slugging Pct:	.316	.327	10
Home Runs:	26		10 (tie)
Stolen Bases:	233		7
ERA:	3.16	3.28	5
Fielding Avg:	.932	.928	5
Runs Scored:	635		12
Runs Allowed:	735		7

Starting Lineup

Cap Anson, 1b
Jim Canavan, 2b
Jiggs Parrott, 3b
Bill Dahlen, ss–3b
Walt Wilmot, lf
Jimmy Ryan, cf
Sam Dungan, rf–lf
George Decker, rf
Jimmy Cooney, ss
Malachi Kittridge, c

Pitchers

Bill Hutchison, sp
Ad Gumbert, sp
Pat Luby, sp

Attendance

109,067 (11th in NL)

Club Leaders

Batting Avg:	Ryan	.293
On–Base Pct:	Ryan	.375
Slugging Pct:	Ryan	.438
Home Runs:	Ryan	10
RBI:	Anson	74
Runs:	Dahlen	114
Stolen Bases:	Dahlen	60
Wins:	Hutchison	37
Strikeouts:	Hutchison	312
ERA:	Hutchison	2.75
Saves:	Hutchison	1

APRIL 4 The Cubs send Fred Pfeffer to Louisville for Jimmy Canavan and $2,000.

Pfeffer was a native of Louisville and wanted to return to his hometown. Anson obliged, but Canavan failed as a replacement. In 439 at–bats, Canavan hit only .166 and had a slugging percentage of just .239. Pfeffer played for the Cubs again in 1896 and 1897.

APRIL 12 In the season opener, the Cubs defeat the Cardinals 14–10 in St. Louis. The Cubs led 9–1 in the fifth inning and 14–5 in the seventh before allowing the Cardinals back in the game.

During the 1891–92 off–season, the American Association folded and four AA teams were incorporated into the National League. The four new NL clubs were the St. Louis Cardinals, Louisville Colonels, Washington Senators, and Baltimore Orioles. With twelve teams and a 154–game schedule, the National League split the pennant race into two halves. The winners of the two halves were Boston and Cleveland, and the two met in a post–season series, with Boston winning. With the exception of the strike–interrupted 1981 campaign, it was the only time that the major league had two pennant races in a season.

APRIL 23 The Cubs lose the season opener by forfeit to Louisville at South Side Park. The Cubs led 4–2 in the ninth inning when many of the 8,000 in attendance began throwing cushions and swarmed the field. Efforts to clear the diamond were unsuccessful, and umpire Jack Sherdian declared the forfeit.

Before the game former Cub Fred Pfeffer was presented with a great floral star with his name in red letters in the center.

MAY 7   Bill Hutchison just misses pitching a no–hitter in an 8–0 win over the Giants at South Side Park. The only New York hit was a scratch single by Jim O'Rourke in the ninth inning.

Hutchison had a record of 37–36 in 1892 and an ERA of 2.76. For the third consecutive year, he led the league in games pitched (75), games started (70), complete games (67), and innings pitched (622). Hutchison accounted for 42 of the Cubs' 84 wins in 1890, 44 of 82 in 1891, and 37 of 70 in 1892. No pitcher since 1892 has accounted for at least 50 percent of his club's victories. The 622 innings that Hutchison piled up in 1892 also made him the last of an era. No pitcher since that season has had more than 500 innings in a season. The last pitcher with at least 400 innings pitched in a season was Ed Walsh of the White Sox in 1908. The last hurler with 300 or more innings was Steve Carlton with the Phillies in 1980.

MAY 21   The Cubs win their 13th game in a row, defeating the Pirates 1–0 at South Side Park. Chicago won despite collecting only two hits off Pud Galvin. Bill Hutchison pitched a three–hit shutout.

The Cubs completed their 13-game winning streak after a 3–11 start to the season. It looked like the club was on the move, but those illusions were dispelled by a 5–18 record in June.

MAY 28   Jimmy Ryan walks five times in five plate appearances during a 10–4 win over the Giants in New York. Amos Rusie issued all five walks.

Ryan hit .293 and scored 103 runs in 1892.

JUNE 6   The Cubs are spanked 23–1 by the Orioles in Baltimore. Pat Luby allowed all 23 runs.

JUNE 30   The Cubs play a 20–inning game against the Reds in Cincinnati that results in a 7–7 tie. The score was 6–6 after three innings, and all 14 runs in the contest were scored by the end of the fifth. Ad Gumbert of

Jimmy Ryan roamed the outfield for the Cubs from 1886 through 1900.

the Cubs and Tony Mullane of the Reds pitched without relief, both throwing shutout ball over the last fifteen innings. The umpire was forced to call the game to allow the Chicago players to catch a train. The time of the game was three hours and twenty minutes.

JULY 1   George Bechtel of the *Chicago Evening News* is punched several times by Jimmy Ryan. The Cubs outfielder was angry about an article Bechtel wrote criticizing his play.

JULY 11   Having clinched the first–half championship, Boston players appear in gingham and calico suits "of the loudest pattern and color" and wear false beards for a game against the Cubs at South Side Park. Boston won the game 3–2.

AUGUST 13   Jimmy Ryan runs his hitting streak to 29 games during a 6–2 loss to Cleveland at South Side Park.

AUGUST 18   Cap Anson collects five hits, including two triples and a double, but the Cubs lose 7–5 to the Dodgers at South Side Park.

AUGUST 25   Bill Hutchison pitches the Cubs to a 1–0 win over Washington at South Side Park.

SEPTEMBER 22   Losing 9–2 to the Pirates in Pittsburgh in the fifth inning, the Cubs resort to stalling tactics to prolong the contest to prevent it from becoming an official game when it looks like rain is forthcoming. Umpire John Gaffney put a stop to the shenanigans by forfeiting the game to the Pirates.

SEPTEMBER 27   The game between the Cubs and the Colonels at Eclipse Park in Louisville is postponed because a fire destroyed most of the ballpark the previous day. Only the bleachers survived the blaze.

SEPTEMBER 28   The Cubs play a double–header before the charred ruins and remains of what is left of Eclipse Park in Louisville following the September 26 fire. Chicago won the first game 5–4, but lost the second tilt 5–3, which was called by darkness after seven innings. Bill Hutchison started and completed both games.

SEPTEMBER 29   Lead–off hitters Jimmy Ryan of the Cubs and Bug Holliday of the Reds begin each half of the first inning with home runs in a 10–4 Cubs win in Cincinnati. Holliday injured his ankle circling the bases and had to leave the game.

OCTOBER 15   Three weeks before Grover Cleveland defeats Benjamin Harrison in the presidential election, the Cubs conclude the 1892 season with a game against the Cardinals played at a neutral site in Kansas City. Chicago won 1–0 behind the pitching of Bill Hutchison.

1893

Season in a Sentence

Cubs fans have little to cheer about in a dreary season as the club sinks to ninth place.

Finish • Won • Lost • Pct • GB

Ninth   56   71   .441   29.0

Manager

Cap Anson

Stats

Stats	Cubs	NL	Rank
Batting Avg:	.279	.280	6
On–Base Pct:	.348	.356	7
Slugging Pct:	.379	.379	6
Home Runs:	32		6 (tie)
Stolen Bases:	255		2
ERA:	4.81	4.66	9
Fielding Avg:	829		6
Runs Scored:	874		9
Runs Allowed:			

Starting Lineup

Malachi Kittridge, c
Cap Anson, 1b
Bill Lange, 2b–cf
Jiggs Parrott, 3b
Bill Dahlen, ss
Walt Wilmot, lf
Jimmy Ryan, cf
Sam Dungan, rf
George Decker, lf–1b–2b
Pop Shriver, c
Lew Camp, 3b–cf–2b

Pitchers

Bill Hutchison, sp
Willie McGill, sp
Hal Mauck, sp
Fritz Clausen, sp

Attendance

223,500 (fourth in NL)

Club Leaders

Batting Avg:	Anson	.314
On–Base Pct:	Anson	.415
Slugging Pct:	Wilmot	.431
Home Runs:	Lange	8
RBI:	Anson	91
Runs:	Dahlen	113
Stolen Bases:	Lange	47
Wins:	McGill	17
Strikeouts:	McGill	91
ERA:	Mauck	4.41
Saves:	Three tied with:	1

APRIL 27   The Cubs lose the season opener 10–1 to the Reds in Cincinnati.

APRIL 28   The Cubs reverse their opening day loss and defeat the Reds 11–1 in Cincinnati.

Three days later, President Grover Cleveland arrived in Chicago to officially open the World's Columbian Exposition in Jackson Park. The fair celebrated the four-hundredth anniversary of Christopher Columbus's arrival in the New World, and attracted 27 million visitors.

MAY 13   The Cubs play their first home game of 1893 and lose 10–8 to the Reds at South Side Park.

MAY 14   The Cubs play on Sunday in Chicago for the first time and lose 13–12 when the Reds score four runs in the ninth.

Sunday games in 1893 were played at newly-built West Side Grounds at Polk and Lincoln (now Wolcott) streets. The rest of the games that season were played at South Side Park, which was maintained for another year because it was nearby the World's Columbian Exposition, and the Cubs hoped to lure to the ballpark some of the millions who came to Chicago to visit the fair. When West Side Grounds was completed, the ballpark held 16,000 in double-decked wooden stands. A balcony of fifty-eight boxes seating about 600 was built above the grandstand between the bases to accommodate the well–to–do. The structure was ornamented with three green towers and a bandstand on the roof. The left field fence was 340 feet down the foul line, the distance center field was a majestic 560 feet, and right field extended 316 feet. The clubhouse, which was painted yellow and had a veranda, was located in the deepest part of center field and was in play. Around 1897, bicycle stands were added to West Side Grounds for fans who traveled to the games on the two–wheeled vehicles. The service was in response to a national mania over bicycling during the 1890s. The love affair with bicycles lasted until shortly after the turn of the century, when the automobile satisfied Americans' craving for private transportation. South Side Park was abandoned after the end of the 1893 season, and West Side Grounds was used exclusively beginning in 1894. It would continue as the home of the Cubs until the end of the 1915 season, when the club moved to Wrigley Field.

MAY 19   The Cubs trounce Louisville 14–9 at South Side Park.

MAY 25   The game at Louisville is postponed when the Cubs' train from Chicago is delayed and the club is unable to arrive on time.

MAY 29   Walt Wilmot bats for Bill Hutchison in the ninth inning of an 18–2 loss at Boston to become the first pinch–hitter in Cubs history.

JUNE 2   On a day in Philadelphia when rain fell during the entire game, the Cubs come from behind with eight runs in the eighth inning to beat the Phillies 11–5.

JUNE 16   Cubs pitchers tie a major league record by hitting six batters in a game, but win 10–9 in eleven innings against the Giants in New York. Starter Sam Shaw hit five batters and reliever Hal Mauck plunked one.

This was Shaw's last major league game. He pitched twice for the Cubs and walked thirteen batters and hit seven in sixteen innings.

JUNE 27   Six days after Lizzie Borden is convicted of the ax murder of her parents, the Cubs score eight runs in the first inning to take an 8–0 lead, but lose 14–13 to the Dodgers at South Side Park. Brooklyn scored nine runs in the fourth inning to pull ahead 12–8.

JULY 3   Bill Hutchison pitches a two–hitter to beat Boston 3–0 at South Side Park. The only hits off Hutchison were singles by Hugh Duffy and Tommy Tucker.

JULY 11   Bill Lange hits a grand slam off Jesse Duryea in the fifth inning of a 15–5 win over Washington at South Side Park.

JULY 21   After taking an 11–3 lead in the fourth inning, the Cubs outlast the Pirates 12–9 at South Side Park.

JULY 29   The Cubs whip the Colonels 14–2 in Louisville.

AUGUST 2   The Cubs clobber Cleveland 17–6 at South Side Park.

AUGUST 6   Jimmy Ryan is injured in a train wreck near Toledo, Ohio, as the Cubs travel
                between Cleveland and Louisville. Ryan was cut badly about the face, head, and
                neck and had to have a piece of glass taken out of his leg.

                *Ryan missed the remainder of the season because of the injuries he sustained in
                the accident.*

AUGUST 9   Sam Dungan circles the bases after hitting an infield grounder, but the Cubs lose
                8–7 in ten innings to the Pirates in Pittsburgh. In the eighth, with the Cubs trailing
                7–6, Dungan grounded to Pirate shortstop George Van Haltren, who threw wildly
                to first base. The ball rolled under the grandstand and into a rat hole, allowing
                Dungan to walk slowly around the bases to tie the score.

AUGUST 24   After incessant rains, the Polo Grounds outfield is flooded with water four to five feet
                deep. With 1,500 fans in the ballpark, the Giants insisted on playing the game. New
                York officials responded by moving the diamond forty-five feet closer to the grand-
                stand for a game against the Cubs. Even after the relocation of the infield, the left and
                right fielders had to stand in water over their knees. Chicago won the game 10–4.

SEPTEMBER 3   Malachi Kittridge hits a grand slam in the fifth inning off Tony Mullane that breaks
                a 4–4 tie in a 9–8 win over the Orioles at West Side Grounds.

SEPTEMBER 4   The Orioles score ten runs in the second inning to take a 10–4 lead, but the Cubs
                score seven runs in the third and rally to win 18–10 at South Side Park.

SEPTEMBER 10   Jiggs Parrott hits a grand slam off Al Maul in the Cubs' seven-run fourth inning
                during a 12–3 over Washington at West Side Grounds.

SEPTEMBER 13   In the second game of a double-header at South Side Park, the Cubs score eight
                runs in the fourth inning to take an 8–3 lead, but allow the Braves to the game 8–8
                before darkness ends the contest at the end of the sixth inning. The Cubs won the
                first game 8–6.

SEPTEMBER 22   Willie McGill pitches the Cubs to a 1–0 win over the Orioles at South Side Park.
                The lone run of the game was scored in the ninth inning on a triple by George
                Decker and an error.

                *McGill made his major league debut at the age of 16 in 1890 with Cleveland in
                the Players League. He became the youngest 20-game winner in major league
                history in 1891 when he was 20–14 with two American Association teams.
                With the Cubs in 1893, McGill was 18–17 as a 19-year-old. He couldn't stay
                away from alcohol, however, and he drifted from team to team because of a
                long series of bar fights. McGill won 71 big league games, but his career was
                over when he was only 22.*

SEPTEMBER 26   Cap Anson puts himself into the game as a pinch-hitter in the tenth inning and col-
                lects the first pinch-hit in Cubs history. Anson's single helped the Cubs score four
                times in the inning to beat the Giants 9–5 at South Side Park.

                *At the age of 41, Anson hit .314 in 1893. Bill Dahlen batted .301 and scored
                113 runs.*

1894

Season in a Sentence

A devastating fire at West Side Grounds, a 42–game hitting streak by Bill Dahlen, and Pop Shriver's catch of a ball dropped from the Washington Monument divert attention from a dreary eighth–place finish.

Finish • Won • Lost • Pct • GB

Eighth   57   75   .432   34.0

Manager

Cap Anson

Stats

Stats	Cubs	NL	Rank
Batting Avg:	.314	.309	4
On–Base Pct:	.380	.379	5
Slugging Pct:	.441	.435	5
Home Runs:	65		3
Stolen Bases:	327		1
ERA:	5.68	5.32	11
Fielding Avg:	.918	.927	11
Runs Scored:	1,041		4
Runs Allowed:	1,066		10

Starting Lineup

Pop Schriver, c
Cap Anson, 1b
Jiggs Parrott, 2b
Charlie Irwin, 3b–ss
Bill Dahlen, ss–3b
Walt Wilmot, lf
Bill Lange, cf
Jimmy Ryan, rf
George Decker, 1b–cf
Malachi Kittridge, c

Pitchers

Clark Griffith, sp
Bill Hutchison, sp
Willie McGill, sp
Scott Stratton, sp
Adonis Terry, sp
Bert Abbey, sp

Attendance

239,000 (fourth in NL)

Club Leaders

Batting Avg:	Anson	.388
On–Base Pct:	Anson	.457
Slugging Pct:	Dahlen	.566
Home Runs:	Dahlen	15
RBI:	Wilmot	130
Runs:	Dahlen	149
Stolen Bases:	Wilmot	74
Wins:	Griffith	21
Strikeouts:	Griffith	71
ERA:	Griffith	4.92
Saves:	None	0

APRIL 20   The Cubs lose the season opener 10–6 to the Reds in Cincinnati. Reds outfielder Bug Holliday hit a grand slam off Bill Hutchison in the sixth inning to break a 6–6 tie. Jiggs Parrott, George Decker, and Hutchison all hit homers for the Cubs.

APRIL 22   Willie McGill walks 11 batters but beats the Reds 5–4 in Cincinnati.

MAY 4   In the home opener, the Cubs win 6–4 over the Reds before 5,000 at West Side Grounds. Chicago scored three runs in the sixth inning to erase a 3–1 deficit. Jimmy Ryan collected four hits, including a double.

> Ryan hit .361 and scored 132 runs in 1894. Cap Anson, playing in 83 games at the age of 42, batted .388. Walt Wilmot batted .330, scored 134 runs, and drove in 130. Bill Dahlen had a batting average of .357, scored 149 runs, and had hitting streaks of 42 and 28 games (see August 7, 1894).

MAY 13   Two days after the start of the violent Pullman railroad car strike in Chicago, the Cubs survive a five–run Louisville ninth inning to win 14–12 at West Side Grounds.

> The 1894 season was the highest–scoring campaign in major league history as National League teams combined to score 14.7 runs per game. The reason was

largely due to lengthening the distance between the pitcher's rubber and home plate to 60 feet, six inches prior to the 1893. Batting averages in the NL jumped from .245 in 1892, to .280 in 1893, to .309 in 1894 as hurlers had trouble adjusting to the new distance.

MAY 30   The Cubs beat the Phillies 12–4 and 12–6 in a Memorial Day double–header in Philadelphia.

JUNE 1   The Cubs are held to one hit by Hank Gastright of the Dodgers during a 5–0 loss at Brooklyn.

JUNE 2   The Cubs' batting slump continues, as Ed Stein of the Dodgers pitches a no–hitter in a game stopped after six innings by rain in Brooklyn. The Dodgers won 1–0.

JUNE 11   The Cubs score seven runs in the ninth inning to take a 14–13 lead, but the Braves score two runs in their half to win 15–14 at Boston.

JUNE 14   The Cubs win 12–11 in twelve innings against the Senators in Washington. The score was 11–11 at the end of the sixth inning. Pop Shriver drove in the winning run with a single.

JUNE 25   The Cubs rout the Orioles 15–8 at West Side Grounds.

JULY 2   The Cubs take a 10–5 lead after three innings, but fall 17–15 to the Phillies at West Side Grounds.

After the July 2 loss, the Cubs had a record of 18–38.

JULY 4   Bats provide the fireworks during a holiday double–header at West Side Grounds, as the Cubs beat the Phillies 16–10 in the first game and lose 12–11 in the second tilt.

JULY 9   The Cubs score seven runs in the second inning and defeat Boston 13–11 at West Side Grounds.

JULY 11   The Cubs rap the Braves 13–1 at West Side Grounds.

JULY 25   The Cubs wallop the Pirates 24–6 at West Side Grounds in a game called at the end of the seventh inning because both teams had to catch a train. Chicago collected 26 hits, including nine doubles, a triple, and two homers, all off Pittsburgh hurler Tom Colcolough. Jimmy Ryan scored six of the runs. Cap Anson had five hits, including three doubles.

JULY 27   Cubs pitcher Scott Stratton hits two homers, but gives up 14 runs in a 14–12 loss to the Reds in Cincinnati. The Cubs made the game close after trailing 12–2 in the second inning.

Even the pitchers hit well in 1894. Cubs hurlers Bill Hutchison, Adonis Terry, and Scott Stratton combined to hit .339 with nine homers and a .502 slugging percentage in 327 at–bats. On the mound, the three were much less successful with a record of 24–32 and an ERA of 5.99. The best pitcher for the Cubs in 1894 was Clark Griffith, who had a record of 21–14 in his first full season in the majors. It was the first of six consecutive seasons of 20 wins or more by Griffith.

JULY 28 After taking an 11–2 lead, the Cubs lose 19–13 to the Reds in another slugging match in Cincinnati.

JULY 29 Walt Wilmot hits a grand slam in the eighth inning of a 16–9 win over the Reds in Cincinnati. The slam was hit off Tom Parrott.

AUGUST 1 Cap Anson and George Decker each collect a homer and a total of five hits during a 26–8 lambasting of the Cardinals at West Side Grounds. Anson's homer was a grand slam off Ernie Mason in the fifth inning. Jimmy Ryan scored five runs.

AUGUST 2 A lost ball leads to a protest in game between the Cubs and the Colonels in Louisville. In the fifth inning, Walt Wilmot knocked a foul ball over the fence. Louisville wanted the ball retrieved and put back into play, a common practice in the nineteenth century when one ball was usually used the entire game. Instead, a new ball was tossed to the Louisville pitcher. New balls introduced in the middle of the game always caused controversy because they traveled father when hit and gave the team at bat an advantage. When the Cubs scored four runs in the fifth with the new ball and won the game 4–3, Louisville Manager Billy Barnie filed a protest with the league.

AUGUST 3 The conflict over baseballs between the Cubs and the Colonels in Louisville leads to Chicago losing a game by forfeit. Cap Anson refused to play with the balls furnished by the Louisville club, claiming they were an inferior lot leftover from the previous year. Anson walked out to the plate with a box of balls, which he handed to umpire Tom Lynch accompanied by a message from NL President Nick Young stating they should be used in the game. Barnie refused to play with the balls supplied by Anson, stating a league rule that stipulated that the home teams had the right to provide the balls. Lynch agreed and forfeited the game to the Colonels.

AUGUST 5 With Cap Anson at bat in the sixth inning and the Cubs leading the Reds 8–1 at West Side Grounds, a fire breaks out in the grandstand. Hundreds were injured as the 10,000 fans stampeded for the exits, tearing down barbed wire that had been put up in front of the stands to prevent the bleacher fans from mobbing the umpire. Cubs players George Decker, Jimmy Ryan, and Walt Wilmot used their bats to force open the barbed wire, helping 1,600 fans in the bleachers to escape onto the field. The cause was variously reported as a cigar stub put into garbage, or from a plumber's stove.

AUGUST 6 With much of West Side Grounds in ruins from the fire the previous day, the Cubs beat the Reds 12–9. The burnt area of the ballpark was fenced off, and the spectators were seated on the left side of the diamond. Bill Dahlen collected a hit to extend his hitting streak to 42 games, a Chicago Cubs record.

AUGUST 7 The Cubs win 13–11 against the Reds at West Side Grounds, but Bill Dahlen's 42-game hit streak comes to an end. Batting second in the lineup, Dahlen was hitless in six at-bats. The pitchers who stopped Dahlen were Chauncey Fisher and Tom Parrott. Parrott's brother Jiggs played second base for the Cubs in the game. Strangely, the hitters surrounding Dahlen in the lineup had big days. Jimmy Ryan, batting leadoff just ahead of Dahlen, collected five hits, and Walt Wilmot, batting behind Dahlen, also had five hits. The Cubs had a total of 18 hits in the game. Wilmot also stole four bases for the second game in a row.

Dahlen's 42–game hit streak is the longest in Cubs history. The second longest is a 30–game streak by Jerome Walton in 1989. The day after Dahlen's 42–game streak ended, he started another one that lasted 28 games, giving him hits in 70 of 71 games. The 28–game hitting streak is the third longest in Cubs history, tied with a similar streak by Ron Santo in 1966. The only players in major league history with a hitting streak longer than 42 games are Joe DiMaggio (56 in 1941), Willie Keeler (44 in 1897), and Pete Rose (44 in 1978).

Fire at the Ballpark

Fire was a constant concern at nineteenth–century ballparks. The grandstands and bleachers were made of wood, and trash piled up for weeks underneath the seats without anyone bothering to dispose of it. The invention of tarpaulins to cover the field during rainstorms was still more than a decade into the future, and teams kept large mounds of sawdust at the ballparks to help dry out the fields. Add thousands of cigar–smoking fans discarding their stogies into the debris below, and you have a potentially lethal mix. In 1894 alone, National League ballparks in Boston and Philadelphia were destroyed by fire, and those in Baltimore and Chicago were severely damaged. The fire at West Side Grounds in Chicago happened on August 5 during a game against the Cincinnati Reds and caused a wild panic among the spectators in which several met with serious injury and a large number of others were cut and bruised in endeavoring to make their exit.

The Cubs were leading the Reds 8–1 in the seventh inning with a crowd of about 10,000 packed in the ballpark. Every available seat in the grandstand and bleachers was occupied. Suddenly a cry of fire was heard from the bleachers, and a thin veil of smoke was seen creeping through the seats from below. In a very short time, a terrible panic ensued. The four exits leading from the park were jammed with anxious fans. The exits were not large enough to permit the terrified throng to go through, and hundreds sought safety by jumping over the barbed wire and onto the field. The four rows of barbed wire were put up to prevent bleachers fans from mobbing the umpire. Many of those who tried to climb the wire became entangled as they tried to crawl through. Their clothing was torn in shreds, and hands and legs were lacerated by the sharp barbs. The crowd was caught between the growing fire and the barbed fence. Cubs players George Decker, Walt Wilmot, and Jimmy Ryan used their bats to pry open the barbed wire, and their efforts along with the pressure of the crowd finally tore the fence down and allowed hundreds to escape the flames. About 500 injuries were reported. Fortunately, two hospitals were nearby to treat the wounded.

When the fire department arrived, the stands on the first base side were a mass of flames. The fire spread with lightning–like rapidity, and the small force of firemen that responded to the first alarm was unable to cope with the raging flames. The fire marshall put in a call for reinforcements. The cedar paving blocks and wooden sidewalks on Lincoln Street (now Wolcott Street) adjacent to the first base stands also caught fire. It was an hour before the blaze was under control. The cause of the fire was thought to be a lighted cigar being thrown among the combustible material under the stands.

Much of the third base side of the ballpark was saved, and a game was played at West Side Grounds the very next day. By the start of the 1895 season, West Side Grounds had been rebuilt, and it served as the home of the Cubs until 1915.

AUGUST 12   The Cubs score seven runs in the
             seventh inning of a 16–5 win over
             Cleveland at West Side Grounds.

AUGUST 22   With the Giants up by six runs over
             the Cubs in the eighth inning in New
             York, Bill Lange comes to the plate
             wielding a five–foot, ten–inch bat
             that had been given to teammate
             Jimmy Ryan by a New York theater
             manager. Neither umpire Jack
             McQuaid nor the Giants objected,
             and Lange, who had struck out twice
             against New York pitcher Jouett
             Meekin, hit a soft grounder to first
             baseman Jack Doyle, who mishan-
             dled it. The Giants won 8–5.

Bill Dahlen enjoyed a career year in 1894, reaching
personal bests in runs, hits, RBIs, homers, and
batting average.

AUGUST 26   On an off day in Washington, Pop
             Shriver of the Cubs catches a ball
             dropped some 500 feet from the top
             of the Washington Monument.

Pop Shriver's Monumental Catch

The Washington Monument was completed in 1885, topping out at 555 feet at a time when an eight–story building was considered a "skyscraper." Baseball players visiting Washington were immediately intrigued by the notion of whether or not it was possible to catch a ball dropped from the top of the shaft. Many players tried and failed to make such a catch, among them Paul Hines, Pop Snyder, Hardy Richardson, and future Hall of Famer Buck Ewing. It was generally believed it was beyond any man's power to catch a ball from such a great height. Furthermore, many argued that anyone who would get his hands on the ball would be seriously injured, if not killed. On August 26, 1894, Cubs catcher Pop Shriver, at the urging of manager Cap Anson, decided to put the idea to the test and became the first to successfully complete the task.

A party including Cubs players Clark Griffith, Jiggs Parrott, George Decker, Scott Stratton, and Bill Hutchison went to the observation platform with a supply of baseballs. Since it was against the law to drop objects from the top of the monument, the group had to proceed with caution.

Griffith dropped the first ball, and Shriver made no attempt to catch it because he wanted to see how high off the ground the ball would bounce to try and gauge the speed at which the ball traveled. When it bounced no higher than the average pop–up, he was encouraged to make a try at the second drop. The signal was given from above, and again a ball was pitched forth. Shriver caught it cleanly to the applause of the spectators who had gathered to watch the event. He didn't get a chance to repeat the act, because the police officer assigned to guard the monument threatened arrest if the players continued.

Washington Senators catcher Gabby Street also caught a ball dropped from the Washington Monument, in 1908. Street missed fourteen balls before he caught one.

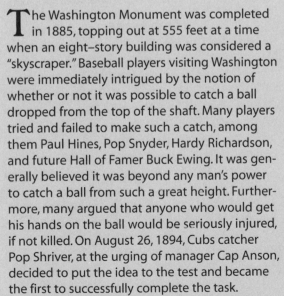

AUGUST 29   The Cubs wallop the Phillies 13–6 at Philadelphia.

SEPTEMBER 1   The Cubs run away with a 17–7 decision over the Braves in Boston.

SEPTEMBER 10   The Cubs are pounded 25–8 by Boston at West Side Grounds. Adonis Terry gave up
                 all 25 runs in pitching a complete game.

SEPTEMBER 11   A day after losing by 17 runs, the Cubs turn the tables and drub Boston 17–2 at
                 West Side Grounds.

SEPTEMBER 15   Bill Dahlen's 28–game winning streak is stopped during a 10–3 win over the
                 Dodgers at West Side Grounds.

SEPTEMBER 20   The Cubs score ten runs in the first inning and rout the Phillies 20–4 at West Side
                 Grounds.

SEPTEMBER 24   The Cubs rout Washington 17–5 at West Side Grounds.

SEPTEMBER 30   The Cubs close the season with a 20–9 loss to the Orioles at West Side Grounds.

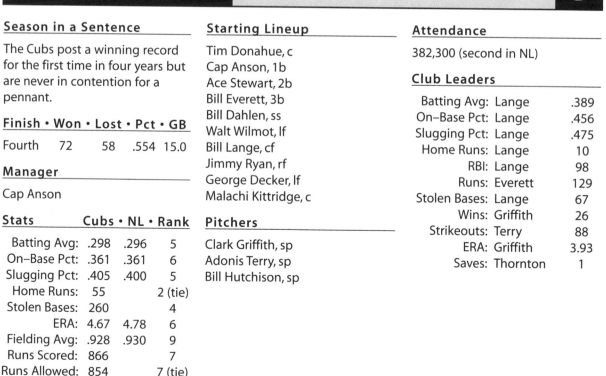

1895   Cubs

Season in a Sentence

The Cubs post a winning record for the first time in four years but are never in contention for a pennant.

Finish • Won • Lost • Pct • GB

Fourth   72   58   .554   15.0

Manager

Cap Anson

Stats

Stats	Cubs	NL	Rank
Batting Avg:	.298	.296	5
On–Base Pct:	.361	.361	6
Slugging Pct:	.405	.400	5
Home Runs:	55		2 (tie)
Stolen Bases:	260		4
ERA:	4.67	4.78	6
Fielding Avg:	.928	.930	9
Runs Scored:	866		7
Runs Allowed:	854		7 (tie)

Starting Lineup

Tim Donahue, c
Cap Anson, 1b
Ace Stewart, 2b
Bill Everett, 3b
Bill Dahlen, ss
Walt Wilmot, lf
Bill Lange, cf
Jimmy Ryan, rf
George Decker, lf
Malachi Kittridge, c

Pitchers

Clark Griffith, sp
Adonis Terry, sp
Bill Hutchison, sp

Attendance

382,300 (second in NL)

Club Leaders

Batting Avg:	Lange	.389
On–Base Pct:	Lange	.456
Slugging Pct:	Lange	.475
Home Runs:	Lange	10
RBI:	Lange	98
Runs:	Everett	129
Stolen Bases:	Lange	67
Wins:	Griffith	26
Strikeouts:	Terry	88
ERA:	Griffith	3.93
Saves:	Thornton	1

APRIL 18   In the season opener, the Cubs win 10–7 over the Cardinals in St. Louis. Playing in his major league debut, Chicago second baseman Ace Stewart hit a home run. Walt Wilmot and Jimmy Ryan also homered for the Cubs.

MAY 2   In the home opener, the Cubs lose 5–4 in ten innings to Louisville at West Side Grounds.

MAY 14   The Cubs suffer an embarrassing 14–1 loss to the Giants at West Side Grounds. In the Giants' half of the third inning with the bases loaded, George Van Haltren took a ball on a 2–2 count. Tom Bannon, the runner on third, believed it was ball four, trotted home, and brushed past catcher Tim Donahue to score a run. The runners on first and second moved up as well, and the Giants were credited with an unmolested triple steal.

MAY 19   Cubs pitcher Adonis Terry collects a homer, a double, and two singles in a 14–9 win over the Dodgers at West Side Grounds. Terry's homer and double were struck during Chicago's eight–run third inning. The homer was a fluke, rolling into a hole near the outfield fence, enabling him to circle the bases.

MAY 20   The Cubs collect 27 hits in a 24–6 win over the Phillies at West Side Grounds. Ace Stewart hit a grand slam off Kid Carsey in Chicago's seven–run eighth inning. For the second day in a row, a pitcher starred with the bat, as Clark Griffith picked up five hits.

            Griffith had a record of 26–14 in 1895 with an ERA of 3.95. Adonis Terry was 21–14.

MAY 22   The Cubs smash the Phillies 14–6 at West Side Grounds.

            The Cubs had a record of 19–10 on May 25.

JUNE 13   Bill Hutchison is an easy mark for Braves batters as he allows all of the runs in a 20–3 loss in Boston.

JUNE 23   With a crowd of 14,000 on hand at West Side Grounds, a pressure group called the "Sunday Observance League," led by Reverend W. W. Clark, holds up play about five minutes in the third inning when the entire Cubs team is arrested for "aiding and abetting the forming of a noisy crowd on a Sunday." Clark had been watching the game from a housetop on Wood Street behind the left field fence and taking the names of the Cubs players in the game. He then secured warrants from Justice Cleveland of Norwood Park. The players filed to the clubhouse in center field, and the warrants were served by five constables. Chicago Owner Jim Hart posted bond, amounting to $100 per player, and the game was resumed. Hart invited Clark to stay for the game, but the reverend declined. The Cubs went on to trounce Cleveland 13–4. (See January 14, 1896.)

JULY 1   The Cubs take a one–sided 17–5 win from the Cardinals at West Side Grounds.

JULY 4   More than 35,000 fans watch a separate admission double–header against the Reds at West Side Grounds. In the first game, before 13,020, the Cubs trailed 7–1 before scoring three runs in the eighth inning, three in the ninth, and one in the tenth to win 8–7. Bill Everett's single, his fifth hit of the game, drove in the game–winner. The second game drew 22,913, which taxed the seating capacity of the ballpark. The outfield was shortened by about 100 feet by the crush of fans surrounding the diamond. The crowd delayed the game several times by surging onto the field. The eighteen policeman on hand were powerless to stop them. A reserve force of eighty officers marched into the ball-park to great cheers and secured the peace, allowing play to continue. Balls hit into the crowd were homers, and there were ten of them in the game, six by the Cubs, even though the contest was called in the seventh inning by darkness. Walt Wilmot hit two homers for Chicago, and Tim Donahue, Cap Anson, Bill Lange, and Bill Everett added one each. Cincinnati pitcher Frank Foreman allowed all six homers and hit two himself. The final score was 9–5 in favor of the Cubs.

Bill Lange's .389 average in 1895 is the team's all–time high.

JULY 17   The Cubs score all 12 of the runs in the fourth inning of a 12–7 win over the Phillies at West Side Grounds. The game was called at the end of the seventh inning to allow the Phillies to catch a train.

AUGUST 6   Cubs players are detained by police following a 6–6 win over the Reds in Cincinnati. Farmer Vaughn of the Reds discovered that one of his bats was missing and received a report that it was taken by a member of the Chicago contingent. Threatened with arrest, Malachi Kittridge of the Cubs surrendered the bat.

AUGUST 24   Jimmy Ryan hits a grand slam in the first inning off Varney Anderson to set the stage for a 9–8 win over the Senators in Washington. The contest was called at the end of the seventh inning by darkness.

AUGUST 27   In the fourteenth inning of the first game of a double–header, Bill Lange hits a ball that bounces off the hands of Senators right fielder Win Mercer and into the bleachers to score Bill Everett from second base for the winning run in a 6–5 win at Washington. Under the scoring rules of the day, Lange was credited with a single instead of a home run because the game ended when Everett crossed home plate. The second tilt ended in a 6–6 tie, which was called on account of darkness after seven innings.

SEPTEMBER 10   The Cubs defeat the Giants 13–2 and 8–6 in a double–header in New York.

SEPTEMBER 14   The Cubs score nine runs in the first inning and defeat the Colonels 14–5 at Louisville. The contest was called by darkness at the end of the seventh inning.

Top hitters for the Cubs in 1895 were rookie third baseman Bill Everett, who batted .358 with 129 runs scored, and Bill Lange, who had a batting average of .389 and scored 120 times. No Cub since 1895 has topped Lange's .389 average.

1896

Cubs

Season in a Sentence

Cap Anson boldly predicts a pennant, but the Cubs slip a notch to fifth place.

Finish • Won • Lost • Pct • GB

Fifth   71   57   .555   18.5

Manager

Cap Anson

Stats

Stats	Cubs	NL	Rank
Batting Avg:	.286	.290	9
On–Base Pct:	.349	.354	9
Slugging Pct:	.390	.387	5
Home Runs:	34		7
Stolen Bases:	332		3
ERA:	4.41	4.38	7
Fielding Avg:	.934	.938	9
Runs Scored:	815		7
Runs Allowed:	799		7

Starting Lineup

Malachi Kittridge, c
Cap Anson, 1b
Fred Pfeffer, 2b
Bill Everett, 3b
Bill Dahlen, ss
George Decker, lf
Bill Lange, cf
Jimmy Ryan, rf
Tim Donahue, c
Barry McCormick, 3b

Pitchers

Clark Griffith, sp
Danny Friend, sp
Adonis Terry, sp
Buttons Briggs, sp

Attendance

317,500 (third in NL)

Club Leaders

Batting Avg:	Dahlen	.352
On–Base Pct:	Dahlen	.438
Slugging Pct:	Dahlen	.553
Home Runs:	Dahlen	9
RBI:	Lange	92
Runs:	Dahlen	137
Stolen Bases:	Lange	84
Wins:	Griffith	23
Strikeouts:	Friend	86
ERA:	Griffith	3.54
Saves:	Briggs	1

JANUARY 14   Ten days after Utah is admitted as the forty–fifth state, a Chicago jury acquits Cubs outfielder Walt Wilmot of charges violating the Sabbath law by playing Sunday baseball. The trial was the result of his arrest during the game at West Side Grounds on June 23, 1895. Charges against the other Chicago players were subsequently dropped, and the way was cleared for Sunday baseball in the Windy City in the future.

APRIL 16   The Cubs win the season opener 4–2 over the Colonels in Louisville. Danny Friend pitched the complete game victory.

APRIL 17   The Cubs score ten runs in the first inning and win 14–3 over the Colonels in Louisville.

              With injuries to his catchers early in the season, Cap Anson moved behind the plate for 10 games even though he was 44 years old and hadn't played the position since he caught two games in 1891. Anson played in 11 more games as a catcher as a 45–year–old in 1897.

APRIL 30   In the first home game of the season, the Cubs win 8–3 over the Cardinals before 7,000 at West Side Grounds.

MAY 3   Bill Dahlen collects three triples during a 16–7 win over the Cardinals at West Side Grounds. The two teams combined for nine triples in the game, five of them by the

Cardinals, even though neither club hit a double or a home run. The unusual situation was created by a large crowd that overflowed the grandstand and ringed the outfield. It was agreed before the game that any ball hit into the crowd would be a ground–rule triple.

MAY 4   Cap Anson hits a two–run walk–off single in the ninth inning to beat the Dodgers 2–1 at West Side Grounds.

MAY 8   A 5–3 win over the Phillies at West Side Grounds ends with an unusual double play. With one out in the ninth and Phillies on first and second, Billy Nash stopped to argue with the umpire over a called strike without calling time. Clark Griffith threw a pitch in the midst of the argument, and it nicked Nash's bat. Catcher Malachi Kittridge picked up the ball, fired to third baseman Barry McCormick to force the lead runner, and McCormick threw to first to retire Nash, who was still at home plate arguing with the ump.

MAY 13   Seven days after the Supreme Court case *Plessy v. Ferguson* approves racial segregation under the "separate but equal" doctrine, a near riot erupts at West Side Grounds over the decisions of umpire Tim Keefe during a game against Boston. In the tenth inning with the score 4–4, Bill Everett of the Cubs lined a ball down the left field line that looked good for a triple. With Keefe's attention focused on the ball, Boston first baseman Tommy Tucker grabbed Everett around the neck and threw him to the ground as he rounded the bag. Everett popped and began to fight with Tucker. During the altercation, second baseman Bobby Lowe retrieved the ball and tagged Everett. Keefe called Everett out, ignoring the obvious interference. At the end of the tenth, with the score still deadlocked, Cap Anson believed that it was too dark to continue and appealed to the umpire to stop play. Keefe thought otherwise and ordered the start of the eleventh inning. The

Bill Everett hit over .300 five years in a row as the Cubs' third sacker.

Cubs did everything they could to prolong the game so that the inning couldn't be completed. Boston scored six runs as the Cubs made one error after another and made no attempts to retire the opposition on the base paths. Keefe finally stopped the game and awarded a forfeit to Boston.

MAY 18   The Cubs score seven runs in the sixth inning, four of them on a grand slam by Bill Lange off Sal Campfield, during a 15–3 win over the Giants at West Side Grounds.

JUNE 3   The Cubs romp to a 14–8 win over the Giants in New York.

JUNE 10   The Cubs score three runs in the ninth inning to beat the Senators 14–13 in Washington.

JUNE 19   The Cubs defeat the Spiders 8–3 in a turbulent game in Cleveland. In the seventh inning, umpire Tom Lynch changed a close call at first base and enraged Cleveland Manager Patsy Tebeau. Lynch ejected Tebeau, but he refused to leave the field. The two began to fight, and a riot nearly ensued. Lynch walked off the field and refused to continue. Players Cy Young of Cleveland and Con Daily of the Cubs served as umpires for the remainder of the contest.

JUNE 25   The Cubs score nine runs in the sixth inning and beat the Pirates 17–10 at West Side Grounds.

JUNE 28   The Cubs score three runs in the ninth to defeat Louisville 4–3 at West Side Grounds.

JULY 1   The Cubs lose 19–7 to Cleveland at West Side Grounds. Pitcher Danny Friend became so disgusted by the misplays made behind him that he walked off the field in the eighth inning and refused to return to the mound. Malachi Kittridge finished the game as a pitcher. It was the only game that Kittridge played at any position other than as a catcher during his eighteen–year major league career.

JULY 4   Bill Lange steals five bases during an 11–6 win over Louisville in the second game of a double–header at West Side Grounds. The Cubs stole 11 bases during the contest. The Cubs also won the first game 8–5.

Lange hit .326, scored 114 runs, and drove in 92 in 1896. Bill Dahlen hit .352 and scored 137 times. Bill Everett had a .320 average and 130 runs. Clark Griffith was the top pitcher, with a 23–11 record and an ERA of 3.54.

JULY 7   Cap Anson drives in seven runs during a 13–11 win over the Orioles at West Side Grounds.

JULY 11   A balk by New York pitcher Jouett Meekin in the twelfth inning allows the winning run to score in a 3–2 Cubs win over the Giants at West Side Grounds.

JULY 13   Ed Delahanty of the Phillies hits four homers at West Side Grounds, but the Cubs survive his heroics to win the game 9–8. Delahanty was the first player in major league history to homer four times in a game. All four were hit off Adonis Terry. Delahanty also hit a single and drove in seven runs. One homer was hit into the bleachers, one cleared the right field wall, and two were inside the park. Both inside–the–park homers were hit over the head of center fielder Bill Lange. One of them bounced behind the clubhouse. Delahanty was applauded wildly by the Cubs fans for his efforts, and the cheering didn't stop until he stepped onto the team omnibus to leave for the hotel.

JULY 16   The Cubs roll to a 17–8 win over Washington at West Side Grounds.

JULY 22   The Cubs win a thrilling 10–9 win over Boston in eleven innings at West Side

Grounds. The Cubs scored seven runs in the seventh inning to take an 8–5 lead, but allowed Boston to score three in the eighth to tie the contest 8–8. Both clubs scored in the tenth. The winning run was scored on a steal of home by Fred Pfeffer while a teammate was trapped between first and second in a rundown.

AUGUST 1   George Decker runs his hitting streak to 26 games during an 8–3 win over Louisville at West Side Grounds.

AUGUST 29   After both teams score five runs in the first inning, the Cubs go on to defeat the Senators 13–11 in Washington. The contest was called on account of darkness after seven innings of play.

AUGUST 31   In the bottom of the tenth inning of a scoreless game between the Cubs and Senators in Washington, Bill Lange makes a diving somersault catch off the bat of Gene DeMontreville. During the same inning, Cubs first baseman George Decker broke his wrist on a throw from third baseman Barry McCormick. Since there was a hospital adjacent to the ballpark, Washington outfielder Kip Selbach used a ladder as a battering ram to knock down several boards of the outfield fence to give Decker a convenient exit. This incident evolved into a popular legend that Lange crashed though the fence making a catch off Selbach. The Senators won the game 1–0 in eleven innings.

1897

Season in a Sentence

In Cap Anson's last season as manager of the Cubs, the club sinks to ninth place.

Finish • Won • Lost • Pct • GB

Ninth   59   73   .447   34.0

Manager

Cap Anson

Stats

Stats	Cubs	NL	Rank
Batting Avg:	.282	.292	8
On–Base Pct:	.347	.354	9
Slugging Pct:	.386	.386	7
Home Runs:	38		4
Stolen Bases:	264		3
ERA:	4.53	4.31	8
Fielding Avg:	.932	.939	10
Runs Scored:	832		4
Runs Allowed:	894		11

Starting Lineup

Malachi Kittridge, c
Cap Anson, 1b
Jim Connor, 2b
Bill Everett, 3b
Barry McCormick, ss–3b
George Decker, lf
Bill Lange, cf
Jimmy Ryan, rf
Bill Dahlen, ss
Nixey Callahan, 2b–p–lf–ss
Walter Thornton, lf–p
Tim Donahue, c

Pitchers

Clark Griffith, sp
Danny Friend, sp
Nixey Callahan, sp
Buttons Briggs, sp
Walter Thornton, sp
Roger Denzer, sp

Attendance

327,160 (fourth in NL)

Club Leaders

Batting Avg:	Lange	.340
On–Base Pct:	Lange	.406
Slugging Pct:	Lange	.480
Home Runs:	Dahlen	6
RBI:	Ryan	85
Runs:	Lange	119
Stolen Bases:	Lange	73
Wins:	Griffith	21
Strikeouts:	Griffith	102
ERA:	Griffith	3.72
Saves:	Griffith	1

APRIL 22   Six weeks after William McKinley is inaugurated as President, the Cubs lose 8–7 in ten innings to the Reds in Cincinnati in the season opener. The Reds scored two runs in the ninth inning to tie the score 6–6. After the Cubs plated a run in the top of the tenth, the Reds rallied again with two runs. Clark Griffith pitched a complete game to take the loss.

MAY 4   Prior to the home opener at West Side Grounds, Cap Anson is presented with a silver service, among other gifts and testimonials, in honor of the start of his twenty-second season with the Cubs. Before 14,960, the Cubs won the game 5–2. Playing as the catcher and batting ninth, Anson had a single in three at-bats.

           Anson had announced before the season that 1897 would be his last as a player. Among those in attendance were comedian Eddie Foy and actors Maurice and Ethel Barrymore. Before the game, the players of both teams stood at attention along the base lines as a band played John Philip Sousa's "El Capitan" march in Anson's honor.

MAY 20   Washington scores five runs in the ninth inning off Buttons Briggs to beat the Cubs 16–14 at West Side Grounds. Briggs pitched the complete game.

MAY 23   In his second straight start, Buttons Briggs allows 16 runs to Washington and wastes another strong offensive performance, taking a 16–12 loss at West Side Grounds. Bill Lange and Senators second baseman John O'Brien came to blows, and both were ejected.

JUNE 14   In the morning at Eastern Park in Brooklyn, a combined team of Cubs and Dodgers plays a visiting team from Australia. The Australians won 11–8 in a contest shortened to five innings. In the afternoon, the Cubs lost to the Dodgers 15–4.

JUNE 29   The Cubs set a major league record by scoring 36 runs in a 36–7 annihilation of the Louisville Colonels at West Side Grounds.

           On July 24, 1882, the Cubs beat Cleveland 35–4, and on July 3, 1883, Chicago won 31–7 over Buffalo. Since 1897, no big league club has scored more than 29 runs in a game. The two highest run totals since then are by the Red Sox, in a 29–4 win over the St. Louis Browns in 1950, and by the White Sox, in a 29–6 triumph over the Kansas City Athletics in 1955.

JULY 4   The Cubs score seven runs in the sixth inning and beat the Senators 16–7 at West Side Grounds.

JULY 17   The Cubs are pounded by the Orioles 20–2 at West Side Grounds.

JULY 19   Bill Lange's two-run, walk-off homer single in the ninth inning beats the Phillies 7–6 at West Side Grounds.

JULY 23   The Cubs score seven runs in the second inning and defeat the Giants 14–3 at West Side Grounds.

JULY 25   In his first game back after suffering a severe spike wound on May 30, Bill Dahlen steals home to account for the only run in a 1–0 victory over the Colonels at West

Side Grounds. Dahlen scored the run in the fourth inning while Louisville pitcher Bert Cunningham and first baseman Perry Werden were carrying on a heated argument without calling time. The game was called by rain in the seventh inning. Nixey Callahan pitched the shutout.

JULY 27   Bill Everett's walk–off homer in the tenth inning beats the Reds 4–3 at West Side Grounds.

AUGUST 8   Cap Anson collects five hits, the last of which drives in the winning run in the ninth inning to lift the Cubs to a 7–6 win over Cleveland at West Side Grounds.

AUGUST 10   The Cubs gallop to a 16–6 win over the Colonels in Louisville.

AUGUST 13   Clark Griffith pitches his first career shutout to beat the Reds 2–0 in Cincinnati. Bill Lange scored both runs.

Cap Anson's skills were eroding by 1897, his final year as a player, though at age 45 he managed to hit .285.

The decision over the Reds was the 104th win of Griffith's career, which began in 1891. He failed to hold a team scoreless prior to 1897 because he believed that shutouts were bad luck. Whenever Griffith went into the eighth or ninth inning of a game with a shutout, he would groove pitches until he allowed a run. With only a two–run lead in the August 13, 1897, contest, Griffith had little margin for error and wound up with the shutout. When no ill will befell him, he eventually began to believe that shutouts weren't bad luck after all. Griffith ended his career with 22 shutouts and led the league in the category in both 1900 and 1901.

AUGUST 30   A pitcher appearing in the outfield wearing a bathrobe, the ejection of a key player, and dwindling daylight highlight a Cubs victory over the Giants in New York. With his team leading 7–5 at the end of the eighth inning, Cap Anson was fined $25 and thumbed by umpire Bob Emslie for arguing too strenuously about the lack of daylight. After the Cubs rallied for three more runs to take a 10–5 lead in the top of the ninth, left fielder George Decker moved to first base to replace Anson in the bottom half. Pitcher Danny Friend, who had already showered and was wearing his street clothes, was summoned to play left. Friend donned his Chicago baseball cap, slipped on a bathrobe, and trotted onto the field. Giants Manager Bill Joyce protested because Friend was out of uniform, and as he and Emslie argued the ump decided was too dark to continue. The top of the ninth was canceled, and the score reverted to a 7–5 Chicago win.

SEPTEMBER 6   The Cubs lose 14–7 and win 12–8 in a Labor Day double–header against the Dodgers in Brooklyn. The second game was called after eight innings by darkness.

SEPTEMBER 25   Bill Lange foils an intentional walk during an 8–1 win over the Pirates in Pittsburgh. In the seventh inning, with the score 1–1 and two runners on base, Lange stepped to the edge of the plate and reached out and poked the ball down the line for a double, which scored two runs for a 3–1 lead. Chicago added five more runs in the eighth before the contest was called by darkness.

SEPTEMBER 28   The Cubs score 11 runs in the fifth inning to take a 15–5 lead in Pittsburgh before the Pirates score five times in the sixth inning and four in the seventh. The final was 15–14 in favor of Chicago before it was called by darkness at the end of the seventh.

OCTOBER 3   In what would prove to be the final two games of Cap Anson's playing career, the Cubs lose 10–9 and win 7–1 against the Cardinals in St. Louis. Batting clean–up and playing first base in the first game, Anson hit two homers. It was his first multi–homer game since 1888. Anson was hitless in three at–bats in the finale.

Before the start of the 1898 season, the Cubs released Anson. (See February 1, 1898.)

1898   Cubs

Season in a Sentence

In their first year without Cap Anson, the "orphaned" Cubs finish 20 games above .500.

Finish • Won • Lost • Pct • GB

Fourth   85   65   .567   17.5

Manager

Tom Burns

Stats

Stats	Cubs	NL	Rank
Batting Avg:	.274	.271	4
On–Base Pct:	.343	.334	4
Slugging Pct:	.350	.347	6
Home Runs:	18		8 (tie)
Stolen Bases:	220		3
ERA:	2.83	3.60	1
Fielding Avg:	.936	.942	10
Runs Scored:	828		5
Runs Allowed:	679		3

Starting Lineup

Tim Donahue, c
Bill Everett, 1b
Jim Connor, 2b
Barry McCormick, 3b
Bill Dahlen, ss
Jimmy Ryan, lf
Bill Lange, cf
Sam Mertes, rf
Jimmy Ryan, rf
Walter Thornton, cf–p
Danny Green, rf
Frank Isbell, cf–p
Frank Chance, c–rf

Pitchers

Clark Griffith, sp
Nixey Callahan, sp
Walter Thornton, sp
Walt Woods, sp
Matt Kilroy, sp
Frank Isbell, sp

Attendance

424,352 (first in NL)

Club Leaders

Batting Avg:	Ryan	.323
On–Base Pct:	Ryan	.405
Slugging Pct:	Ryan	.446
Home Runs:	Lange	5
RBI:	Ryan	79
	Dahlen	79
Runs:	Ryan	122
Stolen Bases:	Ryan	29
Wins:	Griffith	24
Strikeouts:	Griffith	97
ERA:	Griffith	1.88
Saves:	None	0

FEBRUARY 1   The Cubs release Cap Anson as both a player and a manager. Anson had been a
              player with the Cubs since 1876 and player–manager since 1879. He played on six
              NL champions and managed five. Tom Burns, who played for the Cubs from 1880
              through 1891, replaced Anson as manager.

              *Anson was let go following a ninth–place finish and a 59–73 record in 1897,
              which Anson charged was full of "drunkards and loafers." He was never on
              good terms with Jim Hart, who took over as club president in 1891. The two
              grew increasingly antagonistic toward each other as years went on. Hart regarded
              Anson as a relic of the past who was unwilling to change with the times. Anson
              countered that Hart was a meddler who undermined his authority by encouraging
              rebellion among his players. Anson was also angry that Hart was unwilling to
              pay the salaries necessary to build a winning team. Anson served as manager of
              the Giants briefly in 1898, posting a 9–13 record, before resigning because of
              friction with the owners. Until his death at the age of 70 in 1922, Anson was
              involved in a number of business ventures, almost all of which ended badly,
              including a bowling alley, a billiard parlor, and a golf course. He also played for
              and managed a touring semipro club when he was in his late 50s called Anson's
              Colts that failed to generate much interest, and marketed a ginger beer remem-
              bered for its caps, which had an unfortunate tendency to explode off the bot-
              tles. In a brief fling with politics, Anson was Chicago's city clerk for two years
              before losing a re–election bid. He finally found his calling by performing on
              the vaudeville stage, building his act around his fame as a ballplayer in addition
              to some slapstick comedy.*

APRIL 15   Two months after the U. S. battleship *Maine* explodes in Havana harbor, the Cubs
              win the season opener 2–1 over the Cardinals in St. Louis. Clark Griffith pitched
              the complete game, surviving a one–run Cardinal rally in the ninth.

              *With Cap Anson no longer in charge, the Chicago club was nicknamed the
              "Orphans" in the newspapers.*

APRIL 16   Sportsman's Park in St. Louis is destroyed by fire, postponing the game between the
              Cubs and the Cardinals.

              *The ballpark was crowded with 6,000 people when the flames broke out in the
              second inning. The players on both teams did heroic work rescuing many fans
              as the fire, fueled by a strong wind, spread rapidly. At least 100 were burned
              and many suffered broken limbs from jumping from the stands to the grounds.
              The flames also destroyed the saloon and residence of Cardinals Owner Chris
              Von Der Ahe and damaged an adjacent railway depot and the fairgrounds
              across the street. A lit cigar on tarpaulins was the suspected cause.*

APRIL 17   The Cubs score ten runs in the fourth inning and slaughter the Cardinals 14–1 in
              St. Louis.

              *The Cardinals were in no condition to play the game. Club Owner Chris Von
              Der Ahe ordered Manager Tim Hurst and his players to work all night clearing
              debris from the fire the previous day and to help carpenters build 1,700 tempo-
              rary seats.*

APRIL 29   Four days after the United States declares war on Spain, starting the Spanish–American War, the Cubs score nine runs in the seventh inning and blast Louisville 16–2 in the home opener at West Side Grounds. Clark Griffith gave way to his superstition against shutting out the opposition and let the visitors score a couple of runs in the eighth inning. Frank Chance made his major league debut as a substitute for catcher Tim Donahue. Chance allowed two easy pop–ups to fall harmlessly to the earth on order from Griffith, who wanted to avoid the shutout.

Chance remained with the Cubs until 1912. After playing as a catcher during his early years, Chance moved to first base late in the 1902 season, forming one of the most famous infields in big league history with shortstop Joe Tinker and second baseman Johnny Evers. Chance was the manager of the Cubs from 1905 through 1912, leading the club into four World Series including world championships in 1907 and 1908. In fifteen seasons as a Cub, Chance played in 1,274 games and collected 794 runs, 1,266 hits, 200 doubles, 79 triples, a .297 batting average, and an all–time club record 400 stolen bases.

MAY 2   The Cubs outslug Louisville 13–7 at West Side Grounds.

MAY 9   The Cubs splatter the Cleveland Spiders 12–1 at West Side Grounds.

MAY 17   The Cubs roll to a 13–6 win over Cleveland at West Side Grounds.

MAY 18   Cubs pitcher Walter Thornton ties a major league record by hitting three batters in a row with pitches in the fourth inning of an 11–4 loss to the Cardinals at West Side Grounds.

MAY 24   The Cubs score seven runs in the first inning to take a 7–1 lead, but go on to lose 15–13 to the Orioles at West Side Grounds.

MAY 25   The Cubs score seven runs in the fifth inning and defeat the Orioles 20–4 in a contest called after seven innings by darkness.

JUNE 6   Bill Dahlen hits three triples during a 15–2 win over the Dodgers in Brooklyn. Frank Isbell and Bill Everett each collected five singles.

Dahlen batted .290 in 1898. The top hitters were Jimmy Ryan, who hit .323 and scored 122 runs, and Bill Lange, with a .319 average.

JUNE 15   Having overcome his phobia about pitching a shutout, Clark Griffith allows 11 hits and defeats the Cardinals 4–0 at West Side Grounds.

Griffith was 24–10, pitched four shutouts, and led the league in ERA with a 1.88 mark. Nixey Callahan had a 20–10 record and a 2.46 earned run average.

JUNE 26   After rolling up a 13–4 lead in the fifth inning, the Cubs win a 13–10 slugging match with the Dodgers at West Side Grounds.

JUNE 29   Now managing the New York Giants, Cap Anson makes his first appearance in Chicago since his release by the Cubs. A total of 12,000 attended the game. Prior to the contest, which the Cubs won 12–4 at West Side Grounds, Anson was given a huge floral horseshoe to great cheers.

Infielder Jim Connor missed several games in July because of sunstroke.

JULY 4   The day after Theodore Roosevelt and the Rough Riders storm San Juan Hill against Spanish forces in Cuba, the Cubs lose 11–2 and win 4–3 against the Cleveland Spiders in a raucous, separate admission holiday double–header at West Side Grounds. About 12,000 attended the second game, some 500 equipped with firecrackers and revolvers in celebration of the military victory of the previous day. When a great play was made, the armed rooters flashed their guns and shot up in the air. Cleveland right fielder Louis Sockalexis, a Native American, was a target for many of the firecrackers, and stood a big part of the time in a blue haze.

JULY 5   Henry Clarke, a former pitcher with the University of Chicago, wins his debut with the Cubs in a 5–4 decision over the Spiders at West Side Park. Chief Zimmer of Cleveland was ejected for going into the stands in an attempt to assault a fan who had been heckling him.

Despite the win, Clarke never pitched another big league game. Previously, he had an 0–4 record with Cleveland in 1897.

JULY 6   The Cubs score three runs in the ninth inning to defeat Cleveland 6–5 at West Side Grounds.

JULY 15   During a 10–9 loss to the Orioles in Baltimore, Cubs third baseman Barry McCormick accuses first baseman Bill Everett of making a rotten throw, sparking a fistfight on the field. Everett put McCormick in a headlock and punched him repeatedly. While the fight was going on, one of the spectators reached over and tried to separate the combatants, but he got a stiff punch for the trouble. McCormick walked off the field and refused to play any further.

JULY 20   The Cubs score nine runs in the sixth inning and clobber the Phillies 15–5 at Philadelphia.

JULY 30   The Cubs ease past Washington 13–3 at West Side Grounds.

AUGUST 5   Pitcher Frank Isbell commits an unusual balk during a 6–1 loss suffered at the hands of the Orioles at West Side Grounds. With a runner on third base, Isbell's cap fell of his head as he delivered the ball to the plate, and he stopped to adjust his cap in the middle of his motion. The Cubs won the first game 5–0, highlighted by a triple play involving shortstop Bill Dahlen, second baseman Jim Connor, and first baseman Bill Everett.

AUGUST 6   The Cubs win 1–0 in eleven innings over the Phillies at West Side Grounds. The winning run was scored on a line single to center field by Sam Mertes, who swung at a ball two feet over his head. Walter Thornton pitched the complete game shutout.

AUGUST 11   The Cubs defeat the Dodgers 3–2 in fourteen innings at Brooklyn. The winning run was scored on bunt singles by Sam Mertes, Jim Connor, and Tom Donahue.

AUGUST 21 — A week after Spain surrenders, ending the Spanish–American War, Walter Thornton pitches a no–hitter to defeat the Dodgers 2–0 in the second game of a double–header at West Side Grounds. The last out was recorded by a grounder by Fielder Jones to Cubs third baseman Barry McCormick. Thornton walked three and struck out three. The Cubs also won the first game 4–3.

SEPTEMBER 1 — The Cubs hammer the Dodgers 10–0 at West Side Grounds.

SEPTEMBER 6 — The Cubs blow a 7–0 lead and lose 9–8 to the Reds in Cincinnati.

Bill Lange did some damage, quite literally, with a home run during the game. The ball cleared the fence in left center field, bounded high off the granite blocks on Western Avenue, and caromed into a saloon, where it smashed against a mirror, breaking it into smithereens. The horsehide came to rest under a table where a half–dozen men were playing cards.

SEPTEMBER 7 — The Cubs wallop the Reds 13–2 in Cincinnati.

SEPTEMBER 16 — The Cubs lose by forfeit in the first game of a double–header in Philadelphia. With the Cubs leading 2–0 in the fifth inning, Ed McFarland of the Phillies was called safe on a play at the plate. Sam Mertes of the Cubs argued so long that umpire John Gaffney declared the game a forfeit. The second game was completed without incident with the Cubs winning 10–5.

SEPTEMBER 17 — Bill Phyle of the Cubs pitches a shutout in his major league debut, beating the Senators 9–0 in Washington.

In his second start, five days later, Phyle allowed 15 runs in a 15–6 loss to the Orioles in Baltimore. The second game was more typical of Phyle's career. He was 3–9 in two years as a Cub and 10–19 in three seasons as a major leaguer.

SEPTEMBER 22 — The Cubs start a rally with two out and no one on base and score two runs in the eleventh inning to beat the Pirates 5–4 at West Side Grounds. Just six days after making his major league debut, Art Nichols drove in the winning run with a single.

OCTOBER 9 — Cubs pitcher Jack Taylor faces Cardinals pitcher Jack Taylor in the first game of a double–header at West Side Grounds. The Cubs won 5–4 in ten innings. The Cubs also won the second game, called after six innings by darkness, 3–0.

Chicago's Jack Taylor was just beginning a career that lasted until 1907. The Cardinals' Jack Taylor was in the second–to–last season of a nine–year career. He died in February 1900 at the age of 26. The two Jack Taylors met again on April 22, 1899, with the Cubs' Taylor winning 8–4 in Cincinnati when the other Taylor was pitching for the Reds.

1899   Cubs

Season in a Sentence

Tommy Burns is fired after the end of his second season as manager after the Cubs limp to eighth place.

Finish • Won • Lost • Pct • GB

Eighth   75   73   .507   26.0

Manager

Tom Burns

Stats   Cubs • NL • Rank

Batting Avg: .277   .282   9
On–Base Pct: .338   .343   9
Slugging Pct: .359   .366   10
Home Runs: 27   7 (tie)
Stolen Bases: 247   3
ERA: 3.37   3.85   5
Fielding Avg: .935   .942   10
Runs Scored: 812   9
Runs Allowed: 763   6

Starting Lineup

Tim Donahue, c
Bill Everett, 1b
Barry McCormick, 2b
Harry Wolverton, 3b
Gene DeMontreville, ss
Jimmy Ryan, lf
Sam Mertes, cf
Danny Green, rf
Bill Lange, cf
Jim Connor, 2b–3b
Frank Chance, c
George Magoon, ss

Pitchers

Clark Griffith, sp
Jack Taylor, sp
Nixey Callahan, sp
Ned Garvin, sp
Bill Phyle, sp

Attendance

352,130 (third in NL)

Club Leaders

Batting Avg: Everett   .310
On–Base Pct: Ryan   .357
Slugging Pct: Mertes   .467
Home Runs: Mertes   9
RBI: Mertes   81
Runs: Ryan   91
Stolen Bases: Mertes   45
Wins: Griffith 22
Strikeouts: Callahan 77
ERA: Griffith 2.79
Saves: Phyle   1

JANUARY 25   The Cubs trade Bill Dahlen to the Dodgers for Gene DeMontreville.

The trade turned out to be a huge mistake, as Dahlen continued to be a topflight shortstop for several more seasons with the Dodgers and the Giants.

APRIL 14   The Cubs rout the Colonels 15–1 in the season opener at Louisville. Chicago scored during each of the first eight innings. Clark Griffith pitched the complete game.

APRIL 26   Heading into the ninth inning trailing 4–2, the Cubs score five times, then survive a two–run Cardinal rally in the bottom half to win 7–6 in St. Louis.

APRIL 27   In the home opener at West Side Grounds, the Cubs defeat the Reds 4–3.

APRIL 30   A crowd of 27,489 jams into West Side Grounds for a game between the Cardinals and the Cubs. The crowd surrounding the field was so large it was ruled that any ball into the overflow would be a single. Many routine fly balls and drives that normally would have gone for extra bases fell into the crowd for singles. Each team had 12 one–base hits in the game. Cubs pitcher Nixey Callahan did a better job of scattering the hits he allowed and won with a 4–0 shutout.

Callahan had a record of 21–12 in 1899 with an ERA of 3.05. Clark Griffith was again Chicago's leading winner with a 22–14 record and a 2.79 earned run average.

MAY 1   Chicago aldermen, angered because the team put a stop to their free tickets to games, threaten to pass an ordinance banning games on Sundays and to build an alley through the middle of West Side Grounds.

The Cubs figured that granting free admission to elected officials was cheaper than losing the revenue derived from Sunday games or building a new ballpark, so they restored the free passes to the aldermen.

In 1899 Clark Griffith reached the 20–win mark for the sixth straight time, amassing 137 wins during those seasons.

MAY 8   Cubs third baseman Harry Wolverton hits a three–run, inside–the–park walk–off homer to beat Cleveland 8–7 at West Side Grounds.

JUNE 3   The Cubs score five runs in the first inning, seven in the second, and two in the third to take a 14–1 lead, and they go on to beat the Orioles 14–5 in Baltimore.

JUNE 5   Bill Everett collects five hits, including a triple and a double, during a 9–3 win over the Orioles in Baltimore.

JUNE 17   Five days after Butch Cassidy and the Sundance Kid rob a train in Wyoming of $60,000, the Cubs fatten their batting averages with a 12–1 win over the Reds in Cincinnati.

JUNE 23   Before the game against the Dodgers at West Side Grounds, ex–Cub Bill Dahlen is presented with a huge mass of flowers, a diamond stud, a pair of diamond cuff buttons, and $500 in cash. Dahlen went 0–for–4 and the Cubs won the game 3–2.

JUNE 29   The Cubs score a run in the first inning, seven in the second, and nine in the third to take a 17–2 lead and drub the Giants 17–9 at West Side Grounds.

JUNE 30   A Chicago judge issues an injunction restraining the city and James McAndrews, of the Department of Public Works, from interfering with Andrew Brennan and preventing his renting seats on the roof of his building to those who wish to watch Cubs games. Brennan built the seats atop his residence at 783 West Taylor Street. Taylor Street was located behind the right field wall, and Brennan's home was directly across the street from West Side Grounds. Brennan had been selling seats on the roof and the police—at the urging of the Cubs, who were worried about the loss of ticket revenue—sought to stop the practice.

Brennan found plenty of imitators among his neighbors, who also built rooftop bleachers. The practice stopped when a fan fell from one of the roofs to his death in 1908 and the city condemned many of the structures as unsafe. In 1909, the Cubs built a 61–foot wall behind the right field bleachers (the wall eventually reached the height of 80 feet), which blocked the views from the Taylor Street rooftops.

JULY 31   Bill Phyle is scheduled as the starting pitcher against the Senators at West Side Grounds, but he failed to show because he went to St. Louis to attend a boxing match. Jack Taylor started in Phyle's place and lost 8–5.

AUGUST 2   The Cubs trade Gene DeMontreville to the Orioles for George Magoon.

AUGUST 3   The Cubs defeat the Cardinals 1–0 at West Side Grounds. In his first game with the Cubs, George Magoon drove in the lone run with an eighth–inning single. Ned Garvin pitched the shutout.

AUGUST 9   Skel Roach makes his major league debut and pitches the Cubs to a 6–3 win over the Senators in Washington.

              A native of Danzig, Germany, Roach later coached at both Indiana University and the University of Michigan. He used his baseball earnings to work his way through Northwestern University and become an attorney. Roach practiced law for several years in Chicago.

AUGUST 18   In a double–header against the Orioles in Baltimore, the Cubs win the first game 13–12 but lose the nightcap 5–4.

AUGUST 20   The Cubs play both Cleveland and Louisville during an unusual double–header at West Side Grounds. In the first game, the Cubs defeated the Spiders 8–7 in a wild finish. Chicago scored three runs in the eighth inning to take a 5–1 lead, but allowed six tallies to Cleveland in the top of the ninth to fall behind 7–5. The Cubs came back with three in their half to win the game on three walks and a bases-loaded triple by Sam Mertes. The Cubs lost the second game 5–0 to Louisville in a contest called by darkness after six innings.

              The Cleveland Spiders had an abysmal 20–134 record in 1899 and played 112 games on the road because of sparse attendance in Cleveland.

AUGUST 28   Bill Everett hits a grand slam off Charlie Gettig in the fifth inning of an 11–3 win over the Giants in the second game of a double–header at West Side Grounds. New York won the first game 6–4.

AUGUST 31   A clever trick by George Magoon helps the Cubs during a five–run seventh inning, which beats Boston 5–2 at West Side Grounds. Magoon was a base runner on first and Jim Connor was on third when Magoon took off for second on a steal attempt. Magoon had the base stolen, but stopped ten feet short of the bag to get himself caught in a rundown. While the Braves were chasing Magoon, Connor scored from third.

SEPTEMBER 5   The Cubs defeat the Pirates 13–7 in a slugging match at West Side Grounds.

SEPTEMBER 9   The Cubs beat the Spiders 5–2 and 11–0 at West Side Grounds.

SEPTEMBER 13   The Giants score 12 runs in the sixth inning off Chicago pitcher John Malarkey and beat the Cubs 13–2 in New York.

The game was the only one that Malarkey pitched as a member of the Cubs. It was also his first major league appearance since 1896. He didn't pitch in another one until 1902.

SEPTEMBER 16   Umpire Ed Swartwood calls the game between the Cubs and the Dodgers in Brooklyn because of darkness at the end of the seventh inning with the Dodgers leading 9–7. The Cubs believed another inning could have been played, and the umpire was surrounded by Chicago players. According to the newspaper reports, Swartwood was "knocked around a little" by the Cubs, and Bill Lange reached out and "tweaked" the umpire's ear.

SEPTEMBER 18   Bill Lange collects five hits in a game that ends in a 10–10 tie against the Dodgers in Brooklyn. The contest was called after eight innings by darkness.

SEPTEMBER 22   Cubs pitcher Ned Garvin surrenders 13 hits and issues two walks, but shuts out the Braves 3–0 in the first game of a double–header in Boston. The Braves won the second game, called by darkness after eight innings, 8–7.

SEPTEMBER 24   The Cubs go from the sublime to the ridiculous during a double–header against the Reds in Cincinnati, winning the opener 21–5 and losing the second tilt, called by darkness after five innings, 11–1.

OCTOBER 8   The Cubs play both Cleveland and Louisville in a double–header at West Side Grounds. The Cubs beat Cleveland 13–0 and lost to Louisville, in a contest called by darkness in the sixth inning, 7–3.

OCTOBER 15   On the last day of the season, the Cubs play both St. Louis and Louisville in a double–header at West Side Grounds. The Cubs defeated the Cardinals 7–0, then lost to the Colonels 9–5 in a game called on account of darkness after eight innings. Playing in the final two games of his career, Bill Lange was given several ovations from the fans.

A few days earlier, Lange had announced his retirement. At six–foot–one and 190 pounds, Lange was a huge man for his time and today would be called a "five–tool" player. In seven seasons in the majors, all with the Cubs, Lange hit .330, stole 399 bases, and played stellar defense in center field. He quit baseball at the end of the 1899 season when he was only 28 and playing at his peak to wed the daughter of a San Francisco real estate magnate, who forbade her to marry a ballplayer. Lange refused all comeback offers once he left the game, although the marriage ended in divorce. Bill wasn't hurt financially by leaving baseball, as he became wealthy as a real estate and insurance broker. His nephew, George Lange Kelly, played briefly for the Cubs in 1930 and later was elected to the Hall of Fame.

THE STATE OF THE CUBS

The Cubs had a record of 879–592 from 1900 through 1909, a winning percentage of .598. It was the second–best record in the majors during the decade, trailing only the Pittsburgh Pirates. The Cubs won National League pennants in 1906, 1907, and 1908 and the World Series in 1907 and 1908. Others NL pennants were won by the Brooklyn Dodgers (1900), Pirates (1901, 1902, 1903, and 1909), and New York Giants (1904 and 1905). The Cubs and the Giants had an intense rivalry during the last half of the decade and extended through the first half of the 1910s. The 22 matchups between these two teams each season drew capacity crowds and extensive coverage in the national media.

THE BEST TEAM

The 1906 Cubs were 116–36 (.769). No club in major league history won more games. The Cubs stood alone at the top until the Mariners won 116 in 2001, but it took Seattle 162 games to reach that figure. The Cubs' winning percentage of .769 in 1906 remains the best of the modern era.

THE WORST TEAM

The 1901 Cubs were 53–86 (.381). Between the 1900 and 1901 season, the Cubs lost six key players to the American League, and the talent drain was too much to overcome.

THE BEST MOMENT

In 1908, the Cubs win the World Series for the second year in a row, defeating Ty Cobb and the Detroit Tigers. The Cubs haven't won a world championship since.

THE WORST MOMENT

On June 2, 1908, Heinie Zimmerman nearly blinded teammate Jimmy Sheckard by throwing a bottle of ammonia at him.

THE ALL–DECADE TEAM • YEARS WITH CUBS

Johnny Kling, c	1900–08, 1910–11
Frank Chance, 1b	1898–1912
Johnny Evers, 2b	1902–13
Harry Steinfeldt, 3b	1906–10
Joe Tinker, ss	1902–12, 1916
Jimmy Sheckard, lf	1906–12
Jimmy Slagle, cf	1902–08
Wildfire Schulte, rf	1904–16
Three Finger Brown, p	1904–12
Ed Reulbach, p	1905–13
Jack Taylor, p	1898–1903, 1906–07
Orval Overall, p	1906–10

Every member of the 1900's All–Decade Team was a regular on the 1906 club, which won 116 games. The great Chicago Cubs teams of the '00s were paced by some of the best pitching staffs in history. Besides the four pitchers mentioned above, Carl Lundgren (1902–09), Jake Weimer (1903–05), Bob Wicker (1903–06), and Jack Pfiester (1906–11) all played prominent roles. Center fielder Solly Hofman (1904–12, 1916) and right fielder Danny Green (1898–1901) were also among the outstanding Cubs of the decade.

THE DECADE LEADERS

Batting Avg:	Chance	.299
On–Base Pct:	Chance	.397
Slugging Pct:	Chance	.398
Home Runs:	Tinker	21
RBI:	Chance	501
Runs:	Chance	646
Stolen Bases:	Chance	357
Wins:	Brown	135
Strikeouts:	Brown	716
ERA:	Brown	1.51
Saves:	Brown	19

THE HOME FIELD

The Cubs continued to play at West Side Grounds, built in 1894 on a block bounded by Polk, South Lincoln, Taylor, and South Wood. The ballpark was the site of the World Series in 1906, 1907, 1908, and 1910.

THE GAME YOU WISH YOU HAD SEEN

Oddly, most of the big games involving the Cubs during the eventful decade took place outside of Chicago, including the final game on both World Series won by the club. The best game in the Windy City took place on October 4, 1908, when the Cubs kept their pennant hopes alive by defeating the Pirates 5–2 before 30,247 at West Side Grounds, the largest crowd ever to see a game in Chicago up to that time.

THE WAY THE GAME WAS PLAYED

In this decade of pitching and defense, the NL set all-time lows in ERA and batting average. Hit-and-run plays, the stolen base, and sacrificing dominated strategy. In part, this was the result of a 1901 rule change that for the first time counted foul balls as strikes. The merits of the foul-strike rule were hotly debated for years afterward. Offense started a gradual decline that was not reversed until the introduction of the cork-center ball in 1910. The Cubs pitching staff had an astonishingly low team ERA of 2.77 in 1903, 2.30 in 1904, 2.04 in 1905, 1.75 in 1906, 1.73 in 1907, 2.14 in 1908, and 1.75 in 1909.

THE MANAGEMENT

On the field, Frank Selee took over a horrible club when he was hired as manager by James Hart at the end of the 1901 season, succeeding Tom Loftus. He quickly built the Cubs into a contender. The club was on the brink of greatness when Selee was struck by tuberculosis in 1905. Frank Chance succeeded Selee and guided the Cubs to four pennants and two world championships from 1906 through 1910. By that time, Charles Murphy had succeeded Hart as club president. Murphy, with the financial backing of Charles P. Taft, purchased the Cubs in 1905.

THE BEST PLAYER MOVE

The best trade was the one in which the Cubs brought future Hall of Fame pitcher Three Finger Brown to Chicago in a deal with the Cardinals in December 1903.

THE WORST PLAYER MOVE

The Cubs made few mistakes in constructing some of the greatest clubs in history during the latter half of the decade, but they let a boatload of talent get away to the newly established American League in 1901 and 1902, including future Hall of Fame pitcher Rube Waddell.

1900s

1900

Season in a Sentence

An anemic offense dooms the Cubs to a losing season.

Finish • Won • Lost • Pct • GB

Fifth (tie) 65   75   .464 19.0

Manager

Tom Loftus

Stats   Cubs • NL • Rank

Batting Avg:			
On–Base Pct:	.260	.279	8
Slugging Pct:	.317	.339	8
Home Runs:	.342	.366	8
Stolen Bases:	33		3 (tie)
ERA:	189		5
Fielding Avg:	3.23	3.69	2
Runs Scored:	.933	.942	7
Runs Allowed:	635		8
	751		6

Starting Lineup

Tim Donahue, c
John Ganzel, 1b
Cupid Childs, 2b
Bill Bradley, 3b
Barry McCormick, ss
Jack McCarthy, lf
Sam Mertes, cf–rf
Jimmy Ryan, rf–lf
Danny Green, cf–rf
Billy Clingman, ss
Frank Chance, c

Pitchers

Nixey Callahan, sp
Clark Griffith, sp
Ned Garvin, sp
Jack Taylor, sp
Jock Menefee, sp

Attendance

248,577 (fourth in NL)

Club Leaders

Batting Avg:	Green	.298
On–Base Pct:	Mertes	.356
Slugging Pct:	Green	.416
Home Runs:	Mertes	7
RBI:	Mertes	60
Runs:	Mertes	72
Stolen Bases:	Mertes	38
Wins:	Griffith	14
Strikeouts:	Garvin	107
ERA:	Garvin	2.41
Saves:	Taylor	1

FEBRUARY 10   The Cubs purchase Jack McCarthy from the Pirates.

MARCH 8   The National League votes to reduce its membership from twelve teams to eight, dropping Baltimore, Cleveland, Louisville, and Washington. The NL roster of Boston, Brooklyn, Chicago, Cincinnati, New York, Philadelphia, Pittsburgh, and St. Louis remained unchanged from 1900 until the Boston Braves moved to Milwaukee in March 1953.

MARCH 17   At an American League meeting in Chicago, Ban Johnson announces that an AL team will be placed in the Windy City. The club, headed by Charles Comiskey, was formerly located in St. Paul. The other AL franchises were in Buffalo, Cleveland, Detroit, Indianapolis, Kansas City, Milwaukee, and Minneapolis. In an agreement with Cubs owner James Hart, the AL club could not build its ballpark north of 35th Street. The location was four miles from The Loop in what then was a remote part of Chicago, and Hart was convinced Comiskey would attract little patronage. The new club was permitted to use the nickname "White Stockings," formerly used by the NL team and later shortened to White Sox. However, the White Stockings were not permitted to use the word Chicago in its official name. The American League in 1900 was strictly a minor league outfit, but Johnson and his cohorts had greater ambitions (see January 28, 1901).

APRIL 19   The Cubs win the first game of the season 13–10 over the Reds in Cincinnati. Chicago trailed 8–6 before scoring five runs in the seventh inning to take the lead.

The Cubs' new manager in 1900 was Tom Loftus, who replaced Tom Burns. Loftus previously managed the Cincinnati Reds from 1889 through 1891.

APRIL 21   The White Sox play their first game in Chicago and lose 5–4 to Milwaukee in ten innings. The White Sox's ballpark was called South Side Park and was located at 39th and Wentworth.

The White Sox went on to win the American League pennant.

APRIL 27   The Cubs play their home opener and defeat the Cardinals 6–5 before 6,000 at West Side Grounds. The game was tied 5–5 in the eighth inning on a two–run homer by Barry McCormick. The Cubs scored another run later in the inning on a single by pitcher Jack Taylor.

Jack Taylor won 10 games for the 1900 Cubs and picked up 109 victories over eight seasons with the club.

APRIL 28   The Cubs sell Harry Wolverton to the Phillies.

MAY 6   Following a 7–6 win over the Pirates at West Side Grounds, Cubs second baseman Cupid Childs and Pirates player–manager Fred Clarke fight at the train station.

The two nearly came to blows during the game when Clarke twice slid hard into Childs trying to break up a double play. The Cubs and Pirates were scheduled to play each other again the following day in Pittsburgh and travel plans called for the two clubs to board the same train at the Lake Shore Depot. Cupid went looking for Clarke on the platform while the clubs were waiting for the train, and his intent was not to shoot love arrows. Childs cold–cocked Clarke and the fight was on. There was no attempt to break up the battle, as a ring was formed with players on each club urging on their teammate. Childs and Clarke began to pummel each other with a vengeance. Clarke's face was bloodied, but he left several marks on Childs and tore the shirt almost completely off of the Cubs infielder. The proceedings were stopped by policemen. Many Cubs were so disgusted with Childs' behavior that they were rooting for Clarke to win the fight. "Childs made a fool of himself," said outfielder Jimmy Ryan, "and is entitled to no sympathy."

MAY 12   The Cubs topple the Giants 13–3 at West Side Grounds.

MAY 13   Trailing 9–3 at West Side Grounds, the Cubs rally to win 10–9 with five runs in the seventh inning, one in the eighth, and one in the ninth.

Two blazes at different times in the bleachers caused mild panics during the game and necessitated the use of chemical extinguishers by policemen.

MAY 26	Nixey Callahan shuts out the Dodgers 1–0 at West Side Grounds. The lone run of the game was scored on a single by Danny Green in the eighth inning.
MAY 30	Bill Bradley sets a major league record (since tied) for most errors by a third baseman in a double–header with five, four of them in the second game. The Cubs lost both games 5–2 and 13–3 to the Phillies in Philadelphia.
JUNE 9	Sam Mertes leads off a game with a home run for the second day in a row, leading the Cubs to a 6–2 win over the Braves in Boston. The previous day, Mertes led off with a homer in a 6–5 loss in Boston.

Mertes is the only player in Cubs history to lead off a game with a homer two games in a row.

JUNE 19	In a battle of future Hall of Fame pitchers, Clark Griffith outduels Rube Waddell of the Pirates to win 1–0 in fourteen innings at West Side Grounds. Griffith not only pitched a complete game, but he drove in the winning run with a double.
JUNE 29	Clark Griffith pitches a shutout to defeat the Dodgers 1–0 at West Side Grounds. Cupid Childs drove in the winning run with a double in the sixth inning.
JULY 1	The Cubs score three runs in the ninth inning to defeat the Dodgers 6–5 at West Side Grounds. Jack McCarthy drove in the last two runs on a line–drive single to left field.
JULY 4	Approximately 1,000 fans appear at West Side Grounds armed with revolvers and pistols and fire them constantly in celebration of the holiday. The Cubs, meanwhile, shot holes in the Phillies, sweeping the double–header 10–4 and 5–4 in twelve innings. In the second game, the Cubs scored two runs in the ninth to tie 3–3, and after Philadelphia plated a run in the top of the twelfth, Chicago came back with two of their own to win.
JULY 6	The Cubs win their ninth game in a row with a 6–4 decision over the Braves at West Side Grounds.

On July 15, the Cubs were in second place with a 37–32 record, although they were 7½ games behind the Dodgers.

AUGUST 8	Jimmy Ryan steals four bases, but the Cubs lose 5–3 to the Phillies at West Side Grounds.
AUGUST 29	After giving the Cardinals two runs in the tenth inning, the Cubs score two runs in their half and score another in the eleventh to win 6–5 at West Side Grounds. Danny Green scored the winning run on a sacrifice fly after reaching third base on a triple.
SEPTEMBER 5	Bill Bradley collects seven hits, including a double and a homer, in 10 at–bats to lead the Cubs to a 9–4 and 12–1 sweep of the Dodgers in Brooklyn. In the second game, the Cubs scored eight runs in the fifth inning to break a scoreless tie.
SEPTEMBER 6	Nixey Callahan allows 20 runs and 25 hits in a 20–5 loss to the Phillies in Philadelphia.

SEPTEMBER 11   Nixey Callahan is shelled for the second start in a row, surrendering 14 runs and 23 hits in a 14–3 loss to the Giants in New York. The second game resulted in a 3–3 tie, called after nine innings by darkness. Johnny Kling made his major league debut in the second game, and had three hits in four at–bats. Kling remained as a catcher with the Cubs until 1911.

SEPTEMBER 12   In his first two games with the Cubs, shortstop Sammy Strang collects seven hits, including a double, in eight at–bats during a double–header against the Giants in New York. The Cubs won the first game 9–1, and lost the second 7–6.

SEPTEMBER 29   The Cubs score seven runs in the first inning, but go on to lose 10–7 to the Cardinals in the first game of a double–header in St. Louis. The second game ended after seven innings because of darkness with the score 0–0.

OCTOBER 8   The Cubs and the Reds combine for 25 errors during a double–header at West Side Grounds. The Cubs committed 17 of the miscues and lost both of the games to the Reds 13–4 and 9–1. The second game was called after eight innings by darkness.

1901   Cubs

Season in a Sentence

The Cubs lose so many players to the American League that the newspapers call the club the "Remnants."

Finish • Won • Lost • Pct • GB

Sixth   53   86   .381   37.0

Manager

Tom Loftus

Stats

Stats	Cubs	NL	Rank
Batting Avg:	.258	.267	5
On–Base Pct:	.310	.321	5
Slugging Pct:	.326	.348	6
Home Runs:	18		8
Stolen Bases:	137		7
ERA:	3.33	3.32	5
Fielding Avg:	.943	.947	6
Runs Scored:	578		5
Runs Allowed:	699		6

Starting Lineup

Johnny Kling, c
Charlie Dexter, 1b–3b
Cupid Childs, 2b
Fred Raymer, 3b
Barry McCormick, ss
Topsy Hartsel, lf
Danny Green, cf
Frank Chance, rf
Jack Doyle, 1b
Mike Kahoe, c
Pete Childs, 2b
Cozy Dolan, rf
Jock Menefee, rf–p

Pitchers

Jack Taylor, sp
Rube Waddell, sp
Long Tom Hughes, sp
Mal Eason, sp
Jock Menefee, sp

Attendance

205,071 (sixth in NL)

Club Leaders

Batting Avg:	Hartsel	.335
On–Base Pct:	Hartsel	.414
Slugging Pct:	Hartsel	.475
Home Runs:	Hartsel	7
RBI:	Green	61
Runs:	Hartsel	111
Stolen Bases:	Hartsel	41
Wins:	Waddell	14
Strikeouts:	Hughes	225
ERA:	Waddell	2.81
Saves:	None	0

JANUARY 28   The American League formally
organizes as a second major league
with clubs in Baltimore, Boston,
Chicago, Cleveland, Detroit,
Milwaukee, Philadelphia, and
Washington. The AL also
announced plans to raid National
League rosters by offering more
lucrative contracts.

Johnny Kling batted .273 as a rookie catcher for the
Cubs in 1901 on his way to a thirteen-year major
league career.

*Not only would the Cubs
have to compete with a
second major league club
for fan patronage in Chicago,
but the loss of six regulars, a
promising youngster, and a
higher payroll as well. Pitcher
Clark Griffith signed a contract with the White Sox as a
player-manager. Pitcher Nixey
Callahan and outfielder Sam
Mertes also went to the Sox.*
*Third baseman Bill Bradley and outfielder Jack McCarthy signed deals with the
Indians, pitcher Ned Garvin inked a contract with Milwaukee, and catcher
Roger Bresnahan traveled to Baltimore to play for the Orioles.*

APRIL 16   The Cubs purchase Topsy Hartsel from the Reds.

*The Reds parted with Hartsel because they believed at five-foot-five that he
was too small to play regularly in the majors. Batting in the leadoff slot, Topsy
was an immediate sensation with the Cubs, hitting .335 in 1901 with 111 runs
scored and 41 stolen bases. Unfortunately, Hartsel played only one season in
Chicago. In 1902, he bolted to the Philadelphia Athletics in the American
League. He went on to lead the AL five times in walks, twice in on-base
percentage, and once in runs.*

APRIL 18   The Cubs season opener in St. Louis is postponed by rain.

APRIL 19   In the first game of the season, the Cubs defeat the Cardinals 8-7 in St. Louis. The
Cubs trailed 4-0 in the fourth inning before battling back.

APRIL 30   Charlie Dexter hits a bases loaded, two-out double in the ninth inning to score three
runs and lift the Cubs to a thrilling 8-7 win over the Reds at West Side Grounds.

MAY 3   The Cubs purchase Rube Waddell from the Pirates.

*One of the most eccentric players ever to appear in a big league game, Waddell
was cut loose by the Pirates after he jumped the club. Cubs manager Tom Loftus
had previously managed Waddell in the minors at Columbus (Ohio) and Grand
Rapids. According to Waddell biographer Alan H. Levy, the Pirates were so
anxious to get rid of Waddell that Cubs owner James Hart was able to purchase*

Waddell from the Pirates in exchange for a cigar. Waddell had a 14–14 record for the Cubs in 1901.

MAY 5   Rube Waddell pitches his first game with the Cubs. A total of 14,000 paid admission, the largest crowd of the year at West Side Grounds. Before the game, Waddell threw his practice pitches into a wooden board next the dugout, sending loud booms throughout the ballpark. Facing his former teammates, Waddell lost 4–2 but was cheered wildly by the Chicago fans.

Crowds at West Side Grounds were much larger than normal on the days that Waddell pitched in 1901. He just about the only attraction on a club that spent most of the season in last place.

MAY 9   Rube Waddell stars in a 4–1 win over the Cardinals at West Side Grounds. In the top of the fifth inning, Waddell covered a play at first base and was leveled by St. Louis batter Art Nichols. Rube popped up from the collision and turned somersaults on his way back to the mound. In the bottom of the fifth, Waddell hit a three–run homer.

Waddell jumped the club in late August, claiming he was going fishing, and never returned. In September, he pitched for semipro clubs in Gray's Lake, Wisconsin, and Burlington, Illinois. Waddell played with Los Angeles in the Pacific Coast League early in the 1902 season before signing a contract with the Philadelphia Athletics. Waddell harnessed his talent with the A's and had a record of 97–52 from 1902 through 1905. He was elected to the Hall of Fame in 1946.

MAY 11   The Cubs clobber the Cardinals 12–2 at West Side Grounds.

JUNE 22 The Cubs sweep the Dodgers 16–6 and 5–2 in a double–header in Brooklyn. Chicago scored nine runs in the fifth inning of the first game. Danny Green collected seven hits, including a double, in 11 at–bats during the afternoon.

Green batted .313 for the Cubs in 1901. After the season, he signed a contract with the White Sox. Green was one of five 1901 Cubs regulars to play in the American League in 1902, joining Rube Waddell, Topsy Hartsel, Barry McCormick, and Long Tom Hughes.

JUNE 25 The Cubs sell Cozy Dolan to the Dodgers.

JULY 1   Cubs first baseman Jack Doyle, harassed by a New York fan, leaps into the right field stands and assaults a spectator, reinjuring a hand he had broken several weeks before. The Giants won the game 6–4 at the Polo Grounds. Doyle was out of action for a week because of the injury caused by the fight.

JULY 4   With several players sidelined by injuries, the Cubs use 18–year–old amateur player Larry Hoffman at third base during a double–header against the Dodgers at West Side Grounds. Hoffman had four hits, including a double, in eight at bats as the Cubs won twice 5–3 and 10–9.

Hoffman's big league career consisted of eight games in which he batted .318.

JULY 13   The Cubs score all of their runs in a seven–run sixth inning off future Hall of Famer Vic Willis and hang on to defeat the Braves 7–6 at West Side Grounds.

JULY 31   Long Tom Hughes strikes out 15 Reds in a fourteen–inning complete game, but the Cubs lose 5–4 in Cincinnati.

Hughes pitched in hard luck all year, finishing the 1901 season with a 10–23 record. No Cubs pitcher has lost as many as 23 games in a season since then. Hughes went to the American League after the 1901 season and had a 20–7 record for the Red Sox in 1903.

AUGUST 5   Topsy Hartsel hits two inside–the–park home runs, but the Cubs lose 10–7 to the Reds in Cincinnati.

AUGUST 19   Long Tom Hughes strikes out 12 batters, but loses 2–0 to the Reds in Cincinnati.

AUGUST 29   Long Tom Hughes pitches a two–hitter to defeat the Pirates 4–1 in the first game of a double–header in Pittsburgh. The only two Pirates hits were a triple by Ginger Beaumont and a single by Tommy Leach. The Cubs lost the second game 2–1.

SEPTEMBER 3 Jack Doyle collects five hits, including two doubles, in five at bats to lead the Cubs to a 10–4 win over the Giants in New York.

SEPTEMBER 10 Two days after a hurricane in Galveston, Texas, claims 6,000 lives, Topsy Hartsel ties a major league record for most putouts by a left fielder with 11 during a 4–3 win over the Dodgers in Brooklyn.

SEPTEMBER 21 Long Tom Hughes pitches a seventeen–inning shutout, the longest in Cubs history, to defeat the Braves 1–0 at West Side Grounds. Hughes struck out 13 batters. Cupid Childs drove in the winning run with a single.

OCTOBER 6   Long Tom Hughes gives up only four hits, but the Cubs commit nine errors and lose 9–5 to the Pirates at West Side Grounds in the last game of the season. Jock Menefee set a modern major league record (since tied) for most errors by a first baseman in a game, with four.

Menefee was normally a pitcher who occasionally played the outfield between starts. It was only his second big league game at first base.

OCTOBER 30   Frank Selee replaces Tom Loftus as manager of the Cubs.

Selee had just been fired a few weeks earlier as manager of the Boston Braves, ending a successful twelve–year reign. He won five National League pennants in Boston in 1891, 1892, 1893, 1897, and 1898. The Cubs showed immediate improvement under Selee, although he failed to win a pennant in Chicago. Selee was stricken with tuberculosis in 1905 and was forced to retire just as the Cubs were about to become a powerhouse. Frank Chance succeeded Selee as manager and won NL pennants in 1906, 1907, 1908, and 1910, but it was Selee who put those clubs together. In 1999, Frank Selee received a long–overdue induction into baseball's Hall of Fame.

1902 Cubs

Season in a Sentence

The club cleans house as 30 players don a Cubs uniform for the first time in 1902, 20 of whom made their major league debuts.

Finish • Won • Lost • Pct • GB

Fifth 68 69 .496 34.0

Manager

Frank Selee

Stats

Stats	Cubs	NL	Rank
Batting Avg:	.250	.259	5
On-Base Pct:	.307	.312	5
Slugging Pct:	.298	.319	6
Home Runs:	6		6 (tie)
Stolen Bases:	222		1
ERA:	2.21	2.78	1
Fielding Avg:	.946	.949	5
Runs Scored:	530		5
Runs Allowed:	501		2

Starting Lineup

Johnny Kling, c
Frank Chance, 1b
Bobby Lowe, 2b
Germany Schaefer, 3b
Joe Tinker, ss
Jimmy Slagle, lf
Davy Jones, cf
Bunk Congalton, rf
John Dobbs, cf
Charlie Dexter, 3b–1b
Jock Menefee, rf–p
Dusty Miller, lf
Art Williams, rf

Pitchers

Jack Taylor, sp
Pop Williams, sp
Jock Menefee, sp
Carl Lundgren, sp
Bob Rhoads, sp
Jim St. Vrain, sp

Attendance

263,700 (second in NL)

Club Leaders

Batting Avg:	Slagle	.315
On-Base Pct:	Slagle	.387
Slugging Pct:	Slagle	.357
Home Runs:	Tinker	2
	Dexter	2
RBI:	Kling	57
Runs:	Slagle	64
Stolen Bases:	Slagle	40
Wins:	Taylor	23
Strikeouts:	Williams	94
ERA:	Taylor	1.33
Saves:	Taylor	1
	Rhoads	1

MARCH 27 The nickname "Cubs" is coined by the *Chicago Daily News* when an unbylined column notes that manager "Frank Selee will devote his strongest efforts on the team work of the new Cubs this year." The "cubs" referred to in the article were young players, such as Joe Tinker, who were playing on the team for the first time. It took about four years for the new nickname to be used on a consistent basis, however. Chicago's National League club was still called the Orphans and the Colts in the local newspapers for the next few years. Others nicknames for the team which appeared frequently in the Chicago newspapers between 1902 and 1906 were the "Remnants," after the loss of key players to the American League, the "Microbes," due to the high number of players of small stature on the club, and the "Zephyrs," because of the team's location in the Windy City, the "Nationals," and the "Spuds," a reference to team president Charles Murphy and the many Irish players on the club. In 1907, manager Frank Chance insisted that the media call the club the Cubs, and only the Cubs. The nickname was "officially" recognized during the 1907 World Series when new coats were issued to the players sporting a large white bear figure on each sleeve. The Cubs' uniforms in 1908, both at home and on the road, featured a small brown bear holding a bat inside the letter "C."

APRIL 17 The Cubs win the season opener over the Reds in Cincinnati. It was the first game played at a new grandstand in Cincinnati called The Palace of the Fans, which served the Reds from 1902 through 1911.

Playing shortstop, Joe Tinker made his major league debut in the first game of the 1902 season, and had a single in four at–bats. He was purchased by the Cubs from the Portland, Oregon, club in the Pacific Northwest League. As a rookie, he hit .281. Tinker played 1,536 games for Chicago before he was traded to the Reds after the end of the 1912 season. With the Cubs, he collected 1,436 hits, 221 doubles, 93 triples, and 670 RBIs.

APRIL 19   In his major league debut, Reds pitcher Bob Ewing sets a National League record by walking seven batters in one inning during a 9–5 Cubs win in Cincinnati.

APRIL 21   In the home opener, the Cubs defeat the Cardinals 4–3 before 5,000 at West Side Grounds.

APRIL 27   Confused 18–year–old Cubs rookie pitcher Jim St. Vrain runs to third base after hitting a grounder to Pirates shortstop Honus Wagner. Normally a right–handed batter, St. Vrain had trouble hitting Pittsburgh right–hander Deacon Phillippe and decided to bat left–handed. Unfortunately he ran up the third–base line instead of toward first as an astonished Wagner threw him out. The Pirates won 2–0 at West Side Grounds.

MAY 1   The Cubs and the Reds battle to a 0–0 tie, called after twelve innings by darkness at West Side Grounds. Jack Taylor pitched a complete game.

MAY 7   Jack Taylor pitches a two–hitter to defeat the Giants 4–0 at West Side Grounds. The only New York hits were singles by Steve Brodie and Billy Lauder.

Taylor was sensational in 1902. He had a 23–12 record with a league–leading 1.33 ERA. Taylor pitched 324 innings. He completed all 33 of his starts and finished all three of his relief assignments. Between starts, Taylor also filled in at third base for 12 games, right field for three, first base for two, and second base for one. As a batter, he hit .237.

MAY 13   The Cubs collect only one hit off Dodgers pitcher Wild Bill Donovan but win 2–0 at West Side Grounds. The Cubs scored their runs in the sixth inning on a Dusty Miller single, followed by a walk, an error, and a sacrifice.

MAY 15   The Cubs score three runs in the ninth inning and one in the twelfth to defeat the Dodgers 8–7 at West Side Grounds. Jack Taylor pitched four innings of relief and won his own game by driving in the twelfth–inning run with a single. Taylor was also the starting pitcher the next day and shut out the Braves 5–0 in Chicago.

The Cubs were off to a fast start in 1902 and had a 24–12 record on June 2.

JUNE 18   Jack Taylor pitches a shutout and drives in both runs with a double and a single in leading the Cubs to a 2–0 win over the Reds in Cincinnati.

JUNE 22   The Cubs defeat the Pirates 3–2 in nineteen innings at West Side Grounds.

JULY 22   The Cubs score seven runs in the first inning and roll to a 9–1 win over the Reds in Cincinnati.

JULY 30   Jack Taylor pitches a two–hitter to defeat the Braves 1–0 in the first game of a double–header in Boston. The only Braves hits were single by Gene DeMontreville and Ed Gremminger. The Cubs won the second game 3–1 in thirteen innings.

AUGUST 2   The Cubs collect 20 hits and wallop the Phillies 12–0 in Philadelphia.

AUGUST 4   Frank Chance hits a grand slam off Doc White in the twelfth inning of a 7–2 win over the Phillies in Philadelphia.

AUGUST 5   The Cubs win with ease in Philadelphia, defeating the Phillies 11–1.

AUGUST 23 The Cubs score eight runs in the fifth inning off future Hall of Famer Vic Willis and defeat the Braves 14–5 at West Side Grounds. Chicago collected 20 hits in the game.

AUGUST 25 Johnny Kling collects five hits, including a double, in five at–bats in leading the Cubs to a 5–4 win in twelve innings over the Braves at West Side Grounds.

SEPTEMBER 1   Johnny Evers makes his major league debut in a double–header in Philadelphia against the Phillies. Playing shortstop in place of Joe Tinker, who was nursing a broken hand, Evers had a single in seven at–bats as the Cubs lost the first game 11–3 and won the second 6–1. He was purchased from the Troy Cheer–Ups in the New York State League for $500 after Cubs second baseman Bobby Lowe broke his leg.

When Evers made his big league debut, he was five–foot–nine and weighed about 105 pounds. Evers was given the smallest uniform available, but it was much too large for him. His teammates dismissed him and wouldn't allow him aboard the team bus back to the hotel after the games. Evers climbed aboard the roof of the horse–drawn vehicle. Three days later, Evers moved to second base, his primary position for the remainder of a long career. Nicknamed "The Crab" for his manner of moving about the infield and his testy disposition, Evers played for the Cubs until 1913 and appeared in 1,409 games for the club with 742 runs scored and 1,340 hits.

SEPTEMBER 4   Alex Hardy pitches a two–hit shutout in his major league debut to defeat the Dodgers 1–0 in Brooklyn. Jimmy Sheckard's pair of singles were the only Dodgers hits.

SEPTEMBER 13   The Cubs belt the Cardinals 12–0 at West Side Grounds as the famous double–play combination of shortstop Joe Tinker, second baseman Johnny Evers, and first baseman Frank Chance play together for the first time.

Tinker, Evers, and Chance were elected together to the Hall of Fame in 1946.

SEPTEMBER 14   Joe Tinker, Johnny Evers, and Frank Chance turn their first double play during an 8–6 loss to the Reds in the second game of a double–header in Cincinnati. The Cubs also lost the first game 2–1.

SEPTEMBER 28   Jack Taylor earns his 23rd victory of the season with a 4–2 decision over the Cardinals at West Side Grounds.

The Cubs hit only six homers all season in 1902. Just one of those was at West Side Grounds. Although he didn't hit a home run, Jimmy Slagle was the Cubs leading hitter in 1902, batting .315. Slagle was nicknamed "The Human Mosquito" because of his speed and small size of five–foot–seven and 144 pounds. The six homers and .299 slugging percentage are all–time modern Cubs lows for a season.

Jimmy Slagle led the Cubs with a .315 batting average and 64 runs scored in 1902, starting a seven–year run as a regular in the Cubs outfield.

Tinker to Evers to Chance

Franklin Adams left his native Chicago in 1903 as a 21–year–old to work in the newspaper business in New York. By 1910, he had a feature column in the *New York Evening Mail* in which he commented on the issues of the day and won a following with his droll wit. His column often included bits of poetry. In July 1910, one of the poems became the most quoted of the hundreds that he wrote. Titled "Baseball's Sad Lexicon," the poem was inspired by the Cubs infield of shortstop Joe Tinker, second baseman Johnny Evers, and first baseman Frank Chance, which thwarted a Giants rally at a game Adams attended at the Polo Grounds a week earlier.

These are the saddest of all possible words,
Tinker to Evers to Chance,
Trio of bear Cubs and fleeter than birds,
Tinker to Evers to Chance,
Ruthlessly pricking our gonfalon bubble,
Making a Giant hit into a double,
Words that are heavy with
nothing but trouble,
Tinker to Evers to Chance.

According to baseball legend, Adams's immortalization of Tinker, Evers, and Chance catapulted three mediocre infielders into the Hall of Fame. None of this is true. Adams didn't make the trio famous, he wrote about them because they were already famous in 1910. Tinker, Evers, and Chance were not mediocre players in their day, they were stars. If the All–Star Game had existed during their career, it's likely that Chance would have played in five or six of them, and Evers and Tinker between six and eight. Chance also would have been the manager in four of the All–Star Games because he was the manager for four National League pennant winners in Chicago, two of which won the World Series. Furthermore, the poem didn't become well–known until the 1940s, when the players' Hall of Fame credentials were already firmly established in the minds of voters, and the poem became well–known only because Adams became a nationally recognized radio personality.

Tinker, Evers, and Chance played their first game together in the Cubs infield in September 1902, when the club was losing more often than it won. But under manager Frank Selee, the Cubs made tremendous progress and became pennant contenders. Selee had to give up managing the team in July 1905 due to health reasons and was succeeded by Chance. The Cubs won 116 games in 1906, and after a stunning loss in the World Series to the White Sox, rebounded to win the world championship in 1907 and 1908. After finishing a strong second to the Pirates in 1909, the Cubs were on their way to another pennant in the summer of 1910 when Adams wrote "Baseball's Sad Lexicon."

The poem didn't become an instant classic, however. The *New York Evening Mail* was a struggling, minor newspaper which ceased publication a few years later. There was no mass media to speak of in 1910 to disseminate the poem across the country. Since Adams was not a sportswriter and his column didn't appear on the sports page, it's likely that few baseball fans read the lines about Tinker, Evers, and Chance.

It's obvious while reading the literature during the period in which Tinker, Evers, and Chance played, and for decades afterward, that the three were highly thought of as individual players. Articles about any one of the three players rarely mentioned the other two. While researching this book, I could find no references to "Baseball's Sad Lexicon," or even the phrase "Tinker to Evers to Chance," until the 1940s. There are several likely reasons why the poem suddenly took hold some thirty years after it was written. The three former Cubs were among the leaders in the Hall of Fame voting, which began in 1936 and was conducted by the Baseball Writers Association of America. The creation of the Hall of Fame also spurred a greater interest in baseball's history. And, Adams himself became a national figure.

After the *Evening Mail* folded, Adams moved to successively larger New York newspapers and was one of the city's leading literary figures by the 1930s. In 1938, he moved to radio on the program *Information Please*, in which listeners sent questions to try and stump a panel of experts, two of which were on the show every week and one was a guest. Adams was one of the two permanent panelists. The show was a huge hit and Adams won a national following with his vast knowledge and sense of humor.

As a time–filler at the end of the program, Adams sometimes read one of his poems. Given that the poem wasn't widely known until the 1940s, it's probable that "Baseball's Sad Lexicon" was one of those read on the air and that it struck a chord with baseball fans. With radio, the poem had the mass media impetus it lacked in 1910 to become part of baseball legend. Tinker, Evers, and Chance had been retired as players at that point for about thirty years. In the early '40s, the three were as much a part of the recent past as Ernie Banks, Billy Williams, and Ron Santo are today, and Tinker and Evers were still living.

Tinker, Evers, and Chance were elected together to the Hall of Fame by the Committee on Veterans in 1946 and were part of a group of eleven players named by the committee that year for induction into Cooperstown. This followed a BBWAA election in which no one received the necessary 75 percent of the vote necessary for election. In the 1946 writers' vote, Chance finished first, Evers second, and Tinker thirteenth.

How much influence did "Baseball's Sad Lexicon" have on electing Tinker, Evers, and Chance to the Hall of Fame? In studying the voting patterns of the BBWAA from the first election in 1936 through the 1946 balloting along with the information that the poem wasn't well–known until the 1940s, one can reach a few conclusions. It probably had no impact on the election of Chance and Evers. Tinker may have reached the Hall sooner than he might have otherwise. He finished 29th in the voting in 1939, 18th in 1945, and 13th in 1946 and the leap may have been helped by Adams's poem. But, the twenty–eight players ranked ahead of Tinker in 1942 were all elected to the Hall of Fame by the end of the 1950s, with the exception of Ross Youngs, who was inducted in 1972. Tinker, Evers, and Chance would be in the Hall of Fame even if Adams had never written "Baseball's Sad Lexicon."

1903

Cubs

Season in a Sentence

With young stars like Joe Tinker, Johnny Evers, and Frank Chance, the Cubs become pennant contenders.

Finish • Won • Lost • Pct • GB

Third   82   56   .594   8.0

Manager

Frank Selee

Stats	Cubs	NL	Rank
Batting Avg:	.275	.269	3
On–Base Pct:	.340	.331	4
Slugging Pct:	.347	.349	3
Home Runs:	9		7
Stolen Bases:	259		3
ERA:	2.77	3.26	1
Fielding Avg:	.942	.946	6
Runs Scored:	695		4
Runs Allowed:	599		2

Starting Lineup

Johnny Kling, c
Frank Chance, 1b
Johnny Evers, 2b
Doc Casey, 3b
Joe Tinker, ss
Jimmy Slagle, lf
Davy Jones, cf
Dick Harley, rf

Pitchers

Jack Taylor, sp
Jake Weimer, sp
Bob Wicker, sp
Carl Lundgren, sp
Jock Menefee, sp

Attendance

386,205 (second in NL)

Club Leaders

Batting Avg:	Chance	.327
On–Base Pct:	Chance	.439
Slugging Pct:	Chance	.440
Home Runs:	Kling	3
RBI:	Chance	81
Runs:	Slagle	104
Stolen Bases:	Chance	67
Wins:	Taylor	21
Strikeouts:	Weimer	128
ERA:	Taylor	2.45
Saves:	Lundgren	3

JANUARY 10   The National and American League reach a peace accord at a meeting in Cincinnati. The two leagues agreed to refrain from raiding one another's rosters and set up a three–man governing body consisting of the presidents of the two leagues and Cincinnati Reds President Garry Herrmann.

APRIL 12   Joe Tinker and Johnny Kling play an exhibition game with the White Sox against the Kansas City Blues of the American Association in Kansas City.

Tinker and Kling were given permission by the Cubs to take a couple of days off to visit their families in Kansas City. They weren't given permission to play a game with the Cubs' crosstown rivals, however, and were given a stern lecture from manager Frank Selee for the indiscretion.

APRIL 16   In the first game of the season, the Cubs lose 2–1 to the Cardinals in St. Louis.

APRIL 21   The Cubs' scheduled home opener against the Reds is postponed by snow.

APRIL 22   In the first home game of the season before a shivering crowd of 3,000, the Cubs lose 5–3 to the Reds. The high temperature in Chicago on the day was 40 degrees.

APRIL 25   The Cubs score all of their runs in the sixth inning and defeat the Reds 7–3.

APRIL 27   The Cubs collect 20 hits and massacre the Reds 13–5 in Cincinnati.

MAY 6   The Cubs score nine runs in the ninth inning and defeat the Pirates 11–4 in Pittsburgh.

MAY 10   The Cubs defeat the Cardinals 6–3 and 13–8 in a double–header in St. Louis.

MAY 20   Jack Taylor pitches a ten–inning shutout to defeat the Braves 2–0 in Boston.

Taylor had a record of 21–14 and an ERA of 2.45 with the Cubs in 1903. He pitched 312 innings and had 33 complete games.

MAY 22   The Cubs score seven runs in the fifth inning and beat the Phillies 8–4 in Philadelphia.

MAY 23   The Cubs score seven runs in the second inning to take a 9–0 lead and go on to hand the Phillies a 14–1 defeat in Philadelphia.

MAY 31   The Cubs pummel the Cardinals 17–4 in Chicago. Each of Chicago's 17 hits were singles.

The infield of Joe Tinker, Johnny Evers, and Frank Chance starred for the Cubs in 1903. Chance hit .327, Evers .293, and Tinker .291. Catcher Johnny Kling had an average of .293 and set a National League record (since tied) for most triples by a catcher in a season with 13. Jimmy Slagle batted .299 and scored 104 runs. Chance also stole 67 bases, a modern Cubs record for a season.

JUNE 3   The Cubs pile up seven runs in the first inning and rout the Dodgers 11–3 at West Side Grounds.

The Cubs had a 30–13 record on June 3 with a three–game lead in the National League pennant race, but they were bounced out of the top spot with four consecutive losses to the Giants in Chicago from June 4 through June 7. The Cubs never returned to first place in 1903.

JUNE 18   Jake Weimer shuts out the Giants 1–0 in New York. The lone run of the game was scored in the fifth inning when Christy Mathewson walked Jimmy Slagle with the bases loaded.

Weimer was 20–8 for the Cubs in 1903 with an ERA of 2.30.

JUNE 22   In the second game of a double–header, the Cubs score six runs in the ninth inning off Christy Mathewson to defeat the Giants 10–6 in New York. The Giants won the opener 5–4 in ten innings in New York.

Jake Weimer was one of three 20–game winners for the 1903 Cubs.

JUNE 29   Jake Weimer pitches a two–hitter against the Braves in Boston, but the game ends in a scoreless tie when it's called on account of darkness after nine innings. The only Boston hits were singles by Duff Cooley and Charlie Dexter.

JULY 2   Pitcher Jack Doscher makes his major league debut for the Cubs in a 7–2 loss to the Phillies in Philadelphia. His father, Herm Doscher, was a major league third baseman from 1879 through 1902. The Doschers became the first father and son to both play in the major leagues.

This was Jack's only game with the Cubs, but he appeared in 26 more big league contests with the Dodgers and Reds. Other father–son combinations to play for the Cubs include Bobby (1957–59) and Mike (1976–77) Adams; Jimmy (1890–92) and Jimmy (1926–27) Cooney; Marty (1966) and Matt (1986) Keough; Chris (1985–86) and Justin (1998) Speier; Gary (1984–87) and Gary (2000–01) Matthews; and Randy (1966–73, 1976–77) and Todd (2001–02) Hundley.

JULY 4   In the first game of a double–header at West Side Grounds, the Cubs score seven runs in the first inning and defeat the Giants 11–9. The second game was postponed by rain.

JULY 14   Bob Wicker pitches a twelve–inning complete game and drives in the winning run with a walk–off single to defeat the Dodgers 2–1 at West Side Grounds.

Wicker was acquired from the Cardinals in April in a brilliant trade for Bob Rhoads. In his first season with the Cubs, Wicker had a record of 20–9.

JULY 30   Four days after H. Nelson Jackson completes history's first coast–to–coast trip by automobile, the Reds roll to a 15–0 win over the Cubs in Cincinnati.

AUGUST 4   Jock Menefee pitches a 1–0 victory over the Pirates at West Side Grounds. Frank Chance drove in the lone run of the game with a single in the first inning.

AUGUST 12   Pat Moran and Joe Stanley of the Braves both hit grand slams in an 11–10 win over the Cubs in the second game of a double–header at West Side Grounds. The Cubs won the first game 7–4.

SEPTEMBER 7   The Cubs score seven runs in the seventh inning and defeat the Pirates 13–8 in the first game of a double–header in Pittsburgh. The Cubs lost the second game 7–6.

SEPTEMBER 8   The Cubs score four runs in the ninth inning to take a 7–5 lead, then stave off a Pirates rally in the bottom of the inning to win 7–6 in Pittsburgh. The game ended with first baseman Otto Williams making a phenomenal catch of a line drive off the bat of Ginger Beaumont.

SEPTEMBER 18   Chick Fraser of the Phillies pitches a no–hitter to defeat the Cubs 10–0 in the second game of a double–header at West Side Grounds. The Cubs won the first game 6–5.

SEPTEMBER 22   Jake Weimer earns his 20th win of the season, defeating the Giants 6–1 at West Side Grounds.

SEPTEMBER 24   Jack Taylor earns his 21st win of the season, defeating the Braves 7–4 at West Side Grounds.

SEPTEMBER 27   Bob Wicker earns his 20th win of the season, defeating the Braves 10–3 at West Side Grounds.

OCTOBER 1   The Cubs and the White Sox play each other for the first time in a post–season "Chicago City Series." The Cubs won the first game 11–0 at West Side Grounds. The original schedule called for 15 games, with one to be played each day through October 15.

OCTOBER 9   The Cubs win the eighth game of the City Series 1–0 over the White Sox at West Side Park. The lone run of the game was scored in the bottom of the ninth. Carl Lundgren pitched the shutout.

The Cubs won again the following day. After ten days of the City Series, the Cubs had six victories, the White Sox three, and one game was postponed by rain.

OCTOBER 15   The Cubs lose 2–0 to the White Sox at South Side Park, ending the first City Series. Each team won seven games, but no more were played to decide the championship. The White Sox wanted to play a deciding fifteenth game, but the Cubs management refused. The players' contracts expired on October 15, and Cubs President James Hart didn't want to pay the players for another day of work.

DECEMBER 12   Five days before the Wright Brothers' first successful flight, and eighteen days before the terrible Iroquois Theater fire in Chicago claimed the lives of 588 people, the Cubs trade Jack Taylor and Larry McLean to the Cardinals for Three Finger Brown and Jack O'Neill. Taylor was traded because he was accused by Cubs President James Hart of throwing games to the crosstown White Sox in the 1903 City Series. Taylor won his first start 11–0, but lost the next three by scores of 10–3, 9–2, and 4–2. Although the charges were never substantiated, Taylor was hauled before a hearing of the National Commission, then baseball's ruling body, and fined for misconduct. At the time of the trade, Mordecai "Three Finger" Brown was 27 years old and had won only nine big league games. Once in Chicago, he became a star and the acquisition of Brown was one of the most important deals in Cubs history. He played for the club from 1904 through 1912, and again in 1916. Brown had a 188–85 record for the Cubs along with 346 games pitched, 208 complete games, 2,329 innings, 1,043 strikeouts, and a club–record 49 shutouts. His 1.80 ERA is also the best in Cubs history. Brown was elected to the Hall of Fame in 1949. His nickname was the result of an accident he suffered at the age of seven while visiting his uncle's farm in Indiana. Mordecai stuck his right hand in a corn chopper and half of the right index finger was shorn off. The thumb and middle finger were also badly injured. A few weeks later he fell while chasing a hog and further mangled the hand by breaking the third and fourth fingers. As they healed, each finger bent and twisted unnaturally. The disfigured hand gave Brown a unique grip, which aided in Brown's pitching because it gave him an unusual spin on the ball. After he became a renowned pitcher, Brown purchased the corn chopper from his uncle and set it in his garage for display.

The City Series

A largely forgotten aspect of the histories of the Cubs and the White Sox is the Chicago City Series, which was played nearly every fall from 1903 through 1942. The Series was held just after the close of the regular season at the same time as the World Series, and was a highly anticipated event in Chicago. Weekend games usually drew capacity crowds, and those played on weekday afternoons drew well above the regular season figures, even though they were held in the city's fickle October weather. Attendance remained high even in seasons in which both clubs finished with losing records. There were cases in which managers on both clubs either saved their jobs by winning the City Series or wound up unemployed by losing to their crosstown rivals.

The first City Series was played in 1903. The White Sox were founded in 1900, and in 1901 began raiding National League rosters for players, taking several from the Cubs. Naturally, there was a great deal of animosity between the established National League and the upstart American League. It was soothed in part by a peace accord in January 1903 in which each league agreed to respect the player contracts

of the other. At the end of the 1903 season, the Boston Red Sox and Pittsburgh Pirates met in baseball's first World Series. At the same time, the Cubs and the White Sox agreed to play 15 games against each other from October 1 through 15. Bragging rights were at stake, but in the end nothing was settled in that initial City Series, as each team won seven games with another contest postponed by rain and never played.

From 1903 through 1942, the Cubs and the White Sox met in the post–season 26 times, with the White Sox winning 19 times, the Cubs six, and the one draw in 1903. Beginning in 1905, the City Series was played under the same rules that governed the World Series. In 1906, both the Cubs and the White Sox won their league championships and played each other in the World Series. Although fan interest was still high, the last series was played in 1942. Cubs management, led by P. K. Wrigley and Charlie Grimm, hadn't won a City Series since 1930, and were embarrassed by the one–sided nature of the affair and declined to play in any more of them. Wrigley announced that it was a "booby prize" unworthy of the effort.

Following are the results of the series:

The City Series

1903– White Sox 7 games; Cubs 7 games.

1904– No series played.

1905– Cubs 4 games; White Sox 1 game.

1906– White Sox 4 games; Cubs 2 games in the World Series.

1907– No series played (Cubs in World Series).

1908– No series played (Cubs in World Series).

1909– Cubs 4 games; White Sox 1 game.

1910– No series played (Cubs in World Series).

1911– White Sox 4 games; Cubs 0 games.

1912– White Sox 4 games, Cubs 3 games; 2 ties.

1913– White Sox 4 games; Cubs 2 games.

1914– White Sox 4 games; Cubs 3 games.

1915– White Sox 4 games; Cubs 1 game.

1916– White Sox 4 games; Cubs 0 games.

1917– No series played (White Sox in World Series).

1918– No series played (Cubs in World Series).

1919– No series played (White Sox in World Series).

1920– No series played (White Sox roster devastated by Black Sox scandal, which broke in September 1920).

1921– White Sox 5 games, Cubs 0 games.

1922– Cubs 4 games; White Sox 3 games.

1923– White Sox 4 games; Cubs 2 games.

1924– White Sox 4 games; Cubs 2 games.

1925– Cubs 4 games; White Sox 1 game.

1926– White Sox 4 games; Cubs 3 games.

1927– No series played (Cubs declined to participate).

1928– Cubs 4 games; White Sox 3 games.

1929– No series played (Cubs in World Series).

1930– Cubs 4 games; White Sox 2 games.

1931– White Sox 4 games; Cubs 3 games.

1932– No series played (Cubs in World Series).

1933– White Sox 4 games; Cubs 0 games.

1934– No series played (Cubs declined to participate).

1935– No series played (Cubs in World Series).

1936– White Sox 4 games, Cubs 0 games.

1937– White Sox 4 games; Cubs 3 games.

1938– No series played (Cubs in World Series).

1939– White Sox 4 games; Cubs 3 games.

1940– White Sox 4 games; Cubs 3 games.

1941– White Sox 4 games, Cubs 0 game.

1942– White Sox 4 games; Cubs 2 games.

1904

Season in a Sentence

The Cubs win 93 games, the most in club history up to 1904, but it's not enough to compete with the Giants, who become the first team ever to win 106 in a season.

Finish • Won • Lost • Pct • GB

Second   93   60   .608   13.0

Manager

Frank Selee

Stats

Stats	Cubs	NL	Rank
Batting Avg:	.248	.249	5
On–Base Pct:	.295	.306	7
Slugging Pct:	.315	.322	6
Home Runs:	22		5
Stolen Bases:	227		2
ERA:	2.30	2.73	2
Fielding Avg:	.954	.950	3
Runs Scored:	599		5
Runs Allowed:	517		2

Starting Lineup

Johnny Kling, c
Frank Chance, 1b
Johnny Evers, 2b
Doc Casey, 3b
Joe Tinker, ss
Jimmy Slagle, lf
Jack McCarthy, cf
Davy Jones, rf
Shad Barry, rf–3b–1b
Otto Williams, rf–cf–1b–ss
Jack O'Neill, c

Pitchers

Jake Weimer, sp
Buttons Briggs, sp
Carl Lundgren, sp
Bob Wicker, sp
Three Finger Brown, sp
Frank Corriden, sp

Attendance

439,100 (second in NL)

Club Leaders

Batting Avg:	Chance	.310
On–Base Pct:	Chance	.382
Slugging Pct:	Chance	.430
Home Runs:	Chance	6
RBI:	McCarthy	51
Runs:	Slagle	73
Stolen Bases:	Chance	42
Wins:	Weimer	20
Strikeouts:	Weimer	177
ERA:	Brown	1.86
Saves:	Briggs	3

APRIL 14   The Cubs lose 3–2 to the Reds in Cincinnati in the first game of the 1904 season. The Cubs scored two runs in the first inning, but could do no more damage. The Reds plated the winning run in the ninth.

APRIL 20   The Cubs sell Bobby Lowe to the Pirates.

APRIL 21   In the home opener, the Cubs win 4–1 over the Cardinals before 4,200 at West Side Grounds. The Cubs scored all four of their runs in the eighth inning.

MAY 3   The Cubs pound the Pirates 15–3 at West Side Grounds.

MAY 9   Jake Weimer pitches a two–hitter to defeat the Braves 6–0 at West Side Grounds. The only Boston hits were singles by Fred Tenney and Pat Moran.

Weimer was 20–14 with a 1.91 ERA in 1904.

MAY 14   Cubs outfielder Jack McCarthy is forced to leave the game after spraining an ankle by stepping on the umpire's broom during a 12–4 win over the Phillies at West Side Grounds. Three Finger Brown replaced McCarthy in left field, one of only three games that Brown played in the outfield during his 13–year big league career.

McCarthy missed a week of action because of the ankle sprain. As a result of the injury, National League president Harry Pulliam ordered umpires to use pocket–sized whisk brooms to sweep home plate.

MAY 20   The Cubs win their eighth game in a row and take first place with two runs in the ninth inning off Christy Mathewson to defeat the Giants 3–2 at West Side Grounds.

MAY 22   Three Finger Brown pitches a two–hitter to defeat the Giants 3–1 before 26,000 at West Side Grounds. The only New York hits were singles by Bill Dahlen and Dan McGann.

Brown's full name was Mordecai Peter Centennial Brown. He was named Centennial because he was born in 1876, the year the United States celebrated the 100th anniversary of the Declaration of Independence. In his first season as a Cub, Brown had a record of 15–10.

MAY 30   Frank Chance sets a major league record when he's hit five times by Reds pitchers Jack Harper and Win Kellum during a double–header in Cincinnati. The Cubs lost the first game 7–4, but won the second 5–2. Chance emerged from the ordeal with a cut forehead and a black eye. On one of the three occasions he was hit in the first game, Chance lost consciousness when hit in the head.

Throughout his playing days, which took place prior to the use of the batting helmet, Chance paid a high price for crowding the plate. He was hit by pitches 137 times during his 17–year career, never played in more than 140 games in a season, and topped 130 only once, but he refused to back away from the plate. The many beanings he incurred caused deafness in one ear and a stint as an amateur boxer also contributed to head injuries. Blinding headaches ended his playing career and contributed to his death at the early age of 46.

JUNE 6	The Cubs drop out of first place after a 5–2 loss to the Dodgers in Brooklyn.

The Cubs failed to regain the top spot in the league and were out of the race by mid–July as the Giants ran away with the pennant.

JUNE 11	In a sensational performance, Bob Wicker pitches twelve innings and allows only one hit in defeating the Giants 1–0 before 38,805 in New York, the largest crowd in major league history up to that point. Wicker held the Giants hitless through the first nine innings and was deprived of a no–hitter because his teammates failed to score against Joe McGinnity, who entered the contest with a 14–game winning streak. The only New York hit was an infield single by Sam Mertes with one out in the tenth inning that caromed off the hands of Chicago third baseman Doc Casey. Wicker struck out ten batters and walked only one. The lone run of the game was scored when Frank Chance singled, advanced to third base on two infield outs, and scored on a single by Johnny Evers. In appreciation of Wicker's achievement, part of the normally partisan Polo Grounds crowd carried him off the field on its shoulders.

Wicker had a record of 17–9 in 1904. He also played 20 games in the outfield.

JUNE 13	Frank Chance lacks only a single to complete the cycle, as he collects a homer, a triple, and a double in a 3–2 win over the Giants in New York. Chance had three of the Cubs' four hits.

Chance was the Cubs top hitter in 1904 batting .310.

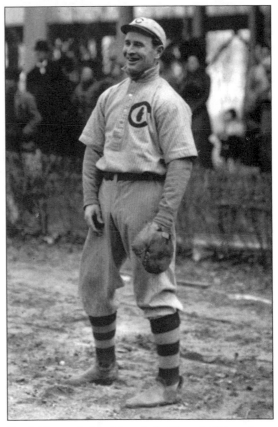

JUNE 18	A fan riot nearly erupts in Cincinnati when hundreds of spectators surround umpire Gus Moran after the Cubs defeated the Reds 4–1. The fans were angered at a sixth–inning call which went against the Reds, and swarmed the field and harassed Moran as he made his way to his dressing room. Park police eventually dispersed the crowd, but not before someone threw a rock through the window of the dressing room. Fortunately, Moran was not injured.

JULY 4	In the second game of a double-header in Pittsburgh, the Pirates and the Cubs set a modern major league record (since tied) for the most triples in a game by two teams with nine. The Pirates had six triples, and the Cubs three, as the Pirates won 11–6. The record wouldn't have been possible if it were not for an overflow crowd that ringed the outfield.

Frank Chance led the Cubs in batting, at .310, and was third in the NL in on–base percentage, at .382, in 1903 at the early stages of his seventeen–year career.

According to the ground rules, any ball hit into the crowd was a triple. The Pirates also won the first game 7–2.

JULY 8   Buttons Briggs wins a 1–0 pitchers' battle with a two–hitter against the Dodgers at West Side Grounds. Briggs also drove in the winning run with a single in the eighth inning. The only two Brooklyn hits were singles by Pop Dillon and Johnny Dobbs.

JULY 14   The Cubs bury the Braves 14–0 at West Side Grounds.

JULY 20   The Cubs trade Frank Corriden and Jack Sutthoff to the Phillies for Shad Barry.

JULY 26   For the second time in 1904, umpire Gus Moran encounters trouble at a Cubs–Reds game, this time in Chicago. Despite a 3–1 Cubs win over the Reds at West Side Grounds, fans reacted violently to calls against the home club by Moran. Frank Chance was ejected after he shoved Moran. A shower of bottles was thrown by fans, and the base lines were soon covered with splintered glass. Several hundred fans waited for Moran after the game, and the umpire was smuggled out of the ballpark by police through a rear gate into a waiting cab.

AUGUST 17   Jack O'Neill hits a grand slam homer off Tom Fisher of the Braves in the third inning of a 6–4 win in the first game of a double–header in Boston. The Cubs lost the first game 6–3.

AUGUST 20   The Cubs collect only two hits but defeat the Braves 1–0 in Boston. Bob Wicker pitched the shutout.

SEPTEMBER 1   Short on pitchers, the Dodgers use Chicago amateur Joe Koukalik in a game at West Side Grounds. Koukalik pitched a credible complete game, but the Cubs lost 3–0. It was the only major league game of Koukalik's career.

SEPTEMBER 17   The Cubs defeat the Reds 2–1 in a long seventeen–inning contest at West Side Grounds. Buttons Briggs of the Cubs and Tom Walker of the Reds both pitched complete games. Jack McCarthy drove in the winning run with a two–out, bases–loaded single. McCarthy also drove in the other Chicago run in the first inning.

SEPTEMBER 26   The Cubs score a double shutout over the Dodgers in Brooklyn. Jake Weimer won the first game 4–0, and Buttons Briggs the second 1–0 in a contest called after six innings on account of darkness.

SEPTEMBER 30   The Cubs score seven runs in the eighth inning to defeat the Giants 12–9 in the first game of a double–header in New York. The Cubs also won the second game, called after seven innings by darkness, 5–3.

OCTOBER 4   Jake Weimer earns his 20th victory of the season, defeating the Braves 4–3 in Boston.

1905

Cubs

Season in a Sentence

The best pitching staff in the league can't compensate for a below–average offense.

Finish • Won • Lost • Pct • GB

Third   92   61   .601   13.0

Managers

Frank Selee (37–28) and
Frank Chance (55–33)

Stats

Stats	Cubs	NL	Rank
Batting Avg:	.245	.255	5
On–Base Pct:	.313	.315	5
Slugging Pct:	.314	.332	7
Home Runs:	12		8
Stolen Bases:	267		2
ERA:	2.04	2.99	1
Fielding Avg:	.962	.954	1
Runs Scored:	667		5
Runs Allowed:	442		1

Starting Lineup

Johnny Kling, c
Frank Chance, 1b
Johnny Evers, 2b
Doc Casey, 3b
Joe Tinker, ss
Wildfire Schulte, lf
Jimmy Slagle, cf
Billy Maloney, rf
Solly Hofman, 2b
Jack O'Neill, c
Jack McCarthy, cf–lf

Pitchers

Ed Reulbach, sp
Jake Weimer, sp
Three Finger Brown, sp
Bob Wicker, sp
Carl Lundgren, sp
Buttons Briggs, sp
Big Jeff Pfeffer, sp

Attendance

509,900 (second in NL)

Club Leaders

Batting Avg:	Chance	.316
On–Base Pct:	Chance	.450
Slugging Pct:	Chance	.434
Home Runs:	Chance	2
	Maloney	2
RBI:	Chance	70
Runs:	Slagle	96
Stolen Bases:	Maloney	59
Wins:	Three tied	18
Strikeouts:	Reulbach	152
ERA:	Reulbach	1.42
Saves:	Weimer	1
	Reulbach	1

APRIL 14   The Cubs win 6–1 over the Cardinals in St. Louis in the first game of the 1905 season. Carl Lundgren allowed only one hit through the first eight innings before being touched for a run and three hits in the ninth.

APRIL 19   In the home opener, the Cubs win 5–1 over the Reds at West Side Grounds.

West Side Grounds was remodeled for the 1905 season, with new boxes on the roof, enlarged bleachers, and a new clubhouse in center field. The new clubhouse, like the old one, was located on the playing field and was in play, although some 500 feet from home plate.

APRIL 23   Three Finger Brown defeats the Pirates 1–0 at West Side Grounds. The run was scored in an unusual manner. With two out in the eighth inning, Brown swung and missed at a Deacon Phillippe pitch, but the ball sailed past Heinie Peitz to the backstop. Brown reached second base by the time Peitz retrieved the horsehide. Doc Casey drove in Brown with a double.

Brown had an 18–12 record and a 2.17 ERA in 1905.

APRIL 26   Center fielder Jack McCarthy ties a major league record for "most assists by outfielder to catcher" and "most double plays started by an outfielder" in a game by nailing three runners on throws to catcher Jack O'Neill during a 2–1 win over the Pirates in Pittsburgh. All three throws went directly from McCarthy to O'Neill without an intervening relay.

MAY 12   Future Hall of Famers Three Finger Brown and Vic Willis battle to a 1–1 tie through ten innings, then fall apart in the eleventh. The Cubs scored four runs and the Braves three to allow Chicago to emerge with a 5–4 victory.

MAY 20   The Cubs sell Shad Barry to the Reds.

MAY 30   Ed Reulbach pitches the Cubs to a 1–0 victory over the Reds in the first game of a Memorial Day double–header in Cincinnati. The lone run of the game was scored on a single by Joe Tinker in the ninth inning. The second game was postponed by rain.

The Cubs were off to a slow start in 1905, and had a 21–24 record on June 4.

JUNE 13   Christy Mathewson pitches a no–hitter at West Side Grounds to lead the Giants to a 1–0 win over the Cubs. Three Finger Brown allowed only one New York hit through the first eight innings when he wilted, surrendering a run and four hits.

JUNE 14   Bob Wicker shuts out Joe McGinnity and the Giants 1–0 at West Side Grounds.

JUNE 24   The Cubs win a long, drawn out eighteen–inning battle by a 2–1 score over the Cardinals in St. Louis. Cubs rookie Ed Reulbach and former Cub Jack Taylor both pitched complete games. The winning run was scored on a triple by Wildfire Schulte and a sacrifice fly by Billy Maloney.

Ed Reulbach tied for the team lead with 18 wins as a rookie in 1905 and was second in the NL in ERA, at 1.42.

Reulbach was 18–14 with five shutouts and a 1.42 ERA in 1905.

JUNE 25   Billy Maloney hits a grand slam off Jack Harper during a nine–run fifth inning as the Cubs trounce the Reds 18–2 at West Side Grounds.

JULY 1   The Cubs score seven runs in the seventh inning to defeat the Reds 13–5 at West Side Grounds.

Frank Chance took over as Cubs manager in place of ailing Frank Selee on this date. Selee was diagnosed with "acute indigestion." A few weeks later, it was learned that Selee had tuberculosis, and on the advice of his physicians he took a leave of absence for the rest of the season to travel to Colorado to recuperate. It was hoped that Selee would recover in time for the start of the 1906 season, but his health worsened and Chance was given the job as manager on a permanent basis. Selee died in 1909 in Denver at the age of 49.

JULY 4   The Cubs sweep the Cardinals 3–2 and 11–1 in a double–header at West Side Grounds.

JULY 12   Three Finger Brown pitches a two–hitter to defeat the Giants 3–1 at the Polo Grounds. The only New York hits were singles by Sam Mertes and Roger Bresnahan.

                Brown is referred to as "Three Finger" Brown in baseball histories, but during his career he was usually called "Three Fingered" Brown.

JULY 17   Jake Weimer pitches a shutout to defeat the Dodgers 1–0 in Brooklyn.

                Weimer was 18–12 with a 2.26 ERA in 1905.

JULY 18   The Cubs belt the Dodgers 12–2 in Brooklyn.

JULY 31   Charles P. Taft, owner of a Cincinnati newspaper and half–brother of future President William Howard Taft, finances Charles W. Murphy's purchase of the Cubs from James Hart with a loan $125,000. Murphy became team president, a position he held until 1914. Before assuming control of the Cubs, Murphy had been a sportswriter in Cincinnati, working under Taft, and publicity director of the New York Giants.

                Murphy had the good fortune to purchase the Cubs just as they were about to emerge as the dominant team in baseball. The franchise became a gold mine as attendance at West Side Grounds soared, and Murphy paid off Taft's loan within twelve months and became a millionaire.

AUGUST 5   Umpire Jim Johnstone is injured by a foul tip in the first game of a double–header, won 6–0 by the Cubs over the Braves at West Side Grounds. Johnstone was unable to continue in the second game, which created a problem since he was the only umpire assigned to officiate. Carl Lundgren of the Cubs and Irv Young of the Braves served as umpires in the second contest, won by the Cubs 5–1.

AUGUST 6   With Jim Johnstone still injured, Sam Mertes of the Giants serves as the umpire as the Cubs defeat the Braves 8–0 at West Side Grounds. The Giants had a day off and were in Chicago to begin a series against the Cubs the following day.

AUGUST 9   The Cubs score in an unusual manner in the seventh inning of a 7–2 win over Giants at West Side Grounds. With Billy Maloney as a base runner on first and Jimmy Slagle on second, Frank Chance hit a drive over the head of right fielder Sammy Strang. Maloney took off running with the crack of the bat, while Slagle held to see whether or not Strang would catch the ball. By the time Slagle started running, Maloney was right on his heels. Slagle, Maloney, and Strang's relay throw arrived at home plate at almost the same moment. Catcher Roger Bresnahan tagged Slagle, but Maloney touched home to score.

AUGUST 13   After losing 2–1 to the Dodgers in the first game of a double–header at West Side Grounds, the Cubs win 15–1 in the nightcap.

AUGUST 21   The Cubs pound the Dodgers 12–2 in Brooklyn.

AUGUST 24   Ed Reulbach pitches twenty innings to defeat the Phillies 2–1 in Philadelphia. Tully Sparks also pitched twenty innings in a losing effort. Both teams scored their first run in the thirteenth inning. In the winning twentieth inning, Jack McCarthy singled, took second on Doc Casey's sacrifice, and scored on Frank Chance's single. It was the second time in 1905 that Reulbach pitched a marathon game on the 24th of the month (see June 24, 1905).

SEPTEMBER 3   The Cubs and the Pirates combine for only 12 hits during a double–header at West Side Grounds. Each team had three hits in each game. The Cubs won the opener 1–0 in eleven innings in a duel between Bob Wicker and Deacon Phillippe. The winning run was scored on a triple by Doc Casey and an error. Pittsburgh took the second game 1–0. It was called after six innings to allow both teams to catch a train.

SEPTEMBER 11   After losing 3–2 to the Reds in the first game of a double–header in Cincinnati, the Cubs take the second contest 12–0, called after six innings by darkness. For the second time in a little over a month, an umpire was unable to officiate in the second game of a Cubs double–header, as George Bausewine was battered by foul tips in the opener and couldn't answer the call in the nightcap. Jake Weimer of the Cubs and Orval Overall of the Reds filled in for Bausewine as arbiters.

SEPTEMBER 13   Joe Tinker and Johnny Evers engage in a fistfight at second base during an exhibition game in Bedford, Indiana, won by the Cubs 15–0.

Evers left for the ballpark in a taxi while leaving his teammates in the hotel lobby. Still seething over the incident, Tinker fired a ball at Evers, who was no more than ten feet away, and Evers punched the Cub shortstop. The pair didn't speak to each other again off the field for over thirty years. The dispute didn't impair their ability to perform together on the field, however. Tinker and Evers played next to each other in the Cubs infield until 1912, a period in which the club appeared in the World Series four times.

SEPTEMBER 23   Carl Lundgren pitches the Cubs to a 1–0 win over the Giants at West Side Grounds. Doc Casey drove in the lone run of the game with a single in the fifth inning.

SEPTEMBER 24   A frenzied crowd of 26,000 watches the Cubs defeat the Giants 10–5 at West Side Grounds. Chicago scored nine runs in the fifth inning off Joe McGinnity to overcome a 4–0 New York lead.

During the wild afternoon in Chicago, an umpire was injured and the crowd staged a riot. Umpire Bob Emslie was hit in the chest by a foul tip in the second inning and dropped to the ground as if he'd been shot. Players rushed to his side while police fought off the curious mob surging from all directions. A physician was called, and Emslie was worked over for twenty minutes before he regained consciousness. He insisted on finishing the game. During the delay, the mob which had overflowed the grandstand and the bleachers onto the field became unmanageable. Police reinforcements came quickly and made an effort to clear the diamond. According to the wire service reports, "clubs were wielded without mercy, and the air was full with flying headgear. Heads were cracked without compunction and the scene looked like a miniature battlefield."

SEPTEMBER 27   Carl Lundgren holds the Dodgers hitless until two are out in the ninth inning before settling for a two–hitter and a 7–2 victory at West Side Grounds. Jimmy Sheckard collected the first Brooklyn hit with a double, which was followed by a Doc Gessler single, a stolen base, and an error which scored the two Dodger runs.

SEPTEMBER 28   All of the gate proceeds from the game between the Cubs and the Braves at West Side Grounds go to Frank Selee to help him in his recovery from tuberculosis. About $4,000 was raised. The Cubs won 7–4.

OCTOBER 11   In the opener of the Chicago City Series against the White Sox, the Cubs win 5–4 at South Side Grounds. The Cubs won the best–of–seven series, four games to one.

DECEMBER 16   The Cubs send Bill Maloney, Jack McCarthy, Doc Casey, Buttons Briggs, and $2,000 to the Dodgers for Jimmy Sheckard. The deal was struck while Cubs President Charles Murphy and Dodgers owner Charles Ebbets walked across the Brooklyn Bridge.

The Cubs gave up four regulars and cash to acquire Sheckard, but it proved to be an excellent trade. Sheckard played for the Cubs for seven seasons and led the National League twice in walks, once in runs scored, and once in on–base percentage.

1906

Season in a Sentence

The Cubs set a major league record by winning 116 games, but lose the World Series to the crosstown White Sox in a shocking upset.

Finish • Won • Lost • Pct • GB

First   116   36   .763 +20.0

World Series–The Cubs lost, four games to two, to the White Sox.

Manager

Frank Chance

Stats

Stats	Cubs	NL	Rank
Batting Avg:	.262	.244	1
On–Base Pct:	.328	.310	2
Slugging Pct:	.339	.310	1
Home Runs:	20		2
Stolen Bases:	283		2
ERA:	1.75	2.62	1
Fielding Avg:	.969	.959	1
Runs Scored:	705		1
Runs Allowed:	381		1

Starting Lineup

Johnny Kling, c
Frank Chance, 1b
Johnny Evers, 2b
Harry Steinfeldt, 3b
Joe Tinker, ss
Jimmy Sheckard, lf
Jimmy Slagle, cf
Wildfire Schulte, rf
Pat Moran, c
Solly Hofman, cf–1b

Pitchers

Three Finger Brown, sp
Jack Pfiester, sp
Ed Reulbach, sp
Carl Lundgren, sp
Jack Taylor, sp
Orval Overall, sp

Attendance

654,300 (first in NL)

Club Leaders

Batting Avg:	Steinfeldt	.327
On–Base Pct:	Chance	.419
Slugging Pct:	Chance	.430
Home Runs:	Chance	3
	Steinfeldt	3
RBI:	Steinfeldt	83
Runs:	Chance	103
Stolen Bases:	Chance	57
Wins:	Brown	26
Strikeouts:	Pfiester	153
ERA:	Brown	1.04
Saves:	Brown	3
	Ed Reulbach	3

Harry Steinfeldt, the answer to trivia questions as the fourth member of the otherwise–famous Cubs infield of the early 1900s, was one of the team's leading hitters.

MARCH 6   The Cubs trade Hans Lobert and Jake Weimer to the Reds for Harry Steinfeldt.

After trading Doc Casey to the Dodgers in the Jimmy Sheckard deal the previous December, the Cubs needed a starting third baseman and had pitching depth to trade. Steinfeldt anchored the left side of the Tinker–Evers–Chance infield in four World Series during his five seasons with the Cubs. In 1906, Steinfeldt hit .327 and led the NL in hits (176) and runs batted in (83).

APRIL 12   The Cubs win the season opener 7–2 in Cincinnati.

APRIL 16   It wasn't a good day for Joe Tinker, Johnny Evers, and Frank Chance as the Cubs lost 3–2 to the Reds in Cincinnati. Evers and Chance were ejected for arguing with the umpires, and Tinker got into a fight with a fan outside the ballpark. Tinker was on the team bus and had enough of the verbal abuse of one fan and jumped from the vehicle to attack the individual. The Cubs shortstop more than met his match, however, and was being beaten badly when pulled away by Chance before police broke up the disturbance.

APRIL 17   In the home opener at West Side Grounds, the Cubs lose 6–3 to the Cardinals before a crowd of 15,000.

APRIL 28   The Cubs use football tactics to steal a 1–0 win from the Reds at West Side Grounds. In the ninth inning with the score 0–0 and Frank Chance a base runner on second base and Joe Tinker on first, Pat Moran grounded to Reds third baseman Jim Delahanty. Delahanty threw to second baseman Miller Huggins to force Tinker, who in turn tackled Huggins and held him to the ground while Chance rounded third with the winning run.

Chance hit .319 and tied for the league lead with 103 runs scored in 1906.

Other Cubs hitters who had an All–Star caliber season were Johnny Kling, who hit .312, Wildfire Schulte, who batted .281 and led the league in triples with 13, and Jimmy Sheckard, who batted .262 and scored 90 runs.

MAY 7   The Cubs win their 10th game in a row by defeating the Pirates 3–2 in Pittsburgh. Frank Chance lost an inside–the–park homer when the return throw from the out-field struck umpire Jim Johnstone. Chance was sent back to third base.

The Cubs had a 6–6 record after their first dozen games in 1906 before breaking loose with the 10–game winning streak.

MAY 8   The Cubs purchase Doc Gessler from the Dodgers.

MAY 16   The Cubs defeat the Phillies 1–0 in ten innings at West Side Grounds behind Carl Lundgren's three–hitter. A single by Wildfire Schulte scored the winning run.

Frank "Wildfire" Schulte played for the Cubs from 1904 through 1916. He appeared in 1,564 games for the club and had 827 runs scored, 1,590 hits, 254 doubles, 117 triples, and 712 RBIs. Schulte got his nickname because of his admiration for famed actress Lillian Russell. In 1908, the Cubs conducted spring training in Vicksburg, Mississippi, at the same time that Russell was in town with her play WILDFIRE. She gave a party for the Cubs, and in apprecia-tion Schulte, who owned racehorses, named one of his trotters "Wildfire." Before long, he too was known by the name.

MAY 20   A crowd of 25,000 watches the Cubs beat the Giants 10–4 at West Side Grounds. The game was delayed for thirty minutes while police got the crowd under control. After the gates to the ballpark were broken, thousands poured in free of charge. Some 2,000 remained on the outside throughout the contest and learned what hap-pened from fans in the top rows who yelled the important plays and scores.

MAY 28   The Cubs take first place with a 4–2 win over the Braves at West Side Grounds. Wildfire Schulte broke the 2–2 tie with a two–run homer in the eighth inning.

Did a hatpin help Schulte hit the homer? One of his idiosyncrasies was the belief that finding a hatpin guaranteed him a base hit. If either prong of the lucky pin was bent, Schulte believed that the hit would go in that direction. In 1906, he led the league in triples with 13 and batted .281.

MAY 30   Jack Pfiester strikes out 17 batters in 15 innings, but the Cubs lose 4–2 to the Cardinals in the first game of a double–header at West Side Grounds. The Cardinals also won the second game 6–1.

Pfiester had a 20–8 record, a 1.51 ERA, and 153 strikeouts in 1906.

JUNE 2   The Cubs send Bob Wicker and $2,000 to the Reds for Orval Overall.

Overall proved to be a tremendous acquisition. From 1906 through 1910, Overall had an 82–39 record for the Cubs and a 1.82 ERA.

JUNE 6   The Cubs score seven runs in the eighth inning and beat the Giants 11–3 in New York.

JUNE 7   The Cubs score 11 runs in the first inning and annihilate the Giants 19–0 in New York. The Cubs scored the 11 first-inning runs off of Christy Mathewson and Joe McGinnity, two of the greatest pitchers of their generation. McGinnity also gave up three runs in the second before he was relieved. Wildfire Schulte collected five of the Cubs' 22 hits. For years afterward, Chicago fans taunted the Giants at West Side Grounds by chanting "Nineteen! Nineteen!"

JUNE 20   The Cubs wallop the Braves 11–1 in Boston.

JUNE 25   Ed Reulbach pitches a one-hitter to defeat the Cardinals 3–1 at West Side Grounds. The only St. Louis hit was a single by Homer Smoot.

             Reulbach was 19–4 with six shutouts and an ERA of 1.65 in 1906.

JUNE 26   Orval Overall shuts out the Cardinals 1–0 at West Side Grounds. Jimmy Slagle drove in the winning run with a single in the third inning.

JUNE 30   Carl Lundgren pitches a two-hitter to defeat the Reds 2–1 at West Side Grounds. The only Cincinnati hits were singles by Jim Delahanty and Admiral Schlei.

JULY 1   Ed Reulbach pitches the Cubs to a 1–0 win over the Reds at West Side Grounds. Joe Tinker drove in the winning run with a sacrifice fly in the seventh inning.

             One the same day, Jack Taylor returned to the Cubs from the Cardinals in a trade for Pete Noonan, Fred Beebe, and cash.

JULY 4   The Cubs win both ends of a double-header in Pittsburgh by scores of 1–0 behind the clutch pitching of Three Finger Brown and Carl Lundgren. Combined with the July 1 win, it was the Cubs' third straight 1–0 victory. It was also Chicago's ninth consecutive game decided by one run, dating back to June 24.

             Three Finger Brown was sensational in 1906 with a record of 26–6 and a microscopic league-leading ERA of 1.04. He also led the NL in shutouts with nine.

Mordecai "Three Finger" Brown was a Cubs ace for eight seasons. His 26 wins in 1906 marked the first of six straight 20-win seasons.

JULY 7   The Cubs break a scoreless tie by scoring five runs in the ninth inning to beat the Pirates 5–0 in Pittsburgh.

JULY 13   The Cubs score three runs in the ninth inning to beat the Phillies 4–3 at West Side Grounds.

JULY 15   Jack Taylor wins his own game by driving in the winning run in the tenth inning with a double, lifting the Cubs to a 4–3 win over the Phillies at West Side Grounds.

AUGUST 3   The Cubs sweep the Phillies 1–0 and 7–0 in Philadelphia behind the pitching of Three Finger Brown and Ed Reulbach.

AUGUST 6   Umpire Jim Johnstone calls Art Devlin of the Giants out at the plate during a 3–1 Cubs victory in New York. After he ejected Giants manager John McGraw, Johnstone became the target of a bottle barrage from Polo Grounds fans. McGraw and Devlin were suspended indefinitely by National League President Harry Pulliam for verbally abusing Johnstone.

AUGUST 7   The Cubs win by forfeit after the Giants refuse to admit umpire Jim Johnstone into the Polo Grounds.

After his disputed call against the Giants the previous day, Johnstone found himself "locked out" of the ballpark. When he showed up for the game between the Giants and the Cubs, he was barred from entering by the gatekeeper and told that police inspector James Sweeney could not ensure his safety. The incident was the work of New York manager John McGraw. Neither Sweeney nor the city police had knowledge of it. Inside the ballpark, the second umpire, Bob Emslie, refused to work without Johnstone. According to National League rules of the day, if no umpires were available, each club appointed a player to serve as umpire. McGraw designated Giants player Sammy Strang as umpire, but Cubs manager Frank Chance refused to play the game without Johnstone and Emslie. Strang then awarded his team a victory by forfeit. Meanwhile, on the outside, Johnstone awarded the Cubs the victory by forfeit. The crowd of 11,000, which had been chanting "Play Ball! Play Ball!" was sent home.

AUGUST 8   With National League President Harry Pulliam backing Jim Johnstone and assigning him to today's game, Giants owner John Brush allows the umpire into the Polo Grounds. Pulliam also called the game the previous day a forfeit in favor of the Cubs. The umpires were applauded by the fans, and this time the game was settled on the field, with the Cubs winning 3–2.

AUGUST 13   Cubs starting pitcher Jack Taylor is knocked out in the third inning of an 11–3 loss to the Dodgers in Brooklyn. It ended a streak in which Taylor completed a major league record 187 starts in a row, dating back to 1901. Taylor also made 15 relief appearances during the streak, and stayed in the game until the finish of each one of them.

SEPTEMBER 1   Umpires Jim Johnstone and Bob Emslie are unable to report to West Side Grounds due to food poisoning. Carl Lundgren of the Cubs and Pete Noonan of the Cardinals served as substitutes, and the Cubs won 8–1 for their 14th win in succession.

SEPTEMBER 6   Three Finger Brown pitches a one-hitter to defeat the Pirates 7–0 at West Side Grounds. The only Pittsburgh hit was a single by Tommy Sheehan.

SEPTEMBER 9   The Cubs score seven runs in the seventh inning to defeat the Pirates 7–2 at West Side Grounds.

SEPTEMBER 13 Three Finger Brown earns his 11th consecutive victory in a 6–2 decision over the Cardinals in St. Louis.

The Cubs stole 283 bases in 1906, a modern club record.

SEPTEMBER 19   The Cubs clinch the pennant with a 3–1 win over the Braves in Boston. It was also the Cubs' 106th victory of the season, which tied the existing record set by the New York Giants in 1905.

SEPTEMBER 24   Three Finger Brown earns his 26th victory of the season with a 6–2 decision over the Giants in New York.

SEPTEMBER 25   Jack Pfiester pitches a ten–inning, one–hitter to defeat the Dodgers 1–0 in Brooklyn. The only Dodger hit was a single by Bill Bergen. The victory was Pfiester's 20th of the season.

Bergen had a batting average of only .159 in 353 at–bats in 1906. The worst hitter in major league history to accumulate at least 2,500 at–bats, Bergen had a career average of .170 in 945 big league games from 1901 through 1911.

OCTOBER 1   Ed Reulbach earns his 12th consecutive victory in a 4–3 decision over the Phillies in the second game of a double–header in Philadelphia that was called by darkness after six innings. The Cubs won the first game 4–0 on a Carl Lundgren two–hitter. The only Philadelphia hits were singles by Sherry Magee and Paul Sentell.

OCTOBER 4   The Cubs win their 116th game of the season with a 4–0 decision over the Pirates in Pittsburgh. The Cubs closed incredibly strong in 1906, winning 55 of their last 63 regular season games to finish with a record of 116–36. The Cubs set major league records for most wins in a season, tied by the Seattle Mariners in 2001, and best winning percentage in the modern era (since 1900) with a mark of .763.

The Cubs' opponents in the World Series were the White Sox, creating the first, and to date only, all–Chicago Fall Classic. It was also the first time that two teams from the same city met in the Series. The 1906 White Sox were known as the "Hitless Wonders" because they won the pennant with a .230 team batting average and only seven home runs, both of which were last in the eight–team American League. The White Sox were also last in the league in slugging percentage and fifth in on–base percentage. Despite these figures, the Sox offense was extremely resourceful and finished third in the league in runs scored. With a 116–36 record by the Cubs, compared to the Sox's mark of 93–58, the Series appeared to be a mismatch, and the National Leaguers were heavy favorites with a betting margin of 3–1.

OCTOBER 9   Amid snow flurries, the White Sox defeat the Cubs 2–1 in the first game of the 1906 World Series before 12,693 at West Side Grounds. The Cubs scored their lone run in the sixth inning when the White Sox had a 2–0 lead. White Sox pitcher Nick Altrock went all the way, allowing four hits, walking one, and striking out three for the win. Despite yielding only four hits and a walk while fanning seven, Three Finger Brown got the loss. Both runs off Brown were unearned, one on his own error.

The game was played on the 35th anniversary of the Great Fire of 1871, which destroyed most of Chicago.

OCTOBER 10   The Cubs bounce back and even the World Series by defeating the White Sox 7–1 in game two before 12,595 fans battered by freezing winds at South Side Park. Ed Reulbach no–hit the White Sox into the seventh inning, when Jiggs Donahue singled. Reulbach ended up with a one–hitter, yielding six walks for the win. The Cubs took a 4–0 lead with three runs in the second inning and one in the third. Harry Steinfeldt was 3–for–3, and Joe Tinker scored three runs.

OCTOBER 11   The autumn cold snap continues, as Ed Walsh two–hits the Cubs, striking out 12, to give the White Sox a 3–0 win in game three of the World Series before 13,667 at West Side Grounds. Walsh held the Cubs hitless over the final eight innings. The Sox managed only four hits, but one was a two–out, bases–loaded sixth–inning triple by George Rohe, driving in all of the game's runs. Jack Pfiester struck out nine, but drew the loss.

Rohe spent most of the 1906 season as a utility infielder. He was playing in the World Series only because of an injury to regular shortstop George Davis.

OCTOBER 12   Pitching continues to dominate, as the Cubs come back once again to even the Series at two games apiece. Three Finger Brown held the "Hitless Wonders" hitless until the sixth inning and allowed only two hits for a 1–0 win before 18,385 at South Side Park. Johnny Evers singled in Frank Chance in the seventh inning for the only run, making a loser of Nick Altrock.

Before the Series, Cubs left fielder Jimmy Sheckard bragged that he would hit .400 against the White Sox. Instead, he was held hitless in 21 at–bats and hit only one ball out of the infield.

OCTOBER 13   The White Sox commit six errors in game five, but win 8–6 to take a three–games–to–two lead in the World Series before 23,257 at West Side Grounds. The Cubs scored three runs in the first inning to take a 3–1 lead, but the White Sox tied the contest with two runs in the third inning and broke the game open with four in the fourth to pull ahead 7–3. It was the fifth straight game in which the visiting team emerged with a victory. Frank Isbell of the Sox hit four doubles, scored three runs, and drove in two. Wildfire Schulte had three hits, including a double, for the Cubs.

The 1906 World Series was the first in which umpires raised their right hand to signal a strike. The innovation was introduced in the minors in 1905 and is credited to Chief Zimmer, who umpired in the Southern League. Previously, umpires used only voice calls to signal balls and strikes, but most fans couldn't hear them and were left in the dark as to whether a pitch was a ball or a strike. The new method of raising a right hand for a strike and making no signal for a ball was immediately popular with fans and players alike, and was universal in baseball by 1907.

OCTOBER 14   The White Sox win the world championship by defeating the Cubs 8–3 before 19,249 at South Side Park. It completed one of the greatest upsets in World Series history. Doc White earned the complete–game win, allowing the Cubs seven hits. The White Sox banged out 14 hits. Three Finger Brown, who was making his third start in six days, was knocked out of the game in the second inning after giving up seven runs. The White Sox offense was led by George Davis and Jiggs Donahue, who each drove in three runs, and Ed Hahn, who collected four hits.

An All–Chicago World Series

Chicago hasn't hosted a World Series since the White Sox met the Dodgers in 1959, when Dwight Eisenhower was president. There hasn't been a Fall Classic at Wrigley Field since 1945, before the existence of television. Neither team has captured a world championship since the Sox won in 1917, prior to the existence of radio. The idea that one of the Windy City teams should reach the Series, much less win one, has been the dream of generations of fans. Any thought of both the Cubs and the White Sox playing each other for a world championship seems preposterous. But it happened in 1906 and resulted in one of the greatest upsets in baseball history. The powerful Cubs, with a record of 116–36, were toppled by a bunch of batters so ineffectual that they were nicknamed "The Hitless Wonders."

The Cubs were hot down the stretch, winning 55 of their last 63 regular season games, and were flawlessly balanced with no glaring weaknesses. The club had an airtight infield with Frank Chance, Johnny Evers, Joe Tinker, and Harry Steinfeldt, a solid outfield, one of the best catchers of the period in Johnny Kling, and a deep pitching staff, headed by Three Finger Brown, which compiled a composite ERA of 1.75. Chance, who was also the manager of the team, said that his biggest job was to persuade his team that the Series wasn't going to be "a walkover."

The White Sox, who were in last place on June 21, looked less than daunting. They appeared to have won 93 games with smoke and mirrors. The team batting average of .230 was dead last in the American League, a full 49 points lower than the third–place Cleveland Indians, who also had a lower team ERA. The Sox were also last in slug-ging percentage with a mark of .286, 18 points lower than the next worst team, and were last in doubles and home runs. The AL champs managed to finish third in runs scored, however, by leading the league in walks and sacrifice hits and finishing third in stolen bases.

In Chicago, the Cubs were between two–to-one and three–to–one betting favorites as the Series began. Even the staunchest White Sox fans really didn't believe that their club had a prayer. Despite what looked like a mismatch, the all–Chicago World Series aroused passion in the Windy City for the dream matchup. The city was at a virtual standstill for the six days in which the two clubs battled for the world title. Two teenage fans, desperate for money so they could buy tickets from scalpers, held up a grocery store. City councilman Charles Martin, a White Sox fan, was arrested after brawling with a drunken Cubs fan.

The 1906 World Series was marked by great pitching performances and bitterly cold weather. The White Sox began the Series without short-stop George Davis, the club's top hitter. But George Rohe, Davis's substitute, hit a key triple in a 2–1 Sox victory in game one amid snow flurries. The Cubs bounced back to win the second game 7–1, but Rohe hit a bases–loaded triple and Ed Walsh pitched a shutout to win game three 3–0. Three Finger Brown evened the Series again with a 1–0 victory in the fourth game. It proved to be the Cubs' last victory. The White Sox won the final two games 8–6 and 8–3 over the stunned Cubs.

Frank Chance vowed that the Cubs would return to the World Series and wouldn't lose again. His club fulfilled the promise by capturing the world championship in 1907 and 1908, both times over the Detroit Tigers.

1907

Season in a Sentence

The Cubs win nine fewer games than in the record–breaking season of 1906 but take a bigger prize by winning the World Series over Ty Cobb and the Detroit Tigers.

Finish • Won • Lost • Pct • GB

First   107   45   .704 +17.0

World Series–The Cubs defeated the Tigers in five games with four victories and a tie.

Manager

Frank Chance

Stats

Stats	Cubs	NL	Rank
Batting Avg:	.250	.308	3
On–Base Pct:	.318	.308	3
Slugging Pct:	.311	.309	4
Home Runs:	13		7
Stolen Bases:	235		2
ERA:	1.73	2.46	1
Fielding Avg:	.967	.960	1
Runs Scored:	574		3
Runs Allowed:	390		1

Starting Lineup

Johnny Kling, c
Frank Chance, 1b
Johnny Evers, 2b
Harry Steinfeldt, 3b
Joe Tinker, ss
Jimmy Sheckard, lf
Jimmy Slagle, cf
Wildfire Schulte, rf
Solly Hofman, rf–ss
Pat Moran, c

Pitchers

Orval Overall, sp
Three Finger Brown, sp
Carl Lundgren, sp
Ed Reulbach, sp
Jack Pfiester, sp
Chick Fraser, sp–rp
Jack Taylor, sp

Attendance

422,550 (second in NL)

Club Leaders

Batting Avg:	Chance	.293
On–Base Pct:	Chance	.395
Slugging Pct:	Chance	.361
Home Runs:	Evers	2
	Schulte	2
RBI:	Steinfeldt	70
Runs:	Sheckard	76
Stolen Bases:	Evers	46
Wins:	Overall	23
Strikeouts:	Overall	141
ERA:	Pfiester	1.15
Saves:	Overall	3
	Brown	3

APRIL 11   The defending National League champion Cubs defeat the Cardinals 6–1 at West Side Grounds in the first game of the season. The Cubs scored single runs in six different innings.

This was the first time that the Cubs played the first game of a season at home since 1881. Cubs management didn't want to open at home during the 26–year interval because of the fickle spring weather in Chicago. Beginning in 1907, the Cubs opened up at home every other year, alternating with the White Sox.

APRIL 18   Three Finger Brown pitches a two–hitter but loses 1–0 to the Pirates in Pittsburgh. The only Pirate hits were singles by Frank Clarke and Honus Wagner.

Brown was 20–6 with six shutouts and a 1.39 ERA in 1907.

APRIL 22   Jack Pfiester pitches 7⅔ innings of shutout relief, allowing only two hits, to lead the Cubs to a 3–2 win over the Reds in Cincinnati.

Pfiester was 14–9 in 1907 and led the NL in ERA with a mark of 1.15.

APRIL 28   Chick Fraser pitches a one–hitter to defeat the Cardinals 1–0 in the second game of a double–header in St. Louis. The only Cardinal hit was a double by Jake Beckley. The Cubs also won the first game 3–2.

MAY 4   The Cubs collect only two hits, both by Solly Hofman, but Carl Lundgren pitches a shutout for a 1–0 win over the Pirates at West Side Grounds. Hofman's single in the fourth inning drove in the only run of the game.

The Cubs had a record of 23–4 on May 18 but were in second place because the Giants were 24–3. Combined with a 110–30 record over the last 140 games of 1906, the Cubs had a record of 133–34 over 167 consecutive regular season games in 1906 and 1907. From April 27, 1906, through August 4, 1907, the Cubs were 181–54 in the regular season, a winning percentage of .770.

MAY 21   The Cubs defeat the Giants 3–2 before a contentious crowd in New York. Over 1,000 followed umpires Bob Emslie and Hank O'Day off the field and threw objects at them. Police fired shots into the air to disperse the crowd. Emslie and O'Day were surrounded by New York players, who escorted them off the field unharmed.

MAY 30   The Cubs win 7–1 and 6–4 over the Pirates at Pittsburgh to take first place. The Cubs remained in first for the rest of the season.

JUNE 20   Orval Overall shuts out the Braves 4–0 at West Side Grounds.

Overall was 23–8 in 1907 with an ERA of 1.68 and a league–leading eight shutouts.

JUNE 21   Three Finger Brown wins his 10th consecutive game with a 2–0 victory over the Cardinals at West Side Grounds. Johnny Kling threw out all four runners trying to steal second.

JUNE 22   For the third game in a row, a Cubs pitcher hurls a shutout as Carl Lundgren blanks the Cardinals 3–0 at West Side Grounds.

JUNE 23   Ed Reulbach wins his own game with an RBI–single in the tenth inning to defeat the Cardinals 2–1 at West Side Grounds.

Reulbach had a record of 17–4 with a 1.69 ERA in 1907.

JUNE 24   The Cubs trade Bill Sweeney and Newt Randall to the Braves for Del Howard.

JULY 8   Frank Chance barely escapes bodily harm from the crowd as the Cubs defeat the Dodgers 5–0 in Brooklyn.

Despite the lead, Chance spent much of the game arguing with the umpires, which agitated the throng at the ballpark. As soon as the Cubs took the field in the ninth inning, some of the fans began throwing pop bottles at Chance. He ignored the first few volleys, but became angry, picked up three of the bottles, and hurled them into the stands. One of these struck a child, and in an instant, a shower of bottles began descending upon Chance. Some of the fans jumped onto the field. Chance stopped to collect more bottles to throw, when Joe Tinker seized him by the arms from behind while other Cubs checked the advance of the mob. Chance was led from the field by police escort. After the game, he had to remain inside the clubhouse for three hours until officers could disperse the angry mob waiting outside. Chance left in an armored police car with three officers. He was suspended for seven days by National League president Harry Pulliam.

JULY 15   Carl Lundgren pitches the Cubs to a 1–0 win over the Phillies in Philadelphia.

           Lundgren had an 18–7 record, a 1.17 ERA, and seven shutouts in 1907.

JULY 19   The Cubs score seven runs in the ninth inning and rout the Giants 12–3 in New York.

JULY 30   The Cubs score three runs in the ninth inning and one in the tenth to beat the Dodgers 7–6 at West Side Grounds. For the second day in a row, Frank Chance drove in the winning run in the tenth inning with a single.

           Chance was the Cubs leading hitter in 1907 with an average of .293.

AUGUST 8   Ed Reulbach pitches a two–hitter to defeat the Phillies 2–0 at West Side Grounds. The only Philadelphia hits were singles by Roy Thomas and Red Dooin.

AUGUST 11 The Cubs defeat the Phillies 1–0 in both games of a double–header against the Phillies at West Side Grounds. The shutouts were pitched by Orval Overall, with ninth–inning relief help from Three Finger Brown, and by Jack Pfiester. The second game was shortened to seven innings to allow both teams to catch a train.

           The Cubs set a club record in 1907 with 32 shutouts, a mark that was tied by the 1909 club. The 1907 pitching staff also set a club record with an earned run average of only 1.73.

AUGUST 16 Orval Overall shuts out the Phillies to win 1–0 in Philadelphia.

           The Cubs and the Phillies played each other in ten consecutive games. The two teams met in six games in Chicago from August 7–11, and four in Philadelphia from August 13–16.

AUGUST 18 The grandstand catches fire prior to a Cubs exhibition game in Bridgeport, Connecticut.

           The fire broke out while the Cubs were warming up. It was started by a cigarette dropped into a pile of refuse under the bleachers. By the time the fire was extinguished forty minutes later the grandstand was almost a total loss. Fortunately, the 5,000 in attendance escaped unharmed. So as not to disappoint the fans, the Cubs played a five–inning exhibition game and won 3–1. A total of 10,000 watched the game, as another 5,000 curious onlookers were added to the original attendees. Several foul balls landed in the still–smoldering ruins.

AUGUST 27 Carl Lundgren pitches a shutout to defeat the Dodgers 1–0 in Brooklyn.

AUGUST 29   Jack Pfiester pitches a two–hitter to beat the Dodgers 5–0 in Brooklyn. The only Dodger hits were singles by Whitey Alperman and Tim Jordan.

SEPTEMBER 1   Ed Reulbach shuts out the Cardinals through eight innings, then allows seven runs in the ninth to lose 7–2 at West Side Grounds.

SEPTEMBER 14   Solly Hofman collects five hits in five at–bats during a 12–5 win over the Reds at West Side Grounds.

Hofman was nicknamed "Circus Solly" for his many circus catches in the outfield.

Jack Pfiester led the NL with a 1.15 ERA in 1907 and pitched the Cubs to a 1–0 lead in the best–of–seven World Series.

SEPTEMBER 23   The Cubs clinch the pennant with a 4–1 win over the Phillies at West Side Grounds. The victory was Three Finger Brown's 20th of the season.

SEPTEMBER 25   Orval Overall earns his 23rd victory of the season with a 4–0 decision over the Phillies at West Side Grounds.

On September 25, the White Sox were only one game behind in the American League pennant race, creating the possibility of a second consecutive all–Chicago World Series. The Sox finished in third place, 5 ½ games out, however.

OCTOBER 2   The Cubs defeat the Giants 13–7 at West Side Grounds, called after eight innings by darkness.

OCTOBER 4   The Cubs smother the Cardinals 12–1 in St. Louis.

OCTOBER 5   The Cubs lose the first game of a double–header to the Cardinals at Robison Field in St. Louis by forfeit. After umpire Cy Rigler called Johnny Evers out at third base in the fourth inning, he was surrounded by Cubs players emphatically questioning the decision. When the Cubs refused to give up the argument, Rigler forfeited the contest to the Cards. The second game went off without a hitch, as the Cardinals won 4–3. Frank Chance, Orval Overall, and Jack Pfiester weren't at the ballpark for the second game, however. They traveled to Sportsman's Park, two blocks away, to scout the Detroit Tigers, who were playing the St. Louis Browns. Overall and Pfiester were scheduled to start the first and second games of the World Series against the Tigers.

The 1907 Tigers were managed by Hughie Jennings and led by 20–year–old Ty Cobb. Detroit had a 92–58 record and beat out the Philadelphia Athletics by 1 ½ games in the pennant race. The Cubs, after losing the World Series in 1906 following a season in which they won 116 games, were looking for redemption.

OCTOBER 8   The 1907 World Series opens before 24,377 at West Side Grounds with a twelve–inning, 3–3 tie, called on account of darkness. The Cubs trailed 3–1 heading into the ninth before rallying with two runs. Frank Chance led off with a single, and then Harry Steinfeldt got hit with a pitch. Johnny Kling popped out, but Johnny Evers reached on an error to load the bases. Wildfire Schulte was retired on a grounder with Frank Chance scoring to make the score 3–2. The other two runners moved up a base. Del Howard pinch–hit for Joe Tinker, and swung and missed at a two–strike pitch on a low curveball, but the Cubs received a huge break when the ball got past Tiger catcher Boss Schmidt, allowing Steinfeldt to score from third base. The inning ended when Johnny Evers was out trying to steal home. Otherwise, the Cubs ran at will, stealing seven bases off Schmidt. The Cubs almost won the game in the tenth inning, when Jimmy Slagle scored from third on another passed ball by Schmidt, but he was ruled out because of interference by batter Steinfedlt. The Cubs also loaded the bases with one out in the eleventh, but failed to score. Wild Bill Donovan, who had a 25–4 record during the regular season, went all the way for the Tigers and fanned 12 batters. For the Cubs, Orval Overall pitched the first nine innings and Ed Reulbach the last three.

After losing three home games in the 1906 World Series, the Cubs believed that their home whites were a jinx and donned their gray road uniforms for game one. The Tigers also wore gray, causing considerable confusion. The only difference in the uniforms was in the caps and stockings. The Cubs had gray caps and blue stockings while the Tigers had black caps and stockings. Curiously, the two clubs wearing the same color uniforms scored the same number of runs, with the contest ending in a 3–3 tie. Garry Herrmann, the president of the National Commission, which was then baseball's governing body, ordered the Cubs to wear white at home for all future games.

OCTOBER 9   With a crowd of 21,901 attending game two of the Series at West Side Grounds, the Cubs top the Tigers 3–1 behind Jack Pfiester's complete–game nine–hitter. The Cubs broke a 1–1 tie in the fourth inning on two runs resulting from a Joe Tinker single, a Pfiester sacrifice, a Jimmy Slagle single, and a Jimmy Sheckard double.

Slagle became the only player in World Series history to become the victim of the hidden–ball trick. In the first inning, Slagle was tagged out by Detroit third baseman Bill Coughlin.

OCTOBER 10   In game three, Ed Reulbach limited the Tigers to six hits in a 5–1 victory before 13,114 at West Side Grounds. The Cubs' 10–hit attack was paced by Johnny Evers, who had three, including two doubles.

OCTOBER 11   The Cubs move within one game of their first world championship with a 6–1 win over the Tigers on a cold, rainy day in Detroit. Orval Overall pitched a five–hitter, and drove in two runs with a single in the fifth inning to give the Cubs a 2–1 lead.

Baseball fanatics in the Chicago suburb of Blue Island, Illinois, resorted to carrier pigeons to receive news of the games at West Side Grounds during the 1907 World Series. Major Gobel, a pigeon fancier, brought 40 of the birds to the ballpark and turned them loose at the end of each inning to carry the news of the game to Blue Island.

OCTOBER 12   A month before Oklahoma becomes the forty–sixth state in the Union, the Cubs win their first world championship with a 2–0 victory over the Tigers before only 7,370 on a cold and snowy Saturday afternoon in Detroit. Three Finger Brown pitched the seven–hit shutout. Harry Steinfeldt had three hits, including an RBI–single in the first to give the Cubs a 1–0 lead, and a triple.

The Cubs stole 18 bases in the five–game series, which still stands as the record in the Fall Classic. Cubs pitchers allowed only six runs, four of them earned, in the five games of the 1907 Series.

1908   Cubs

Season in a Sentence

The Cubs defeat the Tigers in the World Series for the second year in a row after winning one of the most exciting, and controversial, pennant races in history.

Finish • Won • Lost • Pct • GB

First   99   55   .643   +1.0

World Series–The Cubs defeated the Detroit Tigers, four games to one.

Manager

Frank Chance

Stats

Stats	Cubs	NL	Rank
Batting Avg:	.249	.239	2
On–Base Pct:	.311	.299	2
Slugging Pct:	.321	.306	3
Home Runs:	19		4
Stolen Bases:	212		1
ERA:	2.14	2.35	3
Fielding Avg:	.969	.961	1
Runs Scored:	624		2
Runs Allowed:	461		2

Starting Lineup

Johnny Kling, c
Frank Chance, 1b
Johnny Evers, 2b
Harry Steinfeldt, 3b
Joe Tinker, ss
Jimmy Sheckard, lf
Jimmy Slagle, cf
Wildfire Schulte, rf
Solly Hofman, cf–1b–2b
Del Howard, rf–cf
Pat Moran, c

Pitchers

Three Finger Brown, sp–rp
Ed Reulbach, sp
Orval Overall, sp
Jack Pfiester, sp
Chick Fraser, sp–rp
Carl Lundgren, sp–rp

Attendance

655,325 (second in NL)

Club Leaders

Batting Avg:	Evers	.300
On–Base Pct:	Evers	.402
Slugging Pct:	Evers	.375
Home Runs:	Tinker	6
RBI:	Tinker	68
Runs:	Evers	83
Stolen Bases:	Evers	36
Wins:	Brown	29
Strikeouts:	Overall	167
ERA:	Brown	1.42
Saves:	Brown	5

APRIL 14   The Cubs defeat the Reds 6–5 in Cincinnati in the season opener. Heinie Zimmerman hit a pinch–single in the ninth inning to drive in Johnny Evers with the winning run.

APRIL 17   Chick Fraser pitches a shutout to defeat the Reds 1–0 in Cincinnati.

APRIL 22   In the home opener, the Cubs win 7–3 over the Reds before 15,000 at West Side Grounds. There were several hundred others perched on bleachers erected on the roofs of the tall buildings surrounding the ballpark.

The Cubs erected a magnificent new two–story brick entrance off South Lincoln (now known as South Wolcott) in 1908. On the roof were two statues of baseball players, one on each front corner.

MAY 2   Orval Overall pitches a two–hitter to defeat the Cardinals 3–2 at West Side Grounds. The only two St. Louis hits were a home run by Red Murray and a single by Bobby Byrne.

Overall was 15–11 with a 1.92 ERA in 1908.

MAY 17   Three Finger Brown pitches a one–hitter to defeat the Dodgers 5–0 at West Side Grounds. The only Brooklyn base runner was Bill Bergen, who singled in the third inning.

Brown had a 29–9 record, a 1.47 ERA, and nine shutouts in 1908.

MAY 21   The Cubs raise their 1907 world championship banner prior to an 11–3 loss to the Braves at West Side Grounds. The game was preceded by an hour–long concert and a parade of players around the field. Chicago Mayor Frederick Busse threw out the first ball from an upper box.

MAY 25   Joe Tinker hits the ball out of the park with a man on first and the score 7–7 in the tenth inning against the Giants at West Side Grounds but is credited with only a double as the Cubs win 8–7. According to the scoring rules of the day, the game ended as soon as the winning run crossed the plate. The rules changed in 1919, allowing a player who ends a game by hitting the ball out of the ballpark to be awarded a home run.

MAY 30   The Cubs sweep the Cardinals 10–2 and 11–2 in a Memorial Day double–header in St. Louis.

Johnny Evers was the Cubs' top hitter in 1908 with a .300 batting average, .402 on–base percentage, and 83 runs scored.

JUNE 2   During a heated argument in the clubhouse, Heinie Zimmerman throws a bottle of ammonia at Jimmy Sheckard before a 12–4 loss to the Pirates at West Side Grounds. The bottle hit Sheckard in the forehead and exploded. It was feared that he might be permanently blinded. Fortunately, Cook County Hospital was located across the street from the ballpark and medical personnel were able to respond quickly. Prompt action saved his eyesight. Frank Chance tore into Zimmerman, and the two were immediately embroiled in a fistfight. Zimmerman held his own against the manager and appeared to be winning the bout when Cubs players jumped in and beat Zimmerman up so badly that he also had to carted off to the hospital. Both Sheckard and Zimmerman were out of action for a month.

The incident affected Sheckard for years. He batted only .231 in 1908, and his 1909 and 1910 seasons were also well below his usual standards.

JUNE 4   The Cubs and Braves play to a seventeen–inning, 1–1 tie, called on account of darkness in Boston. Jack Pfiester of the Cubs and Vive Lindaman of the Braves pitched complete games. Both teams scored their lone run in the seventh inning.

JUNE 13   Three Finger Brown pitches the Cubs to a 1–0 win over the Phillies in Philadelphia. The only run of the game was driven in on a single by Jimmy Slagle.

JULY 1   Ed Reulbach pitches a two–hitter to defeat the Reds 5–1 in Cincinnati. The only Reds hits were a double by John Ganzel and a single by Rudy Hulswitt.

Reulbach had a record of 24–7, seven shutouts, and a 2.03 ERA in 1908.

JULY 4   Pitching on one day of rest, Three Finger Brown shuts out the Pirates 2–0 in the first game of a double–header in Pittsburgh. It was Brown's fourth consecutive shutout. The Cubs also won the second game 9–3. The two wins put the Cubs into first place.

JULY 17   Joe Tinker's seventh inning homer off Christy Mathewson beats the Giants 1–0 at West Side Grounds. Three Finger Brown pitched the shutout. A fan named William Hudson watched the game from rooftop bleachers built on the top of a four–story building on Taylor Street. In the excitement over Tinker's hit, Hudson fell from his perch and died from a broken neck. A day later, police condemned the stands, which seated more than 1,000.

Tinker batted .266 with six home runs in 1908.

The Cubs get ready to take on the Giants in 1908. The two standing Cub players (in center of photo, profile view) wearing dark ballcaps are (left) Johnny Evers and (right) Frank Chance. A controversial game against the Giants late in the season helped the Cubs win the pennant.

JULY 18   The Cubs score two runs in the ninth inning to beat the Giants 5–4 at West Side Grounds. Joe Tinker's triple drove in both runs.

JULY 30	The Cubs win a double–header 13–4 and 6–3 against the Braves in Boston.
AUGUST 10	Orval Overall pitches a two–hitter but loses 3–2 to the Giants in New York.
AUGUST 13	Ed Reulbach's superstition comes back to haunt him, as the Cubs lose 1–0 to the Pirates in Pittsburgh. Reulbach believed that if he struck out the first man he faced, he would lose the game no matter how well he pitched. After getting two quick strikes on Pirate leadoff batter Roy Thomas, Reulbach threw four pitches wide of the plate. Thomas came around to score following a sacrifice and a single, a run that held up for a Pittsburgh victory.

On August 16, the Cubs had a record of 58–44 and were in third place, six games behind the Pirates.

AUGUST 20	Joe Tinker steals four bases in a 10–2 win over the Braves at West Side Grounds.
AUGUST 23	The Cubs blank the Dodgers twice, both by 2–0 scores, in a double–header at West Side Grounds. Orval Overall pitched a two–hitter in the opener. The only Brooklyn hits were singles by Phil Lewis and John Hummel.

Women of the period made a fashion statement by wearing enormous hats, which often caused problems at the ballpark. According to the August 28 issue of the CHICAGO JOURNAL, *"a girl with a white dress and immense purple hat got behind the catcher" at the August 27 game at West Side Park, "and over 900 fans all lost sight of the game. She stuck for seven innings, amid cries of 'A dollar for a foul tip into the purple lid,' and then left with a contemptuous glare at the wild myriads."*

AUGUST 31	The Cubs win their ninth game in a row with a 2–0 decision over the Cardinals at West Side Grounds.
SEPTEMBER 4	The Cubs lose a controversial 1–0 decision to the Pirates in ten innings in Pittsburgh. In the bottom of the tenth with Three Finger Brown on the mound, two out, and the bases loaded, Pittsburgh's Chief Wilson singled to drive in Fred Clarke with the winning run. Warren Gill, the runner on first, believed the game was over and left the field without touching second base, a common practice at the time. Cubs second baseman Johnny Evers called for the ball from center fielder Jimmy Slagle. Evers touched second and claimed the inning was over by force out. The rules supported Evers' claim, but Hank O'Day, the only umpire assigned to the game that day, said he was focused on making sure that Clarke touched home plate and that Wilson touched first, and he didn't see the play at second.

The Cubs protested the game to National League President Harry Pulliam, who upheld the Pittsburgh victory. O'Day, upon reflection, admitted that he may have made a mistake and vowed that if a similar situation occurred again, he would make certain that he would watch the play at second base. An almost identical situation occurred nearly three weeks later in one of the most famous plays in baseball history (see September 23, 1908).

SEPTEMBER 5	The Cubs walk away with an 11–0 win over the Pirates in Pittsburgh.

SEPTEMBER 12   Johnny Kling hits a grand slam in the twelfth inning off Johnny Lush to lead the Cubs to a 7–3 win over the Cardinals in St. Louis.

SEPTEMBER 18   The Cubs lose 2–1 in ten innings to the Phillies in Philadelphia. The defeat dropped the Cubs 4 ½ games behind the Giants with 16 games to play.

SEPTEMBER 19   With Ed Reulbach pitching a shutout, the Cubs and Phillies play to a 0–0 tie in Philadelphia, called after ten innings by darkness.

SEPTEMBER 22   The Cubs sweep the Giants 4–3 and 3–1 in a double–header in New York. Three Finger Brown saved the first game with 2 ⅔ innings of relief, and pitched a complete game in the second.

The wins put the Cubs only six percentage points behind the Giants. New York had a record of 87–50, the Cubs 90–53, and the Pirates were 1 ½ games back at 88–54.

SEPTEMBER 23   The Cubs and the Giants tie 1–1 at the Polo Grounds in the most controversial game ever played. The score was 1–1 with two outs in the last of the ninth with Jack Pfiester pitching for the Cubs. The Giants' Moose McCormick was on third base and 19–year–old rookie Fred Merkle (subbing for regular first baseman Fred Tenney, who was out with an injured ankle) was on first base. Al Bridwell singled, scoring McCormick. Merkle believed the game was over and turned and headed for the center field clubhouse without touching second base. Center fielder Solly Hofman threw the ball in to Johnny Evers, but the ball was thrown over the head of the Cubs second baseman into the crowd, which overran the field. Giants pitcher Joe McGinnity, who was coaching on third, retrieved the ball and threw it into the crowd. Cubs pitcher Rube Kroh, who was not in the game, pulled the ball away from a fan and handed it to Evers, who stepped on second base. In the midst of the confusion, base umpire Hank O'Day called Merkle out. O'Day ruled the game a 1–1 tie and said that play couldn't continue because the crowd had engulfed the field celebrating the Giants "victory."

SEPTEMBER 24   National League President Harry Pulliam upholds O'Day's decision and declares the previous day's game between the Cubs and the Giants a tie. The Cubs demanded that the game be forfeited to them as the crowd prevented play from continuing, although darkness would have ended it. The Giants claimed they won 2–1. Both teams appealed. Pulliam saw no inconsistency with his ruling on the September 4 game between the Cubs and Pirates, and claimed that he merely upheld his umpire on a question of fact in each case. Meanwhile, the Cubs lost 5–4 to the Giants at the Polo Grounds to fall one game behind in the pennant race.

SEPTEMBER 26   In an extraordinary pitching performance in the thick of a nail–biting pennant race, Ed Reulbach hurls two complete–game, nine–inning shutouts in one day, defeating the Dodgers 5–0 and 3–0 in Brooklyn. Reulbach allowed only five hits in the first game and three in the second, and issued just one walk in the 18 innings. The two games combined consumed two hours and 52 minutes.

Reulbach is the only pitcher in major league history to pitch two shutouts in one day.

Merkle's Boner

The play known as "Merkle's Boner," which occurred in a game between the Cubs and Giants in New York on September 23, 1908, is perhaps the most famous in baseball history. In the bottom of the ninth inning, Giants first baseman Fred Merkle failed to touch second base and turned a New York victory into a tie and eventually cost his club the National League championship. It is still a source of controversy and one of baseball's most enduring legends nearly one hundred years later.

The Cubs, Giants, and Pirates went into September involved in a tight three–way race for the pennant. A game in Pittsburgh on September 4 set the stage for the later drama involving Merkle. In the bottom of the tenth of a scoreless game, the Pirates had the bases loaded and two outs. Owen Wilson lined a clean single to center, and as soon as the ball landed, the winning run scored, and Hank O'Day, umpiring the game alone, started off the field. But the man on first, a recently arrived rookie named Warren Gill, also left the field without going down to touch second, a common practice at the time. Cubs second baseman Johnny Evers called for the ball from the outfield and tagged second for a third–out force, but couldn't get O'Day's attention. The Cubs protested—correctly—that the run shouldn't count, but the league eventually ruled that since O'Day did see a runner score but didn't witness Evers tag second, the result would stand with a 1–0 Pittsburgh victory.

O'Day, upon reflection, admitted that he made a mistake and vowed that if a similar situation occurred again, he would make certain to watch the play at second base. An almost identical situation cropped up nineteen days later.

The Cubs and the Giants squared off in a crucial game on September 23 in New York. The Giants were in first place with a record of 87–50. The Cubs were one–half game behind at 89–53. The Pirates were 1½ games back with a record of 88–54. Giants first baseman Fred Tenney, who had not missed a game all season, was unable to play because of lumbago. He was replaced by little–used rookie Fred Merkle.

The score was 1–1 in the bottom of the ninth. With two out, the Giants had Moose McCormick on third and Merkle, who had just singled, was on first. Al Bridwell lined a Jack Pfiester pitch for a clean single to center. McCormick crossed the plate and much of the overflow crowd of 20,000 poured onto the field in celebration of what appeared to be a 2–1 New York victory.

Merkle, halfway to second, took off for the center field clubhouse believing that the game was won. Cubs second baseman Johnny Evers frantically called for the ball from center fielder Solly Hofman, but Hofman, unable to see Evers clearly in the crowd, overshot the mark with a heave toward third base. Giants pitcher Joe McGinnity, who had been coaching at third, outwrestled Cubs shortstop Joe Tinker for the ball. McGinnity threw the ball far into the crowd beyond third base with Tinker on his back. Rube Kroh, a second–line Cubs pitcher who wasn't even in the game, saw a spectator pick up the ball, demanded it, and slugged the fan when he would not cough it up. Kroh recovered the ball, worked his way through the crowd, and handed it to Evers who tagged second.

The umpire was Hank O'Day, this time working with a partner, Bob Emslie. Chance urged them to call Merkle out, nullifying the run. Surrounded by the crowd, both flustered umpires refused to issue a clear decision. They were hustled off the field by New York police officers after several fans attacked O'Day and punched him repeatedly. Chance also needed police protection to leave the field safely.

That night O'Day filed his report with league president Harry Pulliam, upholding the force play and calling the game a 1–1 tie, citing the precedent set in the September 4 Cubs–Pirates game. He said the game couldn't have continued because the crowd could not be cleared from the field. When the Cubs demanded that the game be declared a forfeit because of lack of crowd control on the part of the Giants, O'Day changed his tune and claimed that darkness prevented further play. The Giants screamed bloody murder over the decision, but Pulliam and the

National League board of directors backed O'Day.

The teams had no mutual open dates left, so Pulliam ruled that the tie be replayed the day after the schedule ended if needed to determine the pennant winner. On Wednesday, October 7, the schedule ended with the Cubs and the Giants tied at 98–55. Pittsburgh was eliminated at 98–56. The "Merkle boner" game would have to be made up. If it had been a Giants victory instead of a tie, the Giants would have been pennant winners by a one–game margin. As it was, a special playoff game would decide the flag.

The Cubs and Giants met at the Polo Grounds in New York on October 8. There were about 35,000 in the ballpark and around twice that many on the surrounding hills. The Cubs won the game 4–2 as Three Finger Brown defeated Christy Mathewson. Chicago went on to the World Series and beat the Tigers in five games. To date, it is the Cubs' last world championship.

Merkle recovered from the debacle to forge a fine career. He played in the majors for sixteen seasons, and was with the Cubs from 1917 through 1920. Merkle played in the World Series with the Giants in 1911, 1912, and 1913, the Dodgers in 1916, and the Cubs in 1918. He played on the losing side all five times, however.

SEPTEMBER 29 The Cubs pass the Giants into first place by a single percentage point after defeating the Reds 6–2 in Cincinnati.

During the game, Joe Tinker hit an unusual home run. The Reds erected light towers at their ballpark in an early experiment in night baseball. One of them was on the playing field in deep center field. Tinker hit a long fly that lodged in one of the towers. He circled the bases while Reds center fielder Dode Paskert tried to fish the ball out of the contraption. The Reds dismantled the towers after playing two night games involving amateur teams in 1909. The first regular season night game in major league history was played in Cincinnati in 1935.

SEPTEMBER 30 The Cubs fall from first place to third place in one day following a 6–5 loss to the Reds in Cincinnati. The Cubs were one–half game behind the Giants and two percentage points in back of the second–place Pirates.

OCTOBER 1 Ed Reulbach pitches a two–hitter to beat the Reds 6–0 in Cincinnati. Dick Egan had both Reds hits with a triple and a double.

The victory was Reulbach's fourth consecutive shutout. He also had a streak of 44 consecutive scoreless innings.

OCTOBER 2 The Cubs defeat the Reds 5–0 in Cincinnati. At the conclusion of the day's action, only one–half game separated the top three teams in the National League. The Pirates were in first, one–half game ahead of the Giants and Cubs. The Cubs trailed the Giants by two percentage points.

OCTOBER 3 The Cubs batter the Reds 16–2 in Cincinnati. Ed Reulbach was the winning pitcher, picking up his 24th victory of the season.

The win put the Cubs one–half game behind the first–place Pirates and one game ahead of the third–place Giants.

OCTOBER 4 The Cubs defeat the Pirates 5–2 before a crowd of 30,247 at West Side Grounds, the largest crowd ever to see a game in Chicago up to that time. Much of the crowd lined the outfield, and balls hit into the overflow were doubles. The game was 2–2 in the sixth inning when Joe Tinker hit a ground–rule double into the outfield crowd with two out. The Pirates walked Johnny Kling to get to pitcher Three Finger Brown, who singled in Tinker with the winning run. Brown shut down the Pirates the rest of the way, earning his 28th victory of the season. When the game ended, thousands poured onto the field in celebration. For fifteen minutes the players, unable to escape to the clubhouse, were carried over the field. There was also excitement in the stands as a woman gave birth during the game.

In Pittsburgh, some 50,000 assembled downtown outside of two newspaper offices, where men with megaphones stood atop the roofs of the buildings and announced each play as it arrived by telegraph. Police had to be called to restore order. With the Giants idle, an electronic scoreboard was set up at the Polo Grounds in New York and 5,000 paid 25 cents to gain entrance into the ballpark to be informed of the play–by–play of the Cubs–Pirates game. At the conclusion of the contest, the Cubs were in first place with a 98–55 record. The Pirates were done for the season at 98–56. The Giants were 95–55 with three games remaining against the Braves in New York on October 5, 6, and 7. If the Giants won all three, they would meet the Cubs in New York on October 8 for the game that would decide the National League pennant.

OCTOBER 5   National League directors comprised of Reds President Garry Herrmann, Dodgers owner Charles Ebbets, and Braves owner George Dovey meet in Cincinnati and back Harry Pulliam, affirming his decision to declare the September 23 game between the Cubs and the Giants a tie.

OCTOBER 7   The Giants defeat the Braves 7–2 to complete a three–game sweep and tie the Cubs for first place.

OCTOBER 8   The Cubs clinch the pennant with a 4–2 win over the Giants before a crowd of between 35,000 and 40,000 frenzied fans at the Polo Grounds. It was Three Finger Brown's 29th win of the season, and his ninth in a row over Giants ace Christy Mathewson, dating back to July 12, 1905.

Police were overwhelmed by the crush of fans heading toward the Polo Grounds. Hundreds gained admission by scaling the walls, even those topped by barbed wire, and knocking down fences. Some even dug holes under the fences and crawled through. Another 60,000 stood atop Coogan's Bluff, which overlooked the Polo Grounds. The elevated tracks outside the ballpark were also packed, and one man fell to his death. According to the NEW YORK TIMES, "his vacant place was quickly filled." The Cubs needed police protection to get in and out of the city. The police failed to protect the Cubs while they were leaving the field at the end of the game, however, and Frank Chance was punched in the neck by a fan who knocked down two officers to get to the Cubs manager. The blow was struck with sufficient force to drop Chance to his knees and leave him gasping for breath. He suffered a broken cartilage in his neck. Pitcher Jack Pfiester, whose nickname was "the Giants Killer" because of his ability to beat the New York club, was also assaulted. Police drew revolvers to help the Cubs reach the clubhouse safely. Once inside, some fans tried to force their way into the building but were driven back by police, who had to dodge stones and pieces of boards. In Chicago, the CHICAGO TRIBUNE *displayed accounts of the game via telegraph on an electric scoreboard set up in the Thomas Orchestra Hall. Among those at the hall was Frank Chance's wife. It was the couple's seventh wedding anniversary.*

The Cubs World Series opponent was the Tigers, for the second year in a row. Detroit had a 90–63 record, and like the Cubs, won a close three–way pennant race. The Tigers finished the season one–half game ahead of the Indians and 1 ½ ahead of the White Sox.

OCTOBER 10   The Cubs defeat the Tigers 10–6 in the first game of the 1908 World Series in Detroit. The game was played in a driving rainstorm with players sloshing through the mud and balls dying in the wet outfield grass. Ed Reulbach had a 5–1 lead in the seventh, but he tired and allowed the Tigers to narrow the gap with three runs in the inning. The Tigers took a 6–5 lead in the eighth with two runs off relievers Orval Overall and Three Finger Brown. The Cubs won the game on six straight hits, which scored five runs in the ninth. Two ground balls went for infield hits as the Tiger infielders slipped in the mud. The big hits in the inning were two–run singles by Solly Hofman and Johnny Kling. Detroit's Ed Summers, a 24–game winner in 1908, gave up all five runs. Summers entered the game in the third inning and had pitched 5 ⅔ innings of scoreless relief before collapsing in the ninth. Jimmy Sheckard had three hits, including two doubles.

OCTOBER 11   Behind Orval Overall, the Cubs win game two of the Series 6–1 before 17,760 at West Side Grounds. Neither team had a hit until the fifth inning. With Wild Bill Donovan pitching for the Tigers, the game was scoreless until Joe Tinker's wind–blown eighth–inning home run into the right field bleachers with Solly Hofman on base began a six–run rally. It was the first homer in a World Series since 1903.

OCTOBER 12   The Tigers bounce back to secure their first win over the Cubs in a World Series game with an 8–3 decision before 14,543 at West Side Grounds. The Cubs had a 3–1 lead in the sixth when the Tigers scored five times. Ty Cobb had four hits, two runs batted in, and two stolen bases. George Mullin was the winning pitcher.

OCTOBER 13   The Cubs move within one game of a world championship as Three Finger Brown pitches a four–hitter to defeat the Tigers 3–0 in Detroit. Harry Steinfeldt and Solly Hofman hit RBI singles in the third inning to put the Cubs up 2–0.

OCTOBER 14   The Cubs become the first team to win back–to–back World Series with a 2–0 win over the Tigers in Detroit. Orval Overall limited Detroit to three hits and struck out 10 batters. In the first inning, Overall became the only pitcher in World Series history to strike out four batters in an inning. The four–strikeout inning was possible because Tigers first baseman Claude Rossman swung at and missed a pitch with two out but reached base when the ball sailed past catcher Johnny Kling. Overall also struck out Charley O'Leary, Ty Cobb, and Germany Schaefer in the inning. The Cubs took a 1–0 lead in the first on singles by Johnny Evers, Wildfire Schulte, and Frank Chance. Evers and Chance each had three hits and an RBI. The attendance was only 6,210, the smallest in World Series history. It was also the shortest game by time in World Series history, lasting only one hour and 25 minutes.

OCTOBER 19   The Cubs and Tigers play an exhibition game in Chicago, with Detroit winning 7–3.

1909

Cubs

Season in a Sentence

The Cubs win 104 games, but finish second to the Pirates.

Finish • Won • Lost • Pct • GB

Second   104   49   .680   6.5

Manager

Frank Chance

Stats

Stats	Cubs	NL	Rank
Batting Avg:	.245	.244	4
On–Base Pct:	.308	.310	5
Slugging Pct:	.322	.314	4
Home Runs:	20		4
Stolen Bases:	187		3
ERA:	1.75	2.59	1
Fielding Avg:	.962	.956	2
Runs Scored:	635		2
Runs Allowed:	390		1

Starting Lineup

Jimmy Archer, c
Frank Chance, 1b
Johnny Evers, 2b
Harry Steinfeldt, 3b
Joe Tinker, ss
Jimmy Sheckard, lf
Solly Hofman, cf
Wildfire Schulte, rf
Pat Moran, c
Del Howard, 1b
Heinie Zimmerman, 2b–3b–ss

Pitchers

Three Finger Brown, sp–rp
Orval Overall, sp
Ed Reulbach, sp
Jack Pfiester, sp
Rube Kroh, sp
Rip Hagerman, sp–rp
Irv Higginbotham, rp–sp

Attendance

633,480 (second in NL)

Club Leaders

Batting Avg:	Hofman	.285
On–Base Pct:	Evers	.369
Slugging Pct:	Tinker	.372
Home Runs:	Tinker	4
	Schulte	4
RBI:	Schulte	60
Runs:	Evers	88
Stolen Bases:	Chance	29
Wins:	Brown	27
Strikeouts:	Overall	205
ERA:	Brown	1.31
Saves:	Brown	7

APRIL 14   In the first game of the season, the Cubs defeat the Cardinals 3–1 at West Side Grounds. Heinie Zimmerman broke a 0–0 tie with a two–run triple in the sixth inning.

The Cubs had to play the 1909 season without one of their key members, as catcher Johnny Kling refused to sign a contract and missed the entire year. Kling spent part of the year as the player–manager of a semi–pro team in his home-town of Kansas City with the Missouri Athletic Club and operated a billiards parlor he owned. In September, Kling took his club to the Windy City to play six games against a semi–pro outfit from Chicago.

MAY 8   Following a 6–3 win over the Reds at West Side Grounds, Joe Tinker and Reds second baseman Dick Egan fight on the field. In the eighth inning, Tinker slid viciously into Egan, who vowed revenge. Egan dressed quickly after the game and spotted Tinker walking across the playing field. The two were soon engaged in fisticuffs. Tinker put Egan in a headlock and wrestled him to the ground before the pair were separated.

MAY 20   The Cubs purchase Pat Ragan from the Reds.

MAY 21   Orval Overall comes within two outs of a no–hitter and defeats the Braves 7–0 at Boston. The only Braves hit was a single by Bill Sweeney with one out in the ninth.

On the same day, the Cubs sold George Browne to the Washington Senators.

MAY 24   An inside–the–park homer by Solly Hofman in the eleventh inning beats the Dodgers 4–3 in Brooklyn. Dodger center fielder Tom Catterson missed a shoestring catch on Hofman's drive and let the ball sail behind him. By the time Catterson retrieved the ball, Hofman circled the bases.

During the 1909 season, the Cubs added an embellishment to the uniforms with the letters "UBS" inside a circular "C." This was the first appearance of the famous Cubs emblem, which has endeared itself to Cubs fans for generations. In 1909, it was used only on the road uniforms. The home uniforms had a brown bear holding a bat inside the letter "C." The "UBS" letters inside the "C" were used on the road again in 1910, disappeared for nine seasons, and returned in 1919. The emblem was used on and off for two decades before becoming a permanent part of the jersey. It has been used on the home uniforms every season since 1937.

MAY 29   President William Howard Taft watches the Cubs score five runs in the ninth inning to defeat the Pirates 8–3 in Pittsburgh. Also in attendance was Secretary of State Philander Knox. Taft sat next to his half–brother Charles, who owned a large share of stock in the Cubs.

JUNE 1   After the Reds plate two runs in the ninth inning to tie the game 3–3, the Cubs score six times in the tenth to win 9–3 in Cincinnati.

JUNE 6   Ed Reulbach pitches a five–hit, twelve–inning shutout to defeat the Phillies 1–0 at West Side Grounds. Solly Hofman drove in the game–winner with a single.

Reulbach had a record of 19–10 in 1909 with a 1.79 ERA.

JUNE 16   The Cubs run into problems raising their 1908 world championship banner at West Side Grounds prior to a 3–1 win over the Dodgers. The flag was hoisted following a parade of both teams around the playing field, headed by a brass band. Just before reaching the top of the pole, however, the rope pulley broke and the pennant blew away behind the bleachers in center field.

JUNE 25   During a 7–0 win over the Reds at West Side Grounds, Joe Tinker hits a foul ball over the grandstand, shattering the window of an automobile. This was probably a first, as there were only 300 autos registered in the city of Chicago at the time.

Tinker hit .256 with four homers in 1909. His double–play partner, Johnny Evers, batted .263 and scored 88 runs.

JUNE 30   The Cubs play in the first game ever at Forbes Field in Pittsburgh and defeat the Pirates 3–1 before 30,388.

JULY 19   Three Finger Brown pitches a two–hitter to defeat the Dodgers 2–0 in Brooklyn. The only Dodger hits were singles by Wally Clement and Tommy McMillan.

Brown was 27–9 in 1909. He led the league in innings pitched with 342⅔, and in complete games with 32. He also had 172 strikeouts, eight shutouts, and a 1.31 ERA.

JULY 31 — Ed Reulbach pitches the Cubs to a 1–0 win over the Phillies at West Side Grounds.

AUGUST 1 — Three Finger Brown pitches a one–hitter to defeat the Phillies 3–0 in the first game of a double–header at West Side Grounds. The only Philadelphia hit was a single by Kitty Bransfield. The Cubs completed the sweep by winning the second game 7–6.

AUGUST 7 — The Cubs collect only two hits off Dodgers pitcher Nap Rucker, but win 3–2 at West Side Grounds. A two–run homer by Wildfire Schulte in the first inning put the Cubs ahead 2–0.

AUGUST 10 — Ed Reulbach wins his 14th consecutive decision with an 8–1 win over the Dodgers at West Side Grounds.

Reulbach missed two weeks during the winning streak with ptomaine poisoning. His 14–game streak is the longest by a Cub pitcher since 1900. It was tied by Rick Sutcliffe in 1984.

AUGUST 18 — Ed Reulbach defeats the Reds 1–0 in Cincinnati. The winning run was scored with two outs in the ninth inning when Reds pitcher Bob Ewing threw a wild pitch that scored Jimmy Sheckard from third base.

AUGUST 21 — Umpire Hank O'Day ejects eight Cubs off the bench for excessive squawking during the second game of a double–header against the Braves in Boston. The Cubs won both games 8–3 and 3–2.

AUGUST 23 — The Cubs score nine runs in the ninth inning to defeat the Braves 11–6 in Boston. The Cubs also tied a major league record with three steals of home during the contest, pulled off by Johnny Evers, Del Howard, and Harry Steinfeldt.

The Cubs tied a major league record for most victories over one club in a season by accumulating a 21–1 record against the Braves in 1909, including 19 in a row. From 1906 through 1912, the Cubs had a 122–34 record against the team from Boston.

AUGUST 27 — Down 5–0 after three innings, the Cubs rally to defeat the Giants 8–6 in New York. The Cubs broke a 6–6 tie with two runs in the ninth.

AUGUST 30 — Jack Pfiester pitches an eleven–inning shutout to defeat the Giants 2–0 in the first game of a double–header in New York. The Giants won the second game 5–0.

Pfiester was 17–6 with a 2.43 ERA in 1909.

SEPTEMBER 1 — Orval Overall pitches a two–hitter to defeat the Dodgers 12–0 in Brooklyn. The only Dodger hits were singles by John Hummel and Bill Bergen.

Overall was 20–11 with a 1.42 ERA in 1909. He led the NL in shutouts with nine, and in strikeouts with 205.

SEPTEMBER 4 — Pitching on two days rest, Orval Overall pitches his second consecutive two–hit shutout, defeating the Reds 3–0 at West Side Grounds. The only Cincinnati hits were singles by Dode Paskert and Frank Roth.

Johnny Evers steals home as one of three Cubs to do so in a 1909 game against the Braves, tying a big–league record. The Cubs beat the Braves 19 times in a row that season.

SEPTEMBER 8   The Cubs score two runs in the ninth inning to defeat the Pirates 4–2 in Pittsburgh.

The Cubs won three of the five games in the series against the Pirates to keep alive their slim hopes of winning a fourth consecutive NL pennant. At the end of the series, the Cubs trailed the Pirates by five games with 28 contests left on the schedule.

SEPTEMBER 14   Three Finger Brown pitches a one–hitter to defeat the Reds 4–0 in Cincinnati. The only Reds hit was a single by Dick Egan.

SEPTEMBER 16   President William Howard Taft takes in a Cubs game for the second time in 1909, this time at West Side Grounds. The Cubs won 2–1 in a duel between Three Finger Brown and Christy Mathewson. Brown was pitching on only one day of rest, and was moved up in the rotation because he wanted to pitch in front of the president.

SEPTEMBER 17   The Cubs lose 4–1 to the Giants at West Side Grounds to all but eliminate Chicago from the pennant race. After the defeat, the Cubs were 7 ½ games behind the Pirates with 19 contests left to play. A ninth–rally Chicago rally was snuffed out by a freak play. With the score 4–0, the Cubs had the bases loaded with none out when Harry Steinfeldt hit a liner toward Giants left fielder Moose McCormick, who completely lost sight of the ball in the sun. McCormick put his hands in front of his face to protect himself, and to his astonishment, the ball stuck in his mitt.

The Cubs finished the season 6½ games behind the Pirates. The Cubs won 104 games in 1909, a major league record for a club which failed to finish a season in first place.

SEPTEMBER 27   A dozen men and women from Japan watch the Cubs defeat the Phillies 4–1 at West Side Grounds. "We heard so much about your Cubs in Japan that we were very anxious to see them play," said Baron Kanda, the leader of the delegation. The victory was Orval Overall's 20th of the season.

OCTOBER 4   Three Finger Brown earns his 27th victory of the season with an 8–2 victory over the Pirates at West Side Grounds.

OCTOBER 6   In his major league debut, Cubs pitcher King Cole pitches a three–hit shutout to defeat the Cardinals 8–0 in the first game of a double–header at West Side Grounds. In addition, Cole had three hits, including a triple, in four at–bats. The Cubs also won the second game 5–1.

Leonard "King" Cole won 39 of his first 50 major league decisions. He had a record of 20–4 in 1910 and was 18–7 in 1911 before arm miseries set in. Ring Lardner gave Cole literary immortality by writing about him in articles for THE SPORTING NEWS, *which later emerged as the Alibi Ike short stories. The Alibi Ike stories first appeared in print in 1915 and were made into three entertaining movies during the 1930s. According to Lardner, Cole was a slow–thinking poker player who was threatened with a $50 fine by Frank Chance unless he quit spoiling poker games on train trips with his erratic playing. Cole's career ended in 1915 with a record of 54–27 when he contracted lung cancer while pitching for the Yankees. He died on January 6, 1916, at the age of 29.*

OCTOBER 8   The Cubs win the first game of the Chicago City Series, defeating the White Sox 4–0 at West Side Grounds.

OCTOBER 15   Three Finger Brown closes out the Chicago City Series with a one–hitter and a 1–0 victory over the White Sox at West Side Grounds. The only White Sox hit was a single by Freddie Parent in the fifth inning. The Cubs won the series, four games to one. The five games drew a total of 74,512 fans.

NOVEMBER 26   With financial help from Charles Murphy, sportswriter Horace Fogel buys the Phillies.

Murphy owned some of the stock in the Phillies, as well as keeping his holdings in the Cubs. At the time, it was legal for an individual to own stock in more than one team. Often at the urging of Murphy, Fogel became an outspoken owner at league meetings and a bitter critic of the NL umpires (see August 12, 1912).

THE STATE OF THE CUBS

The Cubs won their fourth pennant in five years in 1910, then began a slow decline as the roster aged. By 1916, the Cubs fell to fifth place in an eight–team league, but bounced back to win another NL pennant in 1918. Both Cubs pennant winners failed to win the World Series. The Cubs had an overall record of 826–668 during the 1910s, a winning percentage of .553, which was the second best in the National League and the third best in the majors, trailing the New York Giants and Boston Red Sox. The Giants won NL pennants in 1911, 1912, 1913, and 1917. Other clubs that represented the National League in the World Series were the Braves (1914), Phillies (1915), Dodgers (1916) and Reds (1919).

THE BEST TEAM

The 1910 Cubs had a record of 104–50 and won the National League pennant by 13 games, before losing the World Series to the Philadelphia Athletics.

THE WORST TEAM

The 1916 Cubs were 67–86, and were in fifth place, 26½ games off the pace set by the first–place Dodgers.

THE BEST MOMENT

The Cubs clinched the 1918 National League pennant after finishing in fifth place in 1917.

THE WORST MOMENT

The Cubs, conspiring with the Red Sox, nearly went on strike during the 1918 World Series.

THE ALL–DECADE TEAM • YEARS WITH CUBS

Jimmy Archer, c	1909–17
Vic Saier, 1b	1911–17
Johnny Evers, 2b	1902–13
Heinie Zimmerman, 3b	1907–16
Joe Tinker, ss	1902–12; 1916
Jimmy Sheckard, lf	1906–12
Tommy Leach, cf	1912–14
Wildfire Schulte, rf	1904–16
Hippo Vaughn, p	1913–21
Larry Cheney, p	1911–15
Three Finger Brown, p	1904–12; 1916
Claude Hendrix, p	1916–20

The All–Decade Team of the 1910s was a mixture of the players on the 1906–10 teams, which won four NL pennants, and the rebuilding project that began around 1912. Other top players of the decade include right fielder Max Flack (1916–22), first baseman Fred Merkle (1917–20), third baseman Charlie Deal (1916–21), and pitcher Lefty Tyler (1918–21).

THE DECADE LEADERS

Batting Avg:	Zimmerman	.306
On–Base Pct:	Sheckard	.399
Slugging Pct:	Zimmerman	.453
Home Runs:	Schulte	74
RBI:	Zimmerman	530
Runs:	Schulte	534
Stolen Bases:	Schulte	127
Wins:	Vaughn	129
Strikeouts:	Vaughn	977
ERA:	Vaughn	2.08
Saves:	Brown	20

THE HOME FIELD

The Cubs began the decade at antiquated West Side Grounds, which by 1915 was the third best ballpark in Chicago. In 1916, the club moved into Weeghman Park, a facility known today as Wrigley Field.

THE GAME YOU WISH YOU HAD SEEN

Hippo Vaughn of the Cubs and Hod Eller of the Reds teamed up for the only "double no–hitter" in major league history on May 2, 1917, in Chicago. Neither pitcher allowed a hit through the first nine innings. Vaughn surrendered two hits in the tenth and lost 1–0.

THE WAY THE GAME WAS PLAYED

Pitching and defense continued to dominate base-ball. Offense spiked in the early years of the decade after the NL adopted the cork–centered ball in 1910, but by the mid–teens, the league batting average was back around .250. Home runs were at a premium. There were more than twice as many triples as home runs and speedy outfielders were a necessity to cover playing fields that were much larger than those common today. NL pitchers completed 55 percent of their starts, but this was a significant drop from 79 percent during the previous decade. During the 1910s, the strategic use of relief pitching, pinch–hitters, and platooning became an important aspect of the game for the first time.

MANAGEMENT

The Cubs posted the third best winning percentage in the majors during the 1910s, but managerial stability couldn't be cited as a reason for the club's success. From 1912 through 1919, the Cubs had four majority owners (Charles Murphy, Charles P. Taft, Charles Weeghman and William Wrigley Jr.), five presidents (Murphy, Charles Thomas, Weeghman, Fred Mitchell, and Bill Veeck Sr.) and six managers (Frank Chance, Johnny Evers, Hank O'Day, Roger Bresnahan, Joe Tinker, and Mitchell).

THE BEST PLAYER MOVE

The Cubs best trade during the 1910s was made with a minor league club. In 1913, the Cubs sent Lew Richie to Kansas City of the American Association for Hippo Vaughn. The best trade with a major league club brought Grover Alexander from the Phillies on December 11, 1917.

THE WORST PLAYER MOVE

The Cubs traded outfielder Cy Williams to the Phillies in 1917 for Dode Paskert.

1910s

1910  Cubs

Season in a Sentence

The Cubs win their fourth National League pennant in five years, but lose to the Philadelphia Athletics in the World Series.

Finish • Won • Lost • Pct • GB

First   104   50   .675   +13.0

World Series–The Cubs lost to the Philadelphia Athletics, four games to one.

Manager

Frank Chance

Stats

Stats	Cubs	NL	Rank
Batting Avg:	.268	.256	2
On–Base Pct:	.344	.328	3
Slugging Pct:	.366	.338	2
Home Runs:	34		1
Stolen Bases:	173		5
ERA:	2.51	3.02	1
Fielding Avg:	.964	.959	2
Runs Scored:	712		1
Runs Allowed:	499		1

Starting Lineup

Johnny Kling, c
Frank Chance, 1b
Johnny Evers, 2b
Harry Steinfeldt, 3b
Joe Tinker, ss
Jimmy Sheckard, lf
Solly Hofman, cf
Wildfire Schulte, rf
Heinie Zimmerman, 3b–ss–2b
Jimmy Archer, c–1b
Ginger Beaumont, cf–lf

Pitchers

Three Finger Brown, sp–rp
King Cole, sp
Harry McIntyre, sp–rp
Ed Reulbach, sp
Orval Overall, sp
Jack Pfiester, sp
Lew Richie, rp–sp

Attendance

526,152 (first in NL)

Club Leaders

Club Leaders		
Batting Avg:	Hofman	.325
On–Base Pct:	Evers	.413
Slugging Pct:	Hofman	.461
Home Runs:	Schulte	21
RBI:	Hofman	86
Runs:	Schulte	93
Stolen Bases:	Hofman	29
Wins:	Brown	25
Strikeouts:	Brown	143
ERA:	Cole	1.80
Saves:	Brown	7

APRIL 1   Johnny Kling signs a contract to return to the Cubs after sitting out the 1909 season in a salary dispute. He was fined $700 for the holdout. After a training period, Kling played his first game in 1910 on May 8 and finished the season with a .269 batting average.

APRIL 14   The Cubs lose 1–0 in ten innings to the Reds in Cincinnati on Opening Day. Orval Overall lost the pitchers' duel to Fred Beebe.

APRIL 20   The Cubs are saved by the bell in St. Louis. By prior agreement, the game was to end at 5:00 P.M. to allow both teams to catch a train. When the appointed time arrived in the bottom of the eighth, the Cubs led 4–3 and the Cardinals had the bases loaded with one out.

APRIL 21   In the home opener at West Side Grounds, the Cubs beat the Reds 6–1.

APRIL 25   With the Cubs–Pirates game at West Side Grounds postponed by snow, Johnny Kling appears on the stage of a Chicago music hall, demonstrating his skill with a pool cue by playing a match against Cubs legend Cap Anson. During his holdout season in 1909, Kling won the world pocket billiards championship. He also made a speech about how happy he was to be returning to the Cubs. Following Kling's address, motion pictures were shown of the Cubs–White Sox City Series, played the previous October.

APRIL 27   Harry McIntyre pitches the Cubs to a 1–0 win over the Pirates at West Side Grounds.

MAY 2   President William Howard Taft watches the Cubs play for the third time in two years. Taft was accompanied by German ambassador Count Bernstroff at Forbes Field in Pittsburgh. The Cubs lost 5–2.

                The game was originally scheduled for May 5 but was moved up three days to accommodate the president's busy schedule.

MAY 10   Playing shortstop in place of injured Joe Tinker, Heinie Zimmerman makes four errors in the first two innings of a game against the Giants at West Side Grounds but redeems himself with four hits, including a double, in four at–bats. The Cubs won 9–5.

MAY 13   The Cubs trade Doc Miller to the Braves for Lew Richie.

MAY 18   With Chicagoans buzzing about the arrival of Halley's Comet, pitcher Jack Pfiester drives in the winning run in the tenth inning to beat the Dodgers 3–2 at West Side Grounds.

MAY 25   The Cubs take first place with a 6–1 win over the Phillies at West Side Grounds.

                The Cubs started slowly in 1910 with an 11–11 record before running off 11 wins in a row. The club was involved in a tight, three–way pennant race with the Giants and Pirates until early July, when the Cubs began to pull away from the pack.

MAY 26   Orval Overall pitches a one–hitter to beat the Phillies 2–0 at West Side Grounds. The only Philadelphia hit was a single by Sherry Magee.

                Overall sat out the 1911 and 1912 seasons in a salary squabble with Cubs President Charles Murphy. Overall made an unsuccessful comeback in 1913.

MAY 30   The Cubs win their eleventh game in a row with a 6–1 decision over the Cardinals in the first game of a double–header at West Side Grounds. The streak ended with a 3–1 loss in the second game.

JUNE 17   The Cubs defeat the Dodgers 1–0 in thirteen innings in Brooklyn. The only run of the game was scored on Nap Rucker's wild pitch, which scored Harry Steinfeldt from third base. Jack Pfiester (ten innings) and Three Finger Brown (three innings) combined on the shutout.

JUNE 21   The Cubs defeat the Reds 1–0 at West Side Grounds. The Cubs collected only three hits, each of them by Jimmy Sheckard. Ed Reulbach (seven innings) and Three Finger Brown (two innings) combined on the shutout.

                Reulbach missed the early part of the 1910 season because he was suffering from diphtheria.

JUNE 24   First baseman Solly Hofman goes through an entire game without a putout as the Cubs lose 6–5 to the Pirates in Pittsburgh.

Hofman had the best season of his career in 1910, batting .325 with an on base percentage of .406.

JUNE 28   Joe Tinker steals home twice during an 11–1 win over the Reds at West Side Grounds.

Tinker is one of only eleven major leaguers, and the lone Cub, to steal home twice in a game. He hit .288 in 1910.

JUNE 30   The Cubs score five runs in the top of the first, but the Cardinals come back with nine tallies in their half of the inning in St. Louis. The Cards won the game 13–9.

JULY 1   Comiskey Park opens at 35th and Wentworth with the White Sox losing 2–0 to the Browns.

The ballpark was designed by architect Zachary Davis, who later designed Wrigley Field. Comiskey served as the home of the White Sox through the 1990 season. The following year, the new Comiskey opened, and is now known as U. S. Cellular Field.

JULY 11   Entering the game with a one–half game lead over the Giants, the Cubs hold onto first place with a 4–2 win over the New York club at West Side Grounds.

A Giants rally in the eighth inning was stopped by a double play from Joe Tinker to Johnny Evers to Frank Chance. This double play was likely the inspiration for Franklin Adams's famous poem, "Baseball's Sad Lexicon." (See July 18, 1910.)

JULY 17   Ed Reulbach pitches a two–hitter to beat the Dodgers 6–0 in the first game of a double header at West Side Grounds. The only Brooklyn hits were singles by Zack Wheat and Tony Smith. The Cubs completed the sweep with a 7–4 win in the second game.

JULY 18   Franklin P. Adams's poem, "Baseball's Sad Lexicon," which makes "Tinker–to–Evers–to–Chance" a national catchphrase, appears in the *New York Evening Mail*.

JULY 19   Heinie Zimmerman commits four errors at shortstop for the second time in 1910 as the Cubs lose 4–3 to the Dodgers in ten innings at West Side Grounds.

JULY 20   The Cubs defeat the Dodgers 1–0 in twelve innings at West Side Grounds. Jack Pfiester and Harry McIntyre combined on the shutout. Pfiester was forced to leave the game in the ninth inning when he dislocated his thumb trying to catch a line drive off the bat of Ed Lennox.

JULY 26   The Cubs trade Fred Luderus to the Phillies for Bill Foxen.

This deal came back to haunt the Cubs, as Luderus developed into one of the best first basemen in baseball during the 1910s.

JULY 31   King Cole pitches an abbreviated no–hitter in the second game of a double–header against the Cardinals in St. Louis. The game was called with one out in the bottom of the seventh inning with the Cubs leading 4–0 to allow both teams to catch a train. The Cubs also won the first game 9–3.

AUGUST 9   After losing the first game of a double–header in Philadelphia 3–1, the Cubs pound the Phillies 14–1 in the nightcap.

AUGUST 15   The Cubs beat the Dodgers 14–0 in the first game of a double-header in Brooklyn. Three Finger Brown allowed eleven hits in the shutout. The Dodgers turned the tables in the second game, winning 9–1.

AUGUST 17   King Cole pitches a one–hitter to beat the Dodgers 2–0 in the second game of a double–header in Brooklyn. The only Dodgers hit was a single by opposing pitcher Nap Rucker. Shortstop Joe Tinker had a clear shot at catching the pop fly, but he slipped on the grass in short left field while chasing it and cost Cole a shot at a no–hitter. The Dodgers won the first game 7–5.

King Cole led the National League with an .833 winning percentage in 1910, finishing with a 20–4 record.

AUGUST 22   Harry McIntyre hits a three–run homer and pitches a shutout to defeat the Braves 7–0 at West Side Grounds.

> *McIntyre hit only two homers in 615 at–bats during his eight–year major league career. The other homer was in 1905.*

AUGUST 26   Wildfire Schulte and Joe Tinker hit back–to–back homers, a rarity in the dead ball era. It was the first time that two consecutive Cubs batters hit consecutive homers since 1900. Schulte hit two homers in the game, another rarity in the period. He was the first Cub since 1901 to hit multiple homers in a single contest. In another unusual circumstance for the time, all three Cubs runs were scored on solo homers, as the club defeated the Giants 3–1 at West Side Grounds. It was only two days before another Cub hit two homers in a game, and this time two accomplished the feat.

AUGUST 28   Wildfire Schulte and Jimmy Sheckard each hit two home runs during a 10–2 win over the Giants at West Side Grounds. One of Schulte's blasts was the longest ever hit at West Side Grounds up to that time. The ball sailed far over the new steel scoreboard behind the stands in right field. The board, including the billboards that surrounded it, was 61 feet high and the ball cleared it by at least 20 feet. No one saw where Schulte's drive landed.

> *During the 1910 season, major league baseball introduced a new baseball with a cork center that traveled farther than the old version. Schulte was among the first to take advantage of the new ball. Most batters of the dead ball era choked up on bats with thick handles and concentrated on making contact and hitting singles. Schulte used bats with thin handles and placed his hands at the knob to generate better bat speed. In 1910, he hit ten homers to tie for the league lead*

in the category. He also batted .301. (See August 19, 1911.)

The 61–foot–high right field wall was built in part to block the view from the rooftops of the apartments on Taylor Street, where building owners had built bleachers. One of the buildings had bleachers at least 20 rows deep, and judging from the photographs from the period, the seats were constructed precariously at a much steeper angle than the upper deck at new Comiskey Park. In 1911, the Cubs increased the height of the right field wall from 61 to 80 feet.

SEPTEMBER 20   Orval Overall strikes out 13 batters to beat the Dodgers 3–0 in the second game of a double–header in Brooklyn. The Cubs also won the first game 5–4.

OCTOBER 1   Johnny Evers breaks his leg sliding into home plate when his spikes catch in the dirt during the fifth inning of a 9–6 win over the Reds in Cincinnati. It was a compound fracture, and the snap of the breaking bone was heard plainly in the stands.

The injury put Evers out of the World Series. He finished the season with a .263 batting average and a .413 on–base percentage in 1910. Utility infielder Heinie Zimmerman became the starting second baseman for the Fall Classic.

OCTOBER 2   The Cubs pull off a triple play and beat the Reds 8–4 in Cincinnati to clinch the National League pennant.

OCTOBER 3   Heinie Zimmerman hits two balls over the left field wall at the Palace of the Fans in Cincinnati, but the Cubs lose 5–3.

The two homers were the only two balls hit out of the Palace of the Fans in the ten seasons of the ballpark's existence. Prior to that game, no one had even hit the outfield wall on the fly. The Palace opened in 1902. Zimmerman's homers came in consecutive at–bats, both off Cincinnati pitcher George Suggs. There were advertising signs at the Palace atop the left field wall, with a two–foot gap between the wall and the signs. Both of Zimmerman's homers went through the gap.

OCTOBER 7   Three Finger Brown pitches a two–hitter to defeat the Pirates 1–0 in Chicago. The only Pittsburgh hits were singles by Dots Miller and opposing pitcher Lefty Leifield. The victory was Brown's 25th of the season.

Brown had a record of 25–13 with a 1.88 ERA, 295 ⅓ innings in 1910. He not only led the league in complete games with 27 and shutouts with seven, but he topped all major league hurlers in saves as well with seven. Brown made 31 starts and 15 relief appearances.

OCTOBER 9   King Cole walks ten batters and hits another with a pitch, but the Cubs win 4–3 over the Cardinals at West Side Grounds. It was Cole's 20th victory of the season.

OCTOBER 12   On Columbus Day, the Cubs beat the Cardinals 12–2 at West Side Grounds.

The Cubs faced the Philadelphia Athletics in the World Series. It was the beginning of a five–year run for Connie Mack's A's in which the club won four American League pennants and three world championships from 1910 through 1914. The A's had a record of 102–48 in 1910.

OCTOBER 17   The Cubs lose the first game of the 1910 World Series 4–1 to the Athletics before 26,891 in Philadelphia. Future Hall of Fame pitcher Chief Bender allowed the Cubs only three hits. Orval Overall was the losing pitcher.

OCTOBER 18   The Athletics defeat the Cubs 9–3 in Philadelphia in game two. Jack Coombs was the winning pitcher with a complete game. The Cubs left fourteen runners on base. A six–run rally in the seventh inning sent the Cubs and Three Finger Brown to the defeat.

Brown was involved in an auto accident on the way to the game. Although unhurt, he may have been shaken by the ordeal, contributing to his poor performance.

OCTOBER 20   After a day of travel, Jack Coombs pitches again for the Athletics, and defeats the Cubs 12–5 before 26,210 at West Side Grounds to give Philadelphia a three–games–to–none lead in the World Series. The score was 3–3 when the Athletics scored five runs in the third inning off Harry McIntyre and Jack Pfiester. Joe Tinker collected three hits, including a double, for the Cubs.

Frank Chance became the first individual to be ejected from a World Series game when umpire Thomas Connolly chased him for protesting a Danny Murphy home run drive against a sign over the right field bleachers. Chance argued that the drive should have been a ground–rule double. The previous day, one fan on a Chicago street heckled Chance so badly that the Cubs skipper jumped out of his car and attacked him.

OCTOBER 21   Orval Overall announces his retirement at the end of the World Series. "I am just tired of the job," said Overall, "and I don't want any more of it. The life of a big league pitcher is unsatisfactory at best. If you are good you get along all right and nobody has any complaint. But if you are bad, even for a little while, or your arm goes back on you, you are up against it and you can't help yourself." Overall returned to the Cubs in 1913, but was 4–5 in 11 games.

OCTOBER 22   The Cubs stave off elimination with a dramatic ten–inning 4–3 win over the Athletics before 19,150 at West Side Grounds. Down three–games–to–none and trailing 3–2 in the ninth inning with one out, the Cubs tied the score on a Wildfire Schulte double and a Frank Chance triple. They won in the tenth on Jimmy Archer's double and Jimmy Sheckard's two–out single off Chief Bender.

OCTOBER 23   The Athletics claim the world championship with a 7–2 win over the Cubs before 27,374 at West Side Grounds. Philadelphia broke open a close game with five runs in the eighth inning. Jack Coombs won his third game of the series.

With Eddie Plank unavailable because of a sore arm, the Athletics won the World Series by using only two pitchers. Jack Coombs pitched three complete games, and Chief Bender two.

The Best Team in Baseball History

The Cubs dominated during the regular season from 1906 through 1910 like no team during the 20th and 21st centuries. With records of 116–36 in 1906, 107–45 in 1907, 99–55 in 1908, 104–49 in 1909, and 104–50 in 1910, Chicago had a record of 530–235. The winning percentage of .693 is the best over a five–year period of any team since 1900. The Cubs won the National League pennant in 1906, 1907, 1908, and 1910, and took the World Series in 1907 and 1908. The club missed the post–season only in 1909. That season, the Cubs compiled the best record in modern baseball history for a second–place team.

The Top 15 Winning Percentages Over a Five–Year Period Since 1900

Team	Years	Wins	Losses	Pct.	WS Played	WS Won
Chicago Cubs	1906–10	530	235	.693	4	2
Philadelphia Athletics	1928–32	505	258	.662	3	2
St. Louis Cardinals	1941–45	508	261	.661	3	2
New York Yankees	1935–39	498	261	.656	4	4
Pittsburgh Pirates	1901–05	467	257	.645	1*	0
Philadelphia Athletics	1910–14	488	270	.644	4	3
New York Yankees	1949–53	487	280	.635	5	5
New York Yankees	1954–58	486	284	.631	4	2
New York Yankees	1960–64	505	296	.630	5	2
Brooklyn Dodgers	1952–56	484	284	.630	4	1
Cincinnati Reds	1972–76	502	300	.626	3	2
Atlanta Braves	1995–99	495	296	.626	3	1
New York Yankees	1927–31	479	290	.623	2	2
Baltimore Orioles	1969–73	495	303	.620	3	2
New York Yankees	1998–2002	497	309	.617	4	3

* The Pirates won three National League pennants. There was no World Series in 1901 and 1902.

Extending the Cubs record during the era over a ten–year period, the club is still number one. From 1904 through 1913, the Cubs were 986–542 for a winning percentage of .645. The second best ten–year record since 1900 was compiled by the Yankees from 1932 through 1941, when they were 979–546 for a percentage of .642.

1911   Cubs

Season in a Sentence

The Cubs lead the National League for 53 days, the last of which was August 24, before fading out of contention in September.

Finish • Won • Lost • Pct • GB

Second   92   62   .597   7.5

Manager

Frank Chance

Stats

Stats	Cubs •	NL •	Rank
Batting Avg:	.260	.260	5
On–Base Pct:	.341	.335	2
Slugging Pct:	.374	.355	2
Home Runs:	54		2
Stolen Bases:	214		3
ERA:	2.90	3.39	3
Fielding Avg:	.960	.959	4
Runs Scored:	757		1
Runs Allowed:	607		3

Starting Lineup

Jimmy Archer, c
Vic Saier, 1b
Heinie Zimmerman, 2b
Jim Doyle, 3b
Joe Tinker, ss
Jimmy Sheckard, lf
Solly Hofman, cf
Wildfire Schulte, rf
Johnny Evers, 2b

Pitchers

Three Finger Brown, sp–rp
King Cole, sp
Lew Richie, sp
Ed Reulbach, sp
Harry McIntyre, sp–rp

Attendance

576,000 (second in NL)

Club Leaders

Batting Avg:	Zimmerman	.307
On–Base Pct:	Sheckard	.434
Slugging Pct:	Schulte	.534
Home Runs:	Schulte	21
RBI:	Schulte	107
Runs:	Sheckard	121
Stolen Bases:	Sheckard	32
Wins:	Brown	21
Strikeouts:	Brown	129
ERA:	Richie	2.31
Saves:	Brown	13

MARCH 15 The Cubs begin to break up the championship lineup by selling Harry Steinfeldt to the Braves.

The Cubs believed, correctly, that they had better and younger alternatives at third base in Jim Doyle and Heinie Zimmerman.

APRIL 12 In the first game of the season, the Cubs and Cardinals play to a 3–3 tie, called after eleven innings because of darkness before 16,000 at West Side Grounds. The Cardinals scored three runs in the first inning, and the Cubs countered with single runs in the first, sixth, and eighth. Starter Ed Reulbach was knocked out in the first inning. Orlie Weaver pitched 9⅔ innings of relief. Wildfire Schulte hit a home run, the only homer by a Cubs player in the first game of the season between 1895 and 1921.

Two of the first three Cubs games in 1911 ended in a tie. In the third game of the season, played on April 15 in Chicago, the Cubs and Cards played to another 3–3 tie, this one called after ten innings on account of darkness.

APRIL 23 Orlie Weaver pitches a two–hitter to beat the Cardinals 7–0 in St. Louis. The only Cardinal hits were singles by Roger Bresnahan and Lee Magee.

The shutout was the only one of Weaver's career. He finished his two–year stay in the majors with a 6–15 record.

MAY 5   Johnny Evers suffers a nervous breakdown.

A series of personal tragedies struck Evers during the previous eight months. He missed the World Series with a broken leg (see October 1, 1910), and the limb was slow in healing, then he caught pneumonia. In December 1910, Evers lost his life savings when his business partner invested in two shoe stores that went bankrupt. Shortly after the 1911 season started, Evers was the driver in an accident that killed his best friend. Tightly wound and temperamental under the best of circumstances, he couldn't stand the strain. With the exception of one inning in June in a 20–2 laugher, Evers didn't play again until September.

MAY 18   The Cubs pound the Phillies 14–2 in Philadelphia. After the game, about 1,000 Phillie fans made a rush for umpire Jack Doyle, but he was protected by the police and quickly escorted to his dressing room.

Doyle played for the Cubs in 1901 during a seventeen–year career in which he was known as one of baseball's supreme umpire baiters. He lasted only one season as a National League ump.

MAY 29   Carrying the Cubs from St. Louis, the Pennsylvania Railroad sets a speed record, covering the 191 miles from Columbus to Pittsburgh in 215 minutes, breaking the old mark by five minutes.

The train moved quickly to ensure that the Cubs would reach Pittsburgh in time for a game against the Pirates. The train lurched back and forth on the white–knuckle ride. According to the 1912 REACH GUIDE, "it was walking the quarter–deck of a lake steamer in a cyclone to go the length of the car." In the dining car, Cubs trainer Doc Semmons was munching on some roast beef when he was pitched out of his seat, and while lying on the floor, was struck by his drink, silverware, plate, and the remainder of his dinner. The Cubs made it to Pittsburgh in time to defeat the Pirates 4–1.

JUNE 10   The Cubs trade Johnny Kling, Al Kaiser, and Orlie Weaver to the Braves for Cliff Curtis, Wilbur Good, and Bill Collins.

Kling was another key component of the 1906–10 championship clubs to be let go in favor of a younger player. Jimmy Archer became the Cubs catcher. Though 28, Archer was eight years younger than Kling.

JUNE 11   Heinie Zimmerman sets a Cubs record for most runs batted in a game with nine, as the Cubs wallop the Braves 20–2 at West Side Grounds. Zimmerman drove in the nine runs on a pair of three–run homers and two singles. The only other Cub with nine RBIs in a game is Sammy Sosa in 2002. The big inning for the Cubs was the seventh, in which they scored seven runs. Jimmy Sheckard scored five times.

Sheckard led the league in runs scored with 121, in walks with 147, and on–base percentage with a .434 mark in 1911. His batting average was .276. The 147 walks is a club record. In his first season as a regular, Zimmerman hit .307.

JUNE 21	In a batting spree at West Side Grounds, the Cubs rout the Pirates 14–1.
	The Cubs hit a club–record 101 triples in 1911.
JULY 1	Frank Chance collapses on the field before a 3–0 loss to the Reds in Cincinnati because of a blood clot on his brain. Chance's injury was caused by numerous beanings he suffered during his career.
	Chance was hospitalized for nearly a month. Jimmy Sheckard served as acting manager in his absence, and rookie Vic Saier took over as the starting first baseman.
JULY 2	The Cubs rout the Reds 13–3 in Cincinnati.
JULY 4	The Cubs score all eight of their runs in the third inning to defeat the Reds 8–3 in the first game of a double–header at West Side Grounds. During the inning, Wildfire Schulte hits a grand slam off Bobby Keefe. The second game ended in a 2–2 tie, called after ten innings by darkness.
JULY 15	Joe Tinker hits a grand slam off Al Mattern in the seventh inning against the Braves in Boston, but the Cubs lose 17–12.
	Tinker hit .278 in 1911.
JULY 18	Wildfire Schulte hits a grand slam off Lefty Tyler in the sixth inning of a 14–6 win over the Braves in Boston.
JULY 20	Wildfire Schulte is a single shy of a cycle, as he hits a homer, a triple, and a double to lead the Cubs to a 4–3 win over the Phillies in Philadelphia.
JULY 28	The Cubs win their tenth game in a row with a 6–3 decision over the Phillies in Philadelphia.
AUGUST 3	Eddie Zimmerman of the Dodgers hits a ball at West Side Grounds that rolls into a pile of lumber and circles the bases for a freak inside–the–park homer off Lew Richie. Tex Erwin hit Richie's next pitch over the right field wall for another homer. The Dodgers beat the Cubs 5–3.
AUGUST 5	Frank Chance suspends Joe Tinker for two days and fines him $150 for "indifferent play" after the Cubs shortstop misplays two pop flies.
AUGUST 7	In his first game back from his suspension, Joe Tinker has a triple, a double, two singles, and a steal of home, all off Christy Mathewson, to lead the Cubs to an 8–6 win over the Giants at West Side Grounds.
AUGUST 9	The Cubs purchase Kitty Bransfield from the Phillies.
AUGUST 12	A home run by Wildfire Schulte clears the 80–foot–high signboard in right field at West Side Grounds, leading the Cubs to a 9–1 win over the Cardinals.
AUGUST 13	Lew Richie pitches the Cubs to a 1–0 win over the Cardinals at West Side Grounds.

Richie had a record of 15–11 with an ERA of 2.31 in 1911, and followed it up with a 16–8 mark and a 2.95 earned run average in 1912. The Bob Uecker of his day, Richie was one of the funniest players ever to play for the Cubs. A gifted pantomimist, he helped keep the club loose on long train trips with his pranks and humorous stories.

AUGUST 16   During an eight–run fourth inning, Wildfire Schulte connects for a grand slam off Buster Brown to lead the Cubs to a 13–6 win over the Braves in Boston.

The grand slam was Schulte's fourth of the year. The only other Cub with at least four grand slams in a season is Ernie Banks, who had five of them in 1955. They were also the only four grand slams of Schulte's 15–year major league career.

AUGUST 19   Wildfire Schulte hits his 20th home run of the season during a 16–8 win over the Braves in Boston.

Schulte was the first major leaguer to hit 20 homers in a season since Buck Freeman of the Washington Senators had 25 in 1899. Schulte finished the season tied for the league lead in runs batted in with 107, along with 105 runs scored, a .300 batting average, 30 doubles and 21 triples. He became the first player in history to complete a season with at least 20 doubles, 20 triples and 20 home runs. The only other players to accomplish the feat are Jim Bottomley (1928 Cardinals), Jeff Heath (1941 Indians), Willie Mays (1957 Giants), and George Brett (1979 Royals). The 21 triples by Schulte is a Cubs record, matched by Vic Saier in 1913.

Frank "Wildfire" Schulte became the first major leaguer in history to hit at least 20 homers, 20 triples, and 20 doubles in a season.

AUGUST 25   The Cubs fall out of first when they are rained out in Brooklyn while the Giants beat the Pirates.

The Cubs led the National League for 53 days in 1911, but never regained the top spot after August 25 and dropped out of contention quickly in September.

AUGUST 28   Umpire Bill Klem stops a Cubs–Phillies game in Philadelphia twice because a fan used insulting and profane remarks toward Three Finger Brown. Klem threatened to forfeit the game to the Cubs if the fan wasn't removed by Phillies officials. Once the fan was ejected, the Cubs went on to win 8–4.

Brown had a 21–11 record, a 2.80 ERA, and 13 saves in 1911 in the dual role of number one starting pitcher and closer. Brown completed 21 of his 27 starts, and finished 24 of his 26 relief appearances. Not surprisingly, Brown was never again an effective pitcher after that season as the heavy workload took its toll. In 1912 he had a 5–6 record and pitched only 88⅔ innings. The Cubs released Brown at the end of the 1912 season.

SEPTEMBER 17   The Cubs shut out the Dodgers in both ends of a double–header, winning 4–0 and 5–0 at West Side Grounds. Charlie Smith pitched the first game, while Larry Cheney (7⅔ innings) and Lew Richie (1⅓ innings) combined on the second game whitewashing.

Cheney was making his first major league start in the game. He had to leave the contest because he was literally knocked out of the box. Zack Wheat hit a line drive at Cheney's head, driving his thumb into his nose, breaking both. The next year, he couldn't grip the ball tightly and changed his delivery. Cheney dug his fingernails into the ball, creating a knuckler. With the new pitch, Cheney went 26–10 as a 26–year–old rookie in 1912, tying the league lead in wins and leading it with 28 complete games.

SEPTEMBER 20   King Cole pitches a one–hitter to defeat the Phillies 1–0 in the first game of a double–header at West Side Grounds. The only Philadelphia hit was a single by opposing pitcher Earl Moore, who had a .109 batting average in 101 at–bats in 1911. The Cubs lost the second game 4–0.

OCTOBER 3   The Cubs clobber the Cardinals 14–8 in St. Louis.

OCTOBER 9   Three Finger Brown earns his 21st victory of the season with an eleven–inning, 6–5 victory over the Pirates at West Side Grounds.

OCTOBER 13   The Chicago City Series begins at Comiskey Park. The White Sox score three runs in the ninth to defeat the Cubs 4–3.

OCTOBER 15   A crowd of 36,308, the largest ever to see a baseball game in Chicago up to that time, watches the White Sox defeat the Cubs 4–2 at Comiskey Park in game three of the Chicago City Series.

The White Sox swept the Cubs, four games to none, in the 1911 Chicago City Series. The four games drew 99,359.

OCTOBER 22   The White Sox and Cubs play a benefit game for St. Ann's Hospital. The White Sox won 6–2, although the teams exchanged pitchers before the contest. White Sox ace Ed Walsh played for the Cubs, while Lew Richie pitched for the White Sox.

1912

C ubs

Season in a Sentence

Following a third–place finish, the Cubs continue to dismantle an aging team with the departure of Frank Chance, Joe Tinker, Three Finger Brown and Jimmy Sheckard during the 1912–13 off–season.

Finish • Won • Lost • Pct • GB

Third   91   59   .607   11.5

Manager

Frank Chance

Stats

Stats	Cubs	NL	Rank
Batting Avg:	.277	.272	3
On–Base Pct:	.354	.340	2
Slugging Pct:	.387	.369	3
Home Runs:	43		2
Stolen Bases:	164		6
ERA:	3.42	3.40	5
Fielding Avg:	.960	.960	3
Runs Scored:	756		2
Runs Allowed:	668		3

Starting Lineup

Jimmy Archer, c
Vic Saier, 1b
Johnny Evers, 2b
Heinie Zimmerman, 3b
Joe Tinker, ss
Jimmy Sheckard, lf
Tommy Leach, cf
Wildfire Schulte, rf
Ward Miller, lf

Pitchers

Larry Cheney, sp
Jimmy Lavender, sp
Lew Richie, sp–rp
Three Finger Brown, sp–rp
Ed Reulbach, rp–sp
Charlie Smith, rp

Attendance

514,000 (second in NL)

Club Leaders

Batting Avg:	Zimmerman	.372
On–Base Pct:	Evers	.431
Slugging Pct:	Zimmerman	.571
Home Runs:	Zimmerman	14
RBI:	Zimmerman	99
Runs:	Zimmerman	95
Stolen Bases:	Tinker	25
Wins:	Cheney	26
Strikeouts:	Cheney	140
ERA:	Cheney	2.85
Saves:	Reulbach	4

FEBRUARY 1   Cubs third baseman Jim Doyle dies at the age of 30 from blood poisoning following surgery for appendicitis at St. Joseph's Hospital in Syracuse, New York.

APRIL 12   Joe Tinker, Johnny Evers, and Frank Chance play together for the last time as the Cubs lose 3–2 to the Reds in ten innings in Cincinnati.

After the game, Chance announced his retirement as a player. He was suffering from blinding headaches and deafness as a result of the many beanings he suffered through his years as a player (see May 30, 1904, and July 1, 1911). Doctors advised Chance that another blow to the head might be fatal. He never played another game with the Cubs, but appeared in 13 games with the Yankees in 1913 and 1914.

APRIL 20   In the home opener, Jimmy Sheckard hits a walk–off homer in the tenth inning to defeat the Reds 5–4. Sheckard turned and headed for the clubhouse after touching second base, but was reminded by teammates to complete the circuit. The manager of the Reds was Hank O'Day, who was the umpire in 1908 when Fred Merkle failed to touch second base (see September 23, 1908). A native of Chicago's West Side, O'Day was also honored in pre–game ceremonies.

A Chicago restaurant nailed a china plate to the center field fence at West Side Grounds in 1912. Surrounding the fence was an announcement that if Wildfire Schulte broke the plate with a drive, he would be awarded $10,000. Schulte never collected.

MAY 14   Heinie Zimmerman runs his hitting streak to 23 games during a 2–0 win over the Phillies at West Side Grounds.

Zimmerman had a tremendous season in 1912. He led the league in batting average (.372), home runs (14), hits (207), doubles (41), and slugging percentage (.571). Zimmerman also drove in 99 runs.

MAY 28   The Cubs score nine runs in the third inning on the way to a 10–2 win over the Reds at West Side Grounds.

JUNE 3   An unusual double play highlights a 4–3 win over the Braves in Boston. In the Boston sixth, the Braves had two runners on base in Ed McDonald on first and Otto Hess on second. Vin Campbell hit a short fly to left. Jimmy Sheckard could have easily caught the ball, but let it drop on purpose. Sheckard fired the ball to Johnny Evers at second, who stepped on the bag to force McDonald and tagged Hess.

JUNE 6   The Cubs trade King Cole and Solly Hofman to the Pirates for Tommy Leach and Lefty Leifield.

Leach was 34 years old and had played for the Pirates since 1900. Though near the end of a stellar career, Leach gave the Cubs three excellent seasons as a starting center fielder.

JUNE 10   Heinie Zimmerman hits a game–winning homer in the tenth inning on an intentional walk to lift the Cubs to a 9–8 win over the Giants at the Polo Grounds in New York. With the score 7–7 and Joe Tinker on third, Giants pitcher Doc Crandall was ordered to intentionally pass Zimmerman. Heinie took a running jump and swatted a ball high over his head and drove it into the right field stands. Earlier in the game, Zimmerman homered into the left field bleachers.

JUNE 28   Jimmy Lavender stars on the mound with a one–hitter and at bat with three hits, including a double, in three at–bats in a 3–0 win over the Pirates at West Side Grounds. The only Pittsburgh hit was a single by Chief Wilson.

JULY 1   Jimmy Sheckard hits a home run in the twelfth inning to beat the Pirates 1–0 in Pittsburgh. Jimmy Lavender pitched the shutout for the Cubs.

Jimmy Sheckard led the majors with 122 walks in 1912 and hit a walk–off homer to win the home opener.

Lavender had a 16–13 record for the Cubs as a 28–year–old rookie in 1912.

JULY 8 — The Cubs end the 19–game winning streak of Giants pitcher Rube Marquard, the longest single–season streak in major league history, with a 7–2 victory. A crowd of 17,000 turned out on a Monday afternoon at West Side Grounds. Jimmy Lavender was the winning pitcher.

JULY 19 — Phillies manager Red Dooin is ejected from a game, won 4–0 by Philadelphia at West Side Grounds, for putting liniment on the baseball.

The Cubs pitcher was Jimmy Lavender, whose main pitch was a spitball at a time when it was legal for pitchers to use spit on the ball. The Phillies tried to foil Lavender by putting liniment on the ball to make it painful for Lavender to use the spitball. Lavender's technique was to hide the ball in his glove and lick it. The Cubs pitcher took a whiff of the ball, detected the scent of liniment, and showed it to umpire Cy Rigler. The umpire tossed the ball out of play and tossed Dooin from the premises. Dooin and the Phillies tried the same trick on Pirates pitcher Marty O'Toole a few days earlier. O'Toole was forced to leave the game when his tongue was burning from the substance. Lavender and Dooin became involved in another dispute over a baseball two years later (see September 23, 1914).

AUGUST 10 — The Cubs defeat the Braves 11–10 in a hotly–contested match in Boston.

After the game, Johnny Evers and umpire William Finneran continued a quarrel which developed during the game, and exchanged blows. Frank Chance pulled Evers away from the fray. Evers was suspended for five games by National League President Thomas Lynch. The suspension meant that Evers was forced to miss the first two games of a crucial three–game series against the Giants that began on August 15. The Cubs were in second place, 6½ games behind the Giants and gaining ground.

AUGUST 12 — Cubs president Charles Murphy blasts Thomas Lynch for the suspension of Johnny Evers, claiming that Lynch was a mere puppet of Giants owner John Brush. Murphy also accused the Cardinals, managed by former Giant Roger Bresnahan, of failing to give their best against the Giants.

Later, Phillies owner Horace Fogel, who was seen as a front for Murphy, echoed the accusation against Bresnahan and accused NL umpires of fixing the pennant race for the Giants in a letter to the Cubs president. Murphy turned the letter over to the CHICAGO POST for publication. At a league meeting on November 27, Fogel was drummed out of baseball. No charges were made against Murphy, however, but the skids were greased for his departure as well (see February 10, 1914, and February 21, 1914).

AUGUST 17 — Before 30,000 at West Side Grounds, the Cubs defeat the Giants 6–5 in eleven innings to pull within five games of the first–place Giants. The Cubs rallied from a 4–0 deficit. Jimmy Archer drove in the tying run in the ninth with a single and had another RBI single in the eleventh. In his first game back from his suspension, Johnny Evers hit two key doubles.

Evers recovered from his nervous condition (see May 5, 1911) to hit .341 with a .431 on–base percentage in 1912.

AUGUST 22   The Cubs slaughter the Braves 17–5 at West Side Grounds to pull within four
games of the first–place Giants.

*The Cubs could get no closer to John McGraw's Giants, however. Frank
Chance's club had a record of 16–21 from August 23 through the end of the
season and landed in third place, 11½ games behind New York. Chance was
away from the club for most of September because he had surgery to relieve the
pressure of a blood clot on his brain. He suffered from severe and constant
headaches which were especially crippling on hot, sunny days.*

SEPTEMBER 2   A Labor Day double–header between the Cubs and Pirates at Forbes Field is postponed because the Pirates were delayed when their train had to detour around a
bridge that was washed out near Steubenville, Ohio.

SEPTEMBER 8   During a 10–8 loss to the Reds in Cincinnati, Johnny Evers throws dirt at umpire
Brick Owens. Evers drew another five–day suspension from NL president Thomas
Lynch for the infraction.

SEPTEMBER 13   The Cubs score three runs in the ninth inning to defeat the Braves 3–2 in Boston.
The first run of the rally was scored on a home run by pitcher Larry Cheney.

*The homer was the only one Cheney hit during his major league career, which
spanned 617 at–bats over nine seasons.*

SEPTEMBER 19   During a 9–6 loss to the Dodgers in the first game of a double–header in Brooklyn,
Joe Tinker and Johnny Evers fight on the bench. A plainclothes detective assigned
to the game by the New York police department jumped between them and broke
up the fight. The fracas was instigated when Tinker accused Evers of loafing on the
bases during a force play.

SEPTEMBER 26   The Cubs defeat the Reds 11–10 in the first game of a double–header at West Side
Grounds in one of the strangest contests in the history of either franchise. The Cubs
took a 9–0 lead into the ninth inning, but the Reds scored ten times off Jimmy
Lavender, Fred Toney, and Larry Cheney to take a 10–9 lead. The last five Cincinnati
runs were scored on bases–loaded walks. The Cubs came back with two runs in
their half of the ninth, both on bases–loaded walks by Reds pitcher Rube Benton.
Chicago won the second game 10–0, shortened to six innings by darkness.

SEPTEMBER 28   Team president Charles Murphy fires manager Frank Chance.

*As the Cubs faded out of contention in September, Murphy publicly proclaimed
that the club failed to win the pennant because there were too many drunkards
and carousers on the roster. Chance vehemently denied the accusation and
called Murphy a liar. Murphy insisted that the players sign a temperance clause
in their contracts for the 1913 season, and Chance refused to go along with the
idea. It was the culmination of many arguments and disagreements between the
two over the years. Most of them centered on Murphy's refusal to appropriate
funds to acquire new players.*
*Chance became manager of the Yankees in January 1913. The Yankees lost
102 games in 1912, and Chance brought little improvement. He was fired late
in the 1914 season with a 117–168 record at the helm of the club. Chance and*

Murphy later mended fences and tried to purchase the Cubs in 1920, but their offer was turned down by William Wrigley, Jr. Chance was manager of the Red Sox in 1923, but finished in last place and was fired again. His health rapidly declined, and Chance died in September 1924 at the age of 46.

SEPTEMBER 30   In his only career at–bat in his only career game, Cubs catcher George Yantz singles in a 9–3 loss to the Pirates at West Side Grounds, which allows him to retire with a batting average of 1.000.

OCTOBER 2   Cubs catcher Dick Cotter drives in the winning run while batting out of turn to beat the Pirates 6–5 in ten innings at West Side Grounds.

Cotter entered the game as a pinch–hitter in the ninth inning in the ninth spot in the batting order and drove in a run with a single to tie the score 5–5. Cotter remained in the game as a catcher, replacing Jimmy Archer, and the pitcher assumed the eighth slot in the order vacated by Archer. However, Cotter batted in the eighth slot in the tenth inning and hit a two–out single with the bases loaded to win the game. Umpire Brick Owens stayed on the field, expecting an objection from Pirates manager Fred Clarke, but Clarke didn't realize the mistake and walked to the clubhouse. After being informed of the error, Clarke protested to NL president Thomas Lynch, citing a rule which stated that umpires were required to inform managers of rules violations. Lynch upheld the protest, the Cubs lost the victory, and the game was never replayed.

OCTOBER 9   The 1912 Chicago City Series begins at Comiskey Park with a 0–0 tie, called after nine innings by darkness. White Sox pitcher Ed Walsh held the Cubs to one hit.

Game two, played at West Side Grounds on October 11, also resulted in a 3–3 tie, called after 12 innings on account on darkness. After four days of the City Series, neither team had a victory with two rainouts and two ties.
Joe Tinker served as acting manager of the Cubs during the City Series.

OCTOBER 13   A crowd of 30,393, one of the largest ever at West Side Grounds, watches the Cubs defeat the White Sox 4–2 to take a two games to none lead in the City Series.

The crowd became so unmanageable in the early part of the game that it was impossible for a large detail of police to keep them from crowding onto the infield. A dozen or more park attaches and ushers went to the assistance of the police, and when this failed to push the crowd back, the Cubs players, each armed with a bat, went to the rescue. The fans were intimidated by this show of force and were shoved far enough into the outfield to allow play to continue.

OCTOBER 14   The Cubs take a three games to none lead in the City Series with an 8–1 win over the White Sox at Comiskey Park.

After five games, the Cubs had three victories and two ties in the City Series. Incredibly, the White Sox mounted a comeback to win four games in a row to win the championship of Chicago despite the fact that they didn't win a single contest of a best–of–seven series until the sixth game. The Sox clinched the series with a 16–0 trouncing of the Cubs at Comiskey Park on October 18.

OCTOBER 24   Twelve days before the election of Woodrow Wilson as President of the United States, the Cubs elect Johnny Evers as manager for the 1913 season to replace Frank Chance. Evers was given a five–year contract, but he lasted on the job for only a season.

At the same time, Charles Murphy announced plans to build a concrete–and–steel ballpark to replace antiquated West Side Grounds. He said the club would tear down the left–field stands and build a new park along Polk Street opposite Cook County Hospital. Murphy never carried through on his plans.

DECEMBER 11   The Cubs trade Joe Tinker, Grover Lowdermilk, and Harry Chapman to the Reds for Bert Humphries, Red Corriden, Pete Knisely, Art Phelan, and Mike Mitchell. On the same day, the Cubs purchased Al Bridwell from the Braves.

The trade broke up the Johnny Evers–Joe Tinker double play combination, which had been together since 1902. Tinker asked for the trade due to the disappointment of being passed over as manager of the Cubs and grave doubts that he could get along with Johnny Evers due to their long–standing feud. Tinker became manager of the Reds and gave Cincinnati one good season before jumping to the Federal League in 1914. None of the four players the Cubs received in the deal made significant contributions to the club.

1913   Cubs

Season in a Sentence

The rebuilding Cubs feature the best offense in the league, but the pitchers and a shaky defense drag the club into third place.

Finish • Won • Lost • Pct • GB

Third   88   65   .575   13.5

Manager

Johnny Evers

Stats   Cubs • NL • Rank

Stats	Cubs	NL	Rank
Batting Avg:	.257	.262	6
On–Base Pct:	.335	.325	2
Slugging Pct:	.369	.354	2
Home Runs:	59		2
Stolen Bases:	181		4 (tie)
ERA:	3.13	3.20	4
Fielding Avg:	.959	.962	7
Runs Scored:	720		1
Runs Allowed:	630		4

Starting Lineup

Jimmy Archer, c
Vic Saier, 1b
Johnny Evers, 2b
Heinie Zimmerman, 3b
Al Bridwell, ss
Mike Mitchell, lf
Tommy Leach, cf
Wildfire Schulte, rf
Art Phelan, 2b–3b
Ward Miller, lf
Roger Bresnahan, c
Cy Williams, lf

Pitchers

Larry Cheney, sp–rp
Bert Humphries, sp
George Pearce, sp
Jimmy Lavender, sp–rp
Charlie Smith, sp
Orval Overall, sp

Attendance

419,000 (third in NL)

Club Leaders

Batting Avg:	Zimmerman	.313
On–Base Pct:	Leach	.391
Slugging Pct:	Zimmerman	.490
Home Runs:	Saier	14
RBI:	Zimmerman	95
Runs:	Leach	99
Stolen Bases:	Saier	26
Wins:	Cheney	21
Strikeouts:	Cheney	136
ERA:	Pearce	2.31
Saves:	Cheney	11

JANUARY 6   The Cubs purchase Roger Bresnahan from the Cardinals.

> *A future Hall of Famer, Bresnahan was the Cardinals' player–manager the previous four seasons. He played three seasons in Chicago and was player–manager for the Cubs in 1915.*

APRIL 8   The Cubs sell Jimmy Sheckard to the Cardinals.

APRIL 9   The scheduled season opener against the Cardinals at West Side Grounds is postponed by rain. The games on April 10 and 11 were also postponed.

APRIL 12   The Cubs finally get under way and lose the season opener 5–3 to the Cardinals on a damp and chilly day at West Side Grounds.

> *In pre–game ceremonies, Johnny Evers received a chest of silverware and several floral pieces from his admirers.*

APRIL 21   Cubs manager Johnny Evers and Reds manager Joe Tinker face each other as members of the opposition for the first time. The Cubs defeated the Reds 3–2 in Cincinnati.

> *The Cubs had a 12–4 record in April 1913, but an 8–16 May erased any hopes for a pennant.*

APRIL 29   The Reds lose their uniforms before a game against the Cubs in Chicago. Absent–minded trainer and equipment man Doc Semmons forgot to load the trunks containing the uniforms on the train after the April 28 game in St. Louis. Once in Chicago, Semmons hustled across town and borrowed the home uniforms of the White Sox, who were on a road trip. The embarrassed Reds lost 7–2 to the Cubs in their hand–me–down outfits.

> *Ironically, Semmons was the trainer for the Cubs earlier in the month. He left the Cubs for the Reds on April 5 because of his friendship with Joe Tinker.*

MAY 6   The Cubs play the Dodgers at Ebbets Field for the first time and lose 4–3.

> *Ebbets Field was the home of the Dodgers until the club moved to Los Angeles after the 1957 season.*

MAY 10   Johnny Evers Day is celebrated at the Polo Grounds prior to the Cubs 2–1 win over the Giants.

> *About 500 citizens from Evers's hometown of Troy, New York, paraded around the field prior to the game. Evers was presented with a large silver loving cup, a cane, and several floral pieces. Two floral creations were shaped to represent life–size ballplayers.*

MAY 12   Johnny Evers is ejected from a 5–1 loss to the Giants in New York for using obscene language toward umpire Al Orth and for thumbing his nose "in an insulting manner" at umpire Bill Klem.

> *Evers was suspended for three games by the National League for the incident. He denied using obscene language and maintained that a hair in his nose was*

irritating him, and that he was merely scratching his beak.

Evers had a long–standing feud with Klem. In 1909, the two were engaged in a heated argument and Evers said he would leave settlement of the issue with the league office. Klem bet Evers five bucks that he wouldn't show up. Evers showed up, but Klem did not. After that, whenever Klem umpired a Cubs game, Evers would scream about the five dollars Klem owed him and drew the figure "5" in the dirt with his bat at home plate. Finally, the two met on a car of a train between Chicago and Pittsburgh, and Klem paid off. He made Evers write out a receipt, which Klem then proceeded to tear into pieces in front of Evers.

MAY 25   The Cubs score eight runs in the first inning and beat the Cardinals 9–2 at West Side Grounds. Vic Saier hit a grand slam off Bill Steele.

Saier hit .289 with 14 homers 94 runs, 92 RBIs, and a league–leading 21 triples in 1913. Other hitting stars were Heinie Zimmerman, who had a .313 batting average and 95 runs batted in, and Tommy Leach, with 99 runs and a .287 average. Player–manager Johnny Evers hit .285. Larry Cheney topped the pitchers with a 21–14 record, a 2.57 ERA, 305 innings, and 25 complete games in 36 starts. He was also the Cubs' top relief pitcher. In 18 relief appearances, Cheney had a 4–0 record and 11 saves. Bert Humphries led the National League in winning percentage with a 16–4 record.

JUNE 17   Heinie Zimmerman is ejected from a 4–0 win over the Phillies at West Side Grounds for arguing with the umpires. It was the third time in five days that Zimmerman was ejected from a game.

Heinie Zimmerman batted .313 and finished second in RBIs and third in slugging percentage in the National League in 1913.

Two days later, Zimmerman was given half of a $100 bill from an anonymous fan, with Harvey Woodruff, sporting editor of the CHICAGO TRIBUNE, serving as intermediary. Zimmerman was told that he would receive the other half of the bill if he managed to keep from being thrown out of a game for two weeks. Zimmerman made it, but had a narrow escape on July 2, the last day of the two–week probation period, in a game against the Pirates in Chicago. Zimmerman was on third base and attempted to steal home. The throw beat him, and umpire Ernie Quigley called him out. Zimmerman arose to his feet and commenced to argue with the umpire, but suddenly calmed down and walked away. Zimmerman received the other half of the $100 bill before the Cubs–Reds game on July 3. It was presented by umpire Bill Brennan.

JUNE 29   The Reds and Cubs complete a nine–inning game in Cincinnati using only one ball. The Reds won 9–6. The *Cincinnati Enquirer* reported that the ball was "pretty badly battered, but was still in shape for further action in case the Cubs had tied the score in the ninth." Joe Tinker took the ball home as a souvenir.

JULY 6   After winning the first game of a double–header against the Cardinals 6–0 at West Side Grounds, the Cubs lose the second game by forfeit.

By prior agreement, the second game was to end at 5:00 P.M. to allow both teams to catch a train. Five innings had to be played to make it an official game. After the Cardinals took a 3–0 lead in the third, the club began to make outs deliberately in order to keep the game moving so that five innings would be played on time. The Cubs, on the other hand, stalled to take as much time as possible. The last straw for umpire Mal Eason was a play in which Cardinals catcher Ivy Wingo bunted to Ed Reulbach, who threw the ball wildly to first base. Johnny Evers retrieved it, but made no attempt to retire Wingo, who slowly trotted around the bases. Eason declared the game a forfeit. Evers punched Eason, but somehow the Cubs manager escaped a suspension from the National League office.

JULY 23   The Cubs defeat the Pirates 13–8 in Philadelphia.

JULY 27   The Cubs purchase Earl Moore from the Phillies.

AUGUST 5   Cy Williams drives in six runs, including a grand slam in the second inning off Nap Rucker, to lead the Cubs to a 13–2 win over the Dodgers at West Side Grounds.

Williams first attracted attention as an athlete at Notre Dame, where he played football (with Knute Rockne) and baseball while studying architecture. The Cubs were so impressed after seeing him in an exhibition game that the club signed him immediately after graduation in 1912 and brought him directly to the majors.

AUGUST 13   The Cubs acquire Hippo Vaughn from Kansas City of the American Association in exchange for Lew Richie.

James "Hippo" Vaughn was a six–foot–four, 215–pound pitcher who had previous trials with the Yankees and Senators. With the Cubs, Vaughn harnessed his talent and had five seasons in which he won at least 20 games. In nine seasons in Chicago, Vaughn had a 151–105 record with a 2.33 ERA, 2,216 innings, 177 complete games, and 1,138 strikeouts. He's best known for losing the only double no–hitter in major league history (see May 2, 1917).

AUGUST 14   George Pearce pitches a two–hitter to defeat the Braves 5–1 in the second game of a double–header in Boston. The only Braves hits were a double by Bris Lord and a single by Hap Myers.

On the same day, the Cubs traded Ed Reulbach to the Dodgers for Eddie Stack and cash.

AUGUST 15   The Cubs batter the Braves 14–6 in Boston.

AUGUST 18   The Cubs collect nine hits in a row in the ninth inning to score six runs in a 10–4 defeat of the Phillies in Philadelphia. All nine hits came off Phillies pitcher Erskine Mayer. The hits were by Tommy Leach (double), Johnny Evers (single), Heinie Zimmerman (single), Vic Saier (home run), Cy Williams (single), Red Corriden (double), Jimmy Archer (single), and Bert Humphries (single). Corriden was playing in place of Al Bridwell, who was ejected in the sixth inning for throwing dirt in the face of umpire Hank O'Day. Bridwell was suspended for three games for the offense.

AUGUST 31   The Cubs blank the Pirates 10–0 at West Side Grounds.

SEPTEMBER 6   Vic Saier hits a grand slam in the first inning off Chief Johnson of the Reds to lead the Cubs to a 5–3 win at West Side Grounds.

SEPTEMBER 14   Larry Cheney allows 14 hits to the Giants, but the Cubs win 7–0 at West Side Grounds. Cheney's effort set a major league record (since tied) for most hits allowed in a nine–inning shutout.

Johnny Evers was ejected before the first pitch. Before facing the Giants' leadoff hitter, Cheney rubbed the ball in the grass. Umpire Cy Rigler objected, asked for the grass–stained ball, and put a new one in play. Evers threw the new ball over the grandstand, earning a summary dismissal from Rigler. There is no accurate count as to how many times Evers was ejected by the umpires in 1913, but he was probably given the thumb in as many as 20 games.

OCTOBER 8   The White Sox win the first game of the Chicago City Series over the Cubs 4–2 at West Side Grounds. The Cubs won games two and three, but the White Sox rallied with three victories in a row to win the series four games to two.

The sports pages during the 1913–14 off–season centered around the plans of the Federal League, which intended to become a third major league and to raid National and American League rosters with the inducement of more lucrative contracts. The Federal League established franchises in Chicago, Baltimore, Brooklyn, Buffalo, Indianapolis, Kansas City, Pittsburgh, and St. Louis. The Chicago franchise gained immediate credibility by signing Joe Tinker as player–manager. Tinker had just been sold by the Cincinnati Reds to the Brooklyn Dodgers before jumping to the Feds. Nicknamed the Whales, and also known as the Chifeds, the Chicago Federal League club was owned by popular and wealthy Chicago restaurateur Charles Weeghman. The Whales built a new steel–and–concrete ballpark on Chicago's North Side at Clark and Addison streets, called Weeghman Park. Today, the facility is known as Wrigley Field. The Cubs lost shortstop Al Bridwell and outfielder Ward Miller to the Federal League, both to the St. Louis club.

1914

Cubs

Season in a Sentence

With ex-umpire Hank O'Day as manager, the Cubs land in fourth place as attendance plummets.

Finish • Won • Lost • Pct • GB

Fourth   78   76   .506 16.5

Manager

Hank O'Day

Stats

Stats	Cubs	NL	Rank
Batting Avg:	.243	.251	6
On-Base Pct:	.317	.317	5
Slugging Pct:	.337	.334	4
Home Runs:	42		2
Stolen Bases:	164		5
ERA:	2.71	2.78	3
Fielding Avg:	.951	.958	7
Runs Scored:	605		5
Runs Allowed:	638		5

Starting Lineup

Roger Bresnahan, c
Vic Saier, 1b
Bill Sweeney, 2b
Heinie Zimmerman, 3b
Red Corriden, ss
Wildfire Schulte, lf
Tommy Leach, cf
Wilbur Good, rf
Jimmy Archer, c

Pitchers

Hippo Vaughn, sp
Larry Cheney, sp
Jimmy Lavender, sp
Bert Humphries, sp-rp
George Pearce, sp-rp
Zip Zabel, rp

Attendance

202,516 (fourth in NL)

Club Leaders

Batting Avg:	Zimmerman	.296
On-Base Pct:	Saier	.357
Slugging Pct:	Zimmerman	.424
Home Runs:	Saier	18
RBI:	Zimmerman	87
Runs:	Saier	87
Stolen Bases:	Good	31
Wins:	Vaughn	21
Strikeouts:	Vaughn	165
ERA:	Vaughn	2.05
Saves:	Cheney	5

FEBRUARY 10   Charles Murphy announces that Johnny Evers has resigned as manager. Murphy named Hank O'Day to replace Evers. O'Day had been a National League umpire from 1895 through 1911, managed the Reds in 1912, and returned to umpiring in 1913.

Evers hit the roof when he heard the news and denied that he resigned. Evers claimed that he had been fired by Murphy because of disagreements over his managerial style and decision-making. Murphy believed that Evers made decisions based on emotion far too often, instead of with reason. Evers's demand of an increase in salary also led to his dismissal. Before the 1913 season, Evers signed a contract with the Cubs calling for $10,000 a year over four seasons. Charles Weeghman, owner of the Chicago Federal League team, offered Evers a $30,000 bonus and a five-year, $75,000 contract to jump, where he would have been reunited with Joe Tinker. Evers gave the Cubs an opportunity to match the offer, but Murphy refused, considered it a resignation, and released Evers, not only as a manager but as a player as well.

The National League, fighting to maintain as many stars as possible, wouldn't honor the release papers. Instead, National League president John Tener helped negotiate a trade of Evers to the Braves for second baseman Bill Sweeney, which was completed February 11. Evers received a $25,000 bonus from the transaction and an increase in salary to $15,000 a year, and remained a National Leaguer. Evers helped turn the Braves around. Boston had been one of the weakest franchises in the National League, and hadn't had a winning season since 1902.

The Braves were in eighth place as late as July 19 in 1914, when the club put on an incredible rush to win 61 of their last 77 games to capture the pennant, which was followed by a sweep of the heavily–favored Athletics in the World Series.

FEBRUARY 21   Under pressure from his fellow NL owners, Charles Murphy sells his share of the Cubs to Charles P. Taft. Charles Thomas replaced Murphy as club president. Thomas had been the club secretary and worked closely with Murphy.

Impulsive and contentious, Murphy managed to alienate almost every other executive in baseball during his eight years at the head of the Cubs organization. He had been accused by the other National League owners of being dishonest and of being a cheapskate. His dismissal of Johnny Evers gave them an excuse to get rid of Murphy and forced him to sell his stock in the Cubs. Little changed, however. Although he had no official capacity with the Cubs, Murphy continued as an "advisor" to Thomas and Taft. Murphy also left the club a rich man. He invested $15,000 in the Cubs in 1905, and sold his share of stock for $500,000.

MARCH 4   Ground is broken on Weeghman Park at Clark and Addison streets, known today as Wrigley Field. The ballpark was built to house Charles Weeghman's new Federal League franchise (see October 8, 1913) and was called Weeghman Park when opened. The ground –breaking ceremony attracted over 2,000 people. A bottle of wine was broken over the spade that dug the first shovel of earth amid the playing of patriotic music. The ballpark, with about 14,000 seats, was built in seven weeks (see April 23, 1914).

APRIL 14   On Opening Day, the Cubs lose 10–1 to the Reds in Cincinnati. Chicago collected only two hits off Reds pitcher Rube Benton.

APRIL 22   In the home opener, the Cubs lose 4–3 to the Reds. Only 2,000 showed up at West Side Grounds, the smallest crowd ever for an opener in Chicago.

Fans were angry at the club for a variety of reasons. Only Wildfire Schulte remained from the starting lineup of the team that went to the World Series in 1910, as the stars from that club went elsewhere one by one. Charles Murphy was the most unpopular man in Chicago for dismantling a championship club, especially for firing Frank Chance and Johnny Evers. Even though Murphy sold the club, he was still running the show behind the scenes.
In addition, West Side Grounds was an uncomfortable, dilapidated, ramshackle ballpark made entirely of wood. The first concrete–and–steel ballpark in baseball equipped to handle at least 20,000 fans was Shibe Park, built in Philadelphia in 1909. By 1914 nearly every club in the majors had built steel–and–concrete stands, including the White Sox in 1910 and Chicago's Federal League club, which in 1914 opened present–day Wrigley Field. In 1914 and 1915, West Side Grounds was not only one of the worst ballparks in the country, it was only the third best baseball plant in Chicago.

APRIL 23   The Federal League Chicago Whales play their first regular–season game at Weeghman Park (present–day Wrigley Field). Chicago defeated Kansas City 9–1. Art Wilson hit two home runs. The Whales drew a crowd of 21,000. On the same day, the Cubs defeated the Reds before a paltry 800 spectators at West Side Grounds.

MAY 11	Bill Sweeney of the Cubs and Lee Magee of the Cardinals come to blows during a 5–5 tie, called after 13 innings by darkness in St. Louis. In the eleventh inning, Magee tried to steal second base and was greeted by a hard tag from Sweeney in the small of the back. Magee got up and struck at Sweeney, but got the worst of the altercation when the Cubs second baseman dropped him with several punches to the head.
MAY 14	Hippo Vaughn pitches a one–hitter to defeat the Dodgers 5–0 at West Side Grounds. The only Brooklyn hit was a single by Lew McCarty.
	Vaughn had a 21–13 record in 1914 and a 2.05 ERA.
MAY 21	Johnny Evers makes his first appearance in Chicago as an opposing player, as the Braves defeat the Cubs 3–1. Evers had a single in two official at–bats.
MAY 22	In pre–game ceremonies before a 2–0 loss to the Braves at West Side Grounds, Cubs president Charles Thomas is presented by a group of fans with a bear cub shipped from Alaska.
MAY 31	The Cubs score seven runs in the seventh inning and wallop the Cardinals 11–1 at West Side Grounds.
JUNE 19	Tommy Leach's homer in the tenth inning beats the Phillies 8–7 in Philadelphia.
JUNE 30	Two days after the assassination of Archduke Ferdinand of Austria, an event which precipitates the start of World War I in August, Reds manager Buck Herzog picks up a bat and heaves it full force into the West Side Grounds grandstand. Herzog was angry over being ejected by the umpires. Fortunately, no one was injured, but one fan grabbed a bat and charged Herzog before he was restrained. The Cubs won the game 10–7.
	Herzog later played for the Cubs in 1919 and 1920 and was attacked by another Cubs fan (see September 30, 1920).
JULY 1	Larry Cheney pitches a one–hitter to defeat the Reds 7–0 at West Side Grounds. The only Cincinnati hit was a single by Marty Berghammer in the seventh inning.
JULY 23	The Cubs win their eighth game in a row, defeating the Phillies 15–8 at West Side Grounds.
JULY 25	The Cubs record their ninth victory in a row, downing the Braves 5–4 in Boston.
	After the win, the Cubs had a record of 51–37 and were 2 ½ games behind the first–place Giants.
AUGUST 11	Cubs teammates Heinie Zimmerman and Roger Bresnahan fight on the field during a 3–2 loss to the Dodgers in Brooklyn. Playing third base, Zimmerman made a wild throw in the fourth inning that scored two Dodger runs. Bresnahan directed some unkind remarks toward Zimmerman concerning his inability to accurately throw a baseball. Zimmerman took offense and made a rush for Bresnahan and a fight followed along the third–base line. Both were ejected. It wasn't the last time that Zimmerman's fielding inefficiency led to a fight with a teammate (see August 14, 1915).

Zimmerman was the Cubs' best offensive threat in 1914. He batted .296 and drove in 87 runs.

AUGUST 26   Larry Cheney pitches a one hitter to defeat the Braves 1–0 at West Side Grounds. The lone run was scored on a home run in the seventh inning by Vic Saier off Lefty Tyler. The only Boston hit was a single by Hank Gowdy in the sixth inning.

The game was enlivened by a free–for–all fight in the Cubs' half of the seventh inning. The principal participants in the melee were second baseman Johnny Evers, shortstop Rabbit Maranville and first baseman Butch Schmidt of the Braves, and Heinie Zimmerman of the Cubs. All four were ejected. Trying to stretch a single into a double, Zimmerman slid into second and tried to kick the ball out of Evers' hand. Evers resented the intrusion and tagged Zimmerman in the head. Zimmerman jumped up quickly and was punched by Maranville. Schmidt rushed from his position to join in the brawl. It took several minutes for the umpires to quell the disturbance. Zimmerman left the field with blood flowing from his nose.

AUGUST 29   The Cubs defeat the Giants 1–0 in the first game of a double–header at West Side Grounds. Hippo Vaughn pitched the shutout. The lone run was scored in the fourth inning on a single by Wildfire Schulte. The Cubs lost the second game 7–5.

Play was stopped in the first game when the overflow crowd of 20,000, many of whom were ringing the outfield, got out of hand. Mounted policemen were called, and one of them rode blindly through the crowd in center field, scattering fans right and left. Hundreds ran to the infield for protection. After 15 minutes of urging by the players and officers, the mob was pushed back far enough from the diamond to permit play to resume.

SEPTEMBER 5   Wilbur Good hits a three–run walk–off homer in the ninth inning to beat the Pirates 3–2 at West Side Grounds.

On September 8, the Cubs had a 69–59 record and were in third place, only three games out, but were unable to get any closer.

SEPTEMBER 23   A dispute over Jimmy Lavender's use of a trick pitch highlights a 9–4 loss to the Phillies in Philadelphia.

Lavender attached a piece of emery board to the pants leg of his uniform and rubbed the ball against it. There was nothing in the rules to prevent Lavender from doing so, but in the third inning, Phillies manager Red Dooin objected. Umpire Cy Rigler strolled toward the mound, and Lavender walked into right field, refusing to be searched. Rigler declined to chase after the pitcher. The game was delayed until Lavender agreed to have the board cut off of his pants.

Jimmy Lavender won 11 games as one of the Cubs' top starting pitchers in 1914.

SEPTEMBER 29   Larry Cheney allows only three hits, but walks a club record 11 batters as the Cubs lose 3–2 to the Braves in Boston.

> *Cheney had a 20–18 record in 1914, but was worn out after three years of abuse by three different Cubs managers and was never again an effective pitcher. From 1912 through 1914, Cheney won 67 games and recorded 16 saves, but he pitched 919⅔ innings, while making 113 starts and 33 relief appearances.*

OCTOBER 7   In the first game of the Chicago City Series, the White Sox defeat the Cubs 4–2 at Comiskey Park.

OCTOBER 11   In game four of the City Series, the Cubs score two runs in the ninth inning to tie the game 2–2. After the White Sox score in the tenth, the Cubs come back with two tallies to win 4–3 before an overflow crowd of 24,000 at West Side Grounds.

OCTOBER 15   The White Sox take the City Series over the Cubs, four games to three, with a 3–2 win at Comiskey Park.

NOVEMBER 19   Roger Bresnahan is named manager of the Cubs, replacing Hank O'Day.

> *O'Day returned to his former job as National League umpire, a position he held until 1927.*

1915

Season in a Sentence

The Cubs are in first place on July 12 under new manager Roger Bresnahan but stumble to a losing record for the first time in 13 years.

Finish • Won • Lost • Pct • GB

Fourth   73   80   .477   17.5

Manager

Roger Bresnahan

Stats

Stats	Cubs	NL	Rank
Batting Avg:	.244	.248	7
On–Base Pct:	.303	.309	6
Slugging Pct:	.342	.331	1
Home Runs:	53		2
Stolen Bases:	166		2
ERA:	3.11	2.74	7
Fielding Avg:	.958	.964	8
Runs Scored:	570		5
Runs Allowed:	620		7

Starting Lineup

Jimmy Archer, c
Vic Saier, 1b
Heinie Zimmerman, 2b
Art Phelan, 3b
Tom Fisher, ss
Wildfire Schulte, lf
Cy Williams, cf
Wilbur Good, rf
Roger Bresnahan, c

Pitchers

Hippo Vaughn, sp
George Pearce, sp–rp
Jimmy Lavender, sp–rp
Bert Humphries, sp
Larry Cheney, sp
Zip Zabel, rp–sp
Pete Standridge, rp
Karl Adams, rp–sp

Attendance

217,058 (eighth in NL)

Club Leaders

Batting Avg:	Fisher	.287
On–Base Pct:	Saier	.350
Slugging Pct:	Saier	.445
Home Runs:	Williams	13
RBI:	Williams	64
	Saier	64
Runs:	Saier	74
Stolen Bases:	Saier	29
Wins:	Vaughn	20
Strikeouts:	Vaughn	148
ERA:	Humphries	2.31
Saves:	Lavender	4

APRIL 14	In the season opener, the Cubs defeat the Cardinals 7–2 at West Side Grounds.
APRIL 28	Wilbur Good collects five hits, including a double, in five at–bats, leading the Cubs to a 9–8 win in Cincinnati.
MAY 3	Cubs pitcher George Pearce is ejected from a 5–1 win over the Pirates at West Side Grounds for throwing a bat at Pittsburgh hurler Wilbur Cooper after being hit by a pitch. The game was called after five innings by rain.
MAY 14	Seven days after the sinking of the Luisitania by a German submarine, the Cubs collect 25 hits and torpedo the Dodgers 19–4 in Brooklyn. The Cubs scored eight runs in the second inning and had a 15–0 lead after three innings. Chicago outfielder Pete Knisely had five hits in six at–bats.
MAY 19	Bert Humphries pitches the Cubs to a 1–0 win over the Giants in New York. The only run of the game was scored in the first inning on a double steal with Wildfire Schulte swiping home.
MAY 31	The Cubs lose both ends of a double–header to the Pirates in Pittsburgh by 1–0 scores.
JUNE 17	The Cubs defeat the Dodgers 4–3 in a long nineteen–inning battle at West Side Grounds. Zip Zabel was the winning pitcher, hurling 18⅓ innings in the longest relief assignment in major league history. Zabel entered the game for starter Bert Humphries, who left with two out in the first inning when Humphries was hit in the hand by a line drive off the bat of Zack Wheat. Both teams scored in the fifteenth inning, the Cubs tally coming on a Vic Saier home run. The winning run was scored on a single by Tom Fisher, who moved to second on a sacrifice and scored on an error by Brooklyn second baseman George Cutshaw.
	Fisher and Saier were the Cubs' top hitters in 1915. Fisher batted .287, while Saier hit .264 with 11 homers.
JUNE 24	Heinie Zimmerman stars with his bat and his legs as the Cubs score four runs in the ninth inning to beat the Cardinals 14–13 at West Side Grounds. Zimmerman tied the score with a two–run, pinch–hit double, moved to third on an infield out, then stole home to end the game.
	The Cubs were in first place after the games of June 25 with a 33–21 record and a 4½–game lead.
JUNE 27	The second game of a double–header in Cincinnati is held up several minutes when a bullet thrown by a fan in the bleachers strikes the foot of Cubs right fielder Wilbur Good. Good gathered his teammates and the umpires around him to determine if the bullet was likely to detonate. When assured the bullet was harmless, Good stuck it in his pocket and the contest continued. The bad fan who threw the bullet at Good was never apprehended. The Cubs lost the first game 3–0, but won the second 4–1.
JULY 6	The Cubs defeat the Reds 5–4 in fourteen innings in the first game of a double–header at West Side Grounds. The winning run was scored on a triple by Heinie Zimmerman and a single by Pete Knisely. The second game ended in a 2–2 tie after being called on account of darkness after seven innings. Just before the second contest ended, Wilbur

Good slid hard into Cincinnati third baseman Ivy Olson, and the two were ejected after exchanging punches.

JULY 13   The Cubs lose 4–3 to the Giants in New York to drop out of first place.

The Cubs not only failed to regain the top spot in the NL in 1915, they fell so rapidly that the club spent four days in September in last place. A rally during the last week pushed the Cubs into fourth place, though only 3 ½ games ahead of the eighth-place Giants.

JULY 15   In the seventh inning of a 5–2 win over the Giants in New York, Roger Bresnahan engages in an argument with a spectator. Umpire Bill Byron shooed Bresnahan away and stopped the game to lecture the fan on proper ballpark decorum.

AUGUST 9   George Cutshaw of the Dodgers collects six hits off Cubs pitching during a 13–0 Brooklyn win at West Side Grounds.

AUGUST 14   Three weeks after the excursion steamer Eastland capsizes in the Chicago River, killing 835 people, George Pearce and Heinie Zimmerman throw punches at each other on the Cubs bench during a 12–2 loss to the Cardinals in St. Louis. The fight occurred during a discussion over a fumble by Zimmerman that let in two runs. Hippo Vaughn, who attempted the role of peacemaker, emerged with a bleeding lip, but he stopped the fight.

Jim "Hippo" Vaughn's 20 wins and 148 strikeouts paced the Cubs in 1915.

Vaughn had a 20–12 record, 148 strikeouts and a 2.67 ERA in 1915.

AUGUST 15   During a 3–1 win over the Cardinals in the first game of a double-header, Roger Bresnahan has to be stopped by umpire Mal Eason and a police officer from climbing into the stands to attack a heckling fan. Cardinals fans, upset over the calls by Eason's fellow ump Bill Byron, littered the field with pop bottles and vegetables, which halted the contest for five minutes. The Cubs lost the second game 8–1.

AUGUST 18   In the sixth inning of a 9–0 win over the Dodgers in Brooklyn, Wilbur Good becomes the only Cub in history to steal second, third, and home in a single inning.

AUGUST 29   The Cubs trade Larry Cheney to the Dodgers for Joe Schultz.

AUGUST 31   Jimmy Lavender pitches a no–hitter to beat the Giants 2–0 in the first game of a double–header in New York. He walked one and struck out eight. The Giants won the second game 7–1.

Otherwise, it was not a great year for Lavender. He broke a rib in April when he fell while climbing out of a bathtub and had a 10–16 record. The no–hitter was his only shutout.

SEPTEMBER 9   The Cubs purchase Phil Douglas from the Dodgers.

SEPTEMBER 16   Hippo Vaughn pitches a twelve–inning shutout to defeat the Dodgers 1–0 at West Side Grounds. Vaughn allowed only four hits. Vic Saier drove in the winning run with
a single.

OCTOBER 3   In the last regular season game ever played at West Side Grounds, the Cubs beat the Cardinals 7–2. Hippo Vaughn was the winning pitcher, earning his 20th victory of the season.

Charles Murphy continued to hold title to the ballpark and the land on which it was built. West Side Grounds was used by amateur and semi–pro clubs until 1920, when it was torn down. Never one to pass up the possibility of making a buck, Murphy stacked some 1 million board feet of wood from the park and sold it as scrap lumber. It's likely that there are still pieces of West Side Grounds that were used in various construction projects scattered around Chicago. Today, the University of Illinois Medical Center stands on the site of the old West Side Grounds. Murphy also owned Baker Bowl in Philadelphia, which was used as the home field of the Phillies until 1938. Baker Bowl was a decaying, ancient relic, and Murphy refused to put any money into it for upgrades. In 1927, ten rows of seats in right field collapsed.

OCTOBER 6   The White Sox defeat the Cubs 9–5 in game one of the 1915 Chicago City Series. The contest attracted 25,000 to Comiskey Park on a Wednesday afternoon.

OCTOBER 10   The White Sox conclude the City Series with an 11–3 win over the Cubs before 32,000 at Comiskey Park. The Sox won the series, four games to one.

DECEMBER 22   In Cincinnati, the American and National Leagues sign a peace treaty with the Federal League. The NL and AL owners paid $600,000 to the eight owners of the Federal League franchises, and the FL ceased to exist after two seasons.

The deal had a major impact on baseball in Chicago. As part of the agreement, Charles Weeghman, owner of the Federal League Chicago Whales, purchased a controlling interest in the Cubs from Charles P. Taft for $500,000. In addition, all of the Whales players became Cubs, as two clubs were amalgamated into one unit. Joe Tinker, who led the Whales to the Federal League pennant in 1915, became skipper of the Cubs, replacing Roger Bresnahan. The Cubs also abandoned West Side Grounds and moved to Weeghman Park at Clark and Addison on Chicago's North Side. The stadium had been built by Weeghman for the Whales in 1914.

1916

Cubs

Season in a Sentence

Despite the return of Joe Tinker and Three Finger Brown, a new owner, wholesale roster changes, and a move to Chicago's North Side, the decline of the once–mighty Cubs continues.

Finish • Won • Lost • Pct • GB

Fifth   67   86   .438 26.5

Manager

Joe Tinker

Stats   Cubs • NL • Rank

Batting Avg:	.239	.247	7
On–Base Pct:	.298	.303	7
Slugging Pct:	.325	.328	5
Home Runs:	46		1
Stolen Bases:	133		8
ERA:	2.65	2.61	5
Fielding Avg:	.957	.963	7
Runs Scored:	520		5
Runs Allowed:	541		5

Starting Lineup

Jimmy Archer, c
Vic Saier, 1b
Otto Knabe, 2b
Heinie Zimmerman, 3b
Chuck Wortman, ss
Les Mann, lf
Cy Williams, cf
Max Flack, rf
Rollie Zeider, 3b–2b
Wildfire Schulte, lf
Joe Mulligan, ss
William Fischer, c
Joe Kelly, cf–lf
Steve Yerkes, 2b

Pitchers

Hippo Vaughn, sp
Jimmy Lavender, sp–rp
Claude Hendrix, sp–rp
George McConnell, sp
Gene Packard, rp–sp
Mike Prendergast, rp
Tom Seaton, rp–sp

Attendance

453,685 (third in NL)

Club Leaders

Batting Avg:	Williams	.279
On–Base Pct:	Williams	.372
Slugging Pct:	Williams	.459
Home Runs:	Williams	12
RBI:	Williams	66
Runs:	Flack	65
Stolen Bases:	Flack	24
Wins:	Vaughn	17
Strikeouts:	Vaughn	144
ERA:	Vaughn	2.20
Saves:	Packard	5

JANUARY 16   Chewing gum magnate William Wrigley, Jr., becomes a minority stockholder in the Cubs, purchasing a share in the club for $50,000.

Once he bought a piece of the Cubs, Wrigley became a passionate baseball fan and bought larger and larger shares of the club. By 1919, he had controlling interest in the club. Born in 1861 in Philadelphia, Wrigley started in the family soap business. He gave away sticks of chewing gum to housewives as an inducement to buy his wares. Wrigley found the gum to be so popular that he embarked on a business of manufacturing it in 1910 and made a fortune.

APRIL 12   The Cubs win the season opener 7–1 over the Reds in Cincinnati. George McConnell, in his first game with the Cubs, was the winning pitcher with a complete game.

Expectations were high in Chicago in 1916, with the Cubs receiving a major infusion of players from the Federal League. Tinker overestimated the quality of material he brought from the Whales, however, and by the time it became obvious that the Federal League talent was vastly inferior to that of the National League, the Cubs were buried in the second division. George McConnell became the poster boy for the problems with the Cubs during the season. He had a record of

A Toast to Charles Weeghman

The Wrigley Field we see today is largely due to the vision of three generations of the Wrigley family, which operated the Cubs from 1919 through 1981. Credit for selecting the site on which the hallowed ballpark is located, however, goes to Charles Weeghman.

Weeghman was born in 1874 in Richmond, Indiana. After graduation from high school, he came to Chicago as a waiter at $10 a week. Weeghman saved part of his wages, and a few years later opened a restaurant. His aim was to serve as many as possible, as quickly as possible, and soon he had a chain of "quick–lunch" establishments. At Weeghman's eateries, customers sat at one–armed chairs, somewhat like grammar school desks, so that more diners could be squeezed in. At one Weeghman restaurant at Madison and Dearborn downtown, 35,000 were served daily.

Almost instantaneously, Weeghman became a millionaire many times over and was nicknamed "Lucky Charlie." In 1913, he bought the Chicago franchise in the Federal League. A year later, the Federals announced plans to became a third major league and began luring players from the American and National Leagues with promises of higher salaries.

Weeghman needed a place to build a ballpark of his own, and selected an irregular block bounded by Clark, Addison, Waveland, and Sheffield in the growing neighborhood of Lake View. In the 19th century, the site was a picnic ground with a huge bell to summon worshipers to nearby St. Mark's Lutheran Church. From 1891 to 1910, the area was the home of the Theological Seminary of the Evangelical Lutheran Church.

The church chose the property because of its semirural location, but the development of Chicago expanded northward and soon surrounded the seminary. A coal company and a sand and gravel business opened on the Clark Street side. Church officials sought a more pastoral setting, moved the seminary to Maywood, and put the lot up for sale. It was bought by Charles Havenor of Milwaukee for $175,000. Havenor planned to make his money on the property by leasing it to the railroad for switching trains. Over the next three years, however, Havenor sold the lot in pieces to Edward Archambault, who in turn leased it to Weeghman on December 31, 1913. The ninety–nine–year lease cost Weeghman $16,000 per year and specified that Weeghman had to construct modern buildings on the land, and that the land not be used for "immoral or illegal purposes."

One reason he selected the location was that fans could reach the park on the Milwaukee road train and the elevated train from the Loop. Access to public transportation was critical in the era when few people owned private automobiles. Weeghman hired architect Zachary Taylor Davis, designer of Comiskey Park, to plan and build his park. Weeghman stated that he wanted to give Chicagoans "a park which will outshine any other in either the National or American Leagues, with the exception of the one at the Polo Grounds in New York."

Work on his Federal League ballpark began immediately. Four wooden seminary buildings were torn down February 23, 1914, and ground was broken the following week in front of more than 5,000 spectators. With 490 men working around the clock, the ballpark, called Weeghman Park, was open for business on April 23, 1914. It cost a quarter of a million dollars. When Weeghman Park opened, it had 16,000 seats in a single deck, including 2,000 bleacher seats in right field.

Weeghman nicknamed the team the Whales and had two successful seasons at Clark and Addison, but the Federal League folded following the 1915 season. Weeghman then put together a group of ten investors, including gum magnate William Wrigley Jr., to purchase controlling interest in the Cubs. One of Weeghman's first acts was to move the Cubs from decrepit West Side Grounds to the North Side. The first Cubs game at Clark and Addison took place on April 20, 1916.

After purchasing the Cubs, "Lucky Charlie" had nothing but bad luck. Weeghman invested in other ventures, including the movies and the risky commodities market, which weren't successful. In need of cash, he sold shares of the

Cubs in increments to William Wrigley Jr. By 1919, Wrigley was the majority owner, and Weeghman no longer had a financial interest in the club. On August 13, 1920, Weeghman's restaurant business was thrown into the hands of a receiver and he declared bankruptcy. He moved to New York, and opened several restaurants, none of which succeeded. Weeghman was a partner in yet another restaurant when he died in 1938.

25–10 with the Whales in 1915, but was only 4–12 with the Cubs in 1916. The Cubs roster was in constant flux, as forty–six players appeared in a game for the club during the season. Only twelve of those players were with the Cubs in 1915. The amalgamation of the Whales and the Cubs eventually paid dividends, however. Claude Hendrix, Max Flack, Les Mann and Rollie Zeider, each of whom were members of the 1915 Whales, played key roles in winning the 1918 National League pennant for the Cubs.

APRIL 20   The Cubs play their first game at Weeghman Park at Clark and Addison, and defeat the Reds 7–6 in eleven innings before 18,000. The Cubs scored two runs in the eighth and one in the ninth to send the game into extra innings. The ninth–inning run was scored on doubles by Max Flack and Heinie Zimmerman. The winning tally came on a double by Cy Williams and a single by Vic Saier. Reds outfielder Johnny Beall hit the first National League homer at the new ballpark.

First baseman Vic Saier was second on the Cubs in home runs, with 7, and stolen bases, with 20, in 1916.

The first game at present–day Wrigley Field was preceded by a parade from Grant Park through the downtown streets. At the ballpark, flowers were presented to each of the Cubs. Aerial bombs were sent up, with each burst releasing American flags that sailed all over the North Side.

APRIL 22   The Cubs win an 8–7 thriller against the Reds at Weeghman Park. The Cubs led 6–0 after six innings, but allowed the Reds to take a 7–6 lead. The Cubs won it with two runs in the ninth inning, the last one on a suicide squeeze bunt by Mickey Doolan with Heinie Zimmerman on third base.

One of the attractions at Weeghman Park in 1916 was "Joa," a bear cub donated by Cubs minority owner J. Ogden Armour. The bear was housed in a cage outside the park on Addison Street.

MAY 8   The Cubs lose 6–4 to the Pirates in the second game of a double–header despite scoring two runs on a bonehead play by Pittsburgh third baseman Joe Schultz. With Cubs runners on second and third in the third inning, Heinie Zimmerman hit a dribbler to Schultz. Zimmerman didn't run to first base, and instead stayed at the plate to argue with umpire Bill Klem that the ball hit him in the foot and should be ruled a foul ball. During the discussion between Zimmerman and Klem, Schultz threw the ball over the head of the first baseman, allowing both runners to score. The Cubs won the first game 2–1.

MAY 14   Fans at Weeghman Park throw cushions at umpire Cy Rigler at the conclusion of a 6–4 loss to the Giants. The crowd was upset over the call of a third strike on Heinie Zimmerman to end the game.

JUNE 2   The Cubs purchase Charlie Deal from the Browns.

Deal was the Cubs starting third baseman from 1917 through 1921.

JUNE 5   Heinie Zimmerman steals home in the fourth inning for the lone run of the game as the Cubs defeat the Braves 1–0 at Boston. Gene Packard pitched the shutout.

JUNE 27   The Cubs win a double–header 1–0 and 10–4 over the Pirates at Weeghman Park. Mike Prendergast pitched the shutout.

JUNE 28   The Cubs lose both ends of a double–header to the Pirates at Weeghman Park by identical 3–2 scores. The second game went eighteen innings. George McConnell pitched the first seventeen innings before being removed with none out in the eighteenth after allowing a home run to Chief Wilson.

JULY 7   Gene Packard pitches a one–hitter to defeat the Braves 1–0 at Weeghman Park. The only Boston hit was a single by Fred Snodgrass.

The corner of Clark and Addison has a long history as a home run haven. There were 56 home runs hit at Weeghman Park in 1916, more than any other park in the majors. In early July, a ten–foot–high screen was erected in front of the right–field bleachers to hinder the long–ball hitters.

JULY 15   Jimmy Archer's two–run walk–off homer in the ninth inning beats the Dodgers 5–4 at Weeghman Park.

The homer was the only one that Archer hit in 1916. It was also the last of his 16 major league homers struck over a career that lasted from 1904 through 1918.
Archer had the best throwing arm of any catcher of the era, and he came about his renowned arm strength in an unusual manner. His right arm was severely burned by hot tar in a factory accident. When the burns healed, the muscles in his arm shortened, but became particularly strong. This allowed Archer to fire the ball to second base without rising from his squat position behind home plate.

JULY 16   The Cubs and the Dodgers play to a 7–7 tie, called after sixteen innings by darkness. The Cubs tied the game 4–4 with three runs in the ninth. After the Dodgers plated three tallies in the tenth, the Cubs came back with three in their half.

Under the direction of Charles Weeghman, the Cubs in July 1916 became the first club in the major leagues to allow fans to keep baseballs hit into the stands. Previously, fans were expected to return foul balls. Those who kept the baseballs were subject to arrest for theft. Most baseball owners believed that Weeghman was incurring an unnecessary expense. It would be another ten years before the policy of allowing fans to keep balls hit into the stands became universal.

JULY 18   The Cubs lose by a forfeit when Joe Tinker refuses to leave the field. With the score 4–4 against the Dodgers in the tenth inning at Weeghman Park, umpire Bill Byron called a balk on Vaughn for delaying the game after the Cubs pitcher held the ball and refused to throw a pitch. Tinker voiced a violent protest. Byron gave Tinker sixty seconds to leave the field, and when Tinker failed to vacate the premises, Byron awarded the contest to the Dodgers.

JULY 19   Giants center fielder Benny Kauff tags out two Cubs at second base during an 8–6 loss at Weeghman Park. The Cubs loaded the bases with one out. The runners were Cy Williams at first, Les Mann at second and Otto Knabe on third. New York catcher Bill Rariden snapped a throw to shortstop Mickey Doolan, trapping Mann, and Knabe broke for the plate. Doolan switched his attention from Mann to Knabe and threw to the plate, catching Knabe in a rundown between third and home. Knabe scored when Doolan dropped the ball. Kauff came in from the outfield to cover second, took a throw from Doolan, and tagged out both Mann coming back from second and Williams trying to advance from first.

JULY 20   Claude Hendrix pitches a three–hit, ten–inning shutout to defeat the Giants 1–0 at Weeghman Park. The winning run was scored on a single by Rollie Zeider.

Rollie Zeider and Dutch Zwilling are the only two individuals to play for the Cubs, the White Sox, and the Federal League Whales. Zeider played for the White Sox from 1910 through 1913, the Whales in 1914 and 1915, and the Cubs from 1916 through 1918. Zwilling was with the White Sox in 1910, the Whales in 1914 and 1915, and the Cubs in 1916. Zwilling also holds the distinction of being the last player on an alphabetical listing of all of the individuals who have appeared in a big league game.

JULY 29   The Cubs trade Wildfire Schulte and Bill Fischer to the Pirates for Art Wilson and Otto Knabe.

The trade ended Schulte's association with the Cubs, which began in 1904. He had little left, however, and was a backup outfielder until his career ended in 1918.

AUGUST 1   Claude Hendrix pitches a one–hitter against the Phillies, but suffers a 3–2 loss in the second game of a double–header against the Phillies in Philadelphia. The Phillies scored all three of their runs in the first inning on two walks, a sacrifice, two errors, a double steal, and a single by Fred Luderus.

In his next start on August 5 against the Giants in New York, Hendrix pitched a three–hitter, but lost 3–2 despite the fact that the Cubs collected ten hits.

AUGUST 17   Hippo Vaughn pitches a one–hitter to defeat the Giants 1–0 at Weeghman Park. The only run of the game was driven in on a double by Fritz Mollwitz in the first inning.

AUGUST 28   The Cubs trade Heinie Zimmerman and Mickey Doolan to the Giants for Larry Doyle, Herb Hunter, and Merwin Jacobson.

Zimmerman continued to star for the Giants, and led the NL in RBIs in 1917. He was suspended from baseball for life after trying to induce his Giants team-mates to throw a game during the 1919 season (see September 10, 1919). During Prohibition, Zimmerman owned a speakeasy with noted gangster "Dutch" Schultz and in 1935 was indicted for tax evasion. Doyle was one of the best second basemen in the game at the time he was acquired by the Cubs, but he was unhappy in Chicago and was traded after the 1917 season.

SEPTEMBER 4   Cubs pitching icon Three Finger Brown faces Christy Mathewson in the second game of a Labor Day double-header at Weeghman Park. Brown and Mathewson were no longer successful pitchers, but the game attracted interest because of the many legendary matchups between the two when they were the top two pitchers in the National League during the 1900s and early 1910s. Both Brown and Mathewson finished the game, but were unable to shut down the hitters, as the Reds won 10–8.

Mathewson, who was also the Reds manager, never appeared in another game as a player. Brown made only a few more token appearances in 1916 before calling it quits. He pitched successfully in the Federal League in 1914 and 1915 and was one of the players who came to the Cubs in the merger with the Whales, but he pitched only 48 innings for the Cubs in 1916.

SEPTEMBER 10   The Pirates score six runs in the ninth inning to defeat the Cubs 8–7 at Weeghman Park.

SEPTEMBER 14   Scott Perry pitches an eleven-inning shutout to defeat the Braves 2–0 at Boston. A single by Chuck Wortman drove in both runs.

Perry's career with the Cubs lasted only eight games. He had a record of 2–1. The September 14, 1916 game was his only shutout in a Chicago uniform.

OCTOBER 4   The White Sox win 8–2 against the Cubs in game one of the Chicago City Series. The Sox went on to sweep the series, four games to none. It was the sixth consecutive year that the White Sox won the City Series. The Cubs and White Sox didn't meet in the postseason again until 1921, because the White Sox went to the World Series in 1917 and 1919, and the Cubs appeared in the Fall Classic in 1918. The 1920 City Series was canceled because eight White Sox players were suspended just prior to the end of the season for throwing the 1919 World Series.

DECEMBER 14   The Cubs hire 40-year-old Fred Mitchell as manager to replace Joe Tinker.

During the three previous seasons, Mitchell had been the pitching coach for the Boston Braves. He managed the Cubs for four seasons, and won the National League pennant in 1918. Mitchell was the Cubs sixth manager in six years, following Frank Chance (1912), Johnny Evers (1913), Hank O'Day (1914), Roger Bresnahan (1915), and Tinker (1916). Mitchell's given name was Fred Yapp, but he changed it upon entering baseball because in the slang of the day a "yap" was an ignorant or uncouth person. Mitchell was his mother's maiden name.
    Tinker managed in the minor leagues for several seasons before settling in Orlando, Florida. He became quite wealthy developing real estate during the boom years of the 1920s, before the Great Depression of the 1930s wiped out his holdings.

1917

Cubs

Season in a Sentence

The Cubs continue to flounder despite winning 22 of their first 31 games under new manager Fred Mitchell.

Finish • Won • Lost • Pct • GB

Fifth   74   80   .481   24.0

Manager

Fred Mitchell

Stats

Stats	Cubs •	NL •	Rank
Batting Avg:	.239	.249	7
On–Base Pct:	.299	.305	6
Slugging Pct:	.313	.328	7
Home Runs:	17		7
Stolen Bases:	127		7
ERA:	2.62	2.70	3
Fielding Avg:	.959	.964	8
Runs Scored:	552		4
Runs Allowed:	567		5 (tie)

Starting Lineup

Art Wilson, c
Fred Merkle, 1b
Larry Doyle, 2b
Charlie Deal, 3b
Rollie Zeider, ss–3b–2b
Les Mann, lf
Cy Williams, cf
Max Flack, rf–lf
Chuck Wortman, ss
Harry Wolter, rf
Rowdy Elliott, c
Pete Kilduff, ss

Pitchers

Hippo Vaughn, sp
Phil Douglas, sp–rp
Claude Hendrix, sp–rp
Al Demaree, sp
Paul Carter, sp–rp
Mike Prendergast, rp
Vic Aldridge, rp

Attendance

360,218 (second in NL)

Club Leaders

Batting Avg:	Mann	.273
On–Base Pct:	Flack	.325
Slugging Pct:	Merkle	.370
Home Runs:	Doyle	6
RBI:	Doyle	61
Runs:	Merkle	65
	Flack	65
Stolen Bases:	Flack	17
	Zeider	17
Wins:	Vaughn	23
Strikeouts:	Vaughn	195
ERA:	Vaughn	2.01
Saves:	Carter	2
	Aldridge	2

APRIL 2   The Cubs send Jimmy Lavender and cash to the Phillies for Al Demaree.

APRIL 11   The Cubs win the season opener 5–3 against the Pirates at Weeghman Park.

Only five days earlier, the United States declared war against Germany, beginning the country's involvement militarily in World War I. Before the opener, members of the Army and Naval Reserves, with a band at the head of each, paraded on the field playing patriotic songs. A recruiting station was opened at Weeghman Park.

APRIL 15   Vic Saier breaks his leg sliding into home plate in the sixth inning of a 5–3 loss to the Cardinals at Weeghman Park.

The injury put Saier out for the year. The Cubs played pitcher Dutch Ruether at first base for five games until Fred Merkle was purchased by the Dodgers on April 21. Best known for failing to touch second base in a 1908 game that helped the Cubs win the pennant (see September 23, 1908), Merkle was the Cubs' starting first baseman until 1920.

APRIL 21   Hippo Vaughn pitches a two–hitter to defeat the Pirates 2–1 at Forbes Field. The only Pirates hits were doubles, both by ex–Cub Wildfire Schulte.

MAY 1   The Cubs score seven runs in the fourth inning and defeat the Cardinals 9–0 in St. Louis.

MAY 2   At Weeghman Park, Hippo Vaughn and Reds pitcher Fred Toney combine to hurl
             the only game in major league history in which neither team collected a hit through
             the first nine innings. The first hit of the game occurred with one out in the tenth
             inning when Reds shortstop Larry Kopf hit a Vaughn pitch into right field for a
             single. Hal Chase flied to right, but Cubs right fielder Cy Williams muffed an easy
             chance, putting Chase on first and Kopf on third. After Chase stole second, Jim
             Thorpe chopped a hit a few feet in front of home plate. Vaughn raced in and tried
             to throw out Kopf coming in from third base, but catcher Art Wilson dropped the
             throw and Kopf was safe, giving the Reds a 1–0 lead. The advantage held up in the
             bottom of the tenth when Toney retired the Cubs without a hit. Both pitchers
             walked two batters. Vaughn struck out ten while Toney fanned three.

MAY 6   The Cubs are outhit 11–2 by the Pirates, but win the game 3–2 at Weeghman Park.

MAY 14   Phil Douglas pitches a two–hitter to defeat the Braves 6–0 at Braves Field. The only
             Boston hits were infield singles by George Twombly and Fred Bailey.

             *Before the game, Cubs manager Fred Mitchell received a silver tea service from
             his friends in Boston.*

MAY 17   The Cubs earn their tenth win in a row with a 2–1 decision over the Braves in Boston.

             *The win gave the Cubs a 22–9 record and a three–game lead in the pennant
             race under first–year manager Fred Mitchell, but the club lost their next five
             games and quickly faded out of contention.*

JUNE 8   Phil Douglas (eight innings) and Claude Hendrix (one inning) combine on a two–hit-
             ter, but the Cubs lose 1–0 at Weeghman Park. Douglas held the Phillies hitless until
             the eighth inning when Possum Whitted and Fred Luderus collected singles.

JUNE 29   All of the gate receipts from the Cubs–Cardinals game at Weeghman Park are
             donated to the Red Cross. A total of $3,858 was raised for the organization. The
             Cubs lost 9–2.

JULY 2   Three future members of the Pro Football Hall of Fame appear in an 8–5 Reds vic-
             tory over the Cubs at Weeghman Park. Jim Thorpe and Greasy Neale played the
             outfield for the Reds, while Paddy Driscoll started at second base for the Cubs.

             *Driscoll joined the Cubs after starring in both baseball and football at Northwestern
             University. His big league baseball career lasted only thirteen games, in which he
             batted .107. Driscoll was one of the pioneers of the National Football League, play-
             ing from 1920 through 1929 with both the Chicago Bears and Chicago Cardinals.*

JULY 13   Al Demaree pitches a ten–inning shutout to defeat the Phillies 1–0 in the second
             game of a double–header in Philadelphia. Max Flack drove in the game–winning
             run with a single. The Cubs lost the first game 7–0.

             *Demaree was a noted sports cartoonist. After his playing career was ended, his
             work was syndicated in over 200 newspapers and appeared in THE SPORTING*

News for over 30 years.

JULY 17   The Cubs sell Dutch Ruether to the Reds.

                 The Cubs made a blunder in letting Ruether get away. After he left Chicago,
                 Ruether had a major league record of 135–95 and pitched in the World Series
                 with the Reds in 1919 and the Yankees in 1926.

JULY 27   Prior to a 5–1 loss to the Giants at Weeghman Park, the 48th Canadian Highlanders
                 appear with their band and give an exhibition drill to encourage recruiting.

                 World War I had little impact on baseball in 1917 as few players were drafted,
                 but the conflict would have major implications on the sport in 1918.

JULY 31   The Cubs trade Al Demaree to the Giants for Pete Kilduff.

AUGUST 8   Hippo Vaughn pitches a two–hitter to defeat the Dodgers 2–0 at Weeghman Park.
                 The only Brooklyn hits were a double by Jimmy Johnston in the second inning and
                 a single by Ivy Olson in the seventh.

                 Vaughn was 23–13 with a 2.01 ERA, 295 ²/₃ innings and 28 complete games in
                 1917.

SEPTEMBER 9   Phil Douglas pitches the Cubs to a 1–0 win over the Pirates at Weeghman Park.
                 Harry Wolter drove in the winning run with a single in the eighth inning.

SEPTEMBER 24   Hippo Vaughn picks up his 23rd win of the season with a 4–2 decision over the
                 Braves at Weeghman Park.

DECEMBER 11   The Cubs send Mike Prendergast, Pickles Dillhoefer and $60,000 to the Phillies for
                 Grover Alexander and Bill Killefer.

                 The $60,000 price was the largest ever paid for a player up to that time.
                 Alexander had been in the majors for seven years and had a record of 190–88.
                 He was 30–13 in 1917, his third consecutive season of 30 or more victories.
                 The Phillies let Alexander go because it was likely that he would be drafted by
                 the Army before the 1918 season, and owner Bill Baker believed that Alexander's
                 $12,000 was too much to pay in a wartime economy. Charles Weeghman felt
                 that Alexander was just the player to bring the Cubs a pennant and was willing
                 to spend money despite the war. Weeghman was losing the attendance war in
                 Chicago to Charlie Comiskey, as the White Sox drew 684,521 fans to 360,218
                 for the Cubs. The White Sox also won the 1917 World Series.
                 *   Alexander was of little help to the Cubs in 1918, as he was drafted after pitch-*
                 ing just three games. But he returned in 1919 and remained with the club until
                 1926. Although he never reached the peak level he enjoyed with the Phillies,
                 Alexander was an excellent addition. As a Cub, he had a record of 128–83, along
                 with 1,884 ¹/₃ innings, 159 complete games, 24 shutouts, and a 2.84 ERA.

DECEMBER 29   The Cubs trade Cy Williams to the Phillies for Dode Paskert.

                 In the long term, the Cubs made a horrible trade in swapping Williams for

Paskert, who was 36 years old and near the end of his career. Williams was 30 and had seldom produced big numbers in Chicago. But Philadelphia's Baker Bowl had a short right–field fence and a livelier ball was introduced in 1920.
With the combination of the two, Williams became a star with the Phillies. He finished his career in 1930 with 251 homers. Williams was the third player in history, behind Babe Ruth and Rogers Hornsby, to hit at least 250 lifetime home runs.

In the short term, it was a positive trade, however. Paskert had one good season left in his tank, and had a better year than Williams in 1918. Dode was a key contributor in Chicago's drive to the 1918 National League pennant.

1918   Cubs

Season in a Sentence

The Cubs win the pennant and lose the World Series in a season that ends a month earlier than scheduled because of World War I.

Finish • Won • Lost • Pct • GB

First   84   45   .651 +10.5

World Series–The Cubs lost, four games to two, to the Boston Red Sox.

Manager

Fred Mitchell

Stats	Cubs	NL	Rank
Batting Avg:	265	.254	2
On–Base Pct:	.325	.311	2
Slugging Pct:	.342	.328	2
Home Runs:	21		3
Stolen Bases:	159		2
ERA:	2.18	2.76	1
Fielding Avg:	.966	.965	3
Runs Scored:	538		1
Runs Allowed:	393		1

Starting Lineup

Bill Killefer, c
Fred Merkle, 1b
Rollie Zeider, 2b
Charlie Deal, 3b
Charlie Hollocher, ss
Les Mann, lf
Dode Paskert, cf
Max Flack, rf

Pitchers

Hippo Vaughn, sp
Lefty Tyler, sp
Claude Hendrix, sp
Phil Douglas, sp
Paul Carter, rp

Attendance

337,256 (first in NL)

Club Leaders

Batting Avg:	Hollocher	.316
On–Base Pct:	Hollocher	.379
Slugging Pct:	Hollocher	.397
Home Runs:	Flack	4
RBI:	Merkle	65
Runs:	Flack	74
Stolen Bases:	Hollocher	26
Wins:	Vaughn	22
Strikeouts:	Vaughn	148
ERA:	Vaughn	1.74
Saves:	Carter	2
	Douglas	2

JANUARY 4   The Cubs send Larry Doyle, Art Wilson, and $15,000 to the Braves for Lefty Tyler.

Tyler was another building block in Charles Weeghman's dreams of a pennant in 1918. The Cubs president claimed he would continue to spend for top talent and set his sights on stars such as Rogers Hornsby. Weeghman offered the Cardinals two front–line players and $50,000 for Hornsby, but the St. Louis club spurned the offer. Weeghman drew the ire of his fellow National League owners, who accused him of trying to buy a championship. He also angered *the Cubs minority owners, many of whom favored profits over a first place finish and believed that Weeghman's free spending ways put the club on a shaky financial foundation at a time in which the future of the sport was uncertain because of World War I.*

APRIL 16   With Grover Alexander on the mound, the Cubs lose 4–2 to the Cardinals in St. Louis in the first game of the 1918 season.

APRIL 24   In the first game of the season at Weeghman Park, Hippo Vaughn pitches a one–hitter to defeat the Cardinals 2–0. The only St. Louis hit was a single by Rogers Hornsby.

Vaughn had another great season in 1918, with a 22–10 record. He led the NL in ERA (1.74), innings pitched (290⅓) and strikeouts (146), and tied teammate Lefty Tyler for the lead in shutouts with eight. Vaughn completed 27 of his 33 starts.

APRIL 30   Grover Alexander reports for Army duty.

Although the Cubs lost their best pitcher to military service, Alexander was the only Cubs regular who was drafted. Others who went into the Armed Forces in 1918 were reserves such as catcher Rowdy Elliott, infielders Paddy Driscoll and Pete Kilduff, outfielders Morrie Schick and Bill Marriott, and pitchers Harry Weaver and Vic Aldridge.

MAY 3   The Cubs score four runs in the ninth inning and beat the Reds 9–8 at Weeghman Park. Fred Merkle drove in the game–winner with a single.

Merkle had the best season of his career in 1918, batting .297.

MAY 4   Lefty Tyler pitches the Cubs to a 1–0 win over the Reds at Weeghman Park. The only run of the game was driven in on a sacrifice fly by Dode Paskert.

In his first season with the Cubs, Tyler was 19–8 with an ERA of 2.00.

MAY 5   The Cubs run their winning streak to nine games with a 5–3 victory over the Cardinals at Weeghman Park.

The Cubs' infielders, left to right, Fred Merkle, Rollie Zeider, Charlie Hollocher, and Charlie Deal, led them to the 1918 National League pennant.

MAY 15   The Cubs lose 5–3 to the Phillies on "Bat and Ball Day" at Weeghman Park. A quarter of the gate receipts were donated to a fund to purchase baseball equipment for soldiers overseas.

MAY 30   Hippo Vaughn strikes out 12 batters in a 2–1 win over the Reds in the second game of a Memorial Day double–header at Weeghman Park. The Reds won the first game 9–6.

With World War I raging in Europe, Memorial Day should have been one for peaceful reflection, but this one was an exception. Rube Bressler of the Reds lifted a high pop near the plate, that was missed by Cubs catcher Bill Killefer. The ball landed in fair territory, then bounded foul. Greasy Neale of Cincinnati was in the on–deck circle and argued that Killefer touched the ball. The two exchanged words, and Neale punched the catcher. Killefer hit the ground, and Neale leaped upon him and continued to pummel him until pulled away by Hippo Vaughn. Greasy was dragged off the field by his teammates.

JUNE 6   The Cubs take over first place with a 3–0 win over the Phillies in Philadelphia.

Chicago remained in the top spot for the remainder of the season. It was a team without any spectacular stars, winning with a tremendous pitching staff led by Hippo Vaughn, Lefty Tyler, and Claude Hendrix, a team concept, no glaring weakness, the avoidance of major injuries to key regulars, and several batters enjoying career seasons, including Fred Merkle, Charlie Hollocher, Max Flack, and Les Mann. Despite the loss of Grover Alexander, the Cubs were also hurt less by the military draft than the other pennant contenders.

JUNE 11   The Cubs record their ninth win in a row with a 5–3 decision over the Giants in New York. The victory gave the Cubs a record of 31–12.

JUNE 12   Lefty Tyler pitches his second consecutive two–hitter, but loses 1–0 to the Giants in New York. The only run came on a fluke homer. In the first inning, George Burns hit a grounder in right field, but Max Flack slipped on the wet grass and the ball rolled all the way to the fence to allow Burns to round the bases for an inside–the–park homer.

JUNE 19   Phil Douglas pitches the Cubs to a 1–0 win over the Pirates in Pittsburgh.

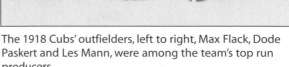

The 1918 Cubs' outfielders, left to right, Max Flack, Dode Paskert and Les Mann, were among the team's top run producers.

JUNE 26   Hippo Vaughn pitches the Cubs to a 1–0 victory over the Cardinals at Weeghman Park. Les Mann drove in the lone run of the game with a double in the first inning.

JULY 4   The Cubs win both ends of a double–header by 1–0 scores against the Cardinals in St. Louis. The first game went ten innings, with Lefty Tyler pitching the shutout. Charlie Deal drove in the winning run with a single. Claude Hendrix hurled the second game whitewashing.

Hendrix had a record of 20–7 for the Cubs in 1918. Hippo Vaughn, Lefty Tyler, and Hendrix had a combined record of 61–25 during the season.

JULY 6   Hippo Vaughn is the whole show in a twelve–inning, 1–0 win over the Giants at Weeghman Park. Vaughn pitched a complete game shutout and drove in the winning run of the game with a walk–off single.

With many young men in the military, the Cubs employed female ushers for the first time in 1918.

JULY 11   Phil Douglas wins both games of a double–header against the Braves at Weeghman Park. Douglas pitched two innings of relief in the first game, won 4–3 in ten innings by the Cubs. In the second game, Douglas pitched a complete game for a 3–2 victory.

Before and during the game, a corps of federal agents guarded the gates of Weeghman Park and every attendee of draft age was forced to show his registration card. A number without cards were held for investigation.

JULY 17   The Cubs defeat the Phillies 2–1 in a marathon twenty–one–inning game at Weeghman Park. Lefty Tyler pitched a complete game, as did Milt Watson of the Phils. The Cubs scored in the first inning, and the Phillies tied it 1–1 in the fourth. For 16 consecutive innings, from the fifth through the twentieth, neither Tyler nor Watson allowed a run. In the twenty–first, Turner Barber pinch–hit for Rollie Zeider and singled. Watson hit Bill Killefer with a pitch, and Bill McCabe, batting for Tyler, beat out a bunt to load the bases. Max Flack then singled, his fifth hit of the game, to end the contest.

AUGUST 1   Hippo Vaughn pitches a one–hitter to down the Giants at the Polo Grounds. The only New York hit was a single by ex–Cub Heinie Zimmerman in the second inning.

On the same day, the National Commission, baseball's governing body, announced that the 1918 season will end on September 2, in order to comply with a draft order issued by the federal government requiring all men of draft age to either enter military service or find a war–related job. Players participating in the World Series received an extension until September 15.

AUGUST 2   The Cubs pound the Giants 11–1 in New York.

AUGUST 13   Between games of a double–header against the Pirates at Weeghman Park, a group of 500 soldiers from Camp Cody in New Mexico, headquartered temporarily in Chicago, entertain the crowd singing. A collection amounting to $182.50 was taken up to purchase cigarettes for the soldiers. The Cubs won the first game 2–1, and lost the second 7–2.

AUGUST 17   The Cubs inflict two shutouts on the Phillies during a double–header at Weeghman Park. Claude Hendrix pitched the first game and Lefty Tyler the second. Charlie Hollocher ran his hitting steak to 20 games during the twinbill.

Hollocher was the Cubs' top hitter in 1918 as a 22–year–old rookie shortstop, batting .316 and leading the league in hits with 161. The promise of a long and prosperous career was ruined by a weird succession of injuries and illnesses. Hollocher played his last game in 1924.

AUGUST 23   The two–run rally in the ninth inning beats the Giants 3–2 at Weeghman Park. A bases–loaded double by Bob O'Farrell drove in both runs.

AUGUST 24   Bill Killefer foils an attempt at an intentional walk during a 3–1 win over the Dodgers in the second game of a double–header at Weeghman Park. With the score 1–1 in the seventh inning, Killefer threw his bat at ball four issued by Larry Cheney and rifled a single into right field, scoring a run from third base. The Cubs won the first game 8–3.

AUGUST 29   The Cubs clinch the pennant with a 1–0 and 6–4 double–header sweep of the Reds at Weeghman Park. Lefty Tyler pitched the first–game shutout. Bill Killefer drove in the lone run of the game with a single in the seventh inning. Claude Hendrix picked up his 20th win of the season in the second game.

The Cubs met the Boston Red Sox in the 1918 World Series. Boston was a dominant team during the 1910s, claiming the world championship in 1912, 1915 and 1916. The Red Sox in 1918 were 75–51 and won the AL pennant by 2½ games. The key to Boston's season was the conversion of Babe Ruth from a pitcher into an outfielder. Ruth still took his regular turn in the pitching rotation, however, and seldom played the outfield when the opposition started a left–handed pitcher. To neutralize Ruth and the other left–handed batters in the Red Sox batting order, Fred Mitchell used only two pitchers, southpaws Hippo Vaughn and Lefty Tyler, as starting pitchers in the Series. Each made three starts in the Series. Ruth started only two games in the Series, both as a pitcher.
      The games in Chicago were played at Comiskey Park, instead of Weeghman Park, a decision that would be unthinkable today. The stands at the Cubs' ballpark had room for only about 16,000 fans, while Comiskey could comfortably hold twice that many. None of the games were sellouts, however, as the war mitigated interest in baseball.

SEPTEMBER 5   In game one of the 1918 World Series, the Red Sox beat the Cubs 1–0 before 19,274 at Comiskey Park. Babe Ruth pitched a complete game six–hitter. The losing pitcher was Hippo Vaughn, who also yielded only six hits. The lone run of the game was scored in the fourth inning on a single by Stuffy McInnis. The game was marked by a fight precipitated when Red Sox coach Heinie Wagner took exception to insults by Vaughn and charged the Cubs' dugout. In game two, Wagner and Vaughn fought again, and Cubs outfielder Les Mann and Sox pitcher Joe Bush also exchanged punches.

Today, flyovers of military aircraft are commonplace before important outdoor sporting events such as the World Series. The first flyover at a World Series game took place before game one in 1918 when sixty Army airplanes flew over the field in military formation. It was only fifteen years after the Wright Brothers' first successful flight.

SEPTEMBER 6 In game two, Lefty Tyler defeats the Red Sox 3–1 before 20,040 at Comiskey Park. Tyler also drove in two runs with a second–inning single off Joe Bush, giving the Cubs a 3–0 lead.

Because of the war–shortened season, the 1918 World Series was played earlier than any other in history. Ironically, if the Series had been played during its normal period in early October, it might have been canceled or postponed due to a flu epidemic. From late September through November, a virulent form of flu struck the nation. Public gatherings in many cities, including Chicago and Boston, were banned by health officials. Estimates are that 20 to 25 percent of the nation's population was struck by the flu. The epidemic caused between 400,000 and 500,000 deaths in the United States and 20 million worldwide.

SEPTEMBER 7 The Red Sox win game three 2–1 in front of 27,054 at Comiskey Park. Hippo Vaughn, pitching on one day of rest, was the losing pitcher. An Everett Scott single in the fourth inning gave the Red Sox a 2–0 lead. In the Cubs half of the inning, Boston left fielder George Whiteman robbed Dode Paskert of a home run with a circus catch. In the bottom of the ninth with two out, Charlie Pick of the Cubs was out on an ill–advised attempt to score from second base on a passed ball. With Turner Barber batting, Boston pitcher Carl Mays shot a pitch past catcher Wally Schang that rolled twenty feet behind the plate. Pick darted for third. Schang made a quick recovery but threw high to third baseman Fred Thomas, who got a glove on the ball and knocked it a few feet into foul territory. Pick tried for home, but was out on a perfect throw from Thomas to Schang.

Fred Merkle appeared in five World Series in eight years and was on the losing end of all five. He played for the Giants in 1911, 1912, and 1913, the Dodgers in 1916 and the Cubs in 1918.

SEPTEMBER 9 After a day off for travel, the Red Sox take a three–games–to–one lead in the Series with a 3–2 win over the Cubs at Fenway Park. Babe Ruth was the winning pitcher. He also contributed with his bat, driving in two runs in the fourth with a triple. In addition, Ruth extended a streak of World Series scoreless pitching, which began in 1916, to 29 ⅔ innings. It ended when the Cubs scored twice in the eighth inning to tie the score 2–2. Boston scored the winning run in the eighth on a single, a passed ball, and an error off Phil Douglas. Cubs outfielder Max Flack became the only player in World Series history to be picked off base twice in a game. Flack led off the game with a single but was picked off when catcher Sam Agnew threw to first baseman Stuffy McInnis for the putout. Flack was nailed again in the fourth inning while on second base when Ruth wheeled and fired to shortstop Everett Scott.

The 1918 World Series is the last one in which neither team hit a home run. The only other years in which there were no home runs were in 1905, 1906, and 1907.

SEPTEMBER 10 The Cubs stay alive in the World Series by defeating the Red Sox 3–0 in game five, as Hippo Vaughn pitches a five–hit shutout in Boston. It was Vaughn's third start in six days. Charlie Hollocher collected three hits in three at–bats, stole a base, and scored two of the three runs.

The game was delayed for an hour because players on both teams discussed going on strike for a larger share of the proceeds from the gate.

The World Series Strike

The 1918 World Series between the Cubs and the Red Sox was an unusual one. It began on September 5 because of a federal government edict which ended the regular season because of World War I. Major leaguers either had to enlist or take war-related jobs. And, the Series almost ended early because prior to the fifth game on September 10 at Fenway Park, players from both teams threatened to strike because the winners' and losers' share of the gate receipts had been drastically reduced.

The players' share in 1918 was less than one-third of what it had been in previous years for a variety of reasons. Attendance at the games was lower than normal because of reduced interest in the games with American troops engaged in heavy fighting in France. Ticket prices were decreased, and baseball earmarked part of the gate money for wartime charities, such as the Red Cross. Also, the second-, third-, and fourth- place clubs received part of the loot for the first time. Much less money had to be split up among many more hands.

Game five was delayed for more than an hour while negotiations were held between representatives of the players and the National Commission, which was baseball's governing body and consisted of Reds President Garry Herrmann, American League President Ban Johnson and National League President John Heydler. Red Sox outfielder Harry Hooper was the official spokesman for the players. The players wanted a guarantee of $2,000 to the winning team and $1,400 to the losing club, figures that were only a little more than half of what the participants in the 1917 Fall Classic received. When this offer was turned down, the players were willing to compromise for $1,500 and $1,000, but the three members of the National Commission, who according to Hooper were all intoxicated, were still unmoved. Boston mayor John F. Fitzgerald, grandfather of future president John F. Kennedy, pleaded with both sides for conciliation. The crowd of 24,694 grew restless and repeated cries of "play ball." Extra police were summoned to the ballpark because of fears that there might be a riot should the contest be called off. Four mounted policemen rode onto the field.

The players backed off on their demands and threats to strike for fear of appearing greedy while the country was fighting a war, particularly in light of the fact that hundreds of wounded soldiers and sailors were seated in the grandstand. Because of the backlash against the players, only 15,238 fans showed up the following day for game six, which the Sox won 2–1 to take the world championship four games to two.

The Red Sox's winning share in 1918 was only $1,103 per player, compared to winning shares of $3,669 in 1917. The Cubs share was just $671, in contrast to $2,442 for the losing Giants the previous season. In 1919, the winning and losing shares were $5,207 and $3,254, respectively.

At the time, players who participated on the winning side in the World Series were given commemorative emblems in the form of stick pins as gifts. The owners withheld the pins from the Red Sox in 1918 in retaliation for the threatened strike. In 1993, the Red Sox bestowed the emblems to the descendants of the 1918 Red Sox in a ceremony at Fenway Park.

SEPTEMBER 11   The Red Sox win the world championship by defeating the Cubs in game six by a 2–1 score in Boston. Carl Mays was the winning pitcher with a three-hitter. Lefty Tyler, making his third start in six days, took the loss. The Red Sox scored both of their runs in the third inning on an error by Max Flack when the outfielder dropped a liner off the bat of George Whiteman with two out and Boston runners on second and third. The Cubs came back with a run in the fourth, but failed to collect a hit over the final five innings.

Despite pitching on short rest, Vaughn and Tyler combined to allow only eight runs in fifty innings of pitching. An anemic offense, which scored only ten runs in six games, cost the Cubs a world championship.

NOVEMBER 11   An armistice is signed with Germany ending World War I.

When the 1918 World Series came to a close, it appeared that there would be no baseball in 1919 because the end of the war was nowhere in sight. But a series of victories by the Allies, led by the United States, Great Britain, and France, led to a conclusion of the war by November 1918. Owners hastily made plans for the 1919 season, but due to the late start in preparing for the campaign and the anticipation of a poor year at the gate, baseball executives shortened the season to 140 games. It was a decision that officials came to regret, as attendance reached record levels in 1919.

NOVEMBER 19   Charles Weeghman steps down as president of the Cubs and is replaced by manager Fred Mitchell.

Weeghman said publicly that he needed to spend more time attending to his chain of restaurants. He soon sold his shares in the Cubs to William Wrigley Jr. who became the majority owner in the Cubs.

1919   Cubs

Season in a Sentence

A punchless offense dooms the defending National League champion Cubs to a third-place finish.

Finish • Won • Lost • Pct • GB

Third   75   65   .536   21.0

Manager

Fred Mitchell

Stats

Stats	Cubs	NL	Rank
Batting Avg:	.256	.258	4
On-Base Pct:	.308	.311	4
Slugging Pct:	.332	.337	5
Home Runs:	21		5
Stolen Bases:	150		3
ERA:	2.21	2.91	1
Fielding Avg:	.969	.967	3
Runs Scored:	454		8
Runs Allowed:	407		2

Starting Lineup

Bill Killefer, c
Fred Merkle, 1b
Charlie Pick, 2b
Charlie Deal, 3b
Charlie Hollocher, ss
Les Mann, lf
Dode Paskert, cf
Max Flack, rf
Lee Magee, cf
Turner Barber, lf
Buck Herzog, 2b

Pitchers

Hippo Vaughn, sp
Grover Alexander, sp
Claude Hendrix, sp
Phil Douglas, sp
Speed Martin, rp-sp
Paul Carter, rp
Sweetbreads Bailey, rp

Attendance

424,430 (third in NL)

Club Leaders

Batting Avg:	Flack	.294
On-Base Pct:	Hollocher	.347
Slugging Pct:	Flack	.392
Home Runs:	Flack	6
RBI:	Merkle	62
Runs:	Flack	71
Stolen Bases:	Merkle	20
Wins:	Vaughn	21
Strikeouts:	Vaughn	141
ERA:	Alexander	172
Saves:	Martin	2

APRIL 23   The opening game of the season, scheduled against the Pirates in Chicago, is post-poned by rain.

With Charles Weeghman no longer president of the Cubs, the ballpark at Clark and Addison ceased to be known as Weeghman Park, and beginning in 1919, the facility was called Cubs Park.

APRIL 24   The Cubs win the first game of the 1919 season, 5–1 before 8,000 at Cubs Park. Hippo Vaughn pitched the complete game victory. All five Chicago runs were scored in the second inning.

Vaughn was 21–14 in 1919, his fifth season of 20 wins or more with the Cubs. He had a 1.79 ERA, 25 complete games, and led the league in innings pitched (306⅔) and strikeouts (141).

MAY 5   Trailing the Reds 6–0 in Cincinnati, the Cubs stage an incredible rally to score six runs in the ninth inning and send the game into extra innings. The Cubs won the game 7–6 with a run in the twelfth.

JUNE 2   The Cubs trade Pete Kilduff to the Dodgers for Lee Magee.

Magee hit .292 in 79 games for the Cubs in 1919, but was released in February 1920 when the Cubs learned that Magee was accused of throwing games in a conspiracy with gamblers while playing with the Reds in 1918 (see June 9, 1920).

JUNE 6   The Cubs honor Braves catcher Hank Gowdy before a 1–0 Boston win at Cubs Park. Gowdy was the first professional baseball player to enlist in the military during World War I. He was presented with a bouquet of American Beauty roses by a delegation of young ladies from a physical culture school.

Charlie Hollocher missed three weeks in June with an injured thumb. He was slated to play in the starting lineup on June 28, but while taking batting prac-tice he was hit in the head by a line drive and knocked unconscious, which put him out for another two weeks. In a game on July 12, Hollocher was running between second and third when he was struck in the neck by a batted ball. He hit .270 for the Cubs in 1919.

JUNE 30   Beer is sold for the last time at Cubs Park until 1933 as Prohibition takes effect in the state of Illinois.

Lefty Tyler pitched only six games in 1919 because of a sore shoulder after a 19–9 record with 269⅔ innings in the war–shortened 1918 season, plus another 23 innings in the World Series. The Cubs sent him to the Mayo Clinic, where he was declared to be in perfect health except for very bad teeth. Tyler had all but three of his teeth extracted, but was never again the same pitcher, and was out of the majors before the end of the 1921 season.

JULY 6   Fred Mitchell resigns as president of the Cubs and is replaced by William Veeck, Sr. Mitchell said that he wanted to devote all of his energies to managing the team on the field.

Veeck was a writer for the CHICAGO AMERICAN until 1918 under the pen name Bill Bailey. He had been one of the many critics of the way the Cubs were operating. Wrigley told Veeck that if he thought he could do better, he should take over the club and offered Veeck a spot as the club's vice president. Veeck accepted and ran the club in the manner of a modern day general manager. Veeck remained as Cubs president from 1919 until his death in 1933.

JULY 23   The Cubs inflict a double blanking on the Dodgers in Brooklyn. The Cubs won the first game 3–0 in eleven innings behind a complete game by Grover Alexander. Charlie Deal drove in all three runs with a bases–loaded double. Phil Douglas pitched the second game, winning 6–0.

The next day, the Cubs traded Douglas to the Giants for Dave Robertson. When sober, Douglas was an effective pitcher but was too often out of condition after one of his many drinking escapades. In 1922, he was suspended for life for writing a letter to ex–Cub teammate Les Mann, then with the Cardinals. Douglas made an ambiguous offer to quit the Giants in the heat of the 1922 pennant in return for "an inducement" from the Cardinals. Robertson gave the Cubs one solid season, with a .300 average and 10 homers in 1920.

JULY 27   Race riots erupt in Chicago after an African–American youngster drifts into the white section of the segregated 29th Street Beach. The youngster drowned after whites threw rocks at him. A week of unrest resulted in the deaths of forty people.

AUGUST 2   With the riots still raging on the South Side, the Cubs lose a double–header at Cubs Park 2–1 in fourteen innings and 4–1 in ten. The second game was interrupted when fans threw bottles at umpire Bill Byron because of decisions made against the Cubs. After the contest, several policemen went onto the field to escort Byron to his dressing room.

On the same day, the Cubs traded Les Mann and Charlie Pick to the Braves for Buck Herzog.

AUGUST 6   The Braves beat the Cubs 2–0 at Cubs Park when Boston pitcher Ray Keating's drive bounces through the hole in the wire fence in front of the bleachers in center field for a home run with a man on base against Grover Alexander. It was Keating's only career homer in 247 at–bats over seven seasons.

AUGUST 14   The Cubs split a double–header against the Dodgers in Brooklyn, winning 2–0 and losing 1–0. The two games were played in just two hours and twenty minutes, the shortest double–header, by time, in National League history.

SEPTEMBER 10 The Giants take a controversial 7–2 win over the Cubs in New York.

During the first inning, Giants third baseman Heinie Zimmerman told pitcher Fred Toney that it would be worth his while not to bear down against the Cubs. Toney relayed the information to manager John McGraw and asked to be taken out of the game. Immediately after the contest, Zimmerman was kicked off the team and never played another big league game.

SEPTEMBER 12   Fred Merkle hits a drive that rolls through a hole in the left field corner for a fluke home run, and participates in a triple play with shortstop Charlie Hollocher to lead the Cubs to a 3–1 win over the Dodgers in the first game of a double–header at Cubs Park. The Cubs lost the second game 5–4.

SEPTEMBER 20   Hippo Vaughn wins his 21st game of the season with a 2–1 decision over the Braves in the first game of a double–header at Cubs Park. The Cubs also won the second game 4–3.

SEPTEMBER 21   The Cubs defeat the Braves 3–0 in a game at Cubs Park that lasts only 58 minutes, the shortest nine–inning game, by time, in Cubs history.

First baseman Fred Merkle led the Cubs in RBIs in 1918 and 1919.

Oddly, it wasn't the shortest game in the majors that day. The Dodgers beat the Reds 3–1 in Cincinnati in 55 minutes. The shortest game in major league history took place seven days later on September 28, when the Giants defeated the Phillies 6–1 in 51 minutes.

OCTOBER 9   The 1919 World Series comes to a conclusion, with the White Sox losing, five games to three, to the Reds amid suspicions that the Sox threw some of the games in collusion with gamblers.

THE STATE OF THE CUBS

The Cubs drifted aimlessly through the early part of the 1920s, and thudded into last place in 1925 under three different managers. After the disastrous season ended, the Cubs hired Joe McCarthy as manager. The club leaped four places to fourth in McCarthy's first season, and in 1929, the Cubs won the National League pennant. Overall, the Cubs had a record of 807–728 during the 1920s, for a winning percentage of .526. It was the fourth best won–lost mark in the eight–team NL, trailing, in order, the New York Giants, Pittsburgh Pirates and St. Louis Cardinals. The Giants won the pennant four consecutive seasons beginning in 1921. Other league championships were won by the Brooklyn Dodgers (1920), the Pirates (1925 and 1927) and the Cardinals (1926 and 1928).

THE BEST TEAM

The 1929 club had a record of 98–54 and won the NL pennant by 10 ½ games before losing the World Series to the Philadelphia Athletics.

THE WORST TEAM

By winning percentage, the worst team of the 1920s was the 1921 club, which was 64–89 and finished in seventh place. The 1925 team won 68 games, but wound up in last place.

THE BEST MOMENT

The Cubs won the 1929 pennant, the first for the franchise in 11 years.

THE WORST MOMENT

Cubs president Bill Veeck, Sr. received a telegram on August 31, 1920, claiming that the Cubs were throwing the game that day against the Phillies in collusion with gamblers.

THE ALL–DECADE TEAM • YEARS WITH CUBS

Gabby Hartnett, c	1922–1940
Charlie Grimm, 1b	1925–36
Rogers Hornsby, 2b	1929–32
Barney Friberg, 3b	1919–25
Charlie Hollocher, ss	1918–24
Riggs Stephenson, lf	1926–34
Hack Wilson, cf	1926–31
Cliff Heathcote, rf	1922–30
Grover Alexander, p	1918–26
Guy Bush, p	1923–34
Charlie Root, p	1926–41
Sheriff Blake, p	1924–31

With the exception of Friberg, Hollocher and Alexander, each of the members of the 1920s All–Decade Team played on the 1929 pennant winner. Other outstanding Cubs players of the decade included catcher Bob O'Farrell (1915–25; 1935), second baseman Sparky Adams (1922–27), first baseman Ray Grimes (1921–24), center fielder Jigger Statz (1922–25), and pitcher Vic Aldridge (1917–18; 1922–24).

THE DECADE LEADERS

Batting Avg:	Stephenson	.342
On–Base Pct:	Stephenson	.419
Slugging Pct:	Wilson	.582
Home Runs:	Wilson	121
RBI:	Wilson	517
Runs:	Wilson	440
Stolen Bases:	Heathcote	117
Wins:	Alexander	110
Strikeouts:	Charlie Root	518
ERA:	Alexander	3.02
Saves:	Bush	18

THE HOME FIELD

At the start of the decade, present–day Wrigley Field was known as Cubs Park and had changed little since it opened as Weeghman Park in 1914. It had only a single deck that held about 16,000 fans. The ballpark was remodeled between the 1922 and 1923 seasons, as the stands were moved back about sixty feet closer to the corner of Clark and Addison. Four years later, the upper deck was added, expanding capacity to 38,396, and the ballpark was renamed Wrigley Field. In 1927, the Cubs became the first team in the National League to draw more than one million fans in a season. In 1929, attendance was 1,485,166, a major league record that stood until it was broken by the Yankees in 1946, and a club record until the Cubs attracted 1,674,993 to Wrigley Field in 1969.

THE GAME YOU WISH YOU HAD SEEN

The Cubs and the Phillies teamed up for the highest-scoring game in major league history. Played in Chicago on August 25, 1922, the Cubs won 26–23.

THE WAY THE GAME WAS PLAYED

Rule changes in 1920 and the emergence of Babe Ruth as a star changed baseball from a low–scoring defensive affair to a high–scoring offensive carnival. This was the first decade that baseball embraced the home run. Teams went from averaging 3.5 runs a game in 1917 to 5.0 runs a game in 1922 to 5.7 per game in 1930. Team batting averages in the NL ballooned from .249 in 1917 to .292 in 1922 and .303 in 1930. Not surprisingly, team ERAs jumped nearly two runs. The 1928 season was the first in National League history in which there were more home runs than stolen bases. There wouldn't be another season in which the number of steals exceeded the number of homers in the NL until 1975. Pitchers completed less than half of their starts in the NL in 1922, the first time that happened, as relief pitching continued to gain in importance.

MANAGEMENT

The Wrigley–Veeck team headed the club during the entire decade, with William Wrigle, Jr. owning the club and William Veeck Sr. as club president. Veeck ran the day–to–day operation of the Cubs. There was a merry–go–round of managers with Fred Mitchell, Johnny Evers, Bill Killefer, Rabbit Maranville and George Gibson running the club on the field until Joe McCarthy took over in 1926.

THE BEST PLAYER MOVE

The best move was the purchase of Gabby Hartnett from Worcester of the Eastern League in 1921. The best trade brought Kiki Cuyler from the Pirates on November 27, 1928, for Sparky Adams and Pete Scott.

THE WORST PLAYER MOVE

The Cubs sold Grover Alexander to the Cardinals on waivers on June 22, 1926. The move may have cost the Cubs the pennant in 1928.

1920s

1920   Cubs

Season in a Sentence

Grover Alexander and Hippo Vaughn combine for 46 wins, but the Cubs fall to fifth place amid allegations that some Cubs players may have been involved in throwing games in conjunction with gamblers.

Finish • Won • Lost • Pct • GB

Fifth   75   79   .487   18.0

Manager

Fred Mitchell

Stats

Stats	Cubs	NL	Rank
Batting Avg:	.264	.270	5
On–Base Pct:	.326	.322	4
Slugging Pct:	.354	.357	5
Home Runs:	34		3
Stolen Bases:	115		5
ERA:	3.27	3.13	5
Fielding Avg:	.965	.966	5
Runs Scored:	619		5
Runs Allowed:	635		5

Starting Lineup

Bob O'Farrell, c
Fred Merkle, 1b
Zeb Terry, 2b–ss
Charlie Deal, 3b
Charlie Hollocher, ss
Dave Robertson, lf
Dode Paskert, cf
Max Flack, rf
Turner Barber, 1b
Buck Herzog, 2b–3b
Bill Killefer, c
Babe Twombly, rf–cf

Pitchers

Grover Alexander, sp
Hippo Vaughn, sp
Lefty Tyler, sp
Claude Hendrix, sp
Speed Martin, rp–sp
Paul Carter, rp

Attendance

424,430 (fourth in NL)

Club Leaders

Batting Avg:	Flack	.302
On–Base Pct:	Flack	.373
Slugging Pct:	Robertson	.462
Home Runs:	Robertson	10
RBI:	Robertson	75
Runs:	Flack	85
Stolen Bases:	Hollocher	20
Wins:	Alexander	27
Strikeouts:	Alexander	173
ERA:	Alexander	1.91
Saves:	Alexander	5

FEBRUARY 9   Baseball's rules committee adopts new regulations that usher in the era of the lively ball. The changes were spurred in part by the owners' recognition of the positive impact of Babe Ruth upon the game. Ruth clubbed a then–record 29 home runs for the Red Sox in 1919 and helped the American League set an all–time attendance record. Baseball's rules committee adopted a more–lively ball, agreed to keep a fresh ball in play at all times, and banned pitchers from using any foreign substances to deface a ball. These included paraffin, resin, powder, emery boards, files, and saliva.

APRIL 14   The Reds defeat the Cubs 7–3 on Opening Day in Cincinnati.

APRIL 22   In the home opener, the Cubs defeat the Reds 4–3 in eleven innings before 10,000 on a soggy field at Cubs Park. Turner Barber's double drove in Buck Herzog with the winning run. Barber's drive was aided by a fierce wind that blew from third base into right field.

              Before the game, a contingent of Marines and players from both teams marched around the field and then out to the flagpole to raise the Stars and Stripes.

MAY 24   Responding to a request by Cubs officials, policemen and private detectives disguised as soldiers, farmers, and bootblacks raid the bleachers at Cubs Park and arrest forty–seven fans for gambling during a 6–0 win over the Phillies.

MAY 28   The Cubs take first place with a 6–2 and 7–0 sweep of the Cardinals at Cubs Park.

MAY 31   Grover Alexander hits a two–out, walk–off homer to beat the Reds 3–2 in the first game of a double–header at Cubs Park. Alexander also drove in a run in the third inning with a single. It was his first homer since 1917. The victory was Alexander's eleventh in a row, running his season record to 11–2, and was the ninth in succession for the Cubs.

Grover Cleveland Alexander led the league in wins, ERA, and strikeouts in 1920, one of the best seasons ever for a Cubs pitcher.

The Cubs nine–game winning ended in the nightcap with a 4–2 loss. That defeat started a ten–game losing streak which knocked Chicago out of first place. The long losing streak ended on June 12 with an 8–1 victory against the Braves in Boston. The victory began which began a six–game winning streak.

JUNE 9   Lee Magee loses his suit against the Cubs in a jury trial in Cincinnati. He had charged that he was released without just cause the previous February and wanted to be paid his 1920 salary of $9,500. The Cubs tore up his contract after learning of Magee's involvement in throwing a game between the Reds and Braves on July 25, 1918, while a member of the Reds. While on the witness stand, he admitted to having bet on the contest. Magee never played in another big league game.

JUNE 16   Hippo Vaughn pitches the Cubs to a 1–0 win over the Braves in Boston. A triple by Charlie Hollocher drove in the only run of the game in the eighth inning.

Vaughn had a record of 19–16 and an ERA of 2.54 in 301 innings in 1920.

JUNE 19   Bob O'Farrell's three–run homer in the twelfth inning beats the Dodgers 5–3 in Brooklyn.

JUNE 28   The Cubs score four runs in the ninth inning to beat the Pirates 5–4 in the second game of a double–header at Cubs Park. Zeb Terry drew a bases loaded walk from Elmer Ponder to score the winning run. The Cubs also won the first game 5–2.

Standing five–foot–eight and weighing 129 pounds, Terry hit .280 in 1920, his first season with the Cubs.

JUNE 30   Hippo Vaughn's one–hitter beats the Pirates 1–0 at Cubs Park. The only Pittsburgh hit was a single by Possum Whitted.

JULY 1   The Cubs win 1–0 for the second day in a row as Grover Alexander defeats the Reds in Cincinnati. Charlie Hollocher's triple in the first inning drove in the only run of the game.

In 1920, Alexander had one of the best seasons ever by a Cubs pitcher with a record of 27–14. He led the National League in wins, ERA (1.91), innings pitched (363⅓), complete games (33), games started (40), strikeouts (173), and strikeouts per nine innings (4.3). Alexander also pitched in six games in relief and earned a victory and five saves.

JULY 4   The Cubs play at Sportsman's Park in St. Louis for the first time, and lose 8–4 to the Cardinals.

The Cardinals played at Sportsman's Park from July 1, 1920, through May 8, 1966. The ballpark was renamed Busch Stadium in 1953. It was built in 1909 for the St. Louis Browns, who occupied the facility jointly with the Cardinals before moving to Baltimore as the Orioles in 1954. From 1893 through 1920, the Cardinals played at Robison Field.

JULY 7   During an 8–5 victory over the Cardinals in St. Louis, Cubs outfielder Dode Paskert tries to climb into the grandstand after engaging in an argument with two hecklers. Paskert stayed in the game, and the offending spectators were escorted from the grounds by police officers.

Charlie Hollocher had another bout with ill health in 1920. He was laid up at the start of the season by a growth on one of his hands that required an operation. In July, Hollocher underwent another operation for appendicitis and missed the remainder of the season.

JULY 14   The fans witness an eventful day at the ballpark as the Cubs lose 3–2 and 4–1 to the Dodgers at Cubs Park.

In the sixth inning of the first game, Ivy Olson of the Dodgers hit a dribbler down the third-base line that hopped into the stands and was ruled a home run by umpire Bill Klem. At the time, any ball which reached the stands at least 235 feet from home plate was a homer. The Cubs maintained the ball rolled out of bounds less than 235 feet from home, entitling Olson to just two bases. Klem asked for a tape measure, which showed that the ball rolled out 241 feet from the plate. Between games, Cubs pitcher Lefty Tyler put on his street clothes and went after a rooter who had been riding him through the first game. The offensive person was stationed directly in back of the Brooklyn bench, and Tyler gave him an invitation to step outside the ball yard and rearrange his face. Club secretary John Seys cooled Tyler off, and the fan was escorted to the elevated station by two policemen. To add to the general excitement, a visitor from Watertown, Wisconsin, lost his young son, and the park was in a turmoil until the lad was found.

JULY 23   Disgusted with his lack of fielding support, Hippo Vaughn walks off the mound in the top of the ninth inning with the Cubs leading the Phillies 6–3 at Cubs Park.

Paul Carter was forced to pitch without warming up, and the Phillies scored seven runs and won the game 10–7.

JULY 28   Hippo Vaughn starts both ends of a double–header against the Braves at Boston. Vaughn lasted only two innings in the first game after allowing six runs, as the Cubs lost 8–4. Hippo pitched a complete game in the nightcap to win 8–2.

AUGUST 15   Lefty Tyler pitches the Cubs to a 1–0 win over the Reds at Cubs Park. Dode Paskert's infield single in the sixth inning drove in the lone run of the game.

AUGUST 28   Two days after women are granted the right to vote with the passage of the nineteenth amendment, Grover Alexander pitches the Cubs to a 1–0 win over the Dodgers at Cubs Park. Zeb Terry drove in the only run of the game with a single in the third inning.

Grover Cleveland Alexander is the only player in major league history to be named after one president and to be portrayed by another in the movies. He was born in 1887 during the first of Grover Cleveland's first terms in office. Alexander was played by Ronald Reagan in the movie biography of his life titled THE WINNING TEAM, *which was released in 1952.*

AUGUST 31   Two hours before the Cubs–Phillies game at Cubs Park, Bill Veeck receives a telegram informing him of heavy betting on the Phillies in betting parlors in Detroit, Cleveland, and Cincinnati. The wire warned Veeck of rumors that the game was fixed. He replaced scheduled starting pitcher Claude Hendrix with Grover Alexander. The Cubs lost 3–0.

According to some reports, Hendrix had bet $5,000 on the Cubs to lose. The Cubs didn't play him for the remainder of the season, and he was released in February 1921. Hendrix never played in another major league game. Buck Herzog played in the 3–0 loss to the Phillies on August 31, but was implicated as one of those involved in the fix and was likewise benched for the rest of the 1920 season, and released during the following off–season (see September 7, 1920, and September 30, 1920).

SEPTEMBER 2   During the 1920 presidential election, the Cubs play an exhibition game in Marion, Ohio, the hometown of Republican Party candidate Warren Harding. In the morning, the Cubs were introduced to Harding on the front porch of the candidate's home in front of a large crowd which gathered on the lawn. Harding also attended the game later in the afternoon.

Harding won the election and served as president from 1921 until his death in 1923. Cubs owner William Wrigley Jr. was a prominent supporter of Harding, as was Albert Lasker, who owned the second largest block of stock in the Cubs. Lasker was a major backroom power in Republican Party politics and helped Harding secure the nomination at the 1920 national convention, which was held in Chicago, after the party was deadlocked over the choice of a candidate. Another minority shareholder in the Cubs was Harry Sinclair, an oil executive who purchased favorable leases on federal land for drilling purposes from Albert Fall, Harding's Secretary of the Interior. The incident became known as the Teapot Dome scandal, and Fall spent time in jail for his role in granting Sinclair the leases.

SEPTEMBER 7   The grand jury of Cook County convenes to investigate gambling in baseball. In addition to investigating the August 31 Phillies–Cubs game, presiding judge Charles McDonald recommended that the grand jury look at the 1919 White Sox–Reds World Series, won by Cincinnati, because of suspicions that the Sox may have thrown the games. The grand jury hearings began on September 22. There wasn't enough evidence to prosecute the Cubs players, and the grand jury focused their attention on the White Sox (see September 28, 1920).

SEPTEMBER 14   Dave Robertson collects five hits, including two doubles and a triple, in five at–bats to lead the Cubs to a 10–2 win over the Dodgers in Brooklyn.

SEPTEMBER 27   The Cubs are hammered 16–1 by the Cardinals at Cubs Park.

SEPTEMBER 28   The grand jury indicts eight White Sox players for conspiring to throw the 1919 World Series. The eight were immediately suspended by Sox owner Charles Comiskey (see August 2, 1921) and became known as the "Black Sox."

SEPTEMBER 30   Buck Herzog is stabbed three times following an exhibition game at Joliet, Illinois.

Herzog climbed into his automobile when an individual jumped on the running board and called the Cubs infielder a "crook," a reference to allegations that Herzog helped throw the game on August 31 in collusion with gamblers. Herzog leaped out of the car to fight with the man, and as the two were rolling in the dirt, one of the man's friends stabbed Herzog twice in the hand and once in the calf with a pen knife. Fortunately, Herzog wasn't seriously injured.

OCTOBER 1   The Cubs defeat the Cardinals 3–2 in seventeen innings at Cubs Park. Grover Alexander and Jesse Haines, two pitchers destined for the Hall of Fame, pitched complete games. Haines held the Cubs hitless for ten consecutive innings from the seventh through the sixteenth before losing the game in the seventeenth. The victory was Alexander's 27th of the 1920 season.

There was no Chicago City Series in 1920 because of the Black Sox scandal and the implication that Cubs players may have also been involved in throwing games.

OCTOBER 10   A National League Football game is played at Clark and Addison for the first time, as the Chicago Cardinals and the Chicago Tigers play to a 0–0 tie before 5,000 at Cubs Park.

The NFL was formed the previous September. The Tigers lasted only one season in the league. The Cardinals are the present–day Arizona Cardinals. The franchise played in Chicago from 1920 through 1959.

OCTOBER 28   The Cubs hire Johnny Evers as manager to replace Fred Mitchell.

Evers played in five World Series, four of them with the Cubs, and it was hoped that he would bring back the glory days. It didn't work. Evers was fired 98 games into the 1921 season when the club had a record of 42–56. Mitchell managed the Braves from 1921 through 1923 and coached at Harvard University from 1924 through 1939.

1921

Cubs

Season in a Sentence

Bringing back Johnny Evers fails to bring back a winning team, as the Cubs compile their worst winning percentage between 1901 and 1948.

Finish • Won • Lost • Pct • GB

Seventh   64   89   .416   30.0

Managers

Johnny Evers (42–56) and Bill Killefer (22–33)

Stats

Stats	Cubs	NL	Rank
Batting Avg:	.280	.289	7
On–Base Pct:	.339	.338	4
Slugging Pct:	.378	.397	7
Home Runs:	37		6 (tie)
Stolen Bases:	70		7
ERA:	4.39	3.78	7
Fielding Avg:	.974	.967	1
Runs Scored:	666		5
Runs Allowed:	773		7

Starting Lineup

Bob O'Farrell, c
Ray Grimes, 1b
Zeb Terry, 2b
Charlie Deal, 3b
Charlie Hollocher, ss
Turner Barber, lf
George Maisel, cf
Max Flack, rf
John Kelleher, 3b–2b
John Sullivan, lf
Babe Twombly, cf

Pitchers

Pete Alexander, sp
Speed Martin, sp
Virgil Cheeves, sp–rp
Buck Freeman, sp–rp
Hippo Vaughn, sp
Elmer Ponder, sp–rp
Lefty York, rp
Percy Jones, rp

Attendance

410,107 (fourth in NL)

Club Leaders

Batting Avg:	Grimes	.321
On–Base Pct:	Grimes	.406
Slugging Pct:	Grimes	.449
Home Runs:	Grimes	6
RBI:	Grimes	79
Runs:	Grimes	91
Stolen Bases:	Flack	17
	Maisel	17
Wins:	Alexander	15
Strikeouts:	Martin	86
ERA:	Alexander	3.39
Saves:	Freeman	3

APRIL 13   The Cubs open the season at home and defeat the Cardinals 5–2 before 20,000 at Cubs Park. Bob O'Farrell contributed a homer, and Grover Alexander was the winning pitcher. Among those in attendance was Kenesaw Landis, who became commissioner of baseball the previous November. Landis remained commissioner until his death in 1944 and maintained his office in Chicago.

Alexander didn't appear in another game until May 10, as he was still feeling the effects of pitching 363⅓ innings the previous season. In early June, Alexander was sent to Youngstown, Ohio, to see James "Bonesetter" Reese, an unschooled former Welsh coal miner who was so skillful as a medical practitioner that the Ohio legislature gave him a special certificate to practice medicine in the state. At a cost of $10, a ligament in Alexander's elbow was snapped back into place. The pitcher finished the season with a 15–13 record and a 3.39 ERA.

APRIL 19   Cubs pitcher Oscar Fuhr gives up nine runs in the ninth inning of a 14–2 loss to the Pirates at Cubs Park.

The game was Fuhr's major league debut and the only contest he played as a member of the Cubs. He didn't appear in another big league game until 1924, when he played for the Red Sox.

MAY 11   The Cubs collect 21 hits and outslug the Phillies 19–8 on a cold and windy day in Philadelphia. Chicago scored seven runs in the seventh inning.

JUNE 12   The Cubs collect 22 hits, but lose 12–9 in ten innings against the Braves at Cubs Park.

JUNE 19   The Giants score nine runs in the first inning, enough for a 9–1 win over the Cubs at Cubs Park.

The starting pitcher in the game was Hippo Vaughn. From 1914 through 1920, Vaughn had a record of 143–94 and an earned run average of just 2.16 for the Cubs, but his long run of success came to a crashing halt in 1921, when he was 3–11 with a 6.01 ERA. Vaughn was suspended for 30 days for insubordination by Johnny Evers in July and never pitched another big league game. Vaughn pitched semi–pro ball in the Chicago area for another fourteen years, however, before finally giving up the game at the age of 47.

JUNE 28   Down 6–1, the Cubs rally to beat the Pirates 8–6 at Cubs Park in the second game of a double–header at Cubs Park. The Cubs also won the first game 2–1.

Charlie Hollocher broke his nose when a grounder took a bad hop in the first game. In the second contest, a drive off the bat of Walter Schmidt hit Cubs pitcher Buck Freeman in the right temple.

JULY 1   The Cubs trade Dave Robertson to the Pirates for Elmer Ponder.

JULY 20   It's feast or famine for the Cubs in a double–header against the Phillies in Philadelphia, with a 10–0 win in the first game and an 8–0 loss in the second.

AUGUST 2   A Chicago grand jury brings in a verdict of not guilty against the eight White Sox player accused of throwing the 1919 World Series. Despite the verdict, commissioner Kenesaw Landis banned all eight from baseball for life.

AUGUST 3   The Cubs fire Johnny Evers as manager and hire Bill Killefer.

Killefer was 33 years old. The 1921 season was his last as a player, and he remained as manager of the Cubs until 1925. Evers had another one–year stint as a manager with the White Sox in 1924.

SEPTEMBER 14   The Cubs collect 20 hits and rout the Phillies 10–0 at Cubs Park.

SEPTEMBER 18   The Cubs sweep a double–header 1–0 and 5–1 over the Dodgers at Cubs Park. Virgil Cheeves pitched the first game shutout.

SEPTEMBER 23   The Cubs score an easy 13–5 win over the Braves at Cubs Park.

SEPTEMBER 25   Cubs rookie outfielder Red Thomas stars in a double–header against the Braves at Cubs Park. Thomas hit a two–run walk–off single in the twelfth inning of the first game to lift Chicago to a 4–3 win. In the second game, Thomas started a twelfth–inning rally with a double and scored the winning run in a 7–6 victory.

The major league career of Red Thomas lasted only eight games, in which he hit .267 in 30 at–bats.

OCTOBER 2   In the final game of the season, the Cubs score seven runs in the third inning to account for all of the runs in a 7–0 win over the Reds in a contest shortened to five innings by darkness. The Cubs also won the first game 7–5 in twelve innings.

OCTOBER 5   The Chicago City Series starts with a 2–0 White Sox win over the Cubs before 16,000 at Comiskey Park. The White Sox won all five games in the best–of–nine series.

1922

Season in a Sentence

In his first full season as manager, Bill Killefer has the Cubs in contention for the pennant in late August as the club improves in all facets of the game.

Finish • Won • Lost • Pct • GB

Fourth   80   74   .519   13.0

Manager

Bill Killefer

Stats

Stats	Cubs	NL	Rank
Batting Avg:	.293	.292	5
On–Base Pct:	.359	.348	3
Slugging Pct:	.390	.404	7
Home Runs:	42		7
Stolen Bases:	97		4
ERA:	4.34	4.10	5
Fielding Avg:	.968	.967	4
Runs Scored:	771		4
Runs Allowed:	808		5

Starting Lineup

Bob O'Farrell, c
Ray Grimes, 1b
Zeb Terry, 2b
Marty Krug, 3b
Charlie Hollocher, ss
Hack Miller, lf
Jigger Statz, cf
Bernie Friberg, rf
Cliff Heathcote, rf–cf
Turner Barber, lf–rf
John Kelleher, 3b
Marty Callaghan, rf

Pitchers

Vic Aldridge, sp
Grover Alexander, sp
Virgil Cheeves, sp–rp
Percy Jones, sp–rp
Tiny Osborne, rp–sp
Tony Kaufmann, rp
George Stueland, rp

Attendance

542,283 (second in NL)

Club Leaders

Batting Avg:	Miller	.352
On–Base Pct:	O'Farrell	.439
Slugging Pct:	Grimes	.572
Home Runs:	Grimes	14
RBI:	Grimes	99
Runs:	Grimes	99
Stolen Bases:	Hollocher	19
Wins:	Aldridge	16
	Alexander	16
Strikeouts:	Osborne	81
ERA:	Aldridge	3.52
Saves:	Osborne	3
	Kaufmann	3

APRIL 12   The Cubs win the season opener 7–3 against the Reds in Cincinnati. Grover Alexander pitched the complete–game victory. Gabby Hartnett made his major league debut and was hitless in three at–bats.

Hartnett batted only .194 in 31 games during his rookie season at the age of 21. Bob O'Farrell remained as the starting catcher, batting .324.

APRIL 14   Cubs icon Cap Anson dies at the age of 70 at St. Luke's Hospital in Chicago following surgery for glandular trouble.

                A public funeral was held for Anson on April 16. Thousands, including some of the top figures in baseball, past and present, filed past his casket where his body lay in state. Anson was laid to rest at Chicago's Oakwood Cemetery.

APRIL 20   The Cubs collect only three hits, but beat the Reds 3–1 in the home opener before 14,781 on a bitterly cold day at Cubs Park.

MAY 6   Cubs pitcher Vic Aldridge collects five hits in five at–bats against the Pirates in Pittsburgh. Aldridge was less effective on the mound, giving up seven runs and 14 hits, but escaped with an 11–7 win.

                Aldridge was 16–15 with a 3.52 ERA in 1922.

MAY 27   Cubs pitchers tie a major league record by allowing nine triples in a double–header, losing 8–1 and 7–6 to the Reds in Cincinnati.

MAY 30   The Cubs trade Max Flack to the Cardinals for Cliff Heathcote.

                The trade was pulled off between games of a separate admission double–header between the Cubs and the Cardinals at Cubs Park. Flack and Heathcote both appeared in the morning game, won 4–1 by the Cubs, traded uniforms, and played for their new teams in the afternoon, a 3–1 Chicago victory. Heathcote was 0–for–3 as a Card and 2–for–4 as a Cub. Flack went 0–for–4 in the first game and 1–for–4 in the second. Flack and Heathcote had remarkably similar careers. Flack played in 1,411 games and Heathcote in 1,415. Flack hit .278 and Heathcote .275. Flack stole 200 bases to Heathcote's 190. Flack had 212 doubles and Heathcote collected 206. Heathcote outhomered Flack 42 to 35. The only other player in major league history besides Flack and Heathcote to play for two teams in one day was Joel Youngblood with the Mets and the Expos on August 4, 1982.

JUNE 7   Umpire Charlie Moran ejects all of the extra players on the Cubs bench during a 9–4 loss to the Giants in New York.

JUNE 16   Ray Grimes hits a home run in the twelfth inning to defeat the Braves 7–6 in Boston.

JUNE 19   Cubs pitcher Tony Kaufmann breaks a 4–4 tie with a two–run homer in the ninth inning, then allows four runs in the bottom half to lose 8–6 to the Phillies in Philadelphia. The game ended on a three–run pinch–hit homer by John Peters.

JUNE 24   Down 7–0 after four innings, the Cubs rally to defeat the Cardinals 10–9 in St. Louis.

JULY 1   The Cubs rally for a 6–5 win at Cubs Park after the Reds score five runs in the first inning.

JULY 4   Vic Aldridge pitches a two–hitter to defeat the Pirates 8–0 in the second game of a double–header at Forbes Field. The only Pittsburgh hits were singles by Rabbit Maranville and Max Carey. The Cubs also won the first game 8–4.

JULY 13 — Heinie Groh of the Giants hits a fluke three–run homer that rolls under the fence at Cubs Park, but the Cubs recover to win 5–4 in twelve innings.

JULY 21 — Grover Alexander pitches the Cubs to a 1–0 win over the Dodgers in a game at Cubs Park that took just one hour and thirteen minutes to play. The only run of the game was driven in on a double by Ray Grimes. It was the fifteenth consecutive game in which Grimes collected a run batted in.

Alexander had a record of 16–13 with a 3.63 ERA.

JULY 23 — Ray Grimes establishes a major league record by driving in a run in his seventeenth consecutive game. Grimes set the mark with a homer in the second inning of a 4–1 win over the Dodgers at Cubs Park.

During the record–breaking seventeen–game streak, Grimes drove in 27 runs and had 29 hits in 67 at–bats for a batting average of .433, along with seven doubles, three triples and three homers. Between games ten and eleven of the streak, Grimes was out of the lineup ten days because of a back injury. During the 1922 season, Grimes hit .354 with 99 RBIs, 45 doubles and 14 homers. He was 28 years old and it looked as though he might have a long and prosperous career, but the back injury flared again in 1923 and he was never again able to play regularly or productively.

AUGUST 4 — The Cubs score three runs in a sensational ninth–inning rally to defeat the Giants 3–2 in the first game of a double–header in New York. The Cubs lost the second game 2–1.

AUGUST 6 — The Cubs explode for eight runs in the tenth inning and defeat the Giants 10–3 in New York.

AUGUST 13 — Charlie Hollocher collects three triples in a 16–5 win over the Cardinals in St. Louis.

Charlie Hollocher had a big year in 1922, batting .340 with 201 hits, but he set a team record by being caught stealing 29 times.

In his first healthy season since 1918, Hollocher collected 201 hits, 37 doubles, and batted .340 in 1922. He struck out only five times in 592 at–bats, but set a club record when he was caught stealing 29 times in 48 attempts.

AUGUST 18 — The Giants score ten runs in the fifth inning of a 17–11 win over the Cubs at Cubs Park.

AUGUST 20 — A crowd of 26,000, nearly 10,000 above the seating capacity at Cubs Park, watches the Cubs lose 5–4 to the Giants. The crowd was angered over the decisions of umpire Barry McCormick and threw bottles and cushions at him. After the game, policemen escorted the arbiter to his dressing room.

The Cubs entered the game with a 65–50 record in third place 3 ½ games behind the Giants. Chicago couldn't pull any closer to first for the remainder of the season, however.

AUGUST 25   In the highest–scoring game in major league history, the Cubs defeat the Phillies, 26–23, at Cubs Park. There were also 51 hits, another record by two teams in a nine–inning game, 26 of them by the Phillies. The hits included 34 singles, 12 doubles, two triples and three homers. Hack Miller had two of the homers, each with two men on base. In addition there were 21 walks and 10 errors by ten different players. The Phils had a total of 16 men left on base, while the Cubs stranded nine. The Cubs scored ten runs in the second inning to take a, 11–3 lead, and fourteen in the fourth to pull ahead, 25–6. The Cubs had a 26–9 advantage after seven innings before the Phillies plated eight runs in the eighth and six in the ninth. The Phillies had the bases loaded when the game ended on a Tiny Osborne strikeout of Bevo LeBourveau. The pitchers who absorbed the pounding were Jimmy Ring and Lefty Weinart of the Phillies and Tony Kaufman, George Stueland, Ed Morris, Uel Eubanks and Osborne for the Cubs. It was Eubanks's second big league game. He never pitched in the majors again. Kaufman was the winning pitcher. The contest lasted three hours and one minute. Marty Callaghan tied a major league record by making three plate appearances in one inning. He had two singles and struck out. Cliff Heathcote tied another mark by reaching base seven times in seven plate appearances with three singles, two doubles and two walks. He scored five runs. Nine different Cubs scored at least two runs, tying another mark. A total of twenty–two different players scored a run, thirteen of them Phillies. There were many Cubs club records set in the game. The 26 runs is the most in one game since 1900. The 23 runs by the Phillies is the most by a Cubs opponent since 1900. Both records have since been tied, but the 14–run fourth–inning is the most runs by a Cubs team in an inning since 1900 and has yet to be matched.

AUGUST 26   The day after the 26–23 run–fest, neither the Cubs nor the Phillies score in the first ten innings of the game at Cubs Park. The Phils scored three runs in the eleventh to win 3–0. The two clubs combined for only 10 hits in the eleven innings.

SEPTEMBER 16   Hack Miller's grand slam in the first inning off Dutch Ruether of the Dodgers paces the Cubs to a 7–5 win in the first game of a double–header at Brooklyn. The Cubs lost the second game 1–0 in ten innings.

Lawrence "Hack" Miller was acquired from Portland in the Pacific Coast League the previous off–season and was an immediate sensation with the Cubs. Although born in New York City, he grew up on the North Side of Chicago within walking distance of the ballpark. Miller's father, a German immigrant, had been a circus strongman and won several weightlifting championships. Miller's sister was also a lifter. To entertain his teammates, Miller drove nails through a two–inch board with his fists protected only by a baseball cap. It is on photographic record that he drove a forty–penny bridge spike through an auto gate at Wrigley Field. Hack could also twist iron bars and uproot trees. He once rescued a woman pinned beneath a touring car on a New York street by lifting the car at one end allowing the woman to be pulled free. Standing a stocky five–feet–nine inches and weighing 200 pounds, Miller batted .352 and slugged 12 homers in 1922. He earned his nickname because of his resemblance to a famous wrestler of the day named Hackenschmidt. Miller's lack of speed hampered him in the outfield, however, and he lasted only two seasons as a regular fading out of the majors by 1925. After his playing career ended, Miller was a longshoreman in Oakland for 25 years.

SEPTEMBER 17   Ray Grimes hits a homer, a triple, and a double in a 6–2 win over the Dodgers in Brooklyn.

SEPTEMBER 29   Tiny Osborne pitches a two–hitter to beat the Cardinals 3–0 at Cubs Park. The only St. Louis hits were a double by Jim Bottomley and a single by Ray Blades.

Ernest "Tiny" Osborne stood six–foot–four and weighed 215 pounds. He pitched for the Cubs from 1922 through 1924.

OCTOBER 3   The Chicago City Series opens with a 6–3 White Sox win over the Cubs before 17,434 at Cubs Park.

OCTOBER 15   The Cubs win the City Series four games to three with a 2–0 win over the White Sox at Cubs Park. Grover Alexander pitched the shutout. The was the first time that the Cubs won the City Series since 1909.

NOVEMBER 8   The Cubs announce plans to enlarge the seating capacity of Cubs Park from 17,000 to 31,000 at a cost of $350,000.

Wrigley commissioned Zachary Davis, the original architect of the plant when it was built in 1914, to plan the renovation to be completed before the start of the 1923 season. The grandstand was cut into three parts. The right and left field wings were separated from the section behind home plate. Eleven sections of the right field wing were retained in its original position. The left field wing was placed under rollers and moved 60 feet northward toward Waveland Avenue. The purchase of a strip of ground more than 100 feet in width from a sand company gave the Cubs the space to expand the size of the ballpark by moving the center section of the stands toward the Clark and Addison corner. Home plate was moved back 68 feet. The playing field was lowered about three feet, and new rows of box seats were installed in front of the existing rows. The new single–deck grandstand held about 26,000 fans. Additionally, temporary bleachers seating another 5,000 were installed in left field to benefit slugging outfielder Hack Miller. The new field dimensions were 325 feet to left field, 447 to center, and 318 to right. During construction, the sod was taken up and re–planted in Lincoln Park to keep it alive during the winter. The sod was brought back to the ballpark in time for Opening Day. Another addition was the construction of a bungalow under the left field stands as a residence for groundskeeper Bobby Dorr.

1923

Cubs

Season in a Sentence

The Cubs win three more games than the previous season, but slip a notch in the standings to fifth place.

Finish • Won • Lost • Pct • GB

Fourth   83   71   .539 12.5

Manager

Bill Killefer

Stats

Stats	Cubs	NL	Rank
Batting Avg:	.288	.286	3
On–Base Pct:	.348	.343	2
Slugging Pct:	.406	.395	2
Home Runs:	90		2
Stolen Bases:	181		1
ERA:	3.82	3.99	3
Fielding Avg:	.967	.966	4
Runs Scored:	756		3
Runs Allowed:	704		3

Starting Lineup

Bob O'Farrell, c
Ray Grimes, 1b
George Grantham, 2b
Barney Friberg, 3b
Sparky Adams, ss
Hack Miller, lf
Jigger Statz, cf
Cliff Heathcote, rf
Charlie Hollocher, ss
Gabby Hartnett, c–1b
John Kelleher, 1b–ss–3b
Allen Elliott, 1b

Pitchers

Pete Alexander, sp
Vic Aldridge, sp
Tony Kaufmann, sp
Tiny Osborne, sp–rp
Vic Keen, rp–sp
Nick Dumovich, rp
Fred Fussell, rp

Attendance

703,705 (second in NL)

Club Leaders

Batting Avg:	Statz	.319
On–Base Pct:	O'Farrell	.408
Slugging Pct:	Miller	.482
Home Runs:	Miller	20
RBI:	Miller	88
	Friberg	88
Runs:	Statz	110
Stolen Bases:	Grantham	43
Wins:	Alexander	22
Strikeouts:	Alexander	72
	Kaufmann	72
ERA:	Kaufmann	3.10
Saves:	Kaufmann	3
	Fred Fussell	3

APRIL 17   In the season opener at remodeled Cubs Park, the Cubs lose 3–2 to the Pirates before 33,000.

After losing the opener, the Cubs won their next seven games, but the club hit a rough patch and was 20–24 by early June.

APRIL 20   Gabby Hartnett hits a walk–off homer to defeat the Pirates 12–11 at Cubs Park. It was Gabby's second homer of the game. The Cubs hit six homers in all. Bernie Friberg also hit two homers, and Cliff Heathcote and Jigger Statz added one each. The Cubs scored seven runs in the eighth inning to take an 11–9 lead before allowing the Pirates to tie the contest in the ninth.

APRIL 24   Vic Aldridge pitches a two–hitter to defeat the Cardinals 2–0 at Cubs Park. The only St. Louis hits were singles by Heinie Mueller and opposing pitcher Jesse Haines.

Aldridge was 16–9 with a 3.48 ERA in 1923.

MAY 4   Marty Callaghan steals home with the winning run in the ninth inning to defeat the Cardinals 2–1 in St. Louis.

MAY 17   Down 4–0, the Cubs score seven runs in the seventh inning, all after two out, to beat the Phillies 7–4 in Philadelphia.

MAY 25   Grover Alexander pitches a two–hitter to beat the Reds 4–0 at Cubs Park. The only Cincinnati hits were singles by George Burns and Pat Duncan.

Alexander had a record of 22–12 and a 3.19 earned run average in 1923. He completed 26 games and walked only 30 batters in 305 innings. During one stretch, Alexander went 51 consecutive innings without issuing a base on balls, a Cub record.

JUNE 3   Tiny Osborne holds the Reds hitless through eighth innings before giving up three runs and three hits in the ninth to survive for a 4–3 win in Cincinnati.

JUNE 6   Thick fog interferes with play during a 6–1 win over the Giants at Cubs Park. At times, it was impossible to see past the infield and on several occasions it was necessary for the umpires to confer as to whether or not batted balls had been caught.

JUNE 7   Charlie Hollocher collects five hits, including a double, in five at–bats during a 9–7 win over the Giants at Cubs Park.

Hollocher missed the first four weeks of the season with the flu and was in and out of the lineup all season with a mysterious stomach ailment. He hit .342, but appeared in only 66 games.

JUNE 9   A base–running error by Gabby Hartnett nearly costs the Cubs a victory. With the score 3–3 and two out in the ninth inning against the Braves at Cubs Park, Hartnett was the runner on first and Cliff Heathcote was on third with Jigger Statz batting. Statz shot a drive to left, scoring Heathcote, but Hartnett started for the clubhouse. The Chicago players rushed toward him, waving, shouting, and pointing toward second base. Hartnett reached the base just before the ball was relayed to secure the 4–3 win.

Jigger Statz scored 110 runs and collected 209 hits in 1923.

JUNE 12   Hack Miller drives in seven runs on a grand slam off Frank Miller in the fifth inning, a two–run homer, and a run–scoring single to lead the Cubs to a 12–11 win over the Braves at Cubs Park. Miller's slam tied the score 7–7.

JUNE 18   Bob O'Farrell drives in six runs on a homer and two singles during a 9–3 win over the Phillies at Cubs Park.

O'Farrell had a .319 batting average and 12 homers in 1923.

Cliff Heathcote tied for third in the National League with 32 stolen bases in 1923.

JUNE 20   The Cubs overwhelm the Phillies 16–1 at Cubs Park.

JULY 15   Bernie Friberg hits a tenth–inning grand slam off Claude Jonnard to defeat the
               Giants 9–5 in New York.

               Friberg batted .318 with 12 homers in 1923.

JULY 21   In a double–header against the Phillies in Philadelphia, the Cubs lose 17–4 before
               recovering to win the second game 16–9. In the sixth inning of the first game, the
               Phillies scored 12 runs off Tiny Osborne and Fred Fussell.

JULY 26   A startling four–run rally in the ninth inning beats the Giants 11–10 in New York.
               Jigger Statz tied the score with a two–run double and scored the winning run on a
               single by Sparky Adams.

               *Standing only five–foot–five, Adams played second base, shortstop, and third
               base during six capable seasons with the Cubs from 1922 through 1927. He led
               the National League in at–bats in 1925, 1926, and 1927.*

AUGUST 3   The Cubs game against the Dodgers in Chicago is postponed to observe a national
               day of mourning following the August 2 death of President Warren Harding, who
               died during a trip to San Francisco. The Cubs game on August 10 was also postponed
               on the day of Harding's funeral. Calvin Coolidge succeeded Harding as president.

               *On the same day, Charlie Hollocher left the club, and didn't return until spring
               training in 1924. He left a note in the clubhouse addressed to Bill Killefer noti-
               fying the Cubs manager of his departure. In the note, Hollocher wrote: "Feeling
               pretty rotten so made up my mind to go home and take a rest and forget base-
               ball for the rest of the year. No hard feelings, just don't feel like playing base-
               ball for the rest of the year."*

AUGUST 11   Gabby Hartnett's walk–off homer in the tenth inning beats the Phillies 5–4 in the
               first game of a double–header at Cubs Park. The Cubs lost the second game 8–6.

               *The first game was delayed while a fire engine pumped water out of the outfield
               from a heavy rain the previous night.*

AUGUST 19   The Cubs trounce the Dodgers 15–3 in Brooklyn.

SEPTEMBER 7   The Cubs score six runs in the first inning which is enough for a 6–4 win over the
               Pirates in Pittsburgh.

SEPTEMBER 16   Umpire Charlie Moran is pelted by bottles during a 10–6 loss to the Giants at Cubs
               Park. Commissioner Kenesaw Landis shook his cane at the angry mob during the fifteen
               minutes play was stopped while the field was cleared of debris. After the game, police
               escorted Moran and the Giants manager, John McGraw, to the clubhouse. Hack Miller
               was the batting hero in the loss with three doubles and a triple in four at–bats.

               *In the morning before the game, a monument was unveiled at the gravesite of
               Cap Anson at Oakwood Cemetery. Anson died on April 14, 1922. Players from
               the Cubs and Giants attended, as did Chicago mayor William Dever and dozens*

of past and present baseball players and executives.

SEPTEMBER 19   Grover Alexander wins his 22nd game of the season with a 5–4 decision over the Pirates at Cubs Park.

SEPTEMBER 29   After the Pirates score two runs in the top of the tenth, the Cubs come back with three in their half to win 5–4 at Cubs Park. Ray Grimes drove in the game–winner with a single.

OCTOBER 10   The fourth–place Cubs defeat the seventh–place White Sox in the first game of the Chicago City Series 5–4 at Cubs Park.

OCTOBER 14   Game Four of the City Series draws a paid crowd of 41,825 to Comiskey Park, the largest ever to see a baseball game in Chicago up to that time. The White Sox won, 5–2 to even the series at two games apiece.

OCTOBER 16   The White Sox win the City Series four games to two with, a 4–2, ten–inning win over the Cubs at Cubs Park.

1924   Cubs

Season in a Sentence

The Cubs are in first place as late as June 14, but fade to fifth by the end of the season.

Finish • Won • Lost • Pct • GB

Fifth   81   72   .529   12.0

Manager

Bill Killefer

Stats

Stats	Cubs	NL	Rank
Batting Avg:	.276	.283	6
On–Base Pct:	.340	.337	4
Slugging Pct:	.378	.392	7
Home Runs:	66		5
Stolen Bases:	137		2
ERA:	3.83	3.87	5
Fielding Avg:	.966	.970	8
Runs Scored:	698		5
Runs Allowed:	699		5

Starting Lineup

Gabby Hartnett, c
Harvey Cotter, 1b
George Grantham, 2b
Bernie Friberg, 3b
Sparky Adams, ss
Denver Grigsby, lf
Jigger Statz, cf
Cliff Heathcote, rf
Charlie Hollocher, ss
Bob O'Farrell, c
Ray Grimes, 1b
Otto Vogel, rf

Pitchers

Vic Aldridge, sp
Vic Keen, sp–rp
Tony Kaufmann, sp
Elmer Jacobs, sp–rp
Grover Alexander, sp
Guy Bush, sp–rp
Sheriff Blake, rp–sp
Rip Wheeler, rp

Attendance

716,922 (fourth in NL))

Club Leaders

Batting Avg:	Grantham	.316
On–Base Pct:	Grantham	.390
Slugging Pct:	Grantham	.458
Home Runs:	Hartnett	16
RBI:	Friberg	82
Runs:	Grantham	85
Stolen Bases:	Heathcote	26
Wins:	Kaufmann	16
Strikeouts:	Kaufmann	79
ERA:	Alexander	3.03
Saves:	Keen	3

APRIL 15 — The Cubs open the season in St. Louis, and lose 6–5 when the Cardinals score three runs in the ninth inning off Vic Aldridge.

Aldridge was one of three Cubs pitchers to win 15 or more games in 1924. Aldridge was 15–12, Vic Keen was 15–14, and Tony Kaufmann had a record of 16–11.

APRIL 23 — In the home opener, the Cubs rout the Cardinals 12–1 at Cubs Park. George Grantham and Ray Grimes hit home runs.

This was the first Cubs game ever broadcast on radio. Hal Totten was at the mike over station WMAQ. Totten broadcast from the Wrigley Field roof, which then had only a single deck. All Cubs home games were on radio during the 1924 season. By the end of the 1920s, Cubs games were on five Chicago radio stations simultaneously. Totten was the broadcaster for both the Cubs and the White Sox until 1944.

APRIL 29 — Grover Alexander pitches an eleven–inning complete game and drives in the winning run with a walk–off double to beat the Pirates 2–1 at Cubs Park.

MAY 14 — In his first game after holding out for the first month of the season, Charlie Hollocher collects three hits, including a homer, but the Cubs lose 6–4 to the Giants in New York. The homer came in the first inning on a ball that rolled through a hole under the grandstand in right field.

Hollocher continued to battle with his stomach problems, but physicians could find nothing organically wrong with him. He played in only 76 games and batted just .245. Hollocher retired after the season was over at the age of 28 because he was convinced that baseball was ruining his health. It's open conjecture as to whether or not Hollocher was suffering from hypochondria, mental illness, or an undiagnosed ailment. In 1940, he died from a self–inflicted gunshot wound in the neck from a newly purchased shotgun.

MAY 25 — The Cubs hammer the Braves 11–0 at Cubs Park.

JUNE 21 — The Cubs beat the Cardinals 4–3 and 1–0 in a double–header at Cubs Park. Tony Kaufmann pitched the shutout and worked out of a bases–loaded jam in the ninth inning.

JUNE 25 — The Cubs allow five runs in the ninth inning to allow the Pirates to tie the score 6–6, and after Chicago scores in the top of the fourteenth, Pittsburgh comes back with two in their half to win 8–7 at Forbes Field. Pirate pitcher Emil Yde drove in the tying run in the ninth with a two–out double and drove in the winning run in the fourteenth with a triple.

The Cubs entered the game in second place with a 36–21 record, 2 ½ games behind the Giants. The Cubs never seemed to recover from the devastating June 25 loss to the Pirates and were never a serious factor in the pennant race after mid–July.

JULY 8 — In the first inning at Cubs Park, the Dodgers score four runs and the Cubs plate seven. Chicago was unable to hold the lead, however, and Brooklyn emerged with a 13–11 win.

JULY 11 — Harvey Cotter of the Cubs ties a record for most chances accepted by a first baseman with 22, on 21 putouts and one assist, but the Cubs lose 9–1 to the Dodgers at Cubs Park.

JULY 19 — Jigger Statz collects seven hits, including two triples, in nine at–bats during a double–header against the Phillies at Cubs Park. Statz was two–for–four in the first game and five–for–five in the second. The Cubs won 7–2 and 9–3.

JULY 23 — In the first inning of a 3–1 loss to the Braves at Cubs Park, a foul tip off the bat of Stuffy McInnis injures Cubs catcher Bob O'Farrell. The blow struck O'Farrell's mask and drove it into his forehead, causing a skull fracture above the right eye.

Absent–mindedness and borrowed equipment contributed to the injury. The clubhouse boy forgot to bring the mask that O'Farrell used on a regular basis to the dugout. O'Farrell sent back for it, but he didn't want to hold up the game, so he put on an old mask that didn't fit him properly, just to catch the inning.

AUGUST 9 — Jigger Statz hits an inside–the–park grand slam down the right field line off Larry Benton during a five–run tenth inning to lift the Cubs to an 11–6 win over the Braves in the first game of a double–header in Boston. The Braves won the second game 6–2.

Left fielder Denver Grigsby suffered facial injuries twice in August. First, he lost a fly ball in the sun and was struck in the face, breaking his sunglasses. Then, he ran face–first into the screen in front of the bleachers at Cubs Park and received an assortment of cuts and abrasions.

SEPTEMBER 20 — Ten days after Chicago teenagers Nathan Leopold and Richard Loeb receive life sentences for the "thrill murder" of 14–year–old Bobby Franks, Grover Alexander earns his 300th career victory. He pitched a twelve–inning complete game to defeat the Giants 7–3 in New York to reach the milestone.

Alexander ended his career in 1930 with a record of 373–208.

OCTOBER 1 — The Chicago City Series opens with the Cubs defeating the White Sox 10–7 before 15,414 at Cubs Park.

OCTOBER 6 — The White Sox win the City Series four games to two, with a 5–3 decision over the Cubs at Comiskey Park.

OCTOBER 27 — The Cubs trade George Grantham, Vic Aldridge and Al Niehaus to the Pirates for Charlie Grimm, Rabbit Maranville, and Wilbur Cooper.

A future Hall of Famer, Maranville was 33–years–old and was acquired to replace retired Charlie Hollocher at shortstop. Maranville lasted only one season with the Cubs, including a turbulent two months as player–manager. Grimm, however was known as "Jolly Cholly," for his light–hearted nature. He played with the Cubs from 1925 through 1936, and spent three different terms as manager (1932–38, 1944–49, and 1960). He played for the Cubs in two World Series as a first baseman (1929 and 1932) and managed the club in three (1932, 1935, and 1945). He was also a coach, scout, consultant, honorary vice–president, and broadcaster with the club. When he died in 1983, his ashes were scattered at Wrigley Field.

1925

Season in a Sentence

In the Cubs 50th season in the National League, the club fires three managers and finishes in last place for the first time in the history of the franchise.

Finish • Won • Lost • Pct • GB

Eighth   68   86   .442   27.5

Managers

Bill Killefer (33–42),
Rabbit Maranville (23–30), and
George Gibson (12–14)

Stats

Stats	Cubs •	NL •	Rank
Batting Avg:	.275	.292	8
On–Base Pct:	.329	.348	8
Slugging Pct:	.397	.414	6
Home Runs:	86		4
Stolen Bases:	94		3
ERA:	4.41	4.27	6
Fielding Avg:	.969	.966	1
Runs Scored:	723		6
Runs Allowed:	773		5

Starting Lineup

Gabby Hartnett, c
Charlie Grimm, 1b
Sparky Adams, 2b
Howard Freigau, 3b
Rabbit Maranville, ss
Art Jahn, lf
Mandy Brooks, cf
Cliff Heathcote, rf
Tommy Griffith, rf
Mike Gonzalez, c
Butch Weis, lf
Pinky Pittenger, 3b–2b
Bernie Friberg, 3b–lf
Jigger Statz, cf
Denver Grigsby, lf–cf

Pitchers

Grover Alexander, sp
Tony Kaufmann, sp
Wilbur Cooper, sp
Sheriff Blake, sp
Guy Bush, rp–sp
Percy Jones, rp–sp

Attendance

622,610 (fourth in NL)

Club Leaders

Batting Avg:	Freigau	.307
On–Base Pct:	Grimm	.354
Slugging Pct:	Hartnett	.555
Home Runs:	Hartnett	24
RBI:	Grimm	76
Runs:	Adams	95
Stolen Bases:	Adams	26
Wins:	Alexander	15
Strikeouts:	Blake	93
ERA:	Alexander	3.39
Saves:	Bush	4

MARCH 15   Four months after the murder of bootlegger Dion O'Banion in his Chicago flower shop, Rabbit Maranville breaks his right leg just above the ankle and suffers torn ligaments during an 8–7 exhibition game win over the Los Angeles Angels of the Pacific Coast League in Los Angeles. Maranville suffered the injury while sliding into third base. He was out of action until late May.

Before the injury, Maranville and Charlie Grimm teamed up for a classic gag photo. Grimm laid on his back with a golf tee holding a ball clenched between his teeth. Above him was Maranville, a golf club poised in his back-swing ready for a follow-through. The picture was snapped, and suddenly Maranville swung the club and knocked the ball down the course, scaring the wits out of the prostate Grimm.

APRIL 14   The Cubs open the 1925 season at home and defeat the Pirates 8–2 before 38,000 at Cubs Park. The Cubs broke a 2–2 tie with six runs in the seventh inning. Grover Alexander pitched the complete game victory, in addition to starring with the bat by collecting a home run, a double, and a single. Gabby Hartnett also belted a home run. Charlie Grimm made his Cubs debut and was hitless in three at–bats.

Alexander had a 15–11 record and a 3.39 ERA in 1925.

APRIL 18   The Cardinals smash the Cubs 20–5 at Cubs Park.

MAY 8   The National League celebrates the fiftieth season in the history of the organization before a game between the Cubs and the Braves in Boston. The celebration was called the Golden Jubilee.

Each team in the NL hosted a Golden Jubilee game in 1925. The first was in Boston on May 8 with the Cubs as the visiting team because the Cubs and the Braves were the only two teams that were members of the league all fifty seasons. George Wright and Jack Manning, who both played for Boston in the first game in the history of the National League on April 22, 1876, were introduced to the crowd. Wright was also a member of the 1869 Cincinnati Red Stockings, baseball's first professional team. Also present were William McLean, who umpired that first game in 1876. Commissioner Kenesaw Landis, National League president John Heydler, Massachusetts Governor Allen Fuller, and Boston Mayor James Curley each made speeches (see June 9, 1925).

MAY 10   The Cubs trade Bob Barrett to the Dodgers for Tommy Griffith.

MAY 22   Percy Jones pitches a one–hitter to defeat the Dodgers 2–0 at Ebbets Field. The only Brooklyn hit was a single by Jimmy Johnston in the first inning. Cubs shortstop Sparky Adams knocked Johnston's hit down, but failed to recover in time to make the out.

Jones pitched for the Cubs from 1920 through 1922, and again from 1925 through 1928, mostly in relief and as a spot starter. In 1928, he was the talk of the baseball world when he reportedly inherited $500,000. Three years later, while pitching for Columbus in the American Association, Jones fell from a third–story window and broke his neck. He spent the rest of his life in a wheelchair. Jones died in 1979 at the age of 79.

MAY 23   The Cubs trade Bob O'Farrell to the Cardinals for Mike Gonzalez and Howard Freigau.

O'Farrell was one of the best catchers in Cubs history, but by 1925 he had lost his job as a starter to Gabby Hartnett, the greatest catcher in Cubs history. The Cuban–born Gonzalez, also a catcher, became the Cubs' first Latin player.

MAY 31   Gabby Hartnett collects a homer, a triple, and a double during an 11–2 win over the Pirates at Cubs Park.

Hartnett hit six home runs in his first six games in 1925, and finished the season with a batting average of .289 and 24 homers.

JUNE 9   The Cubs commemorate the National League's Golden Jubilee prior to a 9–7 loss to the Giants at Cubs Park.

Guests included Deacon White, who played for the 1876 Cubs, Commissioner Kenesaw Landis and NL President John Heydler. Prior to the game, players from both the Cubs and Giants marched around the field and across to the flagpole to hoist the jubilee pennant.

JUNE 13   Charlie Grimm's homers in the third and fifth innings are the only runs in a 2–0 win over the Braves at Cubs Park.

Grimm had only two multihomer games during his twenty-year playing career. The other one was in 1929.

JUNE 15   The Cubs sell Bernie Friberg to the Phillies.

JUNE 20   Grover Alexander collects a homer, a triple and a double, but receives little support from his teammates and loses 3–2 to the Phillies at Cubs Park.

JULY 4   Tony Kaufmann hits two homers and pitches a three-hitter to defeat the Cardinals 9–1 in the second game of a double-header at Cubs Park. The Cubs also won the first game 7–6 in twelve innings.

The two home runs were the only ones that Kaufmann hit in 1925.

JULY 6   The Cubs fire Bill Killefer as manager and replace him with Rabbit Maranville.

The Cubs were 33–42 when the change was made. Killefer was later manager of the St. Louis Browns from 1930 through 1933.
The fun-loving but quick-tempered Maranville was hired despite his propensity for pranks and alcohol, and was clearly the wrong choice to lead a losing club. The fact was made abundantly clear within twenty-four hours of his appointment. Rabbit celebrated his promotion to manager by getting drunk, then poured ice water all over his players sleeping in the Pullman on which they were traveling at the time. Once the Cubs arrived in New York, Maranville got into an altercation with a cab driver and the police. He shared the taxi with infielder Pinky Pittenger and pitcher Herb Brett. When the trio exited the vehicle, the driver mumbled something about the lack of a tip. Maranville was threatening to punch the driver's lights out when police intervened. The new Cubs manager fought with two officers before being subdued and was taken to the station house along with Pittenger and Brett. After they spent a couple of hours in jail, a night court judge dismissed the players. In another incident, Maranville grabbed traveling secretary John Seys and dangled him from a hotel window by his legs. The final straw came in September when Maranville raced through a train anointing passengers with the contents of a spittoon. Rabbit lasted less than two months as manager of the Cubs (see September 3, 1925).

JULY 12   The Cubs defeat the Giants 9–8 in sixteen innings in New York. Charlie Grimm drove in the winning run with a double. The Giants tied the game 8–8 by scoring two runs with two outs in the ninth, the second of which was scored on a glaring error by catcher Gabby Hartnett, who made a careless return throw to pitcher Guy Bush. The ball glanced off Bush's glove, allowing Ross Youngs to score from third base. Bush pitched shutout relief over the final seven innings.

JULY 15   The Cubs score seven runs in the second inning against the Phillies in Philadelphia and win 8–3 in a game shortened to six innings by rain.

JULY 21   The Cubs score nine runs in the fourth inning and defeat the Braves 15–3 in Boston.

AUGUST 5   Two weeks after John Scopes is convicted and fined $100 for teaching evolution following the "Monkey Trial" in Tennessee, the Cubs rally from a 6–2 deficit with three runs in the eighth and two in the ninth to win 7–6 against the Phillies at Cubs Park. The two ninth–inning runs were an outright gift. With two Cubs runners on base and two out in the ninth, Charlie Grimm lifted an easy fly ball toward the outfield, but Philadelphia left fielder Russ Wrightstone dropped the ball and both runners crossed the plate.

Guy Bush won six games as a Cubs rookie in 1925 on his way to 176 career victories.

Part of the left field bleachers at Cubs Park along the foul line and in the power alley was torn down during a road trip in August, reducing seating capacity by about 2,000. The bleachers had been a persistent problem at the ballpark since it was remodeled during the 1922–23 off–season because the seats were too close to home plate, resulting in too many cheap homers, especially by the opposition. There are no reliable figures pertaining to the distance from home plate to the bleachers in the left–center field power alley, but 340 feet is a reasonable guess. From 1923 through 1925, the Cubs hit 153 homers at home and 89 on the road. During those same three seasons, Cubs pitchers allowed 188 homers at home and 89 on the road. Gabby Hartnett benefited the most from the bleachers. He hit 35 homers at home from 1923 through 1925, and 13 on the road. The change dramatically decreased the number of homers struck at Cubs Park. During the 1920s, there were 34 hit at the ballpark in 1920, 60 in 1921, 59 in 1922, 120 in 1923, 101 in 1924, 120 in 1925, 52 in 1926, 56 in 1927, and 58 in 1928, before another jump to 117 in 1929.

Gabby Hartnett led the 1925 Cubs with 24 homers, ranking second in the National League.

AUGUST 9   The Cubs wallop the Braves 8–1 and 13–3 in a double–header at Cubs Park.

AUGUST 24   Eleven Cubs are ejected by umpire Frank Wilson in the first game of a double–header against the Dodgers in Brooklyn for questioning the arbiter's decision–making capabilities. The Cubs lost the first game 13–6 and won the second 11–6.

AUGUST 25   The Cubs collect 22 hits and pound the Phillies 19–10 in Philadelphia. The Phillies took a 6–0 lead in the first inning before succumbing to the Cubs attack. Mandy Brooks hit a grand slam in the ninth inning off Clarence Mitchell.

SEPTEMBER 3   The Cubs fire Rabbit Maranville as manager and replace him with George Gibson.

              Gibson was a Cubs coach and didn't want the job as manager, but he agreed to finish out the season. He had previously managed the Pirates from 1920 through 1922. Maranville remained with the club as a player, but was a seldom–used reserve as Pinky Pittenger became the club's starting shortstop.

SEPTEMBER 20 An old–timers game is played in Cleveland between former Cubs and former Cleveland Indians to raise money for amateur baseball. The game ended in a 6–6 tie, called after eight innings. Among the ex–Cubs to appear in the game were Three Finger Brown, Jimmy Archer, Solly Hofman, and Bill Sweeney.

SEPTEMBER 29 Wrigley Field in Los Angeles opens.

              In addition to owning the Cubs, William Wrigley was also owner of the Los Angeles Angels in the Pacific Coast League. He purchased the club in 1921. In 1925, Wrigley built Wrigley Field in Los Angeles, a ballpark with 22,000 seats at 42nd Street and Avalon. The architect was Zachary Davis, who designed both Comiskey Park and Wrigley Field in Chicago. The Los Angeles version of Wrigley Field served the Angels until 1957 when the franchise passed out of existence after the Dodgers moved to Southern California. Wrigley Field was a major league venue for one season in 1961, when the American League expansion team, also called the Los Angeles Angels, was established. The Angels shared Dodger Stadium with the Dodgers from 1962 through 1965 before moving to Anaheim in 1966. Wrigley Field was demolished in 1966, but can still be seen occasionally on the ESPN Classic network when episodes of Home Run Derby are shown. The series was filmed at Wrigley Field in 1959, were as several feature films over a forty–year period. The Los Angeles version of Wrigley Field was also the backdrop for many Hollywood movies.

OCTOBER 4   The Cubs finish the season in last place with a 7–5 loss to the Cardinals at Cubs Park in the final game of the regular season. The Cubs entered the day in a three–way tie for last with the Phillies and the Dodgers.

              The 1925 season was the first in Cubs history in which the club finished in last place. It didn't happen again until 1948.

OCTOBER 7   The Chicago City Series starts with the Cubs and White Sox playing to a 2–2, nineteen–inning tie at Comiskey Park. The game ended because of darkness. Grover Alexander and Ted Blankenship both pitched complete games. Alexander gave up 20 hits. Neither team scored after the fifth inning. The Cubs won four of the next five games to take the city championship.

OCTOBER 9   The Cubs draft Hack Wilson from the Toledo club in the American Association.

Wilson played for the Giants from 1923 through 1925, but the club dis-missed him because his drinking and happy–go–lucky attitude didn't sit well with John McGraw. Wilson developed into an immediate star with the Cubs. In six seasons in Chicago, he hit 190 homers, drove in 768 runs, and batted .322. In 1930, Wilson collected a major league record 191 runs batted in. He was only five–foot–six and had size six feet, but he was a solid and powerful 190 pounds.

OCTOBER 12   The Cubs hire 35–year–old Joe McCarthy as manager. The announcement came as no surprise, as rumors that McCarthy would be the next Cubs manager had been circulating for months.

McCarthy spent the previous seven seasons as a highly successful manager with Louisville in the American Association. McCarthy never played or managed in the majors before he was hired by the Cubs, and immediately came under fire as a "busher" unfit to manage a big league club. He silenced most of his critics in his first season by lifting the Cubs from last place to fourth, and by 1929, he won the National League pennant.

NOVEMBER 9   The Cubs sell Rabbit Maranville to the Dodgers.

Maranville spent only one year in Brooklyn, and his major league playing career appeared to be over when he was sent to the minors in 1927. Maranville gave up drinking, however, and made it back to the big leagues in 1928 with the Cardinals and helped the club reach the World Series. He played until 1935, but after his experience with the Cubs in 1925, Maranville was never again given the responsibility of managing a big league club.

1926

Season in a Sentence

Under new manager Joe McCarthy, the Cubs leap from eighth place to fourth with the aid of the best pitching staff in the league.

Finish • Won • Lost • Pct • GB

Fourth   82   72   .532   7.0

Manager

Joe McCarthy

Stats

Stats	Cubs	NL	Rank
Batting Avg:	.278	.280	5
On–Base Pct:	.338	.338	4
Slugging Pct:	.390	.386	4
Home Runs:	66		4
Stolen Bases:	85		3
ERA:	3.26	3.82	1
Fielding Avg:	.974	.968	1
Runs Scored:	682		5
Runs Allowed:	602		1

Starting Lineup

Gabby Hartnett, c
Charlie Grimm, 1b
Sparky Adams, 2b
Howard Freigau, 3b
Jimmy Cooney, ss
Riggs Stephenson, lf
Hack Wilson, cf
Cliff Heathcote, rf
Mike Gonzalez, c
Pete Scott, lf–rf
Joe Kelly, lf–rf

Pitchers

Charlie Root, sp
Sheriff Blake, sp–rp
Percy Jones, sp–rp
Tony Kaufmann, sp
Guy Bush, rp–sp
Bob Osborn, rp–sp

Attendance

885,063 (first in NL)

Club Leaders

Batting Avg: Wilson	.321
On–Base Pct: Wilson	.406
Slugging Pct: Wilson	.539
Home Runs: Wilson	21
RBI: Wilson	109
Runs: Heathcote	98
Stolen Bases: Adams	27
Wins: Root	18
Strikeouts: Root	127
ERA: Charlie Root	2.82
Saves: Six tied with:	2

APRIL 13   The Cubs lose 7–6 in ten innings to the Reds on Opening Day in Cincinnati. The Cubs scored five runs in the eighth inning to take a 6–5 lead, but the Reds tied it up in their half before winning in the tenth. Hack Wilson made his debut for the Cubs and tripled in four at–bats. Howard Freigau hit a home run for Chicago.

In his first season with the Cubs, Wilson led the NL in homers with 21. He also had a batting average of .321, 36 doubles and 109 RBIs. The top pitcher for the Cubs in 1926 was Charlie Root. He was 18–17, pitched 271 ⅓ innings, completed 21 starts, and had an ERA of 2.82. It was Root's first season in Chicago.

Charlie Root topped the Cubs staff with 18 victories in 1926, his first year as a Cub. That sent him on his way to 201 wins with the Cubs, making him the all–time leader.

He pitched for the Cubs from 1926 through 1941 and is the club's all–time winningest pitcher with 201 victories. Root's overall record with the Cubs was 201–156. He also leads the Cubs in games pitched (605) and innings pitched (3,137⅓) and is second in strikeouts (1,432).

APRIL 14   Joe McCarthy earns his first win as a manager when the Cubs break up a scoreless game with seven runs in the fifth inning and defeat the Reds 9–2 in Cincinnati.

APRIL 21   In the home opener, the Cubs defeat the Reds 4–2 before 27,400 at Cubs Park.

APRIL 23   The Cubs collected 20 hits and rout the Reds 18–1 at Cubs Park. Chicago scored seven runs in the sixth inning.

MAY 10   The Cubs score seven runs in the eighth inning and defeat the Dodgers 9–0 at Cubs Park.

MAY 22   Grover Alexander is given a $5,500 Lincoln automobile from fans at Cubs Park before the game, then loses 7–1 to the Braves.

MAY 23   The Cubs score seven runs in the eighth inning to defeat the Braves 14–8 at Cubs Park. The fans interrupted the proceedings by throwing bottles at umpire Jim Sweeney for throwing Cubs third baseman Howard Freigau out of the game.

Hack Wilson became the first player to hit a home run off the scoreboard out-side the left–center field wall (then located above the bleachers but in a lower location than today) about 450 feet from home plate. That night, Hack and sev-eral companions were arrested at the apartment of Michael and Lottie Frain, friends of Wilson's, for drinking beer in violation of the Prohibition Act. At 11:00 P.M., four Chicago policemen arrived to put a stop to the illegal drinking. Hack tried to slip out the side door but was nabbed. While other arrests were being made, Mrs. Frain picked up a bookend and fired it at a policeman. Wil-son was fined just $1 for the infraction.

JUNE 7   The Cubs sell Wilbur Cooper to the Tigers.

JUNE 8   Crown Prince Gustavus Adolphus and Princess Louise of Sweden watch the Cubs beat the Giants 2–1 in New York.

JUNE 13   Shortstop Jimmy Cooney, second baseman Sparky Adams and first baseman Charlie Grimm combine for four double plays, but the Cubs lose 6–5 to the Dodgers in Brooklyn.

JUNE 14   Managing in his hometown of Philadelphia for the first time, Joe McCarthy is given a grandfather clock, a trunk and a handbag in pre–game ceremonies. The Cubs defeated the Phillies 9–7.

JUNE 22   The Cubs sell Grover Alexander to the Cardinals.

Alexander constantly feuded with Joe McCarthy and defied the new manager's authority. Alexander showed up drunk six of his last ten days with the club, and twice failed to show up for a game. During one contest, he collapsed on the bench in a drunken stupor. The sale of Alexander had a positive and negative effect. On the positive side, it firmly established McCarthy's authority as the leader of the club. However, Alexander was far from finished as a pitcher, even though he was 39 years old. Bill Killefer had long been a steadying influence on Alexander, both with the Phillies and the Cubs, and without him in 1926, Grover had a difficult time staying away from the bottle. After he was fired by the Cubs after the close of the 1925 season, Killefer was hired as a coach with the Cardinals. Reunited with Killefer, Alexander helped the Cardinals win the 1926 pennant. He was the winning pitcher in game six of the World Series and earned a dramatic save in game seven against the Yankees. Alexander was 21–10 in 1927 and 16–9 in 1928.

JUNE 27
Sheriff Blake pitches a one–hitter to defeat the Cardinals 5–0 in the second game of a double–header at Sportsman's Park. The game was interrupted in the ninth when thousands of bottles descended onto the field after St. Louis fans objected to a call by umpire Charlie Moran. In the first game, Grover Alexander pitched against the Cubs, who sold him five days earlier, and won 3–2 in eleven innings.

JULY 1
Hack Wilson hits a walk–off homer in the eleventh inning to beat the Reds 2–1 at Cubs Park.

JULY 10
Hack Wilson's two–run walk–off homer in the ninth inning beats the Dodgers 6–4 in the first game of a double–header at Cubs Park. The Cubs also won the second game 3–1.

JULY 20
The Cubs bury the Dodgers 16–2 at Cubs Park. Chicago scored seven runs in the third inning to take a 12–1 lead.

AUGUST 4
A home run by Cliff Heathcote in the 11th inning lifts the Cubs to a 7–5 win over the Braves in Boston.

AUGUST 11
The Cubs pound the Giants 11–1 in New York.

AUGUST 17
Guy Bush pitches a two–hitter to defeat the Giants 7–0 at Cubs Park. The only New York hits were singles by Fred Lindstrom and Mel Ott.

Bush played for the Cubs from 1923 through 1934 and had a record of 152–101. He pitched 2,201 ⅓ innings, and completed 127 games. Bush credited much of his success to a "secret dark liniment" applied to his arm by Cubs trainer Andy Lotshaw. Bush swore that the liniment kept his arm loose and pain–free. After Bush was traded to the Pirates in 1935, Lotshaw admitted to Bush that the "secret dark liniment" was Coca–Cola.

AUGUST 29
The Cubs win their eighth game in a row with a 5–1 decision over the Reds at Cubs Park.

AUGUST 31
Sheriff Blake pitches a two–hitter to beat the Reds 1–0 at Cubs Park. A walk–off single by Mike Gonzalez in the ninth inning drove in the lone run of the game. The only Cincinnati hits were singles by Hod Ford and Charlie Dressen.

SEPTEMBER 11
The Cubs score seven runs in the seventh inning and trounce the Phillies 10–6 in

Philadelphia. Pete Scott hit a grand slam in the big inning off Jack Knight.

SEPTEMBER 29   In the first game of the Chicago City Series, the Cubs defeat the White Sox 6–0 at Cubs Park.

OCTOBER 2   In game three of the City Series, Percy Jones pitches the Cubs to a 1–0 win over the White Sox at Cubs Park. Jones also drove in the only run of the game with a single in the eighth inning.

OCTOBER 7   The White Sox win the seventh and final game of the City Series with a 3–0 victory over the Cubs at Cubs Park.

NOVEMBER 16   William Wrigley announces plans to add a second deck to Cubs Park.

The addition of the second deck began in the right field corner and moved around to the left, a process which took over a year. By the time the 1927 season opened, only the portion between the right field corner and home plate was completed. The second deck was finished before the start of the 1928 campaign. In addition, the name of the ballpark was changed from Cubs Park to Wrigley Field.

1927   Cubs

Season in a Sentence

The Cubs lead the National League by six games on August 16, but a stretch of 24 losses in 35 games dooms the club to fourth place.

Finish • Won • Lost • Pct • GB

Fourth   85   68   .556   8.5

Manager

Joe McCarthy

Stats

Stats	Cubs	NL	Rank
Batting Avg:	.284	.282	3
On–Base Pct:	.346	.339	3
Slugging Pct:	.400	.386	4
Home Runs:	74		3
Stolen Bases:	65		7
ERA:	3.65	3.91	4
Fielding Avg:	.971	.968	3
Runs Scored:	750		4
Runs Allowed:	661		3

Starting Lineup

Gabby Hartnett, c
Charlie Grimm, 1b
Clyde Beck, 2b
Sparky Adams, 3b–2b–ss
Woody English, ss
Riggs Stephenson, lf
Hack Wilson, cf
Earl Webb, rf
Cliff Heathcote, rf
Eddie Pick, 3b
Pete Scott, rf

Pitchers

Charlie Root, sp–rp
Sheriff Blake, sp
Hal Carlson, sp
Guy Bush, sp–rp
Bob Osborn, sp–rp
Jim Brillheart, rp–sp
Percy Jones, rp–sp

Attendance

1,159,168 (first in NL)

Club Leaders

Batting Avg:	Stephenson	.344
On–Base Pct:	Stephenson	.415
Slugging Pct:	Wilson	.579
Home Runs:	Wilson	30
RBI:	Wilson	129
Runs:	Wilson	119
Stolen Bases:	Adams	26
Wins:	Root	26
Strikeouts:	Root	145
ERA:	Carlson	3.03
Saves:	Root	2
	Bush	2

APRIL 12   Before a reported crowd of 42,000 at Wrigley Field, the Cubs win the first game of the season 10–1 against the Cardinals. Grover Alexander took the loss for the Cardinals. Charlie Root pitched the complete–game victory for Chicago. Earl Webb, in his first game as a member of the Cubs, hit two homers. They were also Webb's first two big league hits. His previous big league experience consisted of four games with the Giants in 1925. Charlie Grimm also homered in the opener.

Charlie Root, left, and Gabby Hartnett pose with a fan at the Cubs' Catalina Island spring training site in California.

Charlie Root had the best season of his career in 1927, with a 26–15 record. He led the league with 309 1/3 innings pitched, making 36 starts and 12 relief appearances.

APRIL 15   The Cubs collect only two hits off Cardinals pitcher Bill Sherdel but win 1–0 at Wrigley Field. The lone run of the game was a home run by Hack Wilson in the second inning. Percy Jones pitched the shutout.

APRIL 28   The Cubs score nine runs in the second inning to take a 12–0 lead and race to a 16–4 victory over the Pirates in Pittsburgh.

MAY 1   Chuck Tolson hits a pinch–hit grand slam in the seventh inning off Ray Kremer of the Pirates to give the Cubs a 6–5 lead, but Pittsburgh rallies to win 7–6 at Wrigley Field.

MAY 14   The Cubs break open a game against the Braves in Boston with five runs in the eighteenth inning to win 7–2. Guy Bush pitched all eighteen innings for the Cubs. Charlie Robertson went seventeenth and one–third innings for the Braves before being removed during the Cubs late rally. Both teams scored in the twelfth inning. In the bottom of the twelfth, Bush pitched out of a bases loaded, one out jam.

The Braves and Cubs were off on May 15 because games on Sunday were not permitted in Boston, and the contest on the 16th was rained out. This gave the two clubs plenty of rest for another marathon on May 17.

MAY 17   In the longest game in Cubs history, the Cubs defeat the Braves 4–3 in twenty–two innings in Boston. There was no scoring from the seventh inning through the twenty–first. In the twenty–second, Hack Wilson walked, went to second on a sacrifice by Riggs Stephenson, and scored on Charlie Grimm's single. Bobby Smith pitched all twenty–two innings for the Braves. For the Cubs, starter Sheriff Blake pitched seven and one–third innings, Jim Brillheart went two–thirds of an inning, and Bob Osborn the final fourteen. Osborn didn't allow a run.

The games on May 14 and 17, 1927, set a major league record for most innings played in two consecutive games between the same two clubs.

MAY 20   During a 7–5 Cubs win over the Dodgers at Ebbets Field, Brooklyn fans shower umpire Pete McLaughlin with hundreds of bottles. One of them was a bottle of "bootleg" whiskey, a beverage outlawed during Prohibition.

MAY 21   On the day that Charles Lindbergh lands in Paris after his historic solo flight across the Atlantic, the umpires are the target of fans once more in Brooklyn. The Cubs won both games by scores of 6–4 and 11–6. In the second game, the Cubs scored nine runs in the ninth inning off five Dodgers pitchers for the victory. Hack Wilson's bases–loaded triple put the Cubs in the lead. At the conclusion, umpire Frank Wilson was extracted from a threatening crowd with great difficulty by special police and several Brooklyn players.

It was agreed before hand that the game would be called at 5:45 P.M. to allow the Cubs to catch a train. Wilson interpreted that to mean that no inning could start after 5:45. Dodgers Manager Wilbert Robinson believed that the contest would end at precisely 5:45. The ninth inning began at 5:40 and took more than one half–hour to complete. Robinson protested the Cubs victory to National League president John Heydler, but the protest was denied.

MAY 30   Cubs shortstop Jimmy Cooney pulls off an unassisted triple play during a 7–6, ten–inning win over the Pirates in the first game of a double–header in Pittsburgh. The play came in the fourth inning with Lloyd Waner on second and Clyde Barnhart on first as the Pirate baserunners. Cooney snagged Paul Waner's liner, stepped on second to double Paul's brother Lloyd, then tagged Barnhart coming down from first. The Cubs lost the second game 6–5 in ten innings.

This is the only unassisted triple play in Cubs history. There have been only twelve unassisted triple plays in big league history, including the one by Indians second baseman Bill Wambsganss in the 1920 World Series. Oddly, one of them came the day after Cooney's play, when Tiger first baseman Johnny Neun had an unassisted triple killing on May 31, 1927. Cooney's unassisted triple play was the last in the National League until Phillies second baseman Mickey Morandini accomplished the feat in 1992.

JUNE 7   The Cubs trade Tony Kaufmann and Jimmy Cooney to the Pirates for Hal Carlson. Cooney was traded just eight days after completing his unassisted triple play.

JUNE 16   The Cubs run their winning streak to twelve games with a 7–2 decision over the Phillies at Wrigley Field.

At the end of the winning streak, the Cubs had a 34–19 record and were in second place, one game behind the Pirates.
   The top hitters on the Cubs in 1927 were Gabby Hartnett, Riggs Stephenson, and Hack Wilson. Hartnett batted .294 and slugged ten homers. Stephenson had a .344

batting average and collected 199 hits and 46 doubles. Wilson tied for the league lead in homers with 30. He also drove in 129 runs, scored 119, had 12 triples, and batted .318. Sparky Adams set a club record with 165 singles.

JULY 5   During an 8–5 win over the Reds at Wrigley Field, several hundred fans riot after Cincinnati pitcher Pete Donahue becomes engaged in a violent fight with a verbally abusive fan seated next to the Reds dugout. A contingent of 100 police officers was called to subdue the crowd.

Left to right: Chuck Tolson, Riggs Stephenson, Woody English and Sparky Adams, were among the key offensive contributors to the 1927 Cubs' success.

JULY 10   Guy Bush pitches the Cubs to a 1–0 win over the Dodgers in Brooklyn. The only run of the game was scored on a home run by Eddie Pick in the seventh inning off Norman Plitt.

In July, the Cubs purchased pitcher Wayland Dean from the Phillies. Dean claimed that he had a sore arm and pitched only two games for the Cubs. During a trip to New York, Dean disappeared during a drinking binge and was released. He died in 1930 at the age of 28 from tuberculosis.

AUGUST 1   Hack Wilson extends his hitting streak to 26 games during a 6–5 win over the Phillies at Wrigley Field.

The victory put the Cubs back into first place. Chicago held the top spot in the National League continually from August 1 through August 31.

AUGUST 16 Charlie Root shuts out the Dodgers 3–0 in Brooklyn. It was Root's 22nd win of the 1927 season.

With the victory, the Cubs took a six–game lead over their National League rivals with a record of 69–40. The Cubs lost 24 of their next 35 games, however, to fall out of the race.

AUGUST 24 The Cubs allow five runs in the ninth inning to lose 7–6 to the Phillies in the first game of a double–header in Philadelphia. The Cubs recovered to score six runs in the first inning of the second game and cruised to a 13–1 win with 22 hits. Sparky Adams collected five hits, including two doubles, in six at–bats.

SEPTEMBER 1   The Cubs are knocked out of first place with a 4–3 loss to the Pirates in Pittsburgh.

At the end of the day, only two games separated the top four teams in the league, with the Pirates in first, the Cubs in second, the Cardinals in third, and the Giants in fourth. The Cubs faded out of the race, however, while the other three clubs battled to the wire. The Pirates won the pennant, 1½ games ahead of the Cardinals and two games ahead of the Giants.

SEPTEMBER 4   The Cubs purchase Art Nehf from the Reds.

SEPTEMBER 11   A crowd of 45,000 at Wrigley Field watches the Cubs win 7–5 over the Giants. Some of the assemblage ringed the outfield, making hits into the overflow crowd ground–rule doubles. The game was delayed in the sixth inning when a storm of straw hats showered the field and players, ushers, and park attendants gathered the summer headgear.

With the win, there was still some hope for a World Series in Chicago. The Cubs were 2½ games out with eighteen contests left on the schedule.

SEPTEMBER 12   The Cubs lose 7–5 to the Giants at Wrigley Field. Fans vented their frustration with a barrage of bottles thrown on the field. Several of the missiles landed near Giants right fielder George Harper, and one grazed umpire Cy Pfirman.

The loss started a four–game losing streak which put the Cubs out of the pennant race for good. The pennant race did help the Cubs become the first National League club to draw over a million fans in a season. A total of 1,158,168 passed through the Wrigley Field turnstiles in 1927. The only other major league club prior to 1927 to draw over 1,000,000 in a season was the Yankees, who did it six times between 1920 and 1926.

SEPTEMBER 22   After defeating the Phillies 6–4 in the afternoon at Wrigley Field, giving Charlie Root his 26th win of the season, the Cubs go to Soldier Field to watch the Jack Dempsey–Gene Tunney heavyweight boxing match.

SEPTEMBER 23   The Cubs smash the Phillies 10–0 at Wrigley Field.

There was no post–season Chicago City Series between the Cubs and the White Sox in 1927, as the Cubs refused to play in the event. Cubs president William Veeck Sr. issued a vague proclamation stating: "The season of 1927 contained so many possibilities that any series other than a World's Series would be a fitting climax." Veeck and William Wrigley Jr. were roasted by the fans and the press for backing out of the City Series, and it was revived in 1928.

NOVEMBER 28   The Cubs trade Sparky Adams and Pete Scott to the Pirates for Kiki Cuyler.

This proved to be one of the best trades in Cubs history, as Cuyler became a fixture in Chicago for eight seasons. Cuyler was one of the top outfielders in baseball with the Pirates, but was benched during the 1927 season by manager Donie Bush for refusing to move from third to second in the batting order and from right field to center on defense. Cuyler hit .325 as a Cub and joined Riggs Stephenson and Hack Wilson to form the best outfield in club history.

1928

Cubs

Season in a Sentence

For the second straight season, the Cubs are in contention for the pennant in September, only to fall short.

Finish • Won • Lost • Pct • GB

Third   91   63   .591   4.0

Manager

Joe McCarthy

Stats

Stats	Cubs • NL • Rank		
Batting Avg:	.278	.281	5
On–Base Pct:	.345	.344	4
Slugging Pct:	.402	.397	4
Home Runs:	92		3
Stolen Bases:	83		1
ERA:	3.40	3.99	3
Fielding Avg:	.975	.971	1
Runs Scored:	714		4
Runs Allowed:	615		1

Starting Lineup

Gabby Hartnett, c
Charlie Grimm, 1b
Freddie Maguire, 2b
Clyde Beck, 3b–ss
Woody English, ss
Riggs Stephenson, lf
Hack Wilson, cf
Kiki Cuyler, rf
Johnny Butler, 3b
Mike Gonzalez, c

Pitchers

Pat Malone, sp–rp
Sheriff Blake, sp
Charlie Root, sp
Guy Bush, sp–rp
Art Nehf, sp–rp
Percy Jones, rp–sp

Attendance

1,143,740 (first in NL)

Club Leaders

Batting Avg:	Stephenson	.324
On–Base Pct:	Stephenson	.407
Slugging Pct:	Wilson	.588
Home Runs:	Wilson	31
RBI:	Wilson	120
Runs:	Cuyler	92
Stolen Bases:	Cuyler	37
Wins:	Malone	18
Strikeouts:	Malone	155
ERA:	Blake	2.47
Saves:	Carlson	4

APRIL 18   The Cubs lose the home opener 9–6 to the Reds before 46,000 at Wrigley Field. The Cubs scored five runs in the eighth inning to take a 6–5 lead, but Cincinnati tallied four in the ninth to win. Kiki Cuyler and Earl Webb hit homers for the Cubs.

During the 1928 season, a new press box was added to Wrigley Field. It hung behind home plate from the just–completed second deck. The box was glass enclosed and electronically heated.

APRIL 19   Hack Wilson drives in six runs, the Cubs collect 21 hits, and wallop the Reds 13–0 at Wrigley Field. Wilson hit a two–run homer in the first inning and a grand slam off Dolph Luque in the second. Later, Wilson just missed a third homer when his drive struck the top of the screen in front of the right field bleachers just a foot from the top for a double. Sheriff Blake pitched a two–hitter for Chicago. The only Cincinnati hits were singles by Pid Purdy and Hod Ford.

Wilson tied for the league lead in home runs with 31 in 1928. He also drove in 120 runs and batted .313.

MAY 14   While crossing the street outside Wrigley Field to enter a taxicab following an 8–2 Cubs win, Giants manager John McGraw is hit by an automobile and suffers a broken leg. McGraw accepted blame for the accident. The injury kept him out of the dugout for six weeks.

MAY 19   The Cubs win their thirteenth game in a row with a 3–2 decision over the Braves at Wrigley Field.

              The streak gave the Cubs a 22–12 record and a two–game lead in the National League pennant race. Two days later, the Cubs were knocked out of first place, never to return in 1928, but Joe McCarthy kept his club in contention for first place well into September.

JUNE 2   The Cubs score eight runs in the eighth inning to beat the Pirates 10–6 in Pittsburgh.

JUNE 9   The Cubs edge the Phillies in a free–swinging affair by a 13–11 score in Philadelphia. The Phillies led 10–5 at the end of the fifth inning before the Cubs climbed ahead.

JUNE 21   Hack Wilson fights a fan during a double–header against the Cardinals at Wrigley Field. The Cubs won the first game 2–1 behind Sheriff Blake's two–hitter, then lost 4–1. The only St. Louis hits in the opener were a triple by Chick Hafey and a single by Jimmy Wilson.

              After grounding out in the bottom of the ninth in the second game, Wilson climbed into the stands and attacked Edward Young, a milkman who had spent the afternoon hurling insults at the Cubs center fielder. Some 5,000 fans swarmed the field before police and the players, led by Gabby Hartnett and Joe Kelly, succeeded in parting Wilson and Young. After the field was cleared, Riggs Stephenson popped up for the final out. National League President John Heydler fined Wilson $100 and Judge Francis P. Allgretti fined Young $1.

JUNE 30   During the fourth inning of a 7–5 win over the Reds in Cincinnati, Hack Wilson becomes the first right–handed batter to hit a homer into the right field bleachers at Redland Field. The bleachers had been in place since the ballpark opened in 1912. To prove it was no fluke, Wilson hit another homer into the bleachers in the eighth inning. He was also the first batter to drive two balls over the fences in a single game at the Cincinnati ballpark, which was renamed Crosley Field in 1934.

JULY 4   The Cubs and Cardinals celebrate Independence Day with a flurry of runs. St. Louis won the first game 11–6, while the Cubs bagged the second 16–9. The Cubs bagged 21 hits in the nightcap. Riggs Stephenson collected five of the hits, including a homer and a double, in six at–bats.

              Stephenson batted .324 with eight homers in 1928. He played for the Cubs from 1926 through 1934 and compiled a batting average of .336, the highest by any player in club history with at least 2,000 plate appearances. His lifetime on–base percentage as a Cub is .408, second only to Hack Wilson's .412. Stephenson was 28 years old when acquired by the Cubs from Kansas City of the American Association. Previously, he played five seasons with the Indians, mostly as a second baseman, but a shoulder injury suffered while playing foot-ball at the University of Alabama limited his throwing ability. Cleveland sent him to the minors, even though he hit .337 for them. Joe McCarthy brought Riggs back to the majors as an outfielder, and he became a Cubs fixture for nine seasons. His .336 lifetime average ranks 19th all–time by players with a minimum of 4,000 plate appearances. No player since 1900 with a higher average has been denied admission to the Hall of Fame. Stephenson has failed to receive a plaque in Cooperstown because of a relatively short career (1,310 games), little power (63 homers), below–average defense, and only four seasons in which he had as many as 400 plate appearances.

JULY 6   The Cubs collect 20 hits and rout the Dodgers 14–8 at Wrigley Field.

JULY 17   Clyde Beck's grand slam off Jimmy Ring of the Phillies in the fifth inning accounts for all of the Cubs runs in a 4–3 win at Wrigley Field. Chicago trailed 3–0 when Beck connected. It was the eighth win in a row for the Cubs.

JULY 21   The Cubs defeat the Giants in two thrilling extra–inning games during a double–header at Wrigley Field. In the first contest, the Cubs won 2–1 in fifteen innings. Riggs Stephenson drove in the winning run with a single. In the second, the Cubs triumphed 5–4 in ten innings. The deciding run crossed the plate on a triple by Gabby Hartnett.

AUGUST 4   The Cubs collect 22 hits and gallop to a 16–3 win over the Dodgers in Brooklyn. Cubs pitcher Pat Malone had four hits, including a double, in five at–bats.

Pat Malone won 18 games as a rookie in 1928 to lead the Cubs staff.

As a 25–year–old rookie in 1928, Pat Malone lost his first seven decisions, but ended the season with a record of 18–13, an ERA of 2.84 and 155 strikeouts. Malone won 22 games for the Cubs in 1929 and 20 more in 1930. He was unable to continue his success because he loved the nightlife and was a frequent drinking partner of Hack Wilson in many of Chicago's illegal drinking establishments during the Prohibition era. Malone's given name was Perce Lee Malone. During the 1928 season, his roommate on the road was Percy Lee Jones. Despite the similarity in names, Perce Lee and Percy Lee were not a match made in heaven. The arrangement ended when Malone trapped some pigeons off the ledge of a hotel room and placed them in the bed of the sleeping Jones.

AUGUST 15   The Cubs score three runs in the ninth to defeat the Giants 6–5 at Wrigley Field after New York scored two in the top of the inning to take a 5–3 lead. Freddie

Maguire drove in the winning run with a single.

SEPTEMBER 1   Sheriff Blake pitches a one–hitter to beat the Reds 1–0 in Cincinnati. The only Reds hit was a double by George Kelly in the fifth inning. Cliff Heathcote drove in the lone run of the game with a sacrifice fly in the first inning.

Blake was 17–11 with a 2.47 ERA in 1928. Charlie Root was supposed to be the ace of the staff following his 26–win season in 1927, but he reported late to spring training in 1928 after a holdout and was some twenty–seven pounds overweight. Root never shaped up and was 14–18 during the season. He rebounded in 1929 with a 19–6 record in 272 innings.

SEPTEMBER 7   The Cubs sock the Reds 11–1 at Wrigley Field.

SEPTEMBER 9   Guy Bush pitches a two–hitter to beat the Reds 2–0 at Wrigley Field. The only Cincinnati runs were singles by Ethan Allen in the first inning and George Kelly in the fourth.

SEPTEMBER 12   The Cubs defeat the Cardinals 6–1 before a Thursday afternoon crowd of 45,000 at Wrigley Field.

The win put the Cubs only two games back of the first–place Cards. The Cubs were in third place, and the Giants in second, 1½ games out. The Cubs won nine of their last fourteen games, but could pull no closer to St. Louis. The Cubs finished the season four games behind the Cardinals and two games back of the Giants.

SEPTEMBER 17   The Cubs crush the Braves 15–5 in Boston.

OCTOBER 3   In the opening game of the Chicago City Series, the Cubs defeat the White Sox 3–0 before 25,885 at Comiskey Park. Pat Malone pitched the shutout.

OCTOBER 4   The Cubs win game two of the City Series 5–3 in 14 innings at Wrigley Field.

OCTOBER 9   The Cubs win the seventh and deciding game of the City Series 13–2 at Comiskey Park. The seven games drew 184,951 fans.

NOVEMBER 7   The day after Herbert Hoover wins the presidential election against Al Smith, the Cubs send Socks Seybold, Percy Jones, Lou Legett, Freddy Maguire, Bruce Cunningham, and $200,000 to the Braves for Rogers Hornsby.

The trade was agreed to several weeks earlier, but Braves owner Judge Emil Fuchs delayed the announcement until after another election. In Massachusetts, there was an issue on the ballot that would allow the Braves and the Red Sox to play home games on Sunday, and Fuchs didn't want to jeopardize its passage by revealing that Hornsby would be dealt. The trade was announced the day after the issue passed the electorate and Sunday baseball in Boston became a fact. Fuchs was badly in debt and traded Hornsby for the cash necessary to make his franchise financially solvent. The Cubs, on the other hand, had record attendance figures in 1927 and 1928, but just missed winning the pennant, in part because of a weakness at second base. Hornsby was seen as the last piece of the puzzle to vault the Cubs into first place. At the time of the trade, Hornsby was 32 years old, and had a .361 lifetime batting average, .575 slugging percentage, 2,475 hits, and 238 home runs. He was coming off of a season in which he led the NL in batting average (.387), on base percentage (.498), and slugging percentage (.632). Hornsby was brutally blunt, belligerent, and fanatical about baseball. At his previous stops, he quickly wore out his welcome. Hornsby was a Cardinal from 1915 until 1926, but was dealt to the Giants even after delivering a world championship to St. Louis as a player–manager in 1926. After one year in New York, he was traded to Boston, where he was also the player–manager. The Cubs were his fourth team in four years. In Chicago in 1929, Hornsby had one of the greatest offensive years of any player in club history. He batted .380 and led the league in runs (156) and slugging percentage (.679) in addition to hitting 39 homers, 47 doubles, and 229 hits in helping the Cubs win the NL pennant. The batting average, runs and hit totals are still modern Chicago Cubs records for a single season. Beginning in 1930, however, Rogers was hampered by a series of injuries, and his playing time and abilities diminished. From September 1930 through August 1932, Hornsby was also the manager of the Cubs.

Rodgers Hornsby, left, signs a contract with the Cubs as owner William Wrigley looks on. The newly acquired Hornsby was seen as the missing piece expected to lift the Cubs to the 1929 National League pennant.

1929

Cubs

Season in a Sentence

Led by new acquisition Rogers Hornsby, the Cubs soar to the National League pennant for the first time in eleven years, but lose the World Series to the Athletics.

Finish • Won • Lost • Pct • GB

First   98   54   .645 +10.5

World Series–The Cubs lost four games to one to the Philadelphia Athletics.

Manager

Joe McCarthy

Stats

Stats	Cubs	NL	Rank
Batting Avg:	.303	.294	3
On–Base Pct:	.373	.357	2
Slugging Pct:	.452	.426	2
Home Runs:	139		2
Stolen Bases:	103		2
ERA:	4.16	4.71	2
Fielding Avg:	.975	.971	1
Runs Scored:	962		1
Runs Allowed:	758		2

Starting Lineup

Zack Taylor, c
Charlie Grimm, 1b
Rogers Hornsby, 2b
Norm McMillan, 3b
Woody English, ss
Riggs Stephenson, lf
Hack Wilson, cf
Kiki Cuyler, rf
Cliff Heathcote, rf
Clyde Beck, 3b
Mike Gonzalez, c

Pitchers

Pat Malone, sp–rp
Charlie Root, sp
Guy Bush, sp–rp
Sheriff Blake, sp
Art Nehf, rp–sp
Hal Carlson, rp–sp

Attendance

1,485,166 (first in NL)

Club Leaders

Batting Avg:	Hornsby	.380
On–Base Pct:	Hornsby	.459
Slugging Pct:	Hornsby	.679
Home Runs:	Hornsby	39
	Hack Wilson	39
RBI:	Wilson	159
Runs:	Hornsby	156
Stolen Bases:	Cuyler	43
Wins:	Malone	22
Strikeouts:	Malone	166
ERA:	Root	3.47
Saves:	Bush	8

APRIL 16   Two months after seven of Al Capone's rivals are machine–gunned to death in a North Side garage in the St. Valentine's Day Massacre, a crowd reported at 50,000 at Wrigley Field watches the Cubs lose 4–3 to the Pirates on Opening Day. The Pirates scored three of their runs in the first inning. A two–run Cub rally in the ninth fell short. Rogers Hornsby made his Cubs debut, and was 0–for–3 with two walks.

The Cubs were without one of the key components in their lineup all season in 1929 because of an injury to catcher Gabby Hartnett, who hit .302 with 14 homers in 1928. In the second spring training game at Catalina, something snapped in Hartnett's arm when he made a throw to second base. Gabby caught only one game all year (on September 22) and was limited to 22 at–bats, mainly as a pinch–hitter.

APRIL 17   The Cubs break loose and romp to a 13–2 win over the Pirates at Wrigley Field. In his second game as a Cub, Rogers Hornsby hit a grand slam off Fred Fussell in the eighth inning. Hornsby was booed by the crowd of 8,000 when he struck out with the sacks filled in the seventh.

APRIL 23   Two Cubs catchers are injured during a 9–6 loss to the Cardinals at Wrigley Field.

The 1929 Cubs put it all together to win their first National League pennant in eleven years.

Both starter Mike Gonzalez and his replacement, Earl Grace, had to leave the game when they injured their hands. With Gabby Hartnett already out with a sore arm, the Cubs had to finish the April 23 contest with Tom Angley, who was making his major league debut, as the catcher.

APRIL 28   The Cubs score eight runs in the fifth inning against the Reds in Cincinnati, but lose 17–12. The two teams combined for 12 runs in the fifth inning. The score was 16–11 at the end of five innings.

MAY 17   Hack Wilson hits a grand slam off Pete Donohue of the Reds during the sixth inning of a 9–3 Cubs win at Wrigley Field.

Wilson led the NL in RBIs in 1929 with 159 in addition to hitting 39 homers, scoring 135 runs, and batting .345. He was part of one of the best offensive seasons by an outfield in big league history. Riggs Stephenson hit .362 with 17 homers and 110 RBIs. Kiki Cuyler batted .360 and had 15 home runs and 102 runs batted in.

JUNE 5   Held scoreless through eight innings, the Cubs erupt for four runs in the ninth inning to defeat the Dodgers 4–3 at Wrigley Field. The final two runs were scored on a two–run pinch–hit single by Gabby Hartnett.

JUNE 12   Pat Malone strikes out 12 batters to defeat the Phillies 7–3 at Wrigley Field.

Malone had a 22–10 record and a 3.57 ERA in 1929.

JUNE 16   A fracas spreads from Wrigley Field to the police station following a 7–3 Phillies win.

Fresco Thompson and Denny Sothern of the Phillies were alleged to have squirted tobacco juice at a fan who was razzing the players. After the game, the fan demanded an apology and found himself arrested. Other fans followed the officers to the police station where a demonstration took place, and the man was released. Two others refused to quiet down, however, and were taken into custody.

JUNE 18   Hack Wilson drives in six runs, including a grand slam off Hal Haid of the Cardinals during a seven–run fifth inning, leading the Cubs to a 13–6 win at Wrigley Field.

JUNE 28   The Cubs score seven runs in the second inning and defeat the Cardinals 9–5 in St. Louis. The victory put the Cubs into first place.

JUNE 29   Charlie Grimm hits a grand slam in the first inning off Bill Sherdel of the Cardinals to set the pace for a 10–7 win in St. Louis.

JULY 1   The Cubs and the Cardinals play to an 11–11 tie, called after six innings to allow the St. Louis club to catch a train to Pittsburgh. Riggs Stephenson drove in seven runs, four of them on a grand slam off Fred Frankhouse in the first inning. Stephenson later added another homer and a double.

JULY 3   The Reds and the Cubs combine for nine double plays, a National League record for a nine–inning game, in a 7–5 Chicago win at Wrigley Field. The Cubs turned five of the nine double plays.

JULY 4   The Cubs and the Reds split a double–header at Wrigley Field highlighted by a fight between Hack Wilson and Reds pitcher Ray Kolp. The Cubs drop the first game of the holiday twinbill 9–8, and won the second 10–5.

Kolp, whose nickname was Jockey for his ability to insult opponents, had been heckling Wilson mercilessly, and in the sixth inning of the second game the Cub slugger could take no more. After hitting a single, Wilson turned and headed toward the Reds dugout, planting a right to Kolp's jaw. Wilson neglected to call time out and was tagged out by Cincinnati third baseman Charlie Dressen. Later that evening at Union Station, where both teams were boarding a train, Wilson sought out Kolp to either apologize or fight. Pete Donohue, another Cincinnati pitcher, made some unkind remarks about Wilson's behavior at the ballpark, and Hack punched him twice in the face. Donohue fell to the floor after being struck by Wilson and had to have two stitches put in his lip. Wilson was suspended three days by National League President John Heydler.

JULY 6   The Cubs purchase Zack Taylor from the Braves.

Taylor had been a regular catcher with the Dodgers, Giants, and Braves since 1923, and was purchased to fill the gap at the position left by Gabby Hartnett's injury. Taylor caught the majority of the Cubs games for the remainder of 1929 and all five games in the World Series.

JULY 7   The Cubs claw the Braves 15–4 in Boston.

During a stretch in July and August, the Cubs won 35 of 46 games.

JULY 17   The Cubs swamp the Phillies 16–3 in Philadelphia. Rogers Hornsby hit a grand slam in the fourth inning. It was Hornsby's fourth grand slam of the year.

JULY 20   Hack Wilson collects hits in both ends of a double–header against the Dodgers in Brooklyn to run his hitting streak to 27 games. The Cubs won the first game 6–5 in ten innings, and lost the second 4–1.

JULY 24   The Cubs take first place with an 8–7 win over the Giants in New York. The Cubs score four runs in the seventh, three on a Hack Wilson homer, to take the lead.

The Cubs held first place for the rest of the season and turned the race into a runaway. Joe McCarthy's crew advanced their lead to 7 ½ games within two weeks and 14 ½ by the end of August. The Cubs finished the season 10 ½ games in front.

Cubs slugger Hack Wilson poses with ex–Cub Cy Williams, who had been dealt to the Philadelphia Phillies in 1918.

AUGUST 1   Guy Bush pitches the Cubs to a 1–0 win over the Braves at Wrigley Field. The only run of the game was scored in the first inning on a bases–loaded walk issued to Riggs Stephenson by Ben Cantwell.

Bush pitched 270⅔ innings in 1929, making 29 starts and 21 relief appearances. He was 18–7, with an eleven–game winning streak, and recorded eight saves.

AUGUST 3   The Cubs stomp the Dodgers 12–2 at Wrigley Field.

AUGUST 5   The Cubs beat the Dodgers 9–8 in sixteen innings at Wrigley Field. The winning run was scored on Woody English's double and a single by Hack Wilson.

AUGUST 6   The Cubs lose 5–4 to the Dodgers at Wrigley Field in near–riot conditions.

Nearly 29,000 women on Ladies Day and at least 20,000 men overpowered the ticket takers and turnstile keepers before the gates were locked, leaving at least

10,000 more outside. The crowd overran the playing field, stood in the aisles, and sat atop the outfield fences. Some newspapers estimated that 65,000 people were inside Wrigley Field.

AUGUST 19   The Cubs sign 13-year-old Red Solomon, third baseman of the New York Kiwanis Club, to a contract. Solomon is the youngest player ever to be signed to a contract by a major league team. He never played in the majors, however.

AUGUST 20   Hal Carlson pitches the Cubs to a 1–0 win over Carl Hubbell of the Giants in the second game of a double-header in New York. The only run of the game was scored in the fourth inning on a triple by Rogers Hornsby and a sacrifice fly by Hack Wilson.

AUGUST 22   The Cubs romp past the Phillies 16–7 in Philadelphia.

AUGUST 26   The Cubs defeat the Reds 9–5 at Wrigley Field on a freak grand-slam home run by Norm McMillan.

In the eighth inning with the score tied 5–5 and the bases loaded with Cubs, McMillan hit a Rube Ehrhardt pitch down the left field line. Reds left fielder Evar Swanson saw the ball hit an open gutter running along the base of the stands, then lost sight of the ball. He looked in and around the gutter and began to wonder if the horsehide disappeared into thin air. The frantic Swanson spotted the jacket of Cubs pitcher Ken Penner, who was warming up in the bullpen. The Reds outfielder shook the jacket, but still failed to locate the ball. By this time, all of the runners had crossed the plate, and the search was called off. At the start of the ninth inning, Penner entered the game and put on the jacket for the trip from the bullpen to the mound. As he placed his right hand into the sleeve, he found the baseball that Swanson had been looking for in vain.

Home runs such as this were no longer possible after the end of the 1930 season due to a rules change. After 1930, balls that bounced into the stands or into an obstruction, like Penner's jacket, were ground rule doubles.

AUGUST 30   The Pirates massacre the Cubs 15–0 at Wrigley Field.

SEPTEMBER 2   The Cubs beat the Cardinals 11–7 and 12–10 in a separate admission double-header that drew 81,000 to Wrigley Field. The morning game attracted 38,000 and the afternoon tilt drew 43,000.

The Cubs set a major league record in 1929 with an attendance of 1,485,166. The previous record was 1,289,422 by the 1920 Yankees. The 1929 attendance figure by the Cubs remained the major league record until 1946 when the Yankees drew 2,265,512 and the club record until 1969 when 1,674,993 paid their way into Wrigley Field.

SEPTEMBER 7   The Cubs beat the Braves 13–6 and 9–2 in a double-header at Wrigley Field. The Cubs collected ten consecutive hits during the seven-run fourth inning of the first game.

SEPTEMBER 8   The Cubs collect seven runs in the sixth inning, but lose 13–11 to the Braves at Wrigley Field.

SEPTEMBER 17   Kiki Cuyler hits a grand slam in the fifth inning off Dazzy Vance of the Dodgers to put the Cubs up 7–6, but Brooklyn scores two in the ninth to win 8–7 in the first game of a double–header at Wrigley Field. The Cubs also lost the second game 9–6.

The Cubs hit nine grand slams in 1929, a club record.

SEPTEMBER 18   The Cubs lose 7–3 to the Giants at Wrigley Field but clinch the pennant when the Pirates lose to the Braves in Pittsburgh.

SEPTEMBER 19   Pat Malone beats the Giants 5–0 at Wrigley Field for his 22nd victory of the season.

SEPTEMBER 29   Charlie Root pitches the Cubs to a 1–0 win over the Reds at Wrigley Field. Rogers Hornsby's homer off Benny Frey in the fourth inning accounted for the only run of the game. It was one of Hornsby's four hits during the afternoon.

The Cubs played the Philadelphia Athletics, managed by Connie Mack, in the World Series. The Athletics won the American League pennant for the first time in 15 years and had a record in 1929 of 106–46.

OCTOBER 8   In the first game of the 1929 World Series, the Athletics defeat the Cubs 3–1 before 50,740 at Wrigley Field. Connie Mack bypassed 24–game winner George Earnshaw and 20–game winner Lefty Grove to use journeyman pitcher Howard Ehmke as his starting pitcher. Ehmke pitched only 55 innings during the regular season and had a record of 7–2. He responded with an eight–hitter and struck out 13 Cubs batters. Jimmie Foxx broke open a 0–0 game with a solo homer off Charlie Root in the seventh inning. The A's added two runs in the top of the ninth before the Cubs recorded their lone tally.

The game started several minutes late because the umpires failed to arrive on time. Before the contest, two Cubs employees and two Wrigley Field vendors were arrested for threatening and assaulting independent hot dog operators who were selling frankfurters to the thousands lined up outside the ballpark waiting for bleacher seats.

OCTOBER 9   The Athletics, powered by a three–run homer by Jimmie Foxx and a two–run blast by Al Simmons, defeat the Cubs 9–3 in game two of the World Series before 49,987 at Wrigley Field. The Athletics took a 6–0 lead with three runs in the third inning and three in the fourth off Pat Malone. George Earnshaw and Lefty Grove combined to strike out 13 more Cubs batters. Hack Wilson had three hits for the Cubs.

OCTOBER 11   The Cubs bounce back to win game three 3–1 before 29,921 at Shibe Park in Philadelphia. Guy Bush was the winner with a complete game. The Cubs scored all three of their runs in the sixth inning. It was the first win in the Series by a National League team since 1926 and ended a ten–game NL losing streak.

OCTOBER 12   The Cubs blow an 8–0 lead and lose game four 10–8 when the Athletics score ten runs in the eighth inning before 29,921 at Shibe Park. The A's rally was helped by misplays by Hack Wilson, who lost two balls in the sun, one for an inside–the–park home run by Mule Haas that scored three runs. Six of the runs were scored off Charlie Root, two off Art Nehf (in his last major league appearance) and two against Sheriff Blake. It is the only time in World Series history that a team has come from behind to win after trailing by eight runs. Key contributors to the Cubs 8-0 lead were Kiki Cuyler, with three hits, and Charlie Grimm, with a home run.

OCTOBER 14   The Athletics take the world championship with a 3–2 win over the Cubs in game five, played before 29,921 at Shibe Park. Pat Malone pitched shutout ball through eighth innings before coming apart in the ninth as the A's scored three runs to take the title. Mule Haas hit a two–run homer to tie the score. With two out, Al Simmons doubled and Bing Miller drove him the game–winning run. The game was attended by President Herbert Hoover.

Forest Cole of Dallas found that it doesn't pay to bet on the Cubs. He had to pay off a wager with Ernest Luttrell by hitting fly balls from Dallas to Philadelphia. Luttrell accompanied Cole on the journey, furnishing a fungo bat and balls. It took them over three months to complete the excursion.

OCTOBER 27   Two days before the historic stock market crash, which starts the country on the road to the Great Depression, the Cubs purchase Les Bell from the Braves.

Bell was only 28 and was expected to become the Cubs starting third baseman for many years, but he proved to be a huge disappointment.

DECEMBER 19   A proposed prize fight between Hack Wilson and White Sox first baseman Art Shires is called off.

During the fall and winter of 1929, Shires arranged a number of professional boxing matches for himself, and he won all but his contest against George Trafton, center of the Chicago Bears. Shires also challenged Wilson, and Hack readily agreed, but he backed out after Shires lost to Trafton in front of a disappointingly small crowd.

THE STATE OF THE CUBS

The Cubs came into the 1930s as the defending National League champion, having won the pennant in 1929. The Cubs won league titles at three-year intervals, finishing first in 1932, 1935, and 1938. All three 1930s pennants were won with incredible stretch drives in August and September. World Series success was more fleeting, however, as Chicago followed up the loss to the Athletics in 1929 with defeats at the hands of the Yankees in 1932, the Tigers in 1935, and the Yankees again in 1938. In the four Fall Classic appearances from 1929 through 1938, the Cubs had a record of 3–16. Overall, the Cubs had the best record in the National League during the 1930s, and the second best in the majors behind the Yankees, with 889 wins and 648 losses for a winning percentage of .579. The Cubs were in contention for the pennant nearly every season and never had a losing record. Chicago had a winning record for fourteen consecutive seasons from 1926 through 1939. Unfortunately, the Cubs haven't had a winning decade since the 1930s. Besides the three captured by the Cubs, NL pennants were won during the decade by the Cardinals (1930, 1931, and 1934), Giants (1933, 1936, and 1937), and the Reds (1939).

THE BEST TEAM

The 1935 Cubs had a record of 100–54 and were the only club in the decade that won a World Series game, with two victories against the Tigers. The 1932 and 1938 Cubs were swept by the Yankees.

The 1935 Cubs also won the NL pennant with an incredible 21-game winning streak during the stretch drive.

THE WORST TEAM

Even the worst Cubs teams during the decade were moderately successful. Both the 1931 and 1939 outfits were 84–70. The 1931 team finished in third place, 17 games behind, while the 1939 club was fourth and 13 games out.

THE BEST MOMENT

Gabby Hartnett hit a home run on September 28, 1938, against the Pirates to put the Cubs into first place. The clout has forever been known as the "Homer in the Gloamin."

THE WORST MOMENT

Billy Jurges was shot by an ex-girlfriend on July 6, 1932. He was also involved in nearly one major fracas each year on the field. In 1935, Jurges fought a teammate in the dugout during a game following an argument over the Civil War.

THE ALL-DECADE TEAM • YEARS WITH CUBS

Gabby Hartnett, c	1922–40
Charlie Grimm, 1b	1925–36
Billy Herman, 2b	1931–41
Stan Hack, 3b	1932–47
Woody English, ss	1927–36
Augie Galan, lf	1934–41
Hack Wilson, cf	1926–31
Kiki Cuyler, rf	1928–35
Charlie Root, p	1926–41
Bill Lee, p	1934–43, 1947
Lon Warneke, p	1930–36, 1942–43, 1945
Pat Malone, p	1928–34

The 1930s All-Decade team includes four future Hall of Famers in Gabby Hartnett, Billy Herman, Hack Wilson and Kiki Cuyler. Other players with outstanding careers with the Cubs who played key roles during the decade include pitchers Guy Bush (1923–34) and Larry French (1935–41), shortstop Billy Jurges (1931–38, 1946–47), left fielder Riggs Stephenson (1926–34), and right fielder Frank Demaree (1932–38).

THE DECADE LEADERS

Batting Avg:	Stephenson	.329
On–Base Pct:	Stephenson	.394
Slugging Pct:	Hartnett	.492
Home Runs:	Hartnett	149
RBI:	Hartnett	777
Runs:	Herman	794
Stolen Bases:	Hack	100
Wins:	Root	114
Strikeouts:	Root	818
ERA:	Warneke	2.82
Saves:	Root	28

THE HOME FIELD

Wrigley Field was remodeled between the 1937 and 1938 seasons with the addition of new enlarged bleachers, a new scoreboard, and the planting of ivy on the outfield wall.

THE GAME YOU WISH YOU HAD SEEN

It would be hard to top the "Homer in the Gloamin'," but no baseball fan could resist traveling back in time to Wrigley Field for game three of the World Series against the Yankees on October 1, 1932, with a pair of binoculars on Babe Ruth as he stepped to the plate in the fifth inning. Did the Babe "call his shot" by pointing to the center field bleachers before hitting a home run?

THE WAY THE GAME WAS PLAYED

The offensive explosion that changed baseball during the 1920s peaked in 1930 when the National League batting average was .303 and teams averaged 5.7 runs per game. The NL moguls deadened the ball for 1931, and batting averages dipped to .277 and 4.5 runs per game in 1931 and 4.0 runs a game in 1933. From 1934 until 1939, batting averages were generally around .270. There were only 354 stolen bases in the National League in 1938, less than half the total of 1924.

MANAGEMENT

William Wrigley Jr. died in 1932, and William Veeck Sr. passed away a year later. Ownership of the Cubs passed to Wrigley's son, Philip, who continued to own the club until his death in 1977. Philip, better known as P. K., hired Bill Veeck Jr. in 1937 as an $18–a–week office boy in 1937. It was the idea of the junior Veeck to plant the ivy that still adorns the outfield walls of Wrigley Field. Despite the success on the field, the Cubs went through four managers,

twice changing skippers during seasons in which the club won the pennant. The managers during the 1930s were Joe McCarthy, who piloted the club from 1926 through 1930, Rogers Hornsby (1930–32), Charlie Grimm (1932–38), and Gabby Hartnett (1938–40).

THE BEST PLAYER MOVE

The best move was the purchase of Billy Herman from Louisville in the American Association in 1931. The successful Cubs teams of the thirties were built largely on holdovers from the 1920s, and from minor league deals such as the one which brought Herman to Chicago. There were no outstanding trades. The Cubs acquired players such as Dizzy Dean, Chuck Klein, Babe Herman, Burleigh Grimes, Fred Lindstrom, Larry French, and Claude Passeau in trades, but Dean, Herman, Klein, Grimes, and Lindstrom failed to live up to their billing, and the deals that brought French and Passeau to Chicago have to be rated as about even because of the talent the Cubs surrendered in the exchange.

THE WORST PLAYER MOVE

The Cubs had first dibs on Joe DiMaggio, but passed on him after Joe suffered a fractured knee. In the worst trade, the Cubs dealt Dolph Camilli to the Phillies for Don Hurst on June 11, 1934.

1930s

1930

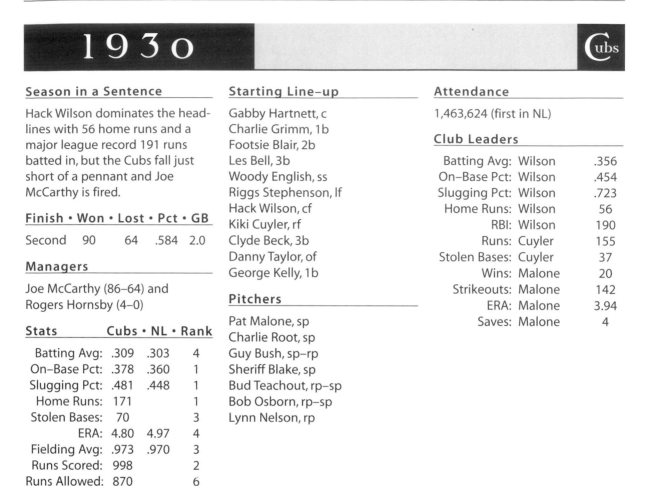

Season in a Sentence

Hack Wilson dominates the headlines with 56 home runs and a major league record 191 runs batted in, but the Cubs fall just short of a pennant and Joe McCarthy is fired.

Finish • Won • Lost • Pct • GB

Second   90   64   .584   2.0

Managers

Joe McCarthy (86–64) and
Rogers Hornsby (4–0)

Stats   Cubs • NL • Rank

Batting Avg:	.309	.303	4
On–Base Pct:	.378	.360	1
Slugging Pct:	.481	.448	1
Home Runs:	171		1
Stolen Bases:	70		3
ERA:	4.80	4.97	4
Fielding Avg:	.973	.970	3
Runs Scored:	998		2
Runs Allowed:	870		6

Starting Line–up

Gabby Hartnett, c
Charlie Grimm, 1b
Footsie Blair, 2b
Les Bell, 3b
Woody English, ss
Riggs Stephenson, lf
Hack Wilson, cf
Kiki Cuyler, rf
Clyde Beck, 3b
Danny Taylor, of
George Kelly, 1b

Pitchers

Pat Malone, sp
Charlie Root, sp
Guy Bush, sp–rp
Sheriff Blake, sp
Bud Teachout, rp–sp
Bob Osborn, rp–sp
Lynn Nelson, rp

Attendance

1,463,624 (first in NL)

Club Leaders

Batting Avg:	Wilson	.356
On–Base Pct:	Wilson	.454
Slugging Pct:	Wilson	.723
Home Runs:	Wilson	56
RBI:	Wilson	190
Runs:	Cuyler	155
Stolen Bases:	Cuyler	37
Wins:	Malone	20
Strikeouts:	Malone	142
ERA:	Malone	3.94
Saves:	Malone	4

APRIL 15   The Cubs win the season opener 9–8 against the Cardinals in St. Louis. The Cubs scored four runs in the eighth to pull ahead 9–4, then survived St. Louis's three runs in the home half of the inning and one more in the ninth.

APRIL 22   The Cubs lose the first home game of the season by an 8–3 score to the Cardinals before 40,000 at Wrigley Field.

MAY 3   Charlie Root pitches ten innings of shut–out ball to beat the Phillies 1–0 at Wrigley Field. Root also started the tenth–inning rally with a double. He scored on a two–base error by Philadelphia second baseman Bernie Friberg.

Root had a 16–14 record in 1930 and a 4.33 ERA. Chicago's top pitcher was Pat Malone with a 22–9 record, a 3.94 ERA, 271⅔ innings pitched and 22 complete games.

MAY 12   The day after Adler Planetaruim opens in Grant Park, the Cubs collect six homers, four of them in the seventh inning, but lose 14–12 to the Giants at Wrigley Field. The Giants led 14–0 before the Cubs came back with one run in the fifth inning, three in the sixth, five in the seventh, one in the eighth, and two in the ninth. The four seventh–inning homers were struck by Clyde Beck, Cliff Heathcote, Hack Wilson, and Cliff Heathcote in a span of seven batters. It was the second homer of the game for Beck and Heathcote. New York pitcher Larry Benton surrendered all six homers. Nine days later, the Giants traded Benton to the Reds.

Beck hit only 12 homers in 1,525 career at–bats. This was the only time he hit more than one homer in a game. The only other time that the Cubs have hit four homers in an inning was on April 27, 2000.

MAY 28   Cubs pitcher Hal Carlson dies suddenly of a hemorrhage of the stomach at 3:35 A.M. in his apartment in a North Side hotel. He was 36 years old.

Carlson arose shortly after 2:00 A.M. after being unable to sleep because of the pain. He called teammates Riggs Stephenson, Kiki Cuyler, and Cliff Heathcote, who in turn summoned Cubs physician Dr. John Davis. Carlson died shortly after Davis arrived. Carlson suffered from stomach ulcers for two years, and often predicted that he would die suddenly of the illness.

MAY 30   Rogers Hornsby breaks his left ankle in the first game of a double–header against the Cardinals at Wrigley Field. The Cubs won both games by scores of 2–0 and 9–8.

Hornsby underwent off–season surgery for bone spurs in his right heel and was unable to play for most of spring training and the month of April. Against doctor's orders, Hornsby put himself into the lineup in early May. The broken ankle occurred because Hornsby favored the sore heel. Sliding into third base, he twisted his body so that his left heel would hit the bag. Instead, Hornsby crashed into Cardinals pitcher Sylvester Johnson, who was covering the base. Hornsby didn't play again until September. He had only 104 at–bats in 1930, and the Cubs were forced to make do with weak–hitting Footsie Blair at second base.
Entering the May 30 double–header, the Cubs had a record of 20–19 and were in fourth place, four games behind the first–place Dodgers. Following the death of Carlson and the injury to Hornsby, the prospects of repeating as National League champions looked bleak, but the Cubs banded together and were hot all through the month of June.

MAY 31   The Cubs come from behind to score three runs in the ninth to beat the Cardinals 6–5 at Wrigley Field. Hack Wilson's single drove in the game–winner.

Wilson had one of the greatest seasons in Cubs history in 1930, rebounding from the indignity of losing two fly balls in the World Series the previous fall. He drove in a major league record 191 runs, which still stands. Wilson also hit 56 home runs, which stood as the National League and Cubs record for 68 years. In addition, Hack scored 146 runs and collected 208 hits.

JUNE 1   The Cubs pillory the Pirates 16–4 at Wrigley Field. Hack Wilson drove in six runs on two homers, a double, and a single.

Guy Bush had a 15–10 record in 1930, but he had an ERA of 6.20 in 225 innings.

JUNE 4   The Cubs keep up their hitting attack with an 18–10 win over the Braves in Boston.

Kiki Cuyler and Riggs Stephenson each collected five hits. Cuyler was five for five with a homer and a double. Stephenson had five hits, including three doubles, in six at–bats.

Cuyler hit .355 in 1930 with 13 homers, 228 hits, 155 runs scored, 50 doubles, and 17 triples. Woody English was another hitting star for the Cubs in 1930, with 214 hits, 14 homers, and a .335 batting average. Stephenson hit .367 in 1930, but was limited to 109 games by injuries.

JUNE 5 The Cubs win their eighth game in a row with a 10–7 decision over the Braves in Boston.

From June 1 through June 6, the Cubs scored 72 runs in five consecutive games.

Kiki Cuyler batted .355 in 1930 and led the Cubs in doubles with 50 and stolen bases with a league–leading 37.

JUNE 6 The Cubs' incredible streak of hitting continues with a 13–0 win over the Dodgers at Ebbets Field. It was also Chicago's ninth win in a row. Charlie Root pitched a two–hitter. The only Brooklyn hits were singles by Johnny Frederick and Babe Herman.

The game drew 51,556 into Wrigley Field, including 30,476 women admitted free on Ladies Day. The crowd led to a change in policy regarding Ladies Day. Women were no longer admitted free when they showed up at the ballpark. Instead, women had to send a postcard to the Cubs' offices to request tickets sent by mail.

JUNE 21 The Cubs raise their 1929 National League pennant at Wrigley Field before winning both ends of a double–header against the Braves. The Cubs won the first game 5–4 in twelve innings and the second 5–4.

JUNE 23 The Cubs collect 24 hits and bury the Phillies 21–8 at Wrigley Field. Hack Wilson led the attack by hitting for the cycle, including two singles. Wilson also scored five runs.

JUNE 25 Gabby Hartnett's walk–off single beats the Phillies 13–12 at Wrigley Field. During the afternoon, Hartnett had two homers, two singles, and six runs batted in. The Cubs scored seven runs in the sixth inning to take an 11–8 lead before allowing the Phillies to come back to tie the game 12–12 with two in the ninth.

After being limited to 22 at–bats in 1929 because of an arm injury, Hartnett came back in 1930 with the best season of his career, with a .339 batting average and 37 home runs.

JUNE 27 Kiki Cuyler strikes a two–out, two–run, walk–off homer in the tenth inning to defeat the Dodgers 7–5 at Wrigley Field.

The Cubs hit 171 homers in 1930, which was the National League record until the Giants hit 221 in 1947, and the club record until the 1958 Cubs hit 182.

JUNE 30   The Cubs score eight runs in the first inning and cruise to a 10–4 win over the Giants at Wrigley Field.

During the month of June, the Cubs were 20–7 and scored 218 runs, an average of 8.1 per game.

JULY 12   The Cubs score four runs in the ninth inning in the second game of a double header against the Braves in Boston, but they don't count because of the Massachusetts Sports Law.

According to the law passed in 1929, games in Boston could not continue past 6:00 P.M. The Braves won the first game of the twin bill 2–1, and were leading the second 3–0 at the end of the eighth inning. The clock struck six during the Cubs' ninth-inning rally, and a police lieutenant came onto the field and notified umpire Ernie Quigley that play must cease. According to NL rules in cases such as this one, the score reverted back to the end of the last full inning played. The game went into the books as a 3–0 Boston victory, called after eight innings by curfew. The Cubs protested to NL President John Heydler, but it was denied.

JULY 16   The Cubs split a boisterous double–header with the Dodgers in Brooklyn, winning 6–4 and losing 5–3.

In the first game, Del Bissonette of the Dodgers tried to stretch a triple into an inside–the–park homer, and in sliding into home he knocked himself unconscious, hitting his head on the plate. Many fans blamed Hartnett for Bissonette's injury and threw bottles at the Cubs catcher. Hartnett tried to charge the stands, but was held back by teammates.

JULY 22   A night game is played for the first time at Wrigley Field in Los Angeles as the Los Angeles Angels of the Pacific Coast League played the Hollywood Stars.

Wrigley Field was built by Cubs owner William Wrigley Jr. in 1925. Night games in the minors were played for the first time in 1930. Night ball reached the majors in 1935 with a game in Cincinnati but wouldn't be played at Wrigley Field in Chicago until 1988.

JULY 26   Hack Wilson hits three homers in a 16–2 win over the Phillies in Philadelphia. The Cubs collected 21 hits in the game and scored seven runs in the second inning. Pat Malone and Gabby Hartnett also homered for the Cubs.

Wilson's salvo was the first three–homer game by a Cubs batter since Cap Anson did it in 1884.

JULY 27   In Cincinnati, Reds pitcher Ken Ash earns all three outs and a victory on one pitch as the Reds pull off one of the strangest triple plays ever in a 6–5 win over the Cubs. All three outs came on the tag of a runner.

Ash took the mound in relief of Larry Benton with none out in the sixth inning, Cubs baserunners Hack Wilson on third and Danny Taylor on first, and the Reds trailing 3–2. On Ash's first pitch, Charlie Grimm hit a routine grounder to second baseman Hod Ford, who saw Wilson breaking for the plate. After Ford's throw to catcher Clyde Sukeforth, Wilson was retired in a rundown between Sukeforth and third baseman Tony Cuccinello. Grimm tried reaching second during the rundown, only to find his teammate Taylor still on the bag. Grimm quickly retreated to first base, and was out on a toss from Sukeforth to first baseman Joe Stripp. Taylor tried to advance to third during the Grimm putout, but was retired on a Stripp–to–Cuccinello throw to complete the unusual triple play. Ash was lifted for a pinch–hitter in the bottom of the sixth, as the Reds scored four times and held on for a 6–5 win.

AUGUST 10   The Cubs polish off the Braves 6–0 and 11–1 in a double–header at Wrigley Field. The Cubs scored eight runs in the second inning of the second game.

The Cubs set club records in 1930 in batting average (.309), runs (998), hits (1,722), total bases (2,648), extra–base hits (548), and slugging percentage (.481). The pitching staff, in this offensive–minded year, allowed a club record 1,642 hits.

AUGUST 15   An overflow crowd of 45,000 at Wrigley Field helps the Cubs defeat the Dodgers 4–3 in ten innings to take a two–game lead in the National League pennant race. The crowd occupied about 25 feet of the outfield, making balls hit into the over-flow ground–rule doubles. Danny Taylor's game–winning drive in the tenth landed in the crowd for a double. It would have been an easy out for Dodgers right fielder Babe Herman on an open field.

AUGUST 16   The Cubs earn a victory and a tie in an exciting double–header at Wrigley Field. In the first game, the Cubs blew an 8–1 lead when the Phillies scored eight runs in the seventh inning, but the home team rallied to win 10–9 with two in the ninth. The second game ended in a 3–3 tie when it was called by darkness after eleven innings. The Cubs wiped out a 3–0 Philadelphia lead with three runs in the ninth, the last two on a Woody English two–out homer. Sheriff Blake (seven innings), Pat Malone (two innings) and Lynn Nelson (two innings) combined on a two–hitter.

AUGUST 19   In his first two games as a Cub, first baseman George Kelly collects seven hits, including a triple, in twelve at–bats during a double–header against the Phillies at Wrigley Field. Kelly was 2–for–4 in the first game, a 9–8 loss, and 5–for–7 in the second, a 6–6 tie called after sixteen innings by darkness. A future Hall of Famer, Kelly was signed after an injury put Charlie Grimm out of the lineup. Kelly batted .331 in 39 games in a Chicago uniform. Despite filling in capably, Kelly was released after the 1930 season was over.

The Cubs and the Phillies played a seven–game series from August 16 through August 20, which included two double–headers, two tie games, and seventy–two innings.

AUGUST 22   Charles Evans Hughes, the chief justice of the United States Supreme Court, watches the Cubs defeat the Giants 12–4 at Wrigley Field.

AUGUST 24   Danny Taylor steals home in the ninth inning to boost the Cubs to a 3–2 win over the Giants at Wrigley Field. Taylor reached on a single, stole second, and went to third on a throwing error by Giants catcher Bob O'Farrell.

On the same day, the Cubs purchased Jesse Petty from the Dodgers.

AUGUST 26   Hack Wilson breaks the National League home run record with his 44th of the season during a 7–5 win over the Pirates at Wrigley Field. Chuck Klein of the Phillies held the previous record with 43 in 1929.

AUGUST 28   The Cubs rally from two desperate situations but lose a twenty–inning battle with the Cardinals 8–7 at Wrigley Field. The Cubs trailed 5–0 with future Hall of Famer Burleigh Grimes on the mound for St. Louis, but rallied with three runs in the seventh inning and two in the eighth. The Cards scored twice in the tenth inning, and the Cubs matched the figure.

AUGUST 29   The Cubs again come from behind when the game appears hopelessly lost, but unlike the previous day, defeat the Cardinals 9–8 in thirteen innings. Held scoreless through eight innings with future Hall of Famer Jesse Haines on the mound for St. Louis, the Cubs erupted for five runs in the ninth to tie the contest 5–5. The Cards scored three times in the eleventh, but the Cubs came back with three in their half. The winning run was scored on a triple by Riggs Stephenson and a single by Les Bell.

AUGUST 30   The Cubs belt the Cardinals 16–4 at Wrigley Field. Hack Wilson hit two homers and a single, and drove in six runs.

At the end of the day, the Cubs had a 77–50 record and held a 5½–game lead in the National League race. The Cubs lost 14 of their next 21 games, however, to sink to third place.

SEPTEMBER 4   Gabby Hartnett hits two homers, one of them in the eleventh inning, to lead the Cubs to a 10–7 win over the Pirates in Pittsburgh.

SEPTEMBER 6   The Cubs win a 19–14 slugfest against the Pirates in Pittsburgh. Down 12–9 after seven innings, the Cubs scored four runs in the eighth inning and six in the ninth.

At the conclusion of the game, the Cubs still had a four–game lead with 19 contests left on the schedule.

SEPTEMBER 11   The Cubs conclude a disastrous three–game series against the Dodgers in Brooklyn with their third loss. Chicago's vaunted batting attack was held to just one run in the series. The Cubs lost by scores of 3–0, 6–0, and 2–1.

SEPTEMBER 12   The Cubs break their losing streak with a 17–4 barrage against the Phillies in Philadelphia. Hack Wilson led the assault with six runs batted in on a homer, two doubles, and two singles in five at–bats.

SEPTEMBER 13   The Cubs fall from first to third in the tight NL pennant race with a 7–5 loss to the Phillies in Philadelphia. The Cardinals were in first place, the Dodgers in second, two percentage points behind, and the Cubs one–half game back.

The Cubs never returned to first place in 1930.

SEPTEMBER 20   The Cubs lose 3–2 to the Braves in Boston to all but eliminate Chicago from the pennant race. Joe McCarthy's club was three games behind the Cardinals with six games to play.

Hack Wilson drove in his 176th run of the season during the game, breaking the major league record of 175 set by Lou Gehrig of the Yankees in 1927.

SEPTEMBER 23   Cubs owner William Wrigley Jr. announces that Joe McCarthy would not return as manager in 1931, and that Rogers Hornsby would succeed McCarthy as the Cubs skipper.

Wrigley was 69 years old and in failing health, and was desperate to add a world championship baseball team to his legacy. "I realize that McCarthy is one of the best managers in baseball," said Wrigley, "but I must have a winner. I have always wanted a world championship team, and I am not sure that Joseph McCarthy is the man to give me that kind of a team." McCarthy came close to a title with the Cubs put couldn't complete the task. In 1927, he had a six–game lead in mid–August, but finished in fourth place. In 1928, McCarthy finished only four games behind the first–place Cardinals. In 1929, the Cubs won the NL pennant, but lost the World Series. And in 1930, McCarthy's Chicago club blew a 5½–game lead in two weeks during late August and early September. Wrigley died before realizing his dream of winning a world championship (see January 26, 1932).

SEPTEMBER 25   Joe McCarthy decides not to wait until the end of the season, and announces his resignation as manager of the Cubs. Rogers Hornsby directed the club during the last four games of the season and in the Chicago City Series against the White Sox.

McCarthy was named manager of the New York Yankees on October 10. He remained on the job until 1946, a period in which he became one of the most successful managers in big league history. Although William Wrigley Jr. believed that McCarthy was not a manager who could deliver a world championship team, Joe won eight American League pennants and seven World Series with the Yankees. He also managed the Red Sox from 1948 through 1950. In 24 seasons as a manager, McCarthy won 2,125 regular–season games with a winning percentage of .615.

SEPTEMBER 27   Hack Wilson hits his 55th and 56th home runs of 1930 during a 13–8 win over the Reds at Wrigley Field. Pat Malone was the winning pitcher, picking up his 20th victory of the season.

Wilson's 56 home runs in 1930 remained the National League record until Mark McGwire hit 70 and Sammy Sosa swatted 66 in 1998.

SEPTEMBER 28   In the final game of the season, the Reds score nine runs in the second inning to take a 9–0 lead, but the Cubs peck away to win 13–11 with five runs in the eighth inning. Hack Wilson drove in two runs to end the season with 191 runs batted in, a major league record.

For nearly seventy years, Wilson's RBI record went into the books with a figure of 190. But researchers discovered that Wilson collected another run batted in during the 1930 season that failed to be recorded, and the mark was revised.

No recent player has come close to Wilson's record. The only two players since 1940 who have driven in as many as 160 runs are Manny Ramirez, who had 165 with the Indians in 1999, and Sammy Sosa, with 160 as a Cub in 2001.

OCTOBER 1   In the first game of the Chicago City Series, the White Sox defeat the Cubs 5–1 at Comiskey Park.

OCTOBER 3   The Cubs take a two–games–to–one lead in the City Series with a 12–1 thrashing of the White Sox at Wrigley Field.

The White Sox won the next three games, however, to take the series, four games to two.

OCTOBER 13   The Cubs trade Wes Schulmerich and Bill McAfee to the Braves for Jimmy Welsh and Bob Smith, and purchase Jakie May from the Reds.

1931 Cubs

Season in a Sentence

The Cubs lead the National League in almost every hitting category, but inconsistent pitching dooms new manager Rogers Hornsby to a distant third–place finish.

Finish • Won • Lost • Pct • GB

Third   84   70   .545   17.0

Manager

Rogers Hornsby

Stats

Stats	Cubs	NL	Rank
Batting Avg:	.289	.277	1
On–Base Pct:	.360	.334	1
Slugging Pct:	.422	.387	1
Home Runs:	84		2
Stolen Bases:	49		4
ERA:	3.97	3.86	6
Fielding Avg:	.973	.971	4
Runs Scored:	828		1
Runs Allowed:	710		6

Starting Lineup

Gabby Hartnett, c
Charlie Grimm, 1b
Rogers Hornsby, 2b
Les Bell, 3b
Woody English, ss
Danny Taylor, lf–cf
Hack Wilson, cf–lf
Kiki Cuyler, rf–cf
Billy Jurges, 3b
Riggs Stephenson, lf
Footsie Blair, 2b–1b
Vince Barton, rf
Rollie Hemsley, c

Pitchers

Charlie Root, sp
Pat Malone, sp
Bob Smith, sp
Guy Bush, sp–rp
Leo Sweetland, sp–rp
Jakie May, rp

Attendance

1,086,422 (first in NL)

Club Leaders

Batting Avg:	Grimm	.331
On–Base Pct:	Hornsby	.421
Slugging Pct:	Hornsby	.574
Home Runs:	Hornsby	16
RBI:	Hornsby	90
Runs:	English	117
Stolen Bases:	Cuyler	13
Wins:	Root	17
Strikeouts:	Root	131
ERA:	Smith	3.22
Saves:	Four tied with	2

APRIL 1   A month after Congress adopts "The Star–Spangled Banner" as the national anthem, the Cubs sell Cliff Heathcote to the Reds.

APRIL 14   The Cubs defeat the Pirates 6–2 in the opening game of the season before 45,000 at Wrigley Field. Gabby Hartnett had a homer, a double, and three RBIs.

APRIL 19   During a 4–1 Cubs win before an overflow crowd in St. Louis, an odd call by umpire Charley Evans triggers a Cardinals protest. Cubs left fielder Riggs Stephenson momentarily held a drive by Jim Bottomley, then dropped it into the crowd. Evans called Bottomley out, claiming that the crowd verbally interfered with Stephenson. The Cardinals filed an official protest with National League President John Heydler, but the protest was denied.

APRIL 24   Rogers Hornsby hits three homers in consecutive at–bats and drives in eight runs to lead the Cubs to a 10–6 win over the Pirates at Forbes Field. Pittsburgh led 5–0 after two innings. Hornsby hit a three–run homer off Larry French in the third inning, another homer with two on in the fifth off French, and a two–run homer off Claude Willoughby.

Hornsby hit .331 in 357 at–bats in 1931, but was slowed down considerably by leg injuries. He played in pain, was slow running the bases, and was unable to slide. Off the field, he walked with a limp. In mid–season, Hornsby moved himself from second base to the less–demanding position of third. During the second half of 1931, Rogers seldom played in more than two games in a row.

MAY 2   Hack Wilson hits his first home run of 1931 during a 6–3 loss to the Cardinals.

It was a trying year for Hack Wilson. After batting .356 with 56 homers and 191 RBIs in 1930, Wilson slumped badly to .261 with 13 homers and 61 runs batted in in 1931. Wilson missed the guidance of Joe McCarthy, who knew the right buttons to push to get the most out of the outfielder. Hack rebelled against the brusque Hornsby, who possessed none of McCarthy's interpersonal skills. Wilson missed the final three weeks of the season under suspension (see September 6, 1931).

MAY 16   The Cubs clobber the Phillies 17–6 in the second game of a double–header in Philadelphia. Woody English collected five hits, including a double, in six at–bats. The Cubs lost the first game 5–1.

English hit .319 with two homers, 117 RBIs, and 202 hits in 1931. His play in the infield was aided by a large pair of hands. As a schoolboy, English was so embarrassed by the size of his hands that he hid them in class by sitting in them.

MAY 31   Bob Smith pitches a two–hitter to beat the Pirates 5–0 at Wrigley Field. The only Pittsburgh hits were singles by Ben Sankey and Gus Suhr.

Smith was 15–12 with a 3.22 ERA in 1931, his first season with the Cubs following a trade with the Braves. He broke into the majors with the Braves as an infielder in 1923 before becoming a pitcher in 1925. Smith remained in the big leagues until 1937.

Riggs Stephenson crosses the plate ahead of Gabby Hartnett after Hartnett's homer helped the Cubs win the 1931 season opener.

JUNE 4   A two–run, walk–off homer by Kiki Cuyler into the center field bleachers beats the Dodgers 6–4 at Wrigley Field.

Cuyler hit .330, collected 202 hits, and scored 110 runs in 1931. Charlie Grimm had the best offensive season of his career during the '31 campaign, hitting .331. The Cubs hit a club–record 340 doubles during the season.

JUNE 13   The Cubs trade Earl Grace to the Pirates for Rollie Hemsley.

JUNE 16   Trailing the Braves 7–0 at Wrigley Field, the Cubs come back with three runs in the fifth inning, one in the sixth, and four in the seventh to win 8–7.

JUNE 27   Hack Wilson is suspended for one day by Rogers Hornsby for violating the midnight curfew prior to a game against the Braves in Boston. Without Wilson, the Cubs scored seventh runs in the eighth inning to break a 2–2 tie. The final score was 12–3.

JUNE 30   Rogers Hornsby drives in seven runs with a three–run homer in the first inning and a grand slam off Clise Dudley in the fifth to lead the Cubs to a 14–3 win over the Phillies in Philadelphia.

JULY 4   Charlie Root pitches a shutout to defeat the Reds 1–0 in the first game of a dou-ble–header at Wrigley Field. Root also drove in the lone run of the game with a sin-gle in the seventh inning. The Cubs lost the second game 6–2.

In the second game, Woody English threw his bat in the air in disgust after a called strike three by umpire Beans Reardon. The bat struck the arm of Charlie Grimm, who was taking a sip of water from the fountain in the dugout.

JULY 7   The Cubs sweep the Cardinals 14–2 and 6–3 in a double–header at Wrigley Field. In the first game, the Cubs scored nine runs in the sixth inning. There were about 45,000 inside Wrigley Field, with another 20,000 milling around outside after the gates were closed. Fifteen people collapsed in the crush. Arthur Breitois of Cornell, Illinois, died of a heart attack after battling his way through the dense throng into the stands.

After the games, the Cubs had a record of 41–32 and were 3 ½ games behind the Cardinals, but Chicago was out of the pennant race by the end of July.

JULY 12   During a double–header in St. Louis, the Cubs and Cardinals combine for a record 32 doubles, 23 of them in the second game. The twin bill attracted a record crowd of 45,715 to Sportsman's Park, many of them encircling the outfield. Balls hit into the overflow were ground–rule doubles, which contributed mightily to the record number of two–baggers. The start of the first game was delayed. At game time, fans were wandering around the field, overwhelming the ushers. Appeals by the umpires to move back were unsuccessful. Police and firemen were needed to put the excess of 8,000 along the outfield walls. The Cubs won the first game 7–5, with nine doubles hit in the contest, five by the Chicago batters. The Cardinals bounced back in the second contest, winning 17–13. There were 23 doubles, the most ever in a single game by two teams. The 13 doubles by the Cardinals is the most by a club in a single game since 1900.

JULY 20   Charlie Root pitches the Cubs to a 1–0 win over the Dodgers at Brooklyn. The only run of the game was scored in the seventh inning on a triple by Danny Taylor and a single by Rollie Hemsley.

Root had a 17–14 record and a 3.48 ERA in 251 innings in 1931.

JULY 27   Riggs Stephenson breaks his ankle during a 7–6 loss to the Phillies at Wrigley Field and is lost for the rest of the season.

On the same day, the Cubs sold Sheriff Blake to the Phillies.

AUGUST 7 Jimmy Archer, who was a catcher for the Cubs from 1909 through 1917, receives a medal by the National Safety Council in Chicago for saving the lives of two men. Archer pulled both from the cab of a truck in the Chicago stockyards when they were overcome by carbon monoxide gas. Archer revived both with first aid.

AUGUST 9 Guy Bush pitches a one–hitter to defeat the Cardinals 1–0 in St. Louis. The only hit of the game was an infield single by George Watkins on a slow roller to shortstop Woody English. Watkins just beat the throw. The only run was scored on a homer by Vince Barton off Paul Derringer in the second inning.

AUGUST 24 During a 2–1 loss to the Giants in the second game of a double–header in New York, Hack Wilson is ejected by umpire Beans Reardon for disputing a called third strike in the fourth inning. Wilson refused to leave, however, and took his place in the outfield pantomiming insults to Reardon. Finally, his own teammates had to pull him off the field so the game could continue.

After the display, Hornsby declared that Wilson would be benched for the remainder of the season.

AUGUST 27   The Cubs score eight runs in the eighth inning to beat the Pirates 11–4 in the second game of a double–header in Pittsburgh. The Cubs lost the first game 3–2. Woody English had six hits, including three doubles, in seven at–bats during the double–header.

AUGUST 29   The Cubs score seven runs in the third inning and defeat the Reds 14–5 at Wrigley Field.

Billy Herman made his major league debut in the game, playing second base. Facing Si Johnson, Herman singled in his first at–bat, but in his second plate appearance, he was knocked out cold by a foul ball. In pulling away from a high inside pitch, Herman kept the bat close to his head, and the ball caromed off the bat and struck him behind the ear. Herman was back in the lineup the next day and remained the Cubs starting second baseman until 1941. The Cubs acquired him from Louisville of the American Association. In his career with the Cubs, Herman played in 1,344 games, scored 875 runs, collected 1,710 hits, 346 doubles, and hit .309. He was elected to the Hall of Fame in 1975. Billy's full name was William Jennings Herman. He was named after Williams Jennings Bryan, who ran unsuccessfully for president on the Democratic Party ticket in 1896, 1900, and 1908.

SEPTEMBER 4   With an injury to Riggs Stephenson, Hack Wilson's benching, and Vince Barton's departure for Toronto to attend his brother's funeral, Rogers Hornsby starts pitcher Bud Teachout in right field during a 12–3 loss to the Reds in Cincinnati. Teachout also started in right the following day, a 4–3, ten–inning loss to the Reds.

SEPTEMBER 6   Hack Wilson is suspended without pay for the remainder of the 1931 season by manager Rogers Hornsby.

The previous day, Wilson went into a drunken tirade on the train from Cincinnati after the Cubs were swept in a six–game series against the last–place Reds. Pat Malone was fined $500 for his actions on the same trip. Malone trapped writers Harold Johnson of the CHICAGO EVENING AMERICAN and Wayne Otto of the CHICAGO HERALD AND EXAMINER in the vestibule between two Pullmans and slugged both with rights to face. Neither writer had a chance to defend himself in the tight quarters. Wilson stood by and egged Malone on to beat up the scribes (see December 9, 1931).

SEPTEMBER 9   The Cubs defeat the White Sox 3–0 in a charity exhibition game before 34,865 at Comiskey Park to benefit the unemployed. A total of $44,489 was turned over to the Illinois State Unemployment Fund. Charlie Root pitched the shutout and drove in all three runs with a double and a single. Al Capone sat in the front row with his bodyguard.

Fans made their opinions known in the Rogers Hornsby–Hack Wilson controversy. Hornsby was the target of lemons thrown from the fans all afternoon, while Wilson, who watched the game from the stands, was cheered.
  Sales of lemons skyrocketed in Chicago during the 1920s and 1930s because they were the weapons of choice for many Cubs fans. It began during the mid–1920s when an anonymous fan attended nearly every game with a bag of lemons and hurled them at players and umpires who displeased him. Soon, others followed the example.

SEPTEMBER 10   The Cubs end a nine–game losing streak with a 17–4 slaughter of the Phillies at Wrigley Field. The Cubs scored nine runs in the fifth inning.

SEPTEMBER 13   Rogers Hornsby and Guy Bush star as the Cubs beat the Braves 11–7 in eleven innings and 8–1 in a double–header at Wrigley Field. In the first game, Hornsby inserted himself into the game in the eleventh as a pinch–hitter with the bases loaded and hit a walk–off grand slam off Bruce Cunningham. In the second game, Bush pitched a one–hitter. The only Boston hit was a single by Earl Sheely in the seventh inning.

SEPTEMBER 16   The Cubs win two tight games in a double–header against the Braves at Wrigley Field by scores of 6–5 and 8–7. In the first game, the Cubs survived a four–run Boston rally in the ninth. In the second game, Chicago trailed 7–2, but won the contest with five runs in the eighth inning and one in the ninth.

SEPTEMBER 17   The Cubs record their eighth win in a row with a 4–3 decision over the Dodgers at Wrigley Field by scoring in the ninth inning on a bases–loaded two–out single by Danny Taylor.

SEPTEMBER 20   The Cubs defeat the Giants 16–6 and 7–6 in a double–header at Wrigley Field. The Cubs scored seven runs in the first inning of the second game and collected 20 hits overall.

It was Gabby Hartnett Day in Chicago. Before the games, Hartnett was presented with a diamond ring. During the twinbill, he had six hits, including two doubles, in eight at–bats and drove in five runs. In 1931, Hartnett batted .282 and hit eight homers.

SEPTEMBER 21   The Giants collect 27 hits and overpower the Cubs 15–7 at Wrigley Field. The Giants had 23 singles, a modern National League record for a nine–inning game.

SEPTEMBER 27   The Cubs close out the 1931 season with 3–1 and 8–4 wins over the Pirates at Wrigley Field. In the second game, Vince Barton hit a grand slam off Erv Brame in the seventh inning.

SEPTEMBER 30   The White Sox win the first game of the Chicago City Series 9–0 against the Cubs at Wrigley Field. The White Sox finished last in the American League in 1931.

Before the game, Gabby Hartnett was photographed chatting with notorious gangster Al Capone while signing a ball for Capone's son. A White Sox fan, Capone had a front–row box at Comiskey Park. When commissioner Kenesaw Landis saw the photograph, he issued an edict barring players from fraternizing with fans at the ballpark. On October 17, Capone was convicted of tax evasion. He spent the next eight years in federal prisons in Atlanta and on Alcatraz Island before dying in Miami in 1947.

OCTOBER 1   Guy Bush pitches the Cubs to a 1–0 win over the White Sox in game two of the City Series at Wrigley Field. Vince Barton drove in the lone run of the game with a single in the ninth inning.

The Cubs took a two–games–to–one lead, but lost the final three games to give the Sox the championship. Game five at Comiskey Park drew a crowd of 41,523.

DECEMBER 9   The Cubs trade Hack Wilson and Bud Teachout to the Cardinals for Burleigh Grimes.

Wilson's awful season in 1931 dictated the trade. He never played a game for the Cardinals, however. Wilson was traded to the Dodgers before the start of the 1932 season. He had a comeback year with the Dodgers, driving in 123 runs, then drifted into alcoholism. Wilson was 48 years old and penniless when he died in 1948. His body went unclaimed for three days because his family refused to pay for the burial. National League President Ford Frick paid the $350 for the funeral. Hack was elected to the Hall of Fame in 1979.

Grimes was the hero of the 1931 World Series with two wins against the Athletics after a 17–9 regular season for the Cardinals. At the time of the trade, he had 257 lifetime wins. Grimes was an extreme disappointment for the Cubs, with a 9–17 record before he was released in July 1933.

1932   Cubs

Season in a Sentence

An August 2 switch in managers from demanding Rogers Hornsby to free-spirited Charlie Grimm proves to be the tonic the Cubs need to win the National League pennant.

Finish • Won • Lost • Pct • GB

First   90   64   .584   +4.0

World Series–The Cubs lost to the New York Yankees four games to none

Managers

Rogers Hornsby (53–46) and Charlie Grimm (37–18)

Stats

Stats	Cubs	NL	Rank
Batting Avg:	.278	.276	4
On–Base Pct:	.330	.328	4
Slugging Pct:	.392	.396	5
Home Runs:	69		5
Stolen Bases:	48		5
ERA:	3.44	3.88	1
Fielding Avg:	.973	.971	2
Runs Scored:	720		4
Runs Allowed:	536		1

Starting Lineup

Gabby Hartnett, c
Charlie Grimm, 1b
Billy Herman, 2b
Woody English, 3b
Billy Jurges, ss
Riggs Stephenson, lf
Johnny Moore, cf
Kiki Cuyler, rf–cf
Stan Hack, 3b

Pitchers

Lon Warneke, sp
Guy Bush, sp
Pat Malone, sp
Charlie Root, sp–rp
Burleigh Grimes, sp–rp
Bob Smith, rp–sp
Bud Tinning, rp

Attendance

974,688 (first in NL)

Club Leaders

Batting Avg:	Stephenson	.324
On–Base Pct:	Stephenson	.383
Slugging Pct:	Moore	.470
Home Runs:	Moore	13
RBI:	Stephenson	85
Runs:	Herman	102
Stolen Bases:	Herman	14
Wins:	Warneke	22
Strikeouts:	Malone	120
ERA:	Warneke	2.37
Saves:	Root	3

JANUARY 26   Cubs owner William Wrigley Jr. dies at the age of 70 at his winter home in Phoenix, Arizona.

With the death of William Wrigley Jr., ownership of the club passed to his 37–year–old son Philip Knight (P. K.) Wrigley. P. K. retained control of the club until his death in 1977. Despite his very public position as head of both the Cubs and the Wrigley Gum Company, Wrigley had a passion for anonymity. He was painfully shy and somewhat of a recluse, with few close friends. Wrigley's huge mansion in Phoenix was built without a guest bedroom because he believed that there was no reason for anyone to stay overnight. P. K. rarely attended games at Wrigley Field, preferring to follow the club on radio, and later television. When he did attend games, it was usually incognito, in which he took a seat among the ordinary fans in the upper deck or the bleachers. P. K. could go unrecognized because he refused to appear on television and didn't like to be photographed. It wasn't unusual for an individual to play for the Cubs for several years and never get an opportunity to meet Wrigley personally. His forty–five–year reign as head of the club was marked by some early success, and the club won four pennants from 1932 through 1945. But that was followed by one losing season after another. During the lean years, Wrigley's devotion to baseball and his competence as an owner came into question. At heart, he possessed no more than a passing interest in baseball, and he didn't have a strong passion for the game. For Wrigley, the idea of attending a baseball game was merely a pleasant way to spend a summer afternoon. He failed to grasp what made the devoted fans of the game tick, or took the time to learn the intricacies of the game. Like many casual fans, Wrigley had some silly notions about what it took to build a winning team. To make matters worse, Wrigley was a contrarian who liked to be different just for the sake of being different. The Cubs lost far more often than they won during his stewardship because this casual and contrary fan was in charge of the club and had the authority to implement his silly notions, such as hiring a swami to sit behind home plate to put a hex on the opposition, and a system of rotating managers tried during the early 1960s. His most controversial decision was a refusal to install lights for night games. On the positive side, Wrigley improved Wrigley Field and transformed it into the most beautiful sports edifice in America.

APRIL 12   Six weeks after the kidnapping of the Lindbergh baby, the Cubs lose the season opener 5–4 in Cincinnati. The Cubs led 4–1 entering the bottom of the ninth, but the Reds scored four runs off Charlie Root and Guy Bush.

The 1932 pitching staff led by, left to right, Larry French, Lon Warneke, Bill Lee, and Charlie Root, led the league in ERA and helped the Cubs win the pennant.

Bush rebounded to have an excellent year in 1932 with a 19–11 record and a 3.21 ERA. The Cubs' top pitcher in 1932 was 23–year–old Lon Warneke, who led the National League in wins and earned run average. He was 22–6 with a 2.37 ERA in 277 innings. Warneke completed 25 of his 32 starts, four of them shutouts.

APRIL 20   In the home opener, the Cubs lose 7–2 to the Reds. Flags were lowered to half–mast in memory of William Wrigley Jr.

APRIL 24   Kiki Cuyler breaks his foot while chasing a fly ball during a 12–5 win over the Pirates at Wrigley Field. Cuyler was out for eight weeks.

The Cubs started 1932 with seventeen wins in their first twenty–three games.

MAY 13   The Cubs score two runs in the ninth to beat the Braves 3–2 at Wrigley Field. With two out and the score 2–2, Rogers Hornsby let pitcher Guy Bush bat for himself, and Bush delivered a game–winning double.

The double was Bush's only extra–base hit in 1931 in 57 at–bats. During his career, he had 888 at–bats and hit .161 with a slugging percentage of .179.

MAY 17   The Cubs score eight runs in the seventh inning to wipe out a 4–1 Phillies lead for a 9–4 win at Wrigley Field.

Gabby Hartnett had another fine season with the Cubs in 1932, with a .271 batting average and 12 homers.

JUNE 8   The Cubs beat the Dodgers 7–5 in fourteen innings in Brooklyn. The Cubs scored three runs in the eighth to tie the score 5–5.

The Cubs tried out a new color scheme with alternative jerseys in 1932 and 1933. They were black and gold instead of the traditional blue and red. The home jerseys had black pinstripes with "Cubs" heavily slanted in script in black and gold on the left breast.

JUNE 9   Ex–Cub Hack Wilson hits a grand slam in the first inning off Pat Malone, his frequent drinking partner, to lead the Dodgers to a 5–2 win over the Cubs in Brooklyn.

JUNE 10   A fistfight between shortstop Billy Jurges of the Cubs and Neal Finn of the Dodgers highlights a 4–3 Chicago loss in Brooklyn. In the first inning, Finn bumped Jurges at second base when the latter was about to try for a double play. As Finn turned away, Jurges made a remark that Finn didn't take kindly, and the two went at it. Third baseman Woody English charged into the fray with a flying tackle that carried both combatants to the ground. Members of both teams rushed up and there was some indiscriminate punching before order was restored.

In late June, the Cubs wore uniform numbers for the first time after the National League passed an edict requiring its club to assign the numbers. The first numbers were issued to Woody English (1), Billy Herman (2), Kiki Cuyler (3), Riggs Stephenson (4), Johnny Moore (5), Charlie Grimm (6), Gabby Hartnett (7), Rollie Hemsley (8), Rogers Hornsby (9), Billy Jurges (11), Charlie Root (12), Guy Bush (14), Pat Malone (15), Burleigh Grimes (16), Lon Warneke (17),

Bob Smith (18), Jakie May (19), Bud Tinning (21), Marv Gudat (22), LeRoy Herrmann (23), Stan Hack (31), Zack Taylor (34), coach Red Corriden (41), coach Charley O'Leary (42), Vince Barton (49), Frank Demaree (51), and Lance Richbourg (56). Numbers 1 through 7 corresponded to the batting order the Cubs used at the time. Number–eight hitter Billy Jurges was given number 11. For reasons unknown, the Cubs didn't issue any numbers ending in zero, such as 10, 20 or 30, until 1937.

JULY 6   In Chicago's Carlos Hotel, a 21–year–old dancer named Violet Popovich Valli shoots Billy Jurges with a .25–caliber pistol. Valli was a former girlfriend of Jurges who was angry because he broke off the relationship.

She intended suicide, and Jurges was wounded trying to wrestle the gun away from her. In the struggle, one bullet caromed off Jurges's ribs and exited near his right shoulder. Another slug grazed the little finger of his left hand. The wounds were superficial, and Jurges was back in the lineup in seventeen days. Jurges refused to press charges because he was convinced that Valli hadn't intended to shoot him. Valli used her notoriety as part of her act, signing a twenty–two–week contract to sing in local nightclubs and theaters. She was billed as Violet (What I Did For Love) Valli, the Most Talked About Girl in Chicago.

AUGUST 2   In a surprise move, the Cubs dismiss Rogers Hornsby as manager and replace him with Charlie Grimm. The move came after the Cubs lost 4–2 to the Dodgers in Brooklyn.

At the time, the Cubs had a record of 53–46 and were five games behind the first–place Pirates. Cubs president Bill Veeck would offer no specifics, other than to say that there was a difference of opinion over how the club would be run. One of the differences centered around Hornsby's insistence that he play more often. Rogers appeared in 19 games in right field and at third base, hit .224, and was stiff as a statue on defense. There were reports of internal strife over Hornsby's martinet methods. He also owed his players several thousand dollars, which he borrowed to cover his gambling debts, including $1,115 to Woody English. The debts were paid when the club deducted money from Hornsby's remaining paychecks. Hornsby subsequently managed the Browns (1933–37 and 1952) and the Reds (1952–53).

Under the easygoing Charlie Grimm, the Cubs won twenty–eight of their first thirty–four games, had an overall record of 37–18 over the remainder of the season, and went on to win the National League pennant. During the stretch run, the Cubs won fourteen games in a row and staged one incredible come–from–behind victory after another (see August 16, 20, and 31, 1932). In Grimm's first thirty–two days as a manager, the Cubs overcame their five–game deficit to the Pirates to take a seven–game lead in the NL race.

AUGUST 4   Playing under Charlie Grimm for the first time, the Cubs score eight runs in the second inning and smash the Phillies 12–1. Grimm contributed two doubles, a single, and three RBIs.

AUGUST 6   In a double–header at Philadelphia, the Cubs win 10–9 and 10–8 in eleven innings. Riggs Stephenson and Billy Herman each had seven hits, including a double.

In his first full season in the majors, Herman batted .314 and collected 214 hits.

AUGUST 11   The Cubs score two runs in the ninth inning and one in the tenth to beat the Pirates 3–2 in Pittsburgh and take over first place.

The Cubs remained in first place for the rest of the season.

AUGUST 16   In a storybook finish, the Cubs score four runs in the ninth inning to defeat the Braves 4–3 at Wrigley Field.

Beginning with this victory, the Cubs ran off a streak of twenty wins in twenty–two games.

AUGUST 17   The Cubs win 3–2 in a nineteen–inning marathon against the Braves at Wrigley Field. The winning run was scored on a one–out, bases–loaded sacrifice fly by pinch–hitter Frank Demaree. The game was scoreless from the eighth inning through the eighteenth. Bud Tinning pitched 12⅔ innings of scoreless relief. Guy Bush, who was on the mound for one inning, was the winning pitcher.

AUGUST 18   A day after the nineteen–inning struggle, the Cubs defeat the Braves 4–3 in fifteen innings at Wrigley Field. Riggs Stephenson drove in the winning run with a single. For the second day in a row, Guy Bush was the winning pitcher with a one–inning relief stint.

AUGUST 20   Trailing the Phillies 5–2 in the ninth inning with two out and no one on base, the Cubs score four runs to win 6–5 at Wrigley Field. The astonishing ninth–inning rally was capped by Mark Koenig's walk–off three–run homer.

Koenig was a shortstop on the 1926, 1927, and 1928 New York Yankee World Series teams. He started the 1932 season in the minors, and was acquired by the Cubs in July after Billy Jurges was shot. Koenig played an important part in the Cubs run for the pennant by hitting .353 in 33 games.

AUGUST 31   Kiki Cuyler stars in a thrilling 10–9, ten–inning win over the Giants, played for the most part in a drizzling rain at Wrigley Field. With the Cubs trailing 5–4 in the ninth, Cuyler singled in a run to send the game into extra innings. The Giants scored four runs in the tenth, but the Cubs came back with five in their half to win, the final three on Cuyler's walk–off homer into the center field bleachers. All five runs were scored with two out. Cuyler finished the game with five hits, including a triple and three singles in addition to the home run. It was also Cuyler's fourth homer in a stretch of five games. The victory was the twelfth in a row for the Cubs.

SEPTEMBER 3   The Cubs record their fourteenth win in a row with a 5–4 decision over the Cardinals in eleven innings in the first game of a double–header at Wrigley Field. The streak ended with a 3–0 loss in the second game.

At the conclusion of the 14–game win streak, the Cubs had a seven–game lead over the Pirates.

SEPTEMBER 15   Kiki Cuyler's eleventh–inning homer beats the Giants 8–7 in New York. The Giants tied it on a two–out homer by Mel Ott in the ninth inning. Both teams scored twice in the tenth. Pitching two innings of relief, Lon Warneke picked up his 22nd win of the season.

This was the third straight extra–inning game between the two clubs. The Cubs lost 3–2 in eleven innings to the Giants in the second game of a double–header on September 13, and lost again 4–3 in ten innings on September 14.

SEPTEMBER 20   The Cubs clinch the 1932 National League pennant with a 5–2 win in the first game of a double–header at Wrigley Field. Ex–Pirate Kiki Cuyler broke a 2–2 tie in the seventh inning with a bases–loaded triple. The Cubs lost the second game 5–0.

The Cubs met the Yankees, under ex–Cub manager Joe McCarthy, in the World Series. It was the first time that the Yankees appeared in the Series since 1928. The 1932 Yankees had a record of 107–47.

SEPTEMBER 21   The Cubs create a controversy by cutting up their World Series shares in a vote among the players.

Despite managing the club for two–thirds of a season, Rogers Hornsby was ignored completely. He protested to Kenesaw Landis, but the commissioner refused to intervene. Mark Koenig was given only one–half a share after hitting .353 and playing a key role in the stretch drive for the pennant. The twenty players on the Cubs who drew a full share earned $4,245 for losing the World Series at a time when only the top stars of the game had salaries of $10,000 or more. The division of shares proved to be a source of contention in the World Series. The Yankees continually razzed the Cubs from the dugout over their snubs of Hornsby and ex–Yankee Koenig. Joe McCarthy, still bitter over being fired by the Cubs two years earlier, further stoked the Yankees hatred of the Cubs.

SEPTEMBER 22   A victory parade is held in Chicago to celebrate the Cubs' 1932 NL championship. The club received congratulations from Mayor Anton Cermak at City Hall. A reviewing stand, decorated with baseballs and tiny teddy bears, was set up on the LaSalle Street side of City Hall. The parade traveled from the Loop to Wrigley Field, with the players waving to fans from open cars.

SEPTEMBER 28   In the first game of the 1932 World Series, the Yankees beat the Cubs 12–6 before 41,459 at Yankee Stadium. Guy Bush retired the first nine Yankee batters before unraveling. In the fourth inning, with the Cubs leading 2–0, Lou Gehrig followed a Babe Ruth single with a two–run homer to set the Yankee attack in motion. Riggs Stephenson had three hits and drove in three runs.

Billy Herman dives back to first base during the first inning of the first game of the 1932 World Series.

SEPTEMBER 29   The Yankees make it two in a row, defeating the Cubs 5–2 before 50,709 at Yankee Stadium. New York broke a 2–2 tie with two runs in the third inning. Lon Warneke took the loss for the Cubs.

OCTOBER 1   Paced by two home runs each by Babe Ruth and Lou Gehrig, the Yankees beat the Cubs 7–5 in game three before 49,986 at Wrigley Field. In the fifth inning, with the score 4–4, Ruth gestured to the Cubs bench and Charlie Root. He then belted a two–strike pitch from Root into the center field bleachers for a homer. Gehrig followed with another homer. Kiki Cuyler and Gabby Hartnett homered for the Cubs.

Ruth's fifth–inning home run has become known as "Ruth's Called Shot."

OCTOBER 2   The Yankees complete their sweep of the demoralized Cubs with a 13–6 win before 49,884 at Wrigley Field. The Cubs scored four runs in the first inning, three on a home run by Frank Demaree, to take a 4–1 lead. The game was tied 5–5 in the sixth inning before the Yankees broke it open. The Yankees collected 19 hits. Tony Lazzeri was the Yankees' big gun with two two–run homers. Earle Combs scored four runs.

The homer by Demaree was his first as a major leaguer. Prior to the 1932 Series, he had played in only 23 games and had just 56 at–bats.
The Yankees outscored the Cubs 37–19 in the four games. The Chicago pitching staff had an ERA of 9.26. Lou Gehrig was the hero in the Series. In 17 at–bats, he had nine hits, including three homers and a double. He scored nine runs and drove in eight.

   ## Ruth's Called Shot

Did Babe Ruth "call his shot" by pointing to center field before homering into the center field bleachers at Wrigley Field in the fifth inning of game three of the 1932 World Series? The question will likely never be solved because there is no reliable film record of the event, and eyewitness, and earwitness, testimony varies. Ruth at first denied calling his shot, then embraced the story and embellished upon it to the point where it became difficult to separate legend from fact.

The 1932 Series between the Cubs and the Yankees was a nasty one filled with what today would be called "trash talking." Much of it centered around Mark Koenig, an ex-Yankee who was acquired from the Cubs in July. Koenig helped the Cubs down the stretch by hitting .353 in 33 games, but was voted only a one-half share of the World Series loot by his Chicago teammates. This angered the Yankees, who taunted the Cubs by calling them "cheapskates."

Ruth was one of the most vocal of the Yankees.

The Yankees won the first two games in New York and the Series shifted to Chicago. Ruth homered in the first inning, and according to *The Sporting News* "there was a lively pantomime as Ruth took his place in left field with the bleacher fans booing and waving their hands in disapproval of the Bambino, while he pointed to the right-center field spot where his home run landed." Some in the crowd heaved lemons at him. In the fourth inning, Ruth stumbled and fell when he missed an attempt shoestring catch. The Cubs began jeering Ruth from their bench, and it escalated when he stepped to the plate in the fifth. The crowd joined in by vociferously booing Ruth. Ruth responded to the taunts by hitting a 2-2 pitch off Cubs pitcher Charlie Root deep into the center field bleachers after making some kind of a motion in the direction of the outfield.

In their reports which appeared the following

day, some newspapermen claimed that Ruth pointed to the fence. Other made no mention of any kind of a gesture whatsoever. Joe Williams's account for the Scripps-Howard chain was among the most emphatic. "With the Cubs riding him unmercifully from the bench," wrote Williams, "Ruth pointed to center and punched a screaming liner to a spot where no ball had ever been hit before." John Drebinger in the *New York Times* said that "Ruth came up in the fifth and in no mistaken motions the Babe notified the crowd that the nature of his retaliation would be a wallop right out of the confines of the park. Root pitched two balls and two strikes while Ruth signaled with his fingers after each pitch to let the spectators know exactly how the situation stood. Then the mightiest blow of all fell." According to Alan Gould of the Associated Press, "The Babe held up one finger and finally two on each hand with the count two and two." *The Sporting News* didn't report any finger-pointing before the blow, but noted that as Ruth circled the bases "he taunted the Cubs."

Ed Burns of the *Chicago Tribune* was among those who wrote nothing of any hand or arm movements by Ruth. The 1933 *Spalding's Official Base Ball Guide* devoted sixteen pages to the 1932 World Series and mentioned nothing extraordinary about the home run, except for the distance it traveled.

Yankee players, eager to maintain Ruth's legend, claimed that he did indeed "call his shot." Most of the Cubs players have a different version. Root and Cubs catcher Gabby Hartnett always denied that Ruth pointed to the mound or the outfield. Root was a notorious headhunter who had no compunction against throwing at hitters, and said that if Ruth pointed he would have thrown a pitch at the Babe's head. Cubs manager Charlie Grimm said that Ruth was gesturing to Guy Bush, who was on the bench and was the scheduled starting pitcher the next day. Bush was among the leaders of the bench jockeys, and according to Grimm, Ruth looked at Bush and pointed toward the mound saying, "You'll be out there tomorrow." Second baseman Bill Herman said, "The only pointing (Ruth) did was at the bench. He held up two fingers," indicating that there were two strikes and he had one left. Home plate umpire Roy Van Graflan said that Ruth looked over at the bench and said, "Let him put this one over and I'll knock it over the wall out there." Cubs public address announcer Pat Pieper, who was stationed in a first row box, backed Van Graflan. "My sight and hearing were perfect," said Pieper.

There is probably a bit of truth in all of these stories. Ruth made some kind of a motion and likely held up two fingers. His dispute seemed to be with the Cubs bench and the crowd, and he was probably not pointing directly at Root, who had a reputation for drilling hitters. Exactly what Ruth said is unknown, although it is possible that the quotes from Grimm and Van Graflan are both correct. Decades after the fact, a grainy film appeared which showed the left-handed hitting Ruth with his right arm outstretched and his bat in his left hand pointed at the ground. From the angle from where the photographer sat or stood, it is impossible to determine exactly where Ruth was pointing.

NOVEMBER 30   Three weeks after the election of Franklin Roosevelt as president, the Cubs send Bob Smith, Rollie Hemsley, Johnny Moore, Lance Richbourg, and $50,000 to the Reds for Babe Herman.

> *At the time of the trade, Herman had a .343 lifetime batting average in seven seasons with the Dodgers and the Reds, although his deficiencies with the glove were legendary. He played two years with the Cubs, and while he played well with a .296 average and 30 home runs in 272 games, he was deemed a failure because he failed to reach his previous numbers. Herman was dealt to the Pirates after the 1934 season. Although Moore had a few good seasons with the Reds and the Phillies, the Cubs didn't give up much to obtain Herman.*

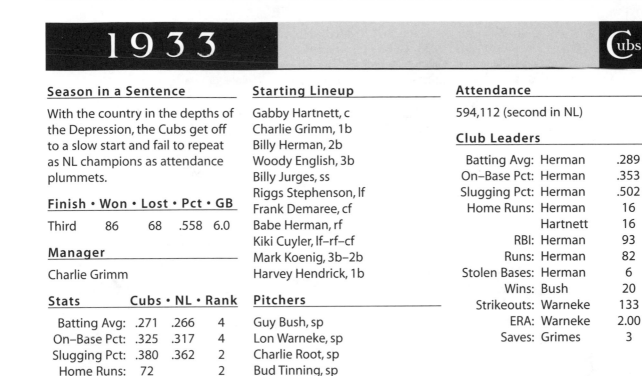

1933

Season in a Sentence

With the country in the depths of the Depression, the Cubs get off to a slow start and fail to repeat as NL champions as attendance plummets.

Finish • Won • Lost • Pct • GB

Third   86   68   .558   6.0

Manager

Charlie Grimm

Stats

Stats	Cubs	NL	Rank
Batting Avg:	.271	.266	4
On–Base Pct:	.325	.317	4
Slugging Pct:	.380	.362	2
Home Runs:	72		2
Stolen Bases:	52		3 (tie)
ERA:	2.93	3.33	2
Fielding Avg:	.973	.973	3
Runs Scored:	646		3
Runs Allowed:	536		3

Starting Lineup

Gabby Hartnett, c
Charlie Grimm, 1b
Billy Herman, 2b
Woody English, 3b
Billy Jurges, ss
Riggs Stephenson, lf
Frank Demaree, cf
Babe Herman, rf
Kiki Cuyler, lf–rf–cf
Mark Koenig, 3b–2b
Harvey Hendrick, 1b

Pitchers

Guy Bush, sp
Lon Warneke, sp
Charlie Root, sp
Bud Tinning, sp
Pat Malone, sp
Lynn Nelson, rp

Attendance

594,112 (second in NL)

Club Leaders

Batting Avg:	Herman	.289
On–Base Pct:	Herman	.353
Slugging Pct:	Herman	.502
Home Runs:	Herman	16
	Hartnett	16
RBI:	Herman	93
Runs:	Herman	82
Stolen Bases:	Herman	6
Wins:	Bush	20
Strikeouts:	Warneke	133
ERA:	Warneke	2.00
Saves:	Grimes	3

MARCH 10 Three weeks after Chicago Mayor Anton Cermak was shot to death in Miami by an assassin who was trying to kill president–elect Franklin Roosevelt, the Cubs survive a Southern California earthquake during spring training. The earthquake struck the Los Angeles area at 5:55 P.M. and resulted in the deaths of 120 people.

Earlier in the day, the Cubs lost to the New York Giants 5–3 at Wrigley Field in Los Angeles. The Cubs were at the Biltmore Hotel in Los Angeles, along with players from Giants, when the earthquake hit. Most of the Cubs were in the upper floors of the hotel dressing for dinner. A few frightened players spent the night in the clubhouse at Wrigley Field, believing that it was safer than the hotel.

MARCH 11 The Cubs defeat the Giants 4–1 at Wrigley Field in Los Angeles, as aftershocks from the previous day's earthquake continue at frequent intervals. At one point, players from both teams huddled around second base as the steel stands of the ballpark swayed.

MARCH 29 Kiki Cuyler breaks his right leg in a spring–training game in Los Angeles. The injury was caused when Cuyler's spikes caught in the dirt during an attempted steal of second base during a 10–8 win over the Hollywood Stars of the Pacific Coast League. Cuyler was out of the lineup until early July.

APRIL 12   Lon Warneke shuts out the Cardinals 3–0 on four hits before 25,000 on Opening Day at Wrigley Field. Gabby Hartnett was the batting star with three hits and two RBIs off Dizzy Dean. The game was the first since 1919 that beer was sold at Wrigley, as Prohibition came to an end.

The game drew less than a capacity crowd. Attendance was a problem all year for the Cubs as the Great Depression made it impossible for many Chicagoans to purchase a ticket. The Cubs drew 594,112 in 1933, a sharp drop from 974,688 in 1932 and 1,463,624 in 1930.

APRIL 29   The Cubs purchase Taylor Douthit from the Reds.

MAY 18   The Cubs raise the 1932 National League pennant between games of a double–header against the Giants at Wrigley Field. The Cubs lost the first game 3–0 and won the second 10–1.

After the first–game loss, the Cubs had a record of 11–17. The Cubs didn't go over the .500 mark to stay until July 5, when they were 39–38.

MAY 25   After a 3–0 Cubs win over the Cardinals at Wrigley Field, umpire Ernie Quigley is knocked unconscious when he brushes against a live wire in the dressing room.

MAY 27   The Cubs postpone their game against the Braves at Wrigley Field because of the opening of the World's Fair in Chicago. The club was afraid that the opening would drain attendance away from the ballpark. The contest was re–scheduled as part of a double–header on May 28.

Charlie Grimm, left, holds ex–teammate Rogers Hornsby on first base in a May 1, 1933, game against the Cardinals.

Called a "Century of Progress," the fair extended over 341 on two man–made islands off Lake Michigan. The fair had a lasting impact on baseball. Arch Ward, sports editor of the CHICA-GO TRIBUNE, proposed an All–Star Game to be played between the best players of the American and National Leagues to coincide with the fair. With the sanction of commissioner Kenesaw Landis, the game was played at Comiskey Park on July 6, 1933. The idea was so successful that it became an annual event.

JUNE 14   Charlie Root pitches a two–hitter to defeat the Reds 7–0 in Cincinnati. The only Reds hits were singles by Sparky Adams in the first inning and Wally Roettger in the fifth.

During the season, the Cubs installed a granite and marble drinking fountain just back of the grandstand near the main entrance as a memorial to William

Wrigley Jr., who died in January 1932.

JUNE 28   On his wedding day, Billy Jurges collects six hits in a double–header as the Cubs defeat the Phillies 9–5 and 8–3 in Philadelphia. In the first game, Billy Herman tied a National League record for most putouts by a second baseman in a game, with 11.

Jurges got married in the morning in Reading, Pennsylvania, to Mary Huyette, then hustled to Philadelphia to play in the two games.

JULY 1   The Cubs hammer the Dodgers 13–3 in Brooklyn.

JULY 6   Cubs players Lon Warneke, Gabby Hartnett, and Woody English play in the first All–Star Game in history, won by the American League 4–2 at Comiskey Park. Warneke allowed one run in four innings on the mound and tripled in his only at–bat.

Warneke hit only two triples in 962 regular season at–bats during his big league career. He is the only pitcher in All–Star Game history to hit a triple. Warneke is also the only individual to play and umpire in the Midsummer Classic. He worked the right field line as a National League ump in the 1952 game.

JULY 13   The Cubs record their eighth win in a row with a 4–1 decision over the Dodgers at Wrigley Field.

The winning streak gave the Cubs a 46–38 record on the season and put them back into the pennant race, just three games back of the first–place Giants.

JULY 20   Babe Herman hits three homers and drives in eight runs in a 10–1 win over the Phillies at Wrigley Field. Herman hit a two–run homer off Ed Holley in the first inning, another two–run shot off Holley in the fifth, and a grand slam in the eighth against Ad Liska.

Herman was benched five days earlier because of a slump. He was in the lineup only because Riggs Stephenson had a cold.

JULY 23   A walk–off pinch–homer by Harvey Hendrick beats the Phillies 9–5 in the first game of a double–header at Wrigley Field. Phillies pitcher Phil Collins walked Charlie Grimm intentionally to load the bases and get to Billy Jurges. Hendrick hit for Jurges. The Cubs also won the first game 3–1.

The two wins put the Cubs only two games behind the Giants in the pennant race, but the Cubs could get no closer.

AUGUST 4   The Cubs sell Burleigh Grimes to the Pirates.

SEPTEMBER 10   The Cubs sweep the Phillies 4–2 and 4–0 at Wrigley Field.

The feature was a near–riot precipitated by Billy Jurges in the fifth inning. After listening to caustic criticism from the opposition about his roughness on the bases, Jurges deliberately pegged two balls into the Philadelphia dugout from his station at shortstop. The entire Phillie squad started out after Jurges, but umpire George Magerkurth and other Cub players persuaded the Phillies to return to the bench. Surprisingly, Jurges was not ejected.

SEPTEMBER 23   A grand slam by Gabby Hartnett in the sixth inning off Ray Kolp is the feature of a 7–1 win over the Reds at Wrigley Field.

Hartnett hit .276 with 16 homers in 1933.

SEPTEMBER 30   Babe Herman hits for the cycle, including a home run off Dizzy Dean, as the Cubs wallop the Cardinals 12–2 in St. Louis. Guy Bush was the winning pitcher, picking up his 20th victory of 1933.

OCTOBER 4   In the first game of the Chicago City Series, the White Sox defeat the Cubs 3–2 at Wrigley Field.

The White Sox went on to sweep the City Series in four games.

OCTOBER 5   Cubs president William Veeck Sr. dies of leukemia at the age of 55.

Veeck had been club president since 1918, and his death left a leadership void that was difficult to fill. Bill Veeck Jr. was a 19–year–old office boy with the Cubs at the time of his father's death and carried on in the family business. Bill Jr. made a lasting imprint on the Cubs by planting ivy on the outfield walls in 1937. He later owned the Cleveland Indians (1946–49), the St. Louis Browns (1951–53), and the White Sox (1959–61 and 1975–80), and became renowned for his outrageous stunts and promotions.

NOVEMBER 21   The Cubs send Ted Kleinhans, Chief Hogsett, Harvey Hendrick, and $65,000 to the Phillies for Chuck Klein.

At the time of the trade, Klein was 29 years old and had a .359 lifetime batting average along with 191 home runs in 823 games. Much of his offensive production was the result of playing his home games in tiny Baker Bowl in Philadelphia, and the move to Chicago and injuries cut sharply into his playing time and batting numbers. Before Klein was traded back to the Phillies in May 1936, he played in 261 games as a Cub with a .297 batting average and 46 home runs. All in all, the trade was a positive one, however, as Klein played well when healthy and the Cubs surrendered almost nothing to acquire him.

DECEMBER 17   The Chicago Bears defeat the New York Giants 23–21 before 26,000 at Wrigley Field in the NFL championship game.

1934

Season in a Sentence

The Cubs win their first seven games, but are out of the pennant race by Labor Day.

Finish • Won • Lost • Pct • GB

Third   86   65   .570   8.0

Manager

Charlie Grimm

Stats

Stats	Cubs	NL	Rank
Batting Avg:	.279	.279	5
On–Base Pct:	.330	.333	5
Slugging Pct:	.402	.394	3
Home Runs:	101		3
Stolen Bases:	59		2
ERA:	3.76	4.06	3
Fielding Avg:	.977	.972	1
Runs Scored:	705		5
Runs Allowed:	639		3

Starting Lineup

Gabby Hartnett, c
Charlie Grimm, 1b
Billy Herman, 2b
Stan Hack, 3b
Billy Jurges, ss
Chuck Klein, lf
Kiki Cuyler, cf
Babe Herman, rf
Woody English, 3b–ss
Tuck Stainback, lf

Pitchers

Lon Warneke, sp
Guy Bush, sp–rp
Bill Lee, sp
Pat Malone, sp–rp
Jim Weaver, sp
Bud Tinning, rp
Charlie Root, rp

Attendance

707,525 (second in NL)

Club Leaders

Batting Avg:	Cuyler	.338
On–Base Pct:	Cuyler	.377
Slugging Pct:	Klein	.510
Home Runs:	Hartnett	22
RBI:	Hartnett	90
Runs:	Cuyler	80
Stolen Bases:	Cuyler	15
Wins:	Warneke	22
Strikeouts:	Warneke	143
ERA:	Warneke	3.21
Saves:	Warneke	3
	Tinning	3

JANUARY 11   William Walker becomes president of the Cubs, succeeding William Veeck Sr., who passed away the previous October.

Walker made his money in the wholesale seafood business and was a substantial shareholder in the group headed by Charles Weeghman that brought the Federal League to Chicago in 1914 and purchased the Cubs in 1916. Walker considered himself to be the world's foremost expert on baseball and alienated almost everyone connected with the Cubs within a few short months. He fired and rehired Charlie Grimm several times and made a horrible trade by sending Dolph Camilli to the Phillies. Walker was gone in less than a year. In October, P. K. Wrigley bought out Walker's share for $191,000 and took over the presidency himself. Wrigley remained as club president until his death in 1977.

JANUARY 12   The Cubs announce a plan for broadcasting the club's games on radio for the 1934 season.

The Cubs allowed any station to broadcast at Wrigley Field with the provision that between the hours of 10 A.M. and 3:30 P.M., each of the stations broadcast five different times a twenty–five–word message advertising the day's game. The stations which took the Cubs up on the offer were WGN, WCFL, WIND, WBBM, and WJJD. Play–by–play announcers included Bob Elson (WGN), Johnny O'Hara (WIND), Pat Flanagan (WBBM), John Harrington (WJJD), and Hal Totten (WCFL).

APRIL 17   In the best Opening Day pitching performance in Cubs history, Lon Warneke throws a one–hitter, strikes out 13 batters, and defeats the Reds 6–0 in Cincinnati. Warneke carried a no–hitter into the ninth inning before Adam Comorosky singled with one out. It was Warneke's second straight Opening Day shutout, following the one he pitched against the Cardinals in 1933. In his first game as a Cub, Chuck Klein hit a home run.

APRIL 22   In his second start of the season, Lon Warneke pitches another one–hitter, defeating the Cardinals 15–2 at Sportsman's Park. The only St. Louis hit was a double by Ripper Collins in the fifth inning.

                Warneke is the only pitcher in Cubs history to hurl one–hitters in consecutive starts. He finished the season with a 22–10 record, 23 complete games, 291 ⅓ innings and a 3.21 ERA. Warneke pitched through a severe cold in May and June that caused him to lose fifteen pounds. Physicians ordered that he go on a diet of eggs and beer to put the weight back on his frame. Guy Bush backed up Warneke with an 18–10 record.

APRIL 24   In the first game of the season at Wrigley Field, the Cubs score three runs in the first inning and defeat the Reds 3–2.

                The Cubs won their first seven games in 1934, the best start in club history.

MAY 7   In his first major league start, Bill Lee pitches a four–hit shutout to defeat the Phillies 2–0 at Wrigley Field.

MAY 12   In his second major league start, Bill Lee pitches his second major league shutout, defeating the Dodgers 5–0 at Wrigley Field. Lee allowed only two hits. Both were singles by Buck Jordan and Lonny Frey.

                Lee is the only Cub to pitch shutouts in his first two major league starts. He played for the Cubs from 1934 through 1943, and again in 1947, and won 139 games in a Chicago uniform. Twice, Lee won 20 or more games in a season. He also pitched in 364 games, completed 153 of his 296 starts, had 25 shutouts, 2,271 ⅓ innings pitched and 874 strike-outs. A tall (six–foot–three) stately Southerner (from Louisiana), he was often referred to as "General" Lee.

In 1934, Bill Lee became the only Cub ever to toss shutouts in each of his first two major league starts. He went on to win 13 games that season.

MAY 21   The Cubs score three runs in the ninth inning to defeat the Dodgers 10–9 in Brooklyn. A pinch–hit homer by Babe Phelps tied the score 9–9, and Chuck Klein drove in the winning run with a single.

                Klein hit .347 with 12 homers in his first 29 games as a Cub, before being slowed down by deep bruises to both hands, back trouble, and a pulled ham-string. He finished the 1934 season with 20 homers and a .301 batting average in 115 games.

JUNE 3   Billy Herman extends his hitting streak to 20 games in a 7–1 win over the Reds in Cincinnati.

JUNE 7   Jim Weaver pitches the Cubs to a 1–0 win over the Cardinals in St. Louis. Babe Herman drove in the lone run of the game with a single in the third inning.

Weaver was purchased from the St. Louis Browns on May 15. A lanky six-foot-six, the tallest player in the majors at the time, he won his first seven decisions as a Cub and finished 1934, his lone season in Chicago, with an 11–9 record.

JUNE 11   The Cubs trade Dolf Camilli to the Phillies for Don Hurst.

This swap of first baseman is one of the worst trades ever made by the Cubs. Although he had a relatively short career (1,490 games), Camilli was one of the top first basemen in the game during the late 1930s and early 1940s with Philadelphia and Brooklyn. He drove in 100 or more runs five seasons, and scored 100 or more in four. Hurst played 51 games as a Cub, and batted .199.

JUNE 12   The Phillies take a 5–0 lead in the third inning at Wrigley Field, but the Cubs battle back to win 6–5.

In June 1934, the Cubs installed netting from the top of the backstop to the front of the second deck to protect fans from foul balls. The club had to replace it within a week, however, because the netting was angled in such a way that those in the press box couldn't see the field clearly.

JUNE 30   The Cubs earn their eighth victory in a row with a 6–4 decision over the Pirates in Pittsburgh.

At the end of June, the Cubs had a 41–26 record and were 1½ games behind the first-place Giants. By the start of September, however, the Cubs were no longer a factor in the pennant race.

JULY 4   Kiki Cuyler collects three doubles and a triple during a 6–2 win over the Cardinals in the second game of the double-header in St. Louis. The Cardinals won the game by the same 6–2 score.

Cuyler missed the first two weeks of the 1934 season because of an infected hangnail, caused when he tried to give himself a clubhouse manicure. Cuyler recovered to hit .338 with a league-leading 42 doubles. Gabby Hartnett had another stellar season with a .299 average and 22 homers.

JULY 21   The day before John Dillinger is killed by FBI agents outside the Biograph Theater in Chicago, the Cubs gun down the Phillies 2–1 and 14–6 in Philadelphia.

AUGUST 8   The Cubs walk over the Pirates 7–4 and 14–3 in a double-header in Pittsburgh.

AUGUST 18   Pat Malone pitches a two–hitter to defeat the Phillies 2–0 at Wrigley Field. The only Philadelphia hits were a double by Dolf Camilli and a single by Bucky Walters.

AUGUST 25   The Cubs score four runs in the ninth inning to defeat the Dodgers 4–3 at Wrigley Field.

AUGUST 29   Pitching on two days' rest, Lon Warneke shuts out the Giants 1–0 at Wrigley Field. The only run of the game was scored on a walk–off double by Kiki Cuyler.

SEPTEMBER 16   In his major league debut, 18–year–old Phil Cavaretta is retired in a pinch–hit appearance during a 12–6 loss to the Dodgers in the first game of a double–header in Brooklyn. The Cubs also lost the second game 5–4.

SEPTEMBER 20   A nighttime wrestling match is held at Wrigley Field. Portable lights were strung up for the world heavyweight wrestling title, pitting Jim Londos against Ed "Strangler" Lewis. It a huge box office success as a total of 35,265 fans paid to attend. Londos pinned Lewis in 49 minutes and 27 seconds.

               There were many wrestling and boxing matches held at night at Wrigley Field during the 1930s, 1940s, and 1950s.

SEPTEMBER 25   Playing in his first game as a Cub in Chicago, and in his first major league start, Phil Cavaretta hits the first pitch of his first plate appearance for a home run. The run held up for a 1–0 Cubs victory over the Reds. It was also Cavaretta's first major league hit. Guy Bush pitched the shutout.

               A first baseman, Cavaretta was only two months past his 18th birthday when he joined the Cubs. A native Chicagoan, Phil attended Lane Technical High School, located on Addison Street, fourteen blocks west of Wrigley Field. He was one of the most popular players ever to play for the Cubs. Cavaretta remained with the Cubs until March 1954. He played in 1,953 games as a Cub, with 968 runs scored, 1,927 hits, 341 doubles, 99 triples, 92 home runs, and 896 runs batted in.

SEPTEMBER 30   On the final day of the season, Lon Warneke wins his 22nd game of 1934 with an 8–2 decision over the Pirates in the first game of a double–header at Wrigley Field. The Cubs completed the sweep with a 7–5 win in the nightcap.

OCTOBER 26   The Cubs trade Pat Malone to the Cardinals for Ken O'Dea.

               Malone was 12–4 for the Yankees in 1936 and pitched in the World Series that season. The hard–drinking Malone didn't have long to live after his playing days ended. He was only 40 when he died of pancreatis.

NOVEMBER 21   The Cubs send Bud Tinning, Dick Ward, and cash to the Cardinals for Tex Carleton.

NOVEMBER 22   The Cubs trade Guy Bush, Babe Herman and Jim Weaver to the Pirates for Larry French and Freddie Lindstrom.

               Overall, the trade had to rank on the positive side of the ledger, but it can't be rated as an overwhelming success. Larry French had a 95–84 record in seven years with the Cubs. Lindstrom was a native Chicagoan and was only 29 at the time of the trade, but he was about done as a player and lasted only a year with the Cubs. Bush, Herman, and Weaver each helped the Pirates as regulars for a year or two.

DECEMBER 19   The Yankees purchase Joe DiMaggio from the San Francisco Seals of the Pacific Coast League for $25,000 and five minor league players.

The Cubs had the option of purchasing DiMaggio before the Yankees or any other big league club, but P. K. Wrigley refused to appropriate the money. DiMaggio suffered a knee injury late in the 1934 season getting out of a cab, and Wrigley believed that he was damaged goods. The owner of the Seals offered Wrigley a money–back guarantee. The Cubs were allowed to try out DiMaggio during spring training in 1935, and if the club believed he wasn't a prospect, Joe could be returned for a full refund of the purchase price. Wrigley still turned down the offer because the Cubs were well–fortified in the outfield with players like Chuck Klein, Kiki Cuyler, Augie Galan, and Frank Demaree. After another season in San Francisco, DiMaggio arrived in the majors in 1936 and was an immediate sensation.

1935   Cubs

Season in a Sentence

The Cubs are 10½ games out of first place in July, but rebound to take the National League pennant with an astonishing 21–game winning streak in September.

Finish • Won • Lost • Pct • GB

First   100   54   .649   +4.0

World Series–The Cubs lost, four games to two, to the Detroit Tigers.

Manager

Charlie Grimm

Stats

Stats	Cubs	NL	Rank
Batting Avg:	.288	.277	1
On–Base Pct:	.347	.331	1
Slugging Pct:	.414	.391	2
Home Runs:	88		3
Stolen Bases:	66		3
ERA:	3.26	4.02	1
Fielding Avg:	.970	.968	2
Runs Scored:	847		1
Runs Allowed:	597		1

Starting Lineup

Gabby Hartnett, c
Phil Cavaretta, 1b
Billy Herman, 2b
Stan Hack, 3b
Billy Jurges, ss
Augie Galan, lf
Frank Demaree, cf
Chuck Klein, rf
Freddie Lindstrom, cf–3b
Ken O'Dea, c
Kiki Cuyler, cf

Pitchers

Lon Warneke, sp–rp
Bill Lee, sp
Larry French, sp
Roy Henshaw, sp–rp
Tex Carleton, sp
Charlie Root, rp–sp

Attendance

692,604 (second in NL)

Club Leaders

Batting Avg:	Hartnett	.344
On–Base Pct:	Hack	.406
Slugging Pct:	Hartnett	.545
Home Runs:	Klein	21
RBI:	Hartnett	91
Runs:	Galan	133
Stolen Bases:	Galan	22
Wins:	Warneke	20
	Lee	20
Strikeouts:	Warneke	120
ERA:	French	2.96
Saves:	Warneke	4

The 1935 Cubs rallied from 10½ games back in July to take the NL title, fueled by a 21–game winning streak.

APRIL 16   In the season opener, the Cubs defeat the Cardinals 4–3 before 15,500 shivering fans at Wrigley Field on a day in which the high temperature in Chicago was only 34 degrees. Dizzy Dean started for the Cardinals, but was knocked out, literally, in the first inning. Fred Lindstrom, in his first at–bat as a Cub, lined a pitch off Dizzy's ankle. Gabby Hartnett's homer in the second inning put the Cubs up 3–0, but the Cards came back to tie the game. Billy Herman's RBI single accounted for the winning run in the eighth.

APRIL 29   The Cubs win a riotous 12–11 contest against the Pirates at Wrigley Field. The Cubs trailed 9–2 heading into the eighth when they scored ten runs, then survived a two–run Pittsburgh rally in the ninth.

In the fifth inning, Cookie Lavagetto of the Pirates slid into second on a double and was spiked by Billy Jurges, who was covering the bag. Lavagetto leaped to his feet with fists flying. Umpires and players from both teams swarmed the field, but before the situation was under control, ex–Cub Guy Bush engaged in a verbal battle with Cubs pitcher Roy Joiner. Bush knocked Joiner to the ground, which brought blood to Joiner's nose and left a six–inch stratch on his left jaw. Charlie Grimm tried to get at Bush, but was restrained. Two days later, Joiner was released and never played another game for the Cubs.

MAY 11   The Cubs rout the Braves 14–7 in Boston.

Charlie Grimm retired as a player after going 35 consecutive at–bats without a hit during spring training, and another eight during the regular season. Phil Cavaretta, who was just 18 years old when the season began, took over as the starting first baseman.

MAY 12   Lon Warneke has a 4–for–4 day at the plate and defeats the Braves 4–1 in Boston.

Warneke had a 20–13 record, a 3.06 ERA, and 20 complete games for the Cubs in 1935. Bill Lee was also a 20–game winner for the Cubs. He had a 20–6 record and a 2.96 earned run average.

MAY 20   Babe Ruth makes his first appearance as a National Leaguer at Wrigley Field during
            a 5–0 Cubs win over the Braves. Ruth was purchased by the Braves from the Yan-
            kees the previous February. The Babe was hitless in two official at–bats, but homered
            the next day during a 4–1 Boston win over the Cubs at Wrigley. Ruth retired as an
            active player two weeks later.

JUNE 12   The Cubs clobber the Phillies 15–0 in the first game of a double–header in Philadel-
            phia, only to lose the second tilt 11–8.

            *At the end of the day, the Cubs had a record of 22–22 and were 8½ games back
            of the first place Giants.*

JUNE 13   Augie Galan hits a three–run, two–out homer in the ninth inning to defeat the
            Phillies 9–7 in the second game of a double–header in Philadelphia. The Cubs also
            won the first game 12–6.

            *In 1935, the Cubs moved Galan from second base to left field because of a
            weak throwing arm and turned him into a switch–hitter to take advantage of
            his speed from the left side of the plate. Galan responded by hitting .314 and
            leading the league in runs scored (133) and stolen bases (22). In 646 at–bats he
            didn't hit into a single double play, although he did hit into a triple play. Galan
            never matched his production in 1935, but remained a solid outfielder for the
            Cubs for the next four seasons.*

JUNE 21   Fred Lindstrom collects five hits, including a double, in six at–bats during an 11–3
            win over the Braves in Boston.

            *Lindstrom was acquired to share time at third base with Stan Hack, but Hack
            established himself as a star in his fourth major league season. In 1935, he hit
            .311. Hack played for the Cubs from 1932 through 1947 and was extremely
            popular with the fans for his pleasant and outgoing disposition. In 1935,
            21–year–old Bill Veeck, working in the Cubs front office, used Hack's perpetual
            smile as a promotional gimmick by selling "Smile With Stan Hack" mirrors at
            Wrigley Field. The NL put a stop to the practice when fans in the bleachers
            were using the mirrors to reflect the sun in the eyes of opposing batters. Hack
            played in 1,938 games for the Cubs, scored 1,239 runs, collected 2,193 hits, 363
            doubles, 81 triples, a batting average of .301, and an on–base percentage of .394.*

JUNE 28   Cubs pitcher Roy Henshaw pitches a one–hitter to defeat the Pirates 8–0 at Wrigley
            Field. A controversial scoring decision cost Henshaw a no–hitter. In the sixth
            inning, a drive by Pittsburgh pitcher Mace Brown just grazed off the glove of center
            fielder Fred Lindstrom after a long run. Lindstrom had both hands on the ball and
            held it for an instant before dropping it. Brown was credited with a double by the
            official scorer. At the time, the Wrigley Field scoreboard did not post scoring deci-
            sions or the number of hits that each club accumulated during the game. At the
            conclusion of the game, players congratulated Henshaw believing that he had pitched
            a no–hitter, and were livid when they learned that Brown's drive was ruled a hit.

            *Standing only five–foot–eight and weighing 155 pounds, Henshaw was 13–5 in
            1935. He earned seven of his victories against the Pirates.*

JUNE 29   Larry French pitches a twelve–inning complete game shutout for the Cubs against his former Pittsburgh teammates to win 1–0 in the first game of a double–header at Wrigley Field. Waite Hoyt also pitched a complete game for Pittsburgh and lost the contest on his own throwing error. The Cubs also won the second game 2–1.

French was 17–10 with a 2.96 ERA in 1935.

JULY 1   The Cubs play at night for the first time and beat the Reds 8–4 at Crosley Field in Cincinnati. It was the third night game in major league history. (The first was on May 24, 1935, with the Phillies visiting Cincinnati.) Charlie Grimm held Gabby Hartnett and Fred Lindstrom out of the lineup because neither had ever seen a night game. Many of the Cubs had played at night in exhibition games or in the minors.

JULY 3   The Cubs release Kiki Cuyler.

Cuyler lost his outfield job to Frank Demaree and appeared to be finished as a player. Cuyler had one good year left, however, and hit .326 for the Reds in 1936.

JULY 5   The Cubs lose 4–0 to the Pirates in Pittsburgh.

At the end of the day, the Cubs had a record of 38–32, were in fourth place, and stood 10½ games back of the first–place Giants, and 12 back in the loss column. From July 6 through September 27, the Cubs had a record of 62–20.

JULY 16   The Cubs win their eighth game in a row with a 2–1 decision over the Phillies in ten innings at Wrigley Field.

JULY 24   Cubs reserve catcher Ken O'Dea clubs a walk–off homer in the eleventh inning to defeat the Dodgers 7–6 in the second game of a double–header at Wrigley Field. O'Dea was in the game because starter Gabby Hartnett was removed for a pinch–runner in the ninth inning, when the Cubs scored two runs to tie the game. Chicago also won the first game 9–3.

JULY 27   Gabby Hartnett slugs a grand slam in the fourth inning off Tony Freitas of the Reds during a 9–8 Cubs win in the first game of a double–header at Wrigley Field. The Cubs completed the sweep with a 12–1 win in the nightcap. The two wins extended the Cubs winning streak to eight games.

Hartnett hit .344 with 13 homers in 1935.

JULY 30   The Cubs defeat the Pirates 9–6 in Pittsburgh for their tenth victory in a row.

During the game, Billy Jurges and third–string catcher Walter Stephenson engaged in a fight in the dugout in clear view of the fans at Forbes Field. The confrontation started when the Brooklyn–born Jurges teased North Carolina native Stephenson about the Confederacy's loss in the Civil War.

JULY 31   The rampaging Cubs run their winning streak to 11 games with a 4–2 decision over the Pirates in the first game of a double–header in Pittsburgh. The streak ended with a 6–5 loss in eleven innings in the second contest.

The Cubs won 24 of 27 from July 6 through July 31. During that period, they gained ten games on the first–place Giants. The Cubs closed July only one–half game behind the Giants, but by mid–August were four games back, seven in the loss column, following a brief slump.

AUGUST 21   The Cubs and the Phillies divide a run–filled double–header in Philadelphia. The Phillies won the first game 13–12, and the Cubs snared the second 19–5. In the second game, the Cubs scored 12 runs in the sixth inning to take an 18–1 lead. Billy Herman had 13 at–bats, to tie a major league record for an eighteen–inning double–header. Chuck Klein tied a National League record by scoring eight runs. Frank Demaree had eight hits, including two doubles, in 12 at–bats. Phil Cavaretta had seven hits, including two doubles, in 11 at–bats.

Billy Herman led the NL in doubles with 57 and hits with 227, while batting .341. The 57 doubles were a club record. He also hit 57 doubles in 1936. Herman's 666 at–bats in 1935 are also a club record.

SEPTEMBER 4   Augie Galan's grand slam in the eighth inning off Jim Bivin of the Phillies helps the Cubs to an 8–2 win at Wrigley Field. Galan also had a solo homer and an RBI–single for a total of six runs batted in.

This was the first of a Cubs record 21 victories in a row. The Cubs entered the game with a 79–52 record and were 2½ games behind the first place Cardinals, four back in the loss column.

SEPTEMBER 11   The Cubs win their eighth game in succession with a 15–3 walloping of the Braves at Wrigley Field. The Cubs score eight runs in the eighth inning.

SEPTEMBER 14   The Cubs take over first place with an 18–14 win over the Dodgers at Wrigley Field. It was the Cubs 11th win in a row. The Cubs scored eight runs in the sixth inning to take a 16–4 lead, then hung on for the victory.

SEPTEMBER 18   The Cubs run their spectacular winning streak to 15 games by collecting 20 hits and crushing the Giants 15–3 at Wrigley Field. The Cubs scored eight runs in the fourth inning.

SEPTEMBER 19   The Cubs complete a four–game sweep of the Giants at Wrigley Field with a 6–1 decision to run the winning streak to 16 games. The four wins extended the Cubs lead over the third–place Giants from 3½ games to 7½. Chicago led the second place Cardinals by 2½ games with seven to play.

SEPTEMBER 22   The Cubs run their winning streak to 18 games with a 2–0 victory over the Pirates at Wrigley Field behind the pitching of Larry French.

The win set the stage for the final five-game series against the Cardinals in St. Louis, beginning on September 25. The Cubs went into the series with a three-game lead over the Cards, and needed one victory for a tie and two to clinch the NL pennant.

SEPTEMBER 25   The Cubs clinch a tie for the pennant with a 1–0 win over the Cardinals at Sportsman's Park. It was Chicago's 19th win in a row. Phil Cavaretta drove in the lone run of the game with a homer in the second inning off Paul Dean. Lon Warneke pitched a two–hitter for his 20th win of the season. The only St. Louis hits were a single by Lynn King in the fourth inning and a double by Ripper Collins in the eighth. Collins was stranded at second when left fielder Augie Galan made a leaping catch at the left field wall on a drive by Leo Durocher.

It was the second season in a row that Cavaretta won a 1–0 game on a home run on the 25th of September.

SEPTEMBER 27   The Cubs clinch the pennant and run their winning streak to 21 games with 6–2 and 5–3 wins over the Cardinals in St. Louis. Bill Lee earned his 20th win of the season in the opener.

The 21–game winning streak is the longest in Cubs history, tying the mark set by the 1880 club. The only longer streak in the majors is the 26–game streak of the 1916 Giants. However, the Giants had a tie game while winning 26 straight. The two longest winnings streaks in big league history uninterrupted by a tie are the pair by the Cubs in 1880 and 1935.

SEPTEMBER 28   The 21–game winning streak comes to an end with a 7–5 loss to the Cardinals in eleven innings in St. Louis. The Cubs scored three runs in the ninth to tie the score 5–5. Joe Medwick's two–run, walk–off homer off Fabian Kowalik decided the issue.

The Cubs faced the Detroit Tigers, managed by Mickey Cochrane, in the World Series. The Tigers had a record of 93–58 in 1935. In 1934, Detroit lost the World Series in seven games to the Cardinals. Heading into the 1935 World Series, the Tigers had yet to win a world championship, and the Cubs hadn't won one since 1908.

OCTOBER 1   In the first game of the 1935 World Series, the Cubs defeat the Tigers 3–0 before 47,391 in Detroit. Lon Warneke pitched a four–hit shutout. The Cubs scored two in the first off Schoolboy Rowe on a double by Augie Galan, a single by Billy Herman, a sacrifice, and a single by Gabby Hartnett. Frank Demaree hit a homer in the ninth.

At the age of 19, Phil Cavaretta was the Cubs first baseman throughout the 1935 World Series. In the history of the Fall Classic, Cavaretta is the youngest first baseman, the second youngest player to appear in a starting lineup, and the fifth youngest overall.

6–foot–4 1/2–inch schoolboy Rowe, left, shakes hands with Cubs pitcher Roy Henshaw, who stood just 5–feet–8. Rowe won 19 regular season games and beat the Cubs once in the series. Henshaw won 13 games in 1935.

Cubs   21 in a Row   Cubs

The Cubs entered the game of September 4, 1935, with a 79–52 record and in second place. Chicago was 2½ games behind the first-place Cardinals and four back in the loss column. The Cubs defeated the Phillies 8–2 that day to start an incredible 21–game winning streak to pull away with the pennant. It is the second-longest winning streak in major league history, trailing only the 1916 New York Giants, who bagged 26 victories in succession.

During the 21–game streak in 1935, the Cubs outscored the opposition 137–53. The pitching staff held the opponents to three runs or less in 20 of the 21 games, including four shutouts. The club won two extra–inning games, five by one run, and swept two double–headers. The 21 wins came in a span of twenty–four days.

The 21-Game Winning Streak

Date	Opponent	Site	Score
September 4	Philadelphia	H	8–2
September 5	Philadelphia	H	3–2 (11 innings)
September 6	Philadelphia	H	3–2 (10 innings)
September 7	Philadelphia	H	4–0
September 9	Boston	H	5–1
	Boston	H	2–1
September 10	Boston	H	4–0
September 11	Boston	H	15–3
September 12	Brooklyn	H	13–3
September 13	Brooklyn	H	4–1
September 14	Brooklyn	H	18–14
September 15	Brooklyn	H	6–3
September 16	New York	H	8–3
September 17	New York	H	5–3
September 18	New York	H	15–3
September 19	New York	H	6–1
September 21	Pittsburgh	H	4–3
September 22	Pittsburgh	H	2–0
September 25	St. Louis	A	1–0
September 27	St. Louis	A	6–2
	St. Louis	A	5–3

OCTOBER 2   In game two, the Tigers even the World Series with an 8–3 win over the Cubs before 46,742 in Detroit. Hank Greenberg drove in two of the four Detroit runs in the first inning with a homer off Charlie Root. Greenberg broke his wrist, however, when he was hit by a Fabian Kowalik pitch in the seventh inning, and didn't play for the rest of the Series.

OCTOBER 4   The Tigers take the lead in the World Series with a 6–5 win in eleven innings before 45,532 at Wrigley Field. Paced by a second–inning home run by Frank Demaree, the Cubs took a 3–1 lead into the eighth, but the Tigers scored four times off Bill Lee and Lon Warneke to take a 5–3 lead. The Cubs came back with two in the ninth on singles by Stan Hack, Chuck Klein, and Ken O'Dea, and a sacrifice fly by Augie Galan. The winning run in the eleventh was scored on a single by Jo–Jo White off Larry French.

Hack played shortstop in the tenth and eleventh inning. He played 16 seasons in the majors, and never played a single game at short during the regular season.

OCTOBER 5   The Tigers take their third victory in a row over the Cubs and come within one win of a world championship with a 2–1 decision in game four of the World Series before 49,350 at Wrigley Field. The Cubs scored first on a home run by Gabby Hartnett in the second inning off General Crowder, but the Tigers came back with single runs in the third and sixth against Tex Carleton.

OCTOBER 6   The Cubs keep their championship hopes alive by defeating the Tigers 3–1 in game five before 49,237 at Wrigley Field. The Cubs took a 2–0 win in the third inning on a triple by Billy Herman and a homer by Chuck Klein. Lon Warneke pitched six shutout innings before leaving the game with a shoulder injury. Bill Lee went the rest of the way.

OCTOBER 7   The Tigers take the world championship be defeating the Cubs 4–3 at Detroit in game six. Billy Herman drove in all three Chicago runs with a single in the third inning and a two–run homer in the fifth. Stan Hack led off the ninth with a triple off Tommy Bridges, but couldn't score. Billy Jurges struck out, Larry French bounced back to the mound, and Augie Galan flied out. Goose Goslin's single with two out in the bottom of the ninth off Larry French won the game.

NOVEMBER 7   James Ridner arrives in Detroit after pushing a baby carriage 550 miles.

Ridner is proof that it doesn't pay to bet on the Cubs to win. He had to push a baby carriage from Kentucky to Michigan because he wagered that the Cubs would defeat the Tigers in the 1935 World Series. To settle the bet, Ridner pushed the carriage from his home in Harlan, Kentucky, to Detroit. Inside the carriage was Arson "Fireball" Stephens, the winner of the wager, along with provisions for the journey. The 550–mile trip took 30 days and ended at home plate at Tiger Stadium. Ridner wore out two baby carriages and three pairs of shoes.

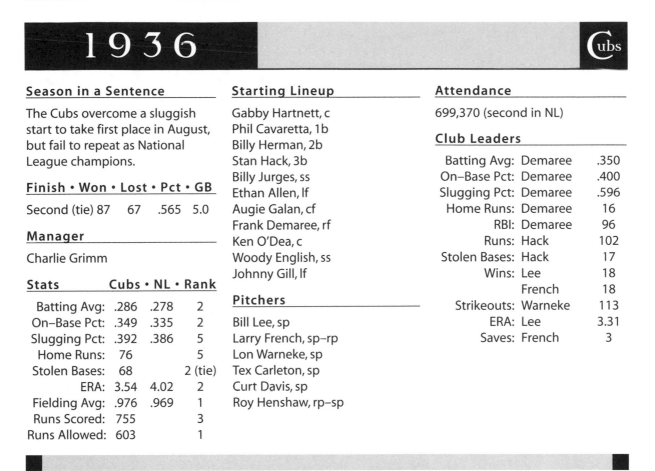

1936   Cubs

Season in a Sentence

The Cubs overcome a sluggish start to take first place in August, but fail to repeat as National League champions.

Finish • Won • Lost • Pct • GB

Second (tie) 87   67   .565   5.0

Manager

Charlie Grimm

Stats

Stats	Cubs	NL	Rank
Batting Avg:	.286	.278	2
On–Base Pct:	.349	.335	2
Slugging Pct:	.392	.386	5
Home Runs:	76		5
Stolen Bases:	68		2 (tie)
ERA:	3.54	4.02	2
Fielding Avg:	.976	.969	1
Runs Scored:	755		3
Runs Allowed:	603		1

Starting Lineup

Gabby Hartnett, c
Phil Cavaretta, 1b
Billy Herman, 2b
Stan Hack, 3b
Billy Jurges, ss
Ethan Allen, lf
Augie Galan, cf
Frank Demaree, rf
Ken O'Dea, c
Woody English, ss
Johnny Gill, lf

Pitchers

Bill Lee, sp
Larry French, sp–rp
Lon Warneke, sp
Tex Carleton, sp
Curt Davis, sp
Roy Henshaw, rp–sp

Attendance

699,370 (second in NL)

Club Leaders

Batting Avg:	Demaree	.350
On–Base Pct:	Demaree	.400
Slugging Pct:	Demaree	.596
Home Runs:	Demaree	16
RBI:	Demaree	96
Runs:	Hack	102
Stolen Bases:	Hack	17
Wins:	Lee	18
	French	18
Strikeouts:	Warneke	113
ERA:	Lee	3.31
Saves:	French	3

APRIL 10   The Cubs arrive in Chicago after enduring a brutal coast–to–coast exhibition trip.

The Cubs played in Los Angeles on March 16, and over the course of nearly a month played in cities from one end of the country to the other, usually stopping to play only one game. The club played in San Antonio, Houston, and New Orleans, the Florida cities of Pensacola, Tallahassee, Lakeland, Tampa, St. Petersburg, Bradenton, Clearwater, Winter Haven, and Sarasota, the Alabama towns of Selma, Dothan, Montgomery, and Birmingham, in addition to Thomasville, Georgia, and Nashville, Tennessee.

APRIL 14   Billy Herman stars in the Cubs 12–7 win in the season opener against the Cardinals in St. Louis. Herman collected five hits, including a homer and three doubles, in five at–bats. Frank Demaree hit two homers, and Gabby Hartnett and Chuck Klein added one each.

Herman was also injured twice in the game. He was knocked dizzy while playing second base when a bad hop struck him and caused a laceration to his face. Later, Herman suffered a deep bruise as the result of sliding with a resin bag in his pocket. Billy had another tremendous season for the Cubs in 1936. He collected 15 doubles in his first 20 games, and finished the year with 57 two–baggers to tie the club record he set in 1935. Herman also had 211 hits and batted .334.

APRIL 17   In the home opener, the Cubs lose 12–3 to the Reds.

Prior to the game, players from both teams marched to the center field flag pole, where the American flag and 1935 National League pennant were raised to the strains of "The Star–Spangled Banner." At the time, the national anthem was played only on special occasions. It did not become routine until the 1942 season, when the United States became involved in World War II.

APRIL 19   The Cubs bury the Reds 16–6 at Wrigley Field.

MAY 16   Phil Cavaretta hits a grand slam off Bucky Walters of the Phillies in the eighth inning of a 7–3 Cubs win in Philadelphia. The drive cleared the right field fence at the foul pole. The Phillies vigorously protested that the ball was foul, to no avail.

MAY 21   The Cubs send Chuck Klein, Fabian Kowalik and $50,000 to the Phillies for Ethan Allen and Curt Davis.

MAY 26   The Cubs score seven runs in the third inning and blast the Reds 10–4 at Wrigley Field.

The Cubs and White Sox home games were on five stations in 1936. Bob Elson was the play–by–play man for WGN, Russ Hodges for WIND, Pat Flanagan for WBBM, Hal Totten on WCFL, and John Harrington on WJJD. In addition, stations in such places as Rock Island, Illinois; Lincoln, Nebraska; Davenport, Iowa; and Des Moines, Iowa, did telegraphic re–creations of Cubs games. In Des Moines, the games were broadcast on station WHO by Ronald (Dutch) Reagan, who would leave the Midwest for a career as a movie actor in 1937. In 1936, THE SPORTING NEWS conducted a reader poll to determine the most popular radio play–by–play broadcaster in the country. Despite the fact that he broadcast no games live and emanated from the relatively small town of Des Moines, Reagan finished ninth in the poll. He fared much better in future elections, winning two terms each as governor of California and president of the United States.

MAY 28   The Cubs score seven runs in the second inning and defeat the Reds 11–5 at Wrigley Field.

The game was punctuated by a bench–clearing brawl in the third. Reds pitcher Lee Stine plunked Woody English with a pitch, and the two swapped punches after an exchange of words. Both benches emptied and a contingent of Chicago police was necessary to quell the battle. The best bout on the card took place between coaches George Kelly of the Reds and Roy Johnson of the Cubs. Kelly connected with a dozen blows and was ejected along with Johnson, Stine, and English.

JUNE 8   During a 3–0 win over the Phillies at Wrigley Field, Cubs trainer Andy Lotshaw leaps from the dugout to attend to a woman who was struck by a foul ball. When he reached the scene, he learned that it was his wife who was hit. Fortunately, Mrs. Lotshaw wasn't seriously injured.

JUNE 12   The Cubs win their ninth game in a row with a 17–1 slaughter of the Braves at Wrigley Field. Ethan Allen and Ken O'Dea each hit bases–loaded triples.

JUNE 21   The Cubs win their 15th game in a row with a 7–2 decision over the Dodgers in the first game of a double–header at Ebbets Field. Brooklyn ended the Cubs' streak in the second game with a 6–4 victory.

When the 15–game winning streak started, the Cubs had a record of 20–21.

JUNE 25   Bill Lee pitches the Cubs to a 1–0 win over the Braves in the first game of a double–header in Boston. Gabby Hartnett drove in the lone run of the game with a single. The Cubs completed the sweep with an 8–4 decision in the second tilt.

JUNE 28   Larry French and Bill Lee both pitch shutouts in a double–header sweep of the Giants in New York. French won the first game 3–0, while Lee captured the second 6–0.

French had a record of 18–9 with a 3.39 ERA in 1936.

JULY 7   Charlie Grimm manages the National League to a 4–3 victory in the All–Star Game, played at Braves Field in Boston. The first run of the game was scored in the second inning when Frank Demaree singled and Gabby Hartnett tripled. Augie Galan hit a homer in the fifth off Schoolboy Rowe. Bill Herman collected two hits. Lon Warneke earned the save with 2 ⅓ innings of shutout ball.

Demaree collected 212 hits and batted .350 with 16 homers for the Cubs in 1936.

JULY 13   Bill Lee pitches the Cubs to a 1–0 win over Carl Hubbell and the Giants at Wrigley Field. The Cubs won with only two hits. Hubbell did not lose again until May 31, 1937, winning his last 16 decisions in 1936 and the first eight in 1937 for a major league record 24 wins in a row.

The victory put the Cubs into first place, three percentage points ahead of the Cardinals.

JULY 25   The Cubs turn back the Phillies 17–4 in Philadelphia.

The victory gave the Cubs a 56–32 record and a three–game lead over the Cardinals in the pennant race.

JULY 26   The day after scoring 17 runs, the Cubs are shutout 4–0 by the Phillies with only two hits in the first game of a double–header in Philadelphia, then bounce back with an 18–5 win in the second contest. In the second game, Frank Demaree collected five hits, including two homers, in five at–bats. Augie Galan, Lon Warneke, Stan Hack, and Ethan Allen also homered for the Cubs. It was Warneke's only homer between 1933 and 1940.

After his playing career ended, Allen developed a tabletop baseball game called All–Star Baseball, which was extremely popular in the days before the advent of video games, and authored several books on baseball–playing technique. Allen later coached at Yale for 23 years. In 1947 and 1948, his Yale teams made it to the NCAA championship game with future President George Bush playing first base.

AUGUST 1   The Cubs win a 1–0 thriller in eleven innings against the Braves in Boston, with Tex Carleton pitching the complete–game shutout. Gabby Hartnett drove in the winning run with a single.

AUGUST 9 — A fight between Dizzy Dean of the Cardinals and Cubs pitcher Tex Carleton highlights a 7–3 loss to the Cardinals in St. Louis. The defeat knocked the Cubs out of first place.

> *In the top of the first with Billy Herman at bat, Dean raced from the mound toward the Cubs dugout in response to taunts from Carleton. Carleton leaped off the bench and met Dean near the first–base line. Dean got Carleton in a headlock and punched him in the face. The two scuffled until members of both teams, aided by the umpires, separated them. Paul Dean, Dizzy's brother, started after Carleton and had to be pulled away. The umpires wanted to eject Dean, but Charlie Grimm pleaded with them to let Dizzy stay in the game in a gesture of sportsmanship that may have cost him the game.*

AUGUST 10 — The Cubs regain first place with a 6–4 win in ten innings against the Cardinals in St. Louis.

AUGUST 22 — The Cubs celebrate the National League's 60th birthday with a celebration prior to a 3–0 win over the Reds at Wrigley Field.

> *A group of amateur players donned 1876 replica uniforms of the Cincinnati and Chicago clubs and played a three–inning game, utilizing the equipment of the day, including no gloves. A 12–foot birthday cake was also wheeled onto the field.*

AUGUST 24 — Billy Jurges fights Gilly Campbell of the Reds during a 2–1 Cubs win in ten innings at Wrigley Field. In the tenth, Campbell slid hard into Jurges, who responded with a punch to Gilly's face. Both were ejected. The Jurges–Campbell feud wasn't over. The two fought each other twice more over the next two weeks.

AUGUST 26 — Bill Lee sets a club record with his 15th consecutive win at Wrigley Field, dating back to September 1935, by defeating the Phillies 4–2 in the first game of a double–header. The Cubs completed the sweep with a 7–4 victory in the second contest.

AUGUST 27 — Roy Henshaw pitches the Cubs to a 1–0 win over the Phillies at Wrigley Field. The lone run of the game was scored in the fifth inning on a sacrifice fly by Stan Hack which scored Billy Jurges.

AUGUST 28 — On Charlie Grimm's 38th birthday, the Cubs score seven runs in the first inning and bury the Braves 18–3 with 21 hits in a game at Wrigley Field.

> *Tex Carleton was the winning pitcher. Seven of his 12 victories in 1936 were against the Braves.*

Cubs third baseman Stan Hack batted .298 in 1936 and led the team with 17 stolen bases. His average was just shy of his career .301 average over sixteen seasons, all with the Cubs.

AUGUST 31 — Lon Warneke beats the Giants 1–0 at Wrigley Field. The only run of the game was scored on a triple by Ethan Allen and a single by Billy Herman in the sixth inning.

Warneke had a record of 16–13 and an ERA of 3.44.

SEPTEMBER 3   Chicago policeman Harry Hanson contributes to a 1–0 loss in ten innings to the Dodgers at Wrigley Field.

In the first inning, Phil Cavaretta sent a drive down the right field line. Hanson, stationed on a bench on the Brooklyn bullpen, believed the ball was foul and tossed it to Dodger right fielder Randy Moore. The umpires sent Cavaretta back to first base. If the ball had gone unimpeded, Cavaretta would have had a double and possibly a triple.

SEPTEMBER 6   The Cubs lose a Labor Day double–header 6–3 and 8–4 to the Reds in Cincinnati, while the first–place Giants win twice. The losses put the Cubs in third place six games back of the Giants with 19 games to play, and ended any realistic hopes of winning the pennant.

SEPTEMBER 20   Burglars break into Wrigley Field and make off with $1,500, which had been placed in a vault.

SEPTEMBER 27   In the final game of the season, the Cubs defeat the Cardinals 6–3 at Sportsman's Park to finish in a tie with St. Louis for second place.

OCTOBER 2   In game one of the Chicago City Series, the White Sox defeat the Cubs 5–1 at Wrigley Field. The White Sox swept the series in four games.

OCTOBER 8   The Cubs trade Lon Warneke to the Cardinals for Roy Parmelee and Ripper Collins.

Warneke gave the Cardinals five effective seasons, while first baseman Collins and pitcher Parmelee failed to live up to expectations for the Cubs.

DECEMBER 2   A month after Franklin Roosevelt wins his second term in office in a landslide over Alf Landon in the presidential election, the Cubs sell Ethan Allen to the Cardinals.

DECEMBER 5   The Cardinals trade Roy Henshaw and Woody English to the Dodgers for Lonny Frey.

DECEMBER 31   The Cubs and the White Sox jointly announce that they will be charging radio stations for the right to broadcast games from Wrigley Field and Comiskey Park in 1937. Previously, stations were permitted to broadcast games free of charge. WGN and WBBM each paid each club $7,500, while WIND, WBBM, and WJJD each paid the two clubs $3,000.

1937

Cubs

Season in a Sentence

Buoyed by the best offense in the league, the Cubs hold a seven-game lead over their rivals in early August, but inconsistent pitching fails the club during the stretch drive.

Finish • Won • Lost • Pct • GB

Second   93   61   .604   3.0

Manager

Charlie Grimm

Stats

Stats	Cubs	NL	Rank
Batting Avg:	.287	.272	1
On–Base Pct:	.355	.332	1
Slugging Pct:	.416	.382	1
Home Runs:	96		3
Stolen Bases:	71		2
ERA:	3.97	3.91	5
Fielding Avg:	.975	.971	1
Runs Scored:	811		1
Runs Allowed:	682		4

Starting Lineup

Gabby Hartnett, c
Ripper Collins, 1b
Billy Herman, 2b
Stan Hack, 3b
Billy Jurges, ss
Augie Galan, lf
Joe Marty, cf
Frank Demaree, rf
Phil Cavaretta, cf–1b
Ken O'Dea, c
Lonny Frey, ss
Tuck Stainback, cf

Pitchers

Bill Lee, sp
Tex Carleton, sp
Larry French, sp–rp
Roy Parmelee, sp–rp
Curt Davis, sp–rp
Charlie Root, rp–sp
Clay Bryant, rp
Clyde Shoun, rp

Attendance

895,020 (second in NL)

Club Leaders

Batting Avg:	Herman	.335
On–Base Pct:	Herman	.396
Slugging Pct:	Demaree	.485
Home Runs:	Galan	18
RBI:	Demaree	115
Runs:	Herman	106
	Hack	106
Stolen Bases:	Galan	23
Wins:	French	16
	Carleton	16
Strikeouts:	Lee	108
ERA:	Carleton	3.15
Saves:	Root	5

APRIL 20   The Cubs lose the season opener 5–0 to the Pirates before 18,940 at Wrigley Field.

During the 1937 season, the Cubs became the first team in baseball to place a bat rack in the dugout. Previously, bats were hazardously spread out in foul territory in front of the bench.

APRIL 24   The Cubs pound out a 13–12 win over the Cardinals in St. Louis.

This was the only Cubs victory in their first six games in 1937. After 32 games, the Cubs were 16–16 before catching fire with a stretch of 44 wins in 60 games from May 28 through August 3.

MAY 5   The Cubs score in eight of the nine innings and pound the Phillies 17–4 in Philadelphia. Frank Demaree hit a grand slam in the sixth inning off Pete Sivess.

Demaree hit .324 with 17 homers, 115 RBIs, 104 runs scored, and 199 hits in 1937. He was one of four Cubs with 100 or more runs scored during the season. Billy Herman batted .335 with 189 hits and 106 runs. Stan Hack batted

.297 and also scored 106 times. Augie Galan scored 104 runs and led the league with 23 stolen bases.

MAY 6 — On the day the German dirigible Hindenburg erupts in flames in Lakehurst, New Jersey, killing thirty–six people, the Cubs beat the Phillies 1–0 in a game shortened to five innings by rain. Bill Lee allowed only one hit. The lone run of the game was scored in the fifth inning on a double by Ripper Collins.

MAY 23 — The Cubs swat the Braves 11–1 at Wrigley Field.

JUNE 4 — The Cubs run their winning streak to eight games with a 6–5 decision over the Giants in eleven innings in the first game of a double–header in New York. The streak ended with a 4–2 loss in the nightcap.

JUNE 18 — A bases loaded walk–off triple down the left field line by Augie Galan wipes out a two–run Phillie advantage to lead the Cubs to an 8–7 win at Wrigley Field.

JUNE 25 — Augie Galan becomes the first Cub switch–hitter to hit homers from both sides of the plate in a game during an 11–2 win over the Dodgers at Wrigley Field. Galan homered off right–hander Fred Fitzsimmons in the fourth inning and lefty Ralph Birkofer in the eighth.

JUNE 29 — The Cubs score three runs in the ninth inning off Dizzy Dean to whip the Cardinals 11–9 in St. Louis. The three runs were scored after Dean struck out the first two batters in the inning. First baseman Ripper Collins went through the entire game without a fielding chance. It was the only time in National League history, and one of only four occasions in the majors, that a first baseman played at least nine innings without a putout or an assist.

Billy Jurges was ejected in the eighth inning for disputing a call by umpire Bill Stewart. After being tossed out, Jurges petulantly kicked dirt onto home plate five times after Stewart swept it off.

JULY 2 — A two–run walk–off homer by Augie Galan beats the Pirates 8–7 at Wrigley Field. The win kept the Cubs in first place, one–half game ahead of the Giants.

JULY 5 — The Cubs win a thrilling double–header 13–12 in fourteen innings and 9–7 against the Cardinals at Wrigley Field. In the first game, the Cardinals led 12–7 before the Cubs scored four times in the eighth inning and one in the ninth. They recorded the winning tally in the fourteenth on a single by Billy Jurges. The Cubs had a total of 23 hits in the contest. Frank Demaree led the assault with six hits, including three doubles, in seven at–bats. He also drew a walk. Demaree is the only Cubs player between 1897 and 1971 to collect six hits in a game. In addition, he had two hits in four at–bats in the second game for a Cub record eight hits in a double–header. Demaree also had eight hits in a twinbill on August 21, 1935.

JULY 15 — Manager Charlie Grimm collapses in pain from back trouble in his Boston hotel room. He was taken several blocks in a wheelchair to a train bound for his hometown of St. Louis, where he was treated by Dr. Robert Hyland. Grimm was away from the club for eleven days. Gabby Hartnett managed the club in the interim.

AUGUST 3   The Cubs take a seven–game lead in the National League pennant race with a 4–1 win over the Phillies at Wrigley Field.

From August 4 through the end of the season, the Cubs had a record of 33–29 and blew the seven–game advantage to finish three games behind the Giants.

AUGUST 4   Gabby Hartnett runs his hitting streak to 24 games, but the Cubs lose 2–1 to the Phillies at Wrigley Field.

At the age of 36, Hartnett hit .354 with 12 homers in 1937.

AUGUST 6   During a 12–6 win over the Braves in the first game of a double–header at Wrigley Field, Gabby Hartnett's homer strikes the head of a workman, who was on the crew constructing the new bleachers in left field. The construction worker was knocked out cold, but wasn't seriously hurt.

The renovations of the bleachers took place during the 1937 season and the 1937–38 off–season. The present–day Wrigley Field bleachers have changed little since they were opened for occupancy on Opening Day in 1938. Originally, the bleachers were supposed to hold 5,000, with the foul lines about 20 to 25 feet closer to home plate than they are today. There were numerous complaints that this would be too much of a home run target, and the size of the bleachers was reduced to 3,000 by creating the curving "cutaways" down the foul lines that are still one of the many unique features at Wrigley Field. The trademark ivy was planted on the buff–brick outfield walls late in the 1937 season. Topping the bleachers was a new scoreboard, which after a few relatively minor modifications, is still in operation. The numerals indicating the uniform number of the batters and the numbers of balls, strikes, and outs were revolutionary magnetic "eyelids," a principle never before employed in scoreboard design that is still in use. The ball and strike openings are 18 inches wide by 30 inches tall. Each is made up of eight rows of four–inch holes. At the throw of a lever, the "eyelids" are lifted from the appropriate openings exposing the white panels beneath. The new bleachers also changed the size of the playing field. The left field line was reduced from 364 feet to 355; the distance from home plate to the center field wall was reduced from 436 feet to 400; and the right field line was increased from 321 feet to 353.

AUGUST 8   The Cubs defeat the Braves 3–0 and 3–2 in a double–header at Wrigley Field. In the first game, Tex Carleton pitched a one–hitter. The only Boston hit was a double by Elbie Fletcher.

Carleton had a 16–8 record and a 3.15 ERA in 1937. He tied for the club lead in wins with Larry French, who was 16–10 with an earned run average of 3.98.

AUGUST 13   The Cubs score nine runs in the third inning and defeat the Reds 22–8 at Wrigley Field.

Before the game, a group of Greek–Americans from Chicago presented Reds second baseman Alex Kampouris with a new Chrysler sedan. During the afternoon, Kampouris committed three errors and struck out twice.

AUGUST 28   Cubs pitcher Clay Bryant hits a grand slam in the tenth inning to break a 6–6 tie in a 10–7 win over the Braves in the second game of a double–header in Boston. The Cubs loaded the bases after the first two batters of the inning were retired. Bryant was allowed to hit for himself, but didn't finish the game. He was removed by Charlie Grimm after allowing a run in the bottom half of the inning. Bryant was one of two Cubs pitchers to homer in the game. Earlier, Charlie Root connected for a home run. The Cubs lost the first game 3–1.

> *Bryant was a good hitting pitcher. He had five homers and a .266 average in 192 career at–bats.*

SEPTEMBER 1   The Cubs are knocked out of first place with a 6–4 loss to the Dodgers in Brooklyn.

> *The Giants stayed in first place for the remainder of the season.*

SEPTEMBER 10   The Cubs coast to a 10–0 win over the Cardinals at Wrigley Field.

SEPTEMBER 23   The Cubs suffer a crucial 8–7 loss to the Giants at Wrigley Field that all but smothers hopes for a World Series in Chicago in 1937. The defeat put the Cubs 3 ½ games behind the Giants with ten contests left on the schedule.

SEPTEMBER 29   Clay Bryant pitches a two–hitter to defeat the Reds 2–0 in Cincinnati before a crowd of only 200. The only Reds hits were singles by Kiki Cuyler in the fourth inning and Ernie Lombardi in the seventh.

OCTOBER 6   The Cubs win the first game of the 1937 Chicago City Series by a 7–3 score at Wrigley Field.

OCTOBER 13   The Cubs lose to the White Sox 6–1 at Wrigley Field in the seventh and deciding game of the City Series.

OCTOBER 28   The Cubs purchase future Hall of Famer Tony Lazzeri from the Yankees. He played only 54 games with the Cubs.

Cubs catcher Gabby Hartnett socks a three–run triple in a September 21, 1937, game against the New York Giants. The 36–year–old Hartnett batted .354 that season with 12 homers and 82 RBIs.

For Love of Ivy

The idea for the ivy adorning the walls of Wrigley Field was a collaboration between P. K. Wrigley and Bill Veeck Jr. as part of the renovation of the ballpark that began in 1937. At the time, Veeck was a 23–year–old front office employee. Wrigley instructed him to create a woodsy motif that suggested a "park" and not a "stadium."

There were two influences that inspired the ivy. Perry Stadium in Indianapolis had ivy–covered walls. The other was a wisteria–covered wall in Pasadena, California, where the White Sox conducted spring training during the 1930s. The Cubs played many exhibition games in Pasadena, and Wrigley had a winter home in the area.

Veeck planned to plant ivy after the end of the 1937 season so that it would be in full bloom by the following spring. But Wrigley called him before the last home series of the season to say that he invited people to the park to see the new ivy. Veeck sprung into action and purchased 350 Japanese bittersweet plants and 200 Boston ivy plants from a North Side nursery. Veeck and the grounds crew ran copper wire up the wall and laced the bittersweet with the ivy. Light bulbs were strung along the wall so they could work all night. By morning the bleacher wall was entirely covered with bittersweet. In time, the ivy took over, becoming a celebrated ornament of the field.

 # 1938

Season in a Sentence

The Cubs trail the Pirates by nine games on August 20 before putting on a rush to win the NL pennant, capped by Gabby Hartnett's "Homer in the Gloamin'."

Finish • Won • Lost • Pct • GB

First   89   63   .586   +2.0

World Series–The Cubs lost, four games to none, to the New York Yankees.

Managers

Charlie Grimm (45–36) and Gabby Hartnett (44–27)

Stats

Stats	Cubs	NL	Rank
Batting Avg:	.269	.267	5
On- Base Pct:	.338	.329	3
Slugging Pct:	.377	.376	5
Home Runs:	65		4 (tie)
Stolen Bases:	49		3 (tie)
ERA:	3.37	3.78	1
Fielding Avg:	.978	.972	1
Runs Scored:	713		3
Runs Allowed:	598		1

Starting Lineup

Gabby Hartnett, c
Ripper Collins, 1b
Billy Herman, 2b
Stan Hack, 3b
Billy Jurges, ss
Augie Galan, lf
Carl Reynolds, cf–lf
Frank Demaree, rf
Phil Cavaretta, rf–1b
Ken O'Dea, c
Joe Marty, cf

Pitchers

Bill Lee, sp
Clay Bryant, sp–rp
Larry French, sp–rp
Tex Carleton, sp
Dizzy Dean, sp
Charlie Root, rp
Jack Russell, rp

Attendance

951,640 (first in NL)

Club Leaders

Batting Avg:	Hack	.320
On–Base Pct:	Hack	.411
Slugging Pct:	Hack	.432
Home Runs:	Collins	13
RBI:	Galan	69
Runs:	Hack	109
Stolen Bases:	Hack	16
Wins:	Lee	22
Strikeouts:	Bryant	135
ERA:	Lee	2.66
Saves:	Root	8

FEBRUARY 4   The Cubs sell Lonny Frey to the Reds.

               The Cubs didn't see any future in Frey as a shortstop, but the Reds converted him into a second baseman, where he became a three-time All-Star.

APRIL 16   The Cubs send Curt Davis, Clyde Shoun, Tuck Stainback, and $185,000 to the Cardinals for Dizzy Dean.

               Three days before the opening game of the season, the Cubs made a huge news splash by trading for Dean. The deal was a complete surprise and was announced with no advance warning. At the time, with his larger than life personality and pitching ability, Dean was among the most well-known individuals in America. From 1932 through 1936, Dean had a record of 120–65 with the Cardinals, which included a 30–7 season in 1934. He slipped to 13–10 in 1937, however, and was out for most of the second half of the season following an injury suffered in the All-Star Game when Earl Averill lined a pitch off his foot that broke his big toe. Dean came back too soon from the injury and hurt his shoulder. The arm was no doubt weakened by an excessive workload before the toe injury. For five consecutive seasons beginning in 1932, Dean averaged 306 innings, 34 starts and 15 relief appearances per year. Dean was only 28 years old when he arrived in Chicago, but his arm never came around. Over four seasons he pitched only 225 innings for the Cubs, although he was reasonably effective when healthy with a 16–8 record and a 3.36 ERA. It proved to be a horrible trade for the Cubs. Not only did they surrender a suitcase full of cash, but pitching talent as well. Over the remainders of their careers, which lasted into the late 1940s, Davis had a record of 100–82 and Shoun was 62–52. Davis won 22 games for the Cardinals in 1939.

APRIL 20   The Cubs score nine runs in the second inning and beat the Reds 10–4 in Cincinnati. Dizzy Dean made his Cubs debut in the game, and allowed two runs and eight hits in six innings.

APRIL 24   Dizzy Dean faces his former Cardinals teammates and pitches a 5–0 complete game shutout before 34,520 at Wrigley Field.

MAY 4   Dizzy Dean is removed from a 5–2 win over the Phillies at Wrigley Field with a sore shoulder. Dean didn't pitch another game until July 17.

Left to right: Charlie Grimm, Phil Wrigley, Charlie Root, Larry French, Carl Reynolds, Joe Marty, and Frank Demaree, of the 1938 Cubs. Grimm was fired as manager in July, even though the team had a 45-36 record at the time.

MAY 5   The Cubs annihilate the Phillies 21–2 at Wrigley Field. The Cubs scored 12 runs in the eighth inning, all off Phillie hurler Hal Kelleher. Philadelphia starter Wayne LaMaster was the losing pitcher, even though he didn't pitch a complete at-bat.

He was taken out of the game with a 3–1 count on Cubs leadoff hitter Stan Hack because of a sore arm. The winning pitcher was 19–year–old Al Epperly, who was making his major league debut. In a strange twist, Epperly played in the majors in the 1930s and 1950s, but not during the 1940s. His big league career consisted of nine games with the Cubs in 1938, and five with the Dodgers in 1950.

MAY 6   The Cubs defeat the Braves 13–9 at Wrigley Field. The Cubs scored their 13 runs on only eight hits, taking advantage of 13 Boston walks and four errors.

MAY 20   The Cubs collect 22 hits and clout the Phillies 16–7 in Philadelphia.

Bill Lee was 19–15 for the Cubs in 1939 in his last good season. From 1935 through 1939, Lee had a record of 93–56 for the Cubs, but averaged 271 innings per season. From 1940 to the conclusion of his career in 1947, Lee's won–lost record was 63–87.

MAY 24   Augie Galan hits a grand slam off Van Mungo of the Dodgers in the fourth inning of a 7–2 win in Brooklyn.

JUNE 3   Bill Lee pitches his third consecutive shutout, and his fourth in five starts, winning 4–0 over the Braves in Boston. Lee also shut out the Pirates 5–0 in Pittsburgh on May 27, and the Reds 3–0 on May 30 in the second game of a double–header at Wrigley Field.

From May 15 through June 20, Lee allowed only seven runs, five of them earned, in a span of 81 innings, an ERA of 0.56. In September, he had a streak of shutouts in four consecutive starts. In 1938, Lee had a total of nine shutouts, and posted a 22–9 record and a 2.66 ERA in 291 innings. The nine shutouts is a modern club record he shares with Three Finger Brown (1906 and 1908), Orval Overall (1909), and Grover Alexander (1919).

JUNE 12   For the second time in fifteen days, the Cubs score all nine of their runs in a single inning as a nine–run eighth defeats the Dodgers 9–3 at Wrigley Field.

In June, Larry French purchased a live bear cub from a fan for $10. French found that the bear was too much to handle and sold it to Ripper Collins. Collins also discovered that bears don't make good pets, and he donated the animal to a New York state conservation camp.

JUNE 21   The Cubs play at Baker Bowl in Philadelphia for the last time, and defeat the Phillies 4–3.

On June 30, the Phillies moved into Shibe Park, a ballpark built in 1909 and owned by the Philadelphia Athletics. The Phillies shared Shibe Park with the Athletics until the Philadelphia American League entry moved to Kansas City in 1955. The Phillies were the lone occupants of the ballpark until Veterans Stadium opened in 1971. Shibe Park was renamed Connie Mack Stadium in 1953.

JULY 1   During an 11–4 win over the Reds in Cincinnati, Joe Marty becomes the first Cub to homer in a night game.

JULY 14   Clay Bryant retires 23 batters in a row from the first inning through the eighth against the Phillies in the first game of a double–header at Wrigley Field. Bryant settled for a three–hitter and a 3–0 win. The Cubs also won the second game 4–1.

Bryant entered the 1938 season as a 26–year–old with only 11 big league victories. But he came out of nowhere to post a 19–11 record in the 1938 pennant chase with a 3.10 ERA on 270⅓ innings. He also led the league in strikeouts (135) and walks (125). After 1938, arm injuries ended Bryant's effectiveness. He pitched only two more seasons and had a 2–2 record and a 5.31 ERA in 57⅔ innings.

JULY 17   Dizzy Dean pitches for the first time in over two months, and defeats the Braves 3–1 in the first game of a double–header at Wrigley Field. Dean retired the first 14 batters he faced. The Cubs also won the second game 4–0.

The Cubs cooled off considerably during the summer of 1938 with the installa-tion of electric fans at both ends of the clubhouse at Wrigley Field.

JULY 20   In a surprise move, the Cubs fire Charlie Grimm as manager and replace him with Gabby Hartnett. The Cubs had a record of 45–36 at the time of the move. P. K. Wrigley believed that Grimm was too easy on his players, and wanted the tougher and gruffer Hartnett in charge. Hartnett continued in his role as the Cubs' starting catcher.

The Cubs had won seven of their previous eight games under Grimm. The club didn't catch fire immediately under Hartnett. In the first 45 games under Gabby, the Cubs had a record of 23–22.

JULY 22   Chicago radio station WBBM hires Grimm as a commentator during Cubs and White Sox home games. In 1939, Grimm moved to WJJD, where he was teamed with former White Sox player Lew Fonseca. Grimm and Fonseca shared the same booth for two years and entertained Chicago baseball fans with a hilarious comedy routine.

JULY 24   The Cubs beat the Giants 5–4 in fifteen innings at Wrigley Field. Stan Hack's walk–off double scored the winning run. It was his fifth hit of the game in eight at–bats.

Hack hit .320 with 195 hits, 109 runs, and a league–leading 109 runs in 1938.

AUGUST 2   Clay Bryant pitches a two–hitter to defeat the Giants 7–0 at the Polo Grounds. The only New York hits were a single by opposing pitcher Carl Hubbell and a double by Mel Ott in the seventh.

AUGUST 11   Carl Reynolds collects five hits, including three doubles, in seven at–bats, but the Cubs lose 8–7 in fourteen innings to the Reds in Cincinnati.

Reynolds was a former star outfielder with several American League clubs, including the White Sox, but he had drifted back to the minors by 1937. The Cubs picked him up at the age of 35, and he contributed to Chicago's 1938 pennant charge with a .302 batting average in 125 games.

AUGUST 20   The Cubs lose 5–2 to the Pirates in Pittsburgh to fall nine games behind in the pen-nant race. The Cubs committed six errors in the loss. At the end of the day, Gabby Hartnett's crew had a record of 59–51 and were in fourth place.

SEPTEMBER 3   The Cubs hopes for a pennant take another jolt with a double–header loss to the Reds 6–0 and 7–5 in Cincinnati. The Cubs were in third place with a 68–61 record and were seven games behind the Pirates. Beginning on September 4, however, the Cubs won 20 of 23 games to take first place.

SEPTEMBER 4   Augie Galan's homer in the eleventh inning beats the Reds 2–1 in Cincinnati. Charlie Root pitched the complete game.

Root also had to contend with a publicity stunt that stopped play in the sixth inning. Root pitched to pilot Douglas Corrigan, who became an overnight celebrity seven weeks earlier on July 17. Federal aviation authorities refused to allow Corrigan to fly his rickety plane to Ireland, so he filed a flight plan from New York to California, then flew across the Atlantic Ocean to Dublin, claiming he got lost due to a faulty compass. Dubbed "Wrong Way" Corrigan, he received a hero's welcome in the United States, and was honored with ticker tape parades, receptions, banquets, and a movie contract. Corrigan arrived at Crosley Field in the sixth inning and, after a short speech, grabbed a bat to face Root. On Root's second pitch, Corrigan tapped the ball back to the mound, and ran to third base to the delight of the crowd.

SEPTEMBER 5   The Cubs win a Labor Day double–header 3–0 and 4–3 against the Pirates at Forbes Field. The wins cut Pittsburgh's first–place margin to five games. Bill Lee pitched the shutout.

SEPTEMBER 11   Bill Lee pitches his second consecutive shutout, beating the Reds 2–0 in Cincinnati. The victory put the Cubs 3 ½ games behind the Pirates with twenty contests left on the schedule.

SEPTEMBER 14   Gabby Hartnett hits a grand slam on a drive down the third base line in the third inning off Lou Fette of the Braves, leading the Cubs to a 6–3 win at Boston. The Braves stormed around umpire George Parker for several minutes after he ruled that the ball left the park in fair territory.

Hartnett hit .274 with 10 homers in 1938.

SEPTEMBER 21   For the third day in a row, both the Cubs and the Pirates are rained out in games scheduled in cities in the Northeast, bringing a brief halt to the National League pennant race. The rain was part of a vicious storm that brought a hurricane to New England and Long Island and resulted in the death of six hundred people.

SEPTEMBER 22   Bill Lee pitches his fourth shutout in a row, and ninth of the season, defeating the Phillies 4–0 in the first game of a double–header in Philadelphia. The Cubs completed the sweep in the second game with a 2–1 victory. The Pirates also won twice. At the end of the day, the Cubs were 3 ½ games behind the Pirates with eleven contests left to play.

SEPTEMBER 23   The Cubs win both ends of a double–header in Philadelphia for the second day in a row by scores of 3–2 and 7–6. In the first game, Augie Galan hit a homer in the eighth to break a 2–2 tie. In the second contest, the Cubs trailed 5–3 heading into the ninth inning and scored four times, three of them on a bases–loaded double by Ripper Collins, then survived a Phillie rally in the ninth. The Pirates lost to the Reds, leaving the Cubs two games out with nine left to play.

SEPTEMBER 26   Bill Lee fails in his bid for a fifth straight shutout, but defeats the Cardinals 6–3 at Wrigley Field.

The Cubs headed into a three-game series against the Pirates in Chicago beginning on September 27, 1½ games behind. The Cubs had six games left to play and the Pirates seven.

SEPTEMBER 27   Suffering from an aching arm and with little on the ball but the cover, Dizzy Dean is the winning pitcher in a 2–1 decision over the Pirates at Wrigley Field. It was Dean's first start since August 20. Dizzy pitched 8⅔ innings, getting last-out help from Bill Lee. With the tying run on third base, Lee fanned Al Todd to end the game. Dean, who led the National League in strikeouts four consecutive seasons from 1932 through 1935, failed to post a single strikeout in the contest as his once devastating fastball was only a memory. It was the Cubs' eighth win in a row, and put them one-half game behind the Pirates.

Dean pitched only 74⅔ innings for the Cubs in 1938, but he was 7–1 with a 1.81 ERA. Pitching to spots and changing speeds, he walked only eight batters during the season and struck out just 22.

SEPTEMBER 28   In the thickening gloom of Wrigley Field, Gabby Hartnett hits a walk-off homer to defeat the Pirates 6–5. The win was the ninth in a row for the Cubs and put the club into first place, one-half game ahead of Pittsburgh. The Pirates broke a 3–3 tie with two runs in the eighth inning, but the Cubs scored twice in their half. With two out and no one on base, Ripper Collins hit a single, Billy Jurges walked, Tony Lazzeri hit a pinch-double to score Collins, Stan Hack walked, and Billy Herman singled to bring across the tying run. Hartnett stepped to the plate against Pirate reliever Mace Brown with two out in the ninth and the score still tied 5–5. If Hartnett was retired, the umpires planned to call the game on account of darkness. Hartnett's game-winning drive came on an 0–2 pitch at 5:37 P.M. While circling the bases, Hartnett had to fight his way through a delirious mob of fans which surged onto the field. The pennant-winning blast has gone into history as the "Homer In The Gloamin'," which is perhaps the greatest moment in Cubs history.

If the Cubs had failed to score in the ninth inning, the game would have ended in a 5–5 tie. The tie would have been played off with a double-header the following day, which would have almost insurmountably handicapped the overtaxed Cubs pitching staff. The club played nine games in seven days from September 22 through 28. A September 29 double-header would have required the Cubs to win both games to take first place.

SEPTEMBER 29   Bill Lee pitches the Cubs to a 10–1 victory over the Pirates to complete the three-game series sweep and run the Cubs' winning streak to 10 games and gave the club their 20th victory in their last 23 games. It was the fourth day in a row in which Lee pitched. He hurled a complete game on September 26, one-third of an inning of relief on the 27th, an inning of relief on the 28th, and another complete game on the 29th, which was his 22nd victory of the 1938 season. The win gave the Cubs a lead of 1½ games. The Cubs had three games remaining, and the Pirates four.

SEPTEMBER 30   The Cubs and the Cardinals play to a 7–7 tie, called by darkness after nine innings in St. Louis. The Cardinals had the bases loaded in the ninth when Joe Medwick popped out to end the game. The Pirates split a double–header with the Reds that allowed the Cubs to maintain their 1 ½–game lead.

OCTOBER 1   The Cubs lose the first game of a double–header 4–3 against the Cardinals in St. Louis, but win the second game 10–3 to clinch the pennant. In the second game, starting pitcher Charlie Root gave up three runs to put the Cubs behind 3–1, but he pitched scoreless ball over the final seven frames. The Cubs broke a 3–3 tie with four runs in the eighth.

The Cubs played the New York Yankees in the World Series. Managed by Joe McCarthy, the Yankees were gunning for their third consecutive world championship. The Yankees had a record of 99–53 in 1938.

The Chicago Cubs ride down LaSalle Street on October 3, 1938, after clinching the NL pennant in St. Louis.

OCTOBER 3   Although he managed the club for over half the season, Charlie Grimm is denied a share of the World Series money in a vote taken during a 55–minute session among the twenty–one players who had been with the club all season. The decision was similar to the one in 1932 when Rogers Hornsby was also denied a share of the World Series loot after he was replaced in mid–season as manager by Grimm.

OCTOBER 5   In the first game of the 1938 World Series, the Yankees defeat the Cubs 3–1 before 43,642 at Wrigley Field. Red Ruffing outdueled Bill Lee for the victory. Stan Hack had three hits for the Cubs.

OCTOBER 6   The Yankees win game two 6–3 before 42,108 at Wrigley Field with Lefty Gomez outdueling Dizzy Dean. The Cubs led 3–2 after three innings with center fielder Joe Marty driving in all three runs on a sacrifice fly in the first inning and a two–run double in the third. Marty also had two singles. The Yankees came back to win on a two–run homer by Frankie Crosetti in the eighth and another two–run shot by Joe DiMaggio in the ninth, both off Dean.

OCTOBER 8   The Yankees move one game from a world championship by defeating the Cubs 5–2 before 55,236 at Yankee Stadium. Joe Marty, who hit only .243 in 235 at–bats during the regular season, was once again the lone bright spot for the Cubs. He had three hits, including a homer, in four at–bats. The Cubs scored only nine runs during the 1938 World Series, and Marty drove in five of them on six hits in 12 at–bats.

OCTOBER 9   The Yankees complete the sweep of the Cubs with an 8–3 win before 59,847 at Yankee Stadium.

DECEMBER 6   Five weeks after Orson Welles fools many Americans into believing Martians are invading New Jersey on his Mercury Theater radio program, the Cubs trade Frank Demaree, Billy Jurges, and Ken O'Dea to the Giants for Hank Leiber, Dick Bartell and Gus Mancuso.

The Cubs traded an outfielder, a shortstop, and a catcher for an outfielder, a shortstop, and a catcher to little positive or negative effect on the team's future. Bartell was one of the better shortstops in baseball during the 1930s, but spent an unhappy season in Chicago in 1939. During spring training, portly sportswriter Ed Burns of the CHICAGO TRIBUNE passed by, and Bartell asked, "What time does the blimp go up?" Burns also served as the official scorer at Wrigley Field, and retaliated by charging Bartell with an error at every opportunity and denying him hits whenever an opposing fielder made the slightest miscue. Bartell was traded to the Tigers shortly after the 1939 season ended.

1939 Cubs

Season in a Sentence

Cubs fans have little to cheer about as the club begins to deteriorate in Gabby Hartnett's first full season as manager.

Finish • Won • Lost • Pct • GB

Fourth   84   70   .545 13.0

Manager

Gabby Hartnett

Stats

Stats	Cubs	NL	Rank
Batting Avg:	.266	.272	5
On–Base Pct:	.336	.335	6
Slugging Pct:	.391	.386	3
Home Runs:	91		4
Stolen Bases:	61		1
ERA:	3.80	3.92	5
Fielding Avg:	.970	.972	8
Runs Scored:	724		3
Runs Allowed:	678		5

Starting Lineup

Gabby Hartnett, c
Rip Russell, 1b
Billy Herman, 2b
Stan Hack, 3b
Dick Bartell, ss
Augie Galan, lf
Hank Leiber, cf
Jim Gleeson, rf
Carl Reynolds, cf
Gene Mancuso, c
Bill Nicholson, rf
Bobby Mattick, ss

Pitchers

Larry French, sp–rp
Claude Passeau, sp
Vance Page, sp–rp
Dizzy Dean, sp–rp
Charlie Root, rp–sp
Earl Whitehill, rp–sp

Attendance

726,663 (third in NL)

Club Leaders

Batting Avg:	Leiber	.310
On–Base Pct:	Leiber	.411
Slugging Pct:	Leiber	.556
Home Runs:	Leiber	24
RBI:	Leiber	88
Runs:	Hack	112
Stolen Bases:	Hack	17
Wins:	Lee	19
Strikeouts:	Passeau	108
ERA:	Passeau	3.05
Saves:	Root	4

MARCH 30   The Cubs release Ripper Collins on his 35th birthday. Rip Russell, a 24–year–old rookie, replaced Collins as the starting first baseman.

APRIL 18   The Cubs' season opener, scheduled against the Reds at Wrigley Field, is rained out. The games on April 19 and 20 against Cincinnati were also postponed by inclement weather.

APRIL 21   The Cubs finally get the 1939 season under way and defeat the Cardinals 4–2 in St. Louis. Joe Marty and Stan Hack homered for the Cubs.

APRIL 24   The first game of the season at Wrigley Field results in a 6–1 whipping of the Pirates before 15,844. Stan Hack had a triple and two singles.

               Hack hit .298, scored 112 runs, and led the league in stolen bases with 17 in 1939. Billy Herman hit .307, scored 111 runs and collected a league–leading 18 triples.

APRIL 26   In his first start as a pitcher, Gene Lillard hurls a complete game to defeat the Pirates 3–1 at Wrigley Field.

               Lillard played 19 games with the Cubs as an infielder in 1936 before being converted into a pitcher. The change of positions didn't help Lillard's career. He pitched 59⅔ innings in the majors and had a 3–6 record with a 7.09 ERA.

MAY 1   The Cubs and the White Sox play a benefit game at Comiskey Park for former White Sox pitcher Monty Stratton, who lost a leg in a hunting accident the previous November. The White Sox won 4–1 before 25,594, raising about $28,000.

MAY 17   The Cubs and the Dodgers play to a 9–9 tie which was called on account of darkness after nineteen innings. There was no scoring during the final ten innings of the contest. The Dodgers tied the game with a run with two out in the ninth. Kirby Higbe pitched the final seven innings for the Cubs, allowing only one hit.

MAY 21   In his first start of the year, Dizzy Dean pitches a three–hit shutout to defeat the Braves 4–0 at Wrigley Field.

MAY 23   The Cubs down the Braves 15–8 at Wrigley Field.

MAY 29   The Cubs send Kirby Higbe, Joe Marty, Ray Harrell, and $35,000 to the Phillies for Claude Passeau. Passeau pitched nine seasons for the Cubs and had a 124–94 record with 22 shutouts, a 2.96 ERA, 143 complete games, and 1,914⅔ innings. The trade has to rated as only a slight success, however, because Higbe had several excellent seasons with the Phillies and the Dodgers.

MAY 30   Larry French and Vance Page both pitch shutouts to defeat the Reds 6–0 and 2–0 in a double–header in Cincinnati.

               This was Page's only big league shutout. He made his major league debut as a 32–year–old in 1938 and pitched four seasons with the Cubs.

Left to right: Pie Traynor and Russ Bauers of the Pirates, with Dizzy Dean and Gabby Hartnett of the Cubs. Hartnett struggled in his first full season as Cubs manager, leading the team to a fourth–place finish, 13 games off the pace.

JUNE 18   Dizzy Dean defeats the Dodgers 1–0 in the first game of a double–header at Wrigley Field. The Cubs collected only two hits, but one was a home run by Gabby Hartnett in the fifth inning off Luke (Hot Potato) Hamlin. The Cubs also won the second game 9–1.

After 52 games, the Cubs had a record of 24–28, offering little hope of another pennant in Chicago in 1939.

JUNE 22   Augie Galan hits a grand slam off Dick Errickson of the Braves in the second inning of a 7–1 win over the Braves at Wrigley Field.

Galan hit .304 for the Cubs in 1939.

JULY 4   Hank Leiber hits three home runs, but the Cubs lose 6–4 in the first game of a double–header against the Cardinals at Sportsman's Park. The homers came in consecutive at–bats off St. Louis pitcher "Fiddler" Bill McGee in the second, third, and sixth innings. The Cubs won the second game 3–2 in ten innings.

JULY 8   Forty–year–old pitcher Charlie Root hits a ninth–inning homer to beat the Reds 7–6 in Cincinnati. The Reds scored five runs off Claude Passeau and Root in the eighth inning to tie the score 6–6.

JULY 11   Gabby Hartnett manages the National League to a 3–1 loss in the All–Star Game, played at Yankee Stadium. Bill Lee gave up all three American League runs in a three–inning relief stint.

JULY 13   Gabby Hartnett is booed and the starting pitchers fight during a 7–5 Cubs win over the Phillies in Philadelphia. Hartnett was booed for failing to play Phillies outfielder Morrie Arnovich in the All–Star Game two days earlier. In the fourth inning, Claude Passeau bunted down the first base line and Phillie hurler Hugh Mulcahy tagged him out. Passeau threw a punch at Mulcahy, who then knocked down the Cubs pitcher with a blow to the jaw. Both were ejected.

Hartnett hit .278 with 12 homers in 1939.

JULY 23   The Cubs score four runs in the ninth inning to defeat the Giants 7–5 in New York.

JULY 28   Rip Russell's walk–off homer in the ninth inning beats the Giants 5–4 at Wrigley Field.

AUGUST 1   Outfielder Bill Nicholson makes his debut as a member of the Cubs and hits a home run during a 6–2 win over the Phillies at Wrigley Field.

Nicholson remained with the Cubs until 1948. Nicknamed "Swish" for his mighty swings, Nicholson hit 195 homers for the Cubs. He led the National League in both homers and runs batted in in both 1943 and 1944. It is ironic that Nicholson had his best years as a player during World War II, because it was his dream as a high school student to be a Naval officer. Nicholson won an appointment to Annapolis, but was rejected on medical grounds because he was color blind.

AUGUST 4   Claude Passeau pitches a shutout to defeat the Braves 1–0 at Wrigley Field. The lone run of the game was scored on a sacrifice fly by Augie Galan in the third inning.

Passeau wore number 13 during his nine years with the Cubs. He was the first Cub to wear the number. Others to wear number 13 for the Cubs include: Hal Manders (1946), Bill Faul (1965–66), Turk Wendell (1993–97), Jeff Fassero (2001–02), Rey Ordonez (2004), and Neifi Perez (2004).

AUGUST 14   In the first regular–season major league night game in the city of Chicago, the White Sox defeat the St. Louis Browns 5–2 at Comiskey Park.

SEPTEMBER 12 Eleven days after Germany invades Poland, triggering a declaration of war from England and France and the start of World War II, Hank Leiber hits a grand slam in the first inning off Bill Posedel of the Braves during an 8–3 win at Wrigley Field.

In 16 games beginning on September 12, Leiber had 31 hits, nine home runs and 31 runs batted in over 69 at–bats. Over the course of the season, Leiber hit .310 with 24 homers and 88 runs batted in over 112 games.

SEPTEMBER 13 The Cubs breeze to a 15–4 win over the Braves at Wrigley Field. Hank Leiber starred for the second day in a row with two homers, two singles, and six RBIs.

SEPTEMBER 14 The Cubs sweep a double–header 13–1 and 5–2 over the Phillies at Wrigley Field.

SEPTEMBER 17 The Cubs and the Dodgers use yellow baseballs during a double–header at Wrigley Field. Brooklyn won both ends of the twinbill 10–4 and 3–2.

Yellow baseballs were the brainchild of Dodgers General Manager Larry MacPhail, who believed that they were easier to see. The yellow balls were used as an experiment during several games in 1938 and 1939, but the idea failed to catch on.

OCTOBER 4   The Chicago City Series starts with a 10–9 Cubs win over the White Sox before 42,767 in a night game at Comiskey Park. Augie Galan drove in the winning run with a single in the ninth inning after Bill Nicholson tied the contest 9–9 with a two–run homer in the ninth.

OCTOBER 7   Hank Leiber's three–run walk–off homer in the ninth inning gives the Cubs a 5–3 win over the White Sox at Wrigley Field and a three–games–to–one lead in the City Series.

The White Sox won the next three games to capture the best–of–seven series. The series drew 128,818 fans.

DECEMBER 6   The Cubs trade Dick Bartell to the Tigers for Billy Rogell.

DECEMBER 8   The Cubs trade Gus Mancuso to the Dodgers for Al Todd.

DECEMBER 29   The Cubs send Steve Mesner, Gene Lillard, and cash to the Cardinals for Ken Raffensberger.

An aerial view of Wrigley Field in 1939, just two years after the legendary ivy was planted on the outfield walls.

THE STATE OF THE CUBS

The 1940s was the first losing decade in club history. The Cubs had only two winning seasons, capturing the National League pennant in 1945 and finishing third in 1946. Other NL pennant winners were the Reds (1940), the Dodgers (1941, 1947, and 1949), the Cardinals 1942, 1943, 1944, and 1946), and the Braves (1948). Overall, the Cubs were 736–802, for a winning percentage of .479. It was the fifth–best winning percentage among the eight teams in the league.

THE BEST TEAM

The Cubs were 98–56 in 1945 and won the National League pennant after five consecutive losing seasons. The Cubs won the pennant largely because they were able to retain players such as Phil Cavaretta, Bill Nicholson, Claude Passeau, Stan Hack, Andy Pafko, and Hank Wyse due to wartime military deferments.

THE WORST TEAM

The Cubs hit bottom in 1949, finishing last for the second year in a row with a record of 61–93.

THE BEST MOMENT

The Cubs play in the 1945 World Series, the likes of which haven't been seen at Wrigley Field since.

THE WORST MOMENT

During the 1945 World Series, P. K. Wrigley ejects the goat of restaurant owner William Sianis, beginning a long–standing "curse."

THE ALL–DECADE TEAM • YEARS WITH CUBS

Clyde McCullough, c	1940–43, 1946–48, 1953–56
Phil Cavaretta, 1b	1934–53
Don Johnson, 2b	1943–48
Stan Hack, 3b	1932–47
Lennie Merullo, ss	1941–47
Peanuts Lowrey, lf	1942–43, 1945–49
Andy Pafko, cf	1943–51
Bill Nicholson, rf	1939–48
Claude Passeau, p	1939–47
Johnny Schmitz, p	1941–42, 1946–51
Hank Wyse, p	1942–47
Hank Borowy, p	1945–48

The Cubs' problems during the 1940s can be best illustrated by the choice of Don Johnson and Lennie Merullo as the double play combination. Merullo was below average both offensively and defensively, and Johnson was little more than a wartime fill–in. The Cubs had three second basemen vastly superior to Johnson in Billy Herman, Eddie Stanky, and Lonny Frey, but traded each of them. Hank Borowy was only 36–34 as a Cub, but he makes the 1940s All–Decade Team because of an 11–2 record during the 1945 pennant drive and a lack of viable alternatives. The strength of the Cubs during the 1940s was in the outfield and at the corner infield positions. Dom Dallesandro (1940–44, 1946–47) was another outfield fixture.

THE DECADE LEADERS

Batting Avg:	Hack	.303
On–Base Pct:	Hack	.402
Slugging Pct:	Nicholson	.472
Home Runs:	Nicholson	200
RBI:	Nicholson	795
Runs:	Nicholson	701
Stolen Bases:	Hack	65
Wins:	Passeau	111
Strikeouts:	Passeau	646
ERA:	Passeau	2.94
Saves:	Passeau	14

THE HOME FIELD

In December 1941, the Cubs had equipment necessary for the installation of lights at Wrigley Field, but after the Japanese attacked Pearl Harbor, P. K. Wrigley donated the light towers to the war effort. By 1948, the Cubs were the only major league team playing all of their home games in the daytime, a distinction they would hold until 1988.

THE GAME YOU WISH YOU HAD SEEN

What is it like to watch the Cubs win a World Series game at Wrigley Field? They last accomplished the feat on October 8, 1945, by defeating the Tigers 8–7 in twelve innings.

THE WAY THE GAME WAS PLAYED

The most significant change in the game was integration in 1947 with the arrival of Jackie Robinson. The Cubs did not integrate their roster until 1953, however. League statistics and averages in 1949 looked very similar to those of 1940, although offense dipped during the war years and there was a surge in home runs at the end of the decade. Home runs in the NL jumped from 562 in 1946 to 1,100 in 1950.

THE MANAGEMENT

P. K. Wrigley continued to run the team with help from general manager Jim Gallagher. Guiding the club from the dugout were Gabby Hartnett (1938–40), Jimmie Wilson (1941–44), Charlie Grimm (1944–49), and Frankie Frisch (1949–51).

THE BEST PLAYER MOVE

The best trade came near the end of the decade when the Cubs acquired Hank Sauer and Frankie Baumholtz from the Reds for Harry Walker and Peanuts Lowrey on June 15, 1949.

THE WORST PLAYER MOVE

The Cubs made two horrible trades by sending second basemen to the Dodgers. Billy Herman went to Brooklyn on May 6, 1941, for Johnny Hudson and Charlie Gilbert, and Eddie Stanky was dealt on June 6, 1944, for Bob Chipman.

1940s

1940   Cubs

Season in a Sentence

The first losing season since 1925 results in the firing of Gabby Hartnett.

Finish • Won • Lost • Pct • GB

Fifth   75   79   .487   25.5

Manager

Gabby Hartnett

Stats

Stats	Cubs	NL	Rank
Batting Avg:	.267	.264	3
On–Base Pct:	.331	.326	3
Slugging Pct:	.384	.376	3
Home Runs:	86		5
Stolen Bases:	63		4
ERA:	3.54	3.85	3
Fielding Avg:	.968	.972	7
Runs Scored:	681		5
Runs Allowed:	636		3

Starting Lineup

Al Todd, c
Phil Cavaretta, 1b
Billy Herman, 2b
Stan Hack, 3b
Bobby Mattick, ss
Bill Nicholson, lf–rf
Jim Gleeson, cf
Hank Leiber, rf–cf
Dom Dallesandro, lf
Rip Russell, 1b
Augie Galan, lf–cf
Zeke Bonura, 1b
Rabbit Warstler, ss–2b

Pitchers

Claude Passeau, sp–rp
Larry French, sp
Vern Olsen, sp–rp
Bill Lee, sp
Ken Raffensberger, rp
Charlie Root, rp

Attendance

534,878 (fourth in NL)

Club Leaders

Batting Avg:	Hack	.317
On–Base Pct:	Hack	.395
Slugging Pct:	Nicholson	.534
Home Runs:	Nicholson	25
RBI:	Nicholson	98
Runs:	Hack	101
Stolen Bases:	Hack	21
Wins:	Passeau	20
Strikeouts:	Passeau	124
ERA:	Passeau	2.50
Saves:	Passeau	5

APRIL 16 The Cubs lose the opener 2–1 in Cincinnati. The only Cubs run was scored on a home run by Augie Galan in the sixth inning that tied the score 1–1. The Reds broke the tie in the eighth.

The Cubs became the first major league team in history to wear sleeveless uniforms in 1940. Baseball uniforms during that period were of loose–fitting flannel to absorb perspiration and to allow for maximum movement. The Cubs' uniforms in 1940 were of a knit material and were skintight. Most of the players hated them and many publicly criticized the jerseys. The lightweight sleeveless vest uniform was abandoned after the 1942 season and the Cubs returned to the more conventional flannel outfits.

APRIL 19 In the home opener, the Cubs defeat the Cardinals 5–0 before 9,029 fans in 41–degree weather at Wrigley Field. Larry French pitched the shutout.

The Cubs installed an automatic sprinkler system at Wrigley Field in 1940 to spread water evenly across the field and help keep the grass green all summer.

APRIL 30 Al Todd's walk–off homer in the tenth inning defeats the Braves 8–7 at Wrigley Field. Todd entered the game in the ninth inning as a replacement for Gabby Hartnett, who took himself out of the game for a pinch–runner.

Todd took over from Hartnett as the starting catcher for the Cubs in 1940. Hartnett played in only 37 games and had just 64 at–bats.

MAY 1 The Cubs game against the Braves at Wrigley Field is postponed when more than an inch of snow falls on Chicago.

MAY 6 A walk–off homer by Billy Herman in the eleventh inning defeats the Phillies 5–4 at Wrigley Field.

MAY 15 Larry French pitches a two–hitter to defeat the Braves 2–0 in Boston. The only Braves hits were singles by Chet Ross and Eddie Miller.

MAY 19 Rip Russell's two–run homer in the tenth inning defeats the Dodgers 7–6 at Ebbets Field. The Cubs trailed 5–1 before scoring two in the eighth, two in the ninth, and two in the tenth, then survived a Brooklyn run in the bottom of the tenth.

JUNE 1 Al Todd's walk–off homer in the twelfth inning defeats the Dodgers 4–3 at Wrigley Field.

On the same day, the Cubs sent Dizzy Dean to the minors. He played for two months with Tulsa in the Texas League and returned to the Cubs in September.

JUNE 4 The Cubs suspend pitcher Clay Bryant indefinitely without pay because he was unable to pitch due to a sore elbow.

Bryant wanted to go to Los Angeles to seek treatment for his arm, but he couldn't afford the trip and the medical bills without a steady paycheck. He appealed the suspension to Kenesaw Landis, but the commissioner told the pitcher that the club was well within its rights to suspend him. P. K. Wrigley wouldn't budge and refused to lift the suspension or pay for Bryant's treatment, but struck on a unique way to help him out. Wrigley hired Bryant's wife Opal at $50 per week for four weeks. Mrs. Bryant's "job" was to accompany her husband to Los Angeles and make certain he received proper attention for his ailing wing. Bryant never pitched another big league game, however, after 1940.

JUNE 9 Five days after 350,000 British troops are evacuated at Dunkirk, the Cubs pound the Braves 7–1 and 15–8 in a double–header at Wrigley Field. The Cubs scored seven runs in the seventh inning of the second game.

JUNE 22 On the day France surrenders to Germany, the Cubs score seven runs in the sixth inning and defeat the Phillies 10–2 in Philadelphia.

JUNE 30 Jim Gleeson hits a grand slam in the fifth inning off Bucky Walters of the Reds, but the Cubs lose 7–4 in Cincinnati.

Gleeson was part of a strong outfield in 1940. He hit .313. Hank Leiber batted .302 with 17 homers. Bill Nicholson had a .297 average and 25 home runs. The threesome helped to make up for the loss of Augie Galan, who fractured his knee on July 31 when he crashed into the wall in Philadelphia.

JULY 2 The Cubs roll to a 10–0 win over the Phillies at Wrigley Field.

JULY 5   Rip Russell's grand slam in the fifth inning off Carl Doyle of the Cardinals is the
                highlight of an 11–5 win in St. Louis.

                *Four days later, Russell underwent an operation to remove his appendix and
                missed the remainder of the season.*

JULY 16   Phil Cavaretta's bases–loaded single in the fourth inning accounts for the only run
                of the game as the Cubs triumph 2–0 over the Giants at Wrigley Field.

JULY 19   Hank Leiber hits a grand slam in the first inning off Whit Wyatt, setting the pace
                for an 11–4 win over the Dodgers at Wrigley Field.

                *In the eighth inning, Claude Passeau was hit in the ribs by Dodgers pitcher
                Hugh Casey. Passeau responded by flinging his bat at the mound, and a fight
                ensued. Passeau and Brooklyn outfielder Joe Gallagher were ejected.*

JULY 22   The Cubs purchase Zeke Bonura from the Senators.

JULY 26   The Cubs take the Giants apart with a 14–1 win in New York. The Cubs scored
                eight runs in the seventh inning.

AUGUST 4   Hank Leiber collects seven hits, including a homer and a double, in nine at–bats in
                a double–header split against the Dodgers in Brooklyn. The Cubs won the first
                game 11–3, and lost the second 7–6 in eleven innings.

AUGUST 10   Vern Olsen pitches the Cubs to a 1–0 win over the Pirates in Pittsburgh. The only
                run of the game was scored on a sacrifice fly by Al Todd in the fourth inning.

AUGUST 17   Down 5–0 in the seventh inning, the Cubs rally to defeat the Pirates 6–5 in thirteen
                innings at Wrigley Field. Stan Hack drove in the tying run with a double and the
                winning run with a single. Billy Herman took part in six double plays. He grounded
                into three of them and participated in three more on defense at second base.

                Hack hit .317 with 101 runs, 191 hits, 38 doubles, and 21 stolen bases in 1940.

AUGUST 25   Dom Dallesandro's bases–loaded double in the tenth scores two runs to defeat the
                Giants 5–4 in the first game of a double–header at Wrigley Field. The Cubs lost the
                second game 12–8.

                *A chunky five–foot–six and 168 pounds, Dallesandro played in the outfield for
                the Cubs from 1940 through 1947, with the exception of the 1945
                pennant–winning season when Dom was in the service.*

AUGUST 30   The Cubs purchase Lou Novikoff from the Los Angeles Angels of the Pacific Coast
                League for $100,000.

                *Novikoff never lived up to his billing as a player, but he became one of the most
                colorful players ever to don a Cubs uniform. Nicknamed "The Mad Russian,"
                Novikoff was born in Glendale, Arizona. He was one of twelve children and
                spoke only Russian until he was 10. Novikoff was a harmonica virtuoso, had a
                booming baritone, and had been a "strongman" and a strip–tease performer.*

Novikoff could hit, but his fielding, throwing and base–running were atrocious. He had no end of excuses for his deficiencies. Novikoff complained he couldn't play left field at Wrigley Field because the foul lines were crooked and was afraid that the ivy on the outfield walls was poisonous. He also claimed he couldn't hit on the road because he was unable to eat a Russian dish of hamburger and cabbage called "hoopsa" that his wife Esther made for him. The lightweight, sleeveless uniforms worn by the Cubs during the early 1940s were also a problem. "No wonder we're in sixth place," complained Novikoff in 1942. "We look so skinny and weak to the other clubs they convince themselves they can blow us down."

SEPTEMBER 7   Bill Nicholson hits a grand slam off Paul Derringer of the Reds in the fourth inning, but the Cubs lose 7–6 at Wrigley Field.

SEPTEMBER 17   Down 7–2, the Cubs score six runs in the eighth inning and go on to defeat the Giants 9–8 in New York.

SEPTEMBER 23   Claude Passeau wins his 20th game of the season in a 10–0 defeat of the Cardinals at Wrigley Field.

Passeau finished the season with a 20–13 record and a 2.50 ERA in 280⅔ innings.

Claude Passeau won 20 games in 1940 and finished second in the NL in wins, ERA, and strikeouts. Passeau won 124 games during his Cubs career.

OCTOBER 1   The Cubs lose the first game of the Chicago City Series 5–3 to the White Sox at Wrigley Field. The White Sox won the best–of–seven series in six games.

NOVEMBER 13   Eight days after Franklin Roosevelt is elected to his third term as president by defeating Wendell Willkie, Philip Wrigley elects to fire Gabby Hartnett as manager. It ended Hartnett's relationship with the Cubs, which began in 1921.

Hartnett signed with the Giants as player–coach on December 10. He played one more season in the majors. Hartnett never managed another big league club.

NOVEMBER 14   Jim Gallagher is named general manager of the Cubs, replacing Charles "Boots" Weber.

A former sportswriter for the CHICAGO HERALD–AMERICAN, Gallagher remained as the Cubs general manager until 1949.

NOVEMBER 18   The Cubs hire Jimmie Wilson as manager.

Wilson was the hero of the 1940 World Series. He was a coach for the Reds, but was pressed into service as a catcher at the age of 40 after Willard Hershberger committed suicide and Ernie Lombardi was injured. Wilson hit .353 as the Reds defeated the Tigers in seven games. P. K. Wrigley was impressed by Wilson's courageous performance in the series and put him at the top of his list of managerial candidates. Previously, Wilson managed the Phillies from 1934 through 1938 and never finished higher than seventh in an eight–team league. Wilson fared little better with the Cubs and was fired in 1944.

NOVEMBER 25   Charlie Grimm gives up his broadcasting job and is hired by the Cubs as a coach.

DECEMBER 4   Four days before the Bears annihilate the Washington Redskins 73–0 in the NFL championship game, the Cubs trade Jim Gleeson and Bobby Mattick to the Reds for Billy Myers.

1941   Cubs

Season in a Sentence

After winning the NL pennant in 1929, 1932, 1935, and 1938, the calendar indicates that the Cubs are due again in 1941, but the club finishes in sixth place.

Finish • Won • Lost • Pct • GB

Sixth   70   84   .455   30.0

Manager

Jimmie Wilson

Stats

Stats	Cubs	NL	Rank
Batting Avg:	.253	.258	5
On–Base Pct:	.327	.326	4
Slugging Pct:	.365	.361	5
Home Runs:	99		2
Stolen Bases:	39		6
ERA:	3.72	3.83	5
Fielding Avg:	.970	.972	5
Runs Scored:	666		5
Runs Allowed:	670		5

Starting Lineup

Clyde McCullough, c
Babe Dahlgren, 1b
Lou Stringer, 2b
Stan Hack, 3b
Bobby Sturgeon, ss
Dom Dallessandro, lf–cf
Phil Cavaretta, cf–1b
Bill Nicholson, rf
Lou Novikoff, lf
Hank Leiber, lf–1b

Pitchers

Claude Passeau, sp
Vern Olsen, sp–rp
Bill Lee, sp
Larry French, sp–rp
Charlie Root, sp
Jake Mooty, rp–sp
Paul Erickson, rp–sp

Attendance

545,159 (fifth in NL)

Club Leaders

Batting Avg:	Hack	.317
On–Base Pct:	Hack	.417
Slugging Pct:	Hack	.427
Home Runs:	Nicholson	26
RBI:	Nicholson	98
Runs:	Hack	111
Stolen Bases:	Hack	10
Wins:	Passeau	14
Strikeouts:	Passeau	80
ERA:	Olsen	3.15
Saves:	Mooty	4

Left to right:
Dom Dallesandro,
Babe Dahlgren, Phil
Cavarretta, and Claude
Passeau. Dallesandro
drove in 85 runs,
Dahlgren knocked 16
homers, and Cavarretta
hit .286 in 1941 while
Passeau led the club in
victories with 14.

APRIL 15

In the first game of the 1941 season, the Cubs defeat the Pirates 7–4 before 17,008 at Wrigley Field. Bill Nicholson was the hitting star with a homer and three RBIs. Claude Passeau was the winning pitcher despite nearly being knocked out of the game in the first inning. Pittsburgh leadoff batter Frankie Gustine smacked a line drive that struck Passeau on the knee. There was a five–minute delay in the game before Passeau was able to resume pitching. The Cubs had four rookies in the starting lineup on Opening Day in catcher Clyde McCullough, shortstop Lou Stringer, first baseman Eddie Waitkus, and left fielder Lou Novikoff. All but McCullough, who played in nine games in 1940, were making their big league debuts.

It wasn't a good day for 23–year–old Lou Stringer. Although he had three hits, including two doubles in his big league debut, Stringer made four errors at shortstop. In four years in the minors, Stringer played exclusively at second base, but Billy Herman was firmly entrenched at the position in the Cub infield. Opening Day in 1941 was Stringer's first regular season game at shortstop in his professional baseball career. Stringer played only seven games at short for the Cubs before he was moved back to his natural position of second base after the Cubs traded Herman (see May 6, 1941). Stringer led all National League second basemen in assists in 1941.

APRIL 25

The Cubs score four runs in the ninth inning to defeat the Pirates 8–7 in Pittsburgh. Augie Galan drove in the winning run with a pinch–hit single.

The Cubs in 1941 became the first team in the majors to install an organ at the ballpark. Also, a clock was added to the top of the Wrigley Field scoreboard. The clock was ten feet in diameter and required a ton of steel to construct.

MAY 6

The Cubs send Billy Herman to the Dodgers for Johnny Hudson, Charlie Gelbert, and $65,000.

Herman didn't fit into the Cubs' youth movement, but the club made a terrible trade, as he helped the Dodgers win the 1941 pennant. Other ex–Cubs who played roles in Brooklyn's pennant were Dolf Camilli, Kirby Higbe, Hugh Casey, Augie Galan, Larry French, and Babe Phelps.

MAY 7   Pitcher Bill Lee hits two homers during an 11–2 win over the Phillies in Philadelphia.

Lee played in the majors until 1947 and never hit another home run. He hit just five homers in 980 at–bats during his big league career.

MAY 12   The Cubs feast on Reds pitching with a 12–1 win in Cincinnati.

MAY 14   The Cubs release Dizzy Dean as a player and sign him as a coach.

With the exception of one game as a publicity stunt with the St. Louis Browns in 1947, Dean never pitched again. He lasted only seven weeks as a coach with the Cubs. On July 5, 1941, Dean signed a deal with radio station KWK as a broadcaster for Browns and Cardinals games. His broadcasting career included the infancy of television and lasted into the 1960s. With his fracturing of English grammar and humorous stories, Dean was enormously popular behind the mike and was an announcer for the national Game of the Week on CBS during the 1950s.

MAY 19   Claude Passeau hits a grand slam off Hugh Casey of the Dodgers in a nine–run Cubs second inning at Wrigley Field. The Cubs won the game 14–1.

MAY 21   Bill Nicholson hits a grand slam off Frank Hoerst of the Phillies in the fifth inning of a 7–3 win at Wrigley Field. Nicholson's homer broke a 2–2 tie.

During the 1941 season, the Cubs roped off a section of the center field bleachers because of complaints from batters that they lost the flight of the ball in the white shirts of fans who sat in their line of vision. The center field section was closed from 1941 through 1947, and opened again from 1948 through 1951. It was closed for good on April 20, 1952, with the exception of the 1962 All–Star Game. The seats were painted dark gray to improve the background and were covered with Astroturf in 1967. Juniper bushes were planted in the area in 1997.

JUNE 1   The Cubs win a double–header 19–5 and 1–0 against the Phillies in Philadelphia. Jake Mooty pitched the second–game shutout. Dom Dallesandro drove in the lone run with a double in the fifth inning.

This was Mooty's only career shutout. He had a lifetime record of 16–23 in seven big league seasons.

JUNE 15   The Cubs purchase Babe Dahlgren from the Braves.

Dahlgren is best known for replacing ailing Lou Gehrig as the Yankee first baseman in 1939. Dahlgren was the Cubs' regular first baseman for the remainder of the 1941 season and hit a respectable .281 with 16 homers.

JUNE 23   Two days after Germany's invasion of the Soviet Union, Claude Passeau pitches the

Cubs to a 1–0 win over the Giants at Wrigley Field. The lone run of the game was scored on a double by Bill Nicholson in the first inning. Hank Leiber was beaned in the game and missed six weeks. It was the third major head injury of his career. Leiber hit just .216 in 53 games in 1941, and retired from the game a year later at the age of 31. Ironically, the injury came three days after the Cubs received a shipment of one–ounce plastic shields which could be inserted into a player's regulation cap to help protect him if hit in the head by a pitch. Leiber refused to wear one, however. The shields were first used by major league clubs during the 1941 season. Batting helmets were not used by big league clubs until the 1950s.

On the same day, Cubs Treasurer Bill Veeck Jr. and coach Charlie Grimm joined forces to purchase the Milwaukee Brewers, then a minor league club in the American Association.

JUNE 30   The Cubs unveil powder–blue road uniforms instead of the traditional gray during a 7–1 loss to the Reds in Cincinnati. When Braves manager Casey Stengel saw them for the first time ten days later he asked, "Doesn't the club offer perfume with those uniforms?"

The Cubs wore the powder–blue road jerseys for the remainder of the 1941 season. "Chicago" was written across the front in white, outlined in dark blue. The numbers on the back were also white outlined in blue. The Cubs returned to the traditional gray in 1942.

JULY 5   Dom Dallesandro hits a grand slam in the seventh inning off Joe Sullivan of the Pirates, but the Cubs lose 9–6 in Pittsburgh.

JULY 8   Claude Passeau surrenders a dramatic three–run, ninth–inning walk–off homer to Ted Williams in the All–Star Game in Detroit, resulting in a 7–5 National League loss.

JULY 14   A squeeze bunt by Dodgers player–manager Leo Durocher results in a 1–0 Cubs loss in Brooklyn. Durocher put himself into the scoreless game as a pinch–hitter and laid down a perfect bunt to the left of the mound with a runner on third. Cubs pitcher Vern Olsen fielded the ball, and when he saw that he had no play at the plate or at first base, he threw the ball over the Ebbets Field grandstand.

Olsen had a streak of 30 consecutive scoreless innings in June.

JULY 29   Bill Nicholson hits a grand slam off Rube Melton of the Phillies in the eighth inning of a 12–4 at Wrigley Field.

AUGUST 8   Rookie pitcher Paul Erickson earns his first major league victory by hurling a one–hitter to defeat the Pirates 1–0 at Wrigley Field. The only Pittsburgh hit was a single by Bob Elliott in the seventh inning. The lone run was scored in the fifth on a single by Clyde McCullough.

AUGUST 10 The Cubs lose 3–1 to the Reds at Wrigley Field on Charlie Root Day.

In pre–game ceremonies, Root was given many gifts, including a station wagon, a desk clock, a casting rod, $50 in gas coupons, and a live pig.

AUGUST 11   Phil Cavaretta, Stan Hack, and Bill Nicholson hit back–to–back–to–back homers in the fifth inning off Lon Warneke, but the Cubs lose 7–5 to the Cardinals in St. Louis.

AUGUST 20   The Cubs sell Larry French to the Dodgers.

French had a 5–14 record for the Cubs in 1941, but bounced back with a 15–4 mark at the age of 34 for the Dodgers in 1942. After the season was over, French went into the Navy to serve in World War II, and after the war announced his retirement from baseball. He went back into the Navy during the Korean War and chose the service as a career. French retired as a captain in the Naval Reserves in 1969.

AUGUST 25   The Cubs sell Augie Galan to the Dodgers.

This was yet another short–sighted transaction. After he was sold by the Cubs, Galan had several excellent seasons with the Dodgers and the Reds.

AUGUST 27   At the age of 42, Charlie Root bags the 200th win of his career with a 6–4 win over the Braves in the second game of a double–header in Boston. Root entered the game as a relief pitcher with one out in the first inning and went the rest of the way. Root helped his own cause as a hitter. With the bases loaded in the ninth and the score 3–3, Root drove in two runs with a single. The Braves walked Lou Stringer intentionally with first base open to get to Root. The Cubs won the first game 6–0.

Root is the only pitcher to win 200 games as a Cub. He finished his career with 201 victories.

SEPTEMBER 14   In his first major league start, Johnny Schmitz collects three singles and a sacrifice in four plate appearances, and pitches a complete game 10–3 win over the Braves in the second game of a double–header at Wrigley Field. The Braves won the first game 6–3.

Schmitz finished his major league career in 1956 with a 93–114 record as a pitcher. He was 69–70 as a Cub. Schmitz played in Chicago in 1941 and 1942, and after three years in the Navy during World War II, again from 1946 through 1951.

SEPTEMBER 20   The Cubs score six runs in the ninth inning, four on Bob Scheffing's grand slam off Howie Krist, to defeat the Cardinals 7–3 in St. Louis. Scheffing's homer came with the score tied 3–3. It was his first big league home run.

OCTOBER 7   The White Sox complete a four–game sweep of the Cubs in the annual Chicago City Series with a 3–1 win over the Cubs at Comiskey Park. The four games drew 66,170 fans.

DECEMBER 4   The Cubs trade Hank Leiber to the Giants for Bob Bowman.

DECEMBER 7   The Japanese attack Pearl Harbor. A day later, the United States declared war on Japan, and on December 11 declared war on Germany.

After the 1941 season ended, P. K. Wrigley purchased material for the installation of lights for night baseball, including 165 tons of steel, 35,000 feet of copper wire, stanchions, and aluminum reflectors, all of which were hidden under the stands. By December 1 it was all assembled and ready for installation. On the day after the attack on Pearl Harbor, Wrigley donated the material to the War Department, where it was used to floodlight a freight yard. The Cubs went into negotiations with the White Sox to play night games at Comiskey Park in 1942 (see February 12, 1942).

Pearl Harbor Douses Wrigley Lights

Were it not for the Japanese attack on Pearl Harbor, the first Cubs game played at night at Wrigley Field would have taken place in 1942, not 1988.

Night baseball in the major leagues began in 1935 in Cincinnati. The Brooklyn Dodgers were the second club to install lights in 1938, and were followed by the Athletics, Phillies, Indians, and White Sox in 1939, the St. Louis Browns and Cardinals in 1940, and Washington Senators in 1941. Cubs owner P. K. Wrigley had been intrigued by the notion of playing at night since it was approved at a National League meeting in December 1934, but the Cubs were among the league leaders in attendance during the 1930s on a yearly basis and there was little need to make any changes in the all-daytime schedule.

Wrigley wasn't so much opposed to night baseball as he was to light towers. He hated the "freight yard" look that light towers had on a ballpark, and was afraid that they would destroy the park-like ambiance of his beloved Wrigley Field. During the 1937-38 renovation of Wrigley Field, he looked into the possibility of installing lights. Wrigley wanted to disguise the light towers as trees, and when that proved too impractical, he sought bids on putting the lights on hydraulic lifts that could be raised for night games and lowered in the daytime. The hydraulics were too expensive, however, and there was no guarantee that the plan would work properly.

The Cubs in 1941 had a record of 70-84, the worst season since 1921, and attendance, which peaked at 1,485,166 in 1929, had fallen to 534,878 in 1940 and 545,159 in 1941. Wrigley decided to install lights for the 1942 season. He bought the lighting equipment under an assumed name at a cost of $185,000 and secretly stored it under-neath the Wrigley Field grandstand. Work was to have begun on December 8, 1941.

The Japanese attacked Pearl Harbor on Sunday, December 7, which sent the entire nation into shock and disarray. With the country suddenly at war, Wrigley called the War Department and offered the 165 tons of steel, 35,000 feet of copper wire, and aluminum reflectors for use in one of the many new military facilities being built across the country.

The Cubs didn't give up on playing home games at night during the 1942 season, however. In January 1942, Wrigley asked the White Sox to allow the Cubs to rent Comiskey Park for the playing of seven games at night. "It would be a considerable blow to our pride to play else-where than in our own park," said Cubs General Manager Jim Gallagher, "but we feel that under the circumstances this would be the only sane and logical thing to do." The plan was scuttled when the White Sox politely refused to allow the Cubs to use Comiskey Park.

Wrigley made another attempt to affix lights at Wrigley Field in the spring of 1944. The end of World War II was nowhere in sight, and in order to purchase the material necessary to erect the lights, it was necessary to file an application with the recreation section of the War Production Board. The request was turned down on May 8, 1944. "While the materials may be available," said George W. McMurphey, chief of the section, "this office also took into consideration that construction could not be completed before August, which would leave only twenty-one weekday dates available to the Cubs in their home park."

McMurphey invited the Cubs to resubmit their application in 1945, but Wrigley failed to do so. Once the war ended in August 1945, he was free of government restrictions on building a lighting system, but he had a complete change of heart with regard to night baseball. Wrigley steadfastly refused to install lights. By 1948, the Cubs were the only team in the majors to play only day games in their home park.

Pleas to have Wrigley reconsider failed to shake his position. In 1962, National League owners pressured him to "review his thinking in regard to night baseball," because attendance at Wrigley Field that season ranked dead last among the twenty major league teams. His answer to them was straight to the point: "Number one, I don't think they're necessary. If you'll check the figures I think you'll see that lights are just a novelty shot in the arm. If you have a winning team I think you'll draw as many people in the long run without lights. Number

two, we're in a residential neighborhood."

Wrigley often went against his "good neighbor" policy, however, by renting out Wrigley Field at night for boxing matches, wrestling matches, political and religious rallies, rodeos, and a Harlem Globetrotters basketball game using portable or temporary lights. During World War II, two All-American Girls Professional Baseball League games were played at Wrigley Field.

P. K. Wrigley died in 1977, and his son William inherited the club. William continued the family policy of refusing to install lights at Wrigley Field, but he was forced to sell the club to the Tribune Company in 1981 to pay huge inheritance taxes. The new owners almost immediately began a campaign to play night games at Wrigley Field, which began in 1988.

1942

Season in a Sentence

The Cubs continue to stagnate and finish sixth for the second season in a row.

Finish • Won • Lost • Pct • GB

Sixth   68   86   .442 38.0

Manager

Jimmie Wilson

Stats

	Cubs	NL	Rank
Batting Avg:	.254	.249	3
On–Base Pct:	.321	.318	4
Slugging Pct:	.353	.343	4
Home Runs:	75		2
Stolen Bases:	63		3
ERA:	3.60	3.31	6
Fielding Avg:	.973	.973	4
Runs Scored:	591		4
Runs Allowed:	665		7

Starting Lineup

Clyde McCullough, c
Phil Cavaretta, 1b–cf
Lou Stringer, 2b
Stan Hack, 3b
Lennie Merullo, ss
Lou Novikoff, lf
Dom Dallesandro, cf–lf
Bill Nicholson, rf
Rip Russell, 1b–3b
Jimmie Foxx, 1b
Charlie Gilbert, cf
Bobby Sturgeon, 2b–ss

Pitchers

Claude Passeau, sp
Bill Lee, sp
Vern Olsen, sp–rp
Lon Warneke, sp
Jake Mooty, sp–rp
Hi Bithorn, rp–sp
Bill Fleming, rp–sp
Johnny Schmitz, rp–sp

Attendance

590,872 (third in NL)

Club Leaders

Batting Avg:	Novikoff	.300
On–Base Pct:	Hack	.402
Slugging Pct:	Novikoff	.476
Home Runs:	Novikoff	21
RBI:	Novikoff	78
Runs:	Hack	91
Stolen Bases:	Merullo	14
Wins:	Passeau	19
Strikeouts:	Passeau	89
ERA:	Passeau	2.68
Saves:	Pressnell	4

JANUARY 15   President Franklin Roosevelt gives baseball commissioner Kenesaw Landis the go–ahead to play ball for the duration of World War II. In his statement, Roosevelt said that he believed the continuation of the sport would be beneficial to the country's morale.

There were three members of the 1941 Cubs in the military by the start of the 1942 season. They were first baseman Eddie Waitkus and pitchers Walt Lanfranconi and Russ Meers.

FEBRUARY 12   The Cubs drop plans to play night games at Comiskey Park in 1942. "We have agreed that in the best interests of the game," said Cubs General Manager James Gallagher, "it would be better to preserve the intense rivalry between the fans of the North and South Sides of Chicago." Two years later, the Cubs again explored the possibility of adding lights to Wrigley Field (see May 8, 1944).

APRIL 14   The Cubs win the season opener 5–4 at Sportsman's Park. The Cubs wiped out a 3–2 St. Louis lead with a three–run sixth. Phil Cavaretta had three hits, including a double, in three at–bats.

APRIL 17   In the first game of the season at Wrigley Field, the Cubs defeat the Reds 3–2 before 10,149.

During the duration of World War II, balls hit into the stands at Wrigley Field were returned by the fans and donated to the recreation departments of the Armed Forces.

APRIL 19   Claude Passeau holds the Reds hitless until one out in the eighth inning, when Harry Craft singles, but the Cubs lose 2–1 in eleven innings at Wrigley Field.

MAY 1   The Cubs win a 13–9 slugfest from the Giants at Wrigley Field.

MAY 13   Jim Tobin of the Braves becomes the only pitcher in major league history to hit three homers in a game during a 6–5 Boston win over the Cubs at Braves Field. Tobin hit two homers off Jake Mooty and one off Hi Bithorn. The previous day, Tobin hit a pinch–hit homer against the Cubs, but Chicago won 9–8.

On the same day, the Cubs sold Babe Dahlgren to the Browns on a conditional basis. He played two games with the Browns and was returned to the Cubs on May 19. The Cubs then sold Dahlgren to the Dodgers.

MAY 27   All of the gate receipts from a Cubs–Reds game at Wrigley Field go to the Army–Navy Relief Fund. A total of 9,966 paid their way into the game, earning the fund $10,455.27. The Reds won the game 10–1. The contest was preceded by a contest between teams from the Great Lakes Naval Training Station and Army's Camp Grant. Great Lakes won 4–1.

JUNE 1   The Cubs purchase Jimmie Foxx from the Red Sox.

At the time of the trade, Foxx was 34 years old and had a .331 lifetime batting average and 524 home runs. To this day, no one has hit 524 career home runs at a younger age than Foxx, but by the time he reached Chicago he was all but finished as a productive major leaguer. With the Cubs, Foxx hit only .191 with three homers in 225 at–bats from 1942 through 1944.

JUNE 13   Seven days after America's victory over Japan in the Battle of Midway, Cubs pitcher Bill Fleming hurls a one–hitter to defeat the Braves 1–0 at Wrigley Field. The only Boston hit was a single by Tommy Holmes in the sixth inning.

Fleming finished his big league career in 1946 with a record of 16–21.

JUNE 30   In a benefit game prior to a 4–1 loss to the Reds in Cincinnati, a combined team of Reds and Cubs plays the Great Lakes Naval Training Station club, managed by Mickey Cochrane. Great Lakes won 3–1.

JULY 8   The Cubs purchase Lon Warneke from the Cardinals.

Warneke was only 33 when he began his second tour of duty with the Cubs, but he was only 10–13 over the remainder of his career.

JULY 15   Angered over taunts from the Brooklyn players, Cubs pitcher Hi Bithorn fires a ball into the dugout during a 10–5 loss at Ebbets Field. The ball narrowly missed hitting Leo Durocher.

JULY 22   Claude Passeau pitches a two–hitter to defeat the Braves 2–1 at Braves Field. The only Boston hits were singles by Max West and Tommy Holmes.

Passeau had a 19–14 record in 1942 with a 2.68 ERA in 278⅓ innings. He completed 24 of his 34 starts.

JULY 26   Clyde McCullough hits three homers in consecutive at–bats off Tommy Hughes of the Phillies, but Hughes throttles the rest of the Cubs lineup in a 4–3 loss in the first game of a double–header at Philadelphia. McCullough homered in the third, fifth, and eighth innings. Despite his heroics in the opener, McCullough didn't start the second game, which the Phillies won 6–1.

AUGUST 9   The Cubs win a wild eighteen–inning encounter by a 10–8 score against the Reds in the first game of a double–header in Cincinnati. The Cubs led 4–0 with a Reds runner on third base and two out in the ninth, when Chicago shortstop Bobby Sturgeon dropped a pop–up. Before the inning was over, the Reds tied the score 4–4. The Cubs scored two in the tenth, but the Reds matched it in their half. Chicago surged ahead once more with two runs in the twelfth, and again the Reds tied the score. After an hour rain delay, the two teams battled until the eighteenth, when the Cubs scored two more runs, which the Reds were unable to counter. The second game ended with a 2–1 Reds win, called after four-and-a-half innings by darkness.

Crosley Field had lights in 1942, but due to a National League rule, they couldn't be turned on to finish the second game. Lights couldn't be used to finish day games until 1950.

AUGUST 13   The Cubs swamp the Cardinals 13–5 at Wrigley Field. Bill Nicholson hit a home run that landed in the ivy and stuck there. He circled the bases before the St. Louis outfielders could fish the ball out of the vines.

The rules were later changed to make drives which stuck in the ivy ground–rule doubles.

AUGUST 22   Bill Nicholson hits a walk–off homer in the eleventh inning to defeat the Reds 5–4 at Wrigley Field. In the top of the eleventh, the Cubs pulled off a triple play. With Cincinnati runners on first and second, Max Marshall popped up an attempted sacrifice, and both runners were retired before they could return to their bases on a triple–killing which went from catcher Clyde McCullough to shortstop Lennie Merullo to first baseman Phil Cavaretta.

AUGUST 23   Claude Passeau and Lon Warneke both shut out the Reds by 3–0 scores at Wrigley Field. Warneke pitched a two–hitter. The only Cincinnati hits off Warneke were a double by Frank McCormick and a single by Lonny Frey.

SEPTEMBER 1   The Cubs defeat the Giants 10–5 on Salvage Day at Wrigley Field. Women who brought two pounds of scrap metal were admitted free.

SEPTEMBER 11   Starting at catcher, Paul Gillespie hits a homer in his first major league at–bat, although the Cubs lose 4–3 to the Giants in New York.

Gillespie's major league career ended in 1945 with six homers in 205 at–bats. He missed the 1944 season while in the military, but returned to baseball in 1945 after being discharged because of a knee injury. Gillespie also homered in his last regular season at–bat in the majors (see September 29, 1945). The only other Cubs with homers in their first major league at–bats are Frank Ernaga in 1957, Cuno Barragan in 1961, Carmelo Martinez in 1983, and Jim Bullinger in 1992. Gillespie is the only one to homer in both his first and last at–bats.

SEPTEMBER 13   Cubs shortstop Lennie Merullo ties a major league record by committing four errors in the second inning against the Braves in the second game of a double–header in Boston. Merullo's four errors came in a span of six batters. He fumbled an easy grounder hit by Clyde Kluttz, mishandled a throw in from outfielder Bill Nicholson on a single by Ducky Detwhiler, bobbled a grounder by Tommy Holmes, and juggled another grounder hit by Al Roberge. The Cubs survived Merullo's miscues to win 12–8 in a contest called after eight innings due to the Sunday closing law in Massachusetts, which stipulated that games must end at 6:00 P.M. Merullo also made an error in the first game, which the Cubs lost 11–6.

Merullo was understandably nervous, because four hours before the start of the first game at a nearby hospital in Boston, his wife gave birth to a son, who was aptly named "Boots."

SEPTEMBER 30   In the Chicago City Series, the White Sox defeat the Cubs 3–0 at Wrigley Field. The White Sox went on to win the series, four games to two. The six games drew 45,818.

This was the last time that the Chicago City Series was played. The Cubs and the White Sox played each other twenty-six times in the post–season between 1903 and 1942, including the 1906 World Series. The White Sox won nineteen of the series and the Cubs six, with another ending in a draw.

NOVEMBER 14   The Cubs purchase Ival Goodman from the Reds.

1943

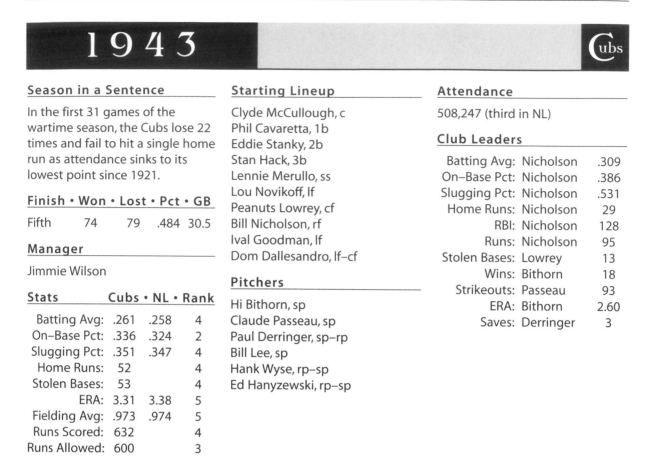

Season in a Sentence

In the first 31 games of the wartime season, the Cubs lose 22 times and fail to hit a single home run as attendance sinks to its lowest point since 1921.

Finish • Won • Lost • Pct • GB

Fifth   74   79   .484   30.5

Manager

Jimmie Wilson

Stats

Stats	Cubs	NL	Rank
Batting Avg:	.261	.258	4
On–Base Pct:	.336	.324	2
Slugging Pct:	.351	.347	4
Home Runs:	52		4
Stolen Bases:	53		4
ERA:	3.31	3.38	5
Fielding Avg:	.973	.974	5
Runs Scored:	632		4
Runs Allowed:	600		3

Starting Lineup

Clyde McCullough, c
Phil Cavaretta, 1b
Eddie Stanky, 2b
Stan Hack, 3b
Lennie Merullo, ss
Lou Novikoff, lf
Peanuts Lowrey, cf
Bill Nicholson, rf
Ival Goodman, lf
Dom Dallesandro, lf–cf

Pitchers

Hi Bithorn, sp
Claude Passeau, sp
Paul Derringer, sp–rp
Bill Lee, sp
Hank Wyse, rp–sp
Ed Hanyzewski, rp–sp

Attendance

508,247 (third in NL)

Club Leaders

Batting Avg:	Nicholson	.309
On–Base Pct:	Nicholson	.386
Slugging Pct:	Nicholson	.531
Home Runs:	Nicholson	29
RBI:	Nicholson	128
Runs:	Nicholson	95
Stolen Bases:	Lowrey	13
Wins:	Bithorn	18
Strikeouts:	Passeau	93
ERA:	Bithorn	2.60
Saves:	Derringer	3

JANUARY 27   Two weeks after Franklin Roosevelt and Winston Churchill begin meetings in Casablanca, Morocco, to formulate strategy for the war in Europe, the Cubs purchase Paul Derringer from the Reds.

Derringer spent three years with the Cubs and won 16 games for the 1945 pennant winners.

FEBRUARY 20   P. K. Wrigley announces the formation of the All–American Girls Professional Baseball League. Wrigley thought that World War II would decimate the major leagues' playing talent, and believed that a women's league would be a way to keep the ballparks busy and the fans entertained. Play began in 1943 with four teams in Rockford, Illinois; South Bend, Indiana; Racine, Wisconsin; and Kenosha, Wisconsin.

MARCH 21   The Cubs open spring training in French Lick, Indiana.

During World War II, teams had to train north of the Ohio River and east of the Mississippi to save on travel expenses. The Cubs shared the French Lick facility with the White Sox. A diamond was laid out between the practice fairway and the parallel 18th fairway of the golf course adjoining the elegant French Lick Springs Hotel, headquarters for both clubs. The Cubs trained at

A League of Their Own

In conjunction with Chicago advertising executive Arthur Meyerhoff, Cubs owner P. K. Wrigley announced the formation of the All-American Girls Professional Baseball League on February 20, 1943. Wrigley thought World War II would decimate the major leagues' playing talent and saw a women's league as a way to keep the ballparks busy and the fans entertained, in addition to serving as a wartime morale booster. Players were paid between $55 and $80 a week, plus expenses and board. The league opened in 1943 with four teams in Rockford, Illinois; South Bend, Indiana; and the Wisconsin cities of Racine and Kenosha. In both 1943 and 1944, the league staged games at Wrigley Field under temporary lights, the first baseball games ever played at night at Clark and Addison. The league had tremendous success and reached its peak in 1948 when ten teams attracted nearly a million spectators, although it remained a regional sport. The league never expanded beyond the borders of Illinois, Wisconsin, Indiana, and Michigan.

Although the women played hard-nosed ball, an emphasis was placed on femininity. Beauty consultant Helena Rubenstein was brought in to talk about makeup, how to walk, how to take off a coat, and deal with male fans. Short hair and slacks were prohibited. The uniforms were short skirts designed to show as much leg as possible within the bounds of decency. Female chaperones lived with the women around the clock, acting as disciplinarians, friends, and surrogate parents. Former major leaguers such as Jimmie Foxx, Max Carey, Dave Bancroft, Bill Wambsganss, Johnny Rawlings, Bert Niehoff, and Leo Murphy served as managers during the league's twelve seasons of existence.

When the league opened in 1943, they played with a 12-inch softball and the pitching mound was 40 feet from home plate. In 1944, the ball was 11½ inches and dropped to 11 inches in 1946 when the mound was moved back to 43 feet. Sidearm pitching was allowed beginning in 1947. A year later, pitchers began throwing overhand from a distance of 50 feet with a ball $10\frac{3}{8}$ inches. The mound was pushed back further to 55 feet in 1951, and the official nine-inch major league baseball was adopted in 1954. Clubs participating in the league were the Rockford Peaches, South Bend Blue Sox, Racine Belles, Kenosha Comets, Milwaukee Chicks, Minneapolis Millerettes, Grand Rapids Chicks, Fort Wayne Daisies, Chicago Colleens, Springfield (Illinois) Sallies, Kalamazoo Lassies, Battle Creek Belles, Muskegon Lassies, and Peoria Redwings.

The league dissolved in 1954. Fewer women were going out for professional baseball in the postwar years, with many potential players opting for marriage, college, or year-round jobs which afforded better pay. Teams mainly had rosters of aging players and second-string talent. Also, the advent of television cut into the league's attendance figures, as fans could stay home and watch major league teams for free. Dozens of men's professional minor league teams also folded during the 1950s, largely because of competition from television.

Ironically, it has been television that has helped to bring the All-American Girls Professional Baseball League back into the public eye. In 1992, a feature film called *A League of Their Own*, directed by Penny Marshall and starring Tom Hanks, Geena Davis, Madonna, and Rosie O'Donnell, followed the exploits of the Rockford Peaches during that inaugural season of 1943. Through television repeats of the film and home video rentals, the long-forgotten story of the league has been revived.

French Lick in 1943, 1944, and 1945, and returned to Catalina Island in California for training in 1946 after the war ended.

APRIL 21   The Cubs lose the season opener 6–0 to the Pirates before 9,044 at Wrigley Field. Rip Sewell pitched the shutout for Pittsburgh.

Members of the 1942 Cubs who were in the military by the start of the 1943 season included pitchers Emil Kush, Vern Olsen, and Johnny Schmitz; catchers Marv Felderman, Bob Scheffing, and Bennie Warren; infielders Cy Block, Lou Stringer, and Bobby Sturgeon; and outfielder Marv Rickert.

MAY 5   The Cubs defeat the Cardinals 2–1 in fourteen innings at Wrigley Field. Catcher Chico Hernandez hit a single to drive in the winning run. Claude Passeau pitched the complete game.

Hernandez and pitcher Hi Bithorn formed the first all–Latin battery in major league history. Hernandez was from Cuba, and Bithorn from Puerto Rico.

MAY 9   The Cubs gallop to a 13–2 and 4–3 sweep of the Reds in Cincinnati.

Bert Wilson began doing the play–by–play on the radio for the Cubs over WIND in 1943, a job he held until his death in 1955 at the age of 44.

MAY 23   The Cubs sweep the Braves 2–1 and 1–0 in Boston. The second game lasted ten innings and Hi Bithorn pitched the complete–game shutout. Dom Dallesandro's sacrifice fly drove in the lone run of the game.

Lou Novikoff held out for over a month past Opening Day and didn't appear in a game until May 26. He hit .279 and failed to hit a home run in 233 at–bats in 1943.

MAY 29   Claude Passeau pitches a thirteen–inning complete game and hits a walk–off single to beat the Braves 4–3 at Wrigley Field.

The Cubs entered the game with a 9–22 record and had yet to hit a single home run. Part of the problem was an inferior batch of baseballs manufactured with different specifications due to wartime shortages. Shortly after the season started, a more resilient ball was rushed into use. The Cubs finished the season with 52 homers, but Bill Nicholson hit 29 of them. Nicholson led the National League in homers. He also led the league in RBIs with 128, and collected 188 hits, scored 95 runs, and batted .309.

Lou Novikoff led the Cubs in hitting with a .300 average in 1942 and followed that with a .279 average in 1943.

MAY 30   In the 33rd game of the season, Bill Nicholson hits the first two Cubs homers of 1943 during a 5–1 win over the Braves at Wrigley Field.

JUNE 22   Paul Derringer pitches the Cubs to a 1–0 win over the Pirates at Wrigley Field. Lennie Merullo drove in the lone run of the game with a single in the seventh inning.

The game started at 11:00 A.M. to make it easier for second–shift workers in war plants to attend the game.

JUNE 25   Hi Bithorn pitches a two–hitter to defeat the Cardinals 6–0 at Wrigley Field. The only St. Louis hits were a single by Johnny Hopp in the second inning and a single by Danny Litwhiler in the seventh inning.

In another wartime experiment with game times, the June 25 game in Chicago started at 6:00 P.M.

JULY 13   Stan Hack collects three hits in five at–bats in the All–Star Game, but the National League loses 5–3 at Shibe Park in Philadelphia.

Hack hit .289 in 1943.

JULY 25   The Cubs defeat the Giants 2–0 in both ends of a double–header at Wrigley Field. Hi Bithorn pitched the shutout in the first game. Ed Hanyzewski (seven innings) and Claude Passeau (two innings) combined for the shutout in the second game.

Bithorn had a record of 18–12 with a 2.60 ERA and seven shutouts in 1943. Hiram Gabriel Bithorn was born in San Juan, Puerto Rico, in 1916, although both of his parents were Dutch. He pitched with the handicap of missing the third and fourth toes on his left foot, which he lost in an accident as a youngster when he roller-skated into a truck. After the 1943 season, Bithorn entered the U.S. Navy, and during two years in the service his weight ballooned from 180 pounds to 225. He was never effective after the war and drifted to the Mexican League. Bithorn was shot to death by a policeman under mysterious circumstances on New Year's Day in 1952 in El Mante, Mexico. The park in San Juan is named Hiram Bithorn Stadium in honor of the former Cubs pitcher. The Montreal Expos played about a quarter of their home schedule there in 2003 and 2004.

JULY 30   The Cubs hit two home runs on two pitches with one baseball during a 12–3 win over the Dodgers at Wrigley Field. Facing Johnny Allen in the sixth inning, Phil Cavaretta homered off the right field foul pole. The ball was retrieved, and Bill Nicholson hit the next pitch out of the ballpark.

Cavaretta was the Cubs' starting first baseman at the age of 18 in 1935, but it wasn't until 1943 that he put together an all–star caliber season when he batted .291 and scored 93 runs.

AUGUST 5   The Cubs trade Bill Lee to the Phillies for Mickey Livingston.

AUGUST 6   In his first at–bat with the Cubs, Mickey Livingston hits a home run, although Chicago loses 9–7 to the Reds at Wrigley Field.

SEPTEMBER 3   Two days before the Allies begin the invasion of the Italian mainland, Phil Cavaretta hits a three–run homer in the tenth inning to defeat the Reds 12–9 in Cincinnati. The Reds tied the score with three runs in the ninth inning.

SEPTEMBER 8   Paul Derringer wins his 200th career game with a 3–2 victory over the Giants at Wrigley Field.

SEPTEMBER 24   A "crowd" of 314 watches the Cubs defeat the Phillies 7–4 at Wrigley Field The game was played in cold temperatures and a freezing drizzle before it was called at the end of five innings. Andy Pafko made his major league debut in the game, and drove in four runs with a double and a single.

Pafko was a fixture in the Cubs lineup as a center fielder and a third baseman from the time he made his major league debut until he was traded to the Dodgers in June 1951.

SEPTEMBER 27   Bill Nicholson hits a walk–off homer in the thirteenth inning to defeat the Giants 10–9 at Wrigley Field. New York led 8–2 in the second inning.

 **1944**

Season in a Sentence

Jimmie Wilson resigns as manager on May 1 during a 13–game losing streak and is replaced by Charlie Grimm, who lifts the Cubs out of the cellar and into fourth place.

Finish • Won • Lost • Pct • GB

Fourth   75   79   .487 30.0

Managers

Jimmie Wilson (1–9),
Roy Johnson (0–1) and
Charlie Grimm (74–69)

Stats

Stats	Cubs	NL	Rank
Batting Avg:	.261	.261	5
On–Base Pct:	.328	.326	5
Slugging Pct:	.360	.363	5
Home Runs:	71		4
Stolen Bases:	53		2
ERA:	3.59	3.61	4
Fielding Avg:	.970	.972	6
Runs Scored:	702		3
Runs Allowed:	669		5

Starting Lineup

Dewey Williams, c
Phil Cavaretta, 1b
Don Johnson, 2b
Stan Hack, 3b
Roy Hughes, ss–3b
Dom Dallesandro, lf
Andy Pafko, cf
Bill Nicholson, rf
Lennie Merullo, ss

Pitchers

Hank Wyse, sp
Claude Passeau, sp
Bob Chipman, sp
Paul Derringer, rp–sp
Bill Fleming, rp–sp
Hy Vandenberg, rp
Paul Erickson, rp–sp
Red Lynn, rp–sp

Attendance

640,110 (second in NL)

Club Leaders

Batting Avg:	Cavaretta	.321
On–Base Pct:	Nicholson	.391
Slugging Pct:	Nicholson	.545
Home Runs:	Nicholson	33
RBI:	Nicholson	122
Runs:	Nicholson	116
Stolen Bases:	Hughes	16
Wins:	Wyse	16
Strikeouts:	Passeau	89
ERA:	Passeau	2.89
Saves:	Passeau	3
	Derringer	3

APRIL 18   The Cubs collect only three hits but win the season opener 3–0 in Cincinnati in a contest that lasts only one hour and 17 minutes. Hank Wyse pitched the shutout.

Following the Opening Day victory, the Cubs lost 13 games in a row.

APRIL 21   In the first game of the season at Wrigley Field, the Cubs lose 4–0 to the Cardinals before a crowd of only 4,783.

Players on the 1943 Cubs who were in the military by the start of the 1944 season included pitchers Hi Bithorn and Lon Warneke, catchers Mickey Livingston and Clyde McCullough, infielder Al Glossop, and outfielders Charlie Gilbert, Peanuts Lowrey, and Whitey Platt. Catcher Joe Stephenson entered the service during the season.

MAY 1   Jimmie Wilson resigns as manager with the club holding a record of 1–9. Coach Roy Johnson was named acting manager until a replacement for Wilson could be hired.

Wilson had a dismal record of 213–258 as manager of the Cubs. He found employment almost immediately as a coach with the Reds. Wilson's son was a pilot during World War II and was killed in India in 1945. Jimmie's health deteriorated following his son's death, and he died of a heart attack in 1947 at the age of 46.

MAY 6   The Cubs hire Charlie Grimm as manager.

This was Grimm's second tour as manager of the Cubs. Previously, he managed the club from 1932 through 1938, which was followed by stints as a broadcaster (1938–40) and coach (1941). From June 1941 through May 1944, he managed the Milwaukee Brewers minor league club in the American Association, where he won a pennant in 1943. Grimm's second term as Cubs manager lasted until 1949 and included an appearance in the World Series in 1945.

MAY 7   In Charlie Grimm's return as manager, the Cubs lose two extra–inning games to the Pirates at Wrigley Field to run Chicago's losing streak to 12 games. The Cubs lost the first game 6–5 in fourteen innings, and the second 3–2 in eleven frames.

MAY 8   The recreation section of the War Production Board turns down the Cubs' application to install lights at Wrigley Field for the purposes of playing night baseball during the 1944 season. But the board invited the Cubs to resubmit their request with a view to construction for 1945.

MAY 10   The Cubs lose their 13th game in a row, dropping a 7–1 decision to the Phillies at Wrigley Field.

MAY 11   The Cubs snap their 13–game losing streak with a 5–3 victory over the Phillies at Wrigley Field.

The Cubs lost their next three games, and fell to 2–16 on the season.

MAY 21   The Cubs break loose with a 15–1 and 14–5 smashing of the Braves in a double–header at Wrigley Field. The second game was called after 7 ½ innings by darkness.

JUNE 6   All major league games are postponed in observance of the D–Day landing in France. President Roosevelt urged Americans to spend the day in prayer at home or in church.

              Unfortunately, the Cubs' front office wasn't idle because they completed one of the worst trades in club history by dealing Eddie Stanky to the Dodgers for Bob Chipman. Stanky was a catalyst on pennant winners on three different clubs. He was the starting second baseman in the World Series for the Dodgers in 1947, the Braves in 1948, and the Giants in 1951.

JUNE 11   Paul Erickson and Bob Chipman both pitch shutouts to defeat the Pirates 5–0 and 1–0 in a double–header at Forbes Field. In the first game, Erickson pitched a two-hitter. The only Pittsburgh hits were singles by Bob Elliott and Jim Russell. Chipman's shutout in the second contest came in his debut as a Cub five days after he was acquired from the Dodgers. It was also Chipman's first career shutout. The lone run of the second game was driven in on a single by Tom York in the seventh inning.

JUNE 28   The Cubs celebrate the return of Stan Hack by defeating the Dodgers 12–6 and 6–2 in a double–header at Wrigley Field. Bill Nicholson hit two homers in the first game, one of them a grand slam off Les Webber in the sixth inning.

              Hack was a holdout during the first third of the 1944 season, in part because of his dislike of Jimmie Wilson. Before the June 28 first game, Charlie Grimm hauled Stan out of the dugout in a wheelbarrow and dumped him at third base. Hack had three hits in eight at–bats in the two games.

JULY 9   The Cubs sweep the Giants 6–2 and 1–0 in a double–header at Wrigley Field. Claude Passeau pitched the second game shutout. Andy Pafko drove in the lone run of the game with a single in the fifth inning.

              Before the double–header, the crowd of 39,434 was encouraged to buy war bonds from a group of ex–Cubs stars, including Three Finger Brown, Jimmy Archer, Rogers Hornsby, Fred Lindstrom, and Hippo Vaughn.

JULY 11   Phil Cavaretta reaches base five times on a triple, a single, and three walks during a 7–1 National League victory in the All–Star Game at Forbes Field in Pittsburgh. Playing with a painfully sore hand, Bill Nicholson drove in a run with a pinch–double in the fifth inning to tie the score 1–1, they scored on a single by Augie Galan to put the NL up 2–1.

              Both Cavaretta and Nicholson had spectacular seasons in 1944. Cavaretta collected a league–

Phil Cavaretta had a big season in 1944, leading the league with 197 hits while batting .321. That set the stage for his MVP year in 1945.

leading 197 hits and batted .321 with five homers. Nicholson lead the league in home runs (33), RBIs (122), and runs (116) and hit .287.

JULY 23   Bill Nicholson hits four home runs and is given an intentional walk with the bases loaded during a double–header against the Giants in New York. The Cubs won the first game 7–4, and lost the second 12–10. After drawing a walk in the second inning, Nicholson homered in the fourth and sixth innings off Bill Voiselle and another in the eighth off Andy Hansen. Combined with the home run he hit in his last plate appearance the previous game against the Giants on July 22, Nicholson homered in four consecutive official at–bats. In the second game of the July 23 double–header, Nicholson connected again in the seventh inning. When he came to bat again in the eighth inning with the bases loaded, two out, and the Giants leading 10–7, New York player–manager Mel Ott ordered Hansen to walk Nicholson intentionally. The strategy worked, as Andy Pafko flied out to end the inning. To add to the drama, Nicholson and Ott were battling for the NL home run leadership. At the end of the day, each had 21 homers.

Nicholson is the only batter in Cub history to homer in four consecutive at–bats. In 13 at–bats over four games on July 21, 22, and 23, 1944, Nicholson hit six homers.

JULY 25   The Cubs pummel the Dodgers 14–6 in Brooklyn.

AUGUST 1   A stoppage of all public transportation in Philadelphia by a trolley, elevated, subway, and bus operators' strike causes a postponement of a double–header between the Cubs and the Phillies. The August 2 single game was also postponed.

AUGUST 5   The Cubs win their 11th game in a row with a 7–2 decision over the Pirates at Wrigley Field.

AUGUST 16 Bill Nicholson hits a grand slam off Woody Rich of the Braves in the third inning of an 11–3 win over the Braves at Wrigley Field.

AUGUST 20 Lennie Merullo hits a grand slam off Harry Feldman of the Giants in the fourth inning of a 7–4 win in the first game of a double–header at Wrigley Field. The Cubs lost the second game 3–1.

AUGUST 29 Four days after Allied troops liberate Paris, the Cubs score seven runs in the first inning of a 15–4 win over the Pirates in the first game of a double–header at Wrigley Field. The Cubs lost the second game 5–4.

SEPTEMBER 21 The Cubs score seven runs in the first inning and defeat the Giants 11–8 in the first game of a double–header in New York. The Cubs completed the sweep with a 6–4 win in the nightcap.

SEPTEMBER 26 The Cubs go from one extreme to the other in a double–header against the Phillies in Philadelphia, winning 15–0 and losing 10–1.

1945

Season in a Sentence

The Cubs are in fifth place and nine games behind in mid–May, before putting on a rush with a stretch of 64 wins in 89 games to move into first place and capture the National League pennant.

Finish • Won • Lost • Pct • GB

First   98   56   .636   +3.0

World Series–The Cubs lost to the Detroit Tigers, four games to three

Manager

Charlie Grimm

Stats   Cubs • NL • Rank

Stats	Cubs	NL	Rank
Batting Avg:	.277	.265	1
On–Base Pct:	.349	.333	2
Slugging Pct:	.372	.364	5
Home Runs:	57		5 (tie)
Stolen Bases:	69		5
ERA:	2.98	3.80	1
Fielding Avg:	.980	.971	1
Runs Scored:	735		4
Runs Allowed:	532		1

Starting Lineup

Mickey Livingston, c
Phil Cavaretta, 1b
Don Johnson, 2b
Stan Hack, 3b
Lennie Merullo, ss
Peanuts Lowrey, lf
Andy Pafko, cf
Bill Nicholson, rf
Roy Hughes, ss–2b
Paul Gillespie, c

Pitchers

Hank Wyse, sp
Claude Passeau, sp
Paul Derringer, sp
Ray Prim, sp–rp
Hank Borowy, sp
Hy Vandenberg, rp
Paul Erickson, rp–sp
Bob Chipman, rp–sp

Attendance

1,036,386 (second in NL)

Club Leaders

Batting Avg:	Cavaretta	.355
On–Base Pct:	Cavaretta	.449
Slugging Pct:	Cavaretta	.500
Home Runs:	Nicholson	13
RBI:	Pafko	110
Runs:	Hack	110
Stolen Bases:	Hack	12
Wins:	Wyse	22
Strikeouts:	Passeau	98
ERA:	Prim	2.40
Saves:	Derringer	4

APRIL 17   The Cubs win the season opener 3–2 over the Cardinals before 11,785 at Wrigley Field. The winning run was scored on a walk–off single by Don Johnson. Bill Nicholson homered in the second inning to give the Cubs a 1–0 lead.

APRIL 25   Claude Passeau hits a home run and pitches a shutout to beat the Reds 4–0 in Cincinnati.

             Passeau had a 17–9 record, a 2.46 ERA, and a league–leading five shutouts in 1945.

APRIL 28   Hank Wyse pitches a one–hitter to defeat the Pirates 6–0 at Wrigley Field. The only Pittsburgh hit was a line single to right field by Bill Salkeld with one out in the eighth inning.

             Wyse had a career year in 1945 with a 22–10 record and a 2.68 ERA in 278 ⅓ innings.

MAY 12   Five days after Germany's surrender closes the European phase of World War II, the Cubs battle back to defeat the Braves 13–12 in Boston after trailing 10–3 in the fourth inning. The Cubs scored six runs in the seventh inning, the last four on a grand slam by Phil Cavaretta that tied the score 12–12. All six runs in the inning were scored after two were out. Bill Nicholson's homer in the ninth broke the tie.

After the victory, the Cubs lost six in a row to drop their season record to 10–13. The club was nine games behind the first place Giants.

JUNE 3   Claude Passeau pitches a two–hitter to defeat the Braves 3–1 in the second game of a double–header at Wrigley Field. The only Boston hits were a double by opposing pitcher Jim Tobin and a single by Phil Masi.

The Wrigley Field scoreboard was painted green in 1945. Previously, it was a reddish brown.

JUNE 23   Two days after Japan surrenders Okinawa to U.S. forces, the Cubs purchase Ray Starr from the Pirates.

JULY 3   Seven days after the signing of the United Nations charter, the Cubs collect 28 hits and bury the Braves 24–2 in Boston. Phil Cavaretta, Don Johnson, and Stan Hack each score five runs. Cavaretta had five hits, including a double, in seven at–bats. Johnson also had five hits, with two doubles, in seven at–bats.

Cavaretta was the National League Most Valuable Player in 1945. He led the NL in batting average with a .355 mark, along with 34 doubles, 10 triples, and six homers. Hack collected 193 hits, scored 110 runs, and hit .323. Andy Pafko also contributed to the offense by batting .298 with 12 homers and 120 RBIs.

JULY 8   The Cubs take first place with a 12–6 and 9–2 double–header sweep of the Phillies in Philadelphia. The victories were the ninth and 10th in a row for the Cubs.

The Cubs remained in first place for the rest of the 1945 season.

JULY 12   The Cubs run their winning streak to 11 games, defeating the Braves 6–1 in the first game of a double–header at Wrigley Field. The streak was stopped with a 3–1 loss in the second game.

After the defeat, the Cubs won their next five to give them 16 wins in 17 games.

JULY 27   The Cubs purchase Hank Borowy from the Yankees for $97,000.

Larry MacPhail purchased the Yankees in April 1945 and took an instant dislike to Borowy, even though he had a 10–5 record on the season at the time he was sold to the Cubs, and a 56–30 career record. MacPhail dismissed Borowy as a "seven–inning pitcher" at a time when starters were expected to finish a majority of their starts. The deal may have won the pennant for the Cubs, as Borowy had a record of 11–2 and a 2.13 ERA over the final two months of the 1945 season. After 1945, however, he had problems with blisters on his fingers and was 25–32 with the Cubs from 1946 through 1948 before he was dealt to the Phillies.

AUGUST 1   A total of 4,044 women are admitted free to Wrigley Field by bringing cakes and cookies for the Chicago Servicemen's Center. The Cubs lost 1–0 to the Pirates.

AUGUST 2   In a reversal of the previous day's game, the Cubs defeat the Pirates 1–0 at Wrigley Field. Paul Derringer pitched the shutout. Don Johnson's double in the sixth inning drove in the only run of the game.

> *Derringer had a 16–11 record in 1945. It was his last year in the big leagues. Derringer turned 39 just after the season ended, and with players returning from the war in 1946, he was considered expendable by the Cubs. Ray Prim was another 38–year–old who was a huge help to the Cubs in 1945. Prim entered the season with a 7–10 lifetime record, but was 13–8 with a 2.40 ERA in the wartime season. Unlike Derringer, Prim returned in 1946, but he won only two games.*

AUGUST 3   Phil Cavaretta stars as the Cubs clobber the Reds 11–5 and 9–1 in a double–header in Cincinnati. He had six hits, including a homer and four doubles, in eight at–bats, scored five runs, and collected eight runs batted in.

AUGUST 11   Five days after the atom bomb was dropped on Hiroshima, the Cubs score eight runs in the fourth inning and wallop the Dodgers 20–6 in Brooklyn. Paul Gillespie hit a grand slam in the fourth inning off Art Herring.

AUGUST 19   Five days after Japan surrenders to end World War II, the Cubs sweep the Giants 3–1 and 8–0 in New York to increase their lead in the National League pennant race to 7½ games over second–place St. Louis. From June 26 through August 19, the Cubs had a record of 45–12. After finishing first in 1942, 1943, and 1944, the Cardinals were gunning for their fourth NL pennant in a row.

> *The wartime pennant won by the Cubs in 1945 was possible because the club was able to put together a semblance of a major league team, with players such as Stan Hack, Phil Cavaretta, Andy Pafko, Bill Nicholson, Peanuts Lowrey, Claude Passeau, Hank Wyse, Paul Derringer, and Hank Borowy, due to medical military deferments issued to those players. The best Cubs players who were in the military during the 1945 season were Clyde McCullough, Johnny Schmitz, Eddie Waitkus, and Marv Rickert. The Cardinals, on the other hand, were without Stan Musial, Enos Slaughter, Walker Cooper, and Howie Pollet, yet they finished just three games behind the Cubs in the 1945 pennant race. If both the Cubs and the Cardinals had been at full strength, Chicago wouldn't have come close to finishing in first place.*

AUGUST 26   The Cardinals complete a three–game sweep of the Cubs at Wrigley Field with a 5–1 win. The three St. Louis victories reduced the Cubs' lead over the second–place Cards to 2½ games.

> *The Cubs had a record of only 6–16 against the Cardinals in 1945.*

AUGUST 30   Stan Hack collects his 2,000th career hit with a single off Preacher Roe, but the Cubs lose 6–4 to the Pirates in Pittsburgh.

SEPTEMBER 3   The Cubs inflict two defeats on the Reds by scores of 7–2 and 7–1 at Wrigley Field. The sweep was set in motion with a grand slam by Andy Pafko in the first inning of the first game off Ed Heusser.

The Cubs had a record of 21–1 against the Reds in 1945, which tied a major league record for most victories over one team in a season. Combined with a win in their last meeting in 1944 and the first three in 1946, the Cubs had a streak of 25 wins in 26 games against Cincinnati.

SEPTEMBER 17   Bill Nicholson sets a National League record for most putouts by a right fielder in an nine–inning game with 10, but the Cubs lose 4–0 to the Dodgers at Wrigley Field.

After the loss to the Dodgers, the Cubs headed to St. Louis for a three–game series against the Cardinals, where they lost two of three. At the end of the September 20 defeat, the Cubs led the Cardinals by two games. Each team had eight contests left on the schedule.

SEPTEMBER 23   Andy Pafko hits a grand slam off Preacher Roe of the Pirates in the third inning of a 7–3 win at Wrigley Field.

With a week left in the season, the Cubs led the Cardinals by 1 ½ games.

SEPTEMBER 25   The Cubs defeat the Cardinals 6–5 at Wrigley Field to increase their lead to 2 ½ games. The Cubs trailed 3–2 before scoring four runs in the seventh inning, then survived a two–run St. Louis rally in the eighth. It was Hank Borowy's 20th win of the season. He won 10 with the Yankees and 10 with the Cubs.

SEPTEMBER 26   The Cardinals keep their slim hopes of winning the pennant alive by beating the Cubs 11–6 at Wrigley Field. Following the loss, the Cubs led the Cardinals by 1 ½ games. The Cubs had five games remaining, and the Cardinals had four left to play.

SEPTEMBER 27   The Cubs defeat the Reds 3–1 and 7–4 in a double–header in Cincinnati to clinch a tie for the pennant with three games remaining. Hank Wyse was the winning pitcher in the first game, earning his 22nd victory of the season.

SEPTEMBER 29   The Cubs sew up the pennant with a 4–3 win over the Pirates in the first game of a double–header at Wrigley Field. Hank Borowy was the winning pitcher. The Cubs also won the second game, called after five innings by darkness, 5–0. In the night-cap, Paul Gillespie hit a home run in what proved to be his final regular season at–bat, although Gillespie had six at–bats in the World Series without a hit.

The Cubs met the Tigers in the World Series. Detroit, managed by Del Baker, had an 88–65 record and nosed out the Washington Senators for the AL pennant by 1 ½ games. With many wartime fill–ins on both rosters, the 1945 Cubs and Tigers were probably the two least–talented teams ever to reach the World Series. "I don't think either one of them can win," said Chicago sportswriter Warren Brown.

OCTOBER 3   The Cubs win the first game of the 1945 World Series 9–0 over the Tigers before 54,637 in Detroit. The Cubs scored four runs in the first inning and three in the third off Hal Newhouser to take a 7–0 lead. Hank Borowy pitched a six–hit shutout. Phil Cavaretta had three hits, including a homer, in four at–bats and scored three runs. Andy Pafko collected two singles, a double, and scored three runs. Bill Nicholson hit a triple and drove in three runs.

OCTOBER 4   The Tigers even the Series with a 4–1 win over the Cubs in game two before 53,838 in Detroit. The Cubs led 1–0 before the Tigers scored four runs in the fifth, three of them on a Hank Greenberg home run off Hank Wyse. Stan Hack had three hits, including a double. Virgil Trucks, who had been out of the Navy for only a week, was the winning pitcher.

OCTOBER 5   In a magnificent pitching performance, Claude Passeau hurls a one–hitter to defeat the Tigers 3–0 in game three before 55,500 in Detroit. The only two Tigers to reach base were Rudy York on a second–inning single and Bob Swift on a sixth– inning walk.

Claude Passeau, left, pitched a one-hitter in the third game of the 1945 World Series. Rudy York, right, singled in the second inning, but the Cubs won 3–0 to take a 2–1 series lead.

OCTOBER 6   The Tigers even the Series again with a 4–1 win in game four over the Cubs before 42,823 at Wrigley Field. Cubs starter Ray Prim retired the first ten Detroit hitters before giving up four runs in the fourth inning.

Chicago restaurant owner Billy Sianis tried to enter the ballpark with his pet goat and was denied admission. Sianis claimed that the Cubs would never play in the World Series again, and "The Curse of the Billy Goat" was born.

OCTOBER 7   The Tigers move within one game of a world championship with an 8–4 decision over the Cubs before 43,463 at Wrigley Field. Detroit broke a 1–1 tie with four runs in the sixth inning off Hank Borowy.

Cubs starting shortstop Roy Hughes missed the game after he was hit in the left ankle by a line drive off the bat of Detroit's Rudy York during batting practice.

OCTOBER 8   The Cubs stay alive in the World Series by beating the Tigers 8–7 in twelve innings before 41,708 at Wrigley Field. The Cubs led 7–3 after seven innings before the Tigers scored four runs in the eighth off Hank Wyse and Ray Prim, who were pitching in relief after Claude Passeau had to leave the game when hit in the finger by a line drive. The score was tied on a two–out homer by Hank Greenberg. Frank Secory, who had a .158 batting average during the regular season, hit a pinch–single with one out in the twelfth inning. Bill Schuster ran for Secory and scored on a two–out double by Stan Hack that bounced over the head of Greenberg in left field. It was Hack's fourth hit of the game. Hank Borowy pitched shutout ball over the final four innings.

The losing pitcher was Dizzy Trout. His son Steve pitched for the Cubs from 1983 through 1987.

OCTOBER 10 The Tigers take the world championship by winning the seventh and deciding game of the World Series 9–3 over the Cubs before 41,590 at Wrigley Field. Charlie Grimm gambled by bringing back Hank Borowy at the starting pitcher, despite his five innings as a starter in game five and a four–inning relief stint in game six two days earlier. Borowy failed to retire a batter as the Tigers scored five runs in the first inning. Phil Cavaretta had three hits in the Chicago comeback bid. It was the seventh World Series loss in a row for the Cubs, following failures in 1910, 1918, 1929, 1932, 1935, and 1938.

Cubs catcher Clyde McCullough is the only player to appear in a World Series game following a regular season in which he didn't play a game. McCullough was discharged by the Navy in September in time for the start of the Series. He pinch–hit in the seventh game and struck out in the ninth inning.

The Billy Goat Curse

Why haven't the Cubs been to the World Series since 1945? Some blame the "The Billy Goat Curse" placed on the club by a Chicago restaurant owner.

In 1945, Billy Sianis owned a restaurant in downtown Chicago called the Billy Goat Tavern. A goat named Sonovia was a mascot of the establishment. Sianis bought two tickets for the fourth game of the 1945 World Series. One was for himself. The other was for Sonovia.

Sianis was denied admission to Wrigley Field unless he left the goat outside. Asked why, Sianis was told "the goat smells." The Cubs went on to lose the Series in seven games. Sianis sent a wire to Cubs owner P.K. Wrigley reading, "Who smells now?"

Sianis put a hex on the Cubs and said they would never play in the World Series again. The Billy Goat Curse was born.

Sianis died during the 1970s, and the Wrigley family sold the Cubs to the Tribune Company in June 1981. At the Wrigley Field opener in 1982, new general manager Dallas Green invited Sam Sianis, Billy's nephew, onto the playing field with another pet goat to lift the curse. Sianis and his goat were brought back in 1994 after the Cubs opened the season with 12 straight losses at Wrigley Field. Thus far, the World Series curse is still intact.

The Billy Goat Tavern became famous for another reason during the 1970s. It was frequented by many members of the comedy troupe Second City, including John Belushi. It became part of a recurring skit on *Saturday Night Live* in which the late comedian hollered, "Cheeseburger! Cheeseburger! Cheeseburger! No Pepsi! Coke! No Fries! Chips!"

1946   Cubs

Season in a Sentence

The "Billy Goat Curse" begins with a third–place finish in the first post–World War II season.

Finish • Won • Lost • Pct • GB

Third   82   71   .536   14.5

Manager

Charlie Grimm

Stats   Cubs • NL • Rank

Batting Avg:	.254	.256	6
On–Base Pct:	.331	.329	4
Slugging Pct:	.346	.355	6
Home Runs:	56		6
Stolen Bases:	43		7
ERA:	3.24	3.41	4
Fielding Avg:	.976	.974	2
Runs Scored:	628		4
Runs Allowed:	581		4

Starting Lineup

Clyde McCullough, c
Eddie Waitkus, 1b
Don Johnson, 2b
Stan Hack, 3b
Bobby Sturgeon, ss
Marv Rickert, lf
Peanuts Lowrey, cf–lf
Phil Cavaretta, rf–1b
Bill Nicholson, rf
Billy Jurges, ss
Andy Pafko, cf
Lou Stringer, 2b
Mickey Livingston, c
Johnny Ostrowski, 3b

Pitchers

Hank Wyse, sp–rp
Johnny Schmitz, sp
Hank Borowy, sp
Claude Passeau, sp
Emil Kush, rp
Bob Chipman, rp
Paul Erickson, rp–sp
Hi Bithorn, rp
Charlie Root, rp

Attendance

1,342,970 (second in NL)

Club Leaders

Batting Avg:	Waitkus	.304
On–Base Pct:	Cavaretta	.401
Slugging Pct:	Cavaretta	.435
Home Runs:	Cavaretta	8
	Nicholson	8
RBI:	Cavaretta	78
Runs:	Cavaretta	89
Stolen Bases:	Lowrey	10
Wins:	Wyse	14
Strikeouts:	Schmitz	135
ERA:	Schmitz	2.61
Saves:	Three tied with:	2

JANUARY 21   The Cubs sell Roy Hughes to the Phillies.

FEBRUARY 22   The Cubs open training camp on Catalina Island. It's the first training camp held in peacetime in five years.

> *The 1946 major league training camps were unique as returning war veterans competed with wartime fill–ins for spots on the roster. The Cubs spring training roster included twenty players who spent the entire 1945 season in the military. Some, like Johnny Schmitz, Eddie Waitkus, Clyde McCullough, Paul Erickson, Marv Rickert, and Emil Kush, were regulars with the Cubs in 1946. Coming off of a pennant–winning season, the Cubs made fewer changes than any other team in baseball in the transition from war to peacetime, however. The only regular from 1945 who was not on the 1946 roster was Paul Derringer.*

APRIL 16   The Cubs score four runs in a sensational ninth–inning rally and defeat the Reds 4–3 at Crosley Field in the season opener.

APRIL 20   The Cubs raise the 1945 pennant prior to the first game of the season at Wrigley Field, but lose 2–0 to the Cardinals before 40,887.

This was the first Cubs game ever telecast. It was carried over station WBKB with Whispering Joe Wilson at the mike. He was known as "Whispering Joe" because of his stage–whisper style while calling bowling tournaments.

MAY 5   Shut out over the first six innings by Phillies pitcher Schoolboy Rowe, the Cubs erupt for 11 runs in the seventh inning and go on to win 13–1 in the first game of a double–header at Wrigley Field. Pitcher Hank Borowy had two doubles and four runs batted in during the big inning. The Phillies recovered to win the second game 7–1.

MAY 15   Clyde McCullough's three–run homer in the thirteenth inning gives the Cubs a 6–3 lead in a 6–4 win over the Phillies in Philadelphia.

MAY 18   The Cubs pummel the Giants 19–3 in New York.

MAY 20   Claude Passeau makes his first error since September 21, 1941, during a 6–4 win over the Braves in Boston. Passeau's record of 273 consecutive fielding chances without an error still stands.

Passeau achieved the record despite wearing the smallest glove in the majors. The small glove was necessary because of a childhood accident that left two fingers of his left hand permanently bent down and almost useless. While riding in the back of a pickup truck, the shotgun he was holding went off and the bullet passed through his hand and went out of his wrist.

MAY 22   The Cubs and the Dodgers fight during a 2–1 Brooklyn win in thirteen innings at Ebbets Field.

Lennie Merullo knocked down Dodger second baseman Eddie Stanky trying to break up a double play in the tenth inning. Stanky wrapped his legs around Merullo's neck in a scissors hold and both punched each other until the umpires and players intervened. During the brawl, Claude Passeau ripped the jersey off Dodgers manager Leo Durocher.

MAY 23   This time, the Dodgers and Cubs fight before the game at Brooklyn.

During batting practice, Dixie Walker of the Dodgers took exception to some remarks Lennie Merullo made to Pee Wee Reese. Walker wrestled Merullo to the ground. Phil Cavaretta came to the rescue and landed a few blows to Walker's body before a squad of police arrived and separated the players. Walker had one tooth knocked out and another one chipped. Merullo was fined $150 and suspended eight days by National League President Ford Frick. Cavaretta was fined $100. Cubs coach Red Smith was suspended for five days because he tried to prevent police from breaking up the fight. The Cubs lost the game 2–1 in eleven innings.

JUNE 6   Frank Secory hits a walk–off, pinch–hit, grand slam homer in the twelfth inning to defeat the Giants 10–6 at Wrigley Field. The Cubs led 6–0 before allowing New York to tie the score with three runs in the eighth inning and three more in the ninth. One month to the day later, Secory was a hero again in a similar situation (see July 6, 1946).

JUNE 7 — Claude Passeau stars with his bat and his arm to defeat the Dodgers 2–0 at Wrigley Field. Passeau not only pitched a four–hit shutout, but he struck a two–run walk–off home run in the ninth inning off Joe Hatten.

JUNE 10 — Coming into the game with a seven–game winning streak, the Cubs take a 7–0 lead after six innings with Hank Borowy cruising with a no–hitter, only to lose 9–8 when the Phillies score a run in the seventh inning, four in the eighth, and four in the ninth.

JUNE 27 — Bill Nicholson hits a two–run pinch–single in the ninth inning with the bases filled to defeat the Pirates 6–5 in Pittsburgh.

Nicholson and Phil Cavaretta each hit only eight homers in 1946, but it was enough to lead the club in the category. It is the only time since 1921 that no Chicago Cubs hitter reached double figures in homers.

JULY 6 — The Cubs beat the Reds with two shutouts in a double–header at Wrigley Field. In the first game, the Cubs won 2–0 in twelve innings with Frank Secory hitting a walk– off, pinch–hit homer with a man on base. The pitchers were Paul Erickson (8 ⅓ innings) and Johnny Schmitz (3 ⅔ innings). In the second contest, Hank Wyse pitched the Cubs to a 1–0 win. The only run of the game scored on a single by Eddie Waitkus. Between games of the double–header, pitcher Paul Erickson injured his right thumb in a fight with a heckler. It required the combined efforts of two ushers and a Chicago police officer to pull Erickson off the spectator.

The Cubs sent Secory to the minors in August. He returned to the majors as a National League umpire, a position he held from 1952 through 1970.

JULY 9 — Charlie Grimm manages the National League to a 12–0 loss in the All–Star Game, played at Fenway Park in Boston.

JULY 12 — Peanuts Lowrey drives in seven runs on a homer and two singles in leading the Cubs to a 13–2 slaughter of the Dodgers at Wrigley Field.

Lowrey played bit parts in several movies. As a youngster, he appeared in the OUR GANG comedy serials. As an adult, Lowrey was in the baseball movies PRIDE OF THE YANKEES (1942), THE STRATTON STORY (1949), and THE WINNING TEAM (1952). Lowrey's scene in THE WINNING TEAM called for him to hit Ronald Reagan, playing Grover Alexander, in the head with a baseball.

Peanuts Lowrey played a role in several baseball movies during the '40s and '50s. He led the Cubs in steals in 1946, with 10.

JULY 17	The Cubs score eight runs in the first inning and coast to a 10–0 win over the Braves at Wrigley Field.
JULY 28	The Cubs score seven runs in the first inning of the first game of a double–header in Philadelphia and roll to a 11–3 and 3–1 sweep of the Phillies.
AUGUST 13	Johnny Schmitz pitches the Cubs to a 1–0 win over the Cardinals at Wrigley Field. Mickey Livingston's single in the second inning drove in the lone run of the game.
AUGUST 18	Paul Erickson pitches a one–hitter to beat the Pirates 8–0 at Wrigley Field. The only Pittsburgh hit was a single by Billy Cox in the seventh inning.
SEPTEMBER 11	The Cubs and the Braves play seventeen innings to a 3–3 tie in Boston. The game was called on account of darkness. Cubs relievers Emil Kush (5 ⅓ innings) and Hank Borowy (seven innings) were brilliant in the contest combining to pitch 12 ⅓ shutout innings while allowing only one hit.
SEPTEMBER 15	The second game of a double–header against the Dodgers is called when a swarm of gnats suddenly invades Ebbets Field in the top of the sixth inning with Brooklyn leading the Cubs 2–0. Dodger hurler Kirby Higbe couldn't deliver a pitch because he was too busy slapping away at the pesky insects. Umpires claimed that the game was called because of darkness, however, not because of the gnats. The Cubs won the first game 4–3 in ten innings.
SEPTEMBER 24	The Cubs score eight runs in the eighth inning to defeat the Pirates 13–3 in the first game of a double–header at Wrigley Field. The Pirates came off the mat to beat the Cubs 13–0 in the second tilt.
SEPTEMBER 29	On the final day of the season, the Cubs defeat the Cardinals 8–3 in St. Louis. The Cardinals needed the victory to clinch the pennant and finished the regular season in a tie for first place with the Dodgers with a 96–58 record. Johnny Schmitz pitched the complete–game victory for the Cubs and didn't allow a hit over the final five innings. The previous day, he was in the hospital with an infected toe.

The Cardinals defeated the Dodgers in a best–two–of–three playoff to advance to the World Series.

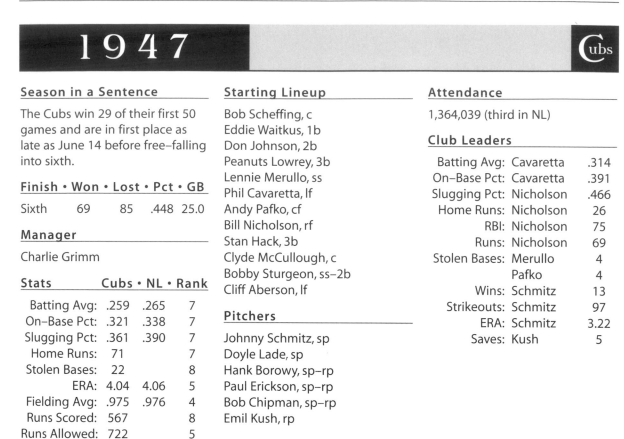

1947

Cubs

Season in a Sentence

The Cubs win 29 of their first 50 games and are in first place as late as June 14 before free–falling into sixth.

Finish • Won • Lost • Pct • GB

Sixth   69   85   .448 25.0

Manager

Charlie Grimm

Stats

Stats	Cubs	NL	Rank
Batting Avg:	.259	.265	7
On–Base Pct:	.321	.338	7
Slugging Pct:	.361	.390	7
Home Runs:	71		7
Stolen Bases:	22		8
ERA:	4.04	4.06	5
Fielding Avg:	.975	.976	4
Runs Scored:	567		8
Runs Allowed:	722		5

Starting Lineup

Bob Scheffing, c
Eddie Waitkus, 1b
Don Johnson, 2b
Peanuts Lowrey, 3b
Lennie Merullo, ss
Phil Cavaretta, lf
Andy Pafko, cf
Bill Nicholson, rf
Stan Hack, 3b
Clyde McCullough, c
Bobby Sturgeon, ss–2b
Cliff Aberson, lf

Pitchers

Johnny Schmitz, sp
Doyle Lade, sp
Hank Borowy, sp–rp
Paul Erickson, sp–rp
Bob Chipman, sp–rp
Emil Kush, rp

Attendance

1,364,039 (third in NL)

Club Leaders

Batting Avg:	Cavaretta	.314
On–Base Pct:	Cavaretta	.391
Slugging Pct:	Nicholson	.466
Home Runs:	Nicholson	26
RBI:	Nicholson	75
Runs:	Nicholson	69
Stolen Bases:	Merullo	4
	Pafko	4
Wins:	Schmitz	13
Strikeouts:	Schmitz	97
ERA:	Schmitz	3.22
Saves:	Kush	5

APRIL 15   The Cubs lose the first game of the season 1–0 to the Pirates before 29,427 at Wrigley Field. Rip Sewell pitched the shutout for Pittsburgh. Hank Greenberg drove in the lone run of the game with a home run off Hank Borowy in the sixth inning. It was Greenberg's first National League game. He was acquired by the Pirates from the Tigers in January 1947.

Among those at Wrigley Field was Bing Crosby, who was part–owner of the Pirates. Crosby sat in a box adjacent to the Buc dugout.

APRIL 16   The Cubs purchase Lonny Frey from the Reds.

On June 25, the Cubs sold Frey to the Yankees.

APRIL 20   Bill Nicholson drives in six runs with two homers to beat the Cardinals 7–4 at Wrigley Field. One of Nicholson's homers was a grand slam off Howie Pollet.

All Cubs home games were televised in 1947 over WBKB with Whispering Joe Wilson and Jack Brickhouse at the mike.

MAY 11   The Cubs score two runs in the ninth inning and one in the tenth to beat the Reds 4–3 in the second game of a double–header in Cincinnati. Andy Pafko's two–run

Left to right, Peanuts Lowery, Andy Pafko, and Bill Nicholson clown around before a game. The three were among the Cubs' offensive leaders in 1947, but they couldn't keep the club over .500.

double tied the score, and Lennie Merullo's double drove in the winning run. The Cubs also won the first game 6–3.

MAY 18 Jackie Robinson makes his Wrigley Field debut. Robinson was hitless in four at–bats, but the Dodgers defeated the Cubs 4–2 before a crowd of 46,572, the largest paid attendance in the history of the ballpark for a single regular season game.

JUNE 14 The Cubs win their fifth straight game with a 6–3 decision over the Phillies at Wrigley Field to take first place.

The Cubs had a record of 29–21 on June 14, but lost 10 of their next 12 games and were 40–64 over the remainder of the season.

JULY 8 The All–Star Game is played at Wrigley Field for the first time, as the American League wins 2–1 before a crowd of 41,123. Johnny Mize put the NL ahead 1–0 with a homer in the fourth inning off Spec Shea, but the AL came back with a run in the sixth inning and another in the seventh. Stan Spence of the Senators drove in the winning run with a single.

JULY 10 Peanuts Lowrey is pelted with debris during a 4–3, ten–inning loss to the Dodgers.

When a homer by Carl Furillo bounded out of the left field bleachers at Ebbets Field, Lowrey tossed it back to the fan, who fired it back at the Cub left fielder. Lowrey angrily threw the ball into the Cub dugout, bringing a cascade of boos and debris from the crowd.

AUGUST 1 Clyde McCullough's two–run, two–out, walk–off homer in the ninth inning beats the Dodgers 10–8 at Wrigley Field. The Dodgers entered the contest with a 13–game winning streak.

The Cubs recorded a club record–low 22 stolen bases in 1947.

AUGUST 8   A walk–off homer by Bill Nicholson in the eleventh inning beats the Reds 2–1 at
              Wrigley Field. Earlier in the at–bat, a fan hindered Cincinnati catcher Ray Mueller's
              attempt to catch Nicholson's pop–up, but umpire George Magerkurth refused to
              call interference. To add to the bizarre afternoon, the Cubs pulled off a triple play
              in the seventh inning, and stranded 17 runners, 16 of them in the first nine innings.

              *Nicholson shook off a two–year slump to hit 26 homers in 1947. After leading
              the NL in homers in 1943 and 1944, Nicholson hit only .235 with 21 homers
              in 855 at–bats in 1945 and 1946. It was later discovered that he suffered from
              diabetes, which affected his eyesight.*

AUGUST 23   With injuries sidelining middle infielders Don Johnson and Lennie Merullo, the
              Cubs activate 39–year–old coach Billy Jurges.

AUGUST 25   Two days after being reactivated as a player, Billy Jurges belts a two–run homer in
              the tenth inning to defeat the Giants 9–7 in New York. The homer was the last of
              the 43 that Jurges struck during a 17–year career.

AUGUST 30   In the last season of his 16–year career, Stan Hack is showered with gifts prior to a
              6–5 loss to the Pirates at Wrigley Field.

              *Among the gifts was a 1948 Cadillac valued at $3,500, a $1,000 television set,
              a freezer, a fishing reel, a rifle, and an engraved mahogany humidor filled with
              50–cent cigars.*

SEPTEMBER 1   Bob Chipman pitches the Cubs to a 1–0 win in the first game of a double–header at
              Wrigley Field. After being shut out in the opener, Cincinnati scored 10 runs in the
              first inning of the second contest and won 13–2. The Chicago starter in the second
              contest was Ox Miller, who was making his Cubs debut and failed to retire any of
              the five batters he faced. Miller previously pitched in the majors for the Senators
              and the Browns.

SEPTEMBER 7   Ox Miller's grand slam in the second inning off Kirby Higbe of the Pirates accounts
              for all of the Cubs runs in a 4–3 win at Pittsburgh. It was Miller's first at–bat as a
              Cub. He wasn't the winning pitcher, however, because he was relieved after allowing
              three runs in the third.

              *This was Miller's only homer in 27 at–bats over a four–season major league
              career. He played in only four games as a Cub, and had a 1–2 record and a
              10.13 ERA.*

SEPTEMBER 9   For the second game in a row, a grand slam accounts for all of the Cubs runs in a
              4–3 victory, this one over the Dodgers at Wrigley Field. Cliff Aberson hit the homer
              off Vic Lombardi, wiping out a 3–0 Brooklyn lead.

SEPTEMBER 17 Bill Nicholson hits a two–run walk–off homer in the ninth inning to defeat the
              Giants 12–10 in the second game of a double–header at Wrigley Field. It was his
              fourth hit of the game. The Cubs took a 10–4 lead with five runs in the eighth
              inning, but allowed the Giants to tie the contest 10–10 with six runs in top of the
              ninth. New York won the first game 9–3.

SEPTEMBER 23   The Cubs score all seven of their runs in the fourth inning of a 7–2 trimming of the Reds in Cincinnati.

> *On the same day, Cubs pitcher Russ Meyer settled a lawsuit in which he paid an undisclosed sum to a Chicago waitress. At a restaurant in June 1947, Meyer asked Kay Gidd for a date, but she spurned his offer. According to Miss Gidd, Meyer bit her on the nose and inflicted other injuries.*

SEPTEMBER 28   On the last day of the season, Hank Borowy acts as a courtesy runner for Bill Nicholson during a 3–0 win over the Cardinals at Wrigley Field. In the third inning, Nicholson tore up a shoe sliding into third base. While Nicholson was replacing his footwear, Borowy ran for him, and Nicholson was allowed to remain in the game with the approval of Cardinals manager Eddie Dyer and the umpires.

OCTOBER 8   The Cubs sell Marv Rickert to the Reds.

1948   Cubs

Season in a Sentence

P. K. Wrigley issues a public apology in September after a youth movement fails and the Cubs collapse into last place with a club record for defeats in a season.

Finish • Won • Lost • Pct • GB

Eighth   64   90   .416   27.5

Manager

Charlie Grimm

Stats

Stats	Cubs	NL	Rank
Batting Avg:	.262	.261	5
On–Base Pct:	.322	.333	6
Slugging Pct:	.369	.383	6
Home Runs:	87		8
Stolen Bases:	39		7
ERA:	4.00	3.95	5
Fielding Avg:	.972	.974	7
Runs Scored:	597		6
Runs Allowed:	706		6

Starting Lineup

Bob Scheffing, c
Eddie Waitkus, 1b
Hank Schenz, 2b
Andy Pafko, 3b
Roy Smalley, ss
Peanuts Lowrey, lf
Hal Jeffcoat, cf
Bill Nicholson, rf
Phil Cavaretta, 1b–lf
Emil Verban, 2b
Clarence Maddern, lf
Clyde McCullough, c
Rube Walker, c
Gene Mauch, 2b–ss

Pitchers

Johnny Schmitz, sp
Russ Meyer, sp
Dutch McCall, sp–rp
Ralph Hamner, sp
Doyle Lade, sp–rp
Jess Dobernic, rp
Hank Borowy, rp–sp
Bob Rush, rp–sp
Cliff Chambers, rp–sp

Attendance

1,237,792 (fifth in NL)

Club Leaders

Batting Avg:	Pafko	.312
On–Base Pct:	Pafko	.375
Slugging Pct:	Pafko	.516
Home Runs:	Pafko	26
RBI:	Pafko	101
Runs:	Waitkus	87
Stolen Bases:	Waitkus	11
Wins:	Schmitz	18
Strikeouts:	Schmitz	100
ERA:	Schmitz	2.64
Saves:	Chipman	4

APRIL 16   In the first game ever telecast over WGN–TV, the White Sox defeat the Cubs 4–1 in
            an exhibition game at Wrigley Field. Jack Brickhouse was at the microphone.

            *WGN–TV began the station's long association with Chicago baseball by tele-
            casting all of the home games of both the Cubs and the White Sox in 1948.
            Brickhouse covered both teams. WIND, with Bert Wilson handling the
            play–by–play, handled the radio broadcasts of the Cubs.*

APRIL 20   In the year's first regular season game, the Cubs lose 3–2 to the Pirates in Pitts-
            burgh. The Cubs took a 2–1 lead in the fourth inning on Phil Cavaretta's home run
            but couldn't hold the advantage.

APRIL 23   Johnny Schmitz pitches a two–hitter, but the Cubs lose 1–0 to the Cardinals in the
            first game of the season at Wrigley Field before a crowd of 26,591. A double by
            Ralph LaPointe in the ninth inning drove in the lone run of the game.

APRIL 24   On the day that the Berlin airlift begins in Germany, Bill Nicholson hits a long
            home run off Al Brazle of the Cardinals during a 6–2 win at Wrigley Field.

            *No one has ever hit the center field scoreboard at Wrigley Field since it was
            erected in 1938, but Nicholson came close. The drive passed the right field side
            of the scoreboard, struck a building, and hit the hood of a southbound car on
            Sheffield Avenue.*

APRIL 25   Russ Meyer pitches a one–hitter to defeat the Cardinals 3–1 at Wrigley Field. The
            only St. Louis hit was a single by Whitey Kurowski in the second inning. Meyer
            retired 22 batters in a row from the second inning through the ninth.

MAY 14   Russ Meyer pitches the Cubs to a 1–0 win over the Reds at Wrigley Field. Andy
            Pafko accounted for the lone run of the game with a home run in the eighth inning
            off Kent Peterson.

MAY 16   The Cubs come from nine runs down to tie the Reds, only to lose 13–11 in ten
            innings at Wrigley Field. Cincinnati led 10–1 in the third inning and 11–7 later in
            the contest before the Cubs scored three runs in the eighth inning and one in the
            ninth to go to extra innings. Andy Pafko collected five hits, including two homers
            and a double, in five at–bats.

MAY 23   Making the first start of his major league career, Cubs catcher Rube Walker suffers
            a concussion in the first inning of the second game of a double–header against the
            Braves in Boston when struck in the head on a pitch by Vern Bickford. Walker was
            carried off the field on a stretcher. The Cubs lost both contests 8–5 and 12–4.

MAY 31   A Wrigley Field record paid attendance of 46,965 watches the Cubs win 4–3 and
            lose 4–2 against the Pirates in a double–header.

JUNE 1   The Cubs play a Chicago police team for the benefit of injured World War II veterans
            at Hines Hospital. The Cubs led 10–0 when the contest was called after seven innings.

JUNE 2   The Cubs and the Phillies battled through ten scoreless innings before the Cubs win
            2–1 in eleven innings. Both teams scored in the eleventh inning. Phil Cavaretta's sin-

gle drove in the winning run. Dutch McCall pitched the first eleven innings and struck out 11 batters.

In his only big league season, McCall won his first two decisions and his last two, but in between he lost a Chicago Cubs record 13 consecutive games to finish the year at 4–13.

JUNE 15
The Detroit Tigers play their first night game at home, leaving the Cubs as the only team in the majors without lights, a distinction they would hold until 1988.

Bob Chipman missed playing time in June and July with an infected foot because he trimmed a callous too closely.

JULY 6
The Cubs win a free–hitting contest 12–10 in St. Louis, called at the end of eight innings at 11:46 P.M. to allow the Cubs to catch a train to Chicago for an afternoon game against the Reds the following day.

JULY 10
Johnny Schmitz pitches a two–hitter to defeat the Pirates 4–2 at Wrigley Field. Clyde Kluttz had both hits with a double and a single and drove in both Pittsburgh runs.

Johnny Schmitz had an 18–13 record and a 2.64 ERA in 1948.

JULY 11
A Cubs pitcher throws a two–hitter for the second game in a row against the Pirates, as Russ Meyer guides the Cubs to a 1–0 win at Wrigley Field. The only Pittsburgh hits were singles by Stan Rojek in the first inning and Frankie Gustine in the seventh. The only run of the game was scored on a home run by Andy Pafko in the seventh inning off Tiny Bonham.

Pafko had a .312 batting average, 26 homers, and 101 RBIs in 1948.

JULY 16
The Cubs win a dramatic 3–2 decision over the Phillies in the first game of a double–header at Wrigley Field. Chicago trailed 2–1 with the bases loaded in the ninth inning when Robin Roberts hit Phil Cavaretta and Andy Pafko with consecutive pitches. Philadelphia won the second game 6–4.

AUGUST 5
Gene Hermanski hits three homers off Cubs pitching during a 6–4 Brooklyn win at Ebbets Field.

AUGUST 26
A near–riot erupts at Wrigley Field when umpire Jocko Conlan credits Phil Cavaretta with a ground–rule double instead of an inside–the–park homer in the third inning of the second game of a double–header with the Braves leading 1–0 on a 95–degree day at Wrigley Field. Cavaretta's drive bounced into the ivy, stuck there for about ten seconds, then fell to the ground. Boston left fielder Jeff Heath didn't see the ball drop and kept looking for it in the ivy when it was actually down by his foot. The ball was in full view of the bleacher fans. Play was held up for twenty minutes as the field was showered with straw hats, hot dog wrappers, fruit, and bottles, and Conlan chewed out a Chicago policeman for not taking action. At one point, there were several hundred fans on the field. When order was restored, Andy Pafko was intentionally walked, setting off another barrage of debris, before Peanuts Lowrey cleared the bases with a triple that Heath had to chase into the left field corner. The Cubs went on to win the contest 5–2. Chicago also won the first game 5–1.

AUGUST 28   The Braves beat the Cubs 5–4 on a fluke three–run homer by Jeff Heath in the ninth inning at Wrigley Field. Center fielder Hal Jeffcoat crashed into the wall chasing the drive and was knocked unconscious. Before left fielder Peanuts Lowrey could retrieve the ball, Heath circled the bases for an inside–the–park homer. It was a memorable day all around for Jeffcoat, because earlier in the day, Jeffcoat's wife presented him with their second son, John Philip Jeffcoat.

Jeffcoat was an outfielder for the Cubs from 1948 through 1953. In 1954, he was converted to pitching and became a successful reliever. In 1955, Jeffcoat had a 2.95 ERA in 50 games for the Cubs before he was traded to the Reds.

AUGUST 30   P. K. Wrigley apologizes to the fans in a paid advertisement published in all of the Chicago newspapers. It read, in part: "The Cub management wants you to know we appreciate the wonderful support you are giving the ball club. We want to have a winning team that can be at the top the kind you deserve. This year's rebuilding job has been a flop. But we are not content to just go along with an eye only to attendance. We want a winner just as you do and will do everything in our power to get one."

AUGUST 31   Hank Borowy pitches a one–hitter to defeat the Dodgers 3–0 in the first game of a double–header before 45,531 at Wrigley Field. The only Brooklyn base runner was Gene Hermanski, who singled in the second inning but was retired on a stolen base attempt. Borowy faced the minimum 27 batters.

SEPTEMBER 6   Emil Verban hits the first homer of his career, although the Cubs lose 3–1 to the Reds in the first game of a double–header in Cincinnati. The home run, struck off Johnny Vander Meer, proved to be the only homer during Verban's career, which spanned 853 games and 2,911 at–bats from 1944 through 1950. In another statistical oddity, Verban drew only 108 walks and struck out just 74 times during his career. He played for the Cubs in 1948 and 1949. The Cubs won the second game, called by darkness after eight innings, 6–2.

Hank Borowy wrapped up his Cubs career with five wins in 1948, including a one–hitter to beat the Dodgers.

SEPTEMBER 21   Andy Pafko hits a three–run homer in the ninth inning and Johnny Schmitz pitches a two–hitter to beat the Giants 3–2 in the second game of a double–header at the Polo Grounds. The win broke a 10–game losing streak. Schmitz had a no–hitter until opposing pitcher Red Webb singled in the eighth. Whitey Lockman homered in the ninth. New York won the first game 3–2.

The losing season inspired a classic painting by Norman Rockwell. On the cover of the September 24, 1948, issue of THE SATURDAY EVENING POST was a Rockwell painting called BOTTOM OF THE NINTH. The painting showed a line of chagrined Cubs slumping in the dugout while fans in the seats above smirked, jeered, and blew raspberries. In the foreground, the Cubs batboy stood forlorn, his cap askew. Behind him in the dugout was the manager, based on Charlie Grimm, holding his huge right hand against his cheek.

SEPTEMBER 25   The Cubs score three runs with two out in the ninth inning to beat the Cardinals 3–2 at Wrigley Field. Emil Verban's RBI single broke the 2–2 tie.

SEPTEMBER 30   Cliff Chambers pitches the Cubs to a 1–0 win over the Reds at Wrigley Field. The lone run of the game was scored on a sacrifice fly by Hal Jeffcoat.

OCTOBER 3   In the final game of the season, Cubs outfielder Carmen Mauro collects his first major league hit with an inside–the–park home run during a 4–3 win over the Cardinals in St. Louis.

The 1948 World Series between the Boston Braves and Cleveland Indians was the first one shown on Chicago television. Only the games from Cleveland were telecast in Chicago, however, because it was not yet possible to transmit images from Boston to the Midwest. The first World Series telecast was in 1947 between the Yankees and Dodgers, but it was seen only on stations in New York, Philadelphia, Washington, and Schenectady, New York.

OCTOBER 4   The Cubs trade Bill Nicholson to the Phillies for Harry Walker.

Nicholson played five more years as a utility outfielder for the Phillies.

OCTOBER 11   The Cubs sell Russ Meyer to the Phillies.

The Cubs gave up on Meyer too soon, largely because of his explosive temper, which earned him the nickname "The Mad Monk." He could pitch when he had his head in the game, however, and was 17–8 for the 1949 Phillies and 15–5 for the pennant–winning Dodgers in 1953.

DECEMBER 8   One month after Harry Truman upsets Thomas Dewey in the presidential election, the Cubs trade Clyde McCullough and Cliff Chambers to the Pirates for Frankie Gustine and Cal McLish.

McLish's chief claim to fame as a Cub is having the longest name in the history of the franchise. His name at birth in 1925 in Anadarko, Oklahoma, was Calvin Coolidge Julius Caesar Tuskahoma McLish.

DECEMBER 14   In the third 1948 off–season deal with the Phillies, the Cubs trade Eddie Waitkus and Hank Borowy to the Phillies for Dutch Leonard and Monk Dubiel.

Waitkus was the Phillies starting first baseman for four years, while Leonard, who was 40 years old on opening day in 1949, was an important part of the Cubs pitching staff for four seasons.

1949
Cubs

Season in a Sentence

The Cubs set a club record for most defeats in a season for the second year in a row.

Finish • Won • Lost • Pct • GB

Eighth   61   93   .396   36.0

Managers

Charlie Grimm (19–31) and Frankie Frisch (42–62)

Stats

Stats	Cubs •	NL •	Rank
Batting Avg:	.256	.262	7
On–Base Pct:	.312	.334	8
Slugging Pct:	.373	.389	7
Home Runs:	97	7	
Stolen Bases:	53	2	
ERA:	4.50	4.04	7
Fielding Avg:	.970	.975	8
Runs Scored:	593		8
Runs Allowed:	773		8

Starting Lineup

Mickey Owen, c
Herman Reich, 1b
Emil Verban, 2b
Frankie Gustine, 3b
Roy Smalley, ss
Hank Sauer, lf
Andy Pafko, cf–3b
Hal Jeffcoat, rf–cf
Phil Cavaretta, 1b
Bob Ramazzotti, 3b
Hank Edwards, rf–lf
Rube Walker, c
Frankie Baumholtz, rf
Harry Walker, lf–rf
Gene Mauch, 2b–ss
Bob Scheffing, c

Pitchers

Johnny Schmitz, sp
Bob Rush, sp
Dutch Leonard, sp
Monk Dubiel, sp–rp
Bob Chipman, rp
Doyle Lade, rp–sp
Warren Hacker, sp
Dewey Adkins, rp

Attendance

1,143,139 (fifth in NL)

Club Leaders

Batting Avg:	Sauer	.291
On–Base Pct:	Pafko	.369
Slugging Pct:	Sauer	.571
Home Runs:	Sauer	27
RBI:	Sauer	83
Runs:	Pafko	79
Stolen Bases:	Jeffcoat	12
Wins:	Schmitz	11
Strikeouts:	Leonard	83
ERA:	Rush	4.07
Saves:	Rush	4
	Dubiel	4

APRIL 19   In the first game of the season, the Cubs lose 1–0 to the Pirates before 29,392 at Wrigley Field. Rip Sewell pitched the Pittsburgh shutout. It was his third Opening Day shutout against the Cubs, following whitewashings in 1943 and 1947. Dutch Leonard pitched the complete game for the Cubs in his debut with the club.

All Cubs home games were on three television stations in 1949. Jack Brickhouse announced the games on WGN, Joe Wilson covered the club on WBKB, and Rogers Hornsby did the play–by–play on WENR (now WLS–TV). There were afternoons when those three stations were the only ones on the air in Chicago, and the Cubs were telecast on all three. By 1952, the competition had fallen aside, and WGN–TV had exclusive rights to Cubs telecasts.

APRIL 23   The Cubs score eight runs in the seventh inning to take an 11–5 lead and go on to defeat the Cardinals 11–7 in St. Louis.

The Cubs integrated their minor league system in 1949 with the signing of African–American pitcher Booker McDaniel. He failed to reach the majors, however. The first African–American to play for the Cubs was Ernie Banks in 1953.

APRIL 30   With the Cubs leading 3–2 with two out in the ninth, Rocky Nelson of the Cardinals is credited with a bizarre home run that produces two tallies and a 4–3 victory over the Cubs at Wrigley Field. Chicago center fielder Andy Pafko, thinking he had made the final out of the game with a diving somersault catch off his shoetops, held the ball while Nelson circled the bases for an "inside–the–glove" homer.

Pafko ran toward the Cubs dugout with the ball, believing that the game was over. Second base umpire Al Barlick, in a delayed call, ruled that Pafko had trapped it. Andy, ignoring his teammates' frantic pleas to throw the ball, raced toward the umpire to protest the decision while Nelson circled the bases as the ball was inside of Pafko's glove. Pafko finally made a belated throw home when Nelson was only steps from the plate, and the Cardinal batter was safe with what proved to be the game–winning run. Arguments by the Cubs delayed the game for ten minutes, and the crowd of 30,775 showed its disapproval by showering the field with debris.

MAY 29   The Cubs score nine runs in the sixth inning and defeat the Reds 10–2 in the second game of a double–header at Wrigley Field. Cincinnati won the first game 4–1.

In 1949, a new electronic scoreboard was added on the front of the left field upper deck for the benefit of bleacher fans.

JUNE 6   The Cubs purchase Bob Muncrief from the Pirates.

JUNE 10   With the Cubs holding a record of 19–31, Frankie Frisch succeeds Charlie Grimm as manager.

Grimm wasn't fired, but instead was promoted to an executive position as vice president in charge of player operations, including the farm system. Jim Gallagher, who had been the general manager, had player operations taken away from his job description and handled only the business side of the operation. A future Hall of Famer, Frisch starred as a second baseman with the Giants and Cardinals from 1919 through 1938 and played in eight World Series. He was the manager of the Cardinals from 1933 through 1938, winning a world championship in 1934. Frisch also managed the Pirates from 1940 until 1946. After leaving the Pirates, Frisch vowed he was "through forever with managing," but he took the Cubs job against the advice of his wife and close friends. The Cubs lost their first six games under Frisch and showed no noticeable improvement before he was fired in 1951.

JUNE 14   Phillies first baseman Eddie Waitkus is shot with a .22–caliber rifle in Room 1297A of the Edgewater Beach Hotel in Chicago by 19–year–old Ruth Steinhagen. The teenager became obsessed with Waitkus while he played for the Cubs and created a shrine dedicated to the ballplayer in her bedroom. Waitkus was taken to Illinois Masonic Hospital with a bullet in the muscles near his spine and a collapsed right lung. He missed the remainder of the 1949 season, but returned to play in 154 games in 1950. Waitkus refused to press changes, and Steinhagen was confined to a mental institution. She was released in April 1952.

JUNE 15   The Cubs trade Harry Walker and Peanuts Lowrey to the Reds for Hank Sauer and Frankie Baumholtz.

> *This was one of the greatest trades in Cubs history. Sauer was an immediate sensation. In his first 38 games with the club, he hit .359 with 15 homers and 47 RBIs. Sauer played for the Cubs until 1955 and hit 198 home runs. After each homer at Wrigley Field, fans in the bleachers threw packages of Hank's favorite chewing tobacco onto the field. (What he couldn't stuff in his pockets, he stashed in the vines.) Sauer's .512 slugging percentage is the third–highest of any Cub with at least 2,000 plate appearances, trailing only Hack Wilson and Sammy Sosa. Sauer was the National League Most Valuable Player in 1952. Baumholtz also played for the Cubs until 1955 and hit .295 in 635 games. A versatile athlete, he played for the Cleveland Rebels in 1946–47 in the inaugural season of the NBA and averaged 14.0 points per game.*

JULY 9   An old–timers game is held at Wrigley Field, including future Hall of Famers Gabby Hartnett, Rogers Hornsby, Max Carey, Red Faber, Ray Schalk, and Ted Lyons. It was part of a scheduled triple–header. The game was preceded by a softball game featuring movie actors Albert Dekker, Eddie Bracken, Sonny Tufts, Buddy Rogers, and William Boyd. A game between city and suburban high school all–stars was postponed by rain.

JULY 20   Hank Sauer drives in all four runs of a 4–3, eleven–inning win over the Phillies in Philadelphia. Sauer hit a two–run homer in the fourth and a solo home run in the sixth, both off Robin Roberts, and a triple off Curt Simmons in the eleventh.

AUGUST 4   The Cubs win 1–0 on a homer by Andy Pafko in the second inning off Larry Jansen against the Giants at Wrigley Field. Johnny Schmitz pitched the shutout and carried a no–hitter into the eighth inning before allowing three hits.

AUGUST 10 Roy Smalley drives in both runs of a 2–0 win over the Pirates at Wrigley Field with a bases–loaded double in the fifth inning. Doyle Lade pitched the shutout.

> *Smalley was a constant source of frustration for Cubs fans while he played for the Cubs from 1948 through 1953. He had solid power for a shortstop with 61 career homers in 2,644 at–bats, but his lifetime batting average was only .227 and he struck out frequently, leading the league in the category in 1950. Defensively, Smalley had great range, but a scatter–gun arm. During the early 1950s, the Cubs' double–play combination was derisively referred to as "Miksis to Smalley to Addison Street." In the only three seasons he played in more than 100 games at shortstop, Smalley led the NL in errors, most of them on throws. In 1950 he became the only Cub in history to join the "20–50" club: 21 home runs and 51 errors.*

AUGUST 15 Frankie Frisch orders the team to take batting practice following a 5–2 loss to the Cardinals at Wrigley Field.

> *The batting drill didn't last very long. Many of the 2,638 youngsters, who were admitted free of charge, remained to watch. They soon swarmed the field despite efforts to stop them and chased after the balls, abruptly ending the practice.*

SEPTEMBER 3   The Cubs explode for nine runs in the eighth inning to take an 11–5 lead and go on to defeat the Pirates 11–7 at Wrigley Field.

SEPTEMBER 9   The Cubs erupt for another high–scoring inning against the Pirates, plating seven runs in the fifth inning for an 8–1 win in Pittsburgh. Andy Pafko hit a grand slam off Ray Poat. It was Pafko's second grand slam in six days. On both of them, Phil Cavaretta, Roy Smalley, and Hank Sauer were on base.

SEPTEMBER 14   The Cubs sell Frankie Gustine to the Athletics.

SEPTEMBER 16   The Cubs win 5–4 against the Giants at Wrigley Field on a tenth–inning run despite two batters hitting out of order.

The mix–up in the Cubs' batting order came after a flurry of pinch–hitters and pinch–runners in the ninth. Relief pitcher Bob Rush should have been batting in the eighth spot and Verban ninth, but Verban batted in the eighth slot in the tenth inning with two out and runners on second and third. Verban walked to load the bases and should have been the third out of the inning since he hit out of turn. Owen, pinch–hitting for Rush and also batting out of order, singled for the win. None of the Giants, including their usually astute manager Leo Durocher, detected the violation, and the victory stood.

OCTOBER 14   Three weeks after President Harry Truman announces that the Soviet Union developed and tested an atomic bomb, the Cubs purchase Paul Minner and Preston Ward from the Dodgers for $100,000.

Despite a 62–79 record in seven seasons as a Cub, Minner was a consistent, above–average pitcher saddled with pitching for some awful clubs. Minner and Ward combined weren't worth $100,000 in 1949 baseball dollars, however, as the Cubs had their pockets picked by Dodgers general manager Branch Rickey.

DECEMBER 14   The Cubs send Gene Mauch and cash to the Braves for Bill Voiselle.

Voiselle's only distinction as a Cub was wearing number 96 on his jersey because he hailed from the tiny town of Ninety–Six, South Carolina.

Wrigley Field wasn't a happy scene for Cubs fans through most of 1949, as the team set a club record for losses with 93.

THE STATE OF THE CUBS

The 1950s was the worst decade in Cubs history. None of the ten teams fielded by the club posted a winning record. Overall, the Cubs were 672–866. The winning percentage of .437 was seventh among the eight teams in the National League. The Pirates ranked eighth, but by the end of the 1950s, Pittsburgh was building a club that would win a world championship in 1960 while the Cubs were still struggling. National League pennant winners during the 1950s were the Phillies (1950), Giants (1951 and 1954), Dodgers (1952, 1953, 1955, 1956, and 1959), and Braves (1957 and 1958).

THE BEST TEAM

The 1952 club was the only one that didn't finish with a losing record, landing in fifth place with a mark of 77–77.

THE WORST TEAM

With plenty to choose from, the worst was the 1956 outfit, which had a record of 60–94.

THE BEST MOMENT

Ernie Banks won his second consecutive Most Valuable Player award in 1959, proving that nice guys can finish first.

THE WORST MOMENT

P. K. Wrigley publicly admonished director of player personnel Wid Matthews during a bizarre press conference in 1952.

THE ALL–DECADE TEAM • YEARS WITH CUBS

Sammy Taylor, c	1958–62
Dee Fondy, 1b	1951–57
Gene Baker, 2b	1953–57
Randy Jackson, 3b	1950–55; 1959
Ernie Banks, ss	1953–71
Hank Sauer, lf	1949–55
Andy Pafko, cf	1943–51
Walt Moryn, rf	1956–60
Bob Rush, p	1948–57
Paul Minner, p	1950–56
Warren Hacker, p	1948–56
Don Elston, p	1953; 1957–64

Banks won two MVP awards and made the Hall of Fame on the first ballot, while no one else on the 1950s All–Decade Team will ever get a whiff of Cooperstown, although Pafko, Rush, Sauer, Baker, Jackson, Moryn, and Elston each played in the All–Star Game. Sauer was the NL MVP in 1952. Outfielder Frank Bamumholtz (1949; 1951–55) was another prominent Cub during the decade. Sammy Taylor played in only 376 games as a Cub, and not very well at that, but makes the team as the catcher because he was the only backstop to hold down the job for more than a year. The Cubs used 22 catchers during the 1950s while changing the starter nearly every year. No one played in at least 100 games in a season as a catcher for the Cubs in consecutive years from the time Gabby Hartnett did it eight years in a row from 1930 through 1937 until Randy Hundley accomplished the feat from 1966 through 1969.

THE DECADE LEADERS

Batting Avg:	Baumholtz	.300
On–Base Pct:	Banks	.355
Slugging Pct:	Banks	.558
Home Runs:	Banks	228
RBI:	Banks	661
Runs:	Banks	582
Stolen Bases:	Fondy	66
Wins:	Rush	95
Strikeouts:	Rush	924
ERA:	Rush	3.65
Saves:	Leonard	28
	Lown	28

THE HOME FIELD

By the 1950s, Wrigley Field was still the most beautiful ballpark in the majors, but it was badly in need of repairs. In a modernization program, new entrances were built to provide better flow in and out of the park. Also, aluminum–and–concrete ticket booths were constructed on both Sheffield and Addison.

THE GAME YOU WISH YOU HAD SEEN

Sam Jones pitched a dramatic no–hitter against the Pirates at Wrigley Field on May 12, 1955. Jones walked the first three batters he faced in the ninth inning, then fanned three in a row.

THE WAY THE GAME WAS PLAYED

The number of home runs continued to rise during the 1950s, with NL teams averaging 140 homers per year, compared to 80 per year in the 1930s. The number of complete games continued to decline, from an average of 62 per club in 1950 to 47 in 1959. Relievers were making more appearances, and the relief specialist emerged, including such Cubs as Dutch Leonard, Turk Lown, and Don Elston. The increased use of relievers to close out victories led to a new statistic called the "save," although it wasn't officially recognized by Major League Base-ball until 1969. Games were also taking longer to play. The average length of a game rose from 2:23 to 2:38. In addition, the Cubs employed African–American players for the first time with the addition of Ernie Banks and Gene Baker to the roster in 1953. Lastly, the first franchise shifts in more than 50 years took place during the decade. In the NL, the Braves moved from Boston to Milwaukee in 1953, and the Dodgers and Giants moved from New York to Califor-nia at the end of the 1957 season.

THE MANAGEMENT

Wid Matthews was in charge of trades and the farm system at the start of the decade and was fired after the 94–loss season in 1956. John Holland suc-ceeded Matthews and held the job until 1975. P. K. Wrigley made the major decisions, however, and the two general managers were often reduced to the role of "yes men" with little authority. Guiding the club in the dugout was Frankie Frisch (1949–51), Phil Cavaretta (1951–53), Stan Hack (1954–56), and Bob Scheffing (1957–59).

THE BEST PLAYER MOVE

The best move by far was the purchase of Ernie Banks from the Kansas City Monarchs of the Negro League in 1953. The best trade with a major league club was made with the Pirates in 1957 and brought Dale Long and Lee Walls to Chicago for Gene Baker and Dee Fondy. That Long and Walls were the best players the Cubs were able to acquire in a trade speaks volumes to the club's lack of success.

THE WORST PLAYER MOVE

The swap of Andy Pafko to the Dodgers in June 1951 is the trade that has lived the longest in the memory of Cubs fans, but the worst deal sent Smoky Burgess to the Reds in October 1951. If he had stayed in Chicago, Burgess would have been the Cubs starting catcher for at least ten years.

1950s

1950

Cubs

Season in a Sentence

The Cubs are on the positive side of .500 in early July, but possess little beyond a home run–hitting lineup, and finish seventh.

Finish • Won • Lost • Pct • GB

Seventh   64   89   .418   26.5

Manager

Frankie Frisch

Stats   Cubs • NL • Rank

Stats	Cubs	NL	Rank
Batting Avg:	.248	.261	8
On–Base Pct:	.315	.336	8
Slugging Pct:	.401	.401	4
Home Runs:	161		2
Stolen Bases:	46		3
ERA:	4.28	4.14	5
Fielding Avg:	.968	.975	8
Runs Scored:	643		8
Runs Allowed:	772		7

Starting Lineup

Mickey Owen, c
Preston Ward, 1b
Wayne Terwilliger, 2b
Bill Serena, 3b
Roy Smalley, ss
Hank Sauer, lf
Andy Pafko, cf
Bob Borkowski, rf–cf
Phil Cavaretta, 1b
Rube Walker, c
Carmen Mauro, rf–lf
Hal Jeffcoat, rf

Pitchers

Bob Rush, sp
Johnny Schmitz, sp–rp
Paul Minner, sp–rp
Monk Dubiel, rp–sp
Frank Hiller, rp–sp
Doyle Lade, rp–sp
Johnny Klippstein, rp–sp

Attendance

1,165,944 (fourth in NL)

Club Leaders

Batting Avg:	Pafko	.312
On–Base Pct:	Pafko	.397
Slugging Pct:	Pafko	.591
Home Runs:	Pafko	36
RBI:	Sauer	103
Runs:	Pafko	95
Stolen Bases:	Terwillnger	13
Wins:	Rush	13
Strikeouts:	Minner	99
ERA:	Rush	3.71
Saves:	Leonard	6

JANUARY 6   Charlie Grimm resigns as vice president to take a job as manager with the Dallas club in the Texas League.

Grimm and Jim Gallagher were essentially dual general managers, with Grimm in charge of playing personnel and Gallagher handling the business end. The partnership failed to work as the two constantly feuded. Grimm also chafed at being confined to an office and missed being on the field. Charlie returned to the major league level as manager of the Braves from 1952 through 1956.

FEBRUARY 10   The Cubs purchase Johnny Vander Meer from the Reds.

FEBRUARY 18   The Cubs hire Wid Matthews as director of player personnel.

Matthews came to the Cubs after working in the Dodgers' front office under Branch Rickey. Matthews possessed unbridled optimism and enthusiasm, and at the end of each season he stated that the Cubs were only a player or two away from a pennant and boldly predicted that success was just around the corner. He announced a "five–year plan" that would bring the Cubs back to contention. Matthews apparently learned little from Rickey on how to build a pennant–winning team, as the Cubs remained stuck at or near the bottom of the standings until Matthews was fired in 1956. His approach was less than scientific. When asked how he sizes up a prospect, Matthews said: "When I shake hands with a boy and he has a good grip, that's one of the essentials. Then I pat him on the shoulder to see how muscular he is."

APRIL 18   Andy Pafko hits two home runs and drives in four runs in a 9–6 win over the Reds on Opening Day in Cincinnati. Preston Ward, in his debut with the Cubs, also homered with two men on base.

On the same day, the Cubs sold Bob Chipman to the Braves.

APRIL 21   The Cubs beat the Cardinals 2–0 before 22,137 in the first game of the season at Wrigley Field. Bob Rush pitched the shutout.

APRIL 30   Johnny Schmitz pitches 13 innings and allows only four hits, but loses 1–0 to the Cardinals in St. Louis. The only run of the game was scored on a walk–off homer by Del Rice. Schmitz retired 20 batters in a row before Rice homered.

MAY 5   Randy Jackson's walk–off homer in the tenth inning beats the Dodgers 7–6 at Wrigley Field. It was Jackson's first major league home run. Hank Sauer tied the score 6–6 with a three–run homer in the ninth with two out.

Hank Edwards started the game in right field for the Cubs, but had to leave when he became violently ill after swallowing his chewing tobacco.

MAY 18   Rube Walker of the Cubs and Monte Irvin of the Giants both hit grand slams in the sixth inning of a 10–4 New York win at the Polo Grounds. The game was called at the end of the sixth by rain. Walker's slam was hit off Clint Hartung.

MAY 26   Roy Smalley's grand slam off Mel Queen accounts for all four runs of a 4–0 win over the Pirates in Pittsburgh.

JUNE 1   Cubs trainer Andy Lotshaw is knocked to the floor when a bolt of lightning strikes the clubhouse at Wrigley Field during a rain delay in a game against the Phillies. Lotshaw was seated on a trunk near the window and was stunned for a few minutes before regaining his faculties.

JUNE 4   The Cubs trounce the Dodgers 13–8 at Wrigley Field.

JUNE 7   The Cubs trade Bob Scheffing to the Reds for Ron Northey.

JUNE 13   Roy Smalley hits a home run in the eleventh inning to beat the Dodgers 6–3 in Brooklyn.

The Cubs faced the problem of playing without their uniforms when they arrived in Brooklyn for the June 13 game. The club's baggage was accidentally placed on the wrong train en route from Chicago, and long–distance calls finally located the equipment in Harrisburg, Pennsylvania. Flown to Brooklyn, the uniforms arrived shortly before game time.

JUNE 25   The Cubs explode for seven runs in the ninth inning to break a 4–4 tie, then survive a four–run Phillie rally to win 11–8 in the first game of a double–header at Shibe Park.

Hank Sauer led the way with two homers and two doubles. Philadelphia won the second game 2–1.

Hank Sauer was one of the Cubs' few stars in 1950. He hit 32 homers, good for third in the NL.

On the same day, the Korean War started when North Korea attacked South Korea. Although the military draft during the war claimed such stars as Ted Williams and Willie Mays, the Cubs weren't adversely affected. Among the Cubs in the service were Carl Sawatski and Preston Ward in 1951 and 1952, and Harry Chiti in 1953.

JUNE 28   Roy Smalley hits for the cycle during a 15–3 win over the Cardinals at Wrigley Field. Smalley homered in the second inning, doubled in the fourth, singled in the seventh, and tripled in the eighth.

JULY 2   The Cubs rout the Reds 16–0 in Cincinnati.

The victory was the high point of the season. The Cubs had a 32–31 record on July 2 but were 32–58 the rest of the way.

JULY 28–29 Andy Pafko hits a home run on two different dates in the same game during a 12–5 win over the Dodgers in Brooklyn that ended at 1:21 A.M. following two rain delays. Pafko homered both before and after midnight.

Pafko hit 36 homers and batted .304 in 1950.

AUGUST 2   Andy Pafko raps three homers good for five runs batted in, but it's not enough to save the Cubs from an 8–6 defeat at the hands of the Giants in the second game of a double–header at the Polo Grounds. All three homers were struck off Larry Jansen in the first, sixth, and eighth inning. New York also won the first game 11–1.

AUGUST 5   The Cubs win 4–2 against the Braves in Boston on thirteenth–inning home runs by Andy Pafko and Carmen Mauro. Hours after getting married, Roy Smalley went hitless in five at–bats.

Smalley and Jolene Mauch married in Brookline, Massachusetts. The couple met in Chicago in 1948 while Jolene was visiting her brother Gene, then an infielder with the Cubs. Roy and Jolene's son, also named Roy, played in the major leagues as a shortstop from 1975 through 1987. Among the younger Smalley's managers was his uncle, Gene Mauch, from 1976 through 1980 with the Twins.

AUGUST 24   Both the Braves and the Cubs score six runs in the ninth inning at Wrigley Field. When the inning began, Boston led 5–3 and emerged with an 11–9 victory.

AUGUST 28   Hank Sauer hits three consecutive homers to lead the Cubs to a 7–5 win over the Phillies in the first game of a double–header at Wrigley Field. All three were hit off Curt Simmons in the second, fourth, and sixth innings. Philadelphia won the second game 9–5.

In seven consecutive games from August 24 through August 28, including two double–headers, Sauer had 14 hits, including seven homers and five doubles, in 27 at–bats. He scored eight runs and drove in 17. During the 1950 season, Sauer batted .274 and hit 32 homers.

SEPTEMBER 7   Bob Rush pitches a two–hitter to defeat the Cardinals 4–2 at Sportsman's Park. Hal Rice had both St. Louis hits with a single and a home run.

In his third season in the big leagues, Rush was 13–20 in 1950. A better–than–average pitcher playing for mediocre teams, Rush had a record of 110–140 with the Cubs from 1948 through 1957. The only two Cubs pitchers since World War II with more wins than Rush are Ferguson Jenkins (167), Rick Reuschel (135), and Greg Maddux (111 through the end of the 2004 season).

SEPTEMBER 19   A two–hit shutout by Frank Hiller and a home run by Hank Sauer off Robin Roberts in the fifth inning gives the Cubs a 1–0 win over the Phillies at Shibe Park. The only Philadelphia hits were singles by Eddie Mayo in the fifth inning and Granny Hamner in the eighth. Each was erased on the base paths, Mayo on a double play and Hamner in a rundown. Hiller faced the minimum 27 batters.

OCTOBER 10   The Cubs send Hank Edwards and cash to the Dodgers for Dee Fondy and Chuck Connors.

The cluelessness of the Cubs front office during the 1950s is evident in this deal, in which the Cubs traded for two first–base prospects to replace Preston Ward, who was purchased ten months earlier from the Dodgers as a first–base prospect. At least Fondy gave the Cubs decent production and was the starter at first from 1952 until he was traded to the Pirates in 1957. Connors played only 67 games in the majors, 66 of them with the Cubs, and hit only two homers along with a .238 batting average, but he had had a long and fascinating life. Before reaching the big leagues in baseball, Connors played for the Boston Celtics from 1946 through 1948. Prior to the first game in Celtics history on November 5, 1946, the six–foot–five Connors shattered the glass backboard in pre–game warm–ups, delaying the contest for a half–hour. While playing in Los Angeles in the Cubs minor league system, he caught the attention of a Hollywood producer and went into acting. Chuck's film debut was in 1952 in the Spencer Tracy–Katherine Hepburn vehicle PAT AND MIKE. Connors was Luke McCain, the lead character on the popular television series THE RIFLEMAN from 1957 through 1962. He appeared in numerous movies and television dramas until his death in 1992, and won critical acclaim in the role of a slave owner in the 1977 mini–series ROOTS.

NOVEMBER 16   The Cubs draft Turk Lown from the Dodgers organization.

1951

Season in a Sentence

Despite a winning record through June 5 and a July 21 managerial change, the Cubs topple back into last place.

Finish • Won • Lost • Pct • GB

Eighth   62   92   .403   34.5

Managers

Frankie Frisch (35–45) and Phil Cavaretta (27–47)

Stats

Stats	Cubs	• NL •	Rank
Batting Avg:	.250	.260	7
On–Base Pct:	.315	.331	7
Slugging Pct:	.364	.390	7
Home Runs:	103		6
Stolen Bases:	63		3 (tie)
ERA:	4.34	3.96	7
Fielding Avg:	.971	.975	8
Runs Scored:	614		7
Runs Allowed:	750		7

Starting Lineup

Smoky Burgess, c
Chuck Connors, 1b
Eddie Miksis, 2b
Randy Jackson, 3b
Roy Smalley, ss
Hank Sauer, lf
Hal Jeffcoat, cf–rf
Frank Baumholtz, rf–cf
Gene Hermanski, rf
Phil Cavaretta, 1b
Wayne Terwilliger, 2b
Andy Pafko, cf
Dee Fondy, 1b
Jack Cusick, ss
Bob Ramazzotti, ss

Pitchers

Bob Rush, sp
Paul Minner, sp
Frank Hiller, sp
Turk Lown, sp–rp
Cal McLish, sp–rp
Bob Schultz, sp–rp
Dutch Leonard, rp
Bob Kelly, rp–sp
Johnny Klippstein, rp–sp

Attendance

894,415 (sixth in NL)

Club Leaders

Club Leaders		
Batting Avg:	Baumholtz	.284
On–Base Pct:	Baumholtz	.346
Slugging Pct:	Sauer	.466
Home Runs:	Sauer	30
RBI:	Sauer	89
Runs:	Jackson	78
Stolen Bases:	Jackson	15
Wins:	Rush	11
Strikeouts:	Rush	129
ERA:	Minner	3.79
Saves:	Leonard	3

APRIL 17   Six days after President Harry Truman removes General Douglas MacArthur from his command in Korea, the Cubs defeat the Reds 8–3 before 18,211 at Wrigley Field. Dee Fondy, in his first major league plate appearance, hit a bases–loaded triple and later added two singles. Andy Pafko had a homer, a triple and a single. Frank Baumholtz also had three hits. Frank Hiller pitched the complete–game victory.

MAY 3   Andy Pafko hits a grand slam off Max Surkont of the Braves in the sixth inning of a 9–3 Cubs win in Boston.

Newly acquired Dee Fondy tripled in his first big–league plate appearance in April 1951. He collected three hits in the game.

During the late–1940s and early–1950s, the owners of the eight Pacific Coast

League franchises wanted to become a third major league. At the time, the league had teams in Los Angeles, Hollywood, San Francisco, Oakland, San Diego, Seattle, Sacramento, and Portland. P. K. Wrigley owned the Los Angeles club and had a vested interest in the outcome. "If I had to choose between selling the Chicago and Los Angeles franchise," said Wrigley in 1951, "I would sell the Chicago Cubs. I believe Los Angeles has the greater future." Wrigley thought that Los Angeles needed to build a first-class public transportation system before it could support a major league team, however. "I've never seen a metropolitan area so dependent on automobiles," said Wrigley.

MAY 12   The Cubs score seven runs in the first inning and defeat the Pirates 8–4 in Pittsburgh.

MAY 18   The Cubs rout the Phillies 18–9 at Wrigley Field. On the way to the win, the Cubs scored seven runs in the fourth inning to take a 17–7 lead. The highlight of the inning was an inside-the-park, grand slam homer by Jack Cusick off Ken Johnson.

Cusick hit only two homers in 242 big league at-bats. Both were inside-the-park jobs and came five days apart. The first one was on May 13, 1951, off Murry Dickson of the Pirates in a 6–0 win at Pittsburgh.

JUNE 6   Smoky Burgess has all three Cubs hits off Robin Roberts in a 9–1 loss to the Phillies in Philadelphia.

The Cubs entered the game with a 21–20 record. Beginning with this loss, Chicago was 41–72 the rest of the way.

JUNE 15   The Cubs trade Andy Pafko, Johnny Schmitz, Rube Walker, and Wayne Terwilliger to the Dodgers for Joe Hatten, Bruce Edwards, Gene Hermanski, and Eddie Miksis.

A Chicago sportswriter insisted the Cubs must have been "chloroformed" into making this deal. That seemed to be the only explanation as the club traded Pakfo, the best player on the team, along with three others, for four players who were sitting on the Dodgers bench. What's more, Edwards reported with a sore arm and was virtually useless. Despite Wid Matthews's inane proclamation that "Miksis will fix us," this was a bad deal all around. Miksis was the only one of the quartet brought from Brooklyn to Chicago to crack the starting lineup, and then only as a light-hitting stopgap at second base and in center field. Pafko remained in the majors until 1959 and played in the World Series for the Dodgers in 1952 and the Braves in 1957 and 1958. With Pafko gone, there was a revolving door in center field at Wrigley Field for the next two decades as no one was able to hold down the position for long. The first player after 1950 to play at least 100 games in center field for the Cubs in consecutive season was Adolpho Phillips from 1966 through 1968.

JUNE 28   Frank Hiller pitches a one-hitter and faces the minimum 27 batters for an 8–0 win over the Cardinals at Sportsman's Park. It was the second time in less than a year that Hiller faced 27 batters in a nine-inning complete game (see September 19, 1950). The only two St. Louis base runners were Tommy Glaviano on a walk in the second inning and Enos Slaughter on a single in the fifth. Both were erased on double plays.

JULY 1   Paul Minner pitches a two–hitter for a 7–0 win over the Reds in the first game of a double–header at Crosley Field. The only two Cincinnati hits were singles by Johnny Pramesa in the third inning and Bob Usher in the eighth. The Cubs completed the sweep with a 7–5 win in eleven innings in the second game.

JULY 21   The Cubs fire Frankie Frisch and hire Phil Cavaretta as manager.

Frisch often berated his players in public with caustic remarks and was clearly unsuited to guide the youth movement the Cubs were undertaking. Frisch's players were close to open revolt over his Captain Bligh methods. "Personally, I think that Frisch has plenty of spirit," said P. K. Wrigley, "but he's used to having a winner, and we've been doing poorly and he's frustrated. Naturally that state of mind produces some friction." Cavaretta was 34 years old and near the end of his playing days, and was the first native Chicagoan to manage the Cubs. In an unusual move, Wrigley announced that Cavaretta would manage the Cubs only through the end of the 1951 season, then go to the minors for further managerial experience. At the end of the 1951 campaign, Wrigley changed his mind and decided to bring Cavaretta back in 1952.

JULY 29   Phil Cavaretta drives in seven runs to pace the Cubs to a 5–4 and 8–6 sweep of the Phillies at Wrigley Field. In the first game, Cavaretta drove in three runs with a triple and a sacrifice fly. In the second game, Cavaretta put himself into the game as a pinch–hitter with the bases loaded in the seventh inning with the score tied 4–4, and he struck a grand slam off future Hall of Famer Robin Roberts.

AUGUST 9 A four–run rally in the ninth inning capped by a two–run, two–out single by Randy Jackson beats the Reds 5–4 at Wrigley Field.

Jackson's given name was Ransom. He resembled actor Gregory Peck, earning Jackson the nickname of "Handsome Ransom." He was also a football star in college as a halfback for the University of Texas.

AUGUST 18 Randy Jackson hits a grand slam off Howie Pollet in the first inning of an 11–5 win over the Pirates in Pittsburgh.

AUGUST 28 Turk Lown pitches the Cubs to a 1–0 win over the Braves in Boston. Lown also scored the only run of the game when he doubled in the fifth inning and crossed the plate on another double by Hal Jeffcoat. It was Lown's only career shutout.

SEPTEMBER 7 The Reds defeat the Cubs 7–6 in an eighteen–inning battle at Crosley Field. The Cubs seemed to have the game in hand when they scored three runs in the top of the fifteenth to take a 6–3 lead, but allowed Cincinnati to tie the contest in their half. During the course of the game, Phil Cavaretta ordered his pitchers to issue an intentional walk to Ted Kluszewski in four consecutive plate appearances.

SEPTEMBER 11 The Cubs defeat the Braves 13–11 at Wrigley Field. The Cubs took a 6–0 lead in the second inning, then fell behind 11–8 before scoring two runs in the seventh inning and three in the eighth.

SEPTEMBER 30 On the final day of the season, the Cubs rally from a 6–0 deficit to defeat the Cardinals 7–6 in the first game of a double–header at Wrigley Field with one run in the sixth inning, five in the eighth and one in the ninth. Hank Sauer's single with the bases loaded drove in the winning run. St. Louis won the second game 3–0.

OCTOBER 4   The Cubs trade Smoky Burgess and Bob Borkowski to the Reds for Johnny Pramesa and Bob Usher. The Reds traded Burgess to the Phillies before the 1952 season started, but reacquired him in another deal with the Phils in 1955.

The trade of Andy Pafko to the Dodgers the previous June gets the hype, but this deal was the worst made by the Cubs during the 1950s and is one of the worst ever. How one-sided was it? After the swap, Burgess played another 16 seasons in the majors in which he appeared in 1,578 games with the Phillies, Reds, Pirates, and White Sox. Pramesa and Usher combined played in only 23 games with the Cubs. Burgess ended his career with a .295 batting average and as the all-time leader in career pinch-hits with 145. A rotund five-foot-eight and 180 pounds, he was also a beloved figure in Chicago because of his numerous key hits coming off the bench for the Sox between 1964 and 1967. Had he remained with the Cubs for the rest of his career, Burgess would have been the starting catcher at least through 1963 and would have retired a beloved figure on the North Side of Chicago instead of on the South Side.

1952   Cubs

Season in a Sentence

Led by Hank Sauer's MVP season, the Cubs' rebuilding project appears to be making progress as the club vaults to fifth place and finishes the season with a .500 record.

Finish • Won • Lost • Pct • GB

Fifth   77   77   .500   19.5

Manager

Phil Cavaretta

Stats   Cubs • NL • Rank

Batting Avg:	.264	.253	2
On-Base Pct:	.321	.323	5
Slugging Pct:	.383	.374	4
Home Runs:	107	4	
Stolen Bases:	50	4	
ERA:	3.58	3.73	3
Fielding Avg:	.976	.976	4
Runs Scored:	628		5
Runs Allowed:	631		3

Starting Lineup

Toby Atwell, c
Dee Fondy, 1b
Eddie Miksis, 2b
Randy Jackson, 3b
Roy Smalley, ss
Hank Sauer, lf
Hal Jeffcoat, cf
Frank Baumholtz, rf–cf
Bill Serena, 3b–2b
Bob Addis, cf–rf
Gene Hermanski, rf
Tommy Brown, ss
Bob Ramazzotti, 2b

Pitchers

Bob Rush, sp
Warren Hacker, sp–rp
Paul Minner, sp
Johnny Klippstein, sp–rp
Turk Lown, sp–rp
Dutch Leonard, rp
Bob Kelly, rp–sp

Attendance

1,024,826 (second in NL)

Club Leaders

Batting Avg:	Baumholtz	.325
On-Base Pct:	Baumholtz	.371
Slugging Pct:	Sauer	.531
Home Runs:	Sauer	37
RBI:	Sauer	121
Runs:	Sauer	89
Stolen Bases:	Fondy	13
Wins:	Rush	17
Strikeouts:	Rush	157
ERA:	Rush	2.70
Saves:	Leonard	11

JANUARY 3   The Cubs trade Frank Hiller to the Reds for Willie Ramsdell.

JANUARY 9   Owner P. K. Wrigley interrupts Wid Matthews with a public admonishment during a bizarre press conference.

At a luncheon with press, radio, and TV correspondents, Matthews began his annual speech about how good the Cubs would be next season. He said that if catcher Bruce Edwards's sore arm responded to treatment, the Cubs could build a winner around him. Wrigley stunned the audience by interrupting and embarrassing Matthews. "I believe it's about time we stopped our daydreaming and wishful thinking and faced things as they are. At the moment I will regard Edwards as no more than a patched–up ballplayer out of whom we hope to get as much service as possible until we can get somebody better. If and when his arm heals, there will be time to celebrate." Wrigley further stated that there was little hope for the fans to expect improvement in 1952.

FEBRUARY 18   Abandoning Catalina Island as a training base, the Cubs begin their first spring training at Rendezvous Park in Mesa, Arizona.

APRIL 15   The Cubs win the season opener 6–5 in ten innings in Cincinnati. The Cubs took a 5–0 lead on a Randy Jackson solo homer in the third inning and a Hank Sauer grand slam off Herm Wehmeier in the fourth, but they allowed the Reds to come back and tie the score. The Cubs won the contest in the tenth when Randy Jackson singled, went to second on a balk, and scored on a pinch–hit single by Gene Hermanski.

The grand slam was the first shot in a season in which Hank Sauer would win the National League Most Valuable Player award. In the first 51 games of 1952, Sauer hit .359 and had 18 homers and 58 RBIs. He finished the campaign by hitting .270 and with league–leading totals in home runs with 37 and runs batted in with 121.

APRIL 18   In the home opener, the Cubs win a thrilling 5–4 decision over the Cardinals with four runs in the ninth inning before 20,396 at Wrigley Field. The tying and winning runs were scored on a pinch–double by Bill Serena. The Cubs scored all four runs before a man was retired.

APRIL 28   Hank Sauer drives in all of the Cubs' runs with a home run, single, and infield out during a 4–3 win over the Cardinals in St. Louis.

APRIL 30   The Cubs score seven runs in the third inning to take a 7–4 lead, but need twelve innings to defeat the Phillies 9–8 at Wrigley Field. Bob Addis drove in the winning run with a single.

MAY 2   Turk Lown holds the Dodgers hitless until the ninth inning, then cracks under the strain, allowing three runs and three hits for a 3–1 loss at Wrigley Field.

MAY 25   Dee Fondy hits a two–run homer in the ninth inning to beat the Pirates 5–4 in Pittsburgh.

From 1952 through 1954, Fondy gave the Cubs three Mark Grace–type seasons, with a .299 average and 37 homers in 1,717 at–bats, before fading.

MAY 30 — Bob Rush retires the first 20 batters to face him and pitches a two-hitter to beat the Reds 11–0 in the second game of a double-header at Wrigley Field. The only Cincinnati hits were a double by Grady Hatton in the seventh inning and a single by Eddie Pellagrini in the eighth. It was Rush's third straight shutout and came during a stretch in which he pitched 32 consecutive scoreless innings. The Cubs also won the first game 7–6.

Rush had the best season of his career in 1952, with a 17–13 record and a 2.70 ERA.

Bob Rush won 17 games to lead the Cubs to a .500 record in 1952, capping off a stretch where he led the Cubs in wins three straight years.

JUNE 11 — Hank Sauer hits three homers to account for all of the Chicago runs in a 3–2 win over the Phillies at Wrigley Field. Sauer clouted homers in the second, sixth, and eighth innings, all off Curt Simmons. Sauer also hit three homers off Simmons in a game on August 28, 1950. Despite the heroics of Sauer, the Cubs would have lost if it weren't for a baserunning blunder by Tommy Brown. With the game tied 1–1 in the fourth and two out, Phillies center fielder Richie Ashburn hit a bases-loaded single that scored two runs and sent Brown from first to third. Brown failed to touch second base, however, negating the two runs.

In yet another inexplicable transaction, the Cubs purchased Brown from the Phillies four days later.

JUNE 14 — Braves pitcher Warren Spahn hits a home run and strikes out 18 Chicago batters, but the Cubs win 3–1 in fifteen innings at Boston. Bill Serena tied the game 1–1 with a homer in the ninth. In the fifteenth, Spahn walked two batters and gave up a triple to Hal Jeffcoat. Willie Ramsdell (seven innings) and Johnny Klippstein (eight innings) combined to allow the Braves only four hits, two off each pitcher.

The victory gave the Cubs a 34–19 record. The club was in third place and 4 ½ games behind the first-place Dodgers, but the next day the Cubs launched a nine-game losing streak.

JUNE 19 — Carl Erskine of the Dodgers pitches a no-hitter to defeat the Cubs 5–0 at Ebbets Field. The only Cubs baserunner was pitcher Willie Ramsdell, who walked on four pitches in the third inning.

JUNE 29 — In one of the most incredible rallies in club history, the Cubs score seven runs in the ninth inning to defeat the Reds 9–8 in the first game of a double-header in Cincinnati. The rally started with two out and no one on base. The first run was scored on a double by Bill Serena, a walk to Roy Smalley, and a pinch-single by Gene Hermanski. Eddie Miksis reached on an error to score Smalley. Hal Jeffcoat walked to load the bases, and Dee Fondy singled in two runs to make the score 8–5. Hank Sauer doubled in Jeffcoat and Fondy to pull the Cubs within a run. After Bruce Edwards walked, pinch–hitter Johnny Pramesa hit a single to drive in the tying and winning runs. The Cubs lost the second game 9–1.

JULY 6   Paul Minner pitches a two–hitter to defeat the Reds 5–1 in the first game of a double–header at Wrigley Field. The only Cincinnati hits were a home run by Bob Borkowski in the third inning and a single by Ted Kluszewski in the seventh. The Cubs completed the sweep with a 2–0 win in the nightcap.

JULY 8   Hank Sauer hits a two–run homer in the fourth inning off Bob Lemon of the Indians to put the National League ahead 3–2 in the All–Star Game at Shibe Park in Philadelphia. It was still 3–2 when the game ended after five innings by rain. Bob Rush gave up two runs in two innings, but was the winning pitcher.

JULY 31   The Cubs break loose with nine runs in the seventh inning and defeat the Giants 11–8 in New York.

AUGUST 10   Phil Cavaretta takes mercy on the woeful Pirates, a club which lost 112 games in 1952, during a game at Forbes Field. Pittsburgh manager Fred Haney used Ed Fitz Gerald and Joe Garagiola as pinch–hitters early in the contest, and when Clyde McCullough tore a nail on his middle finger and could no longer continue, the Pirates had no more catchers. In an act of sportsmanship, Cavaretta let Fitz Gerald re–enter the game. The Cubs came away with a 4–3 victory.

AUGUST 18   Phil Cavaretta's two–run, pinch–hit, walk–off homer caps a three–run Cubs rally in the ninth inning which defeats the Pirates 4–3 at Wrigley Field. It proved to be Cavaretta's last home run as a Cub.

AUGUST 21   Trailing the Giants 6–0, the Cubs rally to win 8–6 with two runs in the fourth inning, three in the fifth, and three in the seventh in the first game of a double–header at Wrigley Field. Hank Sauer led the attack with six runs batted in on a pair of three–run homers. New York won the second game 10–5.

SEPTEMBER 11   The Cubs score seven runs in the fourth inning and defeat the Dodgers 11–7 in Brooklyn.

Many Cubs fans believed the club had turned the corner by finishing with a 77–77 record in 1952, but it was only an illusion. The Cubs avoided a losing season with career years from Hank Sauer, Bob Rush, Warren Hacker, and Toby Atwell. The youth movement begun during the late–1940s was still by and large a failure.

SEPTEMBER 28   On the final day of the season, Stan Musial makes the only pitching appearance of his big league career in a 3–0 Cubs win over the Cardinals in St. Louis.

Musial went into the game with a .336 to .326 lead over Frank Baumholtz in the NL batting race. With one out in the first inning, Musial came in from his center field position to pitch to Baumholtz, while pitcher Harvey Haddix went to the outfield. A right–handed hitter, Baumholtz switched to the left side and hit a weak grounder to shortstop Solly Hemus, who fumbled the ball for an error. Musial returned to the out-field and won the batting championship by going 1–for–3 while Baumholtz was 1–for–4. Musial finished the year at .336 while Baumholtz ended with a .325 average.

DECEMBER 3   A month after Dwight Eisenhower defeats Illinois Governor Adlai Stevenson in the presidential election, the Cubs send Dick Manville and $25,000 to the Pirates for Clyde McCullough.

Frank Baumholtz finished second in the NL batting race in 1952 with a .325 average. He also topped .300 in 1953, marking his two best years in the majors.

1953   Cubs

Season in a Sentence

In another dreary year, any hopes of continued improvement evaporate when the Cubs lose 36 of their first 50 games.

Finish • Won • Lost • Pct • GB

Seventh   65   89   .422   40.0

Manager

Phil Cavaretta

Stats

Stats	Cubs	NL	Rank
Batting Avg:	.260	.266	7
On–Base Pct:	.328	.335	5
Slugging Pct:	.399	.411	7
Home Runs:	137		6
Stolen Bases:	49		2
ERA:	4.79	4.29	7
Fielding Avg:	.967	.975	8
Runs Scored:	633		7
Runs Allowed:	835		7

Starting Lineup

Clyde McCullough, c
Dee Fondy, 1b
Eddie Miksis, 2b
Randy Jackson, 3b
Roy Smalley, ss
Ralph Kiner, lf
Frank Baumholtz, cf–rf
Hank Sauer, rf–lf
Bill Serena, 2b–3b
Joe Garagiola, c
Hal Jeffcoat, cf

Pitchers

Warren Hacker, sp
Paul Minner, sp
Bob Rush, sp
Howie Pollet, sp–rp
Dutch Leonard, rp
Johnny Klippstein, rp–sp
Turk Lown, sp–rp
Bubba Church, rp–sp

Attendance

763,658 (sixth in NL)

Club Leaders

Batting Avg:	Baumholtz	.306
On–Base Pct:	Kiner	.394
Slugging Pct:	Kiner	.529
Home Runs:	Kiner	28
RBI:	Kiner	87
Runs:	Fondy	79
Stolen Bases:	Miksis	13
Wins:	Hacker	12
	Minner	12
Strikeouts:	Hacker	106
ERA:	Minner	4.21
Saves:	Leonard	8

MARCH 17   In the first franchise shift in the major leagues in 50 years, the Boston Braves move 90 miles north of Chicago to Milwaukee.

The Braves drew 1.8 million fans in 1953, which was then a National League record, and attracted over two million each season from 1954 through 1957. With a popular team playing in Milwaukee, the Cubs lost many fans from the state of Wisconsin who shifted their allegiance to the Braves, cutting into the attendance figures at Wrigley Field. In 1957, the Braves drew 2,215,404 fans, compared to 670,629 for the Cubs. Attendance in Milwaukee began to drop in 1958, however, and the club moved to Atlanta following the 1965 season. The Brewers moved to Milwaukee from Seattle, where they were known as the Pilots, in 1970.

APRIL 13   The Cubs open the 1953 season with a 3–2 win over the Reds before 21,222 at Wrigley Field. The Reds led 2–0 before the Cubs scored a run in the sixth inning and two in the eighth. Randy Jackson broke the 2–2 tie with a run–scoring double.

APRIL 25   The Cubs score eight runs in the fourth inning and defeat the Cardinals 10–6 at Wrigley Field. The Cubs collected seven consecutive singles during the inning.

MAY 12   A two–run walk–off homer by Dee Fondy beats the Dodgers 6–4 at Wrigley Field.

JUNE 4   The Cubs send Toby Atwell, Preston Ward, Gene Hermanski, Bob Addis, Bob Schultz, George Freese, and $150,000 to the Pirates for Ralph Kiner, Howie Pollet, Catfish Metkovich, and Joe Garagiola.

Kiner led the National League in home runs seven consecutive seasons from 1946 through 1952. Before he was traded to the Indians at the end of the 1954 season, Kiner hit .284 for the Cubs with 50 home runs in 971 at–bats, but those numbers declined from the batting marks he put up for the Pirates. None of the four players the Cubs gave up to get the 30–year–old Kiner were any great loss, but the trade made no sense for a rebuilding club. The $150,000 paid to purchase Kiner could have been put to better use by investing in the farm system, not to mention his $90,000 salary, then one of the highest in base-ball. Furthermore, whatever Kiner gave the Cubs offensively he took away on defense. With a bad back hampering his mobility, Kiner was only capable of playing left field, and the Cubs already had a slow–footed power–hitter in left field in Hank Sauer, who tied Kiner for the home run leadership in the NL in 1952. Sauer had to move to right field, where he didn't have the arm for the position, and Frank Baumholtz moved from right to center, where he didn't have the speed to cover the vast territory between two corner outfielders who could barely move. With his self–deprecating sense of humor, Kiner got a lot of mileage during his long broadcasting career by joking about how he and Sauer yelled, "You take it, Frankie" to Baumholtz every time a fly ball was hit into the outfield. But it was no laughing matter to Cubs pitchers who watched one catchable fly ball after another drop for extra–base hits. Cubs fans weren't amused either and booed Kiner often during his season–and–a–half in Chicago.

JUNE 14   Ralph Kiner's grand slam in the ninth inning off Carl Erskine of the Dodgers ties the score 6–6 in the second game of a double–header at Ebbets Field. The game ended with the score 6–6 at the end of the ninth when it was called by darkness. At the time, an NL rule stipulated that lights couldn't be turned on to complete games played on Sunday. Brooklyn won the first game 6–3.

JUNE 19   A controversial grand slam by Randy Jackson in the fifth inning off Billy Loes of the Dodgers puts the Cubs ahead 8–6 at Wrigley Field. The Cubs went on to win the game, the first of a double–header, 11–8. Brooklyn won the second game 7–1. The twinbill was played on a day in which temperatures in Chicago reached 102 degrees.

The Dodgers protested Jackson's slam, claiming the drive struck the screen in front of the catwalk in the left field bleachers. The umpires said the ball cleared the screen and was touched by a fan, causing it to bound back onto the field. Pee Wee Reese and Duke Snider were ejected during the argument.

JUNE 20   Playing in 104–degree heat, the highest temperature ever recorded in Chicago history, the Cubs lose 5–3 to the Dodgers at Wrigley Field.

JULY 3   The Cubs break a 3–3 tie with seven runs in the eighth inning and defeat the Cardinals 10–3 at Wrigley Field.

No manager, coach, or player wore uniform number 1 for the Cubs from 1943 through 1953 because it belonged to Joe Heinsen, a printing executive who was an unofficial member of the Cubs family. When the club was at home, Heinsen caught batting practice and filled in whenever the Cubs needed help during pre-game drills.

AUGUST 2   Six days after the signing of the armistice agreement ending the Korean War, Randy Jackson hits a walk–off homer in the eleventh inning to beat the Pirates 7–6 at Wrigley Field.

The Cubs were hurt in 1953 when Hank Sauer and Bob Rush both battled injuries. Sauer hit 19 homers, down from 37 in 1952, and played in only 108 games because he broke three different fingers, one on March 16, another on June 23 and the third on July 18. Rush, after a 17–13 record and a 2.70 ERA in 1952, battled arm problems in 1953 and was 9–14 with an ERA of 4.54.

AUGUST 11   Paul Minner pitches the Cubs to a 1–0 win over the Reds at Wrigley Field. Hal Jeffcoat drove in the lone run of the game with a single in the second inning.

AUGUST 15   Randy Jackson grounds into three double plays during a 2–0 loss to the Braves at Wrigley Field.

AUGUST 31   The Cubs announce that Gene Baker will be called up from the club's Los Angeles farm club when the Pacific Coast League ends on September 13.

Baker became the first African–American player on the Cubs roster, although Ernie Banks became the first to play in a game (see September 17, 1953). Baker played shortstop for Los Angeles for four seasons while putting up superior statistics to those playing short for the Cubs, leading to charges of racism against P. K. Wrigley. While the Cubs dragged their feet in calling up Baker from the minors, only six other major league teams in August 1953 (the Dodgers, Giants, Braves, Indians, White Sox, and Browns) had African–Americans on their roster. Ironically, Baker never played shortstop for the Cubs. After the arrival of Banks, Baker was moved to second base, where he was the club's starter until he was traded to the Pirates in 1957.

Gene Baker was the first African–American on the Cubs roster when he was called up in September 1953. He was a three–year starter at second base.

SEPTEMBER 6 The Cubs score two runs in the ninth, the last one on a steal of home by Dee Fondy, to defeat the Reds 7–6 in the first game of a double–header at Wrigley Field. The Cubs also won the second game 7–3.

SEPTEMBER 8 The Cubs purchase Ernie Banks from the Kansas City Monarchs of the Negro Leagues for $35,000.

The $35,000 was the greatest bargain in Cubs history. Playing for the Cubs until 1971, Banks appeared in 2,528 games (ranking first in club history), hit 512 homers (second to Sammy Sosa), and collected 4,706 total bases (first), 1,636 RBIs (second to Cap Anson), 2,583 hits (second to Anson), 1,305 runs (sixth), 407 doubles (third), 90 triples (seventh), and had a .500 slugging percentage to rank sixth. But what Banks means to Cubs fans cannot be measured in pure statistics. With his genuinely sunny disposition, optimism, and enthusiasm, Banks came to symbolize what was right about baseball and will forever be known as "Mr. Cub."

SEPTEMBER 9 Ralph Kiner hits a three–run walk–off homer to beat his former Pirate teammates 8–7 at Wrigley Field. The winning pitcher was Duke Simpson, the only victory of his big–league career. Simpson was 1–2 lifetime with an 8.00 ERA in 45 innings.

SEPTEMBER 17 Making his major league debut, Ernie Banks is hitless in three at–bats as the Cubs lose 16–4 to the Phillies at Wrigley Field. Ernie was one of four Chicago players in the game to make his major–league debut. The others were center fielder Dale Talbot, starting pitcher Don Elston and reliever Bill Moisan.

SEPTEMBER 20 Ernie Banks hits his first career homer, although the Cubs lose 11–6 to the Cardinals in St. Louis. Banks hit the homer off Gerry Staley off of a knuckleball that hung inside.

SEPTEMBER 22 Ernie Banks and Gene Baker form the first shortstop–second base combination in major league history with two African–Americans during a double–header against the Reds in Cincinnati. The Cubs lost the first game 1–0, but won the second 4–1.

Banks was also the first African–American in major league history to play shortstop on a regular basis.

OCTOBER 17   P. K. Wrigley appoints Bill Veeck as a special advisor "to spearhead the campaign to bring major league baseball to Los Angeles."

Veeck sold the St. Louis Browns three weeks earlier to a group which moved the club to Baltimore, where they were renamed the Orioles. At the time, Wrigley owned the Los Angeles Angels minor league club in the Pacific Coast League. Residents of Los Angeles were clamoring for a major league team. In 1953, big league owners were debating over whether or not to expand the two eight–team leagues to ten clubs, with L.A. as one of the expansion franchises, or to create a third major league with eight teams located in cities west of the Mississippi River. "Bill will not only help Los Angeles get a major league club," said Wrigley, "his job also is to go out and organize the effort so that Los Angeles and possibly other Pacific Coast League cities get top–flight baseball in an orderly and sensible way as soon as it becomes physically possible." Veeck remained with the Cubs until 1955. On March 10, 1959, he purchased a controlling interest in the Chicago White Sox.

DECEMBER 7   The Cubs sell Catfish Metkovich to the Braves.

1954   Cubs

Season in a Sentence

Phil Cavaretta is fired as manager during spring training after telling P. K. Wrigley that the Cubs have no chance to post a winning record, and is proven correct when the club lands in seventh place.

Finish • Won • Lost • Pct • GB

Seventh   64   90   .416 33.0

Manager

Stan Hack

Stats

Stats	Cubs	NL	Rank
Batting Avg:	.263	.265	7
On–Base Pct:	.327	.339	7
Slugging Pct:	.412	.407	4
Home Runs:	159		3
Stolen Bases:	46		4 (tie)
ERA:	4.51	4.07	7
Fielding Avg:	.974	.976	7
Runs Scored:	700		5
Runs Allowed:	766		7

Starting Lineup

Joe Garagiola, c
Dee Fondy, 1b
Gene Baker, 2b
Randy Jackson, 3b
Ernie Banks, ss
Ralph Kiner, lf
Dale Talbot, cf
Hank Sauer, lf
Frank Baumholtz, cf
Walker Cooper, c

Pitchers

Bob Rush, sp
Paul Minner, sp
Howie Pollet, sp
Johnny Klippstein, sp–rp
Dave Cole, sp
Jim Davis, rp–sp
Hal Jeffcoat, rp
Warren Hacker, rp–sp

Attendance

748,183 (fifth in NL)

Club Leaders

Batting Avg:	Sauer	.288
On–Base Pct:	Sauer	.375
Slugging Pct:	Sauer	.563
Home Runs:	Sauer	41
RBI:	Sauer	103
Runs:	Sauer	98
Stolen Bases:	Fondy	20
Wins:	Rush	13
Strikeouts:	Rush	124
ERA:	Rush	3.77
Saves:	Jeffcoat	7

MARCH 20   The Cubs send Roy Smalley to the Braves for Dave Cole and cash.

MARCH 29   Phil Cavaretta is fired as manager of the Cubs and is replaced by Stan Hack. The
              dismissal ended Cavaretta's 20–year association with the Cubs. Since retiring as a
              player in 1947, Hack had been managing in the Cubs system for six seasons, the
              last three at Los Angeles.

> *When Cavaretta was fired, the Cubs had a 5–15 record in exhibition games.
> When asked by P. K. Wrigley for an assessment of the club's chances for
> improving on their 65–89 record of 1953, Cavaretta gave the owner the plain,
> unvarnished facts and stated that the club's chances of posting a winning record
> were almost nonexistent. "The material just isn't there," said Cavaretta. "What
> makes it sadder is that the future looks even worse. There just isn't any good
> new talent coming up." In Cavaretta's estimation, Ernie Banks, Dale Talbot,
> and Gene Baker were the only young stars capable of making an impact. And
> Baker was nearly 29 years old. Wrigley stunned Cavaretta by firing him. "Phil
> seems to have developed a defeatist attitude," said Wrigley. "We don't believe
> he should continue in a job where he doesn't believe success is possible." A few
> days later, Cavaretta signed a contract as a player with the White Sox, as a
> backup first baseman and pinch–hitter. He remained with the White Sox until
> early in the 1955 season and never managed in the majors again.*

APRIL 13   The Cubs wallop the Cardinals 13–4
              on Opening Day in St. Louis. Clyde
              McCullough hit a homer, two dou-
              bles, and a single. Dee Fondy collect-
              ed four
              singles. Randy Jackson and Paul Min-
              ner each drove in three runs. Minner
              also pitched a complete game.

APRIL 15   In the home opener, the Reds smash
              the Cubs 11–5 before 17,271 at
              Wrigley Field. Randy Jackson had
              four hits, including a homer. Hank
              Sauer also homered for Chicago.

APRIL 17   The Cubs wallop the Cardinals 23–13
              at Wrigley Field. Most of the scoring
              was done in the first five innings. The
              Cubs led 9–6 at the end of the third
              inning, then added three more in the
              fourth. After the Cards scored four
              runs in the fifth to close the gap to
              12–10, the Cubs exploded for 10 runs
              in their half to lead 22–10. The Cubs
              had 20 hits, two of them homers, and

Randy Jackson hit .273 with 19 homers in an
otherwise–dismal 1954 season for the Cubs.

              were aided by 12 walks and five errors by the Cardinals.

APRIL 18   In his major league debut, Cubs relief pitcher Jim Davis allows a home run to the
              first batter he faces during a 6–4 loss to the Cardinals at Wrigley Field. The homer

was struck by Tom Alston with two on in the seventh, which turned a 4–3 Cubs lead into a 6–4 deficit.

APRIL 23   The Cubs collect 20 hits, five of them by Randy Jackson, in a 10–3 win over the Reds in Cincinnati. Jackson had a homer and four singles.

In the first eight games of the 1954 season, Jackson had 19 hits, including four homers, in 34 at–bats. Hank Sauer was also off to a hot start, with 10 homers in Chicago's first 18 games. Jackson cooled off, but Sauer ended the year with 41 homers and a .288 batting average.

APRIL 30   The Cubs purchase Steve Bilko from the Cardinals.

A first baseman, Bilko was six–foot–one and weighed between 230 and 260 pounds, depending upon the stage of his most recent diet. He hit only .239 with four homers in 92 at–bats, and was sent to Los Angeles after the season ended. With the minor league Angels, Bilko became a cult hero. From 1955 through 1957, he hit .330 with 148 home runs. The popular television character Sgt. Bilko created by Phil Silvers on the PHIL SILVERS SHOW was named after Steve Bilko. The Cubs sold Bilko to the Reds in October 1957.

MAY 16   Joe Garagiola collects five hits, including a double, in five at–bats in a 12–3 win over the Pirates in the first game of a double–header at Forbes Field. Pittsburgh won the second game 5–1.

Garagiola played 137 games for the Cubs in 1953 and 1954. He retired at the end of the 1954 season and went into a career in broadcasting that lasted over 30 years. Known for his one–liners and humorous anecdotes, Garagiola did the play–by–play in the World Series, the All-Star Game, and on the Saturday after-noon Game of the Week on NBC. He was also the host of the TODAY SHOW from 1969 through 1973 on NBC in addition to hosting game shows, and was a best–selling author of the book BASEBALL IS A FUNNY GAME.

MAY 19   Shut out on only three hits in the first seven innings by Carl Erskine, the Cubs explode for nine runs in the eighth inning and defeat the Dodgers 9–3 in Brooklyn.

On the same day, the Cubs purchased Walker Cooper from the Pirates.

MAY 26   The Cubs score seven runs in the fourth inning and drub the Cardinals 15–5 in St. Louis.

MAY 29   Walker Cooper hits a grand slam off Fred Baczewski of the Reds in the fourth inning of a 6–0 win at Wrigley Field.

MAY 31   The Cubs score seven runs in the fourth inning and smash the Cardinals 14–4 in a game stopped by rain after seven innings at Wrigley Field. Hank Sauer hit two homers for the Cubs, and Ernie Banks, Paul Minner, Randy Jackson, and Bill Serena each added one.

The Cubs were 20–22 at the end of May, but June was one of the worst months in club history as Stan Hack's crew posted a 4–21 record.

JUNE 11 Eddie Miksis homers on the first pitch of the tenth inning off Marv Grissom to beat the Giants 5–4 at Wrigley Field. The winning pitcher was Jim Davis, who was Grissom's nephew.

Davis was 11–7 as a rookie with the Cubs in 1954, but never matched his early success.

JUNE 29 The Cubs drop their 11th game in a row by losing 6–0 to the Braves in Milwaukee.

JULY 18 Walker Cooper hits a grand slam in the fourth inning off Russ Meyer, but the Dodgers defeat the Cubs 12–6 at Wrigley Field.

JULY 22 The Cubs wallop the Giants 13–5 at Wrigley Field.

AUGUST 1 After losing the opener of a twinbill 2–0 to the Pirates in Pittsburgh, the Cubs come back to win the nightcap 12–2.

AUGUST 17 Clyde McCullough's grand slam off Corky Valentine in the sixth inning helps the Cubs to a 5–0 win over the Reds in the first game of a double–header at Wrigley Field. The Cubs completed the sweep with a 6–2 win in the second game.

AUGUST 31 The Cubs smash the Pirates 14–2 and 7–3 in a double–header at Wrigley Field.

SEPTEMBER 3 Coming from behind with one run in the eighth inning and three in the ninth, the Cubs defeat the Cardinals 4–3 in St. Louis. Ernie Banks drove in the last two runs with a double.

In his first full season in the majors, Banks hit .275 with 19 home runs.

SEPTEMBER 30 The Cubs sell Bill Serena to the White Sox.

OCTOBER 1 The Cubs trade Johnny Klippstein and Jim Willis to the Reds for Jim Bolger, Harry Perkowski, and Ted Tappe.

Klippstein was another player the Cubs gave up on too soon. He helped several teams, mainly out of the bullpen, before his career ended in 1967. Bolger, Perkowski, and Tappe were of little use to the Cubs.

NOVEMBER 16 The Cubs send Ralph Kiner to the Indians for Sam Jones, Gale Wade, and $60,000.

Kiner played one more season before retiring. He was elected to the Hall of Fame in 1975. Jones anchored the Cubs rotation for two seasons and pitched a no–hitter (see May 12, 1955).

1955

Cubs

Season in a Sentence

Ernie Banks emerges as a superstar and the Cubs win 32 of their first 53 games, but by the end of the season the club has more losses than wins yet again.

Finish • Won • Lost • Pct • GB

Sixth   72   81   .471   26.0

Manager

Stan Hack

Stats

Stats	Cubs	NL	Rank
Batting Avg:	.247	.259	7
On–Base Pct:	.307	.331	8
Slugging Pct:	.398	.407	6
Home Runs:	164		5
Stolen Bases:	37		7
ERA:	4.17	4.04	6
Fielding Avg:	.975	.976	5
Runs Scored:	626		7
Runs Allowed:	713		6

Starting Lineup

Harry Chiti, c
Dee Fondy, 1b
Gene Baker, 2b
Randy Jackson, 3b
Ernie Banks, ss
Hank Sauer, lf
Eddie Miksis, cf–rf
Jim King, rf
Frank Baumholtz, lf–rf
Bob Speake, lf
Jim Bolger, cf
Lloyd Merriman, cf

Pitchers

Sam Jones, sp
Bob Rush, sp
Warren Hacker, sp
Paul Minner, sp
Hal Jeffcoat, rp
Jim Davis, rp–sp

Attendance

875,800 (fourth in NL

Club Leaders

Batting Avg:	Banks	.295
On–Base Pct:	Banks	.345
Slugging Pct:	Banks	.596
Home Runs:	Banks	44
RBI:	Banks	117
Runs:	Banks	98
Stolen Bases:	Baker	9
	Banks	9
Wins:	Jones	14
Strikeouts:	Jones	198
ERA:	Minner	3.48
Saves:	Jeffcoat	6

APRIL 11   Six days after Richard Daley is elected mayor of Chicago, the Cubs win on Opening Day for the sixth year in a row with a 7–5 triumph over the Reds in Cincinnati. Gene Baker and Harry Chiti hit home runs. It was Chiti's first game since 1952, having spent the previous two seasons in the U.S. Army. Dee Fondy had three hits, including two doubles. The winning pitcher was Sam Jones in five innings of relief. Jones became the first African–American pitcher in Cubs history with the appearance.

APRIL 12   The Cubs win the home opener 14–4 against the Cardinals before 26,153 at Wrigley Field. The Cubs scored five runs in the first inning and six in the second for an 11–1 lead. Randy Jackson homered for Chicago.

APRIL 15   The Cubs run their season record to 3–0, as Randy Jackson and Ernie Banks hit consecutive homers in the tenth inning to beat the Reds 6–4 in Cincinnati.

APRIL 16   Randy Jackson, Ernie Banks, and Dee Fondy each hit two homers, but the Cubs lose 12–11 to the Cardinals in fourteen innings in St. Louis. In the second inning, Jackson, Banks, and Fondy hit back–to–back–to–back homers off Tom Poholsky. In the eleventh, Banks and Fondy hit consecutive homers to put the Cubs up 11–9, but the Cards tied it in their half.

APRIL 17   The Cubs defeat the Cardinals 6–5 with two runs in the ninth inning in the first game of a double–header at Busch Stadium. Lloyd Merriman had a hand in both ninth–inning runs, just one day after he was purchased from the White Sox. Merriman tripled in one run, and scored on a single by Frank Baumholtz. In the second game, St. Louis scored 10 runs in the first inning and defeated the Cubs 14–1.

APRIL 23   The Cubs defeat the Reds 1–0 at Wrigley Field. Frank Baumholtz drove in the lone run of the game with a single in the sixth inning. Warren Hacker (5 ⅔ innings) and Jim Davis (3 ⅓ innings) combined for the shutout.

APRIL 24   Sam Jones pitches a two–hitter to defeat the Reds 2–1 at Wrigley Field. The only Cincinnati hits were a double by Ted Kluszewski and a single by Ray Jablonski.

MAY 1   A two–run, two–out bases–loaded single by Randy Jackson beats the Phillies 8–7 in the first game of a double–header in Philadelphia. The Cubs won the second game 4–2 in a contest that took two days to complete because of the Pennsylvania curfew law which stipulated that games on Sunday must end at precisely 7:00 P.M. The contest was suspended in the ninth inning and completed the next day before the regularly scheduled tilt.

MAY 11   The Cubs break two winning streaks by defeating the Dodgers 10–8 at Wrigley Field. The Dodgers entered the game with an 11–game winning streak. Russ Meyer was the losing pitcher after defeating the Cubs 17 straight times since July 16, 1950. Ernie Banks hit a grand slam off Meyer in the first inning.

            Meyer pitched for the Cubs from 1946 through 1948 and again in 1956. In between his two stints with the club, he posted a 24–3 record against Chicago.

MAY 12   Sam Jones pitches a no–hitter to defeat the Pirates 4–0 before a crowd of only 2,918 at Wrigley Field. In the ninth inning, Jones walked Gene Freese, Preston Ward, and Tom Saffell to load the bases with nobody out. With the tying run at the plate, Stan Hack went to the mound to talk to Jones, and after a brief discussion, decided to leave the pitcher in the game. Jones then proceeded to strike out Dick Groat, Roberto Clemente, and Frank Thomas on 12 pitches, two of which were two–strike foul balls, to end the game. Jones finished the contest with seven walks and six strikeouts. He was the first African–American in major league history to pitch a no–hitter.

            Nicknamed "Toothpick Sam" because he pitched with a toothpick in his mouth, Jones had a 14–20 record for the Cubs in 1955, walking 185 batters and striking out 198 in 242 ⅓ innings. The 185 bases on balls is a Cub record for a season. Jones led the league in walks and strikeouts in both 1955 and 1956, his only two seasons with the Cubs. He was traded to the Cardinals at the end of the 1956 season.

MAY 20   Bob Speake hits a two–run homer in the tenth inning off Warren Spahn to beat the Braves 4–2 in Milwaukee.

MAY 21   Warren Hacker holds the Braves hitless for 8 ⅓ innings before pinch–hitter George Crowe wallops a home run. Hacker twice shook off catcher Harry Chiti's sign for a fastball and threw a knuckler to Crowe. Warren still came away with a one–hitter and a 2–1 win.

On the negative side, Hacker allowed a club–record 38 homers in 1955.

MAY 25   Superb pitching leads the Cubs to a 1–0 and 3–1 sweep of the Cardinals at Wrigley
            Field. Paul Minner pitched the shutout in the first game. The lone run was scored
            on a sixth–inning homer by Bob Speake off Larry Jackson. In the second contest,
            Bob Rush hurled a two–hitter. The only St. Louis hits were a single by Bill Virdon
            and a homer by Rip Repulski.

MAY 27   Gene Baker ties a National League record for most putouts by a second baseman in
            a nine–inning game with 11, but the Cubs lose 7–5 to the Braves at Wrigley Field.

MAY 29   Ernie Banks hits a grand slam off Lew Burdette in the third inning of a 9–6 win
            over the Braves at Wrigley Field.

MAY 30   The Cubs win two extra–inning games in a double–header in St. Louis. The Cubs
            won the first game 9–5 in ten innings, and the second 4–3 when Bob Speake hit a
            home run in the eleventh.

JUNE 5   Frank Baumholtz hits a three–run, pinch–hit homer with two out in the ninth inning to
            beat the Giants in the second game of a double–header at the Polo Grounds. When
            Baumholtz stepped to the plate, Jim Hearn was the pitcher. After Hearn threw two
            balls, Giants manager Leo Durocher brought Marv Grissom in to pitch. Baumholtz hit
            Grissom's first pitch for the homer. New York won the first game 3–2.

            *The Cubs had a 32–21 record on June 9. The club was still in second place in
            early July and was 45–40 at the All–Star break before collapsing.*

JUNE 19   The Cubs lose 1–0 in fifteen innings to the Phillies in the first game of a double–header
            at Wrigley Field, wasting brilliant pitching by Jim Davis (ten innings) and Hal Jeffcoat
            (five innings). The Cubs won the second game, called by darkness after 6 ½ innings, 8–7.

JULY 1   Gene Baker hits a grand slam in the second inning off Brooks Lawrence during an
            11–7 win over the Cardinals at Wrigley Field.

JULY 8   Ernie Banks hits a two–run homer in the eleventh inning to beat the Cardinals 6–4
            in St. Louis. It was Ernie's second home run of the game.

JULY 17   Ernie Banks hits a grand slam homer in the sixth inning off Ron Negray to give the
            Cubs an 11–4 lead, but the Phillies rally to win 12–11 in ten innings in the first game
            of a double–header at Connie Mack Stadium. In the second game, the Cubs led 5–4 in
            the sixth inning when the game was suspended by Pennsylvania's Sunday curfew law.
            The game was completed the next day, and the Cubs wound up losing 9–6.

AUGUST 2   Ernie Banks hits his fourth grand slam of the 1955 season, leading the Cubs to a
            12–4 win over the Pirates at Wrigley Field. The homer was hit off Dick Littlefield in
            the fifth inning.

AUGUST 4   Ernie Banks clubs three homers and drives in seven runs during an 11–10 win over
            the Pirates at Wrigley Field.

AUGUST 8   Gene Baker homers off Don Newcombe in the eighth inning to give the Cubs a 1–0 win over the Dodgers at Wrigley Field. Sam Jones pitched the shutout.

SEPTEMBER 2   The Cubs score eight runs in the second inning and trounce the Cardinals 12–2 at Wrigley Field. Ernie Banks homered in the big inning to become the first shortstop in major league history to hit 40 homers in a season.

SEPTEMBER 4   Willard Schmidt of the Cardinals retires the first 20 Chicago batters to face him, but the Cubs rally to win 4–3 at Wrigley Field with one run in the seventh and three in the eighth.

SEPTEMBER 7   Frank Baumholtz is the only Cub base runner off Bob Friend of the Pirates as the Cubs lose 2–0 at Wrigley Field. Baumholtz's single in the fourth inning was just out of the reach of second baseman Johnny O'Brien.

SEPTEMBER 19   Ernie Banks becomes the first player in major league history to hit five grand slams in a season. The record–breaking blast came off Lindy McDaniel of the Cardinals in the seventh inning at Busch Stadium to give the Cubs a 5–0 lead. St. Louis came back to win, however, 6–5 in twelve innings.

Banks held the major league record for most grand slams in a season until Don Mattingly hit six for the Yankees in 1987. Banks still holds the National League record. The five grand slams in 1955 were the first five of Ernie's career. He didn't hit another one until 1959.

Ernie Banks's second full big–league season was a big one, as he became the first shortstop in major–league history to hit 40 homers in a season and the first player ever to hit five grand slams in a season.

SEPTEMBER 21   Playing left field, Bob Speake ends a 7–5 win over the Cardinals in St. Louis with a spectacular catch. With two out and the bases loaded in the twelfth inning, Speake hauled down an Alex Grammas drive while crashing into the wall. Speake dislocated his wrist and had to be taken off the field on a stretcher.

NOVEMBER 28   The Cubs draft Monte Irvin from the Giants organization.

DECEMBER 9   The Cubs trade Randy Jackson and Don Elston to the Dodgers for Walt Moryn, Don Hoak, and Russ Meyer. The Cubs also sold Frank Baumholtz to the Phillies on the same day.

1956

Cubs

Season in a Sentence

Wid Matthews and Stan Hack are fired after the Cubs finish in last place in the seventh year of Matthews's five–year plan.

Finish • Won • Lost • Pct • GB

Eighth   60   94   .390   33.0

Manager

Stan Hack

Stats

	Cubs	NL	Rank
Batting Avg:	.244	.256	8
On–Base Pct:	.304	.324	7
Slugging Pct:	382	.401	6
Home Runs:	142		5
Stolen Bases:	55		3
ERA:	3.96	3.77	6
Fielding Avg:	.976	.977	6
Runs Scored:	597		6
Runs Allowed:	708		7

Starting Lineup

Hobie Landrith, c
Dee Fondy, 1b
Gene Baker, 2b
Don Hoak, 3b
Ernie Banks, ss
Monte Irvin, lf
Pete Whisenant, cf
Walt Moryn, rf
Eddie Miksis, 3b–cf
Jim King, lf
Solly Drake, cf
Harry Chiti, c

Pitchers

Bob Rush, sp
Sam Jones, sp
Don Kaiser, sp
Warren Hacker, sp–rp
Turk Lown, rp
Jim Davis, rp
Vito Valentinelli, rp
Jim Brosnan, rp–sp

Attendance

720,118 (seventh in NL)

Club Leaders

Batting Avg:	Banks	.297
On–Base Pct:	Banks	.358
Slugging Pct:	Banks	.530
Home Runs:	Banks	28
RBI:	Banks	85
Runs:	Banks	82
Stolen Bases:	Fondy	9
	Drake	9
Wins:	Rush	13
Strikeouts:	Jones	176
ERA:	Rush	3.19
Saves:	Lown	13

MARCH 30   The Cubs trade Hank Sauer to the Cardinals for Pete Whisenant.

Sauer was 39 years old, hit only .211 in 1955, and was deemed expendable by the Cubs front office. Whisenant was 26 and could play center field. Sauer was extremely popular with Cubs fans, however, and the trade was not taken kindly, especially after Whisenant's inadequacies were quickly apparent. Sauer had three more good seasons as a pinch–hitter and spare outfielder, and hit 26 homers for the Giants in 1957.

APRIL 17   The Cubs lose 6–0 to the Braves in Milwaukee in the first game of 1956, played in 39–degree weather. Rain and snow fell intermittently during the last four innings.

Jack Quinlan, Gene Elston, and Milo Hamilton were the radio voices of the Cubs in 1956 over WIND. Quinlan replaced Bert Wilson, who died in November 1955. Wilson is best known for belting out "Bea–oo–tiful Wrigley Field" during each broadcast. Jack Brickhouse, Harry Creighton, and Vince Lloyd covered the Cubs on WGN–TV. Brickhouse and Creighton also telecast the White Sox games. All of the Cubs home games were on television, as well as the Sox home day games. No road games for either of the Chicago clubs were on TV in 1956.

APRIL 20 The Cubs score six runs in the first inning and swamp the Reds 12–1 in the home opener before 13,973 at Wrigley Field. Ernie Banks and Monte Irvin, the latter in his first game as a Cub in Chicago, hit home runs.

MAY 2 The Giants defeat the Cubs 6–5 in seventeen innings in a strange game at Wrigley Field. The two teams combined to use 48 players, 25 of them Giants, including eight pitchers. Cubs third baseman Don Hoak set a National League record and tied a major league mark by striking out six times. Hoak was fanned by six different New York pitchers.

Wrigley Field in 1956 became the first ballpark in baseball to introduce moving ramps to carry fans to the upper deck. It was called the "Speed–Walk," but never worked properly and was removed in 1960.

MAY 12 The Cubs chalk up a 14–10 win over the Cardinals at Wrigley Field.

MAY 27 Jim Davis strikes out four Cardinals batters in the sixth inning of an 11–9 Cubs loss in the first game of a double–header in St. Louis. The feat was possible because Davis's knuckler eluded catcher Hobie Landrith on a third strike to Lindy McDaniel, allowing McDaniel to reach first base. Davis also struck out Hal Smith, Jackie Brandt, and Don Blasingame. St. Louis completed the sweep with a 12–2 win in the second game.

MAY 30 At Wrigley Field, the Cubs and the Braves combine to set a major league record for most home runs in a double–header with 15. The Braves hit nine homers and the Cubs clubbed six. In the first game, won by the Cubs 10–9, there were nine homers. Bobby Thomson hit two for Milwaukee, while Eddie Mathews, Hank Aaron, and Joe Adcock added one each. Gene Baker, Turk Lown, Hobie Landrith, and Dee Fondy went deep for Chicago. The homer by Lown was the only one he hit in 214 at–bats in 11 seasons. In the second contest, which the Braves won 11–9, there were six more homers, four by Milwaukee. Thomson hit two more, giving him four round–trippers on the day, and Mathews and Aaron also homered again. Cubs homers were by Banks and Harry Chiti.

There was also a fight to enliven the day. In the first inning of the first game, Mathews, Aaron, and Thomson hit back–to–back–to–back homers off Russ Meyer. The next hitter was Bill Bruton, who Meyer plunked with a pitch. Bruton rushed the mound, and he and Meyer exchanged punches. Both were ejected.

JUNE 1 A two–run, two–out, walk–off homer by Gene Baker beats the Dodgers 4–2 at Wrigley Field.

During June 1956, following P. K. Wrigley's suggestion, oxygen was placed in the dugout "as a means of speedy restoration of energy after intense periods of exercise." Players were resistant to the idea, however, and it was soon removed.

JUNE 2 Don Kaiser pitches a two–hitter for the Cubs in his first major league start to defeat the Dodgers 8–1 in the first game of a double–header at Wrigley Field. Previously, Kaiser pitched 25 innings of relief over two seasons. The only Brooklyn hits were singles by Duke Snider in the first and ninth innings. The Cubs also won the second game 5–4.

According to a major league rule passed in 1954, any amateur player who signed a contract worth more than $4,000 with a major league club had to *remain on the active roster for two years and could not be farmed out to the minors without waivers. These players became known as "bonus babies." Kaiser was the Cubs' first "bonus baby," signing a deal worth $20,000 in February 1955 just after turning 20. Kaiser's big league career lasted three seasons, and he had a record of only 6–15 with a 4.15 ERA. He was only 22 when he pitched his last game in the majors. Other Cubs "bonus babies" were Moe Drabowsky and Jerry Kindall, signed in 1956. The rule was rescinded in 1957.*

JULY 8   The Cubs score five runs in the ninth inning, the last four on a Monte Irvin grand slam off Gene Conley, to beat the Braves 10–6 in Milwaukee.

JULY 15   Gene Baker hits a grand slam in the third inning off Don Newcombe, but the Cubs lose 10–8 to the Dodgers at Wrigley Field.

JULY 19   Walt Moryn's homer in the ninth inning ties the score 3–3, and Dee Fondy's walk–off homer in the tenth wins the game 4–3 over the Phillies at Wrigley Field.

JULY 25   Roberto Clemente hits a walk–off, inside–the–park, grand slam homer to lift the Pirates to a 9–8 win over the Cubs in Pittsburgh on the only pitch thrown by reliever Jim Brosnan.

JULY 27   A mental lapse during a run–down costs the Cubs a game against the Dodgers in Brooklyn.

Walt Moryn was second on the Cubs in homers with 23 and in batting average at .285 in 1956.

With the score 3–3 in the tenth inning and Dodger base runners Gil Hodges on second base and Sandy Amoros on first, Roy Campanella lifted a pop bunt that was trapped by third base-man Don Hoak. Hoak retired Campanella with a throw to first baseman Dee Fondy and Amoros was caught in a rundown between first and second. While Amoros eluded the tag, the Cubs failed to notice Gil Hodges sprinting across the plate with the winning run.

AUGUST 11   Sidelined with an infected hand, Ernie Banks misses the first game of his career. Banks set a still–standing major league record for most consecutive games played at the start of a career with 424. Jerry Kindall played shortstop in place of Banks in a 3–1 loss to the Cardinals at Wrigley Field. Banks returned to the lineup on August 27 and started another playing streak that reached 717 games before it was stopped in 1961.

Banks hit 28 homers and batted .297 in 1956.

AUGUST 16   Sam Jones strikes out 13 batters in a 4–2 win over the Reds at Wrigley Field. Frank Robinson struck out four times.

SEPTEMBER 1   The Cubs sell Russ Meyer to the Reds.

OCTOBER 11   The Cubs stage a dramatic housecleaning with the firing of manager Stan Hack, director of player personnel Wid Matthews, and business manager Jim Gallagher.

                  Bob Scheffing was hired as the new manager.

NOVEMBER 13   Seven days after Dwight Eisenhower wins his second term in office, defeating Adlai Stevenson in the presidential election, the Cubs trade Don Hoak, Warren Hacker, and Pete Whisenant to the Reds for Ray Jablonski and Elmer Singleton.

DECEMBER 11   The Cubs trade Sam Jones, Hobie Landrith, Eddie Miksis, and Jim Davis to the Cardinals for Jackie Collum, Tom Poholsky, Ray Katt, and Wally Lammers. On the same day, the Cubs purchased Charlie Silvera from the Yankees.

                  John Holland's first two trades after his promotion to Cubs general manager were hardly gems. Jones won 65 games over the next four seasons for the Cardinals and Giants, while none of the four players brought to Chicago from St. Louis were of any help whatsoever.

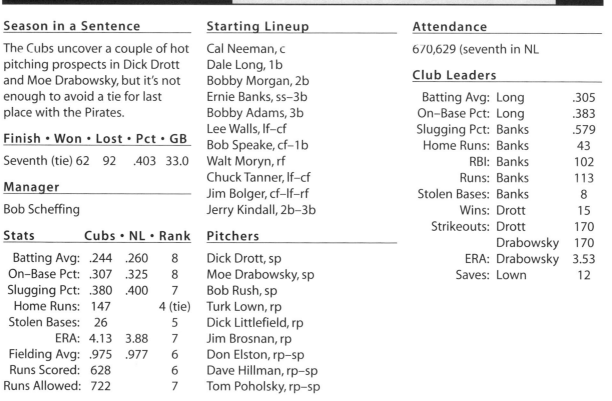

1957   Cubs

Season in a Sentence

The Cubs uncover a couple of hot pitching prospects in Dick Drott and Moe Drabowsky, but it's not enough to avoid a tie for last place with the Pirates.

Finish • Won • Lost • Pct • GB

Seventh (tie) 62   92   .403   33.0

Manager

Bob Scheffing

Stats

	Cubs	NL	Rank
Batting Avg:	.244	.260	8
On–Base Pct:	.307	.325	8
Slugging Pct:	.380	.400	7
Home Runs:	147		4 (tie)
Stolen Bases:	26		5
ERA:	4.13	3.88	7
Fielding Avg:	.975	.977	6
Runs Scored:	628		6
Runs Allowed:	722		7

Starting Lineup

Cal Neeman, c
Dale Long, 1b
Bobby Morgan, 2b
Ernie Banks, ss–3b
Bobby Adams, 3b
Lee Walls, lf–cf
Bob Speake, cf–1b
Walt Moryn, rf
Chuck Tanner, lf–cf
Jim Bolger, cf–lf–rf
Jerry Kindall, 2b–3b

Pitchers

Dick Drott, sp
Moe Drabowsky, sp
Bob Rush, sp
Turk Lown, rp
Dick Littlefield, rp
Jim Brosnan, rp
Don Elston, rp–sp
Dave Hillman, rp–sp
Tom Poholsky, rp–sp

Attendance

670,629 (seventh in NL

Club Leaders

Batting Avg:	Long	.305
On–Base Pct:	Long	.383
Slugging Pct:	Banks	.579
Home Runs:	Banks	43
RBI:	Banks	102
Runs:	Banks	113
Stolen Bases:	Banks	8
Wins:	Drott	15
Strikeouts:	Drott	170
	Drabowsky	170
ERA:	Drabowsky	3.53
Saves:	Lown	12

FEBRUARY 20   P. K. Wrigley sells the Los Angeles Angels franchise in the Pacific Coast League to Brooklyn Dodgers owner Walter O'Malley for a reported $2 million. Wrigley Field in Los Angeles was sold to the Dodgers as part of the deal. In addition to cash, the Cubs received the Dodgers Fort Worth franchise in the Texas League.

The Wrigley family had owned the Los Angeles franchise since 1921. The deal paved the way for the Dodgers to transfer the franchise to L.A., a move which became official in October 1957.

APRIL 16   The Braves defeat the Cubs 4–1 in the season opener before 23,674 at Wrigley Field. Milwaukee scored all of their runs in the fourth inning, and Warren Spahn retired the first 14 Cubs he faced. On the same day, the Cubs traded Ray Jablonski and Ray Katt to the Giants for Dick Littlefield and Don Lennon.

Pinstripes were added to the home uniforms of the Cubs in 1957.

APRIL 20   The Cubs trade Jim King for Bobby Del Greco and Ed Mayer.

APRIL 24   Three Cubs pitchers combine to set a major league record by walking nine batters in one inning during a 9–5 loss to the Reds at Crosley Field. Moe Drabowsky was on the mound at the start of the fifth inning walk–athon. After retiring the first batter, Drabowsky walked four in a row. Jackie Collum relieved, faced five hitters, and walked three. Jim Brosnan replaced Collum, and walked two more. The Reds recorded only one hit in the inning, a single by George Crowe off Collum, and scored seven runs.

APRIL 30   Walt Moryn hits a grand slam in the seventh inning off Clem Labine of the Dodgers to give the club a 9–7 win, but Brooklyn rallies to win 10–9 in ten innings at Ebbets Field. The game ended on a home run by Don Zimmer.

MAY 1   The Cubs trade Gene Baker and Dee Fondy to the Pirates for Lee Walls and Dale Long.

This trade helped the Cubs in the short–term, as both Long and Walls gave the club two commendable seasons. The deal had no long–term value, however, as both Long and Walls were gone by 1960.

MAY 5   The Cubs snap a nine–game losing streak with five tenth–inning runs to beat the Giants 8–3 at the Polo Grounds. New York won the second game 6–2.

MAY 7   The Cubs score four runs in the fourteenth inning to take a 10–6 lead, then stave off a two–run Pirate rally to win 10–8 in Pittsburgh.

MAY 23   The Cubs trade Jackie Collum and Vito Valentinelli to the Dodgers for Don Elston.

This was the second May 1957 trade to work out well for the Cubs. Elston was a mainstay in the Cub bullpen until 1964. His 449 games pitched for the club are the third–highest in Cubs history behind only Charlie Root (605) and Lee Smith (458).

MAY 24   Cubs right fielder Frank Ernaga homers in his first major league at–bat and triples in his second plate appearance during a 5–1 win over the Braves at Wrigley Field. The home run, struck in the second inning, tied the score 1–1. Ernaga's fourth–inning triple, drove in the run which broke the tie. Both hits came off future Hall of Famer Warren Spahn, who won the Cy Young Award in 1957.

MAY 26   Cubs rookie pitcher Dick Drott strikes out 15 batters in a 7–5 win over the Braves in the first game of a double–header at Wrigley Field. Hank Aaron struck out three times. The Cubs also won the second game 5–4 with two outs in the ninth inning.

Dick Drott led the Cubs in wins with 15 as a rookie in 1957. He also struck out 15 in a game.

Drott was only 20 years old on the day of his 15–strikeout performance, and had a 15–11 record with a 3.58 ERA and 170 strikeouts in 229 innings in 1957. He seemed headed for stardom, but the Cubs pushed the youngster far too hard, far too early in his career, and Drott broke down quickly after his fine rookie season. The Cubs gave him up to Houston in the expansion draft following the 1961 season, and Drott's career ended two years later with a 27–46 lifetime record. From 1958 through 1963, Drott had a won–lost record of 12–35 with an ERA of 5.38.

JUNE 1   The Cubs are trounced 22–2 by the Reds in Cincinnati.

JUNE 2   Moe Drabowsky ties a major league record by hitting four batters during a 6–4 loss to the Reds in the first game of a double–header in Cincinnati. The Cubs won the second game 4–2.

JUNE 6   The Cubs–Dodgers game in Brooklyn is postponed by fog. The umpires called time in the second inning when left fielder Bob Speake lost a fly ball, which fell for a double, in the heavy pall. The umps waited one hour and 26 minutes for the atmosphere to clear before calling the game.

JUNE 21   Jim Brosnan has to leave a 12–10 loss to the Giants at Wrigley Field after suffering a pulled tendon during his warm–up tosses.

Brosnan entered the game in the tenth inning with the score 10–10. While warming up, his zipper caught in his jersey, causing him to fall off the mound. Brosnan suffered a sprained Achilles' tendon in his left foot. Dave Hillman was rushed into service to replace Brosnan and allowed the two runs that lost the game.

JULY 2   Lee Walls hits for the cycle, but the Cubs lose 8–6 in ten innings to the Reds at Wrigley Field. Walls had a double in the first inning, a two–run home run in the third, a two–run triple in the fifth, and a single in the seventh.

JULY 11   Bob Rush carries a no–hitter into the eighth inning, but loses 1–0 to the Phillies in eleven innings in the first game of a double–header at Connie Mack Stadium. Rush allowed a total of four hits in the game. In the second tilt, Philadelphia pitcher Jack Sanford retired the first 22 Cubs to face him before Dale Long singled. The Cubs collected three more hits, but lost 3–1.

JULY 14   Bobby Morgan has five hits in six at–bats for the Cubs, but Chicago loses 8–6 in twelve innings to the Giants in New York on a two–run walk–off homer by Willie Mays.

            Morgan was one of eleven third basemen tried by the Cubs in 1957. Even Ernie Banks played 58 games at the hot corner.

JULY 23   Dick Drott strikes out 14 batters to defeat the Giants 4–0 at Wrigley Field.

AUGUST 16   Walt Moryn blasts a two–run walk–off homer in the twelfth inning to defeat the Reds 8–6 at Wrigley Field.

AUGUST 24   The Cubs play the Giants in New York for the last time, and win 4–2 at the Polo Grounds.

            The game was played five days after the Giants announced they were moving to San Francisco at the end of the 1957 season. The Cubs played at the Polo Grounds again in 1962 and 1963, when it was the home of the Mets.

AUGUST 28   The Cubs play the Dodgers in Brooklyn for the last time, and lose 4–3 at Ebbets Field.

            The Dodgers officially announced the move to Los Angeles on October 8.

SEPTEMBER 2   The Braves collect 26 hits and clobber the Cubs 23–10 in the first game of a double–header at Wrigley Field. Frank Torre scored six of the Milwaukee runs to tie a modern major league record. The Braves also won the second game 4–0.

SEPTEMBER 4   Moe Drabowsky pitches a two–hitter to defeat the Reds 1–0 in the first game of a double–header at Wrigley Field. Ernie Banks hit a home run in the fifth inning off Bud Podbielan to account for the lone run of the game. The only Cincinnati hits were a triple by Johnny Temple in the seventh inning and a single by Jerry Lynch in the ninth. The Reds won the second game 7–2.

            Drabowsky was 13–15 as a 21–year–old rookie in 1957. Like Drott, the Cubs wore out young Drabowsky by having him pitch 239⅔ innings. Moe never pitched that many innings again, and never won as many as 13 games again, but he had a big league career that lasted until 1972 with seven clubs, mostly as a reliever. Drabowsky was born in Ozanna, Poland. His family moved to the United States in 1938 and settled in Connecticut.

SEPTEMBER 14   Ernie Banks hits three homers in a 7–3 win over the Pirates in the second game of a double–header at Wrigley Field. Banks homered off Whammy Douglas in the first and fourth innings, and Bob Purkey in the eighth. Pittsburgh won the first game 3–1.

In 12 games from September 7 through September 19, Banks hit nine homers in 40 at–bats. During the 1957 season, Banks hit .285 with 43 homers, 113 runs, and 102 RBIs.

SEPTEMBER 29   Five days after President Eisenhower sends federal troops to Little Rock, Arkansas, to integrate Central High School, Ernie Banks collects five hits, including two doubles, in five at–bats in an 8–3 win over the Cardinals at St. Louis in the last contest of the 1957 season. It was the only five–hit game of Ernie's career.

DECEMBER 2   Two months after the Soviet Union launches the earth satellite Sputnik, the Cubs draft Tony Taylor from the Giants organization.

Taylor was a third baseman in the Giants minor league system. The Cubs moved him to second base, and he became the club's starter at the position in 1958. Taylor played in the majors until 1976.

DECEMBER 5   The Cubs trade Bob Rush, Don Kaiser, and Eddie Haas to the Braves for Sammy Taylor and Taylor Phillips.

1958   Cubs

Season in a Sentence

The Cubs pound out a club–record 182 homers and are in pennant contention in July, but fade to fifth when a youthful and inexperienced pitching staff fails.

Finish • Won • Lost • Pct • GB

Fifth (tie) 72 82 .468 20.0

Manager

Bob Scheffing

Stats

Stats	Cubs	NL	Rank
Batting Avg:	.265	.262	3
On–Base Pct:	.332	.331	4
Slugging Pct:	.426	.408	1
Home Runs:	182		1
Stolen Bases:	39		6
ERA:	4.22	3.96	6
Fielding Avg:	.975	.978	7
Runs Scored:	709		2
Runs Allowed:	725		6

Starting Lineup

Sammy Taylor, c
Dale Long, 1b
Tony Taylor, 2b
Al Dark, 3b
Ernie Banks, ss
Walt Moryn, lf
Bobby Thomson, cf
Lee Walls, rf
Johnny Goryl, 3b–2b
Cal Neeman, c

Pitchers

Taylor Phillips, sp–rp
Dick Drott, sp
Moe Drabowsky, sp
Dave Hillman, sp–rp
John Briggs, sp
Glen Hobbie, rp–sp
Don Elston, rp
Bill Henry, rp

Attendance

979,904 (sixth in NL)

Club Leaders

Batting Avg:	Banks	.313
On–Base Pct:	Walls	.370
Slugging Pct:	Banks	.614
Home Runs:	Banks	47
RBI:	Banks	129
Runs:	Banks	119
Stolen Bases:	Taylor	21
Wins:	Hobbie	10
Strikeouts:	Drott	127
ERA:	Hobbie	3.74
Saves:	Elston	10

APRIL 3   The Cubs trade Bob Speake to the Giants for Bobby Thomson.

                 Thomson was 34 at the time of the trade and gave the Cubs a surprisingly
                 strong season in 1958 as a center fielder with 21 homers and a .283 batting
                 average. At his age, however, he was not a long–term solution to the Cubs
                 never–ending rebuilding project.

APRIL 15   The Cubs win 4–0 in the season opener against the Cardinals in St. Louis. Jim
                 Brosnan pitched six innings for the win, while Don Elston went three innings for
                 the save. Ed Mayer and Dolan Nichols also took the mound for the Cubs in the four–
                 pitcher shutout, but neither retired a batter. The Cardinals left 14 runners on base.

APRIL 18   In the home opener, the Cubs defeat the Cardinals 11–6 before 21,076 at Wrigley
                 Field. The Cubs scored six runs in the fourth inning to break a 2–2 tie. Walt Moryn
                 hit a home run.

                 Lou Boudreau began announcing Cubs games on radio in 1958. Except for a
                 brief fling as Cubs manager in 1960, he remained as a broadcaster until 1990.
                 The radio broadcasts moved to WGN, as the station had the exclusive rights to
                 Cubs games for the first time. The Cubs have been on WGN ever since.

APRIL 22   The Cubs play the Dodgers in Los Angeles for the first time and lose 4–2 at Memorial
                 Coliseum.

APRIL 24   Lee Walls pops three home runs over the left–field screen at Memorial Coliseum in
                 Los Angeles to lead the Cubs to a 15–2 win over the Dodgers. He also collected
                 eight runs batted in. Walls hit a two–run homer off Don Drysdale in the first
                 inning, a three–run shot off Roger Craig in the fifth, and another three–run homer
                 off Ron Negray in the seventh. The winning pitcher was Gene Fodge, in what
                 would prove to be the only victory of his career.

                 Heading into the 1958 season, Walls was 25 years old and had 19 home runs in
                 942 career at–bats. In the first 14 games of 1958, he clubbed nine home runs.
                 Walls finished the season with 24 homers and a .304 batting average. He wasn't
                 able to sustain his success, however, and never hit more than eight homers in
                 any season after 1958.

APRIL 25   The Cubs play the Giants in San Francisco for the first time, and lose 2–0 at Seals
                 Stadium, the Giants home before moving to Candlestick Park in 1960.

MAY 1   Johnny Goryl hits a walk–off homer in the ninth inning to defeat the Braves 3–2 at
                 Wrigley Field.

MAY 2   Walt Moryn's walk–off homer caps a brilliant comeback by the Cubs, resulting in
                 an 8–7 win over the Braves at Wrigley Field. Milwaukee led 7–0 before the Cubs
                 scored one run in the sixth inning, six in the seventh, and one in the ninth on
                 Moryn's homer.

MAY 8   The Reds score eight runs in the ninth inning to stun the Cubs 10–8 at Wrigley
                 Field. Heading into the game, the Cubs were in first place with a 13–7 record. The
                 defeat at the hands of Cincinnati started a seven–game losing streak. By May 27,

the Cubs were 18–23.

> *On the same day, the Cubs traded Turk Lown to the Reds for Hersh Freeman. Freeman flopped with the Cubs, while Lown continued to be an effective reliever for several more seasons. In 1959 with the White Sox, Lown was 9–2 with 15 saves in helping the Sox reach the World Series.*

MAY 13
Moe Drabowsky gives up Stan Musial's 3,000th career hit during a 5–3 Cardinals win at Wrigley Field.

> *Musial was held out of the starting lineup so that he could collect his 3,000th hit in St. Louis, where the Cardinals were scheduled to play the next day. With the Cubs leading 3–1 in the sixth inning and a runner on second base, St. Louis manager Fred Hutchinson brought Musial off the bench, and Stan delivered a run–scoring double.*

MAY 20
The Cubs trade Jim Brosnan to the Cardinals for Al Dark.

MAY 23
The Cubs score seven runs in the fifth inning and defeat the Phillies 11–4 in Philadelphia.

MAY 25
Taylor Phillips pitches the Cubs to a 1–0 win over the Braves and ex–Cub Bob Rush in Milwaukee.

MAY 30
Walt Moryn hits three homers, the third a ninth–inning walk–off blast, to defeat the Dodgers 10–8 in the second game of a double–header at Wrigley Field. The Dodgers led 7–1 when Ernie Banks and Moryn hit back–to–back homers off Don Newcombe. Moryn and Chuck Tanner clubbed consecutive homers off Ed Roebuck in the seventh to tie the score 8–8. Moryn's game–winner in the ninth was hit off Sandy Koufax. The first game of the twinbill was also a thriller, as the Cubs scored three runs in the ninth inning to win 3–2. Moryn doubled in the tying run with a two–out double and scored the winning run on Sammy Taylor's single.

> *The Cubs hit 182 home runs in 1958, breaking the club record of 171 set in 1930. The 1958 mark remained the club record until the 1987 Cubs hit 209 homers.*

JUNE 8
Moe Drabowsky pitches a one–hitter to defeat the Pirates 4–0 at Forbes Field. The only Pittsburgh hit was a broken–bat single by Ted Kluszewski in the second inning.

JUNE 16
Five days after signing a $50,000 contract with the Cubs after graduating from Fresno (Calif.) High School, 18–year–old Dick Ellsworth pitches the Cubs to a 1–0 win over the White Sox in an exhibition game at Comiskey Park.

> *Ellsworth made his regular season major league debut on June 22 as a starting pitcher, but lasted only until the third inning in a 6–2 loss to the Reds in Cincinnati and was immediately sent to the minors. He is the youngest pitcher in Cubs history. Ellsworth returned in 1960 and pitched for the Cubs until 1966, and in the majors until 1971.*

JUNE 20
The Cubs score seven runs in the first inning and race to an 11–3 win over the Reds in Cincinnati in a contest shortened to eight innings by rain.

JULY 1   Entering the game with only one major league homer, Tony Taylor hits two to lead the Cubs to a 9–5 win over the Giants at Wrigley Field. One of Taylor's home runs cleared the wall, while the other was an "inside–the–gutter" homer earned with the ingenious help of his teammates.

Taylor hit a ball just inside the third base line that bounced into the Cub bullpen and then into a rain gutter at the base of the left field line. Cub players leaped off the bullpen bench as Giant left fielder Leon Wagner came charging over. As the Cubs peered under the bench, Wagner scrambled around looking for the ball, which was actually about 40 feet away farther down the line in the gutter. By the time Wagner realized he had been duped, Taylor had circled the bases. Taylor didn't hit more than one homer in a game again until 1970.

JULY 6   Dick Drott (6 ⅓ innings) and Don Elston (2 ⅓ innings) combine for a one–hitter to beat the Dodgers 6–2 at Memorial Coliseum. The only Los Angeles hit was a bloop single by Jim Gilliam in the seventh inning. Drott walked the next three batters, raising his total to eight walks in the game, and was taken out for Elston.

JULY 13   Lee Walls collects hits in seven consecutive at–bats with a home run and six singles during a double–header sweep of the Phillies at Wrigley Field. The Cubs won 3–2 and 2–1.

The next day, Walls homered in his first at–bat giving him eight consecutive hits.

JULY 14   The Cubs earn a dramatic 11–10 win in eleven innings over the Phillies at Wrigley Field. The Phillies led 9–3 before the Cubs scored one run in the fifth inning, one in the seventh and a four–run explosion in the ninth to tie the contest 9–9. Philadelphia scored in the top of the eleventh, but the Cubs came back with two in their half, both scoring on Walt Moryn's walk–off double.

JULY 16   The Cubs sweep a double–header against the Reds at Wrigley Field with two late–inning rallies. In the first game, the Cubs scored three runs in the ninth to win 5–4. The last two runs were scored on a double by Bobby Thomson. In the night-cap, the Cubs plated three runs in the eighth to win 7–5.

After the victories, the Cubs had a record of 45–41 and were in third place, just 2 ½ games behind the first–place Braves. The Cubs lost 29 of their next 39 games, however, and fell into last place before scrambling back to end the season in a tie for fifth.

AUGUST 3   After losing the opener 8–2 to the Phillies in the first game of a double–header in Philadelphia, the Cubs recover to win the second tilt 12–10. The Phillies scored five runs in the first inning to take a 5–0 lead, fell behind 12–5, and scored five more in the ninth in a rally that fell short.

AUGUST 15 Cal Neeman's homer in the tenth inning lifts the Cubs to a 3–1 win over the Giants in San Francisco.

AUGUST 21 Ernie Banks drives in all five Cubs runs with two homers and a double in a 5–3 win over the Pirates at Wrigley Field.

Banks won the first of his two consecutive National League Most Valuable Player awards in 1958. He finished the season leading the NL in home runs (47) and runs batted in (129). Banks also batted .313.

Ernie Banks led the NL in homers, with 47, and RBIs, with 129, in 1958 on the way to his first of two straight NL MVP awards.

AUGUST 23   The Cubs purchase Jim Marshall from the Orioles.

AUGUST 24   In his first two games as a Cub, Jim Marshall hits three home runs during a double–header against the Phillies at Wrigley Field. He clubbed two homers in the first game and one in the second. Despite Marshall's heroics, the Cubs lost twice by scores of 13–8 and 5–3.

Marshall played for the Cubs in 1958 and 1959. He later managed the club from 1974 through 1976.

AUGUST 30   Dale Long's pinch–hit homer in the tenth inning beats the Cardinals 3–1 in St. Louis.

This was the first Cubs road game ever televised in Chicago. The Cubs and White Sox had an agreement that neither club would televise road games so that they would not conflict with other's home games. On this date, the White Sox played a day game at Comiskey Park, and the Cubs contest was televised at night. Regularly scheduled telecasts of Cubs road games began in 1960 but were limited to five games a year through 1967. Beginning in 1968, most of the Cubs road games were on television.

SEPTEMBER 6   Johnny Briggs (7⅔ innings) and Don Elston (1⅓ innings) combine on a two–hitter to defeat the Giants 6–3 at Wrigley Field. The only San Francisco hits were a single by Orlando Cepeda in the seventh inning and a three–run double by Willie Kirkland in the eighth after Briggs walked the bases loaded.

Briggs was one of a corps of young starting pitchers tried out by the Cubs in

1958 that also included Dick Drott, Moe Drabowsky, Taylor Phillips, and Glen Hobbie. Pitchers who were 25 years old or younger on Opening Day of that year started 124 of the Cubs' 154 games. The inexperience showed, as Drabowsky was the Cubs' leading winner among starters with just eight victories. Moe was 8–10 as starter and 1–1 as a reliever. The leading winner overall was Hobbie, who was 10–6. Hobbie had a 4–5 record as a starter and was 6–1 in relief.

SEPTEMBER 20   After the Dodgers score two runs in the ninth to tie the score 2–2, Bobby Thomson hits a walk–off homer in the Cubs half of the inning for a 3–2 victory. Thomson entered the game in the eighth inning as a defensive replacement for Walt Moryn.

SEPTEMBER 27   In the final game of the season, the Cubs score four runs in the ninth inning to beat the Dodgers 7–4 in Los Angeles. The win allowed the Cubs to finish the season in a tie for fifth place with the Cardinals. If the Cubs had lost, they would have finished in seventh behind the Cards and the Dodgers.

1959 Cubs

Season in a Sentence

Bob Scheffing becomes the latest Cubs managerial casualty after the Cubs finish in a tie for fifth for the second straight year.

Finish • Won • Lost • Pct • GB

Fifth (tie)   74   80   .481   13.0

Manager

Bob Scheffing

Stats

Stats	Cubs	NL	Rank
Batting Avg:	.249	.261	7
On–Base Pct:	.319	.328	7
Slugging Pct:	.398	.400	5
Home Runs:	163	3	
Stolen Bases:	32		7 (tie)
ERA:	4.02	3.95	6
Fielding Avg:	.977	.977	4
Runs Scored:	673		5
Runs Allowed:	688		5

Starting Lineup

Sammy Taylor, c
Dale Long, 1b
Tony Taylor, 2b
Al Dark, 3b
Ernie Banks, ss
Walt Moryn, lf
George Altman, cf
Lee Walls, rf
Bobby Thomson, lf–cf–rf
Jim Marshall, 1b
Earl Averill, c
Irv Noren, rf–lf

Pitchers

Glen Hobbie, sp
Bob Anderson, sp
Dave Hillman, sp–rp
Moe Drabowsky, sp
Art Ceccarelli, sp
Bill Henry, rp
Don Elston, rp
John Buzhardt, rp–sp
Bill Henry, rp

Attendance

858,255 (sixth in NL)

Club Leaders

Batting Avg:	Banks	.304
On–Base Pct:	Banks	.374
Slugging Pct:	Banks	.596
Home Runs:	Banks	45
RBI:	Banks	143
Runs:	Banks	97
Stolen Bases:	Taylor	23
Wins:	Hobbie	16
Strikeouts:	Hobbie	138
ERA:	Hillman	3.53
Saves:	Elston	13

MARCH 10   Bill Veeck purchases a controlling interest in the White Sox.

                  *Under Veeck, the White Sox won the 1959 American League pennant. He also
                  stole considerable media attention away from the Cubs with his stunts and pro-
                  motions, and the installation of an exploding scoreboard at Comiskey Park. The
                  White Sox outdrew the Cubs 1,423,144 to 858,255 in 1959, and 1,644,460 to
                  809,770 in 1960. Veeck sold the Sox because of health reasons in June 1961.*

APRIL 10   Three months after Alaska becomes the forty–ninth state, the Cubs home opener
                  against the Dodgers is postponed by snow.

APRIL 11   The Cubs open with a 6–1 win over the Dodgers before 12,288 at Wrigley Field.
                  The temperature at the start of the contest was 42 degrees. Bob Anderson pitched
                  the complete game. Sammy Taylor drove in four runs. On the first pitch of his first
                  major league at–bat, George Altman was hit by a Don Drysdale offering.

APRIL 16   The Cubs score seven runs in the ninth inning to win 11–3 over the Giants in San
                  Francisco.

APRIL 21   Glen Hobbie pitches a one–hitter to defeat the Cardinals 1–0 at Wrigley Field. Hobbie
                  retired the first 20 batters to face him before Stan Musial doubled in the seventh
                  inning. Walt Moryn's double in the second drove in the lone run of the game.

APRIL 30   Ernie Banks hits a home run in the tenth inning to beat the Reds 3–2 in Cincinnati.

                  *Banks won the NL MVP award for the second year in a row by hitting .304
                  with 45 homers and a league–leading 143 runs batted in.*

MAY 4   The Cubs trade Riverboat Smith to the Indians for Randy Jackson.

MAY 10   Earl Averill's home run in the eleventh inning beats the Cardinals 10–9 in the first
                  game of a double–header at Busch Stadium. Bobby Thomson drove in six runs in
                  the game on two homers and a single. St. Louis won the second game 8–7. Relief
                  pitchers Elmer Singleton of the Cubs and Lindy McDaniel of the Cardinals figured
                  in both decisions, each earning a victory and a defeat.

MAY 12   The Cubs score five runs in the ninth inning, the last four on a walk–off, pinch–hit,
                  grand slam home run by Earl Averill off Lew Burdette to defeat the Braves 7–3 at
                  Wrigley Field.

MAY 13   The Cubs score seven runs in the third inning and defeat the Reds 10–0 at Wrigley
                  Field. Ernie Banks hit a home run in the big inning off Bob Purkey.

MAY 17   Roberto Clemente nearly hits the left field side of the Wrigley Field scoreboard with
                  a long home run during a 7–6 Cubs win over the Pirates in the second game of a
                  double–header. Clemente's drive was struck off Bob Henry in the ninth and was
                  estimated to have traveled 500 feet. Pittsburgh won the first game 5–4.

MAY 19   The Cubs score three runs in the ninth inning to defeat the Phillies 8–7 at Wrigley
                  Field. All three runs were charged to Taylor Phillips, who was traded by the Cubs
                  to the Phillies seven days earlier for Seth Morehead.

On the same day, the Cubs traded Charlie King to the Cardinals for Irv Noren.

MAY 28   Dave Hillman sets a Cubs record for most strikeouts in a game by a reliever with 11 in 7⅔ innings during a 7–5 win over the Dodgers in Los Angeles.

MAY 29   The Cubs score eight runs in the fourth inning and defeat the Dodgers 9–4 in Los Angeles.

JUNE 21   John Buzhardt pitches a one–hitter to defeat the Phillies 4–0 at Wrigley Field. The only Philadelphia hit was a single by Carl Sawatski in the third inning.

                Buzhardt was a 22–year–old native of Prosperity, South Carolina, when he threw his one–hitter. At the end of the 1959 season, the Cubs traded him to the Phillies.

JUNE 30   During a 4–1 loss to the Cardinals at Wrigley Field, confusion reigns as two balls wind up in play. *(See below.)*

Two Balls in Play

One of the daffiest situations ever recorded at Wrigley Field took place on June 30, 1959, when two balls were in the play at the same time in a game against the Cardinals. With St. Louis batting in the fourth inning, the count was 3–1 on Stan Musial with Bob Anderson pitching. Anderson's next pitch sailed past Cubs catcher Sammy Taylor, entitling Musial to first base on the walk. Taylor claimed the ball hit Musial's bat and therefore was foul and failed to pursue the ball as it rolled back to the screen. Taylor began arguing with home plate umpire Vic Delmore, and Chicago Manager Bob Scheffing joined Taylor in the discussion. Musial went past first base and headed for second.

Third baseman Al Dark realized the ball was in play and ran full speed toward the backstop where the ball was located. With Dark charging in, the batboy tossed the ball to field announcer Pat Pieper. Pieper acted as though the ball was a hot potato and dropped it to the ground. Dark reached down, grabbed the ball, and threw it to shortstop Ernie Banks.

Meanwhile, Delmore gave Taylor a new ball as the two continued to argue. Anderson, who was also engaged in the debate with the umpire, saw Musial race for second. Anderson grabbed the ball out of Taylor's hand and threw it to second base at almost the precise moment that Dark's throw was headed in the same direction.

Banks fielded Dark's throw on one hop. Anderson's throw sailed into center field. While all this was happening, Musial slid safely into second. Musial saw Anderson's throw head into the outfield and headed for third. Stan didn't take more than two or three steps past second when he was tagged by Banks with the original ball. The second ball was retrieved by center fielder Bobby Thomson, who lobbed it toward the Cubs dugout.

The umpires huddled for ten minutes and ruled that Musial should return to first base. Scheffing protested, and the umps conferred again, this time calling Musial out. Cardinals Manager Solly Hemus protested immediately, claiming interference by the batboy nullified the play. Hemus intended to file a formal protest, but it was never filed because the Cardinals won 4–1.

JULY 7 — Ernie Banks collects two doubles in three at–bats in helping the National League to a 5–4 win in the All–Star Game, played at Forbes Field in Pittsburgh.

This was the first of two All–Star Games in 1959. Two All–Star Games were played each season from 1959 through 1962.

JULY 17 — Art Ceccarelli pitches the Cubs to a 1–0 win over the Reds at Wrigley Field.

JULY 22 — The Cubs score seven runs in the second inning, which is all the club needs to defeat the Dodgers 7–2 in Los Angeles. Earl Averill accounted for four of the runs with a grand slam off Danny McDevitt.

On July 28, the Cubs had a 50–48 record and were in fourth place, 4½ games behind. The Cubs lost their next seven games, however, to erase any pennant hopes.

AUGUST 6 — Billy Williams makes his major league debut. Wearing uniform number 4 (he switched to number 26 in 1961), Williams went hitless in four at–bats and played left field during a 4–2 win over the Phillies at Wrigley Field.

AUGUST 12 — With a 35–mile–per–hour wind sweeping Wrigley Field, the Cubs defeat the Dodgers 11–8. Al Dark hit a grand slam in the first inning off Don Drysdale.

AUGUST 13 — The Cubs hammer out a 20–9 win over the Giants at Wrigley Field. Al Dark hit a grand slam off Mike McCormick in the seventh inning. Rookie outfielder George Altman collected five hits, including two homers, in six at–bats. Dale Long and Tony Taylor also homered for the Cubs.

AUGUST 14 — Dale Long hits a pinch–hit home run for the second day in a row as the Cubs beat the Giants 7–5 at Wrigley Field.

Other Cubs who have hit pinch–hit home runs in consecutive at–bats include Carmen Fanzone (1974), Darrin Jackson (1988), and Henry Rodriguez (2000).

AUGUST 29 — Eight days after Hawaii becomes the fiftieth state, Ernie Banks says "aloha" to a Warren Spahn pitch and drives it for a grand slam home run in the third inning of an 11–4 win over the Braves at Wrigley Field.

SEPTEMBER 6 — Ernie Banks hits a three–run homer off Sandy Koufax in the tenth inning to account for all of the runs in a 3–0 win over the Dodgers in the first game of a double–header in Los Angeles. Art Ceccarelli pitched the complete–game shutout. In the second tilt, Walt Moryn hit a three–run homer in the ninth to give the Cubs a 5–3 win.

SEPTEMBER 16 — A two–run walk–off homer by Tony Taylor in the ninth inning beats the Pirates 4–2 in the second game of a double–header at Wrigley Field. Pittsburgh won the first game 3–2.

SEPTEMBER 17 — Before a crowd of only 598, the Cubs lose 5–2 to the Phillies at Wrigley Field.

SEPTEMBER 22 — The White Sox bring the World Series to Chicago by clinching the American League pennant with a 4–2 win over the Indians in Cleveland.

Earlier in the day, the Cubs had a hand in determining the White Sox's oppo-
nent in the Fall Classic. The Giants entered the game at Wrigley Field one game
behind the Braves and the Dodgers, who were tied for first with five games left
on the schedule. The Cubs defeated the Giants 5–4 when George Altman hit a
two–run, walk–off homer in the ninth off Sam Jones.

SEPTEMBER 23   For the second day in a row, the Cubs diminish the Giants' hope for a pennant with
a walk–off homer when Cal Neeman hits one over the Wrigley Field wall in the
tenth inning to give Chicago a 9–8 win.

SEPTEMBER 26   The Cubs continue to play the role of spoilers in the pennant race by pinning a
12–2 defeat on the Dodgers at Wrigley Field. The loss dropped Los Angeles into a
tie for first place with the Braves with one game remaining on the schedule.

SEPTEMBER 27   On the final day of the regular season, the Dodgers beat the Cubs 7–1 at Wrigley Field.

The Braves also won, forcing a playoff for the NL pennant. The Dodgers won the
playoff, then defeated the White Sox four games to two in the World Series.

SEPTEMBER 28   P. K. Wrigley surprises Cubs fans by firing
Bob Scheffing as manager and replacing him
with 61–year–old Charlie Grimm.

In 1958 and 1959, the Cubs won at least
70 games in back–to–back seasons for
the first time since 1945 and 1946, but it
couldn't save Scheffing's job. (The Cubs
didn't win 70 or more in back–to–back
seasons again until 1963–64). "Managers
are expendable," said Wrigley. "I believe
there should be relief managers just like
relief pitchers." Grimm had been a vice
president in the front office since 1956
after being fired as manager of the
Braves. Previously, Grimm managed the
Cubs from 1932 through 1938 and from
1944 through 1949. "Every time we call
on Charlie, we win a pennant," com-
mented Wrigley. Grimm managed the
Cubs to the World Series in 1932, 1935,
and 1945, but not this time. Just 17
games into the 1960 season, Grimm was
"traded" to WGN for Lou Boudreau

Manager Bob Scheffing and long–time broadcaster Jack Brickhouse shake hands on the
field before a game. Despite winning more
than 70 games in back–to–back seasons,
Scheffing was fired after the 1959 campaign.

(see May 4, 1960). Scheffing later managed the Detroit Tigers from 1961 through
1963 and was general manager of the Mets from 1970 through 1975.

NOVEMBER 21   The Cubs trade Dave Hillman and Jim Marshall to the Red Sox for Dick Gernert.

DECEMBER 1   The Cubs trade Bobby Thomson to the Red Sox for Al Schroll.

DECEMBER 6   The Cubs trade Bill Henry, Lee Walls and Lou Jackson to the Reds for Frank Thomas.

THE
1960s

THE STATE OF THE CUBS

During the 1960s, the Cubs had a record of 735–868 for a winning percentage of .459. It was the worst percentage among the eight pre–expansion teams in the National League. The Cubs posted a modest 82–80 record in 1963, the club's first winning season since 1946. The club slipped back into last place in 1966, however. A revival began in 1967, the first of six consecutive winning seasons, as the Cubs began to build a team around Ernie Banks, Ron Santo and Billy Williams with young players like Ferguson Jenkins, Glenn Beckert, Randy Hundley, Don Kessinger, Bill Hands, and Ken Holtzman. The NL pennant–winners during the 1960s were the Pirates (1960), Reds (1961), Giants (1962), Dodgers (1963, 1965, and 1966), Cardinals (1964, 1967, and 1968), and Mets (1969).

THE BEST TEAM

The 1969 Cubs led the Eastern Division for most of the season and finished with a record of 92–70.

THE WORST TEAM

The clubs in both 1962 and 1966 had records of 59–103. The 1962 team landed in ninth place, and the 1966 team was tenth in a ten–team league.

THE BEST MOMENT

The Cubs took an 8 ½–game lead over the Cardinals and a 9 ½–game lead over the Mets on August 14, 1969.

THE WORST MOMENT

The 1969 Cubs tumbled out of last place and finished the season eight games behind the Mets.

THE ALL–DECADE TEAM • YEARS WITH CUBS

Randy Hundley, c	1966–73; 1976–77
Ernie Banks, 1b	1953–71
Glenn Beckert, 2b	1965–73
Ron Santo, 3b	1960–73
Don Kessinger, ss	1964–75
Billy Williams, lf	1959–74
Adolpho Phillips, cf	1966–69
George Altman, rf	1959–62; 1965–67
Ferguson Jenkins, p	1966–73; 1982–83
Bill Hands, p	1966–72
Dick Ellsworth, p	1958; 1960–66
Ken Holtzman, p	1965–71; 1978–79

Banks, Williams, and Jenkins are all in the Hall of Fame, and Santo should be enshrined at Cooperstown. All twelve of the players on the All–Decade team of the 1960s were part of one youth movement or another in attempt pull the Cubs out of the doldrums. Pitchers Glen Hobbie (1957–64) and Larry Jackson (1963–66) also made significant contributions as the aces of some losing clubs.

THE DECADE LEADERS

Batting Avg:	Williams	.292
On–Base Pct:	Santo	.369
Slugging Pct:	Williams	.494
Home Runs:	Banks	269
RBI:	Santo	937
Runs:	Williams	861
Stolen Bases:	Phillips	66
Wins:	Ellsworth	84
Strikeouts:	Jenkins	917
ERA:	Jenkins	2.95
Saves:	Regan	42

THE HOME FIELD

The upper deck at Wrigley was completely rebuilt between 1968 to 1971 by reinforcing all of the concrete and steel. Plastic, self–rising, wider contour seats replaced folding chairs in the lower deck reserved seating area, and the brickwork in the entire park was renovated. Attendance reached 1,674,993 in 1969, breaking the club record set in 1929. The 1969 figure wouldn't be reached again until 1984.

THE GAME YOU WISH YOU HAD SEEN

No Cubs player made a more spectacular debut than Don Cardwell. On May 15, 1960, just two days after being acquired in a trade with the Phillies, Cardwell pitched a no–hitter at Wrigley Field.

THE WAY THE GAME WAS PLAYED

Baseball was played in several new cities and ball-parks in the 1960s. Candlestick Park, Dodger Stadium, Shea Stadium, Busch Stadium, the Astrodome, and Atlanta–Fulton County Stadium were among the facilities to open. Expansion brought National League baseball back to New York, and major league ball to Houston, San Diego, and Montreal for the first time. The Astrodome, opened in 1965, brought two innovations—indoor baseball and artificial turf. Combined with an expansion of the strike zone in 1963, offense declined in the 1960s until the owners lowered the mound for the 1969 season. The league ERA dipped to 2.99 in 1968, the first time since 1919 it had been below 3.00.

THE MANAGEMENT

Philip Wrigley had some novel ideas, to say the least, in an effort to revive the Cubs after years of losing. John Holland was in charge of trades and the farm system throughout the decade, but Wrigley made the major decisions. Among them was to send manager Charlie Grimm to the radio broadcast booth just seventeen games into the 1960 season, and hire radio announcer Lou Boudreau as manager. When that didn't work, Wrigley employed a rotating group of managers called "The College of Coaches" in 1961 and 1962, which only made a bad situation worse. Bob Kennedy guided the Cubs from the dugout from 1963 through 1965, although with the title "head coach" instead of manager. Leo Durocher was named manager at the end of the 1965 season, and after leading the Cubs to a last place finish in 1966, brought the franchise some much–needed stability.

THE BEST PLAYER MOVE

The Cubs picked up Ferguson Jenkins, Adolpho Phillips, and John Herrnstein from the Phillies for Bob Buhl and Larry Jackson on April 21, 1966.

THE WORST PLAYER MOVE

In a deal which shall live in infamy in the city of Chicago, the Cubs traded Lou Brock, Jack Spring, and Paul Toth to the Cardinals on June 15, 1964 for Ernie Broglio, Bobby Shantz, and Doug Clemens.

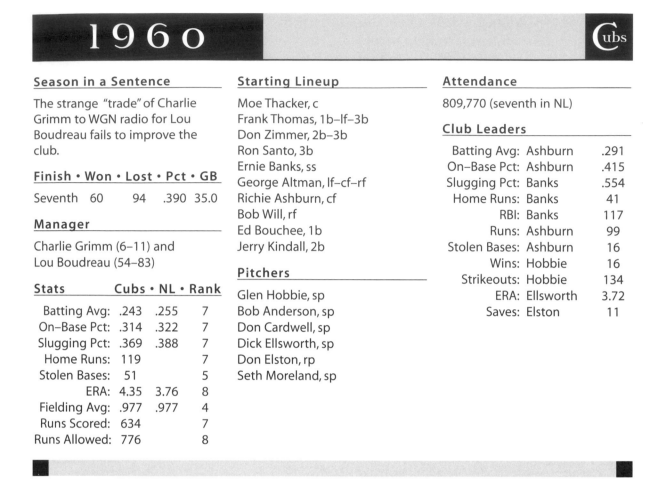

1960   Cubs

Season in a Sentence

The strange "trade" of Charlie Grimm to WGN radio for Lou Boudreau fails to improve the club.

Finish • Won • Lost • Pct • GB

Seventh   60   94   .390 35.0

Manager

Charlie Grimm (6–11) and Lou Boudreau (54–83)

Stats

Stats	Cubs	NL	Rank
Batting Avg:	.243	.255	7
On–Base Pct:	.314	.322	7
Slugging Pct:	.369	.388	7
Home Runs:	119		7
Stolen Bases:	51		5
ERA:	4.35	3.76	8
Fielding Avg:	.977	.977	4
Runs Scored:	634		7
Runs Allowed:	776		8

Starting Lineup

Moe Thacker, c
Frank Thomas, 1b–lf–3b
Don Zimmer, 2b–3b
Ron Santo, 3b
Ernie Banks, ss
George Altman, lf–cf–rf
Richie Ashburn, cf
Bob Will, rf
Ed Bouchee, 1b
Jerry Kindall, 2b

Pitchers

Glen Hobbie, sp
Bob Anderson, sp
Don Cardwell, sp
Dick Ellsworth, sp
Don Elston, rp
Seth Moreland, sp

Attendance

809,770 (seventh in NL)

Club Leaders

Batting Avg:	Ashburn	.291
On–Base Pct:	Ashburn	.415
Slugging Pct:	Banks	.554
Home Runs:	Banks	41
RBI:	Banks	117
Runs:	Ashburn	99
Stolen Bases:	Ashburn	16
Wins:	Hobbie	16
Strikeouts:	Hobbie	134
ERA:	Ellsworth	3.72
Saves:	Elston	11

JANUARY 11   The Cubs trade John Buzhardt, Al Dark, and Jim Woods to the Phillies for Richie Ashburn.

Ashburn was a future Hall of Famer, but he was 33–years–old on Opening Day in 1960 and near the end of his career. Richie gave the Cubs one good season, but it wasn't worth the loss of Buzhardt, who could have helped the Cubs starting rotation for several more years, particularly during the mid–1960s, when he was posting winning records for the cross–town White Sox.

APRIL 5   The Cubs sell Dale Long to the Giants.

APRIL 8   The Cubs send Ron Perranoski, John Goryl, Lee Handley, and $25,000 to the Dodgers for Don Zimmer.

Zimmer was 29 years old and coming off a season in which he hit .165 as a utility infielder, yet the Cubs saw fit to send three prospects and cash to the Dodgers to obtain his services. The trade turned out to be one of the worst ever completed by the Cubs, as Perranoski had a ten–year run of success as one of the premier relief pitchers in baseball with both the Dodgers and the Twins. In addition, Zimmer was acquired to play third base even though Ron Santo was about ready to take over the position and Frank Thomas would have been a better option in the meantime. Zimmer was later moved to second base, and the Cubs dealt Tony Taylor to make room for him in another poorly conceived trade.

APRIL 12   The Cubs open the season in Los Angeles and lose 3–2 to the Dodgers in eleven innings on a walk–off pinch–hit homer by Chuck Essegian off Don Elston. Essegian was one of the heroes of the 1959 World Series, clubbing two pinch–hit home runs for Los Angeles against the White Sox. Don Drysdale pitched the complete game for the Dodgers, and struck out 14. In his first game with the Cubs, Richie Ashburn collected three hits, including a double. Don Zimmer belted a home run in his first at–bat as a Cub.

APRIL 14   Ernie Banks hits a grand slam in the third inning off Jack Sanford to put the Cubs ahead 4–1, during a 6–5 win over the Giants in San Francisco. It was the first game played by the Cubs at Candlestick Park, which opened two days earlier. Frank Thomas hit a double in the ninth which broke the 5–5 tie.

Thomas should have had two doubles in the game. In the eighth, he hit a smash down the left field line. The ball bounced into the bullpen, and Moe Drabowsky, who was warming up, fielded it cleanly. Thomas was ordered back to first base because of Moe's interference.

APRIL 16   Walt Moryn's pinch–hit home run off Sam Jones with two out in the eighth inning is the only Cubs hit in a 6–1 loss to the Giants in San Francisco.

APRIL 22   The Cubs first home game of 1960 is spoiled in a 10–8 loss to the Giants before 26,573 at Wrigley Field. Frank Thomas and George Altman hit home runs.

Cubs home games were telecast in color for the first time in 1960.

APRIL 23   The Giants bombard the Cubs 18–2 at Wrigley Field.

The marquee at the corner of Clark and Addison was painted bright red in 1960. It was added to the ballpark during the 1930s and was originally fern green porcelain. It was painted because the porcelain finish was getting dull.

APRIL 29   The Cardinals score ten runs in the eighth inning and defeat the Cubs 16–6 in St. Louis. Ernie Banks drove in all six Chicago runs with a pair of three–run homers.

MAY 2   The Cubs surrender three runs in the ninth to allow the Phillies to take a 7–5 lead at Wrigley Field, then score three in their half to win 8–7. Don Zimmer's bases–loaded single drove in the game–winner.

MAY 4   P. K. Wrigley makes one of the strangest managerial changes ever made in baseball by calling Lou Boudreau out of the WGN radio booth to manage the Cubs, replacing Charlie Grimm. Wrigley also sent Grimm to replace Boudreau as announcer. At the time of the move, the Cubs had a record of 6–11. Boudreau previously managed the Indians (1942–50), Red Sox (1952–54) and Athletics (1955–57). He had been in the Cubs radio booth since 1958. The Cubs continued to play erratically under Boudreau and landed in seventh place by season's end.

MAY 5   In Lou Boudreau's first game as manager, the Cubs take a 7–2 lead into the seventh inning, but lose 9–7 to the Pirates at Wrigley Field.

MAY 13   The Cubs trade Tony Taylor and Cal Neeman to the Phillies for Ed Bouchee and Don Cardwell.

             Cardwell pitched a no–hitter in his first game as a Cub (see May 15, 1960), but the trade didn't work out well. Taylor remained in the majors until 1976.

MAY 15   Don Cardwell pitches a no–hitter in his first game as a Chicago Cub, leading his new club to a 4–0 win over the Cardinals before 33,542 in the second game of a double–header at Wrigley Field, which followed a 6–1 defeat in the first contest. Alex Grammas, who reached on a walk with one out in the first inning, was the only St. Louis base runner during Cardwell's gem. Cardwell retired the last 26 batters to face him. In the ninth, Carl Sawatski was retired on a leaping catch by George Altman in front of the right field wall. George Crowe flied out to Richie Ashburn in center for the second out. Joe Cunningham followed with a hump back liner on a 3–2 pitch to left field. It looked like a certain hit, but Walt Moryn made a miraculous catch off his shoetops.

             Cardwell was 24 years old with an undistinguished 17–26 lifetime record when he threw the no–hitter. He was 30–44 in three seasons as a Cub and finished his career in 1970 with a mark of 102–138.

MAY 20   The game between the Cubs and the Braves in Milwaukee is stopped because of fog with the score 0–0 in the fifth inning.

             Outfielders on both teams griped incessantly that the heavy fog that blew in from Lake Michigan early in the contest cut their visability to near zero. Finally, in the fifth inning, the three Cubs outfielders got the four umpires to stroll out to center field to inspect the conditions. Frank Thomas, a Cubs player not in the game, stood at home plate and fungoed a fly ball into the outfield. When none of the four umps could see the ball coming their way, they stopped play. After a thirty–minute wait in which the fog got even worse, the game was called.

MAY 23   George Altman's homer in the thirteenth inning beats the Reds 7–6 in Cincinnati.

MAY 28   A run–scoring single by Don Zimmer off Sandy Koufax in the fourteenth inning beats the Dodgers 4–3 at Wrigley Field. Frank Thomas tied the score 3–3 with a home run in the ninth inning.

JUNE 14   Glen Hobbie pitches a two–hitter to defeat the Braves 3–2 at Wrigley Field. The only two Milwaukee hits were home runs by Del Crandall in the eighth inning and Ed Mathews in the ninth.

             Hobbie led the Cubs in victories with 16 in 1960, but he also lost 20 games. He was part of one of the youngest starting pitching staffs in major league history. A total of 147 of the Cubs 156 games in 1960 were started by pitchers who were 25 years old or younger on Opening Day.

JUNE 15   The Cubs trade Walt Moryn to the Cardinals for Jim McKnight.

JUNE 26 — Ron Santo makes his major league debut, as the Cubs sweep a double–header by 7–6 and 7–5 scores over the Pirates in Pittsburgh. In the two games, Santo had three hits, including a double, in seven at–bats, and drove in five runs. Danny Murphy, a 17–year–old outfielder who signed with the Cubs for a signing bonus of $125,000 ten days earlier, also made his debut in the two games. A native of Danvers, Massachusetts, he played center field and had two hits in ten at–bats in the twinbill.

Murphy was rushed too soon and had a .171 batting average in 123 at–bats over three seasons with the Cubs. He later became a pitcher, and was 4–4 with the White Sox in 1969 and 1970.

JULY 3 — Ron Santo collects his first major league homer during a 7–5 win over the Reds at Wrigley Field. The pitcher was Jim O'Toole.

Santo was only four months past his 20th birthday when he struck his first homer. It was the first of 337 home runs that Santo hit as a Cub, which is fourth best all–time behind Sammy Sosa, Ernie Banks and Billy Williams. Santo played in 2,126 games with the club, and had 1,109 runs, 2,171 hits, 353 doubles, 1,290 runs–batted–in, and a .472 slugging average. Ron is also second in walks in Cubs history with 1,071, behind Stan Hack's 1,092.

JULY 9 — A home run by Ernie Banks in the twelfth inning beats the Giants 7–6 in San Francisco.

Banks led the National League in home runs with 41 in 1960. He also drove in 117 runs and hit .271. Early in the season, he hit his 231st homer to pass Gabby Hartnett as the Cubs all–time home run leader. Banks led the Cubs in career homers until Sammy Sosa passed him in 2004.

JULY 11 — Ernie Banks hits a two–run homer and a double during the National League's 5–3 win in the All–Star Game, played at Municipal Stadium in Kansas City.

JULY 20 — Glen Hobbie pitches a two–hitter to defeat the Reds 4–0 in the first game of a double–header at Crosley Field. Hobbie retired the first twenty–one Cincinnati hitters before Wally Post singled leading off the eighth inning. Vada Pinson also singled in the ninth. The Reds won the second game 4–3.

AUGUST 4 — Reds second baseman Billy Martin punches Cubs pitcher Jim Brewer in the face during a brawl at Wrigley Field. Playing in only his fifth big league game, Brewer suffered a fracture of the orbit bone around the right eye. Brewer touched off the incident with a high inside pitch that caused Martin to hit the dirt. Martin swung at the next pitch, but the bat slipped out of his hand and sailed toward the mound, landing about fifteen feet from Brewer. Martin walked out to retrieve the bat, and after an exchange of words, the pair began swinging at each other. The Cubs won the game 5–3.

On August 5, Martin was fined $500 and suspended five days by National League president Warren Giles. Two weeks later, Brewer and the Cubs hit Martin with a $1,040,000 damage suit, inspiring Martin's classic response: "How do they want it? Cash or check?" The claim was settled out of court six years later, with Martin paying an amount reported to be between $10,000 and $25,000.

AUGUST 14   Ron Santo hits a grand slam in the sixth inning off Dallas Green during a 7–3 win over the Phillies in the second game of a double–header in Philadelphia. The Cubs also won the first game 2–1.

AUGUST 17   Ernie Banks hits a walk–off homer in the ninth inning off Don Drysdale to give the Cubs a 1–0 win over the Dodgers at Wrigley Field. Glen Hobbie pitched the shutout.

Bob Will preceded Banks to the plate, and hit a shot through the middle which struck Drysdale in the right (pitching) hand. The ball caromed to first baseman Norm Larker, who caught it in the air for an out. Banks hit the next pitch over the wall.

AUGUST 25   Glen Hobbie wins his own game by hitting a walk–off homer with two out in the ninth off Vinegar Bend Mizell to beat the Pirates 2–1 at Wrigley Field. It was Hobbie's first home run as a major leaguer.

AUGUST 31   The Cubs win at Wrigley Field for the second straight day on a walk–off home run. Bob Will hit a blast in the tenth inning to lift the Cubs to a 5–4 win over the Braves in the first game of a double–header. Don Zimmer hit a two–run, two–out homer in the ninth to tie the score 4–4. Both homers were hit off Lew Burdette. Milwaukee won the second game 11–7.

On the same day, the Cubs sold Dick Gernert to the Tigers.

SEPTEMBER 2   Don Cardwell hits two homers during a 10–4 win over the Cardinals in St. Louis.

Cardwell hit 15 career homers in 698 at–bats.

SEPTEMBER 13   Danny Murphy becomes the youngest Cub ever to hit a home run during an 8–6 loss to the Reds in Cincinnati. Murphy was twenty–one days past his 18th birthday.

OCTOBER 1   Billy Williams hits the first home run of his career during a 4–3 loss to the Dodgers in Los Angeles. The homer was struck off Stan Williams.

Billy Williams hit 426 home runs during his big league career, 392 of them with the Cubs. The only Chicago players with more home runs are Sammy Sosa and Ernie Banks.

OCTOBER 4   Lou Boudreau is fired as manager of the Cubs, and returns to the radio booth.

DECEMBER 21   Seven weeks after John Kennedy is elected president, enigmatic Cubs owner P. K. Wrigley announces a rotating system of managers, which sportswriters dub "The College of Coaches." No one had the title of manager. The individual in charge was called the "head coach."

The eleven coaches in the system during the 1961 season were Bobby Adams, Dick Cole, Rip Collins, Harry Craft, Charlie Grimm, Vedie Himsl, Gordie Holt, Lou Klein, Fred Martin, Elvin Tappe, and Verlon Walker. Himsl, Craft, Tappe, and Klein each took turns as the head coach. At any given time, there were only four or five coaches with the Cubs. The others acted as managers, coaches, or scouts in the minor league system, which also employed rotating head coaches. Martin, Craft, Klein, Collins, Adams, Walker, Himsl, and Cole each took turns managing Cubs farm clubs in Houston, San Antonio, Wenatchee, Washington, and Carlsbad, New Mexico. The plan was greeted with sarcasm, and dismissed as another manifestation of Wrigley's eccentricity. The rotating head coach system lasted two only years, in which the Cubs posted a record of 123–193. Bob Kennedy directed the club from the start of the 1963 season through June 1965, and Klein for the remainder of the 1965 campaign, although the pair were referred to as head coaches and not managers. The hiring of Leo Durocher to run the club from the dugout in October 1965 ended the title of head coach. Durocher insisted on being called the manager.

1961   Cubs

Season in a Sentence

P. K. Wrigley's rotating corps of managers gums up the Cubs and fails to rotate the club out of seventh place.

Finish • Won • Lost • Pct • GB

Seventh 64 90 .416 29.0

Managers (Head Coaches)

Vedie Himsl (5–6),
Harry Craft (4–8),
Himsl (5–12),
El Tappe (2–0),
Craft (3–1),
Himsl (0–3),
Tappe (35–43),
Lou Klein (5–6) and
Tappe (5–11)

Stats

Stats	Cubs	NL	Rank
Batting Avg:	.255	.262	7
On–Base Pct:	.327	.330	7
Slugging Pct:	.418	.405	3
Home Runs:	176		3
Stolen Bases:	35		7
ERA:	4.48	4.03	7
Fielding Avg:	.970	.976	8
Runs Scored:	689		7
Runs Allowed:	800		8

Starting Lineup

Dick Bertell, c
Ed Bouchee, 1b
Don Zimmer, 2b
Ron Santo, 3b
Ernie Banks, ss
Billy Williams, lf
Al Heist, cf
George Altman, rf
Richie Ashburn, cf
Jerry Kindall, 2b–ss
Sammy Taylor, c
Andre Rodgers, 1b–ss

Pitchers

Don Cardwell, sp
Dick Ellsworth, sp
Jack Curtis, sp
Glen Hobbie, sp
Bob Anderson, rp
Don Elston, rp
Barney Schultz, rp
Jim Brewer, rp–sp
Dick Drott, rp

Attendance

673,057 (seventh in NL)

Club Leaders

Batting Avg:	Altman	.303
On–Base Pct:	Santo	.362
Slugging Pct:	Altman	.560
Home Runs:	Banks	29
RBI:	Altman	96
Runs:	Santo	84
Stolen Bases:	Ashburn	7
Wins:	Cardwell	15
Strikeouts:	Cardwell	156
ERA:	Cardwell	3.82
Saves:	Elston	8
	Anderson	8

MARCH 31   The Cubs trade Moe Drabowsky and Seth Morehead to the Braves for Andre Rodgers and Daryl Robertson.

APRIL 6   Vedie Himsl is named the first of the rotating head coaches of the Cubs.

             It was also revealed that Himsl would only be the head coach for the first two weeks of the season, then would go to manage one of the Cubs farm teams. One wag commented that Himsl was the only individual ever to be given his two weeks notice on the day he was hired. Harry Craft, Lou Klein, and El Tappe also served as head coaches during the season. Himsl and Tappe each had three terms as manager, Craft two, and Klein one.

APRIL 11   The Cubs lose the opener 7–1 to the Reds in Cincinnati. Jim O'Toole, the son of a Chicago policeman, pitched the complete game victory for the Reds. Chicago's lone run was on a home run by Andre Rodgers in his first at–bat as a Cub.

             Rodgers grew up playing cricket in the Bahamas and adapted to baseball well enough to last eleven seasons in the majors, mainly as a shortstop. He played for the Cubs from 1961 though 1964.

APRIL 14   In the home opener, Sammy Taylor hits a walk–off, two–run, two–out homer in the ninth inning to beat the Braves 3–2 before 11,299 at Wrigley Field.

APRIL 15   Al Heist hits a walk–off grand slam with two out in the in the ninth inning off Don Nottebart on a 3–2 pitch to lift the Cubs to a 9–5 win over the Braves at Wrigley Field.

             Heist was 32 years old when he made his major league debut in 1960, and played three years in the majors, two of them with the Cubs.

APRIL 22   Six days after the launching of the unsuccessful Bay of Pigs invasion of Cuba, and six days after the Blackhawks win the Stanley Cup, Don Zimmer hits a two–out homer in the eleventh to defeat the Phillies 6–4 in Philadelphia.

APRIL 26   Don Zimmer wins another game with an extra–inning homer, blasting a pitch over the wall at Wrigley Field in the tenth to give the Cubs a 3–2 win over the Reds.

APRIL 30   A seven–run outburst in the second inning sends the Cubs toward a 10–5 win over the Dodgers in the second game of a double–header at Wrigley Field. Los Angeles won the first game 2–1.

MAY 2   Billy Williams collects four hits, including a grand slam off Eddie Fisher in the second inning, to lead the Cubs to a 9–4 win over the Giants at Wrigley Field.

MAY 9   Four days after Alan Shepard becomes the first American in space, the Cubs trade Frank Thomas to the Braves for Mel Roach.

             This deal never achieved lift–off. Thomas had three more seasons as a productive starting outfielder, and hit 34 home runs for the Mets in 1962. Roach played in only 23 games for the Cubs, and batted a measly .128.

MAY 19	Glen Hobbie pitches the Cubs to a 1–0 win over the Cardinals at Wrigley Field. The lone run of the game was scored on a pop fly double by Ernie Banks in the first inning which St. Louis shortstop Daryl Spencer lost in the sun.
MAY 20	The Cubs defeat the Cardinals 1–0 at Wrigley Field for the second day in a row. Dick Ellsworth pitched the shutout. Ed Bouchee accounted for the only run of the game with a walk–off homer in the ninth inning off Larry Jackson.
MAY 23	With a sore knee hampering his mobility, Ernie Banks moves from shortstop to play left field for a game in which the Cubs lose 2–1 to the Phillies at Wrigley Field.

Banks played in 23 games in left field before the Cubs abandoned the experiment in mid–June.

MAY 28	Ernie Banks hits a grand slam in the eighth inning off Stu Miller which ties the score 4–4, but the Cubs lose 6–5 to the Giants in San Francisco.
JUNE 2	Ernie Banks ties a major league record with three sacrifice flies during a 7–6 win over the Reds in Cincinnati.
JUNE 3	The Cubs spot the Reds a 6–0 lead, then score five runs in the seventh inning and five more in the eighth to win 10–7 in Cincinnati.
JUNE 9	The Cubs score two runs in the ninth inning off Warren Spahn to defeat the Braves 11–10 at Wrigley Field. Moe Thacker's single drove in the winning run.
JUNE 16	Ernie Banks plays first base for the first time in his career during a 12–6 win over the Giants in San Francisco. Banks played the previous 23 games in left field. On the day after his 23rd birthday, Billy Williams took over in left and hit a grand slam off Billy Loes in the third inning.

The moves of Banks and Williams had a major impact on the history of the Cubs. Banks played only seven games at first base in 1961, before returning to shortstop, but became a first baseman exclusively beginning in 1962. Williams had been in and out of the line–up from his debut in August 1959 until June 1961. The grand slam was the start of a batting tear that cemented Williams a permanent place in the Cub outfield until he was traded to the Athletics at the end of the 1974 season. As a Cub, Williams played in 2,213 games, third all–time behind only Banks and Cap Anson. He was solid and dependable with a picture perfect swing and an absence of flash. Williams hit 392 homers with the Cubs and had 1,306 runs, 2,510 hits, 402 doubles, 87 triples, 1,353 runs–batted–in, and a .503 batting average. Despite the impressive numbers, Williams was a neglected superstar who never received the recognition he deserved.

JUNE 23	Ernie Banks's streak of 717 consecutive games played, dating back to 1956, comes to an end when he sits out a 5–2 win over the Braves in Milwaukee to rest his ailing knee.

Banks missed 18 games in 1961. He hit 29 homers and batted .278. Other batting leaders were George Altman, with a .303 average and 27 homers, and Ron Santo, who in his first full season in the majors, clubbed 23 homers.

JUNE 28   The Cubs sweep the Reds 16–5 and 7–2 at Wrigley Field. The Cubs scored seven runs in the fifth inning of the first game.

JULY 2   Glen Hobbie hits two home runs in a 10–9 win over the Cardinals at Wrigley Field. Hobbie had a no decision, however, because he allowed seven runs in seven innings.

               The Cubs scored 73 runs in seven consecutive games played from June 27 through July 2.

JULY 4   After being trounced 19–3 by the Giants in the first game of a double–header at Wrigley Field, the Cubs rebound to win the second tilt 3–2.

JULY 11   George Altman hits a home run during the National League's 5–4, ten–inning win in the All–Star Game, played at Candlestick Park in San Francisco.

AUGUST 11   Braves pitcher Warren Spahn records the 300th victory of his career by defeating the Cubs 2–1 in Milwaukee.

AUGUST 20   Seven days after the construction of the Berlin Wall commences, the Cubs defeat the Pirates 1–0 in eleven innings at Wrigley Field. Don Cardwell pitched the complete game shutout. Billy Williams broke the scoreless duel with an RBI–single off Bob Friend, who also went the distance.

Big George Altman found his hitting stroke in 1961, becoming a key power source through 1962.

AUGUST 27   After starting his career with an 0–9 record, Jim Brewer earns his first major league win with a 6–5 decision over the Pirates in the second game of a double–header at Forbes Field. Pittsburgh won the first game 7–3.

SEPTEMBER 1   In his first major league plate appearance, Cuno Barragan hits a home run, although the Cubs lose 4–3 in fourteen innings to the Giants at Wrigley Field. Barragan's homer was struck off Dick LeMay in the first inning and gave the Cubs a 3–0 lead.

SEPTEMBER 10   Lou Brock and Ken Hubbs make their big league debuts in a 14–6 loss to the Phillies at Wrigley Field. Playing second base, Hubbs had two hits in three at–bats. Brock had a hit in five at–bats, and made two errors in center field.

SEPTEMBER 26   The Reds clinch the National League pennant with a 6–3 win over the Cubs at Wrigley Field.

               From 1946 through 1961, every National League team played in the World

Series except the Cubs. The closest the Cubs came to first place during that period was 1959, when they finished in fifth, thirteen games behind the Dodgers.

SEPTEMBER 27   Danny Murphy hits two homers in a 5–2 win over the Cardinals at Wrigley Field. The homers were the only two homers that Murphy hit in 1961, after spending most of the season in the minors. Murphy didn't hit another home run in the majors until 1970.

OCTOBER 10   The Cubs lose Don Zimmer, Ed Bouchee, and Solly Drake to the Mets and Al Heist and Dick Drott to Houston in the expansion draft.

Zimmer was left unprotected after he publicly criticized the "College of Coaches." None of the five drafted by the two new NL clubs was a great loss.

1962   Cubs

Season in a Sentence

Expansion of the National League from eight teams to ten gives the Cubs farther to fall as the club continues its futility with a ninth-place finish and 103 defeats.

Finish • Won • Lost • Pct • GB

Ninth   59   103   .364   42.5

Managers (Head Coaches)

El Tappe (4–15),
Lou Klein (12–18) and
Charlie Metro

Stats

Stats	Cubs	NL	Rank
Batting Avg:	.253	.261	7
On–Base Pct:	.319	.329	9
Slugging Pct:	.377	.393	8
Home Runs:	126	8	
Stolen Bases:	78	4	
ERA:	4.54	3.94	9
Fielding Avg:	.977	.975	4
Runs Scored:	632	8	
Runs Allowed:	827	9	

Starting Lineup

Dick Bertell, c
Ernie Banks, 1b
Ken Hubbs, 2b
Ron Santo, 3b
Andre Rodgers, ss
Billy Williams, lf
Lou Brock, cf
George Altman, rf
Don Landrum, cf–r

Pitchers

Bob Buhl, sp
Dick Ellsworth, sp
Cal Koonce, sp
Don Cardwell, sp–rp
Glen Hobbie, sp–rp
Bob Anderson, rp
Don Elston, rp
Barney Schultz, rp

Attendance

609,802 (tenth in NL)

Club Leaders

Batting Avg:	Altman	.316
On–Base Pct:	Altman	.393
Slugging Pct:	Altman	.511
Home Runs:	Banks	37
RBI:	Banks	104
Runs:	Williams	94
Stolen Bases:	Altman	19
Wins:	Buhl	12
Strikeouts:	Ellsworth	113
ERA:	Buhl	3.69
Saves:	Elston	8

MARCH 25   Five weeks after John Glenn becomes the first American to orbit the earth, the Cubs announce that El Tappe would start the season as the club's head coach.

Tappe was replaced by Lou Klein after the Cubs lost 15 of their first 19 games. Klein was head coach for 30 games before turning the reins over to Charlie Metro for the rest of the season.

APRIL 10   In the first ever regular season major league game played in Houston, the Cubs lose 11–2 to the Colts at Colt Stadium. The Cubs lost all three games of the season–opening series in Houston, scoring only two runs. One of the pitchers who shut out the Cubs was Dean Stone, who was pitching his first big league game in three years.

During the first three years of their existence, the Houston franchise was officially known as the Colt .45s, and informally as the Colts. The nickname was changed to Astros in 1965. Houston played for three years at Colt Stadium, a temporary facility built in what would become the parking lot for the Astrodome, baseball's first indoor stadium, which opened in 1965.

APRIL 13   The Cubs lose the home opener 8–5 in fifteen innings to the Cardinals before 9,750 at Wrigley Field. Lou Brock homered for the Cubs.

Rookie Elder White was the Cubs starting shortstop on Opening Day, as Ernie Banks moved to first base. White's big league career lasted only 23 games in which he hit just .151.

APRIL 17   Rookie second baseman Ken Hubbs collects five hits, including a double, in five at–bats, although the Cubs lose 10–6 to the Pirates at Wrigley Field. Ken's father, who was confined to a wheelchair because of a bout with polio 19 years earlier, attended the game after flying to Chicago from his home in Colton, California.

Ken Hubbs was the National League Rookie of the Year in 1962 and promised to be a Cub fixture for years to come.

Only 20, the ever–hustling Hubbs became an immediate fan favorite in Chicago. In his first season, he batted .260 and set a major league record (since broken) with 78 consecutive errorless games at second base between June and September. At the end of the season, he was named NL Rookie of the Year with 19 out of a possible 20 first–place votes.

APRIL 18   A walk–off home run by Ernie Banks in the tenth inning off Dick Farrell beats Houston 3–2 at Wrigley Field. It also was the 300th home run of Ernie's career and the Cubs' first win of 1962 after starting the season 0–7. It also was the first time that the new Houston expansion franchise played in Chicago.

APRIL 24   Sandy Koufax strikes out 18 Cubs batters in a 10–2 Dodgers victory at Wrigley Field.

APRIL 30   The Cubs trade Jack Curtis to the Braves for Bob Buhl.

As a general rule, no team in the rebuilding mode the Cubs found themselves in during the early 1960s should ever trade a 25–year–old like Curtis for a 33–year–old like Buhl, but this one worked out quite well. Curtis won only four more big league games, while Buhl had 51 victories for some awful Cubs teams in slightly less than four years. In addition, Buhl was sent to the Phillies in a 1966 trade that brought Ferguson Jenkins to Chicago.

MAY 1   Lou Klein replaces El Tappe as head coach before the Cubs take the field against the Dodgers in Los Angeles. The Cubs took a 5–3 lead in the top of the fifteenth inning, only to have the Dodgers score two in their half and another in the sixteenth to win 6–5. It was also the first time that the Cubs played at Dodger Stadium.

As part of the "College of Coaches" system, Tappe remained with the club as a coach. Later in the season, the 35–year–old Tappe was activated as a player and appeared in 26 games as a catcher.

MAY 8   The Mets play in Chicago for the first time and beat the Cubs before a crowd of only 1,369 at Wrigley Field.

MAY 13   Reliever Barney Schultz is the winning pitcher in both ends of a double–header, as the Cubs defeat the Phillies 8–7 and 8–5 at Wrigley Field. Ron Santo started both contests at shortstop in a failed experiment that lasted eight games.

MAY 15   The Cubs play the Mets in New York for the first time and lose 6–5 in thirteen innings at the Polo Grounds.

The Mets played at the Polo Grounds in 1962 and 1963 before moving into Shea Stadium in 1964.

MAY 18   The Cubs belt five home runs and defeat the Phillies 11–8 in Philadelphia. George Altman hit two homers and Ernie Banks, Ron Santo, and Bob Will added one each.

MAY 20   Lou Brock hits a grand slam off Jim Owens in the second inning of a 6–4 win over the Phillies in the first game of a double–header in Philadelphia. Brock also scored the other two Chicago runs. In the second game, Ken Hubbs collected five hits in five at–bats during an 11–2 Chicago win. Hubbs had three hits in the first game to give him eight in the double–header, tying a Cubs record.

MAY 25   Cal Koonce (seven innings) and Don Elston (one inning) combine on a two–hitter, but the Cubs lose 2–1 to the Reds at Crosley Field. The only Cincinnati hits were a single by Johnny Edwards and a double by Frank Robinson in the fourth inning. Ernie Banks was beaned by ex–Cub Moe Drabowsky in the ninth inning and was carried off the field on a stretcher.

MAY 29   In his first game since his May 25 beaning, Ernie Banks hits a double and three con-
          secutive homers, although the Cubs lose 11–9 to the Braves at Wrigley Field. Billy
          Williams, George Altman, and Bob Will also homered for the Cubs. Banks doubled
          in the second inning, then poled homers off Bob Hendley in the third inning, Don
          Nottebart in the fifth and Lew Burdette in the seventh.

          *On the same day, the Cubs hired Buck O'Neill as a coach, thereby becoming
          the first African–American coach in major league history. He remained as a
          coach until 1965, although he spent little time with the Cubs. O'Neill's duties
          consisted mainly of serving as an instructor and scout in the club's minor league
          system. He had been employed by the Cubs as a scout since 1955. Prior to that,
          O'Neill was manager of the Kansas City Monarchs of the Negro Leagues.
          Among his players with the Monarchs were Ernie Banks, George Altman, and
          Elston Howard.*

JUNE 5   Charlie Metro replaces Lou Klein as head coach. Metro remained as head coach for
          the rest of the season.

          *On the same day, Cubs shortstop Andre Rodgers not only blew a chance at an
          unassisted triple play, but he failed to record an out during an 11–4 loss to the
          Giants at Wrigley Field. With Jim Davenport on second, Tom Haller on first,
          and nobody out, the runners were on the move when Jose Pagan whistled a line
          drive straight at Rodgers. But Rodgers dropped the ball as he turned toward
          second. It would have been an easy triple–killing if he made the catch, because
          all he had to do was step on second and tag Haller, who was already moving
          into the bag.*

JUNE 10   In the second game of a double–header at Wrigley Field, Ernie Banks hits a three–
          run pinch–homer with two out in the ninth inning to tie the Mets 4–4. A Billy
          Williams double in the tenth drove in the winning run for a 5–4 victory. New York
          won the first game 2–1.

          *In his first season as a first baseman, Banks hit 37 home runs and drove in 104
          runs. Williams belted 22 homers and hit .298. George Altman also contributed
          with 22 home runs and a .318 batting average.*

JUNE 17   Lou Brock hits a home run into the center field bleachers at the Polo Grounds dur-
          ing an 8–7 win over the Mets in the first game of a double–header. The Cubs also
          won the second game 4–3.

          *The bleachers were constructed in 1923 and were more than 450 feet from
          home plate. The Polo Grounds was the home of the Giants from 1911 through
          1957, and of the Mets in 1962 and 1963. Prior to Brock, the only batter to
          reach the bleachers during a regular season game was Joe Adcock of the Braves
          in 1953. Brock drilled a pitch by Al Jackson approximately 470 feet. Oddly,
          Hank Aaron hit another homer into the bleachers the very next day. No one
          else reached the seats before the ballpark closed at the end of the 1963 season.*

JUNE 19   The Cubs score six runs in the ninth inning to defeat the Phillies 9–5 in Philadelphia.

          Charlie Metro was the head coach, but he wasn't the final authority. Shortly after he took charge, Metro forbade players to shave in the clubhouse, but the other coaches got together for a vote and overruled him. Metro hated the "College of Coaches" system and believed that some of the other coaches rooted against the Cubs to win so that they would get a shot at running the club.

JUNE 24   Lou Brock reaches base nine times in 11 plate appearances during a 4–3 and 8–4 sweep of the Pirates in Pittsburgh. Brock had a triple, two doubles, two singles, and four walks.

JULY 1   Don Cardwell pitches a two–hitter, but loses 1–0 to the Braves at County Stadium. The only Milwaukee hits were doubles by Mack Jones in the third inning and Joe Adcock in the eighth.

JULY 13   Cal Koonce pitches a one–hitter to beat the Reds 1–0 at Wrigley Field. The only Cincinnati hit was a single by Don Blasingame in the fourth inning. The only run of the game was a sacrifice fly by Ron Santo in the sixth inning.

                Koonce was a 21–year–old rookie in 1962, and the July 13 victory gave him a record of 8–2. He finished the season with a 10–10 mark and never reached double figures in wins again. Koonce finished his career in 1971 with a 47–49 record.

JULY 14   With the Cubs and the White Sox playing in Chicago at the same time, WGN–TV carries both games. The station switched back and forth between the two contests, with Vince Lloyd doing the play–by–play at Comiskey Park, and Jack Brickhouse at Wrigley Field. The Cubs defeated the Reds 6–3, while the Sox downed the Tigers 4–2.

JULY 23   A live sports event is telecast from the United States to Europe for the first time, when a small portion of a 5–3 Cubs loss to the Phillies at Wrigley Field is beamed across the Atlantic. Millions on the European continent saw Tony Taylor of the Phillies fly out to George Altman in right field. Fans at Wrigley were informed of the historic program and waved to the camera as it panned over the grandstand.

                The transmission was made possible by the Telstar, the world's first communications satellite, which was sent into space on July 10. In addition to the Wrigley Field scene, Europeans were able to watch a portion of President John Kennedy's press conference and views of the New York skyline, Niagara Falls, San Francisco's Golden Gate Bridge, the U.S.–Mexican border, the Seattle World's Fair, and Mount Rushmore. The program was carried in Austria, Belgium, Denmark, England, Finland, France, Italy, Luxembourg, the Netherlands, Norway, Portugal, Spain, Sweden, Switzerland, West Germany, and Yugoslavia.

JULY 30   The American League wins the All–Star Game 9–4 before 38,359 at Wrigley Field. It was the second of two All–Star Games played in 1962. Rocky Colavito of the Tigers, Pete Runnels of the Red Sox, Leon Wagner of the Angels, and Johnny Roseboro of the Dodgers each hit home runs. P. K. Wrigley wasn't at the game, however, and instead watched on television from his retreat in Lake Geneva, Wisconsin. Wrigley claimed that his presence at Wrigley Field "wasn't necessary."

                There were twenty future Hall of Famers on the rosters of the two teams:

Hank Aaron, Luis Aparicio, Richie Ashburn, Ernie Banks, Yogi Berra, Jim Bunning, Orlando Cepeda, Roberto Clemente, Bob Gibson, Al Kaline, Mickey Mantle, Juan Marichal, Eddie Mathews, Willie Mays, Stan Musial, Brooks Robinson, Frank Robinson, Warren Spahn, Billy Williams, and Hoyt Wilhelm.

AUGUST 26   Three weeks after the death of Marilyn Monroe, four consecutive Cubs batters bunt to score a run during a 4–1 win over the Braves at Wrigley Field. In the sixth inning, Dick Ellsworth reached base on a bunt single. Ken Hubbs followed with an attempted sacrifice, and he and Ellsworth were both safe on a fielder's choice when Milwaukee pitcher Denny Lemaster threw late to second. Ron Santo advanced both runners with a bunt, and Ellsworth scored on a successful squeeze by Don Landrum.

SEPTEMBER 16   Rookie center fielder Nelson Mathews hits a grand slam in the first inning off Stan Williams during a 5–0 win over the Dodgers at Wrigley Field. It was the first extra–base hit of Mathews's career.

SEPTEMBER 21   Four Cubs pinch–hitters strike out during a 4–1 loss to the Mets in New York. The four were George Altman, Bob Will, Don Landrum, and Cuno Barragan.

SEPTEMBER 26   Only 903 fans attend a 6–5 loss to the Phillies at Wrigley Field.

The Cubs finished last in the major leagues in attendance in 1962 with a season total of 609,802. It was also the lowest season attendance for the Cubs between 1943 and the present.

SEPTEMBER 28   Attendance at Wrigley Field is only 595 on a Friday afternoon to watch the Cubs defeat the Mets 3–2. The two teams entered the game with a combined record of 96–220.

SEPTEMBER 29   The Cubs lose their 103rd game of the season, dropping a 2–1 decision to the Mets at Wrigley Field. The 103 losses in 1962 set a club record, which was tied by the 1966 team.

SEPTEMBER 30   On the final day of the season, the Cubs defeat the Mets 5–1 at Wrigley Field. It was the Mets 120th defeat of the season, to set a major league record. The Cubs also pulled off a triple play in the eighth inning. With Joe Pignatano batting, second baseman Ken Hubbs made a spectacular catch running into short right field with his back to the plate. Hubbs threw to Ernie Banks at first base to double Richie Ashburn. Banks then pegged the ball to second in time to triple Solly Drake, who was rounding third base when Hubbs made his catch on what looked like a sure hit.

OCTOBER 17   The Cubs trade George Altman, Don Cardwell, and Moe Thacker to the Cardinals for Larry Jackson, Lindy McDaniel, and Jimmie Schaffer.

This turned out to be an excellent deal as Jackson and McDaniel each gave the Cubs three excellent seasons. McDaniel became the first Cub to save at least 20 games in a season in 1963, and Jackson won 24 times in 1964. In addition, McDaniel and Jackson were used in trades in 1965 and 1966 that brought Ferguson Jenkins, Randy Hundley, and Bill Hands to the Cubs. Altman stopped hitting home runs in St. Louis and had two miserable seasons before returning to the Cubs in 1965.

NOVEMBER 14   Three weeks after America's nerves are frazzled by the Cuban missile crisis, the Cubs hire Bob Kennedy as a coach. On February 20, 1963, Kennedy was named head coach. It was made clear by P. K. Wrigley that Kennedy would lead the club for the entire 1963 season and that the rotation of head coaches had come to an end. Officially, Kennedy's title was head coach, however, and not manager. Kennedy remained as head coach until June 1965.

Kennedy was 42 years old and played in the majors from 1939 through 1957 as an outfielder and third baseman. He also served as a Marine Corps pilot during both World War II and the Korean War.

NOVEMBER 26   The Cubs draft Glenn Beckert from the Boston Red Sox organization.

NOVEMBER 28   The Cubs trade Bob Anderson to the Tigers for Steve Boros.

1963   Cubs

Season in a Sentence

The Cubs junk the rotating head coach system, reach first place in early June, and finish above .500 for the first time since 1946.

Finish • Won • Lost • Pct • GB

Seventh   82   80   .506   17.0

Manager (Head Coach)

Bob Kennedy

Stats

Stats	Cubs	NL	Rank
Batting Avg:	.238	.245	8
On–Base Pct:	.300	.308	8
Slugging Pct:	.363	.364	6
Home Runs:	127		4
Stolen Bases:	68		5
ERA:	3.08	3.29	2
Fielding Avg:	.976	.975	5
Runs Scored:	570		7
Runs Allowed:	578		2 (tie)

Starting Lineup

Dick Bertell, c
Ernie Banks, 1b
Ken Hubbs, 2b
Ron Santo, 3b
Andre Rodgers, ss
Billy Williams, lf
Ellis Burton, cf
Lou Brock, rf
Don Landrum, cf–rf
Nelson Mathews, cf
Merritt Ranew, c

Pitchers

Dick Ellsworth, sp
Larry Jackson, sp
Bob Buhl, sp
Glen Hobbie, sp–rp
Paul Toth, sp–rp
Lindy McDaniel, rp
Don Elston, rp

Attendance

979,551 (fifth in NL)

Club Leaders

Batting Avg:	Santo	.297
On–Base Pct:	Williams	.358
Slugging Pct:	Williams	.497
Home Runs:	Santo	25
	Williams	25
RBI:	Santo	99
Runs:	Williams	87
Stolen Bases:	Brock	24
Wins:	Ellsworth	22
Strikeouts:	Ellsworth	185
ERA:	Ellsworth	2.11
Saves:	McDaniel	22

JANUARY 10   P. K. Wrigley hires Robert Whitlow to man the newly created position of athletic director.

Whitlow was a recently retired Air Force colonel who was the athletic director at the Air Force Academy. His only baseball experience was as a college pitcher at UCLA, and he admitted that he had only seen four or five major league games during the previous five years. Whitlow had many ideas about conditioning, diet, and the use of computers to spot trends and formulate strategy that later became common in baseball, but his lack of experience in the sport gave him no credibility. Whitlow was ignored by general manager John Holland and head coach Bob Kennedy. The colonel resigned in January 1965, and the position of athletic director was abolished.

APRIL 9   The Cubs lose the season opener 5–1 to the Dodgers before 18,589 fans at Wrigley Field in frigid 30–degree weather. The organist played *Jingle Bells* in between innings.

MAY 1   Ernie Banks drives in seven runs on two homers and a single during a 13–8 win over the Cardinals in St. Louis.

Banks suffered through a difficult season in 1963, with 18 homers and a .227 batting average. In September, a blood test revealed that Ernie was suffering from subclinical mumps, a disease that remains in the blood without breaking out in swollen glands.

MAY 8   Bob Buhl ends a streak of 88 consecutive at–bats without a hit by hitting a single off Al McBean in the fifth inning of a 9–5 win over the Pirates at Wrigley Field.

Buhl's hitless streak, which dated back to 1961, is the longest in major league history. In 1962, he was 0–for–70. Buhl finished his career with an .089 batting average in 857 at–bats.

MAY 9   Dick Ellsworth pitches a two–hitter to defeat the Pirates 3–1 at Wrigley Field. The only Pittsburgh hits were singles by Donn Clendenon in the second inning and Dick Schofield in the ninth. Ernie Banks tied a major league record for most putouts in a nine–inning game by a first baseman with 22.

Ellsworth had a terrific season in 1963, with a 22–10 record and a 2.11 ERA with 19 complete games and 185 strikeouts in 290⅔ innings. It followed a 1962 campaign in which Ellsworth was 9–20 with an ERA of 5.02. Dick was 23 years old in 1963, and the heavy workload probably ruined a fine career. From 1964 through 1966, he was 36–55 for the Cubs with an ERA of 3.85. Ellsworth was traded to the Phillies following the 1966 season.

MAY 22   Ken Aspromonte singles in the tying run in the ninth and the winning run in the eleventh to beat the Cardinals 7–6 at Wrigley Field. Aspromonte entered the game as a defensive replacement for Bob Will at first base.

Aspromonte's career as a Cub consisted of 20 games, 34 at–bats, five base hits and a .147 batting average.

MAY 24   Dick Bertell collects five hits, including a double, in six at–bats, but the Cubs lose 6–5 to Houston in twelve innings at Wrigley Field.

Dick Ellsworth had the best year of his career in 1963, winning 22 games and finishing second in the NL with a 2.11 ERA. However, he pitched 290 ²/₃ innings, a workload that might have hurt the rest of his career, although he won 115 games in total.

MAY 30   The Cubs score 10 runs in the first inning and defeat the Mets 12–0 in the first game of a double–header at the Polo Grounds. New York won the second game 2–1.

JUNE 1   Dick Ellsworth pitches a one–hitter to beat the Phillies 2–0 at Connie Mack Stadium. The only Philadelphia hit was a bunt single by Wes Covington in the fifth inning.

The Cubs had a team ERA of 3.08 in 1963, which ranked second in the National League. It's the lowest earned run average of any Cubs staff since 1945.

JUNE 6   Lindy McDaniel is the hero with his bat and his arm in a 3–2 win over the Giants at Wrigley Field. McDaniel entered the game in relief with one out and the bases loaded and the score tied 2–2. He proceeded to pick Willie Mays off second and strike out Ed Bailey. In the bottom of the tenth, McDaniel hit a walk–off home run off Billy Pierce. Lindy hit only three homers during a twenty–one–year major league career. The first was with the Cardinals in 1957. The third came as a Yankee in 1972. McDaniel also set a club record in 1963 with 13 relief wins.

The win put the Cubs into a three–way tie for first place with the Giants and the Cardinals. Each club had a record of 31–23. The Cubs lost six of their next seven games, however, and never reached first place again in 1963.

JUNE 9   Ernie Banks hits three home runs, two of them off Sandy Koufax, but the Cubs lose 11–8 to the Dodgers at Wrigley Field. During the game, Dodgers right fielder Frank Howard missed a fly ball because a bleacher fan dropped the contents of a bag of peanuts on him.

During the road trip following the game, it became more difficult to hit home runs at Wrigley Field because of the "Whitlow fence." At the direction of athletic director Bob Whitlow, a wire fence eight feet high and 64 feet wide was erected on top of the center field wall to provide a better hitting background for batters. The fence was soon covered by Wrigley's trademark ivy. The barrier was torn down between the 1964 and 1965 seasons after Whitlow resigned. It prevented 10 home runs, four for the Cubs and six by the opposition.

JUNE 28   Two weeks after the University of Alabama is integrated by federal troops over the objections of Governor George Wallace, Ron Santo hits a home run in the eleventh inning to defeat the Phillies 4–3 in Philadelphia.

Santo had a .297 batting average, 25 homers, and 99 RBIs in 1963. Billy Williams batted .286 with 25 home runs and 95 runs batted in.

JULY 3   The Cubs score eight runs in the third inning and defeat the Mets 9–2 at Wrigley Field.

JULY 4   Glen Hobbie pitches a two–hitter to defeat the Mets 2–1 in the first game of a double–header at Wrigley Field. The only New York hits were a homer by Jim Hickman in the sixth inning and a single by Ron Hunt in the seventh. The Cubs also won the second game 3–0 on a three–hitter by Paul Toth.

JULY 11   The Cubs shatter a scoreless duel with seven runs in the eleventh inning to beat the Reds 7–0 at Crosley Field. Cincinnati won the second game 7–3.

JULY 16   A home run by Ken Hubbs in the fifth inning off Bob Sadowski beats the Braves 1–0 at Wrigley Field. Bob Buhl (seven innings), Don Elston (1 ⅓ innings), Dick LeMay (one–third of an inning) and Lindy McDaniel (one–third of an inning) combined on a two–hitter. The only Milwaukee hits were a double by Hank Aaron in the seventh inning off Buhl and a single by Mack Jones in the ninth off LeMay.

On July 18, the Cubs had a record of 51–41 and were in second place, 6 ½ games behind the first place Dodgers.

JULY 28   The Cubs beat the Cardinals 5–1 and 16–11 in a double–header at Wrigley Field. The Cardinals led 11–6 in the second game before the Cubs scored four runs in the sixth inning, two in the seventh, and four in the eighth. The twin bill drew a crowd of 40,222, the largest at Wrigley since 1952.

AUGUST 1   Switch–hitter Ellis Burton hits home runs from both sides of the plate during a 10–2 win over the Braves in Milwaukee. Burton was the first Cub since Augie Galan in 1937 to hit switch–hit homers in a game.

AUGUST 2   Trailing 11–5, the Cubs score six runs in the eighth inning and one in the tenth to beat the Giants 12–11 at Wrigley Field. A three–run, pinch–hit homer by Leo Burke narrowed the gap to 11–9, and Ellis Burton tied the score 11–11 with a two–run homer. The winning run was scored on a double by Ron Santo and a single by Jimmie Schaffer.

AUGUST 8   A walk–off homer by Ron Santo in the tenth inning defeats the Dodgers 5–4 at Wrigley Field.

AUGUST 31	Three days after Dr. Martin Luther King Jr. delivers his "I Have a Dream" speech in Washington, the Cubs score five runs in the ninth inning, the last four on a walk–off grand slam by Ellis Burton, to defeat Houston 6–5. Burton's slam was hit off Hal Woodeshick.
SEPTEMBER 2	Glen Hobbie's two–hitter and Ron Santo's grand slam highlight a 6–0 win over the Giants in the second game of a double–header at Candlestick Park. Santo's slam was hit off Eddie Fisher in the fifth inning. He also had a solo homer in the seventh. The only San Francisco hits off Hobbie were a single by Felipe Alou in the third inning and a triple by Willie McCovey in the ninth.
SEPTEMBER 3	Ron Santo makes three errors at third base in the second inning of a 16–3 loss to the Giants in San Francisco.
SEPTEMBER 18	Rookie outfielder Billy Cowan hits a two–run, two–out homer in the ninth inning to beat the Pirates 2–1 in Pittsburgh. It was Cowan's first major league homer.
SEPTEMBER 20	Andre Rodgers hit a home run off Denny Lemaster in the eighth inning to beat the Braves 1–0 at Wrigley Field. Dick Ellsworth pitched the complete–game shutout.
SEPTEMBER 22	Billy Williams's streak of playing in 1,117 consecutive games begins during a 7–3 win over the Braves at Wrigley Field. Williams didn't miss another game until September 3, 1970.
SEPTEMBER 28	The Cubs win their 82nd game of 1963 with a 4–1 decision over the Braves in Milwaukee to clinch the club's first winning season since 1946. Dick Ellsworth was the winning pitcher, earning his 22nd victory of the season.
DECEMBER 13	Three weeks after the assassination of President John Kennedy, the Cubs trade Jim Brewer and Cuno Barragan to the Dodgers for Dick Scott. *This was yet another one–sided trade that retarded the Cubs' rebuilding efforts. At the time of the trade, Brewer was 25 years old and had a 4–13 lifetime record with a 5.66 ERA in 163⅔ innings. He gave little indication he would develop into a solid major league pitcher, but Brewer learned to throw a screw-ball and became one of the best relievers in the majors during his twelve seasons with the Dodgers. After he was traded by the Cubs, Brewer pitched 877 more innings in the majors and posted an ERA of 2.59. He also saved 132 games. In exchange for Brewer, the Cubs obtained Dick Scott, who pitched only three games for the club and had an ERA of 12.46.*
DECEMBER 15	The Cubs trade Nelson Mathews to the Athletics for Fred Norman.
DECEMBER 29	The Bears defeat the New York Giants 14–10 in the NFL championship game before 45,801 at Wrigley Field.

1964

Season in a Sentence

Ken Hubbs dies in a plane crash in February, Lou Brock is traded in June, and the Cubs slip backward again to eighth place.

Finish • Won • Lost • Pct • GB

Eighth   76   86   .469   17.0

Manager (Head Coach)

Bob Kennedy

Stats   Cubs • NL • Rank

Stat	Cubs	NL	Rank
Batting Avg:	.251	.254	5
On–Base Pct:	.316	.313	5
Slugging Pct:	.390	.374	4
Home Runs:	145		3
Stolen Bases:	70		4
ERA:	4.08	3.54	8
Fielding Avg:	.975	.975	4
Runs Scored:	649		7
Runs Allowed:	724		8

Starting Lineup

Dick Bertell, c
Ernie Banks, 1b
Jimmy Stewart, 2b–ss
Ron Santo, 3b
Andre Rodgers, ss
Billy Williams, lf
Billy Cowan, cf
Len Gabrielson, rf
Joey Amalfitano, 2b
Lou Brock, rf

Pitchers

Larry Jackson, sp
Dick Ellsworth, sp
Bob Buhl, sp
Lew Burdette, sp–rp
Ernie Broglio, sp
Lindy McDaniel, rp
Don Elston, rp

Attendance

751,647 (ninth in NL)

Club Leaders

Batting Avg:	Santo	.313
On–Base Pct:	Santo	.398
Slugging Pct:	Santo	.564
Home Runs:	Williams	33
RBI:	Santo	114
Runs:	Williams	100
Stolen Bases:	Cowan	12
Wins:	Jackson	24
Strikeouts:	Jackson	148
	Ellsworth	148
ERA:	Jackson	3.14
Saves:	McDaniel	15

FEBRUARY 13   Ken Hubbs dies at the age of 22 in a plane crash near Provo, Utah, along with lifelong friend Dennis Doyle.

> *Hubbs became fascinated with aviation during Cubs road trips and often sat in the cockpit with the pilot. He purchased a Cessna 172 in November 1963 and began taking flying lessons. Ken obtained his pilot's license two weeks before the crash. He took Doyle to Provo from the pair's hometown of Colton, California, to see Doyle's wife, who was visiting her parents. On the return trip, Hubbs took off in a snowstorm. The single–engine plane went into a spiral and crashed into ice–encrusted Utah Lake five miles from the Provo airport. Hubbs likely lost sight of the horizon in the storm. The bodies of Hubbs and Doyle weren't found until two days later.*

APRIL 14   In the midst of Beatlemania, with the Fab Four holding the top five spots on the *Billboard* chart of top–selling singles, the Cubs break loose with four runs in the tenth inning to beat the Pirates 8–4 in Pittsburgh in the season opener. Andre Rodgers led the batting attack with a homer and two doubles.

APRIL 17   The Phillies defeat the Cubs 10–8 in the home opener before 18,868 at Wrigley Field. There were eight homers in the game, five of them in the fifth inning when Richie Allen, Roy Sievers, and Art Mahaffey went deep for the Phillies, and Lou

Brock and Billy Williams homered for the Cubs. Williams hit two homers in the game, and Ron Santo and Billy Cowan also homered for Chicago.

APRIL 21   The Cubs hit five home runs but score no other runs and lose 8–5 to the Pirates at Wrigley Field. There were nine homers total in the game struck by nine different players. Jimmy Stewart, Andre Rodgers, Ron Santo, Billy Cowan, and Billy Williams connected for the Cubs, while Roberto Clemente, Dick Schofield, Jim Pagliaroni, and Gene Freese homered for Pittsburgh.

Through the first 42 games of 1964, Williams hit .422 with 68 hits and 14 homers in 161 at–bats. He finished the season with a .312 batting average, 33 homers, 100 runs scored, and 98 RBIs.

APRIL 23   The Cubs play at Shea Stadium for the first time and beat the Mets 5–1.

MAY 1   The Cubs score 10 runs in the first inning and go on to win 11–3 in Houston. Billy Williams drove in five runs in the first inning with a grand slam off Joe Hoerner and a single. Williams added another RBI with a double in the ninth. The only other Cub with as many as five RBIs in an inning is Mark Bellhorn in 2002.

MAY 9   In another first–inning outburst against Houston, the Cubs score seven times and win 9–1 at Wrigley Field.

MAY 17   The Cubs score four runs in the ninth inning to defeat the Reds 5–4 in the first game of a double–header at Wrigley Field. The final run was scored on a single by Billy Cowan. Cincinnati won the second game 2–1.

MAY 26   The Mets, losers of 109 games in 1964, stun the Cubs 19–1 at Wrigley Field.

MAY 31   In his first major league starting assignment, 22–year–old rookie Sterling Slaughter pitches seven innings of one–hit shutout ball against the Braves in the second game of a double–header at Wrigley Field. Lindy McDaniel followed with two hitless innings for a 2–0 win. The only Milwaukee hit was a single by Ed Bailey in the fourth inning. The Cubs also won the first game 4–2.

The fine performance in Slaughter's initial start proved to be an aberration. He lasted only one year in the majors, and had a 3–4 record with an ERA of 5.75.

JUNE 2   The Cubs trade Glen Hobbie to the Cardinals for Lew Burdette.

Burdette won 203 regular season games during his career and helped the Braves to a world championship in 1957 with three wins over the Yankees in the World Series. By the time he pitched for the Cubs, however, he was 37 and was about finished. Burdette was 9–11 with a 4.94 ERA in Chicago over two seasons. Hobbie was only 28, but he too was about done and won only one more big league game.

JUNE 8   On a day off in New York, Cubs players attend the World's Fair.

JUNE 12   Joe Amalfitano hits a grand slam in the sixth inning off Roy Face during a 7–1 win over the Pirates at Wrigley Field.

JUNE 15   In one of the most miscalculated trades in club history, the Cubs trade Lou Brock, Paul Toth, and Jack Spring to the Cardinals for Ernie Broglio, Bobby Shantz, and Doug Clemens.

Brock went on to a Hall of Fame career and played in three World Series for the Cards. In three seasons as a Cub, Broglio had a record of 7–19 and an earned run average of 5.40. There was little consternation when the trade was completed, however. Most Cubs fans believed that Chicago got the better of the exchange, and most in St. Louis were outraged. Prior to June 15, 1964, Brock was viewed as a player who could do little but steal a base. He was three days shy of his 25th birthday, had a .257 career batting average with just 20 homers in 1,207 at–bats, and was a liability on defense. Broglio was 28 and had a record of 18–8 and a 2.99 ERA in 1963. He was off to a rough start in 1964, but it was believed that Broglio could return quickly to his winning ways. Within weeks, however, it was apparent to both fans and the Cubs management alike that a horrible miscalculation had been made.

JUNE 21   Larry Jackson pitches a complete game, collects three of the Cubs six hits, and drives in both Chicago runs as the Cubs defeat the Pirates 2–1 in the first game of a double–header in Pittsburgh. Jackson broke a 1–1 tie with an RBI single in the ninth inning. The Cubs completed the sweep with a 7–2 win in the second game.

JUNE 30   Larry Jackson pitches a one–hitter to beat the Reds 1–0 at Wrigley Field. The only Cincinnati base runner was Pete Rose, who singled in the seventh inning to prevent Jackson from throwing a perfect game. Joey Jay allowed only two hits to the Cubs, both by Jimmy Stewart. Stewart drove in the lone run of the game with a single in the sixth inning.

JULY 2   Two days after the passage of the Civil Rights Act, prohibiting racial discrimination in employment and places of public accommodation, Ron Santo hits a three–run homer with two out in the ninth to beat the Braves 4–3 in Milwaukee.

Santo hit .313 in 1964 with 30 homers, 114 RBIs, 94 runs scored, and a league–leading 13 triples. He also led the league in walks with 86.

Third baseman Ron Santo led the NL with 13 triples, 86 walks, and a .401 on–base percentage in 1964 while smashing 30 home runs.

The Trade of Lou Brock

It seemed like a good idea at the time. On June 15, 1964, the Cubs traded Lou Brock, Jack Spring, and Paul Toth to the Cardinals for Ernie Broglio, Bobby Shantz, and Doug Clemens. The deal still rankles Cubs fans, even those who were not yet born in 1964. Brock and Broglio were the principal players in the deal. Brock went on to a Hall of Fame career and played in three World Series for the Cards. In three seasons as a Cub, Broglio had a 7–19 record and an earned run average of 5.40.

At the time the trade was completed, the Cubs were at a crossroads. The club lost 103 games in 1962 but improved to 82–80 in 1963. In mid–June 1964, the Cubs were 27–27, and were only five games behind the first–place Giants in a close race. Cubs general manager John Holland believed that a bold move was necessary to put the Cubs over the hump. "We felt that we were so close to being a top–flight pennant contender," said Holland, "that one good trade might lift us into the thick of the fight. And we believe the deal with the Cardinals has done exactly that. We're taking more than a shot at the flag. We're blasting it with both barrels."

A dependable fourth starter behind Dick Ellsworth, Larry Jackson, and Bob Buhl was the Cubs' greatest need. Those three combined had a record of 23–12 with a 3.28 ERA. The rest of the staff was 4–15 with an earned run average of 5.25.

Ernie Broglio was available because the Cardinals had a surplus of starting pitchers. From 1960 through 1963, he was 60–38 with an ERA of 3.15. Broglio was off to a rough start in 1964, but it was believed that he could return quickly to his winning ways.

The player the Cubs dangled to bring Broglio to Chicago was Lou Brock. Brock made his major league debut in 1961 with predictions that he would soon be a superstar. But the Cubs were growing impatient because he had shown little improvement. At the time of the trade, Brock was viewed as a player who could do little but steal a base. He was three days shy of his 25th birthday, had a .257 career batting average with just 20 homers in 1,207 at–bats, and was a liability on defense. Brock had been tried in center and right field, but didn't possess the fly–ball judgment or arm for those positions. The only place at which he was considered adequate was left field, and the Cubs had no need for a left fielder with Billy Williams on the club.

There was little consternation in Chicago when the trade was made. Most Cubs fans believed that the Cubs got the better of the deal, and most St. Louis followers were outraged. Wrote Bob Smith in the *Chicago Daily News*: "Thank you, thank you, oh you lovely St. Louis Cardinals. Nice doing business with you. Please call again." The St. Louis sportswriters knocked the deal with the complaint, "Who is Lou Brock?"

Brock answered the question in a hurry. From June 15 through the end of the 1964 season, Brock hit .348 with 12 homers and 33 steals in 103 games. The Cardinals overcame a 7½–game deficit with just two weeks remaining to win the National League pennant, then beat the Yankees in the World Series. The Cards returned to the Series in 1967 and 1968 with Brock again as the catalyst at the top of the batting order. The Cubs meanwhile, came close to winning the pennant in 1969, but fell short. The club's greatest needs that season were outfield depth, speed, and a leadoff hitter. Brock could have supplied all three of those qualities.

JULY 7 — Billy Williams hits a home run off John Wyatt of the Athletics in the All–Star Game, played at Shea Stadium in New York. Williams's homer was hit in the fourth and tied the score 1–1. The National League won 7–4 on four runs in the ninth inning, the last three on a walk–off homer by Johnny Callison of the Phillies.

JULY 10 — Jesus Alou of the Giants collects six hits, including a homer, in six at–bats off six different Cubs pitchers as San Francisco wins 10–3 at Wrigley Field. The six pitchers were Dick Ellsworth, Lew Burdette, Don Elston, Dick Scott, Wayne Schurr, and Lindy McDaniel.

JULY 12   The Cubs score four runs in the ninth inning, the last three on a home run by Billy Williams, to defeat the Dodgers 6–3 in the first game of a double–header at Wrigley Field. In the second tilt, Los Angeles scored six runs in the ninth to defeat the Cubs 6–2.

JULY 15   The Cubs commit five errors in the third inning but beat the Mets 4–2 at Wrigley Field. Shortstop Andre Rodgers and catcher Dick Bertell each made two errors, and first baseman Ernie Banks committed one.

JULY 16   A month and a day after being acquired in the Lou Brock trade, Ernie Broglio finally wins his first game as a Cub with an 11–1 win over the Mets at Wrigley Field.

JULY 20   The Cubs score four runs in the ninth inning, the last three on Ron Santo's homer, to beat the Giants 6–4 in San Francisco.

JULY 23   Cubs pitcher Lew Burdette collects four hits, including a homer and a triple, leading the Cubs to a 13–4 win in San Francisco.

AUGUST 15   The Cubs celebrate Ernie Banks Day at Wrigley Field as the crowd of 20,003 pays tribute to Mr. Cub in pre–game ceremonies. Among the gifts presented to Banks was an eleven–transistor oceanic radio, an inscribed sterling silver service, a diamond ring, and a Dodge station wagon. During the game, Banks went hitless in four at–bats, and the Cubs lost 5–4 to the Pirates.

On the same day, the Cubs sold Bobby Shantz to the Phillies.

AUGUST 18   The Cubs defeat the Phillies 4–3 in sixteen innings at Philadelphia. With two out in the sixteenth, Andre Rodgers and Dick Bertell singled, and Joe Amalfitano hit a two–run double. The Phillies scored once in their half of the inning before the Cubs wrapped up the game. Amalfitano entered the game as a defensive replacement in the eighth inning.

AUGUST 29   Ellis Burton, recalled from the minors shortly before the game, hits a game–winning single in the tenth inning to beat the Mets 4–3 at Wrigley Field.

SEPTEMBER 5   The Cubs score all eight of their runs in the second inning of an 8–5 win over the Cardinals at Busch Stadium. Ernie Banks hit a homer and a double in the inning. St. Louis scored four runs in the ninth.

Banks hit 23 homers and drove in 95 runs in 1964.

SEPTEMBER 7   Ellis Burton hits home runs from both sides of the plate during a 10–9 loss to the Braves in the first game of a double–header at Wrigley Field. Milwaukee also won the second game, called after eight innings by darkness, 8–7.

The two homers were the only two that Burton hit as a major leaguer in 1964, and the last two of his big league career. In three seasons as a Cub, Burton hit

14 homers in 467 at–bats, but hit only .216. The only Cubs players with switch–hit homers in the same game are Augie Galan in 1937, Burton in 1963 and again in 1964, and Mark Bellhorn twice in 2002.

SEPTEMBER 13   The Cardinals score in all nine innings and defeat the Cubs 15–2 at Wrigley Field. The Cubs made seven errors in the game.

SEPTEMBER 22   The Cubs defeat Don Drysdale and the Dodgers 1–0 at Wrigley Field. Lew Burdette started the game for the Cubs but had to leave the game after the end of the first inning when he was struck by a batted ball. Cal Koonce followed with eight innings of relief.

SEPTEMBER 24   The Cubs score two runs in the ninth inning without a hit on three walks, an error, and a sacrifice fly to defeat the Dodgers 4–3 before a crowd of only 629 at Wrigley Field.

A lineup mix–up nearly cost the Cubs the game. Bob Kennedy decided to play rookie John Boccabella at first base instead of Ernie Banks, but the Cubs head coach inadvertently listed Banks on the official lineup card. When Boccabella tripled to score Ron Santo in the sixth inning, Dodgers manager Walter Alston protested. Boccabella was ruled out as an improper batter and the run was nullified. According to the scoring rules, Banks was charged with a time at–bat, even though he was sitting idly on the bench.

OCTOBER 4   Seven days after the Warren Commission report is released, declaring that Lee Harvey Oswald acted alone in the assassination of President Kennedy, Larry Jackson earns his 24th win of the season, defeating the Giants 9–2 in San Francisco on the final day of the season.

The 24 wins by Jackson were the most of any Cubs pitcher since Charlie Root won 26 in 1927. The only Cub to win as many as 24 games since 1964 is Ferguson Jenkins, who notched 24 victories in 1971. Jackson posted a 24–11 record in 1964 on a Cubs club that was 76–86. He pitched 297 ⅓ innings and had an ERA of 3.14. The 24–win season was sandwiched in between seasons of 14–18 in 1963 (in which he had an ERA of 2.55) and 14–21 in 1965. Jackson never won more than 15 games in a season after 1964. His previous high in victories was 18 with the Cardinals in 1960.

DECEMBER 9   Five weeks after Lyndon Johnson defeats Barry Goldwater in the presidential election, the Cubs trade Andre Rodgers to the Pirates for Roberto Pena.

1965

Season in a Sentence

Ernie Banks, Ron Santo, and Billy Williams each drive in over 100 runs, but the club continues to flounder and P. K. Wrigley hires Leo Durocher as manager soon after the conclusion of the season.

Finish • Won • Lost • Pct • GB

Eighth   72   90   .444   25.0

Managers (Head Coaches)

Bob Kennedy (24–32) and
Lou Klein (48–58)

Stats   Cubs • NL • Rank

Stats	Cubs	NL	Rank
Batting Avg:	.238	.249	8
On–Base Pct:	.309	.313	8
Slugging Pct:	.358	.374	7
Home Runs:	134		5
Stolen Bases:	65		5
ERA:	3.78	3.54	7
Fielding Avg:	.974	.977	8
Runs Scored:	635		7
Runs Allowed:	723		9

Starting Lineup

Vic Roznovsky, c
Ernie Banks, 1b
Glenn Beckert, 2b
Ron Santo, 3b
Don Kessinger, ss
Doug Clemens, lf–rf
Don Landrum, cf
Billy Williams, rf
Jimmy Stewart, ss–lf
George Altman, lf
Roberto Pena, ss
Chris Krug, c
Ed Bailey, c

Pitchers

Larry Jackson, sp
Dick Ellsworth, sp
Bob Buhl, sp
Cal Koonce, sp–rp
Bill Faul, sp
Ted Abernathy, rp
Lindy McDaniel, rp
Bob Humphreys, rp

Attendance

641,361 (ninth in NL)

Club Leaders

Club Leaders		
Batting Avg:	Williams	.315
On–Base Pct:	Santo	.378
Slugging Pct:	Williams	.552
Home Runs:	Williams	34
RBI:	Williams	108
Runs:	Williams	115
Stolen Bases:	Landrum	14
Wins:	Jackson	14
	Ellsworth	14
Strikeouts:	Jackson	131
ERA:	Koonce	3.69
Saves:	Abernathy	31

JANUARY 15   The Cubs trade Billy Cowan to the Mets for George Altman.

After he was traded by the Cubs after the 1962 season, Altman had two off–seasons with the Cardinals and Mets. The Cubs hoped to revive his career with a return to Chicago, but it didn't work, although he spent two more seasons as a competent fourth outfielder.

MARCH 19   Eleven days after the first U. S. combat troops arrive in Vietnam, Cubs radio broadcaster Jack Quinlan dies in an auto accident near Mesa, Arizona. He was 38.

Quinlan had been in the WGN radio booth since 1956. He was killed while driving to the Cubs team hotel after playing a round of golf in Chandler, Arizona. Quinlan lost control of the rented vehicle and skidded some 100 feet into a parked semi–trailer. Vince Lloyd moved from television to radio to replace Quinlan and work alongside Lou Boudreau. Lloyd Pettit joined Jack Brickhouse for the telecasts of Cubs and White Sox games.

APRIL 12   The Cubs and the Cardinals play to a 10–10 tie on Opening Day before 19,751 at Wrigley Field. The game was called by darkness after eleven innings. The Cubs trailed 9–6 with two out in the ninth inning when Ron Santo walked, George Altman singled, and Ernie Banks homered to deadlock the contest at 9–9. The Cardinals scored in the eleventh, but the Cubs rallied to tie the contest on an RBI double by Santo. Roberto Pena, playing in his major league debut, drove in three runs on a homer, double, and single, but he also made three errors at shortstop. Altman had three hits in his first game as a Cub since 1962.

Bacuse of this tie and one other later in the year, the Cubs played 164 games in 1964. Billy Williams and Ron Santo set a club record by playing in all 164.

APRIL 14   The Cubs purchase Ted Abernathy from the Indians.

There were no Cubs fans rushing to the box office to purchase tickets because of the Abernathy acquisition. After all, he was 32 years old and had a 17–30 lifetime record with an ERA of 5.24. But literally overnight, Abernathy became one of the best relievers in the game. Using his deceptive submarine motion, Abernathy in 1965 pitched in 84 games and 134 innings, had four wins and 31 saves, and an earned run average of 2.58. The 84 appearances as a pitcher is still the Cubs' single–season record, tied by Dick Tidrow in 1980.

APRIL 28   The Cubs lose 3–2 to the Reds in Cincinnati when Ernie Broglio commits a balk with the bases loaded in the fourteenth inning.

APRIL 30   The Cubs play indoors for the first time, and lose 4–3 to the Astros at the Astrodome in Houston.

The Cubs had a two–decade–long stretch of futility at the Astrodome. From 1965 through 1986, the Cubs were 46–97 in the building.

MAY 15   Dick Ellsworth pitches a one–hitter, but the Cubs lose 3–1 to the Dodgers in Los Angeles. Ellsworth had a no–hitter until the eighth, when Al Ferrara hit a three–run pinch–hit homer following an error and a fielder's choice on an attempted sacrifice.

MAY 21   In his first start since losing a one–hitter on May 15, Dick Ellsworth gives up 14 hits to the Dodgers but emerges with a 4–3 win at Wrigley Field.

MAY 23   The Cubs beat the Dodgers 4–3 in sixteen innings at Wrigley Field. Ernie Banks started the winning rally with a double. He moved to third on a wild pitch, and after two intentional walks, Banks scored on an unintentional walk to George Altman.

MAY 29   The Cubs trade Dick Bertell and Len Gabrielson to the Giants for Harvey Kuenn, Ed Bailey, and Bob Hendley.

MAY 30   The Cubs sell Lew Burdette to the Phillies.

JUNE 6   Johnny Callison hits three homers for the Phillies in a 10–9 win over the Cubs in the second game of a double–header at Wrigley Field. Philadelphia also won the first game 2–1.

JUNE 8   The Braves hit four home runs and score six times in the tenth inning to defeat the Cubs 8–2 at Wrigley Field. Joe Torre and Felipe Alou homered against Lindy McDaniel, and Hank Aaron and Gene Oliver went deep on Bob Hendley.

                  On the same day, the first amateur free agent draft was held. The Cubs' first pick was pitcher Rick James from Coffee High School in Florence, Alabama. James reached the majors as a 19–year–old in 1967, but his big league career lasted only three games, in which he had an 0–1 record and a 13.50 ERA. The Cubs made a tremendous selection in the fourth round, however, with the choice of Ken Holtzman, a left–handed pitcher from the University of Illinois. Holtzman arrived in the majors in September 1965 and lasted 15 seasons. Other future major leaguers drafted and signed by the Cubs in the 1965 draft were Ken Rudolph (second round), Gary Jestadt (seventh), Joe Decker (ninth), and Jimy Williams (20th).

JUNE 14   With the Cubs holding a record of 24–32, Lou Klein replaces Bob Kennedy as head coach.

                  Kennedy was moved into the Cubs front office as an administrative assistant. He left the club at the end of the 1965 season to become a coach with the Athletics. Kennedy was manager of the Athletics in 1968, and returned to the Cubs as general manager from 1977 through 1981. Klein had briefly been head coach in 1961 and 1962 in the "College of Coaches" system. The Cubs were 24–16 in their first 40 games under Klein in 1965, but he was dismissed at the end of the 1965 campaign in favor of Leo Durocher after the club returned to its losing ways.

JULY 11   Larry Jackson and Cal Koonce both pitch shutouts and defeat the Cardinals by identical 6–0 scores in a double–header at Wrigley Field.

JULY 13   Ron Santo drives in the winning run in the National League's 6–5 win in the All–Star Game, played at Metropolitan Stadium in Bloomington, Minnesota.

JULY 22   Ed Bailey drives in eight runs on two homers and two singles to lead the Cubs to a 10–6 win over the Phillies at Wrigley Field. One of Bailey's homers was a grand slam off Gary Wagner in the sixth inning.

JULY 29   The Cubs make six errors and lose 14–0 to the Mets in the first game of a double–header at Wrigley Field, but they rebound to win 2–1 in the nightcap on a twelfth–inning, walk–off home run by Ron Santo.

AUGUST 3   Bill Faul pitches a two–hitter to defeat the Phillies 2–0 at Connie Mack Stadium. The only Philadelphia hits were a double by Wes Covington in the second inning and a single by Tony Gonzalez in the third.

                  Purchased from the Tigers in March 1965, Faul was only 7–10 with a 4.07 ERA over two seasons in Chicago, but he will long be remembered as one of the most colorful characters ever to don a Cubs uniform. Faul was a master hypnotist, a karate instructor in the Air Force, had his hands and feet registered as deadly weapons, held a degree as a Doctor of Divinity, preached for the Universal Christian Church, and insisted on wearing uniform number 13. Faul hypnotized himself before each start and insisted that it helped him relax and concentrate.

To put himself in the trance-like state, Faul would walk off the mound, turn his back on the hitter, and wave his hand in front of his face a few times. Faul pitched three shutouts in a span of twenty-seven days in July and August 1965, and his eccentricities were tolerated as long as he was pitching well, but inconsistent performances led to a ticket back to the minors in July 1966.

AUGUST 8   After trailing 8–2 after two innings, the Cubs complete their comeback by scoring six runs in the ninth inning to beat the Mets 14–10 in the second game of a double–header in New York. A single by Billy Williams broke the 10–10 tie. The Cubs also won the first game 7–6.

AUGUST 19   On the fourth day of the Watts riots in Los Angeles, Jim Maloney of the Reds no–hits the Cubs in the first game of a double–header at Wrigley Field. The game lasted ten innings, and Cincinnati came away with a 1–0 win. Maloney walked ten batters, struck out 12, went to a 3–2 count on thirteen hitters, and loaded the bases three times. The Cubs left 10 runners on base. Leo Cardenas provided the only run of the game with a tenth–inning homer off Larry Jackson that caromed off the left field foul pole. Ernie Banks ended the game by hitting into a double play. The Cubs came back from a 4–0 deficit in the second game to win 5–4 on three runs in the eighth inning and two in the ninth. The contest ended on a walk–off homer by Don Landrum.

AUGUST 26   The Cubs play at old Busch Stadium in St. Louis for the last time and lose 7–4 to the Cardinals.

              The Cardinals had played at Busch Stadium since 1920. It was known as Sportsman's Park until 1953. The new Busch Memorial Stadium opened on May 12, 1966.

AUGUST 27   Billy Williams hits a grand slam in the fifth inning off Ken Johnson to power the Cubs to a 5–3 win over the Braves in Milwaukee.

AUGUST 29   Two homers each by Ernie Banks and Ron Santo and one by Billy Williams lead the Cubs to a 10–2 win over the Braves in Milwaukee. This was also the last time that the Cubs played the Braves in Milwaukee. In 1966, the Braves moved to Atlanta.

              Williams, Banks, and Santo each drove in over 100 runs in 1965. Williams hit .315 with 34 homers and 108 RBIs. Banks hit 28 home runs and drove in 106 runs. Santo batted .285 and had 33 homers and 101 runs batted in. And who ranked fourth on the Cubs in RBIs in 1965 behind the three powerhouses in the center of the lineup? It was Don Landrum with only 34 runs batted in.

SEPTEMBER 2   Ernie Banks hits his 400th career homer during a 5–3 win over the Cardinals at Wrigley Field. The victim was Curt Simmons, who was the first pitcher that Banks faced in the majors in 1953.

SEPTEMBER 4   Pitching in relief in the ninth inning, Ken Holtzman gives up a home run on the first pitch he throws in the major leagues. Jim Ray Hart was the batter, and the Cubs lost 7–3 to the Giants at Wrigley Field.

SEPTEMBER 9   Sandy Koufax pitches a perfect game for the Dodgers, and Bob Hendley allows only one hit for the Cubs in a 1–0 Los Angeles win at Dodger Stadium. It is the only major league game in history of nine innings or more in which two teams combined for only one hit. Lou Johnson was the only batter to reach base, collecting a walk and a double. Koufax struck out 14 batters. Hendley had a perfect game until the fifth inning, when the Dodgers scored the only run without a hit. Lou Johnson walked, was sacrificed to second, stole third, and continued home on catcher Chris Krug's high throw. Johnson collected the only hit of the game with a double in the seventh. Koufax struck out the last six men he faced, fanning Ron Santo, Ernie Banks, and Byron Browne in the eighth, and Krug, Joe Amalfitano, and Harvey Kuenn in the ninth. It was the second time that Kuenn made the final out in a no–hitter pitched by Koufax. The other was in 1963 when Kuenn played for the Giants. Amalfitano also played for the Giants in that game. Koufax is the only pitcher to ever throw a perfect game against the Cubs. Through the 2004 season, no one since Koufax has pitched a no–hitter against the Cubs.

Billy Williams was one of the Cubs' three big offensive threats in 1965, leading the team with a .315 batting average, 34 homers, and 108 RBIs.

The Cubs lineup included Byron Browne and Don Young, both making their major league debuts. Chris Krug was a rookie who was named Chris by his parents because he was born on Christmas Day. He also wore uniform number 25 because of his birth on December 25.

SEPTEMBER 14   Sandy Koufax and Bob Hendley match up again. This time Hendley gained revenge for the heartbreaking September 9 defeat, allowing only four hits to win 2–1 at Wrigley Field. A two–run homer by Billy Williams in the sixth inning accounted for both Cubs runs.

SEPTEMBER 16   Only 550 fans attend a 2–0 loss to the Dodgers at Wrigley Field.

SEPTEMBER 21   Ron Santo drives in six runs on two homers and a single in a 7–5 win over the Phillies at Wrigley Field. Attendance was only 892.

The Cubs had the fifth–worst attendance in the majors in 1965, with only 641,361. The four clubs that trailed the Cubs all soon relocated because of low attendance. The four were the Angels, who went from Los Angeles to Anaheim in 1966; the Braves, moving from Milwaukee to Atlanta in 1966; the Athletics, shifting from Kansas City to Oakland in 1968; and the Washington Senators, going to Texas in 1972 where they were renamed the Rangers. The White Sox attracted 1,130,519 to Comiskey Park in 1965, outdrawing the Cubs by nearly a half–million. The Sox drew more fans than the Cubs every season from 1951 through 1967, with the exception of 1958.

SEPTEMBER 27   Billy Williams homers in the eighth inning off Jim Bunning to beat the Phillies 1–0 in Philadelphia. Larry Jackson pitched the shutout.

SEPTEMBER 28   Bill Faul pitches a two–hitter to defeat the Phillies 2–1 at Connie Mack Stadium. Faul also drove in the winning run in the eighth inning. The only Philadelphia hits were a double in the third inning by Cookie Rojas and a single by Tony Gonzalez in the sixth.

OCTOBER 3   The Cubs tie a major league record by completing their third triple play of the 1965 season, but they lose 6–3 to the Pirates in Pittsburgh.

The 1965 Cubs are one of only six teams since 1900 with three triple plays in a season. Oddly, all three were pulled off with Bill Faul on the mound. Faul pitched 96⅔ innings during the season. Shortstop Don Kessinger participated in all three triple plays. The only pitcher besides Faul who has been on the mound for three triple plays in a season was Will White with the Cincinnati Reds in 1882.

OCTOBER 25   Unpredictable P. K. Wrigley shocks the baseball world by announcing the hiring of fiery, blunt, and outspoken 60–year–old Leo Durocher as manager of the long moribund Cubs. Leo's appointment immediately brought hope and excitement to the North Side. Durocher signed a three–year contract, which effectively ended the five–year experiment with head coaches. "If no announcement has been made of what my title is, I'm making it here and now," boomed Leo. "I'm the manager. I'm not a head coach. I'm the manager." At the time of his arrival in Chicago, Durocher hadn't managed a team in more than ten years, but nevertheless he was already a legend and one of the most controversial figures in baseball as well as a national institution and celebrity. His name was familiar to those who didn't follow the game. Durocher lived in a Beverly Hills mansion and hobnobbed with the Hollywood crowd. Leo counted Frank Sinatra, Bob Hope, Dean Martin, Jimmy Durante, George Raft, and George Jessel among his close friends. For a time, Leo was married to actress Laraine Day.

The hiring of Durocher was a departure for P. K. Wrigley, who previously had surrounded himself for the most part with amiable "yes–men" willing to tolerate the owner's eccentricities. In 1958, when asked if he would consider Durocher as a manager, Wrigley said, "No, sir. Wouldn't have him as a gift." By 1965, Wrigley had a change of heart and said that he wanted a "take–charge guy." Leo definitely filled the requirement. With his dynamic, forceful, and dominant personality, Durocher was not someone to take a secondary position to anyone, including the owner of the ballclub. He reached the top of his profession with an often–contradictory combination of ruthlessness and charm, and he aroused considerable antagonism with his insatiable desire to win and lack of diplomacy or tact. Durocher was a slick–fielding, but weak–hitting shortstop who survived for more than ten years as a starter and played for the 1934 world champion St. Louis Cardinals, also known as the "Gas House Gang." He was hired as manager of the Brooklyn Dodgers in 1939 and won the pennant in 1941. Durocher was forced to serve a one–year suspension in 1947, however, because of his relationship with gamblers. He returned to the Dodgers in 1948 but was let go in July and immediately signed as skipper of the New York Giants. Durocher won two more pennants in 1951 and 1954. His 1951 club rallied from a 13½–game deficit to overtake the Dodgers in one of baseball's greatest success stories. The 1954 Giants swept the heavily–favored Cleveland Indians in the World Series. Durocher was fired again by the Giants at the end of the 1955 season and became a broadcaster for NBC. Itching to return to the field, Durocher was hired as a coach with the Dodgers and held the job from 1961 through 1964. In 1965, he returned to television on the national Saturday afternoon Game of the Week.

NOVEMBER 17   General William D. Eckert becomes the new commissioner of baseball, replacing Ford Frick. Eckert was fired in December 1968.

DECEMBER 2   The Cubs trade Lindy McDaniel, Don Landrum, and Jim Rittwage to the Giants for Randy Hundley and Bill Hands.

Leo Durocher realized that the only path to rebuilding the Cubs was to trade veterans for young and promising players in high–risk/high–reward trades. The deal with the Giants for Hundley and Hands was the first positive step in moving the Cubs toward the top of the standings. Hundley was the Cubs' starting catcher from 1966 through 1973, while Hands won 92 games with the club.

1966   Cubs

Season in a Sentence

"This is no eighth–place club," bellows Leo Durocher when hired by the Cubs, and the accuracy of that statement is borne out in a tenth–place finish in his first season at the helm.

Finish • Won • Lost • Pct • GB

Tenth   59   103   .364   36.0

Manager

Leo Durocher

Stats

Stats	Cubs	NL	Rank
Batting Avg:	.254	.256	7
On–Base Pct:	.315	.316	7
Slugging Pct:	.380	.384	6
Home Runs:	140	5	
Stolen Bases:	76	4	
ERA:	4.33	3.61	10
Fielding Avg:	.974	.977	8
Runs Scored:	644	6	
Runs Allowed:	809	10	

Starting Lineup

Randy Hundley, c
Ernie Banks, 1b
Glenn Beckert, 2b
Ron Santo, 3b
Don Kessinger, ss
Byron Browne, lf–cf
Adolfo Phillips, cf
Billy Williams, rf
John Boccabella, c–1b
George Altman, lf

Pitchers

Ken Holtzman, sp
Dick Ellsworth, sp
Bill Hands, sp–rp
Ferguson Jenkins, rp
Cal Koonce, rp
Bob Hendley, rp

Attendance

635,891 (tenth in NL)

Club Leaders

Batting Avg:	Santo	.312
On–Base Pct:	Santo	.412
Slugging Pct:	Santo	.538
Home Runs:	Santo	30
RBI:	Santo	94
Runs:	Williams	100
Stolen Bases:	Phillips	32
Wins:	Holtzman	11
Strikeouts:	Holtzman	171
ERA:	Holtzman	3.79
Saves:	Hendley	7

JANUARY 10   The Cubs trade Doug Clemens to the Phillies for Wes Covington.

FEBRUARY 15   The Cubs sell Ed Bailey to the Angels.

MARCH 5   The Major League Players Association hires Marvin Miller to be the new executive director of the organization. Miller formally took office on July 1. Under Miller's leadership, the association would take actions that led to a revolution in player–owner relations, including free agency beginning in 1976.

The Cubs moved their spring training camp from Mesa, Arizona, to Long Beach, California, for spring training in 1966. Long Beach was planned as a one–year stop, with the club building a training facility in Escondido, California, near San Diego that was scheduled to open in 1967. While in Long Beach, the Cubs were a long way from the other clubs training in the Southwest, however, and had one eight–day road trip and another of seven days during the 1966 exhibition schedule. The Cubs realized the folly of training in Southern California and returned to Arizona in 1967, with a home base in Scottsdale.

MARCH 17   William Schlensky, who owns two shares of stock in the Cubs, files suit against P. K. Wrigley and all members of the board of directors to force the Cubs to play night baseball at Wrigley Field.

Schlensky's suit contended that the Cubs' afternoon games resulted in decreased attendance, the loss of concession income, and limited radio and television audiences that inhibited management from "making expenditures for new player development and new player acquisition." Schlensky lost his suit in the Illinois Appellate Court in a 3–0 decision in March 1968.

APRIL 12   The Cubs lose the season opener 9–1 to the Giants in San Francisco. Juan Marichal retired the first 18 Chicago hitters.

APRIL 14   Leo Durocher earns his first victory as manager of the Cubs, defeating the Giants 9–4 in San Francisco. Ty Cline collected five hits in five at–bats.

Leo Durocher took over as Cubs manager in the 1966 season. His team finished in the cellar that year, but he had them in contention the next season.

Five of Cline's six hits as a Cub were in this game. He played in just seven games with the club and had a .353 batting average in 17 at–bats. Cline was drafted by the Cubs from the Braves organization in November 1965, and was sold back to the Braves on April 28, 1966.

APRIL 19   In the home opener, the Cubs lose 11–10 to the Giants before 15,396 at Wrigley Field. The Cubs led 9–6 after five innings before fading. Byron Browne and Randy Hundley hit home runs.

The Cubs started the 1966 season by losing eight of their first nine games.

APRIL 21   The Cubs trade Larry Jackson and Bob Buhl to the Phillies for Ferguson Jenkins, Adolfo Phillips, and John Herrnstein.

This was another giant step in Leo Durocher's plan to rebuild the Cubs with promising youngsters. It was an extremely risky trade, since the Cubs were trading their number–one and number–three starting pitchers for three unproven youngsters, but it proved to be one of the best ever by the club. Jenkins had pitched only 14⅔ innings in the majors when he was purchased by the Cubs, but he went on to a Hall of Fame career. As a Cub, he was 167–132 and won 20 or more games six consecutive seasons from 1967 through 1972. Among Cubs pitchers, Jenkins is fifth all–time in victories and also ranks first in strike-outs (2,038), first in games started (347), fifth in complete games (154), fourth in shutouts (29), and third in innings (2,673⅔). The only Cubs hurlers since 1900 with a better career in Chicago than Jenkins are Three Finger Brown and Charlie Root, and Ferguson is head and shoulders above anyone who has pitched for the club since 1940. Jenkins was elected to the Hall of Fame in 1991. Jenkins wasn't considered the key player in the April 21, 1966, trade with the Phillies, however. Phillips was the players the Cubs most desired. Adolfo was immediately installed as the starting center fielder, and he held the position until he was traded to the Expos in 1969. Phillips was called "the next Willie Mays" by Leo Durocher and tantalized the Cubs with his natural talent. He became a favorite of the Bleacher Bums, who loved to shout "Ole! Adolfo, Ole!" while giving Phillips a standing ovation after a great play, but he proved to be a disappointment. Phillips was moody, frequently injured, and refused to bat leadoff, where he could best use his ability to steal bases.

APRIL 23   In his debut with the Cubs, Ferguson Jenkins pitches 5⅓ innings of shutout relief and hits a home run off Don Sutton in a 2–0 win over the Dodgers at Wrigley Field.

APRIL 24   In his first major league start, Ken Holtzman pitches six shutout innings. Ted Abernathy followed with three innings of scoreless relief to defeat the Dodgers 2–0 at Wrigley Field.

During the early part of the 1966 season, Holtzman was a commuting college student who pitched for the Cubs on weekends. He attended classes at the University of Illinois at Chicago. Ken's major was French.

APRIL 28   The Cubs purchase Billy Cowan from the Braves.

MAY 3   The Cubs play on Astroturf for the first time and lose 10–2 to the Astros at the Astrodome.

The Astrodome opened in 1965 with a conventional grass field, but fielders lost fly balls in the glare of the glass panels in the roof. The glass had to be painted, which killed the grass. The artificial surface, manufactured by Monsanto and named Astroturf, was the solution to the problem.

MAY 20   The Cubs play the Braves in Atlanta for the first time, and lose 12–2.

Ten of the other nineteen managers in the majors at the start of the season in 1966 once played or coached under Leo Durocher. The ten were Al Dark (Athletics), Eddie Stanky (White Sox), Chuck Dressen (Tigers), Billy Herman (Red Sox), Gil Hodges (Senators), Bill Rigney (Angels), Bobby Bragan (Braves), Herman Franks (Giants), Gene Mauch (Phillies), and Wes Westrum (Mets).

MAY 21   Randy Hundley homers with two out in the tenth inning to beat the Braves 7–6 in Atlanta.

Hundley brought an end to the carousel at the catching position. From 1941 through 1965, the Cubs used fifty different men at catcher. Hundley caught 612 of the Cubs 626 games (including two ties) played from 1966 through 1969. In 1968, Randy set a major league record for most games caught in a season with 160. His durability was due in part to becoming the first big league catcher to adopt the one–handed catching style, in which he protected his bare hand from foul tips by placing it behind his back.

MAY 24   The Cubs play at Busch Memorial Stadium in St. Louis for the first time and defeat the Cardinals 2–0.

MAY 28   Ron Santo hits a three–run, walk–off homer in the eleventh inning to defeat the Braves 8–5 at Wrigley Field. The homer was hit off Ted Abernathy, who earlier in the day was traded by the Cubs to the Braves for Lee Thomas.

MAY 29   For the second day in a row, Ron Santo hits an extra inning, walk–off homer, connecting off Billy O'Dell in the tenth inning to defeat the Braves 3–2 at Wrigley Field.

Santo concluded the 1966 season with 30 homers, 98 runs batted in, and a .312 average. He also led the NL in walks with 98.

JUNE 7   In the amateur draft, the Cubs select Dean Burk, a right–handed pitcher from Highland High School in Highland, Illinois.

Burk never reached the majors, peaking at Triple A. The players drafted and signed by the Cubs in 1966 who did reach the majors were Rich Nye (14th round), Bill Stoneman (31st), and Archie Reynolds (38th). In the secondary phase of the draft, which consisted of previously drafted players who didn't sign with their original team, the Cubs picked up Joe Niekro in the third round.

JUNE 8   Randy Hundley hits a grand slam in the fourth inning off Don Drysdale during an 8–1 win over the Dodgers at Wrigley Field.

In early June, Leo Durocher tried playing Ron Santo at shortstop and Ernie Banks at third base. The experiment lasted only six games.

JUNE 11   Ernie Banks ties a modern major league record by hitting three triples during an 8–2 win over the Astros in Houston.

               Adolfo Phillips struck out nine consecutive times during a three–game span from June 8 through June 11.

JUNE 22   The Cubs purchase Curt Simmons from the Cardinals.

               Simmons was 37 years old and hardly qualified for the Cubs' youth movement, but Leo Durocher felt that the Cubs needed a veteran presence on the pitching staff until the youngsters were ready. Simmons had 184 big league victories when he arrived in Chicago.

JUNE 26   Ron Santo suffers a double fracture of the cheekbone when hit by a pitch from Jack Fisher of the Mets in the fourth inning of a 7–0 win in the first game of a double–header at Wrigley Field. In the at–bat prior to being struck in the face, Santo extended his hitting streak to 26 games. Curt Simmons pitched a complete–game shutout in his first appearance as a Cub. New York won the second game 8–2.

               The Cubs were engaged in a beanball war when Santo was hit. Earlier, Fisher put Adolfo Phillips out of the game by hitting him in the arm, and Simmons retaliated by plunking Ron Hunt. Fisher then turned around and threw at Santo. Leo Durocher and Mets manager Wes Westrum nearly came to blows over the incident. Westrum had to be forcibly restrained by the umpires. Santo submitted to surgery the following day to correct displacement by wiring the cheekbone.

JULY 4   In his first day back in the lineup after fracturing his cheekbone, Ron Santo collects hits in both ends of a double–header against the Pirates at Wrigley Field to extend his hitting streak to 28 games. The Cubs lost the first game 7–5, but won the second 6–4.

               To protect the cheekbone, Santo became the first Cub to wear an earflap on his batting helmet, although he abandoned it when the injury healed. Earflaps became mandatory in the majors in 1971, although anyone in the big leagues prior to that year could opt not to wear one.

JULY 12   Ron Santo drives in a key run in the National League's 2–1 win in the All–Star Game played at Busch Memorial Stadium in St. Louis. In the fourth inning, Santo beat out an infield single that scored Willie Mays from third base and tied the score 1–1.

JULY 13   The Cubs sign Robin Roberts, who was released by the Astros on July 4.

               A future Hall of Famer, Roberts was 39 years old and had 284 career wins when he signed with the Cubs. He pitched 11 games for the club and had a 2–3 record and a 6.14 ERA.

JULY 17   Three days after the bodies of eight student nurses, murdered by Richard Speck, are discovered in Chicago, Billy Williams hits for the cycle, collecting a single, double, triple, and homer in exact order during a 7–2 win over the Cardinals in the second game of a double–header at Busch Memorial Stadium. St. Louis won the first game 4–3 in eleven innings.

JULY 19   The Cubs lose to the Reds 3–2 in an eighteen–inning marathon at Wrigley Field. Don Pavletich drove in the winning run with a homer off Ferguson Jenkins.

JULY 20   Ernie Banks collects his 2,000th career hit with a two–run double off Sammy Ellis, but the Cubs lose 5–4 to the Reds in the first game of a double–header at Wrigley Field. Cincinnati also won the second game, called after seven innings by darkness, 5–1.

AUGUST 5   Ron Santo drives in all four Cubs runs in a 4–3, ten–inning win over the Giants at Wrigley Field. His homer in the second inning put the Cubs up 1–0. Another home run in the eighth tied the score 2–2. After San Francisco scored in the top of the tenth, the Cubs loaded the bases and Santo scored the tying and winning runs with a single.

AUGUST 11   Randy Hundley hits for the cycle in a 9–8 win in eleven innings in the first game of a double–header against the Astros at Wrigley Field. In the eighth inning, Hundley tied the score 8–8 with a homer and completed the cycle with a single in the eleventh that started the game–winning rally. The second game was suspended after seven innings with Houston leading 8–5 to allow both teams to catch a plane for the West Coast. The contest was completed on August 26 in Houston with the Astros winning 9–8.

AUGUST 17   Ernie Banks hits a three–run homer in the tenth inning to put the Cubs ahead 5–2 in a 5–3 win over the Phillies in Philadelphia.

AUGUST 24   Randy Hundley's perfect bunt with the bases loaded caps a two–run ninth–inning rally that beats the Mets 6–5 at Wrigley Field.

AUGUST 26   Leo Durocher rips the phone out of the Cub dugout at the Astrodome in the ninth inning when the animated scoreboard begins making fun of him with various cartoons. Durocher's mood wasn't enhanced by the finish of the game, as Bob Aspromonte hit a walk–off grand slam off Cal Koonce to beat the Cubs 7–4. Leo later received a bill for the damage.

AUGUST 29   The Cubs beat the Braves 4–2 in fourteen innings in Atlanta. George Altman drove in both fourteenth–inning runs with a single. Robin Roberts was the winning pitcher in what proved to be the last of his 286 career victories.

SEPTEMBER 5   A two–run, walk–off home run by Glenn Beckert beats the Phillies 5–4 in the first game of a double–header at Wrigley Field. It was the only homer that Beckert hit during the 1966 season. Philadelphia won the second game 7–2.

SEPTEMBER 11   Glenn Beckert extends his hitting streak to 21 games during a 4–3 win in the first game of a double–header against the Giants in San Francisco. The streak ended in the nightcap, which the Cubs lost 2–0.

SEPTEMBER 22   In his only game as a Cub, Dave Dowling pitches a 7–2 complete game victory over the Reds at Wrigley Field. Dowling's only other big league contest was a one–inning relief appearance with the Cardinals in 1964.

SEPTEMBER 25   Ken Holtzman carries a no–hitter into the ninth inning and emerges with a two–hitter and a 2–1 win over Sandy Koufax and the Dodgers at Wrigley Field. Dick Schofield spoiled the no–hit bid with a single with none out in the ninth and later scored on a single by Maury Wills.

OCTOBER 2   On the final day of the season, the Cubs lose 2–0 to the Cardinals in St. Louis. It was Chicago's 103rd loss of the season, tying the club record set in 1962. The Cubs were also the first team in National League history to finish behind the woeful Mets.

Even though the Cubs had one of the worst seasons in club history, optimism pervaded the North Side of Chicago during the 1966–67 off–season. Fans, players, and management sensed that this was a team on the move with promising young players, like Ferguson Jenkins, Glenn Beckert, Randy Hundley, Adolfo Phillips, Ken Holtzman, Bill Hands, and Don Kessinger, with more on the way in the farm system.

DECEMBER 7   The Cubs send Dick Ellsworth to the Phillies for Ray Culp and cash.

1967   Cubs

Season in a Sentence

Fun and excitement return to Wrigley Field, as the Cubs hold first place briefly in late–July and land in third, a giant leap from the tenth–place finish of 1966.

Finish • Won • Lost • Pct • GB

Third   87   74   .540   14.0

Manager

Leo Durocher

Stats

Stats	Cubs	NL	Rank
Batting Avg:	.251	.249	3
On–Base Pct:	.319	.312	3
Slugging Pct:	.378	.363	3
Home Runs:	128		3
Stolen Bases:	63		6
ERA:	3.48	3.38	7
Fielding Avg:	.981	.978	1
Runs Scored:	702		1
Runs Allowed:	624		6

Starting Lineup

Randy Hundley, c
Ernie Banks, 1b
Glenn Beckert, 2b
Ron Santo, 3b
Don Kessinger, ss
Billy Williams, lf
Adolfo Phillips, cf
Ted Savage, rf
Lee Thomas, rf
Paul Popovich, ss–2b

Pitchers

Ferguson Jenkins, sp
Rich Nye, sp
Joe Niekro, sp–rp
Ray Culp, sp
Curt Simmons, sp
Ken Holtzman, sp
Bill Hands, rp

Attendance

977,226 (seventh in NL)

Club Leaders

Batting Avg:	Santo	.300
On–Base Pct:	Santo	.395
Slugging Pct:	Santo	.512
Home Runs:	Santo	31
RBI:	Santo	98
Runs:	Santo	107
Stolen Bases:	Phillips	24
Wins:	Jenkins	20
Strikeouts:	Jenkins	236
ERA:	Jenkins	2.80
Saves:	Hartenstein	10

MARCH 23   Two months after the Green Bay Packers and the Kansas City Chiefs square off in the first Super Bowl, Leo Durocher's pal Frank Sinatra watches the Cubs lose 2–1 to the Angels in a spring training exhibition game in Palm Springs, California. Sinatra sat next to Durocher on a folding chair adjacent to the Cubs dugout.

APRIL 11   In the season opener, the Cubs defeat the Phillies 4–2 before 16,462 at Wrigley Field. Ferguson Jenkins pitched a complete game and Glenn Beckert hit a home run.

Beckert hit only five home runs in 1967, but he batted .280 and scored 91 runs.

APRIL 18   Adolfo Phillips drops a fly ball that leads to three unearned runs and a 4–3 Phillie lead, but he hits a home run and a triple to help the Cubs to an 8–4 comeback victory in Philadelphia.

Fred Norman opened the 1967 season with the Cubs, pitched one inning in one game, and fanned all three batters he faced. Norman was soon sent packing to the minors, however, and didn't face another major league hitter until 1970.

APRIL 23   On a freezing day with snow flurries swirling at Wrigley Field, Norm Gigon smashes a three–run homer for his first major league hit during a 7–3 win over the Pirates.

This was Gigon's only big league homer. He finished his career with 12 base hits and a .171 batting average.

APRIL 25   The Cubs trade Bob Raudman to the Indians for Dick Radatz.

MAY 4   The Cubs trade Byron Browne to the Astros for Aaron Pointer.

MAY 9   Ron Santo collects five hits in five at–bats during a 10–2 win over the Giants at Wrigley Field.

Santo in 1967 hit .300, collected 31 homers, drove in 98 runs, scored 107, and led the NL in walks with 96.

MAY 14   Billy Williams collects five hits in five at–bats during a 6–3, eleven–inning win over the Dodgers in the second game of a double–header in Los Angeles. The Dodgers won the first game 2–1 in ten innings.

Williams hit .278 with 28 homers and 84 RBIs in 1967.

MAY 15   Billy Williams collects four hits, giving him a club record nine in consecutive games, leading the Cubs to a 9–3 win over the Giants in San Francisco.

MAY 18   Astroturf is installed at Wrigley Field.

Green Astroturf, covering some 5,000 square feet, was placed on the empty seats in the center field bleachers to improve the batters' background. The Astroturf was taken out in 1982, and the benches were painted dark green. Junipers bushes were planted in the bleachers in 1997.

MAY 20   The Cubs maul the Dodgers 20–3 at Wrigley Field. Adolfo Phillips drove in six runs on a pair of three–run homers. Randy Hundley drove in five runs, including a grand slam in the seventh inning off Bob Lee. The 20th run was scored on an inside–the–park homer by Glenn Beckert.

MAY 24   Adolfo Phillips uses his speed to beat the Reds 4–3 in the second game of a double–header at Wrigley Field. In the ninth inning with the score 3–3, Phillips reached on a bunt single, stole second, moved to third on an error, and with the infield pulled in, put on a burst of speed to beat the throw to the plate by Cincinnati shortstop Leo Cardenas for the winning run. The Reds won the first game 4–3.

MAY 30   Ferguson Jenkins strikes out 12 batters and drives in three runs as the Cubs pound out a 12–5 win in the first game of a double–header against the Braves at Wrigley Field.

During his first three off–seasons as a Cub, Ferguson Jenkins played basketball for the Harlem Globetrotters.

Ferguson Jenkins started his run of six straight 20–win seasons with a 20–13 record in 1967, when he led the majors with 20 complete games.

JUNE 5   The Cubs slug their way to a 13–3 win over the Phillies in Philadelphia.

In games through June 6, the Cubs had a record of 24–24.

JUNE 6   With the second overall pick in the 1967 amateur draft, the Cubs select shortstop Terry Hughes from Dorman High School in Spartanburg, South Carolina.

Hughes played only two games as a Cub, both in 1970, and just 54 in his big league career. His lifetime batting average was .209. The only other player chosen by the Cubs in the regular phase of the draft to reach the majors was Mike McMath in the second round. McMath played in only six major league games. In the secondary phase, the Cubs selected Randy Bobb and Darcy Fast, two more players with brief careers in the big leagues.

JUNE 11 | Adolfo Phillips hits four home runs in a double–header, including three in succession in the nightcap, as the Cubs sweep the Mets 5–3 and 18–10 at Wrigley Field. Phillips hit a solo home run in the first game. Following his first at–bat in the second tilt, Adolfo attempted to steal home and was tagged in the head by New York catcher Hawk Taylor. Phillips was knocked dizzy but stayed in the game. In his next three plate appearances, Phillips homered, connecting off Nick Willhite in the third inning with two runners on base, a two–run shot off Chuck Estrada in the fifth, and a solo shot against Don Shaw in the sixth. Phillips added a seventh run batted in with a single in the eighth. The Cubs and the Mets combined for a National League–record 11 home runs in the game. In addition to the three by Phillips, Randy Hundley hit two and Ron Santo and Ernie Banks added one each. The seven home runs by the Cubs is a team record for one game. Ron Swoboda, Jerry Buchek, Jerry Grote, and Bob Johnson hit home runs for the Mets.

JUNE 26 | The Cubs win their seventh game in a row, the club's longest winning streak since 1954, with a 4–2 decision over the Phillies at Wrigley Field.

JULY 2 | The Cubs move into a tie for first place with the Cardinals after defeating the Reds 4–1 before 40,464 at Wrigley Field. After the game, many in the crowd waited until the pennant flags on the scoreboard were rearranged with the Cubs flag placed on the top.

After two decades of hibernation, the Cubs were in first place for the first time during the summer months since 1945.

JULY 3 | The revitalized Cubs maintain their hold on the tie for first place with a 12–6 win over the Braves in Atlanta. The two clubs combined for five homers in the first inning to tie a major league record. Billy Williams, Ron Santo, and Randy Hundley connected for the Cubs, while Rico Carty and Felipe Alou homered for the Braves.

The victory was the 14th in a stretch of 15 games for the Cubs, and their 22nd in a 27–game span. At the conclusion of the July 3 game, the Cubs had a record of 46–29, an astonishing turnaround considering that the club was 59–103 in 1966.

JULY 4 | The Niekro brothers face each other for the first time, with Phil pitching for the Braves and Joe hurling for the Cubs. Phil beat Joe in an 8–3 decision in the first game of a double–header in Atlanta. The Braves also won the second game 4–2.

The double–header defeat started a skid in which the Cubs lost seven games in a row.

JULY 16 | Adolfo Phillips hits a grand slam in the sixth inning off Gaylord Perry, helping the Cubs to a 9–0 win over the Giants in the first game of a double–header in San Francisco. The Cubs completed the sweep with a 3–2 win in the second tilt.

JULY 22 | The day before riots erupt in Detroit, resulting in the deaths of forty people, the Cubs move back into a first–place tie with a dramatic two–run rally in the ninth to beat the Giants 6–5 at Wrigley Field. The runs were scored on a home run by Billy Williams, a triple by Ron Santo, and a single by Randy Hundley.

JULY 24 | After dropping out of first place with a double–header split with the Giants on July

23 at Wrigley Field, the Cubs resume their implausible climb to the top of the league by beating the Cardinals 3–1 in St. Louis to gain a first–place tie once again with a record of 56–40.

JULY 25   The Cubs lose 4–3 to the Cardinals in St. Louis to drop into second place.

Within two weeks, the Cubs were nine games out of first and never regained the top spot again in 1967.

AUGUST 2   The Cubs sell Cal Koonce to the Mets and Curt Simmons to the Angels.

AUGUST 13   The Cubs defeat the Phillies 6–2 and 1–0 in a double–header at Wrigley Field. Ferguson Jenkins pitched the shutout. The only run of the game was scored on a single by Don Kessinger in the third inning.

Ken Holtzman was the winning pitcher in the first game. It was his first appearance in nearly three months. Holtzman was notified in May that his Illinois National Guard unit was to embark on a six–month tour of duty. By August, he was available for weekend passes, and the Cubs dispatched Elvin Tappe, a Cubs coach and former catcher, to work him out during off–duty hours. Holtzman had a 5–0 record when he left for the Army and won four more pitching on weekends in August and September to finish the season at 9–0.

AUGUST 31   Two weeks after the unveiling of the controversial Picasso statue in front of the Richard J. Daley Center in downtown Chicago, an unusual pinch–hit strategy leads to the winning run in a 2–1 win over the Mets at Wrigley Field. With runners on first and second and no one out in the eleventh inning, Ted Savage missed two bunts. With the count 1–2, Leo Durocher put Al Spangler into the game to pinch–hit for Savage. Spangler delivered a single to win the game.

Alderman John Hoellen called the Picasso sculpture a "rusting junk heap" and suggested that it be torn down and replaced by a fifty–foot statue of Ernie Banks, "the symbol of our vibrant city."

SEPTEMBER 4   Ernie Banks hits a homer in the eleventh inning to beat the Dodgers 2–1 at Wrigley Field.

Despite his status as "Mr. Cub," Banks was never one of Durocher's favorites. During spring training in 1967, Banks was 36 years old and coming off of a sub–par season. Durocher believed that Ernie was washed up and spent much of the exhibition schedule looking for someone to replace him at first, but Banks persevered, held his position in the lineup, and hit 23 homers along with 95 runs batted in.

SEPTEMBER 29   Ferguson Jenkins wins his 20th game of the 1967 season with a 4–1 decision over the Reds in Cincinnati. It was the first of seven 20–win seasons for Jenkins in his career, six of which were the Cubs.

Jenkins had a 20–13 record, a 2.80 ERA, 236 strikeouts and a league–leading 20 complete games in 1967. It was the most strikeouts by a Cubs pitcher since Bill Hutchinson fanned 314 in 1892, when the pitcher's mound was only 50 feet from home plate.

SEPTEMBER 30   The Cubs score eight runs in the first inning and beat the Reds 9–4 in Cincinnati.

> *With the Cubs' spectacular leap from tenth place in 1966 to third in 1967, attendance jumped from 635,691 to 977,226. The club's 1967 winning percentage of .540 was the club's best since 1945 and the second–best since 1939. In addition, the future looked bright as the core of the team consisted mainly of players under 30 such as Ron Santo (age 27), Billy Williams (29), Adolfo Phillips (25), Randy Hundley (25), Ferguson Jenkins (23), Glenn Beckert (26), Bill Hands (27), Rich Nye (23), Joe Niekro (22), Chuck Hartenstein (25), Ken Holtzman (21), Don Kessinger (24), Ray Culp (25), and Bill Stoneman (23).*

NOVEMBER 30   The Cubs send Ray Culp to the Red Sox for Bill Schlesinger and cash.

> *After an 8–11 season in 1967, Culp didn't look like a prospect to the Cubs, so the club traded him to the Red Sox for a minor league outfielder. It proved to be a big mistake, as Culp had a record of 50–28 over the next three years while Schlesinger never appeared in another big league game.*

1968   Cubs

Season in a Sentence

The Cubs solidify their position as an up–and–coming team by finishing third again, and they draw over a million fans for the first time since 1952.

Finish • Won • Lost • Pct • GB

Third	84	78	.519	13.0

Manager

Leo Durocher

Stats

Stats	Cubs	NL	Rank
Batting Avg:	.242	.243	5
On–Base Pct:	.300	.302	6
Slugging Pct:	.366	.341	2
Home Runs:	130		1
Stolen Bases:	41		10
ERA:	3.41	2.99	9
Fielding Avg:	.981	.978	1
Runs Scored:	612		1
Runs Allowed:	611		8

Starting Lineup

Randy Hundley, c
Ernie Banks, 1b
Glenn Beckert, 2b
Ron Santo, 3b
Don Kessinger, ss
Billy Williams, lf
Adolfo Phillips, cf
Jim Hickman, rf
Lou Johnson, rf
Al Spangler, rf

Pitchers

Ferguson Jenkins, sp
Bill Hands, sp
Joe Niekro, sp
Ken Holtzman, sp
Rich Nye, sp
Phil Regan, rp
Jack Lamabe, rp

Attendance

1,043,409 (sixth in NL)

Club Leaders

Batting Avg:	Beckert	.294
On–Base Pct:	Santo	.354
Slugging Pct:	Williams	.500
Home Runs:	Banks	32
RBI:	Santo	98
	Williams	98
Runs:	Beckert	98
Stolen Bases:	Kessinger	9
	Phillips	9
Wins:	Jenkins	20
Strikeouts:	Jenkins	260
ERA:	Jenkins	2.63
Saves:	Regan	25

APRIL 6   In the wake of the April 4 murder of Dr. Martin Luther King Jr., the Reds announce that Opening Day, scheduled for April 8 against the Cubs in Cincinnati, will be postponed for two days to avoid conflict with the national day of mourning declared by President Lyndon Johnson for Dr. King's funeral on April 9.

Riots broke out in many of Chicago's African–American neighborhoods in reaction to the assassination. Mayor Richard Daley issued to police a controversial shoot–on–sight order to try and bring a halt to the violence, in which seven people were killed in Chicago and 500 injured.

APRIL 10   The Cubs lose 9–4 in the season opener in Cincinnati. The Reds broke a 1–1 tie with five runs in the fifth inning off starter Joe Niekro. Don Kessinger collected three hits and Randy Hundley drove in three runs.

The Cubs and the White Sox separated their telecasts for the first time in 1968. Previously, WGN–TV telecast both clubs and shared the same announcing team. The White Sox moved to WFLD–TV in 1968 with Jack Drees and Dave Martin doing the play–by–play. The move hurt the Sox because WFLD was a UHF station at a time when many television sets couldn't pick up UHF channels. Jack Brickhouse and Vince Lloyd, who had been handling the telecasts of both Chicago clubs, were now associated exclusively with Cubs. The number of road–game telecasts of the Cubs was increased from five in 1967 to sixty–three in 1968. All away games were telecast except for those from the West Coast.

APRIL 11   The Cubs collect five homers and defeat the Reds 10–3 in Cincinnati. Billy Williams hit two homers, and Ron Santo, Ferguson Jenkins, and Adolfo Phillips each hit one. Jenkins also struck out 12 batters.

Williams hit .288 in 1968 with 30 home runs, 98 RBIs, and 91 runs scored.

APRIL 13   In the home opener, the Cubs take a 4–0 lead in the first inning, but lose 8–5 to the Cardinals before 33,875 at Wrigley Field. Ron Santo hit a three–run homer.

APRIL 23   The Cubs trade Ted Savage and Jim Ellis to the Dodgers for Jim Hickman and Phil Regan.

This turned out to be a steal of a deal for the Cubs, although only in the short term. Regan became the Cubs closer and had a 10–5 record, 25 saves, and a 2.20 ERA for the club in 1968. He followed with a 12–6 mark and 17 saves in 1969. Hickman had two disappointing seasons with the Cubs before breaking loose with an All–Star season in 1970.

MAY 2   Ernie Banks hits a homer off Jim Bunning to lead the Cubs to a 1–0 win over the Pirates in Pittsburgh. Joe Niekro pitched the shutout.

In a revival year, Banks hit 32 homers and drove in 83 runs in 1968.

MAY 5   The Cubs sweep the Mets 3–2 and 1–0 in a double–header in New York. Bill Hands pitched the second–game shutout. The lone run of the game was scored on a double by Jose Arcia.

MAY 16   Rich Nye pitches the Cubs to a 1–0 win over Dodgers in Los Angeles. The only run of the game was scored on a single in the first inning by Ron Santo.

Santo hit 26 homers, drove in 98 runs, and scored 86 times in 1968. He also drew 96 walks to lead the NL in the category for the third straight year.

MAY 18   The Cubs score seven runs in the fourth inning and defeat the Giants 10–7 in San Francisco.

MAY 22   Willie Stargell homers three times for the Pirates during a 13–6 win over the Cubs at Wrigley Field.

MAY 29   Ken Holtzman pitches a two–hitter to defeat the Phillies 9–2 in the first game of a double–header at Connie Mack Stadium. Both Philadelphia hits were singles by Tony Taylor and Don Lock in the first inning. The Phils won the second game 8–3.

JUNE 6   The Cubs select outfielder Ralph Rickey from the University of Oklahoma in the first round of the amateur draft.

Rickey never made it to the majors. Those picked by the Cubs in the regular phase of the draft in 1968 who were signed and did reach the big leagues were Matt Alexander (second round) and Oscar Gamble (16th). In the secondary phase of the draft, the Cubs picked Dave Lemonds, Chris Ward, and Paul Reuschel.

JUNE 8   The game between the Cubs and the Braves at Wrigley Field is postponed because of a national day of mourning declared by President Lyndon Johnson for Senator Robert Kennedy. While campaigning in Los Angeles for the Democratic Party presidential nomination, Kennedy was shot on June 5 and died on June 6.

JUNE 15   The Cubs lose 3–2 to the Braves in ten innings in Atlanta.

The Cubs failed to score in the last eight innings of the June 15 loss, which started a streak of forty–eight consecutive innings in which the Cubs failed to score a run, tying a major league record set by the 1906 Philadelphia Athletics. On June 16, the Cubs lost 1–0 to the Braves in eleven innings in Atlanta. From June 18 through June 20, the Cubs were swept by the Cardinals in St. Louis by scores of 1–0, 4–0, and 1–0. On June 21, the Cubs finally scored in the third inning of a 3–2 win over the Reds at Crosley Field. The runless streak was broken when Cincinnati pitcher George Culver walked the bases loaded and Billy Williams hit a sacrifice fly.

JULY 5   The Cubs lose 4–0 to the Pirates at Wrigley Field.

The defeat represented the low point of the 1968 season, as the Cubs fell to ninth place with a record of 35–45. It looked the massive improvement of 1967 might be a mirage, but Leo Durocher's club won 29 of their next 39 games to vault into second place by August 4 before finishing the season in third.

JULY 7   Ernie Banks hits a grand slam in the first inning off Steve Blass of the Pirates in the first game of a double–header at Wrigley Field. The Pirates rallied to tie the score, but the Cubs won 5–4 on a ninth–inning walk–off homer by Jose Arcia. The Cubs completed the sweep with another walk–off win in the nightcap. With the score 3–3 in the ninth, relief pitcher Phil Regan doubled with two out and scored on a single by Don Kessinger to lift the Cubs to a 4–3 victory. Regan was the winning pitcher in both games.

The homer by Arcia was the only one of the his major league career, which spanned 615 at–bats over three seasons.

JULY 10   The National League votes to divide into two divisions beginning in 1969 because of the addition of expansion teams in Montreal and San Diego. The Cubs were placed in the Eastern Division with Montreal, New York, Philadelphia, Pittsburgh, and St. Louis.

The Cubs were inserted into the Eastern Division in defiance of geographic logic because of Mets Chairman of the Board M. Donald Grant. In 1968, the three biggest road draws in the National League were the Dodgers, Giants, and Cardinals, and Grant insisted that the Mets be placed in the same division with at least one of the three. Thus, St. Louis moved to the Eastern Division, but agreed only if its long–standing rival Cubs were included. That put Cincinnati and Atlanta, two cities east of Chicago and St. Louis, in the West.

JULY 11   In the second game of a double–header at Shea Stadium, Ernie Banks hits a two–run double in the ninth that lifts the Cubs to a 2–0 win. Bill Hands pitched the shutout. New York won the first game 1–0.

From June 9 through July 11, Hands set a major league record (since tied) by striking out in 14 consecutive at–bats. He had an .078 batting average in 472 career at–bats, in which he fanned 249 times.

JULY 14   Billy Williams hits a grand slam off Al McBean in the seventh inning of a 6–2 win over the Pirates in Pittsburgh.

JULY 17   Ernie Banks drives in six runs with two homers and a single to lead the Cubs to an 8–4 win over the Phillies in the first game of a double–header at Connie Mack Stadium. Philadelphia won the second game 8–0.

JULY 22   Glenn Beckert extends his hitting streak to 27 games in a 7–2 win over the Giants in San Francisco.

JULY 24   Ron Santo hits a two–run homer in the ninth inning off Gaylord Perry to beat the Giants 2–0 in San Francisco. Ken Holtzman pitched the shutout.

JULY 27   Ferguson Jenkins strikes out 13 batters in a 2–1 win over the Dodgers at Wrigley Field.

JULY 28   Before 42,261, the largest crowd at Wrigley Field since 1948, the Cubs sweep the Dodgers 8–3 and 1–0 in a double–header. Ken Holtzman pitched the second–game shutout. Randy Hundley drove in the only run of the game with a double in the fifth inning.

AUGUST 2   Ken Holtzman pitches a two–hitter and records his third consecutive shutout, defeating the Cardinals 3–0 at Busch Memorial Stadium. The only St. Louis hits were singles by Julian Javier in the sixth inning and Tim McCarver in the seventh.

Holtzman had a streak of 31 consecutive innings, but overall it was a disappointing year as his record was 11–14. Ken had to leave the club ten times due to calls to active duty by his National Guard unit.

AUGUST 4 On the day that the Stan Musial statue is unveiled at Busch Memorial Stadium, the Cubs defeat the Cardinals 6–5 in thirteen innings. The winning run was driven in on a pinch–single by Lee Elia.

Elia had only three hits in 17 at–bats as a member of the Cubs. He later managed the team in 1982 and 1983.

AUGUST 11 A three–run, two–out, inside–the–park home run by Billy Williams in the fifteenth inning beats the Reds 8–5 in Cincinnati. Williams also homered in the sixth inning. Don Kessinger collected five hits, including a double, in seven innings.

AUGUST 18 Phil Regan is searched by umpire Chris Pelakoudas when he's suspected of throwing an illegal pitch in the second game of a double–header at Wrigley Field. The Cubs lost twice to the Reds 2–1 and 6–3.

Shortly after Regan entered the game in the seventh inning, Pelakoudas went to the mound and inspected Regan's cap and claimed later that he found Vaseline on the inside of the cap. When the game continued, Pelakoudas charged Regan with throwing three illegal pitches "by watching the break of the ball." The ump nullified a fly ball and a strikeout and changed a strike call to a ball. After the strikeout was reversed, Pete Rose hit a single. The result was one of the biggest rhubarbs in Wrigley history as the 30,942 in attendance booed loudly and threw debris on the field. Leo Durocher, Randy Hundley, and Al Spangler were all thrown out of the game. Regan, surprisingly, was allowed to remain in the contest. The Cubs protested the defeat. After a special hearing in Chicago on August 20, NL President Warren Giles disallowed the protest but said that in the future umpires should have better evidence before ruling that a pitch was illegal. Giles also ordered Pelakoudas to apologize to Regan. Trying to find an illegal substance on Regan's person became somewhat of a Holy Grail for National League umpires, however, and games were stopped frequently for several more years for inspections. The frisking stopped in 1971, when Regan stopped winning.

AUGUST 21 Billy Williams drives in nine runs, seven of them in the second game, as the Cubs sweep the Braves 5–4 and 13–5 in a double–header at Wrigley Field. During the two games, Williams had a homer, a double, three singles, and a sacrifice fly.

AUGUST 26 Ken Holtzman is among the Illinois National Guard called to active duty during the Democratic National Party convention, held in Chicago. The National Guard was activated because demonstrators protesting the Vietnam War clashed with Chicago police, resulting in hundreds of arrests and injuries over a period of four days. The Cubs were playing in San Francisco and Los Angeles during the early part of the convention, but returned on Thursday, August 29, as police and demonstrators were still battling on the streets. On August 30, Astros players, arriving for a series against the Cubs, spent a few nervous moments passing through barricades set up by protesters. Arriving at the Conrad Hilton Hotel, the Astros found themselves in the middle of chemical warfare between demonstrators using stink bombs and police using tear gas.

AUGUST 30   Ron Santo drives in all five Cubs runs in a 5–3 win over the Astros at Wrigley Field. Santo hit a three–run homer in the fourth inning and a two–run homer in the sixth, both off Larry Dierker.

SEPTEMBER 1   Ron Santo hits a two–run homer in the seventh inning off Denny Lemaster to account for the only two runs in a 2–0 win over the Astros at Wrigley Field. It was the second time in three days that Santo drove in all of the Cubs runs in a game. Bill Hands pitched the shutout.

Hands had a 16–10 record and a 2.89 ERA in 1968.

SEPTEMBER 7   Nineteen–year–old outfielder Jimmy McMath makes his major league debut during a 4–2 loss to the Phillies at Wrigley Field.

McMath's stay in the big leagues was only a cameo, however, as his career lasted only six games, in which he collected only two hits in 14 at–bats.

Bill Hands finished 16–10 with a 2.89 ERA in 1968 on his way to 92 career victories in a Cubs uniform.

SEPTEMBER 8   Billy Williams hits two homers in a 10–3 win over the Phillies at Wrigley Field.

SEPTEMBER 10   Billy Williams wallops three homers during an 8–1 win over the Mets at Wrigley Field. Williams connected off Dick Selma in the first and sixth innings and Nolan Ryan in the seventh. Each of them were hit with a man on base, giving Williams six runs batted in. Combined with the two homers he struck on September 8, Williams tied a major league record for most home runs in consecutive games with five.

SEPTEMBER 11   Ferguson Jenkins loses 1–0 to the Mets at Wrigley Field. Jenkins lost five games in 1968 by a 1–0 score, which tied a major league record.

Jenkins started 40 games in 1968 and had a record of 20–15 with 309 innings pitched, 260 strikeouts, 20 complete games, and a 2.60 ERA.

SEPTEMBER 15   Ernie Banks plays in his 2,254th career game, breaking the club record for most games played set by Cap Anson. The Cubs defeated the Phillies 4–0 in Philadelphia.

SEPTEMBER 25   Ron Santo hits a walk–off grand slam in the ninth inning off Bill Singer that beats the

Dodgers 4–1 at Wrigley Field. Entering the ninth, Singer had allowed only one hit.

SEPTEMBER 28   Ferguson Jenkins wins his 20th game of the 1968 season with a 4–3 win over the Pirates at Wrigley Field.

The Cubs had a record of 84–78 in 1968, while the White Sox were 67–95. It was the first time since 1950 that the Cubs won more games than the Sox.

OCTOBER 14   Three weeks before the election of Richard Nixon as president over Hubert Humphrey, the Cubs lose six players to the Montreal Expos and San Diego Padres in the expansion draft. The Expos picked Bill Stoneman, Frank Reberger, Gary Jestadt, and John Boccabella, while the Padres chose Jose Arcia and Rick James.

A native of the Chicago suburb of Oak Park, Stoneman proved to be the biggest loss. He pitched well for some awful Expos teams over the next four seasons.

1969   Cubs

Season in a Sentence

The Cubs send their fans on a roller-coaster ride by taking an 8 ½-game lead on August 13, only to blow the chance for the pennant with a late-season nosedive.

Finish • Won • Lost • Pct • GB

Second   92   70   .568   8.0

Manager

Leo Durocher

Stats

Stats	Cubs	NL	Rank
Batting Avg:	.253	.250	5
On–Base Pct:	.326	.321	5
Slugging Pct:	.384	.369	3
Home Runs:	142		2
Stolen Bases:	301		2
ERA:	3.34	3.59	5
Fielding Avg:	.979	.977	4
Runs Scored:	720		3
Runs Allowed:	611		4

Starting Lineup

Randy Hundley, c
Ernie Banks, 1b
Glenn Beckert, 2b
Ron Santo, 3b
Don Kessinger, ss
Billy Williams, lf
Don Young, cf
Jim Hickman, rf
Al Spangler, rf
Willie Smith, lf–1b
Paul Popovich, 2b

Pitchers

Ferguson Jenkins, sp
Bill Hands, sp
Ken Holtzman, sp
Dick Selma, sp–rp
Phil Regan, sp
Ted Abernathy, rp
Hank Aguirre, rp

Attendance

1,674,993 (third in NL)

Club Leaders

Batting Avg:	Williams	.293
On–Base Pct:	Santo	.384
Slugging Pct:	Santo	.485
Home Runs:	Santo	29
RBI:	Santo	123
Runs:	Kessinger	109
Stolen Bases:	Kessinger	11
Wins:	Jenkins	21
Strikeouts:	Jenkins	273
ERA:	Hands	2.49
Saves:	Regan	17

JANUARY 9   Three days before the New York Jets upset the Baltimore Colts in the Super Bowl, the Cubs send Bill Plummer, Clarence Jones, and Ken Myette to the Reds for Ted Abernathy.

The Cubs rectified an old mistake by trading for Abernathy, who they dealt away in May 1966.

FEBRUARY 4   Bowie Kuhn is appointed commissioner to replace William Eckert, who was fired in December 1968. Kuhn remained in office for sixteen years.

APRIL 8   The Cubs win an exciting season opener 7–6 against the Phillies before 40,796 at Wrigley Field. Ernie Banks hit a two–run homer in the first inning and a three–run shot in the third, both off Chris Short, to give the Cubs a 5–1 lead. But the Phillies came back to take a 6–5 lead on one run in the seventh inning, three in the ninth, and one in the eleventh. Don Money drove in five of the six Philadelphia runs. But in the bottom half of the eleventh, the Cubs came back to win on a single by Randy Hundley and a pinch–hit, two–run, walk–off home run by Willie Smith.

The Opening Day win sent Cubs fans into a state of giddiness that lasted until the mid–August collapse. Stereos all over Chicago blared the unofficial theme song of the club with the lyrics, "Hey, hey, holy mackerel, not doubt about it. The Cubs are on their way." The Cubs drew 1,674,993 fans in 1969. As recently as 1966, the Cubs had an attendance of only 635,891. The 1969 figure broke the club record of 1,485,166 set in 1929. It also exceeded the Chicago record of 1,644,460 set by the White Sox in 1960.

APRIL 9   Billy Williams hits four consecutive doubles to tie a major league record during an 11–3 win over the Phillies at Wrigley Field. The Cubs scored seven runs in the seventh inning.

In 1969, Williams hit .293 with 21 homers, 103 runs scored, and 95 RBIs. Ron Santo hit .289 for the Cubs during the season and had a .289 average, 29 homers, 123 RBIs, and 97 runs scored. In his last years as a regular, Ernie Banks had 23 homers and drove in 106 runs. Don Kessinger had the best season of his career, with a .273 average and 109 runs scored.

APRIL 11   The Cubs play the Expos for the first time, and win 1–0 in twelve innings at Wrigley Field. Joe Niekro (nine innings) and Ted Abernathy (three innings) combined on the shutout. Billy Williams drove in the winning run with a two–out single. The victory gave the Cubs a record of 4–0.

APRIL 13   The Cubs score three runs in the ninth to beat the Expos 7–6 at Wrigley Field. A single by Ernie Banks broke the 6–6 tie.

APRIL 16   Ferguson Jenkins pitches the Cubs to a 1–0 win over the Cardinals in St. Louis.

Jenkins was 21–15 with a 3.21 ERA in 1969. He pitched 311 innings and led the league in starts (42, which is also a club record) and strikeouts (273). Bill Hands won 20 games for the only time in his career with a 20–14 record and a 2.49 earned run average. He pitched 300 innings. Ken Holtzman was 17–13 with a 3.59 ERA in 261 innings.

APRIL 19   In the club's first regular season game outside of the United States, the Cubs beat the Expos 6–5 in eleven innings at Jarry Park in Montreal.

APRIL 20   A native of Chatham, Ontario, Ferguson Jenkins pitches in Canada for the first time and defeats the Expos 6–3 in the first game of a double–header in Montreal. The victory gave the Cubs a season record of 11–1. The Expos won the second game 4–2.

APRIL 25   The Cubs trade Joe Niekro, Gary Ross, and Francisco Libran to the Padres for Dick Selma.

Leo Durocher liked power pitchers and didn't believe that Niekro could win in the majors. Joe proved him wrong by winning another 197 big league games after the trade and finished his career in 1988 with a record of 221–204. In fairness to Durocher, Niekro also failed in trials with the Padres, Tigers, and Braves and didn't become an above–average pitcher until 1977, when he played for the Astros and developed a knuckleball taught to him by his brother Phil. Selma became part of Cubs lore in 1969 by regularly leading the Bleacher Bums in cheers from his position in the bullpen.

APRIL 29   The Cubs rout the Phillies 10–0 in Philadelphia.

Hearing that the defending champion Detroit Tigers would play an exhibition game against the Phillies at Connie Mack Stadium on May 1, the day after the Cubs left Philadelphia, Cubs players wrote on the clubhouse blackboard, "See you in the World Series if you can make it." Pennant fever was rampant in Chicago, as Cubs fans anticipated a World Series at Wrigley Field for the first time in a generation.

MAY 3   Four Cubs pinch–hitters strike out to tie a major league record, but the Cubs survive to defeat the Mets 3–2 at Wrigley Field. The four who fanned were Gene Oliver, Willie Smith, Manny Jiminez, and Jim Hickman.

MAY 11   Ken Holtzman shuts out the Giants 8–0 at Wrigley Field.

MAY 12   The Cubs play the San Diego Padres for the first time and win 2–0 at Wrigley Field. Ferguson Jenkins pitched the shutout.

MAY 13   The Cubs wallop the Padres 19–0 at Wrigley Field to tie a club record for the most lopsided shutout since 1900. It was also the third consecutive game in which the Cubs shut out the opposition, with Dick Selma spinning a complete game. Ernie Banks was the hitting star with seven runs batted in on two homers and a double.

MAY 16   The Cubs explode for 10 runs in the seventh inning and defeat the Astros 11–0 in Houston. Ken Holtzman pitched the shutout.

MAY 20   Ken Holtzman pitches his third consecutive shutout and runs his scoreless–innings streak in 33, defeating the Dodgers 7–0 in Los Angeles.

MAY 23   The Cubs play the Padres in San Diego for the first time and emerge with a 6–0 victory.

MAY 24   Ernie Banks hits a grand slam off Jack Baldschun in the fifth inning to give the
              Cubs a 6–4 lead in an eventual 7–5 win over the Padres in San Diego.

MAY 25   After losing the opener of a double–header 10–2 against the Padres in San Diego,
              the Cubs win 1–0 in the nightcap. A homer by Ron Santo off Joe Niekro was the
              game–winner. Bill Hands (six innings) and Ted Abernathy (three innings) combined
              on the shutout. It was the Cubs eighth shutout in a span of 14 games.

MAY 28   Randy Hundley hits a grand slam off Rich Robertson in a seven–run, third inning
              against the Giants in San Francisco. The homer gave the Cubs an 8–0 lead, and the
              club held on to win 9–8.

JUNE 1   The Cubs roll to a 13–4 win over the Braves at Wrigley Field.

JUNE 5   In the amateur draft, the Cubs select shortstop Roger Metzger of St. Edward's High
              School in San Antonio, Texas.

              *Metzger played only one game for the Cubs before he was traded to the Astros
              at the end of the 1970 season. Other future major leaguers drafted and signed
              by the Cubs in 1969 included Larry Gura (second round), Jim Todd (tenth), Bill
              North (12th), and Pat Bourque (33rd). Gura and North were both solid con-
              tributors on World Series teams during their careers, but the Cubs got rid of
              both them before they developed.*

JUNE 6   The Cubs clobber the Reds 14–8 at Wrigley Field.

JUNE 8   Standing outside the Reds clubhouse during a rain delay at Wrigley Field, Reds
              pitcher Jose Pena suffers a broken nose when struck by a ball thrown by a fan.

JUNE 10   Willie Smith homers into the upper deck in Atlanta, a drive estimated at 500 feet,
              during a 3–1 win over the Braves.

JUNE 11   The Cubs trade Adolfo Phillips and Jack Lamabe to the Expos for Paul Popovich.

JUNE 13   With two out in the tenth, the Cubs erupt for six runs to defeat the Reds 14–8 in
              Cincinnati.

JUNE 19   At the age of 63, Leo Durocher marries 40–year–old Lynne Walker Goldblatt in cer-
              emonies at the Ambassador West Hotel in Chicago. Lynne was a Chicago television
              personality and the ex–wife of a Midwest department store executive. It was his
              fourth marriage and her second.

JUNE 22   The Cubs score four runs in the ninth inning to defeat the Expos 7–6 in the first
              game of a double–header at Wrigley Field. Ernie Banks drove in the first two runs
              with a single, and Jim Hickman ended the contest by scoring Banks with a two–run
              walk–off homer. Montreal won the second game, called after six innings by darkness.

JUNE 26   Jim Hickman's home run in the tenth inning defeats the Pirates 7–5 at Wrigley
              Field. The Cubs trailed 1–0, 3–1, and 5–3 before rallying to tie the game on each
              occasion. It was Hickman's second walk–off home run in a span of five days.

On the spur of the moment, Ron Santo leaped in the air and clicked his heels three times on the way to the clubhouse. The victory dance became a hit with euphoric Cubs fans, and it was part of Ron's routine whenever the Cubs won at Wrigley Field. "I'm working on a double-click for the World Series," said Santo. The rest of the league wasn't quite so enthralled, however. Already infuriated by heckling, yellow-hatted Bleacher Bums and Dick Selma's cheerleading routine, opposing players considered Santo's display unprofessional and gave them another reason to loathe the Cubs.

JUNE 29   The Cubs sweep the Cardinals 3–1 and 12–1 on Billy Williams Day before a crowd of 40,060 at Wrigley Field. By playing in both ends of the twin bill, Williams broke Stan Musial's record for consecutive games played. It was Billy's 895th and 896th straight game. In pre-game ceremonies, Williams received a new car, a fishing boat, a trailer, a combination washer-dryer, a watch, a pool table, and a Weimaraner puppy. He was also the center of attraction on the field. Williams had five hits, including two triples and two doubles.

JULY 3   The Cubs score seven runs in the seventh inning and defeat the Expos 8–4 in Montreal.

JULY 8   The Mets score three runs in the ninth inning to defeat the Cubs 4–3 in New York.

Ferguson Jenkins went into the ninth inning with a one-hitter, but the Mets rallied to win in large part because rookie center fielder Don Young misplayed two easy fly balls into two doubles. "Two little fly balls," roared Leo Durocher. "He watches one and lets the other one drop." Ron Santo went into a tirade and berated the defenseless Young. "Young was thinking of himself," complained the Cubs third baseman. "He got his head down worrying about his batting average and not about winning the game. All right, he can keep his head down and he can keep going right out of sight for all I care. We don't need that sort of thing." Although Santo made a public apology the next day, he never really lived it down. Many Cubs fans remained bitter toward Durocher and Santo for years afterward because of their comments about Young.

JULY 9   Tom Seaver retires the first twenty-five Cubs batters, but his hopes for a perfect game are wrecked when rookie center fielder Jimmy Qualls singles with one out in the ninth inning. Seaver had to settle for a one-hit, 4–0 win over the Cubs before a crowd of 59,083 in New York.

Qualls was playing in center field in place of Young, whose defensive lapses cost the Cubs the game the night before. It was Qualls's 43rd major league at-bat. He played only one year with the Cubs and three in the majors, and ended his big league career with 63 games played, 31 hits, and a .223 batting average.

JULY 14   The Cubs defeat the Mets 1–0 in the first game of a three-game series at Wrigley Field. The only run was scored in the sixth inning on a single by Billy Williams. Bill Hands (8⅔ innings) and Phil Regan (one-third of an inning) combined on the shutout.

In what had quickly become part of the routine after victories at Wrigley Field, Ron Santo leaped in the air and clicked his heels several times after the game ended. The Mets won the final two games of the series, and Tom Seaver ran out of the dugout and imitated Santo's heel-click after each one of them. The Cubs still didn't take the Mets seriously, however, despite the two defeats. "If we lose to this club," said Gene Oliver, "we should jump off the Hancock Building."

JULY 20   On the day that Neil Armstrong becomes the first man to walk on the moon, the Cubs sweep the Phillies 1–0 and 6–1 in Philadelphia. Ferguson Jenkins pitched the shutout in the opener. Don Kessinger drove in the only run of the game with a single in the third inning.

JULY 23   The entire Cubs infield of Ernie Banks, Glenn Beckert, Don Kessinger, and Ron Santo appear in the All–Star Game, won by the National League 9–3 at RFK Stadium in Washington, D.C. Kessinger and Santo were starters. The four were hitless in eight at–bats.

JULY 24   The Cubs defeat Don Sutton and the Dodgers 5–3 at Wrigley Field. The win gave the Cubs a 13–0 record against Sutton since his career started in 1966.

JULY 26   Randy Hundley drives in all three Cubs runs, including a walk–off single in the eleventh inning, to left the Cubs to a 3–2 win over the Dodgers at Wrigley Field.

On the day before his 64th birthday, Leo Durocher left the game in the third inning complaining of an upset stomach. A few hours later, Leo appeared in apparent good health at a parents' weekend reception at Camp Ojibwa in Eagle River, Wisconsin, some 400 miles north of Chicago. Durocher went straight from the ballpark and boarded a chartered plane at Meigs Field accompanied by his new bride of five weeks. Her 12–year–old son was enrolled at the camp. P. K. Wrigley nearly fired Durocher over the incident.

JULY 28   Leo Durocher returns to the ball club, and the Cubs score two runs in the tenth inning off Juan Marichal after two are out to beat the Giants 4–3 at Wrigley Field.

JULY 31   The Cubs rout the Giants 12–2 at Wrigley Field.

AUGUST 2   Ken Holtzman pitches a two–hitter to down the Padres 4–1 at Wrigley Field. The only San Diego hits were doubles by Nate Colbert in the sixth inning and Ivan Murrell in the seventh.

AUGUST 4   Ferguson Jenkins strikes out 12 batters in a 9–3 win over the Astros in Houston.

AUGUST 11 The Cubs purchase Ken Johnson from the Yankees.

AUGUST 13 Two days before the start of the Woodstock Music Festival in Bethel, New York, the Cubs are the victims of the first triple play in Padres history, but they win 4–2 in San Diego.

The victory gave the Cubs a 73–43 record, an 8½–game lead over the second–place Cardinals, and a 9½–game edge over the third–place Mets. At the time, the Cards looked like the biggest threat to the Cubs' position in first place. St. Louis won the National League pennant in 1967 and 1968, and on August 13, 1969, had won 28 of their previous 36 games. The Mets in 1969 were in their eighth season of existence after entering the NL as an expansion team in 1962 and had spent much of the first seven years as the universal symbol of failure. Over those seven seasons, the Mets lost 737 games. The Cardinals quickly fell out of contention, however, while the Mets, a club few took seriously, surged forward with a 38–11 record from August 14 through the end of the season.

Over the same period, the Cubs were 19–27 as the dream of winning a pennant for the first time since 1945 turned into a nightmare.

Shortstop Don Kessinger had the best season of his career in 1969 with a .273 average and 109 runs scored as the Cubs held first place for most of the season.

AUGUST 19   Ken Holtzman pitches a no–hitter to defeat the Braves 3–0 before 37,514 on a Tuesday afternoon at Wrigley Field. He threw 112 pitches, walked three, and failed to strike out a single batter. Holtzman was helped by the 16 mile–per–hour wind blowing toward home plate that kept a long drive by Henry Aaron in the seventh inning in the ballpark. Billy Williams caught the ball against the vines. On a normal day, the ball would have landed on Waveland Avenue. In the ninth, Holtzman retired Felipe Alou on a fly ball to short center caught by shortstop Don Kessinger, Felix Millan on a grounder to Ron Santo at third base, and Aaron on a grounder to Glenn Beckert at second. All three Chicago runs were scored on a homer by Santo in the first inning off Phil Niekro.

Randy Hundley had a rare missed start because of an injured thumb. The starting catcher for Holtzman's no–hitter was Bill Heath, who caught only nine games in his career as a Cub. Heath had to leave the game, however, when he broke his hand after it was hit by a foul tip. He was replaced by Gene Oliver. Heath never caught another game in the big leagues.

AUGUST 23   Jim Hickman hits two homers, including a grand slam in the seventh inning off Fred Gladding, during an 11–5 win over the Astros at Wrigley Field.

AUGUST 24   Down 8–2, the Cubs rally to beat the Astros 10–9 in the first game of a double–header at Wrigley Field with one run in the fourth inning, three in the seventh, and four in the eighth. A two–run homer by Ernie Banks put the Cubs in the lead. Houston won the second game 3–2.

AUGUST 26   The Cubs are given authorization by the National League to print playoff tickets.

AUGUST 27   A 6–3 loss to the Reds at Wrigley Field cuts the Cubs' first–place margin over the Mets to just two games.

SEPTEMBER 2 The Cubs defeat the Reds twice 5–4 and 8–2 in Cincinnati to increase the lead over the Mets to five games.

There was little reason to believe that the Cubs would fail down the stretch. Durocher teams had traditionally finished on a high note. Prior to 1969, his clubs had a record of 300–225 in September and October, a winning percentage of .571. This compared to a winning percentage of .539 prior to September 1. In addition, his club had been on both ends of a late pennant surge. In 1942, Durocher's Dodgers had a lead of 10½ games in August, only to finish second to the Cardinals. In 1951, the Durocher–led Giants overcame a 13½–game deficit to the Dodgers to win the NL pennant.

SEPTEMBER 5   Steve Blass of the Pirates allows only four hits to the Cubs, and Billy Williams collects all four with two homers and two doubles. Williams tied a major league record for "most hits comprising all of a club's hits in a game," which was set by Kid Elberfield of the Yankees in 1903. The four extra–base hits by Williams is a modern Chicago Cubs record. The Pirates won the game 9–2 at Wrigley Field.

SEPTEMBER 7   The Pirates complete a three–game sweep at Wrigley Field by defeating the sputtering Cubs 7–5 in eleven innings. The Cubs were one strike from a win. In the ninth inning, Willie Stargell hit a two–out, two–strike pitch off Phil Regan for a home run. The drive was hit into the teeth of a stiff wind and landed on Sheffield Avenue. The loss reduced the Cubs advantage over the Mets to 2½ games.

SEPTEMBER 8   The Mets pull within 1½ games of first place by defeating the Cubs 3–2 in New York. Bill Hands set the tone with his first pitch, which sent Mets leadoff batter Tommie Agee sprawling into the dirt. Agee responded by hitting a two–run homer in the third inning. The Mets broke a 2–2 tie in the sixth inning when a single by Wayne Garrett scored Agee on a close play at the plate, which led to a heated argument by the Cubs, who claimed Randy Hundley tagged Agee.

SEPTEMBER 9   The Mets charge within one–half game of first place with a 7–1 win over the Cubs in New York. During the game, someone released a black cat in front of the Cubs dugout, a fitting metaphor for the luck the Cubs had in September 1969.

SEPTEMBER 10   The wilting Cubs lose 6–2 to the Phillies in Philadelphia while the Mets sweep the Expos 3–2 in twelve innings and 7–1 in a double–header in New York. At the end of the day, the Cubs trailed the Mets by one game. Chicago had been in first place for 155 consecutive days, beginning on Opening Day. The Cubs never returned to first and finished the season eight games behind the Mets.

SEPTEMBER 11   The Cubs suffer through more heartbreak with a 4–3 loss to the Phillies in Philadelphia. The key play of the game happened in the third inning with Dick Selma pitching and the Cubs leading 1–0. Phillie runners were on first and second with two out and a 3–2 count on Richie Allen. Selma figured both runners would be breaking on the pitch and tried to pick off Tony Taylor, the base runner on second, by throwing to third. Ron Santo missed Selma's signal, however, and didn't cover the bag. The ball sailed into the grandstand, and Taylor scored. It was the Cubs' eighth loss in a row.

On the same day, the Cubs sent Terry Bongiovanni and cash to the Yankees for Jimmie Hall.

SEPTEMBER 14   Lou Brock hits a walk–off homer in the tenth inning off Ken Holtzman to beat the

Cubs 2–1 in St. Louis.

SEPTEMBER 15   The Cubs lose for the 11th time in a stretch of 12 games with an 8–2 defeat at the hands of the Expos in Montreal. On the same day, Cardinals pitcher Steve Carlton fanned 19 Mets batters, but the Mets still won the game 4–3 on a pair of two–run homers by Ron Swoboda. The defeat dropped the Cubs 4½ games behind the Mets with 14 games left on the schedule.

SEPTEMBER 19   Ernie Banks collects the 2,500th hit of his career during a 2–1, ten–inning win over the Cardinals at Wrigley Field. The milestone hit was a single off Bob Gibson. The game–winning hit was a disputed double by Jim Hickman. The Cards claimed a fan reached out and touched the ball, preventing Lou Brock from making the catch in left field.

SEPTEMBER 21   Ferguson Jenkins collects his 21st win of the 1969 season with a 4–3 decision over the Cardinals at Wrigley Field.

SEPTEMBER 24   The Mets clinch the Eastern Division pennant with a 6–0 win over the Cardinals in New York.

SEPTEMBER 28   Bill Hands collects his 20th win of the 1969 season with a 3–1 decision over the Pirates in Pittsburgh.

OCTOBER 2   The 1969 season comes to a conclusion with a 5–3 win over the Mets at Wrigley Field.

The devastating fold by the Cubs tore the hearts out of the fans and everyone connected with the club and sent the city into shock. The reasons for the collapse are still hot topics for debate.

NOVEMBER 17   The Cubs trade Dick Selma and Oscar Gamble to the Phillies for Johnny Callison.

Callison was the runner–up in the MVP balloting in 1964 while playing for the Phillies club that blew a 6½–game lead in the final two weeks of the season. Now he was being asked to plug a weak spot in right field on another club that blew a huge lead. Callison, who turned 31 before Opening Day in 1970, proved to be a disappointment in Chicago. Gamble was only 19 when traded by the Cubs and is the last teenager to play for the club. It took him a few years to develop, but he became a valuable platoon outfielder and designated hitter with several American League clubs, including the White Sox.

DECEMBER 4   The Cubs trade Rich Nye to the Cardinals for Boots Day.

Nye was 13–10 as a 22–year–old rookie in 1967, but was only 10–17 for the Cubs in 1968 and 1969. He pitched one more season after the trade to the Cardinals and went back to college to study veterinary medicine. Rich's specialty was rare and exotic birds.

THE STATE OF THE CUBS

The Cubs entered the decade in a state of shock after blowing the 1969 pennant. The nucleus of that club stayed together for several more years, but were unable to finish first, although the Cubs had winning seasons in 1970, 1971, and 1972. The club began to age and atrophy in 1973, the first of eleven consecutive seasons in which the Cubs failed to produce a winning record. Still, the club was in contention late in the year in many of those losing seasons, but something always seemed to happen to cause them to unravel. Overall, the Cubs had a record of 785–827 (.487), seventh best in the National League during the 1970s. The only teams to win less often during the decade were the Padres, the Braves, the Expos, and the Mets. The NL pennant winners in the 1970s were the Reds (1970, 1972, 1975, and 1976), the Pirates (1971 and 1979), the Mets (1973), and the Dodgers (1974, 1977, and 1978). Eastern Division winners were the Pirates (1970, 1971, 1973, 1974, 1975, and 1979), Mets (1973), and Phillies (1976, 1977, and 1978).

THE BEST TEAM

The 1972 team had a record of 85–70 in a last gasp for players like Ron Santo, Billy Williams, Ferguson Jenkins, Don Kessinger, and Glenn Beckert.

THE WORST TEAM

By 1974, the Cubs were almost completely made over, and not for the better. That season, the Cubs were 66–96 and finished in last place.

THE BEST MOMENT

Cubs fans are used to their best moments being followed by extreme disappointment. The best moment of the 1970s was the summer of 1977 when the Cubs were in first place from May 28 through August 4, and the White Sox were in first during the entire month of July. Neither of the Chicago teams, however, came close to winning a pennant.

THE WORST MOMENT

Leo Durocher and his players squared off in an ugly showdown in the clubhouse on August 23, 1971.

THE ALL–DECADE TEAM · YEARS WITH CUBS

Randy Hundley, c	1966–73; 1976–77
Andre Thornton, 1b	1973–76
Manny Trillo, 2b	1975–78; 1986–88
Ron Santo, 3b	1960–73
Don Kessinger, ss	1964–75
Billy Williams, lf	1959–74
Rick Monday, cf	1972–76
Jose Cardenal, rf	1972–77
Rick Reuschel, p	1972–81; 1983–84
Ferguson Jenkins, p	1966–73; 1982–83
Bruce Sutter, p	1976–80
Bill Bonham, p	1971–77

Thornton should have had a long career with the Cubs, but was sent away in an ill–conceived trade. Hundley, Santo, Kessinger, Williams, and Jenkins also made the 1960s All–Decade Team. Jenkins and Williams are in the Hall of Fame. Sutter is eligible on the writer's ballot until 2008 and has an outside chance of election during that time frame. Other key Cubs during the 1970s were pitchers Milt Pappas (1970–73) and Ray Burris (1973–79), third baseman Bill Madlock (1974–76), shortstop Ivan DeJesus (1977–81), and outfielders Jim Hickman (1968–73), Jerry Morales (1974–77; 1981–83), and Dave Kingman (1978–80).

THE DECADE LEADERS

Batting Avg:	Madlock	.336
On–Base Pct:	Madlock	.397
Slugging Pct:	Williams	.523
Home Runs:	Williams	143
RBI:	Williams	498
Runs:	Kessinger	466
Stolen Bases:	Cardenal	129
Wins:	Reuschel	114
Strikeouts:	Reuschel	1,122
ERA:	Jenkins	3.29
Saves:	Sutter	105

THE HOME FIELD

Minor modifications were made to Wrigley Field during the 1970s. The most significant was the wire basket attached to the outfield wall in 1970 to prevent fans from throwing debris onto the field. An innovation of 1978 was a new indicator to inform night travelers of how the Cubs fared that day. A blue light atop the scoreboard signaled victory, and a white one reported defeat. The changes didn't include night baseball, however, as the Cubs continued to be the only club to play home games exclusively in the sunshine.

THE GAME YOU WISH YOU HAD SEEN

Milt Pappas came within one strike of a perfect game in a contest against the Padres at Wrigley Field on September 2, 1972.

THE WAY THE GAME WAS PLAYED

The 1970s were dominated by speed and defense, in part because of new stadiums with more distant fences and artificial turf. Opening in the NL during the 1970s were Riverfront Stadium in Cincinnati, Three Rivers Stadium in Pittsburgh, Veterans Stadium in Philadelphia, and Olympic Stadium in Montreal. The average number of stolen bases per team rose from 87 in 1970 to 124 in 1979, while home runs declined from 140 to 119. The Cubs, however, playing at Wrigley Field, were rooted in the past. Chicago was below the league average in stolen bases every year during the 1970s, and was dead last six times from 1968 through 1979.

THE MANAGEMENT

P. K. Wrigley died in 1977, with the club passing to his son William, then 44. William J. Hagenah became president of the club, while William took the less visible position of chairman of the executive com-

mittee. John Holland, general manager since 1956, went into semi–retirement in 1975. Salty Saltwell served as general manager in 1976 and Bob Kennedy from 1977 through 1981. When the decade started Leo Durocher was in his fifth season as manager of the Cubs. Leo was fired in mid–season in 1972. Finishing out the decade as managers of the club were Whitey Lockman (1972–74), Jim Marshall (1974–76), and Herman Franks (1977–79).

THE BEST PLAYER MOVE

The best move was drafting Rick Reuschel in the third round of the amateur draft in 1970. The best trade brought Bill Buckner and Ivan DeJesus from the Dodgers on January 11, 1977 for Rick Monday and Mike Garman. The Cubs did very well overall in the trade market during the 1970s. The club went from contenders to also–rans during the decade because the farm system produced next to nothing after a series of awful choices in the June amateur draft. How bad was the Cubs farm system? Between the 1964 call–up of Don Kessinger and the 1985 promotion of Shawon Dunston, no non–pitching prospect of the Cubs minor leagues became a day–in and day–out regular on the major league team. The Cubs also did a miserable job of recruiting talent from Latin America. If it weren't for deals which brought players like Monday, DeJesus, Bill Madlock, Jose Cardenal, Manny Trillo, Milt Pappas, Jerry Morales, and Bill Buckner, the situation would have been much worse.

THE WORST PLAYER MOVE

The worst move of the 1970s was perpetrated on May 2, 1975 when the Cubs sent Burt Hooton to the Dodgers for Geoff Zahn and Eddie Solomon.

1970s

1970

Cubs

Season in a Sentence

In an attempt to capture the pennant that eluded them in the 1969 tailspin, the Cubs win 11 in a row in April, lose 12 in a row in June, stay in contention until late–September, and fall five games shy of first place.

Finish • Won • Lost • Pct • GB

Second   84   78   .519   5.0

Manager

Leo Durocher

Stats

Stats	Cubs	NL	Rank
Batting Avg:	.259	.258	8
On–Base Pct:	.335	.332	6
Slugging Pct:	.415	.392	2
Home Runs:	179		2
Stolen Bases:	39		12
ERA:	3.76	4.05	4
Fielding Avg:	978	.977	5
Runs Scored:	806		2
Runs Allowed:	679		3

Starting Lineup

Randy Hundley, c
Ernie Banks, 1b
Glenn Beckert, 2b
Ron Santo, 3b
Don Kessinger, ss
Billy Williams, lf
Jim Hickman, cf–1b–rf
Johnny Callison, rf
Joe Pepitone, cf
Cleo James, cf
Paul Popovich, 2b–ss–3b
Jack Hiatt, c
Willie Smith, 1b

Pitchers

Ferguson Jenkins, sp
Ken Holtzman, sp
Bill Hands, sp
Milt Pappas, sp
Joe Decker, sp
Phil Regan, rp

Attendance

1,642,705 (fourth in NL)

Club Leaders

Batting Avg:	Williams	.322
On–Base Pct:	Hickman	.419
Slugging Pct:	Williams	.586
Home Runs:	Williams	42
RBI:	Williams	128
Runs:	Williams	137
Stolen Bases:	Kessinger	12
Wins:	Jenkins	22
Strikeouts:	Jenkins	274
ERA:	Holtzman	3.38
Saves:	Regan	12

FEBRUARY 27   Nine days after the "Chicago Seven" are found not guilty of conspiring to incite a riot during the 1968 Democratic convention, the FBI arrests Lawrence Bankhead in Chicago, charging him for making threatening phone calls to Ernie Banks. For a few days, Banks received around–the–clock protection from law enforcement agencies while the Cubs were training in Scottsdale, Arizona.

MARCH 29   Ron Santo has to be restrained by teammates from going into the stands in pursuit of a heckler during the sixth inning of a 10–4 win over the Padres in Scottsdale. Santo made repeated efforts to climb over the box seat railing to reach the offensive fan.

APRIL 4   A snowstorm in Chicago moves a two–game exhibition series between the Cubs and the White Sox to Tulsa, Oklahoma. The games were originally scheduled for April 4th and 5th, one at Comiskey Park and the other at Wrigley Field, to conclude spring training. The April 4th contest in Tulsa was postponed, however, because of rain and temperatures in the 30s.

APRIL 7   In the season opener, the Cubs lose 2–0 to the Phillies in Philadelphia. Chris Short pitched the shutout.

APRIL 10   With two out in the ninth inning, Ron Santo singles and Johnny Callison homers to beat the Expos 2–1 in Montreal.

Santo contributed with 26 homers and 114 runs–batted–in during the 1970 season.

APRIL 14   The Cubs survive a four–run Phillie uprising and win 5–4 in the home opener before 38,316 at Wrigley Field.

A rash of fights and general unruly behavior, mostly by teenagers, brought changes at Wrigley Field. Video cameras were installed so that every area of the ballpark could be scanned for trouble spots. It was the first use of cameras at any park in baseball. More importantly, a forty–two–inch mesh screen was constructed around the front wall of the bleachers. It was fastened thirty inches below the top of the wall and angled at forty–five degrees to keep fans from jumping over the wall and throwing debris onto the field. The screen shortened the home run distance at Wrigley by three feet.

APRIL 21   Randy Hundley tears a ligament in his left knee in a jarring collision at the plate with Carl Taylor of the Cardinals during a 7–4 win at Wrigley Field.

Hundley was on the disabled list until July 10.

APRIL 26   Ron Santo hits a grand slam off Larry Dierker in the sixth inning of a 6–3 win over the Astros at Wrigley Field. It was the Cubs tenth win in a row.

Billy Williams, Ron Santo, and Jim Hickman produced 100 home runs and 358 RBIs in 1970 as the heart of a powerful batting order.

APRIL 27   The Cubs post their 11th win in a row, defeating the Pirates 1–0 in Pittsburgh. Joe Decker (8 ⅓ innings), Hank Aguirre (⅓ of an inning) and Phil Regan (⅓ of an inning) combined on the shutout.

The win gave the Cubs a 12–3 record, and seemed to put to rest any lingering doubts about the psychological damage resulting from the collapse of 1969.

APRIL 30   Billy Williams plays in his 1,000th consecutive game, although the Cubs lose 9–2 to the Braves in Atlanta.

Williams was runner–up to Johnny Bench in the Most Valuable Player balloting in 1970 after hitting .322 with 42 homers and 129 runs–batted–in. Williams led the league in hits (205) and runs (137).

MAY 4   Eight days after Ohio National Guardsmen shoot and kill four students at Kent State University, Ernie Banks hits the 500th home run of his career. The milestone home run was hit off Pat Jarvis in the second inning of a 4–3, 11–inning win over the Braves at Wrigley Field. The contest was played under dark clouds with the threat of thunderstorms, and only 5,264 fans were on hand.

After 16 seasons as a starter, Banks was limited to a part–time role in 1970 by aching knees, and appeared in only 72 games.

MAY 10   Billy Williams becomes the first player to homer into the basket in front of the Wrigley Field bleachers during a 7–6 loss to the Reds.

MAY 13   Ernie Banks collects the only Chicago hit off Gary Gentry of the Mets in a 3–0 loss at Wrigley Field. With two out in the eighth inning, left fielder Dave Marshall got his glove on the ball after a long run, but dropped it, and official scorer Jim Enright ruled the play a single.

MAY 19   The Cubs play at Crosley Field for the last time, and lose 3–1 to the Reds.

Crosley Field had been the home of the Reds since 1912. The Cincinnati club moved into Riverfront Stadium on June 30, 1970.

MAY 23   The Cubs batter the Mets 14–8 in New York.

MAY 28   Jim Hickman hits a two–run, walk–off homer in the ninth inning to defeat the Pirates 8–7 at Wrigley Field. Hickman also hit a two–run homer in the seventh.

At the age of 33, Hickman had a year in 1970 that far surpassed any that he had previously experienced. He hit .315 with 32 homers and 115 runs–batted–in. Plus, he did it while learning a relatively new position. He played 74 games at first base, where he played only 49 big league contest prior to 1970, and none since 1967. In what became the dictionary definition of a career year, Hickman never came close to the heights of 1970 again.

MAY 29   The Cubs trade Ted Abernathy to the Cardinals for Phil Gagliano.

This was the second time that the Cubs made a bad deal by trading away Abernathy. He had three more good seasons, while Gagliano was a useless addition.

JUNE 4   The Cubs select outfielder Gene Hiser of the University of Maryland in the first round of the amateur draft.

Hiser played in 206 major league games in which he had one homer, a .202 batting average and a .240 slugging percentage. Tom Lundstedt, picked in the first round of the secondary phase, wasn't any better than Hiser. Rick Reuschel was the only other Cub drafted and signed in 1970 to reach the majors. Chosen in the third round, Reuschel went on to win 135 games with the club, the most of any post–Word War II pitcher except Ferguson Jenkins.

JUNE 5   The Cubs defeat the Giants 12–8 at Wrigley Field.

JUNE 13   The Cubs defeat the Dodgers 7–1 in Los Angeles to take a five–game in the Eastern Division over the Mets and the Pirates. The Cubs had a record of 31–22.

JUNE 24   The Cubs are knocked out of first place with 9–5 and 6–1 losses to the Mets at Wrigley Field. The defeats extended Chicago's losing streak to six games.

The Cubs never got back into first place for the remainder of the season, but stayed in contention for the pennant until late–September.

JUNE 25   The Cubs purchase Milt Pappas from the Braves.

Picked–up off the waiver wire, Pappas proved to be a terrific acquisition. He found a new home in Chicago and revived his career. Milt won ten games for the Cubs in 1970 in little over half a season, and 17 more in both 1971 and 1972. His given name was Militades Stergios Papastedgios.

JUNE 27   Ferguson Jenkins strikes out 14 batters, but the Cubs lose 2–1 to the Pirates in Pittsburgh.

JUNE 28   The Cubs play the Pirates in the last two games ever played at Forbes Field in Pittsburgh. The Pirates won both ends of the double–header 3–2 and 4–1. The two losses extended the Cubs losing streak to ten games.

Forbes Field opened on June 30, 1909. The Cubs were also the opponent on that day. The Pirates played their first game at Three Rivers Stadium on July 16, 1970.

JUNE 29   The Cubs sell Jimmie Hall to the Braves.

JUNE 30   The Cubs lose their 12th game in a row, dropping a 5–4 decision to the Cardinals in St. Louis. The 12–game losing streak dropped the Cubs record to 35–37.

Pitcher Joe Decker was fined for a "defiant attitude" during the loss. When Leo Durocher came to the mound to relieve him in the fourth inning, Decker left the mound before the relief pitcher arrived. Durocher had problems of his own. In the wake of the 12–game losing streak, he was forced to give up a radio talk show he hosted on WIND, probably at the behest of Cubs management. Durocher was being paid $40,000 per year to do the program in a deal signed during the previous off–season. Leo had been using the gig as a forum to blast his players and announce lineup changes.

JULY 1   The 12–game losing streak comes to an end with a 5–0 win over the Cardinals in St. Louis. Ferguson Jenkins pitched the shutout.

The Cubs had a great starting rotation in 1970, especially after Milt Pappas was acquired in late–June. Ferguson Jenkins was 22–16 with a 3.39 ERA, a league–leading 24 complete games, 313 innings and a club record 274 strike–outs. Ken Holtzman had a 17–11 record, 288 innings, 202 strikeouts and a 3.38 earned run average. Bill Hands had an 18–15 mark and an ERA of 3.70. The bullpen was a mess all season, however. The Cubs had a horrible record of 2–15 when the starting pitcher left the game with the score tied.

JULY 3   The Cubs lose 16–14 to the Pirates in a slugfest at Wrigley Field. The Cubs trailed 7–1 in the second inning and pulled ahead 13–10 by the eighth, but the bullpen couldn't hold the Pirates.

JULY 5   A brawl erupts during a 5–2 loss to the Pirates in Pittsburgh.

Pittsburgh pitcher Dock Ellis decked Jim Hickman with a pitch in the eighth inning, and Cubs hurler Jim Colborn buzzed Ellis with a retaliatory pitch in the ninth. Ellis and Leo Durocher began jawing at each other. Both benches emptied and players began swinging at each other until order was restored.

JULY 6   Ron Santo drives in ten runs as the Cubs rip the Expos 3–2 and 14–2 in a double–header at Wrigley Field. Santo drove in two runs in the first game on a two–run homer and eight more in the second. In the nightcap, Ron hit a grand slam off Mike Wegener in the first inning, and later walked with the bases loaded and hit a three–run homer.

JULY 9   The Cubs trade Archie Reynolds to the Angels for Juan Pizarro.

JULY 14   Jim Hickman drives in the winning run in the twelfth inning of the All–Star Game lifting the National League to a 5–4 win at Riverfront Stadium in Cincinnati.

The play is arguably the most famous in All–Star history. Playing in front of his hometown fans, Pete Rose barreled into Indians catcher Ray Fosse at the plate to score the winning run.

JULY 16   Ken Holtzman pitches a two–hitter, but the Cubs lose 2–1 to the Astros in the Astrodome. The only Houston hits were a single by Jim Wynn in the third inning and a double by Cesar Cedeno in the seventh.

JULY 20   In a one–game experiment, Glenn Beckert starts in center field. Beckert misplayed an easy fly ball into a double, and the Cubs lost 5–0 in a game in Atlanta stopped by rain in the sixth inning.

JULY 23   Milt Pappas pitches the Cubs to a 1–0 win over the Reds at Wrigley Field. It was the only time that the Reds were shut out in 1970.

JULY 24   The Cubs breeze to an 11–1 win over the Braves at Wrigley Field.

JULY 26   Glenn Beckert collects five hits in five at–bats in a 7–6 win over the Braves in the second game of a double–header at Wrigley Field. Beckert was also two–for–three in the first game, but the Braves won 8–3 behind three homers by Orlando Cepeda.

JULY 29

Two days after three people are shot during a riot at a Sly and the Family Stone concert in Chicago, the Cubs purchase Joe Pepitone from the Astros. Eight days before the trade, Pepitone walked out on the Astros, and went home to Brooklyn. As part of the deal, the Cubs agreed to send Roger Metzger to the Astros at the end of the season (October 12, 1970).

One of baseball's most colorful characters during a stormy career marked by fines, suspensions, mood swings, and defiance of authority figures, Pepitone became an immediate hit with the Cubs legion of young fans with his flamboyant lifestyle, long hair, and "mod" outfits, including bell–bottoms, open–necked shirts, vests. Joe was the first player to bring a hair dryer into the clubhouse at a time when hair dryers, for men, were practically unheard of. He had previously played on three World Series teams with the Yankees, but never quite reached his potential and drove managers crazy with his eccentricities. Pepitone arrived at Wrigley Field in style in a limousine driven by a chauffeur named "Fabulous Howard," and was the toast of Chicago's nightlife, buying a bar at 12 East Division Street called "Joe Pepitone's Thing." He also sold wigs at a shop he owned in the city, and wore one of his products to conceal his receding hairline. When things were going well, Pepitone kept the clubhouse loose with his sense of humor, but when a club was losing he was a disruptive influence. He could hit when the mood struck him. In 1970 and 1971, Pepitone had 640 at–bats as a Cub and contributed with a .294 batting average with 28 homers and 105 RBIs. But those who buck tradition are tolerated only when they play well, and things began to go south in 1972 when Pepitone was reduced to part–time status and became engaged in a running battle with Leo Durocher. He also sat out two months of the season on the voluntarily retired list. In May 1973, Joe was traded to the Braves.

JULY 31

The Cubs play at Riverfront Stadium in Cincinnati for the first time, and sweep the Reds 7–1 and 11–7. For the second time in a span of six days, Glenn Beckert collected seven hits in a double–header.

AUGUST 6

Angry over being demoted from the clean–up spot to seventh in the batting order during a slump, Ron Santo rips Leo Durocher in a tirade before a game against the Expos in Montreal. Santo responded with four hits, including a homer and a double, in four at–bats to lead the Cubs to a 4–2 victory. Santo was back hitting fourth again the next day.

AUGUST 14

Joe Pepitone hits a grand slam in the first inning off Don Sutton to give the Cubs a 5–0 lead, but the Dodgers rally to win 13–9 at Wrigley Field.

One of Pepitone's favorite pasttimes was showing off a scar on his stomach from a gunshot wound that nearly killed him as a teenager in Brooklyn.

AUGUST 15

The Cubs score seven runs in the third inning and defeat the Dodgers 13–2 in the second game of a double–header at Wrigley Field. Los Angeles won the first game 9–7.

AUGUST 19

The Cubs tie a club record by smashing seven homers and defeat the Padres 12–2 at Wrigley Field. Jim Hickman hit two home runs, with Ferguson Jenkins, Billy Williams, Joe Pepitone, Johnny Callison, and Glenn Beckert adding one each.

AUGUST 21 — Ken Holtzman comes within five outs of a no–hitter as the Cubs clobber the Giants 15–0 at Wrigley Field. The only San Francisco hit was a single by Hal Lanier with one out in the eighth inning.

SEPTEMBER 1 — The Cubs purchase Bob Miller from the White Sox.

SEPTEMBER 2 — The Cubs score eight runs in the fourth inning and defeat the Phillies 17–2 at Wrigley Field. The Cubs collected twenty hits in the contest.

SEPTEMBER 3 — Billy Williams sits out a game for the first time since 1963, ending his streak of consecutive games played at 1,117. The Cubs beat the Phillies 7–2 at Wrigley Field. Cleo James played left field in Billy's place. Williams said that the streak had gone far enough and that he wanted to end the pressure and "get the monkey off my back." He returned to the lineup the next day, and didn't miss another game for the rest of the season. Williams remained remarkably durable. He missed just five games in 1971, six in 1972 and five in 1973.

At the time, Williams had the third–longest consecutive game streak in baseball history, trailing only Lou Gehrig (2,130 games) and Everett Scott (1,307). Williams has since been passed by Cal Ripken, Jr. (2,632) and Steve Garvey (1,207).

SEPTEMBER 7 — The Cubs play at Three Rivers Stadium in Pittsburgh for the first time. In a double–header, the Cubs lost 8–3 to the Pirates, then won 9–2.

SEPTEMBER 13 — With two out in the ninth inning and the Cubs trailing 2–1 at Wrigley Field, Pirates center fielder Matty Alou drops a windblown fly ball hit by Willie Smith. With Smith at second base, the Cubs then rallied for two runs on three singles by Don Kessinger, Glenn Beckert, and Billy Williams to win 3–2.

The win put the Cubs one game back of the Pirates in the Eastern Division race.

SEPTEMBER 16 — The Cubs purchase Tommy Davis from the Athletics.

SEPTEMBER 19 — The Cubs defeat the Expos 8–4 in Montreal. With the victory, the Cubs were 1½ games behind Pittsburgh with a record of 80–71.

SEPTEMBER 21 — The Cubs purchase Hoyt Wilhelm from the Braves.

A future Hall of Famer, Wilhelm was 47 years old when purchased by the Cubs to try and help the club win a pennant. He appeared in only three games with the Cubs, but it was long enough to become the oldest player in club history. Wilhelm was traded back to the Braves in November.

SEPTEMBER 23 — The Cubs suffer a crushing blow to their pennant hopes by losing a double–header by identical 2–1 scores against the Cardinals in St. Louis to drop 2½ games behind the Pirates.

The 1970 Cubs may have been bigger underachievers than the 1969 outfit that blew a 9½-game lead. In 1970, the Cubs outscored the opposition 806–679, the largest run differential in the National League that season. The Cubs scored

31 more runs than the Reds and allowed two fewer, yet Cincinnati won 102 games and Chicago won only 84.

SEPTEMBER 26   The Cubs lose 5–3 to the Phillies in Philadelphia to fall 3 ½ games behind the Pirates with six games left on the schedule and virtually eliminate any chance of winning a pennant in 1970.

With first place on the line, the Cubs lost seven of nine games from September 20 through September 29.

SEPTEMBER 27   The Cubs play at Connie Mack Stadium in Philadelphia for the final time, and defeat the Phillies 5–3.

Veterans Stadium opened on April 10, 1971.

OCTOBER 1   In the final game of the season, Ferguson Jenkins wins his 22nd game of 1970 by pitching a two–hitter to defeat the Mets 2–1 at Shea Stadium. Ken Singleton had the only two New York hits with a pair of doubles in the seventh and ninth innings. The Cubs entered the game in a tie for second place with the Mets, and clinched the runner–up position in the East with the win.

The Cubs outdrew the White Sox 1,642,705 to 495,355 in 1970. It was the lowest attendance figure by a White Sox club since 1942, and quite a contrast to 1965 when the White Sox attracted 1,130,519 to Comiskey Park, while the Cubs drew only 641,361.

OCTOBER 12   The Cubs trade Roger Metzger to the Astros for Hector Torres.

Metzger was 23 years old at the time of the trade, and was Houston's starting shortstop for six seasons from 1971 through 1976. Torres played only 31 games as utility infielder for the Cubs. The trade didn't work out that badly, however, especially since Joe Pepitone was essentially part of the exchange. (See July 29, 1970.) If he had remained in Chicago, it's unlikely that Metzger would have supplanted Don Kessinger, who remained as the starting shortstop until 1975. The Cubs continued to stand pat, heading into the 1971 season while making no significant changes to the central cast that fell short of the pennant in 1969 and 1970.

NOVEMBER 30   The Cubs trade Hoyt Wilhelm to the Braves for Hal Breeden.

DECEMBER 13   The Chicago Bears play at Wrigley Field for the last time and defeat the Green Bay Packers 35–17 before 44,957. The Bears began play at Soldier Field in 1971.

The Bears played their home games at Wrigley Field from 1921 through 1970. They are the only team in NFL history to play home games at one location for 50 consecutive seasons. The Cleveland Browns played at Municipal Stadium from 1946 through 1995, but from 1946 through 1949 the club was in the All–American Football Conference. The Bears record will be broken in 2007, however, when the Packers play their 51st season at Lambeau Field.

1971

Season in a Sentence

An acrimonious feud between Leo Durocher and his players poisons the atmosphere in another frustrating season.

Finish • Won • Lost • Pct • GB

Third   83   79   .512   14.0

Manager

Leo Durocher

Stats

Stats	Cubs	NL	Rank
Batting Avg:	.258	.252	4
On–Base Pct:	.327	.319	4
Slugging Pct:	.378	.366	4
Home Runs:	128		5
Stolen Bases:	441		2
ERA:	3.61	3.47	8
Fielding Avg:	.980	.979	5
Runs Scored:	637		6
Runs Allowed:	648		8

Starting Lineup

Chris Cannizzaro, c
Joe Pepitone, 1b
Glenn Beckert, 2b
Ron Santo, 3b
Don Kessinger, ss
Billy Williams, lf
Brock Davis, cf
Jim Hickman, rf–1b
Johnny Callison, rf
Paul Popovich, 2b

Pitchers

Ferguson Jenkins, sp
Milt Pappas, sp
Bill Hands, sp
Ken Holtzman, sp
Juan Pizarro, sp
Phil Regan, rp

Attendance

1,653,007 (third in NL)

Club Leaders

Batting Avg:	Williams	.301
On–Base Pct:	Williams	383
Slugging Pct:	Williams	.505
Home Runs:	Williams	28
RBI:	Williams	93
Runs:	Williams	86
Stolen Bases:	Kessinger	15
Wins:	Jenkins	24
Strikeouts:	Jenkins	263
ERA:	Jenkins	2.77
Saves:	Regan	6

MARCH 12   Randy Hundley sprains his knee during an 8–7 win over the Angels in an exhibition game in Scottsdale, Arizona. The Cubs had California's Roger Repoz in a rundown between third and home, when Hundley's spikes caught in the dirt and his knee caved in.

Hundley played only nine games in 1971.

APRIL 6   In the season opener, Billy Williams hits a walk–off homer against Bob Gibson in the tenth inning to beat the Cardinals before 41,121 in 39–degree weather at Wrigley Field. Ferguson Jenkins pitched a complete game and allowed only three hits. As a result of age (39) and arthritic knees, Ernie Banks was out of the Opening Day starting lineup for the first time since 1953.

During the previous off–season, Williams became the first Cubs player to sign a contract calling for $100,000 in a season. In 1971, he hit .301 with 26 homers and 93 RBIs. Other offensive contributors were Ron Santo and Glenn Beckert. Santo hit 21 homers and drove in 88 runs. Beckert had the best season of his career, batting .342.

APRIL 9   The Cubs score all six of their runs in the second inning of a 6–0 win over the Astros in Houston.

Amiable Ernie Banks again predicted a pennant for the Cubs, completely ignoring his failure as a prognosticator for the previous 17 years, the length of his service with the Cubs. The April 9 win gave the Banks's Cubs a 2–2 record. By April 19, Chicago was 4–9, and didn't reach the .500 mark again until June 9.

Glenn Beckert was a fan favorite because of his consistent play, particularly during his career year in 1971, when he batted 59 points higher than his lifetime .283 average.

MAY 10 The Cubs play at Veterans Stadium in Philadelphia for the first time, and defeat the Phillies 4–0 behind a 12–strikeout performance by Ferguson Jenkins.

Jenkins was 24–13 for the Cubs in 1971 and won the only Cy Young Award of his career. He had a 2.77 ERA and led the NL in innings pitched (325), games started (39) and complete games (30). He walked only 37 batters. He was backed by Milt Pappas, who had a 17–14 record, a 3.52 ERA, and five shutouts.

MAY 15 Billy Williams hits the 300th home run of his career during a 6–4 win over the Padres at Wrigley Field. The milestone homer was hit off Tom Phoebus.

Jim West replaced Lloyd Pettit in the WGN television booth in 1971, joining Jack Brickhouse. West remained with the Cubs until 1976. Also in 1971, Harry Caray arrived in Chicago as a broadcaster with the White Sox. Previously, he was the play–by–play man with the Cardinals from 1945 through 1969, and with the Athletics in 1970. Caray jumped to the Cubs in 1982.

MAY 16 Down 7–1, the Cubs rally to tie the score 7–7 and force extra innings against the Padres in the first game of a double–header at Wrigley Field. After San Diego scored in the top of the tenth, the Cubs came back again, winning 9–8 on a two–run walk–off homer by Jim Hickman. The second game was suspended after six innings by darkness with the Cubs leading 6–3. It was completed on August 4, with the Cubs winning 6–4.

MAY 19 Billy Williams drives in six runs with two homers and a triple to power the Cubs to a 9–5 win over the Giants at Wrigley Field.

MAY 22 Milt Pappas pitches a complete game to beat the Dodgers 5–2 at Wrigley Field despite being spiked in the first inning, and hit in the head and foot by line drives.

The Cubs closed the month of May with a record of 22–27, and rumors that

Durocher would soon be fired.

JUNE 3

Ken Holtzman pitches a no–hitter to defeat the Reds 1–0 in Cincinnati. Holtzman came into the game with a 2–6 record and a 5.40 ERA, and in his previous start on May 30, allowed eight runs and 11 hits in 3⅔ against the Pirates in Pittsburgh. Holtzman walked four and struck out six, and retired the last eleven men he faced. In the ninth inning, Hal McRae made the first out with a fly ball to Johnny Callison to right field. Holtzman closed out the game by striking out Tommy Helms and Lee May. It was his second career no–hitter, following one he threw against Atlanta in Chicago on August 19, 1969. The lone run of the game was scored in the third inning on a single by Glenn Beckert.

The catcher in Holtzman's no–hitter was Danny Breeden, who played in only 25 games as a Cub and just 28 in his major league career. Danny's brother Hal also played for the Cubs in 1971, to become the first pair of brothers to play for the club at the same time since 1894. Hal's career as a Cub lasted 23 games. Brothers who played for the Cubs at the same time were Larry (1880–85) and Mike (1884) Corcoran; Jiggs (1892–95) and Tom (1893) Parrott; Lew (1893–94) and Kid (1894) Camp; and Rick (1972–81; 1983–84) and Paul (1975–76) Reuschel. Brothers who have played for the Cubs at different times are Ed (1943–45) and Hank (1949–55) Sauer; Mort (1949) and Walker (1954–55) Cooper; Solly (1956) and Sammy (1960–61) Drake; and Jim (1972; 1974–75) and Wayne (1976) Tyrone.

JUNE 4

The Cubs roll to an 11–0 win over the Braves in Atlanta.

Ron Santo was tried for six games in left field during June in a brief experiment.

JUNE 5

Pitching on one day's rest after his no–hitter, Ken Holtzman enters the game as a relief pitcher in the eleventh inning with the Cubs leading 4–3 against the Braves at Atlanta–Fulton County Stadium. Atlanta had two runners on base and one out. The move failed when Holtzman gave up a three–run homer to Mike Lum to lose 6–4. It was Holtzman's only relief appearance during the 1971 season.

The Cubs had 75 complete games in 1971 to lead the NL as Durocher had no faith in his shaky bullpen. The Cardinals were second in complete games with 56. The National League per team average that season was 46.

JUNE 8

In his first start since his no–hitter, Ken Holtzman pitches a twelve–inning shutout and strikes out 12 batters to defeat the Pirates 1–0 at Wrigley Field. Joe Pepitone ended the game with a two–out, walk–off homer off Mudcat Grant into the teeth of a twenty–mile–per–hour wind.

On the same day, the Cubs selected pitcher Jeff Wehmeier from Brebeuf High School in Indianapolis in the first round of the amateur draft. He was the son of former major league pitcher Herm Wehmeier. Jeff never advanced beyond Class A, however. Those chosen and signed by the Cubs in the regular phase of the draft who later played in the majors were Dennis Lamp in the third round, Ron Sperring in the fifth, and Jim Tyrone in the seventh. In the secondary phase, the Cubs came up with a gem in Burt Hooton of the University of Texas. Hooton was originally drafted by the Mets out of high school in 1968, but went to college instead of turning pro (see September 15, 1971). The Cubs did even better in September by signing undrafted pitcher Bruce Sutter.

JUNE 15   Bill Hands pitches a three–hitter and retires the last twenty–three batters he faces in a 3–1 defeat of the Braves at Wrigley Field.

JUNE 17   Don Kessinger collects six hits in six at–bats during a 7–6, ten–inning win over the Cardinals at Wrigley Field. Don's sixth hit of the afternoon started the game–winning, tenth–inning rally.

           Kessinger retired in 1979 after a sixteen–year playing career with a curious stat. He was 0–for–33 as a pinch–hitter.

JUNE 18   The Cubs thrash the Cardinals 15–5 at Wrigley Field.

JUNE 25   The Cubs score ten runs in the seventh inning and defeat the Cardinals 12–0 at Wrigley Field. The Cubs had 20 hits in the game, 19 of them singles. The only extra base hit was a double.

JULY 11   Johnny Callison drives in both runs in a 2–0 win over the Padres in the first game of a double–header in San Diego. Callison hit a home run and a sacrifice fly. Milt Pappas pitched the shutout. San Diego won the second game 7–5.

JULY 15   Down 6–0, the Cubs storm back with one run in the third inning and six in the fourth to win 7–6 over the Phillies at Wrigley Field.

JULY 18   Ray Newman pitches five innings of hitless relief during an 8–4 win over the Expos at Wrigley Field.

JULY 21   Don Kessinger ties a major league record by starting four double plays at shortstop during an 11–7 win over the Mets at Wrigley Field.

JULY 23   Ron Santo reveals that he has been suffering from diabetes for more than a decade.

           Santo kept the fact that he was a diabetic a secret since he was first diagnosed with the illness in 1960, but made the disclosure at the urging of the Diabetes Association of Greater Chicago. The hope was to prove that diabetics could lead an ordinary life, or in the case of Santo, an extraordinary life. He took an insulin shot each day and kept candy bars on the bench in case he felt threatened by a diabetic coma.

JULY 24   Ferguson Jenkins strikes out 14 batters to defeat the Phillies 2–1 in Philadelphia.

AUGUST 5   Juan Pizarro pitches a one–hitter to defeat the Padres 3–0 at Wrigley Field. The only San Diego hit was a single by Ollie Brown in the fifth inning.

           It was the third consecutive shutout thrown by Cubs pitchers. Bill Hands beat the Astros 5–0 at Houston on August 3, and Milt Pappas topped the Padres 3–0 in Chicago on August 4.

AUGUST 16 Ferguson Jenkins pitches a two–hitter to beat the Braves 3–0 at Atlanta–Fulton

County Stadium. The only Atlanta hits were singles by Ralph Garr in the fourth inning and Earl Williams in the fifth inning.

AUGUST 17   Billy Williams collects the 2,000th hit of his career in a 5–4 loss to the Braves in Atlanta.

AUGUST 18   Johnny Callison hits a grand slam off Phil Niekro in the eighth inning of a 7–2 win over the Braves in Atlanta.

AUGUST 20   Ferguson Jenkins wins his 20th game of 1971 with a 3–2 decision over the Astros at Wrigley Field.

The win put the Cubs 4½ games back of the first–place Pirates with a record of 68–55 in the another pressure–packed pennant race. The collapse in 1969 and the near miss in 1970 had made Leo Durocher very hard to live with, and as the Cubs edged closer to the Pirates in 1971, Durocher became impossible for many of the players to tolerate. Riverfront Stadium in Cincinnati had a long bench in the dugout, and during a series from August 13th through 15th against the Reds, Durocher and his coaches sat at one end while the players gathered on the other with a large "de–militarized zone" in between. The tenuous relationship between Leo and the players was about to burst apart.

AUGUST 21   Double–play partners Glenn Beckert and Don Kessinger both play their 1,000th career game, but the Cubs lose 3–0 to the Astros at Wrigley Field.

AUGUST 23   Prior to a 6–3 win over the Reds at Wrigley Field, Leo Durocher and Cubs players square off in an acrimonious clubhouse meeting.

Durocher ripped into Milt Pappas for letting Doug Rader of the Astros hit an 0–2 pitch for a double to drive in the winning run in a 4–3 loss at Wrigley Field the previous day. After Durocher spoke, he told the players they were free to talk and should air their grievances. Joe Pepitone came to Pappas's defense. "He didn't want to do it," said Pepitone. "Why are you always blaming people." Anger and tension, which had been building for years over Durocher's handling of the team, bubbled to the surface. Pappas and Ken Holtzman also spoke up, defiantly blasting the Cubs manager. Durocher responded by ripping into the players one by one in a profanity–laden harangue on what he believed were the deficiencies of the Cubs players. He accused Ron Santo of malingering and front office politics. Santo called Durocher a liar, and had to be restrained from charging Durocher. Despite the losses in the two games prior to the clubhouse explosion, things had been going reasonably well for the Cubs. Since June 1, the Cubs had a record of 46–30, and were only 5½ games out of first place. Any allusions of winning a pennant in 1971 were shattered when the Cubs lost 16 of 21 games from August 24 through September 14 and sank out of contention. (See September 3.) Durocher's relationship with his players was irretrievably damaged, and the Cubs merely went through the motions during the final month.

AUGUST 24   In what would prove to be the last home run of his career, Ernie Banks connects during a 5–4 loss to the Reds at Wrigley Field. The pitcher was Jim McGlothlin.

AUGUST 27   In his first start since the clubhouse shouting match with Leo Durocher, Milt Pappas shuts out the Braves 5–0 in Chicago. The Wrigley Field organist added the theme from *Love Story* to his repertoire because of the player's squabbles with their manager.

AUGUST 28   Cubs fans celebrate the career of their longtime third baseman on Ron Santo Day.

Prior to the game, won by the Braves 4–3, Santo presented a $25,000 check for diabetes research. The star third baseman was given a speedboat, a car, and an all-expenses paid trip to Italy. His wife was presented with a mink coat.

AUGUST 31   Don Kessinger collects five hits in six at-bats, including a walk-off single in the tenth inning, to beat the Expos 7–6 in the first game of a double-header at Wrigley Field. Montreal won the second game 11–2, although it took two days to finish. The contest was suspended after six innings by darkness with the Expos leading 8–1, and completed the next day before the regularly scheduled game.

SEPTEMBER 1   Ferguson Jenkins hits two homers during a 5–2 win over the Expos at Wrigley Field.

Jenkins hit six homers for the Cubs in 1971, to tie a club record for a pitcher in a season. The other two to hit six in a year were John Clarkson in 1887 and Bill Hutchinson in 1894. Jenkins hit 13 career homers, the best of any Cubs pitcher since 1900.

SEPTEMBER 3   P. K. Wrigley takes out an advertisement in all four of Chicago's daily newspapers in which he criticizes his players for their festering quarrel with Leo Durocher that erupted into the stormy August 23 clubhouse meeting.

In the text, Wrigley praised Durocher's role in reviving the Cubs after two decades as a perennial loser and in turning the club into a pennant contender. In the eighth and final paragraph, Wrigley wrote: "Leo is the manager and the 'Dump Durocher Clique' might as well give up. He is running the team, and if some of the players do not like it and lie down on the job, during the off-season, we will see what we can do to find them happier homes." The manifesto was virtually without precedent. An owner, in effect, was threatening to fire the players instead of the manager. At the end of the advertisement, Wrigley added, "P. S. If we could only find more team players like Ernie Banks." The suggestion that Banks was the only team player on the Cubs particularly offended many of the players who believed that they were every bit the team player as Mr. Cub. The players were also angry that Wrigley aired his complaints in the media instead of meeting with them personally. The proclamation by Wrigley failed to revive the Cubs, as the club lost nine of their next 11 games. In the ad, Wrigley carefully avoided committing himself to Durocher beyond the 1971 season, however. (See November 18, 1971.)

SEPTEMBER 10   Ferguson Jenkins breaks Charlie Root's club record for career strikeouts during an 8–7, 12-inning loss to the Cardinals at Wrigley Field.

Jenkins finished his career with 2,038 strikeouts as a Cub, well ahead of Root's 1,432. Root still ranks second on the Cubs all-time strikeout list.

SEPTEMBER 15   In just his second big league start, Burt Hooton strikes out 15 batters to beat the Mets 3–2 in the second game of a double-header at Shea Stadium. Hooton allowed only three hits and had a no–hitter going until two were out in the seventh inning when Mike Jorgensen singled and Ken Singleton homered to tie the score 2–2. The Cubs won the contest on a ninth–inning homer by Billy Williams. The Cubs also won the first game 6–2.

SEPTEMBER 16   Juan Pizarro hits a home run off Tom Seaver in the eighth inning for the only run in a 1–0 victory over the Mets in New York.

The home run by Pizarro was the first one he hit as a major leaguer since 1965 when he played for the White Sox. He never hit another homer before his career ended in 1974, and finished with eight lifetime homers over 18 seasons.

SEPTEMBER 21   In his first start since fanning 15 Mets, and the third of his career, Burt Hooton pitches a two–hitter to beat the Mets 2–0 at Wrigley Field. The only New York hits were singles by Bud Harrelson in the first inning and Mike Jorgensen in the seventh. Ron Santo hit a homer with a man on base off Tom Seaver in the second inning for the only two runs of the contest. It was the 300th homer of Santo's career. (See April 16, 1972.)

SEPTEMBER 26   In the final game at Wrigley Field in 1971, Ernie Banks plays the final game of his major league career. Banks had a single in three at–bats in a 5–1 loss to the Phillies.

Banks played in only 39 games in 1971, and hit .193 with three homers. The end of Ernie's 19–year career as a player came curiously without fanfare. Banks was hired as a coach soon after the season ended, and the possibility that he may play again was left open, but it never happened.

SEPTEMBER 30   In the final game of the season, Ferguson Jenkins wins his 24th game of 1971, defeating the Expos 5–3 in Montreal.

NOVEMBER 18   Leo Durocher signs a contract to manage the Cubs again in 1972.

After the turbulent 1971 season ended, there was considerable speculation as to whether or not Durocher would return for another year because of the battles with his players. For weeks P. K. Wrigley wavered and explained to reporters that a decision had not been reached. Leo finally got a reprieve when Wrigley defied the critics by signing him to boss the Cubs again in 1972. Durocher's contract was renewed with an unusual precedent, however. Hank Aguirre was hired as an "information services coach" to act as a liaison between the acerbic Durocher and the players, and Durocher and the hostile Chicago press corps. Aguirre was in uniform during the games, but had a locker in the player's clubhouse. In addition, all three full–time coaches from 1971 were released. Durocher was 66 years old, however, and unable to change. He remained irascible, profane, and inconsiderate, and controversy continued to swirl around him. Leo was relieved of his duties as Cubs manager in July 1972.

NOVEMBER 29   The Cubs trade Ken Holtzman to the Athletics for Rick Monday.

Despite pitching a no–hitter, Holtzman had a miserable season in 1971 with a 9–15 record and a 4.48 ERA. He was one of Durocher's leading detractors, and was the first key member of the 1969 club to be traded. The Cubs believed that

Burt Hooton could take Holtzman's rotation spot. Monday gave the Cubs five excellent seasons before he was traded to the Dodgers following the 1976 season. The Cubs desperately needed a center fielder, and Rick was the best to play the position for the Cubs in the last 50 years.

DECEMBER 3   The Cubs trade Jim Colborn, Brock Davis, and Earl Stephenson to the Brewers for Jose Cardenal.

Cardenal was 28 and the Cubs were his sixth team, but he filled another need, as the club had been searching for an effective and consistent right fielder for years. Cardenal and Monday also gave the Cubs speed which the club lacked. The Cubs finished last in the NL in stolen bases four straight years from 1968 through 1971. In 821 games over six years, Cardenal hit .296 for the Cubs. In 1975, Cardenal stole 34 bases, the most by any Cub since Kiki Cuyler swiped 37 in 1930.

1972   Cubs

Season in a Sentence

Leo Durocher departs in late July in a season in which the Cubs finish second again, but are never in contention for the pennant.

Finish • Won • Lost • Pct • GB

Second   85   70   .548   11.0

Managers

Leo Durocher (46–44) and Whitey Lockman (39–26)

Stats

Stats	Cubs	NL	Rank
Batting Avg:	.257	.248	4
On–Base Pct:	.332	.318	3
Slugging Pct:	.387	.365	3
Home Runs:	133		4
Stolen Bases:	69		7
ERA:	3.22	3.45	4
Fielding Avg:	.979	.978	5
Runs Scored:	685		4
Runs Allowed:	567		4

Starting Lineup

Randy Hundley, c
Jim Hickman, 1b
Glenn Beckert, 2b
Ron Santo, 3b
Don Kessinger, ss
Billy Williams, lf
Rick Monday, cf
Jose Cardenal, rf
Carmen Fanzone, 3b–1b
Joe Pepitone, 1b

Pitchers

Ferguson Jenkins, sp
Milt Pappas, sp
Burt Hooton, sp
Bill Hands, sp
Rick Reuschel, sp
Jack Aker, rp
Dan McGinn, rp

Attendance

1,299,163 (seventh in NL)

Club Leaders

Batting Avg:	Williams	.333
On–Base Pct:	Williams	.398
Slugging Pct:	Williams	.606
Home Runs:	Williams	37
RBI:	Williams	122
Runs:	Cardenal	96
Stolen Bases:	Cardenal	25
Wins:	Jenkins	20
Strikeouts:	Jenkins	184
ERA:	Pappas	2.77
Saves:	Aker	17

JANUARY 20   The Cubs trade Johnny Callison to the Yankees for Jack Aker.

APRIL 7   The Cubs scheduled season opener against the Expos in Montreal is canceled by
                baseball first player's strike. The Cubs first seven games were eliminated by the
                labor action, which began on April 1 and ended on April 13.

APRIL 15   In the belated season opener, the Cubs lose 4–2 to the Phillies at Wrigley Field.
                Resentment over the strike limited the crowd to 17,401. The Phillies scored two
                runs in the ninth to break a 2–2 tie. Both runs were unearned because right fielder
                Jose Cardenal, playing in his first game as a Cub, dropped a drive hit by Tim
                McCarver with two out.

APRIL 16   In only his fourth career start, Burt Hooton
                pitches a no–hitter to defeat the Phillies on a
                cold and nasty day before 9,583 at Wrigley
                Field. Hooton threw 118 pitches, walked seven
                and struck out seven. A howling wind not only
                helped preserve the no–hitter, but the shutout as
                well, by keeping a seventh–inning drive by Greg
                Luzinski in the ballpark. Rick Monday caught
                the ball at the wall. In the ninth inning, Willie
                Montanez grounded to Glenn Beckert at second
                base, Deron Johnson struck out on a 3–2 pitch,
                and Luzinski fanned with the count 0–2.

Burt Hooton winks at the camera
while holding the ball commemorat-
ing his no–hitter.

                With the help of his unique knuckle–curve,
                Hooton pitched 30 innings in his first four
                major league starts and allowed only five
                earned runs and eight hits. The no–hitter
                was thrown just two months after Hooton's
                22nd birthday. It looked as though the Cubs
                had found another number two starter to
                team with Ferguson Jenkins, but it never
                happened. Hooton struggled after his
                no–hitter, and was traded to the Dodgers in
                1975 with a record of 34–44 as a Cub.

APRIL 26   Directing the club in the absence of Leo Durocher, coach Pete Reiser orders an
                intentional walk to Lee May of the Astros with two out in the tenth inning and no
                one on base. The move backfired when Bob Watson doubled May home with the
                winning run to give the Astros a 5–4 win in Houston. It was the Cubs eighth loss in
                a row, and gave the club a record of 2–9.

                Durocher was in the third day of a five–day stay at Wesley Memorial Hospital
                in Chicago because of "persistent fatigue."

APRIL 28   Jim Hickman drives in six runs with a pair of three–run homers in a 10–8 win over
                the Reds in Cincinnati. Both of the homers were struck off Jack Billingham.

                In 1972, the Cubs joined the conversion from flannel fabrics to the revolution-
                ary new double knits. The first club to wear knit uniforms were the Pirates in

1970. In a one-year experiment, the number on the front of the Cubs road jersey was moved to the center of the shirt, similar to a basketball uniform.

MAY 2   Glenn Beckert hits a homer, triple, and double in a 12–1 win over the Braves at Wrigley Field.

On the same day, Joe Pepitone left the club and asked to be placed on the "voluntarily retired list" because he was "no longer interested in playing professional baseball." Pepitone planned to devote all of his energies to his cocktail lounge "Joe Pepitone's Thing" on the Near North Side. He was 31 years old, and was suffering from gastritis, which had kept him out of the line-up the previous ten days. Under the rules, once a player was placed on the voluntary retired list, he wasn't eligible to return for sixty days. Pepitone returned to the ball club on July 1, as soon as the sixty-day period expired, but his batting production dropped and he was sold by the Cubs to the Braves in May 1973.

MAY 3   The Cubs wallop the Braves 12–1 at Wrigley Field for the second day in a row.

Dan McGinn, who was 0–5 with a 5.86 ERA for the Cubs in 1972, was once a punter for Notre Dame's football team.

MAY 6   Carmen Fanzone, subbing at third base for injured Ron Santo, hits two homers in a 6–4 win over the Astros at Wrigley Field.

Fanzone was a 29-year-old rookie in 1972. He was also a professional trumpet player. In fact, Fanzone's first appearance on the playing field at Wrigley Field was with the Central Michigan University band as part of the halftime show at Bears games in 1963 and 1964. Later, Fanzone played the trumpet in Johnny Carson's Tonight Show *band.*

MAY 16   Rick Monday hits three homers in his first three at-bats, driving in five runs, in an 8–1 win over the Phillies in Philadelphia. He homered off Bill Champion in the first and third innings and Darrell Brandon in the fifth. Monday also singled in the ninth.

JUNE 2   The Cubs sell Phil Regan to the White Sox.

JUNE 6   The Cubs select pitcher Brian Vernoy from LaQuinta High School in Westminster, California, in the first round of the amateur draft.

Vernoy never advanced beyond Class A ball. Players drafted and signed by the Cubs in 1972 who reached the majors were Mike Gordon in the third round, Buddy Schultz in the sixth, Ray Burris in the 17th, and Wayne Tyrone in the 20th. Only Burris had more than a cup of coffee with the Cubs.

JUNE 10   The Cubs score three runs in the ninth inning to defeat the Giants 4–3 in San Francisco. A two-run homer by Rick Monday tied the score 3–3, and a home run by Ron Santo broke the deadlock.

JUNE 14   The Cubs defeat the Padres 12–9 at Wrigley Field. Chicago scored six runs in the sixth inning to break a 6–6 tie.

JUNE 16 — Billy Williams homers for the fourth game in a row, leading the Cubs to a 4–0 win over the Dodgers at Wrigley Field. Williams hit five homers during the streak.

JUNE 18 — One day after the break–in of Democratic Party National Committee offices at the Watergate complex in Washington, Carmen Fanzone plays the National Anthem on the trumpet prior to an eleven–inning, 5–4 win over the Dodgers at Wrigley Field.

JUNE 20 — Randy Hundley hits a grand slam off Don Carrithers in a seven–run first inning against the Giants at Wrigley Field. Hundley also drove in a run with a single giving him five RBIs in the 15–8 Chicago win. Pitching six innings of relief, Rick Reuschel earned his first major league victory.

> *From April 28 through June 20, the Cubs won 32 of 45. With an overall record of 34–22, the Cubs were two games behind the Pirates. But Pittsburgh swept the Cubs in a three–game series at Wrigley Field beginning on June 23, and the Cubs never seriously challenged for the pennant again in 1972.*

JUNE 26 — In his first major league start, Rick Reuschel beats the Phillies 11–1 at Wrigley Field.

> *At a hefty six–foot–three and 235 pounds, Reuschel bore little resemblance to a professional athlete, but posted a record of 135–127 with the Cubs, mostly on clubs that lost more often than they won, and lasted twenty seasons in the majors. On the Cubs all–time list of pitching leaders, Rick ranks 12th in victories, eighth in games pitched (358), second to Ferguson Jenkins in games started (343), sixth in innings (2,290), and third in strikeouts (1,367). Reuschel was traded to the Yankees on June 12, 1981 in a deal which worked to the Cubs disadvantage. He won 79 more games after he left the Cubs for a total of 214 in his career before calling it quits in 1991 at the age of 42. Reuschel pitched in the World Series for the Yankees in 1981 and the Giants in 1989.*

JULY 1 — In his first game back after his "retirement," Joe Pepitone plays first base and hits clean–up in a 4–3 loss to the Pirates in Pittsburgh. Pepitone was hitless in three at–bats.

JULY 11 — Billy Williams collects eight hits in eight at–bats in a double–header against the Astros at Wrigley Field. Williams was three–for–three in the first game, won by Houston 6–5. In the nightcap, he had five hits, including a homer and a double, in five at–bats leading the Cubs to a 9–5 victory.

JULY 14 — The Cubs rally for three runs in the ninth inning to beat the Braves 9–8 at Wrigley Field. Paul Popovich broke the 8–8 tie with an pinch–hit, RBI–single.

JULY 18 — The Reds bring Clay Carroll into the game in relief in the tenth inning, and Billy Williams hits a walk–off homer off Carroll's first pitch to lift the Cubs to a 2–1 win at Wrigley Field.

JULY 21 — Billy Williams drives in six runs with a homer, a double, and two singles during an 11–3 win over the Astros in Houston.

JULY 24 — Leo Durocher steps down as manager and is replaced by Whitey Lockman. The

Cubs had a record of 46–44, lost 22 of their last 34 games, and were ten games behind the first–place Pirates. Durocher closed his stay in Chicago with a 535–526 record as manager, but posted five winning seasons in six full seasons and another winning mark in his partial seventh season. He also presided over a period in which attendance at Wrigley Field boomed, increasing by more than a million between 1966 and 1969.

The five–paragraph press release issued by P. K. Wrigley left open the question as to whether Durocher resigned or was fired, although Wrigley acknowledged the "friction between Leo and his players." Durocher insisted that he "stepped aside" by "mutual agreement" after a meeting with the Cubs owner. But the general interpretation was that Wrigley pressured Durocher for his resignation, and that Leo complied. Wrigley commented that the change "will allow the players, in the remainder of the season, to find out for themselves if they are pennant contenders. If the Cubs don't win now we'll know the players are the ones who are really to blame." In effect, the Cubs owner told players, "you wanted to get rid of Durocher, now see if you can win without him." Durocher wasn't through as a manager, however. He was out of work only five weeks. He was hired by the Astros on August 26 at the age of 67. He had a record of 98–95 in Houston, and resigned at the end of the 1973 season, ending his career in baseball. Durocher died in 1991, and was elected to the Hall of Fame posthumously in 1994.

Lockman was appointed manager the day before his 46th birthday. He had been director of player development in the Cubs organization, and prior to that, had been a coach under Durocher and a minor league manager. He had a distinguished playing career which lasted from 1945 through 1960, and was the first baseman on Durocher's 1951 and 1954 New York Giants pennant winners. The Cubs seemed to respond to Lockman's gentler touch, and were 85–57 under Lockman from the time of his appointment through June 29, 1973. Whitey was saddled with an aging roster, however, and the club ran out of gas during the second half of the 1973 campaign, which brought on a rebuilding project. Lockman was replaced by Jim Marshall in July 1974.

JULY 25   Billy Williams scores the tying run in the ninth inning, helping the National League to a 4–3, ten–inning win in the All–Star Game, played at Atlanta–Fulton County Stadium in Atlanta. Williams led off the ninth with a single, moved to third on a single by Manny Sanguillen, and scored on a ground out by Lee May.

JULY 27   In Whitey Lockman's first game as manager, Ferguson Jenkins pitches a one–hitter to defeat the Phillies 4–0 in the first game of a double–header at Veterans Stadium. The only Philadelphia hit was a double by Willie Montanez in the fourth inning that just eluded Don Kessinger's glove. The Cubs lost the second game 3–2.

AUGUST 3   Bill Hands pitches a one–hitter to defeat the Expos 3–0 in the second game of a double–header at Wrigley Field. The only Montreal hit was a single by Ken Singleton in the seventh inning. The Cubs lost the first game 2–1 in 13 innings.

AUGUST 11 Milt Pappas drives in five runs during a 7–2 win over the Mets at Wrigley Field. Pappas had a homer, a double and a single in three at–bats. The home run was hit with a man on base in the sixth inning and broke a 2–2 tie.

*Pappas finished his seventeen–year major league career with some unusual bat-
ting statistics. Milt hit only .123 and struck out 510 times in 1,073 at–bats, but
he hit 20 home runs.*

AUGUST 14   Ernie Banks plays three innings of a 3–1 Cubs win in an exhibition game against
the White Sox at Comiskey Park. Banks struck out in his only plate appearance.

AUGUST 18   The Cubs trade Tommy Davis to the Orioles for Elrod Hendricks.

AUGUST 26   Ron Santo collects his 2,000th career hit during a 10–9, ten–inning win over the
Giants at Wrigley Field. The milestone hit was a two–run homer in the third inning
off Ron Bryant. The winning run scored when Joe Pepitone was hit by a Randy
Moffitt pitch with the bases loaded. There were a total of five Cubs homers. Santo
and Billy Williams each hit two, and Paul Popovich added another. The home run
was the only one hit by Popovich all year. Williams also had three singles, to give
him five hits in six at–bats.

SEPTEMBER 1   The Cubs score nine runs in the seventh inning of a 14–3 win over the Padres at
Wrigley Field that included a fight between the two clubs. In the fourth inning,
Elrod Hendricks and Carmen Fanzone hit home runs off Bill Greif on consecutive
pitches. Rick Monday was the next batter, and was decked by Greif. Rick became
engaged in an argument with San Diego catcher Pat Corrales, and both dugouts
emptied, leading to a general free–for–all.

*Hendricks hit two homers in the game. They were his only two homers of 1972
and his only two as a Cub. Hendricks had only 43 at–bats in a Chicago uniform, and batted just .116.*

SEPTEMBER 2   Milt Pappas retires the first 26 batters he faces, and pitches a no–hitter to beat the
Padres 8–0 before 11,144 at Wrigley Field. In the ninth, John Jeter hit a fly ball to
Billy Williams in left field. Fred Kendall grounded out to Don Kessinger at short.
This left Pappas one out from becoming the first Cubs pitcher to throw a perfect
game. Larry Stahl pinch–hit for pitcher Al Severinsen, and swung and missed at the
first pitch. Stahl took a ball, than swung and missed again to make the count 1–2.
Pappas now needed only one strike for baseball immortality, but threw three sliders
wide of the plate. The last two were borderline calls, but home plate umpire Bruce
Froemming called them balls. Pappas saved the no–hitter by getting Garry Jestadt
to pop out to second baseman Carmen Fanzone. Milt struck out six and threw 98
pitches.

*Later, Pappas said of Froemming, "I was hoping he would sympathize with me
and give me a call. But they were balls, no question about it." It was the fourth
no–hitter by a Cubs pitcher in a span of four seasons, following two by Ken
Holtzman (in 1969 and 1971) and one by Burt Hooton (earlier in 1972). No
Cub has thrown a no–hitter since Pappas's gem.*

SEPTEMBER 8   Ferguson Jenkins wins his 20th game of the season with a 4–3 decision over the
Phillies in Philadelphia.

SEPTEMBER 15   Jim Hickman hits a grand slam off Gary Gentry in the third inning of a 9–3 win
over the Mets at Wrigley Field.

SEPTEMBER 16   Burt Hooton hits a grand slam off Tom Seaver during a seven–run third inning at
                Wrigley Field. The Cubs won the eventful game 18–5. Altogether, the Cubs hit five
                home runs. In addition to Hooton, Jose Cardenal hit two, and Billy Williams and
                Dave Rosello added one. Elrod Hendricks set a modern club record and tied a
                National League record by drawing five walks. Overall, Mets pitchers walked 15
                batters. Glenn Beckert set a major league record (since tied) by leaving 12 runners
                on base.

                *The homer was Hooton's first as a major leaguer. He hit four home runs in 748
                at–bats during his career. It was also Rosello's first major league homer. He didn't
                hit another one until 1975.*

SEPTEMBER 20   Milt Pappas wins his 200th game as a major leaguer, defeating the Expos 6–2 at
                Wrigley Field. After the game, Montreal manager Gene Mauch challenged Jose
                Cardenal to a fight outside the clubhouse because Mauch claimed Jose called him
                a "bad name." No blows were exchanged, however.

                *Pappas finished his career with a record of 209–164. He never won more than
                17 games in a season, although he won at least 15 seven times.*

SEPTEMBER 23   The Cubs sweep the Cardinals 2–0 and 15–1 in St. Louis.

SEPTEMBER 27   Billy Williams hits a grand slam off Steve Renko in the fifth inning of an 8–0 win
                over the Expos in Montreal.

OCTOBER 1   Milt Pappas wins his 11th consecutive game with a 3–0 decision over the Cardinals
                in St. Louis. Pappas went five innings, leaving the contest when he was hit in the
                cheek by a pitched ball. Joe Decker and Jack Aker combined for four innings of
                shutout relief.

                Pappas had a record of 17–7 in 1972 with an ERA of 2.77.

OCTOBER 2   The Cubs field a starting lineup with eight rookies, and defeat the Phillies 4–3 at
                Wrigley Field.

                *The eight rookies were center fielder Bill North, right fielder Pete LaCock, left
                fielder Gene Hiser, first baseman Pat Bourque, third baseman Carmen Fanzone,
                second baseman Allan Montreuil, shortstop Dave Rosello, and pitcher Rick
                Reuschel. The only veteran in the lineup was catcher Ken Rudolph.*

OCTOBER 4   Billy Williams goes one–for–three on the final day of the season to win the batting
                title with a .333 average. The Cubs lost 2–1 to the Phillies at Wrigley Field.

                *In addition to hitting .333, Williams collected 191 hits, clubbed 37 homers,
                scored 95 runs, and drove in 122. He was runner–up to Johnny Bench in the
                National League Most Valuable Player balloting. Williams also finished second
                to Bench in 1970. Other top Cubs hitters in 1972 were Ron Santo, Jose Cardenal,
                and Don Kessinger. Santo hit .302 with 17 homers. Cardenal also hit 17 homers
                and batted .291. Kessinger had a batting average of .274.*

NOVEMBER 21   Two weeks after Richard Nixon wins the Presidential election over George McGovern, the Cubs trade Billy North to the Athletics for Bob Locker.

Locker gave the Cubs much needed help out of the bullpen, but he wasn't worth the loss of North, who was the Athletics starting center fielder for four years, including two clubs that reached the World Series. North twice led the American League in stolen bases.

NOVEMBER 30   The Cubs trade Bill Hands, Joe Decker, and Bob Maneely to the Twins for Dave LaRoche.

LaRoche was another player acquired to give the Cubs depth in the bullpen, but he was traded away after two ineffective seasons in Chicago. Hands didn't help the Twins, but Decker won 26 games in Minnesota in 1973 and 1974 before blowing out his arm.

1973   Cubs

Season in a Sentence

The Cubs take an eight–game lead on June 29, then lose 33 of their next 42 games in a stunning collapse that brings about the dissolution of most of the last remnants of the 1969 club.

Finish • Won • Lost • Pct • GB

Fifth   77   84   .478   5.0

Manager

Whitey Lockman

Stats   Cubs • NL • Rank

Stats	Cubs	NL	Rank
Batting Avg:	.247	.254	10
On–Base Pct:	.322	.325	7
Slugging Pct:	.357	.376	9
Home Runs:	117		8
Stolen Bases:	65		9
ERA:	3.66	3.66	5
Fielding Avg:	.975	.977	7
Runs Scored:	614		10
Runs Allowed:	655		5

Starting Lineup

Randy Hundley, c
Jim Hickman, 1b
Glenn Beckert, 2b
Ron Santo, 3b
Don Kessinger, ss
Billy Williams, lf
Rick Monday, cf
Jose Cardenal, rf
Paul Popovich, 2b
Ken Rudolph, c
Carmen Fanzone, 3b–1b

Pitchers

Ferguson Jenkins, sp
Burt Hooton, sp
Rick Reuschel, sp
Milt Pappas, sp
Bob Locker, rp
Jack Aker, rp
Dave LaRoche, rp
Bill Bonham, rp–sp

Attendance

1,351,705 (seventh in NL)

Club Leaders

Batting Avg:	Cardenal	.303
On–Base Pct:	Cardenal	.375
Slugging Pct:	Monday	.469
Home Runs:	Monday	26
RBI:	Williams	86
Runs:	Monday	93
Stolen Bases:	Cardenal	19
Wins:	Three tied with:	14
Strikeouts:	Jenkins	170
ERA:	Reuschel	3.00
Saves:	Locker	16

APRIL 6 — Three months after the United States ends its military involvement in Vietnam, the Cubs defeat the Expos 3–2 with two runs in the ninth in the season opener before 40,273 at Wrigley Field. The two runs were scored on bases–loaded walks by Mike Marshall to Randy Hundley and Rick Monday. The starting pitcher was Ferguson Jenkins. It was the seventh consecutive season that Jenkins started the opener for the Cubs.

Tony LaRussa, who entered the game as a pinch–runner for Ron Santo, scored the winning run. It was the only game that LaRussa played as a member of the Cubs, and the last of the 132 contests of his big league career. Santo suffered a tragedy a few weeks earlier when his mother and stepfather were killed in an auto accident on their way to visit him during spring training.

APRIL 17 — Rick Monday smashes a home run off Tom Seaver in the fourth inning and Ferguson Jenkins pitches a two–hitter to lead the Cubs to a 1–0 win over the Mets at Shea Stadium. The only two New York hits were singles by Bud Harrelson in the first inning and John Milner in the fourth.

During the 1972 season, Oakland Athletics owner Charlie Finley paid his players to grow mustaches, beginning the first major leaguers since the turn of the twentieth century to sport facial hair. Several Cubs grew mustaches during the 1973 season, including Billy Williams, Carmen Fanzone, Joe Pepitone, Pete LaCock, Matt Alexander, Bob Locker, Gonzalo Marquez, and Dave Rosello. They were the first Cubs players with facial hair since 1902.

APRIL 18 — In his first major league start, Ray Burris is the winning pitcher in a 1–0 win over the Mets in New York. It was the second game in a row that the Cubs downed the Mets by a 1–0 score. Burris was handed the assignment when Milt Pappas was called to Chicago because his wife was ill. Burris went five innings, while Larry Gura pitched one inning of relief and Jack Aker finished up by hurling the final three.

APRIL 21 — The first eight Cubs collect hits during a six–run first inning against the Pirates at Wrigley Field. The contest was suspended by darkness in the sixth inning with the Cubs leading 10–8. It was completed on July 26 with the Cubs winning 10–9.

APRIL 24 — Cubs pitchers combine to strike out 16 Giants, but lose 4–2 in ten innings at Wrigley Field. Rick Reuschel fanned 12 batters in seven innings, and Bob Locker struck out four hitters in three innings.

APRIL 28 — Rick Monday scores both runs in a 2–0 win over the Padres at Wrigley Field. Monday hit a homer leading off the first inning, and doubled and scored on a single in the third.

Batting out of the lead–off spot, Monday had 21 homers in the Cubs first 75 games in 1973, then went seven weeks without hitting another one out of the ballpark. He finished the season with 26 homers, a .267 batting average, and 93 runs scored.

MAY 6 — A free–for–all highlights an 11–9 Giants win over the Cubs in twelve innings in the first game of a double–header at Candlestick Park. The fight was triggered by a beanball war between Milt Pappas and Jim Barr. Pappas threw a pitch over Barr's head in retaliation for the plunking of Ron Santo by the Giants hurler. Both dugouts emptied, but order was quickly restored. When play resumed Pappas hit Barr with the next pitch, and this time both teams came out swinging. Cubs coach Pete Reiser, who was 54 years old, suffered a broken collarbone and a concussion when he was kicked as he fell to the ground. During the fight, Dave Rader of the Giants, who had been a base runner on first base, circled the bases to score a run. San Francisco also won the second game 4–3.

MAY 8 — Following the ejection of Whitey Lockman, coach Ernie Banks serves as acting manager for the final inning of the Cubs 3–2, twelve–inning win over the Padres in San Diego. Banks became the first African–American to mange a team in major league history. The first African–American to manage a team on a permanent basis was Frank Robinson with the Indians in 1975.

MAY 18 — Glenn Beckert extends his hitting streak to 26 games during a 9–2 win over the Phillies in Philadelphia.

MAY 19 — The Cubs trade Joe Pepitone to the Braves for Andre Thornton.

Pepitone played only three big league games after the trade. Thornton played 271 games as a first baseman for the Cubs before going to Montreal in a trade in 1976.

MAY 29 — As manager of the Astros, Leo Durocher returns to Wrigley Field for the first time, since being let go by the Cubs on July 24, 1972. The Cubs won 7–1.

MAY 31 — The Cubs score ten runs in the first inning and defeat the Astros 16–8 at Wrigley Field. All ten runs were scored after the first two hitters were retired. Twelve consecutive Cubs reached base on six singles, four walks, a hit batsman, and an error.

JUNE 3 — Milt Pappas hits a home run and pitches seven innings of shutout ball to lead the Cubs to a 3–0 win over the Braves at Wrigley Field. Bob Locker went the final two innings for the save.

JUNE 25 — The Cubs score three runs in the ninth inning to beat the Mets 3–2 in New York. Ron Santo doubled in the first two runs, and scored on Don Kessinger's single.

JUNE 27 — Ron Santo has a hand in all six runs in a 6–1 win over the Expos in the first game of a double–header at Wrigley Field. Santo drove in four runs and scored two on a double and two singles. In the second game, Santo tied the score 3–3 in the ninth with a homer. The game was still knotted at 3–3 at the end of twelve innings when it was suspended by darkness, and completed the next day.

JUNE 28 — The game of June 27 against the Expos at Wrigley Field, suspended after twelve innings by darkness, continues. Six more innings were played, and Montreal emerged with a 5–4, eighteen–inning win. Both teams scored in the thirteenth, with Bob Bailey and Ron Santo hitting home runs. Bailey singled in the winning run off Burt Hooton in the eighteenth. The Cubs won the regularly scheduled game 4–2.

Santo hit .267 with 20 homers in 1973, his last year with the Cubs.

| JUNE 29 | The Cubs take an eight–game lead over the second place Expos by defeating the Mets 4–3 in ten innings at Wrigley Field. The score was tied 3–3 in the ninth on the only home run in the 206–game major league career of Gene Hiser. Jose Cardenal drove in the winning run on a bases–loaded single. |

The win gave the Cubs a 46–31 record on the season. The city of Chicago was once again buzzing about the possibility of the Cubs winning a pennant for the first time since 1945, but the club went into an inexplicable tailspin and lost 33 of their next 42 games. Due to playing in an extremely weak division, however, the Cubs still had a remote chance of winning a pennant heading into the last week of the season.

| JULY 1 | Playing before 42,497 at Wrigley Field, the Cubs score three runs in the ninth inning on a walk–off home run by Randy Hundley to beat the Mets 6–5 in the second game of a double–header. Ron Santo had five hits, including a double, in five at–bats. New York won the first game by the same 6–5 score. |

| JULY 4 | A two–run, walk–off homer by Ron Santo in the tenth inning beats the Phillies 3–2 at Wrigley Field. |

| JULY 22 | The Cubs yield first place to the Cardinals after spending eighty–four consecutive days at the top of the Eastern Division with a 4–1 loss to the Giants 4–1 in thirteen innings at Wrigley Field. |

| AUGUST 13 | The Cubs purchase Rico Carty from the Rangers. |

Carty was immediately installed as the Cubs clean–up hitter and left fielder. Billy Williams was moved to first base. Carty lasted only 22 games with the Cubs, and was sold to the Athletics on September 11.

| AUGUST 14 | In a rare display of temperament, Ferguson Jenkins hurls four bats onto the field from the dugout after being lifted for a relief pitcher in the fifth inning of a 6–2 loss to the Braves at Wrigley Field. One of the bats came dangerously close to hitting umpire Jerry Dale. It was the Cubs ninth loss in a row. |

| AUGUST 16 | The Cubs losing streak reaches 11 games with a 10–2 defeat at the hands of the Braves at Wrigley Field. Atlanta scored nine runs in the eighth inning to wipe out a 2–0 Chicago lead. |

| AUGUST 17 | The Cubs defeat the Dodgers 5–1 at Wrigley Field to stop the 11–game losing streak. |

| AUGUST 26 | In trying to steal home during a 4–2 win over the Astros in Houston, Jose Cardenal slams into Ferguson Jenkins, who was batting. Jenkins had to be removed from the game because of a jammed index finger on his pitching hand, suffered when he fell to the ground. |

Cardenal hit .303 with 11 homers for the Cubs in 1973.

AUGUST 31   The Cubs trade Larry Gura to the Rangers for Mike Paul.

              *The Cubs gave up on Gura much too soon in what proved to be a horrible
              trade. Gura won another 123 big league games after leaving Chicago, most of
              them with the Royals. Paul was a complete bust, with an 0–2 record and a 5.21
              ERA as a Cub.*

SEPTEMBER 8   Billy Williams collects five hits, including a double, in five at–bats during an 8–2
              win over the Cardinals at Wrigley Field.

SEPTEMBER 22 Jose Cardenal triples home two runs in the tenth inning, and scored on an error, to
              lead the Cubs to a 5–2 win over the Phillies at Philadelphia to keep alive flickering
              hopes for a pennant in 1973. The Cubs had a record of 75–79 and were in fifth place,
              but were only 2 ½ games behind the first–place Mets, who were 78–77.

SEPTEMBER 23 The Cubs allow five runs in the eighth inning to lose 9–7 to the Phillies in Philadelphia
              and all but douse the chance for Chicago to play into the post–season. The Cubs
              won only two of their last eleven games and finished in fifth place, five games back
              of the Mets.

SEPTEMBER 25 Jose Cardenal's two–run double in the ninth inning beats the Cardinals 4–3 in
              St. Louis.

OCTOBER 1   The Mets clinch the Eastern Division title by beating the Cubs 6–4 at Wrigley Field.

              *With a losing season, the window of opportunity for winning a pennant with
              the aging core of players left from the 1969 Cubs had closed. Time had run out
              on the best Cubs team that has been assembled since World War II. At the end
              of the 1973 season, Billy Williams was 35, Ron Santo 33, Glenn Beckert 32,
              Randy Hundley 31, Don Kessinger 31, and Ferguson Jenkins 29. By Christmas,
              Jenkins, Beckert, Hundley, and Santo would be traded in exchange for much
              younger players.*

OCTOBER 25   Two weeks after Spiro Agnew resigns as vice president due to financial impropri-
              eties, the Cubs trade Ferguson Jenkins to the Rangers for Bill Madlock and Vic
              Harris.

              *Jenkins was the first of four key members of the 1969 Cubs to be traded during
              the 1973–74 off–season. The Cubs believed that Jenkins was finished after he
              posted a 14–16 in 1973. Jenkins proved them wrong when he was 25–12 for
              the Rangers in 1974. He won 17 for the Rangers in 1975, 18 in 1978 and 16 in
              1979. It wasn't a bad trade, however, as the Cubs received equal value in
              return. Madlock hit .336 in three years with the Cubs, including two batting
              titles, before he was dealt to the Giants following the 1976 season. Harris
              played 113 games as a Cub, mostly as a second baseman, and hit only .191
              without a single homer.*

NOVEMBER 3   The Cubs trade Bob Locker to the Athletics for Horacio Pina.

NOVEMBER 7   The Cubs trade Glenn Beckert and Bobby Fenwick to the Padres for Jerry Morales.

Cubs fans hated to see Beckert go, but he was all but through as a player. He appeared in only 73 more games after the trade. It proved to be an advantageous trade, as Morales started in the Cubs outfield for four seasons.

DECEMBER 6   The Cubs continue to unload veterans by trading Randy Hundley to the Twins for George Mitterwald.

Hundley was another player who was nearly finished. Mitterwald wasn't any prize, but he was three years younger and much healthier than Hundley. Mitterwald hit .231 with 26 homers over four seasons as a catcher with the Cubs.

DECEMBER 7   Ron Santo rejects a trade to the Angels which would have brought Andy Hassler and Bruce Heinbechner to the Cubs. Santo had the right to refuse the trade because of a new rule negotiated between the players and the owners in February 1973. Any player with at least ten years of service in the majors and five with one club had the right to turn down a trade. Santo didn't want to leave Chicago, and pleaded with P. K. Wrigley to trade him to the White Sox.

DECEMBER 11   The Cubs trade Ron Santo to the White Sox for Steve Stone, Ken Frailing, Steve Swisher, and Jim Kremmel.

Like Beckert and Hundley, Santo was another player whose days as an effective major leaguer were almost over. Santo played only one more season after the trade, and hit only .221 in 117 games. Stone was the only one of the four players acquired from the White Sox who provided any help to the Cubs. He was 23–20 over three seasons on the North Side before he went back to the Sox as a free agent.

Rick Monday slides into home against the Braves, scoring one of his team–leading 93 runs.

Cubs

Season in a Sentence

The rebuilding Cubs plummet in the standings with eleven rookies on the 25–man roster, a recipe for a 96–loss season and another change of managers.

Finish • Won • Lost • Pct • GB

Sixth   66   96   .407 22.0

Managers

Whitey Lockman (41–52) and Jim Marshall (25–44)

Stats	Cubs	NL	Rank
Batting Avg:	.251	.255	9
On–Base Pct:	.329	.329	6
Slugging Pct:	.365	.367	7
Home Runs:	110		5 (tie)
Stolen Bases:	78		9
ERA:	4.28	3.62	11
Fielding Avg:	.969	.976	12
Runs Scored:	669		6
Runs Allowed:	826		11

Starting Lineup

Steve Swisher, c
Billy Williams, 1b–lf
Vic Harris, 2b
Bill Madlock, 3b
Don Kessinger, ss
Jerry Morales, lf–rf
Rick Monday, cf
Jose Cardenal, rf
Andre Thornton, 1b
George Mitterwald, c
Carmen Fanzone, 3b

Pitchers

Rick Reuschel, sp
Bill Bonham, sp
Steve Stone, sp–rp
Oscar Zamora, rp
Ken Frailing, rp
Dave LaRoche, rp
Burt Hooton, rp–sp
Jim Todd, rp

Attendance

1,015,378 (tenth in NL)

Club Leaders

Batting Avg:	Madlock	.313
On–Base Pct:	Monday	.375
Slugging Pct:	Monday	.467
Home Runs:	Monday	20
RBI:	Morales	82
Runs:	Monday	84
Stolen Bases:	Cardenal	23
Wins:	Reuschel	13
Strikeouts:	Bonham	191
ERA:	Bonham	3.86
Saves:	Zamora	10

MARCH 23   Six weeks after the kidnapping of Patty Hearst, the Cubs trade Jim Hickman to the Cardinals for Scipio Spinks.

APRIL 6   Snow and cold weather wipes out the scheduled season opener against the Expos in Montreal. The wintry atmospheric conditions also postponed the contest on April 7 in the Canadian city, the second of a two–game series.

APRIL 9   The day after Henry Aaron hits the 715th home run of his career to break Babe Ruth's career record, the Cubs finally get underway by playing their first regular season game of 1974. In 40–degree weather, Bill Bonham pitched a complete game shutout to beat the Phillies 2–0 before 30,601 at Wrigley Field. The Cubs scored both of their runs in the first inning.

APRIL 10   Billy Williams hits a two–run single in the ninth inning to carry the Cubs to a 7–6 win over the Phillies at Wrigley Field. Williams also hit a three–run homer in the first.

APRIL 18   In a decided contrast to the 18–9 game of the day before, the Cubs defeat the

Pirates 1–0 at Wrigley Field. The lone run of the game was scored on a sacrifice fly by Billy Williams in the first inning. Ken Frailing (seven innings) and Ray Burris (two innings) combined for the shutout.

APRIL 29   The Cubs batter the Astros 18–2 in Houston.

MAY 3   Rick Monday clouts a two–run walk–off homer in the ninth inning to beat the Reds 6–5 at Wrigley Field. The Reds took a 5–4 lead in the top of the ninth on a homer by Pete Rose.

Monday hit .294 with 20 homers in 1974. Outfield mate Jose Cardenal batted .293 with 13 home runs.

MAY 4   Another walk–off homer beats the Reds, as Billy Williams hits one out of Wrigley Field in the eleventh inning to lift the Cubs to a 3–2 triumph. The Cubs scored two runs in the ninth inning to tie.

The 1974 Cubs bore little resemblance to the recent past. Of the thirty–eight players to appear in a game for the club in 1974, only seven (Bill Bonham, Jose Cardenal, Carmen Fanzone, Don Kessinger, Rick Monday, Rick Reuschel and Billy Williams) played under Leo Durocher, who was let go on July 24, 1972. Kessinger and Williams were the only two remaining from the 1970 Cubs.

MAY 22   Jerry Morales drives in six runs with two homers and a single in a 9–6 win over the Mets in New York. His second circuit clout came with two on and two out in the ninth and the score tied at 6–6.

MAY 24   The Cubs failure to cover home plate during a rundown play in the ninth inning enables the Cardinals to gain a 1–0 victory at Wrigley Field. With Joe Torre on first base and Ted Simmons on third, Tim McCarver grounded to Billy Williams at first. Williams threw home, and catcher Tom Lundstedt closed in on Simmons before tossing the ball to third baseman Matt Alexander. Simmons turned toward the plate, raced past Lundstedt, and scored with Alexander chasing him in vain. Neither pitcher Rick Reuschel nor Williams covered the plate.

JUNE 5   The Cubs select outfielder Scot Thompson from Knox High School in Renfrew, Pennsylvania, in the first round of the amateur draft.

Thompson played in 626 big league games. He was never more than a spare outfielder, who had a .261 batting average and only five homers in 1,273 at–bats. Thompson was the best of a bad lot chosen by the Cubs in the 1974 draft. The only other players drafted and signed to play in the majors were Mike Sember (second round) and George Riley (fourth round).

JUNE 14   The Cubs score seven runs in the seventh inning and defeat the Astros 10–7 at Wrigley Field.

JUNE 16   The Cubs score seven runs in the fourth inning to take a 7–2 lead over the Astros, but wind up losing 8–7 at Wrigley Field when Houston scores a run in the seventh inning and five in the eighth.

JUNE 20   Rick Reuschel allows 12 hits, but shuts out the Pirates 3–0 at Wrigley Field. Pittsburgh had nine singles and three doubles, and left ten men on base.

JUNE 28   The Cubs play 27 innings in a marathon double–header against the Expos in Montreal. The first game went 18 innings with the Cubs winning 8–7. It was 7–7 at the end of the regulation nine. The contest wended its way through eight scoreless innings before Chicago scored in the 18th on a walk to Don Kessinger and a triple by Jerry Morales. Morales was hitless in his first eight at–bats before hitting the game–winning three–bagger. The second game was no contest, as the Expos won 15–0.

JULY 5   Andre Thornton clubs a walk–off homer in the ninth inning to beat the Braves 3–2 in the second game of a double–header at Wrigley Field. The Cubs also won the first game 4–1.

JULY 24   Whitey Lockman resigns as manager and is replaced by Jim Marshall. The Cubs had a record of 41–52 at the time of the switch.

               Lockman remained in the Cubs organization, returning to his old job as director of player development. Marshall had been Lockman's third base coach. He played five seasons in the majors, including a stint with the Cubs in 1958 and 1959, and managed clubs in the Cubs farm system. Marshall was 43 years old at time of his appointment as manager of the club.

JULY 26   Billy Williams hits a grand slam off Jesus Hernaiz in the sixth inning of a 10–7 win over the Phillies at Wrigley Field.

               Williams had a difficult final season with the Cubs, batting .280 with 16 homers in 117 games. In a failed experiment, he played the first two months of the season at first base. On August 19, he went on the disabled list for the first time in his career after he spiked himself on the ankle.

JULY 27   Second baseman Billy Grabarkewitz makes three errors and Don Kessinger adds two more at shortstop during a 3–2 loss to the Cardinals at Wrigley Field.

JULY 31   Bill Bonham strikes out four batters in the second inning, but the Cubs lose 7–4 to the Expos in the first game of a double–header at Wrigley Field. He whiffed Mike Torrez, who reached base on a passed ball by catcher Rick Stelmaszek. Bonham then proceeded to fan Ron Hunt, Tim Foli, and Willie Davis. Montreal also won the second game 4–0.

AUGUST 7   The day before Richard Nixon resigns as President, Reverend Jesse Jackson, national president of Operation PUSH (People United to Save Humanity) accuses the Cubs of racism for the failure to hire Ernie Banks as manager. At the time, there had yet to be an African–American manager in major league history. (Frank Robinson would become the first two months later when hired by the Indians.)

               P. K. Wrigley responded by stating that Banks was "too nice" to be a manager, and that if he wanted the position he would arrange for Banks to serve an apprenticeship in the minors. "All I can say," declared Wrigley, "is that being a major league manager is like being a kamikaze pilot. It's suicide."

AUGUST 18   The Cubs rout the Padres 14–6 at Wrigley Field.

AUGUST 20   Carmen Fanzone hits a grand slam in the eighth inning off Charlie Hough, but the Cubs lose 18–8 to the Dodgers at Wrigley Field. Fanzone entered the game in the sixth as a defensive replacement at third base for Bill Madlock after the Dodgers built an 18–2 lead. Dave Lopes hit three homers, a double and a single for Los Angeles. In the fourth inning, Lopes was sent into the dirt by a Dave LaRoche pitch, and moved slowly toward the mound causing both benches to empty. The umpires stepped in quickly to prevent bloodshed.

AUGUST 23   Rick Reuschel pitches the Cubs to a 1–0 win over the Giants in San Francisco.

AUGUST 28   Bill Madlock hits a grand slam in the eighth inning off Don Sutton to tie the score 6–6, but the Cubs lose 7–6 to the Dodgers in Los Angeles.

Given the difficult assignment of replacing Ron Santo at third base and wearing Glenn Beckert's old number 18, Madlock hit .313 with nine homers in his first season with the Cubs.

Bill Madlock won two batting titles during his short stay with the Cubs 1974–1976.

AUGUST 30   The Cubs win two overtime games in San Diego. Chicago won the first game 5–1 in twelve innings, and the second 4–3 in ten.

SEPTEMBER 8   On the day that President Gerald Ford pardons Richard Nixon, Jerry Morales hits a grand slam in the ninth inning off Larry Christensen of the Phillies, but the Cubs fall short 11–10 at Wrigley Field.

SEPTEMBER 10   Jim Tyrone and Carmen Fanzone both hit pinch–hit homers, but the Cubs lose 12–4 to the Pirates at Wrigley Field.

SEPTEMBER 13   Ron Dunn hits a homer in the eleventh inning to beat the Mets 4–3 in the second game of a double–header at Shea Stadium. New York won the first game 6–0.

SEPTEMBER 14   The Cubs roll to an easy 12–0 win over the Mets in New York.

SEPTEMBER 21   The Cubs humiliate the Cardinals 19–4 in St. Louis. Steve Swisher hit a grand slam off Barry Lersch in the sixth inning.

SEPTEMBER 22   A fight breaks out in the ninth inning of a 6–5 loss to the Cardinals in St. Louis. Nicknamed "The Mad Hungarian," Cardinals reliever Al Hrabosky began each appearance by standing at the back of the mound, meditating for a few seconds to "psyche" himself, pound his glove, then ascend the mound. This aroused the anger of Bill Madlock, who wound up in an argument with St. Louis catcher Ted Simmons that quickly spread into a bench–clearing brawl. Jim Marshall was ejected for "cussing out" the umpires.

SEPTEMBER 30   Bill Bonham loses his 22nd game of 1974 with a 2–1 defeat at the hands of the Pirates in Pittsburgh.

Bonham had a respectable ERA of 3.85 in 1974, but posted an 11–22 record. He is the last Cub pitcher to lose 20 or more games in a season. The 20–game losers since 1900 are Long Tom Hughes (11–21 in 1901), Phil Douglas (14–20 in 1917), Bob Rush (13–20 in 1950), Sam Jones (14–20 in 1955), Glen Hobbie (16–20 in 1960), Dick Ellsworth (9–20 in 1962), Larry Jackson (14–21 in 1965), and Ellsworth again (8–22 in 1966).

OCTOBER 22   Longtime Wrigley Field announcer Pat Pieper dies at the age of 88.

Pieper had been employed by the Cubs since 1904, starting as a vendor at West Side Grounds. In 1916, when the club moved to present–day Wrigley Field, Pieper was hired as the field announcer, carrying a fourteen–pound megaphone and walking up and down in front of the stands to shout the starting lineups. In 1932, an electric public address system was installed, and Pieper was provided a spot almost directly behind the plate. Wearing his trademark brown suit, he launched every game by saying, "Attention! Attention, please! Have your pencils and scorecards ready, and I will give you the correct lineups for today's game." When he was still in his 80s, Pieper moonlighted as a waiter at the Ivanhoe Restaurant twelve blocks south of Wrigley Field, where he walked immediately after the game was over.

OCTOBER 23   The Cubs trade Billy Williams to the Athletics for Manny Trillo, Bob Locker, and Darold Knowles. The deal left Don Kessinger as the only holdover from the 1969 Cubs.

The Cubs continued their policy of trading familiar faces by trading Williams to Oakland. The Athletics won the world championship in 1972, 1973, and 1974, and Williams hoped that the move would allow him to finally play in a World Series, but it didn't work out. He was 36 years old at the time of the trade and played only one more season, mostly as a designated hitter, and the Athletics lost in the American League Championship Series to the Red Sox. Fan reaction to the exchange was vehemently negative, but the trade worked out to the Cubs advantage because Williams was near the end of his career. Although unappreciated by the Wrigley faithful, Trillo was the Cubs starting second baseman for four seasons. Locker, who sat out the 1974 season with arm trouble after the Cubs traded him to the Athletics in December 1973, contributed next to nothing in his second go–around in Chicago, while Knowles was largely ineffective.

1975   Cubs

Season in a Sentence

The Cubs spend 51 days in first place, but the worst pitching staff in the league dooms the club to another losing season.

Finish • Won • Lost • Pct • GB

Fifth (tie) 75   87   .463 17.5

Manager

Jim Marshall

Stats

Stats	Cubs	NL	Rank
Batting Avg:	.259	.257	5
On–Base Pct:	.341	.330	3
Slugging Pct:	.368	.369	6
Home Runs:	95		8
Stolen Bases:	67		9
ERA:	4.49	3.62	12
Fielding Avg:	.972	.976	11
Runs Scored:	712		3 (tie)
Runs Allowed:	827		12

Starting Lineup

Steve Swisher, c
Andre Thornton, 1b
Manny Trillo, 2b
Bill Madlock, 3b
Don Kessinger, ss
Jose Cardenal, lf
Rick Monday, cf
Jerry Morales, rf
Pete LaCock, 1b–rf
George Mitterwald, c

Pitchers

Ray Burris, sp
Bill Bonham, sp
Rick Reuschel, sp
Steve Stone, sp
Darold Knowles, rp
Oscar Zamora, rp
Ken Frailing, rp

Attendance

1,034,819 (eighth in NL)

Club Leaders

Batting Avg:	Madlock	.354
On–Base Pct:	Madlock	.402
Slugging Pct:	Madlock	.479
Home Runs:	Thornton	18
RBI:	Morales	91
Runs:	Monday	89
Stolen Bases:	Cardenal	34
Wins:	Burris	15
Strikeouts:	Bonham	165
ERA:	Reuschel	3.73
Saves:	Knowles	15

APRIL 8   Heavy snow in Chicago prevents the Cubs and Pirates from playing the season opener at Wrigley Field. The April 9 game was also postponed.

APRIL 10   In the first game of the season, the Pirates down the Cubs 8–4 in 37–degree weather before 19,239 at Wrigley Field. Willie Stargell hit two homers for Pittsburgh. The second one broke a 4–4 deadlock in the eighth. Rick Monday had three hits for the Cubs.

APRIL 19   The Cubs beat the Mets 4–2 in New York. It was the Cubs seventh win in a row and ran the season record to 7–1.

APRIL 25   Rick Reuschel ties a major league record during a 4–3 win over the Cardinals at Wrigley Field. In the third inning, Reuschel made all three putouts at first base. He beat Ted Simmons to the bag on a grounder, and took throws from Pete LaCock to retire Keith Hernandez and Ken Reitz.

MAY 2   In a deal known the "The Great Arm Robbery," the Cubs trade Burt Hooton to the Dodgers for Geoff Zahn and Eddie Solomon.

The Cubs believed that Hooton would never develop into a winning pitcher, but made a huge miscalculation. Over the remainder of the 1975 season, Hooton was 18–7, including a 12–game winning streak. As a Dodger from 1975 through 1981, Hooton had a record of 96–63 and he pitched in three World Series. Neither Zahn nor Solomon won a single game in Chicago. Solomon is best known for tossing a chair at a Chicago sportswriter. (The throw was high and outside.) The Cubs released Zahn in 1977, but he went on to pitch several fine seasons in the starting rotations of the Twins and Angels.

MAY 4

The Cubs defeat the Cardinals 8–6 in St. Louis to take a four–game lead in the East over the second place Mets with a record of 15–6.

MAY 20

Bill Bonham pitches a two–hitter to beat the Dodgers 2–1 at Dodger Stadium. The only Los Angeles hits were a single by Ron Cey in the second inning and a homer by Lee Lacy in the fourth.

The relief corps was nicknamed "Gasoline Alley" in 1975. Darold Knowles, Tom Dettore, Oscar Zamora, Ken Frailing, and Milt Wilcox combined to pitch in 212 games and had an ERA of 5.32 in 335 innings.

JUNE 3

Bill Madlock ties the score 5–5 with a homer in the ninth, and doubles in another run in the tenth to lift the Cubs to a 6–5 win over the Giants at Wrigley Field.

With the victory, the Cubs had a record of 27–20 and were in first place 1½ games ahead of the Pirates. But, the Cubs dropped out of first on June 6, ending a stay at the top of the Eastern Division that lasted fifty–one days. The Cubs lost 27 of 38 games from June 6 through July 9 to skid out of contention.

JUNE 9

Heavy rains that flooded roads around the Astrodome cause a 54–minute delay in the start of the game between the Cubs and the Astros. The Cubs won 4–3 in ten innings.

JUNE 15

Bill Bonham strikes out 12 batters in a 4–3 win over the Reds at Wrigley Field.

In four consecutive games from June 13 though June 16, Bill Madlock had 14 hits in 18 at–bats.

JUNE 17

Down 5–0, the Cubs score six runs in the fifth inning and three in the sixth to beat the Phillies 9–5 at Wrigley Field.

JUNE 25

The Cubs surrender ten runs in the seventh inning and lose 12–6 to the Expos in Montreal.

JULY 2

Jose Cardenal is hauled off to jail because of an altercation at O'Hare International Airport.

Cardenal's wife, Patricia, went to the airport to pick him up following a road trip. She was warned three times that her car was illegally parked and told to move. Patricia refused, and by the time her husband arrived, she was in a fierce argument with Patrol Officer Dennis Dickson. According to Dickson, Cardenal took his nightstick from him and clubbed him about the head. Jose was taken to the Jefferson Park police station, and charged with simple battery, assaulting a police officer, and resisting arrest. Cardenal alleged that he was the victim of police brutality. The charges against Jose were later dropped, and his wife was fined $250. In August 1976, Cardenal filed a $750,000 suit against the City of

Chicago, Police Superintendent James M. Rochford, and Dickson. The suit charged Dickson with "physically and verbally abusing" Cardenal and his wife. The case was settled out of court.

JULY 6   The Pirates outslug the Cubs 18–12 at Wrigley Field.

JULY 15   Bill Madlock is the co–MVP of the All–Star Game in a tie vote with the similarly named Jon Matlack, a pitcher with the Mets. At County Stadium in Milwaukee, the contest was tied 3–3 in the ninth when Madlock hit a two–run single off Goose Gossage to give the National League the lead. The NL went on to win 6–3.

JULY 19   Steve Stone allows only one hit in 6⅔ innings, but loses 2–1 to the Padres in San Diego because he issues nine walks. Stone walked five in the sixth inning, and both San Diego runs scored on passes with the bases loaded.

JULY 26   Bill Madlock collects six hits in six at–bats with three RBIs, but the Cubs lose 9–8 to the Mets in ten innings. Madlock tripled in his first at–bat, then picked up five straight singles.

JULY 30   Gary Carter of the Expos rounds the bases on a bunt as the Cubs lose 6–1 at Wrigley Field. Third baseman Bill Madlock fielded the ball and threw it past Pete LaCock at first. By the time that LaCock tracked down the ball, Carter had rounded second. LaCock threw wildly to third, and Carter trotted home.

Steve Stone enjoyed his best season as a Cub in 1975 with a 12–8 record. He won 23 games for the team during his three–year stay.

AUGUST 5   Bill Bonham becomes the only pitcher in major league history to give up hits to the first seven batters he faces, as the Cubs lose 13–5 to the Phillies in Philadelphia. Bonham gave up two homers, two doubles and three singles before being lifted in favor of Ken Crosby. The Phillies tied a major league record for most consecutive hits at the start of a game, with eight, when Crosby gave up a single to the first batter he faced.

                In his next start, on August 11, Bonham retired the first 12 batters he faced, and beat the Braves 9–1 in Atlanta with a complete game five–hitter.

AUGUST 21   Rick and Paul Reuschel become the first pair of brothers in major league history to combine on a shutout. Rick pitched the first 6⅓ innings, but had to leave the game because of a blister on his finger. Paul went the final 2⅔ innings to give the Cubs a 7–0 win over the Dodgers at Wrigley Field.

AUGUST 22   Andre Thornton ties a major league record for first baseman with three assists in an
             inning during a 6–5 win, eleven–inning win over the Astros at Wrigley Field. The
             Astros plated a run in the top of the eleventh, but the Cubs came back with two in
             their half to win. The winning run was scored on a bunt single by Jose Cardenal
             which scored Rick Monday from third base.

             *Thornton hit .293 with 18 homers for the Cubs in 1975. Cardenal batted .317,
             had nine homers, and stole 34 bases.*

SEPTEMBER 3 Pete LaCock hits a grand slam off Bob Gibson in the seventh inning of an 11–6 win
             over the Cardinals at St. Louis. It proved to be the final pitch that Gibson threw as
             a major leaguer.

SEPTEMBER 6 Trailing 5–0, the Cubs rally with one run in the fourth inning, four in the fifth, and
             two in the seventh to defeat the Phillies 7–6 in Philadelphia.

SEPTEMBER 9 Bill Madlock is hit on the thumb by a Bruce Kison pitch in the fifth inning of a 6–5
             win over the Pirates in Pittsburgh.

             *Madlock, who was leading the league in batting with a .362 average, was hit by
             the pitch and missed fifteen days. He played the final week of the season, and
             despite his average dropping to .354, Madlock won the first of his four Nation-
             al League batting titles.*

SEPTEMBER 14 Tim Hosley hits a grand slam in the ninth inning off Randy Lerch, but it's too little,
             too late as the Cubs lose 15–7 to the Phillies at Wrigley Field.

SEPTEMBER 16 The Pirates crush the Cubs 22–0 at Wrigley Field in the most lopsided shutout in
             modern major league history. Pittsburgh scored all 22 runs in the first seven innings
             off Rick Reuschel, Tom Dettore, Oscar Zamora, and Buddy Schultz. Rennie Sten-
             nett collected seven hits in seven at–bats with a triple, two doubles, and four sin-
             gles. The Cubs held the record for most runs allowed in a shutout loss until the
             Yankees tied it in a 22–0 loss to the Indians on August 31, 2004 in New York.

SEPTEMBER 24 Rookie outfielder Joe Wallis foils Tom Seaver's bid for a no–hitter in the ninth
             inning of an exciting 1–0, eleven–inning win over the Mets at Wrigley Field. Seaver
             faced Wallis with two out in the ninth and a no–hitter intact when Wallis rapped an
             0–2 pitch into right field for a single. The game went into extra innings with the
             score 0–0. Seaver gave up two more hits in the tenth, and exited the game in the top
             of the eleventh for a pinch–hitter. The Cubs won the contest in the eleventh when
             Mets reliever Skip Lockwood loaded the bases, then walked Bill Madlock. Rick
             Reuschel (ten innings) and Ken Crosby (one inning) combined on the Chicago
             shutout.

SEPTEMBER 29 In another shocking and off–the–wall decision by P. K. Wrigley, E. R. "Salty"
             Saltwell is appointed as the Cubs general manager to replace John Holland, who
             went into semi–retirement.

             *A longtime Cubs employee, Saltwell seemed to have few qualifications for the
             general manager's job. He had been in charge of Wrigley Field operations, con-
             cessions, and radio and TV contracts when Wrigley tapped him for the post. In*

hiring Saltwell, Wrigley bypassed Blake Cullen and Whitey Lockman, who had been working directly under Holland in player development. It was assumed by nearly everyone connected with the club that either Cullen or Lockman would take over as general manager when Holland retired. Cullen resigned to take a job with the National League office. Saltwell lasted only a year as the g.m. Wrigley gave "Salty" his old job back as director of park operations and hired Bob Kennedy as general manager, (See November 24, 1976.)

OCTOBER 28   The Cubs trade Don Kessinger to the Cardinals for Mike Garman and Bobby Hrapman.

Kessinger left as the last link to the 1969 Cubs. He played another four seasons, but was only a shadow of the player he was in the glory days of the late–1960s and early–1970s. During his last season in 1979, Kessinger was the player–manager for the White Sox. Garman was added to provide bullpen help, but his addition to the bullpen didn't help.

1976   Cubs

Season in a Sentence

The Cubs are ridiculed in the press as "Marshall's Marshmallows" and dismissed by P. K. Wrigley as a "bunch of clowns" during a long summer in which there is little to smile about at Wrigley Field.

Finish • Won • Lost • Pct • GB

Fourth   75   87   .463   26.0

Manager

Jim Marshall

Stats

Stats	Cubs	NL	Rank
Batting Avg:	.251	.255	6
On–Base Pct:	.316	.323	8
Slugging Pct:	.356	.361	5
Home Runs:	105		4
Stolen Bases:	74		10 (tie)
ERA:	3.93	3.50	11
Fielding Avg:	.978	.977	5
Runs Scored:	611		8
Runs Allowed:	728		11

Starting Lineup

Steve Swisher, c
Pete LaCock, 1b
Manny Trillo, 2b
Bill Madlock, 3b
Mick Kelleher, ss
Jose Cardenal, lf
Rick Monday, cf
Jerry Morales, rf
Joe Wallis, cf
George Mitterwald, c
Dave Rosello, ss
Larry Biittner, 1b–lf

Pitchers

Ray Burris, sp
Rick Reuschel, sp
Bill Bonham, sp
Steve Renko, sp
Bruce Sutter, rp
Darold Knowles, rp
Paul Reuschel, rp
Mike Garman, rp

Attendance

1,026,217 (seventh in NL)

Club Leaders

Batting Avg:	Madlock	.339
On–Base Pct:	Madlock	.412
Slugging Pct:	Monday	.507
Home Runs:	Monday	32
RBI:	Madlock	84
Runs:	Monday	107
Stolen Bases:	Cardenal	23
Wins:	Burris	15
Strikeouts:	Reuschel	146
ERA:	Burris	3.11
Saves:	Sutter	10

APRIL 9   The Cubs lose the season opener 5–0 to the Cardinals in St. Louis. Lynn
               McGlothlen pitched the shutout.

APRIL 13   The Cubs beat the Mets 5–4 with a run in the ninth inning in the first 1976 game
               played at Wrigley Field. The game–winning tally was scored on a triple by Manny
               Trillo and a single by Rick Monday. Jerry Morales hit a home run. Attendance was
               44,818.

               *On the same day, the Cubs brought back a Wrigley Field favorite by purchasing
               Randy Hundley from the Padres.*

APRIL 14   In his first game back with the Cubs, Randy Hundley hits a three–run homer in the
               seventh inning to beat the Mets 6–5 at Wrigley Field. Hundley entered the game as
               a defensive replacement in the top of the inning with the Mets leading 5–3.

               *Also in the game, Dave Kingman of the Mets hit the longest home run in
               Wrigley Field history. The drive carried 550 feet over Waveland Avenue, and
               after bouncing a few times, struck the side of a house three doors down from
               the corner on the east side of Kenmore Avenue. The residents of the house
               poured out onto the front porch to see what was knocking at their wall.
               Kingman hit the same house when he was playing for the Cubs in 1979
               with a drive off Ron Reed of the Phillies.*

APRIL 17   Mike Schmidt hits four consecutive homers and drives in eight runs as the Phillies
               rally from an 11–run deficit to defeat the Cubs 18–16 in ten innings at Wrigley
               Field. The Cubs scored seven runs in the second, and led 12–1 after three innings
               and 13–2 after four. The Phillies scored two runs in the fifth inning on Schmidt's
               first homer off Rick Reuschel. Three were added in the seventh, one on Schmidt's
               second home run, again off Reuschel. Philadelphia scored five in the eighth, three
               on Schmidt's third home run, this time off Paul Reuschel. In the ninth inning, the
               Phils scored three times to pull ahead 15–13. The Cubs finally woke up in their half
               to plate two tallies and tie the score 15–15. In the tenth, Schmidt tied a major
               league record for most homers in a game with four by hitting a two–run shot off
               Darold Knowles over the center field wall to make the score 17–15. Each club
               added one more run for the 18–16 final.

APRIL 25   On the 100th anniversary of the first game in Cubs history, Rick Monday rescues
               the American flag during a 5–4, ten–inning loss to the Dodgers in Los Angeles.

               *Playing center field, Monday noticed two fans climb out of the stands and run
               to left–center in the fourth inning. One of them was holding something under
               his arm. As the man unfurled his bundle and spread it on the field, Monday
               recognized that it was an American flag. As he later recalled, "I saw they had a
               can of something and were pouring it over the flag. That's when I started to
               move." Before the men could set the flag on fire, Monday swept in, snatched it
               away, and carried it to the bullpen. As he ran off, security personnel moved in
               and arrested the intruders. The crowd gave Monday a standing ovation, and
               burst out with "God Bless America." Overnight, Monday became a hero in the
               year of the nation's bicentennial, and received more recognition for the flag inci-
               dent than anything else he did during a 19–year playing career. The Illinois leg-
               islature proclaimed a statewide "Rick Monday Day," and he was named grand*

marshall of the Flag Day parade in Chicago. The flag Monday rescued was presented to him by Dodgers vice–president Al Campanis in pre–game ceremonies at Wrigley Field on May 4. The pair who attempted to burn the flag were William Thomas of Eldon, Missouri, and his 11–year–old son, who were protesting the treatment of Native Americans. They were charged with trespassing.

MAY 1   A brawl breaks out during a 3–1 loss to the Giants in San Francisco.

Giants pitcher Jim Barr brushed back Rick Monday in the first inning, Steve Swisher in the second, and nearly hit Jose Cardenal in the head in the third. Jose threw his helmet at Barr. Bill Madlock, hitting next, was hit by a pitch and charged the mound setting off a fight between the two clubs. The Cubs were livid because both Cardenal and Madlock were ejected, while Barr was allowed to stay in the game. The only Giant to be tossed by the umpires was Gary Matthews for punching George Mitterwald, who was striving to pull two other combatants apart. The brawl was especially costly to Randy Hundley, who snapped a disk during the battle, and underwent a cervical fusion operation on June 7. With the exception of two games late in the 1977 season, Hundley never played another game.

MAY 5   With the aid of a thirty–one–mile–per–hour wind, the Dodgers hit seven homers to outslug the Cubs 14–12 at Wrigley Field. Rick Monday hit two homers and a single, drove in six runs, and scored four times. The Cubs collected 21 hits in the loss.

Monday hit 32 homers, scored 107 runs, and batted .272 for the Cubs in 1976. He led off the first inning of eight games with homers, the all–time club record for a season.

MAY 12   The Cubs beat the Giants 1–0 in 11 innings at Wrigley Field. The game was decided on Steve Swisher's RBI–single. Rick Reuschel pitched ten innings and allowed only one hit. Mike Garman picked–up the win with an inning of relief.

MAY 17   The Cubs trade Andre Thornton to the Expos for Steve Renko and Larry Biittner.

Thornton couldn't get along with Jim Marshall, and the Cubs made a foolish trade by dealing a budding star. Renko had an undistinguished two seasons in Chicago, while Biittner was never more than a spare outfielder and first baseman. He could hit, but poor glove work kept him from becoming an every day player. It was said that Biittner was the only player in baseball with two "i's" and no hands.

MAY 21   A 5–4 Cubs win over the Pirates in Pittsburgh is umpired by amateurs because the National League crew refuses to cross a vendor's picket line outside the stadium.

JUNE 4   Rick Reuschel pitches a two–hitter, but loses 1–0 to the Astros in Houston. The run was unearned because of Reuschel's own error, charged when he threw wildly to first base on a Jose Cruz grounder in the first inning.

JUNE 8   The Cubs purchase Joe Coleman from the Tigers.

JUNE 18   Bill Madlock hits a grand slam in the seventh inning off Max Leon during a 6–4 win over the Braves in Atlanta.

JUNE 24   Jerry Morales smashes a walk–off homer in the 13th inning to beat the Pirates 2–1 at Wrigley Field. In the ninth, Morales doubled and crossed the plate on George Mitterwald's single to tie the score 1–1.

JULY 4   On the day the nation celebrates the Bicentennial, the Cubs split a double–header in New York, losing 9–4 to the Mets and winning 4–2.

JULY 5   The Cubs defeat the Padres 1–0 at Wrigley Field. Steve Renko (seven innings) and Joe Coleman (two innings) combined on the shutout.

JULY 6   Steve Stone (six innings) and Bruce Sutter (three innings) combine to shutout the Padres 4–0 at Wrigley Field.

JULY 7   Rick Reuschel pitches a complete game to defeat the Padres 10–0 at Wrigley Field. It was the third straight shutout by Cubs pitchers, all against San Diego.

JULY 15   Before a game against the Dodgers in Los Angeles, comedian Jonathan Winters entertains the Cubs in the visitor's clubhouse. Winters put on a Cubs cap and did a pantomime of a Cubs pitcher giving up a home run, a feeling the real Cubs pitchers knew all too well.

The Cubs hit the low ebb of the season on July 27 with a record of 39–58. From that point for-ward, the club was 36–29. From July 28, 1976 through June 28, 1977, the Cubs were 83–51.

Bruce Sutter emerged in 1976 to become the league's dominant closer, giving the bullpen its first reliable stopper in several years.

JULY 28   Manny Trillo smashes a three–run homer in the eleventh inning to beat the Phillies 5–2 at Veterans Stadium. Philadel-phia walked Pete LaCock intentionally to get to Trillo.

AUGUST 1   The Cubs are held hitless by John Denny of the Cardinals for 7⅔ innings, but rally to win 2–1 in ten innings at Wrigley Field. Pete LaCock drove in the winning run with a single.

AUGUST 6   The Cubs sweep the Expos 6–5 and 1–0 with key homers in a double–header in Montreal. In the first game, Rick Monday homered in the thirteenth inning to give the Cubs the win. In the nightcap, Jerry Morales accounted for the lone run with a ninth–inning circuit clout off Joe Kerrigan. Steve Stone pitched the shutout.

AUGUST 7   Rick Monday hits an extra–inning home run in the first game of a double–header
               for the second day in a row at Olympic Stadium. Monday's two–run homer in the
               eleventh put the Cubs up 4–2. The Expos came back with a run in their half to
               make the final 4–3. Montreal won the second game 7–2.

AUGUST 11   The Cubs score seven runs in the second and lead the Reds 10–1 after three innings
               at Wrigley Field, but blow the nine–run advantage and wind up losing 13–10 in ten
               innings.

AUGUST 14   George Mitterwald drives in both runs on a single and a sacrifice fly during a 2–0
               win over the Dodgers at Wrigley Field. Ray Burris pitched the shutout.

SEPTEMBER 1   The Cubs defeat the Braves 7–5 in fourteen innings in Atlanta. Jerry Morales led
               the way with four hits and four runs–batted–in.

SEPTEMBER 11   Champ Summers hits a three–run, pinch–hit homer in the twelfth inning to defeat
               the Phillies 4–1 in Philadelphia.

SEPTEMBER 16   The Cubs play at Jarry Park in Montreal for the last time, and lose 4–3 to the
               Expos.

               The Expos moved into Olympic Stadium in 1977.

SEPTEMBER 16   Jerry Morales hits a homer off Jim Lonborg in the second inning to defeat the
               Phillies 1–0 at Wrigley Field. Ray Burris pitched the shutout.

SEPTEMBER 26   Bill Madlock is mugged in his room at the Waldorf–Astoria Hotel in New York.
               Two men hit him on the head and took $50. Madlock missed several games with a
               headache and dizziness.

OCTOBER 3   Bill Madlock collects four hits in four at–bats in the final game of the season to win
               his second consecutive batting title. The Cubs defeated the Expos 8–2 at Wrigley
               Field.

               *Going into the final day, Ken Griffey, Sr. of the Reds was batting .337 with
               Madlock at .333. Cincinnati manager Sparky Anderson kept Griffey out of the
               game against the Braves at Riverfront Stadium in order to allow his outfielder
               to preserve his lead in the batting race. In order to pass Griffey, Madlock had to
               pick up four hits in a maximum of five at–bats. In the first inning, Madlock laid
               down a perfect bunt for a hit. In the second, he beat out a roller down the third
               base line. Madlock's third plate appearance came in the fourth inning, and he
               delivered a single into right. He now trailed Griffey .3375 to .3372. Madlock
               took the lead when he laced a single into left in the sixth. Griffey was now the
               pursuer, and Anderson hustled him into the game in Cincinnati as a pinch–hit-
               ter. Griffey struck out, remained in the game, and was retired again. Jim Mar-
               shall lifted Madlock for pinch–hitter Rob Sperring in the eighth. Madlock
               finished the season with a .339 average, while Griffey ended up at .336. It
               proved to be Madlock's last game as a Cub. He was traded to the Giants on
               February 11, 1977.*

NOVEMBER 24   Three weeks after Jimmy Carter is elected president over Gerald Ford, Bob Kennedy replaces "Salty" Saltwell as general manager, and Herman Franks replaced Jim Marshall as manager. A week later, Whitey Lockman was relieved of his duties as director of player personnel. In addition, John Holland went from semi–retirement to permanent retirement.

Kennedy was returning to the Cubs after an absence of twelve years. He served as manager (although his official title was head coach) for the club from 1963 through 1965. Kennedy was a scout for the Cardinals at the time he was chosen by P. K. Wrigley to run the Cubs organization as general manager. Kennedy's first move was to fire Jim Marshall as manager and hire Herman Franks, who turned 63 before spring training started in 1977. Franks was a protégé of Leo Durocher, and like Durocher, was crude, loud, and outspoken.

DECEMBER 6   The Cubs draft Willie Hernandez from the Phillies organization.

DECEMBER 8   The Cubs trade Julio Gonzalez to the Astros for Greg Gross. On the same day, the Cubs were part of a three–team trade in which they sent Pete LaCock to the Royals and received Jim Dwyer from the Mets.

1977

Season in a Sentence

The Cubs electrify the city of Chicago with a 47–22 record and an 8 ½–game lead on June 28, but drop out of first place in early August, ending back at the .500 mark by the end of the season.

Finish • Won • Lost • Pct • GB

Fourth   81   81   .500   20.0

Manager

Herman Franks

Stats

Stats	Cubs	NL	Rank
Batting Avg:	.266	.262	5
On–Base Pct:	.333	.331	5
Slugging Pct:	.387	.396	7
Home Runs:	111		10
Stolen Bases:	64		12
ERA:	4.01	3.91	8
Fielding Avg:	.977	.977	9
Runs Scored:	692		7
Runs Allowed:	739		10

Starting Lineup

George Mitterwald, c
Bill Buckner, 1b
Manny Trillo, 2b
Steve Ontiveros, 3b
Ivan DeJesus, ss
Larry Biittner, lf–1b
Jerry Morales, cf
Bobby Murcer, rf
Greg Gross, lf–cf
Gene Clines, lf
Jose Cardenal, lf
Steve Swisher, c

Pitchers

Rick Reuschel, sp
Ray Burris, sp
Bill Bonham, sp
Mike Krukow, sp
Bruce Sutter, rp
Willie Hernandez, rp
Paul Reuschel, rp

Attendance

1,439,834 (fifth in NL)

Club Leaders

Batting Avg:	Ontiveros	.299
On–Base Pct:	Ontiveros	.390
Slugging Pct:	Murcer	.455
Home Runs:	Murcer	27
RBI:	Murcer	89
Runs:	DeJesus	91
Stolen Bases:	DeJesus	24
Wins:	Reuschel	20
Strikeouts:	Reuschel	166
ERA:	Reuschel	2.79
Saves:	Sutter	31

JANUARY 11   Three weeks after the death of Mayor Richard Daley, the Cubs trade Rick Monday and Mike Garman to the Dodgers for Bill Buckner, Ivan DeJesus, and Jeff Albert.

Monday was traded because his salary demands were deemed excessive by P. K. Wrigley. Rick was 31 and coming off of a terrific season, but his batting numbers tailed off as a Dodger. Although he played eight seasons in Los Angeles, Monday was never more than a spare outfielder and pinch–hitter. Buckner, at first base, and DeJesus, at shortstop, were starters for the Cubs for several years in what proved to be an excellent deal.

JANUARY 19   Ernie Banks is elected to the Hall of Fame in his first year on the ballot. He was formally inducted in ceremonies at Cooperstown on August 8.

FEBRUARY 5   The Cubs send Darold Knowles to the Rangers for Gene Clines and cash.

FEBRUARY 11   The Cubs trade Bill Madlock and Rob Sperring to the Giants for Bobby Murcer, Steve Ontiveros, and Andy Muhlstock.

Like Rick Monday, Madlock was dealt during a salary dispute with Cubs management. Unlike the Monday trade, the Giants deal was a step backward. Madlock won two more batting titles and finished his career in 1985 with a lifetime batting average of .305. Murcer and Ontiveros each gave the Cubs one decent season. Murcer hit 27 homers for the Cubs in 1977, and Ontiveros batted .299. Murcer is also remembered for relaxing in the clubhouse in a rocking chair, which he took on road trips. Ontiveros is best remembered in Chicago for doing testimonials for a scalp treatment clinic that specialized in restoring the hair on the heads of balding men.

MARCH 15   The Cubs trade Joe Coleman to the Athletics for Jim Todd.

APRIL 7   The Cubs lose the season opener 5–3 to the Mets before 39,937 at Wrigley Field. In his first game as a Cub, Steve Ontiveros homered in the fourth inning to put his new club ahead 2–0. In the sixth, the Mets scored four runs, in part because right fielder Bobby Murcer and center fielder Jerry Morales collided chasing a fly ball, which fell for a double. Larry Biittner had three hits.

APRIL 12   P. K. Wrigley dies at the age of 82. He was stricken with a gastro–intestinal hemorrhage while watching the Cubs on television at his Wisconsin retreat.

Wrigley left an estate valued at $60,350,000. Control of the Wrigley empire, including the Cubs, passed to P. K.'s 44–year–old son William. The Wrigley family continued to own the Cubs until 1981 when the ball club was sold to the Tribune Company.

APRIL 17   For the third time in his career, Tom Seaver narrowly misses pitching a no–hitter against the Cubs. The only Chicago hit was a single by Steve Ontiveros in the third inning. The Mets won 6–0 at Wrigley Field.

APRIL 27   The Cardinals overwhelm the Cubs 21–3 at Wrigley Field.

The Cubs finished the month of April with a record of 7–9. It was followed by a surge in which it seemed that the club couldn't lose. The Cubs were 40–13 from May 1 through June 28.

MAY 13   The Cubs play at Olympic Stadium in Montreal for the first time, and defeat the Expos 5–3.

MAY 20   The Cubs rout the Braves 13–4 in Atlanta.

MAY 26   Mike Krukow pitches the Cubs to a 1–0 win over the Expos at Wrigley Field. The lone run of the game was scored in the sixth inning on a bases–loaded walk to Bobby Murcer.

MAY 28   The Cubs move into first place, beating the Pirates 6–3 at Wrigley Field. The five–run fifth inning wiped out a 2–0 Pittsburgh lead.

The Cubs remained in first place until August 4.

MAY 29   Cubs fans, aroused by the possibility of the club's first pennant since 1945, give the players a standing ovation *before* the May 29 game against the Pirates with 39,403 packing Wrigley Field. The Cubs rewarded the fans with two runs in the eighth to defeat the Pirates 3–2. The victory gave the Cubs 21 wins in their last 26 games and an overall season record of 28–14.

JUNE 7   The Cubs select pitcher Randy Martz from the University of South Carolina in the first round of the amateur draft.

Martz pitched three years with the Cubs, and had a record of 17–19. It was another fruitless draft in which the Cubs chose no impact players. The only other athletes drafted and signed by the Cubs in 1977 who reached the majors were Dan Rohn (fourth round), Steve Macko (fifth) and Gary Krug (29th).

JUNE 9   The Cubs beat the Giants 1–0 in eleven innings at Wrigley Field. The winning run was scored on a squeeze bunt by Jose Cardenal which scored Mick Kelleher from third base. Bill Bonham (9 ⅓ innings), and Bruce Sutter (1 ⅔ innings) combined on the shutout.

JUNE 20   Bobby Murcer drives in six runs on a homer and two doubles during a 10–9, twelve–inning win over the Giants in San Francisco. Mick Kelleher drove in the winning run with a triple.

JUNE 25   The never–say–die Cubs score four runs in the ninth inning to defeat the Mets 5–4 at Wrigley Field. Larry Biittner drove in the first two runs with a double, and scored on another double by Bill Buckner. After two walks, a Manny Trillo grounder scored the winning run from third.

JUNE 28   The streaking Cubs win their eighth game in a row with two runs in the tenth to defeat the Expos 4–2 in Montreal.

The win gave the Cubs a record of 47–22 and an 8 ½–game lead in the Eastern Division. Once again, Cubs fans began hallucinating about baseball at Wrigley Field in October.

JULY 2   The Cubs commit seven errors, including five in the first inning, and lose 10–3 to the Cardinals in St. Louis.

JULY 4   The Cubs lose a double–header 19–3 and 7–6 to the Expos at Wrigley Field. Outfielder–first baseman Larry Biittner pitched the last 1⅓ innings, and gave up three homers and six runs.

JULY 13   A blackout of electrical power in New York City strikes during a game between the Cubs and the Mets at Shea Stadium.

The lights went out at 9:31 P.M., with Lenny Randle at bat for the Mets and the Cubs leading 2–1 in the bottom of the sixth. An auxiliary generator kept the public address system and some of the lights in the seating areas operating, but it wasn't powerful enough to keep the field lights turned on. The game was suspended at 10:52 P.M. with the intention of completing it before the regularly scheduled contest the next evening. The Cubs showered and dressed in a dark locker room and went back to the Waldorf-Astoria Hotel. With the elevators out, players had to take the stairs holding candles to their rooms, some as high as the 17th floor. There was also no air conditioning. The next day, the Cubs took their luggage back down stairs, went to Shea Stadium, dressed again in the dark, only to be told that the suspended and regularly scheduled games were called off because power was not yet restored. The Cubs took a bus to Philadelphia, where they lost a double–header on July 15. The suspended game was finished two months later on the Cubs next trip to New York. (See September 16, 1977.)

JULY 22   Rick Reuschel pitches the Cubs to a 1–0 shutout of the Braves at Wrigley Field.

JULY 25   Bill Bonham carries a two–hitter and a 7–0 lead into the eighth inning when the Astros explode for seven runs to tie the score at Wrigley Field. The Cubs came back with two runs in their half of the eighth on a home run by Larry Biittner to win 9–7.

After five years of hard–luck outings for the Cubs, Rick Reuschel became a 20–game winner in 1977.

JULY 28   The Cubs and the Reds combine for 11 homers at Wrigley Field to tie a National League record. Five of the homers were struck in the first inning, to tie another record. The Cubs won 16–15 in thirteen innings. For Chicago, Bill Buckner and George Mitterwald each hit two homers, with Bobby Murcer and Jerry Morales adding one apiece. Pete Rose, Johnny Bench, Mike Lum, Ken Griffey, Sr., and Cesar Geronimo went deep for the Reds. The Reds took a 6–0 lead in the first inning, but the Cubs went ahead 7–6 in the second. The score was 10–10 at the end of four innings. After the Reds took a 14–10 lead, the Cubs scored three runs in the eighth and one in the ninth to knot the skirmish at 14–14. Steve Ontiveros tied the score with an RBI–single with two out. The Reds took the lead 15–14 in the twelfth, but Mitterwald tied it 15–15 with a homer. The Cubs won in the thirteenth on singles by Rick Reuschel, Steve Ontiveros and Dave Rosello. Appearing in relief two days after pitching a complete game shutout, Reuschel was the winning pitching, running his record on the season to 15–3.

The Cubs and the White Sox entered August in first place. It was the first time that both Chicago teams were in first in August since 1907.

AUGUST 3   Bruce Sutter goes on the disabled list with swelling in his shoulder.

With a baffling split–fingered fastball, Sutter was almost unhittable during the early part of the 1977 season. He was the first to use the pitch effectively in the majors. The ball looked like a fastball, but at the last minute, it broke like a curveball. Extreme overwork put Sutter on the shelf for a month just after the 1977 All–Star Game. Without him coming out of the bullpen, the Cubs completely collapsed late in the season. Through the first 88 games of 1977, Sutter was 5–1 with 24 saves and a 1.11 ERA. But he had pitched in 45 games and 81 innings, an unbearable load for a reliever, causing a breakdown. Sutter returned in September, and finished the season with 62 games, 107 innings, a 7–3 record, 31 saves, and a 1.35 earned run average. He learned the split–fingered fastball in 1973 from Cubs minor league pitching coach Fred Martin. At the time, Sutter's career appeared to be going nowhere, but with exceptionally large hands and long fingers, he mastered the pitch well enough to become one of the best relievers in baseball history.

AUGUST 5   The Cubs fall out of first place with an 11–8 loss to the Padres at Wrigley Field. The Cubs had been in first since May 28. The club quickly dropped out of contention during the late–summer of 1977, posting a 16–35 record from August 10 to the end of the season.

On the same day, the Cubs purchase Dave Giusti from the Athletics.

AUGUST 7   The second game of a double–header against the Padres at Wrigley Field is marred by a free–for–all after six–foot–six, 210–pound Dave Kingman of San Diego slams into five–foot–nine, 176–pound Cubs second baseman Mick Kelleher trying to break up a double play. The two got up and started fighting, causing both benches to clear. The Cubs won 9–4. The Padres captured the first tilt 8–6.

AUGUST 10   The Cubs lose an eighteen–inning marathon 2–1 to the Pirates in Pittsburgh. A sacrifice fly by Ed Ott off Pete Broberg drove in the game–winner.

AUGUST 14   The Cubs lose a double–header 10–2 and 4–2 to the Phillies. The twin defeats were part of a four–game sweep of the Cubs at Wrigley Field that left Chicago seven games back of first–place Philadelphia.

AUGUST 16   On the day Elvis Presley dies in Memphis, the Cubs defeat the Pirates 6–5 in fifteen innings at Wrigley Field. Bobby Murcer scored the winning run from second base on a throwing error by Pittsburgh second baseman Rennie Stennett.

AUGUST 18   The Cubs trade Steve Renko to the White Sox for Larry Anderson.

SEPTEMBER 8   Bruce Sutter fans the first six batters he faces in the eighth and ninth innings, then pitches a scoreless tenth to beat the Expos 3–2 at Wrigley Field. In the eighth, Sutter struck out Warren Cromartie, Andre Dawson, and Tony Perez. In the ninth, he fanned Ellis Valentine, Gary Parrish, and Larry Parrish on the minimum nine pitches.

SEPTEMBER 9   A two–run, walk–off, pinch–hit homer by Gene Clines in the ninth inning beats the Mets 10–8 at Wrigley Field.

SEPTEMBER 16   The game interrupted by the July 13 blackout in New York is completed. It was picked up where it left off, with the Cubs leading 2–1 in the bottom of the sixth inning. The Mets tied the score 2–2 in the seventh, but the Cubs won 5–2 with two runs in the eighth and another in the ninth. Ray Burris, who pitched 5 ⅓ innings on July 13 and 3 ⅔ on September 16 was credited a complete game that took sixty–six days to finish. The Cubs and Mets were supposed to play another game after the completion of the suspended contest, but it was rained out.

SEPTEMBER 18   Rick Reuschel wins his 20th game of 1977 with a 6–3 win over the Mets in the first game of a double–header at Shea Stadium. New York won the second game 6–0.

                 Reuschel had a record of 19–5 on August 30 and seemed headed for the Cy Young Award, then lost five of his last six decisions to finish at 20–10. He had an ERA of 2.79.

SEPTEMBER 26   The Cubs collect 20 hits and defeat the Phillies 10–7 at Wrigley Field.

OCTOBER 25   The Cubs trade Jose Cardenal to the Phillies for Manny Seaone.

OCTOBER 31   The Cubs trade Bill Bonham to the Reds for Woodie Fryman and Bill Caudill.

NOVEMBER 30   The Cubs sign Dave Kingman, most recently with the Yankees, as a free agent.

                 Kingman was the Cubs first free agent signing after the system went into place at the end of the 1976 season. Often sullen and moody with streaks of juvenile behavior, Kingman played three seasons for the Cubs and hit 94 homers accompanied by a .278 batting average.

DECEMBER 8   The Cubs send Jerry Morales, Steve Swisher, and cash to the Cardinals for Dave Rader and Hector Cruz.

1978   Cubs

Season in a Sentence

The Cubs hold first place for over a month and become known as the "Grubby Cubbies" after they grow beards to create a new "identity," but are unable to prevent another late-season collapse.

Finish • Won • Lost • Pct • GB

Third   79   83   .488 11.0

Manager

Herman Franks

Stats

Stats	Cubs	NL	Rank
Batting Avg:	.264	.254	1
On-Base Pct:	.334	.323	3
Slugging Pct:	.361	.372	8
Home Runs:	72		11
Stolen Bases:	110		7
ERA:	4.05	3.58	11
Fielding Avg:	.978	.976	7
Runs Scored:	664		5
Runs Allowed:	724		11

Starting Lineup

Dave Rader, c
Bill Buckner, 1b
Manny Trillo, 2b
Steve Ontiveros, 3b
Ivan DeJesus, ss
Dave Kingman, lf
Greg Gross, cf–lf
Bobby Murcer, rf
Larry Biittner, 1b–lf
Gene Clines, lf–rf
Rodney Scott, 3b
Mike Vail, rf

Pitchers

Rick Reuschel, sp
Dennis Lamp, sp
Ray Burris, sp
Mike Krukow, sp
Dave Roberts, sp–rp
Bruce Sutter, rp
Donnie Moore, rp
Willie Hernandez, rp
Lynn McGlothen, rp

Attendance

1,525,311 (sixth in NL)

Club Leaders

Batting Avg:	Buckner	.323
On-Base Pct:	Murcer	.376
Slugging Pct:	Kingman	.542
Home Runs:	Kingman	28
RBI:	Kingman	79
Runs:	DeJesus	104
Stolen Bases:	DeJesus	51
Wins:	Reuschel	14
Strikeouts:	Reuschel	115
ERA:	Lamp	3.30
Saves:	Sutter	27

APRIL 7   The Cubs lose 1–0 on Opening Day to the Pirates in Pittsburgh. Rick Reuschel allowed only three hits. The only run was scored on a ground out by Willie Stargell in the sixth inning that scored Frank Taveras from third base. John Candelaria pitched the shutout.

The Cubs unveiled new road uniforms in 1978 with white pinstripes on a light blue background. A problem developed, because it was nearly impossible to read the royal blue numbers on the Columbia blue background from the stands. The Cubs wore the pinstriped road uniforms through the 1981 season.

APRIL 14   A crowd of 45,777 at Wrigley Field enjoys the home opener as the Cubs defeat the Pirates 5–4 on a walk–off homer by Larry Biittner.

APRIL 26   Bobby Murcer hits a grand slam in the third inning off Steve Carlton to account for all of the Cubs runs in a 4–2 victory over the Phillies in Philadelphia.

MAY 14   On Mother's Day, Dave Kingman blasts three home runs and drives in eight runs as the Cubs outlast the Dodgers for a thrilling 10–7 triumph in fifteen innings in Los Angeles. The first homer was hit off Doug Rau in the sixth inning with a man on base. In the seventh, Kingman drove in a run with a single. The second homer, also with a runner on base, tied the score 7–7 in the ninth. Ex–Cub Mike Garman was the pitching victim. In the fifteenth, Kingman won the game with a three–run homer off Rick Rhoden.

In his first season with the Cubs, Kingman hit 28 homers and batted .266. Ivan DeJesus was another offensive standout in 1978. He led the league in runs scored with 104, and hit .278 with 41 stolen bases.

MAY 24   The Cubs take first place with a 6–4, ten–inning win over the Phillies at Wrigley Field. Manny Trillo ended the game with a two–run homer into the left field bleachers. The contest was tied on a two–run triple by Greg Gross in the ninth inning.

MAY 28   The Cubs win their eighth game in a row with a 2–0 victory over the Cardinals in St. Louis. The contest was called in the sixth inning by rain. Dave Kingman drove in both runs with a first–inning single. Ray Burris pitched the shutout and allowed only two hits.

The win gave the Cubs a record of 24–17 and a 3½–game lead in the East.

JUNE 6   Dave Kingman hits a grand slam in the sixth inning off Oscar Zamora during a 9–4 win over the Astros at Wrigley Field.

JUNE 9   Dennis Lamp pitches a one–hitter to defeat the Padres 5–0 at Wrigley Field. The only San Diego hit was a single by Gene Richards with two out in the sixth inning. The win put the Cubs ten games over .500 at 31–21.

On the same day, the Cubs traded Woodie Fryman to the Expos for Jerry White.

JUNE 10   The Cubs trade Ron Davis to the Yankees for Ken Holtzman.

Cubs fans were excited about the return of Holtzman, but this proved to be a terrible trade. In his second go–around with the Cubs, Holtzman played two years and was 6–12 with an ERA of 5.06. Davis had several outstanding seasons with the Yankees and the Twins as a flame–throwing reliever.

JUNE 15   The Cubs trade Hector Cruz to the Cardinals for Lynn McGlothen.

JUNE 19   The Cubs increase their lead in the Eastern Division to three games with a 6–4, ten–inning win over the Pirates in Pittsburgh.

The Cubs were in first place after June 1 in 1967, 1969, 1970, 1973, 1975, 1977 and 1978, but failed to win a single pennant.

JUNE 25   The Phillies complete a four–game sweep in Philadelphia by defeating the Cubs 4–2. The Cubs went into the series with a two–game lead in the East, and exited two games out.

The Cubs never reached first again in 1978.

JUNE 26   Dave Rader hits a pinch–hit grand slam in the fifth inning off Dale Murray during a

10–9 win over the Mets at Wrigley Field. Rader's slam put the Cubs ahead 9–7.

JUNE 28   A bases–loaded squeeze by Mick Kelleher in the tenth inning scores Dave Kingman from third base, giving the Cubs a 9–8 triumph over the Mets at Wrigley Field.

JULY 11   Bruce Sutter is the winning pitcher in the All–Star Game, played in San Diego. Sutter retired all five batters he faced, including two strikeouts, as the National League won 7–3.

JULY 18   The Giants score twice in the tenth inning, but the Cubs come back with two in their half and another in the eleventh to win 7–6 at Wrigley Field. A sacrifice fly by Greg Gross drove in the winning run.

In 1978, the Cubs led the league in batting average with a .261 mark, but were only 11th in home runs. Chicago had 110 stolen bases and only 72 homers (28 of which were hit by Dave Kingman). The combination of speed and lack of power was unusual for a Cubs team. It was the fewest home runs of any Cubs team since 1947, and the highest number of stolen bases since 1924.

JULY 20   The Cubs–Giants game at Wrigley Field is suspended by darkness in the top of the eighth inning with San Francisco leading 9–8. The game was interrupted three times by rain. The Giants dugout was flooded, and the team had to make their way to the playing field via the stands. The problem was solved when groundskeeper Cotton Bogren dipped his hand down and extracted a paper cup from the drain, and the water swirled out in an instant. The game was completed in San Francisco on July 28 before the regularly scheduled contest. There was no more scoring, and the Giants won 9–8.

JULY 28   Dennis Lamp pitches a shutout to defeat the Giants 1–0 in San Francisco. A single by Jerry White in the seventh inning drove in the lone run.

Lamp pitched in hard luck all year. He had a 3.29 ERA and three shutouts, but with a lack of batting support, he had a record of only 7–15.

AUGUST 6   The Cubs trade Larry Anderson to the Phillies for Davy Johnson.

AUGUST 15   The Cubs bombard the Braves 13–7 at Wrigley Field. Cubs pitcher Dave Roberts gave up back–to–back–to–back homers in the third inning to Gary Matthews, Jeff Burroughs, and Bob Horner.

In August, many of the Cubs grew beards in order to make them look fiercer on the field and to give the team a new "identity." The idea was hatched by Bruce Sutter, and earned the club the nickname "Grubby Cubbies." "If they want to look like idiots that's all right with me," said general manager Bob Kennedy, who was an ex–Marine. "If it helps them win let 'em grow 'em down to the ground." Herman Franks added, "I'll try to grow one myself if we're in first place in September." The beards didn't help, and the Cubs weren't in first place in September.

AUGUST 27   The Cubs complete a three–game sweep of the Reds in Cincinnati with a 7–1 win. The victory put the Cubs only 2 ½ games behind the Phillies with a record of 66–62.

SEPTEMBER 1   The Cubs score in all eight turns at bat, and outlast the Astros 14–11 at Wrigley Field.

SEPTEMBER 3   In his first two at–bats in the major leagues, Scot Thompson drives in runs in both ends of a double–header with pinch–hits to help the Cubs sweep the Astros 3–2 and 4–2 at Wrigley Field.

SEPTEMBER 5   The Cubs and the Expos use 45 players, the most ever by two teams in a nine–inning major league game. Herman Franks put 24 Cubs players into the game, but his club lost 10–8 at Wrigley Field when Montreal scored four times in the eighth inning.

Bill Buckner shows off his many "disco" chains, a trendy fashion in 1978. His .323 batting average led the team that year.

SEPTEMBER 10   Bobby Murcer collects five hits, including two doubles, in five at–bats during a 6–3 win over Expos in Montreal.

SEPTEMBER 11   Bobby Murcer collects three hits, including a homer, in three at–bats leading the Cubs to a 9–4 win over the Mets in New York. Combined with his five–for–five performance the day before, Murcer had hits in eight consecutive at–bats.

SEPTEMBER 15   Cardinals catcher Terry Kennedy, son of Cubs general manager Bob Kennedy, collects his first major league hit and helps beat the Cubs 6–2 in twelve innings at Wrigley Field.

Terry Kennedy went on to enjoy a 14–year major league career which included four selections to the All–Star team.

SEPTEMBER 19   The Cubs suffer a tough 12–11, eleven–inning loss to the Pirates at Wrigley Field. Down 10–2, the Cubs rallied with five runs in the seventh inning, and after the Pittsburgh plated a run in the eighth, the Cubs tied it up 11–11 with four runs in the ninth. The Pirates turned the Chicago comeback into a wasted effort with a run in the 11th.

SEPTEMBER 21   The Cubs tie a National League record by using 27 players during a 3–2, fourteen–inning loss to the Pirates at Wrigley Field.

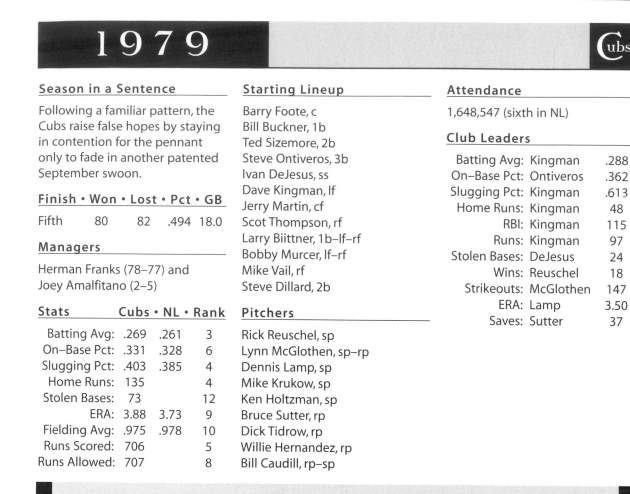

1979   Cubs

Season in a Sentence

Following a familiar pattern, the Cubs raise false hopes by staying in contention for the pennant only to fade in another patented September swoon.

Finish • Won • Lost • Pct • GB

Fifth   80   82   .494   18.0

Managers

Herman Franks (78–77) and Joey Amalfitano (2–5)

Stats

Stats	Cubs	NL	Rank
Batting Avg:	.269	.261	3
On–Base Pct:	.331	.328	6
Slugging Pct:	.403	.385	4
Home Runs:	135		4
Stolen Bases:	73		12
ERA:	3.88	3.73	9
Fielding Avg:	.975	.978	10
Runs Scored:	706		5
Runs Allowed:	707		8

Starting Lineup

Barry Foote, c
Bill Buckner, 1b
Ted Sizemore, 2b
Steve Ontiveros, 3b
Ivan DeJesus, ss
Dave Kingman, lf
Jerry Martin, cf
Scot Thompson, rf
Larry Biittner, 1b–lf–rf
Bobby Murcer, lf–rf
Mike Vail, rf
Steve Dillard, 2b

Pitchers

Rick Reuschel, sp
Lynn McGlothen, sp–rp
Dennis Lamp, sp
Mike Krukow, sp
Ken Holtzman, sp
Bruce Sutter, rp
Dick Tidrow, rp
Willie Hernandez, rp
Bill Caudill, rp–sp

Attendance

1,648,547 (sixth in NL)

Club Leaders

Batting Avg:	Kingman	.288
On–Base Pct:	Ontiveros	.362
Slugging Pct:	Kingman	.613
Home Runs:	Kingman	48
RBI:	Kingman	115
Runs:	Kingman	97
Stolen Bases:	DeJesus	24
Wins:	Reuschel	18
Strikeouts:	McGlothen	147
ERA:	Lamp	3.50
Saves:	Sutter	37

FEBRUARY 23   The Cubs trade Manny Trillo, Dave Rader, and Greg Gross to the Phillies for Barry Foote, Jerry Martin, Ted Sizemore, Dick Botelho, and Henry Mack.

The deal was made at the start of the Cubs first spring training at Mesa, Arizona since 1965. The club moved to Mesa after leaving Scottsdale, Arizona, where spring training was held from 1967 through 1978.

APRIL 5   Five days after the nuclear disaster at Three Mile Island, and two days after Jane Byrne is elected mayor of Chicago, the Cubs lose 10–6 to Mets before 35,615 at Wrigley Field on Opening Day. Winds gusted to 45 miles–per–hour during the game. Dave Kingman hit a three–run homer. It was the first of four consecutive losses to start the 1979 season.

The Cubs rebuilt the dugouts at Wrigley Field in 1979, adding length and depth. The old ones were cramped, and it wasn't unusual for a manager to leap from his seat only to knock himself out by hitting his head on the ceiling. Players complained during the opening series, however, that the footrests were too low and the protective fence was too high. Further modifications were made.

APRIL 20   Dave Kingman hits a grand slam in the third inning off Steve Rogers in the third inning of an 8–5 win over the Expos at Wrigley Field.

APRIL 29   The Cubs stage an incredible finish by scoring six runs in the ninth inning to over come the Braves 6–5 in Atlanta. All six runs were scored with two out. Tim Blackwell drove in two runs with a bases–loaded single, Larry Biittner followed with a pinch–single, and Bobby Murcer capped the explosion with a three–run homer.

MAY 10   The game between the Cubs and the Reds at Wrigley Field is suspended after nine innings with the score tied 7–7 to allow the Cubs to catch a 6:05 P.M. plane for Houston. The contest was completed on July 23.

A riot broke out because of the suspension of the contest. Over 100 fans gathered on the concourse and hurled objects and profanity at the door to the front office, a flight up. One man smashed his fist on the public service department window, breaking it and slightly cutting the eye of secretary Sue Rosberg.

MAY 15   Barry Foote hits a grand slam in the fifth inning off Nino Espinosa during a 7–1 win over the Phillies at Wrigley Field.

MAY 16   The Phillies rout the Cubs 13–0 at Wrigley Field.

MAY 17   A homer with two out in the tenth inning by Mike Schmidt off Bruce Sutter climaxes a scoring marathon at Wrigley Field as the Phillies defeat the Cubs 23–22. Aided by a 20 mile–per–hour wind, the teams combined for eleven homers to tie a National League record. Dave Kingman belted three homers for the Cubs, and drove in six runs. Bill Buckner had seven runs–batted–in on three singles and a grand slam off Tug McGraw in the fifth inning. Steve Ontiveros and Jerry Martin also homered for Chicago. Mike Schmidt hit two homers for the Phillies, and Bob Boone, Randy Lerch, and Garry Maddox added one each. There were a total of 50 hits in the game. The tone was set in the first inning when the Phillies scored seven runs and the Cubs came back with six in their half, three of them on Kingman's first homer. Starting pitchers Lerch and Dennis Lamp each retired only one batter before being replaced. The Phillies led 17–6 after 3 ½ innings, and 21–9 after 4 ½, but the Cubs chipped away at the 12–run lead. After the Cubs scored seven times in their half of the fifth, the score was 21–16. The Cubs scored three more in the sixth and the Phillies one in the seventh. The game was tied 22–22 with three Chicago runs in the eighth. The winning pitcher was Rawly Eastwick, who pitched two perfect innings in the ninth and tenth.

MAY 23   The Cubs trade Ray Burris to the Yankees for Dick Tidrow.

Tidrow, whose nickname was "Dirt," played four seasons with the Cubs as a workhorse out of the bullpen. In 1980 he pitched in 84 games, to tie a club record set by Ted Abernathy in 1965. Tidrow's trademarks were a glowering stare, long hair, a full mustache, a high leg kick, and a sidearm fastball.

JUNE 1   Three days after the crash of a DC–10 kills 275 at O'Hare Airport, the highest death toll in U.S. aviation history, Dave Kingman drives in six runs to power the Cubs to an 8–2 win over the Giants at Wrigley Field. Kingman hit two homers and a double.

In 1979, the Cubs had their first confrontation with a female reporter. Karen Chaderjian of the JOLIET NEWS HERALD was allowed to enter the manager's office, but was denied access to the players' quarters. She appealed to the front office, but found an unsympathetic general manager in Bob Kennedy. "Either grow a beard," growled Kennedy, "or take the club to court."

JUNE 15   The Cubs score two in the ninth to defeat the Padres 3–2 in San Diego and earn their third straight last–at–bat win during a trip to California. On June 13, the Cubs scored in the tenth to beat the Giants 3–2. The next day, they scored twice in the ninth to beat the Giants again 8–6.

JUNE 18   Dave Kingman homers for the fourth game in a row, although the Cubs lose 7–3 to the Dodgers in Los Angeles.

Kingman hit 25 homers in the first 64 games of the 1979 season, and finished the season with 48, the most by a Cubs batter since Hack Wilson clubbed 56 in 1930. Kingman also batted .288, scored 97 runs, drove in 115. In addition to leading the league in home runs, Kingman topped the circuit in slugging percentage with a .613 mark.

JUNE 26   The Cubs trade Bobby Murcer to the Yankees for Pete Semall.

The Cubs traded Murcer for a minor league pitcher to reduce salary. Bobby was the highest paid player on the team, and was among the least productive. He was also the chief target of the "boobirds" at Wrigley Field. Murcer played for the Yankees until 1983 as a spare outfielder, then went into the club's broadcast booth.

Big Dave Kingman provided great power for the Cubs during his three years with the team, but his attitude was not missed by fans after his departure following the 1980 season.

JUNE 27   Jerry Martin homers for the fourth game in a row to help the Cubs beat the Phillies 11–6 at Wrigley Field. Martin homered against the Pirates on June 24, and versus his former Phillies teammates in each of the three game from June 25 through June 27.

JUNE 28   The Cubs purchase Ken Henderson from the Reds.

JUNE 30   Mike Vail hits a pinch–hit grand slam in the eleventh inning off Dale Murray, but it's not enough to beat the Mets at Wrigley Field. New York scored six runs in the top of the eleventh, and the Cubs scored five in a fruitless rally in their half to make the final score 9–8.

JULY 1   The Cubs score three runs in the ninth inning to beat the Mets 5–4 in the first game of a double–header at Wrigley Field. Steve Dillard walked with the bases loaded to force in the winning run. The Cubs completed the sweep with a 8–2 win in the nightcap.

JULY 7   Cubs right fielders combine for eight hits in eight at–bats and six RBIs during a 6–0 and 6–3 double–header sweep of the Astros at Wrigley Field. In the first game, Scot Thompson collected five hits in five at–bats. In the second tilt, Thompson's platoon partner Mike Vail was three–for–three, and had a homer and four runs–batted–in.

JULY 12   Rallying from a 7–0 deficit, the Cubs prevail over the Reds 10–8 in Cincinnati. The Cubs entered the ninth trailing 7–5, and scored five times, the last two on Bruce Sutter's single.

                Sutter won the Cy Young Award in 1979 with a 6–6 record, 37 saves and a 2.23 ERA in 62 games and 101 innings.

JULY 14   The Cubs down the Reds 1–0 in Cincinnati. Steve Ontiveros drove in the only run of the game with a single in the eighth inning. Mike Krukow (7⅔ innings), Dick Tidrow (⅓ of an inning) and Bruce Sutter (one inning) combined on the shutout.

                With the July 14 victory, the Cubs had a record of 47–37 and were two games behind the first–place Expos. From June 6 through July 14, the Cubs were 28–10.

JULY 17   Bruce Sutter is the winning pitcher in the All–Star Game, played at the Kingdome in Seattle. Sutter pitched the eighth and ninth inning and didn't allow a run as the National League won 7–6.

JULY 23   The Cubs win two games against the Reds in unusual fashion at Wrigley Field. The day began with the completion of the suspended game of May 10, which was stopped at the end of the ninth inning with the score tied 7–7 to allow the Cubs to catch a plane. The two clubs resumed the game in the top of the tenth, and it went nine more innings. At the conclusion, the Cubs had a 9–8 win in eighteen innings. Both teams scored in the eleventh. In the 18th, Ken Henderson singled, went to second on a sacrifice, and scored on a single by Steve Ontiveros. In the regularly scheduled game, the Cubs won 2–1 when Dave Kingman hit a two–run walk–off homer in the ninth.

JULY 27   Dave Kingman hits two homers during a 4–2 win over the Mets in New York.

                At the conclusion of the game, the Cubs were just one–half game behind the first place Expos with a record of 54–42. The streaky Cubs lost their next six games, however. As late as August 30, Chicago still had an outside shot at hosting a World Series, with a 71–59 record and 5½ games out of first. But the club lost 23 of their last 32 games.

JULY 28   Dave Kingman whacks three homers after hitting a single in the first inning, although the Cubs lose 6–4 to the Mets in New York. Combined with the two homers the previous day, Kingman tied a major record for most homers in consecutive games with five. Each of his July 28 homers were hit with the bases empty. He went deep off Pete Falcone in the fourth and sixth innings, and Lloyd Allen in the eighth.

AUGUST 3   Ted Sizemore and Dick Tidrow walk out of a team dinner following an August 2, 6–4 loss to the Expos in Montreal.

The August 2 game against the Expos didn't end until 2:40 a.m. on August 3 because of three rain delays. This upset the Cubs travel plans, because planes couldn't fly out of Montreal between midnight and 6:00 a.m., and the Cubs were scheduled to play the Cardinals in Chicago that afternoon. To help soothe frayed nerves due to the loss, the club's sixth in a row, and the difficult travel itinerary, Cubs management treated the players to a dinner at a posh Montreal restaurant. Management placed a two–bottle limit of wine per table (at $40 per bottle), and Sizemore and Tidrow angrily walked out in a tirade because of the restriction placed on their alcohol consumption. Sizemore continued to complain loudly on both the bus ride to the airport and on the flight to Chicago. He was traded two weeks later.

AUGUST 5   Jack Brickhouse is honored in pre–game ceremonies at Wrigley Field on the occasion of his 5,000th broadcast of a major league game in a career began in 1947. Among those attending were Illinois Governor James Thompson and Chicago Mayor Jane Byrne. Brickhouse received a plaque with the names of almost 800 Cubs, a stained–glass replica of Wrigley Field, and a "sofa" made of bats of famous players. The Cubs split a double–header against the Cardinals, winning 3–2 and losing 5–4.

AUGUST 7   The Cubs wallop the Pirates 15–2 at Wrigley Field.

AUGUST 16   The Cubs score eight runs in the seventh inning and thrash the Giants 14–4.

The Cubs in 1979 scored 423 runs in 81 games at Wrigley Field, and 283 in an equal number of contests on the road. Chicago ranked first in the NL in runs scored at home and were last in runs in away games.

AUGUST 17   The Cubs send Ted Sizemore to the Red Sox for Mike O'Berry and cash.

SEPTEMBER 9   Barry Foote hits a grand slam off John Kucek in the fourth inning during a 15–2 laugher over the Phillies at Wrigley Field. Foote also had three singles in the game.

SEPTEMBER 18 Dave Kingman stars in a double–header won by the Cubs 2–0 and 2–1 in eleven innings against the Mets in New York. In the first game, he drove in both runs with a single in the third inning. Rick Reuschel (7⅔ innings) and Bruce Sutter (1⅓ innings) combined on the shutout. In the second contest, Kingman drove in the winning run with a single.

Reuschel had a record of 18–12 with an ERA of 3.62 in 1979.

SEPTEMBER 19 The Cubs defeat the Cardinals 3–2 in the second game of a double–header at Busch Memorial Stadium on three solo homers. Dave Kingman homered in the fourth and ninth innings, and Jerry Martin in the tenth. St. Louis won the first game 6–3.

Ivan DeJesus scored 92 runs and batted .283 in 1979.

SEPTEMBER 23   Herman Franks resigns as manager of the Cubs. Joey Amalfitano was named as interim manager to finish out the last seven games of the season.

Franks left with a parting shot, calling the players selfish, coddled, and uninspired. "I've had it right up to here," said Franks, putting his right hand at his throat. "Some of these players are actually crazy. They don't want to talk to the newspaper people, and they want separate buses for themselves and the reporters. It's silly things like this that get you fed up." Franks singled out Bill Buckner, Ted Sizemore, Barry Foote, and Mike Vail as the "whiners."

SEPTEMBER 25   The Cubs score seven runs in the first inning and defeat the Mets 11–3 at Wrigley Field.

During the September tailspin, Lynn McGlothen said, "That feeling we had in July is gone. I don't want to hear that excuse that day ball killed the Cubs again this year. The Cubs killed the Cubs."

SEPTEMBER 26   Right fielder Larry Biittner loses a ball in his hat during an 8–3 loss to the Mets at Wrigley Field. Biittner raced in to try and catch a sinking line drive by Bruce Bosclair and trapped it. During the chase, Biittner's hat flew off and landed on top of the ball. He ran around in circles looking for the ball, before finding it by lifting up his cap. By this time Bosclair was streaking for second. Biittner fired the ball in that direction, but overthrew the bag, and Bosclair was safe with a double.

OCTOBER 2   Preston Gomez is hired as manager of the Cubs.

A native of Cuba, Gomez was 56 years old and previously managed clubs in San Diego (1969–72) and Houston (1975–75) to a combined record of 308–477, a winning percentage of .392. He had shown absolutely no signs of success as a manager, so his hiring by the Cubs was a complete mystery. It was no surprise that Chicago was 39–51 under Gomez before he was fired in July 1980.

OCTOBER 17   Three weeks before Iranian militants seize U. S. Embassy in Teheran, taking 52 hostages, the Cubs trade Donnie Moore to the Cardinals for Mike Tyson.

THE STATE OF THE CUBS

The Cubs had only two winning seasons during the 1980s, and not only won Eastern Division pennants in both of them, but posted the best record in the National League. In fact, they were the only two winning seasons from 1973 through 1992. The Cubs failed to break the World Series jinx that has existed since 1945, however. In 1984, the Cubs lost the National League Championship to the Padres, and in 1989 to the Giants. Overall, the Cubs were 735–821, a winning percentage of .472, ranking 10th among the 12 National League teams. The only two franchises with fewer wins during the decade were the Braves and the Pirates. The National League pennant winners during the 1980s were the Phillies (1980 and 1983), Dodgers (1981 and 1988), Cardinals (1982, 1985, and 1987), Padres (1984), Mets (1986) and Giants (1989). The Eastern Division winners were the Phillies (1980 and 1983), Expos (1981), Cardinals (1982, 1985, and 1987) and Mets (1986 and 1988).

THE BEST TEAM

The 1984 Cubs were 96–65 and won the East by 6½ games. No Cub team between 1945 and the present has won more games. The 1984 season was also the only time from 1973 through 1988 that the Cubs posted a winning record.

THE WORST TEAM

The 1981 Cubs had a mark of 38–65 in a strike-shortened season. The winning percentage of .369 is the worst of any Cubs team between 1966 and the present.

THE BEST MOMENT

On October 3, 1984, the Cubs took a two–games–to–none lead in the best–of–five National League Championship Series. Just one win in three games in San Diego, and the Cubs would go to the World Series for the first time in thirty–nine years.

THE WORST MOMENT

On October 7, 1984, the Cubs were eight outs from the World Series but lost game five of the NLCS when San Diego rallied for four runs in the seventh to win 6–3.

THE ALL–DECADE TEAM • YEARS WITH CUBS

Jody Davis, c	1981–88
Bill Buckner, 1b	1977–84
Ryne Sandberg, 2b	1982–94; 1996–97
Ron Cey, 3b	1983–86
Shawon Dunston, ss	1985–95; 1997
Gary Matthews, lf	1984–87
Bob Dernier, cf	1984–87
Andre Dawson, rf	1987–92
Greg Maddux, p	1986–92; 2004
Lee Smith, p	1980–87
Rick Sutcliffe, p	1984–91
Scott Sanderson, p	1984–89

The best two Cubs outfielders during the 1980s were right fielders, which kept Keith Moreland (1982–87) from a much deserved spot on the All–Decade Team. Leon Durham (1981–88) also deserves a place on the All–Decade Team of the 1980s, but his time with the Cubs was split between first base and the outfield. Matthews, Dernier, and Sanderson didn't have great careers as Cubs, but they will always be fondly remembered in Chicago for their contributions to the great 1984 team. Dawson is eligible for the Hall of Fame on the writer's ballot until 2016, and Sandberg and Smith until 2017. Each has an excellent chance of induction during that time frame. Maddux is a lock to be elected on the first ballot five years after he retires.

THE DECADE LEADERS

Batting Avg:	Buckner	.302
On–Base Pct:	Sandberg	.341
Slugging Pct:	Dawson	.491
Home Runs:	Sandberg	139
RBI:	Sandberg	549
Runs:	Sandberg	754
Stolen Bases:	Sandberg	250
Wins:	Sutcliffe	76
Strikeouts:	Sutcliffe	850
ERA:	Smith	2.92
Saves:	Smith	180

THE HOME FIELD

Wrigley Field underwent a dramatic change in 1988 when lights were installed for the first time. The first official night game was played on August 9, after the first scheduled nocturnal contest was rained out the previous evening in the fourth inning. In 1989, the mezzanine and old press box and broadcasting booths were replaced by sixty–seven private luxury boxes as well as new facilities for the press and broadcasting personnel at a cost estimated at $6.5 million.

THE GAME YOU WISH YOU HAD SEEN

In what has become known as the "Ryne Sandberg Game," the Cubs second baseman hit game–tying homers in the ninth and tenth innings off Bruce Sutter, and drove in seven runs, to lead the Cubs to a 12–11, eleven–inning win over the Cardinals on June 23, 1984.

THE WAY THE GAME WAS PLAYED

The 1980s had a little something for everybody. Trends surfacing in the 1970s continued, with teams continuing to emphasize speed. Earned run averages hovered around 3.60. But in 1987, offense spiked in a year that combined the speed numbers of the dead ball era with the power numbers of the 1950s. NL teams averaged more than 150 steals and 150 homers, the only time that has ever occurred. But the offensive bubble burst, and the NL experienced its lowest batting averages in twenty years in 1988 and 1989.

THE MANAGEMENT

The 65–year ownership of the Wrigleys ended on June 16, 1981, when the family sold the Cubs to the Tribune Company for $20.5 million. The sale and the up and down nature of the club's fortunes during the 1980s led to numerous changes in management. At the start of the decade, William Wrigley headed the organization chart as Chairman of the Executive Committee. Andrew McKenna was Chairman of the Board from 1981 through 1986, and was succeeded by Dallas Green (1987), John Madigan (1988), and Donald Grenesko (1989–91). The board chairmen were mainly involved with the financial end of the franchise. General managers, in charge of trades and player development, were Bob Kennedy (1977–81), Herman Franks (1981), Green (1981–87) and Jim Frey (1987–91). Field managers were Preston Gomez (1980), Joey Amalfitano (1980–81), Lee Elia (1982–83), Charlie Fox (1983), Frey (1984–86), John Vukovich (1986), Gene Michael (1986–87), Frank Lucchesi (1987), and Don Zimmer (1988–91).

THE BEST PLAYER MOVE

The Cubs stole Ryne Sandberg in a trade with the Phillies on January 27, 1982. Sandberg arrived from Philadelphia with Larry Bowa for Ivan DeJesus.

THE WORST PLAYER MOVE

The Cubs sent Rafael Palmeiro and Jamie Moyer to the Rangers for Mitch Williams and five minor leaguers on December 5, 1988.

1980s

1980

Season in a Sentence

In yet another aimless rebuilding project, the Cubs take a giant step backward with 98 losses, the most in the National League.

Finish • Won • Lost • Pct • GB

Sixth   64   98   .395   27.0

Managers

Preston Gomez (38–52) and
Joey Amalfitano (26–46)

Stats

Stats	Cubs	NL	Rank
Batting Avg:	.251	.259	9
On–Base Pct:	.311	.323	10
Slugging Pct:	.365	.374	9
Home Runs:	107		8
Stolen Bases:	93		11
ERA:	3.89	3.60	11
Fielding Avg:	.974	.978	12
Runs Scored:	614		9
Runs Allowed:	728		12

Starting Lineup

Tim Blackwell, c
Bill Buckner, 1b
Mike Tyson, 2b
Lenny Randle, 3b
Ivan DeJesus, ss
Dave Kingman, lf
Jerry Martin, cf
Mike Vail, rf
Scot Thompson, rf
Larry Biittner, 1b–lf–rf
Steve Dillard, 3b–2b
Barry Foote, c
Jesus Figueroa, cf–lf
Cliff Johnson, 1b

Pitchers

Rick Reuschel, sp
Lynn McGlothen, sp–rp
Mike Krukow, sp
Dennis Lamp, sp
Bruce Sutter, rp
Dick Tidrow, rp
Bill Caudill, rp
Willie Hernandez, rp

Attendance

1,206,776 (eighth in NL)

Club Leaders

Batting Avg:	Buckner	.324
On–Base Pct:	Buckner	.353
Slugging Pct:	Buckner	.457
Home Runs:	Martin	23
RBI:	Martin	73
Runs:	DeJesus	78
Stolen Bases:	DeJesus	44
Wins:	McGlothen	12
Strikeouts:	Reuschel	140
ERA:	Reuschel	3.40
Saves:	Sutter	28

FEBRUARY 25   Bruce Sutter wins an arbitration hearing that nets him a salary of $700,000 for the 1980 season.

> *Sutter wanted to be paid $700,000 while the Cubs were offering $350,000. He made $19,000 in 1976 and $75,000 in 1979. According to the rules, the arbitrator could only choose between one salary or the other, and awarded Sutter the higher figure. The settlement not only shocked the Cubs, but the entire baseball industry. Sutter was entering his fifth season in the majors, and was now one of the highest paid players in the game. Only eight years earlier, Hank Aaron was baseball's top paid player at $200,000. The Cubs immediately began shopping Sutter, and traded him to the Cardinals after the 1980 season ended.*

APRIL 3   Dave Kingman escalates his long–standing feud with the baseball writers by throwing a bucket of ice water on a stunned reporter in Mesa, Arizona.

> *Kingman doused 25–year–old Dan Friske of the suburban Arlington Heights DAILY HERALD. Friske was interviewing Lenny Randle, who was acquired by the Cubs a day earlier, in the clubhouse. "This will give you stories for two*

days," shouted Kingman. Later he said it was a "joke." National League president Charles Feeney dismissed the incident with the warning that Kingman would be punished if it happened again.

APRIL 10   The Cubs lose the season opener 5–2 to the Mets in New York.

Milo Hamilton joined the WGN broadcasting team in 1980 with Jack Brickhouse, Lou Boudreau, and Vince Lloyd.

APRIL 11   The Cubs uncork a five–homer barrage, including two by Dave Kingman, to defeat the Mets 7–5 in New York. Jerry Martin also hit two for the Cubs, and Lenny Randle clouted one.

APRIL 17   In the first game of the season at Wrigley Field, the Cubs defeat the Mets 4–1 before 33,062. Carlos Lezcano hit a two–run homer for his first major league hit.

APRIL 19   The Cubs score seven runs in the eighth inning to overcome the Mets 12–9 at Wrigley Field. New York led 7–0 in the fourth inning. Dave Kingman led the comeback with a two–run homer in the sixth inning and a grand slam off Lloyd Allen in the eighth. Ivan DeJesus, Jerry Martin, and Carlos Lezcano also homered for the Cubs.

APRIL 21   A walk–off grand slam by Barry Foote off Mark Littell beats the Cardinals 16–12 at Wrigley Field. The Cubs collected 23 hits in the game. The Cards led 12–6 in the fifth inning before the Cubs hit the comeback trail. Foote drove in a total of eight runs on two homers, a double, and a single. His solo homer in the eighth tied the score 12–12. Ivan DeJesus hit for the cycle. He had a total of five hits, including two singles, in six at–bats.

Ivan DeJesus provided good defense, a solid bat, and much–needed speed during his five years in Chicago. As a Cub he stole 154 bases.

MAY 2   The Cubs erupt for eight runs in the twelfth to beat the Reds 12–4 in Cincinnati. Lenny Randle had a homer and a double in the inning. Mike Vail contributed a bases–loaded pinch–hit triple.

MAY 3   The Cubs score five runs in the first inning and beat the Reds 7–1 in Cincinnati.

The win put the Cubs into first place with an 11–6 record. The club would soon plummet into the Eastern Division cellar, and remain there for the rest of the season.

MAY 10   Eight days before the eruption of Mt. St. Helens in Washington state, the Cubs out-slug the Giants 15–9 at Wrigley Field.

JUNE 2   Cubs pitchers walk a club record 14 batters in a thirteen–inning, 8–7 loss to the Expos in Montreal. The walks were issued by Mike Krukow (six), Dick Tidrow (one), Bruce Sutter (three), Bill Caudill (two), and Lynn McGlothen (two).

JUNE 3   The Cubs select pitcher Don Schulze of Lake Park High School in the Chicago suburb of Roselle, Illinois, in the first round of the amateur draft.

              Schulze pitched only five games as a Cub at the start of a six–year career. He was 15–25 with a 5.47 ERA in the majors. The only other players drafted and signed by the Cubs in 1980 to reach the majors were Frtiz Connally (seventh round) and Craig Lefferts (ninth round). Lefferts, who was born in Munich, West Germany, was traded by the Cubs following his rookie year in 1983. He had a decent twelve–year career as a reliever and pitched in two World Series.

JUNE 13   Dave Kingman fails to report for a game against the against the Braves at Wrigley Field.

              Kingman was given permission to return home to San Diego on June 12, an open date, because his home was burglarized. He was expected to return for the June 13 game, but didn't show. Kingman was fined $1,250. He returned to Chicago on June 14, was diagnosed with a sore shoulder, and was placed on the disabled list for fifteen days.

JUNE 18   Jerry Martin hits a grand slam off Doug Bair in the seventh inning of a 7–0 win over the Reds at Wrigley Field.

JUNE 23   The Cubs send Mike Pagel to the Indians for Cliff Johnson. On the same day, the Cubs sold Steve Ontiveros to the Seibu Lions of the Japanese League.

              Johnson became an immediate fan favorite with a number of game–winning hits. The only position he was capable of playing, however, was first base, and the Cubs already had Bill Buckner entrenched there. Buckner played 50 games in the outfield in 1980, to make room for Johnson, which wasn't an ideal spot for Buckner's gimpy ankles. Johnson was traded soon after the season ended.

JULY 6   The Cubs lose a twenty–inning marathon 5–4 to the Pirates at Three Rivers Stadium. Pittsburgh led 4–2 before Bill Buckner homered in the eighth and Cliff Johnson followed with another homer in the ninth on a 2–2 pitch with two out to tie the score 4–4. Eight Cubs pitchers combined for 12⅔ consecutive hitless innings. The eight pitchers who contributed to the hitless streak were starter Rick Reuschel (one–third of an inning with the last out in the sixth), George Riley (two innings), Bruce Sutter (two innings), Doug Capilla (one–third of an inning), Dick Tidrow (one–third of an inning), Willie Hernandez (2⅓ innings), Bill Caudill (five innings), and Dennis Lamp (one–third of an inning before Lee Lacy singled with one out in the nineteenth). There were ten consecutive scoreless innings by both pitching staffs before Omar Moreno singled in the winning run in the twentieth off Lamp. The Cubs used 23 of their 24 available players.

JULY 8   Bruce Sutter earns a save in the All–Star Game by pitching a scoreless eighth and
          ninth in the National League's 4–2 win at Dodger Stadium in Los Angeles. Dave
          Kingman started the contest as the NL left fielder, but re–injured his shoulder. He
          was on the disabled list from July 10 through August 12.

          In his final season with the Cubs, Sutter was 5–8 with 28 saves and a 2.65 ERA.

JULY 12   Cliff Johnson hits a grand slam off Stan Bahnsen in the seventh inning to lead the
          Cubs to an 8–6 win over the Expos in the second game of a double–header at
          Olympic Stadium. The Cubs trailed 6–3 when Johnson cleared the bases. Montreal
          won the first game 10–2.

JULY 19   A two–run, two out, walk–off homer by Cliff Johnson in the ninth inning beats the
          Padres 8–7 at Wrigley Field.

          *In July, Chicago radio station WCFL announced plans for a "Snub the Cubs"
          event, urging fans to boycott the game against the Astros on August 29 at
          Wrigley Field. "The idea was to protest the amazing ineptitude of the players
          and front office," explained broadcaster Chuck Swinsky. "We've had thirty–five
          years of awful baseball by the Cubs and the time had come to stage some sort
          of demonstration." The plans for the "Snub the Cubs" day were canceled when
          general manager Bob Kennedy threatened legal action.*

JULY 25   Cubs coach Joe Amalfitano is promoted to manager, replacing Preston Gomez.

          *Gomez, who was hired in October 1979, lasted only 90 games as Cubs manag-
          er in which he was 38–52. Amalfitano was a Cubs coach from 1967 through
          1971, and returned again beginning in 1978. He was interim skipper for seven
          games at the end of the 1979 season. The Cubs needed much more than a
          change in managers, however, and the club played even worse under Amalfitano
          than they had under Gomez.*

JULY 27   The Dodgers outlast the Cubs 3–2 in twelve innings in Los Angeles. Neither team
          issued a walk. It is the longest game in National League history without a walk.
          The six pitchers who combined for the record were Rick Reuschel, Bill Caudill, and
          Dick Tidrow for the Cubs, and Don Sutton, Don Stanhouse, and Steve Howe for
          the Dodgers.

AUGUST 7 The Cubs give away 15,000 Dave Kingman T–shirts as a promotion before an 11–3
          loss to the Pirates at Wrigley Field. Kingman wasn't at the ballpark, however,
          because of his injured shoulder. Instead, he showed up at a city festival where he
          appeared for a fee in a booth to promote the Jet–Ski.

AUGUST 8 Cliff Johnson hits a walk–off grand slam in the fourteenth inning to defeat the
          Expos 8–4 at Wrigley Field. The contest started on May 28, but was suspended at
          the end of ten innings with the score tied 3–3 because of darkness. Both teams
          scored in the twelfth. Ironically, the game started when Johnson was a member of
          the Cleveland Indians. He joined the Cubs on June 23. Montreal won the regularly
          scheduled game 5–2.

AUGUST 23 The Cubs lose 1–0 in seventeen innings in Houston. Astros pitcher Joe Niekro won his own game with a walk–off RBI–single off George Riley.

AUGUST 29   Lenny Randle extends his hitting streak to 21 games, although the Cubs lose 6–5 to the Astros at Wrigley Field.

AUGUST 31   The Cubs break a 13–game losing streak against the Astros, dating back to 1979, by scoring three runs in the ninth inning to win 8–7 at Wrigley Field. Five singles scored the three runs, the last of which was by Tim Blackwell.

SEPTEMBER 1   Lee Smith makes his major league debut with a scoreless fifth inning during a 5–2 loss to the Braves at Wrigley Field.

An intimidating six–foot–six and weighing 235 pounds, Smith retired in 1997 as baseball's all–time leader in saves with 478. He pitched for the Cubs from 1980 through 1987, and is also the club's all–time saves leader with 180. Smith appeared in 458 career games for the Cubs, which ranks second to Charlie Root's 605.

SEPTEMBER 10   Expos rookie pitcher Bill Gullickson strikes out 18 batters to defeat the Cubs 4–2 in Montreal.

SEPTEMBER 12   The Cubs erupt for five runs in the fourteenth inning, the last two on Mike Vail's home run, to defeat the Mets 10–5 in New York.

OCTOBER 5   On the final day of the season, Bill Buckner is hitless in four at–bats during a 1–0 loss to the Pirates in Pittsburgh, but wins the batting title with a .324 average.

Buckner went into the day leading Keith Hernandez of the Cardinals .326 to .321. Cubs manager Joey Amalfitano suggested that Buckner sit the game out to protect his lead, but Buckner insisted on playing. Hernandez was 1–for–4 against the Mets to stay at .321.

OCTOBER 17   The Cubs trade Mike O'Berry to the Reds for Jay Howell.

DECEMBER 8   The Cubs draft Jody Davis from the Cardinals organization.

The minor league draft rarely produces useful players, but Davis was an exception. He was the Cubs starting catcher from 1981 through 1987.

DECEMBER 9   The day after ex–Beatle John Lennon is murdered by a crazed fan, the Cubs trade Bruce Sutter to the Cardinals for Leon Durham, Ken Reitz, and Tye Waller.

Sutter was traded to dump his salary. In the short run, it wasn't a good trade, but over the long haul, it worked out to the Cubs advantage. Sutter played four seasons for the Cardinals, three of them great ones, before his arm gave out. Meanwhile, Lee Smith took over as the Cubs closer, and was as dominating as Sutter. "Bull" Durham was a regular in the Cubs lineup in the outfield and at first base for seven seasons.

DECEMBER 11   The Cubs trade Cliff Johnson and Keith Drumright to the Athletics for Mike King.

1981 — Cubs

Season in a Sentence

The Cubs lose 36 of their first 46 games, the players go on strike for nearly two months, the Wrigley family sells the club, and Chicago has the worst record in the NL for the second straight year.

Finish • Won • Lost • Pct • GB

| * | 38 | 65 | .369 | * |

*The 1981 season was split in two because of the strike. The Cubs were sixth with a 15–37 record in the first half, and fifth with a 23–28 record in the second.

Manager

Joey Amalfitano

Stats

Stats	Cubs	NL	Rank
Batting Avg:	.236	.255	12
On–Base Pct:	.308	.322	12
Slugging Pct:	.340	.364	12
Home Runs:	57		7 (tie)
Stolen Bases:	72		11
ERA:	4.01	3.49	11
Fielding Avg:	.974	.978	11
Runs Scored:	370		11
Runs Allowed:	483		12

Starting Lineup

Jody Davis, c
Bill Buckner, 1b
Steve Dillard, 2b
Ken Reitz, 3b
Ivan DeJesus, ss
Steve Henderson, lf
Jerry Morales, cf
Leon Durham, rf
Bobby Bonds, cf
Tim Blackwell, c
Scot Thompson, cf
Hector Cruz, 3b–rf–lf
Pat Tabler, 2b

Pitchers

Mike Krukow, sp
Rick Reuschel, sp
Doug Bird, sp
Ken Kravec, sp–rp
Dick Tidrow, rp
Doug Capilla, rp
Lee Smith, rp
Randy Martz, rp–sp
Bill Caudill, rp
Rawly Eastwick, rp

Attendance

565,637 (ninth in NL)

Club Leaders

Batting Avg:	Buckner	.311
On–Base Pct:	Henderson	.382
Slugging Pct:	Buckner	.480
Home Runs:	Buckner	10
	Durham	10
RBI:	Buckner	75
Runs:	DeJesus	49
Stolen Bases:	Durham	25
Wins:	Krukow	9
Strikeouts:	Krukow	101
ERA:	Reuschel	3.47
Saves:	Tidrow	9

JANUARY 8   Twelve days before Ronald Reagan is inaugurated as President and the American hostages are released from captivity in Iran, Larry Biittner signs with the Reds as a free agent.

FEBRUARY 17   The Cubs sign Jerry Morales, most recently with the Mets, as a free agent. Morales previously played for the Cubs from 1974 through 1977 as a starting outfielder. In his second tour with the Cubs, Morales served mainly as a pinch–hitter and reserve outfielder.

FEBRUARY 28   The Cubs send Dave Kingman to the Mets for Steve Henderson and cash.

> *The Cubs unloaded a major headache in trading Kingman, who turned off fans, teammates, and the front office with his boorish behavior. Even Pulitzer Prize–winning columnist Mike Royko, a lifelong Cubs fanatic, temporarily became a supporter of the White Sox because of Kingman's churlish character. Royko*

dubbed him "Ding Dong," a play on Kingman's nickname of "King Kong." "I prefer an owner (Bill Veeck) with a wooden leg," wrote Royko, "to a left fielder with a wooden head." Kingman hit 172 home runs in six seasons after leaving the Cubs, but did so with a batting average hovering around the Mendoza line. In 1982, Kingman hit 37 homers for the Mets to lead the National League, but batted only .204.

MARCH 28   Two days before Ronald Reagan is shot by John Hinckley in an assassination attempt, the Cubs trade Dennis Lamp to the White Sox for Ken Kravec.

Lamp played 12 more seasons in the majors as an above average reliever. In 1985, he was 11–0 with the Blue Jays. Plagued by back troubles, Kravec was 2–7 with a 5.31 ERA with the Cubs.

APRIL 9   In the season opener, the Mets beat the Cubs 2–0 before 37,030 at Wrigley Field. Lee Mazzilli accounted for the only runs of the game with a two-run homer off Rick Reuschel in the fourth inning. Ken Reitz was 3-for-3 in his Cub debut.

The Cubs were on cable television in the Chicago area for the first time in 1981. A total of 14 games that were broadcast over the air on WGN–TV were carried over cable.

APRIL 25   Steve Henderson, Leon Durham and Jerry Morales hit three triples in a row in the fourth inning, but the Cubs lose 7–5 to the Phillies at Wrigley Field.

APRIL 26   The Cubs lose their 12th game in a row, dropping a 6–2 decision to the Phillies at Wrigley Field. The loss gave the Cubs a record of 1–13 on the season.

APRIL 27   The Cubs send Barry Foote to the Yankees for Tom Filer and cash.

APRIL 29   The Cubs break their 12–game losing streak with five runs in the eighth inning to defeat the Cardinals 6–1 in the first game of a double–header at Wrigley Field. The second game was suspended after eleven innings because of darkness with the score tied 2–2. It was scheduled to be resumed on July 3, but the players were on strike that day, and the contest eventually went into the books as an eleven–inning tie.

General manager Bob Kennedy said in a television interview in early May, "What difference does it make if I finish fourth, fifth, or sixth? I can't put a winner in here this year, or next year either." The comments upset fans and players alike, and Kennedy was fired less than three weeks later. (See May 22, 1981.)

MAY 4   The Cruz brothers both homer in a 5–4 Astros win at Wrigley Field. Jose Cruz homered in the first inning to give Houston a 3–0 lead. Younger brother Hector went deep for the Cubs in the sixth.

MAY 22   Herman Franks replaces Bob Kennedy as general manager.

Kennedy was fired following his remarks indicating that the immediate future of the Cubs was bleak. Herman Franks, who was manager of the Cubs from 1977 through 1979, took over on an interim basis. At the time, the Wrigley family was negotiating the sale of the Cubs to the Tribune Company (see June 16, 1981), and Franks was hired to ease the transition.

MAY 24   Backed by an unusual double play by first baseman Bill Buckner, the Cubs defeat the Expos 6–2 at Wrigley Field. Buckner caught a pop fly off the bat of Scott Sanderson, then dashed to third base to double up Warren Cromartie, who was headed home on a suicide squeeze.

MAY 25   Overcoming an eight–run deficit, the Cubs prevail the Pirates 10–9 in eleven innings at Wrigley Field. Pittsburgh led 8–0 in the fourth inning and 9–4 after seven before the Cubs scored four in the eighth, one in the ninth and one in the eleventh. The score was tied 9–9 on a homer by Steve Henderson. The winning run crossed the plate following a bases–loaded single by Scot Thompson.

MAY 30   The Cubs score seven runs in the fourth inning and defeat the Mets 10–3 in New York.

JUNE 4   The Cubs purchase Bobby Bonds from the Rangers.

Bonds was 36 years old and had fallen a long way from his peak during the 1970s, when he was one of the best players in baseball. He spent the first two months of the 1981 season with the Rangers farm team in Wichita, where he was hitting just .244. Bonds arrived only an hour before the start of the Cubs June 4 game against the Pirates in Pittsburgh, and was placed in the starting lineup in the clean–up slot, but he didn't last a full inning. Bonds didn't bat in the top of the first, as the Cubs were retired in order. On the fourth pitch of the bottom of the first, he fell trying to reach a short fly to right field to Tim Foli, and broke the little finger on his left hand. The Cubs lost 5–4 in ten innings.

JUNE 8   With the second overall pick, the Cubs select outfielder Joe Carter of Wichita State University in the amateur draft.

The Cubs have a long history of trading promising players far too soon, and Carter is another example. He had a 16–year career, but the Cubs dealt him away after his rookie season in 1983.

JUNE 12   The major league players begin a strike that lasts fifty days and wipes out nearly two months of the 1981 season. The strike reduced the Cubs schedule to 106 games (including three ties). On the same day, the Cubs sent Rick Reuschel to the Yankees for Doug Bird, Mike Griffin, and $40,000.

JUNE 16   William Wrigley sells the Cubs to the Tribune Company for $20.5 million.

The sale ended the 65–year association of the Wrigley family with the Cubs. William was the third generation to run the club, following his grandfather William, Jr. and his father Philip. Estate and inheritance taxes of $40 million led William to sell out. Both of his parents died within two months of each other in 1977. The Tribune Company owned WGN and WGN–TV among its media holdings. The conglomerate saw great financial advantages in combining its ownership of TV and radio stations with the ownership of the team whose games they were broadcasting. Andrew J. McKenna, a lifelong Chicagoan, was *appointed chairman of the board of the Cubs. Previously, McKenna was part owner and member of the board of the White Sox from 1975 until 1980 under the regime of Bill Veeck. The issue of lights at Wrigley Field was one of the immediate questions regarding the end of the Wrigley era. The family had always insisted that there would never be lights at the ballpark as long as they owned the team. The Tribune Company stated that there were no plans to install lights, but fell short of a promise that there would never be lights. Neighborhood activists immediately organized to prevent the addition of night games at Wrigley Field.*

JULY 31   Two days after Prince Charles marries Lady Diana Spencer in London, the players and owners hammer out an agreement that ends the strike.

AUGUST 6   The owners vote to split the 1981 pennant race, with the winners of the two halves of the season meeting in an extra round of playoffs for the division title.

AUGUST 10   The 1981 season resumes with the Cubs losing 7–5 in thirteen innings to the Mets at Wrigley Field before a crowd of 7,551.

                As the only afternoon game on the schedule this day, the Cubs–Mets clash was the first game in the majors following the strike.

AUGUST 15   The Cubs beat the Pirates 4–3 in fifteen innings at Wrigley Field.

                On the same day, the Cubs traded Lynn McGlothen to the White Sox for Bob Molinaro. McGlothen pitched for another year in the majors. He died in a fire in Dubach, Louisiana, on August 14, 1984, at the age of 34.

AUGUST 19   The Cubs end a 4–3 win at Wrigley Field over the Dodgers on a bizarre play. The Dodgers had the bases loaded with one out in the ninth. Reggie Smith grounded sharply to Cubs second baseman Mike Tyson, who threw to shortstop Ivan DeJesus for the force of Pedro Guerrero. Guerrero ran out of the base paths waving his arms to distract DeJesus, and the return throw to first was wild. The tying run was nullified, however, because umpire Jim Quick called Guerrero out for interference.

                On the same day, the Cubs purchased Pat Tabler from the Yankees.

AUGUST 21   In his major league debut, Pat Tabler makes a bonehead play at second base to allow the winning run to score in a 4–3 Giants win at Wrigley Field. With the score 3–3, one out, and San Francisco runners on first and third, Tabler took a throw from Ivan DeJesus for the force of the one runner. But Tabler ran to the dugout believing the inning was over, allowing the other runner to score the tie–breaking run.

AUGUST 26   A two–run walk–off homer by Steve Dillard in the ninth inning beats the Padres 9–7 at Wrigley Field.

SEPTEMBER 7   The Cubs rout the Cardinals 10–0 in St. Louis. Bobby Bonds hit two homers and drove in five runs.

                The split season gave hope to everyone, even the Cubs. On September 11, the Cubs had an overall record of 30–51, but were 15–14 in the second half and only 1 ½ games behind the first place Cardinals. The Cubs lost six of the next seven games, however, and finished the second season with a 23–28 record.

SEPTEMBER 13   Mel Hall's first major league hit is a two–run pinch–homer, but the Cubs lose 10–6 to the Expos at Wrigley Field.

SEPTEMBER 27   The Cubs score seven runs in the fourth inning and defeat the Phillies 14–0 in the second game of a double–header at Wrigley Field. Philadelphia won the first game 5–2.

These were the last games broadcast by Jack Brickhouse at Wrigley Field. Some weeks earlier, it was announced that he would be retiring at the end of the 1981 season. Milo Hamilton, who joined Brickhouse in the broadcasting booth in 1980, was set to take over as the Cubs lead announcer on television, but Hamilton's fate took an unexpected twist two months later when the Cubs hired Harry Caray as the top dog in the booth. (See November 16, 1981.)

OCTOBER 15   The Cubs hire Dallas Green as general manager.

Green resigned as manager of the Phillies to take the job in Chicago. He guided the Phillies to the first (and, to date, only) world championship in the history of the franchise in 1980. Autocratic, heavy–handed, and impetuous, with a nasty temperament, the six–foot–five inch Green wasted no time putting his stamp on the Cubs, adopting a slogan, "Building a New Tradition." Among his first acts was to stir up a furor by demanding that lights be installed at Wrigley Field and threatening to move to a suburban location should the plans for lights be stopped by either city or state legislators. Green believed that lights were a necessity to generate the revenue to attract free agents, and to prevent the common late–season fades by the Cubs because the club was worn down by playing so many games in the heat of the day. Before the lights were installed, Green remade the Cubs with series of controversial, but mostly successful, trades that turned a spiritless, talent–depleted team into a division–winner by 1984. He also cleaned out the Cubs front office. During his first eighteenth months on the job, Green fired nineteen of the twenty–three administrators who were on hand at the end of the Wrigley regime.

OCTOBER 22   Dallas Green hires Lee Elia as manager, replacing Joey Amalfitano.

The gruff and outspoken Elia was Green's third base coach with the Phillies. Elia lasted less than two years as Cubs manager, during a regime highlighted by an unfortunate knack for putting his foot squarely in his mouth.

NOVEMBER 15   Cubs infielder Steve Macko dies of cancer in Arlington, Texas, at the age of 27.

Macko played in only 25 big league games before he was injured in a collision at second base in August 1980. The resulting examination revealed that he had cancer. His father Joe was the equipment manager of the Texas Rangers.

NOVEMBER 16   The Cubs hire Harry Caray as play–by–play announcer.

Caray was hired away from the White Sox, who wanted him to move from

WGN–TV to a new cable venture called Sportsvision. Caray balked at the move and jumped to the Cubs. He almost immediately became a Cubs institution, and with the club's games being carried all over the country through the broadcasts of WGN on its "superstation" cable, Harry became a national institution as well with his bubbling enthusiasm and love of the game. Caray broadcast major league games for 53 years with the Cardinals, Athletics, White Sox, and Cubs. Although just 16 of those 53 years were on the Cubs, he will always be associated with the club and with Wrigley Field.

DECEMBER 8   The Cubs sign Ferguson Jenkins, most recently with the Rangers, as a free agent. On the same day, the Cubs also signed Bill Campbell, most recently a member of the Red Sox, as a free agent. In a third transaction, the Cubs traded Mike Krukow to the Phillies for Keith Moreland, Dickie Noles, and Dan Larson.

Dallas Green began his New Tradition and plans to rebuild with young players by signing Jenkins five days shy of his 38th birthday. Jenkins won 14 games in 1982 and had a 20–24 record in his second tour with the Cubs, which lasted two seasons. The trade with the Phillies brought Moreland, who was the Cubs starting outfielder for six seasons. It was the first of several positive trades with the Phillies over the next few years as Dallas Green dealt with his former employers.

Harry Caray

Harry Caray and the Chicago Cubs are linked forever in the minds of baseball fans all across the country, but he was with the club for only 16 of the 53 years that he was an announcer of major league games on radio and television. Caray didn't move into the Wrigley Field booth until he was 67 years old.

Caray was hired by the Cardinals in 1945 and remained there until 1969. At its peak, the vast Cardinals radio network reached into 14 states on 124 stations. Caray became an extremely popular figure throughout the region, with his unabashed delight at the team's victories and his unvarnished criticism when things weren't going well. Caray described himself as the fan's man in the booth. "I have always contended," said Caray when asked about the key to his success, "that if you put a microphone in front of anyone in the bleachers and told him to start talking about the game he was watching, he would sound very much the way I do."

Caray was fired by the Cardinals at the end of the 1969 season amid rumors that he was carrying on an affair with the wife of the son of Cardinals owner August Busch. After an unhappy year broadcasting Athletics games in Oakland. Caray moved to Chicago in 1971 as the White Sox announcer.

Caray broadcast White Sox games for 11 years. Despite covering teams that lost more often than they won, Caray, through the force of his personality, helped put fans in the seats at Comiskey Park by connecting with the South Side's blue–collar fans. He loved Chicago's abundant nightlife, and his title as the "Mayor of Rush Street," originated during his years with the Sox.

Eddie Einhorn and Jerry Reinsdorf purchased the Sox from Bill Veeck in 1981, and had big changes planned for the club's television package, beginning with the 1982 season. Einhorn and Reinsdorf wanted to drastically reduce the number of games offered to fans for free over WGN–TV in favor of airing the games on a subscription basis on a new cable venture called SportsVision.

Caray bluntly told the two new owners that their plan wouldn't work. Caray believed that Chicago area fans wouldn't pay for the privilege of watching the Sox when nearly every Cubs game was offered for free on WGN. He also believed he'd be losing his connection to much of his core audience, which might not be able to fit pay television into their budget. "Always before," said Caray, "I'd gone into every corner of Chicago, and that's what made it worthwhile—my people. The bartenders, the taxi drivers, the post office guys." Caray was also upset at being offered only a one–year contract extension by the Sox, and that Einhorn and Reinsdorf wanted him to tone down his criticism of the club.

Timing is everything, and the timing for Caray's move from the South Side to the North Side was perfect. He felt that if he continued with the White Sox, it would be the end of his career. Einhorn and Reinsdorf spoke confidentially of wiring 50,000 homes for SportsVision by the start of the 1982 season. Meanwhile, WGN was going national with its "superstation" cable and was available in eight million homes nationwide. The Tribune Company, which owned WGN, had just purchased the Cubs the previous June. And there was an opening in the Cubs broadcasting booth. Jack Brickhouse, who began announcing Cubs games in 1948, retired at the end of the 1981 season, and the Cubs were searching for a replacement.

Hiring Caray wasn't an easy decision for the Cubs front office to make. Many believed that Cubs fans wouldn't accept the outspoken broadcaster who had been long connected with the Cardinals and the White Sox, the Cubs two biggest rivals. "Caray taking over for the retired Jack Brickhouse," wrote Bill Conlin in *The Sporting News*, "figures to have the same shock value as John Belushi showing up as a network anchor man." But Dallas Green, who had just taken over as general manager, persuaded the Cubs board of directors to hire Caray.

Caray was moving from a situation in which he would be seen optimistically in just 50,000 homes in Greater Chicago to eight million across the country. The Cubs were getting an experienced voice who was already well–known in Chicago and had proven that he could connect with the average fan. The announcement that Caray was moving from the Cubs to the White Sox was made on November 16, 1981.

The marriage of Caray and the Cubs took a few years to develop, however. The Cubs of 1982 and 1983 had losing records. Meanwhile, the White Sox were playing winning baseball under manager Tony LaRussa. In 1983, the Sox won 99 games and drew 2,132,821 fans into Comiskey Park. The Cubs won only 71 times and attracted 1,479,717 at Wrigley Field. It also took some time for many Cubs fans to warm–up to Caray. Harry's "shoot from the lip" broadcasting style contrasted sharply with the genteel Brickhouse, who rarely had a bad word in the worst of times.

Everything changed in 1984 when the Cubs won the Eastern Division. With Harry leading the cheers on WGN, the Cubs became a favorite of fans from coast–to–coast as WGN continued expand its coverage. In a bit of irony, Caray left the White Sox because they were making a foray into cable television, but it was cable television, through WGN's nationwide hook–up, that made him famous, as the station was in 28 million homes by the end of the 1980s. Late in his life, Harry Caray became a cult figure as fans as far away as Maine, Florida, Utah, and Oregon caught the contagion of Cubs baseball, partly because of the availability of Cubs telecasts, but in large part to Caray's exuberant personality and showmanship. He was no longer just the Mayor of Rush Street. He was the King of Chicago.

With his huge ego and need for applause, Caray reveled in the attention. Before he moved to the Cubs, Caray could walk through a hotel lobby in a city outside of Chicago and St. Louis and would seldom be recognized. After being hired by the Cubs, he was besieged by autograph seekers who walked past Cubs players to obtain Harry's signature. Through WGN and the Cubs, Harry Caray became a living legend and has remained a broadcasting icon even after his death in 1998.

1982   Cubs

Season in a Sentence

Dallas Green's "New Tradition" looks much like the old one as Cubs fans endure another losing season, although a 33–24 record after July 31 provides some hope for the future.

Finish • Won • Lost • Pct • GB

Fifth   73   89   .451   19.0

Manager

Lee Elia

Stats

Stats	Cubs	NL	Rank
Batting Avg:	.260	.258	6
On–Base Pct:	.319	.322	8
Slugging Pct:	.375	.373	7
Home Runs:	102		7
Stolen Bases:	132		9
ERA:	3.92	3.60	12
Fielding Avg:	.979	.978	5
Runs Scored:	676		6
Runs Allowed:	709		11

Starting Lineup

Jody Davis, c
Bill Buckner, 1b
Bump Wills, 2b
Ryne Sandberg, 3b
Larry Bowa, ss
Keith Moreland, lf
Leon Durham, cf–rf
Jay Johnstone, rf–lf
Gary Woods, cf–lf
Steve Henderson, lf
Junior Kennedy, 2b

Pitchers

Ferguson Jenkins, sp
Doug Bird, sp
Dickie Noles, sp
Randy Martz, sp
Allen Ripley, sp–rp
Lee Smith, rp
Willie Hernandez, rp
Dick Tidrow, rp
Bill Campbell, rp
Mike Proly, rp

Attendance

1,249,278 (tenth in NL)

Club Leaders

Batting Avg:	Durham	.312
On–Base Pct:	Durham	.388
Slugging Pct:	Durham	.521
Home Runs:	Durham	22
RBI:	Buckner	105
Runs:	Sandberg	103
Stolen Bases:	Wills	35
Wins:	Jenkins	14
Strikeouts:	Jenkins	134
ERA:	Jenkins	3.16
Saves:	Smith	17

JANUARY 14   Tim Blackwell signs a free agent contract with the Expos.

JANUARY 27   The Cubs trade Ivan DeJesus to the Phillies for Larry Bowa and Ryne Sandberg.

> The Sandberg trade is the best in Cubs history, and is one of the greatest heists in baseball history. Sandberg was only a throw–in. It was essentially a swap of starting shortstops, and Sandberg was added to even up the deal. At first, the Cubs didn't know where to him play him. "The kid is capable of playing a couple of positions," said Dallas Green of Sandberg. "He can play shortstop, second base, or the outfield." In the Phillies minor league system, Sandberg was a shortstop. Philadelphia included him the trade because the club believed that Julio Franco and Juan Samuel were better prospects. Prior to his arrival in Chicago, Sandberg played in 13 big league games, mainly as a defensive replacement at shortstop and as a pinch–runner, and had six at–bats with one hit. At the beginning of the 1982 season, Sandberg was the Cubs starting third baseman. He moved to second base in September of that season.

FEBRUARY 11   President Ronald Reagan is chosen for membership into the Emil Verban Memorial Society.

In 1982, the Emil Verban Memorial Society had about 175 members. It was a Cubs fan club based in Washington and included several heavy hitters such as Justice Harry Blackman of the Supreme Court, television broadcaster Bryant Gumbel, actor Tom Bosley, and columnists David Broder and George Will. Hillary Clinton, a native of the Chicago suburb of Park Ridge, became a member in 1993. Reagan was chosen because he once broadcast re–creations of Cubs games on radio in Des Moines, Iowa, during the 1930s. The group was founded by six individuals in 1975, headed by lobbyist Bruce Ladd. One of the six original members was Dick Cheney, then White House Chief of Staff under Gerald Ford, and later serving a more prominent position as vice–president. Emil Verban was a second baseman with the Cubs from 1947 through 1949, whose chief claim to fame was batting 2,911 times in the majors with only one home run. The word "memorial" was added even through Verban was still very much alive. "I picked Emil because he was obscure," said Ladd. "We had all seen him play and we could relate to him." At first, Verban was provoked and insulted by the use of him name, but by the time of his death in 1989, he embraced the group, particularly after he was flown to Washington to meet Reagan.

MARCH 26   The Cubs send Paul Mirabella and Paul Semall to the Rangers for Bump Wills.

The son of Maury Wills, Bump was the Cubs starting second baseman at the start of the 1982 season, but didn't live up to expectations, particularly on defense. In September Ryne Sandberg was moved from third base to second and Wills was moved to the bench. In 1983, Bump moved to Japan to play baseball.

APRIL 1   The Cubs sell Bill Caudill to the Yankees.

Neither the Cubs nor the Yankees saw potential in Caudill, but he had several excellent seasons as a closer for the Mariners and Athletics.

APRIL 5   In the season opener, the Cubs beat the Reds 3–2 in Cincinnati in a game shortened to eight innings by rain. Batting in the leadoff spot in his first game as a Cub, Bump Wills hit the second pitch of the season for a home run off Mario Soto. Keith Moreland also had a home run and two singles. Ryne Sandberg made his major league debut in the game, and was hitless in three at–bats.

The Cubs played their road games in royal blue pullover shirts and white pants beginning in 1982. On the front was the same CUBS emblem that appeared on the home jerseys. The blue road uniforms remained part of the club's wardrobe through the 1989 season.

APRIL 9   The Cubs beat the Mets 5–0 in the home opener before 26,091 at Wrigley Field. The game was played in 34–degree temperatures. Ferguson Jenkins, in his first game as a Cub since 1973, was the winning pitcher. Jenkins pitched 6⅔ innings, with Lee Smith going the last 2⅓. Bill Buckner hit a home run.

Among the additions at Wrigley Field in 1982 was an electronic message board across the bottom of the scoreboard. The Cubs made an attempt to reverse the "Billy Goat Curse," placed on the team in 1945 by restaurateur William Sianis, who said the club would never again reach the World Series. His nephew, Sam

Sianis, was brought back to Wrigley Field with another goat to reverse the curse, but so far the effort has been unsuccessful.

APRIL 28   Dickie Noles pitches a one–hitter to defeat the Reds 6–0 at Wrigley Field. The only Cincinnati hit was a single by Eddie Milner in the fourth inning.

MAY 7   Keith Moreland drives in seven runs with a pair of three–run homers and a single as the Cubs beat the Astros 12–6 at Wrigley Field.

               Moreland played defensive back on the University of Texas football team. He started the 1982 season as a catcher, but by early May was moved to the outfield.

MAY 9   Jody Davis hits a three–run walk–off homer in the ninth inning to defeat the Astros 6–3 at Wrigley Field.

MAY 14   The Cubs win the 8,000th game in the history of the franchise, and believe it or not, the winning pitcher is Allen Ripley. The Cubs won 5–0. It was the team's first win at the Astrodome in three years, breaking a 12–games losing streak in Houston. It was Ripley's first start of the season, and he entered the game with a 11.32 ERA in seven relief appearances. Ripley pitched six innings, and Lee Smith went the final three.

MAY 24   Lee Elia and Bill Buckner scuffle during an 8–2 loss to the Padres in San Diego.

               The two fought during the sixth inning in the runway outside the Cubs dugout. The confrontation occurred because Elia felt that Buckner was trying to usurp his managerial authority by asking pitcher Dan Larson to retaliate by throwing at San Diego hitters after Buckner was knocked down by a pitch from Tim Lollar. Larson hit Tim Flannery of the Padres after Buckner went to the mound to confer with the pitcher. No serious blows were struck, but Buckner scratched himself from the May 25 game, claiming he injured his neck during the fracas. Elia stated publicly that he didn't believe the injury was severe enough to keep Buckner out of the lineup.

MAY 25   Ferguson Jenkins records his 3,000th career strikeout, although the Cubs lose 2–1 to the Padres in San Diego. Jenkins reached the goal by fanning Garry Templeton in the third inning.

JUNE 1   The Cubs sign Jay Johnstone as a free agent seven days after he was released by the Dodgers.

JUNE 7   With the first overall pick in the amateur draft, the Cubs select Shawon Dunston of Thomas Jefferson High School in Brooklyn, New York.

               Dunston went on to play 14 seasons in the majors and made two All–Star Game appearances. The draft began in 1965, and Dunston was the first position player chosen by the Cubs to represent the club in an All–Star Game. The only other player drafted and signed by the Cubs in 1982 to reach the majors was fifth–rounder Gary Varsho.

JUNE 13   The Cubs lose their 13th game in a row, dropping a 5–3 decision to the Expos in ten innings in Montreal. Tim Wallach ended the contest with a two–run homer off Willie Hernandez.

It was the longest losing streak by a Cubs team since 1944. At the end of the streak, the Cubs had a record of 21–39.

JUNE 14   The Cubs 13–game losing streak comes to an end with a 12–11 win over the Phillies at Wrigley Field. The Cubs won despite committing six errors. The Phillies nearly pulled it out with four runs in the ninth.

JUNE 17   The Cubs defeat the Expos 12–8 in a slugging match with the Expos at Wrigley Field.

JUNE 18   A bench–clearing brawl erupts during a 4–0 loss to the Expos at Wrigley Field. In the second inning, Gary Carter brushed Bill Buckner at first base while running out a fly ball. The two exchanged several punches, although neither was ejected. The battle stemmed from an incident a week earlier in Montreal when Carter broke Buckner's bat at home plate in retaliation for Buckner smashing Carter's face mask.

Buckner hit .306 with 201 hits, 15 homers and 105 RBIs in 1982. He struck out only 26 times in 637 at–bats. Leon Durham was the Cubs all–around best hitter during the season with a .312 average and 22 home runs and 28 stolen bases. He was the first Cub with at least 20 homers and 20 steals in a season since Wildfire Schulte in 1911.

Leon "Bull" Durham became a starter in 1982 and held a full–time spot in the lineup until he was traded in 1988. A solid run producer during his tenure, he never again approached 1982's .312 batting average or 28 stolen bases.

JULY 5   Lee Smith's first big league base hit is a home run off Phil Niekro, but the Cubs lose 7–5 to the Braves in Atlanta.

                Smith finished his career with only three hits in 84 at–bats for an average of .047. The homer off Niekro was his only extra base hit.

JULY 9   The Cubs humiliate the Reds 12–0 at Wrigley Field.

JULY 10   Dickie Noles pitches the Cubs to a 1–0 win over the Reds at Wrigley Field. Gary Woods drove in the lone run of the game with a double in the fourth inning.

JULY 16   The Cubs beat the Braves 4–3 at Wrigley Field on a tenth–inning rally that takes over 2 ½ hours. It started with a single by Junior Kennedy, followed by a two–hour–and–nineteen–minute rain delay. When play resumed, Kennedy scored on a double by Ryne Sandberg.

                The Cubs ended the month of July with a record of 40–65.

AUGUST 2   The Cubs sell Jay Howell to the Yankees.

                The Cubs have long been horrible judges of relief pitchers, and Howell was no exception. He was a highly effective closer for the Dodgers for many years.

AUGUST 5   Randy Martz pitches a two–hitter to defeat the Mets 5–1 at Wrigley Field. Ron Hodges had both New York hits with singles in the second and eighth innings.

AUGUST 12   The Cubs erupt for eight runs in the seventh inning and defeat the Mets 13–6 in New York.

AUGUST 17   The Cubs–Dodgers game is suspended after seventeen innings by darkness with the score 1–1. The Cubs scored in the first inning and the Dodgers in the second. The contest was completed the next day before the regularly scheduled game.

AUGUST 18   The suspended game of August 17 at Wrigley Field is completed and goes twenty–one innings before the Dodgers defeat the Cubs 2–1. At six hours and ten minutes, it is the longest game by time in Cubs history. Dusty Baker drove in the winning run with a sacrifice fly off Allen Ripley, scoring Steve Sax on a close play at the plate. There were no runs scored from the third inning through the twentieth. Eight Los Angeles pitchers and six Cubs hurlers combined for the eighteen consecutive innings of runless baseball. Both managers were ejected, as well as Cubs coach John Vukovich, who was serving as acting manager. The Dodgers used all twenty–five players on the roster, and pitchers Fernando Valenzuela and Bob Welch played in the outfield. The Dodgers won the regularly scheduled game 7–4.

AUGUST 22   The Cubs retire Ernie Banks's number 14 in ceremonies prior to an 8–7 win over the Padres at Wrigley Field. It was the first number retired by the Cubs.

AUGUST 23   Illinois Governor James Thompson signs legislation prohibiting the Cubs from playing night games at Wrigley Field after 10 P.M. The bill was sponsored by Rep. Ellis B. Levin (D–Chicago) and was specifically written, not to prevent the installation of lights, but as a "noise pollution" measure at outdoor venues. The statute decreed that Illinois cities with more than one million residents (Chicago was the only one in the state) from holding pro sports after 10:00 at night. Through a "grandfather clause," the White Sox, Bears, and Sting (a now defunct soccer team) were exempt. In 1983, a city measure banned night contests on a playing field that was not totally enclosed, that had more than 15,000 seats, and that was within 500 feet of 100 dwelling units. Wrigley Field was the only venue in Chicago that fell under that description.

Soon after the Tribune Company bought the Cubs in June 1981, Wrigleyville and Lake View residents banded together in an organization called CUBS (Citizens United for Baseball in Sunshine). The group began to lobby the Illinois legislature and Chicago city officials to ban lights at Wrigley Field. In 1981, the neighborhood was in a recovery stage after a decline that had lasted about twenty years. Many young professionals began to move into the area during the 1970s and rebuilt what had become a crumbling blue collar area. Real estate values soared and Lake View became one of the most ethnically diverse areas of Chicago. Residents feared that night games would attract a rowdy crowd, threaten their peace and safety, and cause damage to property. "No Lights in Wrigley Field" slogans began appearing on homes and apartments and on T-shirts and automobile bumpers. Cubs management argued that night ball would enhance the club's television revenue and allow more people to attend games.

SEPTEMBER 3   Ryne Sandberg plays second base for the Cubs for the first time during a 3–0 loss to the Padres in San Diego.

Sandberg scored 103 runs during his rookie season, and hit .271 with 32 stolen bases. He had to recover from a dismal start. He was hitless in his first twenty at-bats as a Cub, and had only one hit in his first thirty-two at-bats.

SEPTEMBER 14   Bill Madlock and Richie Hebner both hits grand slams off Cubs pitching during a 15–5 Pirates win in Pittsburgh. Hebner hit his slam off Dickie Noles in the third, and Madlock went deep on Mike Proly in the fourth.

SEPTEMBER 18   Down 7–0, the Cubs score three runs in the sixth inning and seven in the eighth to defeat the Expos 10–7 in Montreal. Bump Wills hit a three-run pinch homer to break the 7–7 tie.

SEPTEMBER 21   Ferguson Jenkins pitches the Cubs to a 1–0 win over the Pirates at Wrigley Field. Jody Davis drove in the lone run of the game with a single in the seventh inning.

Lee Elia wasn't impressed by what he saw in his first year as Cub manager. "There are a lot of guys I hope aren't here next year," said Elia. "You get tired of looking at garbage in your backyard."

DECEMBER 9   The Cubs trade Steve Henderson to the Mariners for Rich Brodi.

DECEMBER 10   The Cubs trade Doug Bird to the Red Sox for Chuck Rainey.

1983   Cubs

Season in a Sentence

Lee Elia lashes out at the Cubs loyal fans in April and is fired in August as the club shows no tangible evidence that better days are in the immediate future.

Finish • Won • Lost • Pct • GB

Fifth   71   91   .438   19.0

Managers

Lee Elia (54–68) and
Charlie Fox (17–22)

Stats   Cubs • NL • Rank

	Cubs	NL	Rank
Batting Avg:	.260	.255	5
On–Base Pct:	.322	.325	8
Slugging Pct:	.401	.376	1
Home Runs:	140		3
Stolen Bases:	84		12
ERA:	4.08	3.63	12
Fielding Avg:	.982	.978	1
Runs Scored:	701		2
Runs Allowed:	719		12

Starting Lineup

Jody Davis, c
Bill Buckner, 1b
Ryne Sandberg, 2b
Ron Cey, 3b
Larry Bowa, ss
Leon Durham, lf–cf
Mel Hall, cf
Keith Moreland, rf
Gary Woods, lf–cf

Pitchers

Chuck Rainey, sp
Dick Ruthven, sp
Steve Trout, sp
Ferguson Jenkins, sp
Dickie Noles, sp
Lee Smith, rp
Bill Campbell, rp
Mike Proly, rp
Warren Brusstar, rp
Craig Lefferts, rp

Attendance

1,479,717 (seventh in NL)

Club Leaders

Batting Avg:	Moreland	.302
On–Base Pct:	Moreland	.378
Slugging Pct:	Davis	.480
Home Runs:	Cey	24
	Davis	24
RBI:	Cey	90
Runs:	Sandberg	94
Stolen Bases:	Sandberg	37
Wins:	Rainey	14
Strikeouts:	Campbell	97
ERA:	Jenkins	4.30
Saves:	Smith	29

JANUARY 20   The Cubs trade Vance Lovelace and Dan Cataline to the Dodgers for Ron Cey.

Cey was past his prime but still had enough left to patch a hole at third base. He was a starter for three years, and all the Cubs gave up were two minor leaguers.

JANUARY 25   The Cubs trade Scott Fletcher, Pat Tabler, Randy Martz, and Dick Tidrow to the White Sox for Steve Trout and Warren Brusstar.

The trade was a controversial one. At the time, teams who lost free agents could enter a draft in which they could choose players from other clubs. Each team could protect twenty–six players. One of those exposed to the draft by the Cubs was Ferguson Jenkins, and the White Sox threatened to select him. In essence, the trade was made to keep Jenkins from being drafted by the White Sox. Fans were angry, believing that the Cubs had been taken, but Trout and Brusstar both became key members of the 1984 division winners. Steve's father, Dizzy Trout, won 170 games in the majors from 1939 and 1957 and pitched for the Tigers against the Cubs in the 1945 World Series. Dizzy Trout was the losing pitcher in the last World Series game the Cubs have ever won.

APRIL 5   The scheduled season opener at Wrigley Field against the Expos is rained out.

APRIL 6   The Cubs get underway with a 3–0 loss to the Expos before only 4,802 at Wrigley Field. The temperature was 40 degrees and the game was played in a constant drizzle. Steve Rogers pitched the shutout, and Al Oliver hit two home runs.

Lee Smith's 1.65 ERA in 1983 was the lowest in his stellar career. He was one of the few bright spots in a dismal year.

Steve Stone moved into the Cubs television booth in 1983 with Harry Caray. Lou Boudreau and Vince Lloyd covered the Cubs on radio, and Milo Hamilton alternated between TV and radio. Also in 1983, the Cubs vastly improved the concession and restroom facilities at Wrigley Field. A new ticket office was added as part of an enlargement and renovation of the team offices. A new clubhouse was built for the players behind the third base dugout under the stands, replacing the old one at the extremity of the left field foul line. The Cubs also experimented with the starting times of home games, beginning seven contests at 3:05 in the afternoon to allow professionals to leave work early and take in a game. It was also designed to avoid early afternoon summer heat and make it easier on players the day after they returned from road trips. The number of 3:05 starts increased to twenty in 1984. Batters disliked the late afternoon starts because of the shadows, which impaired visibility. Many of the 3:05 games had to be suspended because of darkness. One other change met with disapproval. Two Budweiser signs were hung from the bottom of the scoreboard, the first time that advertising appeared inside the park since the 1930s. Complaints that the Cubs were desecrating the old hand–operated board brought the signs down in 1986.

APRIL 9   Dickie Noles is arrested following an 8–4 loss to the Reds in Cincinnati.

Noles was arrested following a tavern brawl. He was charged with assault, resisting arrest, and disorderly conduct. Besides being fined by the Cubs, Noles was named in a $500,000 civil suit by one of the arresting police officers and a $300,000 suit by the doorman at the bar. When the pitcher appeared in court in Cincinnati on July 6, he entered a plea of no contest. The judge sentenced Noles to 180 days, but suspended 150 days. Noles was also credited with the fourteen days he spent at Chicago's Northwestern Memorial Hospital, where he had undergone treatment for alcohol addiction at the club's insistence. Shortly after the season ended, Noles served the remainder of his sixteen–day sentence in jail in Cincinnati. At the same time, Noles donated $1,000 to the Greater Cincinnati Knothole Baseball League.

APRIL 12   After starting the season with six straight losses, the Cubs pick up their first victory of 1983 by blanking the Expos 5–0 in Montreal.

APRIL 17   Four days after the election of Harold Washington, Chicago's first African–American mayor, the Pirates trim the Cubs 7–0 in the first game of a double–header in Pittsburgh. The second tilt is postponed when temperatures dipped below 30 degrees amid snow flurries. "Even Ernie Banks wouldn't want to play two today," said Pirates manager Chuck Tanner.

APRIL 29   Lee Elia delivers a profanity–laced, five–minute tirade against Cubs fans following a 4–3 loss to the Dodgers at Wrigley Field.

Elia was unable to contain his rage after a dozen fans doused Keith Moreland and Larry Bowa with beer as the Cubs trudged to the clubhouse after the defeat. "The 3,000 fans who have been watching us each day have been very negative and expecting too much," said Elia. "Why don't they rip me instead of the ballplayers?

Eighty–five percent of the world is working, but the 15 percent who come out to Wrigley Field have nothing better to do than heap abuse and criticism on the team. Why don't they go out and look for jobs?" The outburst was caught on tape and replayed on radio stations around the country. The forty-six "bleeps" in the tape used to cover the profanity added to the backlash against Elia. Within four months, Elia joined the "15 percent" he said were unemployed. The Cubs fired him on August 22.

MAY 21   Lee Elia slaps umpire Dave Pallone's hand during an 8–4 win over the Reds at Wrigley Field. Elia was ejected and later suspended for one game. The Cubs manager claimed that Pallone provoked the incident by waving his finger in his face.

MAY 22   The Cubs trade Willie Hernandez to the Phillies for Dick Ruthven and Bill Johnson.

Hernandez had been a dependable, but unspectacular, reliever for the Cubs for seven seasons. The Cubs needed a starter, and Ruthven filled the role. The Phillies traded Hernandez in March 1984 to the Tigers, where he suddenly blossomed as a closer. He won the 1984 American League Most Valuable Player Award in leading Detroit to a world championship.

MAY 30   After the Cubs blow a 6–3 lead and lose 9–7 to the Astros at Wrigley Field, Lee Elia shoves WBBM television cameraman Dan Brown in the Cubs clubhouse. Brown suffered a cut on the inside of his mouth when the camera was shoved into his face.

JUNE 3   The Cubs score eight runs in the seventh inning of a 9–3 win over the Pirates at Wrigley Field.

JUNE 8   The Cubs threaten to revoke the media credentials for Chicago rock station WLUP–FM when morning man Jonathan Brandmeier replays Lee Elia's April 29 harangue against Cubs fans everyday for over a month, complete with bleeps, to the team song "Hey, Hey, Holy Mackerel!"

Keith Moreland was the Cubs top hitter in 1983 with a .302 average and 16 homers. After a slow start, Ron Cey hit 24 homers and batted .275. Jody Davis matched Cey's 24 homers and had an average of .271. Lee Smith saved 29 games with a dominating 1.65 ERA.

JUNE 9 The Cubs sign Rick Reuschel after he is released by the Yankees.

Reuschel wasn't effective in his second tour with the Cubs. Over two seasons, he was 6–6 with a 4.54 ERA.

JUNE 12 Jody Davis hits a grand slam in the fourth inning off Bob Forsch in the fourth inning of a 6–3 win over the Cardinals at Wrigley Field. Ryne Sandberg tied a major league record for most assists in a game by a second baseman with 12.

JUNE 18 The Cubs collect 20 hits and defeat the Cardinals 10–1 in St. Louis.

JUNE 19 Dick Ruthven pitches a two–hitter to beat the Cardinals 4–1 at Busch Memorial Stadium. The only St. Louis hits were a single by George Hendrick in the second inning and a homer by Steve Braun in the fifth.

JUNE 20 Bill Campbell is the losing pitcher in both ends of a double–header against the Pirates in Pittsburgh. The Cubs lost the first contest 5–4 in ten innings, and the second 6–5 in thirteen.

JUNE 26 Jody Davis drives in six runs, including a grand slam off Randy Lerch in the second inning, during a 9–5 win over the Expos at Olympic Stadium. Keith Moreland was ejected in the fifth inning when he charged the mound and tackled Montreal pitcher Chris Welsh after a beaning.

JULY 3 The Cubs down the Expos 7–4 at Wrigley Field to pull within a game of the .500 mark.

After a 5–14 start, the Cubs were 38–39 on July 3 in fourth place just two games back of the first-place Expos. The Cubs were 33–52 over the rest of the season, however.

JULY 16 Larry Bowa collects the 2,000th hit of his career with a single during a 7–4 loss to the Dodgers in Los Angeles. The pitching victim was Fernando Valenzuela.

AUGUST 11 Leon Durham belts a grand slam in the third inning off Danny Cox during a 10–5 win over the Cardinals at Wrigley Field.

AUGUST 18 A three–run homer by Jody Davis accounts for all of the runs in a 3–0 win over the Braves at Wrigley Field. Ferguson Jenkins (8⅔ innings) and Lee Smith (⅓ of an inning) combined on the shutout.

AUGUST 22 Carmelo Martinez of the Cubs hits a home run in his first official at–bat in the majors during the fifth inning of a 2–0 win over the Reds at Wrigley Field. Martinez walked in the second inning in his first big league plate appearance.

The game was the first under new manager Charlie Fox. Earlier in the day, Fox replaced Lee Elia, who was fired. The Cubs had a record of 54–69 at the time of the switch. Fox has a special assistant to Dallas Green when he was appointed manager. Previously, Fox managed the Giants (1970–74) and the Expos (1976). He was 17–22 as manager of the Cubs and returned to the front office at his old job under Green at the end of the 1983 season. Elia later was manager of the Phillies in 1987 and 1988.

AUGUST 24   Chuck Rainey comes within one out of a no–hitter during a 3–0 win over the Reds at Wrigley Field. With two out in the ninth, Eddie Milner lined a single into center field. Rainey had to settle for a one–hitter. It was his only complete game in 34 starts in 1983.

AUGUST 29   Mel Hall rips two homers, including a grand slam in the fifth inning off Phil Niekro, to lead the Cubs to a 7–5 win over the Braves in Atlanta. Hall's slam tied the score 4–4, and a solo shot in the seventh deadlocked the game again 5–5. A two–run homer later in the seventh by Keith Moreland scored the winning runs.

SEPTEMBER 1   Nine days after the Soviets shoot down a Korean passenger plane, resulting in the deaths of 269 people, Mel Hall collects two homers and four hits to lead the Cubs to an 8–5 win over the Cardinals at Wrigley Field.

SEPTEMBER 12   The Cubs score seven runs in the sixth inning and defeat the Expos 8–0 at Wrigley Field.

SEPTEMBER 17   Down 6–1, the Cubs rally for two runs in the fifth inning, one in the eighth, and three in the ninth to beat the Mets 7–6 in New York.

SEPTEMBER 18   A two–run double by Gary Woods in the ninth inning lifts the Cubs to a 6–5 win over the Mets in New York.

The Cubs lost the Chicago attendance battle by a wide margin in 1983. The White Sox drew 2,132,821 compared to 1,479,717 for the Cubs. The White Sox won the AL West with a record of 99–63. Beginning with the 1985 season, the White Sox have outdrawn the Cubs only in 1991 and 1992, the first two seasons after the opening of new Comiskey Park.

SEPTEMBER 21   Ferguson Jenkins wins his 284th, and last, major league victory with 1 ⅔ innings of relief in a 7–6 win over the Pirates before only 3,029 at Wrigley Field.

On the same day, Jim Finks was named president and chief executive officer of the Cubs. Finks was a former NFL quarterback, who was general manager of the Minnesota Vikings and the Chicago Bears. Finks resigned his position with the Bears earlier in 1983. His hiring stripped some responsibility from Dallas Green, who in the minds of many in the Tribune Company was spending too much money without significant improvement in the standings. Finks remained with the Cubs until December 1984 when he returned to football as general manager of the New Orleans Saints.

OCTOBER 6   The Cubs hire 52–year–old Jim Frey as manager.

In his first season as a major league manager in 1980, Frey led the Kansas City Royals to the World Series. The Royals lost the Fall Classic to Dallas Green's Phillies. Frey was fired as Kansas City skipper after a slow start in 1981, however, and was a coach with the Mets in 1982 and 1983. In his first season as manager of the Cubs, Frey guided the club to a surprising division title.

NOVEMBER 15   Three weeks after a bomb rips through a Marine compound in Beirut, killing 241, and two weeks after the invasion of Grenada, Charlie Grimm dies at the age of 85. Grimm was associated with the Cubs as a player, manager, broadcaster, and vice–president between 1925 and 1981. According to Charlie's wishes, his wife Marion scattered his ashes over Wrigley Field in April 1984.

DECEMBER 7   In a three–team trade, the Cubs trade Carmelo Martinez, Craig Lefferts, and Fritz Connally to the Padres and receive Scott Sanderson from the Expos.

1984   Cubs

Season in a Sentence

Proving that good things happen to those who wait, Cubs fans are rewarded for their patience when the club reaches the post–season for the first time in thirty–nine years with the best record in the NL, only to suffer a devastating loss in the playoffs to the Padres.

Finish • Won • Lost • Pct • GB

First   96   65   .596   +6.5

National League Championship Series
–The Cubs lost three–games–to–two to the San Diego Padres

Manager

Jim Frey

Stats

Stats	Cubs	NL	Rank
Batting Avg:	.260	.255	4
On–Base Pct:	.333	.322	2
Slugging Pct:	.397	.369	2
Home Runs:	136		2
Stolen Bases:	154		4
ERA:	3.75	3.59	10
Fielding Avg:	.981	.978	2
Runs Scored:	762		1
Runs Allowed:	658		8

Starting Lineup

Jody Davis, c
Leon Durham, 1b
Ryne Sandberg, 2b
Ron Cey, 3b
Larry Bowa, ss
Gary Matthews, lf
Bob Dernier, cf
Keith Moreland, rf

Pitchers

Rick Sutcliffe, sp
Steve Trout, sp
Dennis Eckersley, sp
Scott Sanderson, sp
Dick Ruthven, sp
Rick Reuschel, sp
Chuck Rainey, sp
Lee Smith, rp
Tim Stoddard, rp
Warren Brusstar, rp

Attendance

2,104,219 (second in NL)

Club Leaders

Batting Avg:	Sandberg	.314
On–Base Pct:	Matthews	.410
Slugging Pct:	Sandberg	.520
Home Runs:	Cey	25
RBI:	Durham	96
Runs:	Sandberg	114
Stolen Bases:	Dernier	45
Wins:	Sutcliffe	16
Strikeouts:	Sutcliffe	155
ERA:	Trout	3.49
Saves:	Smith	33

JANUARY 5   The Cubs sign Richie Hebner, most recently with the Pirates, as a free agent.

MARCH 17   The Cubs release Ferguson Jenkins, ending his major league career with a record of 284–226. Jenkins was elected to the Hall of Fame in 1991, his second year on the ballot.

MARCH 26   The Cubs trade Bill Campbell and Mike Diaz to the Phillies for Gary Matthews, Bob Dernier, and Porfi Altamirano.

The Cubs made a brilliant deal, filling two holes in the outfield at a minimal cost as Dernier became the starter in center field and Matthews in left. It also had a ripple effect on the rest of the lineup. Leon Durham moved from the outfield to his natural position of first base, which benched Bill Buckner, who had compiled a batting average of .304 over the previous four seasons. Keith Moreland moved into a platoon situation in right field with Mel Hall. The trade failed to stir Cubs fans at the time it was announced, however. It appeared to be yet another re-arrangement of the deck chairs on a sinking team that lost 90 games in 1983. In the spring training in 1984, the Cubs were awful with a 7–20 record, including an 11–game losing streak. Two fights took place between players on the field. Minor league pitchers Bill Johnson and Reggie Patterson had a punch–up on March 10, and Dick Ruthven and Mel Hall battled on March 20.

APRIL 3   The Cubs open the season in San Francisco, and defeat the Giants 5–3. A two–run double by Jody Davis broke a 2–2 tie in the seventh inning. Keith Moreland and Ron Cey each hit home runs.

The Cubs played their first seven games in California with a 3–4 record against the Giants, Padres and Dodgers.

APRIL 13   In the home opener, the Cubs bash the Mets 11–2 on Friday the 13th before 33,436 at Wrigley Field. Ron Cey, Jody Davis, and Gary Matthews hit home runs.

In his first season with the Cubs, Matthews hit 14 homers, scored 101 runs, and batted .291. Known as "The Sarge," he was also an inspirational force in the clubhouse with his hustle and gung–ho enthusiasm. Matthews drew 103 walks and led the NL in on–base percentage. Cey hit 25 homers and drove in 97 runs. Davis contributed 19 home runs, 94 runs–batted–in. Leon Durham came back from an injury–riddled 1983 season to hit 23 homers with 96 RBIs and a .279 average. But it was Ryne Sandberg who carried the Cubs attack in 1984. He blossomed into a star with a .314 average, 32 stolen bases, a league–leading 114 runs scored, 200 hits, 36 doubles, a league–leading 19 triples, and 19 homers to win the National League Most Valuable Player Award. He came within one triple and one homer of becoming the only player in history to collect at least 200 hits, 20 doubles, 20 triples, 20 homers, and 20 stolen bases in a season.

APRIL 28   Scott Sanderson pitches a two–hitter to defeat the Pirates 7–1 at Three Rivers Stadium. Johnny Ray had both Pittsburgh hits with a double in the first inning and a single in the fourth.

MAY 7   The Cubs score seven runs in the second inning to take a 9–0 lead and hold on to beat the Giants 10–7 at Wrigley Field. Leon Durham hit a home run for the fourth game in a row. He hit a home run in each of the three games against the Padres at Wrigley Field on May 4, 5, and 6.

MAY 8   The Cubs outslug the Giants 12–11 at Wrigley Field. The Cubs scored seven runs in the third inning, four on a grand slam by Ron Cey off Scott Garrelts, to pull ahead 8–2, but San Francisco battled back and tied it 11–11 with two runs in the ninth. The winning run was scored on a pinch–single by Keith Moreland. Leon Durham failed in his bid to hit a homer in his fifth straight game. He walked four times in five plate appearances.

MAY 12   A three–run pinch–homer by Jody Davis in the ninth inning enables the Cubs to prevail 5–4 over the Astros in Houston.

MAY 16   The Cubs take first place with a 10–4 win over the Reds in Cincinnati. The Cubs had a record of 20–14.

MAY 24   Bob Dernier collects five hits in five at–bats during a 10–7 win over the Braves in the first game of a double–header at Wrigley Field. Leon Durham contributed six runs–batted–in with a pair of three–run homers. Dernier didn't start the second game, as Henry Cotto played center field, but the Cubs won 7–5.

MAY 25   The Cubs trade Bill Buckner to the Red Sox for Dennis Eckersley and Mike Brumley.

          Buckner was unhappy over his role as a bench–warmer and went to Boston where he became the Red Sox starting first baseman. Eckersley was 27–26 over three seasons as a Cubs starting pitcher.

MAY 27   A disputed call by third base umpire Steve Rippley triggers a ruckus during a Cubs–Reds game at Wrigley Field.

          In the second inning, Ron Cey struck a Mario Soto pitch down the left field line. which Rippley called a home run. Furious, Soto rushed toward the umpire, and bumped into him. During the course of the argument, the Reds pitcher had to be wrestled to the ground by manager Vern Rapp and catcher Brad Gulden. In the process of restraining Soto, they collided with Cubs coach Don Zimmer, prompting both benches to empty. During the ensuing melee, a vendor threw a bag of ice that struck Soto in the chest. The seething Soto grabbed a bat and tried to climb into the stands, but was stopped before he could inflict bodily harm. Meanwhile, the umpires conferred and reversed the home run ruling, reducing Cey's drive to a mere foul ball. Jim Frey went berserk over the decision, and was ejected along with Soto. In all, the game was delayed for thirty-two minutes. Once play resumed, the Reds won 4–3.

MAY 30   Steve Trout pitches no–hit ball for 7⅔ innings against the Braves in Atlanta before Albert Hall and Rafael Ramirez hit singles. Lee Smith relieved Trout, and preserved a 6–2 Cubs win. For the second time in a week, Bob Dernier had five hits in a game against the Braves.

JUNE 4   With the third overall pick in the amateur draft, the Cubs select pitcher Drew Hall of Morehead State University.

Hall had a 9–12 record and a 5.21 ERA in five seasons in the majors. The Cubs hit the jackpot, however, by drafting Greg Maddux out of Valley High School in Las Vegas, Nevada, in the second round. Another pitcher with an excellent future was chosen in round six, when the Cubs called the name of Jamie Moyer. Jeff Pico was selected in the thirteenth round.

JUNE 10   The Cubs defeat the Cardinals 2–0 in St. Louis, scoring both runs in unusual fashion. In the eighth inning, Ryne Sandberg was hit by a pitch thrown by Joaquin Andujar with the bases loaded. In the ninth, the Cubs pulled off a triple steal, with Leon Durham swiping home, Jody Davis taking third, and Larry Bowa second.

JUNE 13   The Cubs trade Joe Carter, Mel Hall, Don Schulze, and Darryl Banks to the Indians for Rick Sutcliffe, George Frazier, and Ron Hassey. The trade wasn't actually completed until June 19, however, because Dallas Green forgot to put Hall and Carter on waivers, which is required for inter–league deals in mid–season.

Rick Sutcliffe gave the Cubs the ace they needed to win the division in 1984.

On June 13, the Cubs had a record of 34–25, and Dallas Green believed it was time to make a trade to help the Cubs win in 1984 by sacrificing four promising youngsters under the age of 25 for three veterans. Sutcliffe was phenomenal over the remainder of the 1984 season. Utilizing a herky–jerky delivery that kept batters off stride, he was 16–1 with an ERA of 2.69. Sutcliffe won the National League Cy Young Award. Without the trade, it's unlikely the Cubs would have won the division title in 1984, but it hurt the club in the long–term. Carter became a star, and Hall was a productive starter for several clubs.

JUNE 19   On the day the Bulls draft Michael Jordan, Rick Sutcliffe gives up three runs in the ninth inning in his first start with the Cubs, but hangs on to defeat the Pirates 4–3 in Pittsburgh.

JUNE 23   In one of the most dramatic and unforgettable victories in the long history of the Chicago Cubs, Ryne Sandberg hits two homers and three singles and drives in seven runs to spark the Cubs to a thrilling eleven–inning, 12–11 decision over the Cardinals at Wrigley Field. The contest was carried nationally on NBC–TV. The Cardinals took a 7–1 lead in the second and were up 9–3 in the sixth when the Cubs scored five runs. It was still 9–8 when Sandberg faced Bruce Sutter with two out in the ninth. Ryne hit a home run to tie the game 9–9. The Cardinals scored twice in the tenth, and in the bottom of the inning, Sandberg brought the crowd to their feet again with a two–run homer to tie it up again 11–11. The Cubs finally won in the eleventh when Leon Durham singled, reached third on a stolen base and an error, and scored on a pinch–single by Dave Owen.

The Cubs entered the game with a 36–31 record, and had lost six of their previous eight games. The win helped turn the season around. From that point to the end of the regular season, the Cubs were 60–34.

JUNE 24   Rick Sutcliffe strikes out 14 batters as the Cubs blank the Cardinals 5–0 in St. Louis.

JUNE 30   The Cubs score seven runs in the ninth inning to ice the Dodgers 14–4 in Los Angeles. The Cubs collected 20 hits in the game.

The Cubs created considerable consternation around the league by keeping the infield grass cut high to help slow ground to compensate for the lack of range by 38–year–old shortstop Larry Bowa and 36–year–old third baseman Ron Cey. Many Cubs batters were angry because it cost them base hits.

JULY 15   The Cubs trade Chuck Rainey to the Athletics for Dave Lopes.

JULY 21   Prior to an eleven–inning, 4–3 win over the Giants, an Old Timers Game is played between the 1969 Cubs and the 1969 Orioles, two teams stunned by the Mets during that fateful season.

JULY 27   The Cubs lose 2–1 to the Mets in New York. The defeat dropped the Cubs 4 ½ games back of the Mets in the NL East race. Chicago's record was 56–43.

JULY 29   The Cubs sweep the Mets 3–0 and 5–1 in a double–header at Shea Stadium to cut New York's lead in the pennant race to 1 ½ games.

AUGUST 1   The Cubs take over first place from the Mets with a 5–4 win over the Phillies at Wrigley Field. A sacrifice fly by Jody Davis in the ninth inning plated the winning run.

AUGUST 2   The Cubs turn a bizarre double play in the ninth inning to stave off the Expos 3–2 at Wrigley Field. With runners on first and third and one out, Pete Rose hit a liner that bounced off Lee Smith's shoulder to shortstop Dave Owen, who caught the carom. Owen threw to first to double up Don Stanhouse to end the game. The play has gone down in Cubs lore as the "immaculate deflection."

AUGUST 5   A grand slam by Keith Moreland in the third inning off Rick Grapenthin accounts for all of the runs in a 4–3 win over the Expos at Wrigley Field.

AUGUST 8   The Cubs complete a four–game sweep of the Mets at Wrigley Field with a 7–6 victory. The Cubs downed the Mets 9–3 on August 6, and 8–6 and 8–4 in a double–header on August 7. It was a contentious series, as the two teams exchanged beanballs throughout the four games. In the second game of the August 7 twinbill, Keith Moreland rushed the mound and roll–blocked Mets pitcher Ed Lynch, instigating a bench–clearing brawl. The Cubs increased their lead from one–half game to 4 ½ games with the four wins.

AUGUST 30   Trailing 3–0, the Cubs score two runs in the seventh inning, one in the ninth and five in the tenth to beat the Braves 8–3 in Atlanta.

The Cubs rise to the top of the standings created a dilemma because of the absence of lights at Wrigley Field. With the World Series due to open in the

National League park, it would have meant playing the first, second, sixth, and seventh games on weekday afternoons if they Cubs reached the post–season. Under its contract with NBC–TV, midweek games would have cost baseball millions of dollars in revenue because of the reduced advertising income that would have been realized by the network. Each major league team stood to lose between $400,000 and $700,000 as its share of the television proceeds. The Cubs were asked to move the home post–season games to either Comiskey Park or County Stadium in Milwaukee, but the club adamantly refused. The Cubs also vetoed the suggestion to use a portable lighting system at Wrigley Field for the post–season. To solve the situation, commissioner Bowie Kuhn arranged for alternative schedules, which were announced on August 30. They provided for the Fall Classic to start in the American League city if the Cubs won the NL pennant. This would have placed the three games in Chicago on Friday, Saturday, and Sunday afternoon. One Cubs season ticket holder filed a lawsuit in Cook County Circuit Court seeking $1 million in damages against Kuhn and NBC because he might miss a fourth home game if the Series went the limit. The suit was dismissed. The situation became moot when the Cubs lost in the playoffs to the Padres.

SEPTEMBER 3   Rick Sutcliffe strikes out 15 batters in eight innings against the Phillies in Philadelphia. Sutcliffe left the game with the score 3–3, and the Cubs went on to a 4–3 triumph in twelve innings.

SEPTEMBER 8   Rick Sutcliffe strikes out 12 batters, while issuing no walks, to beat the Mets 6–0 in New York.

SEPTEMBER 14   Jody Davis hits a grand slam in the sixth inning off Brent Gaff during a 7–1 win over the Mets at Wrigley Field. It was Rick Sutcliffe's 13th consecutive victory.

SEPTEMBER 15   The Cubs score four runs in the first inning and beat the Mets 5–4 at Wrigley Field to take a 9 ½ game lead in the NL East race.

The Cubs won the Eastern Division title in 1984 mainly with players obtained from other clubs. Among the starting eight position players, Ryne Sandberg, Larry Bowa, Bob Dernier, Gary Matthews, and Keith Moreland came from the Phillies; Leon Durham and Jody Davis from the Cardinals; and Ron Cey from the Dodgers. The starting five in the pitching rotation included Rick Sutcliffe (from the Indians), Dennis Eckersley (Red Sox), Steve Trout (White Sox), Scott Sanderson (Expos), and Dick Ruthven (Phillies). The only two players on the 25–man post–season roster who had spent their entire career in the Cubs organization were close, Lee Smith and reserve outfielder Henry Cotto. The roster had also been almost completely remade since Dallas Green took over in October 1981. The only three players who were on the team during the 1981 season were Smith, Durham, and Davis. Only 14 of the 25 were with the Cubs in 1983.

SEPTEMBER 20   The Cubs go over the two million mark in attendance for the first time, although the home club loses 7–6 to the Pirates.

The Cubs drew 2,104,219 in 1984, shattering the old record of 1,674,993 set in 1969. The Cubs never drew less than two million again with the exception of 1986 and the strike–shortened seasons of 1994 and 1995. The attendance boost was due in large part to a winning club, but also the popularity of Harry Caray and the games being carried nationally over WGN–TV. The number of affiliates on the radio network boomed from eleven in 1983 to sixty–nine in 1986.

SEPTEMBER 23   The Cubs clinch at least a tie for the Eastern Division championship by sweeping the Cardinals 8–2 and 4–2 in a double–header in St. Louis.

SEPTEMBER 24   The Cubs set off an exuberant celebration in Chicago and the popping of champagne corks by clinching their first pennant since 1945 with a 4–1 triumph over the Pirates at Three Rivers Stadium. Rick Sutcliffe pitched a two–hitter and faced the minimum 28 batters. Joe Orsulak had both Pittsburgh hits with a triple in the fourth inning and a single in the sixth. It was Sutcliffe's 14th win in a row, running his record as a Cub to 16–1. Overall, Sutcliffe was 20–6 in 1984, counting his 4–5 mark with the Indians.

SEPTEMBER 30   The Cubs close out the 1984 regular season with a 2–1 win over the Cardinals at Wrigley Field with two runs in the ninth inning. After the game, Jim Frey marched his entire ballclub onto the field and doffed his cap to the Chicago fans. The Cubs finished the season with a record of 96–65, the best in the National League.

The Cubs opponent in the National League Championship Series was the San Diego Padres, who were reaching the post–season for the first time. The Padres were managed by Dick Williams and had a record of 92–70. Heading into the 1984 season, the Cubs and Padres were the only two of the twelve National League clubs who had never reached the NLCS since the division format was established in 1969.

OCTOBER 2   In the first game of the National League Championship Series, the Cubs overwhelm the Padres 13–0 before 36,282 at Wrigley Field. The Cubs hit five home runs, including one by Rick Sutcliffe that cleared the right field bleachers and landed on Sheffield Avenue. Garry Matthews hit two homers and Bob Dernier and Ron Cey added one each. Aided by a 20 mile–per–hour wind, Dernier led off the first inning by belting Eric Show's second pitch for a homer. Sutcliffe pitched seven innings and allowed only two hits.

Ernie Banks threw out the ceremonial first pitch and was allowed to sit on the bench as an honorary coach. The regular National League umpires were on strike when the NLCS began. Amateur umpires were used during the first four games of the series, with Big Ten arbiters handling the games at Wrigley Field. The regular umps returned for Game Five of the NLCS.

OCTOBER 3   The Cubs move within one game of ending their 39–year absence from the World Series with a 4–2 win over the Padres before 36,282 at Wrigley Field. Steve Trout scattered five hits over 8 ⅓ innings, and Lee Smith picked–up the save by retiring the final two batters.

Following the second game, Cubs fan, columnist, and ABC News commentator George Will said, "We all know that means it will be the Padres in five." Mike Royko took the opposite tack, believing that the Cubs were in the World Series after taking two in Chicago. Royko ridiculed San Diego fans in his nationally syndicated column, drawing unflattering comparisons between devoted Cubs followers and laid back Southern Californians. Angered by Royko's column, Padres fans cheered their club loudly and often, breaking all previous decibel levels recorded at San Diego Stadium. Padres players credited the fans with helping them overcome the two–game deficit to win the playoff series.

OCTOBER 4   The Padres unleash their frustration over losing the first two games of the NLCS by defeating the Cubs 7–1 in San Diego. The Cubs led 1–0 before the Padres scored three runs in the fifth inning and four in the sixth. Dennis Eckersley was the losing pitcher.

OCTOBER 6   Steve Garvey's two–run homer in the bottom of the ninth inning off Lee Smith gives the Padres a 7–5 win over the Cubs in San Diego and evens the NLCS at 2–2. The Padres had a 2–0 lead in the fourth inning when Gary Matthews walked and Jody Davis and Leon Durham hit back–to–back homers to put the Cubs ahead 3–2. Garvey tied it with an RBI–single in the fifth and the Padres took a 5–3 advantage with two in the seventh, but the Cubs tied it up 5–5 in the eighth. Keith Moreland drove in a run with a single and scored on Davis's double. The Cubs had the bases loaded in the ninth, but couldn't score. In the bottom half, Tony Gwynn singled and Garvey homered to give the Padres the win. It was Garvey's first home run since August 15. He finished the game with four hits in five at–bats and five runs–batted–in.

OCTOBER 7   The Padres reach the World Series for the first time in the history of the franchise by scoring four runs in the seventh inning to beat the Cubs 6–3 in San Diego. Rick Sutcliffe started the game for the Cubs, carrying a 15–game winning streak into the game including one in the first game of the playoff. Against the Padres in 1984, he had allowed only one earned run in 24 ⅓ innings including the Game One NLCS win. The Cubs took an early 3–0 lead. Leon Durham belted a two–run homer in the first, and Jody Davis contributed a solo blast in the second. The Padres whittled the lead to 3–2 with a pair of runs in the sixth. Although Sutcliffe appeared to be weakening, Jim Frey left him in the game. In the seventh, with a runner on second and one out, and the Cubs just eight outs away from a World Series appearance, a sharp grounder by Tim Flannery rolled through the legs of first baseman Leon Durham. The runner on second scored to tie the game 3–3. Frey gave the second guessers more ammunition by leaving Sutcliffe on the mound to absorb more punishment, as the Padres added three more runs with the aid of a checked–swing single off the end of the bat by Alan Wiggins that looped into right field, and a potential double–play ball hit by Tony Gwynn that took a bad hop over Ryne Sandberg's head for a double which drove in two runs. Goose Gossage shut the Cubs down by pitching scoreless eighth and ninth innings to put San Diego into the World Series against the Tigers. Sutcliffe suffered his first defeat since June 29. The winning pitcher was Craig Lefferts, who held the Cubs hitless in the sixth and seventh. The Cubs traded Lefferts to the Padres on December 7, 1983.

The loss left everyone connected with the Cubs crushed and dumbfounded. Through the first twenty–two innings of the Series, the Cubs outscored the Padres 18–2 and were twelve outs from the World Series with a three–run lead, and eight outs away with a one run advantage, in Game Five. A World Series in Chicago seemed to be in the bag. "We had them by the throat," said Dallas Green, "and let them get away. That's what hurts the most right now."

DECEMBER 18   Six weeks after Ronald Reagan wins a second term as president in an election against Walter Mondale, the Cubs sign Lary Sorensen, most recently with the Athletics, as a free agent.

On the same day, Jim Finks resigned as president and chief executive officer of the Cubs. Dallas Green's title changed from executive vice-president to president.

DECEMBER 19   The Cubs go to court to get lights installed at Wrigley Field.

The Cubs filed a lawsuit against the City of Chicago and Illinois Governor James Thompson, seeking to overturn state and city laws which blocked night games at the ballpark. The lawsuit contended that the laws unfairly singled out Wrigley Field in an effort to block night sporting events there. In October 1985, the Illinois Supreme Court upheld the statutes that kept lights out of Wrigley.

1985   Cubs

Season in a Sentence

The Cubs are in first place in June, but injuries wreck a promising season as the club makes more hospital appearances than the characters on an afternoon soap opera.

Finish • Won • Lost • Pct • GB

Fourth   77   84   .478 23.5

Manager

Jim Frey

Stats

Stats	Cubs	NL	Rank
Batting Avg:	.254	.252	7
On-Base Pct:	.326	.321	4
Slugging Pct:	.390	.374	1
Home Runs:	150		1
Stolen Bases:	182		2
ERA:	4.16	3.59	11
Fielding Avg:	.979	.979	6
Runs Scored:	686		4
Runs Allowed:	729		11

Starting Lineup

Jody Davis, c
Leon Durham, 1b
Ryne Sandberg, 2b
Ron Cey, 3b
Shawon Dunston, ss
Gary Matthews, lf
Bob Dernier, cf
Keith Moreland, rf
Dave Lopes, lf-cf
Chris Speier, ss-3b
Larry Bowa, ss
Thad Bosley, lf
Billy Hatcher, cf-lf

Pitchers

Dennis Eckersley, sp
Steve Trout, sp
Rick Sutcliffe, sp
Ray Fontenot, sp-rp
Scott Sanderson, sp
Dick Ruthven, sp
Lee Smith, rp
George Frazier, rp
Warren Brusstar, rp
Lary Sorensen, rp

Attendance

2,161,534 (fifth in NL)

Club Leaders

Batting Avg:	Moreland	.307
On-Base Pct:	Moreland	.374
Slugging Pct:	Sandberg	.504
Home Runs:	Sandberg	26
RBI:	Moreland	106
Runs:	Sandberg	113
Stolen Bases:	Sandberg	54
Wins:	Eckersley	11
Strikeouts:	Eckersley	117
ERA:	Eckersley	3.08
Saves:	Smith	33

FEBRUARY 28   Rick Reuschel signs a free agent contract with the Pirates.

The Cubs believed that Reuschel was finished at the age of 35, and left him off the 1984 post–season roster. Rick proved them wrong, however, and was 14–8 with a 2.29 ERA on a 1985 Pittsburgh team that lost 104 games. He won 75 more games after 1984 in a career that lasted until 1991.

APRIL 8   The Cubs sign Chris Speier, most recently with the Twins, as a free agent.

During the 1984–85 off–season, the Cubs fired Milo Hamilton as a broadcaster in the WGN television and radio booth. Hamilton went to Houston as announcer for the Astros. DeWayne Staats came from Houston to Chicago to do the play–by–play for the Cubs after the Cubs unsuccessfully tried to hire Brent Musburger away from CBS.

APRIL 9   The Cubs open the season by defeating the Pirates 2–1 before 34,551 at Wrigley Field. Rick Sutcliffe was the winning pitcher. It was his 15th consecutive regular season win over two seasons. Keith Moreland drove in both Chicago runs with a single in the first inning and a homer in the fourth. Leon Durham contributed three hits.

Due to the increased demand for tickets, the Cubs sold bleacher tickets in advance. Prior to 1985, the seats were sold only on the day of the game. In June, additional bleacher capacity was available with the addition of seats on the catwalks down the left and right field lines.

APRIL 14   Rick Sutcliffe extends his regular season winning streak over two seasons to 16 games with a 4–2 win over the Expos at Wrigley Field.

The streak ended with a 5–3 loss to the Expos in Montreal on April 19. Sutcliffe was 5–3 with a 2.11 ERA when he tore his left hamstring on May 19. He was limited to 20 starts in 1985 and had a record of 8–8 with a 3.18 ERA.

APRIL 16   Dennis Eckersley pitches a complete–game, ten–inning shutout to beat the Phillies 1–0 at Wrigley Field. Bob Dernier drove in the winning run with a single.

APRIL 23   Rick Sutcliffe pitches a shutout and hits a home run to defeat the Pirates 5–0 in Pittsburgh.

MAY 4   On a day in which the wind is blowing out at 24 miles–per–hour, the Cubs outslug the Padres 12–8 at Wrigley Field.

MAY 8   Rick Sutcliffe strikes out 12 batters and beats the Giants 1–0 at Wrigley Field. The only run of the game was scored on a home run by Ryne Sandberg off Mike Krukow in the first inning.

MAY 22   With the Cubs trailing the Reds 4–3 in the sixth inning at Wrigley Field, Brian Dayett hits a pinch–hit grand slam off Tom Browning to spark the Cubs to a 7–4 win. It was Dayett's first home run as a Cub and the only one he hit in 1985.

During spring training, a ball thrown by Dayett struck Jim Frey in the face, putting the Cubs manager in the hospital for a few days.

MAY 31   A three–run homer by
          Keith Moreland caps a
          four–run Cubs tenth
          inning in a 6–2 win over
          the Astros in Houston.

          *Moreland hit .307
          with 14 homers and
          106 runs–batted–in
          during the 1985 sea-
          son. Leon Durham
          was another offensive
          star with 21 homers
          and a .282 average.*

In 1985, Keith Moreland had his best season with the Cubs, but he was a productive—and underrated—player throughout his six years with the team.

JUNE 3   In the first round of the
          amateur draft, the Cubs
          select outfielder Rafael
          Palmeiro from Mississippi
          State University.

          *This is the best draft
          in Cubs history to
          date. In the twenty–
          fourth round, the
          Cubs picked up first baseman Mark Grace from San Diego State University.
          Other future major leaguers signed and drafted by the Cubs in 1985 were Greg
          Smith (second round), Rick Wrona (fifth), Doug Dascenzo (twelfth), Joe Kraemer
          (sixteenth), and Kelly Mann (twentieth).*

JUNE 7   Jody Davis hits a home run in the second inning off Jose DeLeon to beat the Pirates
          1–0 at Wrigley Field. Rick Sutcliffe pitched the shutout.

JUNE 11   Leon Durham hits a grand slam in the eighth inning off Gary Lucas boosting the
          Cubs to a 5–3 win over the Expos in Montreal. The Cubs trailed 3–1 when Durham
          cleared the bases.

          *The win gave the Cubs a 34–19 record and a 3 ½–game lead over the Mets. The
          Cubs started a 13–game losing streak on June 12, however, and were 33–59
          from that date through September 19.*

JUNE 25   The Cubs fall 3–2 to the Mets at Wrigley Field to record their 13th loss in a row.

          *The only longer losing streak in Cubs history is 14 games in 1997. The Cubs
          also lost 13 in a row in 1944 and 1982.*

JUNE 26   The Cubs end their 13–game losing streak with a 7–3 victory over the Mets at
          Wrigley Field.

JUNE 29   Ryne Sandberg collects five hits, including a double, in seven at–bats, but the Cubs
          lose 6–5 to the Pirates in 15 innings in Pittsburgh.

Sandberg followed his 1984 MVP season with a .305 average, 26 homers, and 113 runs scored. He also stole 54 bases, the most by a Cub since Frank Chance swiped 57 in 1906.

JULY 3   Ryne Sandberg hits a two–run double in the ninth inning to beat the Phillies 4–3 in Philadelphia.

JULY 19   The Cubs announce that if the team qualifies it will not play World Series games at Wrigley Field because of "the light situation." In a letter sent to season ticket holders, Dallas Green said that "it is also possible" that the Cubs home dates in the National League Championship Series would be moved. The Cubs turned down an offer by the White Sox to play post–season games at Comiskey Park. Instead, St. Louis, Cincinnati, and Pittsburgh were mentioned as alternatives because the Cubs wanted to play in a National League ballpark.

AUGUST 1   A squeeze bunt by Larry Bowa with the bases loaded in the fourteenth inning enables the Cubs to overcome the Cardinals 9–8 at Wrigley Field. The Cubs led 8–2 in the fifth inning before allowing the Cardinals to come back and tie the game.

AUGUST 5   Darryl Strawberry of the Mets slams three homers to beat the Cubs 7–2 at Wrigley Field.

Dave Lopes was 39 years old in 1985 and had only 275 at–bats for the Cubs, but he stole 47 bases in 51 attempts.

AUGUST 6   The Cubs game against the Cardinals in St. Louis is postponed by a strike by the players. The August 7 contest between the same two clubs was also called off. The strike ended on August 8, and both games were made up with double–headers.

AUGUST 12   Thad Bosley stars with two homers in an 8–7 win over the Expos at Wrigley Field. Bosley ripped a three–run, pinch–hit homer in the sixth inning to tie the game 6–6, and remained in the contest in left field. After the Expos pulled ahead 7–6, Bosley hit a two–run homer in the eighth for the win.

Bosley hit .333 as a pinch–hitter in 1985 with 20 hits in 60 at–bats.

AUGUST 13   The Cubs release Larry Bowa.

Shawon Dunston replaced Bowa as the starting shortstop at the beginning of the season, but Dunston was sent to the minors on May 15 after a slow start. Dunston returned on August 13 when Bowa was released. After his release, Bowa played 14 more games with the Mets before his playing career ended. He finished with 2,222 games played at shortstop, ranking fourth all–time behind Luis Aparicio (2,581), Ozzie Smith (2,511), and Cal Ripken (2,302). Bowa became manager of the Padres in 1987.

AUGUST 14   Ron Cey hits a grand slam in the third inning off Bryn Smith to put the Cubs ahead 5–1, but the Expos rally to win 8–7 at Wrigley Field. During the game, Sal Butera and Smith both hit their first major league homers on back–to–back pitches off Ray Fontenot. Butera finished his career with only eight homers, while Smith collected only three.

The Cubs pitching staff was demolished by injuries in 1985. From August 14 through August 23, all five starting pitchers were on the disabled list. Gary Matthews and Bob Dernier also lost time on the disabled list during the season.

SEPTEMBER 1   The Cubs rout the Braves 15–2 at Wrigley Field.

SEPTEMBER 8   Pete Rose ties Ty Cobb in a tie game between the Reds and the Cubs at Wrigley Field. At gametime, Rose had 4,189 career hits, two short of Cobb's record of 4,191. Rose wasn't planning to play in the game because Cubs southpaw Steve Trout was the announced starting pitcher, and Pete hadn't started against a left–handed pitcher all season. Trout was scratched after he injured his elbow falling off a bicycle the night before, however, and Rose penciled himself into the lineup against right hander Reggie Patterson. Rose collected hit number 4,190 with a single in the first inning, and after grounding out in the third, tied Cobb's all–time hit record in the fifth with another single off Patterson. The crowd at Wrigley gave Rose a five–minute standing ovation. Pete went to the plate twice more, and failed to collect a hit. The game ended in a 5–5 tie after nine innings because of darkness. Rose broke the record with a single off Eric Show of the Padres on September 11 in Cincinnati.

SEPTEMBER 17   Jody Davis drills a three–run homer in the sixth inning to account for all of the runs in a 3–0 win over the Expos in Montreal. Dennis Eckersley (seven innings) and Lee Smith (two innings) combined on the shutout.

SEPTEMBER 21   The Cubs score eight runs in the fifth inning and lash the Phillies 9–2 in Philadelphia.

SEPTEMBER 24   Andre Dawson hits three homers and droves in eight runs to lead the Expos to a 17–15 win over the Cubs at Wrigley Field. The Expos scored 12 runs in the fifth inning to take a 15–2 lead. The Cubs made it close with four runs in the eighth and five in the ninth.

SEPTEMBER 28   The Cubs overpower the Phillies 11–10 at Wrigley Field.

OCTOBER 3   The Cubs score eight runs in the sixth inning and defeat the Pirates 13–5 at Wrigley Field.

DECEMBER 11   The Cubs trade Dave Owen to the Giants for Manny Trillo.

DECEMBER 16   The Cubs trade Billy Hatcher and Steve Engel to the Astros for Jerry Mumphrey.

1986

Season in a Sentence

The Cubs fire manager Jim Frey after a 23–33 star and ballgirl Marla Collins after she poses nude in *Playboy*.

Finish • Won • Lost • Pct • GB

Fifth   70   90   .438 37.0

Managers

Jim Frey (23–33),
John Vukovich (1–1) and
Gene Michael (46–56)

Stats

Stats	Cubs	NL	Rank
Batting Avg:	.256	.253	3
On–Base Pct:	.321	.324	10
Slugging Pct:	.398	.380	3
Home Runs:	155		1
Stolen Bases:	132		9
ERA:	4.49	3.72	12
Fielding Avg:	.980	.978	2
Runs Scored:	680		5
Runs Allowed:	781		12

Starting Lineup

Jody Davis, c
Leon Durham, 1b
Ryne Sandberg, 2b
Ron Cey, 3b
Shawon Dunston, ss
Gary Matthews, lf
Bob Dernier, cf
Keith Moreland, rf
Jerry Mumphrey, cf–lf
Dave Lopes, 3b–lf
Chris Speier, 3b–ss
Manny Trillo, 3b

Pitchers

Dennis Eckersley, sp
Scott Sanderson, sp
Rick Sutcliffe, sp
Steve Trout, sp
Ed Lynch, sp
Jamie Moyer, sp
Lee Smith, rp
Ray Fontenot, rp

Attendance

1,859,102 (fifth in NL)

Club Leaders

Batting Avg:	Sandberg	.284
On–Base Pct:	Durham	.350
Slugging Pct:	Durham	.452
Home Runs:	Davis	21
	Matthews	21
RBI:	Moreland	79
Runs:	Moreland	72
Stolen Bases:	Sandberg	34
Wins:	Sanderson	9
	Smith	9
Strikeouts:	Eckersley	137
ERA:	Sanderson	3.19
Saves:	Smith	31

FEBRUARY 17 Three weeks after the space shuttle Challenger explodes, killing six astronauts and teacher Christa McAulliffe, and three weeks after the Bears Super Bowl victory over the Patriots, the 1969 Cubs play the 1969 Mets in an exhibition game in Phoenix. The Mets won the seven–inning contest 11–3.

APRIL 8 In the season opener, the Cubs lose 2–1 to the Cardinals in St. Louis.

APRIL 16 The day after the U.S. bombs Libya in response to terrorist attacks, Shawon Dunston hits a homer in the thirteenth inning to beat the Expos 7–6 in Montreal.

> *Ryne Sandberg was the Cubs top hitter in 1986 with a .284 batting average and 14 home runs.*

APRIL 18 In the home opener before 38,151 at Wrigley Field, the Cubs lose 4–0 to the Pirates.

APRIL 19 Shawon Dunston collects five hits, including a homer and a double, but the Cubs lose 14–8 to the Pirates at Wrigley Field.

APRIL 20   Dave Lopes collects five hits, including a triple and a double, before the game against the Pirates at Wrigley Field is suspended by darkness after thirteen innings with the score 8–8. The game was completed on August 11 with the Pirates winning 10–8 in seventeen innings. The Cubs set a National League record (since tied) by using ten pitchers in the game. Seven were sent to the mound on April 20, and three more on August 11.

APRIL 27   Six days after Geraldo Rivera opens Al Capone's vault on live television, and finds nothing, Jody Davis hits a grand slam off Jeff Reardon in the eighth inning, wipes out a two–run Expos lead, and sparks the Cubs to a 12–10 victory at Wrigley Field.

MAY 3   The Cubs score four runs in the ninth inning to take a 6–4 lead over the Giants, and survive a San Francisco rally in the ninth to win 6–5 at Candlestick Park. Terry Francona broke the 4–4 tie with a two–run single. Ron Cey homered twice for the 300th and 301st homers of his career.

MAY 6   A walk–off homer by Leon Durham in the ninth inning beats the Dodgers 7–6 at Wrigley Field.

MAY 17   Seven Cubs become ill with food poisoning apparently contracted through room service in a Houston hotel.

             In May, National League owners voted unanimously to have the Cubs play home games in St. Louis if they qualified for the playoffs.

JUNE 8   The Cubs score nine runs in the sixth inning and thrash the Cardinals 14–2 in St. Louis. The Cubs collected 20 hits in the contest.

JUNE 12   Jim Frey is fired as manager of the Cubs along with coach Don Zimmer. The Cubs had a record of 23–33. John Vukovich was named interim manager, and guided the Cubs to a double–header split against the Cardinals on June 13.

             Frey won a pennant in his first year as a Cubs manager in 1984 and was 130–83 in his first 213 games with the club, but was 66–98 in his last 164.

JUNE 13   Gene Michael is named manager of the Cubs.

             Michael played in the majors as a shortstop from 1966 through 1975, mostly with the Yankees. He managed the Yankees in 1981 and 1982 to a 90–76 record. Michael was the Yankees third base coach at the time of his hiring by the Cubs.

JUNE 14   Gene Michael is ejected from his first game as Cubs manager, a 1–0 loss to the Cardinals at Wrigley Field. Prior to the game, umpire Eric Gregg warned both managers about pitchers throwing at batters. When a Scott Sanderson pitch sent Terry Pendleton into the dirt, Gregg booted the Cubs pitcher, which according to the rules, also meant an ejection for the manager.

JUNE 23   The Phillies drub the Cubs 19–1 in Philadelphia.

JULY 2   The Cubs defeat the Expos 1–0 at Wrigley Field in a game that took two days to complete. The contest began on July 1, but was suspended after seven innings by darkness with the score 0–0. It continued on July 2, and the Cubs emerged with the 1–0 win with the only run scoring on a single by Jody Davis in the eighth inning. Scott Sanderson (seven innings), Dave Gumpert (one inning), and Lee Smith (one inning) combined on the shutout. The Cubs also won the regularly scheduled game 5–4 on a walk–off homer by Dave Lopes in the ninth inning.

Though past his prime by the time he arrived in Chicago, Gary Matthews was a fan favorite and delivered two respectable seasons—1984 and 1986.

JULY 18   Scott Sanderson (seven innings) and Lee Smith (two innings) combine on a one–hitter to defeat the Giants 2–1 at Wrigley Field. The lone San Francisco hit was a double by Jeffrey Leonard in the fourth inning off Sanderson.

Sanderson and Smith were the leading winners on the Cubs pitching staff with just nine victories each. With the exception of the strike–shortened seasons of 1981 and 1994, it is the only time that no Cubs pitcher reached double digits in wins.

JULY 21   The Cubs trade Dave Lopes to the Astros for Frank DiPino.

JULY 22   The Cubs fire ballgirl Marla Collins for posing nude in *Playboy.*

The 28–year–old Collins began working as a ballgirl at Cubs home games in 1982. Attired in shorts and a Cubs shirt, she occupied a seat near the visitors' dugout and was a familiar sight shagging fouls and keeping the umpire supplied with baseballs. Marla gained a national following among viewers of Cubs broadcasts on cable television and even secured her own athletic shoe endorsement, which was also canceled after her appearance in PLAYBOY. *The eight–page spread was entitled "The Belle of the Ball Club."*

AUGUST 4   During a 4–2 win over the Mets at Wrigley Field, Cubs manager Gene Michael argues with Dave Pallone and turns the umpire's cap around. Michael was suspended for three days for the incident.

AUGUST 13   The Cubs trade George Frazier, Ray Fontenot, and Julius McDougal to the Twins for Ron Davis and Dewayne Coleman.

SEPTEMBER 3 Greg Maddux makes his major league debut, and gives up an eighteenth–inning homer to Billy Hatcher in an 8–7 loss to the Astros at Wrigley Field. The game started on September 2, but was suspended by darkness after fourteen innings with the score 4–4. The contest resumed on September 3, and both teams scored three times in the seventeenth inning before Maddux gave up the game–winning homer. He was the Cubs eighth pitcher of the game. Houston won the regularly scheduled game 8–2. The Cubs used a club record 27 players in the contest.

SEPTEMBER 7 Greg Maddux picks up his first major league win and complete game with an 11–3 win over the Reds in Cincinnati.

SEPTEMBER 8 Rafael Palmeiro makes his major league debut as the Cubs defeat the Phillies 7–4 at Wrigley Field. Palmeiro played left field with a single and an RBI in four at–bats.

SEPTEMBER 9 Leon Durham's two–run walk–off homer in the tenth inning beats the Phillies 8–6 at Wrigley Field. The Cubs trailed 6–1 in the fourth inning. Rafael Palmeiro helped spark the comeback with his first big league homer, a three–run shot off Kevin Gross.

SEPTEMBER 29 The Maddux brothers start against each other in a Cubs–Phillies clash in Philadelphia. Greg came out ahead, defeating his older brother Mike 8–3.

At the end of the 1986 season, in which the Cubs finished last in the league in earned run average, Dallas Green fired pitching coach Billy Connors in a callous manner. Connors was dismissed while in the hospital recovering from hip replacement surgery. Green drove to the hospital, left his car running, went up to Connors's room, fired him, then went back to his car and drove away.

DECEMBER 10 Chris Speier signs with the Giants as a free agent.

The Cubs had a deal in place in December 1986 that would have sent Gary Matthews to the White Sox for Carlton Fisk. The trade fell through when Matthews hurt his knee while exercising.

1987   Cubs

Season in a Sentence

Another power–laden (209 homers), lead–footed (last in NL in stolen bases) team gets off to a fast start (31–23 on June 6), but finishes in last place, resulting in the resignation of Dallas Green as president and general manager.

Finish • Won • Lost • Pct • GB

Sixth   76   85   .472   19.5

Managers

Gene Michael (68–68) and Frank Lucchesi (8–17)

Stats

Stats	Cubs	NL	Rank
Batting Avg:	.264	.261	5
On–Base Pct:	.327	.331	9
Slugging Pct:	.432	.404	2
Home Runs:	209		1
Stolen Bases:	109		12
ERA:	4.55	4.08	11
Fielding Avg:	.979	.979	7
Runs Scored:	720		8
Runs Allowed:	801		11

Starting Lineup

Jody Davis, c
Leon Durham, 1b
Ryne Sandberg, 2b
Keith Moreland, 3b
Shawon Dunston, ss
Jerry Mumphrey, lf
Dave Martinez, cf
Andre Dawson, rf
Rafael Palmeiro, lf
Manny Trillo, 1b–3b
Bob Dernier, cf
Paul Noce, 2b–ss

Pitchers

Rick Sutcliffe, sp
Jamie Moyer, sp
Scott Sanderson, sp–rp
Les Lancaster, sp–rp
Greg Maddux, sp
Lee Smith, rp
Frank DiPino, rp
Ed Lynch, rp
Dickie Noles, rp

Attendance

2,035,130 (sixth in NL)

Club Leaders

Batting Avg:	Sandberg	.294
On–Base Pct:	Martinez	.372
Slugging Pct:	Dawson	.568
Home Runs:	Dawson	49
RBI:	Dawson	137
Runs:	Dawson	90
Stolen Bases:	Sandberg	21
Wins:	Sutcliffe	18
Strikeouts:	Sutcliffe	174
ERA:	Sutcliffe	3.68
Saves:	Smith	36

JANUARY 30   The Cubs trade Ron Cey to the Athletics for Luis Quinones.

FEBRUARY 19   Harry Caray suffers a stroke while playing cards at a country club near his winter home in Palm Springs, California.

Caray didn't return to the television booth until May 19. In the meantime, the Cubs used celebrity announcers on a one–game basis. Brent Musburger did the play–by–play on Opening Day and his successors included Bill Murray, George Wendt, Jim Belushi, Dan Aykroyd, Bob Costas, Ernie Harwell, Dick Enberg, Pat Summerall, Bryant Gumbel, Gary Bender, Jack Buck, Ernie Banks, Mike Royko, George Will, and Stan Musial. There was also a change in the radio booth in 1987 as Jim Frey replaced Vince Lloyd. Frey was fired as manager of the Cubs the previous June.

MARCH 6   The Cubs sign Andre Dawson, most recently with the Expos, as a free agent.

Dawson was considered by many to be the top player in baseball during the *early 1980s, but over time his knees had been ravaged by playing on the artificial turf at Olympic Stadium. He hoped to extend his career by playing on the grass at Wrigley Field. In a successful publicity coup, Dawson's agent Dick Moss advised him to go to the Cubs Arizona camp and to offer his services at a discount. The Chicago newspapers ran photos of Dawson watching the Cubs workouts from behind a chicken-wire fence. Dallas Green was unhappy that Dawson was in Mesa. "If he thinks he can come into my camp and use the press as a springboard, we've got a bad thing going. He can take his dog and pony show elsewhere." Green couldn't disclose the real reason for his refusal to sign Dawson. Some months earlier, major league owners secretly agreed not to sign each other's free agents. (Later an arbitrator would find major league owners guilty of collusion, and they had to pay millions in a settlement with the players.) The Cubs also already had a right fielder in Keith Moreland. When the stalemate between Dawson and the Cubs continued, Moss told Green he would submit a blank contract. Green could fill in the numbers. The contract was left with Green's secretary because he refused to see Moss in person. With public pressure mounting, Green was backed into a corner and collusion agreement or no collusion agreement, he finally gave in and signed Dawson for $500,000, a bargain price at the time. Dawson was the 15th highest paid player on the 1987 Cubs. The Cubs had no reason to regret the decision. Andre won the National League MVP award in 1987 with 49 homers and 137 runs-batted-in, and was the club's starting right fielder for six years.*

MARCH 26   The Cubs trade Thad Bosley and Dave Gumpert to the Royals for Jim Sundberg.

APRIL 7   The Cubs lose the opener 9–3 to the Cardinals before 38,240 at Wrigley Field. The Cubs led 3–0 before the Cardinals scored five runs in the third inning off Rick Sutcliffe. Bob Dernier had three hits, including a triple, in three at-bats.

    Despite the tough start, Sutcliffe rebounded from a 5–14 season in 1986 with an 18–10 campaign and a 3.68 ERA in 1987.

APRIL 11   The Cubs tally seven runs in the first inning and beat the Phillies 9–1 in Philadelphia.

APRIL 13   Jamie Moyer strikes out 12 batters and carries a no-hitter into the ninth inning against the Phillies at Veterans Stadium. The first Philadelphia hit was a single by Juan Samuel leading off the ninth. After a walk and an RBI-single by Mike Schmidt, Lee Smith replaced Moyer on the mound. Smith completed the save for a 5–2 win.

APRIL 17   Rick Sutcliffe pitches a shutout and drives in three runs in a 7–0 win over the Expos at Wrigley Field.

APRIL 22   With the Cubs trailing 3–1, Andre Dawson hits a grand slam in the seventh inning off Todd Worrell, leading Chicago to a 5–4 win over the Cardinals in St. Louis.

APRIL 29   Andre Dawson collects five hits in five at-bats and hits for the cycle during an 8–4 win over the Giants at Wrigley Field. He had a homer in the first inning, a double in the third, a single in the fourth, a triple in the sixth, and another single in the eighth. Dawson also grabbed an apparent hit by Giants pitcher Roger Mason in short right field and threw him out at first base.

MAY 19   Harry Caray returns after a three–month recovery from a stroke. During the first inning of the 9–2 win over the Reds at Wrigley Field, Caray received a congratulatory phone call from President Ronald Reagan. "You've had a lot of celebrities fill in during your recovery," said Reagan, "but there's nothing like the real thing."

MAY 22   The Cubs beat the Braves 7–6 in a sixteen–inning marathon at Wrigley Field. A double by Jerry Mumphrey drove in the winner. Andre Dawson tied the game 6–6 with a two–run, two–out homer in the ninth. The Cubs won despite the fact that the pitchers gave up a club record 14 walks. The bases on balls were issued by Ed Lynch (3), Frank DiPino (1), Dickie Noles (1) Mike Mason (2), Ron Davis (1), and Jamie Moyer (6).

JUNE 1   Andre Dawson hits two homers, including a grand slam in the eighth inning off Julio Solano, and drives in all five Cubs runs, but Chicago loses 6–5 to the Astros in ten innings at Wrigley Field.

JUNE 2   Andre Dawson drives in seven runs with two homers, a triple, and a single during a 13–2 thrashing of the Astros at Wrigley Field. In two consecutive games, Dawson hit four homers and drove in 12 runs.

> *On the same day, the Cubs selected pitcher Mike Harkey from Cal State Fullerton with the fourth over all pick in the amateur draft. Harkey showed some early promise. He was 12–6 with a 3.26 ERA as a 23–year–old rookie in 1990, but ended his career in 1997 with a 36–36 record. Other players drafted and signed by the Cubs in 1987 who reached the majors were Alex Arias (third round), Frank Castillo (sixth), Matt Franco (seventh), Matt Walbeck (eighth), and Tom Thobe (23rd).*

Ryne Sandberg enjoyed a productive year in 1987 and remained the heart of the team. He was as reliable as ever defensively, winning his fifth consecutive Gold Glove.

JUNE 3   The Cubs score nine runs in the first inning and conquer the Astros 22–7 at Wrigley Field. A major league record three grand slams highlighted the contest. Brian Dayett hit a slam off Bob Knepper in the first inning, Billy Hatcher of Houston homered with the bases loaded off Rick Sutcliffe in the fourth, and Keith Moreland did likewise against Julio Solano in the sixth. It was the second time in three days that Solano gave up a grand slam to a Cubs batter. Moreland hit a second homer in the game and drove in a total of seven runs. Jim Sundberg, Ryne Sandberg, and Andre Dawson also homered for the Cubs. The homer gave Dawson five roundtrippers in a span of three games. Jody Davis scored five of the 22 runs.

Sandberg hit .294 with 16 homers in 1987.

JUNE 6   The Cubs beat the Cardinals 6–5 at Wrigley Field to pull within two games of first place.

The Cubs were 31–23 on June 6, but had a record of 45–62 the rest of the way to finish in last place in the NL East.

JUNE 7   The Cubs score seven runs in the fourth inning, but lose 13–9 to the Cardinals at Wrigley Field.

JUNE 8   A two–out, two–run walk–off homer by Manny Trillo beats the Mets 4–2 at Wrigley Field. Trillo entered the game in the seventh inning at third base as part of a double switch.

JUNE 22   A two–run walk–off homer by Keith Moreland off Rick Reuschel enables the Cubs to nip the Pirates 3–2 at Wrigley Field.

JUNE 29   The Cubs score only nine runs on 20 hits, but it's enough to beat the Expos 9–5 in Montreal.

JULY 1   Greg Maddux picks up his first major league shutout defeating the Expos 1–0 at Montreal. The only run of the game was scored on a homer by Jerry Mumphrey in the ninth inning off Bob Sebra, who fanned 14 Cubs.

The Cubs brought Maddux to the majors too soon. He turned 21 shortly after the 1987 season started, and was the youngest player in the majors on an Opening Day roster. During his first two seasons in 1986 and 1987, Maddux was 8–18 with an ERA of 5.58.

JULY 3   Jamie Moyer strikes out seven Giants in a row, but loses 3–1 at Wrigley Field.

JULY 7   During a fight–marred 7–5 win over the Padres at Wrigley Field, Eric Show beans Andre Dawson.

Dawson hit two homers out of the park on July 6 during a 7–0 win over the Padres, and added another off Show in the first inning of the July 7 game. After Show beaned Dawson, Rick Sutcliffe ran out of the dugout after Show and both benches emptied. Dawson remained face down on the ground for a couple of minutes, then he too went after Show and another fight broke out. Five Cubs players, including Sutcliffe and Dawson, manager Gene Michael, and coach

Johnny Oates were ejected. Show wasn't ejected, but had to leave the game because he hurt his foot during the brawl. Dawson suffered a lacerated lip and contusions of his cheekbone and needed 24 stitches to close his wounds.

JULY 8   Down 7–0 in the third inning and 8–4 after seven, the Cubs score eight runs in the eighth inning to beat the Padres 12–8 at Wrigley Field. A pinch–hit grand slam by Jim Sundberg off Lance McCullers highlighted the inning.

JULY 12   The Cubs trade Gary Matthews to the Mariners for David Hartnett. In another deal, the Cubs sent Steve Trout and cash to the Yankees for Bob Tewksbury, Rich Scheid, and Dean Wilkens.

JULY 14   Rick Sutcliffe pitches two scoreless innings and Lee Smith adds three more frames without allowing a run during the National League's 13–inning, 2–0 win in the All–Star Game at Oakland–Alameda County Coliseum in Oakland.

Sutcliffe entered the game in the third inning. Smith came into the contest in the tenth inning and struck out four batters, including Kirby Puckett twice and Mark McGwire once.

AUGUST 1 Andre Dawson hits three homers and drives in all of the Cubs runs in a 5–3 win over the Phillies at Wrigley Field. Dawson hit a three–run homer off Tom Hume, a solo shot off Hume in the fifth, and another in the seventh off Mike Jackson.

AUGUST 3 Andre Dawson's homer in the eleventh inning beats the Pirates 3–2 in Pittsburgh.

Dawson hit 15 homers in August 1987.

AUGUST 13 The Cubs spot the Mets a 5–0 lead, then rally to win 7–5 with three runs in the third inning, two in the fifth, and two in the eighth.

The Cubs retired the number 26 of Billy Williams in 1987. The number was flown from the right field foul pole opposite that of longtime teammate Ernie Banks.

AUGUST 16 The Mets wallop the Cubs 23–10 at Wrigley Field. Pitching in relief, Drew Hall gave up ten runs, all earned, in 1⅔ innings. Jody Davis hit a grand slam for the Cubs off Ron Darling in the fourth inning.

The Cubs led the National League with 209 homers in 1987. It shattered the club record of 182 set in 1958. The only Cub team since that has exceeded the home run total of the 1987 team, was in the 1998 outfit, which went deep 212 times. The 1987 Cubs outhomered the opposition 209–159, but were outscored 801–720. The run disparity was caused in part because the Cubs failed to do little else right. The club was outhit 1,524 to 1,475, and stole 109 bases compared to 169 for opponents. The biggest problem was in walks. Cubs batters walked 504, second worst in the league, while the pitchers issued 628 passes, the most in the NL. Andre Dawson was the MVP but was at the center of much of what was wrong with the Cubs. He hit 49 homers, but walked only 32 times.

AUGUST 21   Andre Dawson hits two homers for the second day in a row, leading the Cubs to a 7–5 victory over the Astros at Wrigley Field.

Dawson homered twice the previous day in a 13–4 loss to the Braves in Atlanta. He added another homer on August 22 during a 5–4 loss to Houston in Chicago, giving Andre five homers in three games.

SEPTEMBER 8   Gene Michael resigns as manager of the Cubs, Frank Lucchesi is appointed interim manager to finish out the season.

The Cubs were 68–68 at the time Michael jumped ship. He would likely have been fired at the end of the season. Michael was too laid back for the intense Dallas Green. Gene didn't go quietly. "I have no respect for Dallas Green," Michael said. "He isn't very sharp and is always covering up for his mistakes. He's a big buffoon with a big mouth. He didn't make a mistake hiring me. His mistake was not listening to me." Lucchesi previously managed the Phillies (1969–72) and Rangers (1975–77). He was 8–17 in his brief tenure with the Cubs.

SEPTEMBER 20   Frank Lucchesi is suspended for three days for bumping umpire Joe West during a 10–2 loss to the Cardinals in St. Louis.

Late in the 1987 season, rookie outfielder Darrin Jackson was diagnosed with cancer, and underwent surgery to remove a growth from his groin area. He recovered, and played in the majors with seven different clubs until 1999.

SEPTEMBER 22   Dickie Noles is traded to the Tigers for a player to be named later.

Noles wound up being traded for himself. He was returned by the Tigers to the Cubs on October 23 as the player to be named later.

SEPTEMBER 30   Darnell Coles of the Pirates hits three homers off Chicago pitching, but the Cubs win 10–8 in the second game of a double–header at Three Rivers Stadium. Pittsburgh won the first game 5–3.

During the last week of the season, Dallas Green apologized to the Cubs fans for the team's performance and said that the players "quit with a capital Q."

OCTOBER 29   Dallas Green unexpectedly resigns as president and general manager of the Cubs.

Green had much of his authority taken away after the Cubs were 76–85 in 1987, the club's third straight losing season. The Cubs had five losing seasons in the six years that Green ran the club, but he left the organization well stocked with young talent through the excellent scouting staff he assembled. When Green submitted his resignation, the Cubs had a long list of players either in the majors or the minors who were productive for many more seasons after 1987 including Greg Maddux, Rafael Palmeiro, Ryne Sandberg, Andre Dawson, Mark Grace, Lee Smith, Jamie Moyer, Shawon Dunston, Rick Sutcliffe, Dave Martinez, Joe Girardi, Rick Wilkins, Bob Tewksbury, Frank Castillo, Darrin Jackson, Dwight Smith, Derrick May, Damon Berryhill, Les Lancaster, and Jerome Walton. Green's successors blew a golden opportunity to build the Cubs into a consistent pennant contender.

NOVEMBER 13   Jim Frey is named general manager of the Cubs.

                  *After being fired by Dallas Green as manager in 1986, Frey returned to the club
                  as a radio broadcaster in 1987.*

NOVEMBER 20   Don Zimmer is named manager of the Cubs.

                  *Zimmer was a high school teammate of Jim Frey at Western Hills High School
                  in Cincinnati. Zimmer served under Frey as coach of the Cubs from 1984
                  through 1986. Previously, Zimmer managed the Padres (1972–73), Red Sox
                  (1976–80), and Rangers (1981–82). He also played for the Cubs in 1960 and
                  1961.*
                  *   To recap, Dallas Green fired Jim Frey as manager and Don Zimmer as
                  coach. Then Frey wound up in the broadcast booth analyzing Green's team.
                  Then Green fired Gene Michael, the man who succeeded Frey as manager. Then
                  the Cubs fired Green. Then the Cubs hired Frey to replace Green as general
                  manager. Then Frey hired Zimmer to manage the club. All of this happened in a
                  span of just seventeen months from June 1986 through November 1987.*

DECEMBER 8   Three weeks after the end of the six–month Congressional hearings investigating the
                  Iran–Contra scandal, and two weeks after the sudden death of Chicago mayor
                  Harold Washington, the Cubs trade Lee Smith to the Red Sox for Al Nipper and
                  Calvin Schiraldi.

                  *Jim Frey was swindled in his first major trade. Smith had another eight seasons
                  ahead of him as one of the top closers in the game. Neither Nipper nor Schiraldi
                  were of any help to the Cubs. The bullpen in 1988 blew 27 saves in 56 chances.*

DECEMBER 19   The Cubs sign Vance Law, most recently with the Expos, as a free agent.

                  *Law gave the Cubs one great season. In 1988, he played in the All–Star Game
                  and hit .293 with 11 homers. Law was the son of former major league pitcher
                  Vern Law. Vance's mother's name was VaNita. His sister was also named
                  VaNita, and he had brothers named Velton, Veryl, Vaughn, and Varlin.*

1988

Cubs

Season in a Sentence

Lights are added to Wrigley Field, but the Cubs continue to look as though they're playing in the dark.

Finish • Won • Lost • Pct • GB

Fourth   77   85   .475   24.0

Manager

Don Zimmer

Stats

Stats	Cubs •	NL •	Rank
Batting Avg:	.261	.248	1
On–Base Pct:	.312	.313	6
Slugging Pct:	.383	.363	2
Home Runs:	113		3 (tie)
Stolen Bases:	120		9
ERA:	3.84	3.46	10
Fielding Avg:	.980	.979	4
Runs Scored:	660		3
Runs Allowed:	694		10

Starting Lineup

Damon Berryhill, c
Mark Grace, 1b
Ryne Sandberg, 2b
Vance Law, 3b
Shawon Dunston, ss
Rafael Palmeiro, lf
Mitch Webster, cf
Andre Dawson, rf
Dave Martinez, cf
Jody Davis, c
Darrin Jackson, cf–rf
Manny Trillo, 1b–3b

Pitchers

Greg Maddux, sp
Rick Sutcliffe, sp
Jamie Moyer, sp
Calvin Schiraldi, sp
Al Nipper, sp
Goose Gossage, rp
Frank DiPino, rp
Les Lancaster, rp
Jeff Pico, rp–sp

Attendance

2,089,034 (fourth in NL)

Club Leaders

Batting Avg:	Palmeiro	.307
On–Base Pct:	Grace	.371
Slugging Pct:	Dawson	.504
Home Runs:	Dawson	24
RBI:	Dawson	79
Runs:	Dawson	78
Stolen Bases:	Dunston	30
Wins:	Maddux	18
Strikeouts:	Sutcliffe	144
ERA:	Maddux	3.18
Saves:	Gossage	13

FEBRUARY 12   The Cubs trade Keith Moreland and Mike Brumley to the Padres for Goose Gossage and Ray Hayward.

Gossage was acquired to replace Lee Smith as the Cubs closer. The trade was a failure, as Gossage had a 4.33 ERA in 46 games with the Cubs.

FEBRUARY 25   The Cubs receive authorization to play night games at Wrigley Field when Chicago City Council votes 29–19 to repeal a 1983 ordinance that barred contests after dark. The decision climaxed a six–year battle by the Tribune Company and the residents of the neighborhood surrounding the ballpark, and others opposed to the installation of lights at Wrigley. Earlier, the Tribune Company threatened to move to the suburbs if permission to use lights was denied. The new ordinance allowed the Cubs to play eight night games in 1988 and eighteen from 1989 through 2002, plus any post–season games or All–Star games. The Cubs also had to stop selling beer at 9:20 p.m. or the end of the seventh inning, whichever came first. The club couldn't schedule night games on Fridays and no more than two Saturdays during the season.

MARCH 31   The Cubs trade Mike Curtis to the Pirates for Mike Bielecki.

Bielecki gave the Cubs one terrific season, going 18–7 in 1989.

APRIL 5   The Cubs beat the Braves 10–9 in thirteen innings in a thrilling season opener in
           Atlanta. The Cubs led 4–1 before the Braves scored seven runs in the fourth inning off
           Rick Sutcliffe. The Cubs tied the game with two runs in the ninth, and won it in the
           thirteenth on a sacrifice fly by Manny Trillo. There were seven home runs in the con-
           test. Ossie Virgil, Ken Oberkfell, Gerald Perry, and Andres Thomas homered for the
           Braves, and Jody Davis, Leon Durham, and Shawon Dunston went deep for the Cubs.

APRIL 7   Installation of the Wrigley Field lights begins when a helicopter lifts the first steel
           girders to workmen on the roof of the upper deck. Six 33–foot towers were erected,
           three down the left field line and three in right field. The latticework of the towers
           was designed to mirror of the vintage architecture of the park. The lighting system
           was built by General Electric of Hendersonville, North Carolina, and cost $5 mil-
           lion. There were no light towers between the left field foul pole and the right field
           foul pole. "We designed the lights," said Cubs president Donald Grenesko, "so you
           could sit in the grandstand and look out at the field and feel nothing had changed."

APRIL 8   Dave Martinez hits a grand slam in the second inning off Floyd Youmans during a
           6–4 win over the Expos in Montreal.

MAY 2   Mark Grace makes his major league debut and collects two hits in five at–bats in a
           5–2 win over the Padres in San Diego.

           *Grace hit .296 as a rookie. He spent thirteen seasons with the Cubs and played
           in 1,910 games with 1,057 runs scored, 2,201 hits, 3,187 total bases, 456 dou-
           bles (second all–time to Cap Anson), 148 home runs, and 1,004 runs–batted–in.*

MAY 3   The Cubs bash the Padres 13–5 in San Diego.

MAY 8   The Cubs batter the Giants 13–7 at Wrigley Field.

MAY 11   Retiring the final 20 batters he faces, Greg Maddux pitches a ten–inning complete
           game shutout to beat the Padres 1–0 at Wrigley Field. The only run of the game
           was scored on a suicide squeeze by Vance Law with the bases loaded and one out.

MAY 19   The Cubs send Leon Durham to the Reds for Pat Perry and cash.

           *With Mark Grace firmly established at first base, the Cubs no longer needed
           Durham, who was traded to Cincinnati, his hometown. There, he remained on
           the bench and was suspended for a substance abuse problem.*

MAY 28   The Cubs vanquish the Astros 14–7 at Wrigley Field.

MAY 31   In his major league debut, Jeff Pico pitches a complete game shutout to defeat the
           Reds 4–0 at Wrigley Field.

           *Pico was the first Cubs pitcher to throw a shutout in his major league debut
           since King Cole in 1909, and the first to pitch a shutout in his first start since
           Bill Lee in 1934. Lee made two prior relief appearances. Pico pitched only one
           more shutout as a major leaguer and finished a three–year career with a 13–12
           record.*

JUNE 1   The Cubs select second baseman Ty Griffin from Georgia Tech in the first round of the amateur draft.

> *Griffin never got higher than Class AA. Overall it was a fruitless draft. The only players who were drafted and signed by the Cubs to reach the majors were Jessie Hollins in the fourth round and Kevin Roberson in the 14th.*

JUNE 12   Pat Perry relieves Greg Maddux with the bases loaded, none out, and a one–run lead, and retires all three batters he faces to preserve a 4–3 win over the Cardinals in St. Louis.

> *At the age of 22, Maddux made the All–Star team. He had a 15–3 record and a 2.15 ERA at the break, but was overworked, pitching 155⅔ innings. In one game in May, Maddux threw 162 pitches, and he was on a pace to throw 297 innings for the season. During the season half, Maddux was 3–5 record with an earned run average of 4.92. Overall, he was 18–8 with a 3.18 ERA and was on the mound for 249 innings.*

Although Greg Maddux returned to the team in 2004 and won 16 games, his move to the Braves in 1993 remains a big regret for Cubs fans. When he left, at age 26, he already had won 95 games.

JUNE 30   Shortly before a midnight deadline, the Illinois legislature passes a $150–million package to finance the construction of a new ballpark for the White Sox. The Sox were poised to move to St. Petersburg, Florida, if the funding for the facility wasn't provided. New Comiskey Park opened in 1991.

JULY 4   The Cubs beat the Giants 3–2 in San Francisco.

JULY 14   The Cubs trade Dave Martinez to the Expos for Mitch Webster.

JULY 25   Cubs players and fans are given an opportunity to preview the new lighting system. The occasion was turned into a festive affair. It began with an autograph session on the field starting at 7:00 p.m. and was followed by a home run hitting contest, which included Ernie Banks and Billy Williams, then batting practice. Approximately 3,000 fans paid $100 apiece to attend, with the gate proceeds going to charity. Shortly before sunset, the field was cleared of spectators, and at 8:45 p.m. the lights were turned on. ABC–TV, which was airing two games nationally, cut away from the telecasts to show portions of the event. Players complained they had trouble seeing the ball in the corners of the outfield, and that there was a glare at second base. The problems were corrected before the first game was played on August 8.

AUGUST 8   The Cubs, formed three years before Thomas Edison's invention of the light bulb, usher in a new era with the introduction of night baseball at Wrigley Field with a game against the Phillies. (See next page.)

AUGUST 9   In the first official night game at Wrigley Field, the Cubs defeat the Mets 6–4 before a crowd of 36,399. The fanfare of the previous night was absent, as well as many of the celebrities and politicians. The Cubs snapped a 2–2 tie with four runs in the seventh inning.

In the tradition of stalwart Cubs backstops such as Gabby Hartnett and Randy Hundley, Jody Davis was a fixture behind the plate through most of the 1980s. Fans admired his toughness and dedication, but the demands of the position took their toll, and by the time he left near the end of 1988, his career as a productive player was over.

AUGUST 23   The Cubs score seven runs in the seventh inning and defeat the Astros 9–3 at Wrigley Field.

Ryne Sandberg hit .264 with 19 homers for the Cubs in 1988.

AUGUST 25   Calvin Schiraldi strikes out 12 batters in a 6–1 triumph over the Braves in Atlanta.

SEPTEMBER 3   In his first major league game, Doug Dascenzo collects three hits, including a double, in five at–bats, although the Cubs lose 6–5 to the Reds at Wrigley Field.

Dascenzo had ten hits in the first 18 at–bats, but it proved to be a mirage. Over his next 196 at–bats covering the remainder of the 1988 season and all of 1989, Dascenzo had only 29 hits, a batting average of just .148. He finished his career with an average of .240 and only five homers in 540 games.

SEPTEMBER 4   The Reds crush the Cubs 17–0 at Wrigley Field.

SEPTEMBER 5   The Cubs score eight runs in the third inning and beat the Phillies 14–3 in the first game of a double–header at Wrigley Field. Philadelphia won the second game 4–3.

Andre Dawson hit .303 with 24 homers for the Cubs in 1988.

SEPTEMBER 13   Damon Berryhill hits a grand slam in the seventh inning off Salome Barojas during a 9–2 win over the Phillies in Philadelphia.

The Night the Lights Went on at Wrigley

Decades of tradition ended on Monday, August 8, 1988, when the Cubs staged their first night game at Wrigley Field. The atmosphere was akin to the World Series, Mardi Gras, and New Year's Eve rolled into one. There were 1.8 million phone calls made to the Cubs ticket office on the day the 8,000 remaining tickets went on sale. A total of 558 media credentials were issued, by far the most ever for a regular season game. The previous record was 275 issued by the Reds in 1985 when Pete Rose broke Ty Cobb's career hit record. There were 109 newspapers and magazines represented, along with 49 television stations, 38 radio stations, and such popular programs as *Good Morning America* and *Entertainment Tonight*. WGN–TV drew a huge national cable audience. Police warned people without tickets not to go near Wrigley Field, but the pleas were largely ignored as thousands sought out scalpers or just wanted to see Wrigley Field lit up even if they couldn't get inside.

At 6:09 P.M., 91–year–old Harry Grossman, a retired tire dealer who attended his first Cubs game in 1906, called for the 540 floodlights of 1,500 watts each on the six banks of light towers to be turned on after 6,852 day games. The crowd joined Grossman as he shouted "1–2–3. Let there be lights." Then he threw the switch, got a hug from the ballgirl and cheers from the 39,008 in attendance. Members of the Chicago Symphony Orchestra, arranged in a semicircle on the dirt next to the backstop, began to play Richard Strauss's "Also Sprach Zarathustra."

The crowd included Illinois governor James Thompson, commissioner Peter Ueberroth, National League president Bart Giamatti, and actors Mark Harmon, Bill Murray, and Dabney Coleman. The opponents were the Philadelphia Phillies. In a bit of irony, the Phillies manager was Lee Elia, who was fired as manager of Cubs in 1983 after criticizing the club's daytime fans as unemployed bums. It was a warm night with the temperature at 91 degrees. Following honorary first pitches by Ernie Banks and Billy Williams, and the National Anthem, sung by public address announcer Wayne Messmer wearing a tuxedo, the game began at 7:01 P.M. Phil Bradley, Philadelphia's lead–off batter, hit the fourth pitch thrown by Rick Sutcliffe over the left field wall and onto Waveland Avenue for a home run. The Cubs came back with Ryne Sandberg clubbing a two–run homer in the bottom of the first and took a 3–1 lead before thunder, lightning and heavy showers halted play in the fourth inning. "Actually, I thought it was a visitation," said Murray on the WGN radio broadcast. "A wrath–of–God type thing. I thought we were all going to be electrocuted for coming to a night game at Wrigley Field."

During the rain delay, many fans surged onto the field, and about twenty were arrested. Jody Davis, Al Nipper, Les Lancaster, and Greg Maddux followed the example and slid headfirst on the water–covered tarpaulin. (Each was fined $500 by general manager Jim Frey for the frolic on the field.) The umpires finally called the game at 10:25 P.M.

The first official night game at Wrigley Field was played the following evening with the Mets as the opponents. Although the contest was televised nationally on NBC–TV, the fanfare of the previous night was absent, as well as many of the celebrities and politicians. The Cubs snapped a 2–2 tie with four runs in the seventh inning and won 6–4.

SEPTEMBER 29   The Cubs trade Jody Davis to the Braves for Kevin Blankenship and Kevin Coffman.

SEPTEMBER 30   President Ronald Reagan makes a visit to Wrigley Field, and throws out the first pitch. He also did an inning of play–by–play with Harry Caray. The Cubs lost 10–9 to the Pirates in ten innings.

OCTOBER 1   Rafael Palmeiro hits a grand slam off Bob Kipper in the fifth inning of a 9–7 win over the Pirates at Wrigley Field.

DECEMBER 5   A month after George Bush defeats Michael Dukakis in the Presidential election, the Cubs trade Rafael Palmeiro, Jamie Moyer, and Drew Hall to the Rangers for Mitch Williams, Paul Kilgus, Steve Wilson, Curtis Wilkerson, Luis Benitez, and Pablo Delgado.

Cubs fans are still harping about the 1964 Lou Brock deal, but this one was much worse. Palmeiro is destined for the Hall of Fame, and Moyer was still good enough in 2003 to post a 21–7 record with the Mariners. Palmeiro was second in the NL in batting average in 1988 with an average of .307, although he hadn't yet developed his power stroke, clubbing just eight home runs. The Cubs traded him, in part, because they didn't believe that he had enough power for a left fielder or a first baseman and was too slow to effectively play the outfield. The trade didn't hurt the Cubs in 1989 as Mitch Williams was effective as a closer, and Dwight Smith filled in capably in Palmeiro's old spot in left field as the Cubs won a division title. In the long run, however, this trade was an unqualified disaster.

DECEMBER 21   Manny Trillo signs with the Reds as a free agent.

1 9 8 9

 Cubs

Season in a Sentence

Given little chance of even posting a .500 record at the beginning of the season, the Cubs astonish their fans by posting the best record in the National League before losing to the Giants in the NLCS.

Finish • Won • Lost • Pct • GB

First   93   69   .574   +6.0

National League Championship Series–The Cubs lost four–games–to–one to the San Francisco Giants

Manager

Don Zimmer

Stats	Cubs	NL	Rank
Batting Avg:	.261	.246	1
On–Base Pct:	.322	.315	2
Slugging Pct:	.387	.365	2
Home Runs:	124		5
Stolen Bases:	136		6 (tie)
ERA:	3.43	3.50	6
Fielding Avg:	.980	.978	5
Runs Scored:	702		1
Runs Allowed:	623		5

Starting Lineup

Damon Berryhill, c
Mark Grace, 1b
Ryne Sandberg, 2b
Vance Law, 3b
Shawon Dunston, ss
Dwight Smith, lf
Jerome Walton, cf
Andre Dawson, rf
Mitch Webster, lf
Lloyd McClendon, lf
Domingo Ramos, ss
Joe Girardi, c

Pitchers

Greg Maddux, sp
Mike Bielecki, sp
Rick Sutcliffe, sp
Scott Sanderson, sp–rp
Paul Kilgus, sp–rp
Mitch Williams, rp
Calvin Schiraldi, rp
Jeff Pico, rp
Steve Wilson, rp
Les Lancaster, rpp

Attendance

2,491,942 (fourth in NL)

Club Leaders

Batting Avg:	Grace.	314
On–Base Pct:	Grace.	405
Slugging Pct:	Sandberg	.497
Home Runs:	Sandberg	30
RBI:	Grace	79
Runs:	Sandberg	104
Stolen Bases:	Walton	24
Wins:	Maddux	19
Strikeouts:	Sutcliffe	153
ERA:	Maddux	2.95
Saves:	Williams	36

MARCH 28   Four days after the Exxon Valdez spills oil into Alaska's Prince William Sound, the Cubs release Goose Gossage.

Even after the Cubs posed a dismal 9–23 record during spring training, it was obvious that Gossage wasn't going to help the club. During a private dinner conversation, Jim Frey and Don Zimmer agreed that if the club won 81 games they would go out and celebrate.

APRIL 4   The Cubs win the season opener 5–4 over the Phillies before 33,681 at Wrigley Field. Andre Dawson hit a two–run homer in the fourth inning that put the Cubs up 3–0. In his debut as a Cub, Mitch Williams loaded the bases with three singles in the ninth, then proceeded to strike out Mike Schmidt, Chris James, and Mike Ryal to end the game. High–wire performances like this one throughout the year earned Williams the nickname "The Wild Thing" as the flaky left–hander became a fan favorite with his off–the–wall personality. "I pitch like my hair is on fire," said

Williams. Rick Sutcliffe, starting in the opener for the fifth straight year, was the winning pitcher. He was the first Cub pitcher to win consecutive openers since Grover Alexander in 1925 and 1926.

During the 1988–89 off–season, the mezzanine level and the old press box and broadcasting booths at Wrigley Field were replaced by 67 luxury boxes as well as new facilities for the press and broadcasting personnel behind home plate at the top of the upper deck.

APRIL 9   In a game played at Wrigley Field in 33–degree temperatures with a wind chill of eight above, 11,387 brave the elements on a Sunday afternoon to watch Rick Sutcliffe strikeout 11 batters and beat the Pirates 8–3.

The Cubs lost two of their first three games in 1989, then won seven in a row to run their record to 8–2. By May 14, however, the Cubs were 17–18 and it looked like another long year for Cubs fans.

APRIL 23   Andre Dawson hits the 300th homer of his career, although the Cubs lose 4–2 to the Mets in New York.

APRIL 25   The 75th anniversary of the opening of Wrigley Field is marked with ceremonies prior to a 4–0 win over the Dodgers. Among the notables attending were Billy Williams, Andy Pafko, Billy Herman, and 97–year–old Bob Wright, who played two games for the Cubs in 1915. Wright also threw out the first ball, tossing a spitball, and blew out the candles on a twelve–foot cake. (Wright died in 1993 at the age of 101.)

APRIL 27   Greg Maddux shuts out the Dodgers 1–0 at Wrigley Field. Gary Varsho drove in the lone run of the game with a triple in the fifth inning off Orel Hershiser.

Maddux was 19–12 with a 2.95 ERA in 1989.

MAY 1   Damon Berryhill hits a homer in the twelfth inning to beat the Giants 4–3 in San Francisco.

MAY 14   Lloyd McClendon hits a three–run homer in his first at–bat as a Cub during a 4–0 win over the Braves at Wrigley Field.

McClendon was acquired in a little noticed trade with the Reds the previous December. At the age of 30, he was one of the many pleasant surprises for the Cubs in 1989, as he hit .286 with 12 homers in 259 at–bats in a utility role in 1989 after starting the season in the minors in Iowa. Other players who had made unexpected contributions for the Cubs during the season included Jerome Walton, Dwight Smith, Mike Bielcki, and Les Lancaster. They all proved to be one–year wonders, however. In 1990, McClendon hit just .159 with one homer in 107 at–bats.

JUNE 4   The Cubs hit six homers and trounce the Cardinals 11–3 in St. Louis. Shawon Dunston and Ryne Sandberg each hit two homers, and Mitch Webster and Vance Law added one each. The game was marred by a brief bench–clearing brawl. Mark Grace charged the mound when he was brushed back by Frank DiPino in the fifth inning. Grace missed the next two weeks because of a shoulder injury suffered in the brawl.

Grace hit .314 with 13 home runs in 1989.

JUNE 5   The Cubs maul the Mets 15–3 at Wrigley Field.

On the same day, the Cubs selected outfielder Earl Cunningham of Lancaster High School in Lancaster, South Carolina, in the first round of the amateur draft. Cunningham was a complete bust, never advancing beyond Class A. In 1991 with Peoria, he hit 19 homers, but struck out 145 times while drawing only ten walks. None of the Cubs picks in 1989 amounted to much. The only ones drafted and signed who reached the majors were Gary Scott (second round), Dave Swartzbaugh (ninth), and Dave Stevens (twentieth).

JUNE 8   Rick Wrona's squeeze bunt in the tenth inning scores Lloyd McClendon from third base to beat the Mets 5–4 at Wrigley Field.

JUNE 18   Jerome Walton steals four bases in a 5–4 win over the Expos in Montreal.

JUNE 21   Lloyd McClendon's sacrifice fly in the 11th inning scores Gary Varsho for the lone run in a 1–0 win over the Pirates in Pittsburgh. Greg Maddux (ten innings) and Mitch Williams (one inning) combined on the shutout.

As a youngster in the 1971 Little League World Series, McClendon hit homers in five consecutive at–bats for a team from Gary, Indiana.

JUNE 29   The Cubs lose 12–2 to the Giants in San Francisco.

The loss dropped the Cubs to 40–37. From that point on, the Cubs had a record of 53–32 in the regular season.

JULY 5   Mark Grace collects a two–run homer and three doubles to lead the Cubs to a 5–3 win over the Padres in San Diego.

JULY 20   Relief pitcher Les Lancaster, an .098 lifetime hitter, bats for himself in the eleventh inning and hits a walk–off RBI–single to defeat the Giants 4–3 at Wrigley Field. The Cubs tied the score with three runs in the ninth.

Lancaster began the year in the minors, but after his recall in June he had a terrific year as a set–up man out of the bullpen with a 1.36 ERA in 72⅔ innings. In July and August, he pitched 30 ⅔ consecutive scoreless innings. In 1990, Lancaster struggled again with an ERA of 4.62 in 109 innings.

JULY 21   Dwight Smith sings the National Anthem before a 4–3 loss to the Giants at Wrigley Field.

Smith could do more than sing. After starting the year in the minors, he was called up on May 31 and took over the left field position hitting .324 with nine homers. Smith couldn't come close to hitting .300 again, though. By 1991, his batting average shrunk to .228.

JULY 30	A two–out, two–run, walk–off homer by Mark Grace beats the Mets 6–4 at Wrigley Field.
JULY 31	Dwight Smith hits a grand slam off Greg Harris in a 10–2 win over the Phillies in the first game of a double–header at Veterans Stadium. Philadelphia took the second game 7–4.
AUGUST 5	A three–run, ninth–inning beats the Pirates 4–2 in Pittsburgh. The win put the Cubs into tie for first place with the Expos. Both teams had a record of 63–47.
AUGUST 6	Jeff King of the Pirates hits a home run in the eighteenth inning off Scott Sanderson to defeat the Cubs 5–4, ending a long afternoon in Pittsburgh. The game took five hours and forty–two minutes.
AUGUST 7	The Cubs take sole possession of first place with a 5–3 win over the Expos at Wrigley Field. A weird incident took place in the fifth inning. Jerome Walton lined a pitch off the arm of Montreal pitcher Pascaul Perez that was caught by second base-man Jeff Huson before it hit the ground. As Perez was on the ground being attend-ed to be the team trainer, the pitcher became annoyed at the needling he received from the Chicago players and suddenly whirled and threw the ball into the Cubs dugout. The ball came flying back out of the dugout aimed at Perez.
AUGUST 10	Ryne Sandberg homers twice, giving him home runs in four games in a row, but the Cubs blow a 10–3 lead and lose 16–13 to the Phillies at Wrigley Field. The Cubs scored eight runs in the third inning.
AUGUST 11	Ryne Sandberg homers in his fifth straight game to tie a club record set by Hack Wilson in 1928. The record–tying homer was struck in a 9–2 win over the Phillies at Wrigley Field. Sandberg hit six homers in the five games. *Sandberg batted .290 with 30 homers in 1989 and led the league in runs scored with 104.*
AUGUST 12	Shawon Dunston drives in six runs with a homer, a double and a single to spark the Cubs to a 9–7 win over the Phillies at Wrigley Field. *Dunston hit .278 with nine home runs in 1989.*
AUGUST 15	Andre Dawson hits a three–run homer in the 12th inning to beat the Reds 5–2 in Cincinnati.
AUGUST 17	A two–run single by Jerome Walton in the ninth inning defeats the Reds 3–2 in Cincinnati. Walton extended his hitting streak to 27 games.
AUGUST 18	Andre Dawson collects his 2,000th career hit, although the Cubs lose 6–5 to the Astros in Houston. Jerome Walton extended his hitting streak to 28 games, tying the modern club record set by Ron Santo in 1966.
AUGUST 20	Jerome Walton extends his hitting streak to 30 games, although the Cubs lost 8–4 to the Astros in Houston. The streak ended in a 10–inning, 6–5 loss to the Reds at Wrigley Field on August 21 when Walton was hitless in five at–bats.

Walton's 30–game hitting streak is the modern Cubs record. As a rookie center-fielder, Walton hit .293 with six homers in 1989. He won the Rookie of the Year Award with 22 out of a possible 24 first–place votes. Dwight Smith, who played alongside Walton in leftfield, was named first on the other two ballots. After his rookie season, Walton proved to be a shooting star who burned out quickly, descending into a steady and mysterious decline. His batting averages fell to .263 in 1990, .219 in 1991, and .127 in 1992.

AUGUST 24   The Cubs trade Pat Gomez and Rick Luecken to the Braves for Paul Assenmacher.

AUGUST 25   Rick Wrona begins his day playing golf in Des Moines, Iowa and ends it with a single that starts a twelfth–inning rally that beats the Braves 4–3 in Atlanta. He was on the ninth hole in the morning when he was informed that he was being recalled to the Cubs from the club's Iowa farm team after Damon Berryhill went down with an injury. Wrona entered the game in the tenth inning as a catcher when Joe Girardi was lifted for a pinch–hitter. The win snapped a six–game losing streak.

AUGUST 29   Down 9–0 to the Astros, the Cubs stage an incredible comeback and win 10–9 in ten innings. The Cubs rallied with two runs in the sixth inning, three in the seventh, four in the eighth and the game–winner in the tenth. Dwight Smith ended the contest with a bases–loaded single. Smith also drove in runs in the sixth and the eighth. He wasn't in the starting lineup. With the score 9–0, all seemed lost, and Don Zimmer took out Andre Dawson to give the slugger a rest and replaced him with Smith in right field.

AUGUST 30   The Cubs trade Darrin Jackson, Calvin Schiraldi, and Phil Stephenson to the Padres for Luis Salazar and Marvell Wynne.

SEPTEMBER 9   In a battle for first place, Luis Salazar drives in the winning run with a single to beat the Cardinals 3–2 on a rainy day at Wrigley Field. The Cubs entered the game with a one–half game lead over St. Louis.

SEPTEMBER 10   After pitching in relief the previous day, Steve Wilson comes back as a starter and strikes out ten batters in five innings as the Cubs beat the Cardinals 4–1 at Wrigley Field. Four Cubs pitchers combined for 18 strikeouts. In addition to Wilson's ten, Scott Sanderson fanned three in one inning, Paul Assenmacher struck out four in 2 ⅓, and Mitch Williams one in ⅔ of an inning.

SEPTEMBER 11   The Cubs end a 4–3 win over the Expos with a trick pick–off play at first base. Jeff Huson was the Montreal runner at first. Playing off the bag, first baseman Lloyd McClendon stuck in behind Huson, received the pick–off throw from Mitch Williams, and applied the tag that closed the contest.

SEPTEMBER 12   Mike Bielecki pitches a two–hitter to defeat the Expos 2–0 at Wrigley Field. The only Montreal hits were singles by Tim Raines in the first inning and Tim Wallach in the second.

Bielecki was a major surprise during the Cubs division–winning season. Entering the season, he was 29 years old with a career record of 12–19 and an ERA of 4.37. But in 1989, using a split–fingered fastball he developed in winter ball, Bielecki had a totally unexpected turnaround and was 18–7 with a 3.14 earned run average. He proved to be a one–year wonder, however. Although he pitched in the majors until 1997, Bielecki never came close to reaching his 1989 level again. The production of most of the other "surprise packages" of 1989, like Lloyd McClendon, Jerome Walton, Dwight Smith, and Les Lancaster, dropped off dramatically during the 1990s. As a result, the Cubs of 1989 won a division title largely with a collection of role players who played over their heads. The club returned to its losing ways in 1990.

SEPTEMBER 15   Shawon Dunston hits a grand slam in the sixth off Bob Patterson during a 7–2 win over the Pirates in Pittsburgh. The win gave the Cubs a 5 ½–game lead with 15 contests left on the schedule.

SEPTEMBER 18   Mitch Williams's first major league hit is a home run, struck during a 10–6 win over the Mets at Wrigley Field.

SEPTEMBER 26   The Cubs clinch the division title with a 3–2 win over the Expos in Montreal.

The Cubs opponent in the National League Championship Series was the San Francisco Giants. The Giants had a record of 92–70 and were managed by Roger Craig.

OCTOBER 4   Will Clark collects four hits in four at–bats and drives in six runs, including a grand slam off Greg Maddux, to lead the Giants to an 11–3 hammering of the Cubs in game one of the NLCS before 39,195 at Wrigley Field. Mark Grace and Shawon Dunston homered for the Cubs. Ryne Sandberg had three hits, including a double.

Those who played for the Cubs in both the 1984 and 1989 NLCS were Sandberg, Rick Sutcliffe, and Scott Sanderson.

OCTOBER 5   The Cubs even the NLCS with a 9–5 win over the Giants before 39,195 at Wrigley Field. The Cubs scored six runs in the first inning. Jerome Walton had two hits in the inning. Mark Grace had three hits in the game and drove in four runs.

OCTOBER 7   With the Cubs leading 4–3, Robby Thompson hits two–run homer in the seventh inning off Les Lancaster giving to give the Giants a 5–4 win in game three at Candlestick Park.

OCTOBER 8   Matt Williams snaps a 4–4 tie in the fifth inning with a homer, and the Giants hold on to defeat the Cubs 6–4 in game four in San Francisco. Andre Dawson struck out with the bases loaded against Steve Bedrosian to end the game. Luis Salazar homered for the Cubs.

OCTOBER 9   The Giants win the National League pennant by defeating the Cubs 3–2 in the fifth game of the NLCS. Will Clark's bases–loaded single in the eighth inning put the Giants up for good.

During the Series, Clark had 13 hits, including two homers, a triple, and three doubles, in 20 at–bats for a .650 batting average. Mark Grace countered with 11 hits, including a homer, a triple, and three doubles, in 17 at–bats for a .647 average.

NOVEMBER 20   Five weeks after an earthquake strikes the San Francisco Bay Area during the World
               Series, the Cubs trade Mitch Webster to the Indians for Dave Clark.

DECEMBER 13   Scott Sanderson signs a free agent contract with the Athletics.

The double–play combination of Shawon Dunston and Ryne Sandberg gave the Cubs a formidable middle–infield
defense. In this photo Dave Magadan of the Mets is forced out.

THE STATE OF THE CUBS

The Cubs struggled to find a winning combination throughout the 1900s and failed to finish in first place. The club did make the post–season as a wild card in 1998. Overall, the Cubs were 739–813 for a winning percentage of .476. Among the twelve clubs that were part of the National League during all ten seasons of the decade (excluding the three expansion teams and the Brewers), only the Phillies posted a lower winning percentage than the Cubs. The NL champions during the decade were the Reds (1990), Braves (1991, 1992, 1995, 1996, and 1999), Phillies (1993), Marlins (1997), and Padres (1998). During the Cubs' last four seasons in the NL East, the champions were the Pirates (1990, 1991, and 1992) and the Phillies (1993). After moving to the Central Division, the leaders were the Reds (1995), Cardinals (1996), and Astros (1997, 1998, and 1999).

THE BEST TEAM

Led by Sammy Sosa's 66 home runs, the 1998 Cubs were 90–73. Chicago won the wild card playoff game against the Giants to reach the post–season for the only time during the 1990s. The Cubs were swept by the Braves.

THE WORST TEAM

The euphoria over playing in the 1998 playoffs didn't last long. The Cubs fell to 67–95 in 1999.

THE BEST MOMENT

The Cubs won a berth in the post–season by defeating the Giants 5–3 in a one–game playoff on September 28, 1998. During the entire month of September, Cubs fans were on the edge as the club battled for the wild card slot in the playoffs, and Sammy Sosa and Mark McGwire staged a race to see who would become the all–time record holder for most home runs in a season.

THE WORST MOMENT

The Cubs lost their 14th game in a row on April 20, 1997, to start the season 0–14.

THE ALL–DECADE TEAM • YEARS WITH CUBS

Rick Wilkins, c	1991–95
Mark Grace, 1b	1998–2001
Ryne Sandberg, 2b	1982–1994; 1996–97
Steve Buechelle, 3b	1992–95
Shawon Dunston, ss	1985–95; 1997
Henry Rodriguez, lf	1998–2000
Brian McRae, cf	1995–97
Sammy Sosa, rf	1992–2004
Greg Maddux, p	1986–1992
Steve Trachsel, p	1993–99
Frank Castillo, p	1991–97
Mike Morgan, p	1992–95; 1998

Andre Dawson (1987–92) was the second best Cubs outfielder of the decade, but he was a right fielder, and Sammy Sosa relegated Dawson to the "bench." The All–Decade Team reflects the Cubs of the 1990s—a handful of stars of the first order surrounded by a sea of mediocrity. The inclusion of Buechele, Morgan, Castillo, Rodriguez, and McRae reflects the problems the Cubs had in fielding competent players at third base, left field, and center field, and in developing a deep pitching staff.

THE DECADE LEADERS

Batting Avg:	Grace	.311
On–Base Pct:	Grace	.385
Slugging Pct:	Sosa	.540
Home Runs:	Sosa	307
RBI:	Sosa	825
Runs:	Grace	843
Stolen Bases:	Sammy Sosa	172
Wins:	Trachsel	60
Strikeouts:	Trachsel	829
ERA:	Maddux	2.98
Saves:	Myers	112

THE HOME FIELD

The Cubs fielded less–than–stellar teams during the 1990s, and the 1994 and 1995 seasons were short-ened by a strike by the players, but the fans kept turning out. The Cubs attracted 17,242,369 to Wrigley Field during the 1980s. Even though the product on the field failed to improve, attendance during the 1990s was 22,948,269.

THE GAME YOU WISHED YOU HAD SEEN

On May 6, 1998, rookie Kerry Wood, in his fifth major league start, pitched a one–hitter and struck out 20 batters to beat the Astros 2–0.

THE WAY THE GAME WAS PLAYED

Baseball experienced one of its pivotal transitions during the 1990s, as offensive numbers soared to new heights. Fueled by the home run, expansion to thirty teams, which weakened the pitching, and newer ballparks with fences closer to home plate, the average number of runs scored per game in the NL jumped from 7.9 runs per game in 1989 to 10.0 in 1999. Teams averaged 114 home runs in 1989 and 181 in 1999. Sammy Sosa was at the center of the home run explosion. He hit 66 home runs in 1998 and 63 more in 1999, yet those figures weren't even enough to lead the league. The trend of the 1970s and 1980s toward artificial turf ended as every new ballpark that opened or was on the drawing boards, had grass fields. The new ballparks also included "retro" features, trying to emulate the older classic venues like Wrigley Field. Four new teams were added in Miami, Denver, St. Petersburg, and Phoenix, and inter–league play began in 1997. Beginning in 1994, there were three divisions in each league, adding a new tier of playoffs.

THE MANAGEMENT

The Tribune Company continued its operation of the Cubs, but management of the club was marked by instability. The organization was headed by Donald Grenesko (1988–91), Stanton Cook (1991–94), and Andy MacPhail (1994–present). General managers were Jim Frey (1988–91), Larry Himes (1991–94), and Ed Lynch (1994–2000). The managers included Don Zimmer (1988–91), Joe Altobelli (1991), Jim Essian (1991), Jim Lefebvre (1992–93), Tom Trebelhorn (1994), and Jim Riggleman (1995–99).

THE BEST PLAYER MOVE

The Cubs traded George Bell to the White Sox for Sammy Sosa and Ken Patterson on March 30, 1992.

THE WORST PLAYER MOVE

The Cubs let Greg Maddux get away to the Braves in 1992 in free agency.

1990s

1990   Cubs

Season in a Sentence

Dom Zimmer loses the magic
touch he possessed in 1989, as
the Cubs lose 52 of their first 88
games and are never a factor in
the pennant race.

Finish • Won • Lost • Pct • GB

Fourth (tie) 77   85   .475 18.0

Manager

Don Zimmer

Stats

Stats	Cubs	NL	Rank
Batting Avg:	.263	.256	2
On–Base Pct:	.316	.324	10
Slugging Pct:	.392	.383	6
Home Runs:	136		5
Stolen Bases:	151		5
ERA:	4.34	3.79	11
Fielding Avg:	.980	.980	5
Runs Scored:	690		6
Runs Allowed:	774		11

Starting Lineup

Joe Girardi, c
Mark Grace, 1b
Ryne Sandberg, 2b
Luis Salazar, 3b
Shawon Dunston, ss
Dwight Smith, lf
Jerome Walton, cf
Andre Dawson, rf
Doug Dascenzo, lf–cf
Domingo Ramos, 3b
Curtis Wilkerson, 3b
Marvell Wynne, cf
Dave Clark, of

Pitchers

Greg Maddux, sp
Mike Harkey, sp
Mike Bielecki, sp
Shawn Boskie, sp
Mitch Williams, rp
Paul Assenmacher, rp
Les Lancaster, rp
Bill Long, rp
Steve Wilson, rp–sp

Attendance

2,243,791 (fifth in NL)

Club Leaders

Batting Avg:	Dawson	.310
On–Base Pct:	Grace	.372
Slugging Pct:	Sandberg	.559
Home Runs:	Sandberg	40
RBI:	Sandberg	100
	Dawson	100
Runs:	Sandberg	116
Stolen Bases:	Dunston	25
Wins:	Maddux	15
Strikeouts:	Maddux	144
ERA:	Harkey	3.26
Saves:	Williams	16

JANUARY 3   The Cubs trade Bryan House to the Rangers for Rey Sanchez.

FEBRUARY 15   The owners lock the players out of spring training because of a lack of progress
                 during negotiations for a new basic agreement.

MARCH 18   The dispute between the players and the owners is resolved.

                 *Spring training camps opened on March 20. The season, scheduled to open April 2,
                 was delayed a week, with the games missed made up on open dates, with double-
                 headers, and by extending the close of the campaign by three days.*

APRIL 10   The Cubs open with a 2–1 win over the Phillies before only 7,791 on a cold and
                 windy day at Wrigley Field. The temperature was 36 degrees with a 26 mile–per–
                 hour wind blowing in from left field. Marvell Wynne's pinch–single with two out in
                 the eighth inning broke the 1–1 tie.

                 *The Cubs had a completely new radio team in 1990 with Thom Brennaman,
                 Ron Santo, and Bob Brenly in the booth.*

APRIL 11	The game between the Cubs and Phillies at Wrigley Field is postponed by snow.
APRIL 17	Lloyd McClendon hits a grand slam in the fifth inning off Sid Fernandez during an 8–6 win over the Mets in thirteen innings in New York. It proved to be the only homer that McClendon hit all year.

Though lacking the power usually associated with first base, Mark Grace held the postion for more than a decade, batting over .300 nine times in thirteen years.

> *The Cubs sported more traditional gray uniforms in 1990, abandoning the navy pullovers worn from 1982 through 1989. The new uniforms had button–down fronts, belt loops, and "Chicago" spelled in block letters across the front.*

APRIL 23	Steve Lyons of the White Sox plays all nine positions in an exhibition game against the Cubs at Wrigley Field. The Cubs lost 6–5.
APRIL 27	Mike Harkey (seven innings) and Mitch Williams (two innings) combine on a two–hitter to win 3–1 over the Padres in San Diego. Harkey held the Padres hitless until Phil Stephenson led off the eighth inning with a home run. Harkey was taken out of the game immediately and replaced by Williams.
APRIL 29	Greg Maddux sets a major league record for pitchers with seven putouts in a 4–0 win over the Dodgers in Los Angeles. Maddux won the first of 13 consecutive Gold Gloves in 1990.
MAY 5	Shawon Dunston hits a two–run, walk–off homer with two out in the ninth to beat the Padres 3–2 in the first game of a double–header at Wrigley Field. San Diego won the second game 6–5.
MAY 8	Andre Dawson ties the game against the Braves at Wrigley Field 8–8 with a homer in the ninth inning, then wins it 10–8 with a two–run, walk–off homer in the eleventh.
MAY 18	Ryne Sandberg ends his major league record streak of consecutive errorless games with a throwing error during a 7–0 win over the Astros in Houston. Sandberg played 123 straight games without an error from June 21, 1989 through May 17, 1990.
MAY 22	Andre Dawson is intentionally walked a major league record five times by Cincinnati manager Lou Piniella during a sixteen–inning, 2–1 win over the Reds at Wrigley Field. The fifth time that Dawson was walked occurred in the sixteenth with runners on first and third. Dave Clark drove in the winning run with a single.
MAY 24	Vice President Dan Quayle throws out the ceremonial first pitch then aids Harry Caray with the TV commentary during a 15–6 loss to the Dodgers at Wrigley Field.
MAY 29	Both the Cubs and White Sox play at home on the same night for the first time in history. The Cubs drew 28,925 for a 6–2 loss to the Giants at Wrigley Field, while

the White Sox attracted 15,353 for a 5–4 win at old Comiskey Park.

JUNE 1   Playing in his major league debut, Hector Villenueva homers in his second at–bat, although the Cubs lose 6–4 to the Cardinals in St. Louis. Villenueva entered the game as a pinch–hitter for the slumping Mark Grace, then remained in the contest at first base.

JUNE 7   The Cubs select Lance Dickson of the University of Arizona in the first round of the amateur draft.

In three minor league stops in the Cubs system in 1990, Dickson was 8–3 with 111 strikeouts and an 0.95 ERA in 76 innings. He was rushed to the majors, made his major league debut at the age of 20 on August 9, but his career lasted but three games in which he was 0–3 with an ERA of 7.24. He never returned to the big leagues, in part because of some bizarre ailments. Dickson had a foot infection in 1990, and suffered a stress fracture of his foot covering first base in 1991. In his first five professional seasons, he was on the disabled list nine times.

For the third straight year, the Cubs failed to draft and sign anyone who developed into a big league regular. The only others picked in 1990 to reach the majors were Ryan Hawblitzel in the second round and Pedro Valdes in the 12th.

JUNE 8   The Cubs score nine runs in the third inning and rout the Phillies 15–2 at Wrigley Field. Shawon Dunston hit a grand slam off Don Carman following an intentional walk to Ryne Sandberg.

Sandberg hit 40 homers with 100 RBIs, 116 runs scored, and a .306 batting average in 1990. He is the only second baseman in history to hit at least 30 homers two seasons in a row. Sandberg is the also the only player besides Barry Bonds with a 40–home run season and a 50–stolen base season during his career. Sandberg stole 52 bases in 1985.

JULY 1   The Cubs score four runs in the eighth inning, the last three on a Luis Salazar home run, to beat the Padres 11–10 in San Diego.

JULY 10   The American League wins the All–Star Game 2–0 before 39,071 at Wrigley Field. The National League was held to only two hits. Both runs scored in the seventh inning on a double by Julio Franco.

JULY 18   Don Zimmer promises to swim across Lake Michigan if Greg Maddux beats the Padres at Wrigley Field.

Maddux entered the game with 13 consecutive starts since May 5 without a victory. He lost eight games and had five no–decisions while compiling an ERA of 6.15. Maddux won the game 4–2. Zimmer showed up at the post-game press interview wearing sun glasses, a life jacket, and a buoy strapped around his leg. Within forty–eight hours Zimmer was inundated with flotation devices. As to swimming the sixty miles across the lake, Zimmer said, "I didn't think anyone would take me seriously. I swim like a rock."

JULY 23   The Cubs win their eighth game in a row with a 3–1 decision over the Cardinals in St. Louis.

The Cubs were 36–52 on July 14, and 41–33 the rest of the way.

JULY 27   The Cubs score two runs in the tenth inning to defeat the Expos 2–0 at Olympic Stadium. Greg Maddux allowed only two hits over nine innings. Bill Long pitched a perfect tenth for the save. The only two Montreal hits were singles by Marquis Grissom in the first and seventh innings.

JULY 28   Shawon Dunston ties a modern major league record with three triples in a 10–7 win over the Expos in Montreal.

Dunston hit six triples overall in 1990. He also had 17 homers and batted .262.

AUGUST 8   Six days after Iraq's invasion of Kuwait, and the day after Operation Desert Storm troops leave for Saudi Arabia, the Cubs beat the Cardinals 4–3 in a thrilling fifteen–inning marathon at Wrigley Field. The score was 0–0 after nine innings. That Cardinals scored twice in the tenth inning and once in the thirteenth, but the Cubs rallied to tie the game each time. Andre Dawson's single with two out drove in the game–winner.

SEPTEMBER 9   In the first Sunday night game ever played at Wrigley Field, Jeff Pico is hit by a line drive that breaks his thumb during a 9–2 loss to the Cardinals.

Pico never pitched another major league game. After the season ended, he married the sister of Mark Grace's wife, Michelle.

SEPTEMBER 11   The Cubs spot the Expos an early 5–0 lead before scoring ten runs in the second inning and going on to win 11–6 at Wrigley Field. All ten runs in the second scored before Montreal retired a batter.

SEPTEMBER 14   Steve Wilson suffers a cut requiring six stitches when he tries to stop an assailant from beating a woman at a restaurant in St. Louis.

SEPTEMBER 22   Andre Dawson collects the 300th stolen base of his career, although the Cubs lose 11–5 to the Mets at Wrigley Field.

The only other players besides Dawson to collects 2,000 hits, 300 home runs, and 300 stolen bases in a career are Willie Mays and Barry Bonds.

NOVEMBER 21   The Cubs sign Danny Jackson, most recently with the Reds, as a free agent.

Jackson had two subpar seasons with the Reds after a 23–8 campaign in 1988. As a Cub, he was 5–14 with a 5.07 ERA. During a stretch of twenty consecutive starts in 1991 and 1992, Jackson had ten losses and ten no decisions.

DECEMBER 6   The Cubs sign George Bell, most recently with the Blue Jays, as a free agent.

Bell gave the Cubs 25 homers and some atrocious defensive play in left field before being sent to the White Sox in a trade for Sammy Sosa.

DECEMBER 14   The Cubs trade Greg Smith to the Dodgers for Jose Vizcaino.

Jose played three seasons with the Cubs and gave WGN–TV viewers plenty of enjoyment listening to Harry Caray try to pronounce Vizcaino.

DECEMBER 17   The Cubs sign Dave Smith, most recently with the Astros, as a free agent

Smith was brought in as a closer, but proved to be a multi–million–dollar boo–boo. He was 36 years old, but he had a career 2.53 ERA in 762 ⅓ career innings and was effective for the Astros in 1990. In 35 games as a Cub in 1991, Smith was 0–6 with an ERA of 6.00 in 35 games. During the 1990–91 off–season, the Cubs spent millions on free agent contracts for Jackson, Bell, and Smith, but received little for their investment.

1991

Season in a Sentence

With the addition of three high–priced free agents in George Bell, Danny Jackson, and Dave Smith, the Cubs seem poised to win the NL East, but the big money doesn't pay off, leading to the firing of two managers.

Finish • Won • Lost • Pct • GB

Fourth   77   83   .481   20.0

Managers

Don Zimmer (18–19),
Joe Altobelli (0–1) and
Jim Essian (59–63)

Stats

Stats	Cubs	NL	Rank
Batting Avg:	.253	.250	5
On–Base Pct:	.309	.318	11
Slugging Pct:	.390	.373	4
Home Runs:	159		2
Stolen Bases:	123		9
ERA:	4.03	3.69	12
Fielding Avg:	.982	.980	3
Runs Scored:	695		3
Runs Allowed:	734		12

Starting Lineup

Rick Wilkins, c
Mark Grace, 1b
Ryne Sandberg, 2b
Luis Salazar, 3b
Shawon Dunston, ss
George Bell, lf
Jerome Walton, cf
Andre Dawson, rf
Chico Walker, 3b–cf
Doug Dascenzo, cf–lf
Hector Villenueva, c
Dwight Smith, rf–cf
Damon Berryhill, c

Pitchers

Greg Maddux, sp
Mike Bielecki, sp–rp
Frank Castillo, sp
Shawn Boskie, sp
Rick Sutcliffe, sp
Paul Assenmacher, rp
Chuck McElroy, rp
Les Lancaster, rp
Heathcliff Slocumb, rp
Bob Scanlan, rp–sp

Attendance

2,314,250 (fourth in NL)

Club Leaders

Batting Avg:	Sandberg	.291
On–Base Pct:	Sandberg	.379
Slugging Pct:	Dawson	.488
Home Runs:	Dawson	31
RBI:	Dawson	104
Runs:	Sandberg	104
Stolen Bases:	Landrum	27
Wins:	Maddux	15
Strikeouts:	Maddux	198
ERA:	Maddux	3.35
Saves:	Smith	17

APRIL 7   Two months after the United States and its allies attack Iraq to start the Persian
               Gulf War, and five weeks after George Bush orders a cease fire to end the same war,
               the Cubs trade Mitch Williams to the Phillies for Chuck McElroy and Bob Scanlan.

               The deal ended two tumultuous seasons for "The Wild Thing" in Chicago.
               Williams pitched three seasons in Philadelphia as the closer, but his last pitch
               with the Phillies will be the one most remembered. In the ninth inning of game
               six of the 1993 World Series, Williams threw a home–run ball to Joe Carter,
               another ex–Cub, which gave the Blue Jays the world championship. After 1993,
               Williams pitched three more seasons with three clubs, and had a 7.96 ERA with
               52 walks in 37 ⅓ innings.

APRIL 9   The Cubs lose the season opener 4–1 to the Cardinals before 31,622 at Wrigley
               Field. St. Louis scored three runs in the eighth inning off Danny Jackson to break a
               1–1 tie. The temperature was 42 degrees on a cloudy day.

APRIL 13   Mike Bielecki drives in four runs with two singles and pitches eight shutout innings
               to lead the Cubs to a 7–3 win at Wrigley Field.

APRIL 19   Andre Dawson's grand slam in the ninth inning off Stan Belinda puts the Cubs
               ahead 4–3, but the Pirates rally with two runs in their half to win 5–4.

APRIL 21   The Pirates stun the Cubs 13–12 in eleven innings at Three Rivers Stadium. The
               Cubs led 7–2 before Pittsburgh scored four runs in the eighth inning and one in the
               ninth. The Cubs seemed to put the game away with five runs in the top of the
               eleventh, four of them on a grand slam by Andre Dawson off Bob Patterson. But
               the Pirates rallied again with six runs in their half of the eleventh off Heathcliff
               Slocumb and Mike Bielecki to win the game.

APRIL 24   Andre Dawson's 350th career homer accounts for the only run in a 1–0 win over
               the Cardinals in St. Louis. The home run was hit in the second inning off Jose
               DeLeon. Mike Bielecki (seven innings) and Paul Assenmacher (two innings) com-
               bined on the shutout.

MAY 13   All three generations of the Caray family are in the WGN–TV booth at Wrigley
               Field when Harry is joined by son Skip and grandson Chip. The Cubs lost 5–3 to
               the Braves.

               Skip had been the Braves announcer since 1976. He was joined by his son Chip
               in 1991. Chip moved to the Cubs in 1998 following his grandfather's death. It
               was also "All in the Family" when the Cubs and Reds played each other from
               1990 through 1995. Thom Brennaman handled the Cubs games on radio and
               TV while his father Marty did the play–by–play for Cincinnati.

MAY 15   A flare–up between the Cubs and Braves highlights a 6–1 Chicago win at Wrigley
               Field. Juan Berenguer hit Andre Dawson with a pitch in the eighth inning. Words
               were exchanged and both benches emptied, but order was restored without inci-
               dent. When play resumed, Luis Salazar hit Berenguer's first pitch for a home run. It
               was Salazar's second homer of the game.

MAY 17   The Cubs go sixteen innings, only to lose 1–0 to the Phillies in Philadelphia. The only run of the game was scored on a two–out single in the sixteenth by Dickie Thon off Les Lancaster.

MAY 20   Just seventeen months after managing the Cubs in the National League Championship Series, Don Zimmer is fired, and coach Joe Altobelli is named interim manager. Altobelli managed the Cubs for just one game, and was ejected in the 8–6 loss to the Mets in New York on May 21. Altobelli was tossed for arguing a call by umpire Steve Rippley.

MAY 22   The Cubs hire Jim Essian as manager.

Essian was 40 years old and was managing the Cubs Class AAA farm club in Iowa. He played in the majors from 1973 through 1985 with four clubs as a catcher. Essian was twenty years younger than Zimmer and was expected to have a better rapport with the players. The Cubs won their first five games under Essian, but reality set in and the club returned to its losing ways. Essian was fired in October and had a 59–63 record as Cubs manager.

MAY 26   Down 6–0, the Cubs score one run in the fifth inning and seven in the seventh to beat the Expos 8–6 at Wrigley Field. The last three runs were scored on a three–run homer by George Bell.

The win was the high point of the season. The Cubs were 23–20 and four games out of first place, but the club lost 18 of 24 from June 4 through June 28.

JUNE 2   Ced Landrum's two–out, two–run single in the ninth inning beats the Expos 4–3 in Montreal. Landrum entered the game in the seventh inning in right field as part of a double switch. Essian ran out of position players, and had to use Greg Maddux as a pinch–hitter in the ninth spot immediately preceding Landrum.

JUNE 13   The day after the Bulls win their first NBA championship in a series with the Lakers, Andre Dawson catches Mike Kingery's fly ball in right field with the bases loaded and two out in the ninth, and throws out Tony Perezchica at home plate to preserve a 4–3 win over the Giants at Wrigley Field.

JULY 4   Mark Grace hits a homer in the eleventh inning to beat the Pirates 9–8 at Wrigley Field. It was Grace's second homer of the game. The Cubs led 8–2 in the seventh inning, but allowed Pittsburgh to rally and force extra innings.

JULY 9   Andre Dawson hits a Roger Clemems pitch over the center field wall in the All–Star Game, played at the Skydome in Toronto. The American League won 4–2. Dawson hit .272 with 31 homers and 104 runs–batted–in in 1991.

JULY 23   Reds pitcher Rob Dibble throws a ball at the legs of Doug Dascenzo during an 8–5 win over Cincinnati at Wrigley Field, after Dascenzo lays down a successful suicide squeeze.

AUGUST 2 Ryne Sandberg hits a two–run homer in the tenth inning to beat the Mets 4–2 in New York.

Sandberg hit .291 with 26 homers, 104 runs scored, and 100 RBIs in 1991.

AUGUST 11   George Bell hits a walk–off homer leading off the fourteenth inning to beat the Mets 3–2 at Wrigley Field.

AUGUST 23   The Cubs score three runs in the ninth inning, the last two on Mark Grace's walk–off double, to defeat the Padres 5–4 at Wrigley Field.

AUGUST 28   Chico Walker hits a grand slam in the fourth inning off Paul McClellan during an 8–6 win over the Giants in San Francisco.

Cleotha (Chico) Walker was 33 years old in 1991, but it was the first time in his career that he spent an entire season in the majors. He spent at least part of every season from 1976 through 1990 in the minors in the organizations of the Red Sox, Angels, Blue Jays, and Cubs. As a pinch–hitter in 1991, Walker was 13–for–32, a .406 average.

SEPTEMBER 2   Ryne Sandberg hits a grand slam in the eighth inning off Jim Lewis during an 10–8 win over the Padres in San Diego.

SEPTEMBER 14   Trailing 5–0, the Cubs rally with three runs in the sixth inning, one in the eighth, one in the ninth, and two in the tenth on Hector Villenueva's walk–off homer to beat the Expos 7–5 at Wrigley Field.

SEPTEMBER 29   The Cubs trade Damon Berryhill and Mike Bielecki to the Braves for Turk Wendell and Yorkis Perez.

OCTOBER 2   The Cubs beat the Phillies 1–0 in Philadelphia. Greg Maddux not only pitched a complete game shutout, but drove in the lone run of the game with a single in the seventh inning. Jose DeJesus held the Cubs hitless before allowing three singles in the seventh.

OCTOBER 5   Ced Landrum ties a modern club record for most steals in a game with four in a 7–5 win over the Cardinals in the second game of a double–header at Wrigley Field. Landrum didn't have a hit in the game, reaching base on two walks. He stole second and third after each base on balls. Landrum also played all three outfield positions in the contest, starting in center field, then moving to right and then left. The Cubs won the first game 3–2.

OCTOBER 18   The Cubs fire Jim Essian as manager.

The Cubs had a 65–62 record on August 29, then lost 21 of their next 29 games, convincing Cubs management that Essian wasn't the answer.

NOVEMBER 14   The Cubs fire Jim Frey as general manager and replace him with Larry Himes.

The Cubs increased their payroll from $14 million in 1990 to $27 million in 1991 without tangible improvement which cost Frey his job, along with some ill–advised trades and a deterioration of the farm system. Himes served as the general manager of the White Sox from 1986 through 1990 and helped build a losing club into a contender. Opinionated and abrasive, he was fired after a personality clash with White Sox majority owner Jerry Reinsdorf. Himes was considered an expert in scouting and developing young players. He was the first individual to head the baseball operations of both Chicago clubs. Frey remained in the organization as an executive vice–president with the understanding that he would be a "consultant," but the phone never rang. The reshuffling of the club also led to an end of Donald Grenesko's term as president. Stanton Cook became the Cubs chairman of the board and was in charge of the financial end of the team.

NOVEMBER 22   The Cubs hire 49–year–old Jim Lefebvre as manager.

Lefebvre was the manager of the Mariners from 1989 through 1991. He took over a club that was 68–93 in 1988, the twelfth losing season in a row. Seattle improved their won–lost record each of the three seasons that Lefebvre managed the club, culminating in a 83–79 mark in 1991, the first winning record in franchise history. Nevertheless, he was fired because of dissension among some of his best players. As a player, he was an infielder with the Dodgers from 1965 through 1972. Lefebvre was the Rookie of the Year in 1965, was an All–Star in 1966, and played in two World Series.

DECEMBER 3   The Cubs sign Mike Morgan, most recently with the Dodgers, as a free agent.

Morgan was 32 years old and had a career record of 67–104 when he was signed by the Cubs, but he had a terrific season in 1992 with a 16–8 record and a 2.55 ERA. At Wrigley Field he was 9–2 with an earned run average of 1.38. But during the rest of his stay with the Cubs, which included the 1993, 1994 and 1995 seasons and a brief stopover in 1998, Morgan was 14–27 with an ERA of 4.75. He played with twelve different teams during his big league career, the most for anyone since 1900. In addition to the Dodgers and Cubs, Morgan pitched for the Athletics, Yankees, Blue Jays, Mariners, Orioles, Cardinals, Reds, Twins, Rangers, and Diamondbacks between 1978 and 2001. His last big league game was in the 2001 World Series with Arizona. It was the only time in his career that he pitched in the Fall Classic.

DECEMBER 19   Rick Sutcliffe signs as a free agent with the Orioles.

Sutcliffe spent more time on the disabled list than on the mound during his last two seasons with the Cubs. He won 16 games for the Orioles in 1992 before the arm miseries returned.

1992

Cubs

Season in a Sentence

The Cubs acquire Sammy Sosa in a brilliant trade, but lose Greg Maddux in a dunderheaded move after he wins his first Cy Young Award.

Finish · Won · Lost · Pct · GB

Fourth   78   84   .481   16.0

Manager

Jim Lefebvre

Stats

Stats	Cubs	NL	Rank
Batting Avg:	.254	.252	5
On–Base Pct:	.328	.330	8
Slugging Pct:	.364	.368	8
Home Runs:	104		6
Stolen Bases:	77		11
ERA:	3.39	3.51	5
Fielding Avg:	.982	.981	5
Runs Scored:	593		10
Runs Allowed:	624		6

Starting Lineup

Joe Girardi, c
Mark Grace, 1b
Ryne Sandberg, 2b
Steve Buechele, 3b
Jose Vizcaino, ss–3b
Derrick May, lf
Doug Dascenzo, cf
Andre Dawson, rf
Rey Sanchez, ss
Sammy Sosa, cf
Luis Salazar, 3b–lf
Rick Wilkins, c
Dwight Smith, cf–rf–lf

Pitchers

Greg Maddux, sp
Mike Morgan, sp
Frank Castillo, sp
Danny Jackson, sp
Shawn Boskie, sp
Bob Scanlan, rp
Paul Assenmacher, rp
Chuck McElroy, rp
Jeff Robinson, rp

Attendance

2,126,720 (fifth in NL)

Club Leaders

Batting Avg:	Grace	.307
On–Base Pct:	Grace	.380
Slugging Pct:	Sandberg	.510
Home Runs:	Sandberg	26
RBI:	Dawson	90
Runs:	Sandberg	100
Stolen Bases:	Sandberg	17
Wins:	Maddux	20
Strikeouts:	Maddux	199
ERA:	Maddux	2.18
Saves:	Scanlan	14

MARCH 2   Ryne Sandberg signs a four–year deal worth $28.4 million, making him the first player in history to earn $7 million in a season.

During spring training, Jim Lefebvre was hit in the face by a Doug Dascenzo line drive while pitching batting practice. The new Cub manager suffered a swollen and blackened eye.

MARCH 30   The Cubs trade George Bell to the White Sox for Sammy Sosa and Ken Patterson.

It didn't look like a great deal at the time, but the Cubs struck gold with this transaction. Bell was still a productive hitter in 1992, while Sosa was a struggling youngster who seemed to be regressing in his development. In 1991 with the White Sox, Sosa hit only .203 with ten homers in 316 at–bats, and struck out 98 times while drawing only 14 walks. He was only 23 when the Cubs acquired him, however, and he became one of the best players of his generation. Bell played only two more seasons after being traded away by the Cubs, mostly as a designated hitter.

When Sosa reported to the Cubs he was assigned the same number 11 worn by George Bell. He switched to number 21 to honor Roberto Clemente. Sosa was number 25 with the White Sox and number 17 with the Rangers.

APRIL 3   Les Lancaster signs as a free agent with the Tigers.

APRIL 7   In the season opener, the Cubs defeat the Phillies 4–3 at Veterans Stadium. Greg Maddux went seven innings for the win and Mark Grace hit a two–run homer to lead the Cubs after Philadelphia took a 4–3 advantage after three innings. Sammy Sosa made his debut with the Cubs. Batting second and playing right field, he had an RBI–double in five at–bats.

The Cubs weren't over the .500 mark again until August 23 when the club was 62–61. In Lefebvre's first season as manager, Chicago was 12–19 on May 11, and peaked at 67–63 before finishing the year with a mark of 78–84.

APRIL 10   The Cubs lose the home opener 2–1 in eleven innings to the Cardinals before 33,659 at Wrigley Field.

The Cubs resurfaced the concourse at Wrigley Field in 1992 with a non–skid, brick–like material.

APRIL 11   Reliever Chuck McElroy hits a triple and a single and pitches a perfect 2 ⅓ innings to close out a 5–1 win over the Cardinals at Wrigley Field.

APRIL 20   With Chicago's Loop paralyzed by flooding after a section of the freight tunnel under the Chicago River caves in, Gary Scott hits a grand slam in the fourth inning off Kyle Abbott in an 8–3 win over the Phillies at Wrigley Field. Scott connected for the slam after fouling off eight pitches. The drive landed in the left field basket with the aid of a 15 mile–per–hour wind.

Scott was the Cubs Opening Day third baseman in both 1991 and 1992, but he proved to be a huge disappointment. In 175 major league at–bats, he hit only three homers and batted .160.

MAY 1   Two days after riots begin in the South Central section of Los Angeles, resulting in the deaths of fifty–two people, the Cubs suffer their fourth shutout loss in a row, dropping a 4–0 decision to the Reds in Cincinnati. The Cubs were swept in Atlanta in a series from April 27 through 29 by scores of 5–0, 1–0, and 8–0.

MAY 2   The Cubs end their streak of 36 consecutive scoreless innings with three runs in the first inning, all on an Andre Dawson homer, and go on to defeat the Reds 10–3 in Cincinnati.

MAY 5   Shawon Dunston goes on the disabled list with a back injury. He didn't play again until September 1993.

MAY 7   Sammy Sosa hits his first home run as a Cub during a 9–2 win over the Astros at Wrigley Field. The home run was hit leading off the first inning. It came in Sosa's 103rd at–bat with the club.

MAY 12   The Cubs defeat the Astros 3–2 at
          the Astrodome in a game in which
          neither team had a hit until the sixth
          inning. Jimmy Jones held the Cubs
          hitless for 7 ⅓ innings, while Mike
          Morgan stopped Houston without a
          hit for 5 ⅓. Both teams finished the
          game with five hits.

MAY 18   Mark Grace drives in the only three
          runs scored in a 3–0 win over the
          Dodgers in Los Angeles with doubles
          in the fourth and eighth inning.

          *Grace collected 185 hits and bat-
          ted .307 in 1992.*

JUNE 1   The Cubs select pitcher Derek
          Wallace from Pepperdine University
          in the first round of the amateur
          draft.

          *Wallace never pitched for the
          Cubs. In two seasons with the
          Yankees and Royals, he was 2–4
          with a 3.82 ERA.*

Journeyman Mike Morgan enjoyed the best season of his twenty–two–year major league career
in 1992, giving the Cubs a strong second starter
behind Greg Maddux.

JUNE 2   Andre Dawson hits a two–run homer in the ninth to tie the game 2–2, and Mark
          Grace drives in the winner with a single in the thirteenth to beat the Padres 3–2 at
          Wrigley Field.

JUNE 8   Cubs relief pitcher Jim Bullinger hits a home run on the first pitch of his first at–bat
          in the major leagues during a 5–2 win over the Cardinals in St. Louis.

          *Bullinger made his big league debut on May 27, but didn't make a plate appear-
          ance until the June 8 game. He was a shortstop when he started his professional
          career in 1986, and became a pitcher in 1989. He finished his career in the
          majors in 1997 with four homers in 165 at–bats.*

JUNE 19   Five days after the Bulls capture their second NBA championship by defeating the
          Portland Trailblazers, Derrick May drives in all five Cubs runs with a pair of
          homers in a 5–2 win over the Phillies in Philadelphia. In attendance were May's
          wife, parents, and about fifty friends and relatives from his hometown of Newark,
          Delaware, a town about forty–five miles from Philadelphia.

JUNE 25   The Cubs score seven runs in the first inning and beat the Mets 9–2 in New York.

JUNE 27   The Cubs trade Mike Sodders to the Dodgers for Kal Daniels.

JUNE 29   The Cubs end a 12–game losing streak to Dwight Gooden, dating back to 1987,
          with a 5–2 triumph over the Mets at Wrigley Field. Gooden retired the first 12 batters

he faced before the Cubs broke through. He entered the game with a 24–3 lifetime record against the Cubs.

JULY 5   Kal Daniels hits a grand slam in the seventh inning off Juan Berenguer during an 8–0 win over the Braves in Atlanta. It was Kal's first homer as a Cub.

JULY 6   Commissioner Fay Vincent orders the Cubs to move to the National League's Western Division beginning with the 1993 season. The Cubs were to move west along with the Cardinals, while the Reds and the Braves were slated to shift to the Eastern Division. Vincent said that he ruled in the best interests of baseball at the urging of many National League owners.

                In March, the National League owners voted 10–2 in favor of moving the four clubs, thus giving the league geographic logic. One of the two negative votes came from the Cubs, who as a directly affected party, had to give their assent before the move became official. Many believed that Vincent exceeded his authority. The Cubs sued the commissioner on July 7 in U.S. District Court and asked for a preliminary injunction barring Vincent from enforcing his decision. The injunction was granted on July 23. Vincent resigned as commissioner on September 7 under pressure from major league owners, and the National League scrapped the realignment plan on September 24. Beginning in 1994, the American and National Leagues split into three divisions, with the Cubs joining the NL Central.

JULY 11   The Cubs trade Danny Jackson to the Pirates for Steve Buechele.

JULY 21   Kal Daniels homers off Tim Belcher in the fourth inning to beat the Reds 1–0 in Cincinnati. Jeff Robinson (4⅔ innings), Ken Patterson (1⅔ innings), Jim Bullinger (two innings) and Bob Scanlan (one inning) combined on the shutout.

JULY 22   Greg Maddux pitches a complete game to shutout the Reds 3–0 in Cincinnati.

JULY 24   For the third game in a row, the Cubs win with a shutout, defeating the Astros 1–0 in Houston. Mike Morgan (eight innings) and Bob Scanlan (one inning) did the pitching. Rick Wilkins hit a homer in the ninth inning off Doug Jones for the lone run of the game.

JULY 27   Sammy Sosa celebrates his return from the disabled list by leading off the first inning with a homer on Doug Drabek's first pitch. The Cubs went on to a 3–2 win over the Pirates at Wrigley Field.

                Sosa was placed on the DL on June 13 with a broken finger suffered when hit by a pitch from Montreal's Dennis Martinez. On August 6, Sosa broke his ankle by fouling off a pitch and was out for the rest of the year. In his first season as a Cub, at the age of 23, Sosa hit .260 with eight home runs in 67 games.

JULY 28   Steve Buechele hits a homer, a triple, and a double during an 11–1 win over the Pirates at Wrigley Field. The big day came just seventeen days after the Pirates traded Buechele to the Cubs. It was his only homer as a Cub during the 1992 season in 239 at–bats.

JULY 29	After going hitless in his first five at–bats, Sammy Sosa hits a two–run, walk–off homer in the eleventh inning to beat the Pirates 6–4 at Wrigley Field.
AUGUST 1	Jeff Robinson (seven innings) and Chuck McElroy (two innings) combine on a two–hitter to beat the Mets 6–1 in the second game of a double–header at Shea Stadium. The only New York hits were doubles by Howard Johnson in the first inning and Chris Donnels in the second. The Mets won the first game 3–0, in which Ryne Sandberg collected four hits in four at–bats. It came during a streak of hits in eight consecutive at–bats beginning with an eleven–inning 6–4 win over the Pirates at Wrigley Field on July 29, and ended in the second game of the August 1 twin bill. *Sandberg scored 100 runs, batted .304, and hit 26 homers in 1992.*
AUGUST 7	The Cubs score seven runs in the fourth inning and beat the Mets 9–1 at Wrigley Field.
AUGUST 16	Greg Maddux pitches the Cubs to a 1–0 win over the Astros at Wrigley Field. *Maddux won the first of four career Cy Young Awards in 1992 with a 20–11 record, 199 strikeouts and a 2.18 ERA in a league–leading 268 innings.*
AUGUST 25	Mike Harkey officially makes it into the box score, but doesn't throw a pitch in the Cubs 7–4 loss to the Padres at San Diego. Harkey strained a groin muscle warming up and was replaced by Jeff Robinson.
AUGUST 30	In his third major league start, Jim Bullinger pitches a one–hitter to beat the Giants 3–1 at Wrigley Field. The only San Francisco hit was a home run by Kirt Manwaring leading off the eighth inning. It was the first one–hitter by a Cubs hurler since Chuck Rainey pitched one in 1983.
SEPTEMBER 4	Andre Dawson collects five hits, including two doubles, in seven at–bats, but the Cubs lose 7–5 in fourteen innings to the Padres at Wrigley Field. *Dawson had just returned to Chicago from Miami, where Hurricane Andrew did $120,000 in damage to his home.*
SEPTEMBER 6	Mike Harkey tears a tendon in his knee trying to do a cartwheel in the outfield during warm–ups prior to a 3–1 loss to the Padres at Wrigley Field. He also dislocated his kneecap. *It wasn't the only unusual injury to a Cubs pitcher during September 1992. Dave Smith was on the disabled list healing from a surgically repaired elbow. He went fishing in the Pacific Ocean on a surfboard and re–injured the elbow when he caught a halibut. Smith went to the emergency room with the cast in shreds and seaweed hanging off of it.*
SEPTEMBER 7	In his second major league start, Cubs shortstop Alex Arias collects five hits, including a double, in five at–bats during an eleven–inning, 6–5 win over the Pirates at Three Rivers Stadium. Derrick May hit a three–run homer in the top of the eleventh before the Cubs withstood a two–run Pittsburgh rally in the bottom half of the inning.

SEPTEMBER 9   Ryne Sandberg hits a grand slam off Danny Cox and gives the Cubs a 7–6 lead, but the Pirates rally to win 13–8 in Pittsburgh.

SEPTEMBER 16   The Cubs score eight runs in the seventh inning and smash the Phillies 14–9 at Wrigley Field.

SEPTEMBER 17   Mike Morgan pitches a two–hitter to beat the Phillies 3–0 at Wrigley Field in a contest interrupted by rain for forty–three minutes in the third inning. The only Philadelphia hits were singles by Ruben Amaro in the fourth inning and Dave Hollins in the seventh.

SEPTEMBER 19   Ryne Sandberg reaches base nine times in nine plate appearances during a double–header against the Cardinals in St. Louis. Sandberg had a home run, a double, three singles, and four walks. The Cubs won the first game 6–5 and lost the second 11–10 in ten innings.

SEPTEMBER 21   Andre Dawson collects the 2,500th hit of his career in a 10–1 victory over the Mets in New York. The milestone hit was a single off Eric Hillman in the first inning.

SEPTEMBER 25   A brawl breaks out during a ten–inning, 3–2 loss to the Phillies at Wrigley Field. In the tenth, Cubs pitcher Bob Scanlan hit Dave Hollins with a pitch. Hollins charged the mound, and he and Scanlan fought as both benches cleared. Scanlan received a four–game suspension.

SEPTEMBER 30   Greg Maddux wins his 20th game of the 1992 season with a 6–0 win over the Pirates at Wrigley Field. It was the first time in Maddux's career that he won 20 games. The contest proved to be his last as a Cub until 2004.

OCTOBER 4   In what would prove to be his last game as a Cub, Andre Dawson hits the 399th home run of his career in a 3–2 win over the Expos at Wrigley Field.

NOVEMBER 17   In the expansion draft, the Rockies select Joe Girardi, Ryan Hawblitzel, and Pedro Castellano from the Cubs. On the same day, the Cubs traded Gary Scott and Alex Arias to the Marlins for Greg Hibbard.

               Hibbard played only one season with the Cubs, and had a record of 15–11.

DECEMBER 8   Five weeks after Bill Clinton defeats George Bush in the presidential election, the Cubs sign Dan Plesac, most recently with the Brewers, as a free agent.

DECEMBER 9   The Cubs lose both Greg Maddux and Andre Dawson to free agency. Maddux signed with the Braves and Dawson with the Red Sox. On the same day, the Cubs signed Randy Myers, most recently with the Padres, as a free agent.

               Maddux, of course, proved to a huge loss. The Cubs should have been able to sign him because Maddux wanted to remain in Chicago, but the star pitcher became angry because general manager Larry Himes took a hard line with his contract. Maddux signed with the Braves for $28 million over five years. He would have been a bargain at twice the price. It's difficult to believe that the Cubs thought they could compete without him. From 1988 through 1992, Maddux was 95–75, a winning percentage of .559. The rest of the staff was 307–331 (.481). With the Braves, Maddux had a won–lost record of 194–88, *led the NL in ERA four times, and won three Cy Young Awards. Dawson had a good year in 1992 with the Cubs, collecting 22 homers and driving in 90 runs with a .277 average, but at 38, the club correctly surmised that he wasn't worth the risk of a long–term contract. Myers gave the Cubs a solid closer. In 1993, he set a National League record with 53 saves accompanied by an ERA of 3.11.*

DECEMBER 11   The Cubs sign Candy Maldonado, most recently with the Blue Jays, as a free agent.

Maldonado was supposed to replace Andre Dawson, but was a complete waste of money, hitting only .186 in 140 at–bats.

DECEMBER 18   The Cubs sign Willie Wilson, most recently with the Athletics, as a free agent.

1993   Cubs

Season in a Sentence

The Cubs post only their third winning season since 1972, but the club still fires Jim Lefebvre as manager.

Finish • Won • Lost • Pct • GB

Fourth   84   78   .519   13.0

Manager

Jim Lefebvre

Stats

Stats	Cubs	NL	Rank
Batting Avg:	.270	.264	6
On–Base Pct:	.328	.330	8
Slugging Pct:	.414	.399	4
Home Runs:	161		3
Stolen Bases:	100		10
ERA:	4.18	4.04	10
Fielding Avg:	.982	.978	5
Runs Scored:	738		5
Runs Allowed:	739		7

Starting Lineup

Rick Wilkins, c
Mark Grace, 1b
Ryne Sandberg, 2b
Steve Buechelle, 3b
Rey Sanchez, ss
Derrick May, lf
Dwight Smith, cf–rf
Sammy Sosa, rf–cf
Jose Vizcaino, ss–3b
Willie Wilson, cf
Kevin Roberson, rf

Pitchers

Greg Hibbard, sp
Jose Guzman, sp
Mike Morgan, sp
Mike Harkey, sp
Frank Castillo, sp
Randy Myers, rp
Bob Scanlan, rp
Jose Bautista, rp
Chuck McElroy, rp

Attendance

2,653,763 (eighth in NL)

Club Leaders

Batting Avg:	Grace	.325
On–Base Pct:	Grace	.393
Slugging Pct:	Wilkins	.561
Home Runs:	Sosa	33
RBI:	Grace	98
Runs:	Sosa	92
Stolen Bases:	Sosa	36
Wins:	Hibbard	15
Strikeouts:	Guzman	163
ERA:	Hibbard	3.96
Saves:	Myers	53

APRIL 5   Five weeks after a terrorist bomb explodes in the parking garage beneath the World
               Trade Center, killing six people, Greg Maddux makes his first regular season
               appearance as an Atlanta Brave and defeats the Cubs 1–0 before 38,218 at Wrigley
               Field in the season opener. Maddux, who was booed loudly by Cubs fans, allowed
               five hits in 8 ⅓ innings before being relieved by Mike Stanton. One fan threw back a
               foul ball that Maddux hit into the stands. Mike Morgan started for the Cubs and
               surrendered only one run in seven innings on the mound.

               *Cubs general manager Larry Himes tried to convince the Braves to push Mad-
               dux back one day in the rotation to boost attendance for the second game of
               the season, but the Braves refused. First Lady Hillary Rodham Clinton was
               scheduled to throw out the ceremonial first pitch, but had to decline because of
               an illness to her father, who died on April 7. Mrs. Clinton handled first pitch
               honors at Wrigley Field in 1994. (See April 4, 1994.)*

APRIL 6   In his Cubs debut, Jose Guzman comes within one out of a no–hitter when Atlanta's
               Otis Nixon hit a single with two out in the ninth. The Cubs won 1–0 at Wrigley
               Field. The lone run of the game was scored on a triple by Mark Grace in the first
               inning.

               *Larry Himes publicly proclaimed that Guzman was just as good a pitcher as
               Maddux, but Jose was 12–10 with a 4.34 ERA for the Cubs in 1993.*

APRIL 24   Five days after the raid on the Branch Davidian compound in Waco, Texas, Chris
               Sabo and Joe Oliver of the Reds both hits grand slams to lead Cincinnati to a 15–5
               win over the Cubs at Wrigley Field. Sabo hit a slam in the first off Greg Hibbard,
               and Oliver connected in the seventh against Dan Plesac.

               *The Cubs put names on the backs of their home uniforms for the first time in
               1993.*

APRIL 26   The Cubs play the Colorado Rockies for the first time, and win 6–3 at Mile High
               Stadium in Denver.

MAY 3   The Rockies play at Wrigley Field for the first time, and beat the Cubs 14–13 in
               eleven innings. The Cubs scored five runs in the ninth inning, the last three on a
               homer by Sammy Sosa, to tie the score 10–10. Colorado plated four runs in the
               eleventh, before the Cubs came back with three in their half, two of them on anoth-
               er homer by Sosa. Sammy also had three singles in the game, giving him five hits in
               six at–bats.

MAY 4   Ryne Sandberg makes his first throwing error since July 4, 1990, in a 3–2 Cubs win
               over the Rockies at Wrigley Field.

               Sandberg was limited to 117 games by injuries, but he hit .309.

MAY 9   Mark Grace hits for the cycle, but it's not enough as the Cubs lose 5–4 to the Padres at
               Wrigley Field. Grace hit a two–run homer in the ninth to complete the cycle.

               *Among those in attendance at the game was actress Janine Turner, who starred
               in the television series* NORTHERN EXPOSURE. *Grace was dating her at the time.*

He finished the 1993 season with 193 hits, a .325 batting average, 14 homers, and 98 RBIs.

MAY 21   The Cubs play the Florida Marlins for the first time, and lose 5–3 at Joe Robbie Stadium in Miami.

MAY 25   Willie Wilson, Derrick May, and Dwight Smith get into an obscenity–filled shoving match after a 5–4 loss to the Giants at Wrigley Field. Wilson lambasted May for not moving a runner, and Smith for misplaying a fly ball. The next day, Wilson was scratched from the starting lineup and fined for showing up only one–half hour before the game. Later in the season, he left the club for a week claiming he had the flu.

JUNE 1   The Cubs trade Heathcliff Slocumb to the Indians for Jose Hernandez.

JUNE 14   The Marlins play at Wrigley Field for the first time, and lose 6–3 to the Cubs.

JUNE 16   The Cracker Jack division of Borden Inc. celebrates the 100th anniversary of the famous candy–coated popcorn and peanut snack with a party at Wrigley Field held before and after the Cubs 6–4 win over the Marlins. A large supply of Cracker Jacks was distributed at the ballpark without charge, and Sailor Jack, the company mascot, threw out the ceremonial first pitch. Cracker Jack was introduced at the Chicago World's fair in 1893 by a local popcorn company. It was inextricably linked to baseball in 1908 when "Take Me Out to the Ballgame" became a music hall hit with the line "Buy me some peanuts and Cracker Jacks."

JUNE 25   Five days after the Bulls win their third straight NBA championship in a series against the Suns, Rick Wilkins hits a three–run homer in the tenth inning to beat the Dodgers 8–5 in Los Angeles.

Wilkins had one of the flukiest seasons of any hitter in Cubs history in 1993. He hit a career–high eight home runs in 1992, but exploded in 1993 with 30 homers and a .303 batting average. The only other catchers in major league history with 30 homers and a .300 batting average in the same season are Gabby Hartnett, Walker Cooper, Roy Campanella, Joe Torre, Mike Piazza, and Ivan Rodriguez. In 1994, Wilkins looked like Bob Uecker, hitting just seven homers with a batting average of only .227. Wilkins was hitting only .191 when he was traded to the Astros in June 1995. He reached double figures in homers only one other time in his career, when he clubbed 14 with the Astros and Giants in 1996.

JULY 2   Sammy Sosa collects six hits, including a double, in six at–bats during an 11–8 win over the Rockies in Denver. The Cubs had a total of 21 hits in the game.

Sosa also had hits in his last three at–bats in the Cubs previous game, a 4–1 win over the Padres in San Diego on June 30. The nine hits in consecutive at–bats is a Cubs record. In 1993, Sosa became the first Cubs with at least 30 homers and 30 stolen bases in a season. He hit 33 home runs and had 36 steals.

JULY 3   Ryne Sandberg's collects his 2,000th hit as a Cub during a 5–4 loss to the Rockies in Denver.

JULY 7	Reds pitcher Tom Browning makes a rooftop visit in Chicago. During the third inning of the Reds 4–3 win over the Cubs at Wrigley Field, Browning left the dugout in uniform, and walked across Sheffield Avenue to sit with a group of Cubs fans on the roof of an apartment building behind the right field bleachers. He was captured on camera by Chicago's WGN television crew with his legs dangling over the edge of the building.

JULY 15 Mike Morgan pitches the Cubs to a 1–0 win over the Rockies at Wrigley Field. Steve Buechele drove in the only run of the game with a double in the fourth inning.

> *The Cubs were the picture of mediocrity in 1993, hovering around the .500 mark all season. The club had a winning percentage of exactly .500 thirty–three times in 1993, beginning with a 1–1 record on April 6 and ending with a 72–72 ledger on September 12. The low point of the year was a 64–70 record on September 2. The Cubs reversed their usual trend and finished strong, winning 20 of the last 28 games to finish at 84–78. The Cubs never had a winning streak longer than five games, or a losing streak longer than four.*

JULY 21 Jose Guzman (seven innings), Bob Scanlan (one inning), and Randy Myers (one inning) combine on a two–hitter to beat the Reds 4–1 at Riverfront Stadium. The only Cincinnati hits were singles by Hal Morris and Joe Oliver in the fifth inning.

JULY 30 The Cubs trade Paul Assenmacher to the Yankees for Karl Rhodes.

AUGUST 2 The Cubs beat the Pirates 12–10 at Wrigley Field in a game spiced by seven homers, brushbacks, a bench–clearing brawl, and six ejections. Pittsburgh led 8–2 before the Cubs tied it with a six–run fifth inning. Chicago added three more in the sixth to pull ahead 11–8 and hung on for the win. Carlos Garcia, who hit two homers for Pittsburgh, was the focal point of the brushbacks that resulted in the sixth–inning brawl. Bob Scanlan threw at Garcia in retaliation for Pirates hurler Blas Minor firing a pitch at Mark Grace. Scanlan was suspended for seven games.

> *The Cubs topped the 2.5 million mark in attendance for the first time in 1993, drawing a total of 2,653,753, although a change in accounting procedures helped the club set the record. Prior to 1993, the turnstile count was used in determining attendance figures. Beginning in 1993, the National League used the number of tickets sold.*

AUGUST 6 The Cubs score three runs in the ninth inning to beat the Cardinals 6–4 in St. Louis. Kevin Roberson put the Cubs ahead with a two–run homer off Lee Smith, and Rick Wilkins added another home run.

AUGUST 17 Jose Guzman strikes out 12 batters in a 7–2 win over the Expos in the first game of a double–header at Wrigley Field. Montreal won the second game 6–4.

> *Wearing uniform number 13, Turk Wendell made his major league debut during the double–header. One of the most colorful players ever to play for the Cubs, Wendell was a bundle of idiosyncrasies. He chewed Brach's black licorice on the mound, and brushed his teeth in between innings. Wendell also talked to the baseball, drew crosses in the dirt on the mound, and leaped side-ways over foul lines. Before he threw his first pitch, he waved to the center*

fielder, and wouldn't turn to face the hitter until the outfielder waved back.

AUGUST 19   The Cubs trade Candy Maldonado to the Indians for Glenallen Hill.

AUGUST 27   Derrick May hits a grand slam in the seventh inning off Mike Stanton to put the Cubs ahead 9–6 in Atlanta. The Cubs won the game 9–7.

AUGUST 30   Rick Wilkins hits a walk–off homer grand slam homer in the eleventh inning off Roger Mason to beat the Phillies 10–6 at Wrigley Field.

SEPTEMBER 4   Shawon Dunston collects his first hit in sixteen months on an eighth–inning pinch–double that ties the game 8–8 against the Mets at Wrigley Field, and scores the winning run on Sammy Sosa's single, lifting the Cubs to a 9–8 victory.

              Dunston was out for over a year following surgery for a herniated disk in his back.

SEPTEMBER 5   Pinch–hitter Glenallen Hill's two–run, walk–off homer with one out in the ninth beats the Mets 2–1 at Wrigley Field.

SEPTEMBER 6   Steve Buechele, Willie Wilson, and Steve Lake hit back–to–back–to–back homers off Roger Mason in the sixth inning to spark the Cubs to a 7–6 win over the Phillies in Philadelphia. It was the only homer that Wilson hit between 1990 and the end of his career in 1994.

SEPTEMBER 8   Trailing 5–1, the Cubs score seven runs in the eighth inning after two are retired to defeat the Phillies 8–5 in Philadelphia. The big inning was high-lighted by a pinch–triple by Kevin Roberson with the bases loaded.

SEPTEMBER 14 Major league baseball announces its three–division alignment, plus an extra round of playoff games, to be put into effect during the 1994 sea-sons. The Cubs were placed in the Central Division with Cincinnati, Houston, Pittsburgh, and St. Louis. Milwaukee was added to the NL Central in 1998 when the club moved into the National League.

Steve Buechele enjoyed a good year in 1993 but did not prove to be a long–term solution to the team's problem at third base.

SEPTEMBER 21 The first seven batters in the Cubs lineup reach base and score in the first inning of a 13–3 win over the Cardinals at Wrigley Field.

SEPTEMBER 22 The Cubs outslug the Cardinals 11–9 at Wrigley Field.

OCTOBER 6   The Cubs fire Jim Lefebvre as manager.

Lefebvre guided the Cubs to the best season since 1989, and was popular with a vast majority of the fans, but it wasn't enough to please Larry Himes. On a Chicago radio show in May, Himes said that the Cubs should be ten games over .500 at the All–Star break, and bickered with Lefebvre all season over the direction of the club.

OCTOBER 13   The Cubs hire 45–year–old Tom Trebelhorn as manager.

Trebelhorn was a Cubs coach in 1992 and 1993. He previously managed the Brewers from 1986 through 1991. Trebelhorn was hired after two days of psychological tests by a professional interviewer. Few things are more psychologically damaging than managing the Cubs, however, and Trebelhorn was fired after only one year on the job.

1994   Cubs

Season in a Sentence

In a season of bad news, the Cubs lose their first 12 games at Wrigley Field, Ryne Sandberg retires, and the players go on strike.

Finish • Won • Lost • Pct • GB

Fifth   49   64   .434   16.5

Manager

Tom Trebelhorn

Stats

Stats	Cubs	NL	Rank
Batting Avg:	.259	.267	11
On–Base Pct:	.326	.336	12
Slugging Pct:	.404	.415	8
Home Runs:	109		8
Stolen Bases:	69		10
ERA:	4.47	4.21	10
Fielding Avg:	.982	.980	5
Runs Scored:	500		11
Runs Allowed:	549		10

Starting Lineup

Rick Wilkins, c
Mark Grace, 1b
Ryne Sandberg, 2b
Steve Buechele, 3b
Shawon Dunston, ss
Derrick May, lf
Glenallen Hill, cf–lf
Sammy Sosa, rf
Rey Sanchez, 2b–ss
Karl Rhodes, cf
Jose Hernandez, 3b–ss
Eddie Zambrano, rf–lf

Pitchers

Steve Trachsel, sp
Willie Banks, sp
Anthony Young, sp
Kevin Foster, sp
Mike Morgan, sp
Randy Myers, rp
Jose Bautista, rp
Dan Plesac, rp
Chuck Crim, rp
Dave Otto, rp
Jim Bullinger, rp–sp

Attendance

1,845,208 (eighth in NL)

Club Leaders

Batting Avg:	Sosa	.300
On–Base Pct:	Grace	.370
Slugging Pct:	Sosa	.545
Home Runs:	Sosa	25
RBI:	Sosa	70
Runs:	Sosa	59
Stolen Bases:	Sosa	22
Wins:	Trachsel	9
Strikeouts:	Trachsel	108
ERA:	Trachsel	3.21
Saves:	Myers	21

JANUARY 14   Eight days after Nancy Kerrigan is attacked by assailants connected to rival skater Tanya Harding, Greg Hibbard signs a free agent contract with the Mariners.

FEBRUARY 1   Dwight Smith signs a free agent contract with the Angels.

Smith closed his career with the Cubs holding the all–time career record for pinch–hits with 50.

MARCH 30   The Cubs trade Jose Vizcaino to the Mets for Anthony Young and Otis Smith.

When Young was acquired by the Cubs, he had a lifetime record of 5–35, including a major league record 27 losses in a row. Young lasted two seasons with the Cubs and posted a record of 7–10.

APRIL 4   With a 22–mile–per–hour gale blowing out at Wrigley Field, Cubs outfielder Karl Rhodes hits three home runs in his first three at–bats on Opening Day, although the Cubs lose 12–8 to the Mets before a crowd of 38,413. Batting lead–off, Rhodes homered in the first, third, and fifth innings, each of them off Dwight Gooden. Karl also walked in the sixth inning and singled in the ninth. The only other player in major league history with three homers on Opening Day is George Bell of the Blue Jays in 1988. Rhodes is the only one to do it in his first three at–bats, however. Entering the 1994 season, he had only five homers in 280 major league at–bats and a .232 batting average. Following his Opening Day explosion, Rhodes returned to obscurity. He had another 306 at–bats in the big leagues, with only five more homers while compiling a batting average of just .206. Rhodes went to Japan, where he became a legitimate home run hitter. In 2001 with the Kintetsu Buffaloes, Rhodes hit 55 homers to tie single–season Japanese League record set by Sadaharu Oh in 1964.

First Lady Hillary Rodham Clinton tossed out the ceremonial first pitch. Wearing a blue Cubs blazer and baseball cap, she threw from the first row of seats on the third base side. She also sang "Take Me Out to the Ballgame" with Harry Caray during the seventh–inning stretch, and smooched the legendary broadcaster at the conclusion of the duet. Her husband Bill threw out the first pitch on the same day in Cleveland at the first game ever played at Jacobs Field. From Cleveland, the president flew to Charlotte, North Carolina, to cheer the University of Arkansas to a 76–72 win over Duke in the NCAA basketball championship game.

APRIL 7   Michael Jordan plays for the White Sox in an exhibition game against the Cubs before 37,825 at Wrigley Field. Jordan collected two singles and played right field. The game ended after ten innings in a 4–4 tie.

A few days later, Jordan reported to the White Sox Class AA farm club in Birmingham, Alabama, where he hit .202 with three homers in 127 games following his "retirement" from basketball. Jordan returned to the Bulls in March 1995.

APRIL 15   Anthony Young gives up consecutive home runs to Fred McGriff, Terry Pendleton, and Tony Tarasco in the first inning of a 19–5 loss to the Braves at Wrigley Field.

APRIL 29   Tom Trebelhorn chats with fans outside Firehouse 78.

Following a 6–5 loss to the Rockies at Wrigley Field, which dropped the Cubs record to 6–15 on the season, and 0–9 at home, Trebelhorn met with about 200 angry fans by standing on a park bench outside the firehouse across Waveland Avenue from the ballpark. He was accompanied by four security guards and responded to questions. The manager was booed when he said, "I have invested more in this and more frustration over what's happening than all of you combined." By the end of the half–hour town meeting, Trebelhorn had won over most of the crowd and was cheered for having the guts to face the fans in the face of defeat. At the finish, the firefighters invited him inside for a broiled chicken dinner.

MAY 3   The Cubs lose their 12th consecutive game at Wrigley Field, falling to the Reds 5–2. The 12 losses in succession, which came in the first 12 home games of the 1994 season, broke the club record of 11, set in 1902 when the Cubs played at West Side Grounds.

MAY 4   The Cubs win their first home game of 1994 after opening the season with 12 consecutive losses at Wrigley Field. The club record home losing streak was stopped with a 5–2 win over the Reds. To help break the streak, Sam Sianis, owner of the Billy Goat Tavern, brought his latest pet goat onto the field at the invitation of Cubs management. The goat, named "Billy," was also accompanied by Ernie Banks.

The Cubs entered the game with a record of 6–18. The club rallied to 22–26 by May 30, then lost ten games in a row.

MAY 6   The Cubs score seven runs in the third inning and hit five homers in the game to beat the Pirates 10–1 in Pittsburgh. Sammy Sosa and Glenallen Hill each hit two homers, and Ryne Sandberg added one.

Sosa batted .300 and hit 25 homers in 105 games in the strike–shortened 1994 season.

MAY 12   The last position player on the bench, Shawon Dunston hits a two–run, pinch–hit homer in the ninth to break a 6–6 tie and beat the Cardinals 8–6 in St. Louis.

The Cubs changed the lettering on their gray road uniforms in 1994, with "Cubs" appearing in blue script trimmed in red and white.

MAY 17   The Cubs score seven runs in the third inning and beat the Cardinals 11–4 at Wrigley Field. On the same day, the Cubs released Willie Wilson.

MAY 24   The Cubs win their eighth game in a row with a 2–0 decision over the Dodgers in Los Angeles.

MAY 29   Batting in the lead–off position, Sammy Sosa swats Tom Glavine's first pitch in the first inning for a home run putting the Cubs on their way to a 4–2 win over the Braves in Atlanta.

MAY 30   Willie Banks (eight innings) and Randy Myers (one inning) combine on a one–hitter to beat the Phillies 3–0 at Wrigley Field. Banks held Philadelphia without a hit until Kim Batiste singled into left field with one out in the eighth inning.

JUNE 2   The Cubs select pitcher Jayson Peterson of East High School in Denver, Colorado, in the first round of the amateur draft.

> *Peterson was another Cubs first round draft choice who never had to worry about being besieged by autograph hounds, as he failed to advance past Class A. The only players drafted and signed by the Cubs in 1994 were Javier Martinez (third round), Steve Rain (11th), Rich Barker (37th), and Kyle Farnsworth (47th).*

JUNE 10   The Cubs lose their tenth game in a row, dropping a 2–1 decision to the Dodgers at Wrigley Field.

> *Mike Morgan suffered through a horrible year. He was 2–10 with a 6.69 ERA and was on the disabled list for three weeks in June with "emotional distress" due to a family matter.*

JUNE 11   The Cubs stop their ten–game losing streak with four runs in the eighth inning to beat the Dodgers 7–4 at Wrigley Field. The Cubs won despite hitting into five double plays, three of them by Mark Grace.

JUNE 13   Ryne Sandberg unexpectedly announces his immediate retirement from baseball at the age of 34.

> *The announcement came without warning and stunned Cubs management, teammates, friends, and everyone in baseball. Sandberg gave no inclination that he intended to hang up his spikes. He said that he had lost the drive that made him a success and that the game was longer "fun." A week later, Sandberg's wife, Cindy, filed for divorce, contending the marriage was "irretrievably broken." Sandberg sat out the rest of the 1994 season and all of 1995 before returning to the game. (See October 31, 1995.)*

JUNE 18   Anthony Young (six innings), Jose Bautista (one inning), Dan Plesac (one inning), and Randy Myers (one inning) combine on a two–hitter to beat the Giants 6–4 at Candlestick Park. The only San Francisco hits were a single by Todd Benzinger and a double by Rikkert Faneyte in the fourth inning. Young gave up four runs on only two hits in part because he walked six batters.

Following an outstanding season in 1993, Randy Myers saved only 21 games in '94 and pitched only 40⅓ innings.

JUNE 23   Suffering from an irregular heartbeat, Harry Caray blacks out and falls face first on the concrete steps of Joe Robbie Stadium in Miami ninety minutes before a 9–3 win over the Marlins. Caray was on his way to the field to conduct a pre–game interview. It was his third fall of the season. In April, Caray slipped and landed on his back on a freshly waxed airport surface in Montreal. In early June, he fell through a coffee table in the manager's office in Philadelphia. Caray didn't return to the broadcast booth until July 23.

JULY 4 — The Cubs play a double–header at Wrigley Field against the Rockies that lasts ten hours and ten minutes, because of three rain delays and a fifteen–inning second game. The Cubs won the first 4–3 with two runs in the ninth. Colorado won the second tilt 4–2.

JULY 16 — Cubs broadcaster Thom Brennaman joins his father Marty as announcers on a regionally televised prime–time contest on ABC–TV. The Reds defeated the Cubs 7–2 in Cincinnati.

AUGUST 10 — In what proves to be the final game of the season, the Cubs lose 5–3 to the Giants at Wrigley Field.

AUGUST 12 — With about 70 percent of the season completed, the major league players go on strike.

The strike, baseball's eighth interruption since 1972, had been anticipated all season. The owners wanted to put a lid on escalating payrolls by capping salaries and revising if not eliminating salary arbitration procedures. The players who were obviously not interested in these reforms had only one weapon once talks broke down: a strike.

SEPTEMBER 9 — The Cubs name Andy MacPhail as president and chief executive officer.

MacPhail had been the general manager of the Twins since 1985, and built a club that won the World Series in 1987 and 1991. His father, Lee, was president of the American League from 1973 through 1984 after serving as general manager of the Orioles and Yankees. His grandfather, Larry MacPhail, had been a general manager of the Reds and Dodgers, and owned the Yankees during the 1930s and 1940s.

SEPTEMBER 14 — The owners of the twenty–eight major league clubs vote 26–2 to cancel the remainder of the season, including the playoffs and the World Series.

OCTOBER 4 — The Cubs demote Larry Himes from general manager to a new job as director of Arizona operations and special assignment scout.

Himes took over in November 1991, and by October 1994, the only two players from the 1991 club left were Mark Grace and Shawon Dunston. Despite the shake–up under Himes, the Cubs failed to improve. He was almost universally disliked by fans, players, the press, and front office employees because of his contentious personality. Himes's term as general manager will be remembered for the trade that brought Sammy Sosa to the Cubs and the loss of Greg Maddux to the Braves.

OCTOBER 11 — The Cubs hire 38–year–old Ed Lynch as general manager.

Lynch was a pitcher with the Mets and Cubs from 1980 through 1986. Prior to becoming the general manager of the Cubs, he worked in the front offices of the Mets and Padres.

OCTOBER 17   The Cubs fire Tom Trebelhorn as manager after only one year on the job.

OCTOBER 21   The Cubs hire Jim Riggleman as manager.

Riggleman managed the Padres from 1992 through 1994 to a record of only 112–179 after serving as a minor league manager for nine years. As a player, he never advanced past Class AA. New general manager Ed Lynch worked with Riggleman in San Diego. Riggleman lasted five seasons with the Cubs, the most of any manager since the end of World War II with the exception of Leo Durocher. From 1979 through 1995, the Cubs had fifteen managers, including four who served on an interim basis.

NOVEMBER 8   Dan Plesac signs a free agent contract with the Pirates.

1995   Cubs

Season in a Sentence

The Cubs stay in the National League's first wild card race until the final weekend and post a winning record under new manager Jim Riggleman.

The Cubs finished in third place in the wild card race, four games behind.

Finish • Won • Lost • Pct • GB

Third   73   71   .507   12.0

Manager

Jim Riggleman

Stats

Stats	Cubs	NL	Rank
Batting Avg:	.265	.263	6
On–Base Pct:	.329	.334	10
Slugging Pct:	.430	.408	3
Home Runs:	158		4
Stolen Bases:	105		9
ERA:	4.13	4.18	8
Fielding Avg:	.979	.980	10
Runs Scored:	693		4
Runs Allowed:	671		8

Starting Lineup

Scott Servais, c
Mark Grace, 1b
Rey Sanchez, 2b
Todd Zeile, 3b
Shawon Dunston, ss
Luis Gonzalez, lf
Brian McRae, cf
Sammy Sosa, rf
Jose Hernandez, ss–2b–3b
Ozzie Timmons, lf
Howard Johnson, 3b
Rick Wilkins, c
Scott Bullett, lf

Pitchers

Jaime Navarro, sp
Frank Castillo, sp
Kevin Foster, sp
Jim Bullinger, sp
Steve Trachsel, sp
Randy Myers, rp
Mike Perez, rp
Turk Wendell, rp
Mike Walker, rp

Attendance

1,918,265 (fifth in NL)

Club Leaders

Batting Avg:	Grace	.326
On–Base Pct:	Grace	.395
Slugging Pct:	Grace	.516
Home Runs:	Sosa	36
RBI:	Sosa	119
Runs:	McRae	92
Stolen Bases:	Sosa	34
Wins:	Navarro	14
Strikeouts:	Foster	146
ERA:	Castillo	3.21
Saves:	Myers	38

JANUARY 13   Major league owners vote to use replacement players during the 1995 season if the strike is not settled.

The Cubs opened training camp at Mesa, Arizona, in February with replacement players and used them until the strike came to an end on April 2.

APRIL 2   The 234–day strike of major league players comes to an end.

The opening of the season, originally scheduled to begin on April 3, was pushed back to April 26 with each team playing 144 games. The replacement players were either released or sent to minor league teams.

APRIL 5   The Cubs trade Geno Morones and Derek Wallace to the Royals for Brian McRae.

APRIL 9   The Cubs sign Jaime Navarro, most recently with the Brewers, as a free agent.

APRIL 13   The Cubs sign Howard Johnson, most recently with the Rockies, as a free agent.

APRIL 26   Seven days after the bombing of a federal office building in Oklahoma City, resulting in the deaths of 168 people, the Cubs win the strike–delayed season opener 7–1 against the Reds in Cincinnati. Brian McRae had three hits in his Cubs debut with his father Hal in uniform as a coach with the Reds. Brian played for his father when the elder McRae was the manager of the Royals from 1991 through 1994. The younger McRae collected a triple, a double, and a single in five at–bats in the opener. Jim Bullinger was the starting pitcher and hurled six shutout innings.

Harry Caray kept a part–time schedule in 1995 because of his age and his health, skipping many of the Cubs road trips.

APRIL 28   In the home opener, the Cubs beat the Expos 4–3 before 32,909 at Wrigley Field. Sammy Sosa hit a home run.

Mike Morgan spent the first month of the season on the disabled list because he broke a rib slipping on a boulder around the swimming pool at his Las Vegas home while playing catch with a football.

APRIL 29   The Cubs run their record to 4–0 on the season with a 5–4 win over the Expos at Wrigley Field. It was Chicago's first 4–0 start since 1969. The contest was delayed for five minutes in the eighth inning when fans littered the field with souvenir magnetic schedules.

MAY 7   The Cubs rout the Pirates 13–5 in Pittsburgh.

MAY 17   Kevin Foster (seven innings) and Mike Perez (two innings) combine on a two–hitter, but the Cubs lose 2–1 to the Giants in San Francisco. Foster retired the first 15 batters to face him before J. R. Phillips singled. Barry Bonds iced the game with a two–run homer in the seventh.

MAY 21   Sammy Sosa's homer in the thirteenth inning gives the Cubs a 2–1 win over the Dodgers in Los Angeles. It was the 9,000th win in the history of the Chicago Cubs franchise.

MAY 22   The Cubs play at Coors Field in Denver for the first time, and lose 9–8 to the Rockies.

MAY 24   The Cubs defeat the Rockies 5–3 in Denver to run their season record to 17–8 with a three–game lead in the NL Central.

MAY 28   The Cubs outslug the Marlins 13–8 at Wrigley Field.

JUNE 1   With the fourth overall pick, the Cubs select pitcher Kerry Wood from Grand Prairie High School in Grand Prairie, Texas, in the first round of the amateur draft.

              Thus far, Wood has proven to be one of the best draft selections in Cubs history. The rest of the draft produced Steve McNichol (second round) and Justin Speier (55th round).

JUNE 5   The Cubs lose 7–5 to the Braves in Atlanta and drop out of first place in the NL Central.

              The Cubs never regained the top spot. From June 14 through the end of the season, the club hovered around the .500 mark, never more than three games over the break–even point (37–34 on July 13) or four games under (39–43 on July 24).

JUNE 10   Shawon Dunston accounts for all of the Cubs runs with a three–run homer off Juan Acevedo in the seventh inning of a 3–0 win over the Rockies at Wrigley Field.

              Dunston hit 14 homers and batted .296 for the Cubs in 1995.

JUNE 14   Mike Benjamin of the Giants collects six hits in helping his club win 4–3 in thirteen innings over the Cubs at Wrigley Field.

JUNE 15   Frank Castillo retires the first 19 batters he faces in a 3–1 win over the Giants at Wrigley Field. Mike Benjamin broke up the perfect game bid with a single in the seventh inning. It was the first of four San Francisco hits.

JUNE 16   Howard Johnson hits a two–run, walk–off homer in the ninth inning to break up a scoreless duel and lift the Cubs to a 2–0 victory over the Dodgers in Los Angeles. Steve Trachsel (seven innings), Mike Perez (1 ⅔ innings), and Bryan Hickerson (⅔ of an inning) combined for the shutout.

Playing his first full season since 1991, and his last full season with the Cubs, Shawon Dunston enjoyed a productive 1995.

On the same day, the Cubs traded Mike Morgan, Paul Torres, and Francisco Morales to the Cardinals for Mike Morgan.

JUNE 22   The Cubs lambaste the Astros 13–2 in Houston.

JUNE 28   Brian McRae hits a grand slam off Mike Dyer in the fourth inning of a 10–3 win over the Pirates at Wrigley Field.

On the same day, the Cubs traded Rick Wilkins to the Astros for Luis Gonzalez and Scott Servais. This was a great trade, but it could have been one of the best in club history if the Cubs didn't let Gonzalez leave via the free agent route at the end of the 1996 season.

JULY 3   Rey Sanchez hits a two–run homer in the eighth inning to defeat the Mets 4–2 in New York. It was his first homer since 1992, a span of 991 at–bats.

JULY 4   Brian McRae scores all three Cubs runs in a 3–0 win over the Mets in New York. McRae homered on the second pitch of the game off Bret Saberhagen, and later added a triple and a double.

JULY 9   Todd Zeile drives in the tying run with an infield single in the ninth inning, and delivers the winner with a sacrifice fly in the thirteenth to beat the Phillies 7–6 in Philadelphia.

JULY 11   Randy Myers earns a save in the All–Star Game by pitching a scoreless ninth to close out the National League's 3–2 victory at The Ballpark in Arlington in Arlington, Texas.

JULY 13   The temperature is 103 degrees for a 7:05 p.m. start in a game against the Reds at Wrigley Field. Cincinnati won 11–5.

JULY 28   Cubs infielder Todd Haney hits his second career homer in a 4–0 win over Phillies at Wrigley Field. He hit his first big league home run exactly one year to the day earlier on July 28, 1994.

Haney played three up–and–down seasons with the Cubs. He batted .162 in 37 at–bats in 1994, .411 in 73 at–bats in 1995, and .134 in 82 at–bats in 1995. He finished his major league career with a .244 average and three homers in 101 games.

JULY 29   Shawon Dunston hits a three–run, two–out, walk–off homer to beat the Phillies 8–7 at Wrigley Field. Philadelphia scored three runs in the top of the ninth to take a 7–5 lead.

Through August 4, 1995, Steve Trachsel had a lifetime record of 13–15. He was 1–12 at Wrigley Field and 12–3 on the road. From August 5, 1995, through the end of the 1999 season when he signed with the Devil Rays as a free agent, Trachsel reversed the trend, and was 31–23 at Wrigley Field and 16–29 on the road.

AUGUST 5   Scott Servais homers off Rich DeLucia in the eighth inning to beat the Cardinals

1–0 in St. Louis. Jim Bullinger pitched the first seven innings, and Randy Myers nailed down the save with a scoreless ninth.

AUGUST 13   Both dugouts and bullpens empty during a 6–3 loss to the Giants in San Francisco when Shawon Dunston charges the mound after being hit by a pitch from Sergio Valdes in the sixth inning.

AUGUST 18   The Cubs explode for a 26–7 victory over the Rockies in Denver. The Cubs tied a post–1900 club record for most runs in a game. The mark was set in the 26–23 win over the Phillies on August 25, 1922. The Cubs scored seven runs in the first inning and led the Rockies 9–1 in the third inning when play was stopped for two hours and 45 minutes by rain. When play resumed, Chicago added six runs in the fifth inning, three in the sixth, four in the seventh, and four in the eighth. Nine different players scored at least two runs to tie a major league record. Luis Gonzalez drove in six runs on a homer, double, and single.

AUGUST 20   Sammy Sosa homers for the fourth game in a row, but the Cubs lose 4–2 in ten innings to the Rockies in Denver.

In a stretch of seven games ending on August 24, Sosa hit seven home runs and drove in 18 runs. He had ten homers in 13 games from August 17 through August 30. Sosa finished the season with 36 homers, 119 RBIs and a .268 batting average.

AUGUST 31   Jose Hernandez hits a grand slam and a solo homer during a 12–3 win over the Marlins in Miami. The slam was hit off Buddy Groom in the fifth inning.

SEPTEMBER 4   Sammy Sosa's two–run homer in the first inning off Bryan Rekar is all the Cubs need to beat the Rockies 2–0 at Wrigley Field. Frank Castillo was the winning pitcher.

Mark Grace hit .326 with 16 homers and 92 RBIs in 1995.

SEPTEMBER 11   The Cubs pummel the Dodgers 12–1 at Wrigley Field.

SEPTEMBER 15   The Cubs beat the Padres 6–2 in San Diego to even their season record at 64–64 and keep alive their slim hopes for a post–season berth. The Cubs were tied for third in the wild card race, four games back of the Dodgers.

SEPTEMBER 22   Kevin Foster (eight innings) and Randy Myers (one inning) combine on a two–hitter to beat the Pirates 6–3 at Wrigley Field. The only Pittsburgh hits were singles by Midre Cummings and Jay Bell in the fourth inning.

SEPTEMBER 24   Brian McRae hits a walk–off homer in the tenth inning to beat the Pirates 3–2 at Wrigley Field.

SEPTEMBER 25   Frank Castillo comes within one strike of a no–hitter in a 7–0 win over the Cardinals at Wrigley Field. With two out in the ninth, Castillo had an 0–2 count on Bernard Gilkey. After the count went to 2–2, Gilkey hit an opposite field triple into right field. Sammy Sosa charged and dove for the ball, but it bounced several feet away. Castillo retired the next batter for a one–hitter. He struck out 13 batters.

SEPTEMBER 27   Kevin Foster strikes out 13 batters in a 5–3 win over the Cardinals at Wrigley Field.

SEPTEMBER 28   The Cubs become the first major league team since 1900 to overcome six different deficits to win a game, defeating the Astros 12–11 in eleven innings at Wrigley Field. The Astros took a 1–0 lead in the first inning. The Cubs surged ahead 5–1 before falling behind again. Houston led 6–5 in the sixth, 7–6 in the seventh, 9–7 in the eighth, and 10–9 in the tenth, but the Cubs rallied to tie the score each time. The Astros took another lead with a run in the eleventh before Chicago scored twice to win.

In the ninth inning, a 27–year–old bond trader named John Murray rushed the mound and attacked Randy Myers after the pitcher allowed a home run. Myers, who often wore combat fatigues and read weapons magazines in the clubhouse, pinned Murray to the ground. "The guy's lucky he's still alive," said Howard Johnson. "Randy's the wrong guy to mess with."

SEPTEMBER 29   The Cubs win their eight game in a row by scoring three runs in the ninth inning and one in the tenth to defeat the Astros 4–3 at Wrigley Field. The winning run was scored on a single by Luis Gonzalez.

With two days left in the season, the Cubs still had a miracle shot at the wild card berth. The Cubs needed to close out the season with two wins over the Astros while the Rockies lost two games, then the Cubs needed to defeat Colorado in a one–game playoff. However, the Cubs lost two while the Rockies won two.

OCTOBER 31   Four weeks after O. J. Simpson is found not guilty of the double murder of his ex–wife and her companion, Ryne Sandberg announces the end of his retirement. In his first season back with the Cubs in 1996, Sandberg shook off the rust and hit .244 with 25 homers. Ryne retired again at the end of the 1997 season.

DECEMBER 14   Randy Myers signs a free agent contract with the Orioles.

DECEMBER 23   Todd Zeile signs a free agent contract with the Phillies.

DECEMBER 26   The Cubs sign Dave Magadan, most recently with the Mets, as a free agent.

DECEMBER 28   The Cubs sign Doug Jones, most recently with the Orioles, as a free agent.

1996

Season in a Sentence

The Cubs are unable to develop any consistency all season, and finish with another losing season after dropping 14 of their last 16 games.

The Cubs finished in seventh place in the wild card race, 14 games behind.

Finish · Won · Lost · Pct · GB

Fourth   76   86   .469 12.0

Manager

Jim Riggleman

Stats

Stats	Cubs	NL	Rank
Batting Avg:	.251	.262	14
On–Base Pct:	.322	.333	13
Slugging Pct:	.401	.408	9
Home Runs:	175		4
Stolen Bases:	108		11 (tie)
ERA:	4.36	4.21	9
Fielding Avg:	.983	.979	1
Runs Scored:	772		5
Runs Allowed:	771		7

Starting Lineup

Scott Servais, c
Mark Grace, 1b
Ryne Sandberg, 2b
Leo Gomez, 3b
Jose Hernandez, ss–3b
Luis Gonzalez, lf
Brian McRae, cf
Sammy Sosa, rf
Rey Sanchez, ss
Dave Magadan, 3b
Scott Bullett, lf–rf

Pitchers

Jaime Navarro, sp
Steve Trachsel, sp
Frank Castillo, sp
Jim Bullinger, sp
Amaury Telemaco, sp–rp
Kevin Foster, sp
Turk Wendell, rp
Bob Patterson, rp
Terry Adams, rp
Kent Bottenfield, rp
Rodney Myers, rp

Attendance

2,219,110 (fifth in NL)

Club Leaders

Batting Avg:	Grace	.331
On–Base Pct:	Grace	.398
Slugging Pct:	Sosa	.564
Home Runs:	Sosa	40
RBI:	Sosa	100
Runs:	McRae	111
Stolen Bases:	McRae	37
Wins:	Navarro	15
Strikeouts:	Navarro	158
ERA:	Trachsel	3.03
Saves:	Wendell	16

JANUARY 8   Shawon Dunston signs a free agent contract with the Giants.

APRIL 1   Mark Grace's tenth–inning single lifts the Cubs to a 5–4 win over the Padres in the season opener before 38,734 at Wrigley Field. Ryne Sandberg, in his first game since his temporary retirement on June 13, 1994, was hitless in three at–bats. Scott Servais and Rey Sanchez each hit home runs. The game–time temperature was 38 degrees with a 17 mile–per–hour wind blowing from the northeast.

               The homer by Sanchez was the only one he hit in 1996 in 289 at–bats.

APRIL 4   The day after "Unabomber" Theodore Kaczynski is arrested in Montana, the Cubs beat snow, sleet, rain, wind, bitterly cold weather, and the Dodgers to win 9–4 on a day unfit for man or beast, much less baseball. The number of tickets sold was 12,626, but only a few thousand brave souls showed up for the game. Game–time temperature was 34 degrees with a 19–mile–per–hour northerly gale that dropped the wind chill to 12 above zero, in addition to a mix of snow and rain. The Wrigley Field aisles were salted to keep people from slipping.

APRIL 5   The Cubs pummel the Dodgers 11–1 on another freezing day at Wrigley Field.

           During the opening six–game homestand, game–time temperatures averaged 38 degrees.

APRIL 8   The Cubs win the road opener for the tenth season in a row, beating the Rockies 9–6 in Denver.

           Pat Hughes joined Ron Santo in the WGN radio broadcasting booth in 1996, replacing Thom Brennaman.

APRIL 17   Sammy Sosa hits a pair of two–run homers, the second a walk–off shot in the tenth, to beat the Reds 8–6 at Wrigley Field.

           The Cubs hit an all–time record low 19 triples in 1996.

APRIL 19   With the wind blowing out at between 17 and 25 miles per hour, the Cubs hit three consecutive homers, and six in the game, to beat the Giants 10–6 at Wrigley Field. Ryne Sandberg hit two homers, and Brian McRae, Mark Grace, Sammy Sosa, and Ozzie Timmons each added one. McRae hit a grand slam in the sixth inning off Allen Watson, which was followed by homers by Sandberg and Grace.

           After the win, the Cubs were 10–6 and in first place. The Cubs lost their next seven games, however, and were 21–31 on May 29. From May 31 through September 13, the club was 53–41 to move into contention for the pennant in a weak division.

MAY 3   Sammy Sosa breaks out of an 0–for–18 slump to hit a three–run, walk–off homer with two out in the ninth to beat the Mets 4–2 at Wrigley Field.

MAY 5   For the second time in three days, Sammy Sosa hits a walk–off homer to beat the Mets at Wrigley Field. Sosa's shot in the ninth broke a 4–4 tie and lifted the Cubs to a 5–4 victory. The shot also broke a window in a building on Waveland Avenue beyond the left field bleachers. It was Sammy's second homer of the game.

           Cubs rookie outfielder Robin Jennings was the first player born in Singapore to reach the major leagues. His father was in the foreign service. Jennings also lived in Geneva, Paris, and Indonesia as a youngster. He graduated from high school in Annandale, Virginia.

MAY 11   The Mets beat the Cubs 7–6 at Shea Stadium in a game interrupted by a long and ugly brawl. There were nine ejections, including four Cubs. In the fifth inning with New York leading 6–3, Terry Adams threw a pitch behind Mets pitcher Pete Harnisch, who then had words with Scott Servais. Harnisch threw a sucker punch at Servais, and both benches and bullpens emptied. The teams exchanged shoves, pushes, and punches for sixteen minutes before order was restored.

MAY 12   Jim Bullinger pitches a two–hitter to defeat the Mets 3–0 at Shea Stadium. The only

New York hits were singles by Jeff Kent in the fifth and eighth innings.

MAY 13   Steve Trachsel pitches a one–hitter to defeat the Astros 6–0 at Wrigley Field. After Brian Hunter opened the game with a double, Trachsel went the rest of the way without giving up a hit.

MAY 16   Sammy Sosa becomes the first Cub to hit two homers in an inning, leading the club to a 13–1 win over the Astros at Wrigley Field. Sosa hit the homers in the Cubs eight–run seventh inning off Jeff Tabaka and Jim Dougherty. Amaury Telemaco made his major league debut and pitched spectacularly, holding Houston hitless for the first 5 ⅔ innings. He allowed one hit and no runs in seven innings.

The only other Cubs with two home runs in an inning is Mark Bellhorn, who accomplished the feat in 2002. Telemaco was only 22 when he made his debut, but failed to repeat the opening performance. In three seasons as a Cub before a trade to the Diamondbacks, Telemaco was 6–11 with an ERA of 5.36.

Steve Trachsel compiled a 3.03 ERA in 1996, giving the team a reliable starter who could keep them in games.

MAY 20   The Braves clobber the Cubs 18–1 in Atlanta.

MAY 24   Ryne Sandberg's grand slam off Greg Swindell in the seventh inning gives the Cubs a 7–4 lead in Houston, but the Astros rally to win with three runs in the ninth inning and one in the tenth to win 8–7.

JUNE 1   Scott Servais hits a home run in the tenth inning to defeat the Marlins 5–4 in Miami.

JUNE 5   Sammy Sosa hits three home runs in consecutive at–bats during a 9–6 win over the Phillies at Wrigley Field. With the Cubs trailing 4–0, Sammy hit a two–run homer in the fourth inning off Terry Mulholland. Sosa later added a solo shot off Mulholland in the sixth and a two–run homer versus Russ Springer in the seventh.

JUNE 8   On a fog–shrouded Saturday night at Wrigley Field, the Cubs defeat the Expos 6–4. Some of the numbers on the scoreboard were nearly unreadable by the sixth inning.

JUNE 9   The fog continues to be a problem at Wrigley Field, obscuring much of the scoreboard and the bleachers during a 4–2 victory over the Expos.

JUNE 13   Terry Shumpert hits a three–run homer in the fourteenth inning to beat the Padres 6–3 at Wrigley Field.

Shumpert had only 31 at–bats as a member of the Cubs and hit two homers.

JUNE 15   The Cubs release Doug Jones.

JUNE 18   Two days after the Bulls defeat the Sonics for the NBA championship following a
               72–10 record in the regular season, rookie Brant Brown hits three homers in a dou-
               ble–header against the Dodgers at Wrigley Field. The home runs were the first three
               of Brown's major league career. The Cubs lost the first game 9–6 and won the
               second 7–4.

JUNE 22   Brant Brown collects five hits, including a homer in the sixteenth inning, in nine
               at–bats during a 9–6 marathon win over the Padres in San Diego.

               In his first 34 big league at–bats, Brown collected 15 hits including four homers.

JULY 2   The Cubs rout the Pirates 15–7 in Pittsburgh. In his first start with the Cubs following
               a trade with the Braves, Tyler Houston collected four hits, including two doubles. The
               Cubs had a total of 22 hits in the contest.

JULY 12   The Cardinals hit seven home runs and defeat the Cubs 13–3 at Wrigley Field.

JULY 15   The Cubs rout the Pirates 12–2 at Wrigley Field.

JULY 23   Down 5–0 after three innings, the Cubs rally to win 9–6 against the Giants in San
               Francisco. Sammy Sosa broke the 3–3 tie with a three–run homer in the seventh
               inning.

JULY 26   Tyler Houston drives in six runs with a homer, a double, and a single in a 17–4
               thrashing of the Rockies in Denver.

AUGUST 9   Two weeks after a bomb explodes in an Atlanta park filled with people attending
               the Olympics, Ryne Sandberg hits a grand slam off Rheal Cormier and a solo
               homer in the ninth to beat the Expos 11–9 in Montreal.

AUGUST 12   The Cubs rout the Mets 11–1 in New York.

AUGUST 18   Jaime Navarro ties a major league record by making three errors in an inning and
               give up six runs in six innings, but emerges as the winning pitcher in a 10–8 deci-
               sion over the Astros at Wrigley Field.

AUGUST 20   Kevin Foster (five innings), Terry Adams (three innings), and Turk Wendell (one
               inning) combine on a two–hitter to defeat the marlins 8–1 at Wrigley Field. The
               only Florida hits were a singles by Luis Castillo in the third inning and Craig
               Grebeck in the fifth.

               *Sammy Sosa broke his right hand in the game when he was hit by a pitch
               thrown by Mark Hutton. The injury ended Sosa's streak of 304 games in a row,
               and he didn't play again in 1996. He ended the season with 40 home runs, 100
               RBIs and a .273 average. Other offensive leaders for the Cubs in 1996 were
               Mark Grace, who hit .331, and Brian McRae, with 11 runs scored, 17 homers,
               and a .276 average.*

| AUGUST 25 | The Cubs play at Atlanta–Fulton County Stadium for the last time, and defeat the Braves 3–2. The Braves moved into Turner Field in 1997. |

The Cubs played eight one–run games in a row from August 23 through August 30. The Cubs won three of the eight games.

| AUGUST 31 | The Cubs clobber the Braves 12–0 at Wrigley Field. |

| SEPTEMBER 13 | The Cubs stay afloat in the NL Central race with a 4–2 win over the Phillies at Wrigley Field. The victory gave the Cubs a 74–72 record, and put them five games behind the Cardinals. The Cubs lost 14 of their last 16 games, however. |

| SEPTEMBER 15 | Benito Santiago hits three homers and drives in all six of the Phillies runs in a 6–1 win over the Cubs at Wrigley Field. |

| SEPTEMBER 20 | Tom Trebelhorn uses five pinch–hitters in a row to produce two runs in the eighth inning, but the Cubs lose 6–4 to the Pirates in Pittsburgh. The five pinch–hitters were Doug Glanville for Jim Bullinger, Ozzie Timmons for Scott Bullett, Ryne Sandberg for Robin Jennings, Leo Gomez for Brant Brown, and Brian McRae for Luis Gonzalez. |

| SEPTEMBER 24 | Willie Greene of the Reds hits three homers as the Cubs lose 6–3 at Wrigley Field. |

| SEPTEMBER 27 | Trailing 9–4, the Cubs rally with one run in the sixth inning, four in the eighth and one in the ninth to beat the Pirates 10–9 in the second game of a double–header at Wrigley Field. Jose Hernandez scored the winning run from second base on a wild pitch and a throwing error. Pittsburgh won the first game 7–4. |

| DECEMBER 2 | Four weeks after Bill Clinton wins his second term as President in an election against Bob Dole, Shawon Dunston rejoins the Cubs after signing a free agent contract. |

| DECEMBER 9 | The Cubs sign Terry Mulholland, most recently with the Mariners, as a free agent. |

| DECEMBER 10 | The Cubs sign Mel Rojas, most recently with the Expos, as a free agent. |

Rojas was expected to be the closer, but was a bust with an 0–4 record and a 4.42 ERA. He spent much of his time with the Cubs looking at the outfield fences after giving up 11 homers in 59 innings before he was traded to the Mets in August.

| DECEMBER 11 | The Cubs sign Kevin Tapani, most recently with the White Sox, as a free agent. On the same day, Jaime Navarro signed a free agent contract with the White Sox. |

Tapani was expected to be the staff's number one starter, but a lingering finger injury led to surgery during spring training in 1997 and he didn't pitch in a regular season game until July. In the long run, the Cubs came out ahead in what was essentially a trade involving Tapani and Navarro. Once healthy, Tapani was 28–12 in his first two seasons as a Cub.

| DECEMBER 19 | Luis Gonzalez signs a free agent contract with the Astros. |

Gonzalez didn't look like a huge loss. He was 29 years old, sported a .270 lifetime batting average, and had never hit more than 15 homers in a season. He was considered to be no more than a platoon outfielder who couldn't hit lefties. In a completely unexpected development with Arizona in 1999, Gonzalez suddenly became one of the most feared hitters in the game. From 1999 through 2003, Gonzalez batted .314 and averaged 34 homers and 115 RBIs a season while the Cubs struggled to find a consistent left fielder to team with Sammy Sosa. Imagine this duo playing the corner outfield positions for the Cubs. In 2001, Sosa hit 64 homers and Gonzalez clubbed 57. One can also ponder the fact that ex–Cub Rafael Palmeiro hit 47 homers for the Rangers that season.

1997   Cubs

Season in a Sentence

In one of the worst seasons in franchise history, the Cubs lose their first 14 games and finish with 94 defeats.

In the wild card race, the Cubs were tied for 10th (last) place, 24 games behind.

Finish • Won • Lost • Pct • GB

Fifth   68   94   .420   16.0

Manager

Jim Riggleman

Stats

Stats	Cubs	NL	Rank
Batting Avg:	.263	.263	5
On–Base Pct:	.323	.336	11
Slugging Pct:	.396	.410	11
Home Runs:	127		13
Stolen Bases:	116		9
ERA:	4.44	4.21	11
Fielding Avg:	.981	.981	5
Runs Scored:	687		12
Runs Allowed:	759		8

Starting Lineup

Scott Servais, c
Mark Grace, 1b
Ryne Sandberg, 2b
Kevin Orie, 3b
Shawon Dunston, ss
Doug Glanville, lf
Brian McRae, cf
Sammy Sosa, rf
Rey Sanchez, ss–2b
Tyler Houston, c
Jose Hernandez, 3b–ss
Dave Hansen, 3b

Pitchers

Steve Trachsel, sp
Jeremi Gonzalez, sp
Kevin Foster, sp
Terry Mulholland, sp
Frank Castillo, sp
Terry Adams, rp
Mel Rojas, rp
Bob Patterson, rp
Kent Bottenfield, rp
Ramon Tatis, rp
Turk Wendell, rp

Attendance

2,190,308 (sixth in NL)

Club Leaders

Batting Avg:	Grace	.319
On–Base Pct:	Grace	.409
Slugging Pct:	Sosa	.480
Home Runs:	Sosa	36
RBI:	Sosa	119
Runs:	Sosa	90
Stolen Bases:	Dunston	29
Wins:	Gonzalez	11
Strikeouts:	Trachsel	160
ERA:	Trachsel	4.51
Saves:	Adams	18

APRIL 1	In the season opener, the Cubs collect only three hits and lose 4–2 to the Marlins in Miami.

The Cubs played their spring training home games at new HoHoKam Park in Mesa, Arizona. It was modeled after Wrigley Field and held 12,500.

APRIL 4   In the first regular season game ever at Turner Field in Atlanta, the Cubs lose 5–4 to the Braves.

The Cubs changed the lettering on their gray uniforms again in 1997. "Cubs" in script across the front was replaced by "Chicago" in capital letters.

With his health declining, beloved announcer Harry Caray retired at the end of the 1997 season after sixteen years in the booth.

APRIL 8   The Cubs drop to 0–7 on the season with a 5–3 loss to the Marlins in the first game of the season at Wrigley Field before a crowd of 35,393.

APRIL 10   The Cubs set a record for the worst start in club history, dropping their eighth straight with a 1–0 loss to the Marlins at Wrigley Field. The only Chicago hit was a single by Dave Hansen with one out in the ninth inning to break–up a no–hit bid by Alex Fernandez. The previous worst start in Cubs history was 0–7 in 1962.

APRIL 11   The game against the Braves at Wrigley Field is postponed by snow.

APRIL 15   The Cubs continue their role as the laughingstock of baseball by losing their 11th straight game with a 10–7 loss to the Rockies at Wrigley Field. The loss set the post–1900 National League record for most consecutive defeats to start a season. The Braves began the 1988 season 0–10.

Ryne Sandberg was injured sitting on the bench during the loss to Colorado. He was struck in the head by a foul ball hit by Brant Brown. Sandberg was taken to the hospital, where he received stitches. He didn't play again for two weeks.

APRIL 16   The Cubs break the all–time National League record for the worst start in a season, losing 4–0 to the Rockies at Wrigley Field. With the defeat, the Cubs fell to 0–12, breaking the 0–11 mark of the 1884 Detroit Wolverines.

APRIL 19   The Cubs lose their 13th straight, dropping a 6–3 decision to the Mets in New York. The losing pitcher was Turk Wendell, who wore number 13. The loss tied the club record for most losses in a row at any point in a season. The Cubs teams in 1944, 1982, and 1985 also lost 13 in a row.

APRIL 20   The Cubs lose a club record 14th game in a row to fall to 0–14 in the first game of a double–header against the Mets at Shea Stadium, then break the streak with a win in the second tilt. The Mets took the opener 8–2. The Cubs finally posted their first 1997 victory in the nightcap winning 4–3, but it wasn't easy. The Mets scored two runs in the ninth.

> *The only team in major league history with a worse start than the 1997 Cubs was the 1988 Orioles, who began the season 0–22. Combining the nose–dive at the end of the 1996 season in which the Cubs lost 14 of their last 16 games with the 0–14 start in 1997, the Cubs had 28 losses in a streak of 30 regular season games.*

APRIL 25   The Cubs thrash the Pirates 11–1 at Wrigley Field.

> *Number 42 was retired in 1997 by every team in baseball in honor of Jackie Robinson. The last Cub to wear number 42 was coach Dan Radison, who switched to number 3.*

APRIL 26   Ryne Sandberg sets a record for most career home runs by a second baseman with his 267th, breaking the all–time record of 266 set by Joe Morgan. The homer came in the second inning off Steve Cooke in a 7–6 win over the Pirates at Wrigley Field.

> *Sandberg finished his career with 282 home runs, 277 of them as a second baseman. He also hit five homers as a third baseman.*

APRIL 28   Brooks Kieschnick drives in six runs with two homers and a single in a 14–8 win over the Expos at Wrigley Field.

> *The six runs–batted–in represented half of Kieschnick's total in 1997. He drove in just 12 runs while batting .200 in 90 at–bats during the season.*

APRIL 29   Terry Mulholland becomes the first left–handed starting pitcher to win a game for the Cubs since Greg Hibbard on September 29, 1993. Mulholland beat the Expos 5–2 at Wrigley Field.

MAY 15   The Cubs hit four triples in a game for the first time since 1968, defeating the Padres 8–2 at Wrigley Field. The triples were hit by Sammy Sosa, Brian McRae, Doug Glanville, and Jose Hernandez.

> *Mark Grace was the Cubs top hitter in 1997 with a .319 average and 13 homers.*

MAY 16   Sammy Sosa drives in six runs on a homer, two singles, and a bases–loaded triple in a 16–7 win over the Padres at Wrigley Field. The Cubs had a total of 21 hits in the contest and scored eight runs in the third inning to take a 13–1 lead.

MAY 18   The Cubs give away 10,000 specially made Beanie Babies to youngsters 13 and under prior to a 5–3 win over the Giants at Wrigley Field. The Beanie Baby was a blue bear named "Cubbie."

MAY 19   The Cubs romp to a 15–4 win over the Giants at Wrigley Field.

MAY 30   Frank Castillo wins a Mercedes–Benz for hitting a home run during batting practice. In

1995, Brian McRae told Castillo that if he ever hit a batting practice home run he would buy him the car. When Castillo homered before a 5–1 loss to the Reds, McRae paid off.

JUNE 13   On the day the Bulls win their fifth NBA championship by defeating the Jazz, the Cubs start inter–league play by opposing an American League club for the first time during the regular season. The Cubs lost 4–2 to the Brewers at Wrigley Field.

The Brewers moved to the National League in 1998.

JUNE 14   It wasn't the World Series, but the Cubs defeat an American League team in a game that counts for the first time since game six of the 1945 Fall Classic, downing the Brewers 9–5 at Wrigley Field.

JUNE 16   The Cubs play the White Sox for the first time in the regular season, and win 8–3 at Comiskey Park. Ex–Cub Jaime Navarro was the losing pitcher. With the exception of the post–season City Series, which was played between the Cubs and White Sox sporadically from 1903 through 1942, it was the first meaningful game between Chicago's two teams since the 1906 World Series.

The White Sox came back to win the final two games of the series, 5–3 on June 17, and 3–0 on June 18, both at Comiskey. The White Sox and Cubs met in just one series in 1997 and 1998. The 1998 games were played at Wrigley Field. Beginning in 1999, the Cubs and White Sox have played each other six times a year, with both clubs hosting three at their home park.

JUNE 27   The Cubs sign Sammy Sosa to a four–year deal worth $42.5 million making him the third–highest–paid player in baseball, behind only Barry Bonds and Albert Belle.

The deal was roundly criticized at the time. In 1997, Sosa was hardly the third–best player in baseball. Although he had 36 homers and 119 RBIs, Sosa hit .251 (the league average was .262) with an on–base percentage of .300 (well below the NL average of .333). He struck out 174 times while drawing only 45 walks. At the end of the 1997 season, Sosa had a career batting average of .257 and an on–base percentage of .308. He was 28 years old, and few players dramatically improve after that age. Other major league clubs were upset with the Cubs front office, because batters with superior statistics to Sammy's wanted more money, causing an upward spike in the salary structure throughout the industry. The contract proved to be a tremendous bargain, however, as Sosa exceeded even his own wildest dreams. Becoming more patient and more selective at the plate, Sosa hit 243 home runs from 1998 through 2001 while batting .310 with an on–base percentage of .395.

JUNE 30   The Cubs play the Royals for the first time in the regular season, and win 8–7 at Wrigley Field. The Cubs trailed 7–3 heading into the eighth inning, then scored five runs, the last three on a pinch–hit homer by Dave Clark.

Clark was 20–for–65 (.308) as a pinch–hitter in 1997 with three homers and 22 RBIs. His 20 pinch–hits tied a club record, set by Thad Bosley in 185.

JULY 13   Jose Hernandez and Kevin Orie both hit pinch–hit homers, but the Cubs lose 11–5 to the Cardinals at Wrigley Field.

JULY 15   The Cubs trade Frank Castillo to the Rockies for Matt Pool.

AUGUST 2   Hours after announcing that he would be retiring at the end of the season, Ryne
                   Sandberg homers in his first two at–bats, then follows with a single, a walk, and a
                   stolen base to lead the Cubs to a 5–1 win over the Dodgers at Wrigley Field.

AUGUST 3   Sammy Sosa hits a two–out, two–run homer in the twelfth inning to beat the
                   Dodgers 4–3 at Wrigley Field.

AUGUST 8   The Cubs trade Brian McRae, Turk Wendell, and Mel Rojas to the Mets for Lance
                   Johnson, Mark Clark, and Manny Alexander. On the same day, the Cubs sold Terry
                   Mulholland to the Giants.

AUGUST 13   The Cubs beat the Giants 6–5 in San Francisco in a game that featured a bench–
                   clearing melee. The battle began in the fourth inning when Jeff Kent was hit in the
                   chest by a pitch from Jeremi Gonzalez, whose pitching Kent publicly ridiculed a
                   week earlier. As Kent walked toward first base, he and Cubs catcher Tyler Houston
                   went nose–to–nose. Home plate umpire Charlie Williams tried to separate them, but
                   Kent ripped off Houston's face mask and the two wrestled to the ground. Houston
                   was given a one–game suspension.

AUGUST 16   The Cubs trade Rey Sanchez to the Yankees for Frisco Parotte.

AUGUST 29   The Cubs play the Indians in the regular season for the first time and lose 7–6 in
                   Cleveland.

AUGUST 30   The Cubs trade Shawon Dunston to the Pirates for a player to be named later.

SEPTEMBER 1   The day after Princess Diana dies following a car accident in Paris, the Cubs play
                   the Twins for the first time in the regular season, and lose 7–6 at Wrigley Field.

SEPTEMBER 16   Kevin Tapani pitches a one–hitter to beat the Reds 5–0 at Wrigley Field. The only
                   Cincinnati hit was a single in the fifth inning by Bret Boone.

SEPTEMBER 20   Ryne Sandberg is honored in ceremonies prior to a 3–2 loss to the Phillies at
                   Wrigley Field. Sandberg was given a five–day skiing vacation in Vail, Colorado, by
                   his teammates and a red Corvette from Cubs management.

SEPTEMBER 21   Ryne Sandberg plays his last game at Wrigley Field. He had a double and a single
                   in three at–bats before being lifted for a pinch–runner. The Cubs defeated the
                   Phillies 11–3.

SEPTEMBER 28   On the final day of the season, Mark McGwire hits his 56th and 57th home runs of
                   the season in a 12–4 win over the Cubs in St. Louis. It was the final game of the
                   career of Ryne Sandberg. He was hitless in two at–bats.

NOVEMBER 18   The Cubs lose Miguel Cairo, Ramon Tatis, and Brooks Kieschnick to the Devil
                   Rays in the expansion draft.

DECEMBER 9   The Cubs sign Jeff Blauser, most recently with the Braves, as a free agent.

Blauser was 32 years old and was coming off of a career year in which he hit .308 with 17 homers for the Braves. He was a colossal failure with the Cubs, hitting just .219 in 1998.

DECEMBER 12   The Cubs trade Miguel Batista to the Expos for Henry Rodriguez.

Rodriguez gave the Cubs 75 homers over three seasons with the club, 31 of them in 1998.

DECEMBER 23   The Cubs trade Doug Glanville to the Phillies for Mickey Morandini.

Morandini provided the Cubs with one good season, batting .296 with nine homers in 1998.

1998   Cubs

Season in a Sentence

In a season of highlights, the Cubs reach the post-season, Sammy Sosa hits 66 home runs, and Kerry Wood strikes out 20 batters in a game.

The Cubs won the wild card berth in a one-game playoff with the San Francisco Giants.

Finish • Won • Lost • Pct • GB

Second   90   73   .552   12.5

National League Division Series- The Cubs lost three-game-to-none to the Atlanta Braves.

Manager

Jim Riggleman

Stats

Stats	Cubs	NL	Rank
Batting Avg:	.264	.262	5
On-Base Pct:	.339	.334	7
Slugging Pct:	.433	.411	4
Home Runs:	212		3
Stolen Bases:	65		15
ERA:	4.47	4.23	11
Fielding Avg:	.984	.981	4
Runs Scored:	831		3
Runs Allowed:	792		11

Starting Lineup

Scott Servais, c
Mark Grace, 1b
Mickey Morandini, 2b
Jose Hernandez, 3b-lf-ss
Jeff Blauser, ss
Henry Rodriguez, lf
Lance Johnson, cf
Sammy Sosa, rf
Brant Brown, cf-lf
Manny Alexander, ss-2b
Tyler Houston, c
Kevin Orie, 3b

Pitchers

Kevin Tapani, sp
Steve Trachsel, sp
Kerry Wood, sp
Mark Clark, sp
Jeremi Gonzalez, sp
Rod Beck, rp
Terry Mulholland, rp
Terry Adams, rp
Marc Pisciotta, rp

Attendance

2,623,000 (sixth in NL)

Club Leaders

Batting Avg:	Grace	.309
On-Base Pct:	Grace	.401
Slugging Pct:	Sosa	.647
Home Runs:	Sosa	66
RBI:	Sosa	158
Runs:	Sosa	134
Stolen Bases:	Sosa	18
Wins:	Tapani	19
Strikeouts:	Wood	233
ERA:	Wood	3.40
Saves:	Beck	51

JANUARY 15   The Cubs sign Rod Beck, most recently with the Giants, as a free agent.

              *Beck gave the Cubs one terrific year in 1998 saving 51 games with an ERA of
              3.02 before arm problems wrecked his effectiveness.*

FEBRUARY 2   The Cubs sign Terry Mulholland, most recently with the Giants, as a free agent.

FEBRUARY 18   Harry Caray dies at the age of 83 of the after effects of a heart attack four days
              after collapsing at a nightclub in Rancho Mirage, California, while having a
              Valentine's Day dinner with his wife.

FEBRUARY 27   More than 1,000 mourners pack Holy Name Cathedral in Chicago for a funeral
              honoring Harry Caray. Among those in attendance were Jim Riggleman, Mark
              Grace, Sammy Sosa, Scott Servais, Ryne Sandberg, Chicago Mayor Richard Daley,
              Illinois Governor Jim Edgar, and former Bears coach Mike Ditka.

MARCH 31   The Cubs play in March for the first time in the regular season, and open the 1998
              campaign with an 11–6 loss to the Marlins in Miami. Kevin Tapani gave up nine
              runs in two innings. Henry Rodriguez hit a home run in his first at–bat with the
              Cubs.

              *Rodriguez was the twelfth opening day left fielder for the Cubs in a span of
              twelve years. The others were Bryan Dayett (1987), Rafael Palmeiro (1988),
              Mitch Webster (1989), Lloyd McClendon (1990), George Bell (1991), Luis
              Salazar (1992), Candy Maldonado (1993), Derrick May (1994), Scott Bullett
              (1995), Luis Gonzalez (1996), and Brant Brown (1997).*

APRIL 2   The Marlins score six runs in the first inning, but the Cubs rally to win 8–7 in
              Miami. Jeff Blauser broke the 7–7 tie with an RBI single in the ninth inning.
              Starting pitcher Jeremi Gonzalez failed to retire any of the seven batters he faced.

              *The Cubs added an alternative third jersey in 1998. It was blue with a red "C"
              outlined in white, and a blue bear, also outlined in white, superimposed over the
              "C." The numbers and names on the back were red outlined in white. It was worn
              only on the road in 1998, and both home and away beginning in 1999.*

APRIL 3   The Cubs defeat the Expos 5–2 before 39,102 in the season opener in Wrigley Field.
              Steve Trachsel was the winning pitcher and drove in three runs with a pair of singles.

              *The Cubs wore a patch with Caray's caricature on the sleeves of their jerseys to
              pay tribute to the late broadcaster. A large caricature of Caray was also placed
              over the broadcast booth at Wrigley Field facing the playing field. In another
              homage to Caray, the club carried on his tradition of leading the crowd in
              singing "Take Me Out to the Ballgame" during the seventh–inning stretch by
              bringing in guests, of widely varied musical abilities and good taste to "con-
              duct" the ballpark anthem. The first such guest, on opening day in 1998, was
              Caray's wife, Dutchie. Standing beside her was her grandson, Chip, who joined
              Steve Stone on the telecasts of Cubs games in 1998.*

APRIL 10   Henry Rodriguez collects five hits, including a three–run homer, in five at–bats in a
              13–0 win over the Expos at Olympic Stadium. It was his first game in Montreal

since his trade from the Expos to the Cubs. The crowd gave Rodriguez a standing ovation after his fifth hit.

The Cubs started the 1998 season with eight wins in the first ten games, a year after beginning the 1997 campaign 0–14.

APRIL 18   Eight runs in the first inning is all the Cubs need to beat the Dodgers 8–1 at Wrigley Field. Kerry Wood won his first major league game with five shutout innings.

MAY 6   In the most dominating pitching performance in Cubs history, Kerry Wood pitches a one–hitter and ties a major league record with 20 strikeouts to shut out the Astros 2–0. The only other pitcher with 20 strikeouts in a nine–inning game is Roger Clemens, who did it in both 1986 and 1996. Wood surpassed the National League record of 19 previously held by four pitchers, and the major league rookie record of 18. The previous Cubs high in strikeouts in a game was by Jack Pfiester who fanned 17 in a fifteen–inning game against the Cardinals on May 30, 1906. The nine–inning record was 16 by John Clarkson in 1886. It was only the fifth major league start for Wood, who was 20 years old. The only other pitcher to strike out as many batters as his age was Bob Feller, who fanned 17 as a 17–year–old with the Indians in 1936. Wood opened the game with five straight strikeouts, and entered the ninth inning with six strikeouts in a row and 18 in the game. In the ninth, Wood struck out Billy Speiers swinging on a 1–2 pitch for his seventh strikeout in succession, retired Craig Biggio on a ground out, and fanned Derek Bell swinging on a 1–2 count. The only two Houston base runners were Ricky Gutierrez on a third–inning single and Craig Biggio, who was hit by a pitch in the sixth.

Wood won the NL Rookie of the Year Award in 1998 posting a 13–6 record and a 3.40 ERA. He struck out 233 batters in 166⅔ innings. Wood broke the Cubs rookie record for strikeouts, set by Tom Hughes, who had 225 in 1901. With the exception of a start in the Division Series against the Braves, Wood didn't pitch after August 31 because of a sprained ulnar collateral ligament in his right elbow. The injury kept him out of the entire 1999 season.

MAY 8   After the Giants score in the top of the fourteenth, the Cubs come back with two in their half to win 5–4 at Wrigley Field. Mark Grace drove in both runs with a bases–loaded single.

MAY 11   The Cubs play the Diamondbacks for the first time and win 4–2 at Bank One Ball-park in Phoenix. Kerry Wood struck out 13 batters in seven innings. Combined with his 20 strikeouts on May 6, Wood set a major league record for most strike-outs in consecutive games with 33.

MAY 12   Mark Grace becomes the first player in major league history to hit a home run into a swimming pool by depositing a drive into the pool just beyond the right field wall at Bank One Ballpark in Phoenix, built to allow fans to frolic during the game. Fans in swimsuits splashed after the souvenir. Grace later drew a bases–loaded walk in the ninth inning to lift the Cubs to a 7–6 win over the Diamondbacks.

Grace hit .309 with 17 homers in 1998.

MAY 14   Henry Rodriguez hits a grand slam in the third inning off John Thomson in a 9–7 win over the Rockies in Denver.

MAY 24   Mark McGwire hits his 24th home run of the season. The Cardinals had played only 48 games to that point. The Cubs had played in 49 contests, and Sammy Sosa had only nine home runs. Sosa was on a pace to finish the 162–game schedule with only 30 homers. From May 25 through June 25, Sosa hit 25 homers in 29 games.

MAY 29   Brant Brown hits a two–run, walk–off homer in the eleventh inning to beat the Braves 5–3 in Atlanta. Kerry Wood struck out 13 batters in seven innings.

The leading winner among Cubs pitchers in 1998 was Kevin Tapani, who had a 19–9 record despite an ERA of 4.85.

JUNE 2   The Cubs select Corey Patterson from Harrison High School in Kennesaw, Georgia, in the first round of the amateur draft. Patterson was the third overall pick in the draft.

Patterson became the Cubs starting center fielder in 2002. David Kelton was drafted in the second round, Will Ohman in the eighth, and Eric Hinske in the 17th.

JUNE 5   The Cubs meet the White Sox at Wrigley Field in the regular season for the first time, and win 6–5 when Brant Brown hits a walk–off homer in the twelfth inning.

JUNE 6   Pinch–hitter Derrick White collects his first major league homer in five years, and his first hit in three years, which puts the Cubs ahead 6–5 in the sixth inning against the White Sox at Wrigley Field. The Cubs went on to win 7–6. It was the Cubs eighth win in a row.

The homer was White's only hit as a Cub in ten at–bats. The homer was also the last of White's 21 big league hits. He batted 13 more times with the Cubs and the Rockies and was 0–for–13. White finished his career with three homers. The other two were with the Twins in 1993.

JUNE 7   The Cubs win their ninth game in a row and complete the three–game sweep of the White Sox at Wrigley Field with a 13–7 win.

JUNE 8   The Cubs win their tenth game in a row with an 8–1 decision over the Twins in Minneapolis. It was the first time that the Cubs played at the Metrodome during the regular season. Sammy Sosa tied a Cubs record by hitting a home run in his fifth consecutive game. Sosa homered against the Marlins on June 3, and against the White Sox on June 5, 6, and 7.

With the victory, the Cubs had a record of 38–24 and were tied for first place with the Astros. The Cubs were within striking distance of first place until early August when Houston pulled away, but Chicago remained in the wild card hunt. From August 8 to the end of the season, the Cubs were never more than one game up or one game out in the wild card race.

JUNE 15   The day after the Bulls win a series against the Jazz for their sixth NBA championship just prior to the second of Michael Jordan's three retirements, Sammy Sosa hits three homers to power the Cubs to a 6–5 win over the Brewers at Wrigley

Field. Sosa hit solo homers off Cal Eldred in the first, third, and seventh inning.

JUNE 18   Brant Brown hits three home runs in a 12–5 win over the Phillies at Wrigley Field. Brown led off the first inning with a homer off Mark Portugal, added another home run off Portugal in the fourth, and completed the hat trick with a blast off Darrin Winston in the eighth. Brown also had a single and drove in five runs.

JUNE 20   Sammy Sosa hits two homers, one a 500–foot blast off Toby Borland, in a 9–4 win over the Phillies in Philadelphia.

JUNE 22   The Cubs play the Indians for the first time at Wrigley Field during the regular season, and lose 3–1. The winning pitcher was Dwight Gooden, who ran his life-time record against the Cubs to 28–4.

JUNE 24   The Cubs play the Tigers, their World Series opponents in 1945, for the first time during the regular season and lose 7–6 in eleven innings at Tiger Stadium.

JUNE 26   The Cubs play the Royals in Kansas City for the first time during the regular season, and lose 6–3.

JUNE 30   Sammy Sosa sets a major league record for most homers in a month with 20 in June of 1998 by going deep in a 5–4 loss to the Diamondbacks at Wrigley Field. The previous record was 18 by Rudy York of the Tigers in August 1937.

JULY 1   Kerry Wood strikes out 13 batters in a 6–4 win over the Diamondbacks at Wrigley Field.

JULY 3   The Cubs defeat the Pirates 12–9 at Wrigley Field.

JULY 5   Down 5–0, the Cubs score two in the seventh and five in the eighth to beat the Pirates 7–6 at Wrigley Field. A two–out, two–run single by Jose Hernandez broke the 5–5 tie.

JULY 6   The Cubs purchase Glenallen Hill from the Mariners.

JULY 9   The Cubs play the Brewers in Milwaukee for the first time, and lose 12–9 at County Stadium. The Cubs previously played at County Stadium against the Milwaukee Braves from 1953 through 1965.

JULY 20   Kevin Tapani hits a grand slam off Denny Neagle in the third inning of an 11–4 win over the Braves in Atlanta. It was the first grand slam by a Cubs pitcher since Burt Hooton in 1972.

JULY 27   Sammy Sosa drives in all of the Cubs runs in a 6–2 win over the Diamondbacks in Phoenix. Sosa tied the game 2–2 with a homer in the sixth, and hit a grand slam off Alan Embree in the eighth.

The grand slam was the first of Sosa's career. It was the 247th home run of his career, setting a record for most home runs at the start of a career without a grand slam. The previous record–holder was Bob Horner with 209. Sosa wasted no time hitting his second career grand slam. (See July 28, 1998.)

JULY 28   Sammy Sosa becomes the only player in Cubs history to hit a grand slam in consecutive games. It happened in the fifth inning off Bob Wolcott in a 7–5 loss to the Diamondbacks in Phoenix.

JULY 31   The Cubs trade Kevin Orie, Justin Speier, and Todd Neal to the Marlins for Felix Heredia and Eve Hoff.

AUGUST 6   Jack Brickhouse, who announced Cubs games on television from 1948 through 1981, dies at the age of 82.

Sammy Sosa took his game to a new level in 1998, becoming one of the biggest stars in baseball. His home run race with Mark McGwire attracted many new fans to the game.

To honor Brickhouse, a blue and white patch with the words "Hey Hey," Brickhouse's signature phrase, was added to the sleeves of the Cubs home and away jerseys. In 1999, letters spelling out "Hey Hey" were placed on the left and right field foul screens at Wrigley Field.

AUGUST 10   With the Cubs trailing the Giants 5–3 in the fifth inning in San Francisco, Sammy Sosa, Mark Grace, and Henry Rodriguez hit back–to–back–to–back homers off Russ Ortiz. Sosa clubbed another homer traveling 480 feet into the center field bleachers in the eighth, and the Cubs won 8–5.

AUGUST 19   At Wrigley Field, the Cubs and Cardinals meet with Sammy Sosa and Mark McGwire tied for the major league lead in homers with 47 apiece. Sammy Sosa hit his 48th home run of the year in the fifth inning, but McGwire delivered the counter punch with his 48th of the year in the eighth inning to tie the game and his 49th in the tenth to beat the Cubs 8–6.

AUGUST 20   With the Cubs trailing the Giants 3–2 at Wrigley Field in the fifth, Glenallen Hill hits a pinch–hit grand slam off Julian Tavarez. The Cubs went on to win the game 7–3. In New York, Mark McGwire hit his 50th and 51st home run of the year during a double–header against the Mets.

On the same day, the Cubs sign Gary Gaetti, most recently with the Cardinals, as a free agent. Gaetti was signed the day after his 40th birthday, and was immediately given the starting third base job. He delivered several key hits during the stretch drive in 1998 with a .320 batting average and eight homers in 128 at–bats.

AUGUST 23   Sammy Sosa hits his 50th and 51st home runs of the season, both off Jose Lima, although the Cubs lose 13–3 to the Astros at Wrigley Field.

AUGUST 25   The Cubs send Scott Downs and cash to the Twins for Mike Morgan.

AUGUST 26   Kerry Wood strikes out 16 batters in eight innings to beat the Reds 9–2 in Cincinnati.

AUGUST 27   After trailing 9–3, the Cubs rally to beat the Rockies 11–10 in ten innings in Denver. The Cubs scored five runs in the seventh and two in the eighth to take a 10–9 lead, and after Colorado tied it up with a run in their half of the eighth, the Cubs came out on top with a tally in the tenth.

AUGUST 31   Sammy Sosa hits his 55th home run of the season in a 5–4 win over the Reds at Wrigley Field. Both Sosa and Mark McGwire finished the month of August with 55 homers, one short of Hack Wilson's National League record 56, set in 1930.

SEPTEMBER 1   Mark McGwire ties and breaks Hack Wilson's National League record for most home runs in a season with his 56th and 57th in a 7–1 Cardinals win over the Marlins in Miami.

SEPTEMBER 2   Sammy Sosa hits his 56th home run of 1998, tying Hack Wilson's Chicago Cubs record for homers in a season, during a 4–2 win over the Reds in an afternoon game at Wrigley Field. The homer was hit off Jason Bere. In a night contest, Mark McGwire hit his 58th and 59th homers of the season in a 14–4 Cardinals win over the Marlins in Miami.

SEPTEMBER 4   Sammy Sosa breaks Hack Wilson's club record with his 57th home run of 1998 during a 5–2 win over the Pirates in Pittsburgh. The homer was hit off Jason Schmidt.

SEPTEMBER 5   Mark McGwire collects number home run 60 in a 7–0 win over the Reds in St. Louis, and Sammy Sosa hits his 58th during an 8–4 win over the Pirates in Pittsburgh. McGwire homered off Dennys Reyes, and Sosa against Sean Lawrence. On the same day, the Cubs signed Orlando Merced, most recently with the Red Sox, as a free agent.

              The Cubs and Cardinals were scheduled to meet in a two-game series in St. Louis on September 7 and 8. The entire nation anticipated the head-to-head match-up between McGwire and Sosa, and their efforts to tie and break Roger Maris's home run record. Most of the attention focused on McGwire, who was one homer away from tying Maris.

SEPTEMBER 7   In the pre-game press conference, Mark McGwire and Sammy Sosa sip bottled water and swap one-liners, seeming to enjoy every minute of the media attention surrounding their race for the home run record. During the contest, McGwire hit his 61st home run of 1998 to tie the all-time record for most home run in a season set by Roger Maris in 1961 during a 3–2 Cardinals win over the Cubs in St. Louis. The home run was struck in the first inning off Mike Morgan. As he crossed the plate, McGwire hugged his 10-year-old son Matthew, who arrived thirty minutes before game time. Also in attendance were McGwire's parents. His father, John, was celebrating his 61st birthday on the day Mark hit his 61st homer. The six children of the late Roger Maris were also in the stands. Their mother was hospitalized with a "heart flutter." After hitting the homer, McGwire saluted in their direction.

The Routes to 66 and 70

Through 1997, only two hitters topped the 60–home run figure in the major leagues. Babe Ruth hit 60 homers in 1927, and Roger Maris surpassed him with 61 in 1961. Maris stood virtually unopposed as the single–season home run king for more than 30 years. Until 1996, his closest challengers were Willie Mays with 52 in 1965, George Foster with another 52–home run season in 1977, and Cecil Fielder, who hit 51 in 1990.

Beginning in the mid–1990s, an offensive explosion gripped baseball that included an increase in home runs. Ken Griffey Jr. struck 49 for the Mariners in 1996 and hit another 56 in 1997. Mark McGwire, who hit 52 homers in 1996 for the Athletics, clouted 58 more in 1997 in a season split between the Athletics and Cardinals.

Both were besieged with questions during spring training in 1998 about the possibility of breaking Maris's home run record. No one was mentioning Maris and Sammy Sosa in the same sentence. After all, Sammy's career high was 40 in 1996. He had 36 in 1997.

McGwire disappointed no one. On May 24, he had 24 homers in 48 games, a pace that would give him 81 homers on the season. On the same day, Sosa had nine homers after 49 games, a pace that would give 30 on the season.

Sosa then embarked on a home–run streak unmatched in baseball history. From May 25 through June 25, he struck 25 homers in 29 games. In the month of June, he hit 20 homers, breaking the old mark for homers in a month set by Rudy York of the Tigers, who hit 18 in August 1937. Suddenly, Sammy became SAMMY!

Tremendous adulation was heaped upon both players. Fans in every ballpark greeted every McGwire plate appearance with a sustained standing ovation, and Sosa won people's hearts with his infectious enthusiasm and public insistence that McGwire was the man of the moment. McGwire, for his part, contended that Sosa deserved to win the league's MVP. As both players approached, and eventually passed,

Maris's mark, baseball enjoyed much greater attention than it had in the past, and extended all across the country, not just in St. Louis and Chicago. The home run chase also helped to win back many fans still jaded by the strike that wiped out part of the 1994 and 1995 seasons. In addition, the Sosa–McGwire competition attracted casual fans and those who previously had little interest in the game.

McGwire and Sosa finished August with 55 homers, one short of Hack Wilson's NL record, set with the Cubs in 1930. McGwire hit two homers on September 1 to break Wilson's record, and his 60th on September 5, tying Babe Ruth's 1927 standard in the Cardinals 142nd game.

The Cubs and the Cardinals met in a two–game series in St. Louis on September 7 and 8. Heading into the series, McGwire had 60 homers and Sosa 58. The obvious affection that the two had for each other was evident in press conferences as they traded one–liners. McGwire rose to the occasion by tying Maris with his 61st homer on September 7 off Mike Morgan, and his 62nd a day later facing Steve Trachsel.

Sosa tied McGwire by hitting his 62nd on September 13. McGwire struck number 62 on the 15th, and Sammy tied him again a day later. McGwire hit number 64 on the 18th and 65 on the 20th. Sosa matched him again, hitting two homers on the 23rd to reach 65, then passed McGwire with his 66th in the Astrodome off Jose Lima on September 25. It was the first time all season that Sosa had more homers than McGwire. Just 45 minutes later in Montreal, the lead evaporated when McGwire hit his 66th. It was the 21st time that the two homered on the same day. In the final two games of the season, played on September 26 and 27, McGwire hit four homers to finish the season with 70. Sosa remained stuck on 66. Ken Griffey, Jr. had a 56 home run season that would have created headlines in any year except 1998.

SEPTEMBER 8   Mark McGwire passes Roger Maris with his 62nd home run of 1998 with a blast
                in the fourth inning off Steve Trachsel of the Cubs during a 6–3 Cardinals win in
                St. Louis. Rounding the bases, McGwire shook hands with the Cubs infielders and
                catcher Scott Servais. Once again, McGwire paused to lift his son in the air and was
                hugged by his friendly rival, Sammy Sosa. McGwire also went to the front row of
                the stands to embrace the Maris family. Sosa went homerless to remain at 58.

SEPTEMBER 11   Sammy Sosa hits his 59th home run of the season, although the Cubs lose 13–11 to
                the Brewers at Wrigley Field. The pitcher was Bill Pulsipher, and the drive landed
                over the right field bleachers onto Sheffield Avenue.

SEPTEMBER 12   Sammy Sosa hits his 60th homer in a thrilling 15–12 win over the Brewers at
                Wrigley Field. The homer was hit in the seventh inning off Valerio De Los Santos
                and ended up on the steps of a house across Waveland Avenue. The Brewers led
                10–2 in the fifth inning and 12–5 in the seventh, but the Cubs rebounded to score
                four runs in the seventh, one in the eighth, and five in the ninth for the extraordi-
                nary win. The game ended on a three–run pinch–homer by Orlando Merced, who
                was purchased from the Red Sox only seven days earlier. Tyler Houston also hit a
                pinch–hit homer during the comeback.

                *Merced had only ten at–bats as a member of the Cubs. This was his only home
                run.*

SEPTEMBER 13   Sammy Sosa hits his 61st and 62nd home runs of the 1998 season during an 11–10,
                ten–inning win over the Brewers at Wrigley Field. The two home runs were hit off
                Brownswell Patrick and Eric Plunk and tied Mark McGwire for the league lead.
                The Cubs tied the score 10–10 with two runs in ninth, one of them on a Sosa home
                run, and won the contest on a walk–off homer by Mark Grace with Sosa on deck.
                After Sosa's second home run, the game was delayed for six minutes and twenty–
                five seconds as the crowd launched into a standing ovation. Sosa took three curtain
                calls. It was the third game in a row in which the Cubs scored at least ten runs.

SEPTEMBER 15   Mark McGwire hits number 63 in an 8–6 Cardinals loss to the Pirates in St. Louis.
                The homer was hit off Jason Christensen in a rare pinch–hitting role.

SEPTEMBER 16   Sammy Sosa's grand slam off Brian Boehringer in the eighth inning breaks a 2–2 tie
                in a 6–3 win over the Padres in San Diego. Sosa drove in all six Cubs runs. The
                homer was Sosa's 63rd of the season, tying him once again with Mark McGwire for
                the league lead.

SEPTEMBER 20   Mark McGwire's 1998 home run total reaches 65 during a 11–6 Cardinals win over
                the Brewers in Milwaukee. McGwire lost another potential home run when a fan
                interfered with a drive into the center field bleachers. In a controversial decision,
                the umpires ruled that the fan reached over the wall, and McGwire was credited with a
                ground–rule double. In Chicago, Sammy Sosa was honored in pre–game ceremonies
                before a crowd of 40,117. The Cubs lost 7–3 to the Reds as Sosa was held without
                a homer.

SEPTEMBER 23   Sammy Sosa breaks out of an 0–for–21 slump by hitting his 64th and 65th homers
                of 1998, tying Mark McGwire again for the league lead, but the Cubs suffer a dev-
                astating 8–7 loss to the Brewers in Milwaukee. The Cubs led 7–0, but the Brewers

battled back. The Cubs held a 7–5 advantage heading into the bottom of the ninth with Rod Beck on the mound. Beck loaded the bases. With two out, Geoff Jenkins lifted a fly ball to Brant Brown, who was put into the contest in the eighth for defensive purposes. Brown seemed to lose the ball in the sun and it dropped out of his glove as all three runners scored to give Milwaukee the win.

At the conclusion of the day, the Cubs were tied for first place in the wild card race with the Mets. The Giants were 1½ games behind. The Cubs and Mets had three games left to play, and the Giants four.

SEPTEMBER 25   Sammy Sosa hits his 66th home run of the season, and forty–five minutes later, Mark McGwire answers with his 66th. The Cubs lost 6–2 to the Astros in Houston. At the conclusion of play, the Cubs, Mets, and Giants were tied for first place in the wild card race, each with 88–72 records.

Brant Brown's troubles didn't end after dropping a fly ball that cost the Cubs a win on September 23. In the September 25 contest at the Astrodome, Brown was attacked in left field by a pigeon, which he swatted with his cap before it disappeared.

SEPTEMBER 26   The Cubs defeat the Astros 3–2 in Houston to maintain a tie with the Giants in the wild card race. The Giants defeated the Rockies 8–4 in Denver. The Mets were one game behind after losing 4–0 to the Braves in Atlanta. In Montreal, Mark McGwire homered twice off Dustin Hermanson and Kirk Bullinger to lift his season total to 68 during a 7–6 Cardinals loss to the Expos in St. Louis.

SEPTEMBER 27   The Cubs blow a 3–1 lead and lose 4–3 in eleven innings to the Astros in Houston, but gain a reprieve when the Giants blow a 7–0 lead and lose 9–8 to the Rockies in Denver. The Mets also lost 7–2 to the Braves in Atlanta. The Mets lost their last five games to blow a chance at the post–season. The Cubs and Giants tied for first in the wild card race, forcing a one–game playoff to be played on September 28 at Wrigley Field for a berth in the Division Series against the Braves. On the same day, Mark McGwire homered twice off Mike Thurman and Carl Pavano in his final game of the season, a 6–3 Cardinals win over the Expos in St. Louis, to give him 70 homers on the season. The Cubs–Giants playoff was considered as a regular season game, so Sammy Sosa had one more chance to add to his season home run total of 66.

SEPTEMBER 28   The Cubs defeat the Giants 5–3 in the wild card playoff game before 39,556 in a night game at Wrigley Field. Gary Gaetti put the Cubs ahead 2–0 with a two–run homer in the fifth. Pinch–hitter Matt Mieske drove in two runs with a single with the bases loaded in the sixth. The Cubs added another run in the eighth and headed into the ninth with a 5–0 lead before the Giants made things interesting with a three–run rally. The game ended when Joe Carter popped up with Jeff Kent on first base and Rod Beck pitching. Starting pitcher Steve Trachsel went 6⅓ and allowed only one hit, but he walked six batters and left after throwing 121 pitches. Trachsel took a no–hitter into the seventh before Brent Mayne doubled with one out.

Sammy Sosa finished the season with 66 homers, a .308 batting average, and 198 hits. He led the league in runs–batted–in with 158 and runs scored with 134. Sosa beat out Mark McGwire for the National League Most Valuable Player Award.

The Cubs moved onto the best–of–five Division Series against the Braves. Managed by Bobby Cox, the Braves had a record of 106–56 in 1998, the best record in the National League. During the regular season, the Cubs beat the Braves six times in nine meetings.

SEPTEMBER 30   In the first game of the Division Series, the Cubs lose 7–1 to the Braves in Atlanta. Michael Tucker got the scoring underway with a two–run homer off Mark Clark in the second inning. In the seventh, Ryan Klesko hit a grand slam off Matt Karchner. The only Cubs run came on a home run by Tyler Houston off John Smoltz in the eighth inning.

OCTOBER 1   The Braves defeat the Cubs in game two of the Division Series 2–1 in ten innings in Atlanta. Behind the pitching of Kevin Tapani and a sixth–inning run, the Cubs went into the ninth with a 1–0 lead that evaporated when Javy Lopez tied the score by drilling a Tapani pitch for a homer. The Cubs had runners on first and third with one out in the tenth, but failed to score. In the bottom of the inning, with Terry Mulholland pitching, the Cubs botched a sacrifice bunt by Tony Graffanino. Mark Grace fielded the ball, but was late making the throw to Mulholland, covering the bag, and the pitcher missed the base for an error. Chipper Jones followed with a game–winning single down the left field line.

OCTOBER 3   The Braves complete a sweep of the Cubs in the Division Series with a 6–2 win before 39,597 at Wrigley Field. Kerry Wood started for the Cubs in his first appearance since August 31 and allowed just one run in five innings. He left the game with the Cubs trailing 1–0. The Braves scored five runs in the eighth to take a 6–0 lead before the Cubs scored two meaningless runs. Greg Maddux went seven innings for Atlanta and was the winning pitcher.

Sammy Sosa failed to homer during the series. He had a single and a double in 11 at–bats for an average of .182.

DECEMBER 8   Mark Clark signs a free agent contract with the Rangers.

DECEMBER 9   The Cubs sign Benito Santiago, most recently with the Blue Jays, as a free agent.

DECEMBER 14   The Cubs trade Brant Brown to the Pirates for Jon Lieber.

If the Cubs didn't trade Brown, Cubs fans in the bleachers would have ridden him unmercifully for dropping the ball that led to the defeat on September 23, 1998. It turned out to be a good trade, as Lieber gave the Cubs four good seasons, including a 20–6 mark in 2001, before running into arm miseries.

1999   Cubs

Season in a Sentence

After starting the season 32–23, the Cubs suffer a monumental collapse losing 63 of their next 87 games.

In the wild card race, the Cubs finished in 12th place, 29.5 game behind.

Finish • Won • Lost • Pct • GB

Fifth 67   95   .414   30.0

Manager

Jim Riggleman

Stats

Stats	Cubs	NL	Rank
Batting Avg:	.257	.269	15
On–Base Pct:	.332	.345	14
Slugging Pct:	.420	.430	13
Home Runs:	189		6
Stolen Bases:	60		16
ERA:	5.27	4.57	15
Fielding Avg:	.977	.980	14
Runs Scored:	747		13
Runs Allowed:	920		15

Starting Lineup

Benito Santiago, c
Mark Grace, 1b
Mickey Morandini, 2b
Gary Gaetti, 3b
Jose Hernandez, ss
Henry Rodriguez, lf
Lance Johnson, cf
Sammy Sosa, rf
Glenallen Hill, lf–rf
Tyler Houston, 3b
Jeff Blauser, 2b–ss–3b
Manny Alexander, ss–3b–2b
Jeff Reed, c
Jose Nieves, ss
Curtis Goodwin, cf–lf

Pitchers

Jon Lieber, sp
Steve Trachsel, sp
Kevin Tapani, sp
Terry Mulholland, sp–rp
Kyle Farnsworth, sp
Terry Adams, rp
Rick Aguilera, rp
Felix Heredia, rp
Scott Sanders, rp
Rodney Myers, rp
Dan Serafini, rp

Attendance

2,813,854 (sixth in NL)

Club Leaders

Batting Avg:	Grace	.309
On–Base Pct:	Grace	.390
Slugging Pct:	Sosa	.635
Home Runs:	Sosa	63
RBI:	Sosa	141
Runs:	Sosa	114
Stolen Bases:	Johnson	13
Wins:	Lieber	10
Strikeouts:	Lieber	186
ERA:	Lieber	4.07
Saves:	Adams	13

JANUARY 18   Scott Servais signs a free agent contract with the Giants.

MARCH 16   A month after Bill Clinton is acquitted following his impeachment trial in the House of Representatives, the Cubs announce that Kerry Wood will miss the entire 1999 season due to elbow surgery.

APRIL 6   The Cubs lose the season opener 4–2 in Houston. Mark Grace was 3–for–3, including a homer. Steve Trachsel took the loss.

APRIL 11   Glenallen Hill collects five hits, including a homer and a double, in five at–bats, but the Cubs lose 9–6 to the Pirates in Pittsburgh.

                Hill hit four pinch–hit homers in 1999, a club record for a season. Hill also holds the career club record for pinch homers with nine.

APRIL 12 The Cubs play the first game of the season at Wrigley Field before 39,092, but lose 7–2 to the Reds.

APRIL 19 Jose Hernandez homers in the tenth inning to beat the Brewers 6–5 in Milwaukee.

APRIL 21 The day after fifteen people die in a shooting at Columbine High School in Littleton, Colorado, Jeff Bagwell hits three homers to lead the Astros to a 10–3 win over the Cubs at Wrigley Field.

APRIL 24 After scheduled starter Jon Lieber is scratched after being hit in the eye by a thrown ball during batting practice, Terry Mulholland answers the call and pitches 6⅓ innings of shutout ball to beat the Mets 2–0 at Wrigley Field with the help of four relievers.

Lieber spent two weeks on the disabled list recovering from the injury.

APRIL 25 On the day in which the Cubs give away "Sammy the Bear" Beanie Babies, Sammy Sosa hits a three–run double to help the Cubs to an 8–4 win over the Mets in New York.

MAY 3 The "friendly confines" of Wrigley Field are less than friendly as seventy–five fans are ejected for rowdy behavior during a 6–1 loss to the Rockies. Play had to be stopped to clear the field of debris, including several empty liquor bottles.

MAY 4 The Cubs hit five homers to take an 8–2 lead, but need two runs in the ninth to beat the Rockies 13–12 at Wrigley Field. The winning run was scored on a single by Mickey Morandini. Henry Rodriguez, Sammy Sosa, Jose Hernandez, Gary Gaetti, and Mark Grace all homered. The homer by Grace came with the bases loaded off Darryl Kile in the third inning. It was Grace's first career grand slam and was hit in his 6,136th career at–bat.

MAY 5 The Rockies score in all nine innings and beat the Cubs 13–6 at Wrigley Field. Combined with runs in the sixth through the ninth innings the day before, Colorado scored in thirteen consecutive innings off Chicago pitching.

Only two teams since 1923 have scored in all nine turns at bat in one game. The Cubs were the victims both times. The other was against the Cardinals on September 13, 1964.

MAY 18 Mark Grace hits a three–run homer in the eleventh inning to beat the Marlins 4–1 in Miami.

MAY 19 Henry Rodriguez hits a two–run homer in the ninth inning to beat the Marlins 8–7 in Miami. The Cubs led 5–0 in the second inning before falling behind 7–6.

MAY 21 Gary Gaetti hits a grand slam off Bruce Chen in the first inning of an 8–4 win over the Braves in Atlanta. The slam gave the Cubs a 4–0 lead, but Atlanta came back to tie the contest before the Cubs scored four runs in the ninth on a pair of two–run homers by Henry Rodriguez and Jeff Blauser.

On the same day, the Cubs traded Kyle Lohse and Jason Ryan to the Twins for Rick Aguilera and Scott Downs.

MAY 26 — Sammy Sosa hits a two–run, walk–off homer in the ninth inning, defeating the Marlins 6–4 at Wrigley Field. Earlier, Sosa hit a two–run single in the seventh to pull the Cubs within a run at 4–3.

> *From May 25, 1998, through June 1, 1999, the Cubs played in 162 games. During that stretch, Sammy Sosa hit 74 home runs.*

MAY 28 — Jim Riggleman employs a four–man outfield, with shortstop Jose Hernandez in right center field, when Mark McGwire comes to bat in a 6–3 win over the Cardinals at Wrigley Field.

JUNE 2 — The Cubs score four runs in the ninth inning, the last three on Sammy Sosa's walk–off homer off Trevor Hoffman, to beat the Padres 9–8 at Wrigley Field. San Diego scored three runs in the top of the ninth to take an 8–5 lead after the Cubs plated four in the eighth to tie the contest 5–5.

> *On the same day, the Cubs selected pitcher Ben Christiansen of Wichita State University in the first round of the amateur draft. There were questions about Christiansen's character because he beaned, and severely injured, an opponent who was standing in the on deck circle during warm–ups pitches. Christiansen was suspended for the remainder of his college career. To date, he has never progressed past Class AA ball.*

Mark Grace exceeds .300 for the fifth year in a row in 1999. A model of consistency throughout his thirteen years as a Cub, Grace remained a fan favorite even after leaving the team in 2001.

© finalshot.com

JUNE 4	Gary Gaetti hits a two–run homer in the ninth inning to beat the Indians 5–4 in Cleveland.

JUNE 8 — Tyler Houston hits a three–run homer with two out in the ninth to beat the Diamondbacks 5–3 in Phoenix.

After the win, the Cubs were 32–23 and only one game behind the Astros in the NL Central, and had the second best ERA in the National League. In an unbelievable free fall, the Cubs had a record of 23–64 from June 9 through September 12, which included a stretch of 40 losses in 50 games. In the 87 games, they gave up 561 runs, an average of 6.4 per game.

JUNE 18 — Sammy Sosa, Henry Rodriguez, and Mark Grace hit back–to–back–to–back homers in the eighth inning, which produces five runs against the Giants in San Francisco. Unfortunately, the Cubs were trailing 8–0 at the time, and finished with 8–5 loss.

JUNE 20 — The Cubs play at 3Com Park (formerly Candlestick Park) in San Francisco for the last time, and lose 7–6 to the Giants.

JUNE 22 — Trailing 9–1 after three innings, the Cubs rally to beat the Rockies 13–12 in Denver. The score was 12–7 in favor of Colorado when the Cubs scored three runs in the seventh inning and three in the eighth. Henry Rodriguez drove in the go–ahead run with a single. The Cubs hit five home runs. They were struck by Rodriguez, Jose Hernandez, Jeff Blauser, Sammy Sosa, and Mark Grace.

Rodriguez hit 26 homers and batted .304.

JUNE 24 — The Cubs survive a five–run Colorado rally in the ninth inning to win 12–10 in Denver.

JUNE 26 — Sammy Sosa hits his 300th career homer during a 6–2 loss to the Phillies at Wrigley Field. The pitcher was Robert Person.

JUNE 27 — The Cubs outslug the Phillies 13–7 at Wrigley Field.

JUNE 30 — With President Bill Clinton watching from a sky box behind home plate, the Cubs beat the Brewers 5–4 at Wrigley Field. Sammy Sosa broke a 4–4 tie with a homer in the seventh inning. It was the fourth game in a row in which he hit a homer.

JULY 1 — The Brewers power past the Cubs 19–12 at Wrigley Field.

JULY 2 — The Cubs lose 14–1 to the Phillies in Philadelphia.

JULY 3 — Cubs pitchers continue to be batting practice fodder in a 21–8 defeat against the Phillies in Philadelphia.

From June 29 through July 3, the Cubs gave up 75 runs in five consecutive games.

JULY 8 — The Cubs sign Jeff Reed, most recently with the Rockies, as a free agent.

JULY 16   In a game that features five lead changes, the Cubs score three runs in the ninth inning to beat the Twins 11–10 at Wrigley Field. Henry Rodriguez hit a single with the bases loaded over a drawn–in outfield to score the winning run.

JULY 31   A seven–run first inning propels the Cubs to a 17–10 win over the Mets at Wrigley Field. Gary Gaetti hit a grand slam in the inning off Octavio Dotel. Sammy Sosa hit two homers. One landed on Sheffield Avenue over the right field bleachers, and the other on Waveland Avenue after clearing the left field bleachers.

On the same day, the Cubs trade Terry Mulholland and Jose Hernandez to the Braves for Micah Bowie, Ruben Quevedo, and Joey Nation.

AUGUST 2   Mark Grace's collects career hit number 2,000 during a 5–1 loss to the Expos at Wrigley Field.

Cubs pitchers set club records for most runs allowed (920) and highest ERA (5.27) in 1999.

AUGUST 6   In his first game with the Cubs, Andrew Lorraine pitches a complete game shutout to beat the Astros 6–0 in the second game of a double–header at Wrigley Field. He was the first Cubs left–hander to pitch a shutout since Jamic Moyer in 1988. Houston won the first game 6–1.

This was Lorraine's only career shutout. In 19 games as a Cub, he had a 3–7 record and a 5.86 ERA.

AUGUST 22 Sammy Sosa hits his 50th and 51st homer of the year in an 8–6 win over the Rockies at Wrigley Field.

AUGUST 26 Trailing 7–2 after three innings and 10–6 at the end of the sixth, the Cubs rally to beat the Giants 11–10 at Wrigley Field. Mickey Morandini's walk–off double ended the game.

AUGUST 29 Kyle Farnsworth pitches a two–hitter to beat the Dodgers 6–0 at Dodger Stadium. Farnsworth had trouble only with hitters that had last names of twelve letters or longer. The Los Angeles hits were singles by Todd Hollandsworth in the fourth inning and Mark Grudzielanek in the ninth.

SEPTEMBER 1 Sammy Sosa's homer in the fourth inning off Sterling Hitchcock gives the Cubs a 1–0 win over the Padres in San Diego. Steve Trachsel (seven innings) and Terry Adams (two innings) combined on the shutout.

On the same day, the Cubs trade Rod Beck to the Red Sox for Mark Guthrie and Cole Liniak.

SEPTEMBER 12 The Cubs play at the Astrodome in Houston for the last time, and lose 7–1 to the Astros.

SEPTEMBER 18 Sammy Sosa becomes the first player in major league history to hit 60 homers two seasons in a row, but he couldn't keep the Cubs from losing 7–4 in fourteen innings to the Brewers at Wrigley Field. Sammy hit number 60 off Jason Bere.

When Sammy hit his 60th homer of 1999, Mark McGwire had 56 on the season.

OCTOBER 3   On the final day of the season, Mark McGwire hits his 65th homer of the season and Sammy Sosa collects his 63rd in a 9–5 Cardinals win over the Cubs in St. Louis, in a contest called by rain after 4 ½ innings. McGwire hit six homers in his final seven games in 1999 to win the McGwire–Sosa home run derby for the second year in a row.

OCTOBER 4   The Cubs fire Jim Riggleman as manager after five seasons.

Riggleman lasted five seasons as manager of the Cubs, and had a record of 374–419.

OCTOBER 7   A deal is finalized to allow the Cubs and Mets to open the 2000 regular season in Tokyo, Japan.

NOVEMBER 1   The Cubs hire Don Baylor as manager. He was the first African–American manager in Cubs history.

Baylor was the manager of the Colorado Rockies from 1993 through 1998. In 1999, he was a coach with the Braves. Baylor had a stellar playing career as an outfielder and a designated hitter from 1970 through 1988. He is the only person to play on three different teams in the World Series in three consecutive seasons. Baylor was on the Red Sox in 1986, the Twins in 1987 and the Athletics in 1988. In addition, he appeared in the American League Championship Series with the Orioles in 1973 and 1974 and the Angels in 1979 and 1982 to become the first of two individuals to play on five different teams in the post–season. (Reggie Sanders became the second in 2004.) Baylor was the AL MVP in 1979.

DECEMBER 12   The Cubs trade Terry Adams, Chad Ricketts, and Brian Stephenson to the Dodgers for Eric Young and Ismael Valdes.

DECEMBER 15   The Cubs sign Joe Girardi, most recently with the Yankees, as a free agent.

DECEMBER 20   The Cubs sign Ricky Gutierrez, most recently with the Astros, as a free agent.

THE STATE OF THE CUBS

Through the first five years of the twenty-first century, the Cubs have a record of 397–413, a winning percentage of .490. The club has seldom been around the .500 mark at the end of the season, however, with records of 65–97, 88–74, 67–95, 88–74 and 89–73. The Cubs won the Central Division title in 2003, were just five outs from reaching the World Series before falling apart in the NLCS against the Marlins. NL champions in the 2000s have been the Mets (2000), Diamondbacks (2001), Giants (2002), Marlins (2003), and Cardinals (2004). NL Central pennant winners are the Astros (2000 and 2001) and Cardinals (2002 and 2004).

THE BEST TEAM

The 2003 Cubs compiled a record of 88–74, won the Central Division, and missed reaching the World Series.

THE WORST TEAM

The 2000 Cubs were 65–97 in Don Baylor's first season as manager.

THE BEST MOMENT

The Cubs move to within one game of the World Series with an 8–3 Game Four win over the Marlins in Miami. All the club had to do to play in the first Fall Classic since 1945 was to win one game out of three.

THE WORST MOMENT

With the aid of an obtrusive fan, the Cubs blow a three–run lead in the eighth inning of the sixth game of the 2003 NLCS.

THE ALL–DECADE TEAM

After only five seasons and a fluid roster, it is much too early to create an All–Decade team for the 2000s, but Sammy Sosa and Kerry Wood have certainly earned positions thus far.

THE DECADE LEADERS

Batting Avg:	Sammy Sosa	.295
On–Base Pct:	Sammy Sosa	.399
Slugging Pct:	Sammy Sosa	.612
Home Runs:	Sammy Sosa	238
RBI:	Sammy Sosa	589
Runs:	Sammy Sosa	542
Stolen Bases:	Eric Young	85
Wins:	Kerry Wood	54
Strikeouts:	Kerry Wood	976
ERA:	Carlos Zambrano	3.25
Saves:	Joe Borowski	44

THE HOME FIELD

The Cubs drew over 3,000,000 fans into Wrigley Field for the first time in 2004. There were safety concerns, however, as chunks of concrete fell from the upper deck during the summer of 2004.

THE GAME YOU WISH YOU HAD SEEN

The Cubs clinched the Central Division title with a 4–2 and 7–2 sweep of the Pirates on September 27, 2003. The players celebrated on the field, and thousands of fans were still in the ballpark an hour after the games ended.

THE WAY THE GAME WAS PLAYED

The offensive explosion baseball experienced during the late–1990s continued into the 2000s, as did the trend toward baseball–only ballparks with grass fields. New ballparks were opened in the NL in Houston, San Francisco, Pittsburgh, Milwaukee, Cincinnati, Philadelphia, and San Diego, with another on the drawing boards in St. Louis. Of the 16 ballparks in use in the NL in 2004, nine have opened since 1995.

THE MANAGEMENT

Andy MacPhail continued to head the front office with the help of general managers Ed Lynch and Jim Hendry. Field managers have been Don Baylor (2000–02), Bruce Kimm (2002), and Dusty Baker (2003–present).

THE BEST PLAYER MOVE

The Cubs signed Moises Alou as a free agent in December 2001.

THE WORST PLAYER MOVE

It's early to speculate as to which player move will be the most harmful to the club's future, but the trade of Dontrelle Willis to the Marlins in 2002 has the potential to rank with the worst in club history.

2000s

2000

Season in a Sentence

The Cubs begin the first season of the new millennium in the Far East and end it far from pennant contention as another new manager, another rebuilding project, and another late–season collapse results in 97 losses.

In the wild card race, the Cubs were tied for 12th place, 29.0 games behind.

Finish • Won • Lost • Pct • GB

Fifth   65   97   .401   30.0

Manager

Don Baylor

Stats

Stats	Cubs	NL	Rank
Batting Avg:	.256	.266	13
On–Base Pct:	.337	.345	12
Slugging Pct:	.411	.432	12
Home Runs:	183		8
Stolen Bases:	93		10
ERA:	5.26	4.63	14
Fielding Avg:	.983	.981	3
Runs Scored:	764		11
Runs Allowed:	904		15

Starting Lineup

Joe Girardi, c
Mark Grace, 1b
Eric Young, 2b
Willie Greene, 3b
Ricky Gutierrez, ss
Henry Rodriguez, lf
Damon Buford, cf
Sammy Sosa, rf
Shane Andrews, 3b
Jeff Reed, c
Jose Nieves, ss–3b
Glenallen Hill, lf

Pitchers

Jon Lieber, sp
Kevin Tapani, sp
Kerry Wood, sp
Scott Downs, sp
Ruben Quevedo, sp
Rick Aguilera, rp
Todd Van Poppel, rp
Tim Worrell, rp
Kyle Farnsworth, rp

Attendance

2,789,511 (ninth in NL)

Club Leaders

Club Leaders		
Batting Avg:	Sosa	.320
On–Base Pct:	Sosa	.406
Slugging Pct:	Sosa	.634
Home Runs:	Sosa	50
RBI:	Sosa	138
Runs:	Sosa	106
Stolen Bases:	Young	54
Wins:	Lieber	12
Strikeouts:	Lieber	192
ERA:	Lieber	4.41
Saves:	Aguilera	29

JANUARY 13   Twelve days after the dawn of the new millennium and the end of worries about the Y2K problem, Steve Trachsel signs a free agent contract with the Devil Rays. On the same day, Lance Johnson signed a free agent contract with the Indians.

Trachsel was up and down during his entire career with the Cubs, which lasted from 1993 through 1999. His season records were 0–2, 9–7, 7–13, 13–9, 8–12, 15–8 and 8–18. In odd–numbered years, Trachsel was 23–45. In even–numbered years, he was 37–24.

JANUARY 27   Mickey Morandini signs a free agent contract with the Expos.

MARCH 29   The Cubs open the 2000 season with a regular season game against the Mets in Tokyo and win 5–3 before 55,000 at the Tokyo Dome. It was the first regular season game ever played outside of North America, and the earliest date for a Cubs opener in club history. Shane Andrews and Mark Grace homered for the Cubs in Don Baylor's debut as Cubs manager. Sammy Sosa delivered a single and a double and walked twice. After the game was over, he met with Crown Prince Naruhito and Princess Masako. The game began at 7:06 p.m. Tokyo time, which was 4:06 a.m. in Chicago. Jon Lieber was the winning pitcher.

MARCH 30   The Mets defeat the Cubs 5–1 in eleven innings in the second of a two–game series in Tokyo. Benny Agbayani drove in the winning runs with a pinch–hit grand slam off Danny Young. It was Young's major league debut.

Young didn't reach the majors until the age of 28 and lasted only four games with the Cubs, posting had an ERA of 21.00.

APRIL 10   After opening the 2000 season on a road trip through Tokyo, St. Louis, and Cincinnati with five losses in seven games, the Cubs finally play at Wrigley Field and win 4–3 against the Braves with a thrilling four–run rally in the ninth before 38,655. Shane Andrews hit a three–run homer to tie the score, and pinch–hitter Jeff Reed singled in Damon Buford with the game–winner.

APRIL 20   Sammy Sosa drives in six runs in a 10–6 win over the Expos in Montreal. Sosa hit a grand slam off Miguel Batista in the sixth inning.

APRIL 23   Kevin Tapani gives up 10 runs, nine of them earned, in a 15–8 loss to the Mets in New York. It was Tapani's 12th consecutive loss over two seasons, one short of the club record. Dutch McCall lost 13 in a row in 1948.

APRIL 25   The Cubs play at Enron Field (now Minute Maid Park) in Houston for the first time and lose 11–7 to the Astros.

APRIL 26   The Cubs outslug the Astros 13–8 in Houston.

APRIL 27   The Cubs hit four home runs in the first inning and defeat the Astros 12–3 in Houston. Eric Young and Ricky Gutierrez led off the first inning with homers. Later, Henry Rodriguez hit a two–run homer and Damon Buford added a solo shot to make the score 5–0. All four homers were hit off Jose Lima. Rodriguez added a grand slam off Lima in the fourth inning.

The only other time that the Cubs hit four homers in an inning was on May 12, 1930.

MAY 2   Kerry Wood pitches for the first time since 1998 after recovering from elbow surgery, and beats the Astros 11–1 at Wrigley Field. He pitched six innings for the victory. On the first pitch of his first at–bat, Wood hit a homer off Jose Lima.

MAY 8   The Cubs edge the Brewers 12–11 in ten innings at Wrigley Field. The Cubs led 9–1 after three innings and 11–7 heading into the ninth but allowed Milwaukee to come back and tie the contest. Shane Andrews drove in the winning run with a single with the bases loaded. There were five Cubs homers by Mark Grace, Sammy Sosa, Eric Young, Ricky Gutierrez, and Andrews.

MAY 10   The Cubs score five runs in the ninth inning to tie the Brewers 8–8 at Wrigley Field, then win 9–8 with a run in the eleventh. Willie Greene drove in the winning run with a single with two outs. The Cubs led 3–1 before Milwaukee scored three runs in the eighth and four in the ninth.

MAY 11	The Cubs and the Brewers set a major league record by playing the longest nine–inning game by time in history. The 14–8 Milwaukee win at Wrigley Field consumed four hours and 22 minutes.
MAY 12	The Cubs trade Mark Guthrie to the Devil Rays for Dave Martinez.
MAY 14	The Expos scored three runs in the ninth inning to beat the Cubs 16–15 at Olympic Stadium. Montreal scored four runs in the eighth inning to surge ahead 13–11, but the Cubs countered with four runs in the top of the ninth to take a 15–13 lead before folding. Eric Young set a post–1900 Cubs record with five stolen bases. Sammy Sosa had five hits, including a double, in six at–bats, and drove in five runs. The Cubs had a total of 21 hits.
MAY 16	A fan punches Chad Kreuter of the Dodgers, then steals his cap, causing a melee between the Dodgers and the fans at Wrigley Field during the ninth inning of a 6–5 Cubs loss. Kreuter was sitting on the bullpen bench when he was hit in the head, and entered the stands to try and stop the assailant. Other members of the Dodgers bullpen crew followed Kreuter before the rest of the team raced over from the dugout. With beer flying and fans and players fighting, it took nine minutes to quell the disturbance. Don Baylor and Rene Lachemann came over to ask the fans to behave. Suspensions and fines were handed to 16 players, three coaches, and the bullpen catcher. Kreuter was suspended for eight days and fined $5,000.
MAY 25	Down 5–0, the Cubs score one run in the seventh inning and five in the eighth to beat the Rockies 6–5 at Wrigley Field. Sammy Sosa paced the comeback with two homers.
MAY 26	The Cubs play at Pacific Bell Park (now SBC Park) in San Francisco for the first time and lose 5–3 to the Giants.
MAY 28	The Cubs complete an unusual double play during a 4–1 win over the Giants in San Francisco. With the bases loaded in the fifth inning, Barry Bonds lifted a full–count pitch straight up. Catcher Joe Girardi, pitcher Kerry Wood and Bonds, all apparently unable to see the ball against the bright sky, barely moved and the runners also held. When the ball landed in fair territory just in front of home plate, Girardi stepped on home for the force and threw out Bonds at first base for the inning–ending double play.
JUNE 2	The Tigers play at Wrigley Field for the first time since the 1945 World Series, and lose 2–0 to the Cubs.
JUNE 6	After the Diamondbacks score two runs in the tenth, the Cubs come roaring back with three in their half of the inning to win 4–3 at Wrigley Field. The game ended on a two–run, two–out double by Jeff Reed.
JUNE 9	The Cubs trade Dave Martinez to the Rangers for Chuck Smith.
JUNE 16	The Cubs score seven runs in the fourth inning to take an 8–5 lead, and hang on to beat the Expos 9–8 at Wrigley Field.
JUNE 17	The Cubs beat the Expos 1–0 at Wrigley Field. The only run was driven in by

starting pitcher Ismael Valdes in the second inning, but he had to leave the game after three innings because of blisters. Steve Rain pitched 3⅔ innings of relief for his first major league win. Rick Aguilera earned the save with a scoreless ninth.

JUNE 28   On the day six–year–old Elian Gonzalez returns to Cuba following a bitter legal battle, Pittsburgh ballboy Kierre Bulls helps the Cubs beat the Pirates 5–4 at Three Rivers Stadium. In the fourth inning, Bulls lunged from his chair along the right field line to deflect a hard–hit ground ball double by Joe Girardi that Bulls thought was foul, but was actually fair. The two–base–hit scored Damon Buford from first base. Umpire Jim McKean didn't see the ball deflect off the ballboy's glove and allowed the run to score. McKean should have ruled interference and returned Buford to third base.

JUNE 30   The Cubs score two runs in the ninth inning to tie the score 4–4, then add three more runs in the fifteenth to beat the Brewers 7–4 in a long evening in Milwaukee. Eric Young tied a club record with five walks, the last with the bases loaded in the 15th to break the 4–4 tie. Young reached base seven times on the five passes and two singles. The only other Cub to reach base seven times in a game was Cliff Heathcote on August 25, 1922.

JULY 3   Jon Lieber pitches a two–hitter to beat the Pirates 3–0 at Wrigley Field. The only Pittsburgh hits were singles by Kevin Young in the second inning and Warren Morris in the sixth.

JULY 8   Jon Lieber strikes out 12 batters in a 9–2 win over the White Sox at Wrigley Field.

JULY 19   Ed Lynch resigns as general manager.

Lynch left after five years on the job. Andy MacPhail took over as general manager in addition to his duties as president and CEO. Jim Hendry was promoted from director of player development and scouting to assistant general manager. Hendry was promoted again to general manager on July 5, 2002.

JULY 21   The Cubs trade Glenallen Hill to the Yankees for Ben Ford and Ozwaldo Mairena.

JULY 26   Mark Grace hits three singles and a homer and drives in six runs in a 14–9 win over the Phillies in Philadelphia. Grace hit a grand slam in the ninth inning off Paul Byrd. The slam capped a six–run inning that broke an 8–8 tie.

JULY 31   Mark Grace drives in both runs with a single in the fourth inning and a homer in the seventh in a 2–0 win over the Rockies at Wrigley Field.

On the same day, the Cubs traded Scott Downs to the Expos for Rondell White, and swapped Henry Rodriguez to the Marlins for Ross Gload and Dave Noyce.

AUGUST 6   Mark Grace collects five hits, including a homer and two doubles, but the Cubs lose 8–6 to the Padres in San Diego.

AUGUST 8   Phil Norton sets a Cubs record for most homers allowed in an inning with four in a 7–5 loss to the Dodgers in Los Angeles. In the fourth inning, Norton surrendered home runs to Kevin Elster, Darren Dreifort, Gary Sheffield, and Shawn Green. This was only Norton's second major league game, and came five days after his debut. He didn't pitch in another big league contest until 2003.

From August 11 through September 20, the Cubs had a record of 7–32, falling from 53–60 to 60–92. Cubs pitchers contributed to the collapse by allowing season club records for homers allowed (231) and walks allowed (658). The Cubs also used a club record 51 players during the year.

AUGUST 21   Sammy Sosa hits a titanic home run in Houston during a 5–4 loss to the Astros at Enron Field. The ball struck a bank of lights 120 to 125 feet above the playing field. It was estimated that the drive would have traveled 457 feet if it didn't hit the lights, but most observers believed that the estimate was far too low.

AUGUST 23   On the day that Richard Hatch is declared the $1 million winner in the first install-ment of *Survivor*, the Cubs rout the Astros 15–5 in Houston.

SEPTEMBER 16   Sammy Sosa hits his 50th home runs for the third year in a row, connecting off Gene Stechschulte in a 7–6 loss to the Cardinals in St. Louis.

Sosa finished the season with 50 homers and led the National League in the cat-egory for the first time. He also drove in 138 runs, scored 106, had 193 hits,

Though he left the team in 2005 on a sour note, Sammy Sosa remains one of the greatest players in Cubs history. His home run production between 1998 and 2004 will remain the benchmark for all Cub sluggers in the future.

© finalshot.com

and batted .320. Otherwise, it was a tumultuous season for Sosa. It began in January when new manager Don Baylor challenged him to run more and upgrade his defensive play. The two had a war of words for months, and Sammy complained about a lack of respect. When negotiations for a contract extension stalled in June, Sosa told the club to either sign him to an extension of the contract due to expire at the end of the 2001 season, or trade him. The Cubs shopped Sosa, but the public outcry against trading the Cubs biggest hero was overwhelming, and the player and the club soon reconciled.

SEPTEMBER 19   Roosevelt Brown hits a grand slam off Juan Acevedo of the Brewers in the sixth inning of a game in Milwaukee. The Cubs trailed 7–0, but scored six runs in the sixth inning, one in the seventh, and one in the eighth to take an 8–7 lead. The Brewers plated two in the ninth, however, to win 9–8. Sammy Sosa missed the game due to lower back stiffness, ending a streak of 388 consecutive games played dating back to 1998.

SEPTEMBER 20   The Cubs play for the last time at County Stadium in Milwaukee, and lose 3–2 to the Brewers in ten innings.

SEPTEMBER 22   Kerry Wood walks eight batters in 1 ⅓ innings as the Cubs lose 5–4 to the Cardinals at Wrigley Field.

SEPTEMBER 27   The Cubs beat the Phillies 1–0 at Wrigley Field. Kerry Wood (eight innings) and Tim Worrell (one inning) combined on the shutout. Wood also scored the lone run of the game in the third inning on a single by Sammy Sosa.

OCTOBER 1   The Cubs play the last baseball game ever at Three Rivers Stadium in Pittsburgh, and beat the Pirates 10–9.

NOVEMBER 19   With the result of the November 7 presidential election between Al Gore and George Bush still in doubt, the Cubs trade Tim Worrell to the Giants for Bill Mueller.

NOVEMBER 20   The Cubs trade Eric Ireland to the Athletics for Matt Stairs.

DECEMBER 8   Mark Grace signs a free agent contract with the Diamondbacks, bringing an end to his thirteen seasons with the Cubs. On the same day, the Cubs signed Jeff Fassero, most recently with the Red Sox, as a free agent.

DECEMBER 13   The day after the U.S. Supreme Court declares George Bush the winner in the Presidential election, the Cubs sign Todd Hundley, most recently with the Dodgers, as a free agent.

Todd's father Randy caught for the Cubs from 1966 through 1973 and again in 1976 and 1977. Todd was born in May of the fateful 1969 season. He signed a four-year contract worth $23.5 million, but his return to Chicago where he spent much of his youth watching his father play for the Cubs was a nightmare. Hundley played in 171 games over two seasons and hit only .199, although he clubbed 28 homers in 512 at-bats. Hundley was booed unmercifully by the Chicago fans before was traded to the Dodgers in December 2002.

DECEMBER 14   The Cubs sign Tom Gordon, most recently with the Red Sox, as a free agent.

2001

Cubs

Season in a Sentence

The Cubs blow a six–game lead, held on June 21, and fail to reach the post–season, but the club wins 23 more games than they did in the 2000 debacle and 21 more than the 1999 edition.

In the wild card race, the Cubs were in fourth place, four games behind.

Finish • Won • Lost • Pct • GB

Third   88   74   .543   5.0

Manager

Don Baylor

Stats

Stats	Cubs	NL	Rank
Batting Avg:	.261	.261	8
On–Base Pct:	.336	.331	6
Slugging Pct:	.430	.425	6
Home Runs:	194		8
Stolen Bases:	671		3
ERA:	4.03	4.36	4
Fielding Avg:	.982	.982	8
Runs Scored:	777		6
Runs Allowed:	701		4

Starting Lineup

Todd Hundley, c
Matt Stairs, 1b
Eric Young, 2b
Ron Coomer, 3b–1b
Ricky Gutierrez, ss
Rondell White, lf
Gary Matthews, cf
Sammy Sosa, rf
Joe Girardi, c
Bill Mueller, 3b
Michael Tucker, cf
Fred McGriff, 1b
Delino DeShields, lf–2b

Pitchers

Jon Lieber, sp
Kerry Wood, sp
Jason Bere, sp
Julian Tavarez, sp
Kevin Tapani, sp
Tom Gordon, rp
Jeff Fassero, rp
Kyle Farnsworth, rp
Todd Van Poppel, rp
Felix Heredia, rp

Attendance

2,779,456 (eighth in NL)

Club Leaders

Batting Avg:	Sosa	.328
On–Base Pct:	Sosa	.437
Slugging Pct:	Sosa	.737
Home Runs:	Sosa	64
RBI:	Sosa	160
Runs:	Sosa	146
Stolen Bases:	Young	31
Wins:	Lieber	20
Strikeouts:	Wood	217
ERA:	Wood	3.36
Saves:	Gordon	27

MARCH 16   Sammy Sosa signs a four–year contract extension worth $72 million for the 2002 through 2005 seasons.

> *Sosa responded with the best season of his career. He hit 64 homers, drove in 160 runs, scored 146 times, hit .328, and had an on–base percentage of .437. Sammy became the first player in baseball history to hit at least 60 homers in a season three times in a career. He set club records for total bases (425), extra–base hits (103), and slugging percentage (.737). Sosa led the majors in RBI, total bases, and runs. He was the first player since Ted Williams in 1949 with at least 300 combined runs and RBI. Sosa's total base figure was the highest since Stan Musial in 1948.*

MARCH 28   The Cubs trade Eric Hinske to the Athletics for Miguel Cairo.

> *Hinske was traded by Oakland to Toronto, where he had a terrific rookie year in 2002. Hinske has regressed since, but this was still a terrible deal by the Cubs.*

APRIL 2   The Cubs lose the season opener 5–4 in ten innings to the Expos before 38,466 at Wrigley Field. The Cubs tied the score 4–4 with three runs in the sixth before taking the loss. Vladimir Guerrero drove in the winning run with a single. Mike Fyhrie, in his debut with the Cubs, was the losing pitcher.

APRIL 6   Todd Van Poppel strikes out all five batters he faces in a relief appearance over the seven and eighth innings during a 3–2 win over the Phillies in Philadelphia.

APRIL 20   The Cubs play at PNC Park in Pittsburgh for the first time and beat the Pirates 8–2. Sammy Sosa capped the victory with a grand slam in the ninth inning off Jose Silva.

The Cubs started the 2001 season with a record of 12–5.

APRIL 27   Kerry Wood strikes out 14 batters in just six innings during a 7–3 win over the Giants in San Francisco.

In 2001, Kerry Wood returned to the dominating form that made him Rookie of the Year in 1998. He struck out 217 batters, fourth best in the National League, in 174 1/3 innings.

APRIL 28   Cubs pitcher Julian Tavarez lashes out at San Francisco fans following a 5–0 loss to the Giants at Pacific Bell Park. Tavarez used profanity and a derogatory term for gays. The Cubs slapped him with a five–figure fine and ordered him to undergo sensitivity training.

MAY 5   The Cubs crush the Dodgers 20–1 at Wrigley Field. The score was a routine 4–1 at the end of six innings before the Cubs erupted for eight runs in the seventh and another eight in the eighth. It was only the fifth time in major league history that a team scored at least eight runs in back–to–back innings, and the only time since 1928.

MAY 7   The Cubs play at Miller Park in Milwaukee for the first time and defeat the Brewers 7–6.

MAY 10   Jeremy Burnitz hits three homers to help the Brewers defeat the Cubs 11–1 in Milwaukee.

MAY 16   Sammy Sosa hits his 400th career homer in the fourth inning of a 6–2 loss to the Astros at Wrigley Field. The pitcher was Shane Reynolds.

MAY 20   The Cubs defeat the Diamondbacks 6–2 in Phoenix. It was a pivotal victory early in the 2001 season, because it ended an eight–game losing streak and began a 12–game winning streak.

               Reserve first baseman Juilo Zuleta decided something drastic needed to be done to break the losing streak. Inspired by the voodoo–practicing Pedro Cerrano from the 1989 film Major League, *and the 1994 and 1998 sequels, Zuleta took the Cubs bats and stuck them handle first through the dugout fencing before the May 20 game. He lit a fire under them, rubbed discarded chicken bones on them, waved apples, bananas, and oranges under them, and chanted to them. Unlike Cerrano in the film, Zuleta stopped short of cutting the heads off of chickens. Nonetheless, the spell worked, and the Cubs didn't lose again for two weeks.*

MAY 24   Jon Lieber pitches a one–hitter to beat the Reds 3–0 at Wrigley Field. Juan Castro collected the only Cincinnati hit with a single in the sixth inning after Lieber retired the first 16 batters he faced. Lieber threw only 79 pitches, and had to wait out 97–minute rain delay in the fourth. It was the first time the Reds had been shutout since 1999, ending a National League record streak of 208 consecutive games scoring at least one run.

               Lieber was 20–6 with a 3.80 ERA in 2002.

MAY 25   For the second straight day, a Cubs pitcher throws a one–hitter as Kerry Wood stops the Brewers 1–0 at Wrigley Field. Wood struck out 14 batters and carried a no–hit bid into the seventh inning before giving a leadoff single to Mark Loretta. Only seven teams since 1900 have had back–to–back one–hitters.

MAY 28   Cubs pitchers combine to strike out 18 batters in a thirteen–inning, 9–6 win over the Reds in Cincinnati. Julian Tavarez struck out four, Kyle Farnsworth four, Tom Gordon one, and Courtney Duncan seven. It was the Cubs eighth win in a row.

MAY 29   The Cubs score seven runs in the fourth inning and beat the Reds 10–5 in Cincinnati. It was Chicago's ninth victory in succession.

JUNE 2   The Cubs win their 12th game in a row with a 10–4 decision over the Brewers in Milwaukee. It was the longest Cubs winning streak since 1936, when the club took

15 in a row. The victory gave the Cubs a 33–20 record and a 3 ½–game lead in the NL Central.

JUNE 3   The 12–game winning streak comes to an end with a 4–2 loss to the Brewers in Milwaukee.

JUNE 5   Julio Zuleta hits a pinch–hit grand slam in the seventh inning off Alan Benes during a 12–6 win over the Cardinals at Wrigley Field.

On the same day, the Cubs selected pitcher Mark Prior from the University of Southern California with the second overall pick in the first round of the amateur draft. Prior was the third excellent first round draft choice by the Cubs in seven seasons, following Kerry Wood (1995) and Corey Patterson (1998). Brendan Harris was chosen in the fifth round of the 2001 draft and Sergio Mitre in the seventh.

JUNE 16   The Cubs hit five homers to beat the Twins 11–4 at Wrigley Field. Sammy Sosa hit two homers and Joe Girardi, Ricky Gutierrez and Eric Young added one each.

Gutierrez hit .290 with ten homers in 2002.

JUNE 17   The Cubs win their 13th game in a row at Wrigley Field with a 5–4 triumph over the Twins.

JUNE 20   Sammy Sosa hits two homers, including a grand slam in the seventh inning off Jason Christiansen during a 9–4 win over the Cardinals in St. Louis. The victory broke a 13–game losing streak by the Cubs at Busch Memorial Stadium dating back to 1999.

JUNE 21   The Cubs take a six–game lead in the NL Central with a 5–2 win over the Cardinals in St. Louis. The Cubs had a record of 43–27.

JUNE 22   The Brewers break the Cubs 13–game winning streak at Wrigley Field by defeating the home team 2–1.

JULY 5   The Cubs score seven runs in the third inning and defeat the Mets 13–4 in New York.

JULY 6   The Cubs play at Comerica Park in Detroit for the first time and win 15–9. The Cubs scored seven runs in the fifth inning to take a 14–9 lead. Roosevelt Brown collected five hits, including a homer and a double, in five at–bats.

On the same day, the Cubs signed Delino DeShields, most recently with the Orioles, as a free agent.

JULY 7   The Cubs reach double figures in runs for the third game in a row, beating the Tigers 10–6 in Detroit.

JULY 12   Ricky Gutierrez hits a grand slam in the eighth inning off Bob Howry to break a 1–1 tie and lift the Cubs to a 5–1 victory over the White Sox at Wrigley Field. Gutierrez gained revenge for an earlier spiking incident. In the fourth inning while covering third base, Gutierrez was hit hard in a spikes–high slide by Chris Singleton.

JULY 20   The Cubs trade Chris Booker and Ben Shaffar to the Reds for Michael Tucker.

JULY 27   The Cubs trade Manny Aybar and Jason Smith to the Devil Rays for Fred McGriff.

                 *On July 16, McGriff evoked the no–trade clause in his contract and refused to
                 come to Chicago, desiring to stay closer to his family in the Tampa area.
                 McGriff relented with an increase in salary. Although he was 37 when he
                 arrived in Chicago, McGriff gave the Cubs two solid seasons. In 195 games and
                 693 at–bats, he had a .276 batting average and 42 homers.*

AUGUST 7   Ex–Chicago Bear Steve McMichael sings "Take Me Out to the Ball Game" during
                 the seventh inning stretch and publicly berates umpire Angel Hernandez during a
                 5–4 win over the Rockies at Wrigley Field. In the sixth inning, Hernandez called
                 out Ron Coomer at home on a close play. With an open mike at his disposal,
                 McMichael told fans "not to worry" about the call because he and Hernandez
                 would "have some speaks" later. Hernandez tossed McMichael out of the ballpark,
                 and the Cubs apologized profusely.

AUGUST 9   Sammy Sosa hits three home runs in consecutive at–bats, but it can't stop the Cubs
                 from losing 14–5 to the Rockies at Wrigley Field. Sosa homered in the third and
                 fifth innings off Mike Hampton and in the seventh off Gabe White. Don Baylor
                 pulled Sosa from the game at the end of the seventh to rest him with the Cubs trail-
                 ing by nine runs.

AUGUST 10   Fred McGriff hits a grand slam in the eighth inning off Aaron Fultz during a 9–3
                 win over the Giants at Wrigley Field.

AUGUST 18   The Cubs drop out of first place with a 5–3 loss to the Diamondbacks in Phoenix.
                 The Cubs failed to regain first for the remainder of the season.

AUGUST 22   Sammy Sosa hits three homers and drives in six runs in a 16–3 win over the Brewers
                 at Wrigley Field. Sosa homered off Mac Suzuki in the first inning and Rocky
                 Coppinger in the fifth and sixth.

AUGUST 26   Sammy Sosa hits his 50th and 51st homers of the season during a 6–1 win over the
                 Cardinals at Wrigley Field. Number 50 was hit off Dustin Hermanson.

AUGUST 30   Bill Mueller hits a walk–off homer in the ninth inning to beat the Marlins 5–4 at
                 Wrigley Field. Fred McGriff tied the score with a three–run homer in the seventh.

SEPTEMBER 1   Sammy Sosa launches a 471–foot homer during a 5–3 win over the Braves in
                 Atlanta.

SEPTEMBER 5   The Cubs suffer a crushing defeat when Preston Wilson hits a three–run, two–out,
                 walk–off homer in the ninth off Tom Gordon to give Marlins a 7–6 win in Miami.
                 The Cubs led 5–1 heading into the bottom of the eighth before folding. The loss put
                 the Cubs five games behind the Astros in the NL Central race with 23 left to play.
                 Chicago was still in first place in the wild card race, however, one–half game up on
                 the Giants.

SEPTEMBER 11   Two hijacked commercial airliners strike and destroy the twin towers of the World Trade Center in New York City in the worst ever terrorist attack on American soil. A third hijacked plane destroyed a portion of the Pentagon and a fourth crashed in Pennsylvania. Some 3,000 people were killed, including about 2,800 at the World Trade Center.

Almost immediately, Bud Selig canceled the slate of games scheduled for that day. Later in the week, he announced that all games through Sunday, September 16, be postponed. They were made up by extending the regular season by a week. When play resumed, an air of heightened security and patriotism enveloped every game. Fans endured close scrutiny by stadium personnel. "God Bless America" replaced "Take Me Out to the Ball Game" as the song of choice at the seventh inning stretch.

SEPTEMBER 18   In the first game back after the September 11 terrorist attacks, the Cubs lose 6–5 in Cincinnati when the Reds score three runs in the ninth inning.

SEPTEMBER 19   The Cubs wallop the Reds 10–0 in Cincinnati.

SEPTEMBER 23   Sammy Sosa hits three home runs in consecutive at-bats, but the Cubs suffer a crucial loss to the Astros by a 7–6 score in Houston. Sosa homered in the first, fourth, and sixth innings off Tim Redding to give the Cubs a 6–4 lead, but Moises Alou hit a three-run homer for Houston in the seventh for the win. The ball hit a ledge above the left field scoreboard and bounced over the fence. The Cubs argued that the drive should have been a ground-rule double, to no avail.

Sosa is the only player in major league history to hit at least three homers in a game three times in a season.

SEPTEMBER 24   The Cubs lead the Pirates 5–0 in the sixth inning, but lose 7–6 to the Pirates in Pittsburgh. Gary Matthews Jr., who was waived by the Cubs on August 10, broke the 6–6 deadlock with a homer in the eighth.

SEPTEMBER 25   The Pirates take a 12–0 lead after three innings and beat the Cubs 13–1 in Pittsburgh. The loss all but eliminated Chicago from wild card contention. The Cubs were five games back of the Cardinals in the wild card race with 11 games left to play.

SEPTEMBER 27   The Cubs play their first home game since the September 11 terrorist attacks. American flags replaced the tribute flags along the roofline and giant flags unfurled from the rooftops as Wayne Messmer sang "The Star-Spangled Banner." Sammy Sosa was up to the occasion, hitting a home run, then taking a small American flag from coach Billy Williams as he rounded first base and waving it around the bases. The Astros won the game 6–5.

SEPTEMBER 29   Fred McGriff, Rondell White, and Todd Hundley hit back-to-back-to-back homers on consecutive pitches off Dave Mlicki in the first inning of a 6–2 win over the Astros at Wrigley Field.

OCTOBER 2   Sammy Sosa hits his 60th home run of the season during a 5–4 loss to the Reds at Wrigley Field. The homer was hit off Lance Davis.

OCTOBER 3   Jon Lieber picks up his 20th win of the season, defeating the Reds 13–7 at Wrigley Field.

Pitching coach Oscar Acosta walked out in the sixth inning. Don Baylor planned to fire him after the season was over, but word leaked out and Acosta resigned in the middle of the game. Pitchers were upset by the firing of Acosta. The Cubs were fourth in the NL in ERA in 2001, the club's highest ranking since 1972.

OCTOBER 4   Todd Hundley hits a two–run homer in the seventh inning that accounts for both runs in a 2–0 win over the Reds at Wrigley Field. The game was called in the top of the eighth by rain.

OCTOBER 6   Julian Tavarez takes a no–hitter into the eighth inning against the Pirates at PNC Park before Mendy Lopez singles in the eighth. The only other Pittsburgh hit in the 13–2 Cubs win was a single in the ninth by Kevin Young off Jeff Fassero. Sammy Sosa hit an inside–the–park homer. It was Sosa's 63rd home run of the season.

OCTOBER 7   On the day that the U.S. launches a sustained air strike campaign in Afghanistan against al–Qaeda, Sammy Sosa hits his 64th home run of the season in the final game of the 2001. The Cubs lost 4–3 against the Pirates at Wrigley Field. The pitcher was Mark Lincoln. On the same day, Barry Bonds hit his 73rd homer of 2001 in the Giants 2–1 win over the Dodger in San Francisco.

At the end of the 2004 season, Sosa has the third–highest (66 in 1998), fifth–highest (64 in 2001), and sixth–highest (63 in 1999) season home runs totals in baseball history. Amazingly, he failed to lead the league in homers in any of those three seasons because Mark McGwire hit 70 home runs in 1998, and 65 more in 1999, and Barry Bonds collected 73 in 2001. Sosa did lead the NL in homers when he hit 50 in 2000 and 49 in 2002.

NOVEMBER 2   The Cubs trade Adam Morrissey to the Athletics for Mark Bellhorn.

Bellhorn proved to be a pleasant surprise, giving the Cubs one terrific season by hitting 27 homers in 2002 while playing all over the infield. He appeared in 77 games at second base, 38 at third, 22 at first, and 12 at shortstop.

DECEMBER 10   The Cubs trade Felix Heredia and James Deschaine to the Blue Jays for Alex Gonzalez.

DECEMBER 19   The Cubs sign Moises Alou, most recently with the Astros, as a free agent. On the same day, the Cubs traded Michael Tucker to the Royals for Shawn Sonnier, and Ricky Gutierrez signed a free agent contract with the Indians.

DECEMBER 21   Rondell White signs a free agent contract with the Yankees.

2002   Cubs

Season in a Sentence

Season in a sentenceThe Cubs come into the season with high expectations, but immediately flop resulting in the mid–season firing of Don Baylor.

In the wild card race, the Cubs were in 11th place, 28.0 games behind.

Finish • Won • Lost • Pct • GB

Fifth   67   95   .414 30.0

Managers

Don Baylor (34–49),
Rene Lachemann (0–1) and
Bruce Kimm (33–45)

Stats

Stats	Cubs	NL	Rank
Batting Avg:	.246	.259	15
On–Base Pct:	.321	.331	14
Slugging Pct:	.413	.410	8
Home Runs:	200		1
Stolen Bases:	631		6
ERA:	4.29	4.11	12
Fielding Avg:	.981	.982	13
Runs Scored:	706		11
Runs Allowed:	759		11

Starting Lineup

Todd Hundley, c
Fred McGriff, 1b
Mark Bellhorn, 2b
Bill Mueller, 3b
Alex Gonzalez, ss
Moises Alou, lf
Corey Patterson, cf
Sammy Sosa, rf
Roosevelt Brown, lf
Chris Stynes, 3b–2b
Joe Girardi, c
Bobby Hill, 2b

Pitchers

Kerry Wood, sp
Matt Clement, sp
Jon Lieber, sp
Mark Prior, sp
Carlos Zambrano, sp–rp
Antonio Alfonseco, rp
Joe Borowski, rp
Jeff Fassero, rp
Kyle Farnsworth, rp
Juan Cruz, rp

Attendance

2,693,071 (seventh in NL)

Club Leaders

Batting Avg:	Sosa	.288
On–Base Pct:	Sosa	.399
Slugging Pct:	Sosa	.594
Home Runs:	Sosa	49
RBI:	Sosa	108
Runs:	Sosa	122
Stolen Bases:	Patterson	18
Wins:	Clement	12
	Wood	12
Strikeouts:	Wood	217
ERA:	Clement	3.60
Saves:	Alfonseca	19

MARCH 27   The Cubs trade Dontrelle Willis, Julian Tavarez, Jose Cueto, and Ryan Jorgensen to the Marlins for Matt Clement and Antonio Alfonseco.

APRIL 1   The Cubs open with a 5–4 loss to the Reds in Cincinnati. A sacrifice fly by Aaron Boone off Jeff Fassero in the ninth inning drove in the winning run. The Cubs tied the score 4–4 with two runs in the eighth.

APRIL 5   The Cubs lose the home opener 2–1 to the Pirates before 40,185 at Wrigley Field. Sammy Sosa's homer in the sixth inning drove in the lone Chicago run.

APRIL 12   Sammy Sosa hits a homer estimated at 484 feet during a 7–3 win over the Pirates in Pittsburgh.

APRIL 13   Matt Clement strikes out 12 batters in seven innings, but the Cubs lose 3–2 to the Pirates in Pittsburgh.

APRIL 15   Sammy Sosa launches another tape measure shot in Montreal during a 6–4 win over the Expos. The drive just missed hitting the 160–foot high concrete rim that surrounds Olympic Stadium, and struck a cable 120–feet above the left field wall.

APRIL 19   Matt Clement strikes out 12 batters in seven innings during a 5–2 win over the Reds at Wrigley Field.

MAY 2   Sammy Sosa hits two homers for the second game in a row during a 6–1 win over the Padres at Wrigley Field. Sosa also homered twice in a 6–4 loss to San Diego in Chicago on May 1.

MAY 5   Mark Bellhorn drives in all three Cubs runs in a 3–0 win over the Dodgers in Los Angeles.

MAY 6   Alex Gonzalez hits a walk–off homer that beats the Cardinals 6–5 at Wrigley Field.

MAY 12   Two Brewers hit grand slams in beating the Cubs 13–4 at Wrigley Field. Paul Casanova connected with the bases loaded against Scott Chiasson in the seventh inning, and Richie Sexson added a slam off Ron Mahay in the eighth inning. Jon Lieber took the loss, ending his 13–game winning streak at Wrigley Field extending back to the previous season.

MAY 22   Mark Prior makes his major league debut, striking out ten batters in six innings while allowing two runs, as the Cubs beat the Pirates 7–4 at Wrigley Field.

MAY 28   Matt Clement pitches a two–hitter to beat the Pirates 3–0 at PNC Park. Clement took a no–hitter into the seventh before Brian Giles singled. The other Pittsburgh hit was a single by Adrian Brown in the eighth. It was Clement's first career complete game. He was cheered by about 100 family members and friends from his hometown of Butler, Pennsylvania.

MAY 30   Mark Bellhorn hits a grand slam off Jimmy Anderson in the fifth inning that gives the Cubs a 7–0 lead over the Pirates at PNC Park. The Cubs withstood a Pittsburgh rally to win 9–8.

JUNE 4   The Cubs select pitcher Bobby Brownlie of Rutgers University in the first round of the amateur draft.

JUNE 7   The Cubs play the Mariners for the first time during the regular season and win 2–0 in Seattle.

> *From June 16, 2001 through June 12, 2002, the Cubs played in 162 games. During that stretch, Sammy Sosa hit 71 home runs.*

JUNE 18   The Cubs play the Rangers for the first time during the regular season and win 4–3 at Wrigley Field on a walk–off homer by Alex Gonzalez off John Rocker.

> *During the series against the Rangers, a four–foot section of ivy in right field starting dying. Conspiracy theories abounded. Some contended that a White Sox fan poisoned the plants when the cross–town rivals played at Wrigley in a series from June 14 through 16.*

JUNE 22   The game between the Cubs and Cardinals at Wrigley Field is postponed because of the sudden death of St. Louis pitcher Darryl Kile. He was found dead in his room in a Chicago hotel due to blockage of the coronary arteries.

JUNE 29   Moises Alou is 4–for–4 with two homers in a 5–4 loss to the White Sox at Comiskey Park.

After three straight .300 seasons with the Astros, Moises Alou came to the Cubs in 2002 but was unable to provide the same level of production. During his three years with the team, however, he was a consistent contributor.

© finalshot.com

JUNE 30   Mark Bellhorn homers from both sides of the plate during a 9–2 win over the White Sox at Comiskey Park. Bellhorn hit a two–run homer right–handed off Mark Buehrle in the sixth inning and a solo hot off Rocky Biddle in the eighth. Matt Clement struck out 12 batters.

JULY 5   The Cubs fire Don Baylor and hire Bruce Kimm as interim manager.

Baylor was fired after the Cubs were off to a 33–49 start to the 2002 season. Kimm was managing the Cubs Class AAA farm club in Iowa at the time he was brought to Chicago to head the Cubs. Rene Lachemann ran the club for one game, a 4–3 loss to the Braves in Atlanta, until Kimm could arrive. On the same day, Jim Hendry was promoted to general manager, taking over duties from Andy Mac Phail.

JULY 12   The Cubs beat the Marlins 5–4 in a sixteen–inning marathon at Wrigley Field.

Angel Echevarria drove in the winning run on a long single with two out. Florida center fielder Preston Wilson ran into the ivy–covered wall and dropped Echevarria's fly ball as he hit the wall running at full speed.

JULY 15   The Cubs beat the Braves 3–2 on "'70s Night" at Wrigley Field. Sammy Sosa donned an Afro wig, sunglasses and a heavy chain before meeting Tony Orlando. Orlando wore a Sosa jersey while singing a pre–game medley of his greatest hits.

AUGUST 1   Alex Gonzalez hits a two–run, two–out, walk–off double off Trevor Hoffman in the ninth inning to beat the Padres 8–7 at Wrigley Field. San Diego led 7–3 before the Cubs closed the gap with three runs in the eighth.

AUGUST 2   Moises Alou hits a two–run, walkoff homer in the twelfth inning to beat the Rockies 6–4 at Wrigley Field. Kerry Wood struck out 13 batters in seven innings.

AUGUST 4   Mark Prior strikes out 13 batters in his first career complete game, leading the Cubs to a 4–1 win over the Rockies at Wrigley Field.

AUGUST 10   Sammy Sosa hits three consecutive three–run homers in three consecutive innings during a 15–1 rout of the Rockies in Denver. Sosa left the game in the sixth inning before having a chance for a major league record fourth homer. Sammy went deep on Shawn Chacon in the third and fourth innings and Mark Corey in the fifth. The nine RBIs by Sosa tied the club record set by Heinie Zimmerman in 1911. It was the sixth three–homer game of Sosa's career, tying the record set by Johnny Mize. Sosa was only the fifth player in history to hit homers in three consecutive innings. The Cubs had a total of 20 hits and six homers in the trouncing of the Rockies. In addition to Sosa's three, Moises Alou hit two homers (along with a double and a single), and Fred McGriff went deep once.

AUGUST 11   A day after driving in nine runs on three, three–run homers, Sammy Sosa hits a grand slam and drives in five runs in a 12–9 win over the Rockies in Denver. The slam was hit off Justin Speier in the seventh. The 14 runs–batted–in by Sosa over two consecutive games set a National League record. It was one shy of the major league record of 15 by Tony Lazzeri of the Yankees in 1936. The Cubs hit a total of five homers in the game. In addition to Sosa, Corey Patterson hit two homers, and Joe Girardi and Fred McGriff each clubbed one. The homer by Girardi was the only one he hit in 2002.

AUGUST 12   The Cubs hit four homers but lose 9–6 to the Astros at Wrigley Field. The home runs by Sammy Sosa, Randy Hundley, Alex Gonzalez, and Corey Patterson gave the Cubs 15 homers in three consecutive game to tie a National League record. During those three games, Sosa hit five homers and drove in 16 runs. His home run on August 12 was his 40th of the season.

AUGUST 15   Mark Prior strikes out 12 batters in six innings, including seven in a row, during a 6–4 win over the Astros at Wrigley Field.

AUGUST 21   The Cubs collect 24 hits and defeat the Astros 14–12 in Houston.

AUGUST 22   The Cubs trade Tom Gordon to the Astros for Russ Rohlicek, Travis Anderson, and Chris Nannini.

AUGUST 24   The Cubs trade Jeff Fassero to the Cardinals for Jason Karmuth and Jared Blasdell.

AUGUST 29   Mark Bellhorn becomes only the second major leaguer to hit home runs from both sides of the plate in a single inning during a 13–10 win over the Brewers in Milwaukee. It happened in the fourth inning when the Cubs broke a scoreless tie by scoring ten runs. Bellhorn hit a homer left–handed off Jose Cabrera and right–handed against Andrew Lorraine. He drove in five runs in the inning, tying a Cub record set by Billy Williams on May 1, 1964. The only other big leaguer in history to hit homers from both sides of the plate in an inning was Carlos Baerga of the Indians in 1993.

AUGUST 30   Just three hours before a 6–3 loss to the Cardinals at Wrigley Field, the players and owners come to a new labor agreement which prevents a strike.

AUGUST 31   The Cubs play a day–night double–header at Wrigley Field for the first time. The opener was scheduled for 12:05 p.m., with the second tilt beginning at 7:05 p.m. The Cubs lose 8–1 and 10–4 to the Cardinals.

SEPTEMBER 2   The Cubs annihilate the Brewers 17–4 at Wrigley Field in the second game of a double–header. The Cubs led 17–0 at the end of the fifth inning. Kerry Wood tied a major league record by striking out four batters in the fourth inning. In the frame, Wood fanned Bill Hall (who reached on a Todd Hundley error), Ryan Thompson, Paul Bako (who reached on a wild pitch), and Andrew Lorraine. In the bottom of the fourth, Wood hit a two–run homer off Lorraine. Milwaukee won the first game 4–2.

SEPTEMBER 3   The Cubs trade Bill Mueller to the Giants for Jeff Verplancke.

SEPTEMBER 9   Alex Gonzalez hits his third walk–off homer of the 2002 season with a solo shot in the ninth inning to beat the Expos 3–2 at Wrigley Field.

SEPTEMBER 12   The Cubs collect 22 hits but lose 15–12 to the Reds in Cincinnati.

SEPTEMBER 15   The Cubs play at Cinergy Field (formerly Riverfront Stadium) in Cincinnati for the last time, and win 6–0.

SEPTEMBER 29   In the last game of the season, Sammy Sosa hits his 49th home run of 2002 and the 499th of his career during a 7–3 win over the Pirates at Wrigley Field. On the same day, the Cubs fired Bruce Kimm after he served as interim manager for the last 78 games of the season.

                 Sosa hit a league–leading 49 homers in 2002 along with 108 RBIs and a .288 batting average in 2002. He also led the NL in runs scored with 122.

NOVEMBER 15   The Cubs hire Dusty Baker as manager.

                 Despite managing the Giants to the World Series in 2002, San Francisco management allowed Baker's contract to expire after disagreements over the future of the ball club. In ten season as San Francisco manager, Baker was 840–715. He became the Cubs 22nd manager, including six who served on an interim basis, since the start of the 1972 season.

DECEMBER 3   The Cubs sign Mike Remlinger, most recently with the Braves, as a free agent.

DECEMBER 4   The Cubs trade Todd Hundley and Chad Hermansen to the Dodgers for Mark
                    Grudzielanek and Eric Karros.

                    Grudzielanek hit .314 for the Cubs in 2003.

DECEMBER 17   The Cubs sign Troy O'Leary, most recently with the Expos, as a free agent.

DECEMBER 20   Fred McGriff signs a free agent contract with the Dodgers.

The Seventh-Inning Stretch

It began as a practical joke at Comiskey Park in 1976. Like many fans, Harry Caray loved to sing "Take Me Out to the Ball Game" during the seventh–inning stretch. And like many fans, Harry sang with a decided lack of musical training. On Opening Day that year, without the announcer's knowledge, Veeck had a microphone set up in the booth and Caray's raspy singing voice was soon bellowing throughout the stadium. The fans loved it, and from that day on Caray's enthusiastic rendering of the song was a Chicago tradition. When Harry moved to Wrigley Field to broadcast Cubs games beginning in 1982, the tradition went with him and soon was eagerly anticipated by television viewers across the country. WGN–TV did not cut away to a commercial until Caray completed the song.

When Caray died in February 1998, the Cubs and the station were faced with a dilemma. How could they keep up the tradition of the sing–along and still preserve Caray's memory? With a stroke of genius, it was decided that guest celebrity "conductors" would lead the fans in the baseball anthem. They have included such diverse individuals and characters as Mike Ditka, Dick Butkus, Denis Savard, Muhammad Ali, Joe Frazier, George Foreman, Randy

Macho Man Savage, Dick Clark, 'NSync, KC and the Sunshine Band, Eddie Vedder, Cyndi Lauper, Ozzie Osborne, Chuck Berry, Kenny Rogers, Vanna White, Barbara Eden, Dawn Wells, Jerry Mathers, Bea Arthur, Mel Gibson, George Will, Roger Ebert, Miss America, Bill Murray, Jim Belushi, Chris Berman, Bozo the Clown, and Barney the Dinosaur.

It's not as easy as it looks. Trained actors have suffered from stage fright and forgotten the words. In fact, the disasters and near disasters are the most fondly remembered. Gibson was so absorbed in singing the song that he was hanging out of the booth with only his legs braced against the windowsill to keep him from falling. Mike Ditka barked the song in 15 seconds after imbibing too much Wrigley Field beer. Bears lineman Steve McMichael used the open mike to blast the umpire, and was tossed out of the ballpark by the umpiring crew. Ozzie Osborne's unintelligible version in 2003 topped them all. According to Rick Reilly in *Sports Illustrated*, Ozzie sounded "like a surgical patient just before anesthesia takes hold." In a 2004 interview for the TV program *Cathedrals of the Game*, Chip Caray, who has seen all of the celebrities come and go since his grandfather's death, called Ozzie's rendition his favorite.

2003

Cubs

Season in a Sentence

The Cubs win the NL Central and reach the National League Championship Series, but the Billy Goat Curse rears its ugly head in the form of an obtrusive fan who helps the Cubs blow a three–run lead just five outs from a World Series.

Division Series–The Cubs defeated the Atlanta Braves three–games–to–two

National League Championship Series–The Cubs lost to the Florida Marlins four–games–to–three

Finish • Won • Lost • Pct • GB

First 88 74 .543 +1.0

Manager

Dusty Baker

Stats   Cubs • NL • Rank

	Cubs	NL	Rank
Batting Avg:	.259	.262	11
On–Base Pct:	.323	.332	13
Slugging Pct:	.416	.417	11
Home Runs:	172		7
Stolen Bases:	73		10
ERA:	3.83	4.28	3
Fielding Avg:	.983	.983	8
Runs Scored:	724		9
Runs Allowed:	683		4

Starting Lineup

Damian Miller, c
Eric Karros, 1b
Mark Grudzielanek, 2b
Aramis Ramirez, 3b
Alex Gonzalez, ss
Moises Alou, lf
Corey Patterson, cf
Sammy Sosa, rf
Ramon Martinez, 2b–3b–ss
Kenny Lofton, cf
Hee Seop Choi, 1b
Paul Bako, c
Troy O'Leary, rf–lf
Thomas Goodwin, cf–rf
Mark Bellhorn, 3b

Pitchers

Mark Prior, sp
Kerry Wood, sp
Matt Clement, sp
Carlos Zambrano, sp
Scott Estes, sp
Joe Borowski, rp
Kyle Farnsworth, rp
Mike Remlinger, rp
Mark Guthrie, rp
Antonio Alfonseca, rp

Attendance

2,962,630 (third in NL)

Club Leaders

Batting Avg:	Grudzielanek	.314
On–Base Pct:	Grudzielanek	.366
Slugging Pct:	Sosa	.553
Home Runs:	Sosa	40
RBI:	Sosa	103
Runs:	Sosa	99
Stolen Bases:	Goodwin	19
Wins:	Pryor	18
Strikeouts:	Wood	266
ERA:	Prior	2.43
Saves:	Borowski	33

JANUARY 8   The Cubs sign Lenny Harris, most recently with the Brewers, as a free agent.

JANUARY 16   The Cubs sign Thomas Goodwin, most recently with the Giants, as a free agent.

MARCH 31   Twelve days after U.S. forces invade Iraq, the Cubs thrash the Mets 15–2 in New York in the opener. Corey Patterson set a Cubs record for most runs–batted–in on Opening Day with seven on two homers and two singles. Mark Grudzielanek was 3–for–3 in his debut with the Cubs, and Mark Bellhorn drove in four runs. Juan Cruz struck out six batters in a row in a relief appearance. The Cubs tied a club record for most runs scored in the first game of the season, matching the 15–1 win at Louisville in 1899.

APRIL 4   Sammy Sosa collects his 500th homer as a major leaguer in a 10–9 loss to the Reds in Cincinnati. The historic homer was hit off Scott Sullivan in the seventh inning. It was the first time that the Cubs played a game at Great American ballpark.

At the age of 34 years and 143 days, Sosa became the third youngest player in history to reach the 500–home run mark behind only Jimmie Foxx (32 years, 337 days) and Willie Mays (34 years 130 days).

APRIL 6   Paul Bako drives in six runs on a triple and two singles in a 9–7 win over the Reds in Cincinnati.

APRIL 8   In the first game of the season at Wrigley Field, the Cubs beat the Expos 6–1 before 29,138.

               The opener proved to be the second smallest crowd of the season. The only time the Cubs drew fewer fans was on April 16 against the Reds when 27,388 purchased tickets.

APRIL 9   The Cubs defeat the Expos 3–0 in a strikeout–filled contest at Wrigley Field. Javier Vasquez of the Expos struck out 14 Cubs batters in seven innings and Mark Prior fanned 12 in a complete game. Neither pitcher allowed a walk.

APRIL 13   Kerry Wood strikes out 13 batters in eight innings in a 4–0 win over the Pirates at Wrigley Field.

APRIL 15   The Cubs pound the Reds 11–1 at Wrigley Field.

APRIL 16   The Cubs shellac the Reds 10–4 at Wrigley Field.

APRIL 17   The Cubs reach double figures for the third game in a row against the Reds at Wrigley Field, winning 16–3.

APRIL 19   The Cubs score five runs in the tenth inning to beat the Pirates 6–1 in Pittsburgh.

APRIL 20   Sammy Sosa leaves an 8–2 loss to the Pirates in Pittsburgh after being hit near the left ear flap by a Salomon Torres pitch. Sosa's helmet was cracked in the frightening beaning, but he wasn't seriously hurt.

APRIL 25   Mark Prior drives in four runs on a homer and a double in an 11–7 win over the Rockies in Denver.

MAY 1   Alex Gonzalez hits a three–run homer and Sammy Sosa adds a solo shot in the tenth inning to sink the Giants 5–1 in San Francisco.

MAY 4   Alex Gonzalez hits a walk–off homer in the tenth inning to beat the Rockies 5–4 at Wrigley Field.

MAY 10   Alex Gonzalez hits a tenth inning home run to beat the Cardinals 3–2 at Wrigley Field. It was his fifth walk–off homer as a Cub in just two seasons. The homer was also the third in extra innings for Gonzalez in a span of ten days.

               The only players in Cubs history with more walk–off homers are Sammy Sosa (9) and Ron Santo (6). Gonzalez is tied with Ernie Banks (1955) and Santo (1966) for most extra–inning homers in a season with three.

MAY 15   Corey Patterson hits a two–run homer in the 17th inning to beat the Brewers 4–2 at Miller Park. Patterson entered the game in the eighth inning. His homer tied the club record for the latest home run. Keith Moreland also homered in the 17th inning on September 2, 1986. Cubs pitchers tied a National League record by combining to strikeout 24 Milwaukee batters. Kerry Wood fanned 13 batters in seven innings and relievers Mike Remlinger (two), Juan Cruz (two), Kyle Farnsworth (four), and Todd Wellemeyer (three) added 11 more over the final ten innings. The game was Wellemeyer's major league debut, and he struck out all three batters he faced. In his first five big league games, Wellemeyer allowed no runs and two hits in 7⅔ innings while striking out 13.

MAY 31   In the longest 1–0 game in Wrigley Field history, the Cubs edge the Astros in a sixteen–inning marathon. It was a blustery day at the ballpark with the temperature standing at 48 degrees accompanied by a 24 mile–per–hour wind blowing in. Sammy Sosa drove in the lone run of the day with a single after striking out five times in his previous six plate appearances. Carlos Zambrano (eight innings), Mike Remlinger (⅔), Antonio Alfonseca (1⅓), Joe Borowski (two), Kyle Farnsworth (two), and Todd Wellemeyer (two) combined on the shutout, allowing just six hits.

              Cubs pitchers set a club record with 1,404 strikeouts in 2003.

JUNE 3   Sammy Sosa is ejected after the umpires find cork in his bat during the first ever Cubs–Devil Rays regular season game, won by Chicago 3–2 at Wrigley Field. Sosa shattered his bat in the first inning on a grounder to second, leading to the discovery of the illegal cork. On the same day, the Cubs selected outfielder Ryan Harvey of Dunedin High School in Florida in the first round of the amateur draft.

              Sosa contended that he used the corked bats for home run exhibitions, and inadvertently selected the bat before his first–inning plate appearance. He was suspended for eight games by major league baseball officials on June 6, but appealed the suspension. After a hearing, the suspension was reduced to seven games on June 11. Tests were made on 76 bats confiscated from Sosa's locker, and no foreign substances were found. Five of his bats at the Hall of Fame were also examined and found to be clean. At the end of the season Sosa had 40 homers, 103 runs–batted–in, and a .279 average.

JUNE 5   The Cubs score seven runs in the third inning and defeat the Devil Rays 8–1 at Wrigley Field.

JUNE 6   The Cubs play the Yankees for the first time during the regular season and lose 5–3 at Wrigley Field.

JUNE 7   Hee Seop Choi suffers a concussion in a violent collision with Kerry Wood during a 5–2 win over the Yankees at Wrigley Field. In the fifth inning, Jason Giambi hit an infield pop–up. Choi and Wood reached toward it, and Wood's glove hit Choi in the face. The first baseman fell hard, slamming the back of his head on the ground. Choi was motionless for several minutes and was taken off the field in an ambulance. Roger Clemens entered the contest with 299 career wins, and took the loss.

              Choi was on the disabled list from June 8 through June 30.

JUNE 8   Sammy Sosa collects his 2,000th career hit with a single off Juan Acevedo during an 8–7 win over the Yankees at Wrigley Field.

JUNE 10   The Cubs play the Orioles for the first time in the regular season and win 4–0 in Baltimore.

JUNE 13   The Cubs play the Blue Jays for the first time during the regular season and lose 5–1 in Toronto.

JUNE 15   Troy O'Leary hits a grand slam in the sixth inning off Cory Lidle to give the Cubs a 4–2 lead, but the Blue Jays rally to win 5–4 in ten innings in Toronto.

JUNE 19   Reds pitcher Paul Wilson and Kyle Farnsworth battle during a 3–1 loss to Cincinnati at Great American ballpark. In the seventh inning, Wilson squared around to bunt and was nearly drilled by an inside pitch from Farnsworth. Wilson charged the mound and was body slammed into the turf by the Cubs hurler. Wilson emerged from the fray with a cut on the bridge of his nose that splattered blood all over his uniform.

JUNE 20   The Cubs trade Mark Bellhorn to the Rockies for Jose Hernandez.

JUNE 24   The Cubs hit six homers, including three in a row, during a 9–1 win over the Reds at Wrigley Field. In the sixth, Kerry Wood, Mark Grudzielanek, and Alex Gonzalez hit consecutive homers. Sammy Sosa added two home runs and Corey Patterson one.

JUNE 26   Mark Prior strikes out 16 batters in eight innings and leaves the game with a 3–2 lead, but Joe Borowski gives up three runs in the ninth to lose 5–3 to the Brewers at Wrigley Field. Prior stuck out the last six batters he faced.

JULY 2   Sammy Sosa homers on the first pitch of the ninth inning and four Cubs pitchers combine on a one–hitter to beat the Phillies 1–0 at Veterans Stadium. The pitchers were Matt Clement (seven innings), Mark Guthrie (⅔), Kyle Farnsworth (1 ⅓), and Joe Borowski. The only Philadelphia hit was an infield hit by David Bell in the fifth inning.

JULY 3   The Cubs play the Phillies at Veterans Stadium in Philadelphia for last time and lose 12–2.

JULY 4   Moises Alou hits three homers and drives in five runs, but the Cubs lose 11–8 to the Cardinals at Wrigley Field. Alou homered off Brett Tomko in the second and sixth innings and Steve Kline in the ninth.

JULY 5   Down 5–0, the Cubs rally to beat the Cardinals 6–5 at Wrigley Field with one run in the second inning, one in the fourth, two in the sixth, one in the seventh, and one in the ninth. An infield single by Alex Gonzalez drove in the game–winning tally.

JULY 9   Kerry Wood strikes out 12 batters to beat the Marlins 5–1 at Wrigley Field.

JULY 19   Kerry Wood pitches a two–hitter to beat the Marlins 1–0 in Miami. The only Florida hits were a double by Ivan Rodriguez in the first inning and a single by Juan Pierre in the sixth. Alex Gonzalez drove in the lone run of the game with a sacrifice fly in the fifth inning.

© finalshot.com

The emergence of Mark Prior in 2003 gave the Cubs a very strong starting rotation. He finished third in the vote for the Cy Young Award that year.

JULY 20   The Cubs collect 20 hits and rout the Marlins 16–2 in Miami.

JULY 21   The Cubs collect 21 hits and smash the Pirates 15–6 at Wrigley Field. Tom Goodwin picked up five hits, including a double, in six at–bats.

JULY 22   The Cubs trade Jose Hernandez, Matt Brubeck, and a player to be named later to the Pirates for Aramis Ramirez and Kenny Lofton.

JULY 26   The Cubs lose 3–1 to the Astros in Houston. The defeat dropped Chicago's record to 51–52 on the season. The club was in third place, 5 ½ games behind first place Houston. From July 27 through September 27, the Cubs were 37–21 to take the division crown.

JULY 29   Matt Clement pitches a two–hitter, and Moises Alou hits a three–run homer in the first inning to beat the Giants at Wrigley Field. The only San Francisco hits were singles by Marquis Grissom in the fourth inning and Andres Galarraga in the seventh. At one point, Clement struck out four consecutive batters (Jose Cruz, Jr., Edgar Alfonso, Damian Moss, and Ray Durham) on the minimum 12 pitches.

JULY 30   The Cubs send Jason Fransz to the Phillies for Doug Glanville.

AUGUST 1   The Cubs beat the Diamondbacks 4–3 in 14 innings at Wrigley Field. Aramis

Ramirez drove in the game–winner with a single. The contest ended almost eight hours after the first pitch because of rain delays and the five extra innings.

AUGUST 2   The Cubs release Lenny Harris.

AUGUST 7   The Cubs play at Qualcomm Stadium in San Diego for the last time and defeat the Padres 9–3.

AUGUST 11   Kerry Wood records his 1,000th career strikeout in a 3–1 loss to the Astros at Wrigley Field. Wood struck out his first 1,000 batters in 853 innings, the fewest of any pitcher in major league history.

AUGUST 19   The Cubs send Enmanual Ramirez and cash to the Rockies for Tony Womack.

AUGUST 22   Carlos Zambrano carries a no–hitter into the eighth inning and Sammy Sosa hits his 499th and 500th homers as a member of the Cubs during a 4–1 win over the Diamondbacks in Phoenix. With two out in the eighth, Shea Hillenbrand dropped a ball down the third base line. Aramis Ramirez charged it and made a throw to first, but umpire Kevin Kelley called Hillenbrand safe to end Zambrano's no–hit bid. TV replays showed Hillenbrand was out. In the ninth, Zambrano gave up two more hits and a run. Both of Sosa's homers were hit off Curt Schilling.

SEPTEMBER 2   Sammy Sosa hits a walk–off home run in the fifteenth inning to beat the Cardinals 4–2 in the first game of a double–header at Wrigley Field. Augie Ojeda, who was 0–for–21 on the season, led off the fifteenth with a single. St. Louis won the second game 2–0.

SEPTEMBER 3   Down 6–0, the Cubs come back to beat the Cardinals 8–7 at Wrigley Field. The Cubs scored three runs in the sixth, three in the seventh, and two in the eighth. Moises Alou broke the 7–7 tie with a run–scoring single. It was his fifth hit of the game in five at–bats. Alou had four singles and a homer in the contest. The tension–filled tilt featured a shouting match between Dusty Baker and Tony LaRussa and starting pitchers Matt Clement and Danny Haren hitting each other with pitches.

On September 8, both the Cubs and the White Sox were in sole possession of first place. It was the first time since 1906 that both Chicago teams were in first in September.

SEPTEMBER 9   The Cubs play the first of a three–game series against the Expos in San Juan, Puerto Rico, and win 4–3.

SEPTEMBER 16   Mark Prior strikes out 13 batters in 8 ⅔ innings during a 3–2 win over the Mets at Wrigley Field.

In his first full season in the majors, Prior was 18–6 with a 2.43 ERA. He struck out 245 batters in 211 ⅓ innings.

SEPTEMBER 21   Mark Prior strikes out 14 batters in 7 ⅔ innings as the Cubs defeat the Pirates 4–1 in Pittsburgh. The win put the Cubs one–half game back of the first place Astros with a week left in the season.

SEPTEMBER 23   Kerry Wood pitches seven innings of shutout ball while allowing only one hit and striking out 14 in a 6–0 win over the Reds in Cincinnati. The only hit off Wood was an infield single by Wily Mo Pena with one out in the seventh inning.

SEPTEMBER 25   The Cubs lose 9–7 to the Reds in Cincinnati and head into the final weekend tied for first place with the Astros. Each club had a record of 86–73.

SEPTEMBER 26   The Cubs game against the Pirates in Pittsburgh is postponed by rain, but Chicago takes sole possession of first place because the Astros lose 12–5 to the Brewers in Houston.

SEPTEMBER 27   The Cubs sweep the Pirates 4–2 and 7–2 in a double–header at Wrigley Field to clinch the NL Central pennant. At the end of the game, Sammy Sosa sprayed fans in the right field bleachers with celebratory champagne. Many of his teammates jogged around the perimeter of the outfield, followed by Dusty Baker in saluting the fans. Thousands stayed in the park for more than an hour after the game as the players celebrated on the field.

The Cubs were paired with the Atlanta Braves in the Division Series beginning on September 30. The Braves were 101–61 in 2003.

SEPTEMBER 28   The Cubs retire Ron Santo's number 10 in ceremonies prior to a 3–2 loss to the Pirates at Wrigley Field. A flag with the number 10 was placed on the left field foul pole.

SEPTEMBER 30   In the first game of the Division Series, the Cubs defeat the Braves 4–2 in Atlanta. The Braves took a 1–0 lead in the third inning on a homer by Marcus Giles off Kerry Wood, which held up until the Cubs scored four times in the sixth. Wood drove in the tying and go–ahead runs with a double off Russ Ortiz. Wood pitched seven innings, allowed one run and two hits, and struck out 11 batters. Joe Borowski earned the save striking out three batters in the ninth.

The victory ended an eight–game, post–season losing streak by the Cubs on the road, dating back to the 1945 World Series.

OCTOBER 1   The Braves even the series in game two with a 5–3 win over the Cubs in Atlanta. The Cubs scored twice in the first inning off Mike Hampton before an out was recorded. The Braves took the lead with single runs in the first, fourth and sixth. The Cubs tied the score 3–3 with a run in the eighth, but Atlanta scored twice in the bottom half off Dave Veres.

OCTOBER 3   The Cubs regain the advantage in game three of the Division Series beating the Braves 3–1 before 39,982 at Wrigley Field. Mark Prior was brilliant, pitching a complete–game two–hitter. The only Atlanta hits off Prior were a single by Marcus Giles in the third inning and a double by Mark DeRosa in the eighth. The Cubs had all the runs they needed with two in the first off Greg Maddux.

The only Cubs in both the 1998 and 2003 post–seasons were Sammy Sosa and Kerry Wood.

OCTOBER 4   The Braves even the series again in game four, defeating the Cubs 6–4 before

39,983 at Wrigley Field. Atlanta broke a 1–1 tie with three runs in the fifth off Matt Clement. Chipper Jones had a pair of two–run homers for the Braves, one from each side of the plate. The game ended on a long drive by Sammy Sosa that was caught by Andruw Jones on the warning track in center field with a runner on first base. Eric Karros had two homers and a single for Chicago. Moises Alou also collected three hits.

OCTOBER 5   The Cubs pull off an upset in the Division Series by defeating the Braves 5–1 in the Atlanta in the fifth and deciding game. Kerry Wood pitched eight innings, allowing one run and five hits. Alex Gonzalez put the Cubs ahead 2–0 with a solo homer in the second inning and Alex Gonzalez made it 4–0 with a two–run shot in the sixth. Joe Borowski closed out the game by pitching a perfect ninth with two strikeouts. Borowski fanned Andruw Jones to end the game.

It was the first post–season series won by the Cubs since the 1908 World Series, ending a streak of ten consecutive losses in a post–season series. Chicago lost the World Series in 1910, 1918, 1929, 1932, 1935, 1938, and 1945, the NLCS in 1984 and 1989, and the Division Series in 1998. The 2003 Cubs moved on to the National League Championship Series against the Marlins, who upset the Giants in the other Division Series. Managed by Jack McKeon, the Marlins were 91–71 in capturing the wild card.

OCTOBER 7   In the first game of the NLCS, the Marlins defeat the Cubs 9–8 in eleven innings before 39,567 at Wrigley Field. The Cubs took a 4–0 lead in the first inning, two of them on a Moises Alou homer, but the Marlins scored five times in the third off Carlos Zambrano. After Florida scored in the sixth, the Cubs tied with two in their half on a homer by Alex Gonzalez. The Marlins went ahead again 8–6 in the ninth, but again the Cubs evened the score with two tallies on a two–out home run by Sammy Sosa that landed on Waveland Avenue. The Marlins put it away in the eleventh on a pinch–hit home run by Mike Lowell off Mark Guthrie, and this time, the Cubs had no answer.

Both the Marlins and the Cubs had a starting shortstop named Alex Gonzalez.

OCTOBER 8   The Cubs bounce back from a heartbreaking loss in the first game of the Series by crushing the Marlins 12–3 before 39,562 at Wrigley Field to even the NLCS at one game apiece. The Cubs led 11–0 at the end of the fifth inning. Alex Gonzalez hit two homers, and Sammy Sosa and Aramis Ramirez added one each. Sosa's homer in the second off Brad Penny traveled 495 feet and banged off of a television camera booth about 100 feet beyond the center field wall. Kenny Lofton collected four hits. Randall Simon added three hits, including a bases–loaded single in the first that put the Cubs ahead 2–0. Mark Prior was the winning pitcher.

OCTOBER 10   The Cubs take game three of the NLCS with a 5–4 win over the Marlins in eleven innings in Miami. In the eleventh, Kenny Lofton hit a one–out single and scored on a pinch–hit triple by Doug Glanville. Randall Simon hit a two–run homer in the eighth to give the Cubs a 4–3 lead before the Marlins tied the contest in their half.

OCTOBER 11   The Cubs come within one game of the World Series with an 8–3 game four win over the Marlins in Miami. Aramis Ramirez paced the attack with two homers, a single, and six runs–batted–in. The first homer by Ramirez was a grand slam off

Dontrelle Willis in the first inning after Willis walked the bases loaded. The Cubs put the game away early with a 7–0 lead after three innings. The winning pitcher was Matt Clement.

OCTOBER 12   With the Marlins facing elimination, Josh Beckett pitches a two–hit shutout to beat the Cubs 4–0 in Miami in Game Five. He struck out 11 and held the Cubs hitless until Alex Gonzalez singled in the fifth inning. The game was scoreless until Carlos Zambrano allowed two runs in the Florida half of the fifth.

OCTOBER 14   The Marlins score eight runs in the eighth inning to defeat the Cubs 8–3 in game six of the NLCS before 39,577 at Wrigley Field. Chicago took a 3–0 with single runs in the first, sixth, and seventh innings. After Mark Mordecai flied out to start the eighth inning, the Cubs were just five outs away from their first World Series since 1945 with a three–run lead, no one on base, and Mark Prior on the mound working on a three–hit shutout. Since August 4, Prior had been 12–1 with an ERA of 1.44 including post–season. Things fell apart in a hurry, however. Juan Pierre started the Florida rally with a double. Luis Castillo, the next batter, hit a foul ball into the left field stands that a fan named Steve Bartman deflected away from Moises Alou. Alou slammed his glove in anger. Castillo walked, and by the time the inning was over, the Marlins had sent 12 batters to the plate and scored eight runs. Prior gave up five of the eight runs.

OCTOBER 15   The Cubs lose an opportunity to reach the World Series with a 9–6 loss to the Marlins in Game Seven before 39,574 at Wrigley Field. The Marlins scored three runs in the first inning on a homer by Miguel Cabrera off Kerry Wood, but the Cubs countered with three in their half, the last two on Wood's home run. Moises Alou put the Cubs ahead 5–3 with a two–run homer in the third. The Marlins zeroed in on Wood, however, scoring three in the fifth and one in the sixth, and then added two in the seventh off Kyle Farnsworth. The last run of the contest came on a Troy O'Leary pinch–hit home run in the seventh. It was Chicago's only hit during the last six innings.

NOVEMBER 25   The Cubs trade Hee Seop Choi and Mike Nannini to the Marlins for Derrek Lee.

DECEMBER 3   The Cubs sign LeTroy Hawkins, most recently with the Twins, as a free agent.

DECEMBER 16   The Cubs acquire Michael Barrett from the Athletics for a player to be named later.

Barrett was a pleasant surprise with 16 homers and a .287 batting average.

DECEMBER 18   The Cubs sign Todd Hollandsworth, most recently with the Marlins, as a free agent.

DECEMBER 23   The Cubs sign Todd Walker, most recently with the Red Sox, as a free agent. On the same day, Kenny Lofton signed a free agent contract with the Yankees.

2 0 0 4

Season in a Sentence

The Cubs finish above the .500 mark two years in a row for the first time in 32 years, but continue to torture their fans by blowing a 1½–game lead in the wild card race with seven losses in their last nine games.

In the wild card race, the Cubs were in third place three games behind.

Finish • Won • Lost • Pct • GB

Third   89   73   .549 16.0

Manager

Dusty Baker

Stats

Stats	Cubs	NL	Rank
Batting Avg:	.268	.263	6
On–Base Pct:	.328	.333	11
Slugging Pct:	.458	.423	1
Home Runs:	235		1
Stolen Bases:	66		11
ERA:	3.81	4.30	3
Fielding Avg:	789		7
Runs Scored:	665		2
Runs Allowed:			

Starting Lineup

Michael Barrett, c
Derrek Lee, 1b
Todd Walker, 2b
Aramis Ramirez, 3b
Ramon Martinez, ss
Moises Alou, lf
Corey Patterson, cf
Sammy Sosa, rf
Mark Grudzielanek, 2b
Jose Macias, rf–3b–2b
Nomar Garciaparra, ss
Todd Hollandsworth, rf

Pitchers

Greg Maddux, sp
Carlos Zambrano, sp
Matt Clement, sp
Kerry Wood, sp
Glendon Rusch, sp
Mark Prior, sp
LeTroy Hawkins, rp
Kyle Farnsworth, rp
Kent Mercker, rp

Attendance

3,170,154 (third in NL)

Club Leaders

Batting Avg:	Ramirez	.318
On–Base Pct:	Ramirez	.373
Slugging Pct:	Alou	.557
Home Runs:	Alou	39
RBI:	Alou	106
Runs:	Alou	106
Stolen Bases:	Patterson	32
Wins:	Maddux	16
	Zambrano	16
Strikeouts:	Clement	190
ERA:	Zambrano	2.75
Saves:	Hawkins	25

JANUARY 12   Doug Glanville signs a free agent contract with the Phillies.

FEBRUARY 18   The Cubs sign Greg Maddux, most recently with the Braves, as a free agent.

Maddux celebrated his return to the Cubs with a record of 16–11 and his 300th career victory.

FEBRUARY 26   A bit of Cubs history is exorcised as the ball Steve Bartman tried to catch in the sixth game of the 2003 National League Championship Series is blown–up at a tent outside Harry Caray's restaurant. The event was nationally televised on MSNBC.

The ball that came to symbolize the Cubs cursed history was reduced to a pile of thread by a Hollywood special effects expert. The stunt was designed by Oscar winner Michael Lantieri, who worked on Jurassic Park and Back to the Future. He used a combination of pressure, heat, and explosives in a bulletproof tank to destroy the ball. In its final hours, the ball was put on display and steak *and lobster were placed in front of it as a "last meal." The Bartman ball was purchased by Grant DePorter at an auction on for $113,824 on behalf of Harry Caray's Restaurant Group.*

APRIL 5   The Cubs defeat the Reds 7–4 in the season opener in Cincinnati. Corey Patterson hit a home run in his first at–bat of the year. Vice President Dick Cheney, one of the founders of the Emil Verban Memorial Society, threw out the first pitch.

The Cubs had a scare coming into Cincinnati when the team plane bounced on one wheel in a stiff wind before landing safely.

Twenty–four–year–old Corey Patterson is one of the future stars of the team, a gifted player who holds much promise for Cubs fans. His 24 homers and 32 stolen bases in 2004 proved his blend of power and speed.

APRIL 9   The Cubs need fifteen innings to beat the Braves 2–1 in Atlanta. Tom Goodwin drove in the winning run with a bases–loaded sacrifice fly. Todd Hollandsworth tied the score 1–1 with a solo homer with two out in the ninth off John Smoltz.

The Cubs hit 235 homers in 2004, breaking the previous mark of 212 set in 1998.

APRIL 11   Kerry Wood ties a Cubs record by striking out seven batters in a row during a 10–2 win over the Braves in Atlanta. Wood fanned a total of 11 batters in seven innings.

The Cubs were third in the National League in team earned run average in 2004 with a mark of 3.81. It was the club's highest finish since the 1963 Cubs were second in the league.

APRIL 12 | The Cubs lose 13–2 in the first game of the season at Wrigley Field before 40,483. In his first start at Wrigley as a Cub since 1992, Greg Maddux allowed six runs in 3⅓ innings. The temperature was 41 degrees with a 16 mile–per–hour wind blowing in from Lake Michigan.

Bill Murray threw out the first ceremonial first pitch and lobbed the ball over the backstop.

APRIL 16 | Sammy Sosa and Moises Alou hit back–to–back homers in the ninth inning to beat the Reds 11–10 at Wrigley Field. The Cubs trailed 9–4 in the sixth inning and 10–7 in the eighth before mounting a comeback.

APRIL 18 | Sammy Sosa becomes the all–time career home run leader in Cubs history, passing Ernie Banks, but the Cubs lose 11–10 to the Reds in ten innings. The homers were number 513 and 514 as a Cub, and 542 and 543 in his career.

During the wild afternoon, both managers were ejected, and umpire Chuck Meriweather left the game with food poisoning.

APRIL 19 | Derrek Lee hits a grand slam off Ryan Wagner of the Reds in the seventh inning of an 8–1 win at Wrigley Field.

APRIL 21 | The Cubs thrash the Pirates 12–1 in Pittsburgh. Corey Patterson collected five hits, including a double, in six at–bats.

APRIL 25 | Mark Clement (eight innings) and Joe Borowski (one inning) combine on a two–hitter to defeat the Mets 4–1 at Wrigley Field. Clement struck out 13 batters and carried a no–hitter into seventh inning before Karim Garcia homered. The other hit was a single by Eric Valent off Clement.

APRIL 28 | The Cubs survive three home runs by Steve Finley to defeat the Diamondbacks 4–3 in Phoenix. Alex Gonzalez broke a 3–3 tie with a homer in the ninth inning.

MAY 6 | Derrek Lee collects five hits, including a home run, in five at–bats during an 11–3 win over the Diamondbacks at Wrigley Field.

MAY 7 | Carlos Zambrano pitches a two–hitter to defeat the Rockies 11–0 at Wrigley Field. The only Colorado hits were singles by Aaron Miles and Matt Holliday.

Zambrano was 16–8 with a 2.75 ERA in 2004.

MAY 14 | Playing at Petco Park in San Diego for the first time, the Cubs defeat the Padres 6–1.

Two days later in San Diego, Sammy Sosa sneezed twice, which brought on back spasms and caused a sprained ligament. Sosa didn't play again until June 18.

MAY 19 | Moises Alou crosses up his father's strategy by hitting a walk–off homer in the tenth inning to defeat the Giants 4–3 at Wrigley Field. With one out, Giants manager Felipe Alou pulled lefty Jason Christiansen and brought in right–hander Jim Brower to face his son. Moises then lined a 3–2 pitch into the bleachers for the win.

MAY 28	Michael Barrett hits a pinch–hit grand slam home run off Mike Johnston of the Pirates in the seventh inning to give the Cubs a 5–4 in the first game of a double–header at PNC Park, but Pittsburgh rallies with five runs in the ninth to win 9–5. The game ended on a grand slam by Rob Makowiak. The Cubs also lost the second tilt on a walk–off homer by Craig Wilson in the tenth inning that lifted the Pirates to a 5–4 victory.
MAY 30	The Cubs break a five–game losing streak by walloping the Pirates 12–1 in Pittsburgh.
JUNE 10	The Cubs score ten runs in the fourth inning and defeat the Cardinals 12–3 at Wrigley Field. The Cubs tied a club record by collecting 11 hits in the inning, nine of which were in succession.
JUNE 11	The Cubs play the Angels during the regular season for the first time and lose 3–2 in Anaheim.
JUNE 13	The Cubs defeat the Angels 6–5 in a fifteen–inning marathon in Anaheim. Todd Walker drove in the winning run with a single. Derrek Lee reached base seven times in seven plate appearances on a home run, a double, three singles, and two walks.
JUNE 18	The Cubs play the Athletics for the first time during the regular season and lose 2–1 at Wrigley Field.
JUNE 19	The Cubs score two runs in the ninth inning on Michael Barrett's walk–off double to defeat the Athletics 4–3 at Wrigley Field.
JULY 1	Sammy Sosa hits a walk–off homer in the tenth inning to defeat the Astros 5–4 at Wrigley Field.
JULY 21	Luis Pujols collects five hits, including three home runs and a double, to lead the Cardinals to an 11–8 win over the Cubs at Wrigley Field. It was a devastating loss for the Cubs, who led 8–2 at the end of the fifth inning. The Cardinals swept the brief two–game series, and the frustration on the part of the Cubs was evident. Carlos Zambrano was suspended for five games because he threw at Jim Edmonds twice on July 20, and LaTroy Hawkins was suspended for three games after an argument with umpire Tim Tschida on July 21. *With the defeat, the Cubs fell ten games behind the division–leading Cardinals with a record of 49–44. Chicago was still very much in the wild card chase, however, three games back of the Giants.*
JULY 22	Greg Maddux wins the 298th game of his career in a 13–2 thrashing of the Reds at Wrigley Field. Aramis Ramirez belted a grand slam in the sixth inning off Mark Wagner. *Over a six–week period in June and July, three chunks of concrete fell from the upper deck. One piece just missed hitting a five–year–old boy on July 16. Mayor Richard Daley threatened to close down sections of the ballpark if the Cubs failed to adequately address the problem before their July 30 home game against the Phillies. A heavy mesh netting was placed under the upper deck to protect fans.*

JULY 23   The Cubs play at Citizens Bank Park in Philadelphia for the first time, and beat the
            Phillies 5–1.

JULY 25   Eric Milton of the Phillies pitches eight scoreless innings in Philadelphia before
            Michael Barrett bloops as double leading off the ninth. The Cubs went on to tie the
            game 2–2, but lost 3–2 when the Phillies scored in their half of the ninth.

JULY 27   Greg Maddux wins the 299th game of his career, defeating the Brewers 4–1 in
            Milwaukee.

JULY 30   Aramis Ramirez hits three homers during a 10–7 win over the Phillies at Wrigley
            Field. Ramirez hit solo homers off Eric Milton in the second and sixth innings and
            another bases–loaded shot against Roberto Hernandez in the seventh.

In his first full season with
the Cubs, Amaris Ramirez
put together an outstand-
ing season. Only 26 years
old, Ramirez could be a fixture at third base for years
to come.

JULY 31   In a complicated, blockbuster trade involving four teams, the Cubs send Alex
            Gonzalez, Francis Beltran, and Brendan Harris to the Expos and Justin Jones to
            the Twins and receive Nomar Garciaparra and Matt Murton from the Red Sox.

            Garciaparra hit .297 for the Cubs in 2004 in only 43 games due to injuries.

AUGUST 1   In an electric atmosphere at Wrigley Field, Greg Maddux bids for his 300th career win and Nomar Garciaparra makes his debut as a Cub. Maddux earned a no decision, but the Cubs won 6–3 over the Phillies. Garciaparra had an RBI–single in four at–bats.

Garciaparra wore number 8 in his first game with the Cubs. Before his second contest with his new club, Nomar swapped numbers with Michael Barrett giving him the number 5 he wore as a member of the Red Sox.

AUGUST 7   Greg Maddux wins the 300th game of his career with an 8–4 decision over the Giants in San Francisco. Maddux gave up four runs in five–plus innings for the victory.

AUGUST 10   The Cubs hit five homers, but lose 8–6 to the Padres at Wrigley Field. Derrick Lee hit two home runs and Sammy Sosa, Moises Alou, and Nomar Garciaparra hit one each.

AUGUST 14   Kerry Wood hits a home run and pitches eight shutout innings to lead the Cubs to a 2–0 win over the Dodgers at Wrigley Field.

AUGUST 18   Corey Patterson hits a two–run homer in the eleventh inning to lift the Cubs to a 7–5 win over the Brewers in Milwaukee.

AUGUST 20   The Cubs hit six homers and defeat the Astros 9–2 in Houston. Mark Grudzielanek hit two home runs, and Sammy Sosa, Nomar Garciaparra, Moises Alou, and Corey Patterson added one each.

AUGUST 24   Moises Alou drives in six runs with a pair of homers during a 13–4 win over the Brewers at Wrigley Field. Derrick Lee hit a grand slam in the second inning off Chris Capuano.

AUGUST 25   Corey Patterson hits a two–run, walk–off homer in the ninth to beat the Brewers 4–2 at Wrigley Field.

AUGUST 27   After giving up six ninth–inning runs in a 15–7 loss to the Astros at Wrigley Field, Kyle Farnsworth is injured kicking an electric fan in the runway on the way to the clubhouse. Farnsworth sprained and bruised his right knee and ended up on the disabled list.

SEPTEMBER 1   The Cubs play the Expos in Montreal for the last time and win 2–1 in eleven innings.

SEPTEMBER 2   The game between the Cubs and Marlins on September 3 in Miami is postponed because of the approach of Hurricane Frances toward Florida's East Coast. The games on September 4 and 5 were also postponed by the hurricane.

SEPTEMBER 6   The Cubs hit home runs and defeat the Expos 9–1 at Wrigley Field. Aramis Ramirez hit two homers, and Derrek Lee, Mark Grudzielanek, and Michael Barrett added one each. Because of a scheduled off day and the three postponements in Miami due to Hurricane Frances, it was the Cubs first game in five days.

In September 2004, the Cubs filed suit against former the HARTFORD COURANT newspaper carrier Mark Guthrie to get back $301,000 in pay that was intended *to go to former pitcher Mark Guthrie. The Cubs and the* COURANT *are owned by the Tribune Company, which deposited the checks in the carrier's account in October 2003 that were intended for the pitcher.*

SEPTEMBER 14   Corey Patterson hits a two–run homer in the eighth inning to tie the score and a walk–off homer in the twelfth to beat the Pirates 3–2 at Wrigley Field.

SEPTEMBER 15   Sammy Sosa hits two home runs, the second one a grand slam in the eighth inning off Mark Corey, during a 13–5 win over the Pirates at Wrigley Field. In the first inning, Derrek Lee, Sosa, and Michael Barrett hit back–to–back–to–back homers against Oliver Perez. Neifi Perez also homered for the Cubs.

SEPTEMBER 16   Aramis Ramirez hits three homers and drives in all five Cubs runs during a 5–4 win over the Reds in Cincinnati. Ramirez also hit a double, tying the club record for most total bases in a game with 14. He hit a two–run home runs of Josh Hancock in the first inning, and a solo shot off Hancock in the fifth. With Cincinnati leading 4–3, Ramirez hit a game–winning two–run homer in the seventh against Ryan Wagner.

Ramirez hit .318 with 36 homers and 103 RBIs in 2004. Moises Alou also had a big year, clubbing 39 homers with 106 runs–batted–in and a .293 batting average.

SEPTEMBER 22   Behind the pitching of Carlos Zambrano (7 ⅓ innings), Kent Mercker (⅔ of an inning), and Mike Remlinger (one inning), the Cubs beat the Pirates 1–0 in Pittsburgh. Zambrano also drove in the lone run of the game on a bases–loaded walk in the fifth inning. Sammy Sosa made a game–saving diving catch in right field with the bases loaded and two out in the eighth.

SEPTEMBER 23   The Cubs defeat the Pirates 6–3 in Pittsburgh to take a one–half game lead in the wild card race over the Giants with ten games left on the schedule.

SEPTEMBER 25   The Cubs suffer a crushing eleven–inning 4–3 loss to the Mets in New York. The Cubs led 3–0 with two Mets on base, two out in the ninth, and two strikes on rookie
Victor Diaz with LeTroy Hawkins pitching. Diaz hit a three–run homer to tie the score. It was only his second big league home run. With Kent Mercker on the mound for the Cubs, the Mets won the game on the first major league homer by Craig Brazell.

The Cubs went into the game having won 13 of their previous 16 games and held a 1 ½ game lead over the Giants in the wild card race. The September 25 loss proved to be the beginning of the end of the Cubs hopes for the post–season.

SEPTEMBER 29   For the second time in a span of five days, LeTroy Hawkins is one strike from a save, but the Cubs wind up losing in extra innings. The Cubs led the Reds 2–1 at Wrigley Field with two out in the ninth and no one base. Hawkins allowed a triple to D'Angelo Jiminez and a two–strike double to Austin Kearns, however, to tie the game. Kearns hit a two–run homer in the twelfth to lift Cincinnati to a 4–2 win. Later in the day, both the Giants and Astros won to drop the Cubs out of first place in the wild card race.

SEPTEMBER 30   For the third time in six days, the Cubs lose an extra inning game, dropping a 2–1, eleven–inning decision to the Reds at Wrigley Field. The Cubs wasted a terrific pitching performance by Mark Prior, who struck out 16 batters in nine innings.

Entering the final three games of the season, the Cubs were in third place in the wild card race, one game behind both the Giants and the Astros.

OCTOBER 2   The Cubs are eliminated from the wild card race with an 8–6 loss to the Braves at Wrigley Field. The Cubs led 6–2 at the end of the fifth inning before the bullpen suffered another meltdown.

OCTOBER 30   In the final day of the season, the Cubs win 10–8 over the Braves at Wrigley Field. Sammy Sosa arrived only seventy minutes before the start of the contest and left fifteen minutes after the first pitch without putting a uniform. Sosa was fined $87,400 by the Cubs for the unexcused absence.

The Cubs never recovered from the crushing loss to the Mets on September 25, losing seven of their last nine games. Close games were a problem all year, as the Cubs had a record of only 19–30 in one–run contests. TV broadcaster Steve Stone was a source of contention during the final weeks, as the front office, Dusty Baker and his coaching staff, and the players were angry because of some of Stone's pointed comments during the season concerning the club's failure to return to the post–season. On the bright side, it was the first time the Cubs had a winning record in consecutive seasons since the club finished above .500 six years in a row from 1967 through 1972. The 2003 and 2004 seasons were the first time the Cubs won at least 88 games in back–to–back years since 1937 and 1938. The combined winning percentage of .546 in 2003 and 2004 was the best over a two–year period since the club had a percentage of .586 in 1945 and 1946. The Cubs also drew over 3,000,000 fans into Wrigley Field for the first time in history with a total of 3,170,154.

NOVEMBER 9   Seven days after George Bush win a second term in the Presidential election against John Kerry, the Cubs sign Bob Brenly as a television analyst to replace Steve Stone, who resigned because the club was unhappy with some of his critical comments about the club.

In early November, a groundskeeper found a rusted hollowed–out shell of a grenade in the right field turf of Wrigley Field. Police bomb investigators were called to examine the device, which they found to be empty and harmless. "It's a dud, just like the Cubs were," said police spokesman Pat Camden. Investigators said there was no way to determine how the device ended up on the field.

NOVEMBER 19   A week after hiring Bob Brenly for the WGN–TV broadcast team, the Cubs hire Len Kasper as the play–by–play voice, replacing Chip Caray.

Ex–Cubs in the World Series

The Cubs haven't been to the World Series since 1945, but that hasn't stopped ex–Cubs from playing in the Fall Classic. The following is a list of former Cubs players on the World Series eligibility rosters of the World Series clubs since 1945.

Former Cubs Players in the World Series Since 1945:

1946 Red Sox– Rip Russell

1947 Dodgers– Hugh Casey, Eddie Stanky

1947 Yankees– Lonny Frey

1948 Braves– Marv Rickert, Eddie Stanky

1950 Phillies– Bill Nicholson, Eddie Waitkus

1951 Giants– Eddie Stanky

1952 Dodgers– Andy Pafko, Rube Walker, Ben Wade

1953 Dodgers– Russ Meyer, Rube Walker, Ben Wade

1955 Dodgers– Russ Meyer, Rube Walker

1956 Dodgers– Randy Jackson, Rube Walker

1957 Braves– Andy Pafko, Carl Sawatski

1958 Braves– Andy Pafko, Bob Rush, Casey Wise

1959 Dodgers– Johnny Klippstein

1959 White Sox– Turk Lown

1960 Pirates– Gene Baker, Smoky Burgess, Don Hoak

1960 Yankees– Dale Long

1961 Reds– Jim Brosnan, Dick Gernert, Bill Henry

1962 Yankees– Dale Long

1963 Dodgers– Lee Walls

1964 Cardinals– Lou Brock, Barney Schultz

1965 Dodgers– Jim Brewer

1965 Twins– Jerry Kindall, Johnny Klippstein

1966 Dodgers– Jim Brewer, Wes Covington

1966 Orioles– Moe Drabowsky, Vic Roznovsky

1967 Cardinals– Lou Brock

1968 Cardinals– Lou Brock

1969 Mets– Don Cardwell, Cal Koonce

1970 Orioles– Moe Drabowsky

1970 Reds– Ty Cline, Jimmy Stewart

1971 Pirates– Bob Miller

1972 Athletics– Ken Holtzman

1972 Reds– Bill Plummer

1973 Athletics– Pat Bourque, Ken Holtzman

1974 Athletics– Ken Holtzman, Bill North

1974 Dodgers– Jim Brewer

1975 Reds– Fred Norman, Bill Plummer

1976 Reds– Fred Norman, Bill Plummer

1976 Yankees– Oscar Gamble, Elrod Hendricks, Ken Holtzman

1977 Dodgers– Mike Garman, Burt Hooton, Rick Monday

1977 Yankees– Ken Holtzman

1978 Dodgers– Burt Hooton, Rick Monday, Bill North

1979 Orioles– Steve Stone

1979 Pirates– Matt Alexander, Bill Madlock, Dave Roberts

1980 Phillies– Manny Trillo

1980 Royals– Jose Cardenal, Larry Gura, Pete LaCock

1981 Dodgers– Burt Hooton, Rick Monday

1981 Yankees– Barry Foote, Oscar Gamble, Dave LaRoche, Bobby Murcer, Rick Reuschel

1982 Cardinals– Bruce Sutter

1983 Phillies– Ivan DeJesus

1984 Padres– Craig Lefferts, Carmelo Martinez, Champ Summers

1984 Tigers– Willie Hernandez, Milt Wilcox

1985 Cardinals– Bill Campbell, Ivan DeJesus

1986 Red Sox– Bill Buckner

1987 Cardinals– Steve Lake

1987 Twins– Joe Niekro

1988 Athletics– Dennis Eckersley, Ron Hassey

1988 Dodgers– Jay Howell

1989 Athletics– Dennis Eckersley, Ron Hassey

1989 Giants– Craig Lefferts, Rick Reuschel

1990 Athletics– Dennis Eckersley, Ron Hassey, Scott Sanderson

1990 Reds– Billy Hatcher, Luis Quinones

1992 Blue Jays– Joe Carter

1992 Braves– Damon Berryhill

1993 Blue Jays– Joe Carter

1993 Phillies– Danny Jackson, Mitch Williams

1995 Braves– Greg Maddux, Dwight Smith

1996 Braves– Mike Bielecki, Greg Maddux

1996 Yankees– Joe Girardi

1997 Indians– Paul Assenmacher

1998 Padres– Randy Myers

1998 Yankees– Joe Girardi

1999 Braves– Jose Hernandez, Greg Maddux, Terry Mulholland

1999 Yankees– Joe Girardi

2000 Mets– Matt Franco, Todd Pratt, Turk Wendell, Todd Zeile

2000 Yankees– Glenallen Hill, Jose Vizcaino

2001 Diamondbacks– Miguel Batista, Luis Gonzalez, Mark Grace, Mike Morgan

2002 Angels– Jose Molina

2002 Giants– Benito Santiago, Tim Worrell

2003 Marlins– Lenny Harris

2004 Cardinals– Julian Tavarez, Tony Womack

2004 Red Sox– Mark Bellhorn, Bill Mueller

Former Cubs Players Who Managed in the World Series Since 1945

1957 Braves– Fred Haney

1958 Braves– Fred Haney

1962 Giants– Al Dark

1986 Mets– Dave Johnson

1988 Athletics– Tony LaRussa

1989 Athletics– Tony LaRussa

1990 Athletics– Tony LaRussa

2004 Red Sox– Terry Francona

2004 Cardinals– Tony LaRussa

2005

JANUARY 4   In his third year on the ballot, Ryne Sandberg is elected into the Hall of Fame, receiving 393 votes from the Baseball Writers' Association of America. He finished second in the balloting to Wade Boggs, earning 76.2% of the votes cast.

Sandberg played 15 years with the Cubs, winning nine Gold Gloves, seven Silver Sluggers, and an NL MVP Award (in 1984). His 277 home runs were the most by a second baseman until Jeff Kent broke the record in 2004. He finished his career with a lifetime .285 batting average, 282 home runs, and 1,062 RBIs, but he was best known for his brilliant defense. His streak of 123 games without an error remains a major league record, and he put together twelve streaks of at least 40 games without an error. He also was known for heady play and quiet leadership and was a key part of the division–winning teams in 1984 and 1989.

Former Cub reliever Bruce Sutter finished third in the balloting with 344 votes (66.7%), too few for election. A minimum of 75% is necessary for election. Andre Dawson, a Cubs outfielder from 1987 through 1992, finished sixth in the voting with 270 votes (52.3%), and Lee Smith, an outstanding Cubs reliever, received 200 votes (38.8%).

JANUARY 10   Left–handed reliever Stephen Randolph is acquired from the Diamondbacks for a player to be named later.

FEBRUARY 2   The Cubs send Sammy Sosa and cash to the Orioles for Jerry Hairston, Jr., Mike Fontenot, and Dave Crouthers.

The front office soured on the one–time franchise player after an off–year in 2004 in which he walked out on the club during the final day of the season. The fans spent much of the season booing Sosa, who was no longer seen as the cuddly figure who clubbed 60 homers a season, and in the view of many Cubs followers, was a narcissistic individual who cared little about the success of the team. Whispers about the possibility of steroid use and his corked bat incident in 2003 also contributed to the change in attitude toward Sosa.

FEBRUARY 9   The Cubs trade Kyle Farnsworth to the Detroit Tigers for pitcher Roberto Novoa, infielder Scott Moore, and outfielder Clarence "Bo" Flowers.

FEBRUARY 23   Plans are announced to retire Ryne Sandberg's number during the 2005 season. Sandberg's No. 23 will be the fourth retired number in club history. Ron Santo (10), Ernie Banks (14), and Billy Williams (29) have also received the honor.

MARCH 3   Plans to expand Wrigley Field are announced after four years of discussion with city officials and residents of the community. The plan calls for adding 1,790 seats to the bleacher section, an expanded parking lot, and a restaurant. Construction will begin after the 2005 season.

CUBS
By the
Numbers

Cubs All-Time Offensive Leaders Since 1876

	Games			Runs			Doubles	
1	Ernie Banks	2,528	1	Cap Anson	1,719	1	Cap Anson	528
2	Cap Anson	2,276	2	Jimmy Ryan	1,410	2	Mark Grace	456
3	Billy Williams	2,213	3	Ryne Sandberg	1,316	3	Ernie Banks	407
4	Ryne Sandberg	2,151	4	Billy Williams	1,306	4	Ryne Sandberg	403
5	Ron Santo	2,126	5	Ernie Banks	1,305	5	Billy Williams	402
6	Phil Cavaretta	1,953	6	Sammy Sosa	1,245	6	Gabby Hartnett	391
7	Stan Hack	1,938	7	Stan Hack	1,239	7	Stan Hack	363
8	Gabby Hartnett	1,926	8	Ron Santo	1,109	8	Jimmy Ryan	362
9	Mark Grace	1,910	9	Mark Grace	1,057	9	Ron Santo	353
10	Sammy Sosa	1,811	10	Phil Cavaretta	968	10	Billy Herman	346
11	Jimmy Ryan	1,660	11	Bill Dahlen	896	11	Phil Cavaretta	341
12	Don Kessinger	1,648	12	Billy Herman	875	12	Sammy Sosa	296
13	Wildfire Schulte	1,564	13	Gabby Hartnett	847	13	Charlie Grimm	270
14	Joe Tinker	1,536	14	Wildfire Schulte	827	14	Wildfire Schulte	254
15	Johnny Evers	1,409	15	Frank Chance	794	15	Bill Nicholson	245
16	Bill Nicholson	1,349	16	George Gore	772	16	Riggs Stephenson	237
17	Billy Herman	1,344	17	Don Kessinger	769	17	Tom Burns	236
18	Charlie Grimm	1,334	18	Woody English	747	18	Bill Buckner	235
19	Frank Chance	1,274	19	Ned Williamson	744	19	Shawon Dunston	226
20	Shawon Dunston	1,254	20	Fred Pfeffer	742	20	Joe Tinker	221
				Johnny Evers	742			

	At-Bats			Hits			Triples	
1	Ernie Banks	9,421	1	Cap Anson	3,055	1	Jimmy Ryan	142
2	Cap Anson	9,173	2	Ernie Banks	2,583	2	Cap Anson	124
3	Billy Williams	8,479	3	Billy Williams	2,510	3	Wildfire Schulte	117
4	Ryne Sandberg	8,379	4	Ryne Sandberg	2,385	4	Bill Dahlen	106
5	Ron Santo	7,768	5	Mark Grace	2,201	5	Phil Cavaretta	99
6	Stan Hack	7,278	6	Stan Hack	2,193	6	Joe Tinker	93
7	Mark Grace	7,156	7	Ron Santo	2,171	7	Ernie Banks	90
8	Sammy Sosa	6,990	8	Jimmy Ryan	2,126	8	Billy Williams	87
9	Jimmy Ryan	6,818	9	Sammy Sosa	1,985	9	Stan Hack	81
10	Phil Cavaretta	6,592	10	Phil Cavaretta	1,927	10	Ned Williamson	80
11	Don Kessinger	6,355	11	Gabby Hartnett	1,867		Bill Lange	80
12	Gabby Hartnett	6,282	12	Billy Herman	1,710		Bill Nicholson	80
13	Wildfire Schulte	5,837	13	Don Kessinger	1,619	13	Frank Chance	79
14	Joe Tinker	5,547	14	Wildfire Schulte	1,590	14	Ryne Sandberg	76
15	Billy Herman	5,532	15	Charlie Grimm	1,454	15	Fred Pfeffer	72
16	Glenn Beckert	5,020	16	Joe Tinker	1,436	16	Don Kessinger	71
17	Charlie Grimm	4,917	17	Glenn Beckert	1,423	17	Tom Burns	69
18	Tom Burns	4,881	18	Johnny Evers	1,340		Billy Herman	69
19	Johnny Evers	4,858	19	Tom Burns	1,325	19	Kiki Cuyler	66
20	Bill Nicholson	4,857	20	Bill Nicholson	1,323		Ron Santo	66

Home Runs

1	Sammy Sosa	545
2	Ernie Banks	512
3	Billy Williams	392
4	Ron Santo	337
5	Ryne Sandberg	282
6	Gabby Hartnett	231
7	Bill Nicholson	205
8	Hank Sauer	198
9	Hack Wilson	190
10	Andre Dawson	174
11	Mark Grace	148
12	Leon Durham	138
13	Andy Pafko	126
14	Jody Davis	122
15	Shawon Dunston	107
16	Rick Monday	106
17	Keith Moreland	100
18	Jimmy Ryan	99
19	Jim Hickman	97
20	Cap Anson	96

Walks

1	Stan Hack	1,092
2	Ron Santo	1,071
3	Cap Anson	952
4	Mark Grace	946
5	Billy Williams	911
6	Sammy Sosa	798
7	Phil Cavaretta	794
8	Ernie Banks	763
9	Ryne Sandberg	761
10	Bill Nicholson	696
11	Gabby Hartnett	691
12	Jimmy Ryan	683
13	Jimmy Sheckard	629
14	Johnny Evers	556
15	Don Kessinger	550
16	Frank Chance	546
17	Woody English	498
18	Bill Dahlen	472
19	Billy Herman	470
20	Ned Williamson	465

Stolen Bases

1	Frank Chance	400
2	Bill Lange	399
3	Jimmy Ryan	369
4	Ryne Sandberg	344
5	Joe Tinker	304
6	Walt Wilmot	292
7	Johnny Evers	291
8	Bill Dahlen	285
9	Fred Pfeffer	263
10	Cap Anson	247
11	Wildfire Schulte	214
12	Jimmy Slagle	198
13	Sammy Sosa	181
14	Bill Everett	179
15	Shawon Dunston	175
16	Stan Hack	165
17	Jimmy Sheckard	163
18	Tom Burns	161
	Kiki Cuyler	161
20	Solly Hofman	154

Runs-Batted-In

1	Cap Anson	1,879
2	Ernie Banks	1,636
3	Sammy Sosa	1,414
4	Billy Williams	1,353
5	Ron Santo	1,290
6	Gabby Hartnett	1,153
7	Ryne Sandberg	1,061
8	Mark Grace	1,004
9	Jimmy Ryan	914
10	Phil Cavaretta	896
11	Bill Nicholson	833
12	Hack Wilson	768
13	Wildfire Schulte	712
14	Charlie Grimm	697
15	Tom Burns	679
16	Fred Pfeffer	677
17	Joe Tinker	670
18	Stan Hack	642
19	Ned Williamson	622
20	Kiki Cuyler	602

Strikeouts

1	Sammy Sosa	1,815
2	Ron Santo	1,273
3	Ryne Sandberg	1,259
4	Ernie Banks	1,236
5	Billy Williams	934
6	Shawon Dunston	770
7	Bill Nicholson	684
8	Gabby Hartnett	683
9	Jody Davis	647
10	Don Kessinger	629
11	Leon Durham	609
12	Phil Cavaretta	585
13	Mark Grace	561
14	Rick Monday	540
15	Randy Hundley	519
16	Ned Williamson	482
17	Woody English	470
18	Stan Hack	466
19	Hack Wilson	461
20	Hank Sauer	454

Batting Average

(minimum 2000 plate appearances)

1	Cap Anson	.339
2	Riggs Stephenson	.336
3	Bill Lange	.330
4	Kiki Cuyler	.325
5	Bill Everett	.323
6	Hack Wilson	.322
7	King Kelly	.316
8	George Gore	.315
9	Jimmy Ryan	.312
10	Frank Demaree	.309
11	Billy Herman	.309
12	Mark Grace	.308
13	Charlie Hollocher	.304
14	Heinie Zimmerman	.304
15	Stan Hack	.301
16	Bill Buckner	.300
17	Bill Dahlen	.299
18	Gabby Hartnett	.297
19	Frank Chance	297
20	Jose Cardenal	.296

On-Base Percentage		Slugging Percentage	
(minimum 2000 plate appearances)		(minimum 2000 plate appearances)	
1 Hack Wilson	.412	1 Hack Wilson	.590
2 Riggs Stepenson.	408	2 Sammy Sosa	.545
3 Bill Lange	.401	3 Hank Sauer	.512
4 Cap Anson	.395	4 Andre Dawson	.507
5 Stan Hack	.394	5 Billy Williams	.503
6 Frank Chance	.394	6 Ernie Banks	.500
7 Kiki Cuyler	.391	7 Gabby Hartnett	.490
8 Mark Grace	.386	8 Kiki Cuyler	.485
9 George Gore	.386	9 Leon Durham	.484
10 Bill Dahlen	.384	10 Ron Santo	.472
11 Jimmy Ryan	.376	11 Bill Nicholson	.471
12 Jimmy Sheckard	.374	12 Riggs Stpehenson	.469
13 Phil Cavaretta	.371	13 Andy Pafko	.468
14 Bill Everett	.371	14 Jim Hickman	.467
15 Dom Dallesandro	.370	15 Rick Monday	.460
16 Gabby Hartnett	.370	16 Bill Lange	.459
17 Charlie Hollocher	.370	17 George Altman	.458
18 Bill Nicholson	.368	18 King Kelly	.453
19 Woody English	.368	19 Walt Moryn	.452
20 King Kelly	.367	20 Ryne Sandberg	.452

The Cubs pennant–winning outfield of 1935, left to right: Augie Galan, Fred Lindstrom, Frank Demaree, and Chuck Klein

Cubs All-Time Pitching Leaders Since 1876

	Wins			Winning Percentage			Games Started	
1	Charlie Root	201		(minimum 100 decisions)		1	Ferguson Jenkins	347
2	Three Finger Brown	188	1	John Clarkson	.706	2	Rick Reuschel	343
3	Bill Hutchison	182	2	Three Finger Brown	.689	3	Bill Hutchison	339
4	Larry Corcoran	175	3	Ed Reulbach	.677		Charlie Root	339
5	Freguson Jenkins	167	4	Larry Corcoran	.673	5	Bill Lee	296
6	Clark Griffith	152	5	Orval Overall	.662	6	Bob Rush	292
	Guy Bush	152	6	Jack Pfeister	.633	7	Hippo Vaughn	270
8	Hippo Vaughn	151	7	Fred Goldsmith	.629	8	Larry Corcoran	262
9	Bill Lee	139	8	Carl Lundgren	.623	9	Clark Griffith	252
10	John Clarkson	137	9	Clark Griffith	.613		Guy Bush	252
11	Ed Reulbach	136	10	Grover Alexander	.607	11	Three Finger Brown	241
12	Rick Reuschel	135	11	Lon Warneke	.602		Greg Maddux	241
13	Grover Alexander	128	12	Guy Bush	.601	13	Dick Ellsworth	236
14	Claude Passeau	124	13	Larry Cheney	.598	14	Claude Passeau	234
15	Pat Malone	115	14	Pat Malone	.593	15	Grover Alexander	223
16	Greg Maddux	111	15	Hippo Vaughn	.590	16	Rick Reuschel	216
17	Bob Rush	110	16	Nixey Callahan	.584	17	Bill Hands	213
18	Jack Taylor	109	17	Claude Passeau	.569	18	Ken Holtzman	209
	Lon Warneke	109	18	Greg Maddux	.563	19	Pat Malone	200
20	Fred Goldsmith	107	19	Charlie Root	.563	20	John Clarkson	1970
			20	Hank Wyse	.561			

	Losses			Games			Complete Games	
1	Bill Hutchison	158	1	Charlie Root	605	1	Bill Hutchison	317
2	Charlie Root	156	2	Lee Smith	458	2	Larry Corcoran	252
3	Bob Rush	140	3	Don Elston	449	3	Clark Griffith	240
4	Ferguson Jenkins	132	4	Guy Bush	428	4	Three Finger Brown	206
5	Rick Reuschel	127	5	Ferguson Jenkins	401	5	Jack Taylor	188
6	Bill Lee	123	6	Bill Hutchison	367	6	John Clarkson	186
7	Dick Ellsworth	110	7	Bill Lee	364	7	Hippo Vaughn	177
8	Hippo Vaughn	105	8	Rick Reuschel	358		Charlie Root	177
9	Guy Bush	101	9	Three Finger Brown	346	9	Fred Goldsmith	164
10	Clark Griffith	96	10	Kyle Farnsworth	343	10	Grover Alexander	159
11	Claude Passeau	94	11	Bob Rush	339	11	Ferguson Jenkins	154
12	Sheriff Blake	92	12	Willie Hernandez	323	12	Bill Lee	153
13	Jack Taylor	90	13	Hippo Vaughn	305	13	Ed Reulbach	149
14	Bill Hands	86	14	Bruce Sutter	300	14	Claude Passeau	143
	Greg Maddux	86	15	Claude Passeau	292	15	Guy Bush	127
16	Larry Corcoran	85	16	Ed Reulbach	281	16	Carl Lundgren	125
	Three Finger Brown	85	17	Paul Assenmacher	279	17	Lon Warneke	122
18	Larry French	84	18	Bill Hands	276	18	Nixey Callahan	116
19	Grover Alexander	83	19	Larry French	272	19	Terry Larkin	113
20	Ken Holtzman	81	20	Glen Hobbie	271	20	Bob Rush	112

Shutouts

1	Three Finger Brown	49
2	Hippo Vaughn	35
3	Ed Reulbach	31
4	Ferguson Jenkins	29
5	Orval Overall	28
6	Bill Lee	25
7	Grover Alexander	24
8	Larry Corcoran	22
	Claude Passeau	22
10	Bill Hutchison	21
	Charlie Root	21
	Larry French	21
13	Carl Lundgren	19
14	Jack Pfeister	17
	Lon Warneke	17
	Rick Reuschel	17
17	Fred Goldsmith	16
	Pat Malone	16
19	John Clarkson	15
	Ken Holtzman	15

Walks

1	Bill Hutchison	1,109
2	Charlie Root	871
3	Guy Bush	734
4	Bob Rush	725
5	Bill Lee	704
6	Sheriff Blake	688
7	Ed Reulbach	650
8	Rick Reuschel	640
9	Hippo Vaughn	621
10	Ferguson Jenkins	600
11	Pat Malone	577
12	Ken Holtzman	530
13	Johnny Schmitz	523
14	Bill Bonham	521
15	Clark Griffith	517
16	Greg Maddux	488
17	Rick Sutcliffe	481
18	Glen Hobbie	480
19	Carl Lundgren	476
20	Claude Passeau	474

Strikeouts/9 Innings

(minimum 1,000 innings pitched)

1	Kerry Wood	10.22
2	Ferguson Jenkins	6.86
3	Rick Sutcliffe	6.46
4	Bill Bonham	6.33
5	Ken Holtzman	6.15
6	Greg Maddux	5.92
7	Orval Overall	5.78
8	Rick Reuschel	5.37
9	Bill Hands	5.18
10	Dick Ellsworth	5.05
11	John Clarkson	4.99
12	Glen Hobbie	4.90
13	Pal Malone	4.84
14	Hippo Vaughn	4.62
15	Bob Rush	4.54
16	Ray Burris	4.46
17	Larry Cheney	4.34
18	Jack Pfeister	4.22
19	Larry Corcoran	4.18
20	Johnny Lavender	4.13

Innings Pitched

1	Charlie Root	3,137.1
2	Bill Hutchison	3,021.0
3	Ferguson Jenkins	2,673.2
4	Larry Corcoran	2,338.1
5	Three Finger Brown	2,329.0
6	Rick Reuschel	2,290.0
7	Bill Lee	2,271.1
8	Hippo Vaughn	2,216.1
9	Guy Bush	2,201.1
10	Clark Griffith	2,188.2
11	Bob Rush	2,132.2
12	Claude Passeau	1,914.2
13	Grover Alexander	1,884.1
14	Ed Reulbach	1,864.2
15	Jack Taylor	1,801.0
16	John Clarkson	1,730.2
17	Greg Maddux	1,654.2
18	Pat Malone	1,632.0
19	Lon Warneke	1,624.2
20	Dick Ellsworth	1,613.1

Strikeouts

1	Ferguson Jenkins	2,038
2	Charlie Root	1,432
3	Rick Reuschel	1,367
4	Bill Hutchison	1,222
5	Kerry Wood	1,209
6	Hippo Vaughn	1,138
7	Greg Maddux	1,088
8	Larry Corcoran	1,086
9	Bob Rush	1,076
10	Three Finger Brown	1,043
11	Ken Holtzman	988
12	John Clarkson	960
13	Rick Sutcliffe	909
14	Dick Ellsworth	905
15	Bill Hands	900
16	Pat Malone	878
17	Bill Lee	874
18	Bill Bonham	811
19	Ed Reulbach	799
20	Claude Passeau	754

ERA

(minimum 1,000 innings pitched)

1	Three Finger Brown	1.80
2	Jack Pfeister	1.85
3	Orval Overall	1.91
4	Ed Reulbach	2.24
5	Larry Corcoran	2.26
6	Hippo Vaughn	2.33
7	Terry Larkin	2.34
8	John Clarkson	2.39
9	Carl Lundgren	2.42
10	Jack Taylor	2.66
11	Larry Cheney	2.74
12	Fred Goldsmith	2.78
13	Lon Warneke	2.84
14	Grover Alexander	2.84
15	Claude Hendrix	2.84
16	Claude Passeau	2.96
17	Jimmy Lavender	3.03
18	Hank Wyse	3.03
19	Bill Hands	3.18
20	Ferguson Jenkins	3.20

Saves

1	Lee Smith	180
2	Bruce Sutter	133
3	Randy Myers	112
4	Don Elston	63
5	Phil Regan	60
6	Rod Beck	58
7	Mitch Williams	52
8	Joe Borowski	44
9	Charlie Root	40
10	Three Finger Brown	39
	Lindy McDaniel	39
	Ted Abernathy	39
13	Terry Adams	37
	Rick Aguliera	37
15	Paul Assenmacher	33
16	Jack Aker	29
17	Dutch Leonard	28
	Turk Lown	28
19	Guy Bush	27
	Tom Gordon	27

February 28, 1941
Dizzy Dean (left) and
Clay Bryant

Cubs All-Time Roster

A

Abbey, Bert	1893-95
Abernathy, Ted	1965-66, 1969-70
Aberson, Cliff	1948-50
Abrego, Johnny	1985
Adair, Jimmy	1931
Adams, Bobby	1957-59
Adams, Mike	1976-77
Adams, Rebel	1915
Adams, Red	1946
Adams, Sparky	1922-27
Adams, Terry	1995-99
Addis, Bob	1952-53
Addy, Bob	1876
Adkins, Dewey	1949
Aguilera, Rick	1999-2000
Aguirre, Hank	1969-70
Aker, Jack	1972-73
Alderson, Dale	1943-44
Aldridge, Vic	1917-18, 1922-24
Alexander, Grover	1918-26
Alexander, Manny	1997-99
Alexander, Matt	1973-74
Alfonseca, Antonio	2002-03
Allen, Nick	1916
Allen, Ethan	1936
Allison, Milo	1913-14
Alou, Moises	2002-04
Altimirano, Porfi	1984
Altman, George	1959-62, 1965-67
Amalfitano, Joey	1964-67
Amor, Vincente	1956
Anderson, Bob	1957-62
Anderson, Jimmy	2004
Andre, John	1955
Andrews, Shane	1999-2000
Andrews, Jim	1890
Andrus, Fred	1876, 1884
Angley, Tom	1929
Anson, Cap	1876-97
Archer, Jimmy	1909-17
Arcia, Jose	1968
Arias, Alex	1992
Arnold, Jamie	2000
Asbell, Jim	1938
Ashburn, Richie	1960-61
Aspromonte, Ken	1963
Assenmacher, Paul	1989-93

Atwell, Toby	1952-53
Averill, Earl	1959-60
Ayala, Bobby	1999
Aybar, Manny	2001

B

Baczewski, Fred	1953
Baecht, Ed	1931-32
Bailey, Ed	1965
Bailey, Sweetbreads	1919-21
Baker, Gene	1953-57
Baker, Ton	1963
Bako, Paul	2003-04
Baldwin, Mark	1887-88
Baller, Jay	1985-87
Balsamo, Tony	1962
Banks, Ernie	1953-71
Banks, Willie	1994-95
Barber, Steve	1970

Ernie Banks

Barber, Turner	1917-22
Barbarie, Bret	1996
Barker, Richie	1989
Barnes, Ross	1876-77
Barragan, Cuno	1961-63
Barrett, Bob	1923-25
Barrett, Dick	1943
Barrett, Michael	2004
Barry, Shad	1904-05
Bartell, Dick	1939
Barton, Vince	1931-32
Bastian, Charlie	1889
Bates, Johnny	1914
Batista, Miguel	1997
Bauers, Russ	1946
Baumholtz, Frank	1949, 1951-55
Baumann, Frank	1965
Bautista, Jose	1993-94
Beals, Tommy	1880
Beard, Dave	1985
Beaumont, Ginger	1910
Beck, Clyde	1926-30
Beck, Rod	1998-99
Becker, Heinz	1943-44, 1946
Beckert, Glenn	1965-73
Beebe, Fred	1906
Bell, George	1991
Bell, Les	1930-31
Bellhorn, Mark	2002-03
Beltran, Francis	2002, 2004
Benes, Alan	2002-03
Benton, Butch	1982
Bere, Jason	2001-02
Berry, Joe	1942
Berryhill, Damon	1987-91
Bertell, Dick	1960-65, 1967
Bielaski, Oscar	1876
Bielecki, Mike	1988-91
Biitner, Larry	1976-80
Bilko, Steve	1954
Bird, Doug	1981-82
Bishop, Bill	1889
Bithorn, Hi	1942-43, 1946
Blackburn, Earl	1917
Blackwell, Tim	1978-81
Bladt, Rick	1969
Blair, Footsie	1929-31
Blake, Sheriff	1924-31
Blankenship, Kevin	1988-90
Blauser, Jeff	1998-99

Block, Cy	1942, 1945-46
Bobb, Randy	1968-69
Boccabella, John	1963-68
Bolger, Jim	1955, 1957-58
Bonds, Bobby	1981
Bonetti, Julio	1940
Bonham, Bill	1971-77
Bonura, Zeke	1940
Borchers, George	1888
Bordi, Rich	1983-84
Borkowski, Bob	1950-51
Boros, Steve	1963
Borowski, Joe	2001-04
Borowy, Hank	1945-48
Boskie, Shawn	1990-94
Bosley, Thad	1983-86
Botelho, Derek	1985
Bottarini, John	1937
Bottenfield, Kent	1996-97
Bouchee, Ed	1960-61
Bourque, Pat	1971-73
Bowa, Larry	1982-85
Bowie, Micah	1999
Bowman, Bill	1891
Bowman, Bob	1942
Bradley, Bill	1899-1900
Bradley, George	1877
Bransfield, Kitty	1911
Breeden, Danny	1971
Breeden, Hal	1971
Brennan, Bill	1993
Bresnahan, Roger	1900, 1913-15
Brett, Herb	1924-25
Brewer, Jim	1960-63
Brewster, Charlie	1944
Bridwell, Al	1913
Briggs, Buttons	1896-98, 1904-05
Briggs, Dan	1982
Briggs, John	1927
Bright, Harry	1965
Brillheart, Jim	1927
Brinkopf, Leon	1952
Broberg, Pete	1977
Brock, Lou	1961-64
Brock, Tarrik	2000
Broglio, Ernie	1964-66
Bronkie, Herman	1914
Brooks, Mandy	1925-26
Brosnan, Jim	1954, 1956-58
Brown, Brant	1996-98, 2000

Brown, Joe	1884		Cannizzaro, Chris	1971
Brown, Jophrey	1968		Capel, Mike	1988
Brown, Jumbo	1925		Capilla, Doug	1979-81
Brown, Lew	1879		Cardenal, Jose	1972-77
Brown, Ray	1909		Cardwell, Don	1960-62
Brown, Roosevelt	1999-2002		Carleton, Tex	1935-38
Brown, Three Finger	1904-12, 1916		Carlsen, Don	1946
Brown, Tommy	1952-53		Carlson, Hal	1927-30
Browne, Byron	1965-67		Carney, Bill	1904
Browne, George	1909		Carpenter, Bob	1947
Brumley, Mike	1987		Carroll, Cliff	1890-91
Brusstar, Warren	1983-85		Carson, Al	1910
Bryant, Clay	1935-40		Carter, Joe	1983
Bryant, Don	1968		Carter, Nick	1916-20
Brynan, Tod	1888		Carty, Rico	1973
Buckner, Bill	1977-84		Caruthers, Bob	1893
Buechelle, Steve	1992-95		Casey, Doc	1903-05
Bues, Art	1914		Casey, Hugh	1935
Buford, Damon	2000-01		Casian, Larry	1995-97
Buhl, Bob	1962-66		Cassidy, John	1878
Bullett, Scott	1995-96		Castillo, Frank	1991-97
Bullinger, Jim	1992-96		Caudill, Bill	1979-81
Burdette, Freddie	1962-64		Cavaretta, Phil	1934-53
Burdette, Lew	1964-65		Ceccarelli, Art	1959-60
Burgess, Smoky	1949, 1951		Cey, Ron	1983-86
Burke, Leo	1963-65		Chambers, Cliff	1948
Burns, Tom	1880-91		Chance, Frank	1898-1912
Burris, Ray	1973-79		Chapman, Harry	1912
Burrows, John	1943-44		Cheeves, Virgil	1920-23
Burton, Ellis	1963-65		Cheney, Larry	1911-15
Burwell, Dick	1960-61		Chiasson, Scott	2001-02
Bush, Guy	1923-34		Childs, Cupid	1900-01
Butler, Johnny	1928		Childs, Pete	1901
Buzhardt, John	1958-59		Chipman, Bob	1944-49
			Chiti, Harry	1950-52, 1955-56
C			Choi, Hee Seop	2002-03
Cairo, Miguel	1997, 2001		Christmas, Steve	1986
Callaghan, Marty	1922-23		Christopher, Lloyd	1945
Callahan, Nixey	1897-1900		Church, Bubba	1953-55
Callison, Johnny	1970-71		Church, Len	1966
Calmus, Dick	1967		Churry, John	1924-27
Camilli, Dolph	1933-34		Clark, Dad	1902
Camp, Kid	1894		Clark, Dave	1990, 1997
Camp, Lew	1893-94		Clark, Mark	1997-98
Campbell, Bill	1982-83		Clarke, Dad	1888
Campbell, Gilly	1933		Clarke, Henry	1898
Campbell, Joe	1967		Clarke, Sumpter	1920
Campbell, Mike	1996		Clarke, Tommy	1918
Campbell, Ron	1964-66		Clarkson, John	1884-87
Campbell, Vin	1908		Clausen, Fritz	1893-94
Canavan, Jim	1892		Clemens, Clem	1916

Clemens, Doug	1964-65	Crosby, George	1884
Clement, Matt	2002-04	Crosby, Ken	1975-76
Cline, Ty	1966	Cross, Jeff	1946
Clines, Gene	1977-79	Cruz, Hector	1978, 1981-82
Clingman, Billy	1900	Cruz, Juan	2001-03
Clymer, Otis	1913	Culler, Dick	1948
Coakley, Andy	1908-09	Culp, Ray	1967
Coffman, Kevin	1990	Cunnane, Will	2002
Cogan, Dick	1899	Cunningham, Bert	1900-01
Coggins, Fred	1972	Curley, Doc	1899
Cohen, Hy	1955	Currie, Clarence	1903
Colborn, Jim	1969-71	Curtis, Cliff	1911
Cole, Dick	1954	Curtis, Jack	1961-62
Cole, King	1909-12	Cusick, Jack	1951
Coleman, Joe	1976	Cuyler, Kiki	1928-35
Collins, Bill	1911	Cvengros, Mike	1929
Collins, Phil	1923		
Collins, Rip	1940		
Collins, Ripper	1937-38		
Collum, Jackie	1957		
Comellas, Jorge	1945		
Compton, Clint	1972		
Congalton, Bunk	1902		
Connally, Fritz	1983		
Connor, Jim	1892, 1897-99		
Connors, Billy	1966		
Connors, Chuck	1951		
Cook, Jim	1903		
Coomer, Ron	2001		
Cooney, Jimmy	1890-92		
Cooney, Jimmy	1926-27		
Cooper, Mort	1949		
Cooper, Walker	1954-55		
Cooper, Wilbur	1925-26		
Corcoran, Larry	1880-85		
Corcoran, Mike	1884		
Corriden, Red	1913-15		
Corridon, Fiddler	1904		
Cosman, Jim	1970		
Cotter, Dick	1912		
Cotter, Hooks	1922, 1924		
Cotrell, Ensign	1912		
Cotto, Henry	1984		
Coughlin, Roscoe	1890		
Covington, Wes	1966		
Cowan, Billy	1963-64		
Cox, Larry	1978, 1982		
Creek, Doug	1999		
Crim, Chuck	1994		
Croft, Harry	1901		

Frank Chance

D

Dahlen, Bill	1891-98
Dahlgren, Babe	1941-42
Daily, Con	1896
Dallesandro, Dom	1940-44, 1946-47
Dalrymple, Abner	1879-86
Daly, Tom	1887-88
Daly, Tom	1918-21
Daniels, Kal	1992
Dark, Al	1958-59
Darling, Dell	1887-89
Darwin, Bobby	1977
Dascenzo, Doug	1988-92
Davidson, Bill	1909
Davis, Brock	1970-71
Davis, Curt	1936-37
Davis, Jim	1954-56
Davis, Jody	1981-88
Davis, Ron	1986-87
Davis, Steve	1979
Davis, Tommy	1970, 1972
Dawson, Andre	1987-92
Day, Boots	1970
Dayett, Brian	1985-87
Deal, Charlie	1916-21
Dean, Dizzy	1938-41
Dean, Wayland	1927
Decker, George	1892-97
Decker, Joe	1969-72
DeFelice, Michael	2004
DeJesus, Ivan	1977-81
Del Greco, Bobby	1957
Delahanty, Jim	1901
Demarais, Fred	1890
Demaree, Al	1917
Demaree, Frank	1932-33, 1935-38
DeMiller, Harry	1892
DeMontreville, Gene	1898
Dempster, Ryan	2004
Dernier, Bobby	1984-87
Denzer, Roger	1897
Derrick, Claud	1914
Derringer, Paul	1943-45
DeShields, Delino	2001-02
Dettore, Tom	1974-76
Dexter, Charlie	1900-02
Diaz, Mike	1983
Dickson, Lance	1990
Dillard, Steve	1978, 1980-81
Dillhoefer, Pickles	1917
Dilone, Miguel	1979

DiPino, Frank	1986-88
Distaco, Alec	1969
Dobbs, John	1902-03
Dobernic, Jess	1948-49
Dolan, Cozy	1900-01
Dolan, John	1895
Dolan, Tom	1879
Donahue, Tim	1895-1900
Donnelly, Ed	1959
Donnelly, Frank	1893
Doolan, Mickey	1916
Dorsett, Brian	1996
Doscher, Herm	1879
Doscher, Jack	1903
Douglas, Phil	1915-18
Douthit, Taylor	1933
Dowling, Dave	1966
Downey, Tom	1912
Downs, Red	1912
Downs, Scott	2000
Doyle, Jack	1901
Doyle, Jim	1911
Doyle, Larry	1916-17
Drabowsky, Moe	1956-60
Drake, Sammy	1960-61
Drake, Solly	1956
Driscoll, Paddy	1917
Drott, Dick	1957-61
Dubiel, Monk	1949-52
Dubois, Jason	2004
Duffy, Hugh	1888-89
Dumovich, Nick	1923
Duncan, Courtney	2001-02
Dunegan, Jim	1970
Dungan, Sam	1892-94, 1900
Dunn, Ron	1974-75
Dunston, Shawon	1985-95, 1997
Dunwoody, Todd	2000
Durbin, Kid	1907-08
Durham, Bull	1981-88
Dwyer, Frank	1888-89

E

Eaddy, Don	1959
Eagan, Bill	1893
Earl, Howard	1890
Earley, Arnold	1966
Eason, Mal	1900-02
Easterwood, Roy	1944
Eastwick, Rawly	1981
Eaves, Vallie	1941-42

Echevarria, Angel	2002		
Eckersley, Dennis	1984-86	**F**	
Eden, Charlie	1877	Fanning, Jim	1954-57
Edens, Tom	1995	Fanzone, Carmen	1971-74
Edwards, Bruce	1951-52, 1954	Farnsworth, Kyle	1999-2004
Edwards, Hank	1949-50	Farrell, Doc	1930
Eggler, Dave	1877	Farrell, Duke	1888-89
Eiteljorge, Ed	1890	Fassero, Jeff	2001-03
Elia, Lee	1968	Fast, Darcy	1968
Elko, Pete	1943-44	Faul, Bill	1965-66
Elliott, Ace	1923-24	Fear, Vern	1952
Elliott, Carter	1921	Felderman, Marv	1942
Elliott, Rowdy	1916-18	Felske, John	1968
Ellis, Jim	1967	Ferguson, Bob	1878
Ellsworth, Dick	1958, 1960-66	Ferguson, Charlie	1901
Elston, Don	1953, 1957-64	Fermin, Felix	1996
Encarnacion, Mario	2002	Fernandez, Frank	1971-72
Engel, Steve	1985	Figueroa, Jesus	1980
English, Woody	1927-36	Filer, Tom	1982
Epperly, Al	1938	Fischer, William	1916
Erickson, Paul	1941-48	Fisher, Cherokee	1877
Ernaga, Frank	1957-58	Fisher, Tom	1914-15
Errickson, Dick	1942	Fitzgerald, Howard	1922, 1924
Estes, Shawn	2003	Flack, Max	1916-22
Estrada, Chuck	1966	Flavin, John	1964
Eubanks, Uel	1922	Fleming, Bill	1942-44, 1946
Everitt, Bill	1895-1900	Fletcher, Scott	1981-82
Evers, Johnny	1902-13	Flint, Silver	1879-89
		Flores, Jesse	1942

Johnny Evers and son

Fluhrer, John	1915		Garriott, Cecil	1946
Flynn, George	1896		Garvin, Ned	1899-1900
Flynn, Jocko	1896		Gassaway, Charlie	1944
Fodge, Gene	1958		Gastfield, Ed	1885
Fondy, Dee	1951-57		Gaw, Chippy	1920
Fontenot, Ray	1985-86		Geisel, Dave	1978-79, 1981
Foote, Barry	1979-81		Geiss, Emil	1887
Fossas, Tony	1998		George, Greek	1941
Foster, Elmer	1890-91		Gerard, Dave	1962
Foster, Kevin	1994-98		Gerberman, George	1962
Foxen, Bill	1910-11		Gernert, Dick	1960
Foxx, Jimmie	1942, 1944		Gessler, Doc	1906
Frailing, Ken	1974-76		Gibson, Robert	1890
France, Ossie	1890		Gigon, Norm	1967
Franco, Matt	1995		Gilbert, Charlie	1941-43, 1946
Francona, Terry	1986		Gill, Johnny	1935-36
Fraser, Chick	1907-09		Gillespie, Paul	1942, 1944-45
Frazier, George	1984-86		Girardi, Joe	1989-92, 2000-02
Freeman, Buck	1921-22		Giusti, Dave	1977
Freeman, Hersh	1958		Glade, Fred	1902
Freeman, Mark	1960		Glanville, Doug	1996-97, 2003
Freese, George	1961		Gleeson, Jim	1939-40
Freigau, Ty	1925-27		Glenalvin, Bob	1890, 1893
French, Larry	1935-41		Glenn, Ed	1902
Frey, Lonny	1937, 1947		Glenn, John	1876-77
Friberg, Bernie	1919-20, 1922-25		Gload, Ross	2000
Friend, Danny	1895-98		Glossop, Al	1946
Friend, Owen	1955-56		Goetz, John	1960
Fryman, Woody	1978		Goldsmith, Fred	1880-84
Fuhr, Oscar	1921		Golvin, Walt	1922
Fussell, Fred	1922-23		Gomez, Leo	1996
Fyhrie, Mike	2001		Gonzalez, Alex	2002-04
			Gonzalez, Jeremi	1997-98
G			Gonzalez, Luis	1995-96
Gabler, Gabe	1958		Gonzalez, Mike	1925-29
Gabrielson, Len	1964-65		Gonzalez, Raul	2000
Gaetti, Gary	1998-99		Good, Wilbur	1911-15
Gagliano, Phil	1970		Goodman, Ival	1943-44
Galan, Augie	1934-41		Goodwin, Curtis	1999
Gamble, Oscar	1969		Goodwin, Tom	2003-04
Gannon, Bill	1901		Gordon, Mike	1977-78
Ganzel, John	1900		Gordon, Tom	2001-02
Garagiola, Joe	1953-54		Gore, George	1879-86
Garbark, Bob	1937-39		Gornicki, Hank	1941
Garces, Rich	1995		Goryl, John	1957-59
Garciaparra, Nomar	2004		Gossage, Goose	1988
Gardner, Jim	1902		Grabarkewitz, Billy	1974
Gardner, Rob	1967		Grace, Earl	1929, 1931
Garibay, Daniel	2000		Grace, Mark	1988-2000
Garman, Mike	1976		Graham, Peaches	1903, 1911
Garrett, Adrian	1970, 1973-75		Grammas, Alex	1962-63

Grammp, Hank	1927, 1929
Grant, Tom	1963
Grantham, George	1922-24
Graves, Joe	1926
Green, Danny	1898-1901
Greene, Willie	2000
Gregory, Lee	1964
Grieve, Ben	2004
Griffin, Hank	1911
Griffin, Mike	1981
Griffith, Clark	1893-1900
Griffith, Frank	1892
Griffith, Tommy	1925
Grigsby, Denver	1923-25
Grimes, Burleigh	1932-33
Grimes, Ray	1921-24
Grimm, Charlie	1925-36
Gross, Greg	1977-78
Groth, Ernie	1904
Grudzielanek, Mark	2003-04
Gudat, Mark	1932
Gumbert, Ad	1888-89, 1891-92
Gumpert, Dave	1985-86
Gura, Larry	1970-73
Gustine, Frankie	1949
Guth, Charlie	1880
Guthrie, Mark	1999-2000, 2003
Gutierrez, Ricky	2000-01
Guzman, Jose	1993-94

H

Haas, Eddie	1957
Hack, Stan	1932-47
Hacker, Warren	1948-56
Hageman, Casey	1914
Hagerman, Rip	1909
Hairston, Johnny	1969
Hall, Drew	1896-88
Hall, Jimmie	1969-70
Hall, Melvin	1981-84
Hallinan, Jimmy	1877-78
Hamilton, Steve	1972
Hamner, Ralph	1947-49
Hands, Bill	1966-72
Haney, Chris	1998
Haney, Fred	1927
Haney, Todd	1994-96
Hankinson, Frank	1878-79
Hanlon, Bill	1903
Hansen, Dave	1997

Hanson, Ollie	1921
Hanyzewski, Ed	1942-46
Harbridge, Bill	1878-79
Hardie, Lou	1886
Hardin, Bud	1952
Hardtke, Jason	1998
Hardy, Alex	1902-03
Hardy, Jack	1907
Hargesheimer, Alan	1983
Hargrave, Bubbles	1913-15
Harkey, Mike	1988, 1990-93
Harley, Dick	1903
Harper, Jack	1906
Harrell, Ray	1939
Harris, Brendan	2004
Harris, Lenny	2003
Harris, Vic	1974-75
Hartenstein, Chuck	1966-68
Hartnett, Gabby	1922-40
Hartsel, Topsy	1901

Ken Holtzman

Hartsock, Jeff	1992	Hiller, Frank	1950-51
Harvey, ZaZa	1900	Hillman, Dave	1955-59
Hassey, Ron	1984	Hines, Paul	1876-77
Hatcher, Billy	1984-85	Hiser, Gene	1971-75
Hatten, Joe	1951-52	Hoak, Don	1956
Hatton, Grady	1960	Hobbie, Glen	1957-64
Hawkins, LeTroy	2004	Hoeft, Billy	1965-66
Hayden, Jack	1908	Hoffman, Guy	1986
Hayes, Bill	1980-81	Hoffman, Larry	1901
Healy, Egyptian	1889	Hofman, Solly	1904-12, 1916
Heath, Bill	1969	Hogg, Brad	1915
Heathcote, Cliff	1922-30	Hollocher, Charlie	1918-24
Hebner, Richie	1984-85	Hollandsworth, Todd	2004
Hechinger, Mike	1912-13	Holley, Ed	1928
Hegan, Jim	1960	Hollins, Jessie	1992
Heist, Al	1960-61	Hollison, Swede	1892
Hemsley, Rollie	1931-32	Holm, Billy	1943-44
Henderson, Ken	1979-80	Holmes, Fred	1904
Henderson, Steve	1981-82	Holtzman, Ken	1965-71, 1978-79
Hendley, Bob	1965-67	Honan, Marty	1890-91
Hendrick, Harvey	1933	Hooton, Burt	1971-75
Hendricks, Elrod	1972	Horne, Trader	1929
Hendricks, Jack	1902	Hornsby, Rogers	1929-32
Hendrix, Claude	1916-20	Hosley, Tim	1975-76
Hennessey, George	1945		
Henry, Bill	1958-59		
Henshaw, Roy	1933, 1935-36		
Heredia, Felix	1998-2001		
Herman, Babe	1933-34		
Herman, Billy	1931-41		
Hermanson, Chad	2002		
Hermanski, Gene	1951-53		
Hernandez, Chico	1942-43		
Hernandez, Jose	1994-99, 2003		
Hernandez, Ramon	1968, 1976-77		
Hernandez, Willie	1977-83		
Hernon, Tom	1897		
Herrman, Leroy	1932-33		
Herrnstein, John	1966		
Herzog, Buck	1919-20		
Hiatt, Jack	1970		
Hibbard, Greg	1993		
Hibbard, John	1884		
Hickerson, Bryan	1995		
Hickey, Eddie	1901		
Hickman, Jim	1968-73		
Higbe, Kirby	1937-39		
Higginbotham, Irv	1909		
Hildebrand, R. E.	1902		
Hill, Bobby	2002-03		
Hill, Glanallen	1993-94, 1998-2000		

Randy Hundley

Houseman, John	1894
Houston, Tyler	1996-99
Howard, Del	1907-09
Howe, Cal	1952
Howell, Jay	1981
Hubbard, Mike	1995-97
Hubbard, Trenidad	2003
Hubbs, Ken	1962-64
Hudson, Johnny	1941
Hughes, Jim	1956
Hughes, Joe	1902
Hughes, Long Tom	1900-01
Hughes, Roy	1944-45
Hughes, Terry	1970
Hughey, Jim	1893
Humphreys. Bob	1965
Humphries, Bert	1913-15
Hundley, Randy	1966-73, 1976-77
Hundley, Todd	2001-02
Hunter, Herb	1916-17
Huntzinger, Walt	1926
Hurst, Don	1934
Huson, Jeff	2000
Hutchinson, Ed	1890
Hutchison, Bill	1889-95
Hutson, Herb	1974

I

Ilsley, Blaine	1994
Irvin, Monte	1956
Irwin, Charlie	1893-95
Isbell, Frank	1898

J

Jackson, Damian	2004
Jackson, Danny	1991-92
Jackson, Darrin	1985, 1987-89
Jackson, Larry	1963-66
Jackson, Lou	1958-59
Jackson, Randy	1950-55, 1959
Jacobs, Elmer	1925-26
Jacobs, Mike	1902
Jacobs, Ray	1928
Jacobs, Tony	1948
Jacobson, Merwin	1916
Jaeckel, Jake	1964
Jaeger, Joe	1920
Jahn, Art	1925
James, Cleo	1970-71, 1973
James, Rick	1967

Jeffcoat, Hal	1954-55
Jelincich, Frank	1941
Jenkins, Ferguson	1966-73, 1982-83
Jennings, Doug	1993
Jennings, Robin	1996-97, 1999
Jestadt, Garry	1971
Jiminez, Manny	1969
Johnson, Abe	1893
Johnson, Ben	1959-60
Johnson, Bill	1983-84
Johnson, Cliff	1980
Johnson, Dave	1978
Johnson, Don	1943-48
Johnson, Footer	1958
Johnson, Howard	1995
Johnson, Ken	1969
Johnson, Lance	1997-99
Johnson, Lou	1960, 1968
Johnston, Jimmy	1914
Johnstone, Jay	1982-84
Joiner, Pop	1934-35
Jones, Charley	1877
Jones, Clarence	1967-68
Jones, Davy	1902-04
Jones, Doug	1996
Jones, Percy	1920-22, 1925-28
Jones, Sam	1955-56
Jones, Sheldon	1953
Jonnard, Claude	1929
Jurges, Billy	1931-38, 1946-47

K

Kahoe, Mike	1901-02, 1907
Kaiser, Al	1911
Kaiser, Don	1955-57
Kane, John	1909-10
Karchner, Matt	1998-2000
Karros, Eric	2003
Katoll, John	1898-1899
Kaufmann, Tony	1921-27
Kearns, Teddy	1924-25
Keating, Chuck	1913-15
Keen, Vic	1921-25
Kelleher, John	1921-23
Kelleher, Mick	1976-80
Kellert, Frank	1956
Kelly, Bob	1951-53
Kelly, George	1930
Kelly, Joe	1916
Kelly, Joe	1926, 1928

Kelly, King	1880-86	Krug, Marty	1922
Kelton, David	2003-04	Krukow, Mike	1976-91
Kennedy, Junior	1982-83	Kuenn, Harvey	1965-66
Kennedy, Snapper	1902	Kunkel, Jeff	1992
Kennedy, Ted	1885	Kush, Emil	1949
Keough, Marty	1966		
Keough, Matt	1986	**L**	
Kerr, Mel	1925	La Russa, Tony	1973
Kessinger, Don	1964-75	LaCock, Pete	1972-76
Kieschnick, Brooks	1996-97	Lade, Doyle	1946-50
Kilduff, Pete	1917-19	Lake, Steve	1983-86, 1993
Kilgus, Paul	1989	Lamabe, Jack	1968
Killefer, Bill	1918-21	Lamers, Pete	1902
Killen, Lefty	1900	Lamp, Dennis	1977-80
Kilroy, Matt	1898	Lancaster, Les	1987-91
Kimball, Newt	1937-38	Landrith, Hobie	1956
Kimm, Bruce	1979	Landrum, Bill	1988
Kindall, Jerry	1956-58, 1960-61	Landrum, Ced	1991
Kiner, Ralph	1953-54	Landrum, Don	1962-65
King, Chick	1958-59	Lanfranconi, Walt	1941
King, Jim	1955-56	Lange, Bill	1893-99
King, Ray	1999	Larkin, Terry	1878-79
Kingman, Dave	1978-80	LaRoche, Dave	1973-74
Kinzie, Walt	1884	LaRose, Vic	1968
Kirby, Jim	1949	Larsen, Don	1967
Kitsos, Chris	1954	Larson, Dan	1982
Kittridge, Malachi	1890-97	Lary, Al	1954, 1962
Klein, Chuck	1934-36	Lauer, Chuck	1890
Kling, Johnny	1900-11	Lavender, Jimmy	1912-1916
Klippstein, Johnny	1950-54	Law, Vance	1988-89
Klugmann, Joe	1921-22	Lazzeri, Tony	1938
Kmak, Joe	1995	Leach, Tommy	1912-14
Knabe, Otto	1916	Lear, King	1918-19
Knisley, Pete	1913-15	Leathers, Hal	1920
Knowles, Darold	1975-76	Lee, Derrek	2004
Koenig, Mark	1932-33	Lee, Don	1966
Koestner, Bob	1914	Lee, Tom	1884
Koonce, Cal	1962-67	Lee, Bill	1934-43, 1947
Korwan, Jim	1897	Lefferts, Craig	1983
Kowalik, Fabian	1935-36	Leiber, Hank	1939-41
Kraemer, Joe	1989-90	Leicester, Jon	2004
Kramer, Randy	1990	Leifield, Lefty	1912-13
Kravec, Ken	1981-82	LeMay, Dick	1963
Kreevich, Mike	1931	Lemonds, Dave	1969
Kreitner, Mickey	1943-44	Lennon, Bob	1957
Kreig, Bill	1885	Lennox, Ed	1912
Kremmel, Jim	1974	Leonard, Dutch	1949-53
Krock, Gus	1888-89	Leslie, Roy	1917
Kroh, Rube	1908-10	Lewis, Darren	2002
Krug, Chris	1965-66	Lezcano, Carlos	1980-81
Krug, Gary	1981	Lieber, Jon	1999-2002

Lillard, Gene	1939	Mahoney, Mike	2000, 2002
Lindstrom, Fred	1935	Mains, Willard	1888
Liniak, Cole	1999-2000	Mairena, Oswaldo	2000
Littlefield, Dick	1957	Maisel, George	1921-22
Littrell, Jack	1957	Maksudian, Mike	1994
Livingston, Mickey	1943, 1945-47	Malarkey, John	1899
Lobert, Hans	1905	Maldonado, Candy	1993
Locker, Bob	1973, 1975	Malone, Pat	1928-34
Lofton, Kenny	2003	Maloney, Billy	1905
Logan, Bob	1937-38	Mancuso, Gus	1939
Long, Bill	1990	Manders, Hal	1946
Long, Dale	1957-59	Mann, Garth	1944
Lopes, Davey	1984-86	Mann, Les	1916-19
Lorraine, Andrew	1999-2000	Manville, Dick	1952
Loviglio, Jay	1983	Maranville, Rabbit	1925
Lowdermilk, Grover	1912	Marquez, Gonzalo	1973-74
Lowe, Bobby	1902-03	Marquez, Luis	1954
Lowery, Terrell	1997-98	Marriott, William	1917, 1920-21
Lown, Turk	1951-58	Marshall, Doc	1908
Lowrey, Peanuts	1942-43, 1945-49	Marshall, Jim	1958-59
Luby, Pat	1890-92	Martin, Frank	1898
Luderus, Fred	1909-10	Martin, Jerry	1979-80
Lum, Mike	1981	Martin, J. C.	1970-72
Lundgren, Carl	1902-09	Martin, Mike	1986
Lundstedt, Tom	1973-74	Martin, Morrie	1959
Lynch, Danny	1948	Martin, Speed	1918-22
Lynch, Dummy	1884	Martin, Stu	1943
Lynch, Ed	1986-87	Martinez, Carmelo	1983
Lynch, Henry	1893	Martinez, Dave	1986-88, 2000
Lynch, Mike	1902	Martinez, Ramon	2003-04
Lynn, Red	1944	Martinez, Sandy	1998-99
Lytle, Dad	1902	Marty, Joe	1937-39
		Martz, Randy	1980-82
M		Mason, Mike	1987
Machado, Robert	2001-02	Massa, Gordon	1957-58
Macias, Jose	2004	Mathews, Nelson	1960-63
Mack, Bill	1908	Matthews, Gary	1984-87
Mack, Ray	1947	Matthews, Gary, Jr.	2000-01
Macko, Steve	1979-80	Mattick, Bobby	1938-40
Madden, Len	1912	Mauch, Gene	1948-49
Maddern, Clarence	1946, 1948-49	Mauck, Hal	1893
Maddux, Greg	1986-92, 2004	Mauro, Carmen	1948, 1950-51
Madlock, Bill	1974-76	Maxwell, Jason	1998
Madrid, Sal	1947	May, Derrick	1990-94
Magadan, Dave	1996	May, Jakie	1931-32
Magee, Lee	1919	May, Scott	1891
Magoon, George	1899	Mayer, Ed	1957-58
Mahay, Ron	2001-02	McAfee, Bill	1930
Maguire, Freddie	1928	McAnany, Jim	1961-62
Mahomes, Pat	2002	McAuley, Ike	1925

McBride, Algie	1896	Meyer, Russ	1946-48, 1956
McCabe, Bill	1918-20	Meyers, Chad	1999-2001
McCall, Windy	1948	Michaels, Ralph	1924-26
McCarthy, Alex	1915-16	Mickelson, Ed	1957
McCarthy, Jack	1900, 1903-05	Mieske, Matt	1998
McCauley, Jim	1895	Mikkelsen, Pete	1967-68
McChesney, Harry	1904	Miklos, Hank	1944
McClellan, Bill	1878	Miksis, Eddie	1951-56
McClendon, Lloyd	1990-91	Miller, Bob	1970-71
McConnell, George	1914, 1916	Miller, Damian	2003
McCormick, Barry	1896-1901	Miller, Doc	1910
McCormick, Jim	1885-86	Miller, Dusty	1902
McCullough, Clyde	1940-43, 1946-48, 1953-56	Miller, Hack	1922-25
McDaniel, Lindy	1963-65	Miller, Curt	1998-99
McDonald, Ed	1913	Miller, Ox	1947
McElroy, Chuck	1991-93	Miller, Ward	1912-13
McFarland, Monte	1895-96	Milstead, George	1924-26
McGill, Willie	1893-94	Minner, Paul	1950-56
McGinn, Dan	1972	Mitchell, Mike	1913
McGinnis, Gus	1893	Mitre, Sergio	2003-04
McGlothlen, Lynn	1978-81	Mitterwald, George	1974-77
McGriff, Fred	2001-02	Moisan, Bill	1953
McIntyre, Harry	1910-12	Molina, Jose	1999
McKnight, Jim	1960, 1962	Molinaro, Bob	1982
McLarry, Polly	1915	Mollwitz, Fritz	1913-14, 1916
McLean, Larry	1903	Monday, Rick	1972-76
McLish, Cal	1949, 1951	Montreuil, Al	1972
McMath, Jimmy	1968	Moolic, George	1886
McMillan, Norm	1928-29	Moore, Charley	1912
McNichol, Brian	1999	Moore, Donnie	1975, 1977-79
McRae, Brian	1995-97	Moore, Earl	1913
McVey, Cal	1876-77	Moore, Johnny	1918-29, 1931-32, 1945
Meakim, George	1892	Mooty, Jake	1940-43
Mears, Russ	1941, 1946-47	Morales, Jerry	1974-77, 1981-83
Meier, Dave	1988	Moran, Pat	1906-09
Mejias, Sam	1979	Moran, Bill	1895
Menefee, Jock	1900-03	Morandini, Mickey	1988-99
Meoli, Rudy	1978	Morehead, Seth	1959-60
Merced, Orlando	1998	Morel, Ramon	1997
Mercker, Kent	2004	Moreland, Keith	1982-87
Meridith, Ron	1984-85	Morgan, Bobby	1957-58
Merke, Fred	1917-20	Morgan, Mike	1992-95, 1998
Merriman, Lloyd	1955	Morgan, Vern	1954-55
Merritt, Bill	1891	Morhardt, Moe	1961-62
Mertes, Sam	1898-1900	Moriarty, George	1903-04
Merullo, Lennie	1941-47	Moroney, Jim	1912
Mesner, Steve	1938-39	Morris, Ed	1922
Metkovich, Catfish	1953	Morrissey, Deacon	1902
Metzger, Roger	1970	Moryn, Walt	1956-60
Metzler, Alex	1925	Moskau, Paul	1983
Meyer, Dutch	1937	Mosolf, Jim	1933

Moss, Mal	1930		Northey, Ron	1950, 1952
Moyer, Jamie	1986-88		Norton, Phil	2000, 2003
Mudrock, Phil	1963		Nottebart, Don	1969
Mueller, Bill	2001-02		Novikoff, Lou	1941-44
Mulholland, Terry	1997-99		Novotney, Rube	1949
Mulligan, Joe	1915-16		Nunez, Jose	1990
Mumphrey, Jerry	1986-88		Nye, Rich	1966-69
Muncrief, Bob	1949			
Munson, Joe	1925-26		**O**	
Murcer, Bobby	1977-79		O'Berry, Mike	1980
Murphy, Danny	1960-62		O'Brien, John	1893
Murray, Calvin	2004		O'Brien, Pete	1890
Murray, Jim	1902		O'Connor, Johnny	1916
Murray, Red	1915		O'Dea, Ken	1935-38
Murray, Tony	1923		O'Farrell, Bob	1915-25
Myers, Billy	1941		O'Hagen, Hal	1902
Myers, Randy	1993-95		O'Leary, Troy	2003
Myers, Richie	1956		O'Neill, Emmett	1946
Myers, Rodney	1996-99		O'Neill, Jack	1904-05
			Ohman, Will	2000-01
N			Ojeda, Augie	2000-03
Nabholz, Chris	1995		Oliver, Gene	1968-69
Nagle, Tom	1890-91		Oliver, Nate	1969
Napier, Buddy	1918		Olsen, Barney	1941
Nation, Joey	2000		Olsen, Vern	1919-42, 1946
Navarro, Jaime	1995-96		Ontiveros, Steve	1977-80
Needham, Tom	1909-14		Ordonez, Rey	2004
Neeman, Cal	1957-60		Orie, Kevin	1997-98, 2002
Nehf, Art	1927-29		Ortiz, Jose	1971
Nelson, Lynn	1930, 1933-34		Osborn, Bob	1925-30
Nen, Dick	1968		Osborne, Donovan	2002
Newkirk, Sailor	1919-20		Osborne, Tiny	1922-24
Newman, Charlie	1892		Ostrowski, Johnny	1943-46
Newman, Ray	1971		Otero, Reggie	1945
Newsom, Bobo	1932		Ott, Billy	1962, 1964
Nichols, Art	1898-1900		Otto, Dave	1994
Nichols, Nick	1958		Overall, Orval	1906-10, 1913
Nicholson, Bill	1939-48		Ovitz, Ernie	1911
Nicol, George	1891		Owen, Dave	1983-85
Nicol, Hugh	1881-82		Owen, Mickey	1949-51
Niekro, Joe	1967-69			
Nieves, Jose	1998-2000		**P**	
Nipper, Al	1988		Packard, Gene	1916-17
Noce, Paul	1987		Pafko, Andy	1943-51
Noles, Dickie	1982-84, 1987		Page, Vance	1938-41
Noonan, Pete	1906		Pagel, Karl	1978-79
Nordhagen, Wayne	1983		Pall, Donn	1994
Noren, Irv	1959-60		Palmeiro, Rafael	1986-88
Norman, Fred	1964, 1966-67		Pappas, Erik	1991
North, Bill	1971-72		Pappas, Milt	1970-73

Parent, Mark	1994-95
Parker, Doc	1893, 1895-96
Parmelee, Roy	1937
Parrott, Jiggs	1892-95
Parrott, Tom	1893
Paskert, Dode	1918-20
Passeau, Claude	1939-47
Patterson, Bob	1996-98
Patterson, Corey	2000-04
Patterson, Ken	1992
Patterson, Reggie	1983-85
Paul, Josh	2003
Paul, Mike	1973-74
Pavlas, Dave	1990-91
Pawelek, Ted	1946
Pearce, George	1912-16
Pechous, Charlie	1916-17
Pedre, Jorge	1992
Pedroes, Chick	1902
Pena, Roberto	1965-66
Penner, Ken	1929
Pepitone, Joe	1970-73
Perez, Mike	1995-96
Perez, Neifi	2004
Perez, Yorkis	1991
Perkowski, Harry	1955
Perlman, Jon	1985
Perry, Pat	1988-89
Perry, Scott	1916
Peters, John	1876-77, 1879
Pettit, Bob	1887-88
Petty, Jesse	1930
Pfeffer, Fred	1883-89, 1891, 1896-97
Pfeffer, Jeff	1905, 1910
Pfiester, Jack	1906-11
Phelan, Art	1913-15
Phelps, Babe	1933-34
Phillips, Adolpho	1966-69
Phillips, Taylor	1958-59
Phoebus, Tom	1972
Phyle, Bill	1898-99
Pick, Charlie	1918-19
Pick, Eddie	1927
Pico, Jeff	1988-90
Pierce, George	1912-16
Pierce, Ray	1924
Piercy, Andy	1881
Piktuzis, Dee	1956
Pina, Horacio	1974
Pisciotta, Marc	1997-98
Pittenger, Pinky	1925

Pizarro, Juan	1970-73
Platt, Whitey	1942-43
Plesac, Dan	1993-94
Plummer, Bill	1968
Poholsky, Tom	1957
Pollet, Howie	1953-55
Ponder, Elmer	1921
Poorman, Tom	1880
Popovich, Paul	1964, 1966-67, 1969-73
Porter, Bo	1999
Porterfield, Bob	1959
Powell, Bill	1912
Powers, Phil	1878
Prall, Willie	1975
Pramesa, Johnny	1952
Pratt, Andy	2004
Pratt, Todd	1995
Prendergast, Mike	1916-17
Pressnell, Tot	1941-42
Prim, Ray	1943-45
Prince, Don	1962
Prior, Mark	2002-04
Proly, Mike	1982-83
Putnam, Ed	1976, 1978
Pyecha, John	1954
Pyle, Harry	1887

Claude Passeau

Q

Qualls, Jim   1969
Quest, Joe   1879-82
Quevedo, Ruben   2000
Quinn, Frank   1899
Quinn, Joe   1877
Quinn, Wimpy   1941
Quinones, Luis   1987

R

Radatz, Dick   1967
Rader, Dave   1978
Raffensberger, Ken   1940-41
Ragan, Pat   1909
Rain, Steve   1999-2000
Rainey, Chuck   1983-84
Ramazzotti, Bob   1949-53
Ramirez, Aramis   2003-04
Ramos, Domingo   1989-90
Ramsdell, Willie   1952
Ramsey, Fernando   1992
Randall, Newt   1907
Randle, Lenny   1980
Ranew, Merritt   1983-84
Rasmussen, Dennis   1992
Raub, Tommy   1903
Raudman, Bob   1966-67
Raymer, Fred   1901
Reberger, Frank   1958
Reed, Jeff   1999-2000
Regan, Phil   1968-72
Reich, Herman   1949
Reilly, Hal   1919
Reilly, Josh   1896
Reis, Laurie   1877-78
Reitz, Ken   1981
Remlinger, Mike   2003
Remsen, Jack   1878-79
Renfroe, Laddie   1991
Renko, Steve   1976-77
Reulbach, Ed   1905-13
Reuschel, Paul   1975-78
Reuschel, Rick   1972-81, 1983-84
Reynolds, Archie   1968-70
Reynolds, Carl   1937-39
Rhoads, Dusty   1902
Rhodes, Karl   1993-95
Rice, Del   1960
Rice, Hal   1954
Rice, Len   1945

Richards, Fred   1951
Richbourg, Lance   1932
Richie, Lew   1910-13
Richmond, Beryl   1933
Richter, Reggie   1911
Rickert, Marv   1942, 1946-47
Riley, George   1979-80
Ripley, Allen   1982
Rivera, Roberto   1995
Roach, Mel   1961
Roach, Skel   1899
Roat, Fred   1892
Roberts, Dave   1977-78
Roberts, Robin   1966
Roberson, Kevin   1993-95
Robertson, Daryl   1962
Robertson, Dave   1919-21
Robertson, Don   1954
Robinson, Jeff   1992
Rodgers, Andre   1961-64
Rodriguez, Bobby   1970
Rodriguez, Freddie   1958
Rodriguez, Henry   1998-2000
Rogell, Billy   1940
Rohn, Dan   1983-84
Rojas, Mel   1997
Roomes, Rolando   1988
Root, Charlie   1926-41
Rosello, Dave   1972-77
Ross, Gary   1968-69
Rowan, Jack   1911
Rowdon, Wade   1987
Rowe, Dave   1877
Roy, Luther   1927
Roznovsky, Vic   1964-65
Rudolph, John   1904
Rudolph, Ken   1969-73
Ruether, Dutch   1917
Rusch, Glendon   2004
Rush, Bob   1948-57
Russell, Jack   1938-39
Russell, Rip   1946-47
Ruthven, Dick   1983-86
Ryan, Jimmy   1885-89, 1891-1900

S

Saier, Vic   1911-17
Salazar, Angel   1988
Salazar, Luis   1989-92
Sanchez, Felix   2003

Sanchez, Jesus	2002	Serena, Bill	1949-54
Sanchez, Rey	1991-97	Servais, Scott	1995-98
Sandberg, Ryne	1982-94, 1996-97	Sewell, Tommy	1927
Sanders, Scott	1999	Shafer, Orator	1879
Sanderson, Scott	1984-89	Shamsky, Art	1972
Santiago, Benito	1999	Shannon, Red	1926
Santo, Ron	1960-73	Shantz, Bobby	1964
Sauer, Ed	1943-45	Shaw, Bob	1967
Sauer, Hank	1949-55	Shaw, Sam	1893
Savage, Ted	1967-68	Shay, Marty	1916
Sawatski, Carl	1948, 1950, 1953	Shealy, Al	1938
Scanlan, Bob	1991-93	Shean, Dave	1911
Schaefer, Germany	1901-02	Sheckard, Jimmy	1906-12
Schaffer, Jimmie	1963-64	Shields, Tommy	1993
Schaffernoth, Joe	1959-61	Shoun, Clyde	1935-37
Scheffing, Bob	1941-42, 1946-50	Shumpert, Terry	1996
Schenz, Hank	1946-49	Sicking, Ed	1916
Schick, Morrie	1917	Signer, Walter	1943, 1945
Schirardi, Calvin	1988-89	Silvera, Charlie	1957
Schlafly, Harry	1902	Simmons, Curt	1966-67
Schmidt, Freddy	1947	Simon, Russell	2003
Schmitz, Johnny	1941-42, 1946-51	Simpson, Duke	1953
Schorr, Ed	1915	Singleton, Elmer	1957-59
Schramka, Paul	1953	Sizemore, Ted	1979
Schrieber, Hank	1926	Skidmore, Roe	1970
Schriver, Pop	1891-94	Slagle, Jimmy	1902-08
Schroll, Al	1960	Slapnicka, Cy	1911
Schult, Art	1959-60		
Schulte, Johnny	1929		
Schulte, Wildfire	1904-16		
Schultz, Barney	1961-63		
Schultz, Bob	1951-53		
Schultz, Buddy	1975-76		
Schultz, Joe	1915		
Schultze, Don	1983-84		
Schurr, Wayne	1964		
Schuster, Bill	1943-45		
Schwenck, Rudy	1909		
Scott, Dick	1964		
Scott, Gary	1991-92		
Scott, Milt	1882		
Scott, Pete	1926-27		
Scott, Rodney	1978		
Seaton, Tom	1916-17		
Secory, Frank	1944-46		
Segelke, Herman	1982		
Seibert, Kurt	1979		
Selma, Dick	1969		
Sember, Mike	1977-78		
Seoane, Manny	1978		
Serafini, Dan	1999		

Ryne Sandberg

Slaughter, Sterling	1964
Sloat, Dwain	1949
Slocumb, Heathcliff	1991-93
Smalley, Roy	1948-53
Smith, Bob	1931-32
Smith, Bobby Gene	1962
Smith, Broadway Aleck	1904
Smith, Bull	1906
Smith, Charley	1969
Smith, Charlie	1911-14
Smith, Dave	1991-92
Smith, Dwight	1989-93
Smith, Earl	1916
Smith, Greg	1989-90
Smith, Harry	1877
Smith, Jason	2001
Smith, Lee	1980-87
Smith, Paul	1958
Smith, Riverboat	1959
Smith, Willie	1968-70
Smyth, Steve	2002
Solis, Marcelino	1958
Solomon, Buddy	1975
Sommers, Pete	1889
Sommers, Rudy	1912
Sorensen, Lary	1985
Sosa, Sammy	1992-2004
Spalding, Al	1876-77
Spangler, Al	1967-71
Speake, Bob	1955, 1957
Speier, Chris	1985-87
Speier, Justin	1998
Sperring, Rob	1974-76
Spongberg, Carl	1908
Spradlin, Jerry	2000
Sprague, Charlie	1887
Spring, Jack	1964
St. Vrain, Jim	1902
Stack, Eddie	1913-14
Stainback, Tuck	1934-37
Stairs, Matt	2001
Staley, Gale	1925
Standridge, Pete	1915
Stanky, Eddie	1943-44
Stanley, Joe	1909
Stanton, Tom	1904
Starr, Ray	1945
Start, Joe	1878
Statz, Jigger	1922-25
Stauffer, Ed	1923
Stedronsky, John	1879

Steenstra, Kennie	1998
Steevens, Morrie	1962
Stein, Ed	1890-91
Stein, Randy	1982
Steinfeldt, Harry	1906-10
Stelmaszek, Rick	1974
Stenzel, Jake	1890
Stephenson, Earl	1971
Stephenson, Joe	1944
Stephenson, John	1967-68
Stephenson, Phil	1989
Stephenson, Riggs	1926-34
Stephenson, Walter	1935-36
Stevens, Dave	1997-98
Stewart, Ace	1895
Stewart, Mack	1944-45
Stewart, Tuffy	1913-14
Stewart, Jimmy	1963-67
Stoddard, Tim	1984

Ron Santo

Stone, Steve	1974-76	Tewksbury, Bob	1987-88
Stoneman, Bill	1967-68	Thacker, Moe	1958, 1960-62
Strain, Joe	1981	Thomas, Frank	1960-61, 1966
Strang, Sammy	1900, 1902	Thomas, Lee	1966-67
Strange, Doug	1991-92	Thomas, Red	1921
Stratton, Scott	1894-95	Thomson, Bobby	1958-59
Stringer, Lou	1941-42, 1946	Thompson, Scot	1978-83
Stueland, George	1921-23, 1925	Thornton, Andre	1973-76
Sturgeon, Bobby	1940-42, 1946-47	Thornton, Walter	1895-98
Sturtze, Tanyon	1995-96	Thorpe, Bob	1955
Stynes, Chris	2002	Tidrow, Dick	1979-82
Sullivan, Bill	1878	Tiefenauer, Bob	1968
Sullivan, John	1921	Timmons, Ozzie	1995-96
Sullivan, Marty	1887-88	Tincup, Ben	1928
Sullivan, Mike	1890	Tinker, Joe	1902-12, 1916
Summers, Champ	1975-76	Tinning, Bud	1932-34
Sunday, Billy	1883-87	Todd, Al	1940-41, 1943
Sundberg, Jim	1987-88	Todd, Jim	1974, 1977
Sutcliffe, Rick	1984-91	Tolson, Chuck	1926-27, 1929-30
Sutcliffe, Sy	1884-85	Tompkins, Ron	1971
Sutter, Bruce	1976-80	Toney, Fred	1911-13
Swartzbaugh, Dave	1995-97	Torres, Hector	1971
Sweeney, Bill	1907, 1914	Toth, Paul	1962-64
Sweetland, Les	1931	Trachsel, Steve	1993-99
Swisher, Steve	1974-77	Tracy, Jim	1980-81
		Traffley, Bill	1878
T		Tremel, Bill	1954-56
Tabb, Jerry	1976	Trillo, Manny	1975-78, 1986-88
Tabler, Pat	1981-82	Triplett, Coaker	1938
Talbot, Dale	1953-54	Trout, Steve	1983-87
Tanner, Chuck	1957-58	Truby, Harry	1895-96
Tapani, Kevin	1997-2001	Tucker, Michael	2001
Tappe, El	1954-56, 1958, 1960, 1962	Turgeon, Pete	1923
Tappe, Ted	1955	Turner, Ted	1920
Tate, Bennie	1934	Twombly, Babe	1920-21
Tatis, Ramon	1997	Tyler, Lefty	1918-21
Tavarez, Julian	2001	Tyree, Earl	1914
Taylor, Chink	1925	Tyrone, Jim	1972, 1974-75
Taylor, Danny	1929-32	Tyrone, Wayne	1976
Taylor, Harry	1932	Tyson, Mike	1980-81
Taylor, Jack	1898-1903, 1906-07		
Taylor, Sammy	1958-62	**U**	
Taylor, Tony	1958-60	Upham, John	1967-68
Taylor, Zack	1929-33	Usher, Bob	1952
Teachout, Bud	1930-31		
Tebeau, Patsy	1887	**V**	
Telemaco, Amaury	1996-98	Vail, Mike	1978-80
Tener, John	1888-89	Valdes, Ismael	2000
Terry, Adonis	1894-97	Valdes, Pedro	1996, 1998
Terry, Zeb	1920-22	Valentinetti, Vito	1956-57
Terwillinger, Wayne	1949-51	Van Haltren, George	1887-89

Van Poppel, Todd	2000-01
Van Zandt, Ike	1904
Vandenburg, Hy	1944-45
Vander Meer, Johnny	1950
VanRyn, Ben	1998
Varga, Andy	1950-51
Varsho, Gary	1998-90
Vaughn, Hippo	1913-21
Verban, Emil	1948-50
Veres, Dave	2003
Veres, Randy	1994
Vernon, Joe	1912
Veryzer, Tom	1983-84
Vickery, Tom	1891
Villanueva, Hector	1990-92
Vizcaino, Jose	1991-93
Vogel, Otto	1923-24
Voiselle, Bill	1950

W

Waddell, Rube	1901
Wade, Ben	1948
Wade, Gale	1955-56
Waitkus, Eddie	1941, 1946-48
Waitt, Charlie	1877
Walbeck, Matt	1993
Walker, Chico	1985-87, 1991-93
Walker, Harry	1949
Walker, Mike	1995
Walker, Roy	1917-18
Walker, Rube	1948-51
Walker, Todd	2004
Wallace, Jack	1915
Waller, Ty	1981-82
Wallis, Joe	1975-78
Walls, Lee	1957-59
Walsh, Tom	1906
Walton, Jerome	1989-92
Ward, Chris	1972, 1974
Ward, Dick	1934
Ward, Preston	1950, 1953
Warner, Hooks	1921
Warner, Jack	1962-65
Warneke, Lon	1930-36, 1942-43, 1945
Warstler, Rabbit	1940
Warwick, Carl	1966
Watson, Doc	1913
Watt, Eddie	1975
Weathers, Dave	2001
Weaver, Harry	1917-19

Weaver, Jim	1934
Weaver, Orile	1910-11
Webb, Earl	1927-28
Webster, Mitch	1988-89
Webster, Ray	1971
Weimer, Jake	1903-05
Weinert, Lefty	1927-28
Weis, Butch	1922-25
Welch, Johnny	1926-29
Wellemeyer, Todd	2003-04
Wendell, Turk	1993-97
Wengert, Don	1998
Wheeler, Rip	1923-24
Whisenant, Pete	1956
White, Deacon	1876
White, Derrick	1998
White, Elder	1962
White, Jerry	1978
White, Rondell	2000-01
Whitehill, Earl	1939
Wicker, Bob	1903-06
Wiedemeyer, Charlie	1934
Wilcox, Milt	1975
Wilhelm, Hoyt	1970
Wilke, Harry	1927
Wilkerson, Curt	1989-90
Wilkins, Dean	1989-90
Wilkins, Rick	1991-95
Will, Bob	1957-63
Williams, Art	1902
Williams, Billy	1959-74
Williams, Brian	2000
Williams, Cy	1912-17
Williams, Dewey	1944-47
Williams, Mitch	1989-90
Williams, Otto	1903-04
Williams, Pop	1902-03
Williams, Wash	1885
Williamson, Ned	1879-89
Wills, Bump	1982
Wills, Jim	1953-54
Wilmot, Walt	1890-95
Wilson, Art	1916-17
Wilson, Hack	1926-31
Wilson, Steve	1989-91
Wilson, Willie	1993-94
Winceniak, Ed	1956-57
Wirts, Kettle	1921-23
Wise, Casey	1957
Wolfe, Harry	1917

Wolter, Harry	1917	Yerkes, Steve	1916
Wolverton, Harry	1898-1900	York, Lefty	1921
Womack, Tony	2003	York, Tony	1944
Wood, Kerry	1998, 2000-04	Yost, Gus	1893
Woodall, Brad	1999	Yoter, Elmer	1927-28
Woods, Gary	1982-85	Young, Anthony	1994-95
Woods, Jim	1957	Young, Danny	2000
Woods, Walt	1898	Young, Don	1968-69
Worrell, Tim	2000	Young, Eric	2000-01
Wortman, Chuck	1916-18		
Wright, Bob	1915	**Z**	
Wright, Dave	1897	Zabel, Zip	1913-15
Wright, Mel	1960-61	Zahn, Geoff	1975-76
Wright, Pat	1890	Zambrano, Carlos	2001-04
Wrona, Rick	1988-90	Zambrano, Eddie	1993-94
Wuertz, Michael	2004	Zamora, Oscar	1974-76
Wynne, Marvell	1989-90	Zeider, Rollie	1916-18
Wyse, Hank	1942-47	Zeile, Todd	1995
		Zick, Bob	1954
Y		Zimmer, Don	1960-61
Yantz, George	1912	Zimmerman, Heinie	1907-16
Yelding, Eric	1993	Zuleta, Julio	2000-01
Yerkes, Carroll	1932-33	Zwilling, Dutch	1916

Billy Williams

Managers

Altobelli, Joe	1991
Amalfitano, Joe	1979, 1980-81
Anson, Cap	1879-97
Baker, Dusty	2003-04
Baylor, Don	2000-02
Boudreau, Lou	1960
Bresnahan, Roger	1915
Burns, Tom	1898-1899
Cavaretta, Phil	1951-53
Chance, Frank	1905-12
Craft, Harry	1961
Durocher, Leo	1966-72
Elia, Lee	1982-83
Essian, Jim	1991
Evers, Johnny	1913, 1921
Ferguson, Bob	1878
Fox, Charlie	1983
Franks, Herman	1977-79
Frey, Jim	1984-86
Frisch, Frankie	1949-51
Gibson, George	1925
Gomez, Preston	1980
Grimm, Charlie	1932-38, 1944-49, 1960
Hack, Stan	1954-56
Hartnett, Gabby	1938-40
Himsl, Vedie	1961
Hornsby, Rogers	1930-32
Johnson, Roy	1944
Kennedy, Bob	1963-65
Killefer, Bill	1921-25
Kimm, Bruce	2002
Klein, Lou	1961-62, 1965
Lachemann, Rene	2002
Lefebvre, Jim	1992-93
Lockman, Whitey	1972-74
Loftus, Tom	1900-01
Lucchesi, Frank	1987
Maranville, Rabbit	1925
Marshall, Jim	1974-76
McCarthy, Joe	1926-30
Metro, Charlie	1962
Michael, Gene	1986-87
Mitchell, Fred	1917-20
O'Day, Hank	1913
Riggleman, Jim	1995-99
Scheffing, Bob	1957-59
Selee, Frank	1902-05
Spalding, Al	1876-77
Tappe, Elvin	1961-62
Tinker, Joe	1916
Trebelhorn, Tom	1994
Vuckovich, John	1986
Wilson, Jimmy	1941-44
Zimmer, Don	1988-91

1932 World Series
Cubs Manager Charlie Grimm and
Yankee Manager Joe McCarthy

Coaches

Acosta, Oscar	2000-01
Adams, Bobby	1961-65, 1973
Aguirre, Hank	1972-74
Alomar, Sandy	2000-02
Altobelli, Joe	1988-91
Amalfitano, Joe	1967-71, 1978-80
Amaro, Ruben	1983-86
Baker, William	1950
Banks, Ernie	1967-73
Becker, Joe	1967-70
Bialas, Dave	1995-99, 2002
Blades, Ray	1953-56
Bloomfield, Jack	1975-78
Burke, Jimmy	1926-30
Clines, Gene	1979-81, 2003-04
Cole, Dick	1961
Collins, Rip	1961-63
Connors, Billy	1982-86, 1991-93
Corriden, Red	1932-40
Cottier, Chuck	1988-94
Cox, Larry	1988-89
Craft, Harry	1960-61
Cuyler, Kiki	1941-43
Dark, Al	1965, 1977
Davis, Spud	1950-53
Dean, Dizzy	1941
DeMerritt, Marty	1999
Dixon, Walt	1964-65
Doolan, Mickey	1926-29
Drabowsky, Moe	1994
Dugey, Oscar	1921-24
Dunlop, Harry	1976
Dyer, Duffy	1983
Ellis, Sammy	1992
Fitzsimmons, Freddie	1957-59, 1966
Foley, Marv	1994
Foxx, Jimmie	1944
Franks, Herman	1970
Freese, George	1964-65
Gamboa, Tom	1998-99
Gibson, George	1925-26
Glynn, Gene	2000-02
Grammas, Alex	1964
Grimm, Charlie	1941, 1961-63
Grissom, Marv	1975-76
Hack, Stan	1965
Harder, Mel	1965
Harmon, Tom	1982
Hartnett, Gabby	1938
Hatton, Grady	1960
Hayworth, Ray	1955
Hiatt, Jack	1981
Himsl, Vedie	1960-64
Holt, Goldie	1961-65
Hornsby, Rogers	1958-59
Hundley, Randy	1977
Jackson, Sonny	2003-04
Jansen, Larry	1972-73
Jenkins, Ferguson	1995-96
Johnson, Roy	1935-39, 1944-53
Jurges, Billy	1947-48
Kelly, Mike	1934
Kennedy, Bob	1963-65
Kim, Wendell	2003-04
Klein, Lou	1960-65
Koenig, Fred	1983
Kranitz, Rick	2002
Lachemann, Rene	2000-02
Land, Grover	1929-30
Lazzeri, Tony	1938
Leonard, Dutch	1954-56
Lockman, Whitey	1965-66
Lopez, John	2003-04
Lowe, Q. V.	1972
Lowrey, Peanuts	1970-71, 1977-79, 1981
MacKenzie, Gordy	1982
Macko, Joe	1964
Marshall, Jim	1974
Martin, Fred	1961-65
Martin, Pepper	1956
Martin, J. C.	1974
Martinez, Jose	1988-94
Matthews, Gary	2003-04
Metro, Charlie	1962
Moss, Les	1981
Mueller, Ray	1957
Muser, Tony	1993-97
Myatt, George	1957-59
Noren, Irv	1975
Oates, Johnny	1984-87
O'Leary, Charley	1931-33
Oliveras, Mako	1995-97
O'Neill, Buck	1962-65
Peden, Les	1965
Pentland, Jeff	1997-2002
Pole, Dick	1988-91, 2003-04
Radison, Dan	1995-99
Regan, Phil	1997-98
Reiser, Pete	1966-69, 1972-74
Roarke, Mike	1978-80
Rojas, Cookie	1978-81

Roof, Phil	1990-91	Spangler, Al	1970-71, 1974
Root, Charlie	1951-53, 1960	Starrette, Herm	1987
Rothschild, Larry	2002-04	Stock, Milt	1944-48
Saul, Jim	1975-76	Tappe, Elvin	1959-65
Schalk, Ray	1930-31	Trebelhorn, Tom	1992-93
Scheffing, Bob	1954-55	Uhle, George	1940
Schulte, Johnny	1933	Vukovich, John	1982-87
Schultz, Barney	1977	Walker, Verlon	1961-70
Shea, Marv	1948-49	Williams, Billy	1980-82, 1986-87, 1999-2001
Smith, Red	1945-48	Wright, Mel	1963-64, 1971
Snyder, Jim	1987	Zimmer, Don	1984-86
Spalding, Dick	1941-43		

Left to right: Charlie Grimm, Phil Wrigley,
Charlie Root, Larry French, Carl Reynolds,
Joe Marty and Frank Demaree

Wrigley Field
1935 World Series

Photos courtesy of George Brace appear on the following pages: 37, 53, 58, 67, 72, 83, 412, 414, 434, 437, 459, 473, 495, 499, 504, 509, 525, 539, 543, 550, 557, 562, 566, 573, 574, 587, 597, 605, 609, 613, 619, 623, 632, 699, 700, 708

Photos courtesy of finalshot.com appear on the following pages: 640, 650, 653, 661, 669, 675, 678, 718

Photos courtesy of Dennis Goldstein appear on the following pages: 9, 13, 117, 123, 126, 130, 132, 144, 177, 190, 198, 207, 231 (both photos), 234, 244, 258, 282, 296, 319, 336, 346, 349, 354, 359, 364, 366, 371, 373, 376, 378, 384, 387, 390, 396, 401, 692, 695, 697, 706, 709, 716, 718

Photos courtesy of Mike Mumby appear on the following pages: 108, 114, 140, 154, 161, 168, 171, 183, 186, 199, 211, 219, 223, 238, 240, 246, 248, 250, 265, 270, 274, 278, 286, 290, 301, 303, 308, 311, 313, 321, 332, 342, 688, 691, 713, 715

Photos courtesy of Transcendental Graphics appear on the following pages: 23, 26, 30, 33, 39, 45, 50, 61, 74, 86, 88, 92, 99, 105, 421, 426, 444, 452, 465, 480, 491, 515, 518, 583, 712

Cubs

For 129 seasons, our heroes have had the right stuff—a mix of heart and humor like no other team in basball, whether it's a clowning Jack Pfiester in 1908, a bashing Derrick Lee in 2004, a winking Burt Hooten in 1972, or a waiting group of pennant-winning pitchers in 1932. There's just something special about the Cubs. That might be what manager Stan Hack is telling his young pitcher, Moe Drabowsky, while pointing into the distance, into the future, where, for all true Cub fans, there is hope.

❖ Books of Interest ❖

BASEBALL BEHIND THE SEAMS

The **Baseball Behind the Seams** series by Rob Trucks presents baseball the way it ought to be: no pouting superstars, no steroids, no players' strikes. Each of the books in this one-of-a-kind series focuses on a single position, exploring it with the kind of depth serious fans crave. Through extensive research, including interviews with more than a hundred players past and present, Trucks has brought together the most original and informative series ever published on the game.

Each book in the series covers

- ◆ The physical and mental qualities of the position
- ◆ The position's history
- ◆ The plays, and how to make them
- ◆ Profiles of the position's top all-time players
- ◆ The best defenders of the position
- ◆ A day in the life of one player, from arriving at the ballpark to the final out
- ◆ Lists of Gold Glovers, MVPs, and Rookies of the Year
- ◆ Fun and quirky facts about the position

THE CATCHER
By Rob Trucks

The Catcher is an in-depth exploration into the most demanding position in baseball. Two-time Gold Glover Charles Johnson of the Colorado Rockies, one of the few African-American catchers in major-league baseball, takes the reader through a game behind the plate. *The Catcher* brims with photos and illustrations, along with profiles of such great catchers as Johnny Bench, Yogi Berra, Bill Dickey, Gary Carter, Mickey Cochrane, and many more.

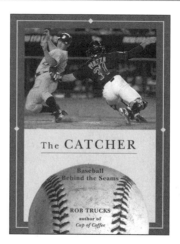

Paperback $14.99
ISBN: 1-57860-164-9

THE STARTING PITCHER
By Rob Trucks

No position on the field receives more attention from fans than the starting pitcher, and yet this is one of the most misunderstood positions in all of baseball. To put the reader behind the seams and into the mind of the man on the mound, Rob Trucks has conducted dozens of in-depth interviews with players, coaches, and scouts to provide a true insider's look at this key position. The "Day in the Life" chapter features Andy Pettitte.

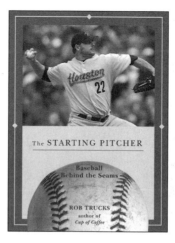

Paperback $14.99
ISBN: 1-57860-163-0

❖   ❖   ❖

To order call: 1(800)343-4499 www.emmisbooks.com
Emmis Books 1700 Madison Road Cincinnati, Ohio 45206